The Princeton Review®

10 Practice Tests for the
SAT®

2023 Edition

The Staff of The Princeton Review

PrincetonReview.com

Penguin
Random
House

The Princeton Review
110 East 42nd St, 7th Floor
New York, NY 10017

ISBN: 978-0-593-45056-7
ISSN: 2377-7273

Editors: Aaron Ricco, Chris Chimera
Production Editors: Sarah Litt, Emma Parker
Production Artist: Tanya Chernyak

Printed in the United States of America.

10 9 8 7 6 5 4 3

2023 Edition

Editorial

Rob Franek, Editor-in-Chief
David Soto, Senior Director, Data Operations
Stephen Koch, Senior Manager, Data Operations
Deborah Weber, Director of Production
Jason Ullmeyer, Production Design Manager
Jennifer Chapman, Senior Production Artist
Selena Coppock, Director of Editorial
Aaron Riccio, Senior Editor
Meave Shelton, Senior Editor
Chris Chimera, Editor
Orion McBean, Editor
Patricia Murphy, Editor
Laura Rose, Editor
Alexa Schmitt Bugler, Editorial Assistant

Penguin Random House Publishing Team

Tom Russell, VP, Publisher
Alison Stoltzfus, Publishing Director
Brett Wright, Senior Editor
Emily Hoffman, Assistant Managing Editor
Ellen Reed, Production Manager
Suzanne Lee, Designer
Eugenia Lo, Publishing Assistant

For customer service, please contact **editorialsupport@review.com**, and be sure to include:

- full title of the book

- ISBN

- page number

Acknowledgments

This edition would not have been possible without the extraordinary talent of and tireless effort by Cynthia Ward and Sara Kuperstein.

The Princeton Review would also like to recognize the sharp eyes and dedicated attention brought to this project by our outstanding production team of Sarah Litt, Emma Parker, and Tanya Chernyak

Amy Minster
Content Director, High School Programs

Contents

Get More
(Free) Content
at **PrincetonReview.com/prep**

As easy as **1·2·3**

1 Go to PrincetonReview.com/prep or scan the **QR code** and enter the following ISBN for your book: **9780593450567**

2 Answer a few simple questions to set up an exclusive Princeton Review account. *(If you already have one, you can just log in.)*

3 Enjoy access to your **FREE** content!

Once you've registered, you can...

- Get our take on any recent or pending updates to the 10 Practice Tests for the SAT 2023 Edition

- Take a full-length practice, SAT and/or ACT

- Get valuable advice about the college application process, including tips for writing a great essay and where to apply for financial aid

- If you're still choosing between colleges, use our searchable rankings of *The Best 388 Colleges* to find out more information about your dream school

- Access comprehensive study guides and a variety of printable resources, including: a bubble sheet and a conversion table

- Check to see if there have been any corrections or updates to this edition

Need to report a **content** issue?

Contact **EditorialSupport@review.com** and include:
- full title of the book
- ISBN
- page number

Need to report a **technical** issue?

Contact **TPRStudentTech@review.com** and provide:
- your full name
- email address used to register the book
- full book title and ISBN
- Operating system (Mac/PC) and browser (Chrome, Firefox, Safari, etc.)

Chapter 1
Your Guide to
Getting the Most
Out Of This Book

WHAT'S INSIDE

Welcome to *10 Practice Tests for the SAT*. As you've probably already guessed, this book contains ten full-length practice tests for the SAT, which we at The Princeton Review have created based off the information released by the College Board. We've rigorously analyzed available tests, and our content development teams have tirelessly worked to ensure that our material accurately reflects what you will see in terms of design, structure, style, and, most importantly, content on test day. We continually evaluate the data on each question to ensure validity and to refine the level of difficulty within each test to match that of the SAT even more closely, and you shouldn't hesitate to reach out to us at EditorialSupport@review.com if you feel something's amiss.

We are confident that if you work through these tests and evaluate your performance with our comprehensive explanations, you'll improve the skills that you need to score higher on the SAT. Register your book at PrincetonReview.com to gain access to detailed, interactive score reports. Alternatively, use the included score-conversion tables to help you to assess and track your overall performance so that you get the most out of your test-prep, as well as in-depth explanations that not only explain how to get the right answer but also why the other choices are incorrect. Through careful self-assessment, you can correct any recurring mistakes, as well as identify any weaknesses or gaps in knowledge that you can then focus your attention on studying.

What Is The Princeton Review?

The Princeton Review is the nation's most popular test-preparation company. We've been at this for almost forty years, and our goal remains to help students everywhere crack the SAT and a bunch of other standardized tests, including the PSAT and ACT as well as graduate-level exams like the GRE and GMAT. We offer courses and private tutoring for all of the major standardized tests, and we publish a series of books to help in your search for the right school. If you would like more information about how The Princeton Review can help you, go to PrincetonReview.com or call 800-2-Review.

HOW TO USE THIS BOOK

Each test is laid out as you'll encounter it on the SAT. While we recommend that you take each test in full, in accordance with the allotted times, and under conditions similar to those that you'll face on the day of the examination, you're welcome to focus on specific sections on which you'd like more practice.

Don't forget to carefully review our detailed explanations! Whether you get a question right or not, its explanation is packed full of our powerful SAT strategies and techniques, and might help you to save time on future questions, or to clarify where you might have gotten a right answer for the wrong reason.

WHEN YOU TAKE A TEST

Here are some suggestions for working through this book:

1. Keep track of your performance. Whether you're working through individual sections or taking each test as a whole, be sure to score yourself either online or with the diagnostic tables beginning on page 909. If you're using the tables in the book, include the time and date with each entry so that you can track your progress.

2.   The SAT is a timed test. You may be a star test-taker when you have all the time in the world to mull over the questions, but can you perform as well when the clock is ticking? Timing yourself will ensure you are prepared for the constraints of the actual test, just as our strategy-filled explanations can help you to discover faster methods for solving questions.

3.   Don't cram it all in at once. It's hard enough to concentrate throughout one SAT—don't burn yourself out by taking multiple tests in a row. You wouldn't run two marathons back-to-back, so why treat your brain (which is like a muscle) in that way? Give yourself at least a couple of months before your anticipated "real" test date so that you can learn from any mistakes that were made on these practice tests.

4.   Accordingly, take time to analyze your performance between tests. As you actively review your work, your mind will be subtly taking notes and tweaking the way it handles future questions of a similar nature, shaving seconds off its processing time as it grows more accustomed to particular wordings or presentations.

Filling In Answers

It's not enough to get the right answer on the SAT quickly—you also have to accurately bubble it into a separate scantron sheet and a surprisingly large number of mistakes can be made at this point, especially if you're skipping over certain questions along the way. To that end, we've included sample scantrons at the end of each test which you can rip out of the book so that you get into the habit of rapidly transferring answers from the test itself to the scantron. (We've also included this in your online student tools, in case you'd rather print out a fresh copy.)

The SAT includes Student-Produced Responses (grid-ins) in the two math sections. We've replicated those on the scantrons so that you can practice correctly filling them in. A version of the following directions should appear on the test itself, but rather than waste valuable time reading it later, take a moment to familiarize yourself with them now.

Directions: A Student-Produced Response question requires you to solve the problem and enter your answer by marking the circles in the special grid, as shown in the examples below. You may use any available space for scratch work.

Answer: $\dfrac{7}{12}$

Write answer in boxes. → ← Fraction line

Grid in → result.

Answer: 2.5

← Decimal point

Answer: 201
Either position is correct.

Note: You may start your answers in any column, space permitting. Columns not needed should be left blank.

- Mark no more than one circle in any column.
- Because the answer document will be machine-scored, **you will receive credit only if the circles are filled in correctly.**
- Although not required, it is suggested that you write your answer in the boxes at the top of the columns to help you fill in the circles accurately.
- Some problems may have more than one correct answer. In such cases, grid only one answer.
- No question has a negative answer.
- **Mixed numbers** such as $3\frac{1}{2}$ must be gridded as 3.5 or 7/2. (If `3 1 / 2` is gridded, it will be interpreted as $\frac{31}{2}$, not $3\frac{1}{2}$.)

- **Decimal Answers:** If you obtain a decimal answer with more digits than the grid can accommodate, it may be either rounded or truncated, but it must fill the entire grid. For example, if you obtain an answer such as 0.6666..., you should record your result as .666 or .667. **A less accurate value such as .66 or .67 will be scored as incorrect.**

Acceptable ways to grid $\dfrac{2}{3}$ are:

GOOD LUCK!

We know that the SAT may seem intimidating at first glance—but then again, after using this book, you'll be taking it at tenth or eleventh glance, so you're headed in the right direction. Also, as you prepare, whether you're stressed or relaxed, remember this key point:

The SAT doesn't measure the stuff that matters. It measures neither intelligence nor the depth and breadth of what you're learning in high school. It doesn't predict college grades as well as your high school grades do, and many colleges know there is more to you as a student—and a person—than how you fare on a single three-hour test administered on a random Saturday, Sunday, or Wednesday morning.

This is a high-stakes test, and you should absolutely work hard and prepare. But don't treat it like it's some mythical monster or world-ending catastrophe. It's just a test, and we at The Princeton Review know tests. We're here for you every step of the way.

Chapter 2
What You Need to
Know for the SAT

GENERAL INFORMATION ABOUT THE SAT

Let's take a moment to discuss some SAT facts. Some of them may surprise you.

Who Writes the SAT?

Even though colleges and universities make wide use of the SAT, they're not the ones who write the test. That's the job of the College Board, the organization that writes the test and decides how it is administered.

They've changed the SAT twice in the last twenty years, and they've admitted that students can and should prepare for the test, which means that the test *can* be beaten, and as they say, practice helps to make perfect.

What's on the SAT?

The SAT is 3 hours long. It includes four tests.

- Reading Test: 65 minutes, 52 questions
- 10-minute break
- Writing and Language Test: 35 minutes, 44 questions
- Math Test (No Calculator): 25 minutes, 20 questions
- 5-minute break
- Math Test (Calculator): 55 minutes, 38 questions

Wait, *Who* Writes This Test?

You may be surprised to learn that the people who write SAT test questions are NOT necessarily teachers or college professors. The people who write the SAT are professional test writers, not superhuman geniuses, so you can beat them at their own game.

The Optional Essay Is No Longer an Option

As of June 2021, the SAT essay is no longer offered for the vast majority of students, and no colleges require it. Only students taking a School Day (not weekend) SAT *may* be given the essay section. If you will be taking a School Day SAT with essay and want to prepare, we've included some sample prompts online in your free Student Tools.

With the exception of a few grid-in questions in the Math sections, everything else is multiple-choice, with four options for each question. Here's a brief rundown of what to expect.

Reading Test

Your score on the Evidence-Based Reading and Writing section of the SAT is comprised of your scores on the Reading Test and the Writing and Language Test. The Reading Test is 65 minutes long and consists of 52 questions, all of which are passage-based and multiple-choice. Passages may be paired with informational graphics, such as charts or graphs, and there will also be a series of questions based on a pair of passages. The selected passages will be from previously published works in the areas of world literature, history/social studies, and science. Questions based on science passages may ask you to analyze data or hypotheses, or to read graphs, while questions about literature passages will concentrate more on literary concepts like theme, mood, and characterization. The main goal is to measure your ability to both understand words in context and find and analyze evidence.

Writing and Language Test

The Writing and Language Test is 35 minutes long and consists of 44 questions, which are also multiple-choice and based on several passages. However, instead of asking you to analyze a passage, questions will ask you to proofread and edit the passage. That means you'll have to correct grammar and word choice and make larger changes to the organization or content of the passage.

Math Test

You'll have a total of 80 minutes to complete the Math Test, which, as we mentioned earlier, is divided into two sections. The No-Calculator portion is 25 minutes and has 20 questions, while the Calculator portion is 55 minutes with 38 questions. Most questions are multiple-choice, but there are also handfuls of student-produced response questions, which are also known as grid-ins. (Instead of choosing from four answer choices, you'll have to work through a question and then enter your answer on your answer sheet by bubbling in the appropriate numbers.) Exactly 13 of the 58 math questions will be grid-ins.

The Experimental Section

The College Board is not straightforward with whether there will be an experimental section on the SAT, and, if so, whether any of the questions within it will actually count toward your score. Therefore, in order to better prepare those students who may see this optional section, the tenth test in this book has an experimental section. This way, you can be more familiar with the test structure if, in fact, you are one of the "lucky" ones.

One final twist: while we know, at least as of the printing of this book, that the experimental section is 20 minutes long, we also know that this section can be on Reading, Writing and Language, or Math. Resist the urge to peek at which one we've included with Practice Test 10; as with each of the tests in this book, you want to emulate testing conditions as closely as possible, and in this case, you're also making sure you're ready to deal with potential testing fatigue. You've got this!

This Just In
The SAT is changing again. In January 2022, College Board announced that the SAT will be going digital and getting a makeover in the process. These changes will go into effect in March 2023 for international students and in March 2024 for students in the U.S. The Princeton Review will be tracking these changes and will continue to offer our students all the tools they need to prepare for this new version of the SAT.

Table of Content
If you're super curious about the content that the Math Test covers, the test developers have cryptically designated the four main areas as (1) Heart of Algebra, (2) Problem Solving and Data Analysis, (3) Passport to Advanced Math, and (4) Additional Topics in Math.

Scoring on the SAT

The SAT is scored on a scale of 400–1600, and also introduces a series of cross-test scores and subscores that analyze various proficiencies. Here's the breakdown:

- **Total score (1):** The sum of the two section scores (Evidence-Based Reading and Writing, Math), ranging from 400 to 1600
- **Section scores (2):** Evidence-Based Reading and Writing, ranging from 200–800; Math, also ranging from 200–800
- **Test scores (3):** Reading Test, Writing and Language Test, Math Test, each of which is scored on a scale from 10 to 40
- **Cross-test scores (2):** Each is scored on a scale from 10 to 40 and based on selected questions from the three tests (Reading, Writing and Language, Math):
  1) Analysis in History/Social Studies
  2) Analysis in Science
- **Subscores (7):** Each of the following receives a score from 1 to 15:
  1) Command of Evidence (Reading, Writing and Language)
  2) Words in Context (Reading, Writing and Language)
  3) Expression of Ideas (Writing and Language)
  4) Standard English Conventions (Writing and Language)
  5) Heart of Algebra (Math)
  6) Problem Solving and Data Analysis (Math)
  7) Passport to Advanced Math (Math)

Scoring Tricks

You will not be penalized for wrong answers on the SAT. This means that you should always guess, even if this means choosing an answer at random. With only four answers to choose from, your odds of getting a right answer are decent and only get better if you use Process of Elimination (POE) to eliminate an answer choice or two.

Because time is at a premium on the test, don't be shy about bubbling in a guess on a question that you don't fully understand so that you can move on to questions that you feel more confident you can answer correctly (and quickly). That being said, try to indicate in your test booklet which questions you've guessed on so that, if you have time left at the end of a test, you can return to those tricky questions and try to get a few extra points.

WHEN IS THE SAT GIVEN?

The SAT schedule for the school year is posted on the College Board website at www.collegeboard.org. There are two different ways to sign up for the test. You can either sign up online by going to www.collegeboard.org and clicking on the SAT hyperlink, or sign up through the mail with an SAT registration booklet, which may be available at your school's guidance counselor's office.

Try to sign up for the SAT as soon as you know when you'll be taking the test. If you wait until the last minute to sign up, there may not be any open spots in the testing centers that are closest to you.

If you require any special accommodations while taking the test (including, but not limited to, extra time or assistance), www.collegeboard.org has information about applying for those. Make sure to apply early; we recommend doing so six months before you plan to take the test.

About the Answer Explanations
The explanations in this book demonstrate The Princeton Review's methods and strategies—like Process of Elimination—in action. If you're looking for a more formal review of content or a specific walk-through of these skills, you can find that information in one of our other books, *SAT Prep*.

Stay on Schedule
Although you may take the SAT at any administration given in your freshman year, most students take it for the first time in the spring of their junior year and possibly retake it in the fall of their senior year. Don't leave it to the last minute: sit down and plan a schedule.

Chapter 3
Practice Test 1

Reading Test

65 MINUTES, 52 QUESTIONS

Turn to Section 1 of your answer sheet to answer the questions in this section.

Each passage or pair of passages below is followed by a number of questions. After reading each passage or pair, choose the best answer to each question based on what is stated or implied in the passage or passages and in any accompanying graphics (such as a table or graph).

Questions 1–10 are based on the following passage.

This passage is excerpted from Mary Shelley, *Frankenstein*, originally published in 1818.

My journey was very melancholy. At first I wished to hurry on, for I longed to console and sympathize with my loved and sorrowing friends; but when I drew
Line near my native town, I slackened my progress. I could
5 hardly sustain the multitude of feelings that crowded into my mind. I passed through scenes familiar to my youth, but which I had not seen for nearly six years. How altered every thing might be during that time! One sudden and desolating change had taken place;
10 but a thousand little circumstances might have by degrees worked other alterations, which, although they were done more tranquilly, might not be the less decisive. Fear overcame me; I dared no advance, dreading a thousand nameless evils that made me
15 tremble, although I was unable to define them. I remained two days at Lausanne, in this painful state of mind. I contemplated the lake: the waters were placid; all around was calm; and the snowy mountains, 'the palaces of nature,' were not changed. By degrees the
20 calm and heavenly scene restored me, and I continued my journey towards Geneva. The road ran by the side of the lake, which became narrower as I approached my native town. I discovered more distinctly the black sides of Jura, and the bright summit of Mont
25 Blanc. I wept like a child. "Dear mountains! My own beautiful lake! How do you welcome your wanderer? Your summits are clear; the sky and lake are blue and

placid. Is this to prognosticate peace, or to mock at my unhappiness?"
30   I fear, my friend, that I shall render myself tedious by dwelling on these preliminary circumstances; but they were days of comparative happiness, and I think of them with pleasure. My country, my beloved country! Who but a native can tell the delight I took
35 in again beholding thy streams, thy mountains, and, more than all, thy lovely lake! Yet, as I drew nearer home, grief and fear again overcame me. Night also closed around; and when I could hardly see the dark mountains, I felt still more gloomily. The picture
40 appeared a vast and dim scene of evil, and I foresaw obscurely that I was destined to become the most wretched of human beings. Alas! I prophesied truly, and failed only in one single circumstance, that in all the misery I imagined and dreaded, I did not conceive
45 the hundredth part of the anguish I was destined to endure. It was completely dark when I arrived in the environs of Geneva; the gates of the town were already shut; and I was obliged to pass the night at Secheron, a village at the distance of half a league from the
50 city. The sky was serene; and, as I was unable to rest, I resolved to visit the spot where my poor William had been murdered. As I could not pass through the town, I was obliged to cross the lake in a boat to arrive at Plainpalais. During this short voyage I saw the
55 lightning playing on the summit of Mont Blanc in the most beautiful figures. The storm appeared to approach rapidly, and, on landing, I ascended a low hill, that I

CONTINUE ➡

might observe its progress. It advanced; the heavens were clouded, and I soon felt the rain coming slowly in
60 large drops, but its violence quickly increased.

While I watched the tempest, so beautiful yet terrific, I wandered on with a hasty step. This noble war in the sky elevated my spirits; I clasped my hands, and exclaimed aloud, "William, dear angel! This is
65 thy funeral, this thy dirge!" As I said these words, I perceived in the gloom a figure which stole from behind a clump of trees near me; I stood fixed, gazing intently: I could not be mistaken. A flash of lightning illuminated the object, and discovered its shape
70 plainly to me; its gigantic stature, and the deformity of its aspect more hideous than belongs to humanity, instantly informed me that it was the wretch, the filthy daemon, to whom I had given life. What did he there? Could he be (I shuddered at the conception) the
75 murderer of my brother? No sooner did that idea cross my imagination, than I became convinced of its truth; my teeth chattered, and I was forced to lean against a tree for support. The figure passed me quickly, and I lost it in the gloom.

1

Which choice best describes the developmental pattern of the passage?

A) A lighthearted description of an adventure

B) A dramatic response to a request for help

C) A profound analysis of an ancient curse

D) A melancholy recounting of a doomed homecoming

2

Which choice best describes what happens in the passage?

A) One character returns home to avenge the death of his brother.

B) One character fears his future in the hometown he left.

C) One character is afraid to return to a city haunted by an unknown monster.

D) One character worries that he won't be welcome at home.

3

As used in line 11 and line 19, "degrees" most nearly means

A) levels.

B) measures.

C) small increments.

D) careful developments.

4

Which emotion does the narrator most feel?

A) He feels joy at returning home.

B) He feels antagonism for the daemon.

C) He feels dread concerning his fate.

D) He feels sorrow over William's death.

5

Which choice provides the best evidence for the answer to the previous question?

A) Lines 34–36 ("Who but . . . lake")

B) Lines 42–46 ("I prophesied . . . endure")

C) Lines 58–60 ("It advanced . . . increased")

D) Lines 74–75 ("Could . . . brother")

6

In the passage, the narrator addresses the tempest with

A) awe, but not fear.

B) ebullience, but not rage.

C) disconsolation, but not anger.

D) insanity, but not regret.

CONTINUE ➡

7

The main purpose of the first paragraph is to

A) represent a journey.

B) embellish an emotion.

C) provide a context.

D) establish a mood.

8

Why does the narrator mention "a thousand little circumstances" (line 10)?

A) He fears a natural disaster and its aftermath.

B) He dreads the effects of a devastating incident.

C) He knows he could have stopped a tragedy.

D) He has incited a revolution to take down the government.

9

Which of the following provides the best evidence for the answer to the previous question?

A) Line 8 ("How altered . . . time")

B) Lines 9–13 ("One sudden . . . decisive")

C) Lines 50–52 ("The sky . . . murdered")

D) Lines 64–65 ("William . . . dirge")

10

As used in line 66, "stole" most nearly means

A) crept.

B) pinched.

C) thieved.

D) displaced.

CONTINUE

Questions 11–20 are based on the following passage.

This passage is an excerpt from Howard Gardner, *Art, Mind, and Brain*. ©1982 by Basic Books.

Twenty years ago psychology seemed a rather remote and sterile area to individuals interested in the full and creative use of the mind. The field harbored a
Line trio of uninviting specializations. There was academic
5 psychology, featuring the use of contrived laboratory apparatus to study the perception of visual illusions or the memorization of long lists of nonsense syllables. Such lines of study bore little evident relationship to human beings engaged in thought. There was
10 behaviorism, the approach that emerged from work with rats and pigeons. Behaviorists claimed that we act in the way we do because we are reinforced for doing so and, given their focus on overt activity, these scholars denied inner life—no thought, no fantasies,
15 no aspirations. Finally, there was psychoanalysis, which offered not only a controversial method of treatment but also an overarching theory of human nature. While psychoanalysis had a grandeur and depth that eluded both academic psychology and behaviorism, it strongly
20 accentuated human personality and unconscious problem-solving.

The cognitive revolution came in two parts. First, there was the frank recognition that one could—one must—take seriously human mental
25 processes, including thinking, problem-solving, and creating. Study of the mind once again became a proper scientific undertaking. Second, there was the demonstration by several researchers that human thought processes were characterized by considerable
30 regularity and structure. Not all of this cogitation took place in full view, nor could such cognitive processes always be either related to external stimuli or confirmed by introspection. But there was structure to thought processes, a structure the careful analyst could
35 help lay bare.

Many of us who were studying the behavioral sciences in the 1960s were swept up—and have remained inspired—by this revolution. For some, the appeal lay in computer programming and
40 artificial intelligence—the design of machines that display intelligence. For others, the thrill came in conducting careful laboratory experiments in which one could trace, on a millisecond-by-millisecond basis, an individual's mental process as he carried out

45 a multiplication problem, reasoned through a logical syllogism, or rotated an image of geometrical form in his head. Still others took roads that went through pedagogy, through anthropology, or through the neurosciences. In my own case, I found especially
50 appealing the approach to the mind put forth by structuralists working in the cognitive regions of several social sciences.

In the opening set of essays I lay out the principal assumption of this structuralist approach as it is
55 exemplified by the developmental psychologist Jean Piaget, the linguist Noam Chomsky, and the anthropologist Claude Levi-Strauss. These thinkers share a belief that the mind operates according to the specifiable rules—often unconscious ones—and that
60 these can be ferreted out and made explicit by the systematic examination of human language, action, and problem-solving. There are many intriguing differences among their approaches as well, and I review several of these; still, one finds throughout a
65 surprisingly (and reassuringly) common vision of what the human mind is like and how it can best be described for scientific purposes.

The structuralist approach to the mind has limitations. Those that are more germane, given my
70 own concern with artistic knowledge, derive from the essentially closed nature of structuralist systems. Though creative thought has not escaped their attention, each of the major cognitive structuralists views the options of human thought as in some way
75 preordained, limited in advance. This makes their work especially problematic for a study of mind where the major focus falls on innovation and creation, as in the fashioning of original works of art.

To my mind the limitation implicit in the standard
80 structuralist stance can be circumscribed by the recognition of one special feature of human thought —its ability to create and sponsor commerce through the use of various kinds of symbol systems. These symbol systems—these codes of meaning—are the
85 vehicles through which thought takes place: by their very nature they are creative, open systems. Through the use of symbols the human mind, operating according to the structuralist principles, can create, revise, transform, and re-create wholly fresh products,
90 systems and even worlds of meaning.

CONTINUE ➡

11

The main purpose of the passage is to

A) review a set of essays on structuralism and creativity.

B) convince scientists to abandon behaviorist thought.

C) emphasize the limitations present in psychology.

D) present the author's view that structuralism allows for creativity.

12

The central claim of the passage is that

A) psychology has evolved since the 1960s before which it was too sedate and impractical for modern scientists.

B) traditional structuralist principles can allow for the possibility of human creativity.

C) behaviorists are limited in their scientific processes and have preordained views that humans act largely on their operant conditioning.

D) the author's opinions on creativity are revolutionary and supported by research in traditional psychology.

13

The author describes the different branches of psychology throughout the passage mainly to

A) guide the reader through a complete historic progression of a science.

B) establish his prominent and novel role within the psychological community.

C) highlight a difference that makes structuralism inferior to behaviorism.

D) show how the revolution of the 1960s affected psychology.

14

Gardner indicates that the cognitive revolution he describes in the passage was

A) a motivation for the author's exploration of creativity and structuralism.

B) a pertinent factor in revitalizing a dying field of science.

C) beneficial for interjecting thoughtful scientists back into the field of psychology.

D) more effective than previous changes to the perspective of psychologists.

15

Which choice provides the best evidence for the answer to the previous question?

A) Lines 8–9 ("Such . . . thought")

B) Lines 27–30 ("Second . . . structure")

C) Lines 36–38 ("Many . . . revolution")

D) Lines 38–41 ("For some . . . intelligence")

16

The author characterizes the branch of psychology that became popular after the cognitive revolution mentioned in line 22 as using both

A) problem-solving and creating.

B) meticulousness and mathematics.

C) regularity and structure.

D) fantasy and aspiration.

17

Which lines best support the previous answer?

A) Lines 11–15 ("Behaviorists . . . aspirations")

B) Lines 23–26 ("First . . . creating")

C) Lines 41–47 ("For others . . . head")

D) Lines 64–67 ("still . . . purposes")

CONTINUE

18

According to the passage, the author references Jean Piaget, Noam Chomsky, and Claude Levi-Strauss because they

A) represent different approaches to a unified belief about the mind.

B) present work that is inherently problematic when used in psychological discussions.

C) are psychologists who support his assumptions about structuralism.

D) published works that do not support the author's opinion on creativity.

19

The "original works of art" mentioned in line 78 mainly serve to emphasize how

A) admiring of artistic knowledge and endeavors the author is.

B) distorted the views of the structural psychologists are.

C) restricted the traditional structuralists' views on creativity are.

D) closed-minded and limited psychology is regarding artistic ability.

20

Which choice most closely captures the meaning of the "symbol systems" referred to in line 84?

A) Thought processes

B) Problematic methods

C) Structured principles

D) Representative expressions

CONTINUE

Questions 21–31 are based on the following passages.

Passage 1 is adapted from Lee Billings, "At Pluto, the End of a Beginning." ©July 2015 by *Scientific American*. Passage 2 is adapted from Caleb A. Scharf, "A New Billion-Mile Journey for New Horizons." ©August 2015 by *Scientific American*. Lee Billings is a science journalist. Caleb Scharf is the Director of Astrobiology at Columbia University.

Passage 1

Early this morning, if all has gone well, the first golden age of interplanetary exploration will have come to a close. At 7:49 Eastern time, NASA's New
Line Horizons spacecraft was slated to reach its primary
5 target, Pluto and its moons, concluding what some call the preliminary reconnaissance of the known solar system.

Though it was conceived in the late 1980s, New Horizons wasn't launched until 2006, after long years
10 of delays, redesigns, and even near-death cancellations. Its unlikely five-billion-kilometer voyage to Pluto has been the work of decades. And yet today, at the climax of its mission, the spacecraft was expected to traverse the expanse of Pluto in less than three
15 minutes, whizzing 12,500 kilometers above the surface at nearly 50,000 kilometers per hour. From the start, the spacecraft was custom-built for speed. Carrying enough fuel to crash into orbit at Pluto would have made New Horizons too bulky, expensive, and slow to
20 even launch in the first place, so instead it will flyby and continue outward, on an endless journey into interstellar night.

During its brief close encounter, New Horizons will be too busy gathering data to immediately phone
25 home, instead using those precious moments to scrutinize the planet with a suite of seven instruments all running on a nightlight's share of electricity. Mission planners will only learn of the flyby's success later tonight, via a radio signal. Or, they could learn of
30 its failure by hearing nothing—the spacecraft has an estimated 1 in 10,000 chance of suffering a destructive high-speed collision with debris while passing through the Plutonian system.

Presuming New Horizons' flyby is successful, its
35 confirmatory signal traveling sunward at the speed of light will reach Earth some 4.5 hours after being transmitted, and is expected to arrive at 8:53 PM. Though the primary encounter is best measured in minutes and hours, the slow data-transmission rate
40 imposed by such vast distances ensures that New Horizons will be beaming its archived images home well into 2017.

Passage 2

What do you do when you've flown 3 billion miles through interplanetary space?
45 You keep going.

Although NASA's New Horizons mission has only just begun to transmit the bulk of the detailed scientific data from its history-making encounter with the Pluto-Charon system (at an excruciatingly slow 2 kilobits per
50 second) the spacecraft team has been hard at work on a critical, and time-sensitive, decision.

It had long been hoped that New Horizons would be able to deploy its instruments to study further objects in the Kuiper belt. But back in early 2014 it
55 wasn't clear that astronomers and planetary scientists were going to be able to find any suitable candidates within the range of trajectories that the mission—with its limited on-board fuel resources—could reasonably adjust to. Despite searching with Earth-bound
60 telescopes it was clear that our understanding of the number of objects smaller than Pluto (but still large enough to study) was incomplete, as candidates were in short supply.

Using the Hubble Space Telescope in the summer
65 of 2014, in what was a bit of a last-ditch attempt, there was huge relief as just five plausible targets finally revealed themselves, with two later confirmed to be good for an intercept.

The first of these, called PT1 (potential target one)
70 or more officially 2014 MU69, has now been chosen as the next goal for New Horizons.

This object is thought to be at most 30 miles across —akin to a cometary nucleus on steroids—and barely 1% the size of Pluto. In other words, it's an entirely
75 different beast than Pluto, but it may be the kind of body that helped form Pluto itself some 4.5 billion years ago, and it's within reach for New Horizons at a mere billion miles further along the interplanetary road.

CONTINUE

21

In line 10, the author of Passage 1 mentions "delays, redesigns, and even near-death cancellations" primarily to

A) indicate why the ship was built for speed.

B) predict that not all may go well with the mission.

C) express concern that the ship may crash.

D) explain the period of time between the plan and its execution.

22

The author of Passage 1 indicates that the flyby over Pluto could have which outcome?

A) Scientists could receive data beginning at 7:49 Eastern time.

B) Scientists could receive no data from the ship.

C) Scientists could learn of the mission's failure through a radio signal.

D) Scientists could receive data after a delay of 3 minutes.

23

Which choice provides the best evidence for the answer to the previous question?

A) Lines 3–7 ("At 7:49 . . . system")

B) Lines 28–29 ("Mission . . . signal")

C) Lines 29–33 ("Or, they . . . system")

D) Lines 34–37 ("Presuming . . . 8:53 PM")

24

As used in line 26, "suite" most nearly means

A) jacket.

B) room.

C) array.

D) candy.

25

What function does the discussion of the measurement of the primary encounter in lines 38–39 serve in Passage 1?

A) It supports a claim made earlier in the text.

B) It undermines an assumption made in the previous paragraph.

C) It emphasizes the relativity of time in measuring space.

D) It highlights the brevity of the encounter versus the slow pace of the documentation.

26

The central claim of Passage 2 is that New Horizons has started to transmit information about Pluto but

A) it will then continue on an endless journey into night.

B) it is also on the way to its next observation.

C) plans for its next task need to be decided upon soon.

D) the preliminary reconnaissance of our solar system is complete.

27

As used in line 53, "deploy" most nearly means

A) mimic.

B) utilize.

C) release.

D) negate.

CONTINUE

28

Which statement best describes the relationship between the passages?

A) Passage 2 expresses concern about the dangers mentioned in Passage 1.

B) Passage 2 revises the interpretation of events described in Passage 1.

C) Passage 2 describes the next chapter in the story depicted in Passage 1.

D) Passage 2 provides qualified support for the successes celebrated in Passage 1.

29

The author of Passage 2 would most likely respond to the discussion of New Horizons' continued journey in lines 21–22, Passage 1, by claiming that the journey

A) will involve at least one further stop.

B) will not take place on a literal road.

C) will be endless.

D) will take a long time before return is possible.

30

Which choice provides the best evidence for the answer to the previous question?

A) Lines 46–51 ("Although . . . decision")

B) Lines 52–54 ("It had . . . belt")

C) Lines 69–71 ("The first . . . Horizons")

D) Lines 74–79 ("In other . . . road")

31

Which point about data transmitted from the New Horizons spacecraft is explicit in Passage 1 and implicit in Passage 2?

A) It will take some time for the data to reach Earth.

B) It would be more useful if scientists were able to interpret it more quickly.

C) It will be valuable only if it offsets the cost of the mission.

D) It is likely to consist primarily of images of objects smaller than Pluto.

CONTINUE

Questions 32–42 are based on the following passage and supplementary material.

This passage is adapted from Grant E. Donnelly, Anne V. Wilson, Ashley V. Whillans, and Michael I. Norton, "Communicating Resource Scarcity and Interpersonal Connection." ©2021 by Grant E. Donnelly, Anne V. Wilson, Ashley V. Whillans, and Michael I. Norton.

People often have the feeling that they lack
enough time and enough money, and this problem
is compounded by the frequency with which other
Line people make demands on both resources. Imagine
5 receiving an invitation to your friend's wedding, a
destination event in Hawaii. You want to celebrate with
your friend, but traveling to Hawaii requires a great
deal of time and money: You have limited remaining
vacation days and money is tight. Given these
10 constraints, you decide that you are not going to attend
the wedding. You know that declining the invitation
will hurt your friend's feelings and may signal that you
do not value the friendship, so your goal is to say "no"
but to limit the negative impact on your friendship.
15 While you could offer no explanation when declining
an invitation people feel compelled to offer a rationale
– for example, by disclosing that they do not have
enough vacation time or enough money.

While receiving a wedding invitation may not be
20 an everyday occurrence, people are regularly invited to
social engagements by friends, family, and co-workers.
In fact, over 25,000 invitations are sent each hour on
Evite, an online invitation service (Evite, 2018). Such
social invitations often necessitate the investment of
25 one's time or money – or both. We propose that people
often turn down social invitations by citing insufficient
time (e.g., "I don't have time to go out to dinner")
or money (e.g., "I don't have money to go out to
dinner"). Despite the commonness of such situations,
30 little is known about the consequences of disclosing
financial or temporal scarcity, particularly with regard
to the downstream consequences of doing so for the
relationship between the inviter and invitee.

Research suggests that consumers might react more
35 favorably to communications about time (vs. money)
scarcity. For example, Liu and Aaker (2008) show that
people respond more generously to charitable requests
for time versus money, because money activates a
value-maximization mindset that is more closely

40 linked to economic utility whereas time engenders an
emotional mindset that is geared toward helping (Liu
& Aaker, 2008).

Similarly, while consumers regularly assess
the value of their money regarding services that
45 they receive in transactional relationships (e.g., a
consumer's relationship with a business; e.g., Fiske,
1992), such comparisons are less common and
are often perceived as inappropriate in communal
relationships (e.g., a consumer's relationship with
50 family and friends; e.g., Fiske, 1992). Thus, citing
insufficient money could make relationships feel
transactional, undermining the communal nature of
the relationship (Kim, Zhang, & Norton, 2019). As
a result, when provided with a rejection to a social
55 invitation, consumers might respond more favorably to
excuses citing a scarcity of time (vs. money).

In contrast, we suggest that communicating
temporal scarcity could lead to more negative
reactions. We propose that time is perceived as more
60 discretionary and under consumers' personal control
than money, which often must be dedicated to non-
discretionary expenses (Bureau of Labor Statistics,
2016a, 2016b). Moreover, consumers tend to see time,
but not money, as more likely to be readily available
65 in the future, regardless of current demands on either
resource (Zauberman & Lynch, 2005). Building on the
literature on "time slack," we suggest that consumers
apply these assumptions when receiving social excuses
such that declining an invitation using a time (vs.
70 money) scarcity excuse will be viewed more negatively
because time is seen as more accessible and the use
of which is more discretionary. In other words, we
propose that excuses citing insufficient time will be
received as a more intentional social slight than citing
75 insufficient money because time is viewed as a more
personally controllable resource. Recipients of time
excuses versus money excuses may therefore perceive
their relationship partner as less invested in the
relationship, resulting in lower feelings of interpersonal
80 closeness and less positive interpersonal behaviors.

CONTINUE ▶

Effects of Time and Money Excuses on
Perceived Closeness in Personal Relationships

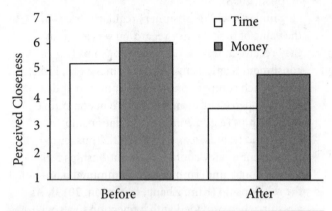

32

The authors most likely use the example in lines 4-9
of the passage ("Imagine . . . tight") to highlight the

A) frequency with which people are invited to
weddings.

B) demands put on one's resources by others.

C) damage done to friendships by declined
invitations.

D) current shortage of vacation time available for
social obligations.

33

The authors indicate that people feel compelled to
explain declining an invitation primarily because they

A) want to avoid harming their friendships.

B) will lose time and money if they don't.

C) would expect the same from their friends.

D) believe they should follow societal customs.

34

Which choice provides the best evidence for the
answer to the previous question?

A) Lines 11-14 ("You know . . . friendship")

B) Lines 23-25 ("Such . . . both")

C) Lines 25-29 ("We propose . . . dinner")

D) Lines 34-36 ("Research . . . scarcity")

35

In line 31, the word "temporal" most nearly means

A) worldly.

B) material.

C) time-related.

D) spiritual.

36

The authors would likely describe the "downstream
consequences" mentioned in paragraph 2 (lines 19-33)
as

A) unrealistic.

B) undetermined.

C) overstated.

D) temporary.

CONTINUE

37

The passage indicates that the assertion made by Kim, Zhang, and Norton in lines 50-53 may be

A) falsified.

B) illogical.

C) unnecessary.

D) inaccurate.

38

Which choice provides the best evidence for the answer to the previous question?

A) Lines 19-21 ("While . . . co-workers")

B) Lines 22-23 ("In fact . . . service")

C) Lines 53-56 ("As a . . . money")

D) Lines 57-59 ("In contrast . . . reactions")

39

As it is used in lines 59, "reactions" most nearly means

A) motivations.

B) responses.

C) transactions.

D) transformations.

40

The authors refer to work by Zauberman and Lynch (line 66) in order to

A) propose a solution.

B) support a theory.

C) discredit an opinion.

D) qualify an assumption.

41

The graph following the passage offers evidence that the perceived closeness in a personal relationship following an excuse is affected by

A) the prior perceived closeness in the friendship.

B) how frequently invitations are rejected.

C) the type of excuse offered.

D) the number of excuses offered in a rejection.

42

The authors would likely attribute the differing effects of time and money excuses on perceived closeness as represented in the graph to

A) decreasing levels of empathy.

B) beliefs about control over resources.

C) resistance to receiving any excuse.

D) the burden of social obligations.

CONTINUE

Questions 43–52 are based on the following passage and supplementary material.

This passage is adapted from Kaitlyn Kunce, "The Second X Chromosome." Originally published in 2016.

Line
    The researchers for The Changing Tides project have been collecting hair and blood samples from female bears along Katmai's coast. Researchers studied the bears during 2015 and 2016, and each bear was
5 assigned a number. The bear's number ended in a "5" if the bear was studied in 2015 (for example, 15, 35, or 115) and ended in a "6" if the bear was studied in 2016 (for example, 16, 66, or 106). Ten collars were dispersed in May of this year on sows and seven of
10 them were recaptured in July. Out of the three that weren't recaptured, one of the sows was in a spot that was inaccessible to the researchers. Another sow's collar was unable to be heard properly to be located. The researchers are careful not to capture sows with
15 spring cubs, also known as cubs of the year. However, sows with older cubs are used in this study. Why this selection of females over males?

    Females are often watched in wildlife populations to determine health. Initial cub nourishment,
20 protection, and teaching are the mother bear's responsibility. Although fall food resources have been shown to influence bear populations, the quality of the early foraging season may have an effect on development of cubs. During the first year, cubs
25 double their weight every two months. They depend exclusively on mom for nourishment for up to six months. This puts a lot of stress on the sow that must re-nourish herself and her cubs after hibernation.

    The coastal areas in Katmai provide an important
30 high quality early-season habitat for bears. The coast is one of the first places that becomes snow-free after winter. Looking at the data from early summer, both this year and last, we can see how important these resources can be for bears along the coast. The sows
35 that were studied gained between 12-140 pounds over two months. Together they averaged about 1.2 pounds a day and only 0.08 pounds of fat a day. During this early summer period the bears are working to gain more muscle than fat. The late summer season is when
40 researchers begin to see more fat gain per day. The salmon season, which runs from July through October, provides a fat-rich food source for the bears. And the salmon season is well-timed for the bears, because the

bigger you get, the more weight and energy you spend
45 to carry that weight around.

    While sows are watched for health of the bear populations, the reason researchers pick females may be a little simpler than that. Throughout the summer as the bears continue to grow, the GPS collars are
50 carefully placed so they won't infringe on the bears movement or growth. Quite often when a bear wakes up and doesn't like the collar, they slide it off within the first two hours. Usually the bears that do that are the males. Temperament may be a key reason researchers
55 pick females over males.

Figure 1
Spring-Summer Weight Gain
2015 and 2016 Changing Tides Project

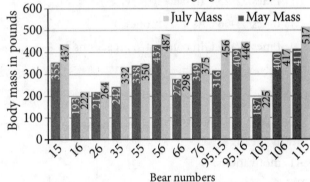

Adapted from The Second X Chromosome by Kaitlyn Kunce. National Parks Service.

Figure 2
Assimilated Body Composition–Bear 035, Bear 105

	Pre-Salmon Foraging Season			
		May 2015	July 2015	Gain/Day
Bear 035	Mass total	242 lbs	332 lbs	2.1 lbs
	Body Fat %	13%	20%	
	Salmon Foraging Season			
		July 2015	Oct 2015	Gain/Day
	Mass total	332 lbs	471 lbs	1.4 lbs
	Body Fat %	20%	39%	
	Pre-Salmon Foraging Season			
		May 2015	July 2015	Gain/Day
Bear 105	Mass total	187 lbs	225 lbs	0.9 lbs
	Body Fat %	2%	7%	
	Salmon Foraging Season			
		July 2015	Oct 2015	Gain/Day
	Mass total	225 lbs	357 lbs	1.4 lbs
	Body Fat %	7%	38%	

Adapted from "Changing Tides – More Questions Than Answers" by Kaitlyn Kunce. National Parks Service

CONTINUE

43

In the first paragraph (lines 1–17), what do the authors claim to be an important concern when selecting bears for the study?

A) The age of a bear's cubs

B) The year of the study

C) The number of bear cubs

D) The accessibility of the area

44

The author's use of the words "double" and "exclusively" in lines 25–26 in the second paragraph functions mainly to

A) underscore the need for sows to find high-quality sources of food during the summer months.

B) provide evidence against the claim that bear cubs double their weight every two months.

C) suggest an explanation for the timing of bears' hibernation during winter months.

D) reinforce the importance of monitoring female bears in order to determine the health of wild bear populations.

45

The author's main purpose of including the information about the Katmai coastal areas is to

A) present the reasoning that led the researchers to choose to study bears in this area.

B) provide an additional argument in favor of studying female rather than male bears.

C) establish that female bears gain more weight in muscle than fat in the summer months.

D) suggest an alternative location more productive for studying bears.

46

A student claims that sows gain weight only during the late summer and fall in preparation for hibernation. Which of the following statements in the passage contradicts the student's claim?

A) Lines 21–24 ("Although . . . cubs")

B) Lines 34–36 ("The sows . . . months")

C) Lines 37–39 ("During . . . fat")

D) Lines 40–42 ("The salmon . . . bears")

47

Based on the passage, the author's statement "the bigger you get, the more weight and energy you spend to carry that weight around" (lines 43-45) implies that a bear

A) requires more energy to catch salmon than to forage for food.

B) mostly gains muscle rather than fat when putting on weight in the early summer months.

C) gains an advantage by putting on more weight during late summer than during early summer.

D) should prioritize eating fatty foods during the months when it is also nourishing cubs.

48

The authors use the word "temperament" in line 54 to indicate that

A) the behavior of male bears accounts in part for researchers' selection of study subjects.

B) researchers study only female bears to avoid the need for locks on the bears' tracking collars.

C) female bears do not often engage in aggressive behavior toward researchers.

D) tracking collars restrict the movements of male bears more significantly than those of females.

CONTINUE

49

Based on figure 2, is the percentage of body fat gained between July and October greater or less than the percentage gained between May and July, and which statement made by the authors is most consistent with that data?

A) Less; "During . . . months" (lines 24–25)

B) Less; "Looking . . . coast" (lines 32–34)

C) Greater; "Together . . . day" (lines 36–37)

D) Greater; "The late . . . day" (lines 39–40)

50

Based on figure 1 and the passage, which choice gives the lowest body mass of a bear measured in July of 2015?

A) 187 pounds

B) 193 pounds

C) 222 pounds

D) 225 pounds

51

Do the data in figure 1 support the author's claim about weight gain among bears in the early summer months?

A) Yes, because for the bears included in the chart, the smallest weight gain was less than 12 pounds, and the largest weight gain was greater than 140 pounds.

B) Yes, because for the bears included in the chart, the smallest weight gain between May and July was 12 pounds, and the largest weight gain was 140 pounds.

C) No, because for the bears included in the chart, the smallest weight gain was less than 12 pounds, and the largest weight gain was greater than 140 pounds.

D) No, because for the bears included in the chart, the smallest weight gain between May and July was 12 pounds, and the largest weight gain was 140 pounds.

52

According to the graph, which of the following pieces of data provide evidence in support of the previous question?

A) Bears 15 and 55

B) Bears 15 and 95.15

C) Bears 55 and 95.15

D) Bears 95.15 and 115

STOP

If you finish before time is called, you may check your work on this section only.
Do not turn to any other section in the test.

No Test Material On This Page

Writing and Language Test

35 MINUTES, 44 QUESTIONS

Turn to Section 2 of your answer sheet to answer the questions in this section.

DIRECTIONS

Each passage below is accompanied by a number of questions. For some questions, you will consider how the passage might be revised to improve the expression of ideas. For other questions, you will consider how the passage might be edited to correct errors in sentence structure, usage, or punctuation. A passage or a question may be accompanied by one or more graphics (such as a table or graph) that you will consider as you make revising and editing decisions.

Some questions will direct you to an underlined portion of a passage. Other questions will direct you to a location in a passage or ask you to think about the passage as a whole.

After reading each passage, choose the answer to each question that most effectively improves the quality of writing in the passage or that makes the passage conform to the conventions of standard written English. Many questions include a "NO CHANGE" option. Choose that option if you think the best choice is to leave the relevant portion of the passage as it is.

Questions 1–11 are based on the following passage.

"Made-Up" Science

When we hear about the opinions of "ten scientists" or "ten dentists," or we hear that things are "clinically proven" or "lab-tested," for **1** example, and we might expect to be reading scientific journals. However, these phrases and statistics are well-known outside of scientific circles because they are so commonly used in a less likely place: advertising. It's not enough for, say, a shampoo to promise clean hair: it seems the only way to sell shampoo is **2** by lowering the price and offering special deals and coupons.

1
A) NO CHANGE
B) example, consequently we
C) example: we
D) example, we

2
Which provides the most relevant detail?
A) NO CHANGE
B) to merge into larger corporations and reduce the number of shampoo brands.
C) by comparing the product to other products customers buy more regularly.
D) to promise 40% more volume and bounce or 60% fewer split ends than other brands.

CONTINUE ▶

These claims are part of what has been called, since 1961, "cosmeutical" science. The word itself combines "cosmetics" and "pharmaceutical." Since the term was coined in 1961, cosmetics companies have been under more pressure to innovate, as competition grows and markets expand outside the United States. This pressure has led to an increased reliance on scientific data as a way to back up the advertisers' claims.

[1] But where exactly do these claims come from? [2] However, if these claims seem absurd at times, it's because they may come from nowhere at all. [3] A recent study of these scientific claims appears in the *Journal of Global Fashion Marketing*. [4] In this study, the researchers looked at over 300 advertisements from fashion magazines like *Elle*, **3** *Vogue*, and *Vanity Fair*. [5] The obvious answer would seem to be "the lab." **4**

To anyone who has ever **5** believed the truth-value of these advertisements (or of advertisements in general), the researchers' findings are probably not surprising. The researchers found that a mere 18% of the claims made in these advertisements were true. 23% of the claims were classified as "outright lies." **6** 42% were considered too vague to classify.

3

A) NO CHANGE
B) *Vogue* and,
C) *Vogue*; and
D) *Vogue*: and

4

To make this paragraph most logical, sentence 5 should be placed
A) where it is now.
B) before sentence 2.
C) before sentence 3.
D) before sentence 4.

5

A) NO CHANGE
B) pondered
C) questioned
D) skepticized

6

The writer is considering deleting the underlined portion. Should the writer do this?
A) No, because it demonstrates the most surprising of the researchers' findings.
B) No, because it completes the discussion of the data and is mentioned again in the passage.
C) Yes, because it is a reminder of how subjective the researchers' study truly was.
D) Yes, because the reader could deduce this information through simple mathematics.

CONTINUE →

These findings are good for a laugh, but [7] they may have more serious implications as well. Although everyone knows that the Food and Drug Administration can [8] reign what goes *into* food and drugs, what is less known is that the FDA can also punish false advertising claims. That sizable 23% that is telling "outright lies" may have a federal agency investigating its claims, and these investigations [9] might have resulted in significant fines and lawsuits.

While this has obvious ramifications for the "outright lies," what can the FDA do [10] from that much larger share of "too vague" claims? These may be safe for the simple reason that they are too vague to be disproven. Whatever the FDA may decide to do, this research should still remind consumers about the potential perils of trusting the word of advertisers. [11] Thus, the claims are often harmless, but consumers want to believe that they are giving their hard-earned money to trustworthy organizations.

7
A) NO CHANGE
B) will have
C) may have
D) might be having

8
A) NO CHANGE
B) regulate
C) name
D) administrate

9
A) NO CHANGE
B) have resulted in significant fine's
C) may result in significant fines
D) may result in significant fine's

10
A) NO CHANGE
B) to
C) by
D) with

11
A) NO CHANGE
B) On the other hand,
C) True,
D) Nevertheless,

CONTINUE

Questions 12–22 are based on the following passage and supplementary material.

Gerry's Salamander

The United States is often lauded for its contributions to democracy in the world. When the process is allowed to work, democracy in the United States is truly admirable, and all of those who vote can feel that they are participating in the process in a significant way. **12** This being the case, there are some abnormalities in the history of U.S. elections that fall short of these expectations.

[1] One notable instance came in a state senate election in Massachusetts in 1812. [2] Unfortunately, it was not the last. [3] Shortly before this election, Elbridge **13** Gerry, then governor of the state, called for a redistricting that was supposed to reflect demographic shifts within the city. [4] To anyone paying attention, however, it **14** will become clear that this redistricting would benefit Gerry's own party, the Democratic-Republicans. [5] It was one of the first and most infamous works of political trickery in the history of the country. **15**

12

A) NO CHANGE
B) Happily,
C) Politically,
D) Unfortunately,

13

A) NO CHANGE
B) Gerry then governor of the state,
C) Gerry, then governor of the state
D) Gerry, then governor, of the state

14

A) NO CHANGE
B) would have become
C) became
D) becomes

15

To make this paragraph most logical, sentence 2 should be placed
A) where it is now.
B) after sentence 3.
C) after sentence 4.
D) after sentence 5.

CONTINUE

Gerry's tactics gave birth to a new term. The *Boston Gazette* poked fun at Gerry's redistricting 16 plan. This newspaper said that the newly created South Essex electoral district resembled a salamander on the map. This image, combined with the governor's name, came to be known by a very specific 17 name: gerrymandering. The practice unfortunately continues to be a tool of political manipulation to this day.

Particularly on the state and local levels, gerrymandering can have a tremendous influence on the outcome of an election. As the below graphic shows, gerrymandering can turn 18 voters against some of the legislative bodies in their state. In a population of 50 people, in which voting blocs lived in contained areas, different districting can result in vastly different outcomes, even where there is a clear advantage for one party. In the redistricting shown below, 19 40% light gray voters can become 60% dark gray districts through the careful manipulation of the districts.

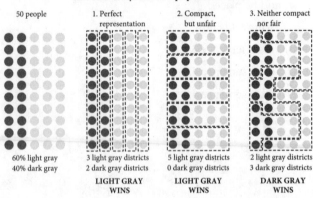

Gerrymandering, explained
Three different ways to divide 50 people into five districts

16
Which choice most effectively combines the two sentences at the underlined portion?
A) plan, when the paper said
B) plan, at which time the paper said
C) plan, saying
D) plan and they said

17
A) NO CHANGE
B) name: which was
C) name;
D) name. And it was

18
Which choice best completes the description of the purpose of gerrymandering?
A) NO CHANGE
B) a series of political factions against one another.
C) elections into long processes with delayed results.
D) electoral disadvantages into electoral advantages.

19
Which choice most accurately and effectively represents information in the figure?
A) NO CHANGE
B) 60% dark gray voters can become 60% light gray districts.
C) 40% light gray voters can become 100% dark gray districts.
D) 60% light gray voters can become 60% dark gray districts.

CONTINUE ➡

Gerrymandering almost always benefits the parties in [20] power, not those out of power, because those are the parties that have the influence necessary to redistrict. Many perfectly viable candidates have been shut out by cruel and unfair districting practices. In this and in other political arenas, it is much easier to stay in power than to gain power.

The real victims of gerrymandering, however, are the voters. The process is used quite often to disenfranchise certain voters by making [21] they're votes less valuable. In "majority-minority" districts in particular, districts with large non-white populations, gerrymandering can discount the importance of particular races or classes of voters, many [22] of whose voting interests may go against those in power. The American voting system works, but only when all voters are given an equal say in the outcome of an election.

20

A) NO CHANGE
B) power usually,
C) power
D) power for the good

21

A) NO CHANGE
B) their
C) there
D) they are

22

A) NO CHANGE
B) voters'
C) of their
D) DELETE the underlined portion.

CONTINUE

Questions 23–33 are based on the following passage and supplementary material.

The Original Condition

If you've ever been to an art museum, you know the basic layout: long hallways and large rooms with paintings hung a few feet apart. You know how the paintings are **23** by certain means marked, and you know that the paintings have been arranged chronologically or thematically.

There's one thing, however, which you've definitely noticed even if you can't quite articulate it. Particularly when looking at old paintings, **24** paintings all have that vividly *new* look, whether they were painted in 1950 or 1450. Even where the subject matter is older, the colors are vibrant, and you're never forced to wonder exactly what the painting must have looked like in its original state. **25** The history of painting is nearly as long as the history of mankind.

23

A) NO CHANGE
B) marked,
C) being marked in a way,
D) by so means of marking,

24

A) NO CHANGE
B) you've surely noticed how *new* all the paintings look,
C) noticing the *new* look of all the paintings is something you can do,
D) the paintings always strike you as very *new* looking,

25

The writer is considering deleting the underlined sentence. Should the sentence be kept or deleted?

A) Deleted, because it strays from the paragraph's major focus by introducing an irrelevant fact.
B) Deleted, because it restates a historical detail that is provided in a later paragraph.
C) Kept, because it is a useful introduction to the topic of this paragraph.
D) Kept, because it provides a humorous anecdote regarding the work of art restorers.

CONTINUE

This incredible feat is the work of a highly specialized group: art restorers. Despite this specialization, the profession has exploded in recent years. **26** Art restoration has been growing steadily since 1930. While the job of an art restorer may seem fairly straightforward **27** when looking, the job is in fact quite complicated. Sometimes, as in the case of Michelangelo's famous sculpture *David*, the cleaning and restoration of artworks is a simple **28** matter, applying chemicals, washing away grime, and scrubbing off the dirt.

26

At this point, the writer wants to add specific information that is consistent with the focus of the paragraph.

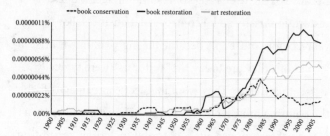

PERCENTAGE OF AMERICAN WORKFORCE IN 3 FIELDS

Which choice most effectively provides a sentence with relevant and accurate information from the graph above?

A) NO CHANGE

B) The number of book restorers who became art restorers tripled in 2000.

C) By the year 2030, it is predicted that art restoration will even eclipse art conservation.

D) From 1970 to 2005, the percentage of people working in art restoration has roughly tripled.

27

A) NO CHANGE

B) beholden,

C) at first glance,

D) under your gaze,

28

A) NO CHANGE

B) matter

C) matter:

D) matter;

CONTINUE

29 With most paintings, however, the process is a good deal more involved because it is not necessarily just a matter of "cleaning" the older paintings. One cannot merely take a scrub brush to a centuries-old great work. Because of the wide range of restoration techniques, art restoration itself can be controversial business. For many years, before museums became the high-volume tourist attractions they are today, art "restorers" were typically artists themselves. They would project some image of what the painting must have looked like originally and apply a variety of techniques, up **30** to and including: repainting, to preserve this "original."

[1] Now, however, more attention is paid to the historical quality of the artworks. [2] Some art historians **31** who is writing today even go so far as to say that dirt and grime themselves are parts of the historical fabric of a painting and thus should be left in. [3] Others argue that the purity of the painting is all that matters. [4] They will restore the original look of a painting, even if that means "fixing" the painting by some non-paint means. **32**

Whatever methods they use, art restorers are more needed **33** for ever, but their work is also less permanent. In order to retain the integrity of the artwork in case the restorers make a mistake, all restoration must now be reversible, a reminder that art "history" is very much a thing of the present and the future.

29

A) NO CHANGE
B) Anyway,
C) In this sense,
D) Alongside cleaning,

30

A) NO CHANGE
B) to, and including,
C) to and including
D) to, and including:

31

A) NO CHANGE
B) who are
C) whom is
D) whom are

32

The writer wants to add the following sentence to the paragraph.

> For example, a recent restoration at Harvard's Art Museums involved precisely calibrated lights that would correct the color damage to a series of murals done by Mark Rothko in the 1960s.

The best placement for the sentence is immediately

A) after sentence 1.
B) after sentence 2.
C) after sentence 3.
D) after sentence 4.

33

A) NO CHANGE
B) by
C) what
D) than

CONTINUE

Questions 34–44 are based on the following passage.

The Rise of *Hyperion*

Literary critics have always paid the most attention to "serious" authors. The great authors of recent memory, especially in American literature, have been distinctly "literary" authors: Toni Morrison, Philip Roth, Thomas Pynchon, and Jonathan Franzen. Often overlooked in this pantheon of great authors are the contributions of authors in non-traditional [34] modes. Specifically overlooked is the genre of science fiction. In some ways, the novel that has hearkened back to the great authors of the Victorian nineteenth century is not Morrison's *Beloved* or Roth's *American Pastoral* but *Hyperion* by Dan Simmons.

Simmons's novel was published in 1989, and it won the Hugo Award for best science-fiction novel that year. [35] All things considered, it is regularly listed among the greatest science-fiction novels of all time. The novel [36] that spawned a series of novels dealing with the same fantastic universe, the first of which was *The Fall of Hyperion*, published in 1990. *Hyperion* tells the story of seven pilgrims who travel to the distant world of Hyperion in an attempt to avert a galaxy-wide war between hostile factions. Because the pilgrims are [37] not sure in a complete way why they've been recruited for this

---

34

Which choice most effectively combines the sentences at the underlined portion?

A) modes, which notably include

B) modes, and overlooked in particular is

C) modes, specifically

D) modes, and one genre suffering neglect is

35

A) NO CHANGE

B) For all that,

C) To this day,

D) Check this out,

36

A) NO CHANGE

B) which,

C) is that which

D) DELETE the underlined portion.

37

A) NO CHANGE

B) not sure in their entirety

C) not entirely sure

D) lacking a complete sureness

CONTINUE ➡

"pilgrimage," they spend the long journey to Hyperion sharing **38** your stories, each of which illuminates the journey **39** while explaining this new fantasy world to the reader.

If this structure **40** of sound familiar, that's because it draws on some of the great classics of literature, most notably *The Canterbury Tales*, which itself is a kind of travel narrative, as it follows **41** pilgrims travel together to the Canterbury Cathedral.

38

A) NO CHANGE
B) their
C) our
D) everyone's

39

A) NO CHANGE
B) when
C) though
D) as if

40

A) NO CHANGE
B) and sounding
C) sounding
D) sounds

41

A) NO CHANGE
B) pilgrim's travels
C) pilgrim's traveling
D) pilgrims traveling

CONTINUE ➡

The name of the novel draws on a long literary history as well: poems by John Keats and novels by Friedrich Hölderlin and Henry Wadsworth Longfellow. **42** With all of these literary tributes, if great works of literature are expressions of, as T.S. Eliot says, "tradition and the individual talent," then *Hyperion* is certainly a great work. **43**

In addition to its incredible achievements in terms of literary history, *Hyperion* is also a truly incredible work of science fiction. The future world it imagines is vivid, and its continuities with the contemporary world **44** is clearly defined. *Hyperion* is awash in literary laurels, but it is also an entertaining novel—quite a combination!

The fact that *Hyperion* is not as well known as some of the more accepted "classics" should make us wonder what we mean by this term "classics." We should also wonder what else we've been missing because it hasn't met our traditional criteria for greatness.

42

Which choice most effectively sets up the information that follows?

A) Dan Simmons must have studied the poems and essays of T.S. Eliot at some point in his life.

B) Even beyond these nominal debts, *Hyperion* pays homage to countless genres, including the war story and the detective novel.

C) But don't worry, there are still plenty of lasers and spaceships in the book, too.

D) Although the critics of the early twentieth century probably would've loved it, many of them died before *Hyperion* was published.

43

At this point, the writer is considering adding the following sentence.

> Some of T.S. Eliot's most famous poems are *The Waste Land* and "The Love Song of J. Alfred Prufrock."

Should the writer make this addition here?

A) Yes, because it helps to put the literary quality of *Hyperion* into its appropriate context.

B) Yes, because it names another series of works that are overlooked for being non-traditional.

C) No, because it introduces a new set of information that does not have a clear link to the rest of the passage.

D) No, because it disagrees with the passage's central claim that *Hyperion* is the greatest work of science fiction.

44

A) NO CHANGE

B) has been

C) being

D) are

STOP
If you finish before time is called, you may check your work on this section only.
Do not turn to any other section in the test.

Math Test – No Calculator

25 MINUTES, 20 QUESTIONS

Turn to Section 3 of your answer sheet to answer the questions in this section.

DIRECTIONS

For questions 1–15, solve each problem, choose the best answer from the choices provided, and fill in the corresponding circle on your answer sheet. **For questions 16–20,** solve the problem and enter your answer in the grid on the answer sheet. Please refer to the directions before question 16 on how to enter your answers in the grid. You may use any available space in your test booklet for scratch work.

NOTES

1. The use of a calculator **is not permitted**.
2. All variables and expressions used represent real numbers unless otherwise indicated.
3. Figures provided in this test are drawn to scale unless otherwise indicated.
4. All figures lie in a plane unless otherwise indicated.
5. Unless otherwise indicated, the domain of a given function f is the set of all real numbers x for which $f(x)$ is a real number.

REFERENCE

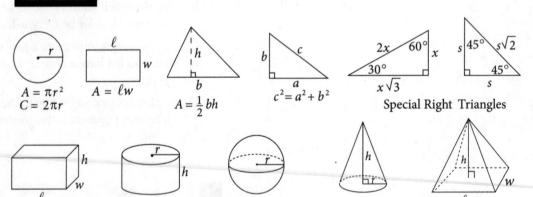

$A = \pi r^2$
$C = 2\pi r$

$A = \ell w$

$A = \frac{1}{2} bh$

$c^2 = a^2 + b^2$

Special Right Triangles

$V = \ell wh$

$V = \pi r^2 h$

$V = \frac{4}{3}\pi r^3$

$V = \frac{1}{3}\pi r^2 h$

$V = \frac{1}{3}\ell wh$

The number of degrees of arc in a circle is 360.
The number of radians of arc in a circle is 2π.
The sum of the measures in degrees of the angles of a triangle is 180.

CONTINUE ➤

1

During a certain week, Jan worked j hours each day for 3 days, and Noah worked n hours each day for 5 days. Which of the following represents the total combined number of hours worked that week by Jan and Noah?

A) $3j + 5n$

B) $5j + 3n$

C) $8jn$

D) $15jn$

2

If $\dfrac{y + 2}{5} = c$ and $c = 4$, what is the value of y?

A) 16

B) 18

C) 20

D) 22

3

For $i = \sqrt{-1}$, what is the sum $(10 - 4i) + (3 + 6i)$?

A) $13 - 10i$

B) $13 + 2i$

C) $7 - 10i$

D) $7 + 2i$

4

$$(ab^2 + 4a^2 + 6a^2b^2) - (-ab^2 + 2a^2b^2 + 4a^2)$$

Which of the following is equivalent to the expression above?

A) $-2a^2b^2$

B) $-2a^2b^2 + 8a^2$

C) $2ab^2 - 2a^2b^2 + 8a^2$

D) $2ab^2 + 4a^2b^2$

CONTINUE

5

$$w = 3,150 + 450l$$

A marine biologist uses the equation above to estimate the weight, w, of a mature great white shark, in pounds, in terms of the shark's fork length, l, in feet. Based on the equation, what is the estimated weight increase, in pounds, for each foot of growth in fork length in a great white shark?

A) 3,150

B) 2,700

C) 1,350

D) 450

6

Juan is a book editor who is given a book to edit. The number of pages that he has left to edit at the end of each hour is estimated by the equation $P = 326 - 12h$, where h represents the number of hours spent editing the book. What is the meaning of the value 326 in this equation?

A) Juan edits pages at a rate of 326 per day.

B) Juan edits pages at a rate of 326 per hour.

C) Juan is given a total of 326 pages to edit.

D) Juan will finish editing the book in 326 hours.

7

If $\dfrac{x}{y} = 3$, what is the value of $\dfrac{12y}{x}$?

A) 4

B) 6

C) 8

D) 12

8

$$2y + x = -17$$
$$5x - 4y = -15$$

What is the solution (x, y) to the system of equations shown above?

A) (−7, −5)

B) (−4, −1)

C) (−3, 0)

D) (5, −11)

CONTINUE

9

$$c = \frac{\dfrac{r}{1,200}}{1 - \left(1 + \dfrac{r}{1,200}\right)^{-N}} M$$

In order to buy a house, a couple takes on a mortgage of M dollars at an annual rate of r percent to be paid off over N months. If the equation above is used to determine the monthly payment, c, that the couple needs to make to pay off the loan, which of the following expressions gives the value of M, in terms of c, r, and N?

A) $M = \left(\dfrac{r}{1,200}\right)c$

B) $M = \left(\dfrac{1,200}{r}\right)c$

C) $M = \dfrac{1 - \left(1 + \dfrac{r}{1,200}\right)^{-N}}{\dfrac{r}{1,200}}c$

D) $M = \dfrac{\dfrac{r}{1,200}}{1 - \left(1 + \dfrac{r}{1,200}\right)^{-N}}c$

10

A line in the xy-plane has a slope of $\dfrac{2}{3}$ and passes through the origin. Which of the following points lies on the line?

A) $\left(0, \dfrac{2}{3}\right)$

B) $(2, 3)$

C) $(6, 4)$

D) $(9, 4)$

11

$$f(x) = cx^2 + 30$$

For the function f defined above, c is a constant and $f(3) = 12$. What is the value of $f(-3)$?

A) -12

B) -2

C) 0

D) 12

CONTINUE

12

$$A = 240 - 20w$$

$$B = 320 - 30w$$

In the equations above, A and B represent the price per night for a room in Hotel A and Hotel B, respectively, w weeks after September 1 last autumn. What was the price per night in Hotel A when it was equal to the price per night in Hotel B?

A) $80

B) $160

C) $180

D) $220

13

If $a - 4b = 18$, what is the value of $\dfrac{3^a}{81^b}$?

A) 81^2

B) 9^6

C) 3^{18}

D) The value cannot be determined from the information given.

14

If $(ax + 3)(bx + 5) = 35x^2 + kx + 15$ for all values of x, and $a + b = 12$, what are the two possible values for k ?

A) 46 and 50

B) 15 and 35

C) 21 and 25

D) 5 and 7

15

If $y > 5$, which of the following is equivalent to

$$\dfrac{1}{\dfrac{1}{y - 4} + \dfrac{1}{y - 3}} ?$$

A) $2y - 7$

B) $y^2 - 7y + 12$

C) $\dfrac{y^2 - 7y + 12}{2y - 7}$

D) $\dfrac{2y - 7}{y^2 - 7y + 12}$

CONTINUE

DIRECTIONS

For questions 16–20, solve the problem and enter your answer in the grid, as described below, on the answer sheet.

1. Although not required, it is suggested that you write your answer in the boxes at the top of the columns to help you fill in the circles accurately. You will receive credit only if the circles are filled in correctly.

2. Mark no more than one circle in any column.

3. No question has a negative answer.

4. Some problems may have more than one correct answer. In such cases, grid only one answer.

5. **Mixed numbers** such as $3\frac{1}{2}$ must be gridded as 3.5 or 7/2. (If  is entered into the grid, it will be interpreted as $\frac{31}{2}$, not as $3\frac{1}{2}$.)

6. **Decimal Answers:** If you obtain a decimal answer with more digits than the grid can accommodate, it may be either rounded or truncated, but it must fill the entire grid.

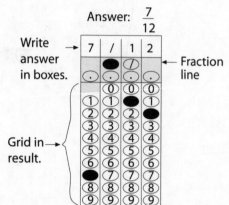

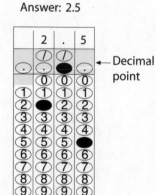

Acceptable ways to grid $\frac{2}{3}$ are:

Answer: 201 – either position is correct

NOTE: You may start your answers in any column, space permitting. Columns you don't need to use should be left blank.

CONTINUE ➡

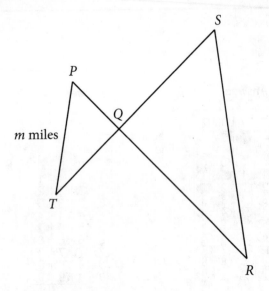

In a certain park, the layout of the six bicycle paths is shown in the figure above. The lengths of $\overline{PQ}$, $\overline{QT}$, $\overline{QS}$, and $\overline{SR}$ are 3 miles, 4 miles, 8 miles, and 10 miles, respectively. Paths $\overline{PR}$ and $\overline{ST}$ intersect at point Q, and $\angle TPQ$ is congruent to $\angle QRS$. What is the value of m ?

If $y > 0$ and $y^2 - 36 = 0$, what is the value of y ?

In a right triangle, one angle measures $d°$, where $\cos d° = \dfrac{5}{13}$. What is $\sin(90° - d°)$?

CONTINUE

19

If $c = 3\sqrt{5}$ and $5c = \sqrt{5z}$, what is the value of z?

20

$$a + b = -10$$
$$2a + b = -33$$

What is the value of b in the system of equations shown above?

STOP

If you finish before time is called, you may check your work on this section only.
Do not turn to any other section in the test.

Math Test – Calculator

55 MINUTES, 38 QUESTIONS

Turn to Section 4 of your answer sheet to answer the questions in this section.

DIRECTIONS

For questions 1–30, solve each problem, choose the best answer from the choices provided, and fill in the corresponding circle on your answer sheet. **For questions 31–38,** solve the problem and enter your answer in the grid on the answer sheet. Please refer to the directions before question 31 on how to enter your answers in the grid. You may use any available space in your test booklet for scratch work.

NOTES

1. The use of a calculator **is permitted**.
2. All variables and expressions used represent real numbers unless otherwise indicated.
3. Figures provided in this test are drawn to scale unless otherwise indicated.
4. All figures lie in a plane unless otherwise indicated.
5. Unless otherwise indicated, the domain of a given function f is the set of all real numbers x for which $f(x)$ is a real number.

REFERENCE

$A = \pi r^2$
$C = 2\pi r$

$A = \ell w$

$A = \frac{1}{2}bh$

$c^2 = a^2 + b^2$

Special Right Triangles

$V = \ell wh$

$V = \pi r^2 h$

$V = \frac{4}{3}\pi r^3$

$V = \frac{1}{3}\pi r^2 h$

$V = \frac{1}{3}\ell wh$

The number of degrees of arc in a circle is 360.
The number of radians of arc in a circle is 2π.
The sum of the measures in degrees of the angles of a triangle is 180.

CONTINUE

1

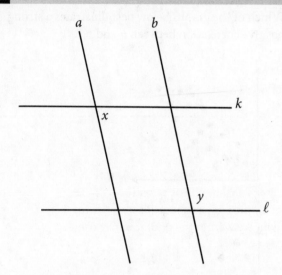

In the figure shown above, lines *a* and *b* are parallel and lines *k* and *ℓ* are parallel. If the measure of ∠*x* is 75°, what is the measure of ∠*y* ?

A)   15°

B)   75°

C)   105°

D)   165°

2

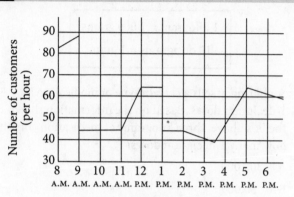

The graph above shows the number of customers per hour at a coffee shop. Over which of the following intervals is the number of customers strictly decreasing then strictly increasing?

A) From 9 A.M. to 12 P.M.

B) From 12 P.M. to 2 P.M.

C) From 2 P.M. to 5 P.M.

D) From 3:30 P.M. to 6:30 P.M.

3

If $y = \dfrac{x}{k}$, where *k* is a constant, and *y* = 5 when *x* = 30, what is the value of *y* when *x* = 42 ?

A)   6

B)   7

C)   10

D)   17

CONTINUE

4

1 kilogram = 1,000 grams

10 decigrams = 1 gram

A pharmacy sells a certain type of medication in 1-decigram doses. Based on the information shown in the box above, three kilograms of medication contain how many 1-decigram doses?

A) 300,000

B) 30,000

C) 3,000

D) 300

5

If $6x - 4$ is 11 less than 25, what is the value of $9x$?

A) 3

B) 8

C) 18

D) 27

6

Which of the graphs below best illustrates a strong positive correlation between h and p ?

A)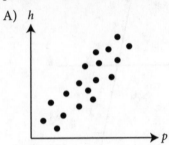

B)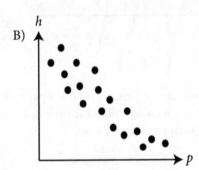

C)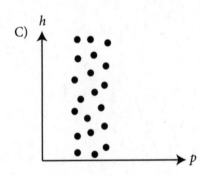

D)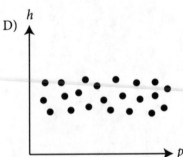

CONTINUE

Questions 7 and 8 refer to the following information.

$$p = 101 + 10.094d$$

The total pressure on an object submerged in the ocean depends on the depth of the object beneath the surface. The formula above shows the relationship between p, pressure, in kilopascals, and d, depth, in meters.

7

At which of the following depths will the total pressure be closest to 200 kilopascals?

A) 8 meters

B) 9 meters

C) 10 meters

D) 11 meters

8

Which of the following formulas expresses depth in terms of pressure?

A) $d = \dfrac{p}{10.094} - 101$

B) $d = \dfrac{10.094}{101 - p}$

C) $d = \dfrac{p + 101}{10.094}$

D) $d = \dfrac{p - 101}{10.094}$

9

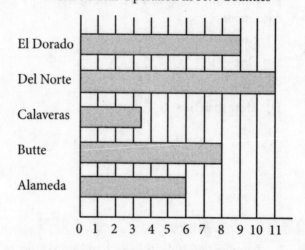

Wind Turbine Operation in Five Counties

The number of wind turbines in use in five counties is shown in the graph above. If there are a total of 3,750 wind turbines operating in these five counties, which of the following is an appropriate label for the horizontal axis of the graph?

A) Number of wind turbines (in tens)

B) Number of wind turbines (in hundreds)

C) Number of wind turbines (in thousands)

D) Number of wind turbines (in tens of thousands)

CONTINUE

10

For how many values of k is it true that $|k - 3| + 2$ is equal to one?

A) None

B) One

C) Two

D) More than two

11

Number of Residents in Each of 14 Apartments

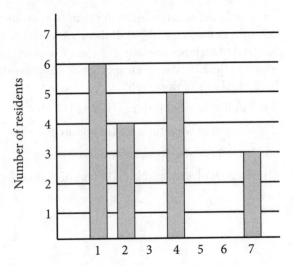

Number of apartments

According to the histogram shown above, which of the following is closest to the average (arithmetic mean) number of residents per apartment?

A) 3

B) 3.25

C) 3.5

D) 4

12

Which of the following integers CANNOT be a solution to the inequality $6x - 4 \leq 7x - 3$?

A) 1

B) 0

C) –1

D) –2

13

Weights of potatoes (in ounces)								
2	3	3	4	4	4	5	5	6
6	7	7	7	7	8	8	9	9

An agriculture class harvested 18 potatoes from the school garden and compiled the weights of the potatoes in the table above. If the 2-ounce measurement is removed from the data, which of the following statistical measures of the values listed will change the least?

A) The mean

B) The median

C) The range

D) The total

CONTINUE

14

$$p + x > y$$
$$r - x < -y$$

In the xy-plane, $(2, 2)$ is a solution to the system of inequalities shown above. Which of the following must be true about p and r?

A) $p < r$

B) $r < p$

C) $p + r = 0$

D) $|p| = |r|$

15

Political Party				
	Liberal	Conservative	Independent	Total
Men	59	74	62	195
Women	82	63	55	200
Total	141	137	117	395

A group of voters in country X responded to a poll that asked which political party they planned to vote for. The table above shows the results of the polling data. Which of the categories below accounts for approximately 15 percent of all poll respondents?

A) Men voting Liberal

B) Men voting Independent

C) Women voting Conservative

D) Women voting Liberal

CONTINUE

Questions 16 and 17 refer to the following information.

Total Cost of Renting a Car by the Day

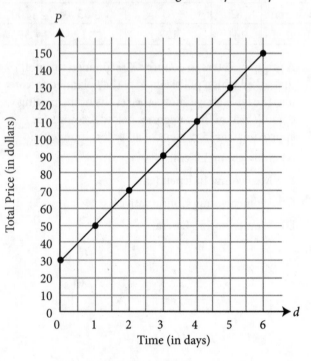

The graph above shows the total price P, in dollars, to rent a car for d days.

Which of the equations below shows the relationship between d and P?

A) $P = 25d$

B) $P = d + 30$

C) $P = 10d + 30$

D) $P = 20d + 30$

What does the slope of the graph represent?

A) The total number of cars rented

B) The initial cost of renting a car

C) The average increase in price to rent a car for each additional day

D) The total number of days for which a car is rented

CONTINUE

18

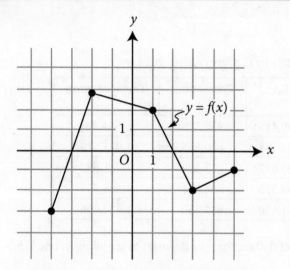

The figure above shows the complete graph of the function f in the xy-plane. For which of the following values of x is $f(x)$ at its maximum?

A) −4

B) −3

C) −2

D) 3

19

The price of a train ticket purchased in the train station or from a conductor is 15 percent less during off-peak hours than it is during peak hours. If a ticket is purchased from the conductor, an 11 percent surcharge is added to the price. Alec purchased a ticket from the conductor during off-peak hours and paid a total of t dollars. Which of the following, in terms of t, represents the price he would have paid if he had purchased the ticket in the train station during peak hours?

A) $\dfrac{t}{0.96}$

B) $0.96t$

C) $\dfrac{t}{(0.85)(1.11)}$

D) $(0.85)(1.11)t$

20

Number of Exercise Sessions per Week

	0–2	3–5	More than 5	Total
Group 1	13	22	15	50
Group 2	11	18	21	50
Total	24	40	36	100

The table above was compiled by a nutrition researcher studying how often people exercise when asked to keep a log of their exercise sessions. Group 1 was comprised of people who regularly eat snacks, and Group 2 was comprised of people who rarely eat snacks. If one person is randomly chosen from among those who exercise fewer than six times per week, what is the probability that this person belonged to Group 1 ?

A) $\dfrac{35}{64}$

B) $\dfrac{50}{64}$

C) $\dfrac{29}{100}$

D) $\dfrac{35}{100}$

21

A service station sells gasoline for $3.25 per gallon and diesel fuel for $3.00 per gallon. On Monday, the service station's revenue from selling a total of 131 gallons of gasoline and diesel fuel was $404.25. How many gallons of diesel fuel did the service station sell on Monday?

A) 35

B) 55

C) 76

D) 86

CONTINUE ➡

Questions 22 and 23 refer to the following information.

Total Budget Spending in One U.S. State by Category, 2010–2014

Year	K-12 education	Higher education	Public assistance	Medicaid	Corrections	Transportation
2014	3,635,265	3,099,112	29,450	2,990,415	930,525	1, 556,244
2013	3,677,428	2,734,615	45,873	3,005,188	820,855	1,873,618
2012	3,715,853	2,550,665	55,645	3,020,012	773,420	1,721,682
2011	3,747,921	2,309,789	54,321	2,984,375	694,011	1,388,904
2010	3,785,200	2,104,214	55,787	3,001,650	632,350	1,434,006

The table above summarizes annual spending, in thousands of dollars, for six categories of spending in one U.S. state, 2010–2014.

22

Of the following, which category's ratio of its 2010 spending to its 2014 spending is nearest to the higher-education category's ratio of its 2010 spending to its 2014 spending?

A) K-12 education

B) Medicaid

C) Corrections

D) Transportation

23

Which of the following is the best approximation of the average rate of change in spending on public assistance from 2012 to 2014 ?

A) $6,000,000

B) $10,000,000

C) $13,000,000

D) $26,000,000

24

A fish leaps vertically upward from the surface of a lake at an initial speed of 9 meters per second. The height h, in meters, of the fish above the surface of the water s seconds after it leaps is given by the equation $h = 9s - 4.9s^2$. Approximately how many seconds after the fish leaps will it hit the surface of the lake?

A) 2.0

B) 2.5

C) 3.0

D) 3.5

25

A circle in the xy-plane is centered at $(3, 0)$ and has a radius with endpoint $\left(1, \dfrac{8}{3}\right)$. Which of the following is an equation of the circle?

A) $(x - 3)^2 + y^2 = \dfrac{10}{3}$

B) $(x + 3)^2 + y^2 = \dfrac{10}{3}$

C) $(x - 3)^2 + y^2 = \dfrac{100}{9}$

D) $(x + 3)^2 + y^2 = \dfrac{100}{9}$

26

A square lawn has a length of 8 feet and a width of 8 feet. Eight researchers each examine a randomly chosen region of the field; all regions are square with length and width of one foot. The researchers count the number of seedlings in each region that have reached a height of at least 2 inches. The table below shows the resulting data.

Region	1	2	3	4
Number of seedlings	82	87	95	99
Region	5	6	7	8
Number of seedlings	102	106	111	115

Which of the following best approximates the number of seedlings that are at least 2 inches high on the entire lawn?

A)   80

B)   640

C)   800

D) 6,400

27

A zoologist is studying the reproduction rates of two different breeds of chinchillas in country Y. He discovered that the Eastern chinchillas in his study produced 30 percent more offspring than the Western chinchillas did. Based on the zoologist's observation, if the Eastern chinchillas in his study produced 143 offspring, how many offspring did the Western chinchillas produce?

A) 100

B) 103

C) 110

D) 186

CONTINUE

28

When polynomial $g(x)$ is divided by $x - 4$, the remainder is 3. Which of the following statements about $g(x)$ must be true?

A) $g(-4) = 3$

B) $g(4) = 3$

C) $x - 4$ is a factor of $g(x)$.

D) $x + 3$ is a factor of $g(x)$.

29

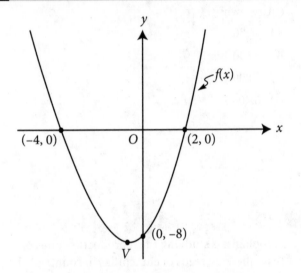

The figure above shows the graph in the xy-plane of the function $f(x) = x^2 + 2x - 8$. Which of the following is an equivalent form of the function f that includes the coordinates of vertex V as constants in the function?

A) $f(x) = (x + 1)^2 - 9$

B) $f(x) = x(x + 2) - 8$

C) $f(x) = (x - 2)(x + 4)$

D) $f(x) = (x + 2)(x - 4)$

30

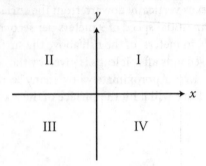

If the system of inequalities $y \geq x + 2$ and $y \geq \dfrac{1}{3}x - 1$ is graphed in the xy-plane shown above, how many quadrants will contain solutions to the system?

A) 4

B) 3

C) 2

D) 1

CONTINUE

DIRECTIONS

For questions 31–38, solve the problem and enter your answer in the grid, as described below, on the answer sheet.

1. Although not required, it is suggested that you write your answer in the boxes at the top of the columns to help you fill in the circles accurately. You will receive credit only if the circles are filled in correctly.

2. Mark no more than one circle in any column.

3. No question has a negative answer.

4. Some problems may have more than one correct answer. In such cases, grid only one answer.

5. **Mixed numbers** such as $3\frac{1}{2}$ must be gridded as 3.5 or 7/2. (If $\boxed{3\ 1\ /\ 2}$ is entered into the grid, it will be interpreted as $\frac{31}{2}$, not as $3\frac{1}{2}$.)

6. **Decimal Answers:** If you obtain a decimal answer with more digits than the grid can accommodate, it may be either rounded or truncated, but it must fill the entire grid.

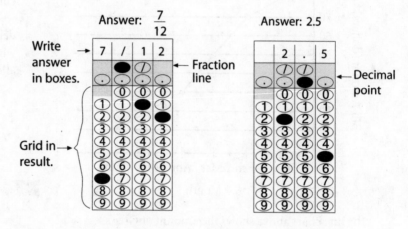

Answer: $\frac{7}{12}$ Answer: 2.5

Write answer in boxes. Fraction line. Grid in result. Decimal point

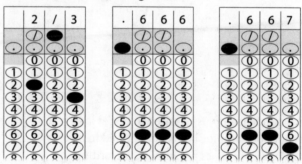

Acceptable ways to grid $\frac{2}{3}$ are:

Answer: 201 – either position is correct

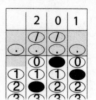 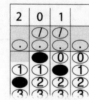

NOTE: You may start your answers in any column, space permitting. Columns you don't need to use should be left blank.

CONTINUE

31

Amount of Greg's Heating Bill Each Month from January to June

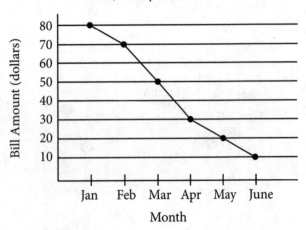

The line chart above shows the amount of Greg's monthly heating bill from January to June. The amount of his bill in April was what fraction of the amount of his bill in February?

32

A worker at a shoe factory is required to box at least 8 pairs of shoes per minute, but is not allowed to box more than 12 pairs of shoes per minute. According to this information, what is a possible amount of time, in minutes, that it could take the worker to box 168 pairs of shoes?

33

Safety regulations in a certain building require that the elevator not carry more than 1,600 pounds. A delivery driver will enter the elevator with a pallet containing a certain number of identical cartons that weigh 45 pounds each. If the combined weight of the delivery driver and the empty pallet is 250 pounds, what is the maximum number of cartons that will be allowed by the building's safety regulations?

34

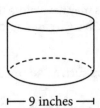

├── 9 inches ──┤

An aluminum can in the shape of a right circular cylinder has a <u>diameter</u> of 9 inches and a volume of 81π cubic inches. What is the height of the can, in inches?

CONTINUE ➡

35

For what value of x is the expression

$$\frac{2}{(x-6)^2 + 4(x-7) + 8}$$ undefined?

36

A train passes through the Appleton train station every 20 minutes. The first train each day passes through at 6:00 A.M., and the last train passes through at 10:40 P.M. How many trains pass through the Appleton station in one day?

Questions 37 and 38 refer to the following information.

Helene purchased a $50 savings bond, issued by city A, which earns interest that is compounded annually. She uses the expression $\$50(1.03)^t$ to find the value of the savings bond after t years.

37

What is the annual interest rate, expressed as a percentage, earned by the savings bond? (Disregard the percent sign when gridding in your answer.)

38

Helene's sister Carolyn purchased a $50 savings bond issued by city B. Carolyn's bond has an interest rate, compounded annually, that is 1 percent greater than the interest rate earned by Helene's bond. After 12 years, the value of Carolyn's bond will be how much greater than the value of Helene's bond? (Round your answer to the nearest cent and disregard the dollar sign when gridding in your answer.)

END OF TEST

DO NOT RETURN TO A PREVIOUS SECTION.

Completely darken bubbles with a No. 2 pencil. If you make a mistake, be sure to erase mark completely. Erase all stray marks.

1.

YOUR NAME: _____
(Print)   Last   First   M.I.

SIGNATURE: _____   DATE: __/__/__

HOME ADDRESS: _____
(Print)   Number and Street

_____
City   State   Zip Code

PHONE NO.: _____
(Print)

IMPORTANT: Please fill in these boxes exactly as shown on the back cover of your test book.

2. TEST FORM

6. DATE OF BIRTH

Month		Day		Year	
○ JAN					
○ FEB	⓪	⓪	⓪	⓪	
○ MAR	①	①	①	①	
○ APR	②	②	②	②	
○ MAY	③	③	③	③	
○ JUN		④	④	④	
○ JUL		⑤	⑤	⑤	
○ AUG		⑥	⑥	⑥	
○ SEP		⑦	⑦	⑦	
○ OCT		⑧	⑧	⑧	
○ NOV		⑨	⑨	⑨	
○ DEC					

3. TEST CODE

4. REGISTRATION NUMBER

⓪	Ⓐ	Ⓙ	⓪	⓪	⓪	⓪	⓪	⓪	⓪	⓪
①	Ⓑ	Ⓚ	①	①	①	①	①	①	①	①
②	Ⓒ	Ⓛ	②	②	②	②	②	②	②	②
③	Ⓓ	Ⓜ	③	③	③	③	③	③	③	③
④	Ⓔ	Ⓝ	④	④	④	④	④	④	④	④
⑤	Ⓕ	Ⓞ	⑤	⑤	⑤	⑤	⑤	⑤	⑤	⑤
⑥	Ⓖ	Ⓟ	⑥	⑥	⑥	⑥	⑥	⑥	⑥	⑥
⑦	Ⓗ	Ⓠ	⑦	⑦	⑦	⑦	⑦	⑦	⑦	⑦
⑧	Ⓘ	Ⓡ	⑧	⑧	⑧	⑧	⑧	⑧	⑧	⑧
⑨			⑨	⑨	⑨	⑨	⑨	⑨	⑨	⑨

7. SEX

○ MALE
○ FEMALE

The **Princeton Review**®

5. YOUR NAME

First 4 letters of last name				FIRST INIT	MID INIT
Ⓐ	Ⓐ	Ⓐ	Ⓐ	Ⓐ	Ⓐ
Ⓑ	Ⓑ	Ⓑ	Ⓑ	Ⓑ	Ⓑ
Ⓒ	Ⓒ	Ⓒ	Ⓒ	Ⓒ	Ⓒ
Ⓓ	Ⓓ	Ⓓ	Ⓓ	Ⓓ	Ⓓ
Ⓔ	Ⓔ	Ⓔ	Ⓔ	Ⓔ	Ⓔ
Ⓕ	Ⓕ	Ⓕ	Ⓕ	Ⓕ	Ⓕ
Ⓖ	Ⓖ	Ⓖ	Ⓖ	Ⓖ	Ⓖ
Ⓗ	Ⓗ	Ⓗ	Ⓗ	Ⓗ	Ⓗ
Ⓘ	Ⓘ	Ⓘ	Ⓘ	Ⓘ	Ⓘ
Ⓙ	Ⓙ	Ⓙ	Ⓙ	Ⓙ	Ⓙ
Ⓚ	Ⓚ	Ⓚ	Ⓚ	Ⓚ	Ⓚ
Ⓛ	Ⓛ	Ⓛ	Ⓛ	Ⓛ	Ⓛ
Ⓜ	Ⓜ	Ⓜ	Ⓜ	Ⓜ	Ⓜ
Ⓝ	Ⓝ	Ⓝ	Ⓝ	Ⓝ	Ⓝ
Ⓞ	Ⓞ	Ⓞ	Ⓞ	Ⓞ	Ⓞ
Ⓟ	Ⓟ	Ⓟ	Ⓟ	Ⓟ	Ⓟ
Ⓠ	Ⓠ	Ⓠ	Ⓠ	Ⓠ	Ⓠ
Ⓡ	Ⓡ	Ⓡ	Ⓡ	Ⓡ	Ⓡ
Ⓢ	Ⓢ	Ⓢ	Ⓢ	Ⓢ	Ⓢ
Ⓣ	Ⓣ	Ⓣ	Ⓣ	Ⓣ	Ⓣ
Ⓤ	Ⓤ	Ⓤ	Ⓤ	Ⓤ	Ⓤ
Ⓥ	Ⓥ	Ⓥ	Ⓥ	Ⓥ	Ⓥ
Ⓦ	Ⓦ	Ⓦ	Ⓦ	Ⓦ	Ⓦ
Ⓧ	Ⓧ	Ⓧ	Ⓧ	Ⓧ	Ⓧ
Ⓨ	Ⓨ	Ⓨ	Ⓨ	Ⓨ	Ⓨ
Ⓩ	Ⓩ	Ⓩ	Ⓩ	Ⓩ	Ⓩ

Test ❶   Start with number 1 for each new section.
If a section has fewer questions than answer spaces, leave the extra answer spaces blank.

Section 1—Reading

1. Ⓐ Ⓑ Ⓒ Ⓓ
2. Ⓐ Ⓑ Ⓒ Ⓓ
3. Ⓐ Ⓑ Ⓒ Ⓓ
4. Ⓐ Ⓑ Ⓒ Ⓓ
5. Ⓐ Ⓑ Ⓒ Ⓓ
6. Ⓐ Ⓑ Ⓒ Ⓓ
7. Ⓐ Ⓑ Ⓒ Ⓓ
8. Ⓐ Ⓑ Ⓒ Ⓓ
9. Ⓐ Ⓑ Ⓒ Ⓓ
10. Ⓐ Ⓑ Ⓒ Ⓓ
11. Ⓐ Ⓑ Ⓒ Ⓓ
12. Ⓐ Ⓑ Ⓒ Ⓓ
13. Ⓐ Ⓑ Ⓒ Ⓓ
14. Ⓐ Ⓑ Ⓒ Ⓓ
15. Ⓐ Ⓑ Ⓒ Ⓓ
16. Ⓐ Ⓑ Ⓒ Ⓓ
17. Ⓐ Ⓑ Ⓒ Ⓓ
18. Ⓐ Ⓑ Ⓒ Ⓓ
19. Ⓐ Ⓑ Ⓒ Ⓓ
20. Ⓐ Ⓑ Ⓒ Ⓓ
21. Ⓐ Ⓑ Ⓒ Ⓓ
22. Ⓐ Ⓑ Ⓒ Ⓓ
23. Ⓐ Ⓑ Ⓒ Ⓓ
24. Ⓐ Ⓑ Ⓒ Ⓓ
25. Ⓐ Ⓑ Ⓒ Ⓓ
26. Ⓐ Ⓑ Ⓒ Ⓓ
27. Ⓐ Ⓑ Ⓒ Ⓓ
28. Ⓐ Ⓑ Ⓒ Ⓓ
29. Ⓐ Ⓑ Ⓒ Ⓓ
30. Ⓐ Ⓑ Ⓒ Ⓓ
31. Ⓐ Ⓑ Ⓒ Ⓓ
32. Ⓐ Ⓑ Ⓒ Ⓓ
33. Ⓐ Ⓑ Ⓒ Ⓓ
34. Ⓐ Ⓑ Ⓒ Ⓓ
35. Ⓐ Ⓑ Ⓒ Ⓓ
36. Ⓐ Ⓑ Ⓒ Ⓓ
37. Ⓐ Ⓑ Ⓒ Ⓓ
38. Ⓐ Ⓑ Ⓒ Ⓓ
39. Ⓐ Ⓑ Ⓒ Ⓓ
40. Ⓐ Ⓑ Ⓒ Ⓓ
41. Ⓐ Ⓑ Ⓒ Ⓓ
42. Ⓐ Ⓑ Ⓒ Ⓓ
43. Ⓐ Ⓑ Ⓒ Ⓓ
44. Ⓐ Ⓑ Ⓒ Ⓓ
45. Ⓐ Ⓑ Ⓒ Ⓓ
46. Ⓐ Ⓑ Ⓒ Ⓓ
47. Ⓐ Ⓑ Ⓒ Ⓓ
48. Ⓐ Ⓑ Ⓒ Ⓓ
49. Ⓐ Ⓑ Ⓒ Ⓓ
50. Ⓐ Ⓑ Ⓒ Ⓓ
51. Ⓐ Ⓑ Ⓒ Ⓓ
52. Ⓐ Ⓑ Ⓒ Ⓓ

Section 2—Writing and Language Skills

1. Ⓐ Ⓑ Ⓒ Ⓓ
2. Ⓐ Ⓑ Ⓒ Ⓓ
3. Ⓐ Ⓑ Ⓒ Ⓓ
4. Ⓐ Ⓑ Ⓒ Ⓓ
5. Ⓐ Ⓑ Ⓒ Ⓓ
6. Ⓐ Ⓑ Ⓒ Ⓓ
7. Ⓐ Ⓑ Ⓒ Ⓓ
8. Ⓐ Ⓑ Ⓒ Ⓓ
9. Ⓐ Ⓑ Ⓒ Ⓓ
10. Ⓐ Ⓑ Ⓒ Ⓓ
11. Ⓐ Ⓑ Ⓒ Ⓓ
12. Ⓐ Ⓑ Ⓒ Ⓓ
13. Ⓐ Ⓑ Ⓒ Ⓓ
14. Ⓐ Ⓑ Ⓒ Ⓓ
15. Ⓐ Ⓑ Ⓒ Ⓓ
16. Ⓐ Ⓑ Ⓒ Ⓓ
17. Ⓐ Ⓑ Ⓒ Ⓓ
18. Ⓐ Ⓑ Ⓒ Ⓓ
19. Ⓐ Ⓑ Ⓒ Ⓓ
20. Ⓐ Ⓑ Ⓒ Ⓓ
21. Ⓐ Ⓑ Ⓒ Ⓓ
22. Ⓐ Ⓑ Ⓒ Ⓓ
23. Ⓐ Ⓑ Ⓒ Ⓓ
24. Ⓐ Ⓑ Ⓒ Ⓓ
25. Ⓐ Ⓑ Ⓒ Ⓓ
26. Ⓐ Ⓑ Ⓒ Ⓓ
27. Ⓐ Ⓑ Ⓒ Ⓓ
28. Ⓐ Ⓑ Ⓒ Ⓓ
29. Ⓐ Ⓑ Ⓒ Ⓓ
30. Ⓐ Ⓑ Ⓒ Ⓓ
31. Ⓐ Ⓑ Ⓒ Ⓓ
32. Ⓐ Ⓑ Ⓒ Ⓓ
33. Ⓐ Ⓑ Ⓒ Ⓓ
34. Ⓐ Ⓑ Ⓒ Ⓓ
35. Ⓐ Ⓑ Ⓒ Ⓓ
36. Ⓐ Ⓑ Ⓒ Ⓓ
37. Ⓐ Ⓑ Ⓒ Ⓓ
38. Ⓐ Ⓑ Ⓒ Ⓓ
39. Ⓐ Ⓑ Ⓒ Ⓓ
40. Ⓐ Ⓑ Ⓒ Ⓓ
41. Ⓐ Ⓑ Ⓒ Ⓓ
42. Ⓐ Ⓑ Ⓒ Ⓓ
43. Ⓐ Ⓑ Ⓒ Ⓓ
44. Ⓐ Ⓑ Ⓒ Ⓓ

Test ❶   Start with number 1 for each new section.
If a section has fewer questions than answer spaces, leave the extra answer spaces blank.

Section 3—Mathematics: No Calculator

1. Ⓐ Ⓑ Ⓒ Ⓓ
2. Ⓐ Ⓑ Ⓒ Ⓓ
3. Ⓐ Ⓑ Ⓒ Ⓓ
4. Ⓐ Ⓑ Ⓒ Ⓓ
5. Ⓐ Ⓑ Ⓒ Ⓓ
6. Ⓐ Ⓑ Ⓒ Ⓓ
7. Ⓐ Ⓑ Ⓒ Ⓓ
8. Ⓐ Ⓑ Ⓒ Ⓓ
9. Ⓐ Ⓑ Ⓒ Ⓓ
10. Ⓐ Ⓑ Ⓒ Ⓓ
11. Ⓐ Ⓑ Ⓒ Ⓓ
12. Ⓐ Ⓑ Ⓒ Ⓓ
13. Ⓐ Ⓑ Ⓒ Ⓓ
14. Ⓐ Ⓑ Ⓒ Ⓓ
15. Ⓐ Ⓑ Ⓒ Ⓓ

16. 17. 18. 19. 20.

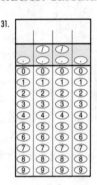
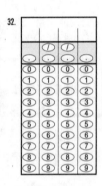
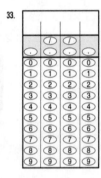
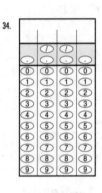

Section 4—Mathematics: Calculator

1. Ⓐ Ⓑ Ⓒ Ⓓ
2. Ⓐ Ⓑ Ⓒ Ⓓ
3. Ⓐ Ⓑ Ⓒ Ⓓ
4. Ⓐ Ⓑ Ⓒ Ⓓ
5. Ⓐ Ⓑ Ⓒ Ⓓ
6. Ⓐ Ⓑ Ⓒ Ⓓ
7. Ⓐ Ⓑ Ⓒ Ⓓ
8. Ⓐ Ⓑ Ⓒ Ⓓ
9. Ⓐ Ⓑ Ⓒ Ⓓ
10. Ⓐ Ⓑ Ⓒ Ⓓ
11. Ⓐ Ⓑ Ⓒ Ⓓ
12. Ⓐ Ⓑ Ⓒ Ⓓ
13. Ⓐ Ⓑ Ⓒ Ⓓ
14. Ⓐ Ⓑ Ⓒ Ⓓ
15. Ⓐ Ⓑ Ⓒ Ⓓ
16. Ⓐ Ⓑ Ⓒ Ⓓ
17. Ⓐ Ⓑ Ⓒ Ⓓ
18. Ⓐ Ⓑ Ⓒ Ⓓ
19. Ⓐ Ⓑ Ⓒ Ⓓ
20. Ⓐ Ⓑ Ⓒ Ⓓ
21. Ⓐ Ⓑ Ⓒ Ⓓ
22. Ⓐ Ⓑ Ⓒ Ⓓ
23. Ⓐ Ⓑ Ⓒ Ⓓ
24. Ⓐ Ⓑ Ⓒ Ⓓ
25. Ⓐ Ⓑ Ⓒ Ⓓ
26. Ⓐ Ⓑ Ⓒ Ⓓ
27. Ⓐ Ⓑ Ⓒ Ⓓ
28. Ⓐ Ⓑ Ⓒ Ⓓ
29. Ⓐ Ⓑ Ⓒ Ⓓ
30. Ⓐ Ⓑ Ⓒ Ⓓ

31. 32. 33. 34. 35.

36. 37. 38.

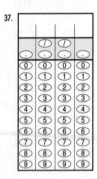

Chapter 4
Practice Test 1:
Answers and
Explanations

PRACTICE TEST 1 ANSWER KEY

Section 1: Reading				Section 2: Writing & Language				Section 3: Math (No Calculator)				Section 4: Math (Calculator)			
1.	D	27.	B	1.	D	23.	B	1.	A	11.	D	1.	C	20.	A
2.	B	28.	C	2.	D	24.	B	2.	B	12.	A	2.	C	21.	D
3.	C	29.	A	3.	A	25.	A	3.	B	13.	C	3.	B	22.	C
4.	C	30.	C	4.	B	26.	D	4.	D	14.	A	4.	B	23.	C
5.	B	31.	A	5.	C	27.	C	5.	D	15.	C	5.	D	24.	A
6.	A	32.	B	6.	B	28.	C	6.	C	16.	5	6.	A	25.	C
7.	D	33.	A	7.	A	29.	A	7.	A	17.	6	7.	C	26.	D
8.	B	34.	A	8.	B	30.	C	8.	A	18.	$\frac{5}{13}$	8.	D	27.	C
9.	B	35.	C	9.	C	31.	B	9.	C			9.	B	28.	B
10.	A	36.	B	10.	C	32.	D	10.	C	19.	225	10.	A	29.	A
11.	D	37.	D	11.	C	33.	D			20.	13	11.	D	30.	B
12.	B	38.	D	12.	D	34.	C					12.	D	31.	$\frac{3}{7},\frac{6}{14},$
13.	D	39.	B	13.	A	35.	C					13.	B		.428,
14.	A	40.	B	14.	C	36.	D					14.	B		or
15.	C	41.	C	15.	D	37.	C					15.	A		.429
16.	B	42.	B	16.	C	38.	B					16.	C	32.	Any value
17.	C	43.	A	17.	A	39.	A					17.	D		from 14
18.	A	44.	A	18.	D	40.	D					18.	C		to 21,
19.	C	45.	A	19.	D	41.	D					19.	C		inclusive
20.	D	46.	B	20.	C	42.	B							33.	30
21.	D	47.	C	21.	B	43.	C							34.	4
22.	B	48.	A	22.	A	44.	D							35.	4
23.	C	49.	D											36.	51
24.	C	50.	D											37.	3
25.	D	51.	B											38.	8.76
26.	B	52.	C												

Go to PrincetonReview.com to score your exam. Alternatively,
for self-assessment tables, please turn to page 909.

PRACTICE TEST 1 EXPLANATIONS

Section 1: Reading

1. **D** The question asks about the developmental pattern of the passage, so it should be answered after the specific questions. Look for clues in the text that indicate the mood and story of the passage. This particular passage moves from glum to foreboding. The narrator is nervous on his journey, but he states that when he sees the city, he foresees his bleak future. Since the narrator discusses the past, he goes further to confirm it: *I prophesied truly, and failed only in one single circumstance, that in all the misery I imagined and dreaded, I did not conceive the hundredth part of the anguish I was destined to endure.* Choice (A) refers to the joy he felt at seeing his native land, but that is only a half-right answer because it does not address the negative mood and events. The passage says nothing about the narrator responding to a request for help, so (B) is incorrect. The author describes the *daemon*, but the passage does not mention an ancient curse, so (C) is incorrect. Choice (D) accurately describes the narrator's mood and final despair. The correct answer is (D).

2. **B** The question asks about what happens in the passage, making it a straightforward question to answer after the specific questions have been answered. Choice (A) goes beyond the information in the passage because there is no mention of any plans the narrator has to avenge his brother's death. Choice (B) accurately addresses the feeling of anxiety the narrator has throughout the passage, as seen in lines 39–42 when he says, *The picture appeared a vast and dim scene of evil, and I foresaw obscurely that I was destined to become the most wretched of human beings.* Keep (B). Choice (C) describes the narrator's fear of returning home to the monster, but the passage discusses how the narrator seems to be more afraid of what has changed and how his future may be affected, so it can be eliminated. Choice (D) addresses how the narrator becomes anxious about returning home, but he says he *longed to console and sympathize with my loved and sorrowing friends,* so it seems that he isn't afraid he will not be welcome. The correct answer is (B).

3. **C** The question asks what the word *degrees* most nearly means in lines 11 and 19. Go back to the text, find the word *degrees* and cross it out. Carefully read the surrounding text to determine another word that would fit in the blank based on the context of the passage. Lines 9–11 say, *One sudden and desolating change had taken place; but a thousand little circumstances might have by degrees worked other alterations.* Lines 19–20 say, *By degrees the calm and heavenly scene restored me.* Therefore, the phrase *by degrees* could be replaced with a phrase such as "little by little." Neither *levels, measures,* nor *careful developments* matches "little by little," so eliminate (A), (B), and (D). Note that (A) and (B) are Could Be True trap answers based on other meanings of d*egrees* that are not supported by the text. By *small increments* matches "little by little," so keep (C). The correct answer is (C).

4. **C** The question asks which emotion the narrator *most* feels. Because the question uses the word *most*, this indicates there may be more than one emotion the narrator feels. The answer to this question is the one that the narrator feels most strongly. Notice that the following question is a best evidence question, so this question and Q5 can be answered in tandem. Look at the answers for Q5 first. The lines in (5A) mention *the delight [the narrator] took,* so look to see if those lines support any answers in Q4. Choice (4A) mentions the *joy...at returning home.* Connect those two answers. Next, consider the lines for (5B). The narrator says that he *prophesied truly... all the misery I imagined and dreaded...anguish I was destined to endure.* Consider the answers to Q4. Choice (4C) mentions *dread concerning his fate,* which matches the lines for (5B). Connect (4C) and (5B). The lines in (5C) mention the coming storm, which does not address what emotion

the narrator feels most. Eliminate (5C). The lines in (5D) mention the narrator's reaction to the daemon, but do not reference any emotion. Eliminate (5D). Without any support from Q5, (4B) and (4C) can be eliminated. Consider the remaining pairs of answer choices in the context of the passage. The emotion the narrator feels *most* is negative, so (4A) and (5A) can be eliminated. The correct answers are (4C) and (5B).

5. **B** (See explanation above.)

6. **A** The question asks about how the narrator addresses the tempest. Find evidence in the text to support how the narrator feels about the storm. He states, *While I watched the tempest, so beautiful yet terrific, I wandered on with a hasty step. This noble war in the sky elevated my spirits; I clasped my hands, and exclaimed aloud, "William, dear angel! This is thy funeral, this thy dirge!* Although the rain is pelting him and lightning is flashing, his spirits are high. Thus, the *awe, but no fear* in (A) looks good. Don't eliminate it. He describes the storm as *violent* and *terrific*, so a word that means "overjoyed" is too positive, making (B) incorrect. While he is sad about William's death, he is not sad about the storm, making (C) incorrect. It is possible that the narrator is a little dramatic, but there is no evidence to prove that he is crazy. Therefore, (D) is incorrect. The correct answer is (A).

7. **D** The question asks about the *main purpose* of the first paragraph, so the correct answer will accurately summarize the paragraph. The author starts the passage by saying *My journey was very melancholy* and later describes his *painful state of mind* to set a tone for what will come. The author's choices create a negative mood for the reader. Choice (A) is incorrect, since the paragraph isn't written to represent anything. Choice (B) says that the author exaggerates the narrator's emotion, but the narrator is feeling a profound sort of dread, so there's no exaggeration. Choice (C) says that the paragraph is there to give context, but the narrator doesn't mention his brother's death explicitly or the daemon until later in the passage. Choice (D) best explains that the paragraph is there to establish the mood as the narrator returns home. The correct answer is (D).

8. **B** The question asks why the narrator uses a particular phrase. Carefully read the window to look for clues to indicate the narrator's meaning. His focus is on how things may have changed in the six years he's been gone (*How altered every thing might be during that time*). Although *one sudden and desolating change had taken place*, the narrator goes on to say that *other alterations* had possibly been worked by those *thousand little circumstances*. Of these little circumstances, he says that *although they were done more tranquilly, [they] might not be the less decisive*. Therefore, although there was only one major change, significant changes could also have come from smaller events that were individually less traumatic but still added up to something big. Choice (A) can be eliminated because the change that happened (the loss of the narrator's brother) was not connected to a natural disaster. Choice (B) is a good paraphrase of the prediction, so don't eliminate it. The narrator never mentions his role in the murder or any way he could have affected the outcome, so eliminate (C). Choice (D) can be eliminated because there is never any mention of politics. The correct answer is (B).

9. **B** Lines 9–13 were used to answer the previous question. The correct answer is (B).

10. **A** The question asks what the word *stole* means in line 66. Go back to the text, find the word *stole*, and mark it out. Carefully read the surrounding text to determine another word that would fit in the blank based on the context of the passage. The passage says, *I perceived in the gloom a figure which stole from behind a clump of trees near me.* The figure is emerging from behind the tree, so *stole* must have something to do with how the figure is moving. The correct answer must mean something like "moved stealthily." Keep (A) because *crept* matches "moved stealthily." Eliminate (B), (C) and (D) because neither *pinched, thieved,* nor *displaced* matches "moved

stealthily." Note that (B) and (C) are Could Be True trap answers based on another meaning of *stole* that is not supported by the text. The correct answer is (A).

11. **D** The question asks about the *main purpose* of the passage. Even though it's the first question for the passage, it should be done at the end. The correct answer should address why the passage was written. In the fourth paragraph, the author does mention *a set of essays*, but this passage is an introduction for those essays, not a review of them. Eliminate (A). Choice (B) is incorrect because the author does not use persuasive language, nor is there an argument for or against any field in this passage. Eliminate it. Choice (C) can be eliminated because, while the author does mention the limitations of Piaget and others, he goes on to reconcile those limitations with his own scientific views, so that's not the main purpose of the passage. Choice (D) sums up the information that the author provides in the passage. He introduces psychology and its fields of study to get to the point of how structuralism has influences on his own work. The correct answer is (D).

12. **B** The question asks about the *central claim* of the passage. This is a general question, so it should be answered after all the specific questions have been answered. The central claim of the passage is related to the main purpose: What is the most important part of the author's argument? The author's main point is that structuralism provided a wider range of avenues for psychologists to explore the mind. Choice (A) does not match this prediction because, while it might make sense that the author thinks pre-1960s psychology was *sedate and impractical*, that isn't actually in the text. Eliminate (A). Choice (B) is supported by the final paragraph, so keep it. Choice (C) is partially true in that behaviorists believe that humans *act in the way we do because we are reinforced for doing so,* but that is not the central claim in this passage. Also, there is no evidence their views are *preordained,* so this choice can be eliminated. Choice (D) can be eliminated because there is no evidence that the author's work is revolutionary. Although that word appears earlier in the passage, it does not refer to the author's work. The correct answer is (B).

13. **D** The question asks about the reason the author *describes different branches of psychology* throughout the passage. In the first paragraph, he mentioned *academic psychology, behaviorism, and psychoanalysis.* He labels these three as *uninviting specializations.* Then he mentions the *cognitive revolution* in the 1960s in the second paragraph, and he goes on to further describe how the revolution *inspired* those in the field who became and remained interested in the *structuralist approach.* The correct answer should address this shift. Choice (A) does not match the prediction because the author's goal is to present the shift, not to simply lay out the history. Choice (B) does not match because there is no evidence that the author is in any way prominent in the scientific community. It can be eliminated. Choice (C) can be eliminated because the author never makes any reference to structuralism being *inferior to behaviorism.* In fact, the author seems to feel more positively about structuralism than behaviorism. Choice (D) is consistent with the prediction. The correct answer is (D).

14. **A** The question asks what the author indicates about the *cognitive revolution* in the passage. Notice that the following question is a best evidence question, so this question and Q15 can be answered in tandem. Look at the answers for Q15 first. The lines in (15A) mention *lines of study* unrelated *to human beings engaged in thought,* so look to see if those lines support any answers in Q14. There is not a link to another answer, so eliminate (15A). Next, consider the lines for (15B). They describe one group's *demonstration,* which is not mentioned in any of the answers to Q14. Eliminate (15B). The lines in (15C) say many *were swept up—and have remained inspired— by this revolution.* Consider the answers to Q14. Choice (14) mentions the author's *motivation,* which suggests being *inspired.* Connect (14A) and (15C). Look at the lines for (15D), which talk about the *appeal* of *machines that display intelligence.* This isn't mentioned in any of the answers to Q14, so eliminate (15D). Only one answer to Q15 matched an answer in Q14. The correct answers are (14A) and (15C).

15. **C** (See explanation above.)

16. **B** The question asks which features of psychology *became popular after the cognitive revolution*. Notice that the following question is a best evidence question, so this question and Q17 can be answered in tandem. Look at the answers for Q17 first. The lines in (17A) bring up *behaviorism*, which features a *focus on overt activity* rather than *inner life*. This doesn't match any answers in Q16, so eliminate (17A). The lines in (17B) mention *thinking, problem-solving, and creating*, which are in (16A). Connect these two answers. Next, consider the lines for (17C). Here, the author describes *the thrill* of *careful laboratory experiments* on individuals doing math problems. *Meticulousness* is similar to being *careful*, so draw a line connecting it to (16B). The lines for (17D) do not mention any features of psychology, so that answer can be eliminated. This leaves two pairs of answers. Choice (17B) might initially look good because the words *problem-solving* and *creating* also show up in (16A), but those words describe mental processes, not the psychology. That pair can be eliminated. The correct answers are (16B) and (17C).

17. **C** (See explanation above.)

18. **A** The question asks about the author's reason for mentioning Piaget, Chomsky, and Levi-Strauss. In the fourth paragraph, the author says these scientists *(psychologist, linguist, and anthropologist)* *exemplify the principal assumption* of the structuralist approach. Choice (A) matches the prediction, so keep it. Choice (B) can be eliminated because their work is not *inherently problematic*; it is just not fully in line with the views of the author. Choice (C) can be eliminated because the author notes that these men are not all psychologists: Chomsky is a linguist and Levi-Strauss is an anthropologist. Choice (D) can be eliminated because there is no evidence that these men have published anything that would not agree with the author's conclusions about creativity and structuralism. The correct answer is (A).

19. **C** The question asks about the author's use of the phrase *original works of art*. In the fifth paragraph, the author discusses the *limitations* of the structural approach. He uses the *original works of art* as an example in which the structuralists' ideas about human thought were *problematic for a study of mind where the...focus falls on innovation and creation*. Choice (A) does not work because it does not address the *limitations*. Eliminate it. Choice (B) can be eliminated because the author makes the point that the structuralists' views are *limited*, but he never argues that the views are *distorted*. Choice (C) is a good paraphrase of the text, so keep it. Choice (D) is too broad in its mention of *psychology* and incorrect in its assessment of psychology as *closed-minded*. The correct answer is (C).

20. **D** The question asks about the meaning of the *symbol systems*. The author states that those systems are *codes of meaning* and *vehicles through which thought takes place*. Choice (A) is incorrect because while the symbol systems are used in thought processes, they are not the thought processes themselves. Choice (B) is incorrect because symbol systems reconcile the issue with creativity and structuralism. Choice (C) is incorrect because the author does not refer to the systems as *principles*, but as a *feature of human thought*. Choice (D) is correct because the symbols are the way the human mind makes meaning. The correct answer is (D).

21. **D** The question asks about the author's purpose in mentioning *delays, redesigns, and even near-death cancellations*. Use the given line reference to find the window in the passage. The earlier part of the sentence makes a contrast between the conception of New Horizon *in the late 1980s* and its launch in *2006*, so look for an answer choice that deals with a time delay. Choice (A) deals with speed, not a span of time. Choices (B) and (C) deal with possible problems with the mission and are thus irrelevant to time delay. Choice (D) deals with a time delay between a plan and its execution. "Plan" matches *conception*, and "execution" matches *launch*. The correct answer is (D).

22. **B** The question asks what outcome the author says could result from the flyby over Pluto. Notice that the following question is a best evidence question, so this question and Q23 can be answered in tandem. Look at the answers for Q23 first. The lines for (23A) say the spacecraft should reach Pluto at *7:49 Eastern time*. Although this is the time in (22A), it does not say when scientists would *receive data*. Eliminate (23A). Next consider the lines for (23B). They mention a *radio signal* that will report *success* from the flyby. Choice (22C) mentions *a radio signal* reporting *the mission's failure*, but these are the right words with the wrong meaning—the text states that scientists will learn of *success* that way. Eliminate (23B). The lines for (23C) states *they could learn of its failure by hearing nothing*. Now consider the answers to Q22. Choice (22B) states that no data might come in, which matches *failure by hearing nothing*. Connect these two answers. The lines in (23D) describe receiving data after a delay of *4.5 hours*. While (22D) also mentions a delay, it specifies only *3 minutes*. Eliminate (23D). The correct answers are (22B) and (23C).

23. **C** (See explanation above.)

24. **C** The question asks what the word *suite* means in line 26. Go back to the text, find the word *suite*, and mark it out. Carefully read the surrounding text to determine another word that would fit in the blank based on the context of the passage. The text describes *seven instruments* being used together. The correct answer should mean something like "group." Choice (A) may recall "suit," which looks like *suite*, but has a different meaning. Choice (B) is one meaning of *suite*, but not in this context. Choice (C) means "arrangement." Keep any unknown words, just in case they are correct, and only eliminate ones that are definitely incorrect. Choice (D) may recall "sweet," which has the same pronunciation as *suite*, but not the same meaning. Since (A), (B), and (D) are wrong, the correct answer must be (C), even if this was a previously unknown word. The correct answer is (C).

25. **D** The question asks why the author discusses the measurement of the primary encounter. Use the given line reference to find the window. The sentence containing *primary encounter* begins with *Though*, so the author is establishing a contrast. Although that encounter *is best measured in minutes and hours*, the sentence goes on to emphasize how long it will take for the data to all be sent to Earth. Look for an answer choice that makes a contrast between a short amount of time and a long amount of time. Choice (A) references an earlier claim that could be supported by this discussion, but no earlier claims are supported by this discussion. Choice (B) refers to an undermined assumption, but there is no assumption, and nothing is undermined. Choice (C) is about time but does not match the prediction. Choice (D) is about time, and it matches the prediction because it indicates a contrast between something fast and something slow. The correct answer is (D).

26. **B** The question asks about the main idea of Passage 2. Because it is a general question, it should be done after all the specific questions. It begins with the first part of a contrast, that *New Horizons has started to transmit information about Pluto*, but then the question ends with a *but*. Find something in the text that contrasts with the idea of New Horizons reaching Pluto. The end of the passage mentions another target for New Horizons *a mere billion miles further along the interplanetary road*. The correct answer will have something to do with further goals for New Horizon. Choice (A) might initially look attractive because New Horizons is going to *continue on...into night*, but (A) has nothing about the next mission. Choice (B) is a solid paraphrase of the prediction, so don't eliminate it. Choice (C) might be true, but it isn't the contrast given in the passage. Eliminate it. Choice (D) is not mentioned in Passage 2. The correct answer is (B).

27. **B** The question asks what the word *deploy* means in line 53. Go back to the text, find the word *deploy*, and mark it out. Carefully read the surrounding text to determine another word that

would fit in the blank based on the context of the passage. The text indicates a hope to use the *instruments to study further objects*. The correct answer must mean something like "use." Look for an answer choice that matches this prediction. Choice (A) might recall the word *decoy*. Choice (B) matches the prediction. Choice (C) does not match the prediction. Choice (D) might recall the word *destroy*. The correct answer is (B).

28. **C** The question asks how the passages relate to each other. Because it is about both passages, it should be done after all the specific and general questions about the individual passages. Both passages inform readers about the objects New Horizons will encounter and study (Pluto, and then something beyond), and both have a positive tone. Choice (A) mentions *concern* and *dangers*, which do not match the prediction. Choice (B) mentions a revision, but there is no revision. Choice (C) is a possible match to the prediction: The *story* could be *the first golden age of interplanetary exploration*, and the *next chapter* could be the search for new objects beyond the solar system. Choice (D) mentions support, but there is no *qualified* support of Passage 1 by Passage 2. The correct answer is (C).

29. **A** The question asks how the author of Passage 2 would most likely respond to something specific in Passage 1. Use the given line reference to find the text in Passage 1. The continued journey is referred to there as an *endless journey into interstellar night*. Notice that the following question is a best evidence question, so this question and Q30 can be answered in tandem. Look at the answers for Q30 first. The lines in (30A) suggest *NASA* needs to make a *critical, and time-sensitive, decision*, which doesn't fit with any of the answers to Q29. Eliminate it. The lines in (30B) describe a *hope* to *study further objects*. Since this is a *hope*, it doesn't really give evidence for any answer choice in Q29, so eliminate this answer as well. Now consider the lines in (30C), which specify a new location as *the next goal for New Horizons*. This matches the answer (29A), which suggests *one further stop*. Connect these two answers. Finally, the lines in (30D) compare the new location to Pluto, which doesn't relate to any answers in Q29, so eliminate it. The correct answers are (29A) and (30C).

30. **C** (See explanation above.)

31. **A** The question asks which *point about data transmitted from the New Horizons spacecraft is explicit in Passage 1 and implicit in Passage 2*. Work through the answer choices, matching each back to both passages. The statement in (A) is explicitly stated in Passage 1: lines 39–42 state, *the slow data-transmission rate imposed by such vast distances ensures that New Horizons will be beaming its archived images home well into 2017*. The statement in (A) is not stated directly in Passage 2, but it is implied in lines 46–50: *NASA's New Horizons mission has only just begun to transmit the bulk of the detailed scientific data from its history-making encounter with the Pluto-Charon system (at an excruciatingly slow 2 kilobits per second)*. Keep (A). Eliminate (B) because neither author states or implies that the data would *be more useful* if people could *interpret it more quickly*. Eliminate (C) because neither author states or implies that the data *will be valuable only if it offsets the cost of the mission*. Eliminate (D) because Passage 1 never mentions that the data will likely include *primarily of images of objects smaller than Pluto*. The correct answer is (A).

32. **B** The question asks what the authors *use the example in lines 4–9 to highlight*. Use the given line reference to find the window. Lines 1–4 state, *People often have the feeling that they lack enough time and enough money, and this problem is compounded by the frequency with which other people make demands on both resources*. The following lines give an example of the types of demands made on time and money: *Imagine receiving an invitation to your friend's wedding, a destination event in Hawaii. You want to celebrate with your friend, but traveling to Hawaii requires a great deal of time and money*. Eliminate answer choices that don't match this answer from the passage.

Choice (A) is a Right Words, Wrong Meaning trap answer: the example is about a wedding, but the authors emphasize *the frequency with which other people make demands on* our time and money; they don't say that people are frequently *invited to weddings*. Eliminate (A). Keep (B) because it matches the passage. Choice (C) is a Right Answer, Wrong Question trap: the authors do discuss the potential *damage done to friendships by declined invitations*, but the purpose of the example in lines 4–9 is to emphasize the demands made on our time and money. Eliminate (C). Choice (D) is a Right Answer, Wrong Question trap: the authors do mention a *shortage of vacation time*, but their purpose is to emphasize the demands placed on time and money, not the lack of vacation time. Eliminate (D). The correct answer is (B).

33. **A** The question asks why *people feel compelled to explain declining an invitation*. This is the first question in a paired set, but it is easy to find, so it can be done on its own. Since there is no line reference, use lead words and the order of the questions to find the window. Q32 asks about lines 4–9, so scan the first paragraph looking for information about *declining an invitation*. Lines 11–14 state, *You know that declining the invitation will hurt your friend's feelings and may signal that you do not value the friendship, so your goal is to say "no" but to limit the negative impact on your friendship.* Eliminate answer choices that don't match this answer from the passage. Keep (A) because it matches the passage. Choice (B) is a Right Answer, Wrong Question trap: the text suggests that people decline invitations because the invitations put demands on their *time and money*, but this is not the reason people feel *compelled to explain* themselves when they decline invitations. Eliminate (B). Choice (C) is a Could Be True trap answer: it may be true that people *would expect the same from their friends*, but the passage doesn't mention this. Eliminate (C). Eliminate (D) because the passage doesn't mention following *societal customs*. The correct answer is (A).

34. **A** The question is the best evidence question in a paired set. Because the previous question was easy to find, simply look at the lines used to answer Q33. Lines 11–14 provided the evidence: *You know that declining the invitation will hurt your friend's feelings and may signal that you do not value the friendship, so your goal is to say "no" but to limit the negative impact on your friendship.* Keep (A) and eliminate (B), (C), and (D). The correct answer is (A).

35. **C** The question asks what the word *temporal* most nearly means as it is used in line 31. Go back to the text, find the word *temporal*, and cross it out. Then read the window carefully, using context clues to determine another word that would fit in its place. The text says, *We propose that people often turn down social invitations by citing insufficient time (e.g., "I don't have time to go out to dinner") or money (e.g., "I don't have money to go out to dinner"). Despite the commonness of such situations, little is known about the consequences of disclosing financial or temporal scarcity.* *Financial* means "related to money," so *temporal* could be replaced by a phrase such as "related to time." Eliminate answer choices that don't match the way the word is used in context. Choices (A) and (B) are Could Be True trap answers based on another meaning of *temporal* that isn't supported by the text. Neither *worldly* nor *material* matches "related to time," so eliminate (A) and (B). Keep (C) because *time-related* matches the way *temporal* is used in context. Eliminate (D) because *spiritual* doesn't match "related to time." The correct answer is (C).

36. **B** The question asks how the *author would likely describe the "downstream consequences" mentioned in paragraph 2*. Use the given line reference to find the window. Lines 29–33 state, *Despite the commonness of such situations, little is known about the consequences of disclosing financial or temporal scarcity, particularly with regard to the downstream consequences of doing so for the relationship between the inviter and invitee.* Eliminate answer choices that don't match this answer from the passage. Eliminate (A) because the passage doesn't indicate that the consequences are not realistic. Keep (B) because *undetermined* matches the statement in the text that

little is known about the consequences. Eliminate (C) because the passage doesn't indicate that the consequences are *overstated* (which means "exaggerated"). Eliminate (D) because the passage doesn't indicate that the consequences are *temporary.* The correct answer is (B).

37. **D** The question asks what the *passage indicates* about *the assertion made by Kim, Zhang, and Norton.* Use the given line reference to find the window. Lines 50–56 cite Kim, Zhang, and Norton's theory that *citing insufficient money could make relationships feel transactional,* and therefore that *when provided with a rejection to a social invitation, consumers might respond more favorably to excuses citing a scarcity of time (vs. money).* However, in lines 57–59 the authors counter this suggestion: *In contrast, we suggest that communicating temporal scarcity could lead to more negative reactions.* Therefore, the authors would disagree with *the assertion made by Kim, Zhang, and Norton.* Eliminate answer choices that don't match this answer from the passage. Eliminate (A) because, although the authors disagree with the assertion, they don't state that it is *falsified,* which would indicate that the researchers were being deceptive. Eliminate (B) because the authors don't indicate that the assertion is not logical; their own research has simply indicated something different. Eliminate (C) because there is no indication that the assertion is not necessary. Keep (D) because *inaccurate* matches the evidence that the authors disagree with the assertion. The correct answer is (D).

38. **D** The question is the best evidence question in a paired set. Because the previous question was easy to find, simply look at the lines used to answer Q37. Lines 57–59 provided the evidence for Q37: *In contrast, we suggest that communicating temporal scarcity could lead to more negative reactions.* Eliminate (A), (B), and (C). The correct answer is (D).

39. **B** The question asks what the word *reactions* most nearly means in line 59. Go back to the text, find the word *reactions,* and cross it out. Then read the window carefully, using context clues to determine another word that would fit in its place. The text says, *As a result, when provided with a rejection to a social invitation, consumers might respond more favorably to excuses citing a scarcity of time (vs. money). In contrast, we suggest that communicating temporal scarcity could lead to more negative reactions.* Since the word *respond* is used in the previous sentence, the word *reactions* could be replaced with "responses." Eliminate answer choices that don't match the way the word is used in context. Eliminate (A) because *motivations* doesn't match "responses." Keep (B) because it matches the use of the word in context. Eliminate (C) because *transactions* doesn't match "responses." Choice (D) is a Could Be True trap answer based on another meaning of *reaction* that isn't supported by the text. Eliminate (D). The correct answer is (B).

40. **B** The question asks why the *authors refer to work by Zauberman and Lynch.* Use the given line reference to find the window. In lines 59–62 the authors explain their theory: *We propose that time is perceived as more discretionary and under consumers' personal control than money, which often must be dedicated to non-discretionary expenses.* In lines 63–66 they state, *Moreover, consumers tend to see time, but not money, as more likely to be readily available in the future, regardless of current demands on either resource (Zauberman & Lynch, 2005).* The reference to *Zauberman and Lynch* is a citation of a study that supports the author's theory. Eliminate answer choices that don't match this answer from the passage. Eliminate (A) because the authors are proposing a theory, not *a solution.* Keep (B) because it matches the use of the citation in the passage. Eliminate (C) because in this paragraph, the authors are supporting their own theory, not discrediting someone else's *opinion.* Eliminate (D) because these lines are about an observation from a study, not an *assumption,* and they don't *qualify* anything (to "qualify" means to "put limits on"). The correct answer is (B).

41. **C** The question references the *graph following the passage* and asks what *the perceived closeness in a personal relationship following an excuse is affected by*. Carefully read the title, variables, and key in the graph. According to its title, the graph shows the *Effects of Time and Money Excuses on Perceived Closeness in Personal Relationships*. The graph gives measurements for *Perceived Closeness* both *Before* and *After* an excuse is given, providing data for both *Time* and *Money* excuses. In the *Before* section of the graph, the perceived closeness measurements for time and money are similar—between 5 and 6 for both. In the *After* section of the graph, the perceived closeness associated with time excuses has dropped below 4, while the perceived closeness associated with money excuses is just below 5. Therefore, the perceived closeness following an excuse is affected by the type of excuse given (time excuse versus money excuse). Keep (C) and eliminate (A), (B), and (D). The correct answer is (C).

42. **B** The question references *the graph* and asks what *the authors would likely attribute the differing effects of time and money excuses on perceived closeness* to. First locate information about *time and money excuses* and *perceived closeness* in the graph. The graph shows a larger decrease in *perceived closeness* associated with *time excuses*, and a smaller decrease associated with *money excuses*. Next, look for evidence in the passage about how the authors would explain the different effects of time excuses and money excuses. Lines 59–62 state, *We propose that time is perceived as more discretionary and under consumers' personal control than money, which often must be dedicated to nondiscretionary expenses*. They go on to suggest that *consumers apply these assumptions when receiving social excuses such that declining an invitation using a time (vs. money) scarcity excuse will be viewed more negatively*. In other words, the authors suggest that people view time excuses more negatively because they believe that people have more control over their time than they do over their money. Eliminate answer choices that don't match this answer from the passage. Eliminate (A) because *empathy* is never discussed. Keep (B) because *control over resources* matches the authors' statements about control over time and money. Eliminate (C) because *resistance to receiving any excuse* does not explain the *differing effects* of time and money excuses. Choice (D) is a Right Answer, Wrong Question trap: the authors do discuss the *burden of social obligations*, but that burden doesn't explain the effects that excuses have on relationships. Eliminate (D). The correct answer is (B).

43. **A** The question asks what the *authors claim to be an important concern when selecting bears for the study*. Use the given line reference to find the window. Lines 14–16 state that *the researchers are careful not to capture sows with spring cubs….however, sows with older cubs are used in this study*. Eliminate answer choices that don't match this answer from the passage. Keep (A) because the *age of a bear's cubs* matches the passage. Eliminate (B) because the *year of the study* is used only to number the bears, not to select the bears that are studied. Eliminate (C) because the *number of bear cubs* a sow has is not mentioned in the passage. Choice (D) is a Right Answer, Wrong Question trap: the *accessibility of the area* is mentioned as a factor in whether researchers could reach a bear at the end of the study, not in their selection of bears for the study. Eliminate (D). The correct answer is (A).

44. **A** The question asks for the main reason the author uses *the words "double" and "exclusively."* Use the given line reference to find the window. Lines 22–28 state *the quality of the early foraging season may have an effect on development of cubs. During the first year, cubs double their weight every two months. They depend exclusively on mom for nourishment for up to six months*, so a sow *must re-nourish herself and her cubs after hibernation*. Eliminate answer choices that don't match this answer from the passage. Keep (A) because it matches the answer from the passage. Eliminate (B) because it is contradicted by the passage, which states that *during the first year, cubs double their weight every two months*. Choice (C) is a Right Words, Wrong Meaning trap answer: the passage mentions *hibernation* but doesn't explain the *timing of* hibernation. Eliminate (C). Choice (D) is a

Right Answer, Wrong Question trap: while the passage does state that *females are often watched in wildlife populations to determine health*, reinforcing that point is not the primary reason the author uses the words *double* and *exclusively*. Eliminate (D). The correct answer is (A).

45.   **A**   The question asks why the author includes *the information about the Katmai coastal areas*. Since there is no line reference, use lead words and the order of the questions to find the window. Q44 asks about lines 25–26, so scan the passage beginning with line 25. The passage states *the coastal areas in Katmai provide an important high quality early-season habitat for bears… Looking at the data from early summer, both this year and last, we can see how important these resources can be for bears along the coast.* The paragraph goes on to describe the researchers' findings about the bears' weight and fat gain during the early summer. Eliminate answer choices that don't match this answer from the passage. Keep (A) because it matches the passage: the study was about weight gain, which is closely tied to foraging for food. Therefore, the fact that *the coastal areas in Katmai provide an important high quality early-season habitat for bears* explains why the researchers chose the Katmai coastal areas for their study. Choice (B) is a Right Answer, Wrong Question trap: in the last paragraph, the author discusses why the researchers chose to study *female rather than male bears*, but that's not the focus of the window for Q45. Choice (C) is a Right Answer, Wrong Question trap: the passage states that bears *gain more muscle than fat* during the early summer months, but this detail is not the reason the author includes the information about *the Katmai coastal areas* providing a good early-season habitat. Eliminate (C). Eliminate (D) because no *alternative location* is suggested. The correct answer is (A).

46.   **B**   The question asks which statement from the passage would contradict a claim that *sows gain weight only during the late summer and fall*. Look at the line references given in the answer choices, and eliminate statements that don't contradict this claim. The lines for (A) say that *the quality of the early foraging season may have an effect on development of cubs*, but this information doesn't address *weight gain*, so eliminate (A). The lines for (B) say, *the sows that were studied gained between 12-140 pounds over two months*, and according to the previous sentence, these two months were during *early summer*, not *late summer*. This information contradicts the claim in the question. Keep (B). The lines for (C) say that in the *early summer period the bears are working to gain more muscle than fat*. This information doesn't directly address whether *weight* is gained, so eliminate (C). The lines for (D) say that the *salmon season…provides a fat-rich food source for the bears*. This information doesn't address weight gain, so eliminate (D). The correct answer is (B).

47.   **C**   The question asks what the statement *the bigger you get, the more weight and energy you spend to carry that weight around* implies. Use the given line reference to find the window. Lines 40–45 state *The salmon season, which runs from July through October, provides a fat-rich food source for the bears. And the salmon season is well-timed for the bears, because the bigger you get, the more weight and energy you spend to carry that weight around.* The statement implies that eating fat-rich food and getting bigger in late summer is advantageous because hibernation follows soon after, and bears don't need to carry the weight around for long. Eliminate answer choices that don't match this answer from the passage. Eliminate (A) because the text doesn't contrast the amount of energy required to procure food from different sources. Eliminate (B) because the statement in the question is about total *weight*, not about the difference between *muscle* and *fat*. Keep (C) because it matches the answer in the text. Eliminate (D) because the passage indicates that a bear must nourish its cubs for at least six months, but the bears prioritize eating fat only during the late summer. Furthermore, this portion of the passage discusses the timing of weight gain in relation to *hibernation*, not in relation to *nourishing cubs*. The correct answer is (C).

48.   **A**   The question asks what the word *temperament* in line 54 indicates. Use the given line reference to find the window. The passage states that *when a bear wakes up and doesn't like the collar, they*

slide it off within the first two hours. Usually the bears that do that are the males. Temperament may be a key reason researchers pick females over males. Therefore, the fact that male bears tend to remove their GPS collars may lead researchers to study female bears. Eliminate answer choices that don't match this answer from the passage. Choice (A) matches the passage, so keep it. Eliminate (B) because the passage doesn't mention *locks* on tracking collars. Choice (C) is a Could Be True trap answer: *aggressive behavior* would be related to *temperament* and would be a logical reason to avoid a bear, but there's no evidence of *aggressive behavior toward researchers* in the text. Eliminate (C). Choice (D) is a Could Be True trap answer: it's possible that the male bears remove their collars because *the collars restrict* their *movements*, but the text doesn't indicate this. Eliminate (D). The correct answer is (A).

49. **D**   The question asks whether the *percentage of body fat gained between July and October* is *greater or less than the percentage gained between May and July*, and which statement from the passage *is most consistent with* the data. First, locate the body fat percentages in figure 2. Bear 35 gained 7% body fat from May to July and 19% body fat from July to October. Bear 105 gained 5% body fat from May to July and 31% body fat from July to October. Therefore, the percentage of body fat gained from July to October is greater; eliminate (A) and (B). Next, evaluate the statements in (C) and (D). The lines for (C) say that the bears studied *averaged about 1.2 pounds a day and only .08 pounds of fat a day.* Although this information is consistent with the fat percentage gained from May to July, it doesn't address the difference in fat gain during the two time periods mentioned in the question. Eliminate (C). The lines for (D) say that *the late summer season is when researchers begin to see more fat gain per day,* which is consistent with the data showing an increase in fat gain between July and October. Keep (D). The correct answer is (D).

50. **D**   The question asks for *the lowest body mass of a bear measured in July of 2015* based on the Figure 1 and the passage. First, locate information about the years of the study in the passage. Lines 3–8 state, *Researchers studied the bears during 2015 and 2016, and each bear was assigned a number. The bear's number ended in a "5" if the bear was studied in 2015 (for example, 15, 35, or 115) and ended in a "6" if the bear was studied in 2016 (for example, 16, 66, or 106).* Next, locate the numbers ending in 5 in Figure 1 and compare the lighter grey bars, which show the bears' masses in *July.* The lowest mass for a bear measured in July of 2015 was 225 pounds for bear 105. Eliminate (A) because the 187-pound measurement was taken in May, not July. Eliminate (B) and (C) because *193 pounds* and *222 pounds* were measurements of bears studied in 2016. Choice (D) matches the information in the figure. The correct answer is (D).

51. **B**   The question asks whether *the data in figure 1 support the author's claim* about bears' *weight gain in the early summer months.* Work through each answer choice using the figure. Eliminate (A) and (C) because the *smallest weight gain* was equal to, not *less than*, 12 pounds (bear 55) and the *greatest weight gain* was equal to, not *greater than*, 140 pounds (bear 95.15). Lines 34–36 state that *the sows that were studied gained between 12-140 pounds over two months.* The data in the figure support this claim, so eliminate (D). The correct answer is (B).

52. **C**   The question asks which data supports the answer to question 51. *Bears 55 and 95.15* had the smallest and largest weight gains, respectively. Eliminate (A), (B), and (D) and keep (C). The correct answer is (C).

Section 2: Writing and Language

1. **D** Punctuation changes in the answer choices, so this question tests how to connect ideas with the appropriate punctuation. The first part of the sentence, *When we hear about the opinions of "ten scientists" or "ten dentists," or we hear that things are "clinically proven" or "lab-tested," for example,* is not an independent clause. The second part of the sentence, *we might expect to be reading scientific journals,* is an independent clause. A comma followed by the word *and* can only be used between two independent clauses, so eliminate (A). A colon must come after an independent clause, so eliminate (C). The word *consequently* does not make the sentence more precise, so there is no reason to include it; eliminate (B). Choice (D) appropriately uses a comma without a transition word to connect the two parts of the sentence. The correct answer is (D).

2. **D** Note the question! The question asks for *the most relevant detail,* so it tests consistency. Eliminate answers that are inconsistent with the purpose stated in the question. The focus of the previous sentence is the *statistics,* so the most relevant choice will contain statistical data. *Lowering the price* is not statistical data, so eliminate (A). *Merge into larger corporations* is not statistical data, so eliminate (B). *Comparing products* is not statistical data, so eliminate (C). *40% more volume* and *60% fewer split ends* is statistical data. The correct answer is (D).

3. **A** Punctuation changes in the answer choices, so this question tests how to connect ideas with the appropriate punctuation. The sentence contains a list of three things: 1) *Elle,* 2) *Vogue,* and 3) *Vanity Fair.* There should be a comma after each item in the list. Keep (A) because it contains a comma after each item. Eliminate (B) because the comma should be before *and,* not after. Eliminate (C) and (D) because a list uses commas, not semicolons or colons. The correct answer is (A).

4. **B** Note the question! The question asks where sentence 5 should be placed, so it tests consistency of ideas. The sentence must be consistent with the ideas that come both before and after it. Sentence 5 says, *The obvious answer,* so it must come after a question. Sentence 1 contains the question, so sentence 5 must follow sentence 1. The correct answer is (B).

5. **C** Vocabulary changes in the answer choices, so this question tests precision of word choice. Look for a word with a definition that is consistent with the other ideas in the sentence. The underlined word describes what people think about *truth-value of these advertisements.* The sentence says that *the findings are probably not surprising,* and the next sentence says that they *found that only 18% of the claims…were true,* so the correct word should mean "doubted." *Believed* means "to accept as true," so eliminate (A). *Pondered* means "to think about," so eliminate (B). *Questioned* means "to doubt," so keep (C). *Skepticized* is not an actual word, so eliminate (D). The correct answer is (C).

6. **B** Note the question! The question asks whether the underlined portion should be deleted, so it tests consistency. If the content of the underlined portion is consistent with the ideas surrounding it, it should be kept; otherwise, it should be deleted. The paragraph contains the statistics about how *true* the advertisements were. The underlined portion contains one of the statistics, so it is consistent and should not be deleted. Eliminate (C) and (D). It is not the *most surprising… finding,* so eliminate (A). It does *complete the discussion of the data,* and the claims that were *too vague to classify,* as the underlined portion says, are discussed later in the passage. The correct answer is (B).

7. **A** Verbs change in the answer choices, so this question tests consistency of verbs. A verb must be consistent with the other verbs in the sentence. The other verb is *are,* which is in the present tense. To be consistent, the underlined verb must also be in the present tense. *May have* is present tense, so keep (A) and (C). *Will have* is future tense, so eliminate (B). *Might be having* is a

progressive tense, so eliminate (D). The difference between (A) and (C) is the presence of the pronoun *they*. The first part of the sentence, *These findings are good for a laugh,* is an independent clause. This clause is followed by a comma and *but*. A comma followed by *but* can only be used between two independent clauses, so the second part of the sentence must also be an independent clause. As written, the second part of the sentence, *they may have more serious implications as well*, is an independent clause, so keep (A). Eliminate (C) because without the word *they*, the second part of the sentence is not an independent clause. The correct answer is (A).

8. **B** Vocabulary changes in the answer choices, so this question tests precision of word choice. Look for a word with a definition that is consistent with the other ideas in the sentence. The meaning of the sentence is that the FDA can "control" *what goes into food and drugs*, so the correct answer must be consistent with that idea. *Reign* means "rule over," so eliminate (A). *Regulate* means "control by law," so keep (B). *Name* means "list" or "state," so eliminate (C). *Administrate* means "manage," so eliminate (D). The correct answer is (B).

9. **C** Verbs change in the answer choices, so this question tests consistency of verbs. A verb must be consistent with the other verbs in the sentence. The other verb at the beginning of the sentence is *may have*, so the correct answer must be consistent with this verb. Eliminate (A) and (B). Apostrophes also change in the answer choices, so this question also tests apostrophe usage. When used with a noun, an apostrophe indicates possession. Nothing belongs to the *fines*, so there is no need to use the apostrophe. Eliminate (D). The correct answer is (C).

10. **D** Prepositions change in the answer choices, so this question tests idioms. Look at the phrase before the preposition to determine the correct idiom. Use POE, and guess if there is more than one answer left. In general, both *do to* and *do with* are both correct idioms, so eliminate (A) and (C). In this context, the correct idiom is *do with*. Eliminate (B). The correct answer is (D).

11. **C** Transitions change in the answer choices, so this question tests consistency of ideas. A transition must be consistent with the relationship between the ideas it connects. The previous sentence discusses *the perils of trusting the word of advertisers*. The sentence that starts with the transition says that *the claims are often harmless*. The second idea is not a conclusion based on the first one, so eliminate (A). The sentence with the underlined transition uses the transition *but* to introduce a counterclaim, so there is not a reason to use a contrasting transition; eliminate (B) and (D). *True* indicates an accepted fact that is then countered. The correct answer is (C).

12. **D** Transitions change in the answer choices, so this question tests consistency of ideas. A transition must be consistent with the relationship between the ideas it connects. The previous sentence describes the merits of democracy *when the process is allowed to work*. This sentence states that *there are abnormalities*, indicating a contrast to the previous sentence. Eliminate (A) because it indicates similar ideas. Eliminate (B) because *elections that fall short* is negative while *happily* is positive. *Politically* does not connect the ideas, so eliminate (C). *Unfortunately* appropriately indicates contrasting ideas, the second of which is negative. The correct answer is (D).

13. **A** Commas change in the answer choices, so this question tests comma usage. The phrase *then governor of the state* is not necessary to the main meaning of the sentence, so it should be set off by commas. Keep (A), which sets off the phrase with commas. Eliminate (B) and (C) because they each only have one comma. Eliminate (D) because the commas set off the wrong phrase. The correct answer is (A).

14. **C** Verbs change in the answer choices, so this question tests consistency of verbs. A verb must be consistent with other verbs in the sentence. The other verbs in the previous sentence are *called* and *was*, which are in simple past tense. To be consistent, the correct answer must be in the sim-

ple past tense. Eliminate (A), which is future tense. Eliminate (B), which is conditional. Keep (C), which is past tense. Eliminate (D), which is present tense. The correct answer is (C).

15. **D** Note the question! The question asks where sentence 2 should be placed, so it tests consistency of ideas. The sentence must be consistent with the ideas that come both before and after it. Sentence 2 says *Unfortunately, it was not the last*, so it must come after an indication of a previous event. Sentence 5 says *It was one of the first*, so sentence 2 must be placed after sentence 5. The correct answer is (D).

16. **C** Note the question! The question asks how to effectively combine the underlined sentences, so it tests precision and concision. The phrase after *plan* changes in the answer choices, so determine which phrase is necessary. The first part of the sentence mentions the *Boston Gazette*, so there's no need to repeat that idea. Eliminate (A) and (B), which each repeat the idea by including *the paper*. Although it's a pronoun, *they* also repeats the idea of the *Gazette* and is less concise than (C), so eliminate (D). Choice (C) is concise and gives a precise meaning to the sentence. The correct answer is (C).

17. **A** Punctuation changes in the answer choices, so this question tests how to connect ideas with the appropriate punctuation. The first part of the sentence, *This image, combined with the governor's name, came to be known by a very specific name*, is an independent clause. The second part of the sentence in (A) and (C), *gerrymandering*, is not an independent clause. A colon can be used after an independent clause, so keep (A). A semicolon can only be used between two independent clauses, so eliminate (C). The colon is used appropriately in (B), but adding the words *which was* does not make the sentence more precise. Eliminate (B) because it is not concise. The extra words in (D) also do not make the sentence more precise, so eliminate (D) as well. The correct answer is (A).

18. **D** Note the question! The question asks which choice *best completes the description of the purpose of gerrymandering*, so it tests consistency. Eliminate answers that are inconsistent with the purpose stated in the question. The previous sentence states that *gerrymandering can have a tremendous influence on the outcome of an election*, and the graphic shows how gerrymandering can turn the losers into the winners. The correct answer will be consistent with these ideas. The graphic does not show the voters changing their votes, so eliminate (A) and (B). There is no indication that the results are *delayed*, so eliminate (C). The graphic does show that disadvantaged dark gray voters can gain an advantage through gerrymandering, so (D) is consistent with the graphic. The correct answer is (D).

19. **D** Note the question! The question asks which choice *most accurately and effectively represents information in the figure*, so it tests consistency. Read the labels on the graph carefully, and look for an answer that is consistent with the information given in the graph. Light gray did not start at 40%, so eliminate (A) and (C). Dark gray did not start at 60%, so eliminate (C). The light gray did start at 60% and the district did become 60% dark gray in division #3. The correct answer is (D).

20. **C** The phrase after *power* changes in the answer choices, so this question tests concision and precision. Select the shortest choice that has the most precise meaning. The phrase *not those out of power* means the same thing as *the parties in power*, so it is not necessary to use both phrases. Eliminate (A). The phrase *usually* means the same thing as *almost always*, so eliminate (B). Keep (C) because it's the most concise and the meaning is clear and precise. The phrase *for the good* means the same thing as *benefits*, so eliminate (D). The correct answer is (C).

21. **B** Pronouns change in the answer choices, so this question tests consistency of pronouns. The underlined pronoun must be consistent with its role in the sentence. *They're* is a contraction of *they are*, which does not work in this context, so eliminate (A) and (D). The *votes* belong to the *voters*, so the possessive pronoun *their* works here; keep (B). *There* indicates location, which does not work in this context; eliminate (C). The correct answer is (B).

22. **A** Pronouns and nouns change in the answer choices, so this question could test precision. There is also the option to DELETE; consider this choice carefully as it is often the correct answer. Removing the underlined portion makes the second part of the sentence, *many voting interests may go against those in power*, an independent clause. The first part of the sentence, *In "majority-minority" districts in particular, districts with large non-white populations, gerrymandering can discount the importance of particular races or classes of voters*, is also an independent clause. The two parts of the sentence are separated by a comma. A comma alone cannot be used between two independent clauses, so eliminate (D). Choices (B) and (C) also make the second part of the sentence an independent clause, so eliminate (B) and (C) as well. Adding the phrase *of whose* means the second part of the sentence is no longer an independent clause, so the comma can be appropriately used. The correct answer is (A).

23. **B** The length of the phrase around the word *marked* changes in the answer choices, so this question tests concision and precision. Select the shortest choice that has the most precise meaning. Choice (B) is most concise and gives a precise meaning to the sentence. The phrase *by certain means* is imprecise, so eliminate (A) and (D). The additional words in (C) do not make the sentence more precise, so eliminate (C). The correct answer is (B).

24. **B** The order of words changes in the answer choices, so this question tests precision. Look for an answer that gives the sentence a clear and precise meaning. The sentence starts with the phrase *Particularly when looking at old paintings*. To communicate the precise meaning, the subject of this phrase must immediately follow the comma. *Paintings* are not *looking*, so eliminate (A) and (D). *You* could be *looking*, so keep (B). *Noticing* cannot be *looking*, so eliminate (C). The correct answer is (B).

25. **A** Note the question! The question asks whether the sentence should be deleted, so it tests consistency. If the content of the sentence is consistent with the ideas surrounding it, then it should be kept. Otherwise, it should be deleted. The focus of the paragraph is the visual appearance of how *new* the paintings look. The underlined sentence discusses the *history of painting*. This is not consistent with the information in the paragraph, so it should be deleted. Eliminate (C) and (D). The sentence does *stray from the major focus*, so keep (A). It does not *restate a historical detail*, so eliminate (B). The correct answer is (A).

26. **D** Note the question! The question asks for *relevant and accurate information from the graph*, so it tests consistency. The correct answer must be consistent with the information in the passage and with the information in the graph. Read the labels on the graph carefully, and look for an answer that is consistent with the information given in the graph. Eliminate (A) because it is not consistent with the graph; art restoration did not start growing in 1930. Eliminate (B) because it is not consistent with either the passage or the graph; there is no indication that *book restorers* became *art restorers*. Eliminate (C) because it is not consistent with the graph; 2030 is not shown. Keep (D) because it is consistent with the passage and true based on the figure. The correct answer is (D).

27. **C** Vocabulary changes in the answer choices, so this question tests precision of word choice. Look for a phrase with a definition that is consistent with the other ideas in the sentence. The sentence contains a contrast: *may seem fairly straightforward* with *in fact quite complicated*. The phrase must help indicate the contrast. *When looking* would need some indication that the other part

of the contrast happened "without looking," which is not the case, so eliminate (A). *Beholden* means "indebted," which does not make sense in this context, so eliminate (B). *At first glance* contrasts with *actually* in the second part of the sentence, so keep (C). The use of *your* in (D) is not consistent with this paragraph, which does not directly address the reader; eliminate (D). The correct answer is (C).

28. **C** Punctuation changes in the answer choices, so this question tests how to connect ideas with the appropriate punctuation. The first part of the sentence, *Sometimes, as in the case of Michelangelo's famous sculpture* David, *the cleaning and restoration of artworks is a simple matter,* is an independent clause. The second part of the sentence, *applying chemicals, washing away grime, and scrubbing away dirt,* is not an independent clause. A comma can sometimes be used this way, so keep (A). Removing the punctuation creates a run-on sentence, so eliminate (B). The colon correctly separates the independent clause from a list that describes *the cleaning and restoration of artworks* mentioned in the first part of the sentence, so keep (C). A semicolon can only be used between two independent clauses, so eliminate (D). The colon more clearly separates the two parts of the sentence than the comma does, so eliminate (A). The correct answer is (C).

29. **A** Transitions change in the answer choices, so this question tests consistency of ideas. A transition must be consistent with the relationship between the ideas it connects. The previous sentence states that the restoration *is a simple matter*. This sentence states that *the process is a good deal more involved*. The ideas are contrasting, to the transitional phrase must be consistent with a contrast. *However* is consistent with a contrast, so keep (A). *Anyway* indicates a completely different idea, so eliminate (B). Both *In this sense* and *Alongside* indicate similar ideas, so eliminate (C) and (D). The correct answer is (A).

30. **C** Punctuation changes in the answer choices, so this question tests how to connect ideas with the appropriate punctuation. The first part of the sentence, *They would project some image of what the painting must have looked like originally and apply a variety of techniques, up to and including,* is not an independent clause. A colon can only be used after an independent clause, so eliminate (A) and (D). There is no need to break up the phrase *up to and including* with a comma, so eliminate (B). No punctuation is necessary. The correct answer is (C).

31. **B** Verbs change in the answer choices, so this question tests consistency of verbs. A verb must be consistent in number with its subject. The subject of the verb is *historians*, which is plural. To be consistent, the underlined verb must also be plural. Eliminate (A) and (C) because *is* is singular. Pronouns also change in the answer choices, so this question also tests consistency of pronouns. The pronoun must be consistent with its role in the sentence. *Who* is a subject pronoun and *whom* is an object pronoun. The pronoun is replacing *historians*, which is the subject of the sentence. To be consistent, the subject pronoun must be used. Eliminate (D). The correct answer is (B).

32. **D** Note the question! The question asks where the new sentence should be added, so it tests consistency. The sentence should be placed where it is consistent with the ideas before and after it. The new sentence gives an *example* of a *recent restoration*. Therefore, the new sentence should be placed after a sentence that discusses a way to restore a painting. Sentence 4 says that they will *restore the original look...by some non-paint means,* so the new sentence must be placed after sentence 4. The correct answer is (D).

33. **D** Prepositions change in the answer choices, so this question tests idioms. Look at the phrase before the preposition to determine the correct idiom. Use POE, and guess if there is more than one answer left. The correct idiom is *more...than*. Eliminate (A), (B), and (C). The correct answer is (D).

34. **C** Note the question! The question asks how to effectively combine the underlined sentences, so it tests precision and concision. The phrase after *modes* changes in the answer choices, so determine which phrase is necessary. The sentence starts with *Often overlooked*, so there's no need to repeat that idea. Eliminate (B), which repeats *overlooked*. *Suffering neglect* also repeats the idea, so eliminate (D). While both (A) and (C) could work, eliminate (A) because it's not as concise as (C). The correct answer is (C).

35. **C** Transitions change in the answer choices, so this question tests consistency of ideas. A transition must be consistent with the relationship between the ideas it connects. The sentence that starts with the underlined portion states that *Simmons's novel was published in 1989, and it won the Hugo Award*. This sentence states that it is *listed among the greatest of all time*. The two sentences both discuss positive views of the novel, so they agree. Eliminate (B) because *for all that* indicates a contrast. *All things considered* would indicate a summing up, which is not consistent with these sentences, so eliminate (A). *To this day* indicates that the two sentences agree, so keep (C). *Check this out* would indicate the introduction of a new idea and is also too informal in tone, so eliminate (D). The correct answer is (C).

36. **D** The length of the phrase changes in the answer choices, so this question tests concision. There is also the option to DELETE; consider this choice carefully as it is often the correct answer. Removing the underlined portion makes the sentence complete and precise: *The novel spawned a series of novels dealing with the same fantastic universe* (the rest of the sentence, after the comma, is a phrase that is not necessary to the main meaning of the sentence). Adding either *which* or *that* makes the sentence incomplete, so eliminate (A) and (B). Choice (C) makes the sentence complete, but the word *that* does not clearly refer to anything, so it should not be included. Eliminate (C). The correct answer is (D).

37. **C** The length of the phrase changes in the answer choices, so this question tests concision and precision. Select the shortest phrase that makes the meaning precise. Since all of the choices mean the same thing, select the shortest choice. Eliminate (A), (B), and (D). The correct answer is (C).

38. **B** Pronouns change in the answer choices, so this question tests consistency of pronouns. A pronoun must be consistent in number with the noun it refers to. The underlined pronoun refers to the noun *pilgrims*, which is plural. To be consistent, the underlined word must be third-person plural. Eliminate (A) because *your* is second person. Keep (B) because *their* is third-person plural. Eliminate (C) because *our* is first person. Eliminate (D) because *everyone's* is singular. The correct answer is (B).

39. **A** Transitions change in the answer choices, so this question tests consistency of ideas. A transition must be consistent with the relationship between the ideas it connects. The sentence states that two things happen together: the story *illuminates the journey* and *explains this new fantasy world*. There is no contrast in the sentence, so eliminate (C). Keep (A) because it uses *while* to show the two things happening together. Although *when* links the two things in time, it indicates a cause-and-effect relationship. This is not the precise meaning of the sentence, so eliminate (B). Eliminate (D) because *as if* would mean that *explaining this new fantasy world* is not actually happening. The correct answer is (A).

40. **D** Verbs change in the answer choices, so this question tests consistency of verbs. A verb must be consistent with other verbs in the sentence. Eliminate (A) because the underlined portion must be a verb, and adding *of* makes *sound* function as a noun. Eliminate (B) because there is nothing in the sentence that *and* would connect to. The other verb in the sentence is *draws*, which is in simple present tense. To be consistent, the correct answer must also be present tense. Eliminate

(C) because *sounding* is not consistent with *draws*. Keep (D) because *sounds* is simple present tense. The correct answer is (D).

41. **D** Apostrophes change in the answer choices, so the question tests apostrophe usage. When used with a noun, an apostrophe indicates possession. In this sentence, the verb form of *travel* must be used with *together*, so nothing belongs to the pilgrims. There's no reason to use the apostrophe, so eliminate (B) and (C). To create a complete sentence, the phrase must modify what the pilgrims are doing, rather than directly state their action. Using *travel* creates an incomplete sentence, so eliminate (A). Using *traveling* creates a modifying phrase, which makes the sentence complete. The correct answer is (D).

42. **B** Note the question! The question asks which choice *most effectively sets up the information that follows*, so this question is testing consistency. Eliminate answers that are inconsistent with the purpose stated in the question. The following sentence says *all of these literary tributes* and mentions *Hyperion*. To be consistent, the correct answer should discuss some *tributes* and mention *Hyperion*. Eliminate (A) because neither of those ideas is mentioned. Keep (B) because it mentions *homage*, which is a type of *tribute*, and *Hyperion*. Eliminate (C) because neither of those ideas is mentioned. Eliminate (D) because, although it mentions *Hyperion*, there is no mention of tributes. The correct answer is (B).

43. **C** Note the question! The question asks whether the new sentence should be added, so it tests consistency. If the content of the new sentence is consistent with the ideas surrounding it, then it should be added. The new sentence introduces *some of T.S. Eliot's most famous poems*. The paragraph is about Simmons's *Hyperion*. Therefore, the information is not consistent, and the sentence should not be added. Eliminate (A) and (B). The new sentence *does not have a clear link to the rest of the passage*, so keep (C). The new sentence does not *disagree with the passage's central claim*, so eliminate (D). The correct answer is (C).

44. **D** Verbs change in the answer choices, so this question tests consistency of verbs. A verb must be consistent with its subject and with the other verbs in the sentence. The subject of the verb is *continuities*, which is plural. To be consistent, the verb must also be plural. Eliminate (A) and (B) because they are singular. The verb *being* creates an incomplete sentence, so eliminate (C). The verb *are* is plural. The correct answer is (D).

Section 3: Math (No Calculator)

1. **A** The question asks for an expression to represent a situation. Write an expression for the number of hours each of the two people has worked. Jan worked *j* hours a day for 3 days, so she worked a total of $3j$ hours. Noah worked *n* hours a day for 5 days, so he worked a total of $5n$ hours. Therefore, the total hours worked by Jan and Noah combined is the sum of these two, which is $3j + 5n$. These are not like terms, so they cannot be combined or simplified further. The correct answer is (A).

2. **B** The question asks for the value of *y* with a given value of *c*. Plug $c = 4$ into the right side of the equation to get $\frac{y + 2}{5} = 4$. Multiply both sides of the equation by 5 to get $y + 2 = 20$. Subtract 2 from both sides to get $y = 18$. The correct answer is (B).

3. **B** The question asks for the sum of two complex numbers (numbers with both a real and imagi-

nary part). Even though this looks complicated, start by combining like terms. Add the real terms, 10 and 3, to get 13. Then, add the imaginary terms, $-4i$ and $6i$, to get $2i$. Add these two to get $13 + 2i$. The correct answer is (B).

4. **D** The question asks for an expression that is equivalent to the given one. Simplify this expression by combining like terms one piece at a time. Start with the ab^2 terms. The $-ab^2$ term from the second polynomial is subtracted from the ab^2 in the first. $ab^2 - (-ab^2) = ab^2 + ab^2 = 2ab^2$. Eliminate any choice that does not include $2ab^2$: (A) and (B). Now look at the a^2 terms. The $4a^2$ term from the second polynomial is subtracted from the $4a^2$ term in the first. $4a^2 - 4a^2 = 0$. Therefore, the correct answer cannot have an a^2 term. Eliminate the remaining choice that does, which is (C). The correct answer is (D).

5. **D** The question asks for the estimated increase in shark weight for each additional foot of fork length. The weight of a mature great white shark is estimated by $w = 3,150 + 450l$, where l is the fork length in feet. To determine this, try out two values for l that show a one-foot increase. First, plug in $l = 2$. If $l = 2$, then $w = 3,150 + 450(2) = 4,050$. Then plug in $l = 3$. If $l = 3$, then $w = 3,150 + 450(3) = 4,500$. The increase is $4,500 - 4,050 = 450$. Therefore, the correct answer is (D).

6. **C** The question asks for the meaning of the number 326 in the equation. The number of pages Juan has left to edit is represented by the equation $P = 326 - 12h$, where h represents the number of hours worked. Since P is a number of pages, 326 must also be a number of pages, so eliminate (D). Choices (A) and (B) each deal with a rate. In order to turn a rate into an amount, the rate must be multiplied by time. Since h represents time, the coefficient on time, 12, must represent the rate rather than 326. Therefore, eliminate (A) and (B). Only (C) remains, so it must be correct. To understand why it is correct, plug in $h = 0$. If $h = 0$, then $P = 326 - 12(0) = 326$. In other words, when he has worked 0 hours, he has 326 pages left to edit. Therefore, the correct answer is (C).

7. **A** The question asks for the value of a fraction with x and y and says that $\frac{x}{y} = 3$. Try some values of x and y that satisfy this equation. Let $x = 6$ and $y = 2$. Plug these values into the expression $\frac{12y}{x}$ to get $\frac{12(2)}{6} = \frac{24}{6} = 4$. Therefore, the correct answer is (A).

8. **A** The question asks for the solution to a system of equations. Test the points in the answer choices by plugging them into the two equations. In order to be the solution of the system of equations, a point must satisfy both equations. Start with (A): $(-7, -5)$. Plug these values into the first equation to get $2(-5) + (-7) = -17$. This is true, so plug the values into the second equation to get $5(-7) - 4(-5) = -15$. Since this is also true, the correct answer is (A).

9. **C** The question asks for the value of M in a very complicated equation. The variable M is not part of the fraction but rather the value that is being multiplied by the fraction. In order to isolate a variable that is multiplied by a fraction, multiply both sides by the reciprocal of the fraction. On the right side of the equation, the fractions cancel, isolating M. On the left side, the reciprocal is multiplied by c to get $\dfrac{1 - \left(1 + \dfrac{r}{1,200}\right)^{-N}}{\dfrac{r}{1,200}}c$. Therefore, the correct answer is (C).

10. **C** The question asks about a point on a line in the xy-plane. Any such line can be defined by the equation $y = mx + b$, in which m is the slope and b is the y-intercept. The question says that the slope is $\frac{2}{3}$, so $m = \frac{2}{3}$. The question also says that the line passes through the origin, which is the point $(0, 0)$. Since the y-intercept is the point at which the x-coordinate is 0, the origin must be the y-intercept, so $b = 0$. Thus the equation of the line is $y = \frac{2}{3}x + 0$, or $y = \frac{2}{3}x$. Try the points in the answer choices in this equation. Start with (A). Plug in the values from (A) to get $\frac{2}{3} = \frac{2}{3}(0)$. Since this is false, eliminate (A). Try (B). Plug in the values from (B) to get $3 = \frac{2}{3}(2)$. Since this is false, eliminate (B). Try (C). Plug in the values from (C) to get $4 = \frac{2}{3}(6)$. This becomes $4 = 4$, which is true. The correct answer is (C).

11. **D** The question asks for the value of $f(-3)$ for the given function f. Begin by finding the value of constant c. Since $f(3) = 12$, plug this into the function to get $f(3) = c(3)^2 + 30 = 12$. Therefore, $9c + 30 = 12$. Subtract 30 from both sides to get $9c = -18$. Divide both sides by 9 to get $c = -2$. Plug this into the original equation to get $f(x) = -2x^2 + 30$. The question asks for $f(-3)$, so plug in $x = -3$ to get $f(-3) = -2(-3)^2 + 30 = -2(9) + 30 = -18 + 30 = 12$. The correct answer is (D).

12. **A** The question asks for the price per night when it was the same for both hotels. Since the two equations given are for the price per night in the two hotels, set the two expressions for the prices equal: $240 - 20w = 320 - 30w$. Add $30w$ to both sides to get $240 + 10w = 320$. Subtract 240 from both sides to get $10w = 80$. Divide both sides by 10 to get $w = 8$. This represents the number of weeks, but the question asks for the price per night. Plug this value of w into the equation for A, which becomes $A = 240 - 20(8) = 240 - 160 = 80$. The correct answer is (A).

13. **C** The question asks for the value of $\frac{3^a}{81^b}$. To divide numbers with exponents, the bases must be the same. Convert the denominator to a base of 3: since $81 = 3^4$, $81^b = (3^4)^b$. When raising a number with an exponent to an exponent, multiply the exponents, so $81^b = (3^4)^b = 3^{4b}$. Therefore, $\frac{3^a}{81^b} = \frac{3^a}{3^{4b}}$. When dividing numbers with exponents and the same base, subtract the exponents, so $\frac{3^a}{3^{4b}} = 3^{a-4b}$. The question also says that $a - 4b = 18$, so $3^{a-4b} = 3^{18}$. Therefore, the correct answer is (C).

14. **A** The question asks for the value of k in an equation that contains a quadratic in both factored and expanded form. Get them in the same form by expanding the factored quadratic on the left side. Use FOIL (First, Outer, Inner, Last) on $(ax + 3)(bx + 5)$. Multiply first terms to get $(ax)(bx) = abx^2$. Compare this to the x^2 term on the right side, $35x^2$. Therefore, $ab = 35$. Since $ab = 35$, consider the factors of 35. There are two pairs of factors: 1, 35 and 5, 7. Since the question says that $a + b = 12$, a and b must be 5 and 7, but there is no way to determine the order. Therefore, consider both $a = 5$, $b = 7$ and $a = 7$, $b = 5$. If $a = 5$ and $b = 7$, the equation becomes $(5x + 3)(7x + 5) = 35x^2 + kx + 15$. To get the value of k, determine the coefficient on the x-term of the quadratic expression on the left. To do this, find the product of the outer terms and the product of the inner terms, which

are $25x$ and $21x$, respectively. Add these products to get $25x + 21x = 46x$, so, in this case, $k = 46$. Eliminate any choice that does not include 46: (B), (C), and (D). Therefore, the correct answer is (A). (To determine the other possible value, plug in $a = 7$ and $b = 5$ to get $(7x + 3)(5x + 5)$. Multiply outer terms to get $35x$. Multiply inner terms to get $15x$. Add the products to get $50x$, so $k = 50$.)

15. **C** The question asks for an expression equivalent to the given fraction. Rather than dealing with complicated fractions, simplify things by putting in a number for y. The question says that $y > 5$, so plug in $y = 6$ to get $\dfrac{1}{\frac{1}{6-4} + \frac{1}{6-3}}$. The fraction simplifies to $\dfrac{1}{\frac{1}{2} + \frac{1}{3}}$. Now, add the fractions in the denominator, using the common denominator of 6. Therefore, the original fraction is equivalent to $\dfrac{1}{\frac{3}{6} + \frac{2}{6}} = \dfrac{1}{\frac{5}{6}}$. When dividing by a fraction, flip the bottom fraction and multiply. Therefore, $\dfrac{1}{\frac{5}{6}} = \dfrac{\frac{1}{1}}{\frac{5}{6}} = \dfrac{1}{1} \times \dfrac{6}{5} = \dfrac{6}{5}$, so $\dfrac{6}{5}$ is the target number.

Plug $y = 6$ into the answer choices and eliminate any choice that is not equal to $\dfrac{6}{5}$. Since (A) and (B) are not fractions, eliminate them immediately. Try (C). The expression becomes $\dfrac{y^2 - 7y + 12}{2y - 7} = \dfrac{6^2 - 7(6) + 12}{2(6) - 7} = \dfrac{36 - 42 + 12}{12 - 7} = \dfrac{6}{5}$, so keep (C). Try (D). The expression becomes $\dfrac{2y - 7}{y^2 - 7y + 12} = \dfrac{2(6) - 7}{6^2 - 7(6) + 12} = \dfrac{5}{6} \neq \dfrac{6}{5}$, so eliminate (D). The correct answer is (C).

16. **5** The question asks for the value of m on the figure, so label the given information on the figure. Label $\overline{PQ}$ with length 3, $\overline{QT}$ with length 4, $\overline{QS}$ with length 8, and $\overline{SR}$ with length 10. When a question involves two triangles, determine whether they are similar. Similar triangles, by definition, have three pairs of congruent corresponding angles. However, since the measures of the angles in all triangles have a sum of 180°, it is only necessary to show that two pairs of corresponding angles are congruent. The question says that $\angle TPQ$ is congruent to $\angle QRS$. Also, $\angle PQT$ and $\angle SQR$ are vertical angles, so they are also congruent. Thus, the two triangles are similar. Similar triangles have a consistent proportion between corresponding sides (sides that are opposite congruent angles). The question asks for the value of m, or the length

of $\overline{PT}$, which corresponds with $\overline{SR}$. Use the lengths of another pair of corresponding sides, $\overline{QT}$ and $\overline{QS}$, to set up a proportion: $\dfrac{m}{10} = \dfrac{4}{8}$. Cross-multiply to get $8m = 40$. Divide by 8 to get $m = 5$. Therefore, the correct answer is 5.

17. **6** The question asks for the value of y in the equation $y^2 - 36 = 0$. Add 36 to both sides to get $y^2 = 36$. Take the square root of both sides to get $y = \pm 6$. However, the question specifies that $y > 0$, so $y = 6$. The correct answer is 6.

18. $\dfrac{5}{13}$ The question asks for the value of a sine function in a right triangle. There is no figure, so draw the right triangle. Label one of the non-right angles with measure $d°$. Since $\cos = \dfrac{\text{adjacent}}{\text{hypotenuse}}$ and $\cos d° = \dfrac{5}{13}$, label the side adjacent to d as 5 and the hypotenuse 13. Using the Pythagorean Theorem (or the 5:12:13 Pythagorean triple), the missing side has length 12. Since the angles in a triangle have a sum of 180, label the missing angle x and set up the equation $d + x + 90 = 180$. Subtract 90 from both sides to get $d + x = 90$, and subtract d from both sides to get $x = 90 - d$. The question asks for the sine of this angle. Since $\sin \theta = \dfrac{opp}{hyp}$, find the side opposite this angle, which is 5, and the hypotenuse, which is 13, to get $\sin(90° - d°) = \dfrac{5}{13}$. Alternatively, note that the angle of measure $(90° - d°)$ is the complement of the angle of measure $d°$. The sine of an angle is equal to the cosine of its complement. Therefore, $\sin(90° - d°) = \cos d° = \dfrac{5}{13}$. Either way, the correct answer is $\dfrac{5}{13}$.

19. **225** The question asks for the value of z. The second equation, $5c = \sqrt{5z}$, is in terms of c and z, so plug in the value of c to get $5\left(3\sqrt{5}\right) = \sqrt{5z}$. Simplify the left side to get $15\sqrt{5} = \sqrt{5z}$. Since the equation involves square roots, square both sides to get $\left(15\sqrt{5}\right)^2 = \left(\sqrt{5z}\right)^2$. Square each factor to get $(15)^2\left(\sqrt{5}\right)^2 = \left(\sqrt{5z}\right)^2$ and $(225)(5) = 5z$. Divide both sides by 5 to get $225 = z$. The correct answer is 225.

20. **13** The question asks for the value of b in a system of equations, so find a way to cancel the a terms. To do this, make sure that the a term coefficients are opposites so that they will disappear when the equations are added together. Multiply the first equation by -2 to get $-2a - 2b = 20$. Stack this below the second equation, $2a + b = -33$, and add the two equations.

$$\begin{array}{r} 2a + b = -33 \\ \underline{-2a - 2b = 20} \\ 0a - b = -13 \end{array}$$

Therefore, the new equation is $0 - b = -13$ or $b = 13$. Thus, the correct answer is 13.

Section 4: Math (Calculator)

1. **C** The question asks for the measurement of an angle on the figure. When two parallel lines are intersected by a third line, or by two or more parallel lines, the following is true: all the small angles are the same, all the big angles are the same, and any small angle + any big angle = 180°. "Small" angles are less than 90°, and "big" angles are greater than 90°. In this question, x is a small angle, and y is a big angle, so $x + y = 180°$. Substitute the given value: $75° + y = 180°$. Subtract 75° from both sides to get $y = 105°$. The correct answer is (C).

2. **C** The question asks for the interval that shows the number of customers decreasing then increasing. Work through the answer choices one at a time. For (A), the number of customers stays the same from 9:00 A.M.–11:00 A.M., then increases from 11:00 A.M.–12:00 P.M., so eliminate (A). For (B), the number of customers stays the same from 12:00 P.M.–1:00 P.M., drops suddenly, then stays the same from 1:00 P.M.–2:00 P.M., so eliminate (B). Choice (C) looks good; the number of customers decreases from 2:00 P.M.–3:30 P.M., then increases from 3:30 P.M.–5:00 P.M. Finally, in (D), the number of customers increases from 3:30 P.M.–5:00 P.M., then decreases from 5:00 P.M.–6:30 P.M. This is a trap answer that does the opposite of what the question asks for, so eliminate (D). The correct answer is (C).

3. **B** The question asks for the value of y given a certain value of x. Start by plugging in the values given for x and y, then solve for k. If $5 = \dfrac{30}{k}$, then $5k = 30$ and $k = 6$. It is given that k is a constant, which means that its value doesn't change (whereas x and y are variables, so their values do change). Now plug in the values for the second scenario: $y = \dfrac{42}{6}$, so $y = 7$. The correct answer is (B).

4. **B** The question asks for the number of 1-decigram doses in three kilograms of medicine. When given conflicting units, set up a proportion. First, convert the 3 kilograms into grams: $\dfrac{1\,\text{kg}}{1,000\,\text{g}} = \dfrac{3\,\text{kg}}{x\,\text{g}}$, so $x = 3(1,000) = 3,000$ grams. Next, convert the 3,000 grams into decigrams: $\dfrac{1\,\text{g}}{10\,\text{dg}} = \dfrac{3,000\,\text{g}}{x\,\text{dg}}$, so $x = 10(3,000) = 30,000$ decigrams. The correct answer is (B).

5. **D** The question asks for the value of $9x$ in a certain situation. The simplest way to solve this question is to translate it into an equation and solve for x. The statement *6x – 4 is 11 less than 25* can be translated as $6x - 4 = 25 - 11$. Simplify the right side: $6x - 4 = 14$. Add 4 to both sides: $6x = 18$. Divide by 6: $x = 3$. Be careful not to fall for (A); read the full question! The question asks for the value of $9x$, and $(9)(3) = 27$. The correct answer is (D).

6. **A** The question asks for a graph that shows a positive correlation between the variables. When a question contains a scatterplot, draw a line of best fit through the dots, so that roughly half the dots are above the line, and half are below. If the line of best fit has a positive slope, it means that h and p have a *positive correlation* (the question might say "association" rather than "correlation"). If the line has a negative slope, it means that the two quantities have a *negative correlation*, as in (B). If there is no clear relationship between the variables, there is *no* correlation. If the dots in the scatterplot are packed relatively closely, the correlation is *strong*; if they are far apart, the correlation is *weak*. Fortunately, there's no need to choose between strong and weak here. The correct answer is (A).

7. **C** The question asks for the depth that will result in a pressure of 200 kilopascals. In the given equation, plug in 200 for p and solve for d: $200 = 101 + 10.094d$. Subtract 101 from both sides: $99 = 10.094d$. Divide both sides by 10.094 to get $d = 9.808$. The question asks for the closest answer, so round to the closest integer, which is 10. The correct answer is (C).

8. **D** The question asks for the formula for pressure p to be rearranged to express depth d. The fastest way to solve this question is to use algebra. Start by isolating the term that contains d by subtracting 101 from both sides: $p - 101 = 10.094d$. Divide by 10.094: $\frac{p - 101}{10.094} = d$. Now simply write the expression in reverse so that d is on the left side: $d = \frac{p - 101}{10.094}$. This matches (D), so that's the correct answer. Another way to do this would be to try real numbers in the equation. Plug in 2 for d and solve for p: $101 + (10.094)(2) = 121.188 = p$. Now plug these values into the answers and pick the one that works. The correct answer is (D).

9. **B** The question asks for the best label for a graph of the number of wind turbines. The answers differ only in the units, so compare the graph to the information given. Add up the number of wind turbines shown on the graph: $9 + 11 + 3.5 + 8 + 6 = 37.5$. Now try the answer choices. Start with (B) or (C), then move higher or lower if the first choice doesn't work. Try (C): $37.5 \times 1,000 = 37,500$, which is too big. Try (B): $37.5 \times 100 = 3,750$, which matches the information on the graph. The correct answer is (B).

10. **A** The question asks for the number of values of k that will make an expression equal to one. When the SAT mixes math symbols and words, try translating the words into a math equation. In this question, the phrase $|k - 3| + 2$ *is equal to one* translates to $|k - 3| + 2 = 1$. To isolate the absolute-value expression, subtract 2 from both sides to get $|k + 3| = -1$. Here's the tricky part of the question: an absolute-value expression can never be negative, so no values of k would make this expression true. Therefore, the correct answer is (A).

11. **D** The question asks for the average number of residents per apartment based on the graph. There are 14 apartments: 1 apartment with 6 residents, 2 with 4 residents, 4 with 5 residents, and 7 with 3 residents. Add up all the residents: $6 + 4 + 4 + 5 + 5 + 5 + 5 + 3 + 3 + 3 + 3 + 3 + 3 + 3 = 55$. Divide by the number of apartments: $\frac{55}{14} = 3.929$. This is closest to 4. The correct answer is (D).

12. **D** The question asks for the number that CANNOT be a solution to an inequality. There are two ways to tackle this question: solve algebraically or use the answers. To solve algebraically, subtract $6x$ from both sides to get $-4 \leq x - 3$. Then add 3 to both sides to get $-1 \leq x$ or $x \geq -1$. Since x must be -1 or greater, -2 cannot be a solution, so the answer is (D). To try out the answers, start with (B) or (C). Here, it makes more sense to start with (B), because 0 is a very easy number to plug in. Plugging in 0 gives $-4 \leq -3$, which is true, so eliminate (B). Now try (C): $-10 \leq -10$, which is true, so eliminate (C). Finally, try (D): $-16 \leq -17$, which is false. The correct answer is (D).

13. **B** The question asks for the statistical measure that will change the least when a data point is removed. To calculate (or estimate) mean, median, or range, it's best to save mean for last, since it's usually the most time-consuming to calculate. Start with the easiest part: the total. If 2 is removed, the total will change by 2. The range is the difference between the largest and smallest term. The range now is $9 - 2 = 7$, but if 2 is removed, the smallest term will be 3, so the range

will be 9 − 3 = 6, and the range changes by 1. To find the median in a set with an even number of terms, take the average of the two middle terms. Here, the two middle terms are both 6, so 6 is the median. If 2 is removed, there will be 17 terms, so the 9th term will be the median. Since the new 9th term will be 6, the median will not change at all. This makes it unnecessary to calculate the average. The average is the total divided by the number of things, so if 2 is removed from the total and 1 from the number of things, the average will change. Therefore, the correct answer is (B).

14. **B** The question asks for the relationship between p and r in a system of inequalities. Since a point is given as a solution, use that in the inequalities. Put (2, 2) in for x and y, and solve for p and r. In the first inequality, $p + 2 > 2$, so $p > 0$. In the second inequality, $r − 2 < −2$, so $r < 0$. Since r is negative and p is positive, r must be less than p. The correct answer is (B).

15. **A** The question asks for the category that accounts for approximately 15% of the people who responded to a poll. When a question says *approximately*, go ahead and approximate. The total, 395, is close to 400, so 15% of 400 = $\frac{15}{100} \times 400 = 60$. Often, this would be enough to find the correct answer, but in this case there are two answers, 59 and 62, that are very close, so try them both. $\frac{59}{395} \times 100 = 14.94\%$. That looks good, but try (B), just to be safe: $\frac{62}{395} \times 100 = 15.7\%$, which rounds to 16%, which is not correct. The correct answer is (A).

16. **C** The question asks what the slope of a line represents in a given situation. Slope is rise divided by run, or vertical change divided by horizontal change. For each additional day, the price increases by $20, so the slope, $\frac{20}{1}$, is equivalent to the average daily price increase. The correct answer is (C).

17. **D** The question asks for the relationship between two variables, so it is asking for an equation. In this case, it's the equation of a line, and all the answer choices are in slope-intercept form. The slope is 20 (as calculated for the previous question). Notice on the graph that when $d = 0$, $P = 30$, so the y-intercept is 30. The equation of a line in slope-intercept form is $y = mx + b$, where m is the slope and b is the y-intercept. In this question, $m = 20$ and $b = 30$, so the equation is $y = 20d + 30$. Plugging in values from the graph can also determine the correct equation. Either way, the correct answer is (D).

18. **C** The question asks for the value of x at which $f(x)$ has its maximum. In the xy-plane, $f(x) = y$. The maximum y-value on this line graph is 3, and when $y = 3$, $x = −2$. In this type of question, if they ask for an x-value, the corresponding y-value is likely to be a trap answer. In this case, (D) is the trap. The correct answer is (C).

19. **C** The question asks for an expression to represent the price of a ticket bought in the train station during peak hours. There is a lot of abstract information in this question, so make up some numbers. Start from the simplest price, which is a peak ticket bought in the station. Let's say that price is $100. In that case, an off-peak ticket purchased in the station will be 15% off, or $85. For an off-peak ticket purchased from the conductor, there is an 11% surcharge, so $\frac{11}{100} \times 85 = 9.35$, and $85 + $9.35 = $94.35. This is the value of t, and the question is asking for the value of a peak ticket bought in the station, which is $100. Now plug $t = $94.35 into the answer choices, and choose the one that equals $100. The correct answer is (C).

20. **A**   The question asks for the probability that a chosen person who exercises fewer than 6 times per week belonged to Group 1. In most SAT questions, all the information matters. But, once in a while, there will be unnecessary information designed to create confusion. In this question, it is not necessary to know the total number of people, nor whether they eat snacks or not. A person is being randomly chosen from *among those who exercise fewer than six times per week*, so only the first two columns in the table matter. There are a total of 24 + 40 people who exercise fewer than 6 times per week and, of those people, 13 + 22 = 35 of them are in Group 1. Use the probability formula: probability = $\frac{\text{want}}{\text{total}}$ = $\frac{35}{64}$. The correct answer is (A).

21. **D**   The question asks for the number of gallons of diesel fuel sold by the gas station on Monday. This question can be solved two ways: as a system of equations or by trying out the answers.

To solve with equations, start by assigning variables. Make g the number of gallons of gasoline and d the number of gallons of diesel. Now write two equations: $3.25g + 3d = 404.25$ and $g + d = 131$. To get the value for d, try to make the g-values disappear. Multiply the second equation by -3.25 to get $-3.25g - 3.25d = -425.75$. Stack and add the two equations to get

$$
\begin{aligned}
3.25g + 3d &= 404.25 \\
\underline{-3.25g - 3.25d} &= \underline{-425.75} \\
-0.25d &= -21.5
\end{aligned}
$$

Divide by -0.25 to find that $d = 86$. The correct answer is (D).

A safer method is to use the answers. Start with (C). If the station sold 76 gallons of diesel, then the station sold $131 - 76 = 55$ gallons of gasoline. The revenue from diesel would be $76 \times \$3 = \$228$, and the revenue from gasoline would be $55 \times \$3.25 = \$178.75$, for a total of $\$228 + \$178.75 = \$406.75$, which doesn't match the total sales of \$404.25 given by the question. Since the total was too high, move to (D), where more of the cheaper diesel fuel was sold: if the station sold 86 gallons of diesel, then the station sold $131 - 86 = 45$ gallons of gasoline. The revenue from diesel would be $86 \times \$3 = \$258$, and the revenue from gasoline would be $45 \times \$3.25 = \$146.25$, for a total of $\$258 + \$146.25 = \$404.25$, which matches the total sales given by the question. The correct answer is (D).

22. **C**   The question asks for the category in which the ratio of 2010 to 2014 spending was closest to that of the same ratio for higher education. With the ugly numbers in the chart, approximation is helpful here. The ratio of 2010 higher-education spending to 2014 higher-education spending can be estimated as 2.1 million to 3.1 million, or even more approximately as 2:3. The only other column that is close is corrections, which can be estimated as 630,000 to 930,000, also fairly close to 2:3. The correct answer is (C).

23. **C**   The question asks for the approximate rate of change in public assistance spending from 2012 to 2014. When questions ask for an approximate value, round the numbers to avoid unnecessary math. Round public assistance spending in 2012 to \$56,000 and round 2014 spending to \$30,000. Subtract to get an approximate difference of \$26,000. Divide by two to get an average of \$13,000. Read carefully: the chart values are in *thousands of dollars*, so multiply by 1,000 to get the actual rate of change of \$13,000,000. The correct answer is (C).

24. **A**   The question asks for the number of seconds it will take for the jumping fish to hit the surface of the lake. At that time, the height will be 0, so plug 0 into the equation: $0 = 9s - 4.9s^2$. From here, the

easiest thing to do is plug in the answer choices. Start with (C): $(9)(3) - (4.9)(3^2) = 27 - 44.1 = -17.1$. This negative value means that the fish has gone 17 meters below the surface. Choice (C) is too big, so try (B). It's also too big, so the answer must be (A). Double check to be sure: $9(2) - (4.9)(2^2) = 18 - 19.6 = -1.6$. The question is asking for an approximate answer, and (A) is closest. The question can also be solved by factoring $h = 9s - 4.9s^2$ into $h = s(9 - 4.9s)$. The solutions for s in this equation are $s = 0$ (the time when the fish began the leap) and $9 - 4.9s = 0$ (the time when the fish hit the water). Solve the latter for s: $9 = 4.9s$, so $s = \dfrac{9}{4.9} = 1.84$ seconds. Either way, the correct answer is (A).

25. **C** The question asks for the equation of a circle with a given center and radius endpoint. The equation of a circle centered at (h, k) is $(x - h)^2 + (y - k)^2 = r^2$. Therefore, the left side of the equation must be $(x - 3)^2 + y^2$. Eliminate (B) and (D). To narrow it down further, find the radius by drawing a triangle and finding the legs to plug into the Pythagorean Theorem (this is safer than trying to remember the distance formula).

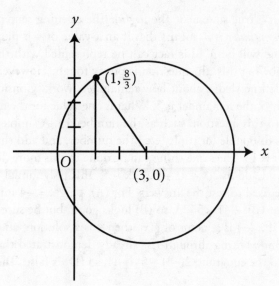

The base is 2 and the height is $\dfrac{8}{3}$, so use the Pythagorean Theorem to find the radius. $2^2 + \left(\dfrac{8}{3}\right)^2 = r^2$, so $4 + \dfrac{64}{9} = r^2$, or $\dfrac{36}{9} + \dfrac{64}{9} = \dfrac{100}{9} = r^2$. It's not necessary to take the square root, because the only piece missing from the circle formula is r^2. The correct equation is $(x - 3)^2 + y^2 = \dfrac{100}{9}$. The correct answer is (C).

26. **D** The question asks for the number of seedlings on a square lawn that are at least 2 inches high. When dealing with area questions, always calculate the areas—don't make assumptions. The area of the lawn is $8 \times 8 = 64$ square feet. There are 8 samples, and each sample is $1 \times 1 = 1$ square foot, so the total area sampled is $\dfrac{8}{64} = \dfrac{1}{8}$ of the total area. Next, since the question asks for approximation, approximate the total number of seedlings. The middle values are very close to 100, and the highest and lowest values are almost equidistant from 100, so the average number of seedlings in a sample is about

100. Therefore, the total number of seedlings in all the samples is approximately $100 \times 8 = 800$, and the total number of seedlings on the lawn is approximately $800 \times 8 = 6,400$. The correct answer is (D).

27. **C** The question asks for the number of offspring of the Western chinchillas. The easiest approach will be to use the answer choices. Start with (B). If there were 103 Western chinchilla offspring, then the Eastern chinchilla produced $103 \times \dfrac{30}{100} = 30.9$ more offspring than the Western chinchilla, totaling 133.9. Since 133.9 does not match the 143 offspring specified by the question, eliminate (B) and move to a larger number. Try (C). If there were 110 Western chinchilla offspring, then the Eastern chinchilla produced $110 \times \dfrac{30}{100} = 33$ more offspring than the Western chinchilla, totaling 143, which matches the number specified in the question. Therefore, the correct answer is (C).

28. **B** The question asks for a true statement about $g(x)$. The opening sentence, *when polynomial g(x) is divided by x – 4, the remainder is 3,* means that if an x-value of 4 is plugged into the polynomial, the corresponding y-value will be 3. This fact can be represented with the equation $g(4) = 3$, so (B) is correct. Without knowing this, the question is pretty tough. However, it is possible to try out some numbers with a little knowledge about how remainders work. Consider an easier question: when a number is divided by 5, the remainder is 3. What is one value for the number? It's fairly easy to come up with an answer to this question, such as the number 13. A simple way to find a quotient with a certain remainder is to double (or triple, etc.) the number, and add the remainder. So, double 5 and add 3, and the result is 13. The same thing can be done in this more difficult question. The divisor is $x - 4$, so double it and add 3: $2(x - 4) + 3 = 2x - 5$. This polynomial meets the requirements of the question and can be used to test the answers. For (A), plug $x = -4$ into the polynomial: $2(-4) + 5 = -3$, so (A) is false. For (B), $2(4) - 5 = 3$, so (B) looks good, but be sure to check all four answers. For (C), remember that if $x - 4$ is a factor of $g(x)$, then 4 is a solution, and plugging 4 into the equation should yield zero. But working through (B) already demonstrated that $2(4) - 5 = 3$, so (C) is false. For (D), plug -3 into the equation: $2(-3) - 5 = -11$, so (D) is false. The correct answer is (B).

29. **A** The question asks for the equation in vertex form based on the equation in standard form, which is $y = ax^2 + bx + c$. The vertex form of a parabola is $y = a(x - h)^2 + k$. It's called "vertex form" because the vertex of the parabola is at (h, k). The x-coordinate of the vertex will always be the average of the x-coordinates of any two points that have the same y-value. The graph gives two points on the y-axis (these are the *solutions* or *zeros* of the equation), so find the average of the x-coordinates: $\dfrac{-4 + 2}{2} = -1$, so $h = -1$. From the graph, it also looks like the y-coordinate of the vertex is -9, so $k = -9$, making the vertex $(-1, -9)$. Now look at the answers. Choice (A) is in "vertex form," and the vertex it shows is $(-1, -9)$. The correct answer is (A).

30. **B** The question asks for the number of quadrants that will contain part of the solution to a system of inequalities. To answer this question, use the provided quadrant drawing to make a quick sketch

with both equations drawn. It is not necessary to make a perfectly accurate graph; just get the general idea. For this system of inequalities, any solutions must be above *both* lines (because the solutions must be greater than both $y \geq x + 2$ and $y \geq \frac{1}{3}x - 1$), so shade in this area as shown below:

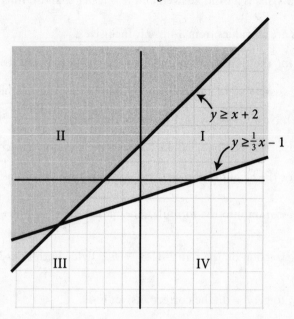

As the sketch shows, some areas are shaded in light gray to represent the graph of just one of the inequalities. The light gray area in the lower left only applies to $y \geq x + 2$, and the other light gray area only applies to $y \geq \frac{1}{3}x - 1$ The dark gray area of overlap shows the solution to the system of inequalities, as only points in that region will satisfy both inequalities. This dark gray area shows solutions in Quadrants I, II, and III, but not in IV. The correct answer is (B).

31. $\dfrac{3}{7}, \dfrac{6}{14}, \dfrac{9}{21}$, .428, or .429

The question asks for a fraction based on the amounts of Greg's April and February bills. Locate the values for April and February, and write them as a fraction: $\dfrac{30}{70}$. This fraction won't fit into the grid-in box, so either reduce it or convert it into a decimal. The correct answers include all equivalent fractional or decimal forms of $\dfrac{3}{7}$.

32. **Any value from 14 to 21, inclusive**

The question asks for a possible amount of time needed for the worker to box 168 shoes. If the worker boxes 8 pairs of shoes per minute, it will take $\dfrac{168}{8} = 21$ minutes to box all the shoes. If the worker boxes 12 pairs per minute, the same task will take $\dfrac{168}{12} = 14$ minutes. Therefore, any answer from 14 to 21 is valid. An easy way to solve a question like this is to just plug in a value within the given range. Suppose the worker boxes 10 pairs per minute. In that case, it will take $\frac{168}{10} = 16.8$ minutes to complete the task. This is a valid answer, and it is faster than finding the boundaries of the range. The correct answers are all values from 14 to 21, inclusive.

33. **30** The question asks for the maximum number of cartons a delivery driver can take in an elevator within the building's safety regulations. Begin by subtracting the weight of the driver and the pallet: $1,600 - 250 = 1,350$. Now divide by the weight of the boxes: $\frac{1,350}{45} = 30$. Therefore, 30 is the maximum number of boxes that can be safely loaded into the elevator. The correct answer is 30.

34. **4** The question asks for the height of the can. The formula for the volume of a cylinder is $V = \pi r^2 h$, so plug the given information into the formula. The radius is $\frac{9}{2}$, so $81\pi = \pi \left(\frac{9}{2}\right)^2 h$. Divide both sides by π and square the fraction on the right: $81 = \frac{81}{4} h$. Divide both sides by $\frac{81}{4}$, which is the same as multiplying by $\frac{4}{81}$, to get $h = 4$. The correct answer is 4.

35. **4** The question asks for the value of x that will cause an expression to be undefined. A fraction is undefined if the denominator is zero, so set the denominator equal to zero: $(x - 6)^2 + 4(x - 7) + 8 = 0$. Now solve for x by using FOIL (First, Outer, Inner, Last) and distributing where necessary. The equation becomes $x^2 - 12x + 36 + 4x - 28 + 8 = 0$. Combine like terms to get $x^2 - 8x + 16 = 0$. Factor the equation as $(x - 4)^2 = 0$, then take the square root of both sides to get $x - 4 = 0$. Add 4 to both sides to get $x = 4$. The correct answer is 4.

36. **51** The question asks for the number of trains that pass through Appleton each day. The trains arrive at 6:00, 6:20, 6:40, then 7, 7:20, 7:40, then 8, 8:20, 8:40, and so on. There are three trains per hour, so count the number of hours—using a pencil to keep track if necessary. There are 17 hours, and $17 \times 3 = 51$. The correct answer is 51.

37. **3** The question asks for the interest rate earned by a savings bond, expressed as a percent. For this question, it helps to know the compound interest formula, which is $A = P\left(1 + \frac{r}{n}\right)^{nt}$, where A is the total amount, P is the principal or initial amount, r is the interest rate (expressed as a decimal), n is how many times per year the rate is compounded, and t is the number of years. That may seem complicated, but usually the interest is compounded once a year, so $n = 1$, and the formula can be simplified to $A = P(1 + r)^t$. Therefore, the interest rate expressed as a decimal is 0.03. Multiply by 100 to express the interest rate as a percentage: $(0.03)(100) = 3$. The correct answer is 3.

38. **8.76** The question asks for the difference in value between Carolyn's bond and Helene's bond after 12 years. It helps to solve question 37, the easier question of the pair, before solving this one. Helene's interest rate, from the answer to question 37, is 3%, so to find her total after 12 years, use the formula given above: $A = 50(1.03)^{12} = 71.29$. Carolyn earns 1% more, so her total is $A = 50(1.04)^{12} = 80.05$. Subtract the first total from the second to get 8.76. The correct answer is 8.76.

Chapter 5
Practice Test 2

Reading Test

65 MINUTES, 52 QUESTIONS

Turn to Section 1 of your answer sheet to answer the questions in this section.

DIRECTIONS

Each passage or pair of passages below is followed by a number of questions. After reading each passage or pair, choose the best answer to each question based on what is stated or implied in the passage or passages and in any accompanying graphics (such as a table or graph).

Questions 1–10 are based on the following passage.

This passage is excerpted from Miguel de Cervantes, *Don Quixote*, originally published in 1605 and translated by John Ormsby in 1885.

At this point they came in sight of thirty or forty windmills that are on that plain.

"Fortune," said Don Quixote to his squire, as soon as he had seen them, "is arranging matters for us better
5　than we could have hoped. Look there, friend Sancho Panza, where thirty or more monstrous giants rise up, all of whom I mean to engage in battle and slay, and with whose spoils we shall begin to make our fortunes. For this is righteous warfare, and it is God's good
10　service to sweep so evil a breed from off the face of the earth."

"What giants?" said Sancho Panza.

"Those you see there," answered his master, "with the long arms, and some have them nearly two
15　leagues* long."

"Look, your worship," said Sancho. "What we see there are not giants but windmills, and what seem to be their arms are the vanes that turned by the wind make the millstone go."
20　"It is easy to see," replied Don Quixote, "that you are not used to this business of adventures. Those are giants, and if you are afraid, away with you out of here and betake yourself to prayer, while I engage them in fierce and unequal combat."
25　So saying, he gave the spur to his steed Rocinante, heedless of the cries his squire Sancho sent after him, warning him that most certainly they were windmills

and not giants he was going to attack. He, however, was so positive they were giants that he neither heard the
30　cries of Sancho, nor perceived, near as he was, what they were.

"Fly not, cowards and vile beings," he shouted, "for a single knight attacks you."

A slight breeze at this moment sprang up, and the
35　great vanes began to move.

"Though ye flourish more arms than the giant Briarus**, ye have to reckon with me!" exclaimed Don Quixote, when he saw this.

So saying, he commended himself with all his
40　heart to his lady Dulcinea, imploring her to support him in such a peril. With lance braced and covered by his shield, he charged at Rocinante's fullest gallop and attacked the first mill that stood in front of him. But as he drove his lance-point into the sail, the wind whirled
45　it around with such force that it shivered the lance to pieces. It swept away with it horse and rider, and they were sent rolling over the plain, in sad condition indeed. Sancho hastened to his assistance as fast as his ass could go, and when he came up found him unable
50　to move, with such a shock had Rocinante fallen with him.

"God bless me!" said Sancho, "did I not tell your worship to mind what you were about, for they were only windmills? And no one could have made any
55　mistake about it but one who had mills of the same kind in his head."

CONTINUE ➤

"Hush, friend Sancho" replied Don Quixote, "the fortunes of war more than any other are liable to frequent fluctuations; and moreover I think, and it is 60 the truth, that the same sage Friston*** who carried off my study and books, has turned these giants into mills in order to rob me of the glory of vanquishing them, such is the enmity he bears me; but in the end his wicked arts will avail but little against my good sword."

*	seven miles
**	a hundred-armed giant from Greek mythology
***	the magician (El Sabio Frestón), an imaginary character who Quixote imagines as the thief of his books and the enchanter of the windmills

1

Which choice best summarizes the passage?

A) An adventure goes awry when two young men decide to pretend they are in a great battle due to their longing for adventure.

B) A great warrior and his faithful steed single-handedly vanquish an army of giants in a mystical tale.

C) Two knights find themselves in an argument over what is really happening in their immediate surroundings.

D) A knight with an altered perception of reality engages in what he believes to be a battle of good versus evil.

2

The main purpose of the opening sentence of the passage is to

A) inform the reader of the true setting of the story for later plot purposes.

B) elaborate on the importance of technological advances during the Middle Ages.

C) describe the field on which a great battle is about to take place.

D) provide detailed imagery to enhance the mood of the following story.

3

During the course of the first six paragraphs (lines 1–24), the main character's focus shifts from

A) recollection of past victories to the prospect of imminent defeat.

B) reflection on the role of money in warfare to the role of God in battle.

C) generalization of how to wage a successful battle to specific rules of combat.

D) evaluation of an enemy before him to an argument with his faithful companion.

4

The phrase "sweep so evil a breed from off the face of the earth" at the end of the second paragraph mainly has which of the following effects?

A) It establishes the story as a horror story that will primarily focus on the evil in the world.

B) It informs the reader that Don Quixote is in fact a prophet who receives orders from God to go into battle.

C) It indicates the grandiose view that Don Quixote has of the battle he is about to undertake.

D) It demonstrates to the reader the dangers of taking religious fanaticism to the point of violence.

5

The passage indicates that Don Quixote would characterize his charge into battle as

A) ridiculous.

B) insane.

C) unexceptional.

D) brave.

CONTINUE

6

The passage indicates that Sancho views Don Quixote as a

A) boss who endangers his employees.

B) superior who needs looking after.

C) skillful leader to follow into battle.

D) pious man who requires help.

7

Which choice provides the best evidence for the answer to the previous question?

A) Lines 5–8 ("Look . . . fortunes")

B) Lines 20–21 ("It is . . . adventures")

C) Lines 25–28 ("So saying . . . attack")

D) Lines 41–43 ("With . . . him")

8

The passage indicates that Don Quixote does not believe Sancho's description of the "giants" (line 17) because

A) Sancho's eyesight is not as good as Don Quixote's.

B) Don Quixote claims Sancho is not as brave as he is when it comes to battle.

C) Don Quixote knows more about Friston's schemes than Sancho does.

D) Don Quixote believes Sancho is too busy praying to pay attention.

9

Which choice provides the best evidence for the answer to the previous question?

A) Lines 13–15 ("Those . . . long")

B) Lines 16–19 ("Look . . . go")

C) Lines 21–24 ("Those . . . combat")

D) Lines 32–33 ("Fly not . . . you")

10

At the end of the passage, the reference to Friston mainly has the effect of

A) giving the reader greater insight into how Don Quixote perceives reality.

B) revealing the evil in the world that Don Quixote is fighting his battle against.

C) explaining to the reader the detailed history of how Don Quixote came to see things.

D) illustrating for the reader the evil that can come from personal misunderstandings.

CONTINUE

Questions 11–20 are based on the following passage.

This passage is adapted from Susan B. Anthony's 1873 address to Post Office Districts of Monroe on women's suffrage.

Friends and Fellow-citizens: I stand before you tonight, under indictment for the alleged crime of having voted at the last Presidential election, without
Line having a lawful right to vote. It shall be my work this
5 evening to prove to you that in thus voting, I not only committed no crime, but, instead, simply exercised my *citizen's right,* guaranteed to me and all United States citizens by the National Constitution, beyond the power of any State to deny.

10   Our democratic-republican government is based on the idea of the natural right of every individual member thereof to a voice and a vote in making and executing the laws. We assert the province of government to be to secure the people in the
15 enjoyment of their unalienable rights. We throw to the winds the old dogma that governments can give rights. Before governments were organized, no one denies that each individual possessed the right to protect his own life, liberty and property. And when 100 or
20 1,000,000 people enter into a free government, they do not barter away their natural rights; they simply pledge themselves to protect each other in the enjoyment of them, through prescribed judicial and legislative tribunals. They agree to abandon the methods of brute
25 force in the adjustment of their differences, and adopt those of civilization.

    Nor can you find a word in any of the grand documents left us by the fathers that assumes for government the power to create or to confer rights.
30 The Declaration of Independence, the United States Constitution, the constitutions of the several states and the organic laws of the territories, all alike propose to protect the people in the exercise of their God-given rights. Not one of them pretends to bestow rights.

35   "All men are created equal, and endowed by their Creator with certain unalienable rights. Among these are life, liberty and the pursuit of happiness. That to secure these, governments are instituted among men, deriving their just powers from the consent of the
40 governed."

    Here is no shadow of government authority over rights, nor exclusion of any from their full and equal enjoyment. Here is pronounced the right of all men, and "consequently," as the Quaker preacher said, "of
45 all women," to a voice in the government. And here,

in this very first paragraph of the declaration, is the assertion of the natural right of all to the ballot; for, how can "the consent of the governed" be given, if the right to vote be denied. Again:

50   "That whenever any form of government becomes destructive of these ends, it is the right of the people to alter or abolish it, and to institute a new government, laying its foundations on such principles, and organizing its powers in such forms as to them shall
55 seem most likely to effect their safety and happiness."

    Surely, the right of the whole people to vote is here clearly implied. For however destructive in their happiness this government might become, a disfranchised class could neither alter nor abolish it,
60 nor institute a new one, except by the old brute force method of insurrection and rebellion. One-half of the people of this nation today are utterly powerless to blot from the statute books an unjust law, or to write there a new and a just one. The women, dissatisfied as
65 they are with this form of government, that enforces taxation without representation,—that compels them to obey laws to which they have never given their consent,—that imprisons and hangs them without a trial by a jury of their peers, that robs them, in
70 marriage, of the custody of their own persons, wages and children,—are this half of the people left wholly at the mercy of the other half, in direct violation of the spirit and letter of the declarations of the framers of this government, every one of which was based
75 on the immutable principle of equal rights to all. By those declarations, kings, priests, popes, aristocrats, were all alike dethroned, and placed on a common level politically, with the lowliest born subject or serf. By them, too, men, as such, were deprived of their
80 divine right to rule, and placed on a political level with women. By the practice of those declarations all class and caste distinction will be abolished; and slave, serf, plebeian, wife, woman, all alike, bound from their subject position to the proud platform of equality.

CONTINUE →

11

The central problem that Anthony explains in the passage is that women have been

A) prevented from voting, which is a violation of their human rights.

B) prevented from participating in Congress, which has led to the creation of unjust laws.

C) too kind and just, while men are cruel and unfair.

D) denied equal access to schools, which has prevented them from attending college.

12

Anthony uses the phrase "grand documents" (lines 27–28) mainly to refer to the

A) paper the Declaration of Independence was written on.

B) letters from a grand jury.

C) President's personal notes.

D) important legislation the country was founded on.

13

Anthony claims that which of the following was a purpose of the Declaration of Independence?

A) The protection of human rights

B) The bestowal of human rights

C) The creation of human rights

D) The prevention of violence

14

Which choice provides the best evidence for the answer to the previous question?

A) Lines 4–9 ("It shall . . . deny")

B) Lines 27–29 ("Nor can . . . rights")

C) Lines 30–34 ("The Declaration . . . rights")

D) Lines 56–57 ("Surely . . . implied")

15

As used in line 33, "the exercise" most nearly refers to

A) an activity.

B) a workout.

C) a use or application.

D) a process.

16

It can be reasonably inferred that "natural right" (line 47) was a term generally intended to

A) describe the right of men and women to vote.

B) criticize the right of women to run for office.

C) advocate for the right to bear arms.

D) introduce the origin of the Fifth Amendment.

17

As used in line 59, "class" most nearly means

A) subject.

B) group.

C) genus.

D) stylish.

18

The situation Anthony describes in the passage suggests that the U.S. government has

A) established laws denying women's suffrage.

B) denied participating in an unjust system.

C) considered women superior to men.

D) dethroned kings for political equality.

CONTINUE

19

Which choice provides the best evidence for the answer to the previous question?

A) Lines 1–4 (*"Friends . . . vote"*)

B) Lines 35–40 ("All men . . . governed")

C) Lines 50–55 ("That . . . happiness")

D) Lines 75–78 ("By those . . . serf")

20

Lines 61–75 of the seventh paragraph are primarily concerned with establishing a contrast between

A) those with power and those without.

B) poor men and rich men.

C) social customs and religious customs.

D) laws and guidelines.

CONTINUE

Questions 21–30 are based on the following passage and supplementary material.

This passage is adapted from the U.S. Geological Survey, "Ground Water." ©1999 by the U.S. Department of the Interior.

Although there are sizable areas where ground water is being withdrawn at rates that cause water levels to decline persistently, as in parts of the dry
Line Southwest, this is not true throughout the country. For
5   the Nation as a whole, there is neither a pronounced downward nor upward trend. Water levels rise in wet periods and decline in dry periods. In areas where water is not pumped from aquifers in excess of the amount of recharge to the aquifer—particularly in the
10 humid central and eastern parts of the country—water levels average about the same as they did in the early part of the twentieth century.

A major responsibility of the U.S. Geological Survey is to assess the quantity and quality of the
15 Nation's water supplies. The Geological Survey, in cooperation with other Federal, State, and local agencies, maintains a nationwide hydrologic-data network, carries out a wide variety of water-resources investigations, and develops new methodologies for
20 studying water. The results of these investigations are indispensable tools for those involved in water-resources planning and management. Numerous inquiries concerning water resources and hydrology are directed to the Survey and to State water-resources
25 and geological agencies.

To locate ground water accurately and to determine the depth, quantity, and quality of the water, several techniques must be used, and a target area must be thoroughly tested and studied to identify hydrologic
30 and geologic features important to the planning and management of the resource. The landscape may offer clues to the hydrologist about the occurrence of shallow ground water. Conditions for large quantities of shallow ground water are more favorable under
35 valleys than under hills.

Rocks are the most valuable clues of all. As a first step in locating favorable conditions for ground-water development, the hydrologist prepares geologic maps and cross sections showing the distribution and
40 positions of the different kinds of rocks, both on the surface and underground. Some sedimentary rocks may extend many miles as aquifers of fairly uniform permeability. Other types of rocks may be cracked and broken and contain openings large enough to carry
45 water. Types and orientation of joints or other fractures

may be clues to obtaining useful amounts of ground water. Some rocks may be so folded and displaced that it is difficult to trace them underground.

Next, a hydrologist obtains information on
50 the wells in the target area. The locations, depth to water, amount of water pumped, and types of rocks penetrated by wells also provide information on ground water. Wells are tested to determine the amount of water moving through the aquifer, the
55 volume of water that can enter a well, and the effects of pumping on water levels in the area. Chemical analysis of water from wells provides information on quality of water in the aquifer.

Evaluating the ground-water resource in developed
60 areas, prudent management of the resource, and protection of its quality are current ground-water problems. Thus, prediction of the capacity of the ground-water resource for long-term pumpage, the effects of that pumpage, and evaluation of water-
65 quality conditions are among the principal aims of modern-day hydrologic practice in achieving proper management of ground water.

Ground water, presently a major source of water, is also the Nation's principal reserve of fresh water. The
70 public will have to make decisions regarding water supply and waste disposal-decisions that will either affect the ground-water resource or be affected by it. These decisions will be more judicious and reliable if they are based upon knowledge of the principles of
75 ground-water occurrence

Historical Groundwater Levels and Population for Santa Clara Valley

Adapted from SCVWD.

CONTINUE ▶

21

As used in line 6, "trend" most nearly means

A) style.

B) result.

C) tendency.

D) preference.

22

Based on information in the passage, it can reasonably be inferred that ground water occurrence

A) is produced only by the flow of rain water through permeable rock in a valley.

B) could be located by proximity to landscape features such as hills and existing wells.

C) might be relatively constant across large landscapes but is affected by seasonal variables.

D) achieves roughly the same depth regardless of the occurrence and persistence of surface water.

23

Which choice provides the best evidence for the answer to the previous question?

A) Lines 6–12 ("Water . . . century")

B) Lines 26–31 ("To locate . . . resource")

C) Lines 31–35 ("The landscape . . . hills")

D) Lines 36–41 ("As a . . . underground")

24

According to the Geological Survey, the capability to assess the nation's water supplies is significant primarily because

A) the study of such supplies will provide information critical to water-resource administration.

B) the study of water supplies will allow agencies to increase the efficiency of crop irrigation.

C) it will enable researchers to develop improved methods of chemical analysis.

D) it will enable scientists to verify the maximum depth of rock layers.

25

Which choice provides the best evidence for the answer to the previous question?

A) Lines 1–4 ("Although . . . country")

B) Lines 20–22 ("The results . . . management")

C) Lines 41–43 ("Some...permeability")

D) Lines 56–58 ("Chemical . . . aquifer")

26

The third paragraph (lines 26–35) serves mainly to

A) propose a subject for future research.

B) introduce a process for finding a natural resource.

C) describe a recent discovery and suggest its implications.

D) relate the sequence of a series of events.

27

As used in line 75, "occurrence" most nearly means

A) plan.

B) happening.

C) event.

D) presence.

CONTINUE

28

In the graph, the maximum water-level elevation in feet is closest to

A) 125.

B) 1.75.

C) 0.75.

D) −25.

29

Which concept is supported by the passage and by the information in the figure?

A) Groundwater levels tend to decrease during drier years and increase during wetter years on average.

B) The amount of water pumped from aquifers may have an impact on groundwater levels.

C) Humid regions tend to experience smaller average declines in groundwater levels than do drier regions.

D) Recharge to aquifers and water pumped from aquifers may balance one another in the long run.

30

How does the figure support the author's point that the public may impact and be impacted by groundwater levels?

A) It provides evidence that waste disposal decisions affect the water supply.

B) It shows a relationship between increasing population and decreasing groundwater level.

C) It highlights the extent to which rapid population growth affects water quality.

D) It suggests a correlation between human-made landscape changes and availability of shallow groundwater.

CONTINUE

Questions 31–41 are based on the following passage and supplementary material.

This passage is adapted from Chester Lloyd Jones, "Bananas and Diplomacy." ©1913 by *The North American Review.*

To those in world-trade, names of countries and regions suggest their products. It has always been so. The East Indies four hundred years ago meant spice; two hundred years ago China meant silks and tea;
Line
5   Canada meant fur. The Caribbean to Queen Elizabeth meant gold—it was the route of the treasure ships of Spain—to Washington it meant sugar and molasses, and to our children it will mean bananas.

The Panama Canal has so occupied our attention
10 for the last decade that we have overlooked a significant economic change taking place independently of the forces which promise so radically to change the transportation routes of world commerce. Economists tell us that the trend of Caribbean diplomacy will be
15 determined by the banana crop. At the beginning of the twentieth century, there are food products that will exercise an influence upon international politics unconnected with the Panama Canal and of an importance which can be measured only in prophesy.
20 The market for bananas in the United States was developed largely through the efforts of one man. Forty years ago, Captain L. D. Baker was engaged in trade between the Orinoco River and Boston. On one trip he called at Port Morant, Jamaica, for a cargo of
25 bamboo for paper-making and carried back a few bunches of bananas, then a curiosity in the New England markets. The venture proved profitable and the captain thereafter made several trips a year to Port Antonio, Jamaica, to take cargoes of bananas to
30 Boston.

How important the trade has become is illustrated by the figures of exports. In 1911 there were sent from Caribbean countries in the export trade 52,936,963 bunches, which, on the average of 140 bananas to
35 the bunch, represents a total of over 7,400,000,000 bananas. In 1912 the continental United States alone consumed 44,520,539 bunches, or over sixty bananas for each man, woman, and child. Two facts appear from the following figures: with the exception of the
40 Canary Islands, all the countries producing large quantities of bananas for export border the Caribbean, and the United States consumes 85 percent of all bananas exported—five times as much as all the rest of the world.

Banana Supply of the United States 1912

Jamaica	15,467,918
Honduras	7,151,178
Costa Rica	7,053,664
Panama	4,581,500
Cuba	2,478,581
Nicaragua	2,270,100
Guatemala	2,017,650
Colombia	1,542,988
Mexico	817,006
British Honduras	557,160
Dominican Republic	304,000
Dutch Guiana	261,548
Others	17,246
Total	44,520,539

The world supply in 1911 as shown by the same records was:

Country of Origin	*Quantity (Bunches)*
Dominican Republic	404,000
Mexico (Frontera Province)	750,000
Honduras	6,500,000
Costa Rica	9,309,586
Jamaica	16,497,385
Colombia	4,901,894
Panama	4,261,500
Canary Islands	2,648,378
Cuba	2,500,000
Nicaragua	2,225,000
Guatemala	1,755,704
British Honduras	525,000
Dutch Guiana	387,516
Others	250,000
Total	52,915,963

45 The business, especially when the fruit must be sent long distances, demands organization for collecting fruit from small planters and large capital for steamers with refrigerating appliances. In fact, reliance on private planters has proven unsatisfactory and the
50 big banana-marketing companies now own extensive plantations throughout the West Indies and on the mainland.

CONTINUE

The increased production of the banana in its natural state and the diversification of its uses promise
55 to introduce a new and hitherto neglected factor in our food supply. If present development continues, it will raise the Caribbean region from its dependence on foreign markets for food to one of the regions from which an important part of the world's food-
60 supply will be drawn. The wheat fields of the Dakotas and Manitoba will meet as one of their competitors in feeding the world the banana plantations of the American Mediterranean.

These figures show that the world is just awakening
65 to the value of the banana as food. If the present development continues, the acreage devoted to banana-growing must rapidly increase. Improved refrigeration and quick steam service will continue to widen the area in which the product can be marketed.
70 The development of the banana-flour industry also promises to open a market for the product of areas too distant to profit by the demand of fresh fruit, just as the perfection of the manufacture of copra, the dried meat of the coconut, has opened up a new industry reaching
75 to the farthest islands of the Pacific.

Great as the blessings of the Panama Canal will be to the trade of the world and to that of the United States in particular, we must not let the new markets which it will develop beyond the Isthmus make us
80 forget that region so rich in possibilities which lies this side of the continental divide and so much nearer our own markets. Friendship with our near neighbors is no less important than the good will of people over wide seas. One of the most important, and from our past
85 experience let us remember, one of the most delicate problems with which our men of state have to deal is the diplomacy of the Caribbean.

31

The main purpose of the passage is to

A) examine the impact of an export on the global economy.

B) posit that bananas will become the new gold standard.

C) consider a dilemma brought about by global economics.

D) argue that international politics bars the Caribbean from gaining financial independence.

32

The main purpose of the second paragraph (lines 9–19) is to

A) illustrate how exports will skyrocket with the completion of the Panama Canal.

B) introduce an idea not widely associated with a familiar region.

C) prove that bananas will dominate the economy of the twentieth century.

D) provide support that economists correctly prophesy that the Panama Canal will radically change world commerce.

33

As used in line 17, "exercise" most nearly means

A) operate.

B) exert.

C) train.

D) maneuver.

34

Which choice best supports the author's claim that bananas are likely to play a significant role in the global economy?

A) Lines 1–5 ("To those . . . fur")

B) Lines 13–15 ("Economists . . . crop")

C) Lines 42–44 ("United . . . world")

D) Lines 60–63 ("The wheat . . . Mediterranean")

35

As used in line 82, "friendship" most nearly means

A) affection.

B) fondness.

C) collusion.

D) cooperation.

CONTINUE

36

The main idea of the final paragraph (lines 76–87) is that

A) friendship is important and often overlooked in the global economy.

B) the Panama Canal has proven to be a great blessing in international trade.

C) new markets will emerge beyond the Isthmus, calling for change in the global economy.

D) the Caribbean may prove to be an important component of the global economy in coming decades.

37

In the passage, the author anticipates which of the following potential difficulties for the banana industry?

A) Transporting bananas large distances requires certain technology to be successful.

B) Steamers are the best way to transport large quantities of bananas.

C) Banana flour is produced in areas too distant to be reached.

D) The banana industry will be surpassed by copra exports.

38

Which choice provides the best evidence for the previous question?

A) Lines 15–19 ("At the . . . prophesy")

B) Lines 45–48 ("The business . . . appliances")

C) Lines 48–52 ("In fact . . . mainland")

D) Lines 70–75 ("The development . . . Pacific")

39

Data in the tables provide most direct support for which idea in the passage?

A) Although it is a major banana importer, the United States is not the only nation that imports bananas.

B) The increased production of the banana is the beginning of an economic revolution in the Caribbean.

C) Acreage toward banana-growing must increase to accommodate increased production.

D) The export numbers in the tables show an upward trend in banana consumption.

40

Data in the tables indicate that the difference between the number of bananas supplied to the U.S. in 1912 and the number of bananas supplied to the world in 1911 was greatest for which country?

A) Honduras

B) Panama

C) Jamaica

D) Nicaragua

41

Data in the table of the world supply in 1911 most strongly support which of the following statements?

A) Panama and Colombia combined supplied more bananas than did Jamaica in 1911.

B) The profits earned from bananas did not fluctuate.

C) Dutch Guiana produced the fewest bananas in 1911.

D) Colombia exported more bananas in 1911 than did Cuba.

CONTINUE

Questions 42–52 are based on the following passages.

Passage 1 is adapted from Bret Stetka, "Where's the Proof That Mindfulness Meditation Works?" ©2017 by Scientific American. Passage 2 is adapted from Matthieu Ricard, Antoine Lutz, and Richard J. Davidson, "Neuroscience Reveals the Secrets of Meditation's Benefits." ©2014 by Scientific American.

Passage 1

Research in recent decades has linked mindfulness practices to a staggering collection of possible health benefits. Yet many psychologists, neuroscientists and
Line meditation experts are afraid that hype is outpacing
5 the science. In an article released in *Perspectives on Psychological Science*, 15 prominent psychologists and cognitive scientists caution that despite its popularity and supposed benefits, scientific data on mindfulness are woefully lacking. Many of the studies
10 on mindfulness and meditation, the authors wrote, are poorly designed—compromised by inconsistent definitions of what mindfulness actually is, and often void of a control group to rule out the placebo effect.

The new paper cites a 2015 review published in
15 *American Psychologist* reporting that only around 9 percent of research into mindfulness-based interventions has been tested in clinical trials that included a control group. The authors also point to multiple large placebo-controlled meta-analyses
20 concluding that mindfulness practices have often produced unimpressive results. A 2014 review of 47 meditation trials, collectively including over 3,500 participants, found essentially no evidence for benefits related to enhancing attention, curtailing substance
25 abuse, aiding sleep or controlling weight.

Lead author of the report Nicholas Van Dam, a clinical psychologist and research fellow in psychological sciences at the University of Melbourne, contends potential benefits of mindfulness are being
30 overshadowed by hyperbole and oversold for financial gain. Mindfulness meditation and training is now a $1.1-billion industry in the U.S. alone. "Our report does not mean that mindfulness meditation is not helpful for some things," Van Dam says. "But the
35 scientific rigor just isn't there yet to be making these big claims."

Van Dam acknowledges that some good evidence does support mindfulness. The 2014 analysis found meditation and mindfulness may provide modest
40 benefits in anxiety, depression and pain. He also cites a 2013 review published in *Clinical Psychology Review* for mindfulness-based therapy that found similar results.

Behavioral and social sciences professor and
45 director of Brown University's Mindfulness Center Eric Loucks, agrees there are multiple definitions of mindfulness. But it is the trickiness in bringing a rich spiritual concept into a standardized framework for testing and advising patients that he feels might be
50 tough to tackle.

"One element in defining mindfulness, if considering its roots in Buddhism, is…the Buddha's recommendation that descriptions of concepts like 'mindfulness' are like a finger pointing at the moon,"
55 he explains. "It is important not to confuse the finger for the moon. There will always be variations in people's understanding of mindfulness. It is a personal experience."

Passage 2

The goals of meditation overlap with many of the
60 objectives of clinical psychology, psychiatry, preventive medicine and education. As suggested by the growing compendium of research, meditation may be effective in treating depression and chronic pain and in cultivating a sense of overall well-being.
65 Staying aware of an unpleasant sensation can reduce maladaptive emotional responses and help one to move beyond the disagreeable feeling and may be particularly useful in dealing with pain. In our Wisconsin lab, we have studied experienced
70 practitioners while they performed an advanced form of mindfulness meditation called open presence. In open presence, sometimes called pure awareness, the mind is calm and relaxed, not focused on anything in particular yet vividly clear, free from excitation
75 or dullness. The meditator observes and is open to experience without making any attempt to interpret, change, reject or ignore painful sensation. We found that the intensity of the pain was not reduced in meditators, but it bothered them less than it did
80 members of a control group.

Several studies have documented the benefits of mindfulness on symptoms of anxiety and depression and its ability to improve sleep patterns. By deliberately

CONTINUE

monitoring and observing their thoughts and emotions
85 when they feel sad or worried, depressed patients
can use meditation to manage negative thoughts and
feelings as they arise spontaneously and so lessen
rumination. In 2000 clinical psychologists John
Teasdale, then at the University of Cambridge, and
90 Zindel Segal of the University of Toronto showed that
for patients who had previously suffered at least three
episodes of depression, six months of mindfulness
practice, along with cognitive therapy, reduced the risk
of relapse by nearly 40 percent in the year following
95 the onset of a severe depression. More recently, Segal
demonstrated that the intervention is superior to a
placebo and has a protective effect against relapse
comparable to standard maintenance antidepressant
therapy.

42

As used in line 11, "compromised" most nearly means

A) accommodated.

B) shaped.

C) divided.

D) undermined.

43

According to the author of Passage 1, what do aiding
sleep and controlling weight have in common?

A) Neither has been convincingly linked to
meditation.

B) Neither is a potential benefit of mindfulness
practices.

C) They are challenging health goals to achieve.

D) They are well understood by medical researchers.

44

The author of Passage 1 indicates that the positive
effects of meditation practice are currently

A) increasing practitioners' productivity.

B) benefitting growing numbers of people.

C) exaggerated for the sake of profit.

D) not worth the cost of research.

45

The analogy in the final paragraph of Passage 1 has
primarily which effect?

A) It illustrates a challenge involved in applying a
particular concept.

B) It uses elegant imagery to mask a theory's
shortcomings.

C) It refers to nature to lend a sense of credibility.

D) It applies familiar language to simplify a technical
procedure.

46

The author of Passage 2 indicates which of the
following about the use of mindfulness meditation
practice?

A) It should generally be discouraged.

B) It reduces practitioners' impulsive behaviors.

C) It should be researched further.

D) It does not affect pain sensation directly.

CONTINUE

47

Which choice provides the best evidence for the answer to the previous question?

A) Lines 68–71 ("In our . . . presence")

B) Lines 77–79 ("We found . . . meditators")

C) Lines 81–83 ("Several . . . patterns")

D) Lines 95–99 ("More . . . therapy")

48

The author of Passage 2 refers to "open presence" to suggest that disagreeable sensation may be less troublesome to those who

A) can take their minds off their discomfort.

B) understand the source of their emotions.

C) remain aware of the sensation without judging the experience.

D) seek treatment for their pain.

49

The main purpose of each passage is to

A) provide an evaluation of the potential health benefits of mindfulness practices based on research.

B) make a case for revising standard approaches to researching psychology and daily habits.

C) present findings on the attention spans of people with varying amounts of mindfulness training.

D) contrast anxiety levels of those who meditate for spiritual reasons with those who meditate for health benefits.

50

Which choice best describes the relationship between the two passages?

A) Passage 2 provides anecdotal evidence that coincides with experimental evidence given in Passage 1.

B) Passage 2 examines in detail one of the topics which Passage 1 explores more broadly.

C) Passage 2 cites research supporting claims that are questioned in Passage 1.

D) Passage 2 suggests an alternative explanation for the results discussed in Passage 1.

51

On which of the following points would the authors of both passages most likely agree?

A) Meditators tend to sleep more soundly than those who do not meditate.

B) Those who practice meditation for spiritual reasons are unlikely to participate in research trials.

C) Mindfulness meditation and training attract interest because they are profitable fields.

D) Including a control group in research can yield important evidence about potential treatments.

52

Which choice provides the best evidence that the author of Passage 1 would agree to some extent with the claim made in lines 61–64, Passage 2?

A) Lines 1–3 ("Research . . . benefits")

B) Lines 3–5 ("Yet many . . . science")

C) Lines 38–40 ("The 2014 . . . pain")

D) Lines 47–50 ("But it . . . tackle")

STOP

If you finish before time is called, you may check your work on this section only.
Do not turn to any other section in the test.

No Test Material On This Page

Writing and Language Test

35 MINUTES, 44 QUESTIONS

Turn to Section 2 of your answer sheet to answer the questions in this section.

DIRECTIONS

Each passage below is accompanied by a number of questions. For some questions, you will consider how the passage might be revised to improve the expression of ideas. For other questions, you will consider how the passage might be edited to correct errors in sentence structure, usage, or punctuation. A passage or a question may be accompanied by one or more graphics (such as a table or graph) that you will consider as you make revising and editing decisions.

Some questions will direct you to an underlined portion of a passage. Other questions will direct you to a location in a passage or ask you to think about the passage as a whole.

After reading each passage, choose the answer to each question that most effectively improves the quality of writing in the passage or that makes the passage conform to the conventions of standard written English. Many questions include a "NO CHANGE" option. Choose that option if you think the best choice is to leave the relevant portion of the passage as it is.

Questions 1–11 are based on the following passage.

Streaming Something Beyond Hard Work

There is no question that the American workforce has changed, regardless of whether one believes it has changed for better or worse. In the 1940s, the United States led the world in most economic categories, and its businesses were some of the most praised in the world. By the 1980s, however, the dominance of the United States had been challenged by industries the world over, and the economy was measured in terms of global effects rather than national ones.

This **1** growing and enlarging competition has unfortunately led to a loosening of companies' responsibilities toward their employees. Retirement

1

A) NO CHANGE
B) increased competition
C) increased competing among countries
D) larger spirit of competitiveness for all

CONTINUE

pensions are largely a thing of the past. **2** Moreover, whereas someone born in the 1940s might have expected to spend his or her entire career with a single company. Many of whom now swap through four or five "careers" throughout a single working life.

This trend has intensified recently, particularly in **3** Silicon Valley startups. One of the major success

Which choice most effectively combines the underlined sentences?

A) Moreover, whereas someone born in the 1940s might have expected to spend his or her entire career with a single company; many workers now swap through four or five "careers" throughout a single working life over the course of it.

B) Swapping jobs is, moreover for instance, a thing that new workers do now, whereas those in the 1940s would have been more likely to work for a single company for their entire careers.

C) Moreover, whereas someone born in the 1940s might have expected to spend his or her entire career with a single company; many workers now swap through four or five "careers" throughout a single working life.

D) Moreover, whereas someone born in the 1940s might have expected to spend his or her entire career with a single company, now the norm has workers swapping through four or five "careers" throughout a single working life.

At this point, the author is considering adding the following information.

the fast-paced, forward-thinking, occasionally ruthless world of

Should the writer make the addition here?

A) Yes, because it shows the author's ability in finding apt adjectives.

B) Yes, because it creates a richer description of the company discussed in the essay.

C) No, because it lengthens the sentence unnecessarily with information that is given elsewhere.

D) No, because it is not the kind of thing that would be acceptable to say in the workplace.

CONTINUE ➡

stories from among these many-sided companies [4] that is Netflix, the streaming and DVD-mailing giant, which may have been singlehandedly responsible for ending the lifespans of both the video store and the DVD in only a few short years. Netflix's compulsively innovative methods have changed the way that those living in the United States and in many other parts of the globe interact with visual media, especially in movie theaters, on home entertainment systems, and on [5] computers.

[6] For all this, Netflix has become famous (or infamous) for changing its employees' relationship to the workplace. Netflix's staff is relatively lean, and employees are incredibly well-treated. Their salaries are higher than those of other Silicon Valley businesses, and the employees are given *unlimited* (yes, you read that correctly) vacation time. Furthermore, as Netflix continues to push beyond the traditional boundaries of film and TV, the company affords its employees the opportunity to be on the cutting edge of change.

4

A) NO CHANGE
B) that are
C) is
D) are

5

A) NO CHANGE
B) machines used for computing.
C) PCs and Macs with the capacity to stream.
D) intelligent machines.

6

A) NO CHANGE
B) Regardless,
C) Thus,
D) Furthermore,

CONTINUE

All of Netflix's success comes at a price, however. **7** Just putting seriously all of it right out there, employees at Netflix are warned not to think of the job as one that they will keep "for life." Netflix is not concerned with traditional ideas of "hard work": **8** to come to work on time, staying late, and showing loyalty to the company. Instead, Netflix is concerned only with *results*. Just ask the computer programmers who started Netflix's streaming service and then were let go when the service became so successful that Netflix had to use Amazon.com's servers instead. While these employees had done about as good a job as they could do, **9** yet they were fired the moment they were no longer needed.

Indeed, as companies continue to tighten their belts and their responsibility to be profitable remains, they will demand more of their employees and withdraw some of the comfortable **10** premising that the employees of earlier eras relied on. **11** This may be the workplace of the future, and we can only hope that employees will adapt as well as they have to past changes.

7

Which choice most effectively sets up the idea given in the second part of this sentence?

A) NO CHANGE

B) Turned off by the company's rudeness,

C) Having no idea what they're walking into,

D) From the first day on the job,

8

A) NO CHANGE

B) coming

C) come

D) workers coming

9

A) NO CHANGE

B) and

C) because

D) DELETE the underlined portion.

10

A) NO CHANGE

B) premise

C) promises

D) promising

11

Which statement most clearly ends the passage with a restatement of the writer's primary claim?

A) NO CHANGE

B) This is the end of employment as we know it, and we should all head for the hills.

C) You can try to get a job at Netflix, but they're not really hiring all that often.

D) If you've ever been fired or laid off from a job, you know how difficult it can be.

CONTINUE ➡

Questions 12–22 are based on the following passage.

Television—Not So Bad After All?

— 1 —

A mere ten years ago, surveys recorded data that showed the average American viewer to watch four hours of television a day. Television was a central part of the American household. Now that the Internet has come to supplant television's central role in American culture (as people spend more time watching short videos on TikTok, reading short posts on Facebook and Twitter, and [12] they send quirky photos and videos on Snapchat), the complaints that had always been made about television can seem rather quaint. Those who critiqued television as a dangerous influence on society have since changed to new and, as they would see it, worse targets on the [13] web and are not much interested in television anymore.

— 2 —

Television certainly had its harmful effects on those who watched it for those four hours a day. There could be no "couch potatoes" without TVs, and the scourge of reality TV would never have been thrust upon the American viewing public. [14] As aforementioned, shining light in your eyes for many hours at a time can wreak havoc on one of [15] your most important senses: vision.

12

Which choice most closely matches the stylistic pattern established earlier in the sentence?

A) NO CHANGE

B) the sending of quirky photos and videos features prominently on Snapchat),

C) sending quirky photos and videos on Snapchat),

D) they send quirky photos on Snapchat and videos),

13

A) NO CHANGE

B) web,

C) web, they

D) web, the images on the Internet

14

A) NO CHANGE

B) However,

C) That said,

D) Moreover,

15

A) NO CHANGE

B) you're most important senses,

C) you're most important senses;

D) your most important senses;

CONTINUE

— 3 —

However, television accomplished some incredible things as well. Drawing on the networks that **16** radio creates throughout the entire country, television provided something truly national for the first time. In 1964, over 70 million people, or a third of the United States population at the time, watched The Beatles make their American debut on *The Ed Sullivan Show*. **17** While young people were already fawning over the rock band, the televised performance fueled the subsequent "Beatlemania" that brought together Americans of all ages during a time of major social anxieties.

— 4 —

A large component of this "big world" was the presence of non-white faces. **18** Especially African Americans, non-white people, who parroted and parodied the patterns of Black speech, were represented on the radio by white actors. While African Americans were the most frequently targeted group, Asian Americans and those of all ethnicities were similarly lampooned in the national media. The popularity of television actually ended up forcing these media into a kind of progressivism: the

16

A) NO CHANGE
B) radio created
C) radios' create
D) radio's creation

17

At this point, the writer is considering adding the following sentence.

> The Beatles had many hits, including "She Loves You" and "I Wanna Hold Your Hand," that continue to influence the course of rock and roll to the present day.

Should the writer make this addition here?

A) Yes, because it helps to explain why the music of The Beatles can help to prevent crime.
B) Yes, because it gives the reader additional context that helps to explain the importance of television.
C) No, because it suggests that television's only function was to broadcast musical performances.
D) No, because it adds a detail that is irrelevant to the paragraph's main focus.

18

A) NO CHANGE
B) For many years, non-white people, especially African Americans, were represented on the radio by white actors, who parroted and parodied the patterns of Black speech.
C) African Americans were non-white people especially who for many years parroted by white actors and parodied in speech patterns.
D) White actors parroted especially African Americans from non-white actors in their patterns of Black speech, which were parodied for many years.

Chinese American character on *Have Gun Will Travel*
[19] and some of the other shows set in the old West would
no longer work as racial masquerades. As a result, some of
the earliest leading roles for non-white actors and actresses
came on television, earlier than in film and theater in many
cases.

— 5 —

Television may not play the central role in American
culture that it once did, but many of the things that it
achieved, both good and bad, remain in the culture today.

— 6 —

This national reach could occasionally lead to
conformity and sensationalism, but it also showed
[20] many in the American public, just how diverse the
American scene had become. People still had to have
a certain amount of wealth to travel physically outside
of their [21] hometowns. They were usually filled with
citizens who had the same basic backgrounds and
attitudes. Television could show them just how big the
world outside was.

**Question [22] asks about the previous passage as a
whole.**

19

Which choice gives a second supporting example
that is most similar to the example already in the
sentence?

A) NO CHANGE

B) who was played by Ben Wright on the radio show

C) and even some of the shows that weren't so
popular on radio

D) or the African American character on *The Beulah
Show*

20

A) NO CHANGE

B) many, in the American public

C) many in the American public

D) many, in the American public,

21

Which choice most effectively combines the sentences
at the underlined portion?

A) hometowns: they

B) hometowns, and theirs

C) hometowns with what

D) hometowns, which

**Think about the previous passage as a whole as you
answer question 22.**

22

To make the passage most logical, paragraph 6 should
be placed

A) where it is now.

B) before paragraph 2.

C) before paragraph 3.

D) before paragraph 4.

CONTINUE ➡

Questions 23–33 are based on the following passage and supplementary material.

The Noise Is Not for the Birds

Even if you love the vibrant life of the city, there are probably times when you crave silence. Even the busiest lives need some calm once in a while for some of life's basic, private tasks. In fact, this doesn't only describe human lives. While untouched nature is usually prized for the way it *looks*— **23** there greenery, scurrying animals, and placidity—nature is actually just as much characterized by the way it *sounds*.

24 Thus, when we build highways through thriving natural habitats, we don't just change the way they look. **25** You've certainly been somewhere remote enough that there aren't any cars around, or you've been woken up some morning by the sound of a car horn or a revving engine. Although the sound of the car is the sound of our day-to-day life, that does not change the fact that car traffic is remarkably loud.

23

A) NO CHANGE
B) their
C) it's
D) its

24

A) NO CHANGE
B) Thence,
C) Whereas,
D) This being so,

25

At this point, the writer is considering adding the following sentence.

　　We also change the way they sound.

Should the writer make this addition here?

A) Yes, because it reminds the reader of the beauty of birds' songs.
B) Yes, because it completes the idea started in the previous sentence.
C) No, because it shifts the emphasis of the paragraph to sound rather than sight.
D) No, because it disagrees with the thesis developed in the paragraph as a whole.

Furthermore, while we have become relatively [26] weakened to the sounds of cars on our "quiet" residential streets, not all animals have. A recent study checked the effect of [27] raising the highway volume on local bird populations. This might seem like an easy study with all the new highway construction going on in the United States all the time, but the researchers [28] at the Intermountain Bird Observatory in Idaho and wanted to study the effects without becoming part of the problem. Instead of building new roads, the researchers opted to produce the *sound* of roads, creating a fake, [29] or, a "phantom," road with 15 pairs of speakers playing the sounds of traffic noise.

26

A) NO CHANGE

B) inured

C) hip

D) keen

27

A) NO CHANGE

B) the noise being more on highways

C) increased highway noise

D) highways exhibiting more noise levels

28

A) NO CHANGE

B) who work at the Intermountain Bird Observatory in Idaho, where they wanted to

C) at the Intermountain Bird Observatory in Idaho wanted to

D) at the Intermountain Bird Observatory in Idaho, they wanted to

29

A) NO CHANGE

B) or a "phantom," road

C) or a "phantom"; road

D) or a "phantom" road,

CONTINUE

[1] The results were telling. [2] According to the study, the mere *sounds* of **30** traffic, "reduced avian populations by a third and cut species diversity by a significant amount. [3] Birds, it seems, need to spend as much time as possible with their heads down—hunting and pecking, feeding their young, and fattening up for their various migrations. [4] This is bad news for avian life in the deep South, where the Interstate Highway Commission **31** has announced plans to eradicate avian and other wildlife populations between Natchez, Augusta, Savannah, and Knoxville. **32**

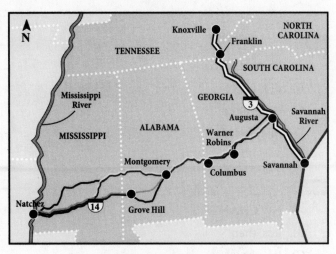

Proposed Interstate Routes

While this study will, the scientists hope, discourage new road construction within the national parks and other forested areas, it can also have effects where the roads are already present. With lower speed limits and rubberized asphalt, **33** the roads won't be quite so noisy, and the native fauna might feel just a little bit freer to roam.

30

A) NO CHANGE

B) traffic reduced

C) traffic, reduced

D) traffic—reduced

31

Which choice offers an accurate interpretation of the data in the figure?

A) NO CHANGE

B) will push avian populations northeast into North Carolina and northwest into western Tennessee.

C) has planned an east-west route from Savannah to Knoxville and a north-south route from Augusta to Natchez.

D) has planned a north-south route from Savannah to Knoxville and an east-west route from Augusta to Natchez.

32

Where is the most logical place in the paragraph to add the following sentence?

> When there is so much distraction from outside noise, however, birds are more likely to be looking up than down, casting a cautious eye on their potentially perilous surroundings.

A) After sentence 1

B) After sentence 2

C) After sentence 3

D) After sentence 4

33

A) NO CHANGE

B) there won't be so much noise,

C) they won't be so noisy,

D) there won't be all the noisy roads,

CONTINUE

Questions 34–44 are based on the following passage.

A "Failed" Search for the American Southwest

Sometimes it really *is* about the journey rather than the destination. Francisco Vázquez de Coronado, an early Spanish explorer and [34] conquistador; died believing that he had failed in his mission, but his pursuit of that mission has been just as significant to history as it would have been had he achieved his goal. Coronado's experience is an excellent window into the difficulty of assessing the Spanish explorers, [35] but also we can see the blurring of the line between hero and villain. In much the same way that Columbus is still praised as being the "discoverer" of the United States but reviled for the atrocities he [36] eviscerated against the native populations, Coronado presents a historical challenge.

Coronado's aims were [37] fewer than noble. He didn't particularly care about making history. He was

34

A) NO CHANGE

B) conquistador

C) conquistador,

D) conquistador—

35

A) NO CHANGE

B) wherein

C) just as

D) so too

36

A) NO CHANGE

B) did

C) committed

D) manifested

37

A) NO CHANGE

B) less, then

C) less then

D) less than

CONTINUE

much more interested in making something 38 else, altogether: money. Coronado, 39 who grew up in a noble family in Spain, came to New Spain (present-day Mexico) when he was 25 years old. Within four years of his arrival, Coronado had become intoxicated by the circulating rumors of the Seven Cities of Gold. As rumor had it, these cities were richer than any place in the world and were waiting for someone to 40 arise to the challenge of claiming their bounty.

Of course, there were no such places, neither in Cíbola, a city just west of modern-day Albuquerque, nor in Quivira, a town in central Kansas. Coronado's disappointment was absolutely unforgiving and vicious: many fellow travelers died on these expeditions, and 41 many Zuni families in the region were slaughtered as a result of Coronado's greed.

38

A) NO CHANGE

B) else:

C) else, nevertheless:

D) else, and it was:

39

A) NO CHANGE

B) he grew

C) growing

D) whom grows

40

A) NO CHANGE

B) rise to

C) arise

D) rising to

41

Which choice provides information that best supports the claim made by this sentence?

A) NO CHANGE

B) the journeys were long and arduous.

C) medical care was very limited at the time.

D) no one stopped to see the sites.

CONTINUE ➡

[1] However, Coronado's journey was not entirely without merit. [2] That's a lot of territory to cover in the middle of the sixteenth century! [3] Notice how far we have traveled in this short essay alone. [4] We started in Spain, then went to Mexico, then to New Mexico, then to Kansas **42** after that. [5] Thus, while Coronado's tactics were vicious and his goals less than noble, he was nonetheless one of the first to provide reliable information on the terrains of vast stretches of the American West. [6] His expedition provided the first European sightings of the Grand Canyon, the Colorado River, and many of the lands along his route. **43**

Though Coronado's expedition may have been fraught with unpleasantness and we may balk at the idea of calling his sightings "discoveries," Coronado's contributions to the course of American history were nonetheless significant. His influence is all around us. **44** While Coronado may not have achieved his stated goal, we have his "failure" to thank for a large swath of the contemporary United States.

42

A) NO CHANGE

B) en route.

C) while we were there.

D) DELETE the underlined portion, and end the sentence with a period.

43

To make this paragraph most logical, sentence 2 should be placed

A) where it is now.

B) before sentence 1.

C) before sentence 4.

D) before sentence 5.

44

At this point, the writer is considering adding the following sentence.

> A small island off the coast of San Diego bears his name, as does a high school halfway across the country in Lubbock, Texas.

Should the writer make this addition here?

A) Yes, because it names some of the places of which Coronado was most fond.

B) Yes, because it cites some of the contemporary places that were influenced by Coronado.

C) No, because it disagrees with the paragraph's central claims regarding Coronado's cruelty.

D) No, because it introduces a tangent into the American Southwest that is not further elaborated.

STOP
If you finish before time is called, you may check your work on this section only.
Do not turn to any other section in the test.

No Test Material On This Page

Math Test – No Calculator

25 MINUTES, 20 QUESTIONS

Turn to Section 3 of your answer sheet to answer the questions in this section.

DIRECTIONS

For questions 1–15, solve each problem, choose the best answer from the choices provided, and fill in the corresponding circle on your answer sheet. **For questions 16–20,** solve the problem and enter your answer in the grid on the answer sheet. Please refer to the directions before question 16 on how to enter your answers in the grid. You may use any available space in your test booklet for scratch work.

NOTES

1. The use of a calculator **is not permitted**.
2. All variables and expressions used represent real numbers unless otherwise indicated.
3. Figures provided in this test are drawn to scale unless otherwise indicated.
4. All figures lie in a plane unless otherwise indicated.
5. Unless otherwise indicated, the domain of a given function f is the set of all real numbers x for which $f(x)$ is a real number.

REFERENCE

The number of degrees of arc in a circle is 360.
The number of radians of arc in a circle is 2π.
The sum of the measures in degrees of the angles of a triangle is 180.

CONTINUE

1

The cost C, in dollars, that a catering company charges to cater a wedding is given by the function $C = 20wt + 300$, where w represents the number of workers catering the wedding and t represents the total time, in hours, it will take to cater the wedding using w workers. Which of the following is the best explanation of the number 20 in the function?

A) A minimum of 20 workers will cater the wedding.

B) The cost of every wedding will increase by \$20 per hour.

C) The catering company charges \$20 per hour for each worker.

D) There will be 20 guests at the wedding.

2

If $12x + 4 = 20$, what is the value of $6x + 5$?

A) 4

B) 6

C) 10

D) 13

3

$$5x - 4y = 36$$
$$-x - y = 0$$

Which of the ordered pairs (x, y) below is a solution to the system of equations shown above?

A) $(-5, 4)$

B) $(-4, 4)$

C) $(4, -4)$

D) $(5, -4)$

4

In the equation $y - \sqrt{4x^2 + 28} = 0$, $x > 0$ and $y = 8$. What is the value of x ?

A) 3

B) 4

C) 5

D) 6

CONTINUE

5

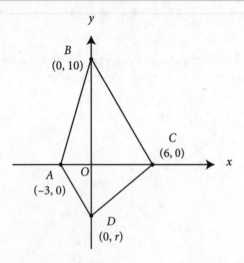

The figure above shows quadrilateral *ABCD* in the *xy*-plane. If $\overline{BC}$ is parallel to $\overline{AD}$, what is the value of *r* ?

A) −6

B) −5

C) −3

D) −2

6

Which of the following expressions is equivalent to $16x^6 - 24x^3y^3 + 9y^6$?

A) $(16x^2 - 9y^2)^3$

B) $(16x^3 - 9y^3)^2$

C) $(4x^3 - 3y^3)^2$

D) $(4x - 3y)^6$

7

$$S = 180(n - 2)$$

The measure *S*, in degrees, of the sum of the angles in a polygon is related to the number of sides, *n*, of the polygon by the formula above for all $n > 2$. If the sum of the angles of a polygon is greater than 2,000°, then what is the least number of sides it can have?

A) 11

B) 12

C) 13

D) 14

8

The graph of line *k* in the *xy*-plane has a *y*-intercept of −8 and contains the point (4, 4). The graph of line *m* contains the points (1, 5) and (5, −3). If lines *k* and *m* intersect at the point (*s*, *t*), what is the value of $s - t$?

A) 2

B) 3

C) 4

D) 5

CONTINUE

9

$$\left(k^{x^2 + xy}\right)\left(k^{y^2 + xy}\right) = k^{25}$$

In the equation above, $k > 1$ and $x = 3$. What is the positive value of y ?

A) 1

B) 2

C) 4

D) 5

10

$$F = \frac{D}{E - D}$$

A factory tracks quality control by using the formula above to determine a fault rating, F, based on the number of defective parts, D, and the number of acceptable parts, E. Which of the following expresses D, in terms of F and E ?

A) $D = \dfrac{E}{1 - F}$

B) $D = \dfrac{E}{1 + F}$

C) $D = \dfrac{FE}{1 - F}$

D) $D = \dfrac{FE}{1 + F}$

11

The graph in the xy-plane of the function g has the property that y is always greater than or equal to -2. Which of the following could be g ?

A) $g(x) = x^2 - 3$

B) $g(x) = (x - 3)^2$

C) $g(x) = |x| - 3$

D) $g(x) = (x - 3)^3$

12

Which of the following complex numbers is equivalent to $\dfrac{1 + 10i}{6 - 3i}$? (Note: $i = \sqrt{-1}$)

A) $\dfrac{1}{6} + \dfrac{10i}{3}$

B) $-\dfrac{1}{6} + \dfrac{10i}{3}$

C) $\dfrac{8}{15} + \dfrac{7i}{5}$

D) $-\dfrac{8}{15} + \dfrac{7i}{5}$

CONTINUE

13

The estimated value of a truck declines at an annual rate of 7 percent. If the original value of the truck was \$35,000, which of the functions v best models the value of the truck, in dollars, t years later?

A) $v(t) = 0.07(35,000)^t$

B) $v(t) = 0.93(35,000)^t$

C) $v(t) = 35,000(0.07)^t$

D) $v(t) = 35,000(0.93)^t$

14

$$\frac{6x - 1}{x + 4}$$

Which of the following is equivalent to the expression above?

A) $6 - \dfrac{25}{x + 4}$

B) $6 - \dfrac{1}{x + 4}$

C) $6 - \dfrac{1}{4}$

D) $\dfrac{6 - 1}{4}$

15

$$3k^2 - 18k + 12 = 0$$

What is the product of all values of k that satisfy the equation above?

A) 3

B) 4

C) $3\sqrt{5}$

D) $6\sqrt{5}$

CONTINUE

DIRECTIONS

For questions 16–20, solve the problem and enter your answer in the grid, as described below, on the answer sheet.

1. Although not required, it is suggested that you write your answer in the boxes at the top of the columns to help you fill in the circles accurately. You will receive credit only if the circles are filled in correctly.

2. Mark no more than one circle in any column.

3. No question has a negative answer.

4. Some problems may have more than one correct answer. In such cases, grid only one answer.

5. **Mixed numbers** such as $3\frac{1}{2}$ must be gridded as 3.5 or 7/2. (If 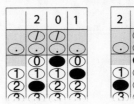 is entered into the grid, it will be interpreted as $\frac{31}{2}$, not as $3\frac{1}{2}$.)

6. **Decimal Answers:** If you obtain a decimal answer with more digits than the grid can accommodate, it may be either rounded or truncated, but it must fill the entire grid.

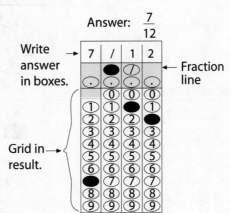

Acceptable ways to grid $\frac{2}{3}$ are:

Answer: 201 – either position is correct

NOTE: You may start your answers in any column, space permitting. Columns you don't need to use should be left blank.

16

In the equation $3(x - 5)^2 + 7 = ax^2 + bx + c$, a, b, and c are constants. If the equation is true for all values of x, what is the value of c ?

17

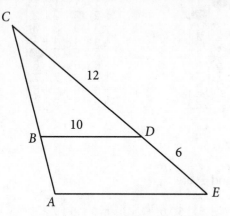

In the figure above, $\overline{BD} \parallel \overline{AE}$. What is the length of $\overline{AE}$?

18

At the end of a card game, Eve has a pile of red and blue chips that is worth $120. If red chips are worth $5 and blue chips are worth $20, and Eve has at least one red chip and at least one blue chip, what is one possible number of red chips Eve has?

19

$$\frac{1}{2} x + ay = 16$$
$$bx + 4y = 48$$

In the system of equations shown above, a and b are constants. If there are infinitely many solutions for this system, what is the value of $a + b$?

CONTINUE

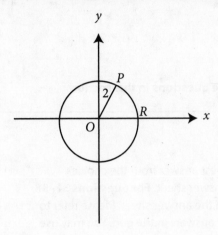

The *xy*-plane above shows the circle with center *O* and radius 2. If the measure of $\angle POR$ is $\dfrac{\pi}{3}$ radians, what is the *x*-coordinate of point *P*?

STOP
If you finish before time is called, you may check your work on this section only.
Do not turn to any other section in the test.

Math Test – Calculator

55 MINUTES, 38 QUESTIONS

Turn to Section 4 of your answer sheet to answer the questions in this section.

$A = \pi r^2$
$C = 2\pi r$

$A = \ell w$

$A = \frac{1}{2} bh$

$c^2 = a^2 + b^2$

Special Right Triangles

$V = \ell wh$

$V = \pi r^2 h$

$V = \frac{4}{3}\pi r^3$

$V = \frac{1}{3}\pi r^2 h$

$V = \frac{1}{3}\ell wh$

The number of degrees of arc in a circle is 360.
The number of radians of arc in a circle is 2π.
The sum of the measures in degrees of the angles of a triangle is 180.

CONTINUE

1

A contractor creates a mosaic floor pattern in which there are 9 blue tiles for every 80 tiles in total. At this rate, how many blue tiles will there be in a floor pattern of 4,800 tiles?

A) 700

B) 620

C) 540

D) 480

2

$$c = 120 + 75d$$

A couple rents a car for their vacation. When a particular car is rented for d days, the total cost will be c dollars as shown in the equation above. What is the value of d when c is 345 ?

A) 25,995

B) 354

C) 75

D) 3

3

An artist creates prints of her latest painting to sell. The artist earns \$50 for each large print she sells and \$35 for each small print she sells. Which of the following expressions represents the amount, in dollars, that the artist earns for selling l large prints and s small prints?

A) $50l + 35s$

B) $50l - 35s$

C) $35l + 50s$

D) $35l - 50s$

4

When 6 times a number y is subtracted from 15, the result is 33. What number results when 3 times y is added to 19 ?

A) −3

B) 7

C) 10

D) 28

CONTINUE

Questions 5 and 6 refer to the following information.

A television store's revenue is directly proportional to the number of televisions it sells. The store earns $1,440 on a day in which it sells 6 televisions.

5

The store pays the factory 39% of the money earned from the sale of each television. The rest of the money earned is the store's profit. What is the profit the store makes on a day in which it sells 6 televisions?

A) $390.00

B) $561.60

C) $690.00

D) $878.40

6

How much revenue will the store earn on a day in which it sells 9 televisions?

A) $960

B) $2,160

C) $8,640

D) $12,960

7

A record collector is looking to buy records that cost either $20 or $35 each. Let a be the number of $20 records and b be the number of $35 records. The collector can buy a maximum of 25 records and can spend up to $750. Which of the following systems of inequalities accurately describes this relationship?

A) $\begin{cases} a + b \le 750 \\ 20a + 35b \le 25 \end{cases}$

B) $\begin{cases} 20a + 35b \le 750 \\ a + b \le 750 \end{cases}$

C) $\begin{cases} \dfrac{a}{20} + \dfrac{b}{35} \le 750 \\ a + b \le 25 \end{cases}$

D) $\begin{cases} 20a + 35b \le 750 \\ a + b \le 25 \end{cases}$

8

$$y = x^2 - 12x + 35$$

The equation above is a quadratic equation. Which of the following equivalent forms of the equation displays the x-intercepts of the parabola in the xy-plane as constants or coefficients?

A) $y + 1 = (x - 6)^2$

B) $y - 35 = x^2 - 12x$

C) $y = (x - 5)(x - 7)$

D) $y = x(x - 12) + 35$

CONTINUE

9

In a certain quiz game, each player begins with p points, loses 3 points for every question answered incorrectly, and cannot increase his or her score. If a player who answers 15 questions incorrectly has a score of 165, which of the following is the value of p ?

A) 210

B) 180

C) 140

D) 0

10

Number of hours per day Albert expects to devote to typing the document	4
Number of units in the document	21
Number of words Albert types per minute	85
Number of sections in the document	145
Number of pages in the document	725
Number of words in the document	181,235

Albert needs to type a long, prewritten document. The table above shows information about the document, Albert's typing speed, and the number of hours he expects to devote to typing the document each day. If Albert types at the rates provided in the table, which of the following is closest to the number of days Albert would expect to take in order to type the entire document?

A) 9

B) 36

C) 148

D) 2,132

11

At 9:00 A.M. on Monday, a trash can with a capacity of 20 cubic feet contains 8 cubic feet of garbage. Each day after Monday, 3 cubic feet of garbage are added to the trash can. If no garbage is removed and d represents the number of days after Monday, which of the following inequalities describes the set of days for which the trash can is full or overflowing?

A) $12 \geq 3d$

B) $8 + 3d \geq 20$

C) $20 - 3 \leq d$

D) $20 \leq 3d$

12

In function m, $m(4) = 6$ and $m(6) = 10$. In function n, $n(6) = 4$ and $n(10) = 2$. What is the value of $m(n(6))$?

A) 2

B) 4

C) 6

D) 10

CONTINUE

13

The circumference of Earth's equator is approximately 40,000 kilometers. Earth rotates completely around its axis in one day. Which of the following is the closest approximation of the average speed, in kilometers per minute, of a point on Earth's equator, as the Earth rotates about its axis?

A) 18

B) 20

C) 28

D) 56

14

A theater owner wanted to determine whether local residents were more interested in seeing operas or symphonies. The theater owner asked 85 people who were in a shopping mall on a Sunday and 5 people declined to respond. Which of the following factors is the greatest flaw in the theater owner's methodology in reaching a reliable conclusion about the local residents' performance-viewing preferences?

A) The size of the sample

B) The location in which the survey was given

C) The population of the area

D) The residents who declined to respond

15

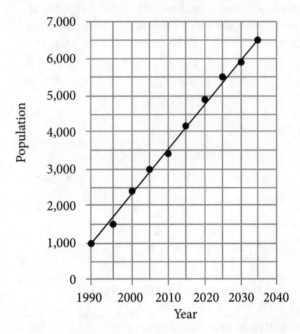

Population of Town T from 1990
Projected Through 2035

According to the line of best fit in the scatterplot above, which of following best approximates the year in which the population of Town T is projected to reach 5,000 ?

A) 2017

B) 2022

C) 2028

D) 2033

16

The half-life of an unknown isotope is approximately 25% less than that of carbon-14. The half-life of carbon-14 is 5,730 years. Which of the following best approximates the half-life, in years, of the unknown isotope?

A) 1,400

B) 4,300

C) 5,705

D) 7,200

CONTINUE

17

A company's accounting department took a survey of its employees' salaries and found that the mean salary was $80,000 and that the median salary was $45,000. Which of the following could explain the difference between the mean and the median salary in the company?

A) Many of the employees' salaries are between $45,000 and $80,000.

B) The employees have salaries that are close to each other.

C) There are a few employees with salaries that are much lower than the rest.

D) There are a few employees with salaries that are much higher than the rest.

18

Results of Interview for Applicants to College C

	Accepted by College C	Rejected by College C
Completed interview	15,700	34,300
Did not complete interview	9,300	40,700

The table above summarizes the results of the 100,000 applicants to College C. If an accepted student is randomly chosen, what is the probability that the student did <u>not</u> complete an interview?

A) $\dfrac{93}{1,000}$

B) $\dfrac{1}{4}$

C) $\dfrac{93}{250}$

D) $\dfrac{157}{250}$

19

Mathias saves an average of d dollars per month, where $d > 300$. The actual amount he saves per month varies, but is always within $20 of the average amount. If Mathias saved k dollars this month, which of the following inequalities expresses the relationship between k, the amount he saved this month, and d, the average amount he saves per month?

A) $d - k < 20$

B) $d + k < 20$

C) $-20 < d - k < 20$

D) $-20 < d + k < 20$

CONTINUE

Questions 20 and 21 refer to the following information.

The class president chose 200 students at random from each of the junior and senior classes at her high school. Each student was asked how many hours of homework he or she completed in an average school night. The results are shown in the table below.

Number of hours	Junior class	Senior class
1	25	30
2	80	70
3	50	60
4	35	35
5	10	5

There are a total of 600 students in the junior class and 400 students in the senior class.

20

What is the median number of hours of homework in an average night for all the students surveyed?

A) 2

B) 3

C) 4

D) 5

21

Based on the survey data, which of the following statements accurately compares the expected total number of members of each class who complete four hours of homework?

A) The total number of students who complete four hours of homework in the junior class is 35 more than in the senior class.

B) The total number of students who complete four hours of homework in the senior class is 35 more than in the junior class.

C) The total number of students who complete four hours of homework in the junior class is 200 more than in the senior class.

D) The total number of students who complete four hours of homework is expected to be the same in both classes.

22

The equation of circle P in the xy-plane can be represented as $x^2 + y^2 - 6x + 8y = -9$. What is the radius of circle P?

A) 2

B) 4

C) 8

D) 16

CONTINUE

Questions 23 and 24 refer to the following information.

$$G = \frac{ab}{d^2}$$

The gravitational force, G, between an object of mass a and an object of mass b is given by the formula above, where d represents the distance between the two objects.

23

Which of the following expressions represents the square of the distance between the two objects in terms of the masses of the objects and the gravitational force between them?

A) $d^2 = \dfrac{Gb}{a}$

B) $d^2 = \dfrac{Ga}{b}$

C) $d^2 = \dfrac{G}{ab}$

D) $d^2 = \dfrac{ab}{G}$

24

Objects k and m have the same masses, respectively, as do objects a and b. If the gravitational force between k and m is 9 times the gravitational force between a and b, then the distance between k and m is what fraction of the distance between a and b ?

A) $\dfrac{1}{243}$

B) $\dfrac{1}{81}$

C) $\dfrac{1}{9}$

D) $\dfrac{1}{3}$

CONTINUE

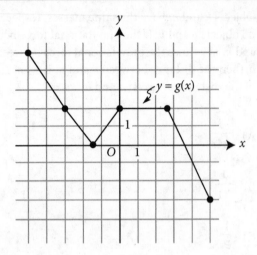

The figure above shows the complete graph of the function g in the xy-plane. Which of the following must be true?

    I. $g(-3) = 2$

    II. $g(2) = -3$

    III. $g\left(\dfrac{1}{2}\right) = g(2)$

A) III only

B) I and II only

C) I and III only

D) I, II, and III

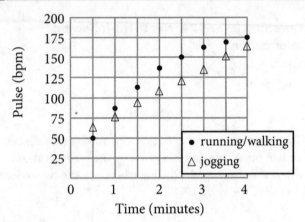

Two athletes have their pulses, in beats per minute (bpm), monitored while they exercise. One athlete alternates brisk running with walking, while the other athlete jogs at a constant pace. The graph above shows the athletes' heart rates at 30-second intervals. Which of the following statements accurately compares the average rates at which the pulses of the two athletes change?

A) In the interval from 1 to 2 minutes, the rate of change of pulse for the athlete who alternates running and walking is of lesser magnitude than the rate of change of pulse for the athlete who jogs only, whereas in the interval from 3 to 4 minutes, the rate of change of pulse for the athlete who jogs only is of lesser magnitude.

B) In the interval from 1 to 2 minutes, the rate of change of pulse for the athlete who jogs only is of lesser magnitude than the rate of change of pulse for the athlete who alternates running and walking, whereas in the interval from 3 to 4 minutes, the rate of change of pulse for the athlete who alternates running and walking is of lesser magnitude.

C) In every 30-second interval, the rate of change of pulse for the athlete who alternates running and walking is of lesser magnitude than it is for the athlete who jogs only.

D) In every 30-second interval, the rate of change of pulse for the athlete who jogs only is of lesser magnitude than it is for the athlete who alternates running and walking.

CONTINUE

27

The graph in the *xy*-plane of linear function *g* has an *x*-intercept at $(s, 0)$ and a *y*-intercept at $(0, t)$. If $t - s = 0$, $t \neq 0$, and $s \neq 0$, which of the following must be true about the graph of *g* ?

A) It has a positive slope.

B) It has a negative slope.

C) It has a slope of zero.

D) It has no slope.

28

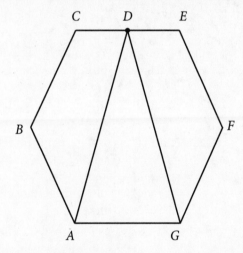

In the figure above, *ABCEFG* is a regular hexagon and *D* is the midpoint of $\overline{CE}$. If the area of the hexagon is $864\sqrt{3}$ square feet, what is the area, in square feet, of triangle *ADG* ?

A) 144

B) 432

C) $288\sqrt{3}$

D) $432\sqrt{3}$

29

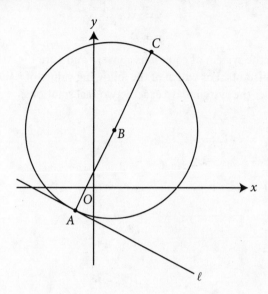

In the *xy*-plane above, $\overline{AC}$ is the diameter of the circle centered at *B*, and the coordinates of points *A* and *C* are $(-1, -1)$ and $(3, 7)$, respectively. If line ℓ is tangent to the circle at point *A*, which of the following is an equation of line ℓ ?

A) $y = -\dfrac{1}{2}(x + 3)$

B) $y = -\dfrac{1}{2}x + 3$

C) $y = -2x + 1$

D) $y = -2x - 3$

CONTINUE

30

$$y = rx^2 + s$$
$$y = -2$$

In the system of equations above, r and s are constants. For which of the following values of r and s does the system have exactly two real solutions?

A) $r = -2, s = -1$

B) $r = -1, s = -2$

C) $r = 2, s = -2$

D) $r = 3, s = 1$

CONTINUE

DIRECTIONS

For questions 31–38, solve the problem and enter your answer in the grid, as described below, on the answer sheet.

1. Although not required, it is suggested that you write your answer in the boxes at the top of the columns to help you fill in the circles accurately. You will receive credit only if the circles are filled in correctly.

2. Mark no more than one circle in any column.

3. No question has a negative answer.

4. Some problems may have more than one correct answer. In such cases, grid only one answer.

5. **Mixed numbers** such as $3\frac{1}{2}$ must be gridded as 3.5 or 7/2. (If  is entered into the grid, it will be interpreted as $\frac{31}{2}$, not as $3\frac{1}{2}$.)

6. **Decimal Answers:** If you obtain a decimal answer with more digits than the grid can accommodate, it may be either rounded or truncated, but it must fill the entire grid.

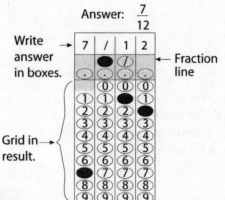

Answer: $\frac{7}{12}$ — Write answer in boxes. — Fraction line — Grid in result.

Answer: 2.5 — Decimal point

Acceptable ways to grid $\frac{2}{3}$ are:

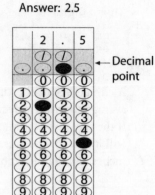

Answer: 201 – either position is correct

NOTE: You may start your answers in any column, space permitting. Columns you don't need to use should be left blank.

CONTINUE →

31

If 560 minutes is equal to z hours and 20 minutes, what is the value of z ?

32

A climate scientist estimates that a certain state's average snowfall is decreasing by 0.4 inch per year. If the scientist's estimate is accurate, how many years will it take for the average annual snowfall to be 6 inches less than it is now?

33

Dave was charged a fine for returning a number of overdue books to the library. Each week after he incurred the fine, he paid the library a fixed amount until the fine was paid off. The equation $C = 12 - 1.5w$, where $C \geq 0$, models the amount C, in dollars, that Dave owes w weeks after he incurred the fine. According to this model, how much money, in dollars, did Dave initially owe the library? (Disregard the $ sign when gridding in your answer.)

34

$$g(x) = 2x^2 - kx + 14$$

In the xy-plane, the graph of the function above contains the point $(4, -2)$. What is the value of k ?

CONTINUE

35

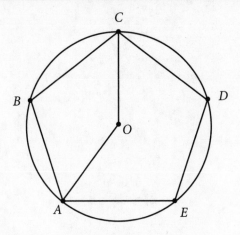

In the figure above, the circle is centered at point O, $ABCDE$ is a regular pentagon, and $ABCO$ is a quadrilateral. If the length of arc $\overset{\frown}{ABC}$ is 24, what is the circumference of circle O ?

36

Satya ate a breakfast sandwich and an order of fried potatoes, and consumed a total of 910 calories. If the breakfast sandwich contained 240 more calories than the fried potatoes, how many calories did the breakfast sandwich contain?

Questions 37 and 38 refer to the following information.

$$P_{t+1} = P_t + 0.3(P_t)\left(1 - \frac{P_t}{C}\right)$$

A certain species of deer on an isolated island has a current population of 4,200. The estimated population of deer next year, P_{t+1}, is related to the population this year, P_t, by the formula above. In this formula, the constant C represents the maximum number of deer the island is capable of supporting.

37

Suppose that environmental conditions on the island changed suddenly, and there was a resultant decrease in the maximum number of deer the island is capable of supporting. If the number of deer increases from 4,200 this year to 4,704 next year, what would be the maximum number of deer the island is capable of supporting?

38

If $C = 10,500$, and the given formula is accurate, what will the population of deer be 2 years from now? (Round your answer to the nearest whole number.)

END OF TEST

DO NOT RETURN TO A PREVIOUS SECTION.

The
Princeton
Review®

Completely darken bubbles with a No. 2 pencil. If you make a mistake, be sure to erase mark completely. Erase all stray marks.

1.

YOUR NAME: _____
(Print)   Last   First   M.I.

SIGNATURE: _____   DATE: ___ / ___ / ___

HOME ADDRESS: _____
(Print)   Number and Street

_____
City   State   Zip Code

PHONE NO.: _____
(Print)

IMPORTANT: Please fill in these boxes exactly as shown on the back cover of your test book.

2. TEST FORM

6. DATE OF BIRTH

Month	Day		Year	
◯ JAN				
◯ FEB	⓪	⓪	⓪	⓪
◯ MAR	①	①	①	①
◯ APR	②	②	②	②
◯ MAY	③	③	③	③
◯ JUN		④	④	④
◯ JUL		⑤	⑤	⑤
◯ AUG		⑥	⑥	⑥
◯ SEP		⑦	⑦	⑦
◯ OCT		⑧	⑧	⑧
◯ NOV		⑨	⑨	⑨
◯ DEC				

3. TEST CODE   **4. REGISTRATION NUMBER**

7. SEX
◯ MALE
◯ FEMALE

The
Princeton
Review®

5. YOUR NAME

| First 4 letters of last name | | | | FIRST INIT | MID INIT |

Test ❷

Start with number 1 for each new section.
If a section has fewer questions than answer spaces, leave the extra answer spaces blank.

Section 1—Reading

1. Ⓐ Ⓑ Ⓒ Ⓓ
2. Ⓐ Ⓑ Ⓒ Ⓓ
3. Ⓐ Ⓑ Ⓒ Ⓓ
4. Ⓐ Ⓑ Ⓒ Ⓓ
5. Ⓐ Ⓑ Ⓒ Ⓓ
6. Ⓐ Ⓑ Ⓒ Ⓓ
7. Ⓐ Ⓑ Ⓒ Ⓓ
8. Ⓐ Ⓑ Ⓒ Ⓓ
9. Ⓐ Ⓑ Ⓒ Ⓓ
10. Ⓐ Ⓑ Ⓒ Ⓓ
11. Ⓐ Ⓑ Ⓒ Ⓓ
12. Ⓐ Ⓑ Ⓒ Ⓓ
13. Ⓐ Ⓑ Ⓒ Ⓓ
14. Ⓐ Ⓑ Ⓒ Ⓓ
15. Ⓐ Ⓑ Ⓒ Ⓓ
16. Ⓐ Ⓑ Ⓒ Ⓓ
17. Ⓐ Ⓑ Ⓒ Ⓓ
18. Ⓐ Ⓑ Ⓒ Ⓓ
19. Ⓐ Ⓑ Ⓒ Ⓓ
20. Ⓐ Ⓑ Ⓒ Ⓓ
21. Ⓐ Ⓑ Ⓒ Ⓓ
22. Ⓐ Ⓑ Ⓒ Ⓓ
23. Ⓐ Ⓑ Ⓒ Ⓓ
24. Ⓐ Ⓑ Ⓒ Ⓓ
25. Ⓐ Ⓑ Ⓒ Ⓓ
26. Ⓐ Ⓑ Ⓒ Ⓓ
27. Ⓐ Ⓑ Ⓒ Ⓓ
28. Ⓐ Ⓑ Ⓒ Ⓓ
29. Ⓐ Ⓑ Ⓒ Ⓓ
30. Ⓐ Ⓑ Ⓒ Ⓓ
31. Ⓐ Ⓑ Ⓒ Ⓓ
32. Ⓐ Ⓑ Ⓒ Ⓓ
33. Ⓐ Ⓑ Ⓒ Ⓓ
34. Ⓐ Ⓑ Ⓒ Ⓓ
35. Ⓐ Ⓑ Ⓒ Ⓓ
36. Ⓐ Ⓑ Ⓒ Ⓓ
37. Ⓐ Ⓑ Ⓒ Ⓓ
38. Ⓐ Ⓑ Ⓒ Ⓓ
39. Ⓐ Ⓑ Ⓒ Ⓓ
40. Ⓐ Ⓑ Ⓒ Ⓓ
41. Ⓐ Ⓑ Ⓒ Ⓓ
42. Ⓐ Ⓑ Ⓒ Ⓓ
43. Ⓐ Ⓑ Ⓒ Ⓓ
44. Ⓐ Ⓑ Ⓒ Ⓓ
45. Ⓐ Ⓑ Ⓒ Ⓓ
46. Ⓐ Ⓑ Ⓒ Ⓓ
47. Ⓐ Ⓑ Ⓒ Ⓓ
48. Ⓐ Ⓑ Ⓒ Ⓓ
49. Ⓐ Ⓑ Ⓒ Ⓓ
50. Ⓐ Ⓑ Ⓒ Ⓓ
51. Ⓐ Ⓑ Ⓒ Ⓓ
52. Ⓐ Ⓑ Ⓒ Ⓓ

Section 2—Writing and Language Skills

1. Ⓐ Ⓑ Ⓒ Ⓓ
2. Ⓐ Ⓑ Ⓒ Ⓓ
3. Ⓐ Ⓑ Ⓒ Ⓓ
4. Ⓐ Ⓑ Ⓒ Ⓓ
5. Ⓐ Ⓑ Ⓒ Ⓓ
6. Ⓐ Ⓑ Ⓒ Ⓓ
7. Ⓐ Ⓑ Ⓒ Ⓓ
8. Ⓐ Ⓑ Ⓒ Ⓓ
9. Ⓐ Ⓑ Ⓒ Ⓓ
10. Ⓐ Ⓑ Ⓒ Ⓓ
11. Ⓐ Ⓑ Ⓒ Ⓓ
12. Ⓐ Ⓑ Ⓒ Ⓓ
13. Ⓐ Ⓑ Ⓒ Ⓓ
14. Ⓐ Ⓑ Ⓒ Ⓓ
15. Ⓐ Ⓑ Ⓒ Ⓓ
16. Ⓐ Ⓑ Ⓒ Ⓓ
17. Ⓐ Ⓑ Ⓒ Ⓓ
18. Ⓐ Ⓑ Ⓒ Ⓓ
19. Ⓐ Ⓑ Ⓒ Ⓓ
20. Ⓐ Ⓑ Ⓒ Ⓓ
21. Ⓐ Ⓑ Ⓒ Ⓓ
22. Ⓐ Ⓑ Ⓒ Ⓓ
23. Ⓐ Ⓑ Ⓒ Ⓓ
24. Ⓐ Ⓑ Ⓒ Ⓓ
25. Ⓐ Ⓑ Ⓒ Ⓓ
26. Ⓐ Ⓑ Ⓒ Ⓓ
27. Ⓐ Ⓑ Ⓒ Ⓓ
28. Ⓐ Ⓑ Ⓒ Ⓓ
29. Ⓐ Ⓑ Ⓒ Ⓓ
30. Ⓐ Ⓑ Ⓒ Ⓓ
31. Ⓐ Ⓑ Ⓒ Ⓓ
32. Ⓐ Ⓑ Ⓒ Ⓓ
33. Ⓐ Ⓑ Ⓒ Ⓓ
34. Ⓐ Ⓑ Ⓒ Ⓓ
35. Ⓐ Ⓑ Ⓒ Ⓓ
36. Ⓐ Ⓑ Ⓒ Ⓓ
37. Ⓐ Ⓑ Ⓒ Ⓓ
38. Ⓐ Ⓑ Ⓒ Ⓓ
39. Ⓐ Ⓑ Ⓒ Ⓓ
40. Ⓐ Ⓑ Ⓒ Ⓓ
41. Ⓐ Ⓑ Ⓒ Ⓓ
42. Ⓐ Ⓑ Ⓒ Ⓓ
43. Ⓐ Ⓑ Ⓒ Ⓓ
44. Ⓐ Ⓑ Ⓒ Ⓓ

Test 2

Start with number 1 for each new section.
If a section has fewer questions than answer spaces, leave the extra answer spaces blank.

Section 3—Mathematics: No Calculator

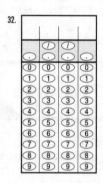
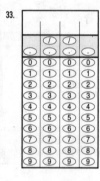
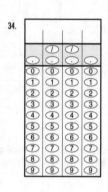

Section 4—Mathematics: Calculator

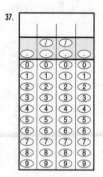

Chapter 6
Practice Test 2:
Answers and
Explanations

PRACTICE TEST 2 ANSWER KEY

Section 1: Reading				Section 2: Writing & Language				Section 3: Math (No Calculator)				Section 4: Math (Calculator)			
1.	D	27.	D	1.	B	23.	D	1.	C	11.	B	1.	C	20.	A
2.	A	28.	A	2.	D	24.	A	2.	D	12.	D	2.	D	21.	A
3.	D	29.	A	3.	B	25.	B	3.	C	13.	D	3.	A	22.	B
4.	C	30.	B	4.	C	26.	B	4.	A	14.	A	4.	C	23.	D
5.	D	31.	A	5.	A	27.	C	5.	B	15.	B	5.	D	24.	D
6.	B	32.	B	6.	D	28.	C	6.	C	16.	82	6.	B	25.	C
7.	C	33.	B	7.	D	29.	B	7.	D	17.	15	7.	D	26.	B
8.	B	34.	B	8.	B	30.	B	8.	A	18.	4, 8, 12, 16, or 20	8.	C	27.	B
9.	C	35.	D	9.	D	31.	D	9.	B			9.	A	28.	C
10.	A	36.	D	10.	C	32.	C	10.	D			10.	A	29.	A
11.	A	37.	A	11.	A	33.	A			19.	$\dfrac{17}{6}$ or 2.83	11.	B	30.	A
12.	D	38.	B	12.	C	34.	C					12.	C	31.	9
13.	A	39.	A	13.	A	35.	B					13.	C	32.	15
14.	C	40.	C	14.	D	36.	C			20.	1	14.	B	33.	12
15.	C	41.	D	15.	A	37.	D					15.	B	34.	12
16.	A	42.	D	16.	B	38.	B					16.	B	35.	60
17.	B	43.	A	17.	D	39.	A					17.	D	36.	575
18.	A	44.	C	18.	B	40.	B					18.	C	37.	7,000
19.	A	45.	A	19.	D	41.	A					19.	C	38.	5,741
20.	A	46.	D	20.	C	42.	D								
21.	C	47.	B	21.	D	43.	D								
22.	C	48.	C	22.	D	44.	B								
23.	A	49.	A												
24.	A	50.	C												
25.	B	51.	D												
26.	B	52.	C												

Go to PrincetonReview.com to score your exam. Alternatively, for self-assessment tables, please turn to page 909.

PRACTICE TEST 2 EXPLANATIONS

Section 1: Reading

1. **D** The question asks for the main idea of the passage. Because this is a general question, it should be done after all the specific questions have been completed. The passage tells the story of a knight, Don Quixote, and his squire Sancho Panza. They encounter a field of windmills, which Don Quixote believes to be giants he must battle. Eliminate any answers that aren't consistent with this idea. Eliminate (A) because neither Don Quixote nor Sancho Panza *decide[s] to pretend* that he is entering battle. Choice (B) can be eliminated because the giants are not actually there. Choice (C) might initially look good, because the two men do have an argument. However, the text identifies Sancho as Don Quixote's squire, not another knight, so eliminate (C). Choice (D) includes the battle of the second half of the passage as well as the different perception of reality of the first half (and the very end). The correct answer is (D).

2. **A** The question asks about the function of the opening sentence. Carefully read the sentence and the surrounding window to determine the function of the sentence: *At this point they came in sight of thirty or forty windmills that are on that plain.* The author tells the reader that these are windmills, not giants, as Don Quixote thinks, so the function of the sentence is to let the reader know the reality of the situation. Choice (A) mentions the *true setting*, which is consistent with this prediction, so keep it. Choice (B) mentions *technological advances* and their importance, which are not discussed in this passage. The first half of (C) might initially look attractive because it describes the field, but the answer can be eliminated because there is no *great battle.* Choice (D) can be eliminated because there is no *detailed imagery.* The correct answer is (A).

3. **D** The question asks how the main character's focus changes from paragraph 1 to paragraph 6. Carefully read the window to determine how Don Quixote's focus changes. At the beginning of the window, Don Quixote sees the windmills, calling them *monstrous giants*, and telling Sancho he intends to *engage in battle.* When Sancho tries to tell him that they are in fact *not giants but windmills*, Don Quixote calls him a coward. Eliminate any answer choices that aren't consistent with that change in focus. Eliminate (A) because there are no *recollections of past victories* or *prospects of imminent defeat* in the text. Choice (B) mentions *money* and *God*, neither of which are consistent with the prediction. Choice (C) can be eliminated because neither *generalizations about successful battle* nor *specific rules of combat* are part of Don Quixote's focus. Choice (D) mentions an *evaluation of an enemy*, which is consistent with Don Quixote misidentifying the windmills as giants, and an *argument with his faithful companion.* The correct answer is (D).

4. **C** The question asks about the effect of the phrase *sweep so evil a breed from off the face of the earth.* Locate the phrase and carefully read the window. Don Quixote explains that he intends to fight the "giants," sweeping them *from the face of the earth.* Don Quixote's exaggerations show that he sees himself as a brave and powerful knight, regardless of what the truth might be. Eliminate any answer choices that aren't consistent with the idea of Don Quixote having an inflated view of himself. Choice (A) can be eliminated because the story is not *a horror story.* Eliminate (B) because Don Quixote is not *a prophet,* nor has he received any *orders from God.* Choice (C) is consistent with the prediction, so keep it. Eliminate (D) because Quixote is not presented as a religious fanatic. The correct answer is (C).

5. **D** The question asks how Don Quixote would characterize his charge into battle. He says he plans to *engage [the giants] in fierce and unequal combat.* The battle will be *unequal* because there are

30 or 40 of them, and he is only *a single knight*. He also calls the giants *cowards*. Don Quixote would likely characterize his charge as "bold" or "heroic." Eliminate any answer choices that aren't consistent with that prediction. Choice (A), *ridiculous*, might be consistent with what Sancho Panza thinks, but the question asks about Don Quixote, so eliminate (A). Choice (B), *insane*, can be eliminated for the same reason. Choice (C), *unexceptional*, is not consistent with the prediction, so eliminate it. Choice (D), *brave*, fits the prediction. The correct answer is (D).

6. **B** The question asks how Sancho Panza views Don Quixote. Notice the next question is a best evidence question, so Q6 and Q7 can be answered in tandem. Look at the answers for Q7 first. The lines in (7A) show that Don Quixote views Sancho as a *friend*, but the question asks how Sancho views Don Quixote. Eliminate (7A). Choice (7B) again shows how Don Quixote views Sancho Panza, so it can also be eliminated. Choice (7C) shows Sancho yelling after Don Quixote that they *most certainly were windmills and not giants*. Those lines support (6B), so draw a line connecting those two answers. Choice (7D) describes Don Quixote's charge at the windmills but does not mention Sancho, so eliminate (7D). Without support from Q7, (6A), (6C), and (6D) can all be eliminated. The correct answers are (6B) and (7C).

7. **C** (See explanation above.)

8. **B** The question asks why Don Quixote does not believe Sancho Panza's description of the "giants." Use the line reference to carefully read the window. Panza says they are windmills, and in lines 21–22, Quixote says that Panza is *not used to this business of adventures* and suggests that he might be *afraid*. Look for an answer that is consistent with the idea that Don Quixote believes Sancho is afraid. Choice (A) mentions *eyesight*, which does not fit the prediction, so eliminate it. Choice (B) mentions *not as brave*, which is consistent with *afraid*. Keep (B). Although Don Quixote mentions Friston's schemes, he never indicates whether he believes Sancho also knows about the schemes, so (C) can be eliminated. Choice (D) can be eliminated because Quixote suggests that Panza might start praying, not that he is doing so now. The correct answer is (B).

9. **C** The question is a best evidence question, so simply refer back to the lines used to predict the answer to the previous question. Lines 21–22 were used to answer the question. The correct answer is (C).

10. **A** The question asks about the main effect of referring to Friston. Use that name as a lead word to locate the window. Carefully read to determine the effect of referring to Friston. Quixote says that this same Friston *who carried off my study and books* has also *turned these giants into mills in order to rob me of the glory of vanquishing them*. Referring to Friston shows how Quixote can maintain his ideas about his own reality: even though he can now see that the things he attacked are really windmills, his fanciful view of the world has not changed. Choice (A) mentions that the reader gains insight into how Quixote perceives reality. This is consistent with the prediction, so keep it. Choice (B) says mentioning Friston reveals the *evil in the world*. Since it is unclear whether Friston is even real, and since the author does not say Friston is evil, eliminate (B). Choice (C) can be eliminated because there is no *detailed history* provided. Choice (D) again mentions how evil results from *personal misunderstandings*. This is not supported by the passage and can be eliminated. The correct answer is (A).

11. **A** The question asks about the central problem women have had, according to Anthony. Since this is a general question, do it after all the specific questions have been completed. According to Anthony, women have been denied the right to vote, *in direct violation of the spirit and letter of the declarations of the framers of this government, every one of which was based on the immutable principle of equal rights to all*. Eliminate any answer choices that aren't consistent with this prediction. Choice (A) is consistent, so keep it. Choice (B) can be eliminated because she is not concerned

about whether or not women are allowed to participate in Congress. Eliminate (C) because her concerns are not about the differences in the temperaments of men and women. Choice (D) mentions *equal access*, but Anthony's concern is about voting, not schools. Eliminate (D). The correct answer is (A).

12. **D** The question asks what the author means by *grand documents*. Use the given line reference to find the window and read carefully. The passage mentions the *Declaration of Independence, the United States Constitution*, and other documents, so choose an answer that means *important documents from U.S. history*. Choice (A) is too literal and too specific. Choice (B) does not match the prediction, so eliminate it. Choice (C) can also be eliminated because there's no mention of *personal notes*. Choice (D) refers to *important legislation the country was founded on*, which matches the prediction. The correct answer is (D).

13. **A** The question asks what Anthony claimed to be a purpose of the Declaration of Independence. Use the lead words *Declaration of Independence* to find the window and read carefully. Lines 32–34 say that the Declaration of Independence, along with other documents, *propose to protect the people in the exercise of their God-given rights*. This is directly stated by (A), so keep that answer choice. Choice (B) can be eliminated because it's the opposite of what the text says. Choice (C) can be eliminated for the same reason. There is no mention of *prevention of violence*, so eliminate (D). The correct answer is (A).

14. **C** The question asks for the best evidence for the answer to Q13. Lines 32–34 were used to answer the previous question. The correct answer is (C).

15. **C** The question asks what the phrase *the exercise* means in line 33. Go back to the text, find *the exercise*, and mark it out. Carefully read the surrounding text to determine another word that would fit in the blank based on the context of the passage. The text says that the documents *protect the people in the exercise of their...rights*. The missing word must mean something like "the practice." Choice (A), *an activity*, can be eliminated because there is no activity discussed. Eliminate (B) because there is no *workout*. Choice (C) is consistent with the prediction, so keep it. Choice (D) can be eliminated because *process* is not consistent with *practice* in this context. The correct answer is (C).

16. **A** The question asks for a logical inference regarding the general function of the term *natural right*. Use the line reference to find the window and read carefully. The complete phrase is *natural right of all to the ballot*, and the sentence ends with a mention of the *right to vote*. The phrase refers to the idea that all humans should be able to vote, regardless of gender. Choice (A) is consistent with this prediction, so keep it. Choice (B) can be eliminated because there is no criticism implied in the phrase. Eliminate (C) because there is no discussion about the *right to bear arms*, and (D) can also be eliminated because there is no mention of the *Fifth Amendment*. The correct answer is (A).

17. **B** The question asks what the word *class* means in line 59. Go back to the text, find *class*, and mark it out. Carefully read the surrounding text to determine another word that would fit in the blank based on the context of the passage. Anthony is discussing how women are not allowed to vote, so they are a *disenfranchised class*. A word that means *"crowd"* or *"part of society"* would make sense, so eliminate anything that isn't consistent with that prediction. Choice (A), *subject*, can be eliminated because there is no discussion of a ruling class. Choice (B) is consistent with the prediction, so keep it. Choice (C) can be eliminated because this is not a discussion of scientific classifications. Eliminate (D) because it's a definition of *class* that isn't consistent with the context. The correct answer is (B).

18. **A** The question asks what the *situation* described by Anthony suggests *the U.S. government* has done. Notice that the following question is a best evidence question, so it can be answered in tandem with Q19. Look at the answers for Q19 first. The lines in (19A) mention that the author is accused of the *crime of having voted…without having a lawful right to vote*, so look to see if those words support any answers in Q18. Choice (18A) mentions *laws denying women's suffrage*. Since "suffrage" means "the right to vote," connect those two answers. Next, consider the lines for (19B). The speaker quotes selections from the Declaration of Independence about being *created equal* and having *rights* such as *life, liberty, and the pursuit of happiness*. This is not referenced in any choices in Q18, so eliminate (19B). The lines in (19C) refer to the need for revolution when any government becomes repressive. This may weakly support (18D), so connect those two answers. Next, consider lines for (19D). These lines do not discuss the U.S. government and therefore do not answer Q19. Eliminate (19D). Without any support from Q19, (18B) and (18C) can be eliminated. Consider the remaining pairs of answer choices in the context of the passage. While both (18A) and (18D) seem to be something that the author says that the government has done, the question asked what the author says about the government given the situation described in the text. Since that situation is the government unjustly barring women from voting, eliminate (18D) and its support in (19C). The correct answers are (18A) and (19A).

19. **A** (See explanation above.)

20. **A** The question asks for the primary contrast in paragraph 7. Carefully read the given lines. They begin with *the whole people* and then state that *one-half of the people* have been made powerless by *the other half*. Choice (A) is a clear paraphrase of the text, so keep it. Choice (B) can be eliminated because the contrast is about power, not money. Choice (C) does not contrast people, nor does (D), so both of those answers can be eliminated. The correct answer is (A).

21. **C** The question asks what the word *trend* most nearly means as used in line 6. Go back to the text, find the word *trend* and cross it out. Carefully read the surrounding text to determine another word that would fit in the blank based on the context of the passage. The text says, *For the Nation as a whole, there is neither a pronounced downward nor upward trend. Water levels rise in wet periods and decline in dry periods.* Therefore, the word *trend* could be replaced with a word such as "pattern." Neither *style, result,* nor *preference* matches "pattern," so eliminate (A), (B), and (D). Note that (A) is a Could Be True trap answer based on another meaning of *trend* that is not supported by the text. Keep (C) because *tendency* matches "pattern." The correct answer is (C).

22. **C** The question asks what the passage states about the occurrence of ground water. Notice that this is the first question in a paired set, so it can be done in tandem with Q23. Consider the answers to Q23 first. The lines for (23A) reference how water levels *rise in wet periods and decline in dry periods* and *average about the same as they did in the early part of the twentieth century*, especially in the *humid central and eastern parts of the country*. This supports (22C), so connect those two answers. The lines for (23B) discuss techniques for finding ground water. These lines don't support any of the answer choices for Q22, so eliminate (23B). The lines for (23C) mention using the *landscape* and *hills* to find ground water. Choice (22B) mentions using landscape features to locate water, so connect (23C) and (22B). The lines for (23D) discuss *locating favorable conditions for ground-water development* by mapping the *distribution and positions of the different kinds of rocks*. This evidence does not support any of the choices in Q22, so eliminate (23D). Look at the remaining pairs of answer choices and use the text to make a decision about which pair best answers the question. Choice (22B) is not actually supported by the text, because the *landscape features* mentioned in the text are *hills* and *valleys*, rather than *existing wells*. This eliminates (22B) and (23C). The correct answers are (22C) and (23A).

23.   **A**   (See explanation above.)

24.   **A**   The question asks why *the capability to assess the nation's water supplies is significant*. Notice that this is the first question in a paired set, so it can be answered in tandem with Q25. Consider the answers to Q25 first. The lines for (25A) indicate that *ground water is being withdrawn at rates that cause water levels to decline* in some, but not all, areas of the country. These lines don't mention assessing the nation's water supplies, so eliminate (25A). The lines for (25B) say that the results of the investigations are *indispensable...for those involved in water-resources planning*. These lines support (24A), so draw a line connecting those two answers. The lines for (25C) are about *sedimentary rocks*. These lines don't mention assessing the nation's water supplies, so eliminate (25C). The lines for (25D) say that chemical analysis on the wells provides information on the *quality of water*. Although this is information about the water, these lines don't connect with any answers in Q24. Eliminate (25D). Without support from Q25, (24B), (24C), and (24D) can all be eliminated. The correct answers are (24A) and (25B).

25.   **B**   (See explanation above.)

26.   **B**   The question asks for the main purpose of the third paragraph. Read a window around the given line reference. The second paragraph discusses the importance of assessing water resources. The third paragraph mentions how to locate ground water, and the fourth paragraph continues to discuss locating ground water using clues from rocks. The third paragraph is included because it introduces how a water resource can be found and assessed. Eliminate answers that don't match this prediction. Eliminate (A) because the third paragraph describes how something is currently done, not a *subject for future research*. Keep (B) because it matches the prediction. Eliminate (C) because the paragraph doesn't mention a *recent discovery*. Eliminate (D) because the paragraph doesn't describe *events* nor relate things done in *sequence*. The correct answer is (B).

27.   **D**   The question asks what the word *occurrence* means in line 75. Go back to the text, find *occurrence*, and mark it out. Carefully read the surrounding text to determine another word that would fit in the blank based on the context of the passage. The text indicates that *decisions regarding water supply will be more reliable...if they are based upon the knowledge of the principles of ground-water occurrence*. Therefore, the word *occurrence* could be replaced with a word such as "existence." Neither *plan*, *happening*, nor *event* matches "existence," so eliminate (A), (B), and (C). Note that (B) and (C) are Could Be True trap answers based on another meaning of *occurrence* that isn't supported by the text. Choice (D), *presence*, means "existence." The correct answer is (D).

28.   **A**   The question asks for an approximation of the *maximum water-level elevation in feet* according to the graph. First, use the key to identify that the solid line shows *water-level elevation*. Then carefully read the labels on the graph's axes to determine that *water level elevation* is on the left axis. Next, find the highest point for the solid line and read its measurement on the left axis. The *maximum water level elevation* is between 100 and 150 feet. Keep (A) and eliminate (B), (C), and (D). The correct answer is (A).

29.   **A**   The question asks which *concept is supported by the passage and by the information in the figure*. Work through each answer choice using the figure. Keep (A) because the solid line indicating water level elevation generally trends downward in the sections of the figure marked "dry" and upward in the sections marked "wet." Choice (A) is also supported by lines 6–7 of the passage: *Water levels rise in wet periods and decline in dry periods*. Eliminate (B) because the graph doesn't include information on the *amount of water pumped from aquifers*. Eliminate (C) because the graph doesn't compare *humid regions with drier regions*. Eliminate (D) because the graph doesn't include information on *water pumped from aquifers*. The correct answer is (A).

30. **B**   The question asks how *the figure* supports *the author's point that the public may impact and be impacted by groundwater levels*. Work through each answer choice using the figure. Eliminate (A) because the figure doesn't include information about *waste disposal decisions*. Keep (B) because the dotted line indicating *population* increases steadily, while the solid line indicating *water-level elevation* decreases overall. Eliminate (C) because the figure doesn't include information about the *quality* of the water. Eliminate (D) because the figure doesn't include information about *landscape changes*. The correct answer is (B).

31. **A**   The question asks about the main idea of the passage, so it should be done after all the specific questions have been completed. The passage describes the impact of exports on the global economy, specifically focusing on the banana and its potential impact on the Caribbean. This supports (A). Choice (B) can be eliminated because there is no evidence that the author believes the banana will become *the new gold standard*. The passage is focused specifically on bananas rather than *global economics* as a whole, so eliminate (C). Choice (D) can be eliminated because the Caribbean is not barred *from gaining economic independence*. The correct answer is (A).

32. **B**   The question asks about the main purpose of the second paragraph. Carefully read the second paragraph to determine its purpose. In the first sentence, the author says that the Panama Canal has *so occupied our attention* that we have *overlooked a significant...change taking place*. The paragraph goes on to describe that change. The correct answer will have something to do with a new change in economics or the emergence of the banana as an influential economic player. Choice (A) recycles *the completion of the Panama Canal,* but it is not the main idea of the paragraph, nor is it a true statement based on the passage, so it can be eliminated. Choice (B) matches the prediction, so don't eliminate it. Choice (C) is extreme because the passage never indicates that bananas will *dominate the economy*, and (D) is not the main point of the passage, so both of these choices should be eliminated. The correct answer is (B).

33. **B**   The question asks what the word *exercise* means in line 17. Go back to the text, find *exercise*, and mark it out. Carefully read the surrounding text to determine another word that would fit in the blank based on the context of the passage. The window mentions the food products having an *influence upon international politics,* so the products are "placing" or "pushing" influence. Although (A), (C), and (D) are all synonyms for *exercise*, based on the context and prediction, (B), *exert,* is the only answer consistent with the text. The correct answer is (B).

34. **B**   The question asks which lines best support the author's claim that *bananas are likely to play a significant role in the global economy*. Carefully read each set of given lines and eliminate any that don't answer the question. Choice (A) can be eliminated because the lines do not mention bananas at all. The lines for (B) refer to economists' predictions that *Caribbean diplomacy will be determined by the banana crop*, which show a *significant role* for bananas. Keep (B). The lines for (C) show the banana's popularity in the U.S., but do not address a role in the *global economy*. Eliminate (C). The lines for (D) describe how the Caribbean can become self-sustaining with the banana. There is no mention of the *global economy*, so eliminate (D). The correct answer is (B).

35. **D**   The question asks what the word *friendship* means in line 82. Go back to the text, find *friendship*, and mark it out. Carefully read the surrounding text to determine another word that would fit in the blank based on the context of the passage. The passage mentions *near neighbors* and *diplomacy of the Caribbean*, so the missing word must mean something like "positive relations with neighboring countries." Choices (A) and (B) might be good synonyms for *friendship*, but neither matches the context of the passage. Eliminate both of those choices. *Collusion* does mean working together, but with an illegal or fraudulent goal. This doesn't match the prediction, so eliminate (C). Choice (D), *cooperation,* matches the prediction. The correct answer is (D).

36. **D** The question asks for the main idea of the final paragraph. The final paragraph highlights the importance of the Caribbean and the diplomatic importance of exports. Choice (A) is incorrect because it is too literal. While the word *friendship* does show up in the final paragraph, it is not a literal reference to being friends. It's a reference to diplomacy, which is not mentioned in (A). Eliminate (A). Choice (B) is mentioned, but it is not the main point of the paragraph. Choice (C) recycles words, so it might look good at first glance. However, a careful reading of (C) shows that although the words look familiar, they aren't put together in a way that matches the prediction. Eliminate (C). Choice (D) matches the prediction. The correct answer is (D).

37. **A** The question asks which potential difficulty for the banana industry is anticipated by the author. Notice that this is the first question in a paired set, so it can be done in tandem with Q38. Consider the answers to Q38 first. Choice (38A) refers to *food products* in general exercising *an influence upon international politics*. There is no mention of the banana or any potential problems, so eliminate (38A). Choice (38B) mentions the demand for organizing fruit collection *from small planters* and *large capital for steamers with refrigerating appliances*. This supports (37A), so draw a line connecting those two answer choices. Choice (38C) mentions that companies *own extensive plantations* but does not mention any potential problems, so eliminate (38C). Choice (38D) compares the potential of the banana market to the expansion of the coconut market. There's no potential difficulty here, so eliminate (38D). Without support from Q38, (37B), (37C), and (37D) can all be eliminated. The correct answers are (37A) and (38B).

38. **B** (See explanation above.)

39. **A** The question asks which *idea in the passage* is most directly supported by *the data in the tables*. Work through each answer choice using the tables. Choice (A) is supported by the tables, which show that the U.S. imported a total of 44,520,539 bunches of bananas in 1912, while the world supply of bananas in 1911 was 52,915,963 bunches. The world banana supply exceeds the number of bunches consumed by the U.S. by more than eight million, suggesting that countries other than the U.S. probably also imported bananas. (Although the tables are based on two different years, they are close enough in time that it is reasonable to make this inference.) The passage also supports (A): lines 42–44 state that *the United States consumes 85 percent of all bananas exported—five times as much as all the rest of the world.* Keep (A). Choice (B) is not supported by the tables because the tables do not contain any information about *an economic revolution.* Eliminate (C) and (D) because the tables do not compare banana supply for the same two regions in 1911 and 1912, so there is no basis to say whether there was *increased production* or an *upward trend in banana consumption.* The correct answer is (A).

40. **C** The question asks which country has the greatest difference in banana supply in 1911 compared to the number of bananas sent to the United States from that country in 1912. Simply check the exports from each of these countries to see which shows the greatest increase or decrease in exports to the United States. Jamaica has the greatest difference between those two data points. The correct answer is (C).

41. **D** The question asks which answer is most strongly supported by data from the table. Choices (A), (B), and (C) are untrue statements according to the chart. From the numbers in the chart, (D) is true because Colombia exported more bananas than Cuba in 1911. The correct answer is (D).

42. **D** The question asks what the word *compromised* most nearly means in line 11. Go back to the text, find the word *compromised*, and cross it out. Then read the window carefully, using context clues to determine another word that would fit in its place. The text says, *Many of the studies on mindfulness and meditation, the authors wrote, are poorly designed—compromised by inconsistent definitions of what mindfulness actually is, and often void of a control group to rule out the placebo*

effect. Therefore, *compromised* could be replaced by a word such as "weakened." Eliminate answer choices that don't match the way the word is used in context. Choice (A), *accommodated*, is a Could Be True trap answer based on a different meaning of *compromised* that is not supported by the text. *Accommodated* means "made allowances for" or "made room for" and does not match "weakened," so eliminate (A). *Shaped* does not match "weakened," so eliminate (B). *Divided* also does not match "weakened," so eliminate (C). *Undermined* means "weakened," so keep (D). The correct answer is (D).

43.   **A**   The question asks what *aiding sleep and controlling weight have in common*, according to the author of Passage 1. Since there is no line reference, use lead words and the order of the questions to find the window. Q42 asks about line 11, so scan the passage beginning with line 11, looking for the lead words *aiding sleep* and *controlling weight*. Starting in line 21, the passage states, *A 2014 review of 47 meditation trials, collectively including over 3,500 participants, found essentially no evidence for benefits related to enhancing attention, curtailing substance abuse, aiding sleep or controlling weight.* Hence, what *aiding sleep and controlling weight have in common* is that these *meditation trials* didn't find *benefits related to* either of them. Eliminate answer choices that don't match this answer from the passage. Keep (A) because it is a good paraphrase of what the passage states. Choice (B) is a Mostly Right/Slightly Wrong trap answer: each of the goals mentioned in the question is referenced as *a potential benefit of mindfulness practices* even though there is no convincing evidence linking either to mindfulness practices, so eliminate (B). Choice (C) is a Could Be True trap answer: even though one might assume that the goals mentioned in the question are *challenging health goals to achieve*, the passage does not state this, so eliminate (C). Eliminate (D) since the passage does not state that the goals mentioned in the question *are well understood by medical researchers*. The correct answer is (A).

44.   **C**   The question asks what the author indicates about the *positive effects of meditation practice*. Since there is no line reference, use lead words and the order of the questions to find the window. Q43 asks about *aiding sleep* and *controlling weight*, which were mentioned in line 25, so scan the passage beginning with line 26, looking for the lead words *positive effects of meditation practice* or synonyms for those words. On lines 26–31, the passage states that *Nicholas Van Dam, a clinical psychologist and research fellow in psychological sciences at the University of Melbourne, contends potential benefits of mindfulness are being overshadowed by hyperbole and oversold for financial gain.* Eliminate answer choices that don't match this answer from the passage. Choice (A) is a Could Be True trap answer: even though one might assume that meditation could increase *practitioners' productivity*, the passage provides no evidence for this; eliminate (A). Choice (B) is another Could Be True trap answer, since the passage does not indicate that meditation is *benefitting growing numbers of people*; eliminate (B). Choice (C) is a good paraphrase of the passage's claim that the *potential benefits of mindfulness are being overshadowed by hyperbole and oversold for financial gain*, so keep (C). Eliminate (D) because there is no indication that the benefits of meditation are *not worth the cost of research*, even if the benefits are unclear; eliminate (D). The correct answer is (C).

45.   **A**   The question asks about the *effect* of the *analogy in the final paragraph of Passage 1*. Use the given paragraph reference to find the window. Lines 47–50 state, *But it is the trickiness in bringing a rich spiritual concept into a standardized framework for testing and advising patients that* [Eric Loucks] *feels might be tough to tackle.* The final paragraph goes on to quote Eric Loucks: "*…descriptions of concepts like 'mindfulness' are like a finger pointing at the moon…It is important not to confuse the finger for the moon. There will always be variations in people's understanding of mindfulness. It is a personal experience.*" The effect of the analogy is to better explain the *trickiness in bringing a rich spiritual concept into a standardized framework for testing and advising patients*. Eliminate

answer choices that don't match this answer from the passage. Choice (A) is a good match: the *particular concept* is *mindfulness* and the *challenge* is bringing this type of personal experience into *a standardized framework* for research and treatment, so keep (A). Choice (B) is a Mostly Right/Slightly Wrong trap answer: although the *finger pointing at the moon* could be considered *elegant imagery*, the analogy makes no attempt to *mask a theory's shortcomings*, so eliminate (B). Choice (C) is also a Mostly Right/Slightly Wrong trap answer: though the analogy does *refer to nature* to some extent in referencing the moon, the purpose is not *to lend a sense of credibility*, so eliminate (C). Choice (D) is yet another Mostly Right/Slightly Wrong trap answer: the analogy does *apply familiar language* but does not *simplify a technical procedure*, so eliminate (D). The correct answer is (A).

46. **D** The question asks what Passage 2 indicates about *the use of mindfulness meditation practice*. This is the first question in a paired set, so it can be done in tandem with Q47. Look at the answer choices for Q47 first, reading with the question in mind. The lines for (47A) state that *we have studied experienced practitioners while they performed an advanced form of mindfulness meditation called open presence*. While the lines do mention *mindfulness meditation*, they don't provide much information about its *use*, nor do they support any of the answers to Q46, so eliminate (47A). The lines for (47B) say, *we found that the intensity of the pain was not reduced in meditators*. This is information about *the use of mindfulness meditation practice*, so check the answer choices for Q46 to see whether any of the choices are supported by these lines. The information matches (46D), which states that mindfulness meditation *does not affect pain sensation directly*; draw a line connecting (47B) and (46D). The lines for (47C) state, *Several studies have documented the benefits of mindfulness on symptoms of anxiety and depression and its ability to improve sleep patterns*. Though this information does address the task of Q46, it does not support any of the answer choices to Q46, so eliminate (47C). The lines for (47D) state that *Segal demonstrated that the intervention is superior to a placebo and has a protective effect against relapse comparable to standard maintenance antidepressant therapy*. While these lines do address the task of Q46 indirectly, they do not support any of the answers to Q46, so eliminate (47D). Without any support from Q47, (46A), (46B), and (46C) can be eliminated. The correct answers are (46D) and (47B).

47. **B** (See explanation above.)

48. **C** The question refers to the mention of *"open presence"* in Passage 2 and asks what may make *disagreeable sensation less troublesome*. Since there is no line reference, use lead words and the order of the questions to find the window. The lines for (47A), lines 68–71, mentioned *open presence*, so read the second paragraph as the window for Q48. Lines 65–80 state, *Staying aware of an unpleasant sensation can reduce maladaptive emotional responses and help one to move beyond the disagreeable feeling and may be particularly useful in dealing with pain. In our Wisconsin lab, we have studied experienced practitioners while they performed an advanced form of mindfulness meditation called open presence...The meditator observes and is open to experience without making any attempt to interpret, change, reject or ignore painful sensation. We found that...[the pain] bothered them less than it did members of a control group*. Eliminate answer choices that don't match this answer from the passage. Eliminate (A) because it is contradicted by the passage. The passage says that *staying aware of an unpleasant sensation* can help, so it wouldn't help people to *take their minds off their discomfort*. Eliminate (B) because the passage doesn't mention understanding *the source of their emotions*. Keep (C) because it matches the passage, which states that *staying aware of an unpleasant sensation* can help. Additionally, the phrase *without judging the experience* matches *without making any attempt to interpret, change, reject or ignore painful sensation*. Eliminate (D) because there is no mention of *seeking treatment* in the window for this question. The correct answer is (C).

49. **A** The question asks for the *main purpose of each passage*. Because this question is about both passages, it should be done after the questions that ask about each passage individually. The main idea of Passage 1 can be found in lines 1–5: *Research in recent decades has linked mindfulness practices to a staggering collection of possible health benefits. Yet many psychologists, neuroscientists and meditation experts are afraid that hype is outpacing the science.* The main idea of Passage 2 can be found in lines 61–64: *As suggested by the growing compendium of research, meditation may be effective in treating depression and chronic pain and in cultivating a sense of overall well-being.* Eliminate answer choices that don't match both passages. Keep (A) because both passages *provide an evaluation—one negative and one positive—of the potential health benefits of mindfulness practices.* Eliminate (B) because the passages are not about the research *approaches* used. Eliminate (C) because people's *attention spans* are not the main focus of either passage. Eliminate (D) because neither passage *contrasts anxiety levels of those who meditate for spiritual reasons with those who meditate for health benefits.* The correct answer is (A).

50. **C** The question asks about the *relationship between the two passages*. Because this question is about both passages, it should be done after the questions that ask about each passage individually. The main idea of Passage 1 can be found in lines 1–5: *Research in recent decades has linked mindfulness practices to a staggering collection of possible health benefits. Yet many psychologists, neuroscientists and meditation experts are afraid that hype is outpacing the science.* The main idea of Passage 2 can be found in lines 61–64: *As suggested by the growing compendium of research, meditation may be effective in treating depression and chronic pain and in cultivating a sense of overall well-being.* Therefore, the two passages essentially take opposing views about the evidence that mindfulness practices result in health benefits. Eliminate answer choices that don't match both passages. Eliminate (A) because Passage 2 does not provide *anecdotal evidence* related to an experiment in Passage 1. Eliminate (B) because Passage 2 doesn't examine the topics from Passage 1 *in more detail*; it presents a contrasting point of view. Keep (C) because it matches the contradictory relationship between the passages. Eliminate (D) because Passage 2 does not provide an *alternative explanation* of results from Passage 1; instead it provides other studies that suggest an opposing conclusion. The correct answer is (C).

51. **D** The question asks for a point both authors would *most likely agree* on. Because this question is about both passages, it should be done after the questions that ask about each passage individually. Eliminate answer choices that don't match both passages. Eliminate (A) because Passage 1 states that there is *essentially no evidence for benefits related to…aiding sleep.* Eliminate (B) because neither passage discusses who is likely *to participate in research trials.* Eliminate (C) because only Passage 1 addresses profitability. Keep (D) because it is supported by both passages. Lines 14–21 of Passage 1 state, *The new paper cites a 2015 review published in American Psychologist reporting that only around 9 percent of research into mindfulness-based interventions has been tested in clinical trials that included a control group. The authors also point to multiple large placebo-controlled meta-analyses concluding that mindfulness practices have often produced unimpressive results.* Lines 95–99 of Passage 2 state, *More recently, Segal demonstrated that the intervention is superior to a placebo and has a protective effect against relapse comparable to standard maintenance antidepressant therapy.* Each of these references suggests that *including a control group in research can yield important evidence.* The correct answer is (D).

52. **C** The question asks which choice provides evidence that *the author of Passage 1 would agree to some extent* with a certain claim made in Passage 2. Because this question is about both passages, it should be done after the questions that ask about each passage individually. First, use the given line reference to find the claim from Passage 2. Lines 61–64 state, *As suggested by the growing compendium of research, meditation may be effective in treating depression and chronic pain and in cultivating a sense of overall well-being.* Look at the line references given in the answer

choices, and eliminate the statements that don't indicate the author's agreement with this claim. The lines for (A) state, *Research in recent decades has linked mindfulness practices to a staggering collection of possible health benefits.* However, these lines don't represent the author's opinion, so eliminate (A). The lines for (B) say, *Yet many psychologists, neuroscientists and meditation experts are afraid that hype is outpacing the science.* These lines indicate potential disagreement with the claim in the question, so eliminate (B). The lines for (C) state, *The 2014 analysis found meditation and mindfulness may provide modest benefits in anxiety, depression and pain.* This matches the claim that *meditation may be effective in treating depression and chronic pain,* so keep (C). The lines for (D) say, *But it is the trickiness in bringing a rich spiritual concept into a standardized framework for testing and advising patients that he feels might be tough to tackle.* These lines do not address the benefits of meditation, so eliminate (D). The correct answer is (C).

Section 2: Writing and Language

1. **B** The length of the phrase changes in the answer choices, so this question tests concision. Check the shortest answer first. Choice (B) makes the meaning of the sentence precise, so keep (B). *Growing* and *enlarging* mean the same thing, so there is no need to use both words; eliminate (A). The previous sentence states that *the dominance of the United States had been challenged the world over,* so there is no need to repeat that idea; eliminate (C) because it repeats that the competition is *among countries.* Choice (D) unnecessarily repeats that the competition is increasing *for all,* so eliminate (D). The correct answer is (B).

2. **D** Note the question! The question asks how to effectively combine the underlined sentences, so it tests precision and concision. Three of the answer choices—(A), (C), and (D)—begin with an identical phrase. The first part of the sentence in those three choices, *Moreover, whereas someone born in the 1940s might have expected to spend his or her entire career with a single company,* is not an independent clause, so it cannot be connected to the second part of the sentence with a semicolon. Both (A) and (C) use a semicolon to connect the two parts of the sentence, so eliminate (A) and (C). Choices (B) and (D) are both complete sentences, but (B) includes phrases like *moreover for instance* and *a thing that new workers do now,* which are less concise phrases than those included in (D). Choice (D) is both grammatically correct and concise. The correct answer is (D).

3. **B** Note the question! The question asks whether a phrase should be added, so it tests consistency. If the content of the new phrase is consistent with the ideas that surround it, then it should be added. The paragraph describes the *compulsively innovative methods* of *Netflix,* and the subsequent paragraph notes that *Netflix has become famous (or infamous) for changing its employees' relationship to the workplace.* The proposed new phrase describes the *world* of *Silicon Valley startups,* like Netflix, as *fast-paced, forward-thinking,* and *occasionally ruthless.* This description is consistent with the ideas discussed elsewhere in the passage, so the phrase should be added: eliminate (C) and (D). Choice (A) states that the phrase *shows the author's ability in finding apt adjectives;* this rationale is unrelated to the consistency of ideas in the passage, so eliminate (A). Choice (B) notes that the phrase *creates a richer description of the company discussed,* which is consistent with the relationship between the phrase and the rest of the paragraph; keep (B). The correct answer is (B).

4. **C** Verbs change in the answer choices, so this question tests consistency of verbs. A verb must be consistent in number with its subject. The subject of the underlined verb is *One of the major success stories,* which is singular. To be consistent, the underlined verb must be singular as well. Eliminate (B) and (D), because *are* is a plural verb. The addition of the word *that* is unnecessary

in this sentence, because the subject of the verb *is* does not need to be repeated with a pronoun; eliminate (A). The correct answer is (C).

5. **A**   The length of the phrase changes in the answer choices, so this question tests concision. Check the shortest answer first: (A), *computers*, makes the meaning of the sentence precise, so keep it. Now consider whether any additional information is required for the sentence to make sense. The word *computers* already means "machines that can store, process, and communicate information," so any longer answer choice would need to include additional and relevant detail in order to be a better answer than (A). Choice (B), *machines used for computing*, is a less concise way to describe computers, so eliminate (B). Choice (D), *intelligent machines,* suggests that the computers themselves have intelligence, which is not a necessary claim for the focus of the essay. Eliminate (D). Choice (C) names two subsets of computers and identifies a specific kind of processing ability, *the capacity to stream,* but this choice is less concise and no more precise than (A). Eliminate (C). The correct answer is (A).

6. **D**   Transitions change in the answer choices, so this question tests consistency of ideas. A transition must be consistent with the relationship between the ideas it connects. The sentence before the transition states that *Netflix's compulsively innovative methods have changed the way that those living in the United States and in many other parts of the globe interact with visual media.* The sentence that begins with the underlined transition explains that *Netflix has become famous (or infamous) for changing its employees' relationship to the workplace.* The second sentence provides an additional example of how Netflix's methods affect people, so the correct answer should reflect that relationship between the sentences. *For all this* and *regardless* both suggest that the second sentence is in contrast to the idea of the first sentence, which is inconsistent with the passage; eliminate (A) and (B). Choice (C), *Thus,* implies that the second sentence is a consequence of the first sentence. Both sentences describe the consequences of Netflix's practices, but the first sentence does not have to be true in order for the second sentence to be true, so eliminate (C). Choice (D), *Furthermore,* reflects the correct relationship between the two sentences. The correct answer is (D).

7. **D**   Note the question! The question asks which choice *most effectively sets up the idea given in the second part of this sentence*, so it tests consistency of ideas. Eliminate answers that are inconsistent with the purpose stated in the question. The second part of the sentence states that *employees at Netflix are warned not to think of the job as one that they will "keep for life."* Choice (A), *Just putting seriously all of it right out there,* is inconsistent in tone with the rest of the passage, and the phrase is not precise: it is not clearly describing either the *employees* or the people who warn the employees. Eliminate (A). Choice (B), *Turned off by the company's rudeness,* does not set up the situation described in the second part of the sentence so much as it describes one possible outcome of the warning. Eliminate (B). Choice (C), *Having no idea what they're walking into,* is inconsistent with the passage's statement that Netflix is famous for its employment approach, and describing the employees' ignorance does not clearly set up the fact that they are warned not to expect to keep their jobs for life. Eliminate (C). Choice (D), *From the first day on the job,* gives a clear context for the employees' being warned about the possibility of losing their jobs. The correct answer is (D).

8. **B**   Verbs change in the answer choices. The underlined portion is part of a list in the sentence, so this question tests consistency. All items in a list must be consistent with one another. The other items in the list are phrases that start with an *-ing* verb—*staying late* and *showing loyalty to the company*—so the third item must have the same form. Eliminate (A) and (C) because they do not include the correct verb form. Neither of the other items in the list includes a pronoun, so eliminate (D), which includes the pronoun *they*. The correct answer is (B).

9. **D** Transitions change in the answer choices, so this question tests consistency of ideas. There is also the option to DELETE; consider this choice carefully, as it is often the correct answer. The first part of the sentence, *While these employees had done about as good a job as they could do*, is not an independent clause; the part of the sentence that follows the underlined transition, *they were fired the moment they were no longer needed*, is an independent clause. A comma followed by a coordinating conjunction such as *and* or *yet* can only be used between two independent clauses, so eliminate (A) and (B). Adding *because* would make the entire sentence an incomplete idea, so eliminate (C). The underlined word should be deleted. The correct answer is (D).

10. **C** Vocabulary changes in the answer choices, so this question tests precision of word choice. The sentence states that companies attempting to *tighten their belts* will *demand more of their employees* and *withdraw some of the comfortable* perks *that employees of earlier eras relied* on, so the correct answer should mean something like "commitments." *Premise* means "assumption" or "statement," while *promise* means "assurance" or "guarantee." The better term in this sentence is *promise*, so eliminate (A) and (B). The underlined word is modified by *some*, so the word should be a plural noun: eliminate (D), because *promising* is a singular noun. The correct answer is (C).

11. **A** Note the question! The question asks which choice *most clearly ends the passage with a restatement of the writer's primary claim*, so it tests consistency of ideas. Eliminate answers that are inconsistent with the purpose stated in the question. The paragraph states that *as companies continue to tighten their belts and their responsibility to be profitable remains, they will demand more of their employees*. Choice (A) restates the earlier idea that the situation described *may be the workplace of the future*, so keep (A). Choice (B) departs dramatically from the tone and content of the rest of the passage by suggesting that *we should all head for the hills*, so eliminate (B). Choice (C) states that Netflix is *not really hiring all that often*, which contrasts with the earlier description of Netflix's frequent employee turnover, so eliminate (C). Choice (D) describes *how difficult it can be* to be fired, which is not an issue the passage addresses, so eliminate (D). The correct answer is (A).

12. **C** Note the question! The question asks which answer *most closely matches the stylistic pattern established earlier in the sentence*, so it tests consistency. The underlined phrase is an item in a list. All items in a list must be consistent with each other. The first two items in the list are *watching short videos on TikTok* and *reading short posts on Facebook and Twitter*, so the third item should also be a verb phrase without a subject pronoun. Eliminate (A) and (D), because these choices include the pronoun *they* at the beginning of the phrase. Choice (B) introduces the word *the* before *sending*, which is inconsistent with the pattern in the other items: eliminate (B). Choice (C) matches the format of the earlier items in the list. The correct answer is (C).

13. **A** The length of the phrase following *web* changes in the answer choices, so this question tests concision. Check the shortest answer first. Choice (B) does not give a precise meaning to the sentence. The first part of the sentence, *Those who critiqued television as a dangerous influence on society have since changed to new and, as they would see it, worse targets on the web*, is an independent clause. The second part of the sentence, *are not much interested in television anymore*, is not an independent clause. Choice (B) does not make the relationship between the two parts of the sentence clear, so eliminate (B). Choices (C) and (D) both make the second part of the sentence into an independent clause. A comma on its own cannot be used between two independent clauses, so eliminate (C) and (D). Removing the comma and adding the word *and* to the sentence makes it clear that the idea in the second part of the sentence, *are not much interested in television anymore*, is the second item in a list that describes *those who have critiqued television*. The correct answer is (A).

14. **D** Transitions change in the answer choices, so this question tests consistency of ideas. A transition must be consistent with the relationship between the ideas it connects. The sentence before the

transition states that *There could be no "couch potatoes" without TVs, and the scourge of reality TV might never have been thrust upon the American viewing public.* The sentence that begins with the underlined transition states that *shining light in your eyes for hours at a time can wreak havoc* on vision. These are separate examples of the negative effects of watching television, so the correct transition will reflect that relationship. Choice (A), *As aforementioned,* incorrectly suggests that the bad effects of light were mentioned earlier in the paragraph, so eliminate (A). Choices (B), *However,* and (C), *That said,* indicate that the idea of the second sentence is in contrast to the idea of the first sentence, which is inconsistent with the relationship between the two sentences: eliminate (B) and (C). Choice (D), *Moreover,* reflects that the idea in the second sentence is an additional example of the trend indicated in the first sentence, which is consistent with the passage: keep (D). The correct answer is (D).

15. **A** Punctuation and apostrophes change in the answer choices, so this question tests apostrophe usage and how to connect ideas using appropriate punctuation. When used with a pronoun, an apostrophe indicates a contraction. *You're* is equal to "you are," which is not necessary in this sentence: eliminate (B) and (C). The difference between (A) and (D) is that (A) uses a colon to connect the first part of the sentence to the word *vision,* while (D) uses a semicolon. The first part of the sentence, *shining light in your eyes can wreak havoc on one of your most important senses,* is an independent clause, while the second part of the sentence, *vision,* is not an independent clause. A semicolon can only be used between two independent clauses, so eliminate (D). The correct answer is (A).

16. **B** Apostrophes change in the answer choices, so this question tests apostrophe usage. When used with a noun, an apostrophe indicates possession. In this sentence, nothing belongs to *radios,* so there is no need for an apostrophe. Eliminate (C) and (D). The difference between (A) and (B) is in the tense of the verb. A verb must be consistent in tense with the other verbs in the sentence. The other verb in the sentence is *provided,* which is in the past tense, so the correct verb must also be in the past tense. Eliminate (A) because *creates* is in the present tense. The correct answer is (B).

17. **D** Note the question! The question asks whether a sentence should be added, so it tests consistency. If the content of the new sentence is consistent with the ideas that surround it, then it should be added. The paragraph describes how *television provided something truly national for the first time,* and claims that during the *first American performance of The Beatles on* The Ed Sullivan Show, it seemed that *Everyone, literally everyone, was watching TV.* The new sentence states that *The Beatles had many hits* that *continue to influence the course of rock and roll to the present day,* so it is not consistent with the focus of the ideas in the rest of the paragraph. The sentence should not be added. Eliminate (A) and (B). Choice (C) states that the new sentence *suggests that television's only function was to broadcast musical performances,* which does not accurately describe the sentence: eliminate (C). Choice (D) accurately states that the new sentence *adds a detail that is irrelevant to the paragraph's main focus.* The correct answer is (D).

18. **B** The order of phrases in the sentence changes in the answer choices, so this question tests precision and consistency of ideas. The sentence before this one describes the *presence of non-white faces,* and the following sentence describes how *African Americans were the most frequently targeted group,* but *Asian Americans and those of all ethnicities were similarly lampooned,* suggesting that the underlined sentence will describe a problematic form of representing African Americans. Look for the answer choice that clearly presents such a description. The order of phrases in (A) suggests that *non-white people* were those *who parroted and parodied the patterns of Black speech,* while that description seems most logically to characterize the *white actors.* Eliminate (A). Choice (B) correctly makes *non-white people* the subject of the verb *were represented,* and it

identifies the *white actors* as those who *parroted and parodied*, so keep (B). Choice (C) describes African Americans as those *who for many years parroted by white people and parodied in speech patterns*, which is not a complete thought, so eliminate (C). Choice (D) suggests that the white actors' parroting of *patterns of Black speech* were *parodied for many years*, which is not a claim indicated elsewhere in the paragraph, so eliminate (D). The correct answer is (B).

19. **D** Note the question! The question asks which choice gives *a second supporting example that is most similar to the example already in the sentence*, so it tests consistency of ideas. Eliminate answers that are inconsistent with the purpose stated in the question. The example given earlier in the sentence is of the *Chinese American character on* Have Gun Will Travel. Both (A) and (C) describe general numbers of *shows*, which is not similar to the specific example provided earlier in the sentence, so eliminate (A) and (C). Choice (B) describes the actor who played the character *on the radio show*, which elaborates on the earlier example instead of providing a *second supporting example*, so eliminate (B). Choice (D) names another character, *the African American character on* The Beulah Show, which is consistent with the earlier example. The correct answer is (D).

20. **C** Commas change in the answer choices, so this question tests comma usage. The phrase *in the American public* is necessary to the main meaning of the sentence, so it should not be separated from the rest of the sentence by commas: eliminate (D). The phrase *in the American public* modifies the word *many*, so the phrase and the word should also not be separated by a comma: eliminate (B). Inserting a single comma after *public* suggests that the *national reach* of television was showing *many in the American public*, instead of showing to those many Americans *just how diverse the American scene had become*: the comma is inconsistent with the main idea of the sentence, so eliminate (A). No commas are necessary in this underlined phrase. The correct answer is (C).

21. **D** Note the question! The question asks how to effectively combine the sentences, so it tests precision. The pronoun *they* could refer to *people* or *hometowns*, so it is not precise: eliminate (A). Choice (B) also uses the imprecise pronoun *they*, though this phrase makes the pronoun possessive: it is unclear who *theirs* refers to, so eliminate (B). Choice (C) states that when people had the *wealth to travel physically outside of their hometowns*, those people traveled *with what were usually filled with citizens*: this phrasing doesn't make sense, so eliminate (C). Choice (D) uses the pronoun *which*, which clearly refers to the *hometowns* and not to the *people*: this is the most precise option, so keep it. The correct answer is (D).

22. **D** Note the question! The question asks where paragraph 6 should be placed, so it tests consistency of ideas. The paragraph must be consistent with the ideas that come both before and after it. Paragraph 6 describes how *this national reach could occasionally lead to conformity and sensationalism*, so it must come after a description of the *national reach* of television. Paragraph 3 introduces the fact that television *provided something truly national for the first time*, so eliminate (B) and (C). Paragraph 6 also claims that *television could show* Americans who had not traveled much *just how big the world outside was*, so it must come before the reference to *this "big world"* in paragraph 4. Eliminate (A). The correct answer is (D).

23. **D** Pronouns change in the answer choices, so this question tests consistency of pronouns. A pronoun must be consistent in number with the noun it refers to. In this case, the pronoun refers to *untouched nature*, which is singular, so the pronoun must also be singular. Eliminate (B), because *their* is a plural pronoun. *There* identifies a specific place, which is not consistent with this sentence, so eliminate (A). The difference between (C) and (D) is an apostrophe. When used with a pronoun, an apostrophe indicates a contraction. *It's* means "it is," which is incorrect in this sentence, so eliminate (C). Choice (D), *its*, provides the possessive form of a singular pronoun. The correct answer is (D).

24. **A** Transitions change in the answer choices, so this question tests consistency of ideas. A transition must be consistent with the relationship between the ideas it connects. The sentence before the transition states that *nature* is *characterized* not just by *the way it* looks but also *by the way it* sounds. The sentence that begins with the underlined transition states that *when we build highways through thriving natural habitats, we don't just change the way they look.* This second statement builds on the idea of the previous statement, so the correct transition will reflect that relationship. Keep (A), because *thus* reflects the idea that the second statement is a logical consequence of the first statement. *Thence* means "in that place," which is inconsistent with the relationship between the ideas, so eliminate (B). Eliminate (C) because *whereas* suggests that the second sentence is a departure from the idea of the first sentence. While (D), *This being so*, reflects the correct relationship between the ideas, it is less concise than (A), so eliminate (D). The correct answer is (A).

25. **B** Note the question! The question asks whether a sentence should be added, so it tests consistency. If the content of the new sentence is consistent with the ideas that surround it, then it should be added. The paragraph describes how building highways does not *just change the way* that *natural habitats* appear, and it also states that *car traffic is remarkably loud*. The new sentence states that *We also change the way they sound.* This statement is consistent with and builds on the ideas in the previous sentence, so it should be added: eliminate (C) and (D). Choice (A) states that the new sentence *reminds the reader of the beauty of birds' songs*, which is inconsistent with the content of the new sentence: eliminate (A). Choice (B) notes that the sentence *completes the idea started in the previous sentence*, which is accurate: keep (B). The correct answer is (B).

26. **B** Vocabulary changes in the answer choices, so this question tests precision of word choice. Look for a word whose definition is consistent with the other ideas in the sentence. The sentence says that *while we have become relatively* accustomed to *the sounds of cars on our "quiet" residential streets, not all animals have*, so the correct answer must mean something like "used to" or "accustomed." *Weakened* means "made less intense," so eliminate (A). *Inured* means "accustomed to," so keep (B). *Hip* means "aware of" and *keen* means "eager for;" neither is consistent with the idea of the passage, so eliminate (C) and (D). The correct answer is (B).

27. **C** The length of the phrase changes in the answer choices, so this question tests concision. The rest of the sentence states that *a recent study checked the effect* of a change in volume *on local bird populations*, so the focus of the underlined portion should be on the increase in noise. Check the shortest answer first: *increased highway noise* is consistent with the focus of the sentence, so keep (C). The next shortest answer, *raising the highway volume*, suggests that the researchers were increasing the sound of particular highways, which is inaccurate, so eliminate (A). Choice (B), *the noise being more on highways,* and (D), *highways exhibiting more noise levels*, are both less concise and less precise than (C): eliminate them. The correct answer is (C).

28. **C** The length of the phrase changes in the answer choices, so this question could test concision. The first part of the sentence, *This might seem like an easy study with all the new highway construction going on in the United States all the time*, is an independent clause, and it is connected with a comma and the word *but* to the second part of the sentence: in order for the non-underlined part of the sentence to be correct, the second part of the sentence must also be an independent clause. Choice (C) is the shortest option, and it appropriately makes the second part of the sentence an independent clause: *the researchers at the Intermountain Bird Observatory in Idaho wanted to study the effects without becoming part of the problem.* As written, the second part of the sentence is not an independent clause, so eliminate (A). Choice (B) also fails to make the second part of the sentence an independent clause, so eliminate (B). The addition of the word *they* in (D) does not make the sentence more precise, so eliminate (D). The correct answer is (C).

29. **B** Punctuation changes in the answer choices, so this question tests how to connect ideas with the appropriate punctuation. The sentence describes the creation of a *fake* road, which is also called a *"phantom"* road. The phrase *or a "phantom"* should be set off from the rest of the sentence using commas, because it provides an alternative to the term *fake* and is therefore not necessary to the main meaning of the sentence. The non-underlined portion of the sentence already includes a comma before *or*, so look for the answer choice that includes a comma after *"phantom."* Eliminate (C) and (D). There is no need for an additional comma after *or*, so eliminate (A). The correct answer is (B).

30. **B** Punctuation changes in the answer choices, so this question tests how to connect ideas with the appropriate punctuation. Choice (A) includes an opening quotation mark, but there is no corresponding closing quotation mark later in the sentence, so eliminate (A). The first part of the sentence, *According to the study, the mere sounds of traffic*, is not an independent clause. A single dash in a sentence can only be used after an independent clause, so eliminate (D). The subject of the whole sentence is *sounds of traffic*, and the main verb is *reduced*, so these words should not be separated by any piece of punctuation: eliminate (C), which separates the words with a comma. No punctuation is necessary. The correct answer is (B).

31. **D** Note the question! The question asks which answer *offers an accurate interpretation of the data in the figure*, so it tests consistency. Read the labels on the figure carefully, and look for an answer that is consistent with the information given in the figure. The figure offers no data about the locations of *avian populations* or *other wildlife populations*, so the statements in (A) and (B) are not consistent with the figure: eliminate (A) and (B). Choice (C) describes a plan for *an east-west route from Savannah to Knoxville and a north-south route from Augusta to Natchez*, but the direction of travel between Savannah and Knoxville is north-south, according to the figure, and the direction of travel between Augusta and Natchez is east-west. Eliminate (C). Choice (D) matches the cities with the correct directions of travel in the proposed interstates. The correct answer is (D).

32. **C** Note the question! The question asks where the new sentence should be placed, so it tests consistency of ideas. The sentence must be consistent with the ideas that come both before and after it. The new sentence describes how *birds are more likely to be looking up than down* when there is *so much distraction from outside noise*. Sentence 3 explains that birds *need to spend as much time as possible with their heads down*, so the new sentence must appear after sentence 3. Eliminate (A) and (B). Sentence 4 states that *This is bad news for avian life in the deep South*; while sentence 3 ends with a description of the benefits of birds' looking down, including *feeding their young* and *fattening up for their various migrations*, the new sentence explains that the time spent looking up means that birds are *casting a cautious eye on their potentially perilous surroundings*. The word *This* in sentence 4 refers to the situation in the new sentence, so the new sentence must appear before sentence 4: eliminate (D). The correct answer is (C).

33. **A** Pronouns and nouns change in the answer choices, so this question tests precision. A pronoun can only be used if it is clear what it refers to. The pronoun *they* in (C) could refer to *speed limits*, *roads*, or *effects*, so (C) is not a precise statement. Eliminate (C). The statements in (B) and (D) are too general to be consistent with the specific details mentioned earlier in the sentence: the *lower speed limits* and *rubberized asphalt* will not mean that *there won't be so much noise* generally, or that *there won't be all the noisy roads*, but rather that roads with those specific characteristics won't be so noisy. Eliminate (B) and (D) because they are too general. Choice (A) states that *the roads won't be quite so noisy*, which is consistent with the focus of the sentence. The correct answer is (A).

34.   **C**   Punctuation changes in the answer choices, so this question tests how to connect ideas with the appropriate punctuation. The first part of the sentence, *Francisco Vázquez de Coronado, an early Spanish explorer and conquistador*, is not an independent clause. The second part of the sentence, *died believing that he had failed in his mission, but his pursuit of that mission has been just as significant to history as it would have been had he achieved his goal*, is also not an independent clause. A semicolon can only be used between two independent clauses, so eliminate (A). A single dash in a sentence must come after an independent clause, so eliminate (D). The phrase *an early Spanish explorer and conquistador* is not necessary to the main meaning of the sentence, so it should be set off from the rest of the sentence using commas. Eliminate (B) because it lacks a comma after *conquistador*. The correct answer is (C).

35.   **B**   Transitions change in the answer choices, so this question tests consistency of ideas. A transition must be consistent with the relationship between the ideas it connects. The first part of the sentence containing the transition states that *Coronado's experience is an excellent window into the difficulty of assessing the Spanish explorers*, and the second part of the sentence states that *we can see the blurring of the line between hero and villain*. The second part of the sentence provides more detail on what is meant by the description in the first part of the sentence. The correct transition will reflect this relationship. *But also* suggests that the second part of the sentence is in contrast to the first part of the sentence, so eliminate (A). *Wherein* means "in which," which does suggest that the second part of the sentence provides further explanation of the first part of the sentence: keep (B). Choices (C), *just as*, and (D), *so too*, both suggest that the situation in the second part of the sentence is equivalent to the first part of the sentence, which is inconsistent with the ideas of the sentence: eliminate (C) and (D). The correct answer is (B).

36.   **C**   Vocabulary changes in the answer choices, so this question tests precision of word choice. Look for a word with a definition that is consistent with the other ideas in the sentence. The sentence says that *Columbus is still praised as being the "discoverer" of the United States but reviled for the atrocities* that he enacted *against the native populations*, so the correct answer will mean something like "performed." *Eviscerated* means "tore violently apart;" while the atrocities might have eviscerated the native populations, in this sentence, the subject of the underlined verb is Columbus, not the atrocities, so this meaning is inconsistent with the idea of the sentence. Eliminate (A). *Did* and *committed* both mean something like "performed," so keep (B) and (C). *Manifested* means "showed plainly," so eliminate (D). Although *did* seems tempting, *committed* is a word also associated with perpetrating crimes and is a word frequently used with *atrocities*, so (C) more closely matches the tone of the sentence. The correct answer is (C).

37.   **D**   Vocabulary changes in the answer choices, so this question tests precision of word choice. Look for a word with a definition that is consistent with the other ideas in the sentence. The word *then* is used to indicate time, while the word *than* is used to make a comparison. The sentence makes a comparative judgment about *Coronado's aims*, so *than* is the appropriate word. Eliminate (B) and (C). *Fewer* means "smaller in number," while *less* means "to a smaller extent." The word *noble* cannot be described as "smaller in number," so eliminate (A). The correct answer is (D).

38.   **B**   The punctuation and length of the phrase following *else* changes in the answer choices, so this question tests both how to connect ideas with appropriate punctuation and concision. The first part of the sentence, *He was much more interested in making something else*, is an independent clause. The second part of the sentence, *money*, is not an independent clause. A colon can be used to separate these two ideas, and the shortest answer, (B), makes the meaning of the sentence precise, so keep (B). Adding the transition word *altogether* or *nevertheless* does not make the sentence more precise, so eliminate (A) and (C). Adding the phrase *and it was* to the first part of the sentence means it is no longer an independent clause. A colon can only be used after an independent clause, so eliminate (D). The correct answer is (B).

39. **A** Verbs and pronouns change in the answer choices, so this question tests consistency of verbs and pronouns. A verb must be consistent with its subject and with the other verbs in the sentence. In this case, the other verbs in the sentence are *came* and *was,* which are both past tense, so the underlined phrase should also include a past tense verb. Eliminate (C) and (D), because they do not contain past tense verbs. The difference between (A) and (B) is a difference of pronouns. The phrase that includes the underlined portion is a description of *Coronado* that is set off from the rest of the sentence by commas. This descriptive phrase should not be an independent clause. The subject pronoun *he* makes it an independent clause, so eliminate (B). The pronoun *who* does not make it an independent clause. The correct answer is (A).

40. **B** Verbs change in the answer choices, so this question tests verbs. The answer choices contain two options: *rise* and *arise.* The word *arise* means "wake up," while *rise* means "move upward." In this sentence, the word *rise* is needed because it involves moving upward to tackle a challenge, not waking up. Eliminate (A) and (C). Before the blank is the word "to." The correct phrase is "to rise," not "to rising," so eliminate (D). The correct answer is (B).

41. **A** Note the question! The question asks which choice gives *information that best supports the claim made by this sentence,* so it tests consistency of ideas. Eliminate answers that are inconsistent with the purpose stated in the question. The sentence states that *Coronado's disappointment was absolutely unforgiving and vicious,* and it already includes the example that *many fellow travelers died on these expeditions.* Choice (A) provides another example of how people *were slaughtered as a result of Coronado's greed,* which precisely supports the claim that Coronado's disappointment was *unforgiving and vicious,* so keep (A). Choice (B) states that *the journeys were long and arduous,* which does not provide further evidence of how Coronado behaved in response to disappointment, so eliminate (B). Choice (C) focuses on how *very limited* was *medical care* during the time of Coronado's expeditions, which is also inconsistent with the focus of the rest of the sentence, so eliminate (C). Choice (D) states that *no one stopped to see the sites,* which is irrelevant to the discussion of Coronado's *disappointment:* eliminate (D). The correct answer is (A).

42. **D** The length of the phrase changes in the answer choices, so this question tests concision. There is also the option to DELETE; consider this choice carefully, as it is often the correct answer. The sentence describes the geography covered over the course of the essay: *We started in Spain, then went to Mexico, then to New Mexico, then to Kansas.* The word *then* already implies that Kansas is the last stop in the essay's travel, so there is no need to repeat that idea: eliminate (A). Both (B) and (C) suggest that visiting Kansas occurred during the travels described earlier in the sentence, which is inconsistent with the trajectory of the essay, so eliminate (B) and (C). Choice (D) is concise and makes the sentence precise. The correct answer is (D).

43. **D** Note the question! The question asks where sentence 2 should be placed, so it tests consistency of ideas. The sentence must be consistent with the ideas that come both before and after it. Sentence 2 states that *That's a lot of territory to cover,* so it must come after a description of a lot of travel. Sentences 3 and 4 outline *how far we have traveled in this short essay alone,* then list the places traveled, so sentence 2 should come after sentence 4. Eliminate (A), (B), and (C). The correct answer is (D).

44. **B** Note the question! The question asks whether a sentence should be added, so it tests consistency. If the content of the new sentence is consistent with the ideas that surround it, then it should be added. The paragraph states that Coronado's *influence is all around us,* and that we have *his "failure" to thank for a large swath of the contemporary United States.* The new sentence states that *A small island off the coast of San Diego bears his name, as does a high school halfway across the country in Lubbock, Texas.* The idea of the new sentence is consistent with the focus of the rest of the

paragraph, so it should be added: eliminate (C) and (D). Choice (A) states that the new sentence *names some of the places of which Coronado was most fond*; the sentence does not mention whether Coronado even knew about these locations, let alone was fond of them, so eliminate (A). Choice (B) states that the sentence *cites some of the contemporary places that were influenced by Coronado*, which is consistent. The correct answer is (B).

Section 3: Math (No Calculator)

1. **C** The question asks for the meaning of the number 20 in the equation. Label the pieces of the equation, and use Process of Elimination. The w represents the number of workers, and t represents the total time in hours. Therefore, the 20 must have something to do with the cost of the workers' hourly wage. Eliminate (A) because nothing is mentioned about a minimum number of workers. Eliminate (B) because it is unrelated to the workers. Choice (C) relates to the hourly wage, so keep it, but check (D) just in case. Choice (D) can be eliminated because the number of wedding guests is unrelated to the cost and unrelated to the workers and their time. The correct answer is (C).

2. **D** The question asks for the value of an expression. Manipulate the given equation to match the expression. Subtract 4 from both sides of the equation to get $12x = 16$. Divide the entire equation by 2 to get $6x = 8$. Therefore, $6x + 5 = 8 + 5 = 13$. The correct answer is (D).

3. **C** The question asks for the solution to a system of equations. Since there are ordered pairs in the answers, try out those points in the equations, starting with (B). In (B), $x = -4$ and $y = 4$. Plug those values into the first equation to get $5(-4) - 4(4) = 36$. Distribute on the left side of the equation to get $-20 - 16 = 36$, and $-36 = 36$. Since the values do not work in the first equation, eliminate (B). Next, try (C). In (C), $x = 4$ and $y = -4$. Plug those values in the first equation to get $5(4) - 4(-4) = 36$. Distribute on the left side of the equation to get $20 - (-16) = 36$, and $36 = 36$. Next, try the same numbers in the second equation: $-4 - (-4) = 0$. Simplify the left side of the equation to get $-4 + 4 = 0$, and $0 = 0$. The coordinate pair works in both equations. The correct answer is (C).

4. **A** The question asks for the value of x in the equation for a given value of y. Put $y = 8$ into the equation to get $8 - \sqrt{4x^2 + 28} = 0$. Therefore, $\sqrt{4x^2 + 28} = 8$. Now try the answers in the equation to see which value of x works. In (B), $x = 4$, making the square root $\sqrt{4(4)^2 + 28} = \sqrt{4(16) + 28} = \sqrt{92}$, which is not equal to 8. A smaller number is needed, so eliminate (B), (C), and (D). The correct answer is (A).

5. **B** The question asks for the value of r, the y-coordinate of a point on the diagram of a quadrilateral. There are parallel lines, which have the same slope. Since the question asks for the y-coordinate of a point on $\overline{AD}$, which is parallel to $\overline{BC}$, start by finding the slope of $\overline{BC}$. Use the slope formula $\dfrac{y_2 - y_1}{x_2 - x_1}$ to get $\dfrac{10 - 0}{0 - 6} = \dfrac{10}{-6} = \dfrac{5}{-3}$. Now use this slope to find the value of r: $\dfrac{5}{-3} = \dfrac{0 - r}{-3 - 0}$ or $\dfrac{5}{-3} = \dfrac{-r}{-3}$. Therefore, $5 = -r$, so $r = -5$. The correct answer is (B).

6. **C** The question asks for an expression that is equivalent to the given one. Rather than factoring, expand out the answers one piece at a time and use Process of Elimination. Focus on just the first term in the expression given, which is $16x^6$. In (A), the first term in the expanded version of the expression would be $(16x^2)^3 = 4{,}096x^6$. Eliminate (A). In (B), the first term in the expanded version of the expression would be $(16x^3)^2 = 256x^6$. Eliminate (B). In (C), the first term of the expanded expression would be $(4x^3)^2 = 16x^6$. This is correct, so either expand out the rest of (C) or check the first term on the expression in (D) to be sure. The second option is easier: $(4x)^6 = 4{,}096x^6$, so (D) can be eliminated. The correct answer is (C).

7. **D** The question asks for the least number of sides in a polygon. Use the values in the answers, starting with the smallest answer choice. Plug in $n = 11$ from (A) and see if $S > 2{,}000$ as stated in the question. The equation becomes $S = 180(11 - 2) = 1{,}620$. This is not greater than $2{,}000$, so eliminate (A). A larger value for n is needed to make the sum of the angles greater than $2{,}000$. Try (C) to get $S = 180(13 - 2) = 1{,}980$. This is still too small. The correct answer is (D).

8. **A** The question asks for the value of $s - t$, where (s, t) is the point of intersection of two lines. First, define the equations for both of the lines. The slope-intercept form of a line is $y = mx + b$, where x and y are the coordinates of a point on the line, m is the slope, and b is the y-intercept. Plug in the point $(4, 4)$ and a y-intercept of -8 into the slope-intercept equation to get $4 = (m)(4) - 8$. Add 8 to both sides to get $12 = 4m$, then divide both sides by 4 to get $m = 3$. Therefore, the equation for line k is $y = 3x - 8$. Next, find the equation of line m. Given two points, use the point-slope formula to find the line: $y - y_1 = m(x - x_1)$. To find the slope, m, use the slope formula $\frac{y_2 - y_1}{x_2 - x_1}$. For line m, the slope is $\frac{-3-5}{5-1} = \frac{-8}{4} = -2$. Therefore, plugging the point $(1, 5)$ into the point-slope formula results in $y - 5 = -2(x - 1)$. Distribute the -2 to get $y - 5 = -2x + 2$. Add 5 to both sides of the equation to get $y = -2x + 7$. To find the point of intersection for the two lines, set the two line equations equal to each other to get $3x - 8 = -2x + 7$. Add 8 and $2x$ to both sides of the equation to get $5x = 15$, then divide both sides by 5 to get $x = 3$. Plug $x = 3$ into the equation for line k to get $y = 3(3) - 8 = 1$. Therefore, the point of intersection (s, t) is $(3, 1)$ and $s - t = 3 - 1 = 2$. The correct answer is (A).

9. **B** The question asks for the positive value of y in an equation with exponents. When multiplying variables with the same base and different exponents, add the exponents. The equation becomes $k^{x^2 + xy + y^2 + xy} = k^{25}$. Combine like terms to get $k^{x^2 + 2xy + y^2} = k^{25}$. Therefore, $x^2 + 2xy + y^2 = 25$. Factor the quadratic to get $(x + y)^2 = 25$. Take the square root of both sides to get $x + y = \pm 5$. Substitute 3 for x to get $3 + y = \pm 5$. Since the question asks for the positive value of y, the equation to use is $3 + y = 5$, so $y = 2$. The correct answer is (B).

10. **D** The question asks for a variable expressed in terms of other variables in the equation. Rather than doing complex algebra, try out some numbers for the variables on the right side of the equation. Let $D = 2$ and $E = 5$, so the equation becomes $F = \frac{2}{5 - 2} = \frac{2}{3}$. Plug these values for D, E, and F into the answer choices to see which answer works. Choice (A) becomes $2 = \dfrac{5}{1 - \frac{2}{3}}$. Simplify the denominator on the right side of the equation to get $2 = \dfrac{5}{\frac{1}{3}}$, then multiply the top and the bottom of the fraction by 3 to get $2 = 15$. Eliminate (A). Choice (B) becomes $2 = \dfrac{5}{1 + \frac{2}{3}}$

Simplify the denominator on the right side of the equation to get $2 = \dfrac{5}{\frac{5}{3}}$, then multiply the top and the bottom of the fraction by $\dfrac{3}{5}$ to get $2 = 3$. Eliminate (B). Choice (C) becomes $2 = \dfrac{\frac{2}{3}(5)}{\frac{10}{3}}$.

Simplify the denominator on the right side of the equation to get $2 = \dfrac{\frac{3}{1}}{\frac{1}{3}}$, then multiply the top and the bottom of the fraction by 3 to get $2 = 10$. Eliminate (C). Only (D) is left, and checking it by plugging in the values gives $2 = \dfrac{\frac{2}{3}(5)}{\frac{10}{1+\frac{2}{3}}}$. Simplifying the denominator on the right side of the equation results in $2 = \dfrac{\frac{3}{1}}{\frac{5}{3}}$, then multiplying the top and the bottom of the fraction by $\dfrac{3}{5}$ results in $2 = 2$. The correct answer is (D).

11. **B** The question asks for a function for which y is always greater than or equal to -2. Since calculator use is not allowed on this section, graphing and checking each function is not an option. Try out some values of x instead. Usually, zero is a number to avoid, since it messes things up, but the goal here is to find what could be true, so messing things up helps. If $x = 0$, (A) becomes $0^2 - 3 = -3$. This is not greater than or equal to -2, so eliminate (A). Choice (B) becomes $(0 - 3)^2 = 9$, which is greater than -2, so keep it for now. Choice (C) becomes $|0| - 3 = -3$, and (D) becomes $(0 - 3)^3 = -27$. Neither of these values is greater than -2, so eliminate them. The correct answer is (B).

12. **D** The question asks for an equivalent expression to the fraction given. When a fraction has imaginary numbers in the denominator, multiply the numerator and denominator of the fraction by the complex conjugate of the denominator. The complex conjugate of $(6 - 3i)$ is $(6 + 3i)$. The original expression becomes $\dfrac{(1 + 10i)(6 + 3i)}{(6 - 3i)(6 + 3i)}$. Use FOIL (First, Outer, Inner, Last) to multiply it out to get $\dfrac{6 + 3i + 60i + 30i^2}{36 + 18i - 18i - 9i^2}$. Combine like terms to get $\dfrac{6 + 63i + 30i^2}{36 - 9i^2}$. Since $i = \sqrt{-1}$, $i^2 = -1$. Plug this into the expression, which becomes $\dfrac{6 + 63i + 30(-1)}{36 - 9(-1)} = \dfrac{6 + 63i - 30}{36 + 9} = \dfrac{-24 + 63i}{45}$. Split this into two fractions, as seen in the answer choices, to get $\dfrac{-24}{45} + \dfrac{63i}{45} = \dfrac{-8}{15} + \dfrac{7i}{5}$. The correct answer is (D).

13. **D** The question asks for the equation that best models the decreasing value of the truck over time. The decay formula states that $decay = original(1 - r)^t$, where r is the rate of decay and t is time. Therefore, the value of the truck after t years is $35{,}000(0.93)^t$. The correct answer is (D).

14. **A** The question asks for an equivalent expression to the one given. Rather than trying to do some messy algebraic manipulation, try out a simple number like $x = 2$. The expression becomes

$\frac{6(2)-1}{2+4} = \frac{11}{6}$. Now plug $x = 2$ into the answer choices to see which one equals $\frac{11}{6}$. Choice (A) becomes $6 - \frac{25}{2+4} = 6 - \frac{25}{6} = \frac{36}{6} - \frac{25}{6} = \frac{11}{6}$. That matches, but check the other answer choices to be sure. None of them equals $\frac{11}{6}$ when $x = 2$. The correct answer is (A).

15. **B** The question asks for the product of all values of k that satisfy the quadratic. The product of the roots of a quadratic $ax^2 + bx + c = 0$ is $\frac{c}{a}$. In the given quadratic, $c = 12$ and $a = 3$, so the product is $\frac{12}{3} = 4$. Without this handy trick, another way to solve this is to use the quadratic formula to find the roots, then multiply them together. The quadratic formula is $x = \frac{-b \pm \sqrt{b^2 - 4ac}}{2a}$. The values of a and c are 3 and 12, respectively, and $b = -18$. The solutions are $x = \frac{-(-18) \pm \sqrt{(-18)^2 - 4(3)(12)}}{2(3)} = \frac{18}{6} \pm \frac{\sqrt{180}}{6} = 3 \pm \sqrt{5}$. The product is $\left(3 + \sqrt{5}\right)\left(3 - \sqrt{5}\right) = 9 - 5 = 4$. Either way, the correct answer is (B).

16. **82** The question asks for the value of c in a quadratic. To compare the two sides of the equation, expand the left side of the equation to get $3(x - 5)(x - 5) + 7$. Use FOIL (First, Outer, Inner, Last) on the binomials of the quadratic to get $3(x^2 - 10x + 25) + 7$. Distribute the 3 to get $3x^2 - 30x + 75 + 7 = 3x^2 - 30x + 82$. Therefore, $c = 82$. This is the correct answer.

17. **15** The question asks for the length of line segment $\overline{AE}$ on the diagram. Because $\overline{BD}$ and $\overline{AE}$ are parallel, triangles ACE and BCD are similar triangles (all of their corresponding angles are equal to each other). Therefore, the lengths of their sides are proportional. To solve for the length of $\overline{AE}$, set up the following proportion: $\frac{10}{12} = \frac{AE}{18}$. Cross-multiply to get $12AE = 180$. Divide both sides of the equation by 12 to get $AE = 15$. This is the correct answer.

18. **4, 8, 12, 16,** or **20**

The question asks for the number of red chips Eve has in a game. Rather than writing equations, try out different numbers. Start by testing whether a single red chip could work. If Eve has one red chip, then she has $120 – $5 = $115 worth of blue chips, which does not divide by 20 for an integer number of blue chips. If Eve had 2 red chips, she would have $110 worth of blue chips, which still won't work. If Eve had $20 worth of red chips, though, she would have $100 left for exactly 5 blue chips. She would need 4 red chips to equal $20, so 4 is one possible answer. Any number of red chips that gave Eve a multiple of $20 would also work, so 8, 12, 16, and 20 are also correct answers.

19. $\frac{17}{6}$ or **2.83**

The question asks for the value of $a + b$, where a and b are constants in a system of equations. If the system of equations has infinitely many solutions, it means that the two equations are the same line. Therefore, seek to make the two equations look the same. Multiply the top equation

by 3 to get $\frac{3}{2}x + 3(ay) = 48$. To make the bottom equation the same, it must be true that $b = \frac{3}{2}$,

and $3a = 4$. Divide both sides of the second equation by 3 to get $a = \frac{4}{3}$. Therefore, $a + b =$

$\frac{4}{3} + \frac{3}{2} = \frac{17}{6}$. The correct answer can be entered as $\frac{17}{6}$ or 2.83.

20. **1**   The question asks for the x-coordinate of point P on the circumference of the circle. Convert

the given angle measurement of $\frac{\pi}{3}$ radians to degrees by multiplying by $\frac{180}{\pi}$. This becomes

$\frac{\pi}{3}\left(\frac{180}{\pi}\right) = 60$. Therefore, the angle $POR = 60°$. Next, draw a straight line from P to the x-axis,

and mark the angles as follows:

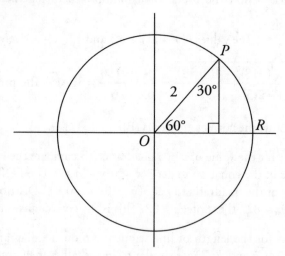

The sides of a 30-60-90 triangle are in a ratio of $1:\sqrt{3}:2$. Given that 2 is opposite the 90° angle, the length opposite the 30° angle is 1, and the x-value of P is therefore also 1. The correct answer is 1.

Section 4: Math (Calculator)

1. **C**   The question asks for the number of blue tiles in a floor pattern in which there are 9 blue tiles for every 80 tiles. The question says *at this rate*, so set up a proportion. Make sure to have like units on the top and like units on the bottom:

$\frac{9 \text{ blue}}{80 \text{ total}} = \frac{b \text{ blue}}{4{,}800 \text{ total}}$. Cross-multiply to get $80b = 43{,}200$. Divide both sides by 80 to get $b = 540$. The correct answer is (C).

2. **D**   The question asks for the value of d when $c = 345$. Plug this value of c into the equation, $c = 120 + 75d$, to get $345 = 120 + 75d$. Subtract 120 from both sides to get $225 = 75d$. Divide both sides by 75 to get $d = 3$. The correct answer is (D).

3. **A**   The question asks for the amount of money the artist will earn if she sells l large prints and s small prints. Translate the given information into algebraic expressions. The question states that

the artist makes $50 for each large print. Since the artist sells l large prints, she earns a total of $50l$ for all the large prints. The artist also earns $35 for each small print. Since the artist sells s small prints, she earns a total of $35s$ for all of the small prints. The amount she earns will be equal to the sum of the two amounts, which is $50l + 35s$. The correct answer is (A).

4. **C** The question asks for the result when 3 times y is added to 19. To figure this out, start by translating the first sentence into an equation. The expression *6 times a number y* translates to $6y$. This term *subtracted from 15* translates to $15 - 6y$. The term *the result is 33* translates to $= 33$, so the whole sentence translates to $15 - 6y = 33$. Solve for y. Subtract 15 from both sides to get $-6y = 18$. Divide both sides by -6 to get $y = -3$. Now translate the question into an equation. The term *what number* translates to a variable. Use x. The term *results* translates to $=$. The term *3 times y* translates to $3y$. The term *is added to* translates to $+$. Therefore, the question translates to $x = 3y + 19$. Since $y = -3$, plug this into the equation to get $x = 3(-3) + 19 = -9 + 19 = 10$. The correct answer is (C).

5. **D** The question asks for the profit the store makes when it sells 6 televisions. It also defines "profit" as the amount of money left after paying 39 percent of the money earned. According to the information given, the total revenue from selling 6 televisions is $1,440. To determine how much the store paid the factory, take 39% of this by entering $\frac{39}{100} \times 1,440$ on a calculator to get $561.60. To find the profit, subtract this amount from the revenue: $1,440.00 - $561.60 = $878.40. The correct answer is (D).

6. **B** The question asks for the revenue the store will earn if it sells 9 televisions. The information given for this set of questions uses the term *directly proportional*, so set up a proportion in the form $\frac{x_1}{y_1} = \frac{x_2}{y_2}$. The information above the question says the store makes a profit of $1,440 when the store sells 6 televisions. Set up the proportion: $\frac{\$1,440}{6 \text{ televisions}} = \frac{x}{9 \text{ televisions}}$. Be sure to put like units in the numerators and like units in the denominators. Cross-multiply to get $6x = \$12,960$. Divide both sides by 6 to get $x = \$2,160$. The correct answer is (B).

7. **D** The question asks for a system of inequalities to describe the situation. Figure out one small piece at a time and use Process of Elimination. The question says the collector can buy a maximum of 25 records, so the total number of records must be less than or equal to 25. Come up with an expression to determine the total number of records. The number of $20 records is a and the number of $35 records is b, so the total number of records must be $a + b$. Therefore, the correct choice must include the inequality $a + b \leq 25$. Eliminate any choice that does not include this: (A) and (B). The other equation in both remaining answers involves an expression set less than or equal to 750. Find 750 in the question. The question states that the collector can spend up to $750, so come up with an expression for what the collector spends. To find the cost of the $20 records, multiply the number of these records, a, by 20 to get $20a$. Similarly, to find the total cost of the $35 records multiply b by 35 to get $35b$. Therefore, the total cost of all the records is this sum: $20a + 35b$. This sum must be less than or equal to $750, so the answer must include the inequality $20a + 35b \leq 750$. Eliminate the remaining choice that doesn't include this inequality: (C). Therefore, the correct answer is (D).

8. **C** The question asks for the form of a quadratic equation that shows the x-intercepts of the parabola. The x-intercepts, by definition, are the x-coordinates of the points at which $y = 0$, so set $y = 0$ in the equation to get $0 = x^2 - 12x + 35$. Factor the right side of the equation by finding a pair of numbers with a product of 35 and a sum of -12. This pair is -5 and -7. The factored form of

the equation, therefore, is $0 = (x - 5)(x - 7)$. Set both factors equal to 0 to get $x - 5 = 0$ and $x - 7 = 0$. Solve each equation to get $x = 5$ and $x = 7$. Select the answer that includes both the numbers 5 and 7, which is (C). Alternatively, know that the x-intercepts are the same as the solutions. To find the solutions, put the equation in factored form. Either way, the correct answer is (C).

9.   **A**   The question asks for the value of p, which is the number of points a player has at the start of a game. A player loses 3 points for every question answered incorrectly. If a player answers 15 questions incorrectly, he or she loses $15 \times 3 = 45$ points. If this player has 165 points remaining, he or she must have started with $165 + 45 = 210$ points. Since the player started with p points, p must equal 210. Therefore, the correct answer is (A).

10.   **A**   The question asks for the number of days it would take Albert to type the entire document. The table provides the number of pages, sections, and units in the document. However, it does not provide any way to determine the amount of time it would take to type a page, section, or unit, so ignore this information. The table does, however, provide the number of words in the document and the number of words Albert can type per minute. Use the formula: *Amount = Rate × Time*. The amount is 181,235 words, and the rate is 85 words per minute. Set up the equation $181,235 = 85t$. Divide both sides by 85 on a calculator to get approximately 2,132 minutes (it's okay to round a bit, since the question asks for the closest answer). However, the question asks for days. Each day, Albert expects to devote four hours to typing the document. 2,132 minutes is equal to $\frac{2,132}{60} = 35.533$ hours. At 4 hours per day, 35.533 hours of typing can be completed in $\frac{35.533}{4} = 8.88$ days. Select the closest choice, which is 9. The correct answer is (A).

11.   **B**   The question asks for the number of days at which the trash can with a capacity of 20 cubic feet will be full or overflowing. In other words, it asks when the amount of garbage in the trash can is at or above capacity. First, come up with an expression for the amount of garbage in the trash can. Each day, 3 cubic feet is added. Therefore, after d days, $3d$ cubic feet has been added. This amount is added to the original amount, which is 8, so the amount of garbage in the trash can after d days is $8 + 3d$. The question asks for when this amount is at or above capacity, which is 20. Therefore, the inequality is $8 + 3d \geq 20$. The correct answer is (B).

12.   **C**   The question asks for the value of $m(n(6))$. For compound functions, start on the inside and work to the outside. The inside is $n(6)$. According to the information in the question, $n(6) = 4$. Therefore, $m(n(6)) = m(4)$. According to the information in the question, $m(4) = 6$. Therefore, $m(n(6)) = m(4) = 6$. The correct answer is (C).

13.   **C**   The question asks for the average speed of a point on the Earth's equator. The speed will be measured in kilometers per minute, so determine distance and time in kilometers and minutes, respectively. The circumference of Earth's equator is about 40,000 kilometers, so this is the distance. Earth completes a rotation in one day, which is 24 hours. However, the question asks for minutes, so convert hours to minutes with the proportion $\frac{1 \text{ hour}}{60 \text{ min}} = \frac{24 \text{ hours}}{x \text{ min}}$. Cross-multiply to get $x = 1,440$. To determine speed, divide distance by time to get $\frac{40,000 \text{ km}}{1,440 \text{ min}} \approx 28$. The correct answer is (C).

14.   **B**   The question asks for the greatest flaw in a survey conducted by a theater owner who is trying to determine whether local residents would prefer to see operas or symphonies by surveying people at a mall on a Sunday. Go through each choice and determine which one describes the cause of a flaw in the theater owner's methodology. Choice (A) is the size of the sample. While it's possible that this

sample size is too small, there is no information about the area's population to determine whether this is a sufficiently or insufficiently large sample. Eliminate (A). Choice (B) is the location in which the survey was given. The location causes a flaw, because it creates a bias toward people who are likely to visit a shopping mall. Keep (B). Choice (C) is the population of the area. There is no information about the population of the area, so it is impossible to determine whether this creates a problem. Eliminate (C). Choice (D) is the residents who declined to respond. There is no reason to think that this significantly hurts sample size or creates a bias. Eliminate (D). The correct answer is (B).

15. **B** The question asks for the year the population on the graph is projected to reach 5,000. Population is expressed by the vertical axis, so find 5,000 on that axis. Trace the line across the graph until reaching the line of best fit. Then, follow downward until reaching the horizontal axis somewhere between 2020 and 2025. The only choice between these two is 2022. The correct answer is (B).

16. **B** The question asks for the half-life of an element. The half-life of the unknown element is approximately 25% less than that of carbon-14. Take 25% of the half-life of carbon-14, which is $\frac{25}{100} \times 5,730 = 1,432.50$. Since it's 25% less, subtract this number from 5,730 to get 5,730 − 1,432.50 = 4,297.50, which is closest to 4,300. The correct answer is (B).

17. **D** The question asks for the reason there is a difference between the mean and median salary at the company. The question states that the mean salary of the employees is $80,000 and the median salary is $45,000. The mean refers to the average (the sum of the salaries divided by the number of employees), and the median refers to the middle salary when listed in order. If the median is $45,000, there must be an equal number of employees with salaries greater than $45,000 and less than $45,000. If the average is greater than the median, it must mean that the salaries at the top half have a greater effect on the average than the ones at the bottom half, which would happen if a few employees had significantly higher salaries. This is (D). Alternatively, come up with a simple example that describes the situation. For example, there could be three employees with salaries of $20,000, $45,000, and $175,000. The median is $45,000 and the mean is $80,000. Go through the choices and eliminate any choice that doesn't describe this situation. Choice (A) says that many employees' salaries are between $45,000 and $80,000. In this case, there are no salaries between $45,000 and $80,000. Eliminate (A). Choice (B) says the employees' salaries are close to each other. In this case, the salaries are far apart from each other. Eliminate (B). Choices (C) and (D) are opposites. Choice (C) says a few salaries are much lower than the rest, and (D) says a few salaries are much higher than the rest. In this example, the low salary is much closer to the median than the high salary, so eliminate (C). The correct answer is (D).

18. **C** The question asks for the probability that a chosen student did not complete an interview. Probability is defined as $\frac{\text{want}}{\text{total}}$. The question says *an accepted student* is chosen, so the *total* is the number of accepted students, which is 15,700 + 9,300 = 25,000. The question asks for the probability that *the student did not complete an interview*, so this number represents the *want*. Make sure to only count the students who did not complete an interview and were accepted, which is 9,300. Therefore, the probability is $\frac{\text{want}}{\text{total}} = \frac{9,300}{25,000} = \frac{93}{250}$. The correct answer is (C).

19. **C** The question asks for an inequality to represent the relationship between the amount Mathias saved this month and the amount he usually saves on average. Try using some numbers for the variables. Let d = 400 and k = 390. Plug these values into the answer choices to see which answer works.

Choice (A) becomes 400 − 390 < 20, which is true. Keep (A). Choice (B) becomes 400 + 390 < 20. This isn't true, so eliminate (B). Choice (C) becomes −20 < 400 − 390 < 20. This is also true, so keep (C). Choice (D) becomes −20 < 400 + 390 < 20. Eliminate (D). Now plug in some different numbers to try to eliminate (A) or (C). Try d = 390 and k = 400. Choice (A) becomes 390 − 400 < 20, and (C) becomes −20 < 390 − 400 < 20. Both of these are still true. When that happens, try using some numbers that *don't* work—the correct answer will prove false and an incorrect answer may still be true. Try d = 400 and k = 450, which don't work because they are more than $20 apart. Choice (A) becomes 400 − 450 < 20, which is still true, so eliminate it. The correct answer is (C).

20. **A** The question asks for the median number of hours spent on homework. The median is the middle number when all the numbers are listed in order. However, in this case, there are too many numbers to list them in order. Instead, think in terms of what the middle number would be. Half the numbers should be greater than the median and the other half of the numbers should be less than the median. Since the president polled 200 students each from the junior and senior classes, a total of 400 students were polled. Therefore, in this case, there should be 200 greater than and 200 less than the median. Therefore, the median is the average of the 200th and 201st numbers. Find the 200th and 201st numbers in the ordered list. Start with the smallest numbers. In the combined junior and senior classes, there are 25 + 30 = 55 students who complete one hour of homework a night. The median must be greater than this. In the combined junior and senior classes, there are 80 + 70 = 150 students who complete two hours of homework. Therefore, there must be a total of 55 + 150 = 205 students with 1 or 2 hours. Since the tally is greater than 201, the 200th and 201st students must be part of the group of students who complete two hours of homework. Therefore, the average of the 200th and 201st (the median) must be 2. The correct answer is (A).

21. **A** The question asks how to compare the number of students who complete four hours of homework in the two classes. The number in the table for both classes is 35, which would seem to point to (D). However, these numbers do not represent the entirety of the two classes but rather a random sample of 200 from each class. Use proportions to determine the actual expected amounts. Since there are 600 students in the junior class, set up the proportion $\frac{35}{200} = \frac{x}{600}$. Cross-multiply to get $200x$ = 21,000. Divide both sides by 200 to get x = 105 students in the junior class who complete four hours of homework per night. Since there are 400 students in the senior class, set up the proportion $\frac{35}{200} = \frac{x}{400}$. Cross-multiply to get $200x$ = 14,000. Divide both sides by 200 to get x = 70 students in the senior class who complete four hours of homework per night. Therefore, the junior class has 105 − 70 = 35 more students who complete four hours of homework than does the senior class. The correct answer is (A).

22. **B** The question asks for the radius of a circle in the xy-plane. The equation of a circle is $(x − h)^2 + (y − k)^2 = r^2$, where r stands for radius. Start by reordering the equation to get $x^2 − 6x + y^2 + 8y = −9$. To solve for the radius, it is necessary to complete the squares. Take the coefficient on the x-term, divide it in half, and square that to complete the square for the x-terms. This value is 9. Do the same to complete the square for the y-terms, adding 16. Anything that gets added to one side of the equation must be added to the other, so the full equation is now $(x^2 − 6x + 9) + (y^2 + 8y + 16) = −9 + 9 + 16$. Therefore, $r^2 = −9 + 9 + 16 = 16$, and $r = 4$. The correct answer is (B).

23. **D** The question asks for the square of the distance expressed in terms of the other variables, so solve the equation for d^2. First, multiply both sides of the equation by d^2 to get $Gd^2 = ab$. Then, divide by G to get $d^2 = \frac{ab}{G}$. Therefore, the correct answer is (D).

24. **D** The question asks for the relationship between the distances of two pairs of objects with the same mass and one pair with 9 times the gravitational force of the other pair. Start by putting in the same mass for k, m, a, and b. Let $k = m = a = b = 2$. The gravitational force between k and m is 9 times the force between a and b, so plug in $G_{km} = 81$ and $G_{ab} = 9$. Square numbers will work well here, since the distance is squared in the formula. Use these values in the formula to find the distance between the given objects. The gravitational force for k and m becomes $81 = \dfrac{(2)(2)}{(d_{km})^2}$, so $81(d_{km})^2 = 4$, and $(d_{km})^2 = \dfrac{4}{81}$. Take the square root of both sides to get $d_{km} = \dfrac{2}{9}$. Follow the same steps to find the gravitational force for a and b: $9 = \dfrac{(2)(2)}{(d_{ab})^2}$, then $9(d_{ab})^2 = 4$, so $(d_{ab})^2 = \dfrac{4}{9}$, and $d_{ab} = \dfrac{2}{3}$. Now make the fraction: $\dfrac{d_{km}}{d_{ab}} = \dfrac{\frac{2}{9}}{\frac{2}{3}} = \dfrac{2}{9} \times \dfrac{3}{2} = \dfrac{1}{3}$. The correct answer is (D).

25. **C** The question asks for a true statement or statements about the graph of a function in the xy-plane. Check out each statement and eliminate as needed. For any graph, $f(x)$ or $g(x) = y$. The graph shows that when the x-value is -3, the y-value is 2. Therefore, statement (I) is true. Eliminate (A). The graph shows that when the x-value is 2, the y-value is 2. Therefore, statement (II) is false. Eliminate (B) and (D). Only one answer remains, so there is no need to check the third statement. The correct answer is (C).

26. **B** The question asks for a statement that accurately compares the heart rates of two runners. Use Process of Elimination to get rid of answers that don't match the graph. The graph of the athlete who only jogs is linear, which is to say the rate of change is consistent throughout time, while the rate of change for the athlete who alternates running/walking is represented by a curve—it flattens out during minutes 3 and 4. Based on this, eliminate (C) and (D) since the rate of change is not consistent for the running/walking athlete. Eliminate (A) because the rate of change is greater for the athlete who jogs during minutes 3 and 4. The correct answer is (B).

27. **B** The question asks for a true statement about the graph of linear function g in the xy-plane. The points of intercept are given with variables in them, so try out some numbers instead. Pick values for s and t that make the statement $t - s = 0$ true, such as $t = 5$ and $s = 5$. Therefore, the points $(0, 5)$ and $(5, 0)$ are on the line. The answers all refer to the slope of the line, so plug these points into the slope formula: $\dfrac{y_2 - y_1}{x_2 - x_1}$. This becomes $\dfrac{0 - 5}{5 - 0} = \dfrac{-5}{5} = -1$. The correct answer is (B).

28. **C** The question asks for the area of a triangle within a hexagon. Rather than trying to remember the formula for the area of a hexagon, ignore triangle ADG for now and divide the hexagon up into triangles, like this:

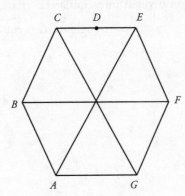

Because the hexagon is a regular one, each of these six triangles is the same. The area of each triangle is $\frac{1}{6}$ of the hexagon, or $144\sqrt{3}$. Each internal angle in a regular hexagon is $120°$, so each triangle is equilateral.

Use this information to find the length of a side of the hexagon. Isolate one triangle to work with, and divide it in half to form two $30°:60°:90°$ triangles.

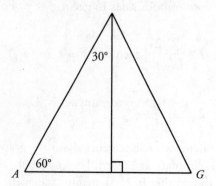

To more easily use the relationships of the $30°:60°:90°$ triangle's sides, label $\overline{AG}$ as $2x$, so the height of the equilateral triangle is $x\sqrt{3}$.

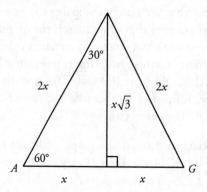

The area of a triangle is $A = \frac{1}{2}bh$, so plug the information into the formula to get $144\sqrt{3} = \frac{1}{2}(2x)(x\sqrt{3})$. Simplify the right side to get $144\sqrt{3} = x^2\sqrt{3}$, then divide both sides by $\sqrt{3}$ to get $144 = x^2$. This means that $x = 12$, and $\overline{AG} = 2x = 24$. This is the base of triangle ADG. To find the height, go back to the hexagon divided into equilateral triangles. The height of each equilateral triangle is $x\sqrt{3}$ or $12\sqrt{3}$, and the height of triangle ADG is equal to 2 of these heights, or $24\sqrt{3}$.

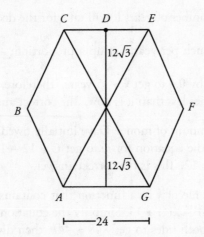

Plug these values into the area formula to get $A = \frac{1}{2}(24)(24\sqrt{3}) = 288\sqrt{3}$. Another way to approach this question is to Ballpark—the area of triangle ADG is about one-third of the area of the hexagon. Dividing $864\sqrt{3}$ by 3 results in $288\sqrt{3}$. Either way, the correct answer is (C).

29. **A** The question asks for the equation of line l in the xy-plane. Start by using Process of Elimination to get rid of equations that have the wrong slope or y-intercept. The diagram shows that line l has a negative slope and a negative y-intercept. All the answers have lines with negative slopes, but only (A) and (D) have negative y-intercepts. Eliminate (B) and (C). Since line l is tangent to the circle at point A, line l is perpendicular to the line containing $\overline{AC}$. Perpendicular lines have slopes that are negative reciprocals, so find the slope of $\overline{AC}$. The slope formula is $\frac{y_2 - y_1}{x_2 - x_1}$, which becomes $\frac{7 - (-1)}{3 - (-1)} = \frac{8}{4} = 2$ for $\overline{AC}$. Therefore, the slope of line l is $-\frac{1}{2}$. The correct answer is (A).

30. **A** The question asks for the values of constants r and s in a system of equations that will result in two real solutions to the system. The solutions to a system of equations are the points the equations share. The line $y = -2$ is the straightforward equation, so y must be -2 in the other equation. Plug the values given in each answer choice for r and s, along with -2 for y, into the first equation, and solve for x. The answer that yields two real solutions for x will be the correct answer. Choice (A) becomes $-2 = -2x^2 - 1$. Add 1 to both sides to get $-1 = -2x^2$. Divide both sides by -2 to get $\frac{1}{2} = x^2$. Take the square root of both sides of the equation to get $\pm\sqrt{\frac{1}{2}} = x$. Therefore, (A) has two real solutions: $\left(-\sqrt{\frac{1}{2}}, -2\right)$ and $\left(\sqrt{\frac{1}{2}}, -2\right)$. The correct answer is (A).

31. **9** The question asks for the value of z in a time scenario. There are 60 minutes in an hour. To convert minutes into hours, divide the number of minutes by 60. $\frac{560}{60} = 9.\overline{3}$ or nine and one-third hours. Therefore, 560 minutes is equal to 9 hours and 20 minutes, and $z = 9$. This is the correct answer.

32. **15** The question asks for the number of years it will take for the decrease in snowfall to equal 6 inches. The rate of decrease is 0.4 inch per year. Set up a proportion: $\frac{0.4 \text{ inch}}{1 \text{ year}} = \frac{6 \text{ inches}}{x}$. Cross-multiply to get $6 = 0.4x$, then divide by 0.4 to get $x = 15$ years. Therefore, it will take 15 years for the average annual snowfall to be 6 inches less than it is now. The correct answer is 15.

33. **12** The question asks for the amount of money Dave initially owed the library. He incurred the initial fine at week 0. Plug 0 into the equation for w to get $C = 12 - 1.5(0)$. Simplify the right side of the equation to get $C = 12 - 0 = 12$. This is the correct answer.

34. **12** The question asks for the value of k in a function that contains the point $(4, -2)$. Put $(4, -2)$ into the function to get $-2 = 2(4)^2 - k(4) + 14$. Simplify the equation to get $-2 = 32 - 4k + 14$, and $-2 = 46 - 4k$. Subtract 46 from both sides to get $-48 = -4k$, then divide both sides by -4 to get $k = 12$. This is the correct answer.

35. **60** The question asks for the circumference of the circle on the diagram. Because the angle COA faces two of the five sides of the pentagon, angle COA is $\frac{2}{5}$ of the circle. The length of the arc made by this angle is 24, so set up an equation: $24 = \frac{2}{5} \times circumference$. Multiply both sides by $\frac{5}{2}$ to get *circumference* = 60. This is the correct answer.

36. **575** The question asks for the number of calories in the breakfast sandwich. Translate the information into equations. Let b represent the number of calories in the breakfast sandwich and f represent the number of calories in the fried potatoes. The information in the question can then be translated into the following equations: $b + f = 910$ and $b = f + 240$. Solve the second equation for f by subtracting 240 from both sides to get $f = b - 240$. Plug this value for f into the first equation to get $b + b - 240 = 910$. Solve for b by combining like terms to get $2b - 240 = 910$. Add 240 to both sides to get $2b = 1,150$, then divide both sides by 2 to get $b = 575$. This is the correct answer.

37. **7,000** The question asks for the maximum number of deer the island can support, given the populations for two years. According to the question, $P_t = 4,200$ and $P_{t+1} = 4,704$. Plug these values into the equation to get $4,704 = 4,200 + 0.3(4,200)\left(1 - \frac{4,200}{C}\right)$. Simplify the right side of the equation to get $4,704 = 4,200 + 1,260\left(1 - \frac{4,200}{C}\right)$. Subtract 4,200 from both sides of the equation to get $504 = 1,260\left(1 - \frac{4,200}{C}\right)$. Divide the equation by 1,260 to get $0.4 = 1 - \frac{4,200}{C}$. Subtract 1 from both sides to get $-0.6 = -\frac{4,200}{C}$, then multiply both sides by C to get $-0.6C = -4,200$. Divide both sides by -0.6 to get $C = 7,000$. This is the correct answer.

38. **5,741** The question asks for the deer population 2 years from now. According to the question, $C = 10,500$ and $P_t = 4,200$. Therefore, $P_{t+1} = 4,200 + 0.3(4,200)\left(1 - \dfrac{4,200}{10,500}\right)$. Solve the equation to get $P_{t+1} = 4,200 + 1,260(1 - 0.4) = 4,200 + 756 = 4,956$. That's the deer population after one year, but the question asks for the population after two years, so do it again. Plug 4,956 into the equation as the new P_t to get the deer population two years from now: $P_{t+1} = 4,956 + 0.3(4,956)\left(1 - \dfrac{4,956}{10,500}\right)$. Solve the equation to get $P_{t+1} = 4,956 + 1,486.8(1 - 0.472) = 4,956 + 785.03 \approx 5,741$. Only round at the last step to make sure the answer is as accurate as possible. The correct answer is 5,741.

Chapter 7
Practice Test 3

Reading Test

65 MINUTES, 52 QUESTIONS

Turn to Section 1 of your answer sheet to answer the questions in this section.

DIRECTIONS

Each passage or pair of passages below is followed by a number of questions. After reading each passage or pair, choose the best answer to each question based on what is stated or implied in the passage or passages and in any accompanying graphics (such as a table or graph).

Questions 1–10 are based on the following passage.

This passage is adapted from Oscar Wilde, "Lord Arthur Savile's Crime," originally published in 1887.

It was Lady Windermere's last reception before Easter, and Bentinck House was even more crowded than usual. Six Cabinet Ministers had come on from
Line the Speaker's Levée in their stars and ribands, all the
5 pretty women wore their smartest dresses, and at the end of the picture-gallery stood the Princess Sophia of Carlsrühe, a heavy Tartar-looking lady, with tiny black eyes and wonderful emeralds, talking bad French at the top of her voice, and laughing immoderately
10 at everything that was said to her. It was certainly a wonderful medley of people. Gorgeous peeresses chatted affably to violent Radicals, popular preachers brushed coat-tails with eminent sceptics, a perfect bevy of bishops kept following a stout prima-donna from
15 room to room, on the staircase stood several Royal Academicians, disguised as artists, and it was said that at one time the supper-room was absolutely crammed with geniuses. In fact, it was one of Lady Windermere's best nights, and the Princess stayed till nearly half-past
20 eleven.

As soon as she had gone, Lady Windermere returned to the picture-gallery, where a celebrated political economist was solemnly explaining the scientific theory of music to an indignant virtuoso
25 from Hungary, and began to talk to the Duchess of Paisley. Lady Windermere looked wonderfully beautiful with her grand ivory throat, her large blue forget-me-not eyes, and her heavy coils of

golden hair. *Or pur* ("pure gold") they were—not
30 that pale straw colour that nowadays usurps the gracious name of gold, but such gold as is woven into sunbeams or hidden in strange amber; and they gave to her face something of the frame of a saint, with not a little of the fascination of a sinner. She was
35 a curious psychological study. Early in life she had discovered the important truth that nothing looks so like innocence as an indiscretion; and by a series of reckless escapades, half of them quite harmless, she had acquired all the privileges of a personality. She had
40 more than once changed her husband; indeed, Debrett credits her with three marriages; but as she had never changed her lover, the world had long ago ceased to talk scandal about her. She was now forty years of age, childless, and with that inordinate passion for pleasure
45 which is the secret of remaining young.

Suddenly she looked eagerly round the room, and said, in her clear contralto voice, 'Where is my chiromantist?'

'Your what, Gladys?' exclaimed the Duchess, giving
50 an involuntary start.

'My chiromantist, Duchess; I can't live without him at present.'

'Dear Gladys! you are always so original,' murmured the Duchess, trying to remember what
55 a chiromantist really was, and hoping it was not the same as a chiropodist.

'He comes to see my hand twice a week regularly,' continued Lady Windermere, 'and is most interesting about it.'

CONTINUE ➡

60 'Good heavens!' said the Duchess to herself, 'he is a sort of chiropodist after all. How very dreadful. I hope he is a foreigner at any rate. It wouldn't be quite so bad then.'

'I must certainly introduce him to you.'

65 'Introduce him!' cried the Duchess; 'you don't mean to say he is here?' and she began looking about for a small tortoise-shell fan and a very tattered lace shawl, so as to be ready to go at a moment's notice.

'Of course he is here; I would not dream of giving 70 a party without him. He tells me I have a pure psychic hand, and that if my thumb had been the least little bit shorter, I should have been a confirmed pessimist, and gone into a convent.'

'Oh, I see!' said the Duchess, feeling very much 75 relieved; 'he tells fortunes, I suppose?'

'And misfortunes, too,' answered Lady Windermere, 'any amount of them. Next year, for instance, I am in great danger, both by land and sea, so I am going to live in a balloon, and draw up my dinner in a basket 80 every evening. It is all written down on my little finger, or on the palm of my hand, I forget which.'

1

Which choice best summarizes the passage?

A) A woman tries to introduce a guest to the practice of chiromancy.

B) A woman hosts a large party and engages another woman in conversation.

C) A detailed description of a party and its host.

D) A woman hosts her last party before fleeing danger.

2

As used in line 5, "smartest" most nearly means

A) most fashionable.

B) most clever.

C) most painful.

D) brightest.

3

The description of "gorgeous peeresses…violent Radicals, popular preachers…eminent sceptics" and "a perfect bevy of bishops" (lines 11–14) mainly serves to

A) contrast political and artistic types of people.

B) illustrate the variety of people attending the reception.

C) compare the women to the men.

D) underscore the discrepancy between social classes.

4

The narrator implies that Lady Windermere's reception is

A) sparsely attended.

B) a dignified affair.

C) a reckless escapade.

D) a success.

5

As presented in the passage, Lady Windermere is best described as having

A) kind intentions but tactless actions.

B) innocent looks but a mischievous personality.

C) an extravagant spirit but frugal practices.

D) warm friendships but a shy nature.

6

As used in line 50, the word "start" most nearly means

A) opening.

B) commencement.

C) twitch.

D) procedure.

CONTINUE

7

The narrator indicates that the chiromantist is

A) a mysterious foreign visitor.

B) a charlatan preying on partygoers.

C) a well-known professional.

D) a frequent visitor at Lady Windermere's home.

8

Which choice provides the best evidence for the answer to the previous question?

A) Lines 53–56 ("Dear . . . chiropodist")

B) Lines 57–59 ("He comes . . . it")

C) Lines 60–61 ("Good . . . dreadful")

D) Lines 74–75 ("Oh, I . . . suppose")

9

The passage most clearly implies that Lady Windermere is

A) nearing the end of her hostessing days.

B) uninterested in discussions of political economy.

C) less gracious than the Duchess of Paisley.

D) less serious about fortune-telling than she claims.

10

Which choice provides the best evidence for the answer to the preceding question?

A) Lines 1–3 ("It was . . . usual")

B) Lines 46–48 ("Suddenly . . . chiromantist")

C) Lines 69–70 ("Of course . . . him")

D) Lines 77–81 ("Next . . . which")

CONTINUE

Questions 11–20 are based on the following passage and supplementary material.

This passage is adapted from Michael W. Kraus and Bennett Callaghan, "Noblesse Oblige? Social Status and Economic Inequality Maintenance among Politicians." ©2014 by Public Library of Science.

The United States is in the midst of unprecedented levels of economic inequality. These large scale economic disparities place the most strain on those at the bottom of the social hierarchy—poor and working class families—who must contend with increased poverty, unemployment, problems with health and social support, and homelessness. Americans have few options to combat economic inequality, but they can turn to the democratic system to enact social and fiscal policies that protect individuals from growing wealth disparities. Given that political participation is one of the only avenues available for individuals to combat this economic trend, investigations into the factors that predict whether politicians will support the reduction or increase of economic inequality remain an important area of research.

Social status is broadly defined as the rank-based value of individuals, and can be measured by one's leadership role in organizations, by assessing levels of socioeconomic status (SES; e.g., occupation prestige, annual income), or by one's membership in one or more social categories—such as one's race or gender. However social status is measured, most research finds that higher status confers greater benefits than lower status. For example, when compared to high SES individuals, men, and European Americans, lower status individuals (i.e., low SES individuals, women, and African Americans) experience stereotype threat —anxiety about confirming negative stereotypes about their low status group—that impedes their academic performance. In general, individuals belonging to higher status positions in society benefit from greater access to material and social resources, increased workplace opportunities, and reduced discrimination based on their social status. High status individuals also tend to hold public office more than their low status counterparts, and as a result, have unique access to decision-making power on matters related to economic policy and wealth distribution.

Status disparities force high status individuals to explain why they hold a potentially unfair advantage in society relative to their low status counterparts. Recent research indicates that when faced with explaining their elevated social positions, high status individuals endorse meritocratic beliefs. Specifically, high status individuals, motivated to maintain their elevated social positions and the benefits they bestow, are particularly likely to explain their many social advantages in terms of a fair application of effort, talent, and skill.

Several lines of empirical evidence suggest that high status individuals endorse meritocratic beliefs more than their low status counterparts. For instance, people with higher status are happier when they believe that positive outcomes in society are based on merit and high-performing members of a group are more likely to advocate dividing resources based solely on merit. In a recent online survey, individuals with higher income and who subjectively ranked themselves higher in the social class hierarchy in society— using rungs of a ladder based on ascending levels of education, income, and occupation status—reported a greater belief that the world is fair and that society's structure is based on merit than did their lower status counterparts.

The present research aligns with mounting evidence suggesting that an individual's social status is a reliable predictor of support for economic inequality in society. That social status predicts support for economic inequality among members of Congress—individuals with direct access to creating and implementing policies that shape the future of economic inequality in the US—is a potentially important piece of information for US citizens to consider in future elections.

CONTINUE

Panel A

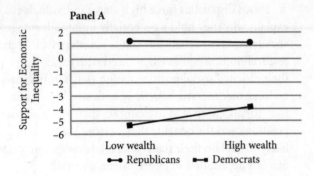

Support for Economic Inequality

Low wealth — High wealth

●—● Republicans   ■—■ Democrats

Panel B

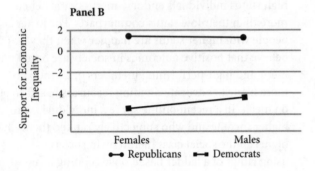

Support for Economic Inequality

Females — Males

●—● Republicans   ■—■ Democrats

Relationships between social status and the tendency to sponsor legislation supporting economic inequality

11

What function does the first paragraph (lines 1–16) serve in the passage as a whole?

A) It advocates embracing the trend supported by subsequent research in following paragraphs.

B) It illustrates a practice favored by the authors that should be implemented according to correlational research.

C) It acknowledges that a discrepancy exists and offers solutions to the problem based on research results.

D) It gives an overview of a discrepancy and indicates why research on that discrepancy might be important.

12

Which choice do the authors explicitly cite as an advantage of individuals with higher socioeconomic status?

A) Stereotype threat

B) Increased workplace opportunities

C) Political activism

D) Discrimination

13

Which choice provides the best evidence for the answer to the previous question?

A) Lines 2–7 ("These . . . homelessness")

B) Lines 23–25 ("However . . . status")

C) Lines 25–31 ("For example . . . performance")

D) Lines 31–35 ("In general . . . status")

14

Which choice best supports the conclusion that members of Congress are likely to be of high social status?

A) Lines 35–39 ("High . . . distribution")

B) Lines 50–52 ("Several . . . counterparts")

C) Lines 52–57 ("For instance . . . merit")

D) Lines 65–68 ("The present . . . society")

CONTINUE

15

The central idea of the third paragraph (lines 40–49) is that

A) some individuals with higher socioeconomic status cite reasons other than socioeconomic status for their perceived advantage.

B) the world is fair and society's structure is based on merit for both high and low socioeconomic status individuals.

C) individuals of high socioeconomic status seek to keep those of lower socioeconomic status from succeeding.

D) socioeconomic status predicts social inequality in most societies.

16

Which choice provides the best evidence for the answer to the previous question?

A) Lines 17–19 ("Social . . . organizations")

B) Lines 40–42 ("Status . . . counterparts")

C) Lines 42–45 ("Recent . . . beliefs")

D) Lines 57–64 ("In a . . . counterparts")

17

As used in line 47, "bestow" most nearly means

A) withhold.

B) grant.

C) earn.

D) promote.

18

As used in line 65, "aligns" most nearly means

A) arranges.

B) straightens.

C) agrees.

D) focuses.

19

Which choice is supported by the data in the figure?

A) Males are slightly less likely to sponsor legislation supporting economic inequality than females.

B) The number of individuals polled who identify as low socioeconomic status is higher than the number of individuals who identify as high socioeconomic status.

C) The number of Republicans endorsing legislation that supports economic inequality, and the number of Democrats supporting such legislation is roughly the same.

D) A female Democrat self-reporting a lower wealth status is most likely to vote for legislation reducing economic inequality.

20

Taken together, the two figures suggest that most people who are likely to sponsor legislation supporting economic inequality

A) are employed and have upward mobility with increased work opportunities.

B) are from all socioeconomic backgrounds and social categories.

C) are Democrats who identify as female and low wealth.

D) are Republicans, regardless of gender.

CONTINUE

Questions 21–30 are based on the following passage.

This passage is adapted from PLoS, "No Rest for the Weary: Migrating Songbirds Keep Their Wits without Sleep." ©2004 by Public Library of Science.

Every spring and fall, billions of songbirds fly thousands of miles between their summer breeding grounds in North America and their wintering grounds in the more hospitable climates of southern California, Mexico, and Central and South America. While some birds fly during the day, most, including the white-crowned sparrow, fly under cover of night. Many aspects of this remarkable voyage remain obscure, especially if, and how, nocturnal migrators get any sleep at night.

A tracking study of the Swainson's thrush found that the roughly seven-inch birds flew up to seven hours straight on six of seven nights, racking up over 930 miles. While the study didn't track their daytime behavior, the birds' migratory pace—as well as the increased activity required to sustain migrations—suggests little time for sleep. Yet field observations indicate that presumably sleep-deprived fliers appear no worse for wear, foraging, navigating, and avoiding predators with aplomb. Researchers are left trying to reconcile this observation with the vast body of evidence linking sleep deprivation to impaired neurobehavioral and physiological function. How do songbirds cope with so little sleep? Do they take power naps? Have they taken "sleep walking" to new heights? Or have they managed to selectively short-circuit the adverse effects of sleep deprivation during migratory stints?

To investigate these questions, Ruth Benca and colleagues studied cognitive and sleep behaviors in captive white-crowned sparrows over the course of a year. The sparrows fly nearly 2,700 miles twice a year between their Alaska and southern California homes. In laboratory cages, the birds' migratory instincts manifest as increased restlessness at night during the migratory season, with lots of hopping around and wing flapping.

Niels Rattenborg et al. characterized the birds' activity levels with motion-detection measurements and video recordings, and placed sensors on their brains to monitor their seasonal sleep patterns. The brain recordings showed a marked seasonal difference in both the amount and type of sleep during a 24-hour period. Cognitive tests—birds performed a task that involved pecking a key in exchange for seed—revealed that birds in the nonmigrating state suffered cognitive deficits when sleep-deprived but displayed an "unprecedented" ability to maintain cognitive function in the face of ongoing sleep loss in the migratory state.

These results suggest that wild songbirds drastically reduce sleep time during migration, though Benca and colleagues concede it's impossible to know for sure without recording the birds in action. Such an ability to temporarily circumvent the need for sleep, however, could prove useful for humans in situations that demand continuous performance.

Whatever the mechanism, the unprecedented imperviousness of migrating songbirds to sleep deprivation, the authors conclude, clearly warrants further testing. But it also raises interesting questions about the role of sleep, which recent studies suggest is required to incorporate novel perceptions into the brain's memory banks. If this is true, how do songbirds consolidate memories of migratory events with so little sleep?

Understanding the mechanisms that power the sleepless flight of songbirds promises to unravel one of the longstanding mysteries of their improbable journey. It may also shed light on the origins of sleep-related seasonal disorders and the much-debated role of sleep itself.

21

Which choice best reflects the overall sequence of events in the passage?

A) A phenomenon is observed and a series of experiments seek to explain it, yet further research is necessary to fully understand the data found.

B) An anomaly is observed and recorded; the results are analyzed and declared inconclusive.

C) A new discovery revolutionizes a current theory, disproving old assumptions, and a new hypothesis is formed.

D) An unexpected finding arises during a study, spawning a secondary study; both studies are interpreted and summarized.

CONTINUE

22

As used in line 21, "reconcile" most nearly means

A) reunite.

B) appease.

C) clarify.

D) integrate.

23

Which statement best captures an assumption Ruth Benca made in setting up her research?

A) The acquisition of sleepwalking from their evolutionary ancestors allows songbirds to travel great distances while migrating.

B) The tendency for songbirds to hop and flap their wings indicates increased cognitive function.

C) Songbirds' ability to fly long distances without sleeping is key to their survival.

D) Songbirds in a controlled research setting will exhibit sleep patterns similar to those of songbirds in the wild.

24

Which choice provides the best evidence for the answer to the previous question?

A) Lines 6–7 ("While . . . night")

B) Lines 14–17 ("While . . . sleep")

C) Lines 32–33 ("The sparrows . . . homes")

D) Lines 50–53 ("These . . . action")

25

In the fourth paragraph (lines 38–49), the results of Niels Rattenborg's findings mainly serve to

A) show how unexpected results can upset an entire hypothesis.

B) reinforce the findings of Ruth Benca's laboratory research and previous field observations.

C) introduce a component of previous research on the songbirds' migration patterns.

D) underscore certain differences between other researchers and Benca's research.

26

After researchers noted the "'unprecedented' ability to maintain cognitive function" during migratory state, (line 48), they

A) concluded that it was impossible to know how the birds maintain normal levels of cognition during migratory seasons.

B) acknowledge that the correlation raises other questions about how the birds function during migration.

C) observed the birds' cognitive deficits when sleep-deprived in a nonmigratory state.

D) consulted other researchers in the field to compare their results.

27

The passage identifies which of the following as a factor necessitating that the team of researchers concede that further research is necessary?

A) The speed at which the birds flapped and hopped

B) The birds' increased activity levels

C) The controlled environment of the study

D) The decreased cognitive levels during sleep-deprived, nonmigratory states

28

As used in line 68, "improbable" most nearly means

A) dubious.

B) unconvincing.

C) remarkable.

D) supposed.

CONTINUE

What can reasonably be inferred about songbirds from the passage?

A) Their activity levels may correlate to migratory seasons.

B) Their activity levels while migrating are similar to those of sleepwalkers.

C) Their mechanisms of migration are impossible to fully understand.

D) Their cognition and memories increase during migration.

Which choice provides the best evidence for the answer to the previous question?

A) Line 25 ("Have . . . heights")

B) Lines 34–37 ("In laboratory . . . flapping")

C) Lines 57–60 ("Whatever . . . testing")

D) Lines 60–63 ("But it . . . banks")

CONTINUE

Questions 31–41 are based on the following passages.

Passage 1 is adapted from Carol Boston, "High School Report Cards. ERIC Digest," originally published in 2003. Passage 2 is adapted from Winnie Hu, "Report Cards Give Up A's and B's for 4s and 3s," originally published in 2009.

Passage 1

Most states have embraced standards-based education, a process that requires them to identify what specific knowledge and skills students are
Line expected to master at each grade level and then align
5 curriculum, teaching, and testing with those standards. Some schools are now experimenting with changes in their report cards to better reflect student progress toward achieving the standards.

Rather than the familiar A through F in each
10 subject, standards-based report cards might feature numbers or phrases that represent whether students have reached, exceeded, or not yet met various specific performance expectations. As an example, a third-grade mathematics grade might include a number or
15 phrase that would denote whether students exceed, meet, approach, or begin to achieve standards in comparing, adding, and subtracting fractions and identifying place values. Such a report card actually provides more detailed, specific information than a
20 traditional grade, though parents and students may find the change disconcerting, and concerns have been expressed about how colleges might evaluate report cards that don't show traditional grade point averages (Manzo, 2001).

25 Report cards that combine traditional grades and information about progress toward standards are also an option. Wiggins (1994) advocates a performance-based report card that plots overall student achievement against norms and standards,
30 identifies strengths and weaknesses in specific areas, and also includes teacher judgments about students' academic progress, growth, intellectual character, and work habits. Marzano (1998) shows an example report card that includes a transcript indicating how many
35 times each standard has been assessed, the average score obtained, as well as the highest, lowest, and most recent scores.

Passage 2

Thomas R. Guskey, a professor at Georgetown College in Kentucky and an author of *Developing*
40 *Standards-Based Report Cards*, a book that is soon to be released, said the new approach was more accurate, because it measures each student against a stated set of criteria, rather than grading on a curve, which compares members of a class with one another. "The
45 dilemma with that system is you really don't know whether anybody has learned anything. They could all have done miserably, just some less miserably than others."

The executive director of the National Association
50 of Secondary School Principals, Gerald Tirozzi—who supports standards-based report cards—said that many educators and parents were far from ready to scrap letter grades, especially for older students, in part because they worry about the ripple effects on
55 things like the honor roll and class rank. "I think the present grading system—A, B, C, D, F—is ingrained in us," Mr. Tirozzi said. "It's the language which college admissions officers understand; it's the language which parents understand."

60 Outside San Francisco, the San Mateo-Foster City district delayed plans to expand standards-based report cards to its four middle schools from its elementary schools, where they have been used since 2006, after parents packed school board meetings and
65 collected more than 500 signatures in opposition . . . .

Addressing these parental complaints, Pelham district officials said they planned to change the system next year to use benchmarks for each marking period—rather than a year-end standard—to give
70 more timely snapshots of students' progress (and allow many more students to earn 4's from the beginning). They also plan to bring back teacher comments, and are looking for ways to recognize student effort and attitude.

31

As used in line 10, "feature" most nearly means

A) present.

B) attribute.

C) report.

D) promote.

32

It can be inferred that the author of Passage 1 believes that a standards-based report card

A) will be challenging for colleges and universities to evaluate.

B) provides a more specific way for teachers to evaluate students.

C) is unnecessarily complicated compared to a traditional report card.

D) is more effective for a student in third grade than a student in high school.

33

Which choice provides the best evidence for the answer to the previous question?

A) Lines 6–8 ("Some . . . standards")

B) Lines 9–13 ("Rather . . . expectations")

C) Lines 13–18 ("As an . . . values")

D) Lines 18–23 ("Such . . . averages")

34

Passage 2 states that the new approach to grading

A) introduces a dilemma into the system.

B) does not truly measure whether learning has occurred.

C) is supported by experts in educational theory.

D) does not compare members of a class to each other.

35

Which choice provides the best evidence for the answer to the previous question?

A) Lines 38–44 ("Thomas . . . another")

B) Lines 44–46 ("The dilemma . . . anything")

C) Lines 46–48 ("They . . . others")

D) Lines 72–74 ("They . . . attitude")

36

As used in line 53, "scrap" most nearly means

A) save.

B) fragment.

C) discard.

D) detach.

37

According to the author of Passage 2, the use of standards-based report cards in elementary schools

A) led to plans for expansion into higher grades.

B) encountered much resistance.

C) has proven more accurate than other systems.

D) has been successfully implemented.

38

The author of Passage 2 includes the quote by Thomas Guskey (lines 44–48) in order to address which concern not mentioned in Passage 1?

A) Colleges might favor traditional report cards over standards-based report cards.

B) Students might be disconcerted by a change from letter grades to number grades.

C) Student learning might be less accurately measured on a curve than by set criteria.

D) Traditional report cards might not provide information as specific as that in a standards-based report card.

CONTINUE

39

Which best describes the overall relationship between
Passage 1 and Passage 2?

A) Passage 2 examines different responses to the
argument presented in Passage 1.

B) Passage 2 strongly challenges the point of view in
Passage 1.

C) Passage 2 draws alternative conclusions from the
evidence presented in Passage 1.

D) Passage 2 elaborates on the proposal presented in
Passage 1.

The authors of both passages would most likely
agree with which of the following statements about
standards-based report cards?

A) Parental insistence on including traditional
information has helped to improve the new
system.

B) Despite encountering some resistance, standards-
based report cards may provide more information
than do previous systems.

C) Standards-based report cards remove the flawed
system of grading on a curve.

D) Although concerns are understandable, standards-
based report cards are superior to the alternatives.

How would the author of Passage 1 most likely
respond to the points made in the final paragraph
(lines 66–74) of Passage 2?

A) The author of Passage 1 would sympathize with
the parental worries.

B) The author of Passage 1 would caution against the
use of benchmarks.

C) The author of Passage 1 would agree with the
proposed changes.

D) The author of Passage 1 would insist that
intellectual character be included.

CONTINUE

Questions 42–52 are based on the following passage and supplementary material.

This passage is adapted from Nadav S. Bar, Sigurd Skogestad, Jose M. Marçal, Nachum Ulanovsky, and Yossi Yovel, "A Sensory-Motor Control Model of Animal Flight Explains Why Bats Fly Differently in Light Versus Dark," published in 2015 by the Public Library of Science. A series of flight experiments are performed with live and simulated bats.

Animal flight requires fine motor control. However, it is unknown how flying animals rapidly transform noisy sensory information into adequate *Line* motor commands. Here we developed a sensorimotor 5 control model that explains vertebrate flight guidance with high fidelity. This simple model accurately reconstructed complex trajectories of bats flying in the dark.

To test our model, we used behavioral data 10 from Egyptian fruit bats (*Rousettus aegyptiacus*)— flying mammals that possess an advanced biosonar (echolocation) system, as well as an excellent visual system. We found that a simple model, which considers only the angle-to-target and its derivative, 15 was able to reconstruct complex, several-meter-long flight trajectories very accurately—with an average error of only 14.6 cm.

In reality, however, all organisms have sensory errors. To assess the effect of this sensory noise, 20 we tested two models of angle-dependent additive Gaussian noise, which mimic the sensory errors found in the auditory system of several vertebrates. As expected, sensory noise had strong implications for the convergence of the model: in many trials, adding the 25 noise resulted in increased maneuvering errors, and oftentimes led to complete failure to converge.

We therefore hypothesized that the bat must use a noise-suppression strategy and integrate (average) over several sensory measurements to overcome the 30 noise. An exponentially decaying integrator, which only takes into account the three to four most recent measurements, was found to outperform uniform and linearly decaying integrators. This simple exponential integrator exhibited successful noise suppression 35 and reproduced the bat's flight trajectories with high fidelity.

An important prediction of our model is that sensory noise determines motor performance. To test this hypothesis, we conducted new experiments in 40 which the same individual bats (five of the six bats) flew under a light level that is considered optimal for bat vision (1 lux), while performing the same landing task. We found that, as we hypothesized, the simulated bat exhibited significantly larger gain parameters in 45 light versus dark. Further, the simulated bat exerted significantly stronger forces when flying in the light. Moreover, flight trajectories in light conditions were more direct than in darkness, as quantified by their higher straightness index.

50 Taken together, these results imply the surprising conclusion that the highly curved flight trajectories often exhibited by bats in the dark are due to sensory limitations—not motor limitations.

The Effect of Noise on Sensorimotor Control

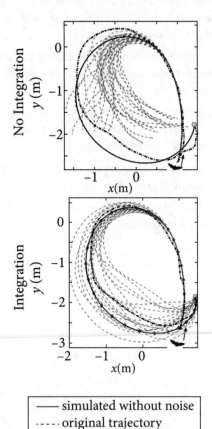

— simulated without noise
---- original trajectory
---- simulated with noise

The figure above indicates the results of the experiments described in the 3rd and 4th paragraphs of the passage.

CONTINUE ▶

42

The words "must," "exhibited," and "reproduced" in the fourth paragraph (lines 27–36) have what impact on the tone of the paragraph?

A) They display a hopeful tone that demonstrates the authors want the reader to agree with their uncertain results.

B) They display a confident tone that demonstrates the authors have faith in some elements of their conclusions.

C) They display an argumentative tone that demonstrates the authors disagree with researchers who conclude that bats do not use a noise-suppression strategy.

D) They display a commanding tone that demonstrates the authors desire to instruct others in the reproduction of simulated bat trajectories.

43

In line 49, the passage indicates that particular experiments resulted in a "higher straightness index." According to the passage, which of the following choices represents the theory these experiments were performed in order to verify?

A) In order to maintain experimental control conditions, it is vital to use the same bats in both the original and later experiments.

B) Inaccurate perceptions caused by common sensory errors have a significant detrimental impact on physical movements and coordination.

C) Mathematical models designed to test average measurements should always avoid uniform or linearly decaying integrators.

D) Bats which fly under light conditions that differ significantly from 1 lux, either brighter or darker, will not likely demonstrate optimal gain parameters.

44

Which choice provides the best evidence for the answer to the previous question?

A) Lines 30–33 ("An exponentially . . . integrators")

B) Lines 37–38 ("An important . . . performance")

C) Lines 38–43 ("To test . . . task")

D) Lines 43–45 ("We found . . . dark")

45

It can be inferred from the passage that including a simple exponential integrator countered what inaccuracy in the described experiments?

A) It can replace information the bats lose when they fly.

B) It accounted for sub-optimal light conditions.

C) It combined sensory input data for more accurate predictions.

D) It increased errors due to sensory noise.

46

Which choice provides the best evidence for the answer to the previous question?

A) Line 1 ("Animal . . . control")

B) Lines 6–8 ("This . . . dark")

C) Lines 33–36 ("This . . . fidelity")

D) Lines 50–53 ("Taken . . . limitations")

47

As used in line 36, "fidelity" most nearly means

A) an accurate reproduction of the significant details.

B) a consistent performance of lower quality.

C) a complete perfection in all areas.

D) a rough, approximate similarity.

48

The main purpose of the fourth paragraph
(lines 27–36) is to

A) describe a theory and experimental verification
regarding the method a bat uses to handle
imperfect perception.

B) suggest a trial in which three to four
measurements are taken of several vertebrates to
assess noise reduction.

C) introduce the probable pitfalls of the earlier theory
briefly summarized in the following paragraph
(lines 37–49).

D) detail the resulting data of a test that supports the
authors' claim involving the accuracy of uniform
integrators as applied to bat trajectories.

49

Before the study, the authors assumed that highly
curved flight trajectories

A) are atypical of the *Rousettus aegyptiacus*.

B) never straighten for any brief period of time.

C) were not replaced by significantly straighter
trajectories by bats flying in bright light.

D) were caused by physical limitations of the bat.

50

The passage and the figures are in agreement that
the addition of a noise-suppression strategy to trials
simulated with noise resulted in convergence with the
original trajectory in

A) all trials.

B) only one trial.

C) roughly half of the trials.

D) none of the trials.

51

Based on the data in the figure, which of the following
trajectories most nearly matched the original
trajectory?

A) The simulated trajectory with no noise and no
integration

B) The simulated trajectory with no noise and
integration

C) The simulated trajectory with noise and
integration

D) The simulated trajectory with noise and no
integration

52

Is the claim made by the authors that bat flight
trajectories under optimal light conditions are more
direct supported by the information in the figure?

A) Yes, because the simulated trajectories most nearly
like the original trajectory are some of the 30 of
those trajectories that included both noise and
integration.

B) Yes, because the simulations with and without
integration demonstrate that sensory noise caused
bats to develop a compensating factor.

C) No, because they do not provide comparative
data regarding the flights under optimal light
conditions.

D) No, because the simulations with and without
integration fail to clarify whether noise was a
causal factor.

STOP
**If you finish before time is called, you may check your work on this section only.
Do not turn to any other section in the test.**

No Test Material On This Page

Writing and Language Test

35 MINUTES, 44 QUESTIONS

Turn to Section 2 of your answer sheet to answer the questions in this section.

DIRECTIONS

Each passage below is accompanied by a number of questions. For some questions, you will consider how the passage might be revised to improve the expression of ideas. For other questions, you will consider how the passage might be edited to correct errors in sentence structure, usage, or punctuation. A passage or a question may be accompanied by one or more graphics (such as a table or graph) that you will consider as you make revising and editing decisions.

Some questions will direct you to an underlined portion of a passage. Other questions will direct you to a location in a passage or ask you to think about the passage as a whole.

After reading each passage, choose the answer to each question that most effectively improves the quality of writing in the passage or that makes the passage conform to the conventions of standard written English. Many questions include a "NO CHANGE" option. Choose that option if you think the best choice is to leave the relevant portion of the passage as it is.

Questions 1–11 are based on the following passage.

The Agents of the FDA

When you go to the grocery store, **1** can't it be fun to go with your friends and family? Why do you trust the chicken that you buy from the grocery store more than the chicken you could buy off the back of some guy's truck? Beyond common sense, the answer is pretty simple: the Food and Drug Administration, or FDA. The **2** agency's beginnings came in 1906, when politicians and consumer

1

Which choice provides the most appropriate introduction to the passage?

A) NO CHANGE

B) which way do you take when you drive or walk?

C) how is it possible to buy only the things that you need?

D) how do you know what you're buying is safe?

2

A) NO CHANGE

B) agency's beginning's

C) agencies beginnings

D) agencies' beginnings'

CONTINUE →

advocates began to realize how harmful unregulated food, cosmetics, and drugs could be. The FDA **3** for we know it today was formally created in 1930.

   The FDA is everywhere in American culture. **4** In fact, the FDA regulates nearly $1 trillion worth of American consumer goods. This $1 trillion constitutes approximately 25% of all that is bought and sold in the United States. A large portion of this money is devoted to goods imported into the United States. The FDA operates on a budget of nearly $5 billion a year, much of which is generated by user fees, **5** which come primarily from pharmaceutical companies, whose drugs require FDA approval.

3

A) NO CHANGE
B) how
C) as
D) DELETE the underlined portion.

4

In context, which choice best combines the underlined sentences?

A) In fact, the FDA regulates nearly $1 trillion worth of American consumer goods, approximately 25% of all that is bought and sold in the United States.

B) The FDA, in fact, which regulates nearly $1 trillion worth of American consumer goods, moreover regulates what amounts to 25% of all that is bought and sold.

C) A quarter of all that is bought and sold in the United States, which amounts to $1 trillion dollars approximately, is approved in some way by the FDA.

D) The $1 trillion dollars of goods in the United States, the same goods that constitute 25% of United States trade, are regulated by the FDA.

5

A) NO CHANGE
B) thus coming
C) those come
D) they come

CONTINUE

[6] Still, while many people are familiar with the FDA's warning labels and health warnings, few know who actually *works* there. After all, an "agency" requires some agents, and the FDA must be a huge operation with all the food and pharmaceutical drugs needed in a population of hundreds of millions. The FDA is certainly large: [7] you've almost certainly seen its approvals on some of the products you use.

While the largest group of FDA employees comprises consumer safety officers, the central work of the FDA is conducted by scientists. [8] Relying on scientists makes sense, since the science of acceptable food is something most of us never think about. But how is it possible to know whether a type of food is safe for general consumption?

6

A) NO CHANGE
B) Stunningly,
C) Therefore,
D) For safety's sake,

7

Which choice best supports the statement made in the first part of the sentence?

A) NO CHANGE
B) it has played a large role in reducing the amount of tobacco use in the United States.
C) Teddy and Franklin Roosevelt were proud of it, and you should be too.
D) it has over 200 offices in the United States and employs many thousands of people.

8

At this point, the writer is considering adding the following sentence.

> The FDA employs nearly 1,000 chemists, 500 biologists, 300 pharmacologists, 40 epidemiologists, and many, many more.

Should the writer make this addition here?

A) Yes, because it lists the employment statistics for the FDA last year.
B) Yes, because it gives some data that will be elaborated upon later in the paragraph.
C) No, because it interrupts the paragraph's discussion of consumer safety officers.
D) No, because it does not account for the non-scientists who work at the FDA.

CONTINUE

How can one possibly be confident that a packaged good on a supermarket shelf will be safe **9** with confidence? This can't be a matter of taste: it must be a matter of chemistry, **10** biology, and a matter of physics. The average consumer simply does not have the knowledge to be able to assess the quality of food. The same goes for drugs. Imagine you were taking five prescription drugs at once—if the pills got mixed up, what would you do?

In short, the FDA is omnipresent in American life, even if it is a bit hidden. The truly remarkable thing about the FDA, other than its high rates of success, **11** are being the collection of expertise it has amassed among its workforce. Perhaps no other government agency requires such an incredible amount of brainpower on the cutting edge of scientific thought.

9

A) NO CHANGE

B) certainly?

C) with sureness?

D) DELETE the underlined portion and end the sentence with a question mark.

10

A) NO CHANGE

B) biology, including some

C) biology, and

D) biological sciences, and

11

A) NO CHANGE

B) have had

C) is

D) are

CONTINUE →

Questions 12–22 are based on the following passage.

Drop the Puck!

For anyone aspiring to play ice hockey professionally, the National Hockey League (NHL) represents the pinnacle of hockey greatness in North America, if not the world. But how did the NHL rise to these remarkable ranks?

The story begins with that elusive trophy: the Stanley Cup. In many ways, this goal is as old as the history of professional hockey **12** its self. It was commissioned in 1892 as the Dominion Hockey Challenge Cup and was given to Canada's top-ranking amateur team each year. The name was later changed to commemorate the contributions of then-Governor General of Canada, Lord Stanley of Preston, **13** who did a great deal to grow the sport in the country.

12

A) NO CHANGE
B) themselves
C) itself
D) himself

13

Which choice provides the most logical conclusion to the sentence?

A) NO CHANGE
B) who was born in London and educated at Eton and Sandhurst.
C) who served as Governor General under British Queen Victoria.
D) DELETE the underlined portion and end the sentence with a period after the word *Preston*.

One of the early contenders for this prize was the National Hockey Association (NHA). When the NHA folded in 1917, it was replaced by the NHL that same year. Despite the name change, the NHL followed from the NHA in just about every way. Just as the NHA had before, **14** also competing annually for the Stanley Cup. This competition came against a variety of other professional and amateur teams and leagues, most notably the Pacific Coast Hockey Association (PCHA), which had formalized its relations with the NHA in 1915. The Boston Bruins, established in **15** 1924; they began the NHL's expansion into the United States.

By 1926, however, all other competing leagues had folded or merged, and the only remaining league was the NHL. **16** While other leagues and teams have issued challenges for the Cup, no non-NHL team has played for the Cup since that time. The NHL's sole dominion over Lord Stanley's Cup also symbolized its **17** supremacy in the world of professional hockey.

14

A) NO CHANGE
B) so too did the NHL compete
C) so too competed
D) so too was competing

15

A) NO CHANGE
B) 1924,
C) 1924. They
D) 1924:

16

The writer is considering deleting the previous sentence. Should the writer make this change?

A) Yes, because it breaks with the logical flow of the previous paragraph.
B) Yes, because it provides a topic sentence that would be better placed elsewhere in the passage.
C) No, because it contains the central argument of the passage as a whole.
D) No, because it provides a logical introduction and relevant information for this paragraph.

17

Which choice best maintains the tone established in the passage?

A) NO CHANGE
B) awesomeness
C) tyranny
D) swagger

CONTINUE

This high position was firmly cemented in the 1940s when the "Original Six" NHL franchises competed with one another each year. 18 There were two Canadian teams that were especially ascendant, even dominant, and many of the players from the era are still considered all-time greats. The league has only continued to expand. Six more teams were added during the first expansion of 1967. Today, the league has 30 teams. 19

18

A) NO CHANGE

B) Ascendant, even dominant, were the Canadian teams especially,

C) Canadian teams were especially ascendant, even dominant,

D) Canadian teams especially were dominant,

19

Which choice most logically follows the previous sentence?

A) There are even plans to expand the league to 32, with teams in Las Vegas and Quebec City.

B) My personal favorite team is the Philadelphia Flyers, who were part of the 1967 expansion.

C) Many of the "Original Six" teams have won the Stanley Cup in recent years.

D) It can seem a little bit odd to have hockey teams in places with no natural ice, but that's the way it goes.

CONTINUE

Since the early days of professional [20] hockey, but other leagues have come and gone. There are other [21] leagues. These, however, are "minor leagues," where young players develop the skills necessary for NHL play, or where players spend whole careers waiting for their chance at the big leagues. Still, while the NHL, made up of players from all over the world, [22] hold the sway that it does, the short history given here provides the important reminder that leagues come and go. The only thing that remains, the only unadulterated constant, is the passion both men and women have for the game.

A) NO CHANGE
B) hockey,
C) hockey;
D) hockey:

The writer is considering revising the underlined portion of the sentence to read:

> leagues, such as the AHL, OHL, and QMJHL.

Should the writer add this information here?

A) Yes, because it lays the groundwork for the shift in this paragraph's focus.
B) Yes, because it provides examples of some current leagues other than the NHL.
C) No, because it suggests that the NHL is not such an important league after all.
D) No, because it provides details that should be given earlier in the passage.

A) NO CHANGE
B) holds the sway that they do,
C) hold the sway that they do,
D) holds the sway that it does,

CONTINUE →

Questions 23–33 are based on the following passage and supplementary material.

Is Sitting the New Smoking?

[1] Health scientists have a new warning: "Sitting is the new smoking." [2] However, excessive sitting and stillness, particularly when it is uninterruptedly sedentary, can have terrible consequences for health. [3] Indeed, now that many Americans have accepted the health risks of smoking and **23** puffed away from that deadly pastime, researchers worry that the sedentary lifestyle of many Americans may have replaced smoking as a national health risk. [4] This may sound odd because everyone has to sit at some point, whether at a job, in class, or in a car. **24**

25 Nearly 20 studies conducted in about as many years have confirmed this grim conclusion, and these studies have covered over 800,000 people overall. While this number does not cover the entire population, it is safely representative as a sample. In one study, researchers found a 46 percent increase in deaths from any cause among people who sat for more than four hours a day while watching television, **26** which is as compared to people who sat for only two. Other studies found links between excessive sitting and obesity, diabetes, and heart problems.

23

A) NO CHANGE
B) run
C) fired
D) veered

24

To make this paragraph most logical, sentence 4 should be placed
A) where it is now.
B) at the beginning of the paragraph.
C) before sentence 2.
D) before sentence 3.

25

Which choice most effectively combines the underlined sentences?
A) 800,000 is safely representative of the entire population, and that's precisely the number that nearly 20 studies used to confirm the grim conclusion that was mentioned above.
B) 20 tests used 800,000 subjects over the course of twenty or so years to confirm the grim conclusion and did so with a representative sample that was safe.
C) Nearly 20 studies conducted in about as many years have confirmed this grim conclusion, and these studies have covered over 800,000 people overall, a safely representative sample.
D) 800,000 people were safe from the grim conclusion of representative samples, as they were the 20 experiments of people in their 20s.

26

A) NO CHANGE
B) having
C) this is
D) DELETE the underlined portion.

CONTINUE

The problem, it seems, is that the human body has not evolved for this kind of idleness. Consider our primate [27] ancestors for example, if they were not incredibly active at all times, they would not have survived. Even many humans throughout history had to live actively— not just as hunters, but as farmers or machinists. Now, as most white-collar jobs involve sitting at a desk, human bodies aren't sure what to do with all the free time. And there is a lot of it, with some estimates showing that the average American is upright and active [28] for only 8 hours of a day. This data shows that the sitting epidemic is not restricted to the workplace: [29] standing desks have become increasingly popular in the American workplace.

How Sedentary is the Typical American Each Day?

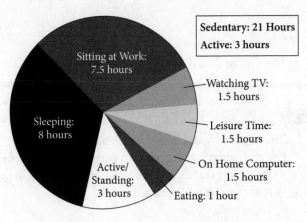

Sedentary: 21 Hours
Active: 3 hours

Sitting at Work: 7.5 hours
Sleeping: 8 hours
Watching TV: 1.5 hours
Leisure Time: 1.5 hours
On Home Computer: 1.5 hours
Active/ Standing: 3 hours
Eating: 1 hour

27

A) NO CHANGE
B) ancestors. For example,
C) ancestors, for example,
D) ancestors, for example:

28

Which choice offers an accurate interpretation of the data in the graph?
A) NO CHANGE
B) for only 3 hours of the 24-hour day.
C) for nearly one-third of an average day.
D) for less than an hour a day.

29

Which choices offers an accurate interpretation of the data in the graph?
A) NO CHANGE
B) the sitting done at work accounts for more than half of all sedentary time on an average day.
C) the average American also eats far too much, sometimes for hours at a time.
D) less than half of all sedentary time during an average day is done at work.

CONTINUE

There may be a message of hope in this news, however. For one, this research suggests that much of the American obesity epidemic could be solved with a change in sitting habits rather than a change in eating habits. More walking (not to mention more running, biking, or other strenuous activity) can reduce weights significantly over time.

Also, the mantra that "sitting is the new smoking" may not apply to those **30** that, of all things, fidget. Researchers in the U.K. tracked the habits of nearly 13,000 women over the course of 12 years. In controlling for other factors, they found that the women who fidgeted—who moved their hands and feet in small, seemingly negligible ways—were less at risk for the perils of sitting than those who **31** sit perfectly still. The leader of the study, Janet Cade, says that fidgeting may not help with body-mass index, but it could improve metabolism.

Thus, while sitting is not likely to come with a warning label, we can see some of **32** their detrimental effects. We can also see, however, how easy those detrimental effects are to counteract. Perhaps you can't avoid sitting down on the job, but you can do yourself all kinds of favors by standing up, stretching out, or tapping your toes. **33** You don't have to take this national health threat sitting down.

30
A) NO CHANGE
B) who
C) we
D) which

31
A) NO CHANGE
B) went
C) are
D) sat

32
A) NO CHANGE
B) its
C) it's
D) they're

33
The writers wants a conclusion that acknowledges the problem of sitting but also encourages the reader to use this research in a proactive way. Which choice best accomplishes this goal?
A) NO CHANGE
B) You should also really go to the gym once in a while.
C) You might consider applying for a job that allows you to go outside sometimes.
D) There's not all that much you can do, frankly.

CONTINUE

Questions 34–44 are based on the following passage.

It's So Rustic It's Chic

For many people, "fashion"—the latest lines of shoes, suits, dresses, or [34] furniture; refers to new things. Increasingly, however, the new things are considered *less* fashionable than the old ones. Granted, "retro" has been popular for a long time, as people have sported the clothes and [35] furnished their homes with the knick-knacks of yesteryear. The newest style of all is both newer and older than mere "retro." This new style, rustic chic, rooted in the various attempts by the stylish to glorify old things, [36] seeks to take its proponents back even further to… well, no one's quite sure.

34

A) NO CHANGE
B) furniture
C) furniture,
D) furniture—

35

A) NO CHANGE
B) have furnished
C) furnish
D) furnishing

36

A) NO CHANGE
B) has sought
C) seek
D) seeking

CONTINUE

Poking fun at this trend, the creators of a popular comedy [37] show IFC's *Portlandia*, changed their early theme song "The Dream of the '90s is Alive in Portland." Framed by men riding nineteenth-century bicycles, chipping their own ice, curing their own meats, and coiffing their handlebar [38] mustaches; these parts of the song jokes that the dream of the 1890s is alive in Portland. In fact, this joke is rooted in reality. Go into many coffee shops, restaurants, clothing stores, and furniture stores, and [39] the results may surprise you; salvaged furniture repainted in such a way that its age shows, handmade goods from artisans and craftspeople, and facial-hair configurations last seen on William Howard Taft.

This concept of "rustic chic" may seem a little odd. First, there's the question of economics. [40] Why, for instance, would anyone want to pay good money for a piece of furniture that is not only out of style but shows its signs of age? Or why would someone want to pay *more* money for something that is worn and broken than for something that is new?

37

A) NO CHANGE
B) show, IFC's *Portlandia*,
C) show, IFC's, *Portlandia*
D) show, IFC's, *Portlandia*,

38

A) NO CHANGE
B) mustaches, the song
C) mustaches. These parts of the song
D) mustaches. The song

39

Which choice most effectively sets up the examples that follow?
A) NO CHANGE
B) you'll notice something peculiar:
C) you'll see the look of yesteryear:
D) everything will be curiously expensive;

40

At this point, the writer is considering adding the following sentence.

> The effect of "rustic chic" on the American gross domestic product is yet to be determined.

Should the writer make this addition here?
A) Yes, because it adds a note of economic seriousness to the passage.
B) Yes, because the passage goes on to describe the global economy.
C) No, because it is not relevant to the main focus of the passage.
D) No, because it contradicts information given in the following paragraph.

CONTINUE ➜

Moreover, "rustic chic" is difficult to understand because it does not have a clear **41** interest. At least we know that hippies are trying to dress like people from the 1960s and flappers are trying to dress like people from the 1920s. How about people who are interested in the rustic chic aesthetic? When people plan barn weddings, they do so because they want to get married like "they" did. **42** Why do you think people are getting married later now?

[1] These questions may be unanswerable, but that does not mean that we cannot speculate as to why rustic chic has become such a popular style. [2] Wear the clothes that men and women did *before* the existence of the fashion industry. [3] The simple answer would seem to be this: people want authenticity, so they want to free themselves of all the things that would seem to have created our contemporary, inauthentic world. [4] Have corporations ruined everything? [5] Buy from individual sellers and farmers. [6] Has the fashion industry ruined everything? **43**

In a culture wherein advertisements tell us every day to be ourselves, many have found that command to be restricting rather than liberating. Truly being yourself is the work of a lifetime. Even so, rustic chic provides one way to **44** prevent the capitalist system from turning us all into drones, though depending on whose side you're on, you might just think of it as a different type of clutter.

41
A) NO CHANGE
B) choice.
C) fashion.
D) source.

42
The writer wants to link this paragraph with the ideas that follow. Which choices best accomplishes this goal?
A) NO CHANGE
B) But who are "they"?
C) As it was famously said, "There's no accounting for the public's taste."
D) It's one thing to have a beard, but who actually likes mustaches?

43
To make this paragraph most logical, sentence 2 should be placed
A) where it is now.
B) after sentence 4.
C) after sentence 5.
D) after sentence 6.

44
A) NO CHANGE
B) reduce some of the clutter of contemporary life,
C) halt the military-industrial complex of today,
D) go off the grid and live a pure life,

STOP
If you finish before time is called, you may check your work on this section only.
Do not turn to any other section in the test.

Math Test – No Calculator

25 MINUTES, 20 QUESTIONS

Turn to Section 3 of your answer sheet to answer the questions in this section.

$A = \pi r^2$
$C = 2\pi r$

$A = \ell w$

$A = \frac{1}{2}bh$

$c^2 = a^2 + b^2$

Special Right Triangles

$V = \ell w h$

$V = \pi r^2 h$

$V = \frac{4}{3}\pi r^3$

$V = \frac{1}{3}\pi r^2 h$

$V = \frac{1}{3}\ell w h$

The number of degrees of arc in a circle is 360.
The number of radians of arc in a circle is 2π.
The sum of the measures in degrees of the angles of a triangle is 180.

CONTINUE

1

If $4s = 28$, what is the value of $8s + 13$?

A) 7

B) 56

C) 69

D) 84

2

Which of the following is equal to $b^{\frac{3}{4}}$, for all values of b ?

A) $\sqrt[4]{b^3}$

B) $\sqrt[4]{b^{\frac{1}{3}}}$

C) $\sqrt[4]{b^{\frac{1}{4}}}$

D) $\sqrt[4]{b^4}$

3

A landscaper will sod p plots of land with the same dimensions with a particular type of grass. The landscaper charges based on the equation $Cost = pGlw$, where p is the number of plots, G is a constant in dollars per square meter, l is the length of a plot in meters, and w is the width of a plot in meters. If the customer asks the landscaper to use a cheaper type of grass for sodding, the value of which of the following would change?

A) p

B) G

C) l

D) w

4

$$3x + 2y = -21$$
$$5x + 6y = -35$$

If (x, y) is a solution to the system of equations above, what is $x + y$?

A) −14

B) −7

C) 14

D) 56

CONTINUE

5

The number of countries that were members of the European Union in 2008 was three times the number of countries in the European Union (then called the European Communities) in 1974. If the European Union had 27 members in 2008 and m members in 1974, which of the following equations is true?

A) $m + 27 = 3$

B) $\dfrac{m}{3} = 27$

C) $3m = 27$

D) $27m = 3$

6

If $\dfrac{7}{y} = \dfrac{17}{y + 30}$, what is the value of $\dfrac{y}{7}$?

A) $\dfrac{1}{3}$

B) 3

C) 7

D) 21

7

$$cx - 6y = 8$$
$$3x - 7y = 5$$

In the system of equations shown above, c is a constant and x and y are variables. For what value of c will the system of equations have no solution?

A) $\dfrac{24}{5}$

B) $\dfrac{18}{7}$

C) $-\dfrac{18}{7}$

D) $-\dfrac{24}{5}$

8

x	$g(x)$
0	2
1	5
3	-1
7	0

The function g is defined by a polynomial. Some of the values of x and $g(x)$ are shown in the table above. Which of the following must be a factor of $g(x)$?

A) $x - 1$

B) $x - 2$

C) $x - 3$

D) $x - 7$

CONTINUE

9

The line $y = cx + 6$, where c is a constant, is graphed in the xy-plane. If the point (r, s) lies on the line, where $r \neq 0$ and $s \neq 0$, what is the slope of the line, in terms of r and s?

A) $\dfrac{r - 6}{s}$

B) $\dfrac{6 - s}{r}$

C) $\dfrac{6 - r}{s}$

D) $\dfrac{s - 6}{r}$

10

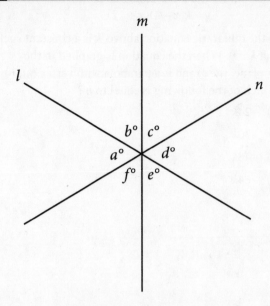

Note: Figure not drawn to scale.

In the figure above, lines l, m, and n intersect at a single point. If $a + b = c + d$, which of the following must be true?

I. $b = c$

II. $e = f$

III. $a = e$

A) I and II only

B) II and III only

C) I and III only

D) I, II, and III

CONTINUE

11

$$y = k(x - 4)(x + 12)$$

In the quadratic equation above, k is a constant such that $k \neq 0$. When the equation is graphed in the xy-plane, the graph is a parabola with vertex (m, n). Which of the following is equal to n ?

A) $-24k$

B) $-36k$

C) $-48k$

D) $-64k$

12

In the xy-plane, a parabola defined by the equation $y = (x - 8)^2$ intersects the line defined by the equation $y = 36$ at two points, P and Q. What is the length of $\overline{PQ}$?

A) 8

B) 10

C) 12

D) 14

13

$$F(C) = \frac{9}{5}C + 32$$

The function above describes the relationship between temperatures measured in degrees Fahrenheit, F, and in degrees Celsius, C. Based on the function, which of the following must be true?

   I. A temperature decrease of 1.8 degrees Celsius is equivalent to a temperature decrease of 1 degree Fahrenheit.

  II. A temperature decrease of 1 degree Celsius is equivalent to a temperature decrease of $\frac{9}{5}$ degrees Fahrenheit.

 III. A temperature decrease of $\frac{5}{9}$ degree Fahrenheit is equivalent to a temperature decrease of 1 degree Celsius.

A) I only

B) II only

C) II and III only

D) I, II, and III

CONTINUE

14

$$\frac{80x^2 + 84x - 13}{kx - 4} = -16x \ -4 - \frac{29}{kx - 4}$$

The equation above is true for all values of $x \neq \dfrac{4}{k}$, where k is a constant. What is the value of k?

A) −5

B) −2

C) 2

D) 5

15

What are the solutions to $5x^2 + 30x + 15 = 0$?

A) $x = -2 \pm 2\sqrt{6}$

B) $-2 \pm \sqrt{6}$

C) $x = -3 \pm \dfrac{\sqrt{60}}{10}$

D) $x = -3 \pm \sqrt{6}$

CONTINUE

DIRECTIONS

For questions 16–20, solve the problem and enter your answer in the grid, as described below, on the answer sheet.

1. Although not required, it is suggested that you write your answer in the boxes at the top of the columns to help you fill in the circles accurately. You will receive credit only if the circles are filled in correctly.

2. Mark no more than one circle in any column.

3. No question has a negative answer.

4. Some problems may have more than one correct answer. In such cases, grid only one answer.

5. **Mixed numbers** such as $3\frac{1}{2}$ must be gridded as 3.5 or 7/2. (If [3 1 / 2] is entered into the grid, it will be interpreted as $\frac{31}{2}$, not as $3\frac{1}{2}$.)

6. **Decimal Answers:** If you obtain a decimal answer with more digits than the grid can accommodate, it may be either rounded or truncated, but it must fill the entire grid.

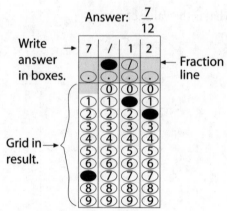

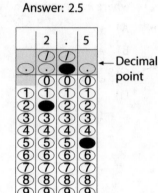

Acceptable ways to grid $\frac{2}{3}$ are:

Answer: 201 – either position is correct

NOTE: You may start your answers in any column, space permitting. Columns you don't need to use should be left blank.

CONTINUE

16

If $\dfrac{21}{25}z - \dfrac{16}{25}z = \dfrac{1}{2} + \dfrac{3}{10}$, what is the value of z ?

17

$$y^3(y^2 - 10) = -9y$$

If $y > 0$, what is one possible solution to the equation above?

18

At a music school, each long session lasts twenty minutes longer than each short session. If 3 long sessions and 4 short sessions last a total of 270 minutes, how many minutes does a long session last?

19

In triangle UVW, the measure of $\angle U$ is 90°, $WV = 39$, and $UV = 36$. Triangle XYZ is similar to triangle UVW, where $\angle X$, $\angle Y$, and $\angle Z$ correspond to $\angle U$, $\angle V$, and $\angle W$, respectively. If each side of triangle XYZ is $\dfrac{3}{5}$ the length of its corresponding side of triangle UVW, what is the value of $\cos Z$?

20

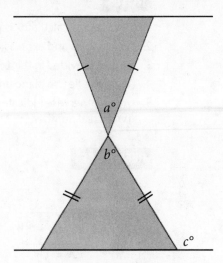

Note: Figure not drawn to scale.

Two isosceles triangles are shown above. If $b = 180 - 4a$ and $a = 35$, what is the value of c ?

STOP
If you finish before time is called, you may check your work on this section only.
Do not turn to any other section in the test.

Math Test – Calculator

55 MINUTES, 38 QUESTIONS

Turn to Section 4 of your answer sheet to answer the questions in this section.

DIRECTIONS

For questions 1–30, solve each problem, choose the best answer from the choices provided, and fill in the corresponding circle on your answer sheet. **For questions 31–38,** solve the problem and enter your answer in the grid on the answer sheet. Please refer to the directions before question 31 on how to enter your answers in the grid. You may use any available space in your test booklet for scratch work.

NOTES

1. The use of a calculator **is permitted**.
2. All variables and expressions used represent real numbers unless otherwise indicated.
3. Figures provided in this test are drawn to scale unless otherwise indicated.
4. All figures lie in a plane unless otherwise indicated.
5. Unless otherwise indicated, the domain of a given function f is the set of all real numbers x for which $f(x)$ is a real number.

REFERENCE

$A = \pi r^2$
$C = 2\pi r$

$A = \ell w$

$A = \frac{1}{2}bh$

$c^2 = a^2 + b^2$

Special Right Triangles

$V = \ell wh$

$V = \pi r^2 h$

$V = \frac{4}{3}\pi r^3$

$V = \frac{1}{3}\pi r^2 h$

$V = \frac{1}{3}\ell wh$

The number of degrees of arc in a circle is 360.
The number of radians of arc in a circle is 2π.
The sum of the measures in degrees of the angles of a triangle is 180.

CONTINUE

1

| | Eye color | | Total |
Species	Yellow	Brown	
Grey wolf	16	2	18
Coyote	7	5	12
Total	23	7	30

The table above shows the distribution by species and eye color for the 30 canids living in a nature conservancy. If one canid is selected at random, what is the probability that it will be either a grey wolf with yellow eyes or a coyote with brown eyes?

A) $\dfrac{11}{30}$

B) $\dfrac{17}{30}$

C) $\dfrac{21}{30}$

D) $\dfrac{23}{30}$

2

The graph below shows U.S. military spending, in billions of dollars, each year from 1992 through 2006.

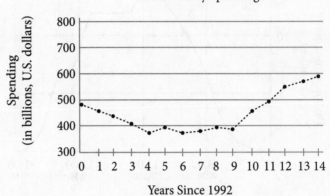

U.S. Military Spending

Years Since 1992

Based on the graph, which of the following best describes the overall trend in U.S. military spending from 1992 through 2006 ?

A) Spending generally decreased in every year since 1992.

B) Spending generally increased in every year since 1992.

C) Spending generally remained constant in every year from 1992 through 2006.

D) Spending decreased until 1996 and increased after 2001.

CONTINUE ➡

3

Eddie's Bike Ride

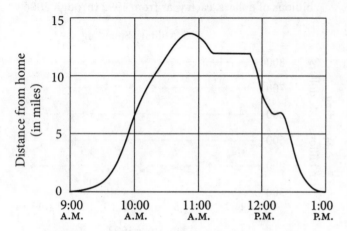

The graph above represents Eddie's distance from home during a 4-hour bike ride. He stopped for 40 minutes during his bike ride to repair a flat tire. According to the graph, which of the following is nearest to the time he finished repairing his flat tire and continued on his ride?

A) 11:10 A.M.

B) 11:50 A.M.

C) 12:10 P.M.

D) 12:50 P.M.

4

At the Acme automobile factory, approximately 4 percent of male employees and 6 percent of female employees received performance bonuses last month. If there were 648 male employees and 519 female employees at the Acme automobile factory last month, which of the following is closest to the total number of male and female employees at the Acme automobile factory who received performance bonuses last month?

A) 26

B) 31

C) 57

D) 113

5

What is the sum of the polynomials $4x^2 + 3x - 2$ and $2x^2 - 8x + 9$?

A) $6x^2 - 5x - 7$

B) $6x^2 - 5x + 7$

C) $6x^4 - 5x - 7$

D) $6x^4 - 5x + 7$

CONTINUE ▶

6

k	1	2	3	4	5
$g(k)$	–3	1	5	9	13

The table above shows selected values of the linear function g. Which of the following best defines g ?

A) $g(k) = k - 1$

B) $g(k) = 2k - 4$

C) $g(k) = 3k - 5$

D) $g(k) = 4k - 7$

7

The total annual rainfall, in inches, in Brown County from 2005 to 2015 can be modeled by the equation $y = -0.14x + 7.8$, where x is the number of years since 2005 and y is the total annual rainfall. Which of the following best describes the meaning of the number -0.14 in the equation?

A) The total annual rainfall in 2005

B) The total annual rainfall in 2015

C) The estimated difference between the total rainfall in 2005 and the total rainfall in 2015

D) The estimated decrease in the average rainfall per year from 2005 to 2015

8

An insect crawls 30 inches in 16.3 minutes. If the insect continues to crawl at the same rate, approximately how many inches will it crawl in 6 hours?

A) 200

B) 300

C) 650

D) 960

CONTINUE

9

$$\frac{8}{5}v = \frac{7}{4}$$

In the equation above, what is the value of v ?

A) $\dfrac{56}{20}$

B) $\dfrac{35}{32}$

C) $\dfrac{32}{35}$

D) $\dfrac{20}{56}$

10

The function g has four distinct zeros. Which of the following could be the complete graph of g in the xy-plane?

A)

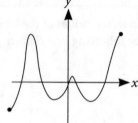

B)

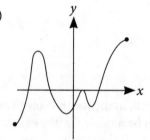

C)

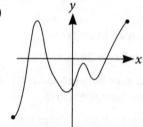

D)

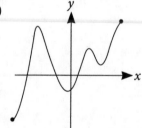

CONTINUE

Questions 11 and 12 refer to the following information.

Substance	Specific heat capacity $\left(\dfrac{J}{g}\right)$
Aluminum	0.90
Copper	0.39
Glass	0.67
Gold	0.13
Olive oil	1.79
Porcelain	1.08
Rubber	1.25
Water	4.18

The chart above gives approximations for the specific heat capacity, in joules per gram $\left(\dfrac{J}{g}\right)$, for eight common substances. The heat energy required to raise the temperature of a substance by 1° Celsius can be represented by the expression $Q = mC$, where Q is heat energy measured in joules (J), m is the mass of the substance measured in grams (g), and C is the specific heat capacity measured in $\dfrac{J}{g}$.

11

A piece of copper has a mass of 75 grams. How much heat energy, in joules, is needed to raise the temperature of the piece of copper by 1° Celsius?

A) 29.25

B) 50.25

C) 111.95

D) 192.30

12

A piece of porcelain requires 80 joules of heat energy to raise its temperature by 1° Celsius. If a piece of another substance with the same mass requires approximately 67 joules of heat energy to raise its temperature by 1° Celsius, the piece could be composed of which substance?

A) Aluminum

B) Glass

C) Olive oil

D) Rubber

CONTINUE

13

A medical study was conducted in order to determine whether product K could help people with hearing loss improve their hearing. The administrators of the study selected 200 subjects at random from a large group of people who had severe hearing loss. Half of the subjects were randomly assigned to be given product K and half were not. The resulting data demonstrated that subjects who were given product K had significantly improved hearing compared to those who were not given product K. Based on this study, which of the following conclusions is most appropriate?

A) Product K will enable all people who take it to significantly improve their hearing.

B) Product K is more effective than all other hearing-improvement products.

C) Product K will help people significantly improve their hearing.

D) Product K is likely to help people with severe hearing loss improve their hearing.

14

A car accelerates for t seconds at a constant rate of a meters per second squared $\left(\dfrac{m}{s^2}\right)$ until it reaches a velocity of v meters per second. The distance in meters the car travels is given by $d = vt - \dfrac{1}{2}at^2$. Which of the following gives a, in terms of v, d, and t ?

A) $a = 2\left(v - \dfrac{d}{t}\right)$

B) $a = 2\left(v + \dfrac{d}{t}\right)$

C) $a = 2\left(\dfrac{v}{t} - \dfrac{d}{t^2}\right)$

D) $a = 2\left(\dfrac{v}{t} + \dfrac{d}{t^2}\right)$

15

A certain type of ribbon costs $0.15 per inch. Which of the equations below gives the total price, p, in dollars, for y yards of ribbon? (1 yard = 36 inches)

A) $p = 0.15y + 36$

B) $p = 0.15(36y)$

C) $p = \dfrac{0.15y}{36}$

D) $p = \dfrac{36y}{0.15}$

CONTINUE

Questions 16 and 17 refer to the following information.

$$C(q) = 60q + 300$$

$$R(q) = 75q$$

The cost of producing a product and the revenue earned from selling a product are functions of the number of units sold. The functions shown above are the estimated cost and revenue functions for a certain product. The function $C(q)$ gives the total cost, in dollars, of producing a quantity of q units of the product, and the function $R(q)$ gives the total revenue, in dollars, earned from selling a quantity of q units of the product.

16

How will the total cost of producing q units change if the quantity is decreased by 20 units?

A) The total cost will decrease by $1,200.

B) The total cost will decrease by $320.

C) The total cost will decrease by $20.

D) The total cost will increase by $1,200.

17

At what quantity will the cost of producing q units equal the revenue earned from selling q units?

A) 2

B) 15

C) 20

D) 45

18

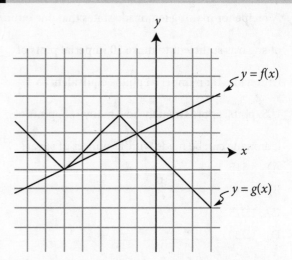

The figure above shows the graphs of the functions f and g in the xy-plane. For which of the following values of x is it true that $f(x) + g(x) = 1$?

A) −5

B) −4

C) −3

D) −2

19

Of the four types of depreciation shown below, which one would yield exponential decay in the value of an item?

A) The item loses 5% of its initial value in each successive year.

B) The item loses 6% of its current value in each successive year.

C) The value of the item decreases by $50 in each successive year.

D) The value of the item decreases by $60 in each successive year.

CONTINUE

20

A recipe for making lemonade states that one ounce of sugar is sufficient to make 30 imperial pints of lemonade. If an imperial pint is equivalent to $1\frac{1}{4}$ U.S. pints, approximately how many U.S. pints of lemonade can be made with 17 ounces of sugar?

A) 515

B) 640

C) 1,015

D) 1,280

21

Horizontal Distance versus Vertical Distance

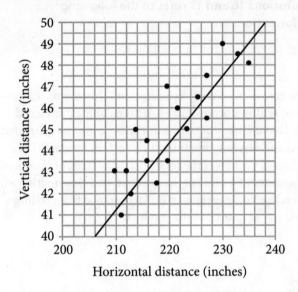

For a physics experiment, Hussain made 18 long jumps, and his classmates recorded the results. The scatterplot above shows both the vertical and horizontal distance of each jump. A line of best fit for the data is also shown. For the jump with a horizontal distance of 230 inches, the vertical distance was approximately how many inches more than the distance predicted by the line of best fit?

A) 1.5

B) 3

C) 4.5

D) 6

CONTINUE

22

Mrs. Warren has b boxes of Girl Scout cookies that she wants to distribute to the members of her troop. If she gives each girl 4 boxes, she will have 11 boxes left over. If she wanted to give each student 5 boxes, she would need an additional 12 boxes. How many girls are in Mrs. Warren's Girl Scout troop?

A) 12

B) 23

C) 27

D) 32

23

When three numbers are added together, the result is 665. The largest number is four-thirds the sum of the other two numbers. What is the value of the largest number?

A)   95

B) 245

C) 350

D) 380

24

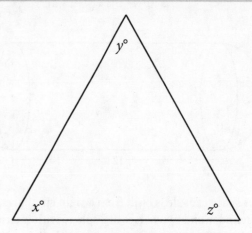

Note: Figure not drawn to scale.

In the triangle shown above, $\cos(x°) = \sin(z°)$. If $x = 3j - 19$ and $z = 5j - 15$, what is the value of j ?

A)   8.5

B) 15.5

C) 34.5

D) 51.5

25

The length of a rectangle is decreased by 25 percent, and the width of the rectangle is increased by k percent. If the area of the rectangle increases by 5 percent, what is the value of k ?

A) 25

B) 30

C) 35

D) 40

CONTINUE

26

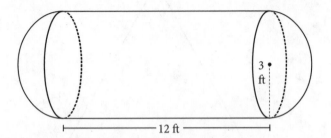

A space capsule is built from a right circular cylinder and two halves of a sphere with internal measurements as shown in the figure above. Which of the following is closest to the volume, in cubic feet, of the capsule?

A) 339.9

B) 396.3

C) 452.4

D) 565.6

27

The graph of line ℓ in the xy-plane passes through the origin and the points $(p, 4)$ and $(9, p)$. Which of the following is a possible value for p ?

A) –6

B) –3

C) 0

D) 12

28

	Decaffeinated	Caffeinated
Tea		
Coffee		
Total	28	116

The partially completed table above shows all the drinks that were sold on one day at a coffee shop. The shop sold 3 times as many cups of caffeinated tea as it did decaffeinated tea, and it sold 5 times as many cups of caffeinated coffee as it did decaffeinated coffee. If 28 cups of decaffeinated beverages and 116 cups of caffeinated beverages were sold, and one cup is selected at random out of all the caffeinated beverages that were sold, which of the following is closest to the probability that this cup contains coffee?

A) 0.508

B) 0.583

C) 0.672

D) 0.690

CONTINUE

29

$$4x + j = 7x - 9$$
$$4y + k = 7y - 9$$

In the system of equations shown above, j and k are constants, and j is k plus $\frac{3}{2}$. Which of the following must be true?

A) x is y minus $\frac{1}{2}$

B) x is y plus $\frac{1}{2}$

C) x is y minus $\frac{3}{2}$

D) x is y plus $\frac{9}{2}$

30

Banerji currently owns 6,500 baseball cards. He is gradually selling his collection and estimates that the number of cards he owns will decrease by 20 percent every 6 months. Which of the following expressions best models Banerji's estimate of the number of baseball cards he will own m months from now?

A) $6,500(0.2)^{\frac{m}{6}}$

B) $6,500(0.2)^{6m}$

C) $6,500(0.8)^{\frac{m}{6}}$

D) $6,500(0.8)^{6m}$

CONTINUE

DIRECTIONS

For questions 31–38, solve the problem and enter your answer in the grid, as described below, on the answer sheet.

1. Although not required, it is suggested that you write your answer in the boxes at the top of the columns to help you fill in the circles accurately. You will receive credit only if the circles are filled in correctly.

2. Mark no more than one circle in any column.

3. No question has a negative answer.

4. Some problems may have more than one correct answer. In such cases, grid only one answer.

5. **Mixed numbers** such as $3\frac{1}{2}$ must be gridded as 3.5 or 7/2. (If $\boxed{3\ 1\ /\ 2}$ is entered into the grid, it will be interpreted as $\frac{31}{2}$, not as $3\frac{1}{2}$.)

6. **Decimal Answers:** If you obtain a decimal answer with more digits than the grid can accommodate, it may be either rounded or truncated, but it must fill the entire grid.

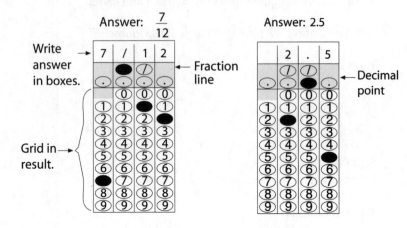

Acceptable ways to grid $\frac{2}{3}$ are:

Answer: 201 – either position is correct

NOTE: You may start your answers in any column, space permitting. Columns you don't need to use should be left blank.

CONTINUE

31

If the expression $(6x^2 - 7x + 5) - 3(x^2 - 5x + 4)$ is written in the form $ax^2 + bx + c$, what is the value of a ?

32

At a grocery store, potatoes are $0.30 each, and onions are $0.50 each. If Emeril plans to spend at least $2.00 but no more than $2.50 on p potatoes and 1 onion, what is one possible value for p ?

33

Height of 12 Infants in Mrs. Graham's Daycare Program

Student	Height	Student	Height
Angela	25	Letitia	22
Benjamin	22	Moishe	26
Charles	23	Nancy	30
Denise	27	Sasha	21
Elaine	24	Tormund	27
Johanna	30	Walter	25

The table above shows the heights, in inches, of 12 infants between the ages of 3 months and 6 months. According to the table, what is the mean height, in inches, of these infants? (Round your answer to the nearest tenth.)

34

In a certain course, students take 8 exams that are graded on a scale from 0 to 100, inclusive. Jacob received an average score of 65 on his first 4 exams. What is the lowest score he can receive on his 5th exam and still be able to score an average of 75 for all 8 exams?

CONTINUE

35

$$y \leq 20x + 3,500$$
$$y \leq -8x$$

The graph in the *xy*-plane of the solution set of the system of inequalities above contains the point (j, k). What is the greatest possible value of k ?

36

In the circle centered at P, the measure of central angle QPR is $\dfrac{7\pi}{6}$ radians. The length of the arc defined by central angle QPR is what fraction of the circumference of the circle?

Questions 37 and 38 refer to the following information.

According to a well-known statistics theorem, if patients enter a medical clinic at a rate of m patients per minute and each stays at the clinic an average of W minutes, the average number of patients, L, in the clinic at any point in time is given by $L = mW$.

The manager of the Kind Care clinic estimates that when the clinic is open, an average of 4 patients per minute enter the clinic and that on average, each of them stays 45 minutes. The manager uses the above theorem to estimate that at any point in time, there are 180 patients in the clinic.

37

A rival clinic, the Speedy Care clinic, recently opened across the street. The manager of this clinic estimates that, when the clinic is open, an average of 324 patients per <u>hour</u> enter the clinic and that, on average, each of them stays 40 minutes. The average number of patients in the Speedy Care clinic at any point in time is what percent greater than the average number of patients in the Kind Care clinic at any point in time? (Note: Disregard the percent sign when gridding in your answer. For example, if your answer is 38.4%, enter 38.4.)

CONTINUE

38

The theorem above may be applied to any part of the clinic, such as the waiting room or a particular office. The manager observes that, when the clinic is open, approximately 36 patients per hour are being treated by a doctor, and that each of these patients spends an average of 15 minutes with his or her doctor. At any time when the clinic is open, approximately how many patients, on average, are being treated by a doctor at the Kind Care clinic?

▲

END OF TEST

DO NOT RETURN TO A PREVIOUS SECTION.

Completely darken bubbles with a No. 2 pencil. If you make a mistake, be sure to erase mark completely. Erase all stray marks.

1.

YOUR NAME:
(Print) _____
Last   First   M.I.

SIGNATURE: _____ DATE: __ / __ / __

HOME ADDRESS:
(Print) _____
Number and Street

_____
City   State   Zip Code

PHONE NO.:
(Print) _____

IMPORTANT: Please fill in these boxes exactly as shown on the back cover of your test book.

2. TEST FORM

3. TEST CODE

4. REGISTRATION NUMBER

5. YOUR NAME

First 4 letters of last name | FIRST INIT | MID INIT

6. DATE OF BIRTH

Month	Day	Year
JAN		
FEB	0 0	0 0
MAR	1 1	1 1
APR	2 2	2 2
MAY	3 3	3 3
JUN	4 4	4
JUL	5 5	5
AUG	6 6	6
SEP	7 7	7
OCT	8 8	8
NOV	9 9	9
DEC		

7. SEX
- MALE
- FEMALE

The Princeton Review®

Test ③ Start with number 1 for each new section.
If a section has fewer questions than answer spaces, leave the extra answer spaces blank.

Section 1—Reading

1. A B C D
2. A B C D
3. A B C D
4. A B C D
5. A B C D
6. A B C D
7. A B C D
8. A B C D
9. A B C D
10. A B C D
11. A B C D
12. A B C D
13. A B C D
14. A B C D
15. A B C D
16. A B C D
17. A B C D
18. A B C D
19. A B C D
20. A B C D
21. A B C D
22. A B C D
23. A B C D
24. A B C D
25. A B C D
26. A B C D

27. A B C D
28. A B C D
29. A B C D
30. A B C D
31. A B C D
32. A B C D
33. A B C D
34. A B C D
35. A B C D
36. A B C D
37. A B C D
38. A B C D
39. A B C D
40. A B C D
41. A B C D
42. A B C D
43. A B C D
44. A B C D
45. A B C D
46. A B C D
47. A B C D
48. A B C D
49. A B C D
50. A B C D
51. A B C D
52. A B C D

Section 2—Writing and Language Skills

1. A B C D
2. A B C D
3. A B C D
4. A B C D
5. A B C D
6. A B C D
7. A B C D
8. A B C D
9. A B C D
10. A B C D
11. A B C D
12. A B C D
13. A B C D
14. A B C D
15. A B C D
16. A B C D
17. A B C D
18. A B C D
19. A B C D
20. A B C D
21. A B C D
22. A B C D

23. A B C D
24. A B C D
25. A B C D
26. A B C D
27. A B C D
28. A B C D
29. A B C D
30. A B C D
31. A B C D
32. A B C D
33. A B C D
34. A B C D
35. A B C D
36. A B C D
37. A B C D
38. A B C D
39. A B C D
40. A B C D
41. A B C D
42. A B C D
43. A B C D
44. A B C D

Completely darken bubbles with a No. 2 pencil. If you make a mistake, be sure to erase mark completely. Erase all stray marks.

Test ③ Start with number 1 for each new section.
If a section has fewer questions than answer spaces, leave the extra answer spaces blank.

Section 3—Mathematics: No Calculator

1. Ⓐ Ⓑ Ⓒ Ⓓ
2. Ⓐ Ⓑ Ⓒ Ⓓ
3. Ⓐ Ⓑ Ⓒ Ⓓ
4. Ⓐ Ⓑ Ⓒ Ⓓ
5. Ⓐ Ⓑ Ⓒ Ⓓ
6. Ⓐ Ⓑ Ⓒ Ⓓ
7. Ⓐ Ⓑ Ⓒ Ⓓ
8. Ⓐ Ⓑ Ⓒ Ⓓ
9. Ⓐ Ⓑ Ⓒ Ⓓ
10. Ⓐ Ⓑ Ⓒ Ⓓ
11. Ⓐ Ⓑ Ⓒ Ⓓ
12. Ⓐ Ⓑ Ⓒ Ⓓ
13. Ⓐ Ⓑ Ⓒ Ⓓ
14. Ⓐ Ⓑ Ⓒ Ⓓ
15. Ⓐ Ⓑ Ⓒ Ⓓ

16. 17. 18. 19. 20.

Section 4—Mathematics: Calculator

1. Ⓐ Ⓑ Ⓒ Ⓓ
2. Ⓐ Ⓑ Ⓒ Ⓓ
3. Ⓐ Ⓑ Ⓒ Ⓓ
4. Ⓐ Ⓑ Ⓒ Ⓓ
5. Ⓐ Ⓑ Ⓒ Ⓓ
6. Ⓐ Ⓑ Ⓒ Ⓓ
7. Ⓐ Ⓑ Ⓒ Ⓓ
8. Ⓐ Ⓑ Ⓒ Ⓓ
9. Ⓐ Ⓑ Ⓒ Ⓓ
10. Ⓐ Ⓑ Ⓒ Ⓓ
11. Ⓐ Ⓑ Ⓒ Ⓓ
12. Ⓐ Ⓑ Ⓒ Ⓓ
13. Ⓐ Ⓑ Ⓒ Ⓓ
14. Ⓐ Ⓑ Ⓒ Ⓓ
15. Ⓐ Ⓑ Ⓒ Ⓓ
16. Ⓐ Ⓑ Ⓒ Ⓓ
17. Ⓐ Ⓑ Ⓒ Ⓓ
18. Ⓐ Ⓑ Ⓒ Ⓓ
19. Ⓐ Ⓑ Ⓒ Ⓓ
20. Ⓐ Ⓑ Ⓒ Ⓓ
21. Ⓐ Ⓑ Ⓒ Ⓓ
22. Ⓐ Ⓑ Ⓒ Ⓓ
23. Ⓐ Ⓑ Ⓒ Ⓓ
24. Ⓐ Ⓑ Ⓒ Ⓓ
25. Ⓐ Ⓑ Ⓒ Ⓓ
26. Ⓐ Ⓑ Ⓒ Ⓓ
27. Ⓐ Ⓑ Ⓒ Ⓓ
28. Ⓐ Ⓑ Ⓒ Ⓓ
29. Ⓐ Ⓑ Ⓒ Ⓓ
30. Ⓐ Ⓑ Ⓒ Ⓓ

31. 32. 33. 34. 35.

36. 37. 38.

Chapter 8
Practice Test 3:
Answers and
Explanations

PRACTICE TEST 3 ANSWER KEY

Section 1: Reading				Section 2: Writing & Language				Section 3: Math (No Calculator)				Section 4: Math (Calculator)			
1.	B	27.	C	1.	D	23.	D	1.	C	11.	D	1.	C	20.	B
2.	A	28.	C	2.	A	24.	C	2.	A	12.	C	2.	D	21.	A
3.	B	29.	A	3.	C	25.	C	3.	B	13.	B	3.	B	22.	B
4.	D	30.	B	4.	A	26.	D	4.	B	14.	A	4.	C	23.	D
5.	B	31.	A	5.	A	27.	D	5.	C	15.	D	5.	B	24.	B
6.	C	32.	B	6.	A	28.	B	6.	B	16.	4	6.	D	25.	D
7.	D	33.	D	7.	D	29.	D	7.	B	17.	1 or 3	7.	D	26.	C
8.	B	34.	D	8.	B	30.	B	8.	D	18.	50	8.	C	27.	A
9.	D	35.	A	9.	D	31.	D	9.	D	19.	$\frac{5}{13}$	9.	B	28.	D
10.	D	36.	C	10.	C	32.	B	10.	A			10.	B	29.	B
11.	D	37.	A	11.	C	33.	A			20.	110	11.	A	30.	C
12.	B	38.	C	12.	C	34.	D					12.	A	31.	3
13.	D	39.	D	13.	A	35.	A					13.	D	32.	5 or 6
14.	A	40.	B	14.	B	36.	A					14.	C	33.	25.2
15.	A	41.	C	15.	B	37.	B					15.	B	34.	40
16.	C	42.	B	16.	D	38.	B					16.	A	35.	1,000
17.	B	43.	B	17.	A	39.	C					17.	C	36.	$\frac{7}{12}$ or .583
18.	C	44.	B	18.	D	40.	C					18.	C		
19.	D	45.	C	19.	A	41.	D					19.	B	37.	20
20.	D	46.	C	20.	B	42.	B							38.	9
21.	A	47.	A	21.	B	43.	D								
22.	D	48.	A	22.	D	44.	B								
23.	D	49.	D												
24.	D	50.	A												
25.	B	51.	C												
26.	B	52.	C												

Go to PrincetonReview.com to score your exam. Alternatively, for self-assessment tables, please turn to page 909.

PRACTICE TEST 3 EXPLANATIONS

Section 1: Reading

1. **B**   The question asks for the best summary of the passage. Do this question after answering the specific questions. Look for an answer choice that matches the passage as a whole; eliminate answer choices that are true but too specific. The first paragraph describes the party, the second paragraph gives the back story of the woman Lady Windermere is talking to, and the rest of the text relates their conversation. Choice (A) is true, but only refers to the last part of the text. Eliminate (A). Choice (B) could be true, as it reflects all three parts of the text. Keep (B) for now. Choice (C) is true, but only refers to the first part of the text. Eliminate (C). Choice (D) uses the right words but has the wrong meaning: this is her last reception before Easter, not her last reception ever, and she only jokingly refers to the need to flee danger. Eliminate (D). The correct answer is (B).

2. **A**   The question asks what the word *smartest* means in line 5. Go back to the text, find the word *smartest*, and mark it out. Carefully read the surrounding text to determine another word that would fit in the blank based on the context of the passage. Here, *smartest* has to do with a "nice appearance." Choice (A), *most fashionable*, is possible; keep it for now. Choice (B), *most clever*, is another meaning of *smartest*. Eliminate (B). Choice (C), *most painful*, recalls another meaning of the verb "to smart." Eliminate (C). Choice (D), *brightest*, is another potential meaning for *smartest* but does not relate to appearance. Eliminate (D). The correct answer is (A).

3. **B**   The question asks about the purpose of the description of *gorgeous peeresses…violent Radicals, popular preachers…eminent sceptics* and *a perfect bevy of bishops*. Look for that description in context. It is located in paragraph 1, following this sentence: *It was certainly a wonderful medley of people. Medley* means *blend*, and so the description seems to support the claim that it was a wonderful mix of people. Choice (A) could be true, since political and artistic types are indeed two different groups. Choice (B) is even better, since the phrase *variety of people* can refer to *peeresses, Radicals, preachers, sceptics,* and *bishops*. Eliminate (A) for being too narrow in scope. Choice (C) is also narrow in scope, reducing the list to women and men, which is not the point of the description. Eliminate (C). Choice (D) can be eliminated because there is no explicit difference set up between any classes in the text. The correct answer is (B).

4. **D**   The question asks what the narrator implies about Lady Windermere's reception. Use lead words and the order of the questions to find the window. Q3 asks about lines 11–14, so scan the first paragraph looking for information about *Lady Windermere's reception*. The first paragraph indicates that it was Lady Windermere's last reception before Easter and that the house was *even more crowded than usual*. Several of the guests are described, and lines 18–19 state, *it was one of Lady Windermere's best nights*. Eliminate answer choices that don't match the prediction. Eliminate (A) because *sparsely attended* means that "few people came," and this is contradicted by the passage. Eliminate (B) because there is no evidence that the reception was *dignified*; in fact, one guest is described as *talking bad French at the top of her voice, and laughing immoderately*. Choice (C) is a Right Answer, Wrong Question trap: the passage later mentions *a series of reckless escapades*, but those were things Lady Windermere did when she was young. This phrase doesn't describe the *reception*, so eliminate (C). Keep (D) because the reception is described as *was one of Lady Windermere's best nights*; therefore, it was *a success*. The correct answer is (D).

5.   **B**   The question asks what *Lady Windermere is best described as having*. Use lead words and the order of the questions to find the window. The answer to question 4 came from lines 18–19, so scan the second paragraph looking for information describing *Lady Windermere*. Lines 26–34 describe Lady Windermere as *beautiful*, with blue eyes and *heavy coils of golden hair* that *gave to her face something of the frame of a saint, with not a little of the fascination of a sinner*. Lines 35–39 say, *Early in life she had discovered the important truth that nothing looks so like innocence as an indiscretion; and by a series of reckless escapades, half of them quite harmless, she had acquired all the privileges of a personality*. Eliminate answer choices that don't match the passage. Eliminate (A) because nothing in the passage suggests that Lady Windermere was *tactless*. Keep (B) because it matches the passage. Eliminate (C) because there is no evidence that Lady Windermere is *frugal*, which means "careful about spending money." Eliminate (D) because nothing in the passage suggests that she is *shy*. The correct answer is (B).

6.   **C**   The question asks what the word *start* means in line 50. Go back to the text, find the word *start*, and mark it out. Carefully read the surrounding text to determine another word that would fit in the blank based on the context of the passage. The Duchess is showing that she is surprised by something. *Start* must mean something like "surprise." Choices (A), *opening*, and (B), *commencement*, refer to another meaning of "start." Eliminate (A) and (B). Choice (C), *twitch*, refers to a movement that one might make when surprised, so keep it for now. Choice (D), *procedure*, is irrelevant, so eliminate (D). The correct answer is (C).

7.   **D**   The question asks what the *narrator indicates about the chiromantist*. This is the first question in a paired set, but it is easy to find, so it can be done on its own. Use lead words and the order of the questions to find the window. Question 6 asks about line 50, so start with line 51 and scan the passage for the lead word *chiromantist*. In lines 51–59, Gladys (who is Lady Windermere) says of the chiromantist, "*I can't live without him*" and "*He comes to see my hand twice a week regularly*." Eliminate answers that don't match the passage. Eliminate (A) because there is no evidence that the chiromantist is *foreign*. Eliminate (B) because there is no evidence that the chiromantist is *preying on the partygoers*. Eliminate (C) because there is no evidence that the chiromantist is *well-known*. Keep (D) because Lady Windermere says that the chiromantist comes to see her *twice a week regularly*, which suggests that he is a *frequent visitor* at her home. The correct answer is (D).

8.   **B**   The question is the best evidence question in a paired set. Because the previous question was easy to find, simply look at the lines used to answer Q7. Line 57 provided the evidence for the previous question: "*He comes to see my hand twice a week regularly*." Eliminate (A), (C), and (D). The correct answer is (B).

9.   **D**   The question asks about Lady Windermere. Notice that the following question is a best evidence question, so this question and Q10 can be answered in tandem. Look at the answers for Q10 first. The lines for (10A) reference Lady Windermere's *last reception before Easter*, which could connect to *the end of her hostessing* in (9A). Draw a line between them. In the lines for (10B), Lady Windermere asks a question. The text does not support any of the answers for Q9, so eliminate it. The lines in (10C) support the idea that Lady Windermere is serious about the fortune-teller, which is not an idea presented in Q9, so eliminate (10C). The lines in (10D) show Lady Windermere's off-hand response to the Duchess's question about the chiromantist's fortunes. Her response is not serious, so (10D) could connect with (9D). Read the two remaining pairs closely, looking for the one that best answers the question. Notice that (9A) says Lady Windermere is *nearing the end of her hostessing days*, while the text simply says it's the *last reception before Easter*. These two answers don't accurately support each other, so eliminate (9A) and (10A). The correct answers are (9D) and (10D).

10. **D** (See explanation above.)

11. **D** The question asks how the first paragraph fits in with the rest of the passage. This requires understanding of the whole passage, so do it last. The opening paragraph gives an overview of the growing disparity between individuals of high and low socioeconomic status. Eliminate (A) and (B), since neither mentions a disparity or discrepancy. Choice (C) does acknowledge a discrepancy, but there are no solutions offered throughout the course of the passage, making this choice incorrect. Choice (D) highlights the discrepancy and mentions the research that permeates the rest of the passage, so keep it. The correct answer is (D).

12. **B** The question asks for an *advantage of individuals with higher socioeconomic status* that is *explicitly* stated. This is the first question in a paired set, but it is a specific question, so it can be done on its own. Use the order of the questions to find the window. Q11 asks about the first paragraph, and Q13 asks about the third paragraph, so scan the second paragraph, looking for information about advantages of people with high socioeconomic status. Lines 31–35 state that *individuals belonging to higher status positions in society benefit from greater access to material and social resources, increased workplace opportunities, and reduced discrimination based on their social status.* Eliminate answers that don't match this prediction. Choice (A) is a Deceptive Language trap answer: the passage states that *stereotype threat* is experienced by *lower status individuals*, rather than by higher status individuals. Eliminate (A). Keep (B) because it matches the prediction. Choice (C) is a Deceptive Language trap answer: the passage states that higher status individuals are more likely to *hold public office*, not to engage in *political activism*. Eliminate (C). Choice (D) is a Deceptive Language trap answer: the passage states that higher status individuals *benefit from...reduced discrimination*; it doesn't state that *discrimination* is an advantage. Eliminate (D). The correct answer is (B).

13. **D** The question is the best evidence question in a paired set. Because the previous question was a specific question, simply look at the lines used to answer Q12. Lines 31–35 provided the prediction for Q12: *individuals belonging to higher status positions in society benefit from...increased workplace opportunities...based on their social status.* Eliminate (A), (B), and (C). The correct answer is (D).

14. **A** The question asks for evidence that *supports the conclusion that members of Congress are likely to be of high social status.* Use the line references given in the answer choices to find a statement that supports this claim. The lines for (A) state, *High status individuals also tend to hold public office more than their low status counterparts.* A seat in *Congress* is a *public office*, so this statement supports the conclusion; keep (A). The lines for (B) discuss the *beliefs* of high-status individuals, but they don't indicate that *members of Congress are likely to be of* high status. Eliminate (B). The lines for (C) discuss high-status individuals' beliefs and what they are likely to *advocate* for, but they don't indicate that *members of Congress are likely to be of* high status. Eliminate (C). The lines for (D) indicate that *social status is a reliable predictor of support for economic inequality*, but they don't indicate that *members of Congress are likely to be of* high status. Eliminate (D). The correct answer is (A).

15. **A** The question asks for the function of the third paragraph. Look for clues in that window. The text discusses high socioeconomic status and explains *why they hold a potentially unfair advantage* from their viewpoint. These individuals have *meritocratic beliefs*, attributing their successes to *a fair application of effort, talent, and skill*. This fits (A), which states that these individuals cite reasons other than socioeconomic status for their success. Choice (B) states that there is equal opportunity for both high and low socioeconomic status, which contradicts the passage. Choice

(C) is extreme and offensive, implying that the high socioeconomic status individuals purposely repress those less fortunate, and (D) is too strong and over encompassing as well. Eliminate (B), (C), and (D). The correct answer is (A).

16. **C**   Lines 42–45 were used to answer the previous question. The correct answer is (C).

17. **B**   The question asks what the word *bestow* means in line 47. Go back to the text, find the word *bestow*, and mark it out. Carefully read the surrounding text to determine another word that would fit in the blank based on the context of the passage. This part of the text talks about the *benefits* of *elevated social positions*. The correct answer should mean something like "give." Eliminate (A) because it's the opposite of *give*. Choice (B) might work, so hang on to it. Choice (C) might initially look attractive, but a closer reading of the window shows that these individuals try to explain their benefits as something earned, but they actually aren't. Eliminate (C). Choice (D) does not match the prediction. The correct answer is (B).

18. **C**   The question asks what the word *aligns* means in line 65. Go back to the text, find the word *aligns*, and mark it out. Carefully read the surrounding text to determine another word that would fit in the blank based on the context of the passage. The text talks about the *present research* doing something with *mounting evidence* about *reliable predictors*. The missing word must mean something like "agree." Now use the prediction to go through the answer choices and eliminate anything that doesn't match the prediction. Choice (A) can be eliminated because *arranges* has nothing to do with *agrees*. Choice (B) does not match the prediction and can be eliminated. Choice (C) matches the prediction. Keep it. Choice (D) can be eliminated. The correct answer is (C)

19. **D**   The question asks about data in the figure. Go straight to the figure and use the data points to POE. Find precise data points on the figure to support keeping or eliminating answer choices. Choice (A) can be eliminated because Panel B shows clearly that Democratic males are more likely to support the legislation than their female counterparts. Choices (B) and (C) are both incorrect because no information is given about the number of individuals who answered the polls to obtain this data. Choice (D) is supported by both Panel A and Panel B. The correct answer is (D).

20. **D**   The question asks what the figures suggest about people *likely to sponsor legislation supporting economic inequality*. The figures show an elected official's tendency to support or not support legislation supporting economic inequality, so a positive number would be more likely to support such legislation, while a negative number would be less likely to support it. Consistently, Republicans are in the positive range, while the Democrats are in the negative range, supporting (D). Choice (A) is incorrect because, while it may be true based on the passage, it is not supported by the figures. Several socioeconomic and social categories are mentioned in these figures, but they are not equally supporting or opposing such legislation. Choice (C) is also incorrect because Democratic females and individuals with low wealth are the most likely to *oppose* such legislation, not support it. The correct answer is (D).

21. **A**   The question asks about the sequence of events in the passage. This is a general question, so save it until after the specific questions are answered. The passage begins with the songbirds' migration and then discusses experiments about the migration that provided some information but left other questions unanswered. Choice (A) works because the observed phenomenon is the birds' nocturnal migration and decreased sleep need during migratory states. There is more research to be done, as the lab is a controlled environment and migration happens in the wild. Choice (B) is partially true, but the portion about inconclusive results makes it incorrect, since the study did reveal strong findings. Choice (C) is incorrect because nothing is revolutionized

or disproved. Similarly, (D) is incorrect because there is never a second study mentioned in the passage. The correct answer is (A).

22. **D** The question asks what the word *reconcile* means in line 21. Go back to the text, find the word *reconcile*, and mark it out. Carefully read the surrounding text to determine another word that would fit in the blank based on the context of the passage. This part of the text talks about researchers trying to bring together conflicting observations that *sleep-deprived fliers appear no worse for wear* and that there's *evidence linking sleep deprivation to impaired neurobehavioral and physiological function*. The missing word must mean something like "bring together." Choices (A) and (B) are both definitions of *reconcile*, but neither works in this context. Eliminate both of those answers. Choice (C) might initially sound good, because *clarify* might help researchers figure out the disparity between the observations, but it doesn't fit the context of needing to *bring together* the theories. Choice (D), *integrate*, does mean *bring together*. The correct answer is (D).

23. **D** The question asks which statement *best captures an assumption Ruth Benca made in setting up her research*. This is the first question in a paired set, so it can be done in tandem with Q24. Look at the answer choices for Q24 first. The lines for (24A) indicate that when migrating, most birds *fly under cover of night*. This statement is not an assumption of Ruth Benca's research, and it doesn't support any of the answers to Q23. Eliminate (24A). The lines for (24B) discuss the results of a *study*, but it is not Ruth Benca's study. Therefore, (24B) does not provide evidence for Q23. Eliminate (24B). The lines for (24C) indicate that the sparrows studied by Ruth Benca *fly nearly 2,700 miles twice a year between their Alaska and southern California homes*. This statement is given as an established fact; it is not an *assumption* made by Benca, nor does it support any of the answers for Q23, so eliminate (24C). The lines for (24D) state, *These results suggest that wild songbirds drastically reduce sleep time during migration, though Benca and colleagues concede it's impossible to know for sure without recording the birds in action*. This statement indicates that Benca made an assumption that the birds she studied in the laboratory were exhibiting behavior similar to that of birds in the wild. These lines support (23D). Draw a line connecting (23D) and (24D). Without any support in the answers from Q24, (23A), (23B), and (23C) can be eliminated. The correct answers are (23D) and (24D).

24. **D** (See explanation above.)

25. **B** The question asks about Neils Rattenborg's findings and what they serve to do. Carefully read the fourth paragraph to see what Rattenborg found. His tests found that birds in the *nonmigrating state suffered cognitive deficits when sleep-deprived* but were able to *maintain cognitive function* when faced with *ongoing sleep loss in the migratory state*. These findings dovetail nicely with what Benca observed in the field. Eliminate any answers that have nothing to do with this prediction. Choice (A) can be eliminated because the results support the hypothesis rather than upset it. Choice (B) is almost exactly what the prediction is, so keep it. Choice (C) can be eliminated, because no previous research was introduced. Choice (D) can be eliminated because there are no differences that are underscored. The correct answer is (B).

26. **B** The question asks about the researchers' reaction to the birds' *unprecedented ability to maintain cognitive function*. Use the line reference to find the window for this question. The passage says that *Benca and colleagues concede it's impossible to know for sure without recording the birds in action*. The answer must have something to do with conceding a lack of information. Choice (A) might initially look good because it contains the word *impossible*, but that answer choice is too extreme. It's not impossible to know, just impossible to know without additional information. Eliminate (A). Choice (B) mentions still having *other questions*, which is a good paraphrase of the prediction, so keep it. Choice (C) can be eliminated because that observation of *cognitive*

deficits happened before, not after as a reaction. Choice (D), *consulted other researchers*, is not mentioned anywhere in the text. The correct answer is (B).

27. **C**   The question asks about a factor that would necessitate further research. Using chronology, the answer to this question must come after the noted results from the research, so look around lines 50–56. The text says that the additional answers to the cognition question would be *impossible to know for sure without recording the birds in action*. The study tested the birds in a lab setting, so further research must require birds actually flying and migrating. Choice (C) is the only answer that addresses this. The correct answer is (C).

28. **C**   The question asks what the word *improbable* means in line 68. Go back to the text, find the word *improbable*, and mark it out. Carefully read the surrounding text to determine another word that would fit in the blank based on the context of the passage. This part of the text talks about *the longstanding mysteries of the sleepless flight* of the migrating birds, indicating that their migration is something of notable interest because of its unusual nature. The correct answer must mean something like "unlikely" or "impressive." Choices (A), (B), and (D) could be possible meanings for *improbable* in other contexts, but the other meanings imply the journey isn't real. Only (C), *remarkable*, fits the context of the passage. The correct answer is (C).

29. **A**   The question asks what can *be inferred about songbirds*. Notice that the following question is a best evidence question, so this question and Q30 can be answered in tandem. Look at the answers for Q30 first. The line for (30A) asks about *sleep walking*. This makes (29B) look good, but there is no mention of actual sleepwalkers in the passage. Eliminate (30A). Next, consider the lines for (30B). The text refers to *increased restlessness at night during the migratory season*. This matches the idea about *activity levels* in (29A). Connect answers (29A) and (30B). The lines in (30C) mention songbirds' *imperviousness* to *sleep deprivation* (which means that they are not affected strongly by sleep deprivation). This doesn't support any answers in Q29, so eliminate it. The lines in (30D) talk about the *role of sleep*, not songbirds, so eliminate it too. The correct answers are (29A) and (30B).

30. **B**   (See explanation above.)

31. **A**   The question asks what the word *feature* means in line 10. Go back to the text, find the word *feature*, and mark it out. Carefully read the surrounding text to determine another word that would fit in the blank based on the context of the passage. The text mentions *report cards* with *numbers or phrases* on them. The correct answer must mean something like "show." Notice that the word is used as a verb. Choice (A), *present*, might look like the noun, but as a verb, it matches the prediction, so keep it. Choice (B), *attribute*, does not fit the prediction, so eliminate it. Choice (C), *report*, matches the prediction, so keep it. Choice (D), *promote*, does not fit the prediction, so eliminate it. Consider the remaining answer choices, (A) and (C). *Report* means to tell, to convey information; *present* more generally means to give or to show. Although these might initially seem very close, the report cards are not reporting the phrases. They are using the phrases to communicate performance expectations. Eliminate (C). The correct answer is (A).

32. **B**   The question asks for a reasonable inference about what the authors of Passage 1 believe about a standards-based report card. Notice that the following question is a best evidence question, so this question and Q33 can be answered in tandem. Look at the answers for Q33 first. The lines in (33A) mention report card *changes*, but not details, so eliminate it. The lines in (33B) refer to *performance expectations* on standards-based report cards. This describes the report cards but doesn't express a belief about them, so eliminate it. The lines in (33C) mention *third-grade mathematics*, which makes (32D) look good, but it doesn't mention *high school* in comparison. Eliminate (33C). Now consider the lines for (33D). They state: *Such a report card actually pro-*

vides more detailed, specific information than a traditional grade. This corresponds to the *specific way for teachers to evaluate students* as in (32B), so connect these answers. The correct answers are (32B) and (33D).

33. **D** (See explanation above.)

34. **D** The question asks what Passage 2 states about the new approach to grading. Notice that the following question is a best evidence question, so this question and Q35 can be answered in tandem. Look at the answers for Q35 first. The lines in (35A) refer to a contrast between the new approach's criterion-based grading versus grading on a curve. This supports (34D), so draw a line connecting them. The lines in (35B) are deceptive: they refer to a dilemma, which would seem to support (34A), but the dilemma refers to the old, curve system, not the new one. Eliminate (35B). The lines in (35C) again refer to the inferiority of the old, curve system. Eliminate (35C). The lines in (35D) refer to plans to bring back teacher comments, and to recognize student effort and attitude. This does not support anything in Q34, so eliminate it. Only one pair of connected answers is remaining. The correct answers are (34D) and (35A).

35. **A** (See explanation above.)

36. **C** The question asks what the word *scrap* means in line 53. Go back to the text, find the word *scrap*, and mark it out. Carefully read the surrounding text to determine another word that would fit in the blank based on the context of the passage. The text refers to *letter grades* as something people are *far from ready* to change to *standards-based report cards*. The correct answer must mean something like "get rid of." Choices (A), *save*, (B), *fragment*, and (D), *detach*, do not fit this prediction, although they do recall the noun form meanings of the word *scrap*. Only (C), *discard*, fits the prediction. The correct answer is (C).

37. **A** The question asks what the author of Passage 2 says about the use of standards-based report cards in elementary schools. Since it is not clear from what part of the passage the answer will come, this question can be answered later. Look for discussion of elementary schools in particular. There is no mention of elementary schools until paragraph 3, and elementary schools are not mentioned again in paragraph 4, so the correct answer has to be a restatement of something said in paragraph 3. Choice (A) matches paragraph 3's mention of *plans to expand standards-based report cards to its four middle schools from its elementary schools, where they have been used since 2006,* even though the paragraph is about the delay of such plans. Keep it for now. Choice (B) is the right answer to the wrong question, because it matches the resistance encountered to instituting the report cards in the middle school, rather than the elementary school. Eliminate (B). Choice (C) is too strong: there is no comparison between the standards-based report cards and other systems in Passage 2. Eliminate (C). Choice (D) goes too far. They have been implemented, but the text does not specify whether they have been successfully implemented in grade schools. Eliminate (D). The correct answer is (A).

38. **C** The question asks which concern not mentioned in Passage 1 is addressed by the given quote used by the author of Passage 2. First, locate the quote in context and predict an answer based on the text. The quote describes a weakness of the older system of grading on a curve, namely how it's hard to know *whether anybody has learned anything.* Because they are just compared to each other, *they could all have done miserably, just some less miserably than others.* Eliminate any answer choices that don't address this issue. Choice (A) is about report cards rather than grading on a curve, so eliminate (A). Choice (B) is about letter grades versus number grades, so eliminate that answer. Choice (C) mentions students *graded on a curve,* so keep (C). Choice (D) contrasts *traditional report cards* with *standards-based report cards.* Eliminate (D). The concern about grading on a curve is not mentioned in Passage 1. The correct answer is (C).

39. **D**   The question asks about the general relationship between Passage 1 and Passage 2. Answer it after answering the specific questions about Passage 1 only and Passage 2 only. First, consider the tone and opinions of both passages. Both of them report on new report cards and have a neutral-to-positive tone. Eliminate answer choices that misrepresent these facts. Choice (A) indicates a match in tone, but Passage 1 does not contain an argument, and Passage 2 does not contain responses to that argument. Eliminate (A). Choice (B) is completely wrong in tone, so eliminate (B). Choice (C) could match in tone, but there are no alternative conclusions drawn in one passage versus the other. Eliminate (C). Choice (D) matches in tone, and Passage 2 does contain further information about the new report cards, so select (D). The correct answer is (D).

40. **B**   The question asks what the authors of both passages would likely agree on regarding standards-based report cards. To answer it, consider what the authors of both passages actually say about these report cards, and base the prediction on that evidence. Choice (A) references *parental insistence*, which sounds something like the parental complaints mentioned in Passage 2. But the only thing Passage 1 says about parents is that they *may find the change disconcerting*. Because Passage 1 provides no evidence about possible agreement with Passage 2 on this point, (A) can be eliminated. Choice (B) references *some resistance*, which both Passages 1 and 2 also do, and (B) states that the new report cards may provide more information than previous systems; both Passages 1 and 2 also do this. Since both passages state these things explicitly, it is reasonable to assume that both authors would agree on this point. Keep (B), but also keep checking, in case something better comes along. Choice (C) references *grading on a curve*, which is not mentioned in Passage 1, so eliminate (C) on that basis. Also, it is not known whether the new report cards *remove* the other system, so (C) is wrong on that count as well. Choice (D) sounds reasonable up to the comma, but the claim that the new report cards are *superior* to alternatives is not supported by statements in either passage. Eliminate (D). The correct answer is (B).

41. **C**   The question asks how the author of Passage 1 would most likely respond to points made in the final paragraph of Passage 2. To answer this question, first review the final paragraph of Passage 2, which talks about responding to parental complaints by introducing benchmarks for each marking period, bringing back teacher comments, and looking for ways to recognize student effort and attitude. Then consider what the author of Passage 1 actually says that is relevant to these points. In the second paragraph of Passage 1, the author states that a standards-based report card provides more information than does a traditional report card, which shows clear support for the new system. But in the third paragraph of Passage 1, the author also shows support for report cards *that combine traditional grades and information about progress toward standards* and cites a researcher who supports including *teacher judgments about students' academic progress, growth, intellectual character, and work habits*. Based on this evidence, it seems the author of Passage 1 would support the changes mentioned in the fourth paragraph of Passage 2. Choice (A) could be true, but there isn't strong textual support for such sympathy. Keep (A) for now, just in case. Choice (B) can be eliminated: the author of Passage 1 would likely support the use of benchmarks, not oppose it. Choice (C) looks good, as it fits the evidence-based prediction made above, so keep it, and eliminate (A), as (C) is better. Choice (D) is too strong: the author of Passage 1 cites an author who supports including intellectual character. This is not the same thing as the author of Passage 1 *insist[ing]* that this factor be included. Eliminate (D). The correct answer is (C).

42. **B**   The question asks about the impact of the words *must, exhibited,* and *reproduced* on the tone of the paragraph. Look for specific evidence in the text indicating the authors' goal of the paragraph. The paragraph is informational—the authors give straightforward information about a hypothesis and the observed results of the experiments. Choice (A) can be eliminated because the authors aren't *hopeful* or trying to convince readers of *uncertain results*. Choice (B) goes

along with the prediction based on the text, so don't eliminate it. Choice (C) can be eliminated because the authors are straightforward but not argumentative. Choice (D) does not work because there is no indication that the authors want to *instruct others in the reproduction of simulated bat trajectories*. The correct answer is (B).

43. **B**   The question asks about the theory *experiments were performed in order to verify*. Notice that the following question is a best evidence question, so this question and Q44 can be answered in tandem. Look at the answers for Q44 first. The lines in (44A) mention one *integrator* that outperformed others. Although (43C) also mentions *integrators*, the text is giving information, not outlining a theory. Eliminate (44A). Next, consider the lines in (44B). They state: *An important prediction of our model is that sensory noise determines motor performance*, describing the predicted theory in full. This idea is paraphrased in (43B), where *sensory errors* affect *movements*. Connect these two answers. The lines in (44C) describe the *new experiments* without mentioning the theory again. Eliminate (44C). The lines in (44D) talk about *gain parameters in light versus dark*. This sounds like the *light conditions* and *gain parameters* in (43D). However, (43D) refers to *optimal gain parameters*, whereas the text is referring to *a light level that is considered optimal*. Since (44D) doesn't fully support any answer from Q43, eliminate it. The correct answers are (43B) and (44B).

44. **B**   (See explanation above.)

45. **C**   The question asks about the inaccuracy addressed by the *single exponential integrator*. Find this phrase in the text, and read the window to determine what the integrator does. According to the text, the exponential integrator models bats' *noise suppression* strategy better than others. The answer should have something to do with an error of *noise suppression*. Choice (A) can be eliminated because information is not lost. Choice (B) can be eliminated because it's too specific. The integrator deals with all sensory noise, not just *sub-optimal light*. Choice (C) can be kept because it's a solid rewording of the prediction. Choice (D) can be eliminated because it's the opposite of the prediction. The correct answer is (C).

46. **C**   Lines 33–36 were used to answer the previous question. The correct answer is (C).

47. **A**   The question asks what the word *fidelity* means in line 36. Go back to the text, find the word *fidelity*, and mark it out. Carefully read the surrounding text to determine another word that would fit in the blank based on the context of the passage. The text states the *integrator* was *successful* at showing the *bat's flight trajectories*. The correct answer must mean something like "closely imitating the original." Choice (A) could work, so keep it. Choice (B) can be eliminated because the results were not *lower quality*. Choice (C) can be eliminated because there is no evidence of *complete perfection*. Choice (D) might look okay on its own, but (A) is better, because the correct answer should be as close to *really accurate* as possible. The *reproduction of details* matches the text's description that the integrator *reproduced…trajectories with high fidelity*. The correct answer is (A).

48. **A**   The question asks about the *main purpose* of the fourth paragraph. Read the paragraph to determine what the main idea is. The researchers hypothesized that the bats were using *a noise-suppression strategy…to overcome the noise*. Then they determined this strategy was the *simple exponential integrator*. Choice (A) completely describes this, so keep it. Choice (B) is deceptive, using several words and phrases from the text without actually matching the prediction. Eliminate it. No *pitfalls of a theory* are mentioned, so eliminate (C). Choice (D) does not match the text since the authors found the simple exponential integrator outperformed the uniform integrator. The correct answer is (A).

49. **D**   The question asks about the assumption made about *highly curved flight trajectories*. In the final sentence of the passage, the authors summarize their findings as a *surprising conclusion* that the

curved trajectories *are due to sensory limitations—not motor limitations.* Therefore, the flight patterns are a result of a limitation the bat deals with. Choice (A) can be eliminated, because the trajectories were normal for bats with the introduction of sensory noise. Choice (B) can be eliminated because it's too extreme and not supported by the text. Choice (C) doesn't make sense. The researchers compared flight trajectories of bats in light and dark, but no flight trajectory replaced another one. Choice (D) matches the prediction because the authors were surprised that sensory limitations rather than motor limitations caused the curved trajectory, so they must have previously thought the curved trajectories were caused by the physicality of the bat. The correct answer is (D).

50.   **A**   The question asks about the effect of adding a *noise-suppression strategy to trials simulated with noise*, based on both the passage and the figures. The figures do not include the phrase *noise-suppression strategy*, so look for that phrase in the text. Lines 27–30 state, *We therefore hypothesized that the bat must use a noise-suppression strategy and integrate (average) over several sensory measurements to overcome the noise.* Based on these lines, the trials with the *noise-suppression strategy* must be in the figure labeled *Integration*, so look at the second figure. According to the key, the light grey dotted lines represent tests *simulated with noise*, so focus on those lines. There are many of the light grey dotted lines, and they all *converge* (come together at a point) with the original trajectory. Therefore, the figures support (A). The passage also supports (A): lines 33–36 state, *This simple exponential integrator exhibited successful noise suppression and reproduced the bat's flight trajectories with high fidelity.* Keep (A) and eliminate (B), (C), and (D). The correct answer is (A).

51.   **C**   The question asks about the trajectory that most nearly *matches the original trajectory.* The *original trajectory* line is the dotted black line. Find the line that most closely follows that one. The *Integration* lines are all much closer to the original trajectory than any of the *No Integration* lines, so eliminate (A) and (D). Look to see which line most closely lines up with the *original trajectory* line in the *Integration* graphic. It's one of the gray lines, which are *simulated with noise*. The correct answer is (C).

52.   **C**   The question asks if the graph supports the authors' claim that bat flights in *optimal light conditions are more direct.* There is no evidence in the figure to show *optimal light conditions.* Eliminate (A) and (B). Choice (C) addresses the lack of information about optimal light conditions in the figure. Keep it. Choice (D) does not address optimal light specifically. Eliminate (D). The correct answer is (C).

Section 2: Writing and Language

1.   **D**   Note the question! The question asks which choice *provides the most appropriate introduction*, so it tests consistency of ideas. Determine the subject of the passage and find the answer that is consistent with that idea. The passage asks why people *trust the chicken…from the grocery store* and states that it is because of the FDA. Eliminate (A), (B), and (C) because they are not consistent with the passage's focus on *trust* and the FDA. Keep (D) because *safe* is consistent with the idea of *trust* that the passage says the FDA provides. The correct answer is (D).

2.   **A**   Apostrophes change in the answer choices, so this question tests apostrophe usage. When used with a noun, an apostrophe indicates possession. In this sentence, the *beginnings* belong to the agency, so there should be an apostrophe on *agency*. Eliminate (C). Nothing belongs to *beginnings* in this sentence, so no apostrophe is needed on that word; eliminate (B) and (D). The correct answer is (A).

3. **C** Prepositions change in the answer choices, so this question tests idioms. There is also the option to DELETE; consider this choice carefully as it is often the correct answer. A preposition is necessary to complete the sentence, so eliminate (D). Look at the phrase after the preposition to determine the correct idiom. Use POE and guess if there is more than one answer left. The correct idiom is *as we know it*. Eliminate (A) and (B). The correct answer is (C).

4. **A** Note the question! The question asks how to best combine the underlined sentences, so it tests precision and concision. The order of phrases changes in the answer choices, so look for the one with the most precise meaning. Choice (A) combines the ideas effectively, so keep it. Choice (B) uses the word *regulates* twice. There is no reason to repeat that verb, so eliminate (B). Choice (C) expresses the same idea as (A), but is less concise, so eliminate (C). Choice (D) uses the word *goods* twice, so eliminate (D). The correct answer is (A).

5. **A** Transitions and pronouns change in the answer choices, so this question could test consistency of pronouns or consistency of ideas. A transition must be consistent with the relationship between the ideas it connects. There is no conclusion in the second part of the sentence, so the word *thus* is not consistent with the sentence; eliminate (B). The pronouns in (A), (C), and (D) are all consistent with *fees*, the noun the underlined pronoun refers to. The first part of the sentence, *The FDA operates on a budget of nearly $5 billion a year, much of which is generated by user fees*, is an independent clause. As written, the second part of the sentence, *which come primarily from pharmaceutical companies, whose drugs require FDA approval*, is not an independent clause. Choice (A) correctly links these two ideas with a comma. Changing the pronoun from *which* to either *those* or *they* makes the second part of the sentence an independent clause. A comma alone cannot be used between two independent clauses, so eliminate (C) and (D). The correct answer is (A).

6. **A** Transitions change in the answer choices, so this question tests consistency of ideas. A transition must be consistent with the relationship between the ideas it connects. The paragraph before the transition explains the scope of the FDA and its budget. This paragraph talks about the people who *work* at the FDA. These ideas contrast with each other because the author indicates that people *are familiar with the FDA's warning labels* but that they don't know *who actually works there*. Choice (A) can indicate a contrast, so keep it. Eliminate (B), (C), and (D) because they are not contrasting transitions. The correct answer is (A).

7. **D** Note the question! The question asks which choice *best supports the statement made in the first part of the sentence*, so it tests consistency. Eliminate answers that are inconsistent with the purpose stated in the question. The first part of the sentence says *The FDA is certainly large*. Eliminate (C) because it is inconsistent with the idea that the FDA is *large*. Choices (A), (B), and (D) are all consistent with the idea of *large*, but neither the FDA's *approvals* nor its *role in reducing tobacco use* is consistent with the focus of the paragraph, which is about the people who work at the FDA. Eliminate (A) and (B). Choice (D) is consistent with both the first part of the sentence and the paragraph. The correct answer is (D).

8. **B** Note the question! The question asks whether a sentence should be added, so it tests consistency. If the new sentence is consistent with the ideas surrounding it, then it should be added. The paragraph discusses the *employees* of the FDA and *scientists* specifically. The new sentence lists types of scientists, so it is consistent with the main idea of the paragraph. Eliminate (C) and (D). Eliminate (A) because it does not accurately describe the new sentence. Choice (B) accurately states that the new sentence *gives some data that will be elaborated upon later in the paragraph*. The correct answer is (B).

9. **D** Vocabulary changes in the answer choices, so this question tests precision of word choice. There is also the option to DELETE; consider this choice carefully as it is often the correct answer. The sentence already contains the word *confident*, so there is no reason to repeat that word or idea. Eliminate (A). *Certainly* and *sureness* mean the same thing as *confident*, so eliminate (B) and (C). Choice (D) is concise and gives the sentence a precise meaning, so the underlined portion should be deleted. The correct answer is (D).

10. **C** The number of words changes in the answer choices, so this question tests concision. The sentence contains a list of three things: 1) *chemistry*, 2) *biology*, and 3) *physics*. The sentence says *a matter of* before the list, so there is no reason to repeat that phrase; eliminate (A). Eliminate (B) because the word *and* is needed to join the last item in the list. Keep (C) because it is concise, and it correctly lists the three items. Eliminate (D) because it uses the phrase *biological sciences*, which is inconsistent with the words *chemistry* and *physics*. The correct answer is (C).

11. **C** Verbs change in the answer choices, so this question tests consistency of verbs. A verb must be consistent with its subject and with the other verbs in the sentence. The subject of the verb is *thing* in the phrase *the truly remarkable thing about the FDA*, which is singular. To be consistent, the underlined verb must also be singular. Eliminate (A), (B), and (D) because they are all plural. The correct answer is (C).

12. **C** Pronouns change in the answer choices, so this question tests consistency of pronouns. A pronoun must be consistent in number with the noun it refers to. The underlined pronoun refers to the noun *professional hockey*, which is singular. To be consistent, the underlined pronoun must also be singular. Eliminate (B) because *themselves* is plural. *Professional hockey* is not a person, so it should be referred to as *it*, not *him* or *her*, so eliminate (D). Eliminate (A) because *its self* is incorrect; the correct way to write this idea is *itself*. The correct answer is (C).

13. **A** Note the question! The question asks which choice *provides the most logical conclusion to the sentence*, so it tests consistency of ideas. There is also the option to DELETE; consider this choice carefully as it is often the correct answer. Determine the subject of the first part of the sentence and find the answer that is consistent with that idea. The first part of the sentence states that *the name* of the hockey cup was changed *to commemorate the contributions of* Lord Stanley. Keep (A) because it explains why Lord Stanley was important to the sport of hockey. Eliminate (B) and (C) because they are not consistent with the paragraph's focus on hockey. Eliminate (D) because deleting the underlined portion makes the sentence less precise. The correct answer is (A).

14. **B** The number of words changes in the answer choices, so this question could test concision. Check the shortest answer first: (A) makes the sentence incomplete: *Just as the NHA had before, also competing annually for the Stanley Cup*. Eliminate (A). Choices (C) and (D) similarly make the sentence incomplete, so eliminate (C) and (D) as well. Choice (B) makes the sentence complete by adding a subject: *Just as the NHA had before, so too did the NHL compete annually for the Stanley Cup*. The correct answer is (B).

15. **B** Punctuation changes in the answer choices, so this question tests how to connect ideas with the appropriate punctuation. The first part of the sentence, *The Boston Bruins, established in 1924*, is not an independent clause. Eliminate (A) and (C) because semicolons and periods can only be used between two independent clauses. Eliminate (D) because a colon can only come after an independent clause. Choice (B) appropriately places a comma after the descriptive phrase *established in 1924* to separate it from the rest of the sentence. The correct answer is (B).

16. **D** Note the question! The question asks whether a sentence should be deleted, so it tests consistency. If the content of the sentence is consistent with the ideas surrounding it, then it should not be

deleted. The sentence explains that the NHL was *the only remaining league*, which is consistent with the idea later in the paragraph that the NHL had *dominion* over the hockey cup. The sentence should not be deleted, so eliminate (A) and (B). Eliminate (C) because this sentence does not *contain the central argument of the passage as a whole*. Choice (D) accurately states that the sentence is *relevant* to the ideas in this paragraph. The correct answer is (D).

17. **A** Note the question! The question asks which choice *best maintains the tone established in the passage*, so it tests consistency. Eliminate answers that are inconsistent with the purpose stated in the question. The first paragraph of the passage describes the NHL as *the pinnacle of hockey greatness*, and *the NHL's sole dominion* is described just before this sentence. The passage is also written with a formal tone. Choice (A), *supremacy*, is a good match with these ideas and tone, so keep it. Eliminate (B) and (D) because *awesomeness* and *swagger* are too informal for the tone of the passage. Eliminate (C) because *tyranny* is a very negative word suggesting that the author does not support the NHL, which is not consistent with the passage's tone.

18. **D** The length of the phrase around *Canadian teams* changes in the answer choices, so this question tests concision. The words *ascendant* and *dominant* have very similar meanings in this context, so there is no need to use both terms. Eliminate (A), (B), and (C). Choice (D) is concise and gives a precise meaning to the sentence. The correct answer is (D).

19. **A** Note the question! The question asks which choice *logically follows the previous sentence*, so it tests consistency. Eliminate answers that are inconsistent with the purpose stated in the question. The previous sentence states that *the league has 30 teams* today. Choice (A) is consistent with the idea of the number of teams in the league. Keep (A). Eliminate (B) because the author's *favorite team* is not consistent with the idea of how many teams are in the league. Eliminate (C) because information about which teams *have won the Stanley Cup in recent years* does not relate to the number of teams in the league. Eliminate (D) because *places with no natural ice* is inconsistent with the number of teams. The correct answer is (A).

20. **B** Punctuation changes in the answer choices, so this question tests how to connect ideas with the appropriate punctuation. The first part of the sentence, *Since the early days of professional hockey*, is not an independent clause. The second part of the sentence, *other leagues have come and gone*, is an independent clause. Eliminate (A) because a comma followed by the word *but* can only link two independent clauses. Keep (B) because a comma alone can link these two types of clauses. Eliminate (C) because a semicolon can also only be used between two independent clauses. Eliminate (D) because a colon can only come after an independent clause, and the first part of the sentence is not an independent clause. The correct answer is (B).

21. **B** Note the question! The question asks whether a phrase should be added, so it tests consistency. If the content of the phrase is consistent with the ideas surrounding it, then it should be added. The phrase gives examples of *other leagues*, which is consistent with the sentence and the rest of the paragraph. Adding the examples makes the sentence more precise, so the phrase should be added; eliminate (C) and (D). Eliminate (A) because the paragraph does not *shift its focus*. Keep (B) because the phrase does provide *examples of some current leagues*. The correct answer is (B).

22. **D** Verbs and pronouns change in the answer choices, so this question tests consistency of verbs and pronouns. A verb must be consistent in number with its subject. The subject of the underlined verb is *the NHL*, which is singular. To be consistent, the underlined verb must also be singular. Eliminate (A) and (C) because they use the plural verb *hold*. In (B) and (D), the pronouns differ. A pronoun must be consistent in number with the noun it refers to. The underlined pronoun refers to the noun *the NHL*, which is singular. To be consistent, the underlined pronoun must also be singular. Eliminate (B) because *they* is a plural pronoun. The correct answer is (D).

23. **D**   Vocabulary changes in the answer choices, so this question tests precision of word choice. Look for a word with a definition that is consistent with the other ideas in the sentence. The sentence states that *many Americans have accepted the health risks of smoking*, and it contrasts the fact that people may be smoking less but have another health risk that has *replaced smoking*. The answer should suggest that Americans have "changed" *from that deadly pastime. Puffed* means "breathe," so eliminate (A). *Run* means "hurry," so eliminate (B). *Fired* means "stimulated" or "dismissed," so eliminate (C). *Veered* means "changed direction," so keep (D). The correct answer is (D).

24. **C**   Note the question! The question asks where sentence 4 should be placed, so it tests consistency of ideas. The sentence must be consistent with the ideas that come both before and after it. Sentence 4 says *this may sound odd* and *everyone has to sit*. The word *this* refers to an idea in the sentence before that *may sound odd*. Eliminate (A) because there is nothing *odd* about what is stated in sentence 3. Eliminate (B) because the sentence cannot begin the paragraph since it needs to come after something that is *odd*. Keep (C) because the quote in sentence 1 could seem *odd* before the author explains more. The word *however* at the beginning of sentence 2 also logically follows sentence 4 because there is a contrast between it sounding *odd* and having *terrible consequences*. Eliminate (D) because sentence 3 says *indeed*, which means it must build on the previous point, and it is more of a contrast with what is stated in sentence 4. The correct answer is (C).

25. **C**   Note the question! This question asks how to effectively combine the underlined sentences, so it tests precision and concision. Check the shortest answer first. Choice (D) is the shortest option, but the meaning is not precise: the people should not be described as being *safe*; rather, the original sentence states that this sample size is *safely representative*. The people are also not described as being *in their 20s*; eliminate (D). Choice (B) is the next shortest option, but the word *safe* is used to describe *sample* instead of the *sample* being described as *safely representative* as in the original. Eliminate (B) because the meaning is not precise. Choice (A) does not indicate that time frame over which the studies took place, so eliminate (A). Choice (C) gives a precise meaning to the sentence. The correct answer is (C).

26. **D**   The length of the phrase changes in the answer choices, so this question tests concision. There is also the option to DELETE; consider this choice carefully as it is often the correct answer. Deleting the underlined portion makes it clear that there is a comparison in the sentence between people *who sat for more than four hours a day* and those *who sat for only two*, so keep (D). Choices (A), (B), and (C) do not add any information that makes the meaning of the sentence more precise, so eliminate them. The correct answer is (D).

27. **D**   Punctuation changes in the answer choices, so this question tests how to connect ideas with the appropriate punctuation. Choice (B) splits the sentence after *ancestors*. In this case, the first part of the sentence, *Consider our primate ancestors*, is an independent clause. The second part of the sentence, *for example, if they were not incredibly active at all times, they would not have survived*, is also an independent clause. A period can be used between two independent clauses, but the phrase *for example* is not necessary to the main meaning of the sentence and should have a comma after it. Eliminate (B). Choice (D) puts a colon after *example*. In this case, the first part of the sentence, *Consider our primate ancestors, for example*, is an independent clause. The second part of the sentence is *if they were not incredibly active at all times, they would not have survived*, which is also an independent clause. A colon can connect two independent clauses, so keep (D). Eliminate (A) and (C) because the sentence contains two independent clauses, which must be linked with some type of punctuation other than a comma alone. The correct answer is (D).

28. **B**   Note the question! The question asks which choice *offers an accurate interpretation of the data in the graph*, so it tests consistency. Read the labels on the graph carefully, and look for an

answer that is consistent with the information given in the graph. The first part of the sentence is describing when Americans are *upright and active*. Look for that on the graph. According to the graph, people are *active/standing* for 3 hours each day. This supports (B). Eliminate (A), (C), and (D) because they don't match with this information. The correct answer is (B).

29. **D** Note the question! The question asks which choice *offers an accurate interpretation of the data in the graph*, so it tests consistency. Read the labels on the graph carefully, and look for an answer that is consistent with the information given in the graph. Choice (A) is not consistent with the figure because the figure never mentions *standing desks*. Eliminate (A). According to the graph, *sitting at work* is 7.5 hours, and out of the whole day 21 hours are sedentary. That means that work time is not *more than half of all sedentary time on an average day*, so eliminate (B). The graph does not give any information about how much *the average American…eats*, so eliminate (C). Choice (D) is consistent with the graph. The correct answer is (D).

30. **B** Pronouns change in the answer choices, so this question tests consistency of pronouns. A pronoun must be consistent with other pronouns in the sentence. The underlined pronoun refers to *those*, which represents people, since it is the subject of the verb *fidget*. The words *that* and *which* cannot refer to people, so eliminate (A) and (D). The word *who* can refer to people, so keep (B). The pronoun *we* does refer to people, but the phrase *those we…fidget* makes the meaning of the sentence unclear, so eliminate (C). The correct answer is (B).

31. **D** Verbs change in the answer choices, so this question tests consistency of verbs. A verb must be consistent in tense with other verbs in the sentence. The sentence contains the past-tense verbs *found*, *fidgeted*, and *were*. To be consistent, the underlined verb should also be in the past tense. Eliminate (A) and (C) because they are both present tense. Eliminate (B) because to say that people *went…still* is not precise. Choice (D), *sat…still* is more precise since the sentence is talking about *sitting*. The correct answer is (D).

32. **B** Pronouns change in the answer choices, so this question tests consistency of pronouns. A pronoun must be consistent in number with the noun it refers to. The underlined pronoun refers to *sitting* since the passage describes the *detrimental* (negative) *effects* of sitting. *Sitting* is singular, so the underlined pronoun must be singular. Eliminate (A) and (D) because *their* and *they're* are plural pronouns. Apostrophes also change in the answer choices, to this question also tests apostrophe usage. Eliminate (C) because *it's* means "it is," and *it is detrimental effects* does not make sense in the context of the sentence. Choice (B) appropriately uses the possessive pronoun *its*. The correct answer is (B).

33. **A** Note the question! The question asks which choice is *a conclusion that acknowledges the problem of sitting but also encourages the reader to use this research in a proactive way*, so it tests consistency. Eliminate answers that are inconsistent with the purpose stated in the question. Choice (A) is consistent with the purpose stated in the question because it suggests that the reader could do something about the *threat*. Keep (A). Choice (B) *encourages the reader* to be healthy, but it does not *acknowledge the problem*, so eliminate (B) because it is not fully consistent with the purpose stated in the question. Choice (C) also does not *acknowledge the problem*, so eliminate it. Choice (D) does not *encourage the reader* to be *proactive*, as it suggests that the reader can't do anything, so eliminate it because it is not consistent with the purpose stated in the question. The correct answer is (A).

34. **D** Punctuation changes in the answer choices, so this question tests how to connect ideas with the appropriate punctuation. The first part of the sentence, *For many people, "fashion"—the latest lines of shoes, suits, dresses, or furniture*, is not an independent clause. The second part of the sentence, *refers to new things*, is also not an independent clause. Eliminate (A) because a semicolon

can only be used between two independent clauses. Note that the non-underlined portion of the sentence has a dash after "fashion." The phrase *the latest lines of shoes, suits, dresses, or furniture* is not necessary to the main meaning of the sentence, so it must be set off from the rest of the sentence. Since the phrase has a dash before it, it needs another dash after. Eliminate (B) and (C) because they do not include a dash. The correct answer is (D).

35.   **A**   Verbs change in the answer choices, so this question tests consistency of verbs. A verb must be consistent with its subject and with other verbs in the sentence. The underlined portion is part of a list of two things in the sentence. The first verb in the list is *have sported*, which is in present perfect tense, so the underlined portion needs to be in the same tense. Eliminate (C) and (D) because they are both present tense. Choice (B) appears to match with *have sported*; however, the word *have* before *sported* can refer to both verbs in the list. It is not necessary to repeat the word *have* before *furnished*. Eliminate (B). Choice (A) is concise and gives a precise meaning to the sentence. The correct answer is (A).

36.   **A**   Verbs change in the answer choices, so this question tests consistency of verbs. A verb must be consistent with its subject and with other verbs in the sentence. The subject of the sentence is *this new style*, which is singular. To be consistent, the underlined portion must also be singular. Eliminate (C) because *seek* is a plural verb. The previous sentence also describes *the newest style* and uses the present tense verb *is*, so this sentence should be in present tense. Eliminate (B) because *has sought* is past tense. Choice (A) is present tense and singular, so keep it. Eliminate (D) because it makes the sentence incomplete. The correct answer is (A).

37.   **B**   Commas change in the answer choices, so this question tests comma usage. The phrase *IFC's Portlandia* is not necessary to the main meaning of the sentence, so it should be set off by commas. Eliminate (A) because it lacks a comma before the phrase. Keep (B) because it correctly places commas before and after the phrase. Eliminate (C) because it lacks a comma after the phrase. Eliminate (D) because it has an extra comma after *IFC's*. The correct answer is (B).

38.   **B**   Punctuation changes in the answer choices, so this question tests how to connect ideas with the appropriate punctuation. The first part of the sentence, *Framed by men riding nineteenth-century bicycles, chipping their own ice, curing their own meats, and coiffing their handlebar mustaches*, is not an independent clause. The second part of the sentence, *these parts of the song jokes that the dream of the 1890s is alive in Portland*, is an independent clause. Choice (B) appropriately uses a comma to connect the two parts of the sentence. Both periods and semicolons can only be used between two independent clauses, so eliminate (A), (C), and (D). Choice (B) also appropriately uses the singular noun *the song*, which is consistent with the non-underlined verb *jokes*. The correct answer is (B).

39.   **C**   Note the question! The question asks which choice *most effectively sets up the examples that follow*, so it tests consistency of ideas. Eliminate answers that are inconsistent with the purpose stated in the question. The examples that follow are *salvaged furniture repainted in such a way that its age shows, handmade goods from artisans and craftspeople, and facial-hair configurations last seen on William Howard Taft*. Eliminate (A) and (B) because while these things may be *surprising* or *peculiar*, these answer choices are not precise about why the examples are unusual. The word *yesteryear* in (C) is consistent with the ideas of *age* and *last seen on William Howard Taft*, so keep (C). Eliminate (D) because the examples in the sentence are not described as being *expensive*. The correct answer is (C).

40.   **C**   Note the question! The question asks whether a sentence should be added, so it tests consistency. If the content of the new sentence is consistent with the ideas surrounding it, then it should be added. The paragraph discusses *rustic chic* and specifically *the question of economics*, which the

author describes as paying *more* for something that is old. The new sentence mentions *American gross domestic product*, which has to do with economics but not in the sense that economics is used in this paragraph. Since this is not consistent with the ideas in the paragraph, the sentence should not be added. Eliminate (A) and (B). Choice (C) accurately states that the new sentence *is not relevant to the main focus of the passage*. The new sentence does not *contradict information given in the following paragraph*, so eliminate (D). The correct answer is (C).

41.   **D**   Vocabulary changes in the answer choices, so this question tests precision of word choice. Look for a word with a definition that is consistent with the other ideas in the sentence. The sentence explains why rustic chic is *difficult to understand*. The author goes on to say that *we know* whom *hippies* and *flappers* are *trying to dress like*. This suggests that we do not know whom *rustic chic* is imitating. Thus, the word in the sentence should mean something like "person they're trying to be like." *Interest* means "object of attention," which could work, so keep (A). *Choice* means "decision," so eliminate (B). *Fashion* means "style," so eliminate (C). *Source* means "where something comes from," which gives a precise meaning to the sentence, so keep (D). *Interest* is less precise than *source*, so eliminate (A). The correct answer is (D).

42.   **B**   Note the question! The question asks which choice could *link this paragraph with the ideas that follow*, so it tests consistency of ideas. Determine the subjects of these paragraphs and find the answer that is consistent with those ideas. This paragraph explains that rustic chic is *difficult to understand* because it does not have a clear referent, meaning people whom fans of rustic chic are trying to be like. The next paragraph says that *these questions may be unanswerable*. Choice (A) does ask a question, but *getting married later* is not consistent with the idea in this paragraph, so eliminate (A). Choice (B) asks a question and *"they"* is consistent with this paragraph, so keep (B). Choice (C) does not ask a question, so it is inconsistent with the statement at the beginning of the next paragraph. Eliminate it. Choice (D) does ask a question, but *beards* and *mustaches* are not consistent with the idea in this paragraph, so eliminate (D). The correct answer is (B).

43.   **D**   Note the question! The question asks where Sentence 2 should be placed, so it tests consistency of ideas. The sentence must be consistent with the ideas that come both before and after it. Sentence 2 offers a suggestion to wear clothes *that men and women did before the existence of the fashion industry*. Sentence 4 asks a question, and Sentence 5 offers a suggestion in response to that question. Sentence 6 asks another question, but this sentence does not have a parallel suggestion that would respond to it. Thus, Sentence 2 should go after Sentence 6 as the response to that question. The correct answer is (D).

44.   **B**   The subject of the underlined phrase changes in the answer choices, so this question tests consistency. Choose the answer that is consistent with the rest of the sentence. The first part of the sentence says *rustic chic provides one way to*, so the underlined portion should be something rustic chic provides. The later part of the sentence says that *depending on whose side you're on, you might just think of it as more clutter*. The *capitalist system* is not consistent with this sentence, so eliminate (A). The word *clutter* in (B) is consistent with that idea at the end of the sentence, so keep (B). Neither *the military-industrial complex* nor going *off the grid* are consistent with the non-underlined portions of the sentence, so eliminate (C) and (D). The correct answer is (B).

Section 3: Math (No Calculator)

1.   **C**   The question asks for the value of $8s + 13$, so determine the value of s. Since $4s = 28$, divide both sides by 4 to get $s = 7$. Therefore, $8s + 13 = 8(7) + 13 = 56 + 13 = 69$. Alternatively, since $4s = 28$, $8s = 2(4s) = 2(28) = 56$. Therefore, $8s + 13 = 56 + 13 = 69$. Using either method, the correct answer is (C).

2. **A** The question asks which choice is equal to $b^{\frac{3}{4}}$. By rule, fractional exponents express roots. Let the denominator of the fraction equal the root taken. Since the denominator is 4, take the 4th root. The numerator of the fraction remains as the exponent. Therefore, $b^{\frac{3}{4}} = \sqrt[4]{b^3}$. The correct answer is (A).

3. **B** The question asks for the value that will change if a cheaper type of grass is used. The only thing that has changed is that the customer has asked for a cheaper type of grass. A cheaper type of grass does not change the number of plots, the length of a plot, or the width of any plot, so the values p, l, and w do not change. Eliminate (A), (C), and (D). Only (B) remains. Alternatively, note that it is only the price that changes and the only value whose units involve dollars is G, so this must be the value that changes. The correct answer is (B).

4. **B** The question asks for the value of $x + y$ in a system of equations. When there is a system of equations, stack and add or subtract the two equations to solve. The goal is to find an equation in which the coefficients on x and y are the same as in the expression the question asks for the value of. In this case, since the question asks for $x + y$, the coefficients on x and y should be equal. Stack and add the two equations to get $8x + 8y = -56$. Divide both sides by 8 to get $x + y = -7$. The correct answer is (B).

5. **C** The question asks for an equation related to the number of countries in the European Union and says that the number of countries in the European Union in 2008 was three times the number of countries in 1974. Translate this into an equation. Since the question says that the European Union had 27 members in 2008, translate *the number of countries in the European Union in 2008* to 27. Translate *was* to =. Translate *three times* to 3( ), leaving room between the parentheses for whatever follows in the sentence. What follows is *the number of countries in the European Union (then called the European Communities) in 1974*, which the question later says is m. Therefore, the sentence translates to $27 = 3(m)$, or $3m = 27$. The correct answer is (C).

6. **B** The question asks for the value of $\frac{y}{7}$, so solve for y. Since $\frac{7}{y} = \frac{17}{y + 30}$, cross-multiply to get $7(y + 30) = 17y$. Distribute the 7 to get $7y + 210 = 17y$. Subtract $7y$ from both sides to get $210 = 10y$. Divide both sides by 10 to get $21 = y$. Therefore, $\frac{y}{7} = \frac{21}{7} = 3$. The correct answer is (B).

7. **B** The question asks for the value of c that will cause the system of equations to have no solution. Since there are no exponents on x or y in either equation, the equations are linear. A system of linear equations has no solution if the two lines represented by the equations are parallel. Two lines are parallel when they have the same slope. To determine the slope of the lines, get each line in slope-intercept form: $y = mx + b$. Start with the second equation, $3x - 7y = 5$. Subtract $3x$ from both sides to get $-7y = -3x + 5$. Divide both sides by -7 to get $y = \frac{3}{7}x - \frac{5}{7}$. In slope-intercept form, the slope is equal to m, so the slope of this line is $\frac{3}{7}$. Now get the slope of the other line, $cx - 6y = 8$. Subtract cx from both sides to get $-6y = -cx + 8$. Divide both sides by -6 to get $y = \frac{c}{6}x - \frac{8}{6}$, so the slope of this line is $\frac{c}{6}$. Since these two slopes have to be equal, set $\frac{3}{7} = \frac{c}{6}$. Cross-multiply to get $7c = 18$. Divide both sides by 7 to get $c = \frac{18}{7}$. The correct answer is (B).

8. **D**   The question asks for an expression that must be a factor of polynomial function g. A factor of a polynomial is used to find a solution, or a value of x for which the corresponding value of the function is 0. When a function in factored form is set equal to 0, each factor can be set equal to 0 to get each solution. Since, according to the table, $g(7) = 0$, $x = 7$ is one solution of g. Therefore, it must also be the solution to an equation made by setting one of the factors equal to 0. To find this factor, get the equation $x = 7$ into the form of an equation with one side equal to 0. Subtract 7 from both sides to get $x - 7 = 0$. Therefore, $x - 7$ is one of the factors of g. The correct answer is (D).

9. **D**   The question asks for the slope of the line in terms of r and s, the coordinates of a point on the line. A line whose equation is in the form $y = mx + b$ has slope m and y-intercept b. In the equation $y = cx + 6$, the slope is c. Plug the point (r, s) into the equation to get $s = cr + 6$. To find the slope, solve for c. First, subtract 6 from both sides to get $s - 6 = cr$. Now, divide both sides by r to get $c = \dfrac{s - 6}{r}$. The correct answer is (D).

10. **A**   The question asks for true statements based on the figure and gives three pairs of congruent angles. Start with the vertical angles. Vertical angles are non-adjacent angles formed by intersecting lines. The pairs of vertical angles in this figure are $a°$ and $d°$, $b°$ and $e°$, and $c°$ and $f°$. Since vertical angles are always congruent, $a = d$, $b = e$, and $c = f$. The question also states that $a + b = c + d$. Since $a = d$, it must also be the case that $b = c$. This shows that statement (I) is true, so (B) can be eliminated. Since $b = c$, $b = e$, and $c = f$, then e must also equal f. Statement (II) is true, so eliminate (C). Statement (III) says that $a = e$. It has been determined that $b = c = e = f$ and that $a = d$, but so far nothing has shown that $a = e$. To be sure, try out a value for e. Let $e = 30$. If $e = 30$, then $b = c = f = 30$, so $b + c + e + f = 30 + 30 + 30 + 30 = 120$. Since $a + b + c + d + e + f = 360$, then $a + d + 120 = 360$ and $a + d = 240$. Since $a = d$, then a and d are both equal to 120. Therefore, $a \neq e$. Cross off (III) and eliminate (D). The correct answer is (A).

11. **D**   The graph asks for the y-coordinate of the vertex, which is the point of the parabola on the axis of symmetry. Therefore, the axis of symmetry is the line $x = m$. To determine the value of m, find a pair of points with the same y-coordinate, and get the midpoint of the segment between them. To make this easy, let $y = 0$ to get $0 = k(x - 4)(x + 12)$. Set each factor equal to 0 to get $k = 0$, $x - 4 = 0$, and $x + 12 = 0$. Since the question says $k \neq 0$, reject the first equation. Solve the second equation, $x - 4 = 0$, by adding 4 to both sides to get $x = 4$. Solve the third equation, $x + 12 = 0$, by subtracting 12 from both sides to get $x = -12$. Therefore, the points $(4, 0)$ and $(-12, 0)$ are on the parabola. The midpoint of $(4, 0)$ and $(-12, 0)$ is $\left(\dfrac{4 + (-12)}{2}, 0\right) = \left(\dfrac{-8}{2}, 0\right)$ $= (-4, 0)$. Therefore, $m = -4$. Since (m, n) is a point on the parabola, $n = k(m - 4)(m + 12)$. To find n, plug in $m = -4$ to get $n = k(-4 - 4)(-4 + 12) = k(-8)(8) = -64k$. Another option would be to make up a value for k to get a quadratic, then complete the square on the x-terms to get the equation into the vertex form. Either way, the correct answer is (D).

12. **C**   The question asks for the length of a line segment between the parabola and the line's points of intersection. Points of intersection are solutions to both equations. Since $y = (x - 8)^2$ and $y = 36$, set $(x - 8)^2 = 36$. To solve, take the square root of both sides to get $x - 8 = \pm 6$. Always remember to use $\pm$ when taking the square root of both sides of an equation. Consider both possible equations. If $x - 8 = 6$, add 8 to both sides to get $x = 14$. If $x - 8 = -6$, add 8 to both sides to get $x = 2$. Therefore, points P and Q are at coordinates $(2, 36)$ and $(14, 36)$. Since the endpoints of $\overline{PQ}$ share y-coordinates, the length of the segment is the difference in the x-coordinates of the endpoints. Therefore, $PQ = 14 - 2 = 12$. The correct answer is (C).

13. **B** The question asks for a true statement about the relationship between measurements in Celsius and Fahrenheit. Test each of these statements by putting in actual numbers. Statement (I) refers to a decrease of 1.8 degrees Celsius. Use a simple example of such a decrease. Try $C = 1.8$ and $C = 0$. Since the formula includes fractions, convert 1.8 into a fraction in order to do the arithmetic. Rewrite the fraction as $\frac{1.8}{1.0} = \frac{18}{10} = \frac{9}{5}$, so $1.8 = \frac{9}{5}$. If $C = \frac{9}{5}$, then $F\left(\frac{9}{5}\right) = \frac{9}{5}\left(\frac{9}{5}\right) + 32 = \frac{81}{25} + 32 = 3\frac{6}{25} + 32 = 35\frac{6}{25}$. If $C = 0$, then $F(0) = \frac{9}{5}(0) + 32 = 32$.

Since this is a decrease of more than 1, cross out (I) and eliminate any choice that includes (I): (A) and (D). Now look at the remaining choices. Since both remaining choices include (II), (II) must be true, so test (III) only. Statement (III) refers to a decrease of $\frac{5}{9}$ degree Fahrenheit. Pick two easy values for F with a difference of $\frac{5}{9}$. $F = \frac{5}{9}$ and $F = 0$ might appear easy, but the first step to solving will be to subtract 32, which is not convenient with $F = \frac{5}{9}$. Instead, use $F = 32\frac{5}{9}$ and $F = 32$. If $F = 32\frac{5}{9}$, then $32\frac{5}{9} = \frac{9}{5}C + 32$. Subtract 32 from both sides to get $\frac{5}{9} = \frac{9}{5}C$. Multiply both sides by $\frac{5}{9}$ to get $\frac{25}{81} = C$. If $F = 32$, then $32 = \frac{9}{5}C + 32$. Subtract 32 from both sides to get $0 = \frac{9}{5}C$. Multiply both sides by $\frac{5}{9}$ to get $0 = C$. Since this a decrease of less than 1, cross off (III) and eliminate (C). The correct answer is (B).

14. **A** The question asks for the value of constant k in an equation. This is a complicated algebra question, so look for a way to use an actual number instead. Since no calculator is allowed on this section, it is especially important to pick an easy number. Try $x = 1$. If $x = 1$, then $\frac{80(1)^2 + 84(1) - 13}{k(1) - 4} = -16(1) - 4 - \frac{29}{k(1) - 4}$. Simplify to get $\frac{80 + 84 - 13}{k - 4} = -16 - 4 - \frac{29}{k - 4}$ and $\frac{151}{k - 4} = -20 - \frac{29}{k - 4}$. Add $\frac{29}{k - 4}$ to both sides to get $\frac{151}{k - 4} + \frac{29}{k - 4} = -20$. Since the fractions on the right have the same denominator, add both the numerators to get $\frac{180}{k - 4} = -20$.

Multiply both sides by $(k - 4)$ to get $180 = -20(k - 4)$. Distribute on the right side to get $180 = -20k + 80$. Subtract 80 from both sides to get $100 = -20k$. Divide both sides by -20 to get $k = -5$. The correct answer is (A).

15. **D** The question asks for the solutions to the given quadratic. To find the solutions to a quadratic equation, the first option is to factor. First, since 5 is a factor of each term, factor 5 to get $5(x^2 + 6x + 3) = 0$. Divide both sides by 5 to get $x^2 + 6x + 3 = 0$. However, as the answer choices hint, factoring this equation further will be difficult, so use the quadratic formula: $x = \frac{-b \pm \sqrt{b^2 - 4ac}}{2a}$.

The standard form of a quadratic equation is $ax^2 + bx + c = 0$, so $a = 1$, $b = 6$, and $c = 3$.

Therefore, $x = \dfrac{-b \pm \sqrt{b^2 - 4ac}}{2a} = \dfrac{-6 \pm \sqrt{6^2 - 4(1)(3)}}{2(1)} = \dfrac{-6 \pm \sqrt{36 - 12}}{2} = \dfrac{-6 \pm \sqrt{24}}{2}$. Simplify the square root by finding a perfect square factor. Since $24 = 4 \times 6$, $\sqrt{24} = \sqrt{4} \times \sqrt{6} = 2\sqrt{6}$, so $x = \dfrac{-6 \pm 2\sqrt{6}}{2}$. Simplify the fraction by dividing both terms in the numerator by 2 to get $x = -3 \pm \sqrt{6}$. The correct answer is (D).

16. **4** The question asks for the value of x in the equation. To solve this equation, start by combining like terms on the left side. Since the denominators are the same, subtract the numerators to get $\dfrac{5}{25}z = \dfrac{1}{2} + \dfrac{3}{10}$. Simplify the fraction on the left side of the equation to get $\dfrac{1}{5}z = \dfrac{1}{2} + \dfrac{3}{10}$. Now eliminate the fractions by multiplying both sides by a common multiple of all three denominators, such as 10. The result is $2z = 5 + 3$. Simplify the right side to get $2z = 8$. Divide both sides by 2 to get $z = 4$. The correct answer is 4.

17. **1 or 3** The question asks for one possible solution to the equation. To solve a polynomial, get one side of the equation equal to 0. To do that in this case, add $9y$ to both sides to get $y^3(y^2 - 10) + 9y = 0$. Distribute y^3 to get $y^5 - 10y^3 + 9y = 0$. Since each term on the left includes y, factor y to get $y(y^4 - 10y^2 + 9) = 0$. Now factor $(y^4 - 10y^2 + 9)$. This resembles a quadratic of the form $ax^2 + bx + c$ but with the exponents doubled. It can be factored the same way. The quadratic $(y^2 - 10y + 9)$ factors to $(y - 9)(y - 1)$, so $(y^4 - 10y^2 + 9)$ factors to $(y^2 - 9)(y^2 - 1)$. Each of these factors is a difference of squares, so $(y^2 - 9) = (y - 3)(y + 3)$ and $(y^2 - 1) = (y - 1)(y + 1)$. Therefore, the equation $y(y^4 - 10y^2 + 9) = 0$ factors to $y(y - 3)(y + 3)(y - 1)(y + 1) = 0$. Set each of these factors equal to 0 to get $y = 0$, $y - 3 = 0$, $y + 3 = 0$, $y - 1 = 0$, and $y + 1 = 0$. Solve these equations to get $y = 0$, $y = 3$, $y = -3$, $y = 1$, and $y = -1$, respectively. Since the question specifies that $y > 0$, the only remaining possible solutions are $y = 3$ and $y = 1$. The correct answer is 1 or 3.

18. **50** The question asks for the length of a long session in minutes. To answer this question, translate each statement into an equation. Let L represent the length of a long session and S represent the length of a short session. Each long session lasts 20 minutes longer than each short session. *Each long session* translates to L. The word *lasts* is the main verb of the sentence, so it translates to =. The phrase *20 minutes longer* translates to ___ + 20, leaving room on the left for whatever follows. What follows is *each short session*, which translates to S. Therefore, the first sentence translates to $L = S + 20$. Now translate the second sentence. The term *3 long sessions* translates to $3L$. The word *and* translates to +. The term *4 short sessions* translates to $4S$. The term *last a total of* translates to =. Therefore, the second sentence translates to $3L + 4S = 270$. To solve this system of equations, substitute $L = S + 20$ into the second equation to get $3(S + 20) + 4S = 270$. Distribute 3 to get $3S + 60 + 4S = 270$. Combine like terms to get $7S + 60 = 270$. Subtract 60 from both sides to get $7S = 210$. Divide both sides by 7 to get $S = 30$. This is not the answer. Don't forget to read the question, which asks for the length of a *long* session. Since $L = S + 20$, $L = 30 + 20 = 50$. The correct answer is 50.

19. $\dfrac{5}{13}$ The question asks for the value of $\cos Z$. By definition, corresponding angles in similar triangles are congruent. Since $\angle Z$ corresponds to $\angle W$ in a similar triangle, $\angle Z$ is congruent to $\angle W$. Since congruent angles have equal cosines, $\cos Z = \cos W$. Therefore, this question can be answered by ignoring triangle XYZ and working exclusively with triangle UVW to determine the value of $\cos W$, and thus the value of $\cos Z$. Draw triangle UVW, filling in $WV = 39$ and $UV = 36$.

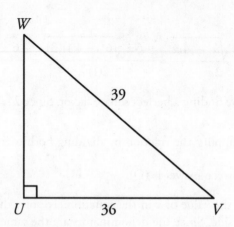

By definition, $\cos W = \dfrac{\text{adjacent}}{\text{hypotenuse}}$. The hypotenuse is 39, but the adjacent side isn't given. The adjacent side can be solved for using the Pythagorean Theorem, but this is difficult with numbers this large and no calculator. Instead, look for a Pythagorean triple. The ratio 36:39, can be reduced by a factor of 3 to 12:13, so this is a 5:12:13 right triangle. Therefore, the missing side, $\overline{UW}$, must have a length of $3 \times 5 = 15$. Thus, the adjacent side is 15, and $\cos W = \dfrac{15}{39} = \dfrac{5}{13}$. The correct answer is $\dfrac{5}{13}$.

20. **110** The question asks for the value of c on the diagram. Start with the equation $b = 180 - 4a$. Since $a = 35$, $b = 180 - 4(35) = 180 - 140 = 40$. Therefore, the two base angles of the lower triangle have a sum of $180° - 40° = 140°$. Since the two base angles are opposite equal sides, they must be equal, so each is 70°. The angle with measure c combines with the base angle on the right to form a straight angle. Therefore, $70° + c° = 180°$, and $c = 110$. The correct answer is 110.

Section 4: Math (Calculator)

1. **C** The question asks for the probability that a randomly selected canid fits either of two categories.

   Find the probability of each category. The probability of selecting a grey wolf with yellow eyes is $\dfrac{16}{30}$, and the probability of selecting a coyote with brown eyes is $\dfrac{5}{30}$. Therefore, the probability of selecting one or the other is $\dfrac{16}{30} + \dfrac{5}{30} = \dfrac{21}{30}$. The correct answer is (C).

2. **D** The question asks for the trend in military spending as shown on the graph. Use Process of Elimination. From 1992 to 1996, the graph shows a downward slope, which indicates a decrease in military spending. Therefore, eliminate (B) and (C). In 2001, the graph shows an upward slope, which indicates an increase in military spending. Eliminate (A). The correct answer is (D).

3. **B** The question asks for the time at which Eddie finished fixing his flat and started riding again. During the 40 minutes that Eddie stops to repair his bike, his distance does not change. On the graph, this time period would be shown as a flat horizontal line. The only flat horizontal portion of the graph occurs from about 11:10 A.M. to just before noon. Therefore, he finished repairing his bike just before noon. The correct answer is (B).

4. **C** The question asks for the total number of employees who received performance bonuses. Work through the information one piece at a time. Translate "4 percent" of the 648 male employees into math and calculate: $\frac{4}{100}(648) = 25.92$ male employees who received bonuses. Do the same for the female employees: $\frac{6}{100}(519) = 31.14$ female employees who received bonuses. Add these together to get $25.92 + 31.14 = 57.06$, which is close to 57. The correct answer is (C).

5. **B** The question asks for the sum of two polynomials. Rather than do all the work before looking at the answers, do just one piece at a time. Start by adding the x^2 terms: $4x^2 + 2x^2 = 6x^2$. Eliminate (C) and (D). Next, since the x terms are the same in the remaining answers, add the constants: $-2 + 9 = 7$. Eliminate (A). Therefore, the correct answer is (B).

6. **D** The question asks for the definition of function g based on a table of values. Use the given values to test out the equations in the answers. According to the table, when $k = 1$, $g(k) = -3$. Plug in 1 for k in the answers and eliminate any answers that do not return a value of -3. Choice (A) becomes $1 - 1 = 0$. Eliminate (A). Choice (B) becomes $2(1) - 4 = -2$. Eliminate (B). Choice (C) becomes $3(1) - 5 = -2$. Eliminate (C). Choice (D) becomes $4(1) - 7 = -3$. Therefore, the correct answer is (D).

7. **D** The question asks for the meaning of -0.14 in the equation. Use Process of Elimination. Since x represents the number of years since 2005, the -0.14 must somehow be related to the number of years. Eliminate (A) and (B) since the question states that y represents the rainfall in any given year. Choice (C) would be represented by the y-value for 2005 minus the y-value for 2015, so eliminate (C). The correct answer is (D).

8. **C** The question asks for the approximate number of inches an insect will crawl in 6 hours. There are $60(6) = 360$ minutes in 6 hours. To calculate the distance the insect crawls, set up the following proportion: $\frac{30 \text{ inches}}{16.3 \text{ min}} = \frac{x}{360 \text{ min}}$. Cross-multiply: $16.3x = 30(360)$. Do the multiplication on the right side to get $16.3x = 10,800$, then divide both sides by 16.3 to get $x = 662.577$. The question asks for an *approximate* answer, so choose the closest answer. The correct answer is (C).

9. **B** The question asks for the value of v in the equation. To isolate v, multiply both sides of the equation by $\frac{5}{8}$, resulting in $v = \frac{7}{4} \times \frac{5}{8} = \frac{35}{32}$. The correct answer is (B).

10. **B** The question asks for the graph of function g, which has four distinct zeros. The term *zero* means an x-intercept (a point where the curve crosses the x-axis). The only graph showing a curve that crosses the x-axis four times is (B). The correct answer is (B).

11. **A** The question asks for the amount of heat energy needed to raise the temperature of copper. According to the information given, $Q = mC$ where $C = \frac{J}{g}$. The chart shows that the heat capacity $\left(\frac{J}{g}\right)$ for copper is 0.39, and the mass is 75. Therefore, $Q = 75(0.39) = 29.25$. The correct answer is (A).

12. **A** The question asks about the substance that makes up a piece of material with the same mass but a different heat capacity as compared to porcelain. According to the information given, $Q = mC$. The table indicates that for porcelain, $C = 1.08$. Find the mass of the porcelain by plugging in 80 for Q and 1.08 for C, resulting in $80 = m(1.08)$. Divide both sides of the equation by 1.08 to get $m \approx 74$. To find the unknown substance, plug in 67 for Q and 74 for m, resulting in $67 = 74C$. Divide both sides of the equation by 74 to get $C \approx 0.9054$. This approximates the value given for aluminum in the chart. The correct answer is (A).

13. **D** The question asks for the most appropriate conclusion based on the study. Read each answer and use Process of Elimination. The study was done on 200 people with severe hearing loss. Eliminate (A) because the study population doesn't deal with all people; it only deals with people who have severe hearing loss. Because no other hearing-improvement products were mentioned in the question, eliminate (B). In comparing (C) and (D), (C) is too broad, because it applies to people generally, rather than just to the people with severe hearing loss who were studied. Therefore, eliminate (C). The correct answer is (D).

14. **C** The question asks for an equation expressed in terms of a, so rearrange the formula so that a is alone on one side. First, subtract vt from both sides, resulting in $d - vt = -\frac{1}{2}at^2$. Next, multiply both sides by -2, resulting in $-2(d - vt) = at^2$, then divide both sides by t^2, resulting in $\frac{-2(d - vt)}{t^2} = a$. To make the equation look like the answer choices, flip it around so the a is on the left and apply the t^2 in the denominator to each part of the binomial in the parentheses. The equation becomes $a = -2\left(\frac{d}{t^2} - \frac{vt}{t^2}\right)$, and the second fraction can be reduced, resulting in $a = -2\left(\frac{d}{t^2} - \frac{v}{t}\right)$. Finally, apply the negative sign in front of the 2 to the terms in the parentheses and switch their order: $a = 2\left(\frac{v}{t} - \frac{d}{t^2}\right)$. The correct answer is (C).

15. **B** The question asks for the total price for y yards of ribbon. The price is given in inches, and there are 36 inches in a yard, so the ribbon costs $0.15(36) = \$5.40$ per yard. Now pick a number of yards of ribbon. If $y = 2$, then $p = 2(5.40) = 10.80$. Plug 2 in for y in the answers to see which answer returns a value of 10.80. Choice (A) becomes $0.15(2) + 36 = 36.30$. Eliminate (A). Choice (B) becomes $0.15(36)(2) = 10.8$. Keep (B), but check (C) and (D) just in case. Choice (C) becomes $\frac{0.15(2)}{36} \approx 0.008$. Eliminate (C). Choice (D) becomes $\frac{36(2)}{0.15} = 480$. Eliminate (D). The correct answer is (B).

16. **A** The question asks for the change in the total cost of production if 20 fewer units are produced. Try actual numbers in the equation to see what happens to the cost. If $q = 40$, then $C = 60(40) + 300 = 2,700$. Now decrease q by 20 units: if $q = 20$, then $C = 60(20) + 300 = 1,500$. The change in cost is $2,700 - 1,500 = 1,200$. The correct answer is (A).

17. **C** The question asks for the quantity for which revenue will equal cost. To find this, set the equations equal to each other: $60q + 300 = 75q$. Subtract $60q$ from each side to get $300 = 15q$, and divide both sides by 15 to find that $q = 20$. The correct answer is (C).

18. **C** The question asks for the value of x that will make $f(x) + g(x) = 1$. Look up the values for $f(x)$ and $g(x)$ for each of the x-values in the answer choices and see which pair adds up to 1. For (A), $f(-5) = -1$ and $g(-5) = -1$, and the sum of these values is -2. Eliminate (A). For (B), $f(-4)$ is a small negative number and $g(-4) = 0$, and the sum of these values is negative, so eliminate (B). For (C), $f(-3) = 0$ and $g(-3) = 1$, and the sum of these values is 1. The correct answer is (C).

19. **B** The question asks for the situation that yields exponential decay, which provides increasingly greater or smaller changes in values as time progresses. Try out some numbers to see what would happen in each situation. Let the initial value of the item equal $100. For (A), the item would lose $100 \times 0.05 = \$5$ every year. Eliminate (A), because the amount of value the item loses would be the same every year. For (B), the item would lose $100 \times 0.06 = \$6$ the first year. Therefore, the new item value would be $100 - 6 = \$94$. The second year, the item would lose $94 \times 0.06 = \$5.64$, and the new item value would be $94 - 5.64 = \$88.36$. Each successive year, the loss would be less than the loss the year before. This is an exponential decay. The correct answer is (B).

20. **B** The question asks for the number of U.S. pints of lemonade that can be made using 17 ounces of sugar. First, calculate the number of imperial pints that can be made with 17 ounces of sugar. Set up the following proportion: $\dfrac{1 \text{ ounce}}{30 \text{ I. pints}} = \dfrac{17 \text{ ounces}}{x}$. Cross-multiply to get $x = 510$ imperial pints.

    Next, calculate the number of U.S. pints that are equivalent to 510 imperial pints by setting up the following proportion: $\dfrac{1 \text{ I. pint}}{1\frac{1}{4} \text{ U.S. pints}} = \dfrac{510 \text{ I. pints}}{x}$. Simplify the left side of the equation to $\dfrac{1}{\frac{5}{4}} = \dfrac{510}{x}$, or $\dfrac{4}{5} = \dfrac{510}{x}$. Cross-multiply, resulting in $4x = 2,550$. Divide both sides by 4 to get $x = 637.5$. The closest approximation for 637.5 is 640. The correct answer is (B).

21. **A** The question asks for the difference between the predicted and actual vertical distances for the jump with a horizontal distance of 230 inches. The actual plotted point at a horizontal distance of 230 inches is a vertical distance of 49 inches. However, the line of best fit at 230 inches equals 47.5 inches. The difference is $49 - 47.5 = 1.5$. The correct answer is (A).

22. **B** The question asks for the number of girls in the Girl Scout troop. This is a specific value and the answers are numbers, so try out the answers to see which one works. Start with (B). If there are 23 girls in the troop, then Mrs. Warren currently has $23(4) + 11 = 103$ boxes. If she were to give 5 boxes to each girl, she would need $23(5) = 115$. Therefore, she is $115 - 103 = 12$ boxes short. This matches the information given in the problem. The correct answer is (B).

23. **D** The question asks for the largest number of three numbers and gives the relationship of the numbers. Translate the information into equations. Let l represent the largest number and s represent the sum of the other two numbers. According to the question, $l = \dfrac{4}{3}s$. Divide both sides by $\dfrac{4}{3}$ to get $\dfrac{3}{4}l = s$. Now check the answers, starting with (B). If the largest number is 245, the sum of the other two numbers is $\dfrac{3}{4}(245) = 183.75$. The sum of all three numbers would be $245 + 183.75 = 428.75$.

Eliminate both (A) and (B) because these values are too small. Try (C). If the largest number is 350, then the sum of the other two numbers is $\frac{3}{4}$(350) = 262.5, and the sum of all three numbers is 350 + 262.5 = 612.5. Eliminate (C). The correct answer is (D).

24. **B** The question asks for the value of j, a constant that is used to express the measurement of two angles in a triangle. Use the values in the answer choices to determine the measurements of x and y. Start with (B) and make j = 15.5. The value of x would then be 3(15.5) − 19 = 27.5, and the value of z would be 5(15.5) − 15 = 62.5. Now use a calculator to check if cos (27.5°) = sin (62.5°). Both equal 0.887. The correct answer is (B).

25. **D** The question asks for the value of k, a percent by which the width of a rectangle changes. No measurements are given, so make up a length and a width for the rectangle. Let l = 12 and w = 10. The area of this rectangle can be calculated as $A = lw$ = (12)(10) = 120. In the new rectangle, the length is reduced by 25% or $\frac{1}{4}$, making the new length $12 - \left(\frac{1}{4}\right)(12) = 9$. The area of 120 is increased by 5%, so the new area is $120 + \left(\frac{5}{100}\right)(120) = 120 + 6 = 126$. Plug these new numbers into the area formula to get 126 = 9w, then divide both sides by 9 to get w = 14. The width increased from 10 to 14, but the question asks for the percent increase, which is calculated as $\frac{\text{difference}}{\text{original}} \times 100$. In this case, that value is $\frac{14-10}{10}(100) = \frac{4}{10}(100) = 40$, so k = 40%. The correct answer is (D).

26. **C** The question asks for the volume of the capsule, which is made of a cylinder and two halves of a sphere. Find the volume of each piece separately, using the formulas in the reference box, then add the volumes together. The formula for the volume of a cylinder is $V = \pi r^2 h$. For the figure shown, r = 3 and h = 12. The volume of the cylinder portion of the capsule is $V = \pi(3^2)(12) = 108\pi$. The two ends of the capsule make up one complete sphere. The formula for the volume of a sphere is $V = \frac{4}{3}\pi r^3$. Again, r = 3. Therefore, the volume of the spherical portion of the capsule is $V = \frac{4}{3}\pi(3)^3 = 36\pi$. The volume of the entire figure is $108\pi + 36\pi = 144\pi \approx 452.4$. The correct answer is (C).

27. **A** The question asks for the value of p, a coordinate in two points on the line. Any two points on the line can be used to calculate the slope, and all slope calculations must give the same result. Given two points on a line, the slope is calculated as $\frac{y_2 - y_1}{x_2 - x_1}$. Use the points (0, 0) and (p, 4) to find the slope of the line: $\frac{4-0}{p-0} = \frac{4}{p}$. Next, use the points (0, 0) and (9, p) to find the slope of the line: $\frac{p-0}{9-0} = \frac{p}{9}$. Set the two expressions equal to each other to get $\frac{4}{p} = \frac{p}{9}$. Cross-multiply to get $p^2 = 36$. Take the square root of both sides of the equation to get $p = \pm 6$. Only the −6 value appears in the answers. The correct answer is (A).

28. **D** The question asks for the probability that a randomly selected caffeinated beverage will be coffee, but the table is incomplete. To fill in the table, write a system of equations using the information given. Call the number of decaffeinated teas x, so the number of caffeinated teas is $3x$. Call the number of decaffeinated coffees y, so the number of caffeinated coffees is $5y$. The two equations that can be written from this information and the table are $x + y = 28$ and $3x + 5y = 116$. When dealing with systems of equations, look for a way to stack and add the equations to eliminate one variable and solve for another. To do this, multiply the first equation, $x + y = 28$, by -3 to get $-3x - 3y = -84$. Now stack and add the equations:

$$3x + 5y = 116$$
$$\underline{-3x - 3y = -84}$$
$$2y = 32$$

Divide by 2 to get $y = 16$. This means that $x = 28 - y = 28 - 16 = 12$. Use these values to fill in the chart.

	Decaffeinated	Caffeinated
Tea	$x = 12$	$3x = 36$
Coffee	$y = 16$	$5y = 80$
Total	28	116

Now find the probability that a caffeinated beverage chosen at random is a coffee. Divide the number of caffeinated coffees, 80, by the total number of caffeinated beverages, 116, to get a probability of 0.69. The correct answer is (D).

29. **B** The question asks for a true statement given a complicated system of equations. Start by consolidating like terms. The top equation becomes $j = 3x - 9$, and the bottom equation becomes $k = 3y - 9$. In the first equation, replace j with $k + 1.5$ to get $k + 1.5 = 3x - 9$. Subtract 1.5 from both sides of the equation to get $k = 3x - 10.5$. Set the two equations equal to each other to get $3y - 9 = 3x - 10.5$. Add 10.5 to both sides to get $3y + 1.5 = 3x$. Divide the entire equation by 3 to get $y + 0.5 = x$. Another approach would be to try out numbers for j and k and then solve for x and y. Either way, the correct answer is (B).

30. **C** The question asks for the equation that will best estimate the number of baseball cards after m months. The fastest way to solve this is to use the decay formula: *final amount = original amount*$(1 - r)^t$. In this case, the *original amount* = 6,500 and $r = 0.2$. The *final amount* = $6,500(1 - 0.2)^t = 6,500(0.8)^t$. Eliminate (A) and (B). Next, try a value for m. If $m = 12$, then because the value of the baseball cards decreases every 6 months, $t = \frac{12}{6} = 2$. For $m = 12$, the exponent in (C) will equal 2. Of course, this question can also be solved without the formula, though not as quickly. Pick a value for m that will make the number of baseball cards easy to calculate, such as $m = 6$. Banerji starts with 6,500 cards, and he will sell off 20% of them in those 6 months. Calculate 20% of 6,500, which is 1,300, then subtract that from 6,500 to get 5,200 cards. Now put $m = 6$ in each of the answer choices to see which one equals 5,200. Either way, the correct answer is (C).

31. **3** The question asks for the value of a when a quadratic is written in the form $ax^2 + bx + c$. Start by distributing -3 to get $6x^2 - 7x + 5 - 3x^2 + 15x - 12$. Combine like terms to get $3x^2 + 8x - 7$. Therefore, $a = 3$. The correct answer is 3.

32. **5 or 6** The question asks for the one possible value of p, the number of potatoes. One onion costs $0.50. Subtract that from the total amounts that Emeril might spend to find that he can spend between $1.50 and $2 on potatoes. If he spends $1.50 on potatoes that cost $0.30 each, he can buy 5 potatoes. If he spends closer to $2.00 on potatoes, he can get 6 for $1.80. He can't get 7 potatoes, as that would put him over his $2 potato budget, so Emeril can get 5 or 6 potatoes. The correct answers are 5 or 6.

33. **25.2** The question asks for the mean height of the infants in the daycare program. The mean of a list is the total divided by the number of items in the list. Here, the total of all the heights is 302, and there are 12 infants in the program. $\frac{302}{12} = 25.1\overline{6}$. The question asks for the mean rounded to the nearest tenth. Therefore, the correct answer is 25.2.

34. **40** The question asks for the lowest score Jacob can receive on the 5th exam while still maintaining an average of 75. For averages, use the formula $T = AN$, in which T is the total, A is the average, and N is the number of things. For an average score of 75 on all 8 exams, Jacob needs to score a total of $T = 75 \times 8 = 600$ points. Over the first 4 exams, he has already scored $65 \times 4 = 260$ points. To find the minimum score allowable for the 5th exam, maximize the scores on all of the other remaining exams. The most he can score on an exam is 100. If he got 100 on the 6th, 7th, and 8th exams, that would be a total of 300 points. Add this to his current points: $300 + 260 = 560$ points, which means that on the 5th test, he would need to score a minimum of $600 - 560 = 40$. The correct answer is 40.

35. **1,000** The question asks for the greatest value of k, the y-coordinate of a point in the solution to a system of inequalities. Draw a rough sketch of the graph of this system of inequalities to figure out what is going on here. It would look something like this:

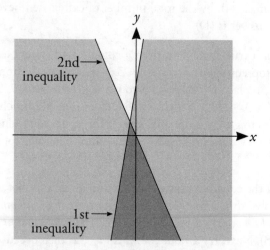

The area included in both inequalities represents the solution to the system. The question asks for the greatest value of k, which is the y-coordinate, so it would happen as close to the top of the graph as possible. For the area of overlap representing the solution, this happens at the point of intersection of the two lines. Find this point of intersection by setting the two equations, $y = 20x + 3,500$ and $y = -8x$, equal to each other to get $20x + 3,500 = -8x$. Add $8x$ to both sides to get $28x + 3,500 = 0$, then subtract 3,500 from both sides to get $28x = -3,500$. Dividing both sides by 28 results in $x = -125$. This is the value for j, and it can be plugged back into either equation to get the value of k, the y-coordinate at that point. Use the easier equation, $y = -8x$, to get $k = -8(-125) = 1,000$. The correct answer is 1,000.

36. $\dfrac{7}{12}$ or **.583**

The question asks for the fractional part of the circumference that an arc defines. There is a proportional relationship between the arc length, degree measure, and area of a section of a circle formed by two radii. For this question, the important aspects of the circle are the given angle measure of $\dfrac{7\pi}{6}$ radians and the arc the question asks about. Set up a proportion: $\dfrac{\text{arc}}{\text{circumference}} = \dfrac{\text{angle measure}}{\text{total radians}}$.

This fractional part of the circumference in the first part of the proportion is what the question is asking for, so focus on the second part. The angle measure is given, and the total number of radians in a circle is 2π. Fill in the second fraction to get $\dfrac{\text{arc}}{\text{circumference}} = \dfrac{\frac{7\pi}{6}}{2\pi}$. Dividing by a number is the same as multiplying by the reciprocal of the number, so the second fraction becomes $\dfrac{7\pi}{6} \times \dfrac{1}{2\pi} = \dfrac{7}{12}$. The correct answer is $\dfrac{7}{12}$ or .583.

37. **20** The question asks for a comparison of the number of patients in the two clinics at any given time. Start by calculating the average number of patients in the Kind Care clinic. According to the information provided, $m = 4$ and $W = 45$. Therefore, Kind Care has an average of $4(45) = 180$ patients in its clinic. Speedy Care sees 324 patients "per hour," so set up a proportion: $\dfrac{324 \text{ patients}}{60 \text{ minutes}} = \dfrac{m \text{ patients}}{1 \text{ minute}}$.

Cross-multiply to get $60m = 324$, then divide by 60 to get $m = 5.4$ patients per minute. Therefore, the average number of patients in the Speedy Care clinic can be calculated as $L = 5.4(40) = 216$. To calculate a "percent greater than," use the following percent change formula: $\dfrac{\text{difference}}{\text{original}} \times 100$. In this case, the smaller number is the original, so the percent change is $\dfrac{216 - 180}{180} \times 100 = 20\%$. The correct answer is 20.

38. **9** The question asks for the average number of patients being treated by a doctor at the Kind Care clinic at any given time. According to the question, the rate at which patients enter the clinic is defined as m patients per minute. This question gives the rate of 36 patients "per hour," so set up a proportion: $\dfrac{36 \text{ patients}}{60 \text{ minutes}} = \dfrac{m \text{ patients}}{1 \text{ minute}}$. Cross-multiply to get $60m = 36$, then divide by 60 to get $m = 0.6$ patients per minute. Each stays with the doctor an average of 15 minutes, so to find the average number of patients being treated, L, use the formula to get $L = (0.6)(15) = 9$. The correct answer is 9.

Chapter 9
Practice Test 4

Reading Test

65 MINUTES, 52 QUESTIONS

Turn to Section 1 of your answer sheet to answer the questions in this section.

Each passage or pair of passages below is followed by a number of questions. After reading each passage or pair, choose the best answer to each question based on what is stated or implied in the passage or passages and in any accompanying graphics (such as a table or graph).

Questions 1–10 are based on the following passage.

This passage is adapted from Ayn Rand, *Anthem*. ©1938. The protagonist, a street sweeper named Equality 7-2521, lives in a society in which the word "I" is forbidden.

Note: Because the word "I" is forbidden in this society, the narrator refers to himself as "we."

And as we all undress at night, in the dim light of the candles, our brothers are silent, for they dare not speak the thoughts of their minds. For all must agree
Line with all, and they cannot know if their thoughts are the
5 thoughts of all, and so they fear to speak. And they are glad when the candles are blown for the night. But we, Equality 7-2521, look through the window upon the sky, and there is peace in the sky, and cleanliness, and dignity. And beyond the City there lies the plain, and
10 beyond the plain, black upon the black sky, there lies the Uncharted Forest. We do not wish to look upon the Uncharted Forest. We do not wish to think of it. But ever do our eyes return to that black patch upon the sky. Men never enter the Uncharted Forest, for there is
15 no power to explore it and no path to lead among its ancient trees which stand as guards of fearful secrets. It is whispered that once or twice in a hundred years, one among the men of the City escape alone and run to the Uncharted Forest, without call or reason. These
20 men do not return. They perish from hunger and from the claws of the wild beasts which roam the Forest. But our Councils say that this is only a legend. We have heard that there are many Uncharted Forests over the land, among the Cities. And it is whispered that
25 they have grown over the ruins of many cities of the

Unmentionable Times. The trees have swallowed the ruins, and the bones under the ruins, and all the things which perished. And as we look upon the Uncharted Forest far in the night, we think of the secrets of the
30 Unmentionable Times. And we wonder how it came to pass that these secrets were lost to the world.
    We have heard the legends of the great fighting, in which many men fought on one side and only a few on the other. These few were the Evil Ones and they were
35 conquered. Then great fires raged over the land. And in these fires the Evil Ones and all the things made by the Evil Ones were burned. And the fire which is called the Dawn of the Great Rebirth, was the Script Fire where all the scripts of the Evil Ones were burned, and with them
40 all the words of the Evil Ones. The words of the Evil Ones... The words of the Unmentionable Times... What are the words which we have lost? May the Council have mercy upon us! We had no wish to write such a question, and we knew not what we were doing till we
45 had written it. We shall not ask this question and we shall not think it. We shall not call death upon our head.
    And yet . . . And yet . . . There is some word, one single word which is not in the language of men, but which had been. And this is the Unspeakable Word,
50 which no men may speak nor hear. But sometimes, and it is rare, sometimes, somewhere, one among men find that word. They find it upon scraps of old manuscripts or cut into the fragments of ancient stones. But when they speak it they are put to death.
55 There is no crime punished by death in this world, save this one crime of speaking the Unspeakable Word.

CONTINUE ➔

1

In the passage, the narrator's focus shifts from

A) fear of exploring frontiers to preparation for it.

B) disquiet about the unknown to curiosity about it.

C) acknowledgment of an ancient city to dismissal of it.

D) repetition of the Council's rules to acceptance of them.

2

Which choice provides the best evidence for the answer to the previous question?

A) Lines 1–3 ("And as . . . minds")

B) Line 22 ("But our . . . legend")

C) Lines 35–37 ("And in . . . burned")

D) Lines 47–49 ("And yet . . . been")

3

As used in lines 3–4, "all must agree with all" most nearly means

A) truth is true.

B) language must be accurate.

C) thought must be uniform.

D) words match their meaning.

4

The sentence in lines 12–14 ("But ever . . . sky") mainly serves to

A) confirm that the narrator's job is to guard against outside threats.

B) show that some people find an object of mystery to be of recurring interest.

C) indicate that members of the narrator's society know everyone keeps looking at the horizon.

D) illustrate a repeated action stemming from a confusion about an unexplainable phenomenon.

5

The narrator states that a person who wished to navigate the Uncharted Forest would find

A) no source of electricity.

B) it impossible to locate objects within.

C) answers to many long-forgotten questions.

D) no clear trail through.

6

Which choice provides the best evidence for the answer to the previous question?

A) Lines 14–16 ("Men never . . . secrets")

B) Lines 20–21 ("They . . . Forest")

C) Lines 26–28 ("The trees . . . perished")

D) Lines 37–40 ("And the . . . Ones")

7

Which of the following most accurately expresses the narrator's perspective about exploring the secrets of the past?

A) Compelling but dangerous

B) Easily pursuable but illegal

C) Unavoidable but unexpectedly challenging

D) Appealing but inauthentic

8

The statement the narrator makes in lines 26–28 ("The trees . . . perished") can be most clearly inferred to mean that

A) people who ask questions in the narrator's society are banished to the Forest.

B) the trees grew in the streets of cities in the Unmentionable Times.

C) the visible traces of the past have been completely obscured.

D) the city buries its dead in the Forest.

CONTINUE

As used in lines 30–31, "how it came to pass" most nearly means

A) what crossed each other.

B) what went in circles.

C) what happened historically.

D) how time elapsed.

As used in line 39, "scripts" most nearly means

A) clothes.

B) habits.

C) screenplays.

D) writings.

CONTINUE

Questions 11–21 are based on the following passage and supplementary material.

This passage is adapted from James Ellsmoor, "Smart Cities: The Future Of Urban Development." ©2019 by James Ellsmoor.

As the world becomes increasingly interconnected and technology-dependent, a new wave of smart applications is changing how we approach everyday
Line activities. Utility appliances such as intelligent fridges
5 (yes, you read that right), personal assistants like Amazon's Alexa or smart home security applications create opportunities for more efficient living. While the idea of "Smart Cities" has been proposed as the future of urbanism, the question remains: how do
10 we connect this new technology for the ultimately "efficient" society? Smart cities bring together infrastructure and technology to improve the quality of life of citizens and enhance their interactions with the urban environment. But how can data from areas
15 such as public transport, air quality meters and energy production be integrated and effectively used?

The Internet of Things (IoT), could have some of the answers. Created as part of the smart technology movement, the IoT enables various objects and
20 entities to communicate with each other through the internet. By creating a network of objects capable of smart interactions, the door is opened to a wide range of technological innovations that could help improve public transport, give accurate traffic reports
25 or provide real-time energy consumption data. By rendering more technology capable of communicating across platforms, IoT generates more data that can help improve various aspects of daily life. Cities can identify both opportunities and challenges in real-time,
30 reducing costs by pinpointing issues prior to their emergence and allocating resources more accurately to maximize impact.

By investing in public spaces, smart cities can be places where people want to spend more time. The
35 city of Barcelona has adopted smart technologies by implementing a network of fiber optics throughout the city, providing free high-speed Wi-Fi that supports the IoT. By integrating smart water, lighting and parking management, Barcelona saved €75 million of city funds
40 and created 47,000 new jobs in the smart technology sector. The Netherlands have tested the use of IoT-based infrastructure in Amsterdam, where traffic flow, energy usage and public safety are monitored and adjusted based on real-time data. Meanwhile, in the
45 United States, major cities like Boston and Baltimore have deployed smart trash cans that relay how full they are and determine the most efficient pick-up route for sanitation workers.

The Internet of Things has led to a plethora
50 of opportunities for cities willing to implement new smart technology to improve the efficiency of operations. Furthermore, tertiary institutions are also looking into maximizing the impact of integrated smart technology. Places such as university campuses
55 and island communities provide smaller laboratories to implement technology in a more manageable environment that can be then replicated on a larger scale. Universities are essentially smaller, more condensed versions of cities, often boasting their own
60 transport systems, small businesses as well as their own citizens (students). This makes campuses the perfect testing ground as Manchester Metropolitan University's IT portfolio manager Tori Brown explains in The Guardian: "The smart campus idea was first
65 floated in spring 2016. As more projects and initiatives kept coming to light, it felt right to bring these together to tell a story around student engagement and how we can use technology to support this."

Brown illustrates how smart technology could go
70 even further in improving efficiency by tracking the movements and actions of students: "It's a continually evolving plan. There are possibilities around smart kiosks with personalized information, true cross-campus digital and personalized wayfinding. These
75 include wearable tech like smartwatches and phones." On campus, your phone or smartwatch could remind you of a class and how to reach it, give you updates on your assignment due dates as well as warn you about overdue books you have borrowed from the library.
80 Whilst these may seem like small improvements compared to the ones implemented in various cities worldwide, they can help form a blueprint for future development that can be upscaled to fit larger developmental needs.
85 As smart technology continues to improve and urban centers expand, both will become interconnected. For example, the United Kingdom has plans to integrate smart technology in future development and use big data to make better
90 decisions to upgrade the country's infrastructure.

CONTINUE ➡

Better decisions could be a boom to the economy. The potential to improve several aspects of public service systems as well as quality of life and reduce costs has driven the demand for smart cities. By taking a step
95 towards the future, we will improve not only how we interact with our general environment but how cities interact with us, ensuring that we receive the best quality options and waste fewer resources.

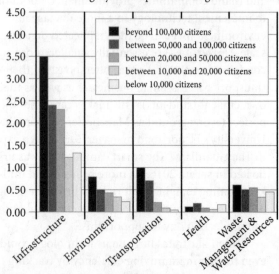

Mean Values of Implemented Actions Per Category and Population Range

Legend:
- beyond 100,000 citizens
- between 50,000 and 100,000 citizens
- between 20,000 and 50,000 citizens
- between 10,000 and 20,000 citizens
- below 10,000 citizens

Categories of actions

Charalabidis, Yannis & Alexopoulos, Charalampos & Vogiatzis, Nikolaos & Kolokotronis, Dimitris. (2019). A 360-Degree Model for Prioritizing Smart Cities Initiatives, with the Participation of Municipality Officials, Citizens and Experts. 10.1007/978-3-319-89474-4_7.

The graph above shows the number of smart cities developments and actions per identified smart city category and population category.

11

Which choice best summarizes the first two paragraphs of the passage (lines 1–32)?

A) Smart cities are a good idea, but making them a reality is a complicated problem.

B) The Internet of Things can help smart appliances, such as intelligent fridges and personal assistants, communicate with each other.

C) Smart cities integrate infrastructure and technology to make more efficient decisions about cost management.

D) The Internet of Things can make smart cities a reality by providing a network for various technologies to connect.

12

As used in line 13, "enhance" most nearly means

A) emphasize.

B) enrich.

C) convey.

D) increase.

13

According to the passage, which aspect of the city's infrastructure did Barcelona improve through integration with the IoT?

A) Lighting

B) Traffic flow

C) Trash cans

D) Energy

14

The passage implies that universities using smart technology

A) implemented smart technology before cities.

B) practice implementing technology in laboratories before implementing it on campuses.

C) have infrastructure needs similar to those of cities.

D) can serve as models for cities.

15

Which choice provides the best evidence for the answer to the previous question?

A) Lines 52–54 ("Furthermore . . . technology")

B) Lines 54–58 ("Places . . . scale")

C) Lines 69–71 ("Brown . . . students")

D) Lines 76–79 ("On campus . . . library")

CONTINUE

16

As used in line 65, "floated" most nearly means

A) buoyed.

B) suggested.

C) suspended.

D) claimed.

17

According to the passage, which choice best describes a potential effect of implementing smart technology in cities?

A) Rising employment due to a spike in building projects

B) Lack of housing due to rapid growth in population

C) Increased efficiency due to the improved responsiveness of cities

D) Growing privacy concerns due to increased tracking by smart devices

18

Which choice provides the best evidence for the answer to the previous question?

A) Lines 85–87 ("As smart . . . interconnected")

B) Lines 87–90 ("For example . . . infrastructure")

C) Line 91 ("Better . . . economy")

D) Lines 91–94 ("The potential . . . cities")

19

In relationship to the passage, the information in the chart provides

A) an illustration of drawbacks that the author fails to mention.

B) historical perspective on the developments the author examines.

C) a comparison of some of the applications mentioned by the author.

D) analysis of the effectiveness of the author's proposed solutions.

20

According to the chart, cities with between 20,000 and 50,000 citizens implemented

A) an almost equal number of projects in infrastructure and environment.

B) fewer projects in four of the categories of action than cities with 50,000 to 100,000 citizens.

C) more projects in the transportation category than the environment category.

D) fewer than half of the number of projects in infrastructure compared to cities with beyond 100,000 citizens.

21

The chart suggests which of the following about smart cities developments?

A) Cities with the largest populations implemented more projects than cities with the smallest populations.

B) More money was spent on waste-management projects than on projects in the environment category.

C) Projects in the health category were implemented more often than were projects in the environment category.

D) Infrastructure projects were better received than were waste-management projects.

CONTINUE

Questions 22–32 are based on the following passage and supplementary material.

This passage is adapted from Schmitt et al., "Identifying the Volcanic Eruption Depicted in a Neolithic Painting at Çatalhöyük, Central Anatolia, Turkey." ©2014 by PLOS ONE.

A mural excavated at the Neolithic Çatalhöyük site (Central Anatolia, Turkey) has been interpreted as the oldest known map. Dating to around 6600 B.C.E.,
Line it putatively depicts an explosive summit eruption of
5 the Hasan Dağı twin-peaks volcano located about 130 km northeast of Çatalhöyük, and a birds-eye view of a town plan in the foreground. This interpretation, however, has remained controversial not least because independent evidence for a contemporaneous
10 explosive volcanic eruption of Hasan Dağı has been lacking.

Here, we document the presence of andesitic pumice veneer on the summit of Hasan Dağı, which we dated using (U-Th)/He zircon geochronology.
15 Collectively, our results reveal protracted intrusive activity at Hasan Dağı punctuated by explosive venting, and provide the first radiometric ages for a Holocene explosive eruption which was most likely witnessed by humans in the area. Geologic and
20 geochronologic lines of evidence thus support previous interpretations that residents of Çatalhöyük artistically represented an explosive eruption of Hasan Dağı volcano.

Starting from the discovery of the Neolithic
25 settlement of Çatalhöyük in the early 1960s by British archaeologist James Mellaart, the excavations at this location have provided unique insights into the living conditions of humans at the transition from hunter-gatherer to settled agriculture societies.
30 One outstanding find is a mural from level VII of Çatalhöyük famously described by its discoverer as depicting a volcanic eruption.

Similar interpretations, differing in detail, have been put forward since then, implicating this painting
35 not only as the oldest depiction of a volcanic eruption, but as a contender for being the first graphical representation of a landscape or a map. Detailed volcanological interpretations of the painting include reconstructions of the eruptive style with the summit
40 region showing "falling volcanic 'bombs' or large semiliquid lava." According to these interpreters, the most likely candidate for the erupting volcano depicted in the upper register of the painting is the twin-peak

volcano of Hasan Dağı, located about 130 km NE of
45 Çatalhöyük.

This view, however, has been contested, largely because of the extraordinary age of the mural, and the absence of any other landscape art or map until much later in history. The depiction of a leopard skin
50 underlain by geometric patterns has been proposed instead.

A testable prediction of the volcanic eruption hypothesis for the Çatalhöyük mural is a geologic record of an eruption that would fall into, or briefly
55 predate, the time when the Çatalhöyük mural was painted.

Protracted periods of oral tradition over 250 generations have been proposed for prehistoric native North American myths following the Mount Mazama
60 eruption at around 5700 B.C.E. For the Çatalhöyük map (and volcano) hypothesis to be plausible, however, we surmise that a brief line of oral tradition, or even an eyewitness portrayal, is perhaps more likely than tradition of a myth that detached itself from its
65 inspiration in the physical world. This is not to say that realism must prevail in Neolithic art, but many of the apparent details can be reasonably expected to become lost or obscured during a long period of oral tradition. A tradition that predated the settlement of Çatalhöyük
70 thus appears very unlikely, and hence we would predict a time period for the eruption between 7400 and 6600 B.C.E. based on the ^{14}C chronology of the Çatalhöyük cultural strata.

Neither proponents nor opponents of the "volcano"
75 hypothesis for the Çatalhöyük painting have thus far scrutinized if and when such a volcanic eruption might have occurred. The radiometric age, and the following geologic evidence, corroborates the "volcano" hypothesis.

CONTINUE ➤

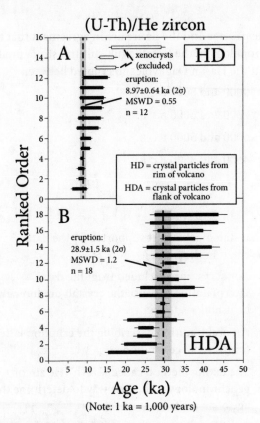

(U-Th)/He zircon

xenocrysts (excluded)

A — **HD**

eruption:
8.97±0.64 ka (2σ)
MSWD = 0.55
n = 12

HD = crystal particles from rim of volcano

HDA = crystal particles from flank of volcano

B

eruption:
28.9±1.5 ka (2σ)
MSWD = 1.2
n = 18

HDA

Ranked Order

Age (ka)

(Note: 1 ka = 1,000 years)

This table shows the (U-Th)/He zircon dated ages of sample particles removed from the rim and the flank of the Hasan Dağı volcano.

22

The main purpose of the passage is to

A) describe periods in Turkey's ancient geologic history.

B) explain the ways scientists use radiometric aging.

C) describe opposing views regarding an ancient mural and cautiously endorse one view.

D) explain how andesitic pumice veneer forms after volcanic eruptions.

23

Over the course of the passage, the focus shifts from

A) an explanation of a theory to a response to criticism of this theory.

B) a depiction of an event to its proof in oral history.

C) the use of (U-Th)/He zircon geochronology to a new method.

D) the use of radiometric aging to an examination of andesitic pumice veneer.

24

Which choice provides the best evidence for the answer to the previous question?

A) Lines 12–14 ("Here . . . geochronology")

B) Lines 46–49 ("This . . . history")

C) Lines 69–70 ("A tradition . . . unlikely")

D) Lines 77–79 ("The radiometric . . . hypothesis")

25

The author uses the phrase "it putatively depicts" (line 4) most likely to

A) detail the hands-on nature of the work done by those who study science.

B) emphasize the fact that scientists must always question theories.

C) underscore the need for clarification of the work of scientists.

D) bolster the idea that the evidence to support the claim is imperfect.

26

Where does the author indicate the Neolithic volcanic eruption most probably was located?

A) Near Central Anatolia, in Turkey

B) In the British Isles

C) In the Middle East

D) In the central region of North America

CONTINUE ▶

27

Which choice provides the best evidence for the answer to the previous question?

A) Lines 1–6 ("A mural . . . Çatalhöyük")

B) Lines 24–29 ("Starting . . . societies")

C) Lines 57–60 ("Protracted . . . B.C.E.")

D) Lines 60–65 ("For the . . . world")

28

As used in line 65, the phrase "This is not to say" implies that

A) the lost details are crucial for proving the truth.

B) oral traditions describe stories but not real events.

C) the scientists don't expect the mural to be completely true to life.

D) Neolithic artists used realism to portray the natural world.

29

Which choice best supports the claim that the mural was painted near the time of the volcanic eruption?

A) Lines 7–11 ("This . . . lacking")

B) Lines 49–51 ("The depiction . . . instead")   .

C) Lines 65–68 ("This . . . tradition")

D) Lines 74–77 ("Neither . . . occurred")

30

According to the data, the youngest Holocene eruption age for Hasan Dağı is approximately

A) 1.2 ka.

B) 8.97 ka.

C) 18 ka.

D) 28.9 ka.

31

The passage and the figure are in agreement that the chronology of the Çatalhöyük cultural strata predicts that the Hasan Dağı volcano erupted between

A) 9000 and 8000 B.C.E.

B) 7000 and 6000 B.C.E.

C) 6000 and 5000 B.C.E.

D) 4500 and 3500 B.C.E.

32

What statement is best supported by the data presented in the figure?

A) Xenocrysts are excluded from the data interpretation because the crystals are too new to be useful.

B) An oral tradition describing the eruption lasted for over 250 generations.

C) The dating method called (U-Th)/He zircon geochronology is the best way to determine the age of an artifact.

D) Particles on the rim of a volcano are more likely to be from recent eruptions than particles on the flank of the volcano.

CONTINUE ➤

Questions 33–42 are based on the following passages.

Passage 1 is excerpted from Edmund Burke, *Reflections on the Revolution in France*, originally published in 1790. Passage 2 is excerpted from Thomas Paine, *Common Sense*, originally published in 1776.

Passage 1

A few years ago I should be ashamed to overload a matter so capable of supporting itself by the then unnecessary support of any argument; but this
Line seditious, unconstitutional doctrine is now publicly
5 taught, avowed, and printed.

The people of England will not ape the fashions they have never tried, nor go back to those which they have found mischievous on trial. They look upon the legal hereditary succession of their crown as among
10 their rights, not as among their wrongs; as a benefit, not as a grievance; as a security for their liberty, not as a badge of servitude. They look on the frame of their commonwealth, *such as it stands*, to be of inestimable value; and they conceive the undisturbed succession of
15 the crown to be a pledge of the stability and perpetuity of all the other members of our Constitution.

I shall beg leave, before I go any further, to take notice of some paltry artifices which the abettors of election as the only lawful title to the crown are
20 ready to employ, in order to render the support of the just principles of our Constitution a task somewhat invidious. These sophisters substitute a fictitious cause, and feigned personages, in whose favor they suppose you engaged, whenever you defend the inheritable
25 nature of the crown. It is common with them to dispute as if they were in a conflict with some of those exploded fanatics of slavery who formerly maintained, what I believe no creature now maintains, "that the crown is held by divine, hereditary, and indefeasible
30 right."

These old fanatics of single arbitrary power dogmatized as if hereditary royalty was the only lawful government in the world, just as our new fanatics of popular arbitrary power maintain that a popular
35 election is the sole lawful source of authority. The old prerogative enthusiasts, it is true, did speculate foolishly, and perhaps impiously too, as if monarchy had more of a divine sanction than any other mode of government; and as if a right to govern by inheritance
40 were in strictness *indefeasible* in every person who should be found in the succession to a throne, and under every circumstance, which no civil or political right can be.

Passage 2

But it is not so much the absurdity as the evil of
45 hereditary succession which concerns mankind. Did it ensure a race of good and wise men it would have the seal of divine authority, but as it opens a door to the FOOLISH, the WICKED, and the IMPROPER, it hath in it the nature of oppression. Men who look upon
50 themselves born to reign, and others to obey, soon grow insolent; selected from the rest of mankind their minds are early poisoned by importance; and the world they act in differs so materially from the world at large, that they have but little opportunity of knowing its true
55 interests, and when they succeed to the government are frequently the most ignorant and unfit of any throughout the dominions. Another evil which attends hereditary succession is, that the throne is subject to be possessed by a minor at any age; all which time the
60 regency, acting under the cover of a king, have every opportunity and inducement to betray their trust. The same national misfortune happens, when a king worn out with age and infirmity, enters the last stage of human weakness. In both these cases the public
65 becomes a prey to every miscreant, who can tamper successfully with the follies either of age or infancy.

The most plausible plea, which hath ever been offered in favour of hereditary succession, is, that it preserves a nation from civil wars; and were this true,
70 it would be weighty; whereas, it is the most barefaced falsity ever imposed upon mankind. The whole history of England disowns the fact. Thirty kings and two minors have reigned in that distracted kingdom since the conquest, in which time there have been
75 (including the Revolution) no less than eight civil wars and nineteen rebellions. Wherefore instead of making for peace, it makes against it, and destroys the very foundation it seems to stand on. ... In short, monarchy and succession have laid (not this or that kingdom
80 only) but the world in blood and ashes.

CONTINUE →

33

In Passage 1, Burke indicates that the argument of those who support elected leaders is characterized by its

A) weakness and dishonesty.

B) universality and fanaticism.

C) antiquity and irrelevance.

D) hypocrisy and innovation.

34

As used in line 1, "overload" most nearly means

A) burden excessively.

B) cause to burst.

C) express emotionally.

D) short circuit.

35

As used in line 20, "employ" most nearly means

A) hire.

B) utilize.

C) reimburse.

D) work.

36

Passage 2 most strongly suggests that Paine believes leaderships by right of birth to be

A) illegitimate failures that cause devastating results.

B) useful means by which to avoid dangerously inferior governance.

C) complicated and passionate methods for expressing opinions.

D) valuable despite some historical setbacks.

37

In response to Burke's statement in lines 22–25 ("These . . . crown"), what would Paine most likely say?

A) He would indicate that it is important to address all possible reasons for supporting an unjust cause.

B) He would state that the argument against the divine right to rule is less important than the tendencies of rulers to arbitrarily provide favors to their supporters.

C) He would clarify that the argument against an accepted form of rule is based on results, not redirection.

D) He would deny that the old belief in an inherently granted right to rule a state has completely disappeared.

38

Which choice provides the best evidence for the answer to the previous question?

A) Lines 49–51 ("Men who . . . insolent")

B) Lines 57–59 ("Another . . . age")

C) Lines 67–69 ("The most . . . wars")

D) Lines 71–72 ("The whole . . . fact")

39

Which of the following types of responses would Burke most likely make to Paine's statements in the final paragraph of Passage 2?

A) One of disagreement, because conflicts do not necessarily indicate an unstable structure

B) One of agreement, because civil wars are a burden on a nation

C) One of acceptance, because excessive violence demonstrates a failure of a system

D) One of doubt, because Paine failed to provide details and dates of the wars and rebellions he cites

CONTINUE

40

Which choice provides the best evidence for the answer to the previous question?

A) Lines 6–8 ("The people . . . trial")

B) Lines 12–16 ("They . . . Constitution")

C) Lines 31–35 ("These . . . authority")

D) Lines 35–39 ("The old . . . government")

41

Which choice best states the relationship between the two passages?

A) Passage 2 underscores the concerns raised by Passage 1.

B) Passage 2 argues a point dismissed by Passage 1.

C) Passage 2 presents another method for resolving the issues delineated in Passage 1.

D) Passage 2 expands on the main position expressed and advocated in Passage 1.

42

The main purpose of both passages is to

A) evaluate the various benefits of parliamentary forms of government.

B) seek compromise on a passionately debated issue of importance.

C) reject an opposing view and a particular position.

D) prove that history is based on false beliefs.

CONTINUE

Questions 43–52 are based on the following passage.

This passage is adapted from Shouguang Jin, University of Florida, "Explainer: CRISPR technology brings precise genetic editing—and raises ethical questions," originally published by *The Conversation*: https://theconversation.com/.

A group of leading biologists earlier this month called for a halt to the use of a powerful new gene editing technique on humans. Known by the acronym
Line CRISPR, the method allows precise editing of genes
5 for targeted traits, which can be passed down to future generations.

Scientists have long sought after this sort of genome editing tool for living cells. Two other technologies, called zinc-finger nucleases and TALEN (transcription
10 activator-like effector nuclease) are available to achieve the same result. However, the CRISPR technology is much easier to generate and manipulate. This means that most biological research laboratories can carry out the CRISPR experiments. As a result, CRISPR
15 technology has been quickly adopted by scientists all over the world and put into various tests. It has been demonstrated to be effective in genome editing of most experimental organisms, including cells derived from insects, plants, fish, mice, monkeys and humans.

20 Such broad successes in a short period of time imply we've arrived at a new genome editing era, promising fast-paced development in biomedical research that will bring about new therapeutic treatments for various human diseases. The CRISPR
25 technology offers a novel tool for scientists to address some of the most fundamental questions that were difficult, if not impossible, to address before. For instance, the whole human genomic DNA sequence had been deciphered many years ago, but the majority
30 of information embedded on the DNA fragments are largely unknown. Now, the CRISPR technology is enabling scientists to study those gene functions. By eliminating or replacing specific DNA fragments and observing the consequences in the resulting cells,
35 we can now link particular DNA fragments to their biological functions.

Recently, cells and even whole animals with desired genome alterations have successfully been generated using the CRISPR technology. This has proven highly
40 valuable in various biomedical research studies, such as understanding the cause and effect relationship between specific DNA changes and human diseases. Studying DNA in this way also sheds light on the

mechanisms underlying how diseases develop and
45 provides insights for developing new drugs that eliminate specific disease symptoms.

With such profound implications in medical sciences, many biotech and pharmaceutical companies have now licensed the CRISPR technology to develop
50 commercial products. For example, a biotech company, Editas Medicine, was founded in 2013 with the specific goal of creating treatments for hereditary human diseases employing the CRISPR technology. However, products derived from the use of CRISPR technology
55 are yet to hit the market with FDA approval.

With the CRISPR technology, scientists can now alter the genome composition of whole organisms, including humans, through manipulating reproductive cells and fertilized eggs or embryos. Those particular
60 genetic traits are then passed down through generations. This brings hope to cure genetic defects that cause various hereditary human diseases, such as cystic fibrosis, haemophilia, sickle-cell anemia, Down syndrome and so on.

65 Unlike the current approaches of gene therapy which temporarily fix defective cells or organs through the introduction of corrected or functional genes, the CRISPR technology promises to correct the defect in the reproductive cells, producing progenies that
70 are free of the defective gene. In other words, it can eliminate the root causes of hereditary human diseases.

In theory, then, hereditary features that people consider advantageous, such as higher intelligence, better body appearance and longevity, can be
75 introduced into an individual's genome through CRISPR mediated reproductive cell modifications as well. However, scientists do not yet fully understand all the possible side effects of editing human genomes. It is also the case that there is no clear law to regulate
80 such attempts.

That's why groups of prominent scientists in the field have recently initiated calls for ethical guidelines for doing such modifications of reproductive cells, the fear being that uncontrolled practice might bring
85 about unforeseen disastrous outcomes in the long run. The guidelines call for a strong discouragement of any attempts at genome modification of reproductive cells for clinical application in humans, until the

CONTINUE ▶

social, environmental, and ethical implications of such
90 operations are broadly discussed among scientific and
governmental organizations.

    There is no doubt that the exciting and
revolutionary CRISPR technology, under the guidance
of carefully drafted and broadly accepted rules, will
95 serve well for the well-being of humankind.

43

The primary purpose of the passage is to

A) contrast competing theories in a scientific field.

B) detail the findings of a study.

C) outline the history of a scientific discovery.

D) evaluate the prospects of a technological
advancement.

44

The author's attitude toward CRISPR technology is
best described as

A) unconcerned ambivalence.

B) cautious optimism.

C) restrained fear.

D) unqualified exuberance.

45

As used in line 21, "editing" most nearly means

A) abridging.

B) altering.

C) revising.

D) polishing.

46

According to the passage, which of the following is
true of DNA fragments?

A) The majority of the information embedded in
them has been discovered.

B) They are a mechanism underlying how diseases
develop.

C) Their sequence was deciphered using gene editing
technology.

D) Their purposes may be revealed through the use
of CRISPR technology.

47

Which choice provides the best evidence for the
answer to the previous question?

A) Lines 27–31 ("For instance . . . unknown")

B) Lines 33–36 ("By eliminating . . . functions")

C) Lines 43–46 ("Studying . . . symptoms")

D) Lines 72–77 ("In theory . . . well")

48

What does the author suggest about current
approaches to gene therapy?

A) They do not prevent people from passing on
diseases to their offspring.

B) They are obsolete now that CRISPR technology is
available.

C) They include introducing corrected genes derived
from insects, plants, and fish.

D) They are the only safe alternatives to the use of
CRISPR technology.

CONTINUE

49

Which choice provides the best evidence for the answer to the previous question?

A) Lines 1–3 ("A group . . . humans")

B) Lines 16–19 ("It has . . . humans")

C) Lines 65–70 ("Unlike . . . gene")

D) Lines 70–71 ("In other . . . diseases")

50

The reference to "higher intelligence, better body appearance and longevity" in lines 73–74 most likely serves to

A) support a theory.

B) counter an argument.

C) provide illustrative examples.

D) summarize a key point.

51

Which of the following does the author suggest about the "ethical guidelines" mentioned in line 82?

A) They may discourage scientists from achieving further advances.

B) Scientists hope such guidelines will end human genome modification.

C) They were not in place when CRISPR technology was developed.

D) They are needed despite scientists' deep understanding of human genome modification.

52

The word "revolutionary" (line 93) most directly suggests that

A) CRISPR technology will have a profound effect on human gene therapy.

B) human health has been dramatically improved by CRISPR technology.

C) a significant shift in thinking was required to develop the CRISPR technique.

D) new ethical guidelines have fundamentally changed CRISPR's potential applications.

STOP
If you finish before time is called, you may check your work on this section only.
Do not turn to any other section in the test.

No Test Material On This Page

Writing and Language Test

35 MINUTES, 44 QUESTIONS

Turn to Section 2 of your answer sheet to answer the questions in this section.

DIRECTIONS

Each passage below is accompanied by a number of questions. For some questions, you will consider how the passage might be revised to improve the expression of ideas. For other questions, you will consider how the passage might be edited to correct errors in sentence structure, usage, or punctuation. A passage or a question may be accompanied by one or more graphics (such as a table or graph) that you will consider as you make revising and editing decisions.

Some questions will direct you to an underlined portion of a passage. Other questions will direct you to a location in a passage or ask you to think about the passage as a whole.

After reading each passage, choose the answer to each question that most effectively improves the quality of writing in the passage or that makes the passage conform to the conventions of standard written English. Many questions include a "NO CHANGE" option. Choose that option if you think the best choice is to leave the relevant portion of the passage as it is.

Questions 1–11 are based on the following passage.

The New American Renaissance

Since 1970 or so, the shape of the humanities has changed significantly. Before that time, it was rare to read books, look at paintings, or **1** watch plays by anyone other than white male European-American artists. While a bias still remains, there is no question that the canon, the group of accepted "classic" **2** works; has become much

1
A) NO CHANGE
B) rarer still was watching
C) to watch
D) DELETE the underlined portion.

2
A) NO CHANGE
B) works—
C) works
D) works,

CONTINUE ➡

more diverse. Still, in the United States, some groups have been **3** more vocal than others. There is no better example of such a marginalization than that of Native Americans.

Each century has had its figures—William Apess was a minister and autobiographer in the nineteenth century and Zitkala-Sa was a story writer and memoirist in the early twentieth. Still, these figures were never able to reach audiences as broad as those of their white contemporaries. Today, however, as the reclamation of heritage gains more traction, this public marginalization may be changing.

Literary critic Kenneth Lincoln identifies the change and **4** outlined a kind of historical timeline in his 1983 book *Native American Renaissance*. Throughout the nineteenth century, Native Americans were systematically eradicated throughout all parts of the growing United States. Much of their **5** repartee with white Americans came in the form of military campaigns. When the wars subsided, the American government started a similarly cruel program of assimilation, **6** often this involved the movement of Native American children from their homes to "Indian schools" that sought to remove any trace of tribal inheritance.

3

Which choice most effectively sets up the information that follows?

A) NO CHANGE

B) successful despite the obstacles.

C) forced to stay on the periphery.

D) content to stay out of the public eye.

4

A) NO CHANGE

B) outlining

C) was outlining

D) outlines

5

A) NO CHANGE

B) contact

C) chatting

D) banter

6

A) NO CHANGE

B) it often involved

C) this type of thing often involved

D) often involving

CONTINUE

[7] There were lots of anti-war demonstrations in the 1960s and 1970s, an era of cultural reclamation, when the emphasis on "melting-pot"-style assimilation shifted toward an attitude of "multicultural society." [8] At this time, people from all races began to think it possible to live in the United States while at the same time identifying with a particular racial group. Around this time, after many of the "Indian schools" had closed, Native American children could gain English-language education closer to home. [9] However, they could continue to identify with their cultural heritage while gaining an "American" education.

7

Which choice connects the sentence with the previous paragraph?

A) NO CHANGE

B) Kenneth Lincoln was just a young man

C) This practice of assimilation had begun to change

D) Many important things happened

8

At this point, the writer is considering adding the following sentence.

> This was not always the case as many groups have been marginalized throughout American history.

Should the writer make this addition here?

A) Yes, because it gives an important reminder that the United States is always changing.

B) Yes, because it shows that Native American writers have not always been popular.

C) No, because it makes a historical claim that the passage contradicts.

D) No, because it repeats information from earlier in the passage that is already implied in this paragraph.

9

A) NO CHANGE

B) Nevertheless,

C) Because,

D) Moreover,

CONTINUE ➤

This shift led to more Native Americans attending colleges and universities, and more empathetic attitudes among the literary establishment allowed more **10** of them space for publication of poetry and fiction. **11** The result was an efflorescence of Native American writers, particularly in the 1970s and 1980s. During this period, writers like Leslie Marmon Silko, Gerald Vizenor, and Paula Gunn Allen became popular. These writers are now among the most respected in the country, and they have influenced countless others. While the literary establishment may have been centuries late in acknowledging the significant contributions that Native American culture can make to the world, we should nonetheless be glad that this influence is finally more widely available.

10

A) NO CHANGE
B) Native American writers
C) of these
D) from it

11

Which choice most effectively combines the underlined sentences?

A) Particularly in the 1970s and 1980s, writers like Leslie Marmon Silko, Gerald Vizenor, and Paula Gunn Allen became popular, a resultant efflorescence of Native American writers.

B) The result was an efflorescence of Native American writers, particularly in the 1970s and 1980s; in these decades, popularity was earned for writers including Leslie Marmon Silko, Gerald Vizenor, and Paula Gunn Allen.

C) Leslie Marmon Silko, Gerald Vizenor, and Paula Gunn Allen were three of the writers who became popular in this period of the 1970s and 1980s amid the resulting efflorescence of Native American writers.

D) The result, particularly in the 1970s and 1980s, was an efflorescence of Native American writers including Leslie Marmon Silko, Gerald Vizenor, and Paula Gunn Allen.

CONTINUE →

Questions 12–22 are based on the following passage.

Make Like a Tree and Change Leaves

Anyone who lives in the Mid-Atlantic or New England **12** knows the flowering of spring and the lush greens of summer. The four seasons in these areas are most evident in the look of the trees. This is never more true than **13** when people are in the case of fall, when the trees are covered with beautiful swatches of red, yellow, and orange as the leaves change color. For many, this fall foliage represents the Northeast in **14** the state in which it is most pure.

People in this region have taken to the idea. Now, foliage tourism is as much a part of the region as beach season is for those on the coast. Many business **15** owners including, restaurant owners, hoteliers, and farmers, throughout the region depend on a boom in October and November.

12
A) NO CHANGE
B) bodes
C) foretells
D) indicates

13
A) NO CHANGE
B) considering
C) with the consideration
D) DELETE the underlined portion.

14
A) NO CHANGE
B) its purest state.
C) which it is in the purest possible state.
D) the state of purity rather than impurity.

15
A) NO CHANGE
B) owners, including
C) owners, including,
D) owners including:

CONTINUE

However, there is a problem. Except in very odd circumstances, it will *always* be beach season in July and August. Foliage season, however, is a bit more difficult to predict. It is clear, **16** for instance, that the leaves tend to change in the last few months of the year, but when they change and how vivid their colors will be has long remained a mystery. Of course, many people would certainly like to know the cause. **17** Because of it, fall without the foliage is like a whole season of rainy beach days, at least from a tourism perspective.

A recent study published in *Proceedings of the National Academy of Sciences* has begun to uncover some of the factors behind the change. Scientists **18** have long known that climate conditions influence the changing of the leaves, but no one has ever been sure which aspect of the weather to privilege—moisture, temperature, frost, etc. **19** No previous explanation has been able to say why in one year the leaves were still a vibrant yellow on the first of November while the next year they had all fallen already.

16

A) NO CHANGE
B) nevertheless,
C) for all that,
D) on the other hand,

17

A) NO CHANGE
B) Subsequently,
C) After all,
D) Additionally,

18

A) NO CHANGE
B) long knows
C) long know
D) are long knowing

19

At this point, the writer is considering adding the following sentence.

> The Mount Washington Observatory reports that the average rainfall in the New Hampshire region is approximately 6–9 inches, depending on the month.

Should the writer make this addition here?

A) Yes, because it provides support for the passage's main claim that fall foliage can now be accurately predicted.

B) Yes, because it adds an important detail regarding the expected moisture levels in one region.

C) No, because it introduces the work of an organization that is not discussed elsewhere in the passage.

D) No, because it is not relevant to the paragraph's description of the general factors that influence fall foliage.

CONTINUE

The answer, it seems, is that [20] their is different factors in different places. This group of scientists analyzed two different New England ecosystems, one along the coast and one in the highlands. They found that both reacted to frosts in the fall, but only the highlands reacted to frosts in the spring. [21]

Combining these findings with climate-change predictions for the next century, [22] having suggested that the changes will come later in the year for the highlands and perhaps a bit earlier for the coasts. Should these predictions turn out to be true, it could be a major boon for the tourism industry in these areas and for the tourists who visit them.

20

A) NO CHANGE

B) their's

C) their are

D) there are

21

At this point, the writer wants to add another detail that adds to the findings described in this paragraph. Which choice most effectively accomplishes this goal?

A) The forests along the coast, perhaps not surprisingly, were particularly sensitive to rain and other types of moisture.

B) The leaves fall from the trees after they have changed, thus giving the name "fall" to the season.

C) Except for the ocean breezes, temperatures along the water tend to be a bit higher than in the mountains.

D) The leaves do not change color in the same way in the spring, but the blossoms of the trees create their own kind of beauty.

22

A) NO CHANGE

B) to suggest

C) suggesting

D) the researchers suggest

CONTINUE

Questions 23–33 are based on the following passage and supplementary material.

(Almost) The Fifty-First State

When people refer to the "fifty-first state," they are usually referring to Puerto Rico or one of the contemporary U.S. holdings outside the fifty states. What many don't realize, however, is that the idea of extra states, particularly within U.S. borders, **23** is mainly the concern of academics. One early case is the state of Franklin. On a modern map, the state of Franklin would be bound by Tennessee to the west and south, Virginia to the north, and North Carolina to the southeast. **24**

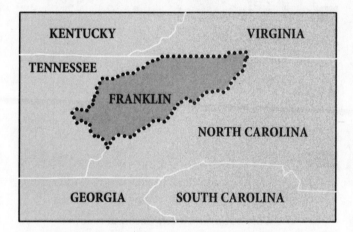

North Carolina, one of the original thirteen colonies, offered a few of its westernmost counties to the federal **25** government as payment for debts; those that had been incurred—for manpower and ammunition—during the Revolutionary War. As Congress decided what to do with the land, the North Carolinian legislature decided that the western counties were too valuable to let go, and the state soon retracted **26** it's offer of its' western counties.

23

Which choice most effectively completes the contrast in the sentence and is consistent with the information in the rest of the passage?

A) NO CHANGE

B) presents a fun historical challenge.

C) is actually quite an old idea.

D) is rather outdated in this day and age.

24

The writer wants the information in the passage to correspond as closely as possible with the information in the map. Given that goal and assuming that the rest of the previous sentence would remain unchanged, in which sequence should the three state names be discussed?

A) NO CHANGE

B) Virginia, Tennessee, North Carolina

C) North Carolina, Virginia, Tennessee

D) North Carolina, Tennessee, Virginia

25

A) NO CHANGE

B) government as payment for debts:

C) government as payment for debts

D) government—as payment for debts,

26

A) NO CHANGE

B) it's offer of its

C) its offer of it's

D) its offer of its

CONTINUE ➡

In the meantime, though, the counties in the northwest corner of the state had been developing a kind of regional identity. The three counties now called the State of Franklin **27** having been attempted to secede from North Carolina. Encouraged by the new federal government's quick creation of states from ceded lands, the three counties issued a declaration of **28** independence, yet their independence was rooted in particular in their distance from North Carolina's state capital.

[1] The secession was not recognized by Congress, and John Sevier and the leaders of the Franklin movement eventually took oaths of allegiance to the state of North Carolina. [2] This time, Congress acted quickly and accepted North Carolina's offer, interested as it was in pushing statehood further west from the thirteen colonies along the Atlantic coast. [3] Sevier and others led the administration of the ceded territories. [4] These territories were eventually granted statehood in 1796, though this time as something more recognizable—as the northeastern **29** boarder to the modern-day state of Tennessee. **30**

27

A) NO CHANGE
B) was attempting
C) were attempting
D) is attempting

28

A) NO CHANGE
B) independence, which
C) independence. Independence
D) independence, and independence

29

A) NO CHANGE
B) boarder from
C) border to
D) broader than

30

To improve the cohesion and flow of this paragraph, the writer wants to add the following sentence.

> In 1789, however, North Carolina renewed its offer of the western counties to the federal government.

The sentence would most logically be placed after

A) sentence 1.
B) sentence 2.
C) sentence 3.
D) sentence 4.

CONTINUE

Today, Franklin is a distant memory, but its short-lived history provides a unique look into some of the early machinations of the newly formed American government. The contemporary fifty states may seem like they have always existed, but that is certainly not the case—just as national borders are artificial creations, **31** so too are state borders, and as such, they are always subject to change. It may have been nearly 150 years since a state, West Virginia, was carved out of another existing state, Virginia, but that does not mean that the map as it is drawn now will forever be so. The State of Franklin may be a mere historical **32** curiosity to some, but to others, it is a reminder that even a powerful, federally oriented nation is **33** usually made up of 50 or so states.

31

A) NO CHANGE

B) being

C) but also are

D) the same can be said of

32

The writer wants to convey an attitude of genuine interest and to avoid the appearance of mockery. Which choice best accomplishes this goal?

A) NO CHANGE

B) stumper

C) thing

D) mind-blower

33

Which choice most effectively concludes the sentence and paragraph?

A) NO CHANGE

B) very important in the world and in history.

C) a living, breathing thing, ever subject to change.

D) home to many things of historical interest.

CONTINUE

Questions 34–44 are based on the following passage.

What's So Civil About Engineers Anyway?

No matter where you live, you see their work everywhere. Whether you cross a bridge or drive on a highway, you `34` see the work of civil engineers. Civil engineering as a profession is centuries old and has long been necessary for the functioning of modern government. `35` As long as people need to get to school or work, civil engineers will continue to be `36` beginnings of modern societies.

`34`
A) NO CHANGE
B) saw
C) have been seeing
D) sees

`35`
At this point, the writer is considering adding the following sentence.

Few governments in the modern world could function without the work of civil engineers.

Should the writer make this addition here?

A) Yes, because it supports the information contained in the following paragraph.
B) Yes, because it provides an important reminder that governments are not made up of politicians alone.
C) No, because it is a mere restatement of an idea expressed in the previous sentence.
D) No, because it is a digression from the main point of the paragraph.

`36`
A) NO CHANGE
B) cornerstones
C) basics
D) footings

CONTINUE

The American Society of Civil Engineers defines the profession as "the design and maintenance of public works such as roads, bridges, water, and energy systems as well as public facilities like ports, railways, and airports." [37] In other words, civil engineers design and maintain the components of energy and transportation systems in the modern world. The projects can be [38] large—like the Hoover Dam, the Holland Tunnel, or the interstate system that covers the whole country—or small—like local roads and power stations. Civil engineers see these projects through from start to finish: from the earliest stages of design and analysis to the final stages of completion and beyond.

37

A) NO CHANGE
B) On the other hand,
C) Nonetheless,
D) In the abstract,

38

A) NO CHANGE
B) large; like the Hoover Dam, the Holland Tunnel, or the interstate system that covers the whole country;
C) large: like the Hoover Dam, the Holland Tunnel, or the interstate system that covers the whole country,
D) large: like the Hoover Dam, the Holland Tunnel, or the interstate system that covers the whole country—

[1] Civil engineers collaborate on large projects. [2] Their backgrounds tend to **39** vary—however, specialties can range from architecture to environmental engineering, from ecology to urban planning. [3] Those who want a greener country draw on the expertise of civil engineers in designing windmills and other sustainable sources of energy. [4] Environmental engineering has been particularly popular of late on both sides of the environmental debate. [5] Those who are less concerned with long-term energy sources have drawn on the help of civil engineers in mining oil and gas and in **40** creating delivery mechanisms that they make to get those resources all over the country. **41**

39

A) NO CHANGE
B) vary however specialties
C) vary, however, specialties
D) vary, however. Specialties

40

A) NO CHANGE
B) creating delivery mechanisms
C) creating delivery mechanisms by making them
D) fabricating and making mechanisms for delivery

41

To make this paragraph the most logical, sentence 3 should be

A) placed where it is now.
B) placed after sentence 4.
C) placed after sentence 5.
D) DELETED from the paragraph.

CONTINUE

In either case, civil engineering is a fascinating field, and it is **42** full of interesting people. The Bureau of Labor Statistics predicts that the field will grow by nearly 20% between 2012 and 2022. The field offers incredible job security—regardless of changes in political power, civil engineering will continue to occupy a central place in the world. With every new development in energy or transportation, a civil engineer faces a new set of problems that **43** they have to solve for the country to reap the full benefits of these developments.

44 Should you so choose the work of civil engineering it may not have the glory of political leadership, but it certainly does present opportunities to make a tangible difference in the city, state, or country in which you live. The work of civil engineers is always about the future. After all, it wouldn't make sense to build a bridge if it were only meant to stand for your own lifetime. The work of civil engineers is a gift to future generations in a way that few other types of work can be.

42

Which choice results in a sentence that best supports the point developed in this paragraph?

A) NO CHANGE

B) very complicated.

C) constantly growing.

D) difficult to describe.

43

A) NO CHANGE

B) they must solve

C) all of them really have to solve

D) he or she must solve

44

A) NO CHANGE

B) The career they call civil engineering

C) Civil engineering

D) Opting for a career in civil engineering

STOP
If you finish before time is called, you may check your work on this section only.
Do not turn to any other section in the test.

Math Test – No Calculator

25 MINUTES, 20 QUESTIONS

Turn to Section 3 of your answer sheet to answer the questions in this section.

DIRECTIONS

For questions 1–15, solve each problem, choose the best answer from the choices provided, and fill in the corresponding circle on your answer sheet. **For questions 16–20**, solve the problem and enter your answer in the grid on the answer sheet. Please refer to the directions before question 16 on how to enter your answers in the grid. You may use any available space in your test booklet for scratch work.

NOTES

1. The use of a calculator **is not permitted**.
2. All variables and expressions used represent real numbers unless otherwise indicated.
3. Figures provided in this test are drawn to scale unless otherwise indicated.
4. All figures lie in a plane unless otherwise indicated.
5. Unless otherwise indicated, the domain of a given function f is the set of all real numbers x for which $f(x)$ is a real number.

REFERENCE

$A = \pi r^2$
$C = 2\pi r$

$A = \ell w$

$A = \frac{1}{2} bh$

$c^2 = a^2 + b^2$

Special Right Triangles

$V = \ell wh$

$V = \pi r^2 h$

$V = \frac{4}{3}\pi r^3$

$V = \frac{1}{3}\pi r^2 h$

$V = \frac{1}{3}\ell wh$

The number of degrees of arc in a circle is 360.
The number of radians of arc in a circle is 2π.
The sum of the measures in degrees of the angles of a triangle is 180.

CONTINUE

1

In the function $g(x) = \dfrac{5}{3}x + k$, k is a constant. If $g(9) = 12$, what is the value of $g(-3)$?

A) −12

B) −8

C) −3

D) 2

2

$$3(k + 2) = h$$
$$\dfrac{h}{k} = 5$$

If the solution set to the system of equations shown above is (h, k), what is the value of k?

A) 1

B) 3

C) 6

D) 15

3

Which of the following expressions is equal to 1 for some value of y?

A) $|2 - y| + 2$

B) $|y - 2| + 2$

C) $|y + 2| + 2$

D) $|2 - y| - 2$

4

If $\dfrac{x + y}{x}$ is equal to $\dfrac{6}{5}$, which of the following is true?

A) $\dfrac{y}{x} = \dfrac{1}{5}$

B) $\dfrac{y}{x} = \dfrac{11}{5}$

C) $\dfrac{x + y}{x} = \dfrac{1}{5}$

D) $\dfrac{x - 2y}{x} = -\dfrac{1}{5}$

CONTINUE

5

$$g(x) = -4x - 7$$

The function g is shown above. Which of the following is equal to $g(-2x)$?

A) $8x - 7$

B) $8x + 7$

C) $8x^2 - 21x$

D) $-8x - 7$

6

Which of the following expressions is equivalent to $4(3x - 2)(5x - 2)$?

A) $12x$

B) $7x^2 + 15x$

C) $60x^2 + 16x$

D) $60x^2 - 64x + 16$

7

If $k = 1$, which of the following is the solution set for $x - 7 = \sqrt{x - k}$?

A) $\{1\}$

B) $\{5\}$

C) $\{10\}$

D) $\{5, 10\}$

8

While preparing for a weightlifting competition, Alexei plans a training program in which his heaviest lift of each day increases by a constant amount. If Alexei's training program requires that his heaviest lift on day 6 is 180 pounds and his heaviest lift on day 24 is 225 pounds, which of the following most accurately describes how the amount Alexei lifts changes from day 6 to day 24 in his training program?

A) Alexei increases the weight of his heaviest lift by 2 pounds every 5 days.

B) Alexei increases the weight of his heaviest lift by 2 pounds per day.

C) Alexei increases the weight of his heaviest lift by 2.5 pounds per day.

D) Alexei increases the weight of his heaviest lift by 5 pounds per day.

CONTINUE

9

$$y = -4x - 6$$

Which of the following is the equation of a line that is parallel to the line with the equation shown above?

A) $4x - y = 9$

B) $4x + 2y = 8$

C) $6x + 3y = 12$

D) $12x + 3y = 10$

10

$$y = (x - 7)(3x + 4)$$
$$x = 3y - 1$$

The solution set for the system of equations shown above contains how many ordered pairs?

A) Infinitely many

B) 2

C) 1

D) 0

11

Peggie and Joan each purchased a bouquet of flowers from a florist. The price of Peggie's bouquet was d dollars, and the price of Joan's bouquet was $4 less than the price of Peggie's bouquet. If Peggie and Joan split the cost of the bouquets equally, and each paid 15% sales tax on her share, which of the following expressions gives the amount, in dollars, that each of them paid?

A) $1.15d - 2.3$

B) $2d - 1.15$

C) $2.15d - 2$

D) $2.3d - 4.6$

12

$$\frac{z - 3}{z + 3} = 8$$

What is the value of z in the equation above?

A) $-\dfrac{27}{7}$

B) $-\dfrac{7}{2}$

C) -3

D) $-\dfrac{21}{9}$

CONTINUE

13

In the quadratic equation $x^2 - 3t = \dfrac{v}{3}x$, t and v are constants. What are the solutions for x?

A) $x = \dfrac{v}{3} \pm \dfrac{\sqrt{v^2 + 4t}}{3}$

B) $x = \dfrac{v}{3} \pm \dfrac{\sqrt{v^2 + 36t}}{6}$

C) $x = \dfrac{v}{6} \pm \dfrac{\sqrt{v^2 + 108t}}{6}$

D) $x = \dfrac{v}{6} \pm \dfrac{\sqrt{v^2 + 4t}}{6}$

14

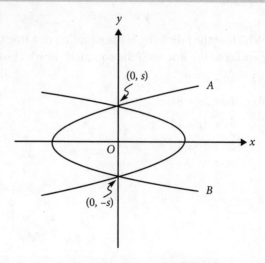

Two equations, A and B, defined by $x = 18y^2 - 2$ and $x = -18y^2 + 2$, respectively, are graphed in the xy-plane above. The graphs of A and B intersect at the points $(0, s)$ and $(0, -s)$. What is the value of s?

A) 3

B) 1

C) $\dfrac{1}{3}$

D) $\dfrac{1}{9}$

CONTINUE

15

In the equation $\dfrac{18 + i}{4 + 3i} = a + bi$, where a and b are real numbers, what is the value of a ?

(Note: $i = \sqrt{-1}$)

A)   2

B)   3

C) $\dfrac{18}{4}$

D) $\dfrac{11}{2}$

CONTINUE

DIRECTIONS

For questions 16–20, solve the problem and enter your answer in the grid, as described below, on the answer sheet.

1. Although not required, it is suggested that you write your answer in the boxes at the top of the columns to help you fill in the circles accurately. You will receive credit only if the circles are filled in correctly.

2. Mark no more than one circle in any column.

3. No question has a negative answer.

4. Some problems may have more than one correct answer. In such cases, grid only one answer.

5. **Mixed numbers** such as $3\frac{1}{2}$ must be gridded as 3.5 or 7/2. (If [3 1 / 2] is entered into the grid, it will be interpreted as $\frac{31}{2}$, not as $3\frac{1}{2}$.)

6. **Decimal Answers:** If you obtain a decimal answer with more digits than the grid can accommodate, it may be either rounded or truncated, but it must fill the entire grid.

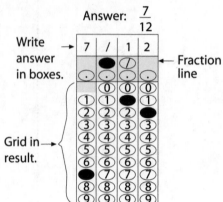

Answer: $\frac{7}{12}$ — Write answer in boxes. — Fraction line — Grid in result.

Answer: 2.5 — Decimal point

Acceptable ways to grid $\frac{2}{3}$ are:

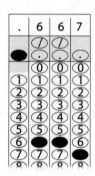

Answer: 201 – either position is correct

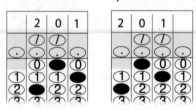

NOTE: You may start your answers in any column, space permitting. Columns you don't need to use should be left blank.

CONTINUE ▶

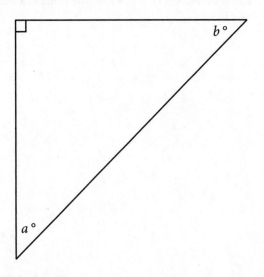

In the triangle above, the cosine of $a°$ is 0.625. What is the sine of $b°$?

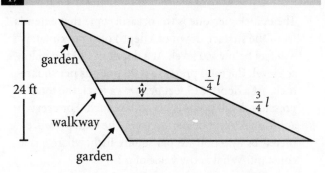

Bridget owns a triangular patch of land. She decides to convert it into a garden with a paved walkway, as shown above. The long sides of the walkway are parallel to each other and to the base of the triangular patch of land. What is the width, w, in feet, of the walkway?

$$8x - 5y = 27$$
$$5x + 10y = 30$$

The solution set of the system of equations above is (x, y). What is the value of y ?

CONTINUE

19

The epipelagic zone is the oceanic zone that extends from the surface down to a depth of approximately 650 feet below sea level. At a depth of 170 feet below sea level, the total pressure is 90 pounds per square inch. At a depth 215 feet below sea level, the total pressure is 110 pounds per square inch. For every additional 5 feet below sea level, the total pressure increases by p pounds per square inch, where p is a constant. What is the value of p ?

20

If $x^3 - 4x^2 + 3x - 12 = 0$, what real value is a solution for x ?

STOP
**If you finish before time is called, you may check your work on this section only.
Do not turn to any other section in the test.**

No Test Material On This Page

Math Test – Calculator

55 MINUTES, 38 QUESTIONS

Turn to Section 4 of your answer sheet to answer the questions in this section.

DIRECTIONS

For questions 1–30, solve each problem, choose the best answer from the choices provided, and fill in the corresponding circle on your answer sheet. **For questions 31–38,** solve the problem and enter your answer in the grid on the answer sheet. Please refer to the directions before question 31 on how to enter your answers in the grid. You may use any available space in your test booklet for scratch work.

NOTES

1. The use of a calculator **is permitted**.
2. All variables and expressions used represent real numbers unless otherwise indicated.
3. Figures provided in this test are drawn to scale unless otherwise indicated.
4. All figures lie in a plane unless otherwise indicated.
5. Unless otherwise indicated, the domain of a given function f is the set of all real numbers x for which $f(x)$ is a real number.

REFERENCE

$A = \pi r^2$
$C = 2\pi r$

$A = \ell w$

$A = \frac{1}{2} bh$

$c^2 = a^2 + b^2$

Special Right Triangles

$V = \ell wh$

$V = \pi r^2 h$

$V = \frac{4}{3}\pi r^3$

$V = \frac{1}{3}\pi r^2 h$

$V = \frac{1}{3}\ell wh$

The number of degrees of arc in a circle is 360.
The number of radians of arc in a circle is 2π.
The sum of the measures in degrees of the angles of a triangle is 180.

CONTINUE

1

To make the high school football team, Walter must be able to run a 40-yard dash in under 6 seconds. Walter currently runs the 40-yard dash in 7.2 seconds, and believes that with training he can reduce his time by 0.2 seconds per week. Which of the following represents the number of seconds in which Walter believes he will be able to run the 40-yard dash *w* weeks from now?

A) 0.2 – 7.2*w*

B) 6.0 – 0.2*w*

C) 7.2 + 0.2*w*

D) 7.2 – 0.2*w*

2

A piece of yarn 4 yards long is cut in half, and each half is cut into fourths. What is the length, in inches, of each of the pieces of yarn? (1 yard = 36 inches)

A) 8

B) 18

C) 24

D) 36

3

A ride-sharing service charges a base fee of $2.40 per ride. The cost of gas is included in the base fee, but there is an additional charge of $0.30 per mile. For one ride, Edward paid $3.60. How many miles long was Edward's ride?

A) 2

B) 3

C) 4

D) 5

4

Yesterday, Tiki cycled 13 fewer miles than Irina. If the two of them cycled a total of 51 miles yesterday, how many miles did Irina cycle?

A) 19

B) 32

C) 38

D) 64

CONTINUE

5

The resistance of a circuit is equal to the voltage applied to the circuit divided by the number of amps flowing through the circuit. How many amps are flowing through a circuit with a resistance of 9 ohms if 54 volts are applied to the circuit?

A) 486

B) 45

C) 6

D) 0.167

6

Florence interviewed a random sample of her first-year classmates in medical school to determine the statistical distribution of blood types among the students. Of the 75 students she interviewed, 38.7% had O-positive blood type. Based on this result, about how many of the 265 students in Florence's first-year class would be expected to have O-positive blood type?

A) 40

B) 80

C) 100

D) 110

CONTINUE

Number of Viewers by Favorite Television Network

Network	Age (years)					Total
	18–24	25–34	35–44	45–64	65 and older	
A	3,729	11,471	12,758	4,164	3,284	35,406
B	5,731	19,879	23,480	7,999	5,466	62,555
C	3,798	12,360	15,252	4,643	3,685	39,738
D	2,984	8,975	12,084	3,676	3,053	30,772
Total	16,242	52,685	63,574	20,482	15,488	168,471

A survey asked television viewers to name their one favorite network: *A*, *B*, *C*, or *D*. The table above displays the number of surveyed viewers, categorized by age group and favorite network. According to the table, if a viewer who was 35-to-64 years old at the time of the survey is chosen at random, which of the following is nearest to the probability that the viewer preferred network *D* ?

A) 0.20

B) 0.35

C) 0.50

D) 0.75

CONTINUE

8

Custom Furniture Made in 2015

Wood species	Furniture type				
	Beds	Chairs	Desks	Tables	Total
Cherry	9	7	0	15	31
Maple	12	6	9	0	27
Walnut	3	1	11	2	17
Total	24	14	20	17	75

The table above shows the 75 pieces of furniture that a custom furniture maker made in 2015, categorized by furniture type and wood species. What proportion of the furniture pieces are desks made of maple?

A) $\dfrac{2}{25}$

B) $\dfrac{3}{25}$

C) $\dfrac{4}{15}$

D) $\dfrac{9}{25}$

9

The graph of line m in the xy-plane passes through Quadrants I, II, and III, but not Quadrant IV. Which of the following must be true about the slope of line m ?

A) It is positive.

B) It is negative.

C) It is undefined.

D) It is zero.

10

The graph of the function g in the xy-plane has x-intercepts at –2, 2, and 5. Which of the following could be the function g ?

A) $g(x) = (x - 2)^2(x - 5)$

B) $g(x) = (x - 2)(x + 2)(x + 5)$

C) $g(x) = (x + 2)^2(x + 5)$

D) $g(x) = (x - 5)(x - 2)(x + 2)$

CONTINUE

Questions 11 and 12 refer to the following information.

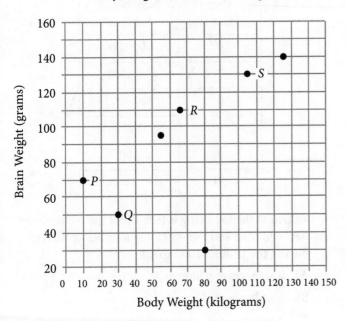

Body Weight Versus Brain Weight

A researcher at a university made the scatterplot above to illustrate the relationship between the body weight and brain weight of 9 species of animals.

11

What is the brain weight, in grams, of the animal that has the greatest body weight?

A) 70

B) 125

C) 140

D) 160

12

Of the points labeled *P*, *Q*, *R*, and *S*, which point represents the species whose ratio of brain weight to body weight is the least?

A) *P*

B) *Q*

C) *R*

D) *S*

CONTINUE

13

Which of the scatterplots below illustrates a relationship that is best modeled by the function $f(x) = \left(\dfrac{j}{x}\right)^k$, where j is a positive constant and k is a constant less than -1 ?

A)

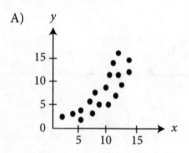

B)

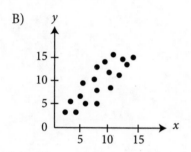

C)

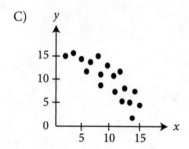

D)

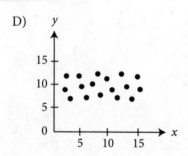

14

The estimated number of bacteria in a laboratory culture over a span of 10 hours is shown in the table below.

Time (hours)	Number of bacteria
0	1,000,000
2	100,000
4	10,000
6	1,000
8	100
10	10

Which of the following is true about the relationship between time and the estimated number of bacteria during the 10-hour time span?

A) It is increasing linearly.

B) It is decreasing linearly.

C) It is increasing exponentially.

D) It is decreasing exponentially.

CONTINUE

15

The expression $20,000\left(1 + \dfrac{p}{400}\right)^4$ shows the value, in dollars, one year after purchase, of a savings bond that has an initial value of $20,000 and that pays an interest rate of p percent, compounded quarterly. If Roger purchased a bond that pays an interest rate of 4 percent and Pete purchased a bond that pays an interest rate of 6 percent, which of the following expressions represents how much more Pete earned than Roger earned, after one year?

A) $20,000\left(1 + \dfrac{6-4}{400}\right)^4$

B) $20,000\left(1 + \dfrac{\frac{6}{4}}{400}\right)^4$

C) $20,000\left(1 + \dfrac{6}{400}\right)^4 - 20,000\left(1 + \dfrac{4}{400}\right)^4$

D) $\dfrac{20,000\left(1 + \dfrac{6}{400}\right)^4}{20,000\left(1 + \dfrac{4}{400}\right)^4}$

Questions 16 and 17 refer to the following information.

Stella is planning a vacation and deciding which travel package to purchase. The table below shows the cost of airfare, hotel, and car rental for three different travel packages.

Travel package	Cost of air-fare, A (in dollars)	Cost of hotel, H (in dollars per day)	Cost of car rental, R (in dollars per day)
P	400	85	60
Q	550	75	50
R	500	80	70

The total cost, $f(x)$, of a travel package for x days is given by the function $f(x) = A + H(x - 1) + Rx$, where $x \geq 2$.

16

If the relationship between the total cost, $f(x)$, of airfare, hotel, and car rental with travel package R and the number of days, x, for the package is graphed in the xy-plane, the slope of the graph represents which of the following?

A) The combined daily cost of the hotel and car rental

B) The daily cost of the hotel

C) The daily cost of the car rental

D) The total cost of airfare

CONTINUE

17

For how many days, x, will the total cost of travel package Q be less than or equal to the total cost of travel package P?

A) $x \leq 8$

B) $x \geq 8$

C) $x \leq 9.4$

D) $x \geq 9.4$

18

A well-known projection known as Moore's law states that the maximum number of transistors that can be placed on an integrated circuit doubles every two years. Which of the following graphs is an accurate representation of Moore's law? (Note: In each graph below, O represents $(0, 0)$.)

A)
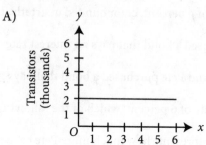

B)
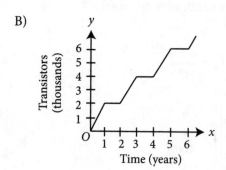

C)
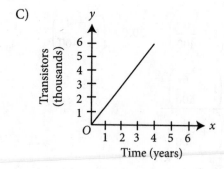

D)
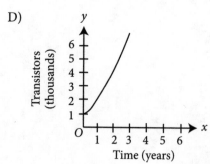

CONTINUE

19

Bob has a number of identical right circular cylindrical buckets, each with an inside diameter of 1 foot. He pours oil from a 55-gallon drum into each bucket until it is full. If the height of the oil in each bucket is approximately 1.5 feet, what is the greatest number of full buckets Bob can pour from one 55-gallon drum of oil? (Note: There are 0.133 cubic feet in 1 gallon.)

A) 6

B) 7

C) 9

D) 10

20

If $2x + 5 \leq 9$, what is the greatest possible value of $2x - 5$?

A) −3

B) −1

C) 0

D) 2

21

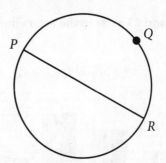

In the figure above, $\overline{PR}$ is a diameter. If the length of arc $\overparen{PQR}$ is 18π, what is the length of $\overline{PR}$?

A) 6

B) 12

C) 18

D) 36

CONTINUE

23

Questions 22 and 23 refer to the following information.

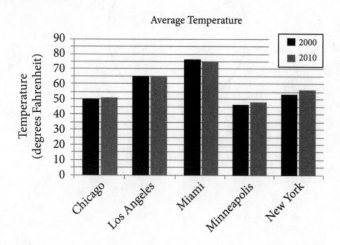

The bar graph above shows the average temperature in degrees Fahrenheit for five select cities in 2000 and 2010.

22

In a scatterplot of this data where the average temperature of each city in the year 2000 is plotted along the x-axis and the average in the year 2010 is plotted along the y-axis, how many data points would be below the line $y = x$?

A) 1

B) 2

C) 3

D) 4

23

Of the following, which best approximates the percent increase in the average temperature of New York from 2000 to 2010 ?

A)   0.5%

B)   1%

C)   6%

D)   12%

CONTINUE

24

The tables below show the distribution of scores of recent quizzes in English and Physics given to the same 33 students of a particular class.

English Quiz

Score	Frequency
1	5
2	7
3	8
4	7
5	6

Physics Quiz

Score	Frequency
1	1
2	2
3	3
4	22
5	5

Which of the following is true about the data provided for the 33 students?

A) The standard deviation of the scores on the English quiz is larger.

B) The standard deviation of scores on the Physics quiz is larger.

C) The standard deviation of the scores on the English quiz is the same as that of the Physics quiz.

D) The standard deviation for the scores on the two quizzes cannot be calculated from the data provided.

25

Let a and b be numbers such that $b < a < -b$. Which of the following must be true?

    I. $a < 0$

    II. $b < 0$

    III. $a < |b|$

A) I only

B) III only

C) I and II only

D) II and III only

26

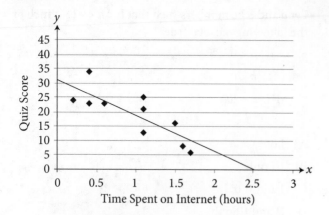

Time Spent on Internet (hours)

The scatterplot above shows scores on a recent quiz in a particular class and the number of hours the student spent on the Internet the day before. The line of best fit is also shown and can be described as $y = -12.408x + 31$. Which of the following best describes how the number 31 in the equation relates to the scatterplot?

A) On the quiz, even students who spend very little time on the Internet are unlikely to score above 31 on the quiz.

B) On the quiz, even students who spend very little time on the Internet never score above 31 on the quiz.

C) On the quiz, the lowest score was about 31% of the highest score.

D) On the quiz, the highest score on the test was 31.

27

$$r(x) = 3x^3 + 24x^2 + 21x$$
$$s(x) = x^2 + 8x + 7$$

The polynomials $r(x)$ and $s(x)$ are defined above. Which of the following polynomials is divisible by $3x + 4$?

A) $a(x) = r(x) + s(x)$

B) $b(x) = r(x) + 2s(x)$

C) $c(x) = r(x) + 4s(x)$

D) $d(x) = 2r(x) + 4s(x)$

28

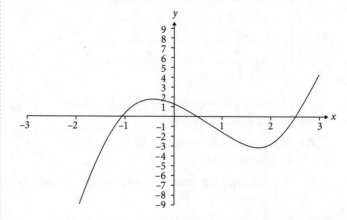

The function $g(x) = x^3 - 2x^2 - 2x + \dfrac{4}{3}$ is graphed in the

xy-plane above. If c is a constant such that $g(x) = c$ has

one real solution, which of the following could be the

value of c ?

A)   3

B)   1

C)   0

D)   −1

CONTINUE

29

$$g(x) = (x - 10)(x + 4)$$

Which of the following is an equivalent of the function g shown above in which the minimum value of g appears as a constant or coefficient?

A) $g(x) = (x + 3)^2 - 31$

B) $g(x) = (x - 3)^2 - 49$

C) $g(x) = x^2 - 6x - 40$

D) $g(x) = x^2 - 40$

30

If a is the average (arithmetic mean) of $4x$ and 7, b is the average of $5x$ and 6, and c is the average of $3x$ and 11, what is the average of a, b, and c, in terms of x ?

A) $x + 4$

B) $x + 8$

C) $2x + 4$

D) $4x + 8$

CONTINUE

DIRECTIONS

For questions 31–38, solve the problem and enter your answer in the grid, as described below, on the answer sheet.

1. Although not required, it is suggested that you write your answer in the boxes at the top of the columns to help you fill in the circles accurately. You will receive credit only if the circles are filled in correctly.

2. Mark no more than one circle in any column.

3. No question has a negative answer.

4. Some problems may have more than one correct answer. In such cases, grid only one answer.

5. **Mixed numbers** such as $3\frac{1}{2}$ must be gridded as 3.5 or 7/2. (If ⬚ is entered into the grid, it will be interpreted as $\frac{31}{2}$, not as $3\frac{1}{2}$.)

6. **Decimal Answers:** If you obtain a decimal answer with more digits than the grid can accommodate, it may be either rounded or truncated, but it must fill the entire grid.

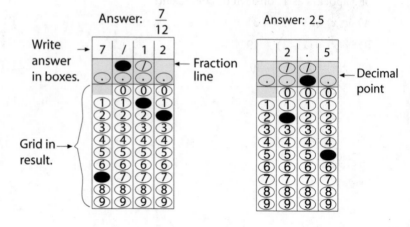

Answer: $\frac{7}{12}$ — Write answer in boxes. — Fraction line — Grid in result.

Answer: 2.5 — Decimal point

Acceptable ways to grid $\frac{2}{3}$ are:

Answer: 201 – either position is correct

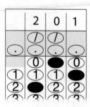 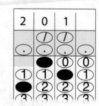

NOTE: You may start your answers in any column, space permitting. Columns you don't need to use should be left blank.

CONTINUE ➤

31

The target heart rate during moderate activity R, in beats per minute, for an adult who is y years old can be estimated using the equation $R = \dfrac{3(220 - y)}{5}$. According to this estimate, for every increase of 2 years in age, by how many beats per minute will the target heart rate for adults engaged in moderate activity decrease?

32

At 1:00 P.M., a truck driver is 200 miles into a long journey to make a delivery. The driver continues on the journey and travels at an average speed of 60 miles per hour. How many total miles into the journey will the driver be at 8:00 P.M. ?

33

$$d = \frac{1}{2}at^2$$

The displacement d of an object in a vacuum, starting from rest with an acceleration a, can be found using the formula above, where t is the time the object has been moving. A physics student uses the formula to determine the displacement of an object in a vacuum accelerating from rest for time t and an object with the same acceleration from rest for time $2.5t$. What is the ratio of the displacement of the object that accelerated for more time to the displacement of the object that accelerated for less time?

34

The *deben*, an ancient Egyptian unit of weight, is approximately equal to 3.21 ounces. It is also equivalent to 12 smaller Egyptian units called *shematies*. Based on these relationships, 488 shematies is equal to how many pounds, to the nearest hundredth? (16 ounces = 1 pound)

CONTINUE

35

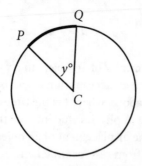

Note: Figure not drawn to scale.

The circle above has center C and has a radius of 20. If the length of arc $\overset{\frown}{PQ}$ (shown in bold) is between 15 and 16, what is one possible <u>integer</u> value of y ?

36

A toy store keeps marbles in the closet of its stock room. In the closet, 230 marbles are blue and 370 marbles are red. If 110 red marbles are added, how many blue marbles must be added to the closet so that $\dfrac{2}{5}$ of the marbles in the closet are blue?

Questions 37 and 38 refer to the following information.

A CD account contains $5,400 today. The account earns an annual interest of 7% for each of the next four years. The bank uses the equation $A = 5,400(r)^y$ to determine the amount of money in the account, A, after y years if no other deposits or withdrawals are made.

37

What numerical value should the bank use for r ?

38

To the nearest dollar, how much money will be in the CD account at the end of the four years? (Note: Disregard the $ sign when gridding your answer.)

END OF TEST

DO NOT RETURN TO A PREVIOUS SECTION.

The Princeton Review®

Completely darken bubbles with a No. 2 pencil. If you make a mistake, be sure to erase mark completely. Erase all stray marks.

1.

YOUR NAME: _____
(Print)   Last   First   M.I.

SIGNATURE: _____   DATE: ___/___/___

HOME ADDRESS: _____
(Print)   Number and Street

_____
City   State   Zip Code

PHONE NO.: _____
(Print)

IMPORTANT: Please fill in these boxes exactly as shown on the back cover of your test book.

2. TEST FORM

6. DATE OF BIRTH

Month		Day		Year	
○ JAN					
○ FEB	⓪	⓪	⓪	⓪	
○ MAR	①	①	①	①	
○ APR	②	②	②	②	
○ MAY	③	③	③	③	
○ JUN		④	④	④	
○ JUL		⑤	⑤	⑤	
○ AUG		⑥	⑥	⑥	
○ SEP		⑦	⑦	⑦	
○ OCT		⑧	⑧	⑧	
○ NOV		⑨	⑨	⑨	
○ DEC					

3. TEST CODE

⓪ Ⓐ Ⓙ ⓪
① Ⓑ Ⓚ ①
② Ⓒ Ⓛ ②
③ Ⓓ Ⓜ ③
④ Ⓔ Ⓝ ④
⑤ Ⓕ Ⓞ ⑤
⑥ Ⓖ Ⓟ ⑥
⑦ Ⓗ Ⓠ ⑦
⑧ Ⓘ Ⓡ ⑧
⑨

4. REGISTRATION NUMBER

⓪ ⓪ ⓪ ⓪ ⓪ ⓪ ⓪ ⓪ ⓪
① ① ① ① ① ① ① ① ①
② ② ② ② ② ② ② ② ②
③ ③ ③ ③ ③ ③ ③ ③ ③
④ ④ ④ ④ ④ ④ ④ ④ ④
⑤ ⑤ ⑤ ⑤ ⑤ ⑤ ⑤ ⑤ ⑤
⑥ ⑥ ⑥ ⑥ ⑥ ⑥ ⑥ ⑥ ⑥
⑦ ⑦ ⑦ ⑦ ⑦ ⑦ ⑦ ⑦ ⑦
⑧ ⑧ ⑧ ⑧ ⑧ ⑧ ⑧ ⑧ ⑧
⑨ ⑨ ⑨ ⑨ ⑨ ⑨ ⑨ ⑨ ⑨

7. SEX

○ MALE
○ FEMALE

The Princeton Review®

5. YOUR NAME

First 4 letters of last name				FIRST INIT	MID INIT
Ⓐ	Ⓐ	Ⓐ	Ⓐ	Ⓐ	Ⓐ
Ⓑ	Ⓑ	Ⓑ	Ⓑ	Ⓑ	Ⓑ
Ⓒ	Ⓒ	Ⓒ	Ⓒ	Ⓒ	Ⓒ
Ⓓ	Ⓓ	Ⓓ	Ⓓ	Ⓓ	Ⓓ
Ⓔ	Ⓔ	Ⓔ	Ⓔ	Ⓔ	Ⓔ
Ⓕ	Ⓕ	Ⓕ	Ⓕ	Ⓕ	Ⓕ
Ⓖ	Ⓖ	Ⓖ	Ⓖ	Ⓖ	Ⓖ
Ⓗ	Ⓗ	Ⓗ	Ⓗ	Ⓗ	Ⓗ
Ⓘ	Ⓘ	Ⓘ	Ⓘ	Ⓘ	Ⓘ
Ⓙ	Ⓙ	Ⓙ	Ⓙ	Ⓙ	Ⓙ
Ⓚ	Ⓚ	Ⓚ	Ⓚ	Ⓚ	Ⓚ
Ⓛ	Ⓛ	Ⓛ	Ⓛ	Ⓛ	Ⓛ
Ⓜ	Ⓜ	Ⓜ	Ⓜ	Ⓜ	Ⓜ
Ⓝ	Ⓝ	Ⓝ	Ⓝ	Ⓝ	Ⓝ
Ⓞ	Ⓞ	Ⓞ	Ⓞ	Ⓞ	Ⓞ
Ⓟ	Ⓟ	Ⓟ	Ⓟ	Ⓟ	Ⓟ
Ⓠ	Ⓠ	Ⓠ	Ⓠ	Ⓠ	Ⓠ
Ⓡ	Ⓡ	Ⓡ	Ⓡ	Ⓡ	Ⓡ
Ⓢ	Ⓢ	Ⓢ	Ⓢ	Ⓢ	Ⓢ
Ⓣ	Ⓣ	Ⓣ	Ⓣ	Ⓣ	Ⓣ
Ⓤ	Ⓤ	Ⓤ	Ⓤ	Ⓤ	Ⓤ
Ⓥ	Ⓥ	Ⓥ	Ⓥ	Ⓥ	Ⓥ
Ⓦ	Ⓦ	Ⓦ	Ⓦ	Ⓦ	Ⓦ
Ⓧ	Ⓧ	Ⓧ	Ⓧ	Ⓧ	Ⓧ
Ⓨ	Ⓨ	Ⓨ	Ⓨ	Ⓨ	Ⓨ
Ⓩ	Ⓩ	Ⓩ	Ⓩ	Ⓩ	Ⓩ

Test ④

Start with number 1 for each new section.
If a section has fewer questions than answer spaces, leave the extra answer spaces blank.

Section 1—Reading

1. Ⓐ Ⓑ Ⓒ Ⓓ
2. Ⓐ Ⓑ Ⓒ Ⓓ
3. Ⓐ Ⓑ Ⓒ Ⓓ
4. Ⓐ Ⓑ Ⓒ Ⓓ
5. Ⓐ Ⓑ Ⓒ Ⓓ
6. Ⓐ Ⓑ Ⓒ Ⓓ
7. Ⓐ Ⓑ Ⓒ Ⓓ
8. Ⓐ Ⓑ Ⓒ Ⓓ
9. Ⓐ Ⓑ Ⓒ Ⓓ
10. Ⓐ Ⓑ Ⓒ Ⓓ
11. Ⓐ Ⓑ Ⓒ Ⓓ
12. Ⓐ Ⓑ Ⓒ Ⓓ
13. Ⓐ Ⓑ Ⓒ Ⓓ
14. Ⓐ Ⓑ Ⓒ Ⓓ
15. Ⓐ Ⓑ Ⓒ Ⓓ
16. Ⓐ Ⓑ Ⓒ Ⓓ
17. Ⓐ Ⓑ Ⓒ Ⓓ
18. Ⓐ Ⓑ Ⓒ Ⓓ
19. Ⓐ Ⓑ Ⓒ Ⓓ
20. Ⓐ Ⓑ Ⓒ Ⓓ
21. Ⓐ Ⓑ Ⓒ Ⓓ
22. Ⓐ Ⓑ Ⓒ Ⓓ
23. Ⓐ Ⓑ Ⓒ Ⓓ
24. Ⓐ Ⓑ Ⓒ Ⓓ
25. Ⓐ Ⓑ Ⓒ Ⓓ
26. Ⓐ Ⓑ Ⓒ Ⓓ
27. Ⓐ Ⓑ Ⓒ Ⓓ
28. Ⓐ Ⓑ Ⓒ Ⓓ
29. Ⓐ Ⓑ Ⓒ Ⓓ
30. Ⓐ Ⓑ Ⓒ Ⓓ
31. Ⓐ Ⓑ Ⓒ Ⓓ
32. Ⓐ Ⓑ Ⓒ Ⓓ
33. Ⓐ Ⓑ Ⓒ Ⓓ
34. Ⓐ Ⓑ Ⓒ Ⓓ
35. Ⓐ Ⓑ Ⓒ Ⓓ
36. Ⓐ Ⓑ Ⓒ Ⓓ
37. Ⓐ Ⓑ Ⓒ Ⓓ
38. Ⓐ Ⓑ Ⓒ Ⓓ
39. Ⓐ Ⓑ Ⓒ Ⓓ
40. Ⓐ Ⓑ Ⓒ Ⓓ
41. Ⓐ Ⓑ Ⓒ Ⓓ
42. Ⓐ Ⓑ Ⓒ Ⓓ
43. Ⓐ Ⓑ Ⓒ Ⓓ
44. Ⓐ Ⓑ Ⓒ Ⓓ
45. Ⓐ Ⓑ Ⓒ Ⓓ
46. Ⓐ Ⓑ Ⓒ Ⓓ
47. Ⓐ Ⓑ Ⓒ Ⓓ
48. Ⓐ Ⓑ Ⓒ Ⓓ
49. Ⓐ Ⓑ Ⓒ Ⓓ
50. Ⓐ Ⓑ Ⓒ Ⓓ
51. Ⓐ Ⓑ Ⓒ Ⓓ
52. Ⓐ Ⓑ Ⓒ Ⓓ

Section 2—Writing and Language Skills

1. Ⓐ Ⓑ Ⓒ Ⓓ
2. Ⓐ Ⓑ Ⓒ Ⓓ
3. Ⓐ Ⓑ Ⓒ Ⓓ
4. Ⓐ Ⓑ Ⓒ Ⓓ
5. Ⓐ Ⓑ Ⓒ Ⓓ
6. Ⓐ Ⓑ Ⓒ Ⓓ
7. Ⓐ Ⓑ Ⓒ Ⓓ
8. Ⓐ Ⓑ Ⓒ Ⓓ
9. Ⓐ Ⓑ Ⓒ Ⓓ
10. Ⓐ Ⓑ Ⓒ Ⓓ
11. Ⓐ Ⓑ Ⓒ Ⓓ
12. Ⓐ Ⓑ Ⓒ Ⓓ
13. Ⓐ Ⓑ Ⓒ Ⓓ
14. Ⓐ Ⓑ Ⓒ Ⓓ
15. Ⓐ Ⓑ Ⓒ Ⓓ
16. Ⓐ Ⓑ Ⓒ Ⓓ
17. Ⓐ Ⓑ Ⓒ Ⓓ
18. Ⓐ Ⓑ Ⓒ Ⓓ
19. Ⓐ Ⓑ Ⓒ Ⓓ
20. Ⓐ Ⓑ Ⓒ Ⓓ
21. Ⓐ Ⓑ Ⓒ Ⓓ
22. Ⓐ Ⓑ Ⓒ Ⓓ
23. Ⓐ Ⓑ Ⓒ Ⓓ
24. Ⓐ Ⓑ Ⓒ Ⓓ
25. Ⓐ Ⓑ Ⓒ Ⓓ
26. Ⓐ Ⓑ Ⓒ Ⓓ
27. Ⓐ Ⓑ Ⓒ Ⓓ
28. Ⓐ Ⓑ Ⓒ Ⓓ
29. Ⓐ Ⓑ Ⓒ Ⓓ
30. Ⓐ Ⓑ Ⓒ Ⓓ
31. Ⓐ Ⓑ Ⓒ Ⓓ
32. Ⓐ Ⓑ Ⓒ Ⓓ
33. Ⓐ Ⓑ Ⓒ Ⓓ
34. Ⓐ Ⓑ Ⓒ Ⓓ
35. Ⓐ Ⓑ Ⓒ Ⓓ
36. Ⓐ Ⓑ Ⓒ Ⓓ
37. Ⓐ Ⓑ Ⓒ Ⓓ
38. Ⓐ Ⓑ Ⓒ Ⓓ
39. Ⓐ Ⓑ Ⓒ Ⓓ
40. Ⓐ Ⓑ Ⓒ Ⓓ
41. Ⓐ Ⓑ Ⓒ Ⓓ
42. Ⓐ Ⓑ Ⓒ Ⓓ
43. Ⓐ Ⓑ Ⓒ Ⓓ
44. Ⓐ Ⓑ Ⓒ Ⓓ

Completely darken bubbles with a No. 2 pencil. If you make a mistake, be sure to erase mark completely. Erase all stray marks.

Test 4 Start with number 1 for each new section.
If a section has fewer questions than answer spaces, leave the extra answer spaces blank.

Section 3—Mathematics: No Calculator

1. Ⓐ Ⓑ Ⓒ Ⓓ
2. Ⓐ Ⓑ Ⓒ Ⓓ
3. Ⓐ Ⓑ Ⓒ Ⓓ
4. Ⓐ Ⓑ Ⓒ Ⓓ
5. Ⓐ Ⓑ Ⓒ Ⓓ
6. Ⓐ Ⓑ Ⓒ Ⓓ
7. Ⓐ Ⓑ Ⓒ Ⓓ
8. Ⓐ Ⓑ Ⓒ Ⓓ
9. Ⓐ Ⓑ Ⓒ Ⓓ
10. Ⓐ Ⓑ Ⓒ Ⓓ
11. Ⓐ Ⓑ Ⓒ Ⓓ
12. Ⓐ Ⓑ Ⓒ Ⓓ
13. Ⓐ Ⓑ Ⓒ Ⓓ
14. Ⓐ Ⓑ Ⓒ Ⓓ
15. Ⓐ Ⓑ Ⓒ Ⓓ

16. 17. 18. 19. 20.

Section 4—Mathematics: Calculator

1. Ⓐ Ⓑ Ⓒ Ⓓ
2. Ⓐ Ⓑ Ⓒ Ⓓ
3. Ⓐ Ⓑ Ⓒ Ⓓ
4. Ⓐ Ⓑ Ⓒ Ⓓ
5. Ⓐ Ⓑ Ⓒ Ⓓ
6. Ⓐ Ⓑ Ⓒ Ⓓ
7. Ⓐ Ⓑ Ⓒ Ⓓ
8. Ⓐ Ⓑ Ⓒ Ⓓ
9. Ⓐ Ⓑ Ⓒ Ⓓ
10. Ⓐ Ⓑ Ⓒ Ⓓ
11. Ⓐ Ⓑ Ⓒ Ⓓ
12. Ⓐ Ⓑ Ⓒ Ⓓ
13. Ⓐ Ⓑ Ⓒ Ⓓ
14. Ⓐ Ⓑ Ⓒ Ⓓ
15. Ⓐ Ⓑ Ⓒ Ⓓ
16. Ⓐ Ⓑ Ⓒ Ⓓ
17. Ⓐ Ⓑ Ⓒ Ⓓ
18. Ⓐ Ⓑ Ⓒ Ⓓ
19. Ⓐ Ⓑ Ⓒ Ⓓ
20. Ⓐ Ⓑ Ⓒ Ⓓ
21. Ⓐ Ⓑ Ⓒ Ⓓ
22. Ⓐ Ⓑ Ⓒ Ⓓ
23. Ⓐ Ⓑ Ⓒ Ⓓ
24. Ⓐ Ⓑ Ⓒ Ⓓ
25. Ⓐ Ⓑ Ⓒ Ⓓ
26. Ⓐ Ⓑ Ⓒ Ⓓ
27. Ⓐ Ⓑ Ⓒ Ⓓ
28. Ⓐ Ⓑ Ⓒ Ⓓ
29. Ⓐ Ⓑ Ⓒ Ⓓ
30. Ⓐ Ⓑ Ⓒ Ⓓ

31. 32. 33. 34. 35.

36. 37. 38.

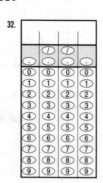
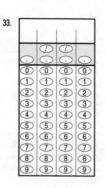
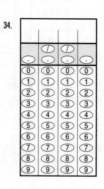

Chapter 10
Practice Test 4:
Answers and
Explanations

PRACTICE TEST 4 ANSWER KEY

Section 1: Reading		Section 2: Writing & Language		Section 3: Math (No Calculator)		Section 4: Math (Calculator)	
1. B	27. A	1. A	23. C	1. B	11. A	1. D	20. B
2. D	28. C	2. D	24. A	2. B	12. A	2. B	21. D
3. C	29. C	3. C	25. B	3. D	13. C	3. C	22. A
4. B	30. B	4. D	26. D	4. A	14. C	4. B	23. C
5. D	31. B	5. B	27. C	5. A	15. B	5. C	24. A
6. A	32. D	6. D	28. B	6. D	16. $\frac{5}{8}$ or	6. C	25. D
7. A	33. A	7. C	29. C	7. C	.625	7. A	26. A
8. C	34. A	8. D	30. A	8. C	17. 3	8. B	27. C
9. C	35. B	9. D	31. A	9. D	18. 1	9. A	28. A
10. D	36. A	10. B	32. A	10. B	19. $\frac{20}{9}$ or	10. D	29. B
11. D	37. C	11. D	33. C		2.22	11. C	30. C
12. B	38. D	12. A	34. A		20. 4	12. D	31. 1.2
13. A	39. A	13. D	35. C			13. A	32. 620
14. D	40. B	14. B	36. B			14. D	33. $\frac{25}{4}$,
15. B	41. B	15. B	37. A			15. C	$\frac{50}{8}$,
16. B	42. C	16. A	38. A			16. A	or
17. C	43. D	17. C	39. D			17. B	6.25
18. D	44. B	18. A	40. B			18. D	34. 8.16
19. C	45. B	19. D	41. B			19. A	35. 43,
20. B	46. D	20. D	42. C				44, or
21. A	47. B	21. A	43. D				45
22. C	48. A	22. D	44. C				36. 90
23. A	49. C						37. 1.07
24. B	50. C						38. 7,078
25. D	51. C						
26. A	52. A						

> Go to PrincetonReview.com to score your exam. Alternatively,
> for self-assessment tables, please turn to page 909.

PRACTICE TEST 4 EXPLANATIONS

Section 1: Reading

1. **B**   The question asks about the narrator's shift in focus through the passage. Because this is the first question in a paired set, it can be done in tandem with Q2. Consider the answers for Q2 first. Choice (2A) can be eliminated because those lines don't refer to the narrator's focus. Choice (2B) could refer to the *disquiet about the unknown*, but there's no support for a shift. Eliminate (2B). Choice (2C) does not refer to the narrator at all, so eliminate it. Choice (2D) contains the phrase *and yet,* which indicates a change. In context, the lines show the narrator shifting from *we shall not ask this question* to wondering about that very question. This supports Q1, so (2D) is correct. Now check the answers for Q1 to see which answers the question and is supported by (2D). Eliminate (1A) because the narrator never prepares to explore a frontier. Choice (1B) refers to a shift from *disquiet* to *curiosity*, which not only answers Q1 but can be supported with the lines from (2D). Keep (1B). Choice (1C) might look good initially, because the narrator does acknowledge the ancient city. He never dismisses it, though, so eliminate (1C). Choice (1D) can be eliminated because although the narrator mentions the Council's rules, there's no shift from *repetition...to acceptance.* The correct answers are (1B) and (2D).

2. **D**   (See explanation above.)

3. **C**   The question asks what the phrase *all must agree with all* means in lines 3 and 4. Go back to the text, find the phrase *all must agree with all*, and mark it out. Carefully read the surrounding text to determine another phrase that would fit in the blank based on the context of the passage. The text further explains the brothers are silent because they don't know if their *thoughts are the thoughts of all.* The correct answer should mean something like "all in agreement." Choice (A) can be eliminated because there's nothing in the text about whether the thoughts are actually true or not. Choices (B) and (D) can be eliminated for similar reasons because the text never talks about the accuracy or meaning of language. The brothers must simply agree, regardless of the truth. Choice (C) matches the prediction. The correct answer is (C).

4. **B**   The question asks about the role of the indicated sentence. Use the given line reference to find the window. Before the sentence, the narrator mentions the *Uncharted Forest* and says *we do not wish to look upon...we do not wish to think of it. But ever do our eyes return to that black patch.* The *but* indicates a contrast, showing that even though the narrator may not wish to think about it, he definitely does. After the indicated sentence, the narrator provides evidence that the people know very little about the Uncharted Forest, and the only things he has heard have been dismissed as legend. Choice (A) can be eliminated because there is no indication that the Forest is an immediate threat or that the narrator's job is to guard anything. Choice (B) matches the prediction, so don't eliminate it. Choice (C) does match the part that the narrator keeps looking at the horizon, but it doesn't address *why* he is looking in that direction. Eliminate (C). Choice (D) might initially look good because there is a repeated action and something unexplainable, but there's nothing in the text to support *confusion*. Eliminate (D). The correct answer is (B).

5. **D**   The question asks about what a *person who wished to navigate the Uncharted Forest would find.* Because this is the first question in a paired set, it can be done in tandem with Q6. Consider the answers for Q6 first. Choice (6A) indicates that the Uncharted Forest has *no power* and *no path*, which supports both (5D) and Q5. Keep (6A). Choices (6B) (*wild beasts that roam the forest*), (6C) (*bones*), and (6D) (*fires* and *Evil Ones*) may support Q5, but none of them connect to

Q5 answer choices, so eliminate them. As the sole remaining pair, the correct answers are (5D) and (6A).

6. **A** (See explanation above.)

7. **A** The question asks about the narrator's view of the secrets of the past. He knows the secrets exist, but he doesn't know the secrets themselves. He pays attention and wonders about the legends and stories. He equates seeking answers to the questions with *calling death upon our head*. The narrator is fascinated by the secrets of the past but also afraid of this curiosity because it is forbidden. Choice (A) matches this prediction, so keep it. Choice (B) can be eliminated because the text makes it clear that the answers to the secrets are not *easily pursuable*. Choice (C) does not match the prediction because the narrator is doing a very good job of avoiding exploring the secrets. Choice (D) can be eliminated because there is no mention of authenticity in the text. The correct answer is (A).

8. **C** The question asks about the inference that can be made from the given line. Find the line and carefully read the window around it to determine what clues are in the text about the meaning of the line. The Uncharted Forests have *grown over the ruins of many cities* and the *trees have swallowed...all things which perished*. The narrator means that anything that existed in the ancient cities is now covered up and destroyed by the growth of the Forests. Choice (A) can be eliminated because there's no stated connection in these lines between people in the narrator's society and the ancient cities. Choice (B) can be eliminated because the trees mentioned in the lines are covering the ancient cities, not living within them. Choice (C) matches the prediction, so don't eliminate it. Choice (D) can be eliminated because the text indicates that the Forest is forbidden, and there is no evidence that the Forest is used for any literal purpose. The correct answer is (C).

9. **C** The question asks what the phrase *how it came to pass* means in lines 3 and 4. Go back to the text, find the phrase *how it came to pass*, and mark it out. Carefully read the surrounding text to determine another phrase that would fit in the blank based on the context of the passage. The correct answer should mean something like "what happened back then." Choices (A) and (B) can be eliminated because nothing is crossing anything else or going in a circle. Choice (C) matches the prediction. Choice (D) might initially look good because it connects to the passage of time, but the original phrase refers to what actually happened in the past, not how time moved from the past to the present. The correct answer is (C).

10. **D** The question asks what the word *scripts* means in line 39. Go back to the text, find the word *scripts*, and mark it out. Carefully read the surrounding text to determine another word that would fit in the blank based on the context of the passage. The author refers to the *words of the Unmentionable Times*, so the correct answer should mean something like "written words." Eliminate (A) and (B). There is no evidence in the text that the words are specifically screenplays, or even that there are movies at all, so (C) can be eliminated. The correct answer is (D).

11. **D** The question asks for a summary of *the first two paragraphs of the passage*. Use the given line reference to find the window. Lines 11–14 say, *Smart cities bring together infrastructure and technology to improve the quality of life of citizens and enhance their interactions with the urban environment*, while lines 17–25 add that the *Internet of Things (IoT)* empowers Smart cities by enabling *various objects and entities to communicate with each other through the internet*, which creates *a network of objects capable of smart interactions*. Eliminate answer choices that don't match the text of the first two paragraphs. Eliminate (A) because while the author does pose a possible *complicated problem*, (*how do we connect this new technology for the ultimately "efficient" society?*) the focus of the first two paragraphs is a viable solution via the *IoT*. Choice (B) includes a true detail from the second paragraph but does not *summarize* the first two paragraphs, making (B) a Right Answer,

Wrong Question trap answer. Eliminate (B). Like (B), (C) is a Right Answer, Wrong Question trap answer, as it matches the idea that *cities* are *reducing costs by pinpointing issues prior to their emergence* (lines 28–32) but does not provide a *summary* of the first two paragraphs. Eliminate (C). Choice (D) matches the text, so keep it. The correct answer is (D).

12. **B** The question asks what the word *enhance* most nearly means in line 13. Go back to the text, find the word *enhance*, and cross it out. Then read the window carefully, using context clues to determine another word that would fit in its place. The text says that *smart cities bring together infrastructure and technology to improve the quality of life of citizens and enhance their interactions with the urban environment.* Therefore, *enhance* could be replaced by a word such as "improve." Eliminate answer choices that don't match the way the word is used in context. *Emphasize* does not match "improve," so eliminate (A). *Enrich* matches *"improve,"* so keep (B). Neither *convey* nor *increase* matches "improve," so eliminate (C) and (D). Note that (A) and (D) are Could Be True trap answers based on alternate meanings of *enhance* that are not supported by the text. The correct answer is (B).

13. **A** The question asks *which aspect of the city's infrastructure Barcelona* improved *through integration with the IoT.* Since there is no line reference, use lead words and the order of the questions to find the window. Q12 asks about line 13, so scan the passage beginning with line 13, looking for the lead word *Barcelona*. Lines 38–41 state, *By integrating smart water, lighting and parking management, Barcelona saved €75 million of city funds and created 47,000 new jobs in the smart technology sector.* Eliminate answer choices that don't match this answer from the passage. Choice (A), *lighting*, matches the text, so keep it. *Traffic flow, trash cans,* and *energy* do not match the text, so eliminate (B), (C), and (D). Each of these is a Right Answer, Wrong Question trap, since the passage mentions them as projects done in other cities. The correct answer is (A).

14. **D** The question asks what *the passage implies* about *universities using smart technology.* This is the first question in a paired set, so it can be done in tandem with Q15. Look at the answer choices for Q15 first, reading with the question in mind. The lines for 15(A) state that *tertiary institutions are also looking into maximizing the impact of integrated smart technology.* While *universities* would qualify as *tertiary institutions*, this information does not match any of the answer choices from Q14. Eliminate (15A). The lines for (15B) state, *Places such as university campuses and island communities provide smaller laboratories to implement technology in a more manageable environment that can be then replicated on a larger scale.* These lines directly address Q14, so check the answer choices for Q14 to see whether any of the choices are supported by these lines. This information matches (14D), which states that these *universities can serve as models for cities.* Draw a line connecting (15B) with (14D). The lines for (15C) indicate that *smart technology could go even further in improving efficiency by tracking the movements and actions of students.* These lines do not match any answer choices for Q14, so eliminate (15C). The lines for (15D) say, *On campus, your phone or smartwatch could remind you of a class and how to reach it, give you updates on your assignment due dates as well as warn you about overdue books you have borrowed from the library.* These lines do not match any answer choices for Q14, so eliminate (15D). Without any support in the answer choices from Q15, (14A), (14B), and (14C) can be eliminated. The correct answers are (14D) and (15B).

15. **B** (See explanation above.)

16. **B** The question asks what the word *floated* most nearly means in line 65. Go back to the text, find the word *floated*, and cross it out. Then read the window carefully, using context clues to determine another word that would fit in its place. The text says, *The smart campus idea was*

first floated in spring 2016. Therefore, *floated* could be replaced by a word such as "proposed." Eliminate answer choices that don't match the way the word is used in context. *Buoyed* does not match "proposed," so eliminate (A). *Suggested* matches "proposed," so keep (B). *Suspended* doesn't match "proposed," so eliminate (C). *Claimed* does not match "proposed," so eliminate (D). Note that (A) and (C) are Could Be True trap answers based on other meanings of *floated* that are not supported by the text. The correct answer is (B).

17. **C** The question asks about *a potential effect of implementing smart technology in cities.* This is the first question in a paired set, so it can be done in tandem with Q18. Look at the answer choices for Q18 first, reading with the question in mind. The lines for (18A) say, *As smart technology continues to improve and urban centers expand, both will become interconnected.* These lines do not support any of the answer choices for Q17, so eliminate (18A). The lines for (18B) indicate that *the United Kingdom has plans to integrate smart technology in future development and use big data to make better decisions to upgrade the country's infrastructure.* These lines do not support any of the answer choices for Q17, so eliminate (18B). The lines for (18C) state, *Better decisions could be a boom to the economy.* These lines do not support any of the answers for Q17, so eliminate (18C). The lines for (18D) state, *By taking a step towards the future, we will improve not only how we interact with our general environment but how cities interact with us, ensuring that we receive the best quality options and waste fewer resources.* This information describes *increased efficiency* and *responsiveness* quite well, so draw a line connecting (17C) and (18D). Without any support in the answer choices from Q18, (17A), (17B), and (17D) can be eliminated. The correct answers are (17C) and (18D).

18. **D** (See explanation above.)

19. **C** The question asks what *the information in the chart provides.* Work through each answer choice using the figure. Eliminate (A) because the *drawbacks* of the various applications are not mentioned in the chart. Eliminate (B) because this chart doesn't examine *historical* comparisons, only a snapshot in time. Keep (C) because the chart provides *a comparison of some of the applications* of smart technology that are mentioned in the passage. Eliminate (D) because the chart doesn't measure *effectiveness* of the solutions, only the extent of their implementation. The correct answer is (C).

20. **B** The question asks what was implemented by *cities with between 20,000 and 50,000 citizens.* Make sure to read the *x*-axis, the *y*-axis, and the legend carefully. The *x*-axis measures the five different categories of projects that are being compared. The *y*-axis measures the mean values of the number of measures implemented. The legend contains the range of different populations measured. Work through each answer choice using the figure. Eliminate (A) because, for cities with *between 20,000 and 50,000 citizens,* the difference in number of projects between *infrastructure* and *environment* is nearly 2.0. Keep (B) because for *infrastructure, environment, transportation,* and *health,* cities with populations *between 20,000 and 50,000* implemented fewer projects than did cities with populations *between 50,000 and 100,000.* Eliminate (C) because cities with populations *between 20,000 and 50,000* measure nearly 0.5 on the *y*-axis in the *environment* category, while cities with the same population range measure barely 0.25 in the *transportation* category. This contradicts what is stated by the answer choice. Eliminate (D) because cities with *between 20,000 and 50,000 citizens* implemented a mean of about 2.25 projects in the *infrastructure* category, while cities with *beyond 100,000 citizens* implemented a mean of nearly 3.5 projects, and 2.25 is more than half of 3.5. The correct answer is (B).

21. **A** The question asks for a statement *about smart cities developments* that is suggested by the *chart.* Work through each answer choice using the figure. Choice (A) is accurate because, in each of the five categories, the cities with populations of more than *100,000 citizens* implemented more

projects than the cities with fewer than *10,000 citizens*. Keep (A). Eliminate (B) because the figure doesn't measure how much *money* was spent on the projects. Eliminate (C) because the number of projects in the *environment* category is greater than the number of projects in the *health* category for every population category. Eliminate (D) because the figure doesn't measure how well-received the projects were. The correct answer is (A).

22. **C** The question asks about the main purpose of the passage. Because this is a general question, it should be done after all the specific questions. The main purpose of the passage is to discuss how the authors investigated whether an ancient mural in Turkey depicts an actual eruption by proving that there was an eruption nearby at approximately the same time. Choice (A) can be eliminated because the passage doesn't discuss multiple geologic ages. Choice (B) can be eliminated because although the passage mentions radiometric aging, it never explains the ways in which it was used. It's also not the main idea. Choice (C) closely matches the prediction, so keep it. Choice (D) similarly doesn't explain how the pumice veneer forms, nor is this the main idea, so this answer can be eliminated. The correct answer is (C).

23. **A** The question asks how the focus of the passage shifts. Because this is the first question in a paired set, it can be done in tandem with Q24. Consider the answers for Q24 first. Choice (24A) does not support a shift and can be eliminated. The *view...contested* in (24B) not only supports Q23 but also connects to the turn toward *criticism of this theory* in (23A). Connect (24B) and (23A). The lines in (24C) state, *A tradition that predated the settlement of* Çatalhöyük *thus appears very unlikely.* These lines do not indicate a shift in focus, nor do they support any of the answers to Q23. Eliminate (24C). Choices (24D) and (23D) follow the same pattern: both mention *radiometric aging* but fail to address Q23. After eliminating (24C) and (24D), (23A) and (24B) remain the only possible pairing. The correct answers are (23A) and (24B).

24. **B** (See explanation above.)

25. **D** The question asks about the phrase *it putatively depicts* in the context of the passage. Use the given line reference to find the window. The context reveals that it's not clear whether the mural shows an actual volcano or not, since *independent evidence...has been lacking.* Another word or phrase that could go into the passage here might be "possibly" or "theoretically." Choice (A) describes what scientists do and has nothing to do with the doubt relayed, so it can be eliminated. Choices (B) and (C) are closer in that they mention the need for clarification and certainty that scientists rely upon, but they're both too general. Choice (B) says theories must *always* be questioned, but the text only discusses one theory. Choice (C) refers to *the work of scientists*, which is again too broad. Only (D) addresses the idea that this specific claim does not have enough evidence to be proven with a reasonable amount of satisfaction. The correct answer is (D).

26. **A** The question asks about the probable location of the Neolithic volcanic eruption. Because this is the first question in a paired set, it can be done in tandem with Q27. Consider the answers for Q27 first. Choice (27A) states that a *mural* found at the *Neolithic* Çatalhöyük *site (Central Anatolia, Turkey)* shows *an explosive summit eruption*, which supports both Q26 and (26A). Choice (27B) may reference a *British archaeologist*, but it provides no support that an eruption happened either in the *British Isles* (26B) or anywhere else. Eliminate (27B). Choice (27C) lays a similar trap, noting *North American* traditions that may appear connected to (26D) without any direct support for a *Neolithic eruption.* Eliminate (27C). Last, (27D) mentions the same volcanic site as (27A) but without any indication of its location, leaving (26A) and (27A) as the only possible pairing. The correct answers are (26A) and (27A).

27. **A** (See explanation above.)

28. **C**   The question asks about the meaning of the phrase *This is not to say* in the context of the passage. Use the given line reference to find the window. Prior to this sentence, the passage states, *For the* Çatalhöyük *map (and volcano) hypothesis to be plausible, however, we surmise that a brief line of oral tradition, or even an eyewitness portrayal, is perhaps more likely than tradition of a myth that detached itself from its inspiration in the physical world.* Basically, for the map to be somewhat accurate, someone would have to have seen the eruption himself or the description could only have been relayed a couple times. *This is not to say* clarifies that they wouldn't expect a Neolithic map to be completely accurate, but it should have details specific to that type of volcano. Choice (A) can be eliminated because it isn't stated that details were lost, nor does the passage state that details from the mural are crucial for proving the truth. Choice (B) is tempting since this sentence is near the discussion of oral histories, but the passage doesn't say that oral histories don't describe real events. Choice (C) closely matches the prediction, so don't eliminate it. Choice (D) is the opposite of the prediction, since the passage says *realism must not prevail in Neolithic art*, meaning that it wasn't important to the scientists that the drawing be realistic. The correct answer is (C).

29. **C**   The question asks about evidence that supports the claim that the *mural was painted near the time of the volcanic eruption*, so find evidence in the passage to support that. Although this question might initially look like a best evidence paired question, notice that the lines in the answers are all answers for this question. It is most efficient to work backwards, using the lines given in the answers. Choice (A) does address the volcanic eruption, but it does not connect the eruption to the mural at all. Eliminate (A). Choice (B) has nothing to do with the volcano or the mural, so it can be eliminated. Choice (C) does connect time with accuracy, saying *but many of the apparent details can be reasonably expected to become lost or obscured during a long period of oral tradition.* That is, if the eruption happened and was described over many generations, the truth about the details would gradually change. Thus, the eruption must have happened close to the time of the painting of the mural. While it might not initially look perfect, there's no clear reason to eliminate it, so keep (C). Choice (D) focuses on the volcano and does not connect the eruption to the mural, so (D) can be eliminated. The correct answer is (C).

30. **B**   The question asks about an eruption age. On the table, two eruptions are marked: A and B. Notice the eruptions are labeled with the *ka* unit, which is defined as *age in thousands of years.* Therefore, the two eruptions are 8.97 ka, or 8,970 years old, and 28.9 ka, or 28,900 years old. The question asks about the *youngest* eruption, which would be the smallest number. The correct answer is (B).

31. **B**   The question asks when the Hasan Dağı is predicted to have erupted. The passage states *we would predict a time period for the eruption between 7400 and 6600 B.C.E.* and the table indicates the eruption is roughly 8,970 years old. Going back in time just under 9,000 years would put the eruption roughly around 6900 B.C. The correct answer is (B).

32. **D**   The question asks about which statement would be supported by the data, so use the data to go through each of the four statements. Choice (A) is the opposite of what is in the table. The xenocrysts were older than the other particles. Eliminate (A). Choice (B) can be eliminated because there is nothing about the oral tradition in the graphic. Choice (C) does reference the dating method used for the crystals, but this answer can be eliminated because there is no indication that it's the *best way* to determine the age of an artifact. Choice (D) matches the data, indicating that the particles from HDA (the flank of the volcano) are older than the particles taken from the rim. The correct answer is (D).

33.　**A**　The question asks about Burke's opinion of the argument of those who support electing officials. In the text, Burke says that they use *paltry artifices* and *substitute a fictitious cause, and feigned personages*, thereby using weak or untrue arguments. Choice (A) matches that prediction, so don't eliminate it. Choice (B) can be eliminated because even though Burke mentions *fanatics*, he isn't referring to the *sophisters*, and though *universality* might be understood, there's no support for it in the text. Choice (C) doesn't work because the argument, though weak, is current, not antiquated. Eliminate (C). Choice (D) can be eliminated because there is no mention anywhere of *innovation*. The correct answer is (A).

34.　**A**　The question asks what the word *overload* means in line 1. Go back to the text, find the word *overload*, and mark it out. Carefully read the surrounding text to determine another word that would fit in the blank based on the context of the passage. There is a time contrast in the sentence between *a few years ago* and *now* that can be used for context. Burke says *a few years ago* he would have been *ashamed to overload a matter...*with *unnecessary support* but now the doctrine is *publicly taught, avowed, and printed*. The correct answer should mean something like "unnecessarily support." Choice (A) is a clear synonym of that phrase, whereas (B), (C), and (D) don't have anything to do with "unnecessarily support." The correct answer is (A).

35.　**B**　The question asks what the word *employ* means in line 20. Go back to the text, find the word *employ*, and mark it out. Carefully read the surrounding text to determine another word that would fit in the blank based on the context of the passage. The correct answer should mean something like "use," since the abettors are employing the artifices *in order to render the support... invidious*. POE anything that has nothing to do with *use*. The correct answer is (B).

36.　**A**　The question asks about Paine's beliefs about *leadership by right of birth*. He clearly has a negative view, as evidenced throughout Passage 2 with phrases such as *the evil of hereditary succession, minds early poisoned by importance,* and *monarchy and succession have laid but the world in blood and ashes*. Eliminate anything positive, including (B) because Paine does not view hereditary succession as useful and (D) because Paine does not see hereditary succession as valuable. Compare (A) and (C). Choice (A) might initially look extreme, but remember that a correct answer can contain extreme wording if the text has equally strong wording. Choice (C) can be eliminated because Paine doesn't believe leadership is about *expressing opinions*. The correct answer is (A).

37.　**C**　The question asks about Paine's likely response to Burke's statement in lines 22–25. Because this is the first question in a paired set, it can be done in tandem with Q38. Consider the answers for Q38 first. Choice (38A) talks about men who consider themselves *born to reign* who *soon grow insolent*. While this might be an excellent argument against the crown, these lines don't support any of the answers to Q37. Eliminate (38A). Choice (38B) is another specific example of problems with the hereditary crown, but none of the answers for Q37 deal with specific examples. Choice (37A) is the closest thing, but that answer says *address all possible reasons* and that answer is just one reason. Eliminate (38B). Choice (38C) is an argument for the hereditary crown, which is the opposite of Paine's point. Eliminate it. Choice (38D) refers to an entire country denying a fact and believing something false. This supports (37C), so connect those two answers. Without any support from Q38, (37A), (37B), and (37D) can all be eliminated. The correct answers are (37C) and (38D).

38.　**D**　(See explanation above.)

39.　**A**　The question asks about Burke's likely response to Paine's statements in the final paragraph of Passage 2, including *...monarchy and succession have laid (not this or that kingdom only) but the* *world in blood and ashes.* Because this is the first question in a paired set, it can be done in tandem with Q40. Consider the answers for Q40. Choice (40A) has nothing to do with either qualifying the negative statements about the monarchy from Q39 or the link between stability and *conflicts* in (39A). Eliminate (40A). Choice (40B) states that the people of England *conceive the undisturbed succession of the crown to be a pledge of the stability and perpetuity...of our Constitution*, which supports the idea that monarchy can be a stabilizing force. Connect (40B) to (39A). As part of a contrast, (40C) mentions the *fanatics* who support the monarchy but does not include any support for (39A) or Q39. Eliminate (40C). Choice (40D) continues focusing on the monarchy *enthusiasts* and can also be eliminated. With no support, (39B), (39C), and (39D) can all be eliminated, leaving only one pair of answers. The correct answers are (39A) and (40B).

40. **B** (See explanation above.)

41. **B** The question asks about the relationship between the passages. The two passages do not agree, so (A) and (D) can be eliminated. Neither passage presents a method for *resolving the issues*, so (C) can be eliminated. Passage 2 discusses the specifics of England's violent history in relation to hereditary monarchy, a topic never discussed by Burke in Passage 1. The correct answer is (B).

42. **C** The question asks for the main purpose of the passages. Because this is a general question, it should be done after all the specific questions. Both of these passages deal with hereditary succession and views about the validity of a crown passed down through families. However, this is not all they do. Burke argues for a hybrid of monarchy and elected officials (which is what Paine wants). As a result, their disagreement isn't really so extreme. Burke concedes, especially in the last paragraph, that pure hereditary monarchy is not all it's cracked up to be, while Paine addresses those who support the idea and explains why they are wrong. The correct answer is (C).

43. **D** The question asks for the *primary purpose* of the passage. Since this is a general question, it should be done after the specific questions. The passage discusses the promise of CRISPR technology as well as concerns about how CRISPR technology might be used if it is not well-understood and regulated. Look for an answer that matches this prediction. Eliminate (A) because the passage does not discuss *competing theories*. Eliminate (B) because the passage does not focus on the details of one *study*. Eliminate (C) because the passage does not focus on the *history* of CRISPR technology's *discovery*; instead it focuses on its potential applications. Keep (D) because the passage does *evaluate the prospects* (both positive and negative) of the CRISPR technology. The correct answer is (D).

44. **B** The question asks how the *author's attitude toward CRISPR technology* could best be described. Since this is a general question, it should be done after the specific questions. The author is hopeful that CRISPR technology *will serve well for the well-being of humankind.* However, he also discusses the need for regulation and understanding of *the social, environmental, and ethical implications* of the technology. Look for an answer that matches this prediction. Eliminate (A) because the author is not *unconcerned*. Keep (B) because it matches the prediction; the author is optimistic but recognizes the need for caution. Eliminate (C) because the author's primary attitude is optimism; although he supports caution, he does not express *fear*. Eliminate (D) because the author's positive view is balanced with caution; he does not show *unqualified exuberance*. The correct answer is (B).

45. **B** The question asks what the word *editing* most nearly means as used in line 21. Go back to the text, find the word *editing*, and mark it out. Then read the window carefully, using context clues to determine another word that would fit in the text. The text says, *Such broad successes in a short period of time imply we've arrived at a new genome editing era...By eliminating or replacing specific*

DNA fragments and observing the consequences in the resulting cells, we can now link particular DNA fragments to their biological functions. Therefore, *editing* must mean something like "changing." Eliminate (A) because *abridging* means "making shorter" and does not match "changing." Keep (B) because *altering* matches "changing." Although (C) may be tempting, *revising* means "reviewing" or "creating an improved version;" it does not match the context of eliminating or replacing DNA fragments to learn about them, so eliminate (C). Eliminate (D) because *polishing* does not match "changing." The correct answer is (B).

46. **D** The question asks which statement about *DNA fragments* is true. This is the first question in a paired set, but it is a specific question, so it can be done on its own. Since there is no line reference, use chronology and lead words to find the window for the question. Q45 asks about line 21, so beginning with line 24, scan the passage looking for the lead words *DNA fragments*. Lines 29–36 state, *the majority of information embedded on the DNA fragments are largely unknown. Now, the CRISPR technology is enabling scientists to study those gene functions. By eliminating or replacing specific DNA fragments and observing the consequences in the resulting cells, we can now link particular DNA fragments to their biological functions.* Look for an answer that matches this prediction. Choice (A) is a Mostly Right/Slightly Wrong trap answer: the passage states that *the majority of information embedded* on the fragments is *unknown*; it has not *been discovered*; eliminate (A). Choice (B) is a Right Words, Wrong Meaning trap answer: the passage states that *Studying DNA…sheds light on the mechanisms underlying how diseases develop*. It does not say that DNA fragments are *a mechanism underlying how diseases develop*; eliminate (B). Choice (C) is also a Right Words, Wrong Meaning trap answer: the passage states that the *human genomic DNA sequence* has been *deciphered* and that gene editing technology will help scientists learn more about DNA fragments. It does not say that gene editing technology was used to decipher *the sequence of DNA fragments*; eliminate (C). Keep (D) because it matches the prediction that *CRISPR technology is enabling scientists to…link particular DNA fragments to their biological functions*. The correct answer is (D).

47. **B** The question is the best evidence question in a paired set. Because Q46 was a specific question, simply look at the lines used to answer Q46. Lines 29–36 were used to answer Q46. Of these lines, only lines 33–36 are given as an answer choice for Q47. The correct answer is (B).

48. **A** The question asks what the author suggests about *current approaches to gene therapy*. This is the first question in a paired set, so it can be done in tandem with Q49. Look at the answer choices for Q49 first. The lines for (49A) say that a group of biologists called for a halt to the use of a new gene editing technique on humans. These lines discuss a *new* gene editing technique, not *current approaches* to gene therapy. These lines do not answer Q48, so eliminate (49A). The lines for (49B) say that CRISPR technology *has been demonstrated to be effective in genome editing of most experimental organisms, including cells derived from insects, plants, fish, mice, monkeys and humans.* Look to see whether these lines support any of the answers to Q48. Some of the same words appear in (48C), but the lines for (49B) do not state that *corrected genes* from insects, plants, and fish are currently used in *gene therapy*. The lines for (49B) do not support any of the answers for Q48, so eliminate (49B). The lines for (49C) contrast CRISPR technology with *the current approaches of gene therapy which temporarily fix defective cells or organs.* Unlike the current approaches, the CRISPR technology *promises to correct the defect in the reproductive cells*, producing offspring that do not have the defective gene. This implies that current approaches to gene therapy are not able to protect offspring from receiving a defective gene. Therefore, the lines for (49C) support (48A); draw a line connecting (48A) and (49C). The lines for (49D) state that CRISPR technology promises to *eliminate the root causes of hereditary human diseases*; it may be tempting to connect these lines with (48B), but the passage indicates that CRISPR technology is not yet available. It

is also too extreme to say that the current approaches would be completely obsolete once the CRISPR technology is available, so eliminate (49D). Without support in the answers for Q49, (48B), (48C), and (48D) can be eliminated. The correct answers are (48A) and (49C).

49. **C** (See explanation above.)

50. **C** The question asks for the purpose of the *reference to "higher intelligence, better body appearance and longevity"* in lines 73–74. Use the given line reference to find the window. Lines 72–74 mention *hereditary features that people consider advantageous, such as higher intelligence, better body appearance and longevity*. The author uses *higher intelligence, better body appearance and longevity* as examples of the kinds of *hereditary features that people consider advantageous*. Look for an answer that matches this prediction. Although the text uses the phrase *in theory*, the author does not give the examples to support a theory; instead they are used to illustrate the kinds of traits the author is discussing. Eliminate (A). The author is not making a counterargument, so eliminate (B). Keep (C) because it matches the prediction. Eliminate (D) because these are only examples; they do not *summarize* any point. The correct answer is (C).

51. **C** The question asks what the author suggests about the "ethical guidelines" mentioned in line 82. Use the given line reference to find the window. Lines 81–83 indicate that *prominent scientists in the field have recently initiated calls for ethical guidelines* for using CRISPR technology on reproductive cells. Eliminate answers that are not consistent with the text. Choice (A) is a Right Words, Wrong Meaning trap answer: the text says the guidelines would discourage modifying *reproductive cells for clinical application in humans, until the...implications of such operations* are discussed. It does not say that the guidelines will discourage *further advances*, so eliminate (A). Choice (B) is a Mostly Right/Slightly Wrong trap answer: the text does not say that scientists hope the guidelines will *end human genome modification*, only that they hope it will discourage modification of *reproductive cells* until the implications are discussed. Eliminate (B). Choice (C) is a logical inference from the text. Since the calls for ethical guidelines were *recently initiated*, it's reasonable to assume that the ethical guidelines did not already exist when the CRISPR technology was first developed. Keep (C). Choice (D) is a Mostly Right/Slightly Wrong trap answer: the text says that *scientists do not yet fully understand all the possible side effects of editing human genomes*. Therefore, they do not have a *deep understanding* of this kind of modification. Eliminate (D). The correct answer is (C).

52. **A** The question asks what is suggested by the use of the word *"revolutionary."* Use the given line reference to find the window. The final paragraph states, *There is no doubt that the exciting and revolutionary CRISPR technology, under the guidance of carefully drafted and broadly accepted rules, will serve well for the well-being of humankind.* The word *revolutionary* indicates the author's belief that CRISPR technology will create significant positive changes. Keep (A) because it matches this prediction. Choice (B) is a Mostly Right/Slightly Wrong trap answer: the passage indicates that CRISPR technology is not yet approved for treating humans. Although the technology shows great promise, the text does not say that it has already *dramatically improved human health*. Eliminate (B). Choice (C) is a Could Be True trap answer: it is possible that developing the CRISPR technology required a shift in thinking, but this is not discussed in the passage, so eliminate (C). The passage indicates that the *new ethical guidelines* are not in place yet, so they could not have changed CRISPR's *potential applications*. Eliminate (D). The correct answer is (A).

Section 2: Writing and Language

1. **A** Verbs change in the answer choices. The underlined portion is part of a list in the sentence, so this question tests consistency. There is also the option to DELETE; consider this choice carefully as it is often the correct answer. All items in a list must be phrased in the same way to be consistent with each other. The first two items in the list are verb phrases—*read books* and *look at paintings*—so the third item must also be a verb phrase. Eliminate (D), since deleting the underlined portion eliminates the verb from the phrase. Eliminate (B), as the verb phrase *was watching* is not consistent in form with *read* and *look*. Both (A) and (C) use *watch*, which is consistent with the other items in the list, but (C) also includes *to*. The addition of *to* is not necessary, so eliminate (C). The correct answer is (A).

2. **D** Punctuation changes in the answer choices, so this question tests how to connect ideas with appropriate punctuation. The first part of the sentence, *While a bias still remains, there is no question that the canon, the group of accepted "classic" works*, is not an independent clause. The second part of the sentence, *has become much more diverse*, is also not an independent clause. A semicolon can only be used between two independent clauses, so eliminate (A). The phrase *the group of accepted "classic" works* is not necessary to the main meaning of the sentence—it provides a further definition of the word *canon*—so that phrase should be set off by commas. Choice (B) uses a dash to set off the end of the phrase, which is inconsistent with the punctuation earlier in the sentence, so eliminate (B). Choice (C) does not separate the end of the phrase from the rest of the sentence, so eliminate (C). Choice (D) correctly separates the unnecessary phrase from the rest of the sentence using a comma. The correct answer is (D).

3. **C** Note the question! The question asks which choice *most effectively sets up the information that follows*, so it tests consistency. Eliminate answers that are inconsistent with the purpose stated in the question. The sentence following the underlined phrase claims that there is *no better example of such a marginalization than that of Native Americans*. Look for an answer choice that is consistent with the idea of marginalization. Choice (A) describes the groups as *more vocal than others*, which is inconsistent with the idea of *marginalization*, so eliminate (A). Choice (B), *successful despite the obstacles*, emphasizes success rather than the obstacle of marginalization, so eliminate (B). Choice (C), *forced to stay on the periphery*, is consistent with the idea of *marginalization*, so keep (C). Choice (D), *content to stay out of the public eye*, characterizes the groups as *content* with their marginalization, which is inconsistent with the tone and claims of the rest of the passage, so eliminate (D). The correct answer is (C).

4. **D** Verbs change in the answer choices, so this question tests consistency of verbs. A verb must be consistent in tense with the other verbs in the sentence. The first part of the sentence explains that in his book, Kenneth Lincoln *identifies the change*, which is a present tense verb. To be consistent, the underlined verb must also be in the present tense. Eliminate (A), (B), and (C) because they are not in the present tense. The correct answer is (D).

5. **B** Vocabulary changes in the answer choices, so this question tests precision of word choice. Look for a word with a definition that is consistent with the other ideas in the sentence. The sentence says that, in the nineteenth century, *much of* Native Americans' interactions *with white Americans came in the form of military campaigns*, so the correct word should mean something like "meetings" or "communication." *Repartee* and *banter* both mean "quick, witty conversation," which is a kind of interaction, but these choices are inconsistent with the tone of the sentence, which describes the interactions as usually *in the form of military campaigns*. Eliminate (A) and

(D). *Chatting* means "casual talking," which is also inconsistent with the tone of the sentence, so eliminate (C). *Contact* means "communication," and is general enough to include both verbal communication and military conflict, so keep (B). The correct answer is (B).

6. **D**   The number of words changes in the answer choices, so this question could test concision. Check the shortest answer first, which is (D). Choice (D) makes the sentence complete: *When the wars subsided, the American government started a similarly cruel program of assimilation, often involving the movement of Native American children from their homes to "Indian schools" that sought to remove any trace of cultural inheritance.* Keep (D). The underlined phrase follows a comma; (A), (B), and (C) add a new subject and verb to the underlined portion, making the second half of the sentence an independent clause. The first part of the sentence, before the underlined portion, is also an independent clause. A comma cannot connect two independent clauses, so eliminate (A), (B), and (C). The correct answer is (D).

7. **C**   Note the question! The question asks which choice *connects the sentence with the previous paragraph*, so it tests consistency of ideas. Determine the subject of the rest of the sentence and find the answer that connects this idea with the previous paragraph. The sentence says that the time period of the *1960s and 1970s* was *an era of cultural reclamation, when the emphasis on "melting-pot"-style assimilation shifted toward an attitude of "multicultural society."* The previous paragraph describes *cruel* methods *of assimilation*, including reeducation, so the correct answer will connect the description of these methods with the shift toward *cultural reclamation* in the later part of the twentieth century. Choice (A) introduces the subject of *lots of anti-war demonstrations*, which is inconsistent with the focus on the status of Native Americans' cultural heritage, so eliminate (A). Choice (B) focuses on the biography of *Kenneth Lincoln*, the literary critic, and is thus inconsistent with the main idea of the previous paragraph, so eliminate (B). Choice (C) references *This practice of assimilation*, and explains that it *had begun to change*, which is consistent with the idea that *the 1960s and 1970s* saw a shift away from the previously described approach to reeducating Native American children; keep (C). Choice (D) claims that *many important things happened* in the 1960s and 1970s, which is too general a claim to be consistent with the purpose of the question: eliminate (D). The correct answer is (C).

8. **D**   Note the question! The question asks whether a sentence should be added, so it tests consistency. If the content of the new sentence is consistent with the ideas surrounding it, then it should be added. The paragraph discusses how, in the 1960s and '70s, *the emphasis on "melting-pot"-style assimilation shifted* and *people from all races began to think it possible to live in the United States while at the same time identifying with a particular racial group*. The new sentence discusses how *many groups had been marginalized throughout American history*; this idea is not consistent with the main idea of this paragraph, so it should not be added. Eliminate choices (A) and (B). Eliminate (C), because the sentence does not *make a historical claim that the passage contradicts*; the claim is one that the passage confirms. Choice (D) accurately states that the new sentence *repeats information from earlier in the passage that is already implied in this paragraph*, so keep (D). The correct answer is (D).

9. **D**   Transitions change in the answer choices, so this question tests consistency of ideas. A transition must be consistent with the relationship between the ideas it connects. The sentence before the transition states that *Native American children could gain English-language education closer to home*, and the sentence that starts with the underlined transition states that *they could continue to identify with their cultural heritage while gaining an "American" education*. The second sentence provides a positive continuation of the idea in the first sentence, so eliminate (A) and (B), which contain contrasting transitions. Choice (C), *Because*, makes the second sentence incomplete by

introducing a transition word that should not be followed by a comma; eliminate (C). Choice (D), *Moreover*, indicates that the ideas in the two sentences agree with each other, and it does not introduce an incorrect comma. The correct answer is (D).

10. **B** Pronouns and nouns change in the answer choices, so this question tests precision. A pronoun can only be used if it clearly refers to a specific noun earlier in the sentence. The pronoun *them* could refer to *Native Americans*, *colleges and universities*, or *more empathetic attitudes*, so that pronoun is not precise: eliminate (A). Choice (C), *these*, is similarly imprecise: eliminate (C). The pronoun *it* could refer to *This shift* or to *the literary establishment*, so it is also imprecise: eliminate (D). Choice (B), *Native American writers*, is the most precise choice. The correct answer is (B).

11. **D** Note the question! The question asks how to effectively combine the underlined sentences, so it tests precision and concision. The first sentence makes clear that the *efflorescence of Native American writers* who became popular in *the 1970s and 1980s* was the result of increased space for Native writers in literary publications, and the second sentence introduces the list of writers *Leslie Marmon Silko, Gerald Vizenor, and Paula Gunn Allen* as examples of that *efflorescence*; the correct answer should maintain that relationship between the components of the sentences. Choice (A) suggests that these writers' becoming popular was *a resultant efflorescence of Native American writers*, which erases the idea that the efflorescence was the result of increased publishing opportunities; eliminate (A). Choice (B) maintains the correct relationship between the ideas of the sentence, but there is no need to repeat the idea *in those decades*, and the phrase *popularity was earned for writers* is not concise, so eliminate (B). Choice (C) emphasizes the popularity of the three specific writers *in this period of the 1970s and 1980s*, which is not consistent with the original sentences' focus on the overall *efflorescence of Native American writers*, so eliminate (C). Choice (D) most effectively combines the sentences by keeping the focus on *the result* of the publishing shift and by introducing the three writers as examples of *an efflorescence of Native American writers*. The correct answer is (D).

12. **A** Vocabulary changes in the answer choices, so this question tests precision of word choice. Look for a word that is consistent with the other ideas in the sentence. The sentence says that *Anyone who lives in the Mid-Atlantic or New England* will be familiar with *the flowering of spring and the lush greens of summer*, so the correct answer should mean something like "recognizes" or "knows about." *Knows* is consistent with this idea, so keep (A). *Bodes* and *foretells* both mean "predicts," which is inconsistent with the idea of the sentence, so eliminate (B) and (C). *Indicates* means "shows," which is a better description of what the leaves do than what *anyone who lives* in these regions might do, so eliminate (D). The correct answer is (A).

13. **D** The length of the phrase after *never more true than* is changing in the answer choices, so this question tests precision and concision. There is also the option to DELETE; consider this choice carefully, as it is often the correct answer. The sentence already uses the phrase *in the case of fall*, so there is no need to repeat the idea that *fall* is the particular situation under consideration. Choices (A), (B), and (C)—*when people are*, *considering*, and *with the consideration*—all repeat the idea that this case will be particularly significant, so eliminate (A), (B), and (C). Choice (D) is concise and gives the sentence a precise meaning. The correct answer is (D).

14. **B** The length of the phrase after *represents the Northeast in* is changing in the answer choices, so this question tests precision and concision. All four answer choices include the idea that the foliage is representing the Northeast in a state of *purity*, so look for the answer choice that states this idea in the fewest possible words. Choice (B), *its purest state*, is the shortest answer and gives the sentence

a precise meaning, so keep (B). Choice (A) describes the state as *most pure*, and (C) describes it as *the purest possible* state, both of which include unnecessary repetition of the idea of purity: eliminate (A) and (C). Describing the Northeast in a state of purity implies that it is not in a state of impurity, so (D) repeats this idea unnecessarily; eliminate (D). The correct answer is (B).

15. **B** Punctuation changes in the answer choices, so this question tests how to connect ideas with the appropriate punctuation. The word *including* introduces a list of *business owners*; the list is not necessary to the main meaning of the sentence, so the list, as well as the word *including*, should be set off from the rest of the sentence by commas. Eliminate (A) and (D), because they do not use a comma to separate *owners* from *including*. There is no need for a comma between *including* and *restaurant*, so eliminate (C). The correct answer is (B).

16. **A** Transitions change in the answer choices, so this question tests consistency of ideas. A transition must be consistent with the relationship between the ideas it connects. The sentence before the transition states that *foliage season* is *a bit more difficult to predict* than *beach season*; the sentence that includes the underlined transition states that *it is clear* that *leaves tend to change* toward the end of the year, *but when they change and how vivid their colors will be has remained a mystery*. The second sentence provides a more specific example of the general situation described in the first sentence, so the transition word should reflect that relationship between ideas. Choice (A), *for instance*, correctly reflects the relationship between the sentences, so keep (A). Eliminate (B), (C), and (D) because they all contain contrasting transitions, which are inconsistent with the relationship between the sentences. The correct answer is (A).

17. **C** Transitions change in the answer choices, so this question tests consistency of ideas. A transition must be consistent with the relationship between the ideas it connects. The sentence before the transition states that *many people would certainly like to know the cause* of leaf change, and the sentence that begins with the underlined transition explains that *fall without the foliage is like a whole season of rainy beach days*. The second sentence explains a *perspective* underlying the statement in the first sentence, so the correct answer should reflect that relationship between the ideas. Choice (A), *Because of it*, suggests that the second sentence is caused by the fact that *many people would certainly like to know the cause* of foliage changes; this is inconsistent with the ideas of the sentences, so eliminate (A). Choice (B), *subsequently*, suggests that the actions of the second sentence occur later than the events of the first sentence, which is also inconsistent with the ideas of the paragraph: eliminate (B). Choice (C), *After all*, correctly indicates that the perspective represented in the second sentence underlies the idea represented in the first sentence. Keep (C). Choice (D), *Additionally*, suggests that both sentences are examples of the same phenomenon, rather than that the second sentence explains the idea of the first sentence from *a tourism perspective*; eliminate (D). The correct answer is (C).

18. **A** Verbs change in the answer choices, so this question tests consistency of verbs. A verb must be consistent with its subject and with the other verbs in the sentence. The subject of the verb is *Scientists*, which is plural. To be consistent, the underlined verb must also be plural. Eliminate (B), *long knows*, because it is singular. The other main verb in the sentence is *has ever been sure*, which is in the past tense. To be consistent, the underlined verb must also be in the past tense. Eliminate (C), *long know*, and (D), *are long knowing*, because they are in the present tense. The correct answer is (A).

19. **D** Note the question! The question asks whether a sentence should be added, so it tests consistency. If the content of the new sentence is consistent with the ideas surrounding it, then it should be added. The paragraph explains that *no one has ever been sure which aspect of the weather to privilege* in order to understand how *climate conditions influence the changing of the leaves*, and it goes

on to state that *no previous explanation has been able to say why* leaves' changes vary from year to year. The new sentence discusses a report from the *Mount Washington Observatory*, which noted that *the average rainfall in the New Hampshire region is approximately 6–9 inches, depending on the month*. This specific example focuses on one *aspect of the weather* and does not provide a connection between that aspect and the changing of leaves, so it is not consistent with the ideas in the text: the sentence should not be added. Eliminate (A) and (B). While the sentence does introduce *the work of an organization that is not discussed elsewhere*, that work is not the reason the sentence is inconsistent with the main idea of the paragraph: eliminate (C). Choice (D) correctly asserts that the example *is not relevant to the paragraph's description of the general factors that influence fall foliage*. The correct answer is (D).

20. **D** Pronouns change in the answer choices, so this question tests precision. *Their* is a possessive pronoun, so it can only be used in a sentence when it is describing a noun that belongs to multiple other people or things. In the underlined phrase, the pronoun is not describing a noun that belongs to anything—it is referring to *different factors*—so *their* is not the correct pronoun to use. Eliminate (A), (B), and (C). Choice (D), *there are*, correctly uses the word *there* with a plural verb to describe the *factors*. The correct answer is (D).

21. **A** Note the question! The question asks which choice most effectively *adds to the findings described in this paragraph*, so it tests consistency. Eliminate answers that are inconsistent with the purpose of the question. The paragraph states that the group of scientists found that *different factors* affect foliage *in different places*, then mentions how coastal ecosystems and highland ecosystems *reacted* differently to different seasonal frosts. Look for an answer choice that is consistent with the discussion of the scientists' analysis of ecosystems and seasonal change. Choice (A) describes *forests along the coast* as *particularly sensitive to rain and other types of moisture*, which is consistent with the findings mentioned earlier in the paragraph, so keep (A). Choice (B) describes the origin of *the name "fall,"* which is not consistent with the main idea of the paragraph; eliminate (B). Choice (C) describes the difference between *temperatures along the water* and those *in the mountains*, which continues the description of differences between the ecosystems the scientists studied, but the statement in (C) does not add new information to the scientists' findings regarding how ecosystems respond to specific factors, so eliminate (C). Choice (D) describes *the blossoms of the trees* in the spring, which is not consistent with the paragraph's focus on how ecosystems react to frost or other precipitation in different seasons, so eliminate (D). The correct answer is (A).

22. **D** The number of words changes in the answer choices, so this question could test concision. Check the shortest answer first: (C), *suggesting*, makes the sentence incomplete: *Combining these findings with climate-change predictions for the next century, suggesting that the changes will come later in the year for the highlands and perhaps a bit earlier for the coasts*. Eliminate (C). Choices (A) and (B) are the next shortest answers, but neither answer makes the sentence complete, so eliminate (A) and (B). Only choice (D) makes the sentence complete, by adding a subject and a verb to the second half of the sentence: *Combining these findings with climate-change predictions for the next century, the researchers suggest that the changes will come later in the year for the highlands and perhaps a bit earlier for the coasts*. The correct answer is (D).

23. **C** Note the question! The question asks which choice *most effectively completes the contrast in the sentence and is consistent with the information in the rest of the passage*, so it tests consistency of ideas. Determine the subject of the passage and find an answer that is consistent with that idea. The sentence containing the underlined phrase is set up in contrast to the previous sentence, which explains that people referring to *the "fifty-first state"* are usually talking about *Puerto Rico or one of the contemporary U.S. holdings outside the fifty states*. The next sentence in this paragraph describes *the state of Franklin* as *one early case* of *the idea of extra states*, and later paragraphs

describe historical events surrounding the suggestion of forming such a state. Choice (A) claims that *the idea of extra states* is *mainly the concern of academics*, which is not consistent with the focus of the rest of the passage, so eliminate (A). The statement in (B) that the *idea of extra states presents a…challenge*, is not consistent with the rest of the passage, so eliminate (B). Choice (C), *is actually quite an old idea*, asserts that the idea has a long history, while the word *actually* also clearly contrasts with the previous sentence. Keep (C). Choice (D) claims that the idea of a fifty-first state *is rather outdated*, which is not consistent with the rest of the paragraph, so eliminate (D). The correct answer is (C).

24. **A**   Note the question! The question asks for the best *sequence* for *the three state names* so the *information in the passage will correspond as closely as possible with the information in the map*, so it tests consistency. The previous sentence explains that *the state of Franklin would be bound* by one state *to the west and south*, another state *to the north*, and a third state *to the southeast*. Look for the answer choice that is consistent with the map and names the correct states in the correct order. According to the map, *Tennessee* is to the west and south of Franklin, so *Tennessee* should be discussed first in the passage: eliminate (B), (C), and (D) because they do not list *Tennessee* first. The correct answer is (A).

25. **B**   Punctuation changes in the answer choices, so this question tests how to connect ideas with the appropriate punctuation. The first part of the sentence, *North Carolina, one of the original thirteen colonies, offered a few of its westernmost counties to the federal government as payment for debts*, is an independent clause. The second part, *those that had been incurred—for manpower and ammunition—during the Revolutionary War*, is not an independent clause. A semicolon can only be used between two independent clauses, so eliminate (A). A colon can be used after an independent clause, so keep (B). Choice (C) does not provide any punctuation to connect the two ideas, which is incorrect: eliminate (C). Choice (D) introduces an unnecessary dash between *government* and *as*, so eliminate (D). The correct answer is (B).

26. **D**   Apostrophes change in the answer choices, so this question tests apostrophe usage. When used with a pronoun, an apostrophe indicates a contraction. *Its'* is not a word that occurs in English, so eliminate (A). *It's* is the contraction of the words *it is*, which is not needed in the sentence, so eliminate (B) and (C). Choice (D) appropriately uses the possessive pronoun *its* to indicate that both the *offer* and the *western counties* belong to *the state*. The correct answer is (D).

27. **C**   Verbs change in the answer choices, so this question tests consistency of verbs. A verb must be consistent with its subject and with the other verbs in the sentence. The subject of the verb is *the three counties*, which is plural. To be consistent, the underlined verb must also be plural. Eliminate (B), *was attempting*, and (D), *is attempting*, because those verbs are singular. The other verbs in the paragraph, *had been developing* and *issued*, are in the past tense. To be consistent, the underlined verb must also be in the past tense. While (A), *having been attempted*, is in the past tense, it makes the sentence incomplete, so eliminate (A). Choice (C), *were attempting*, is in the past tense. The correct answer is (C).

28. **B**   Punctuation and the number of words after the word *independence* change in the answer choices, so this question tests how to connect ideas with appropriate punctuation and concision. The first part of the sentence, *Encouraged by the new federal government's quick creation of states from ceded lands, the three counties issued a declaration of independence*, is an independent clause. As the sentence is written, the second part, *their independence was rooted in particular in their distance from North Carolina's state capital*, is also an independent clause. A comma followed by *yet* can be used between two independent clauses, so keep (A). Choices (C) and (D) have an independent clause in the second part of the sentence and also have appropriate punctuation between the two parts

of the sentence. The second part of the sentence in (B) is not an independent clause, and again, it uses appropriate punctuation to connect the two ideas. All four answer choices use correct punctuation to connect the two parts of the sentence, so nothing can be eliminated on that basis. There is no need to repeat the word *independent* in the second part of the sentence, so eliminate (A), (C), and (D). Choice (B) uses correct punctuation, is concise, and gives the sentence a precise meaning. The correct answer is (B).

29. **C** Vocabulary changes in the answer choices, so this question tests precision of word choice. Look for a word whose definition is consistent with the ideas in the sentence. The sentence says that the *territories were eventually granted statehood in 1796, though* not as the state of Franklin, but as *something more recognizable—as the northeastern* edge of *the modern-day state of Tennessee*. The correct word should mean something like "edge" or "limit." *Boarder* means "someone who pays to stay and eat somewhere," so eliminate (A) and (B). *Border* does mean "edge," so keep (C). *Broader* means "wider," so eliminate (D). The correct answer is (C).

30. **A** Note the question! The question asks where the new sentence should be placed *to improve the cohesion and flow of this paragraph*, so it tests consistency of ideas. The sentence must be consistent with the ideas that come both before and after it. The new sentence describes an event *in 1789*, when *North Carolina renewed its offer of the western counties* to the government, so it must come before sentence 2, which describes how *This time, Congress acted quickly and accepted North Carolina's offer*. Therefore, the new sentence should follow sentence 1. The correct answer is (A).

31. **A** Transitions and length of the phrase change in the answer choices. There is a comparison in the sentence, so this question tests consistency. When two things are compared, the verbs used to describe them should be consistent with each other. The first item in the comparison is the phrase *national borders*, which the sentence says *are artificial creations*. In order for the comparison of *national borders* to *state borders* to be consistent, *state borders* should also be the subject of a verb, and the verb describing the state borders should be consistent in tense with the verb *are*. Eliminate (B), because *being* is not consistent with *are*. Eliminate (D), because *state borders* are not the subject of the phrase *the same can be said of*. The beginning of the comparison is *just as*, which suggests that there is a similarity between the status of *national borders* and the status of *state borders*; eliminate (C), because the transition *but also* indicates a contrast rather than a comparison. The correct answer is (A).

32. **A** Note the question! The question asks which choice *best accomplishes* the goal of representing *an attitude of genuine interest* and avoiding *the appearance of mockery*, so it tests consistency in tone. Eliminate answers that are inconsistent with the purpose stated in the question. The sentence suggests a contrast between the *State of Franklin* seeming like *a mere historical* oddity to some people and its representing, for others, a *reminder* of the complexities of *even a powerful, federally oriented nation*. *Stumper* and *mind-blower* do not match the passage's tone and suggest mockery or dismissal, so eliminate (B) and (D). Choice (C), *thing*, is too general to convey *an attitude of genuine interest*, so eliminate (C). Choice (A), *curiosity*, is consistent with the tone of the sentence and with the purpose of the question. The correct answer is (A).

33. **C** Note the question! The question asks which choice *most effectively concludes the sentence and paragraph*, so it tests consistency. Earlier, the paragraph states that the history of Franklin *provides a unique look into some of the early machinations of the newly formed American government* and that it is an example of how, *just as national borders are artificial creations*, so *state borders* are also *always subject to change*. The sentence including the underlined phrase suggests that Franklin is a *reminder* of an aspect of *a powerful, federally oriented nation*; look for an answer that is consistent with the example of Franklin in relation to the larger-scale example of a nation overall. Choice

(A) is inconsistent with the main idea of the paragraph, focusing on the number of *states* instead of how Franklin is a reminder of the artificiality of borders, so eliminate (A). Choice (B), *very important in the world and in history*, is not consistent with the rest of the paragraph, which is that a federally oriented nation is subject to change, so eliminate (B). Choice (C) describes the nation as *a living, breathing thing, ever subject to change,* which is consistent with the rest of the paragraph, so keep (C). Choice (D) describes the nation as *home to many things of historical interest,* which does not clarify how the example of Franklin relates to the changeable status of the nation overall, so eliminate (D). The correct answer is (C).

34. **A** Verbs change in the answer choices, so this question tests consistency of verbs. A verb must be consistent with its subject and with the other verbs in the sentence. The subject of the verb is *you,* which is a second-person pronoun. To be consistent, the underlined verb must also be in a second-person form. Eliminate (D), because *sees* is not a second-person verb form and does not work with *you.* The other verbs in the sentence containing the underlined portion are *cross* and *drive,* which are present-tense verbs. To be consistent, the underlined verb must also be in the present tense. Eliminate (B) and (C), because they are not in the present tense. The correct answer is (A).

35. **C** Note the question! The question asks whether a sentence should be added, so it tests consistency. If the content of the new sentence is consistent with the ideas surrounding it, then it should be added. The paragraph describes the importance of *civil engineers,* claiming that their field of work *has long been necessary for the functioning of modern government.* The new sentence repeats the idea that *few governments in the modern world could function without the work of civil engineers,* so it should not be added. Eliminate (A) and (B). Choice (C) accurately notes that the new sentence restates *an idea expressed in the previous sentence,* so keep (C). Choice (D) incorrectly claims that the new sentence would be *a digression from the main point of the paragraph,* so eliminate (D). The correct answer is (C).

36. **B** Vocabulary changes in the answer choices, so this question tests precision of word choice. Look for a word whose definition is consistent with the other ideas in the sentence. The sentence identifies the role *civil engineers will continue to* fill in *modern societies* for as long as *people need to get to school or work,* so the correct word must mean something like "important people." *Beginnings* means "starting points," so eliminate (A). *Cornerstones* means "important point" and can be used to describe people, so keep (B). *Basics* means "essential elements" but cannot be used to describe people, so eliminate (C). *Footings* means "concrete bases of a wall," so eliminate (D). The correct answer is (B).

37. **A** Transitions change in the answer choices, so this question tests consistency of ideas. A transition must be consistent with the relationship between the ideas it connects. The sentence before the transition provides a definition of the *profession* of civil engineers as *"the design and maintenance of public works,"* while the sentence that begins with the underlined transition states that *civil engineers design and maintain components of energy and transportation systems.* The second sentence restates the definition provided as a quotation in the first sentence. Keep (A), *In other words,* because this transition is consistent with the relationship between the two sentences. Choices (B), *On the other hand,* and (C), *Nonetheless,* suggest that the two ideas are in contrast to one another, which is inconsistent with the relationship between the ideas: eliminate (B) and (C). Choice (D), *In the abstract,* suggests that the second sentence provides a less-concrete definition of civil engineering than does the first sentence, which is not accurate; eliminate (D). The correct answer is (A).

38. **A** Punctuation changes in the answer choices, so this question tests how to the connect ideas with the appropriate punctuation. The phrase *like the Hoover Dam, the Holland Tunnel, or the interstate system that covers the whole country* is not necessary to the main meaning of the sentence, so it should be set off using a pair of matching punctuation marks. Choice (A) correctly uses the same punctuation mark, a pair of dashes, at the beginning and the end of the list. Eliminate (B) because semicolons cannot be used to set a phrase off from the rest of the sentence. Eliminate (C) and (D) because they both use a colon at the beginning of the list and a different type of punctuation at the end of the list. The correct answer is (A).

39. **D** Punctuation changes in the answer choices, so this question tests how to connect ideas with the appropriate punctuation. The first part of the sentence, *Their backgrounds tend to vary*, is an independent clause. The second part of the sentence, *specialties can range from architecture to environmental engineering, from ecology to urban planning*, is also an independent clause. The word *however* would not affect either part of the sentence, whether it is included at the end of the first part or at the beginning of the second part. Two independent clauses must be separated by some type of punctuation other than a comma alone, so eliminate (B) and (C). Choice (A) places *however* at the beginning of the second part of the sentence, which would indicate a contrast between the two parts of the sentence. The ideas in both parts of the sentence agree, so eliminate (A). Choice (D) appropriately uses a period between the two independent clauses and places *however* at the end of the first independent clause. This makes it clear that the contrast is between the first sentence of the paragraph and this sentence. The correct answer is (D).

40. **B** The length of the underlined phrase changes in the answer choices, so this question tests concision. *Creating, fabricating*, and *making* all mean the same thing in this context, so it is not necessary to use more than one term; eliminate (A), (C), and (D). Choice (B) is concise and gives a precise meaning to the sentence. The correct answer is (B).

41. **B** Note the question! The question asks where sentence 3 should be placed, so it tests consistency of ideas. There is also the option to DELETE; consider this choice carefully, as it is often the correct answer. The sentence must be consistent with the ideas that come both before and after it; if it is inconsistent with the entire paragraph, it should be deleted. Sentence 3 says that people *who want a greener country draw on the expertise of civil engineers in designing windmills and other sustainable sources of energy*. This topic is consistent with ideas discussed throughout the paragraph, so eliminate (D): the sentence should not be deleted. Because sentence 3 introduces *those who want a greener country*, a group with a specific stance on environmental issues, it should not come before sentence 4, which states that *Environmental engineering has been particularly popular of late on both sides of the environmental debate*. Eliminate (A). Sentence 5 introduces another group with a specific environmental stance, but it describes that group as *less concerned with long-term energy sources*; the word *less* suggests that this group is being compared to another, already-described group that is *more* concerned with sustainable energy. Sentence 3 names just such a group, so sentence 3 should come after sentence 4 but before sentence 5: eliminate (C). The correct answer is (B).

42. **C** Note the question! The question asks which choice *results in a sentence that best supports the point developed in this paragraph*, so it tests consistency. Eliminate answers that are inconsistent with the purpose stated in the question. The paragraph states that the field of civil engineering is expected to *grow by nearly 20% between 2012 and 2022* and that *every new development in energy or transportation* presents *a new set of problems* for engineers to tackle, so look for an answer choice that is consistent with the idea that the field is expanding. Choice (A) mentions

that the field is *full of interesting people* but does not directly support the idea that the field is growing, so eliminate (A). Choice (B) focuses on how *complicated* the field already is, not on its expansion, so eliminate (B). Choice (C), *constantly growing*, is consistent with the main idea of the paragraph, so keep (C). Choice (D) claims that the field is *difficult to describe*, which is inconsistent with the paragraph: eliminate (D). The correct answer is (C).

43.   **D**   Pronouns change in the answer choices, so this question tests consistency of pronouns. A pronoun must be consistent in number with the noun it refers to. The underlined pronoun refers to the noun *a civil engineer*, which is singular. To be consistent, the underlined pronoun must also be singular. Eliminate (A) and (B), because they contain the plural pronoun *they*. Choice (C) also contains the plural pronoun phrase *all of them*, so eliminate (C). Choice (D) appropriately uses the singular pronouns *he or she*. The correct answer is (D).

44.   **C**   The length of the phrase surrounding *civil engineering* changes in the answer choices, so this question tests precision and concision. *Civil engineering* is the name of the profession, so there is no need to repeat the idea that civil engineering is a *career* or a type of *work*. Eliminate (A), (B), and (D). Choice (C) is concise and makes the meaning of the sentence precise. The correct answer is (C).

Section 3: Math (No Calculator)

1.   **B**   The question asks for the value of $g(-3)$. Solve for k first by plugging in 9 for x into the function to get $\frac{5}{3}(9) + k = 12$. Do the multiplication on the left side to get $15 + k = 12$, then subtract 15 from both sides of the equation to get $k = -3$. Therefore, $g(x) = \frac{5}{3}x - 3$, and $g(-3) = \frac{5}{3}(-3) + (-3) = -5 - 3 = -8$. The correct answer is (B).

2.   **B**   The question asks for the value of k in the system of equations. Get rid of the fraction in the second equation by multiplying both sides of the equation by k to get $h = 5k$. Substitute $5k$ for h in the first equation to get $3(k + 2) = 5k$. Distribute the 3 to get $3k + 6 = 5k$. Subtract $3k$ from both sides of the equation to get $6 = 2k$, so $3 = k$. The correct answer is (B).

3.   **D**   The question asks for the expression that is equal to 1. Set the expressions in each of the answer choices equal to 1 and solve for y. Choice (A) becomes $|2 - y| + 2 = 1$ or $|2 - y| = -1$. The result of an absolute value is always greater than or equal to 0, so this doesn't work. Eliminate (A). The same thing happens with (B) and (C). Only (D) works: $|2 - y| - 2 = 1$ or $|2 - y| = 3$, which happens when $y = -1$ or 5. Therefore, the correct answer is (D).

4.   **A**   The question asks for a true statement given that $\frac{x + y}{x} = \frac{6}{5}$. Pick an easy value for x, such as $x = 5$, and solve for y. The equation becomes $\frac{5 + y}{5} = \frac{6}{5}$, so $5 + y = 6$ and $y = 1$. Try these values in the answer choices to see which one works. Choice (A) becomes $\frac{1}{5} = \frac{1}{5}$. This is true, so

keep (A), but check the rest of the answers to be sure. Choice (B) becomes $\frac{1}{5} = \frac{11}{5}$, (C) becomes

$\frac{5+1}{5} = \frac{1}{5}$, and (D) becomes $\frac{5 - 2(1)}{5} = -\frac{1}{5}$. None of these are true, so eliminate (B), (C), and

(D). The correct answer is (A).

5. **A** The question asks for the expression that is equal to $g(-2x)$. Put $-2x$ in for x in the function to get $g(-2x) = -4(-2x) - 7 = 8x - 7$. The correct answer is (A).

6. **D** The question asks for an expression that is equivalent to a factored quadratic. Use FOIL (First, Outer, Inner, Last) to expand the quadratic to get $4(15x^2 - 6x - 10x + 4)$. Focus on distributing the 4 just to the first part in parentheses to see that the first term is $4(15x^2) = 60x^2$. Eliminate (A) and (B). Likewise, the last term must be $4(4) = 16$. Therefore, eliminate (C). The correct answer is (D).

7. **C** The question asks for the solution set for the equation. Put 1 in for k to get $x - 7 = \sqrt{x - 1}$. Now try the values in the answer choices to see if they make the equation true. Start with $x = 5$ since 5 appears in two of the answers. If $x = 5$, the equation becomes $5 - 7 = \sqrt{5 - 1}$. Simplify both sides of the equation to get $-2 = \sqrt{4}$. The square root of a number is always a positive value. Therefore, this expression is untrue. Eliminate (B) and (D). Next, try $x = 1$. If $x = 1$, the equation becomes $1 - 7 = \sqrt{1 - 1}$. Simplify both sides of the equation to get $-6 = \sqrt{0}$. This is also untrue, so eliminate (A). The correct answer is (C).

8. **C** The question asks for the best description of how Alexei's weightlifting changed over the course of his training program. All the answers refer to a number of pounds, and three of them are pounds per day, so calculate his increase in pounds per day. According to the question, Alexei increased the amount he lifted by $225 - 180 = 45$ pounds over $24 - 6 = 18$ days. Calculate his daily increase to get $45 \div 18 = 2.5$ pounds per day. The correct answer is (C).

9. **D** The question asks for the equation of a line that is parallel to the given line. In the slope-intercept from of an equation, $y = mx + b$, m represents the slope. Therefore, the slope of the given line is -4. In the standard form of the equation $Ax + By = C$, the slope equals $-\frac{A}{B}$. For (A), the slope is $\frac{-4}{-1} = 4$. Eliminate (A). In (B), the slope is $-\frac{4}{2} = -2$. Eliminate (B). In (C), the slope is $-\frac{6}{3} = -2$. Eliminate (C). The correct answer is (D).

10. **B** The question asks for the number of solutions to the system of equations. The first equation is a parabola, because if the factors were multiplied out, it would contain an x^2 term. The second equation is a line, because there is no exponent attached to x. The two can, at most, have two points of intersection, so eliminate (A). Next, draw a rough sketch of the parabola. Start by finding the roots of the equation by setting each of the binomials in the parentheses equal to 0. If $x - 7 = 0$, then $x = 7$. Therefore, one point on the parabola is $(7, 0)$. If $3x + 4 = 0$, then $3x = -4$,

and $x = -\dfrac{4}{3}$. Therefore, a second point on the parabola is $\left(-\dfrac{4}{3}, 0\right)$. Lastly, plug in 0 for x to get

$y = (0 - 7)[3(0) + 4] = (-7)(4) = -28$. Therefore, a third point on the graph is $(0, -28)$. Connecting the three points should yield a graph like this:

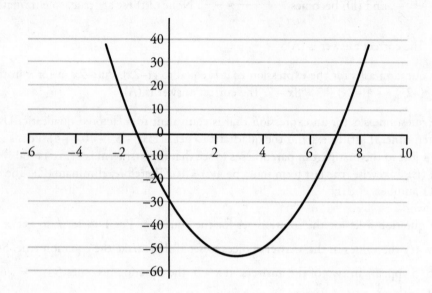

Next, draw the line. Rearrange the equation into slope-intercept form, $y = mx + b$, where m stands for the slope and b stands for the y-intercept. This is $y = \dfrac{1}{3}x + \dfrac{1}{3}$. Therefore, the line has a slope of $\dfrac{1}{3}$, and a y-intercept of $\dfrac{1}{3}$. A rough sketch of the line would look like this:

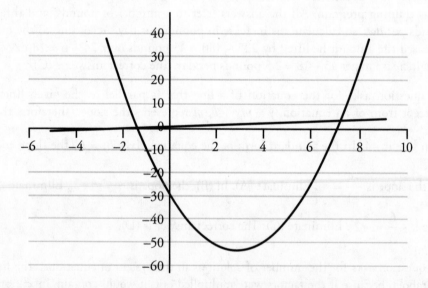

It is clear from a rough drawing of the two equations that the line must cross the parabola twice. The correct answer is (B).

11.   **A**   The question asks for the expression that represents how much Peggie and Joan each paid. The information about the prices is given in terms of the variable d, so pick a value for d. If $d = 10$, then Joan's bouquet costs $10 - 4 = \$6$. The combined cost of both bouquets is $10 + 6 = \$16$,

which means that each of them paid $16 ÷ 2 = $8 for the bouquets before the tax was added. The tax on each share is $8 × 0.15 = $1.20, which means that each of them paid a total of $8 + $1.20 = $9.20. Put 10 in for d in each of the answers to see which answer equals the target of $9.20. Choice (A) becomes 1.15(10) – 2.3 = 11.50 – 2.3 = 9.2. This matches the target, but check the remaining answers just in case. Choice (B) becomes 2(10) – 1.15 = 20 – 1.15 = 18.85. Eliminate (B). Choice (C) becomes 2.15(10) – 2 = 21.5 – 2 = 19.5. Eliminate (C). Choice (D) becomes 2.3(10) – 4.6 = 23 – 4.6 = 18.4. Eliminate (D). Therefore, the correct answer is (A).

12. **A** The question asks for the value of z in the equation. Get rid of the fraction by multiplying both sides of the equation by $(z + 3)$ to get $z - 3 = 8(z + 3)$. Distribute the 8 to get $z - 3 = 8z + 24$. Add 3 to both sides of the equation to get $z = 8z + 27$, then subtract $8z$ from both sides to get $-7z = 27$. Finally, divide both sides by -7 to get $z = -\dfrac{27}{7}$. The correct answer is (A).

13. **C** The question asks for the solutions for x in the quadratic. There is a lot going on here, so pick some numbers for the variables. It isn't easy to pick numbers for all three and have the equation work, so just pick numbers for two variables. Let $x = 3$ and $v = 6$. The equation becomes $(3)^2 - 3t = \dfrac{6}{3}(3)$. Solve for t to get $9 - 3t = 6$, and $t = 1$. In the answers, plug in 6 for v and 1 for t to see which answer could return a value of 3 for x. Choice (A) becomes $\dfrac{6}{3} \pm \dfrac{\sqrt{6^2 + 4(1)}}{3} = 2 \pm \dfrac{\sqrt{40}}{3}$, which will not come out to an integer like 3. Eliminate (A). Choice (B) becomes $\dfrac{6}{3} \pm \dfrac{\sqrt{6^2 + 36(1)}}{6} = 2 \pm \dfrac{\sqrt{72}}{6}$, which won't be an integer either. Eliminate (B). Choice (C) becomes $\dfrac{6}{6} \pm \dfrac{\sqrt{6^2 + 108(1)}}{6} = 1 \pm \dfrac{\sqrt{144}}{6} = 1 \pm \dfrac{12}{6} = 1 \pm 2 = 3$. Keep (C), but check (D) just in case. Choice (D) becomes $\dfrac{6}{6} \pm \dfrac{\sqrt{6^2 + 4(1)}}{6} = 1 \pm \dfrac{\sqrt{40}}{6}$. This won't be an integer, either. The correct answer is (C).

14. **C** The question asks for the value of s on a figure for which two equations intersect at points $(0, s)$ and $(0, -s)$. To find the value of s, plug either of these points into either equation and solve for s. It is easier to use the first point in equation A to avoid having to deal with negative signs. Plugging $(0, s)$ into $x = 18y^2 - 2$ results in $0 = 18s^2 - 2$. Add 2 to both sides to get $2 = 18s^2$, then divide both sides by 18 to get $\dfrac{2}{18} = s^2$ or $\dfrac{1}{9} = s^2$. Take the square root of both sides to find that $s = \dfrac{1}{3}$. The correct answer is (C).

15. **B** The question asks for the value of a when a complex number is written in the form $a + bi$. To get i out of the denominator of a fraction, multiply by the complex conjugate of the denominator. Multiply the top and bottom of the fraction by $(4 - 3i)$ to get $\dfrac{(18 + i)(4 - 3i)}{(4 + 3i)(4 - 3i)} = \dfrac{72 - 54i + 4i - 3i^2}{16 - 9i^2}$. Because $i = \sqrt{-1}$, $i^2 = -1$. Substitute -1 for i^2 to get $\dfrac{72 - 54i + 4i - 3(-1)}{16 - 9(-1)}$

$$= \frac{72 - 50i + 3}{16 + 9} = \frac{75 - 50i}{25}.$$ The full equation becomes $3 - 2i = a + bi$. Therefore, $a = 3$. The correct answer is (B).

16. $\dfrac{5}{8}$ or **0.625**

The question asks for the sine of $b°$, where b is an angle measurement marked on the figure. In a right triangle with angles $a°$ and $b°$, $\cos a = \sin b$. Knowing this fact about the complementary angles of a right triangle makes questions like this easier. Without that knowledge, trying out some numbers can help. Convert 0.625 to a fraction, which is $\dfrac{5}{8}$. Cosine is defined as $\dfrac{\text{adjacent}}{\text{hypotenuse}}$, so label the side next to a as 5 and the hypotenuse as 8. Sine is defined as $\dfrac{\text{opposite}}{\text{hypotenuse}}$, and the side opposite b is the side that is 5. Therefore, $\sin a° = \dfrac{5}{8}$, or 0.625. Either one can be entered into the grid as the correct answer.

17.   **3**   The question asks for the width of the walkway on the diagram. Imagine the triangle as a right triangle with a height of 24 feet and a hypotenuse of $l + \dfrac{1}{4}l + \dfrac{3}{4}l = 2l$. The proportions that hold for the hypotenuse also hold for the height. To solve for the width, set $2l = 24$, which means that $l = 12$, and $\dfrac{1}{4}l = \left(\dfrac{1}{4}\right)(12) = 3$. This is the correct answer.

18.   **1**   The question asks for the value of y in the system of equations. Try to get one of the variables to disappear. Multiply the first equation by 2 to get $16x - 10y = 54$. Stack the two equations on top of each other and add them together to get:

$$\begin{array}{r} 16x - 10y = 54 \\ + \ \underline{5x + 10y = 30} \\ 21x \qquad\quad = 84 \end{array}$$

Divide both sides of this answer by 21 to get $x = 4$. Plug 4 in for x into the second equation to get $5(4) + 10y = 30$. This becomes $20 + 10y = 30$. Subtract 20 from both sides to get $10y = 10$, so $y = 1$. This is the correct answer.

19. $\dfrac{20}{9}$ or **2.22**

The question asks for the change in pressure for every additional 5 feet in depth below sea level. The difference in the values given for p is $110 - 90 = 20$. The difference in the depths for which the values of p are known is $215 - 170 = 45$ feet. Therefore, the pressure increase for every one foot of depth is $\dfrac{20}{45}$, which reduces to $\dfrac{4}{9}$. The question asks for the increase every 5 feet, though, so multiply this value by 5 to get $\frac{20}{9}$, or 2.22. Either one can be entered into the grid as the correct answer.

20. **4** The question asks for the value of x in a fourth-degree polynomial. Look for ways to factor things out of pairs of terms. Factor x^2 out of the first two terms to get $x^2(x-4) + 3x - 12 = 0$. Factor a 3 out of the last two terms to get $x^2(x-4) + 3(x-4) = 0$. Pulling out the $(x-4)$ from both parts will leave the x^2 and the 3, so the equation becomes $(x^2 + 3)(x - 4) = 0$. Therefore, one of the solutions to the equation is $x - 4 = 0$. Solve for x to get $x = 4$. The other solutions come from $x^2 + 3 = 0$, so $x^2 = -3$. This will yield imaginary solutions, so the only real solution is 4. This is the correct answer.

Section 4: Math (Calculator)

1. **D** The question asks for the expression that represents the time Walter will take to run the 40-yard dash after w weeks. No value is given for w, so pick a number. Let $w = 2$. In two weeks, his training time will be $7.2 - (0.2)(2) = 7.2 - 0.4 = 6.8$ seconds. Plug 2 in for w in each of the answers to see which answer equals the target answer of 6.8. Choice (A) becomes $0.2 - 7.2(2) = 0.2 - 14.4 = -14.2$. Eliminate (A). Choice (B) becomes $6.0 - 0.2(2) = 6.0 - 0.4 = 5.6$. Eliminate (B). Choice (C) becomes $7.2 + 0.2(2) = 7.2 + 0.4 = 7.6$. Eliminate (C). Check (D) just to be sure: $7.2 - 0.2(2) = 7.2 - 0.4 = 6.8$. Therefore, the correct answer is (D).

2. **B** The question asks for the length of each piece of yarn, in inches. Start by converting the yards to inches by setting up the following proportion: $\frac{1 \text{ yard}}{36 \text{ inches}} = \frac{4 \text{ yards}}{x \text{ inches}}$. Cross-multiply to get $x = (36)(4) = 144$ inches. After the first cut, the yarn's length is $144 \div 2 = 72$. After the second cut, the yarn's length is $72 \div 4 = 18$. The correct answer is (B).

3. **C** The question asks for the length of Edward's ride, in miles, based on the price he paid. Start by subtracting the base fee to get $3.60 - 2.40 = 1.20$. Divide this amount by the cost per mile to get $1.20 \div 0.30 = 4$ miles. The correct answer is (C).

4. **B** The question asks for the number of miles Irina cycled. Translate the information into equations. Let T represent the number of miles Tiki cycled and I represent the number of miles Irina cycled. According to the question, $T + I = 51$, and $T = I - 13$. Substitute the second equation into the first to get $(I - 13) + I = 51$. Combine like terms to get $2I - 13 = 52$, then add 13 to both sides to get $2I = 64$. Therefore, $I = 32$. Another approach is to plug in the answers. Either way, the correct answer is (B).

5. **C** The question asks for the number of amps flowing through a certain circuit. According to the question, resistance = voltage applied ÷ number of amps. Plug the numbers given into the equation to get $9 = 54 \div x$. Solve for x to get $x = 6$. The correct answer is (C).

6. **C** The question asks for the expected number of students with O-positive blood type based on the results of a random sample. According to the sample, 38.7% of the class would be expected to have O-positive blood. Multiply the total by the percent to get $265 \times 0.387 \approx 103$. This is close to 100. Therefore, the correct answer is (C).

7. **A**   The question asks for the probability that a randomly selected viewer aged 35 to 64 would prefer network D. Probability is defined as the number that fit the requirements divided by the total. The total number of 35- to 64-year-old viewers is $63{,}574 + 20{,}482 = 84{,}056$. The total number of viewers in that age range who preferred network D is $12{,}084 + 3{,}676 = 15{,}760$. Therefore, the probability that a viewer in this age group preferred network D is $\dfrac{15{,}760}{84{,}056} \approx 0.2$. The correct answer is (A).

8. **B**   The question asks for the proportion of pieces of furniture that were desks made of maple. According to the table, there were 75 total pieces of furniture made, of which 9 were desks made of maple. Therefore, the proportion of maple desks is $\dfrac{9}{75} = \dfrac{3}{25}$. The correct answer is (B).

9. **A**   The question asks for a true statement about the slope of a line that goes through Quadrants I, II, and III only. Draw an xy-plane, labeling the quadrants going counter-clockwise from the upper right quadrant. Then draw the line going through quadrants I through III. It should look like this.

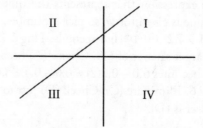

From the drawing, it is clear that the line has a positive slope. The correct answer is (A).

10. **D**   The question asks for a possible equation for the function g based on the x-intercepts. For the graph to have x-intercepts at -2, 2, and 5, the expression must equal 0 when $x = -2$, $x = 2$, and $x = 5$. For each answer choice, set each binomial equal to 0 to see if it results in these values for x. For (A) and (C), there is a squared binomial times another binomial. For (A), if $(x - 2) = 0$, $x = 2$, but that root will appear twice, leading to only 2 distinct roots. For this reason, eliminate (A) and (C). For (B), the first root is 2, then $(x + 2) = 0$ gives a root of $x = -2$, and $(x + 5) = 0$ gives a root of -5. Eliminate (B). The roots for (D) will be 5, 2, and -2, respectively. The correct answer is (D).

11. **C**   The question asks for the brain weight of the animal with the greatest body weight. That animal is represented by the point furthest to the right along the x-axis, so the animal weighs approximately 125 kilograms. Look to the y-axis to see that the same animal has a brain weight of 140 grams. Therefore, the correct answer is (C).

12. **D**   The question asks for the species whose brain weight to body weight ratio is the smallest. The brain weight is given in grams but the body weight is given in kilograms, and 1 kilogram = 1,000 grams. Calculate the ratio of each of the points given in the answers in grams. The ratio in (A) is $\dfrac{70}{10(1{,}000)} = \dfrac{7}{1{,}000} = 0.007$. The ratio in (B) is $\dfrac{50}{30(1{,}000)} = \dfrac{5}{3{,}000} = 0.001\overline{6}$. Since this is less than the ratio in (A), eliminate (A). The ratio in (C) is $\dfrac{110}{65{,}000} = 0.00169$. Since this is bigger than (B), eliminate

(C). The ratio in (D) is $\dfrac{130}{105,000} = 0.00124$. Since this is smaller than (B), eliminate (B). The correct

answer is (D).

13. **A** The question asks for the scatterplot that could represent the function f. First, because an exponent other than 1 is applied to the fraction, the function is not a linear function. Because the scatterplots in (B) and (D) suggest a linear relationship between x and y, eliminate (B) and (D). Next, plug in some numbers to see what happens when x gets larger. If $x = 1$, $j = 4$, and $k = -2$,

the function becomes $f(1) = \left(\dfrac{4}{1}\right)^{-2} = 4^{-2} = \dfrac{1}{4^2} = \dfrac{1}{16}$. If $x = 100$, $j = 4$, and $k = -2$, the function

becomes $f(100) = \left(\dfrac{4}{100}\right)^{-2} = \left(\dfrac{1}{25}\right)^{-2} = 625$. Therefore, according to the function, as x increases, y

also increases. Of the remaining answer choices, this is not true for (C). Eliminate (C). The correct answer is (A). Another option would be to choose some values for the variables j and k and then graph the function on a graphing calculator.

14. **D** The question asks for the relationship between time and the number of bacteria in a lab culture. Over time, the estimated number of bacteria is clearly decreasing. Therefore, eliminate (A) and (C), which both indicate an increase. If the number of bacteria were decreasing linearly, then it would be decreasing by the same amount every hour. However, between hours 0 and 2, the number of bacteria decreased by 900,000, whereas between hours 2 and 4, the number of bacteria decreased by only 90,000. Since the rate of decrease is not the same every hour, eliminate (B). The correct answer is (D).

15. **C** The question asks for the difference in value between two savings bonds after one year, so find the

value of each savings bond. The value of Pete's bond after one year would be $20,000\left(1 + \dfrac{6}{400}\right)^4$,

and the value of Roger's savings bond after one year would be $20,000\left(1 + \dfrac{4}{400}\right)^4$. The difference in

the value of their two bonds would be $20,000\left(1 + \dfrac{6}{400}\right)^4 - 20,000\left(1 + \dfrac{4}{400}\right)^4$. Since both of them

started with savings bonds in the same amount and held them over the same time period, the difference in the value of the bonds is equal to the difference in their earnings. The correct answer is (C).

16. **A** The question asks for the factor that is represented by the slope of a graph. To see what's happening here, pick two values for x, for example, $x = 2$ and $x = 3$, and find the corresponding y-values. When $x = 2$, then $f(x) = 500 + 80(2 - 1) + 70(2) = 720$. When $x = 3$, then $f(x) = 500 + 80(3 - 1) + 70(3)$ $= 870$. Two points on the graph would then be $(2, 720)$ and $(3, 870)$. Next, calculate the slope:

$\dfrac{y_2 - y_1}{x_2 - x_1} = \dfrac{870 - 720}{3 - 2} = 150$. Now check the answer choices. For (A), the combined daily cost of the

hotel and car rental is $70 + 80 = 150$. This matches the value for the slope. The correct answer is (A).

17. **B** The question asks for the number of days at which the cost of package Q will be less than or equal to the cost of package P. According to the equation given, the total cost of package P is $400 + 85(x - 1)$ $+ 60x$, and the total cost of package Q is $550 + 75(x - 1) + 50x$, where x is the number of days traveled. Pick a number of days to try out, and eliminate answers accordingly. Try $x = 8$ days. The cost

cost of package $P = 400 + 85(8 - 1) + 60(8) = 400 + 595 + 480 = 1,475$, and the cost of package $Q = 550 + 75(8 - 1) + 50(8) = 550 + 525 + 400 = 1,475$. The cost of the two packages is the same at 8 days, which fits the requirements of the question. Eliminate (D), since that range does not include 8. Now try a different value such as $x = 7$. Package P would cost $400 + 85(6) + 60(7) = 1,330$, and package Q would cost $550 + 75(6) + 50(7) = 1,350$. Travel package Q is not less than or equal to the total cost of travel package P, so eliminate ranges that include 7. This eliminates (A) and (C). The correct answer is (B).

18. **D** The question asks for the graph the fits the description of Moore's law. Use Process of Elimination. According to Moore's Law, the maximum number of transistors that can be placed on a circuit each year doubles. If there was 1 transistor to start, the next year there would be 2, then 4, then 8, then 16. The number of transistors would increase more and more rapidly over the years, which indicates exponential growth. Choice (A) is a flat, horizontal line, showing no growth at all, and (B) has flat sections, showing periods of no growth. Eliminate (A) and (B). Choice (C) shows growth, but it is a line, which indicates growth at a constant rate. Eliminate (C). Only (D) shows growth that increases exponentially. The correct answer is (D).

19. **A** The question asks for the greatest number of buckets Bob can fill from a drum of oil. Start by determining the volume of the oil he has in cubic feet. The volume of a cylinder can be calculated as $V = \pi r^2 h$. According to the information given, the radius of each bucket is 0.5 feet and the height of the oil in each bucket is 1.5 feet. Therefore, the volume of the oil in each bucket is $\pi(0.25)(1.5) \approx$ 1.1781 cubic feet. Set up the following proportion: $\dfrac{1 \text{ gallon}}{0.133 \text{ feet}^3} = \dfrac{x \text{ gallons}}{1.1781 \text{ feet}^3}$. Cross-multiply to get $0.133x = 1.1781$. Divide both sides of the equation by 0.133 to get $x = 8.858$ gallons per bucket. Bob has 55 gallons of oil, so he can fill $55 \div 8.858 \approx 6.2$ buckets. Only round at the last step to ensure a correct answer when the choices are close together. The question asks for the number of full buckets, so round this down to 6. The correct answer is (A).

20. **B** The question asks for the greatest possible value of $2x - 5$, so there is no need to solve all the way for x. Just make the first inequality look like the second one. Start by subtracting 5 from both sides of the inequality to get $2x \le 4$. Subtract 5 from each side again to get $2x - 5 \le 4 - 5$ or $2x - 5 \le -1$. Therefore, the greatest possible value is -1. The correct answer is (B).

21. **D** The question asks for the length of $\overline{PR}$, which is a diameter, and it says that the length of arc $\overset{\frown}{PQR}$ is 18π. An arc formed by the diameter is a semicircle. The length of a semicircle is equal to half the circumference of the circle, so the circumference of the circle is $18\pi \times 2 = 36\pi$. The formula for the circumference of a circle is $C = \pi d$, so $36\pi = \pi d$. Divide both sides by π to get $36 = d$. The correct answer is (D).

22. **A** The question asks which data points on a scatterplot are below the line $y = x$. To see what happens when a point is below a line, sketch a line on the coordinate plane and a point below it. The y-coordinate of the point is lower than the y-coordinate of the line at that same value of x. In the case of the line $y = x$, a point is below the line if its y-value is less than its x-value. According to the question, the y-value is equal to a city's average temperature in 2010 and the x-value is equal to the city's average temperature in 2000, so find cities in which the average temperature in 2010 is less than its average temperature in 2000. The only city on the chart for which this is true is Miami. The correct answer is (A).

23. **C** The question asks for the approximate percent increase in New York's temperature from 2000 to 2010, so an estimate will be enough. The top of the 2000 bar is between the 50 and 55 line,

closer to 55, so call the average temperature 53. The top of the 2010 bar is between the 55 and 60 line, closer to 55, so call the average temperature 57. To calculate percent change, use the formula $\frac{\text{difference}}{\text{original}} \times 100$. The difference is $57 - 53 = 4$. Since the question asks for a percent *increase*, the original is the smaller value, which is 53. Therefore, the percent increase is about $\frac{4}{53} \times 100 \approx 7.55\%$.

The closest choice is 6%. Therefore, the correct answer is (C).

24. **A** The question asks for a true statement about the data in the tables, and the answer choices refer to standard deviation. All that is needed to compute standard deviation is the individual scores. Since this is provided by the table, eliminate (D). The formula to calculate standard deviation is very long and complicated. However, it is not necessary to use the formula here. Just understand that the standard deviation is a measure of how far apart the values are spread out. A strong majority of students received a 4 on the Physics quiz. Since most of the students got the same score, the scores are not very spread out. Since the distribution of scores on the English quiz is more even, these scores are more spread out. Therefore, the standard deviation is higher for the English quiz. The correct answer is (A).

25. **D** The question asks for an inequality that *must be true*, so try some real numbers. Make sure to pick a value for b such that $b < -b$. Let $b = -3$. If $b = -3$, then $-3 < a < 3$. Let $a = 2$. Go through each statement. Statement (I) says $a < 0$. Since $a = 2 > 0$, cross out (I) and eliminate the choices that include (I): (A) and (C). Since both remaining choices include (III), (III) must be true, so only worry about (II). Since $b = -3$, (II) is true, so keep (II) at least for now. Try to come up with a value of b that will satisfy the inequality but make (II) false. Try a positive number. If $b = 4$, then $4 < a < -4$. Since 4 is not less than -4, do not use $b = 4$. In fact, any positive value for b will lead to the same problem. Try $b = 0$. If $b = 0$, then $0 < a < 0$. Again, 0 is not less than 0, so do not use $b = 0$. Since positive numbers and 0 do not satisfy the inequality, only negative numbers do. Therefore, (II) must be true. Eliminate the remaining answer that does not include (II), which is (B). The correct answer is (D).

26. **A** The question asks how the number 31 relates to the scatterplot. The number 31 is the y-intercept of the line, or the point at which $x = 0$. The x-axis refers to the number of hours spent on the Internet, and the y-axis refers to the score on the quiz. Therefore, a student who spends no time on the Internet would be expected to score around a 31. Go through the answer choices. Choice (A) says that even students who spend very little time on the Internet are unlikely to score above a 31. This matches the prediction. Also, only one of the data points is above 31. Keep (A). Choice (B) says that even students who spend very little time on the Internet will never score above 31. This is more extreme than the prediction. Also, there is a data point above 31. Eliminate (B). Choice (C) says the lowest score was about 31% of the highest score. This doesn't match the prediction. Also, the highest score is about 34 and the lowest score is about 6, so the lowest score is $\frac{6}{34} \times 100 \approx 18\%$ of the highest score. Eliminate (C). Choice (D) says the highest score on the test was 31. Similar to (B), this is more extreme than the prediction. Also, there is a data point above 31. Eliminate (D). The correct answer is (A).

27. **C** The question asks for the polynomial that is divisible by $3x + 4$. Rather than do complicated polynomial division or factoring, pick a value for x, such as $x = 2$. If $x = 2$, then $r(x) = r(2) = 3(2)^3 + 24(2)^2 + 21(2) = 162$, $s(x) = s(2) = 2^2 + 8(2) + 7 = 27$, and $3x + 4 = 3(2) + 4 = 10$. The question asks which choice is divisible by $3x + 4$, plug in $x = 2$ to each choice and eliminate any choice that isn't divisible by 10. Choice (A) is $r(2) + s(2) = 162 + 27 = 189$. This is not divisible by 10, so eliminate (A). Choice

(B) is $r(2) + 2s(2) = 162 + 2(27) = 216$. This is not divisible by 10, so eliminate (B). Choice (C) is $r(2) + 4s(2) = 162 + 4(27) = 270$. This is divisible by 10, so keep (C). Choice (D) is $2r(2) + 4s(2) = 2(162) + 4(27) = 432$. This is not divisible by 10, so eliminate (D). The correct answer is (C).

28.   **A**   The question asks for the value of c that will cause $g(x) = c$ to have one real solution. Since c is on the other side of the equals sign, it is the y-value. Therefore, if $g(x) = c$ has one real solution, it will intersect the line $y = c$ exactly once. Let each answer choice equal c and draw the line $y = c$. Draw $y = 3$, $y = 1$, $y = 0$, and $y = -1$. Each line should be a horizontal line crossing the y-axis at 3, 1, 0, and -1, respectively. The lines $y = 1$, $y = 0$, and $y = -1$ cross the graph of g at three points each. Therefore, if c is any of these values, $g(x) = c$ has three real solutions. The line $y = 3$ crosses g exactly once, so $g(x) = 3$ has exactly one real solution. Therefore, the correct answer is (A).

29.   **B**   The question asks for the form of a quadratic in which the minimum value appears. A parabola reaches its minimum (or maximum) value at its vertex, so get the equation into vertex form, which is $y = a(x - h)^2 + k$, where (h, k) is the vertex. Choice (C) is not in this form, so eliminate it. To get g into vertex form, expand using FOIL (First, Outer, Inner, Last) to get $(x - 10)(x + 4) = x^2 + 4x - 10x - 40 = x^2 - 6x - 40$. Eliminate (D), which is not equivalent to this. Get the quadratic into vertex form by completing the square. The coefficient on the x term is -6. Cut this value in half to get -3, and square the result to get 9. Add 9 to both sides (without combining like terms) to get $y + 9 = x^2 - 6x + 9 - 40$. Factor $(x^2 - 6x + 9)$ to get $y + 9 = (x - 3)^2 - 40$. Subtract 9 from both sides to get $y = (x - 3)^2 - 49$. Thus, the vertex is $(3, -49)$ and the minimum value is -49. The correct answer is (B).

30.   **C**   The question asks for the average of three numbers that are in terms of x, so pick a value for x. Let $x = 2$. The question states that a is the average of $4x$ and 7. The sum of $4x$ and 7 is $4(2) + 7 = 15$, so the average is $\frac{15}{2} = 7.5$. The question also states that b is the average of $5x$ and 6. The sum of $5x$ and 6 is $5(2) + 6 = 16$, so the average is $\frac{16}{2} = 8$. Finally, the question states that c is the average of $3x$ and 11. The sum of $3x$ and 11 is $3(2) + 11 = 17$, so the average is $\frac{17}{2} = 8.5$. The question asks for the average of a, b, and c. The sum of a, b, and c is $7.5 + 8 + 8.5 = 24$, so the average is $\frac{24}{3} = 8$. Circle 8; this is the target number. Go through the answer choices and eliminate any choice that is not equal to 8. Choice (A) is $x + 4 = 2 + 4 = 6$, so eliminate (A). Choice (B) is $x + 8 = 2 + 8 = 10$, so eliminate (B). Choice (C) is $2x + 4 = 2(2) + 4 = 8$, so keep (C). Choice (D) is $4x + 8 = 4(2) + 8 = 16$, so eliminate (D). The correct answer is (C).

31.   **1.2**   The question asks how much of a decrease in target heart rate will occur if the person's age increases by 2 years. Try two values of y that are 2 years apart. Start with $y = 20$. If $y = 20$, then $R = \frac{3(220 - 20)}{5} = 120$. Now try $y = 22$. If $y = 22$, then $R = \frac{3(220 - 22)}{5} = 118.8$. To determine the decrease, subtract the two values of R to get $120 - 118.8 = 1.2$. This is the correct answer.

32.   **620**   The question asks how many miles into the journey the driver will be at 8:00 P.M. From 1 P.M. to 8 P.M., the driver travels for 7 hours. To determine the distance traveled, use *distance = rate × time* to get $d = rt = (60 \text{ miles per hour})(7 \text{ hours}) = 420 \text{ miles}$. This is not the answer. Note that at 1:00 P.M. the driver is already 200 miles into his journey. Therefore, the driver has traveled a total of 200 miles + 420 miles = 620 miles. The correct answer is 620.

33. $\dfrac{25}{4}$, $\dfrac{50}{8}$, or **6.25**

The question asks for the ratio of the displacement of two objects accelerating for different amounts of time. Since the variables are given in relation to one another, pick values for them to see what happens. Let the first object travel at an acceleration of $a = 4$ for a time of $t = 10$. The displacement is $d = \dfrac{1}{2}(4)(10)^2 = 200$. The second object also has an acceleration of $a = 4$ but for a time of $2.5t = 2.5(10) = 25$. This displacement is $d = \dfrac{1}{2}(4)(25)^2 = 1,250$. The question asks for the ratio of the velocity of the object that traveled for more time to the velocity of the object that traveled for less time. This is $\dfrac{1,250}{200}$. This requires more than four spaces on the answer sheet, so reduce the fraction to get $\dfrac{25}{4}$. Note that $\dfrac{50}{8}$ is also an acceptable answer, as is 6.25. Any of these three values can be entered into the grid as the correct answer.

34. **8.16**   The question asks for the number of pounds that are equivalent to 488 shematies. The question states that 12 shematies is equivalent to 1 deben, so set up the proportion $\dfrac{12 \text{ shematies}}{1 \text{ deben}} = \dfrac{488 \text{ shematies}}{x \text{ debens}}$. Cross-multiply to get $12x = 488$. Divide by 12 to get $x = 40.\overline{66}$, so 488 shematies is equivalent to $40.\overline{66}$ debens. The question also says that a deben is approximately equal to 3.21 ounces, so set up the proportion $\dfrac{3.21 \text{ ounces}}{1 \text{ deben}} = \dfrac{y \text{ ounces}}{40.66 \text{ debens}}$. Cross-multiply to get $y = 130.54$, so 488 shematies is equivalent to 130.54 ounces. Finally, the question states that 16 ounces is equivalent to one pound, so set up the proportion $\dfrac{16 \text{ ounces}}{1 \text{ pound}} = \dfrac{130.54 \text{ ounces}}{z \text{ pounds}}$. Cross-multiply to get $16z = 130.54$. Divide both sides by 16 to get $z = 8.15875$. The question asks for the answer to the nearest hundredth, which is 8.16. This is the correct answer.

35. **43, 44,** or **45**

The question asks about arc, the degree measure of a central angle in a circle, based on the arc length. The parts of a circle are proportional such that $\dfrac{\text{arc}}{\text{circumference}} = \dfrac{\text{angle}}{360}$. The radius is 20, so use the circumference formula to get that the circumference is $C = 2\pi r = 2\pi(20) = 40\pi$. The arc is between 15 and 16, so start with an arc of 15 to get $\dfrac{15}{40\pi} = \dfrac{y}{360}$. Cross-multiply to get $5,400 = 40\pi y$. Divide both sides by 40π to get $y = \dfrac{5,400}{40\pi} = \dfrac{135}{\pi} = 42.9718$. Now try an arc of 16 to get $\dfrac{16}{40\pi} = \dfrac{y}{360}$. Cross-multiply to get $5,760 = 40\pi y$. Divide both sides by 40π to get $y = \dfrac{5,760}{40\pi} = \dfrac{144}{\pi} \approx 45.8366$.

The angle is, therefore, in between these two values of y. The question specifies that the answer must be an integer. Therefore, the correct answers are 43, 44, or 45.

36. **90**   The question asks how many blue marbles must be added so that $\frac{2}{5}$ of the marbles are blue. At the beginning, there are 230 blue marbles and 370 red marbles, so there are a total of 230 + 370 = 600 marbles. Then 110 red marbles are added, so there is now a total of 370 + 110 = 480 red marbles and 600 + 110 = 710 total marbles. If b blue marbles are added, there will be 230 + b blue marbles and 710 + b total marbles. Set up the equation $\frac{230 + b}{710 + b} = \frac{2}{5}$. Cross-multiply to get 5(230 + b) = 2(710 + b). Distribute to get 1,150 + 5b = 1,420 + 2b. Subtract 2b from both sides to get 1,150 + 3b = 1,420. Subtract 1,150 from both sides to get 3b = 270. Divide both sides by 3 to get b = 90. This is the correct answer.

37. **1.07**   The question asks for the value of r in the bank's interest formula. Interest is a type of exponential growth. The formula for this is *final amount = original amount*$(1 + rate)^{number\ of\ changes}$. The original amount is $5,400 and the rate of interest is 7%. In the formula, rate is in decimal form rather than percent form, so the rate is 0.07. The bank pays annual interest, so the number of changes is the number of years, which is y. The final amount is the amount in the bank after y years, which is A. Plug these into the exponential growth formula to get $A = 5,400(1 + 0.07)^y$ or $A = 5,400(1.07)^y$. This is now in the same form as the equation provided by the question, $A = 5,400(r)^y$. The value in parentheses in the same position as r in the provided equation is 1.07. This is the correct answer.

38. **7,078**   The question asks for the value of the CD account after four years. As discussed in the explanation for Q37, the value of r is 1.07, so the formula becomes $A = 5,400(1.07)^y$. The number of years is 4, so the formula becomes $A = 5,400(1.07)^4$. Enter this into a calculator to get about $7,078.29. The question asks for the value to the nearest dollar (disregarding the dollar sign), which is 7,078. Without the formula, it is still possible to get the answer. Just add 7% of 5,400 to get the value after one year, 7% of that new value to get the value after two years, and do that two more times to get the value after four years. Either way, the correct answer is 7,078.

Chapter 11
Practice Test 5

Reading Test

65 MINUTES, 52 QUESTIONS

Turn to Section 1 of your answer sheet to answer the questions in this section.

Questions 1–10 are based on the following passage.

This passage is excerpted from Robert Louis Stevenson, *Treasure Island,* originally published in 1883. The narrator and his parents own an inn on the English coast.

The stranger kept hanging about just inside the inn door, peering round the corner like a cat waiting for a mouse. Once I stepped out myself into the road, but
Line he immediately called me back, and as I did not obey
5 quick enough for his fancy, a most horrible change came over his tallowy face, and he ordered me in with an oath that made me jump. As soon as I was back again he returned to his former manner, half fawning, half sneering, patted me on the shoulder, told me I
10 was a good boy and he had taken quite a fancy to me. "I have a son of my own," said he, "as like you as two blocks, and he's all the pride of my 'art. But the great thing for boys is discipline, sonny—discipline. Now, if you had sailed along of Bill, you wouldn't have stood
15 there to be spoke to twice—not you. That was never Bill's way, nor the way of sich as sailed with him. And here, sure enough, is my mate Bill, with a spy-glass under his arm, bless his old 'art, to be sure. You and me'll just go back into the parlour, sonny, and get
20 behind the door, and we'll give Bill a little surprise—bless his 'art, I say again."

So saying, the stranger backed along with me into the parlour and put me behind him in the corner so that we were both hidden by the open door. I was very
25 uneasy and alarmed, as you may fancy, and it rather added to my fears to observe that the stranger was certainly frightened himself. He cleared the hilt of his

cutlass and loosened the blade in the sheath; and all the time we were waiting there he kept swallowing as if
30 he felt what we used to call a lump in the throat.

At last in strode the captain, slammed the door behind him, without looking to the right or left, and marched straight across the room to where his breakfast awaited him.
35 "Bill," said the stranger in a voice that I thought he had tried to make bold and big.

The captain spun round on his heel and fronted us; all the brown had gone out of his face, and even his nose was blue; he had the look of a man who sees a
40 ghost, or the evil one, or something worse, if anything can be; and upon my word, I felt sorry to see him all in a moment turn so old and sick.

"Come, Bill, you know me; you know an old shipmate, Bill, surely," said the stranger.
45 The captain made a sort of gasp.

"Black Dog!" said he.

"And who else?" returned the other, getting more at his ease. "Black Dog as ever was, come for to see his old shipmate Billy, at the Admiral Benbow Inn. Ah,
50 Bill, Bill, we have seen a sight of times, us two, since I lost them two talons," holding up his mutilated hand.

"Now, look here," said the captain; "you've run me down; here I am; well, then, speak up; what is it?"

"That's you, Bill," returned Black Dog, "you're
55 in the right of it, Billy. I'll have a glass of rum from this dear child here, as I've took such a liking to; and we'll sit down, if you please, and talk square, like old shipmates."

CONTINUE ➡

When I returned with the rum, they were already
60 seated on either side of the captain's breakfast-table—
Black Dog next to the door and sitting sideways so
as to have one eye on his old shipmate and one, as I
thought, on his retreat.

He bade me go and leave the door wide open.
65 "None of your keyholes for me, sonny," he said; and I
left them together and retired into the bar.

For a long time, though I certainly did my best to
listen, I could hear nothing but a low gattling; but at
last the voices began to grow higher, and I could pick
70 up a word or two, mostly oaths, from the captain.

"No, no, no, no; and an end of it!" he cried once.
And again, "If it comes to swinging, swing all, say I."

1

Which choice is the best synopsis of what happens in
the passage?

A) Two characters make a plan to surprise a third
character.

B) One character shows another character how to
properly behave in a parlour.

C) One character unpleasantly surprises another
character with an unexpected reunion.

D) Two characters reminisce about their time
together on a ship.

2

Which choice best describes the developmental
pattern of the passage?

A) A detailed analysis of an enthusiastic encounter

B) An inaccurate dictation of a notable conference

C) An apprehensive account of a contentious meeting

D) A dismissive description of an important
homecoming

3

As it is used in line 5 and line 10, "fancy" most nearly
means

A) elaboration.

B) impatience.

C) imagination.

D) preference.

4

Which emotion does the narrator most sense from
the stranger regarding his imminent meeting with the
captain?

A) The stranger is fearful about the captain's reaction
to seeing him.

B) The stranger is overjoyed to reunite with the
captain.

C) The stranger is worried the captain won't
remember him.

D) The stranger is concerned the captain will be more
interested in his breakfast than in conversation.

5

Which choice provides the best evidence for the
answer to the previous question?

A) Lines 24–27 ("I was . . . himself")

B) Lines 31–34 ("At last . . . him")

C) Lines 43–44 ("Come . . . stranger")

D) Line 71 ("No, no, . . . once")

6

In the passage, the stranger addresses the narrator
with

A) respect but not friendliness.

B) violence but not anger.

C) disgust but not hatred.

D) affection but not trust.

CONTINUE

7

The main purpose of the first paragraph is to

A) introduce a character.

B) criticize a belief.

C) describe a relationship.

D) investigate a discrepancy.

8

As it is used in line 51, "talons" most nearly means

A) weapons.

B) claws.

C) fingers.

D) hooks.

9

Why does the narrator describe the captain's face as something from which "all the brown had gone out of" (line 38)?

A) The captain has grown pale after being on land so long.

B) The captain has washed his face before the meal.

C) The captain has become ill during his walk.

D) The captain has gone pale with fright.

10

Which choice provides the best evidence for the answer to the previous question?

A) Lines 22–24 ("So saying . . . door")

B) Lines 39–42 ("he had . . . sick")

C) Lines 52–53 ("Now, look . . . it")

D) Lines 59–63 ("When . . . retreat")

CONTINUE

Questions 11–21 are based on the following passage and supplementary material.

This passage is adapted from Russell W. Belk, "It's the Thought that Counts." ©1976 by University of Illinois at Urbana-Champaign.

The phenomenon of selecting an object or service "X" to present as a gift to person "Y" on occasion "Z" is a unique and important act of consumer behavior.
Line Not only must the gift giver attempt to infer the
5 recipient's tastes, needs, desires, and reactions, the gift selection may also be affected by the information which it would appear to convey about the giver and the giver-recipient relationship. The ancient practice of gift-giving is still pervasive and significant in modern
10 cultures. For instance, Lowes, Turner, and Willis (1971) cite a series of British Gallup Polls from 1963–1967, in which it was found that over 90 percent of the adult population did some Christmas gift-giving each year. Another limited sample of middle and upper
15 income families in Montreal, Caron and Ward (1975) found that third- and fifth-grade children received an average of between five and six gifts for Christmas. Both because of its prevalence and because of its strong interpersonal meanings, gift-giving offers a potentially
20 rich area for consumer behavioral explanation.

Gift-giving has been treated from a variety of related theoretical perspectives, focusing primarily on the functions and effects of giving. The preeminent theoretical analysis of the gift-giving process is an essay
25 by French anthropologist-sociologist Marcell Mauss (1923). Based on his examination of gift-giving among numerous primitive, remote, or ancient societies, Mauss concluded that gift-giving is a self-perpetuating system of reciprocity. More specifically, Mauss outlined
30 three types of obligations, which perpetuate gift-giving:
    1. The obligation to give,
    2. The obligation to receive,
    3. The obligation to repay.
The obligation to give may be based on moral
35 or religious imperatives, the need to recognize and maintain a status hierarchy, the need to establish or maintain peaceful relations, or simply the expectation of reciprocal giving. These motives, which do not admit purely selfless giving, become institutionalized
40 in a society so that under appropriate conditions an individual is socially obligated to give. Receiving is seen as similarly obligatory, and avoiding or refusing gifts is construed as an unfriendly or even hostile act. Mauss noted however that there is a certain tension
45 created in receiving a gift since acceptance is an implicit recognition of dependence on the giver. This tension may then be reduced by fulfilling the third obligation, the obligation to repay. Failure to repay or failure to repay adequately results in a loss of status
50 and self-esteem. Adequate or overly adequate repayment, on the other hand, creates an obligation to repay on the part of the original giver, and the cycle is reinitiated.

Schwartz (1967) noted that beyond the functions
55 served by the general process of gift exchange, the characteristics of the gift itself also act as a powerful statement of the giver's perception of the recipient. He also suggested that acceptance of a particular gift constitutes an acknowledgment and acceptance of the
60 identity that the gift is seen to imply. Among children this may lead to lasting changes in self-perceptions, but presumably gifts have less influence on the self-concept of an adult.

Nevertheless, the importance of this symbolic
65 function of gift selection appears clear enough in a gift shop's recent advertisement, which asks, "Do you want your gifts to tell someone how creative you are, how thoughtful you are, or just how big your Christmas bonus was? Do you buy with a specific
70 price or a specific personality in mind?" While the answers to such basic questions about gift selection may be personally evident, the underlying behavioral questions have not been addressed by empirical research.

75 There can be little doubt that gift-giving is a pervasive experience in human life and consumer behavior. Despite the additional variables which gift-giving introduces to conceptions of consumer behavior (e.g., characteristics of the recipient, gifter-
80 receiver similarity, nature of the occasion), the present findings suggest that preference for cognitive balance is a concept which can go far toward explaining gift selection and evaluation.

CONTINUE

GIFT-GIVING AS COMMUNICATION

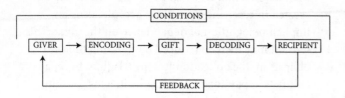

11

The author most likely uses the examples in lines 10–17 of the passage ("For instance . . . Christmas") to highlight the

A) recent increase in consumerism around Christmas time.

B) discrepancies in gift-giving between ancient and modern times.

C) apprehension between gift-givers and receivers.

D) pervasiveness of gift-giving on special occasions.

12

In line 20, the word "rich" most nearly means

A) opulent.

B) embellished.

C) fertile.

D) saccharine.

13

The passage indicates that the gift-giving described in lines 28–29 may be:

A) oppressive to gift recipients.

B) repeated between the same two people.

C) one-sided in most cases.

D) the result of deception.

14

Which choice provides the best evidence for the answer to the previous question?

A) Lines 38–41 ("These . . . give")

B) Lines 50–53 ("Adequate . . . reinitiated")

C) Lines 58–60 ("He also . . . imply")

D) Lines 70–74 ("While . . . research")

15

The author indicates that Marcell Mauss believes people's reasons for giving gifts may

A) be based somewhat on their own needs.

B) shift over the course of their lifetimes.

C) differ from culture to culture.

D) influence the timing of gift-giving.

16

Which choice provides the best evidence for the answer to the previous question?

A) Lines 21–23 ("Gift-giving . . . giving")

B) Lines 23–26 ("The preeminent . . . 1923")

C) Lines 34–38 ("The obligation . . . giving")

D) Lines 41–43 ("Receiving . . . act")

17

Schwartz, mentioned in paragraph 4 (lines 54–63), would likely describe the process of gift-exchanging as

A) stressful.

B) unnerving.

C) intentional.

D) symbolic.

CONTINUE

18

As it is used in line 65, "function" most nearly means

A) purpose.

B) tradition.

C) occasion.

D) occupation.

19

The author refers to a gift shop's recent advertisement (lines 65–66) in order to

A) question a former claim.

B) offer a motive.

C) introduce a counter explanation.

D) support an argument.

20

The graph and the passage offer evidence that the communication process of gift-giving predicts that a gift will demonstrate

A) the receiver's self-concept.

B) the amount the gift-giver spent.

C) encoded meaning.

D) the thoughtfulness of the gift-giver.

21

The author would likely explain the encoding phase represented in the figure in part as the gift-giver's attempt to convey information about

A) the occasion for gift-giving.

B) the giver's personal preferences.

C) the location where the gift was purchased.

D) the relationship between giver and receiver.

CONTINUE

Questions 22–31 are based on the following passage and supplementary material.

This passage is adapted from Nils Ekholm, "On the Variations of the Climate of the Geological and Historical Past and Their Causes." ©1901 by *Quarterly Journal of the Royal Meteorological Society*. Ekholm's studies are based on new mathematical calculations that show discrepancies among earlier scientists' findings in the study of historical changes in climate.

The atmosphere plays a very important part of a double character as to the temperature at the earth's surface. Firstly, the atmosphere may act like the glass of
Line a green-house, letting through the light rays of the sun
5 relatively easily, and absorbing a great part of the dark rays emitted from the ground, and it thereby may raise the mean temperature of the earth's surface. Secondly, the atmosphere acts as a heat store placed between the relatively warm ground and the cold space, and thereby
10 lessens in a high degree the annual, diurnal, and local variations of the temperature.

There are two qualities of the atmosphere that produce these effects. The one is that the temperature of the atmosphere generally decreases with the height
15 above the ground or the sea-level, owing partly to the dynamical heating of descending air currents and the dynamical cooling of ascending ones, as is explained in the mechanical theory of heat. The other is that the atmosphere, absorbing but little of the
20 insolation and most of the radiation from the ground, receives a considerable part of its heat store from the ground by means of radiation, contact, convection, and conduction, whereas the earth's surface is heated principally by direct radiation from the sun through
25 the transparent air.

It follows from this that the radiation from the earth into space does not go on directly from the ground, but on average from a layer of the atmosphere having a considerable height above sea-level. The
30 height of that layer depends on the thermal quality of the atmosphere, and will vary with that quality. The greater is the absorbing power of the air for heat rays emitted from the ground, the higher will that layer be. But the higher the layer, the lower is its temperature
35 relatively to that of the ground; and as the radiation from the layer into space is the less the lower its temperature is, it follows that the ground will be hotter the higher the radiating layer is.

Now if we are able to calculate or estimate how
40 much the mean temperature that layer is lower than the mean temperature of the ground, we may apply Table I for calculating the mean temperature of the ground, as soon as we know by direct measurements the quantity of solar heat absorbed by the ground.
45 Owing to the clouds and dust floating in the atmosphere, this heat is probably only about a third of that derived by using Langley's solar constant; and is thus about 360 calories per square centimeter during twenty-four hours. This gives, by means of Table I,
50 a temperature of –31°C to the radiating layer. But, according to Arrhenius's estimate, this is at a height of about 7600 meters; and assuming a corresponding decrease of 0.6°C per 100 meters, we find its temperature to be 46°C lower than that of the ground,
55 and thus the mean temperature of the ground equal to 15°C, as it is according to observations.

The table shows the loss of heat by radiation into space from a perfectly black body of the temperature $t°$ centigrade. In gram-calories per square centimeter per
60 24 hours at 7600 meters.

t	Loss of Heat	t	Loss of Heat	t	Loss of Heat
100	2023	20	770	–60	215
80	1624	0	581	–80	145
60	1285	–20	428	–100	94
40	1003	–40	308	–120	57

22

A student claims that over half of solar radiation influences the ground temperature on the earth's surface. Which of the following statements in the passage contradicts the student's claim?

A) Lines 3–7 ("Firstly . . . surface")

B) Lines 13–18 ("The one . . . heat")

C) Lines 45–49 ("Owing . . . hours")

D) Lines 49–50 ("This . . . layer")

CONTINUE ➤

23

In the first paragraph (lines 1–11), what does the author claim is the atmosphere's importance to the temperature of the earth's surface?

A) The trapping of all hot air and energy from the sun

B) Controlling the heat energy that is admitted and released

C) The enclosure of all the earth's heat-producing mechanisms

D) The free passage of heat energy to and from the surface

24

The author uses the word "green-house" in line 4 to indicate that

A) the heat on the ground and in the atmosphere of the earth is provided exclusively by solar radiation.

B) most of the heat in the atmosphere comes from radiation from the ground.

C) the agricultural and botanical sectors of the economy are those most affected by climate fluctuations.

D) solar heat enters the atmosphere relatively unobstructed but the same does not apply as it leaves.

25

Based on the passage, the author's statement "the earth's surface is heated principally by direct radiation from the sun through the transparent air" (lines 23–25) implies that

A) when the sun is obscured by clouds, the ground is heated principally by other sources of energy.

B) heat generated independently by the ground and by the sun is held in the atmosphere and released as cool air.

C) the heat from the sun that warms the ground must be partially absorbed by the earth's atmosphere.

D) the solar heat reflected back from the earth does not account for all the heat in the atmosphere.

26

The author's use of the words "if," "may," and "as soon as" in lines 39–43 functions mainly to

A) provide definitive evidence that the author's mathematical calculations predict the span of global warming with accuracy.

B) demonstrate that many of the author's conclusions rely on both observable and non-observable factors.

C) support the hypothesis that ground temperatures are warmer than higher temperatures.

D) warn against the indiscretion of earlier scientists who made incorrect claims with insufficient evidence.

27

The author's main purpose in noting the observations of ground temperature is to

A) indicate that the mathematical calculations given in this paragraph correspond to data recorded by others.

B) show the limitations of mathematical formulas in providing precise measurements of observable phenomena.

C) provide an example of one place in which the global temperature has risen because of human activity.

D) underline the importance of mathematical calculations in determining the influence of solar radiation.

28

Based on the table and passage, which choice gives the correct temperature on the ground when the loss of heat is approximately 300 gram-calories per square centimeter for 24 hours?

A) 40°C

B) 6°C

C) –6°C

D) –40°C

CONTINUE

29

Does the data in the table support the author's claim regarding the atmosphere as a heat store?

A) Yes, because at each given temperature, as the temperature decreases, the heat loss decreases as well but by larger and larger intervals.

B) Yes, because at each given temperature, as the temperature decreases, the heat loss decreases as well but by smaller and smaller intervals.

C) No, because at each given temperature, as the temperature decreases, the heat loss fluctuates according to an irregular pattern and series of intervals.

D) No, because at each given temperature, as the temperature decreases, the heat loss increases by larger and larger intervals.

30

According to the table, which of the following pairs of heat-loss values at different temperatures provide evidence in support of the answer to the previous question?

A) 2023 to 1624 and 2023 to 57

B) 1003 to 581 and 581 to 94

C) 1003 to 770 and 770 to 581

D) 308 to 94 and 581 to 57

31

Based on the passage and the table, does the temperature of the atmosphere of the earth stay the same or does it vary with distance from the earth, and which statement made by the authors is most consistent with this data?

A) The same; "Secondly . . . temperature" (lines 7–11)

B) The same; "It follows . . . sea-level" (lines 26–29)

C) It varies; "Now if . . . ground" (lines 39–44)

D) It varies; "But, according . . . observations" (lines 50–56)

CONTINUE

Questions 32–41 are based on the following passage.

This passage is adapted from Frederick Douglass's speech "On Women's Suffrage" delivered in 1888 to a gathering of women's suffrage activists.

Mrs. President, Ladies and Gentlemen:— I come to this platform with unusual diffidence. Although I have long been identified with the Woman's Suffrage
Line movement, and have often spoken in its favor, I am
5 somewhat at a loss to know what to say on this really great and uncommon occasion, where so much has been said.

When I look around on this assembly, and see the many able and eloquent women, full of the subject,
10 ready to speak, and who only need the opportunity to impress this audience with their views and thrill them with "thoughts that breathe and words that burn," I do not feel like taking up more than a very small space of your time and attention, and shall not.
15 I would not, even now, presume to speak, but for the circumstance of my early connection with the cause, and of having been called upon to do so by one whose voice in this Council we all gladly obey. Men have very little business here as speakers, anyhow;
20 and if they come here at all they should take back benches and wrap themselves in silence. For this is an International Council, not of men, but of women, and woman should have all the say in it. This is her day in court. I do not mean to exalt the intellect of woman
25 above man's; but I have heard many men speak on this subject, some of them the most eloquent to be found anywhere in the country; and I believe no man, however gifted with thought and speech, can voice the wrongs and present the demands of women with
30 the skill and effect, with the power and authority of woman herself. The man struck is the man to cry out. Woman knows and feels her wrongs as man cannot know and feel them, and she also knows as well as he can know, what measures are needed to redress them.
35 I grant all the claims at this point. She is her own best representative. We can neither speak for her, nor vote for her, nor act for her, nor be responsible for her; and the thing for men to do in the premises is just to get out of her way and give her the fullest opportunity
40 to exercise all the powers inherent in her individual personality, and allow her to do it as she herself shall elect to exercise them. Her right to be and to do is as full, complete and perfect as the right of any man on earth. I say of her, as I say of the colored people, "Give
45 her fair play, and hands off." There was a time when, perhaps, we men could help a little. It was when this woman suffrage cause was in its cradle, when it was not big enough to go alone, when it had to be taken in the arms of its mother from Seneca Falls, N.Y., to
50 Rochester, N.Y., for baptism. I then went along with it and offered my services to help it, for then it needed help; but now it can afford to dispense with me and all of my sex. Then its friends were few—now its friends are many. Then it was wrapped in obscurity—now it is
55 lifted in sight of the whole civilized world, and people of all lands and languages give it their hearty support. Truly the change is vast and wonderful.

There may be some well-meaning people in this audience who have never attended a woman suffrage
60 convention, never heard a woman suffrage speech, never read a woman suffrage newspaper, and they may be surprised that those who speak here do not argue the question. It may be kind to tell them that our cause has passed beyond the period of arguing. The demand
65 of the hour is not argument, but assertion, firm and inflexible assertion, assertion which has more than the force of an argument. If there is any argument to be made, it must be made by opponents, not by the friends of woman suffrage. Let those who want
70 argument examine the ground upon which they base their claim to the right to vote. They will find that there is not one reason, not one consideration, which they can urge in support of man's claim to vote, which does not equally support the right of woman to vote.

32

The main purpose of the passage is to

A) qualify the credentials of a speaker.

B) provide support for the suffrage movement.

C) argue for the equal rights of women.

D) compare the sufferings of women to those of African Americans.

CONTINUE ➡

33

The central claim of the passage is that

A) women should have the floor at this assembly.

B) men should act for women in this movement.

C) women and men have the same justification for voting.

D) the suffrage movement should be less obscure.

34

Douglass uses the word "cause" throughout the passage mainly to

A) clarify his early connection to the suffrage movement.

B) explain why the suffrage movement deserves support.

C) compare the suffrage movement to a baby in a cradle.

D) describe the suffrage movement.

35

According to the passage, Douglass is hesitant to speak at the gathering because

A) he had an early association with the suffrage movement.

B) he believes that women should be the featured speakers.

C) he does not consider himself an eloquent and forceful speaker.

D) it is improper to speak from the back benches.

36

Douglass indicates that men

A) should not be speakers in such a movement.

B) should not take too much time and attention.

C) should primarily listen at such a gathering.

D) should voice the wrongs of women publicly.

37

Which choice provides the best evidence for the answer to the previous question?

A) Lines 8–14 ("When I . . . not")

B) Lines 15–18 ("I would . . . obey")

C) Lines 18–21 ("Men have . . . silence")

D) Lines 27–31 ("and I . . . herself")

38

Douglass characterizes the "demands of women" in line 29 as related to injuries that

A) women can best describe and suggest solutions for.

B) men should speak about more eloquently.

C) the civilized world should support heartily.

D) men and women should both be responsible for.

39

Which choice provides the best evidence for the answer to the previous question?

A) Lines 25–27 ("but I . . . country")

B) Lines 32–34 ("Woman . . . them")

C) Lines 42–44 ("Her right . . . earth")

D) Lines 45–46 ("There . . . little")

CONTINUE

40

Which choice most closely captures the meaning of the figurative "cradle" referred to in line 47?

A) Nest

B) Rock

C) Hold

D) Beginnings

41

The surprise referred to in lines 58–74 mainly serves to emphasize how

A) some attendees may have expected different sorts of speeches.

B) male attendees may have expected more arguments than assertions.

C) audience members may not have expected speeches on women's suffrage.

D) speakers may have presented unexpected arguments for the right to vote.

CONTINUE

Questions 42–52 are based on the following passages.

Passage 1 is adapted from Michael B. McElroy and Xi Li, "Fracking's Future." ©2013 by *Harvard Monthly*. Passage 2 is adapted from Natural Resources Defense Council, "Unchecked Fracking Threatens Health, Water Supplies." ©2015.

Passage 1

Supplies of natural gas now economically recoverable from shale in the United States could accommodate the country's domestic demand for natural gas at current levels of consumption for more
5   than a hundred years: an economic and strategic boon, and, at least in the near term, an important stepping-stone toward lower-carbon, greener energy.

The first step in extracting gas from shale involves drilling vertically to reach the shale layer, typically a
10   kilometer or more below the surface. Drilling then continues horizontally, extending a kilometer or more from the vertical shaft, and the vertical and horizontal components of the well are lined with steel casing, cemented in place. The horizontal extension of the
15   casing is then perforated, using explosives; thereafter, water, carrying sand and proprietary chemicals, is injected into the well at high pressure. The water encounters the shale through the perforations, generating a series of small fractures in the rock (hence
20   the nickname, "fracking"); the sand in the water keeps the cracks open, while the chemicals enhance release of gas from the shale. The injected water flows back up to the surface when the pressure in the well is released following completion of the fracking procedure. Then
25   the well starts to produce natural gas.

As many as 25 fracture stages (per horizontal leg) may be involved in preparing a single site for production, each requiring injection of more than 400,000 gallons of water—a possible total of more than
30   10 million gallons before the well is fully operational. A portion of the injected water flows back to the surface, heavily contaminated with the fracking chemicals and others it has absorbed from the shale. Depending on the local geology, this "return water" may also include
35   radioactive elements.

Drillers developing a well must take exceptional care to minimize contact between the wellbore and the surrounding aquifer—often the source of nearby residents' fresh water. Serious problems have arisen
40   in the past from failures to isolate the drilling liquids,

including cases where well water used for drinking became so contaminated that human and animal health was threatened. It is essential that monitoring be in place to ensure the continuing integrity of the seal
45   isolating the well from the aquifer even *after* the well has been fully exploited and abandoned.

Passage 2

The oil and gas industry is rapidly expanding production across the nation, as new technology makes it easier to extract oil or gas from previously
50   inaccessible sites. Over the last decade, the industry has drilled hundreds of thousands of new wells all across the country. These wells are accompanied by massive new infrastructure to move, process, and deliver oil and gas, together bringing full-scale
55   industrialization to often previously rural landscapes.

The sector's growth is spurred by the use of hydraulic fracturing, or fracking, in which often-dangerous chemicals are mixed with large quantities of water (or other base fluid) and sand and injected
60   into wells at extremely high pressure. Unconventional development using advanced fracking methods poses threats to water, air, land, and the health of communities. Studies have shown dangerous levels of toxic air pollution near fracking sites; and oil and
65   gas extraction have caused smog in rural areas at levels worse than downtown Los Angeles. Oil and gas production have been linked to increased risk of cancer and birth defects in neighboring areas; as well as to a risk of increased seismic activity.
70   Constant massive truck traffic associated with large-scale development disrupts communities and creates significant hazards. The millions of gallons of water used in fracking operations not only strain water resources, but end up as vast amounts of contaminated
75   wastewater. Fracking has been reported as a suspect in polluted drinking water around the country. And methane—a potent climate change pollutant—leaks rampantly throughout the extraction, processing, and distribution of oil and gas.
80   Weak safeguards and inadequate oversight have allowed oil and gas producers to run roughshod over communities across the country with their extraction and production activities for too long, resulting in

CONTINUE →

contaminated water supplies, dangerous air pollution,
85 destroyed streams, and devastated landscapes. Our
state and federal leaders have failed to hold them to
account, leaving the American people unprotected.
Many companies don't play by the few rules that do
exist; and industry has used its political power at every
90 turn to gain exemptions from environmental laws
designed to protect our air and water.

42

The author of Passage 1 indicates that fracking could
have which positive effect?

A) It could support small, local economies that do
not have other sources of income.

B) It could alter the way scientists understand the
shale layer of the Earth.

C) It could provide resources that meet the needs of
contemporary consumers.

D) It could lower the price that large-scale industrial
firms pay for natural gas.

43

Which choice provides the best evidence for the
answer to the previous question?

A) Lines 1–5 ("Supplies . . . years")

B) Lines 17–22 ("The water . . . shale")

C) Lines 22–25 ("The injected . . . gas")

D) Lines 30–35 ("A portion . . . elements")

44

In lines 26–30, the author of Passage 1 mentions the
number of gallons of water primarily to

A) warn of the inevitable dangers of industrial
fracking in small communities.

B) show the variety of ways that natural gas can be
extracted from shale.

C) expand upon the idea that fracking uses only a few
basic elements.

D) establish the size and scope of a fracking
operation.

45

What function does the discussion of the aquifer in
lines 36–46 serve in Passage 1?

A) It outlines one significant risk involved in the
process described in earlier paragraphs.

B) It addresses and disputes the concerns of those
whose attitude toward fracking is cautious.

C) It extends a discussion of a significant term that
begins in the previous paragraph.

D) It presents an unexpected new finding that
undermines industry arguments for a certain
practice.

46

As used in line 44, "integrity" most nearly means

A) morality.

B) impermeability.

C) moisture.

D) confidence.

47

The central claim of Passage 2 is that fracking mines
useful resources but

A) the wells that have been built are not sufficiently
productive to justify all the cost.

B) some experts believe that natural gas can be
acquired just as easily from other sources.

C) it may lead some industry executives to believe
that they can mine resources from any place they
choose.

D) it is currently not sufficiently regulated in a way
that is safe for local populations.

CONTINUE

48

As used in line 80, "oversight" most nearly means

A) error.

B) planning.

C) regulation.

D) omission.

49

Which statement best describes the relationship between the passages?

A) Passage 2 undermines the optimistic confidence of the author of Passage 1.

B) Passage 2 expands upon some of the concerns expressed less explicitly in Passage 1.

C) Passage 2 argues for certain regulations of which the author of Passage 1 does not approve.

D) Passage 2 describes the process discussed in Passage 1 but does so with more detail and statistics.

50

The author of Passage 2 would most likely respond to the discussion of drillers in lines 36–46, Passage 1, by claiming that these drillers

A) cite their successes in having grown the mining industry throughout the country.

B) often come from small towns themselves and are not likely to abuse the land.

C) have already caused irreparable harm to the American landscape.

D) can be difficult to contact when their work is conducted so far underground.

51

Which choice provides the best evidence for the answer to the previous question?

A) Lines 47–52 ("The oil . . . country")

B) Lines 56–60 ("The sector's . . . pressure")

C) Lines 66–72 ("Oil and . . . hazards")

D) Lines 80–85 ("Weak . . . landscapes")

52

Which point about the potential effects of fracking is implicit in Passage 2 and explicit in Passage 1?

A) The pollution caused by fracking can affect both the water and the air.

B) The process of fracking requires the use of many billions of gallons of water.

C) The process can contaminate drinking water and thus harm both animals and humans.

D) The economic costs of preparing wells can often cost more than the profits gained from mining.

STOP
If you finish before time is called, you may check your work on this section only.
Do not turn to any other section in the test.

No Test Material On This Page

Writing and Language Test

35 MINUTES, 44 QUESTIONS

Turn to Section 2 of your answer sheet to answer the questions in this section.

DIRECTIONS

Each passage below is accompanied by a number of questions. For some questions, you will consider how the passage might be revised to improve the expression of ideas. For other questions, you will consider how the passage might be edited to correct errors in sentence structure, usage, or punctuation. A passage or a question may be accompanied by one or more graphics (such as a table or graph) that you will consider as you make revising and editing decisions.

Some questions will direct you to an underlined portion of a passage. Other questions will direct you to a location in a passage or ask you to think about the passage as a whole.

After reading each passage, choose the answer to each question that most effectively improves the quality of writing in the passage or that makes the passage conform to the conventions of standard written English. Many questions include a "NO CHANGE" option. Choose that option if you think the best choice is to leave the relevant portion of the passage as it is.

Questions 1–11 are based on the following passage.

A Horse of a Different Doctor

Although medical science has made huge bounds in understanding many parts of the body, the brain remains a kind of mystery. A heart attack, for instance, is much easier to identify and prevent than a brain stroke. And mental illness aside, **1** the variety of neurological disorders can make specific brain diagnoses complicated and often unreliable. As a result, the therapeutic resources available to neurologists and those with neurological disorders must necessarily be as vast and diverse as the patient base itself. Disciplines like art therapy, aromatherapy, and horticultural therapy have begun to gain some traction in the popular imagination. Some fields, however, are still awaiting **2** the okay from the people, although their achievements and successes are just as significant. One such field is that of hippotherapy.

1
A) NO CHANGE
B) the variety of different kinds of neurological disorders
C) the differing variety of disorders in neurology
D) disorders that show a variety of differences

2
A) NO CHANGE
B) broader public acceptance
C) something elusive from the public
D) a public to give the thumbs up

CONTINUE

Hippotherapy positions itself at the intersection of physical, occupational, and speech therapy. In this discipline, the characteristic movements of a horse (*hippo-* in Greek) **3** is used to build a foundation for improvements in human neurological functions and sensory processing. Its main difference from therapeutic horseback riding is that hippotherapy uses the movement of the horse as a way to treat a specific ailment. **4** Thus, it is more concerned with learning a skill set and establishing a bond between rider and horse.

3

A) NO CHANGE

B) has been used

C) are used

D) used

4

At this point, the writer is considering adding the following sentence.

> Therapeutic horseback riding teaches riding skills and is more concerned with emotional and behavioral disabilities.

Should the writer make this addition here?

A) Yes, because it makes the argument that hippotherapy is the more effective of the two disciplines.

B) Yes, because it further clarifies the difference between the two disciplines discussed in this paragraph.

C) No, because it undermines the point the author is trying to make about the validity of hippotherapy.

D) No, because a discussion of therapeutic horseback riding has no place in this particular paragraph.

CONTINUE

[1] Many fields use the basic tenets of hippotherapy, but they each provide a unique spin on the practice. [2] Physical therapists may incorporate hippotherapy to manage a variety of disabilities and, hopefully, cure diseases. [3] Occupational therapists use many of the same features of the horse's movement, but they [5] are similarly plagued by the lack of laboratory support. [4] The research on the effectiveness of hippotherapy is still in the early stages of development, but therapists in a variety of fields, even including speech and language pathology, regularly achieve success with this technique and [6] eagerly to recommended it to their patients. [5] As the name suggests, these therapists are concerned mainly with the movement of the horse as it relates to physical aspects such as balance, posture, and strengthening the core. [7]

The American Hippotherapy Association can provide certification for those wishing to work in the discipline. Physical therapists, occupational therapists, and speech-language pathologists must have practiced for at least three years and had 100 hours of hippotherapy practice before they can sit for the Hippotherapy Clinical Specialty Certification Exam, and the certification lasts for five years. Because the discipline is relatively [8] new, certified, hippotherapists have stringent requirements for staying current on the research within the field.

5

Which choice provides a supporting example that reinforces the main point of the sentence?

A) NO CHANGE

B) use the therapy to develop the cognitive and fine motor skills.

C) work on different maladies and different parts of the body.

D) have a whole different set of requirements and backgrounds.

6

A) NO CHANGE

B) eager recommending of

C) eagerly recommending

D) eagerly recommend

7

To make this paragraph most logical, sentence 5 should be placed

A) where it is now.

B) before sentence 1.

C) before sentence 3.

D) before sentence 4.

8

A) NO CHANGE

B) new, certified

C) new, and certified

D) new; certified

CONTINUE

Just as medical science is constantly evolving, [9] so are its alternatives. Hippotherapy may seem a bit out of the ordinary, but if it provides effective relief or treatment for people in pain, the skeptics [10] between doctors and researchers will not hesitate to embrace it. [11] Becoming a hippotherapist is pretty hard, as evidenced by all those hours one has to spend keeping up with the literature.

9

A) NO CHANGE
B) so too are its alternatives.
C) its alternatives also are.
D) its alternatives are, too.

10

A) NO CHANGE
B) above
C) within
D) among

11

The writer wants a concluding sentence that restates the main argument of the passage. Which choice best accomplishes that goal?

A) NO CHANGE
B) Hippotherapy has positioned itself at the crossroads of many disciplines, and it may just be the practice to provide relief in ways the other therapies have not done yet.
C) Many people used bloodletting and radiation regularly before the medical establishment showed how unsafe these practices were.
D) It makes you wonder whether the medical profession is ready for such a crazy discovery.

CONTINUE

Questions 12–22 are based on the following passage and supplementary material.

The Call of the Wilderness

The way science textbooks teach about different ecosystems [12] elicit responses primarily from our visual and tactile senses. We have all seen pictures of the silent sands of the desert and can almost feel the heat radiating from the sands. We all know the ballet of fish and marine life coursing through the vast ocean. Some recent studies, however, have expanded our ideas about these ecosystems by incorporating another one of our senses: sound.

[13] It was Marco Polo who crossed the desert on his way to China, he described the sound he heard as "a variety of musical instruments." Researchers now understand that the curious sound that Polo heard, that odd confluence of pipe organ and [14] cello, probably resulted from the wind blowing across the sand dunes. In a study conducted in the deserts of California, scientists found that the "singing" dunes had dry, tightly packed layers of sand, with dry sand on top of layers of damp sand. This variation creates an effect similar to that of a musical [15] instrument, a tonal quality coming from the trapping and release of certain frequencies.

---

[12]

A) NO CHANGE
B) elicits responses
C) illicit responses
D) illicits responses

[13]

A) NO CHANGE
B) Marco Polo crossed the desert
C) They called him Marco Polo, he who crossed the desert
D) As Marco Polo crossed the desert

[14]

A) NO CHANGE
B) cello;
C) cello—
D) cello: it has

[15]

A) NO CHANGE
B) instrument; a tonal quality coming
C) instrument, a tonal quality that is said to be coming
D) instrument, this quality comes

CONTINUE

16 From among the world's countless ecosystems and throughout that world, the ocean, too, has recently been given a kind of "voice." Although Jacques Cousteau referred to this body of water as *le monde du silence*—"the silent world"—recent research has shown the ocean to be anything but silent. University of Washington biologist Kate Stafford has, for the past five years, recorded sounds in the deep waters of the Bering Strait. **17** For Stafford, sound provides advantage that sight cannot: one can continue to record sound at night or underneath ice cover, and the challenges of deep-sea sound-recording are not nearly as problematic as those of deep-sea diving.

16

Which choice most smoothly and effectively introduces the writer's discussion of the sounds of the ocean in this paragraph?

A) NO CHANGE

B) Ecosystems are filled with sound, and one such sound in one such ecosystem is the "voice" of the ocean.

C) Another place that has recently been given a kind of "voice" is the ocean.

D) DELETE the underlined sentence.

17

At this point, the writer is considering adding the following sentence.

> If you go far enough from the coast, the only sounds you will hear are those of distant ships passing in the night.

Should the writer make this addition here?

A) Yes, because it creates a poetic image that complements the main idea of the paragraph.

B) Yes, because it supports the main idea of the passage as a whole.

C) No, because it is not consistent with the main point of the paragraph.

D) No, because it would be more appropriately placed at the beginning of the paragraph.

CONTINUE

According to Stafford's research, one of the most interesting aspects of the sound of the ocean is **18** its unwillingness to **19** not act so weird. Stafford's team found inconsistencies among the sounds at any particular time of year. This may help to explain the **20** lack of any consistency in whale migrations during 2012–2013 as compared to previous seasons. Data from the 2012–2013 season shows that on many days the number of whales migrating was **21** more than twice the ten-year average. This gives some hint as to how marine animals are currently adapting to climate change, and how they may adapt in the future. It seems that those with the most flexibility will be those who are least affected.

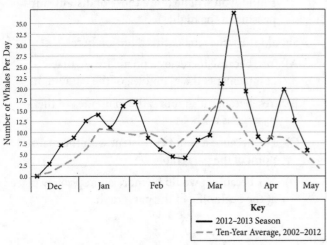

2012–2013 Season, Compared to the Average of the Previous Ten Seasons

Key
—— 2012–2013 Season
– – – Ten-Year Average, 2002–2012

18

A) NO CHANGE
B) it's
C) their
D) they're

19

A) NO CHANGE
B) follow any discernible patterns.
C) chill out and be normal for a second.
D) play nice with others.

20

Which choice offers the most accurate interpretation of the data in the chart?

A) NO CHANGE
B) definable inverse relationship
C) absolute confluence
D) notable increases

21

Which choice offers an accurate interpretation of the data in the chart?

A) NO CHANGE
B) more than ten times the ten-year average.
C) less than half of the ten-year average.
D) more than twice the number of shorebirds migrating.

CONTINUE

The work that Stafford and others are doing adds another dimension to how we understand different ecosystems. [22] Sound may clarify the processes of these ecosystems in ways that were not available to researchers before.

The writer wants a conclusion that points toward the role that sound might play in future research into different ecosystems. Which choice results in the passage having the most appropriate concluding sentence?

A) NO CHANGE

B) This is not, of course, to say that no research has ever been done on sound before; that would be an overstatement.

C) Researchers may have missed this sound component, but you have to hand it to them for covering the other parts as thoroughly as they have.

D) The vividness of soundscapes is nowhere more evident than in the experiences of the blind, who can use sound in much the way that sighted people use sight.

CONTINUE

Questions 23–33 are based on the following passage.

Roosevelt's 100 Days

In the 1932 presidential election, up-and-comer Franklin D. Roosevelt [23] won— in a landslide over the incumbent Herbert Hoover, who had done little to avert the crisis that would become known as the Great Depression. [24] And Hoover took office in 1929, the unemployment rate was a mere 3.2%. By 1932, that rate had skyrocketed to 25%.

[25] Roosevelt took office with a clear mandate for action. Even so, no one was quite ready for the legislative whirlwind that would follow. This period became known as Roosevelt's "100 Days." Roosevelt's first action came on March 5, 1933, when an executive order shut down all the nation's banks. At that time, he sent government workers to inspect each bank, [26] although determining which banks would be safe and sustainable to reopen. Four days later, the banks reopened and started business anew.

23

A) NO CHANGE
B) won;
C) won,
D) won

24

A) NO CHANGE
B) Because
C) When
D) DELETE the underlined portion and begin the sentence with a capital letter.

25

Which choice most effectively sets up the paragraph?
A) NO CHANGE
B) Politics could move a bit more quickly in those days.
C) That unemployment rate is remarkably low.
D) Hoover had given up all hope of ending the Depression.

26

A) NO CHANGE
B) for
C) thereby
D) whereupon

CONTINUE

Roosevelt's main goal was to lift the country from depression and to get the **27** economy operating again. In the 100 days, Roosevelt established programs to aid the poor, such as the $500 million Federal Emergency Relief Association. The Civilian Conservation Corps was established to give unemployed men six-month job assignments on environmental projects, such as national parks. In agricultural regions, Roosevelt sought to control supply as a way to level **28** with demand, and certain projects were geared toward electrifying until-then remote regions. The Tennessee Valley Authority (TVA) brought dams to the non-coastal southern states, **29** including Tennessee itself, of course, but also the northern parts of Alabama and Mississippi.

27

Which choice provides the most specific information on the areas that Roosevelt hoped to stimulate?

A) NO CHANGE

B) industrial and agricultural sectors

C) whole thing

D) money flowing and the economy

28

A) NO CHANGE

B) on

C) off

D) to

29

Which choice gives an additional supporting detail that emphasizes the importance of the TVA in Roosevelt's larger economic project?

A) NO CHANGE

B) taking account of the fact that farming is difficult without a reliable large body of water.

C) establishing not only more reliable sources of water and work but electricity for millions of Americans.

D) one of many impressive public-works projects completed throughout Roosevelt's tenure.

CONTINUE ➡

Many of the programs, including the Tennessee Valley Authority, continue to exist to this day. Roosevelt's 100 Days were unique in that they not only jumpstarted the American economy at a time when a stimulus was most needed but also laid the groundwork for programs that could persist into the [30] future, past their own moment. Indeed, Roosevelt's "New Deal" remains new even though, at this point, [31] it's more than eighty years old.

Still, Roosevelt's 100 Days remain the subject of controversy. In Roosevelt's day, there was widespread criticism from those who thought government should play a smaller rather than a larger role in [32] people's day-to-day lives. For many others, Roosevelt's government interventions are a model for how governments should aid citizens in times of need. [33] Clearly, Roosevelt's unadulterated successes would seem odd in an era of political wrangling characterized by gridlock rather than swift action.

[30]

A) NO CHANGE
B) future.
C) future, which is to say after the present.
D) future, many years beyond when they were created.

[31]

A) NO CHANGE
B) its
C) they're
D) there

[32]

A) NO CHANGE
B) peoples'
C) peoples
D) peoples's

[33]

The writer wants to conclude the paragraph effectively without dismissing the debate described in this paragraph. Which choice best accomplishes this goal?

A) NO CHANGE
B) Unfortunately, even Roosevelt's obvious failures can
C) In either case, Roosevelt's achievements in the first 100 Days of his presidency
D) Both sides are obviously unfounded, but everyone can agree that Roosevelt's 100 Days

CONTINUE

Questions 34–44 are based on the following passage.

Setsuko Hara: In and Out of the Tokyo Spotlight

One of the [34] hammiest board-treaders in the history of Japanese cinema was also one of the most mysterious. Setsuko Hara died in September 2015 at the age of 95, and while she is remembered as perhaps the most formidable actress in Japan's long cinematic tradition, no one had seen her in anything since the 1960s. The actress went into seclusion after the death of her longtime collaborator, the director Yasujiro Ozu.

Hara's first acting role came when she was only 15. The Japanese film industry had divided loyalties at the time, [35] despite its obvious debt to American cinema amid the increasing international tensions with the United States and others that would lead to World War II. Hara's first film, a German-Japanese production called *The Daughter of the Samurai* (1937), emerged among these tensions, [36] using the conventions of the American melodrama to promote an early version of what would become Axis propaganda. After her success in this film, Hara became one of the faces of the Japanese propaganda effort during the Second World War.

34
A) NO CHANGE
B) most exquisite thespians
C) most emotive of histrionists
D) greatest actresses

35
A) NO CHANGE
B) as evidenced by
C) contrasting with
D) enabled by

36
The writer is considering deleting the underlined portion (ending the sentence with a period). Should the writer make this deletion?

A) Yes, because the information is provided in the previous sentence.
B) Yes, because the underlined portion undermines the paragraph's description of the Axis propaganda effort.
C) No, because the underlined portion gives a specific example of how the Axis powers conducted their propaganda campaign.
D) No, because the underlined portion provides information that clarifies an idea central to this paragraph.

CONTINUE

After Japan's defeat in the war, however, Hara's career changed significantly. Directors and audiences discovered her incredible talent acting in quieter dramas. The masterpieces in this mode were Ozu's *Late Spring* (1949) and *Tokyo Story* (1953), in which Hara plays a woman who is torn between the demands of various family members, who in turn **37** represented different generational expectations. Hara could reveal incredible emotion through subtle, almost imperceptible facial expressions and voice modulations. **38** Moreover, her compelling and unique beauty kept screen audiences eagerly engaged.

The subtle conflicts in *Late Spring* capture Hara's particular **39** style of acting in films. Even in the 1940s, Hollywood films were characterized by grand conflicts and even grander emotions. The films of Ozu's late period, especially his collaborations with Hara, however, worked with a much smaller canvas, usually with very few sets, limiting the scenes to a character's **40** office kitchen, living room, or garden. In *Late Spring*, Hara's character

37

A) NO CHANGE
B) would represent
C) had represented
D) represent

38

A) NO CHANGE
B) In sum,
C) Nevertheless,
D) Meanwhile,

39

A) NO CHANGE
B) acting style.
C) acting methods that were unique to her.
D) acting style in film and presumably in the theater.

40

A) NO CHANGE
B) office, kitchen, living,
C) office, kitchen, living
D) office, kitchen living,

CONTINUE ▶

Noriko is twenty-seven years old and has not married. Against the **41** council of her friends and family, she has instead chosen to care for her aging widowed father. The conflict and plot are that simple, **42** and Ozu's cinematography and Hara's expressive face show that sometimes the simplest and smallest domestic conflicts can have profound implications.

[1] Hara never formally announced her retirement, though she made her last film in 1963. [2] Rumors have always circulated about Hara's mysterious disappearance from the screen, and viewers' many theories show **43** their grief at having lost such a bright star. [3] Some believe that she had been going blind and did not want to do so in the public eye. [4] In either case, Hara left an indelible mark on the shape of world cinema. [5] Especially in a moment when all cinematic achievement seems to point toward bigger and louder, Setsuko Hara provides the important reminder that smaller and quieter can be just as powerful. **44**

41

A) NO CHANGE
B) council from
C) counsel with
D) counsel of

42

A) NO CHANGE
B) for
C) so
D) yet

43

A) NO CHANGE
B) one's
C) his
D) your

44

The writer plans to add the following sentence to this paragraph.

> Others believe that her grief over Ozu's death in 1963 kept her from returning to the cinema.

To make this paragraph most logical, the sentence should be placed

A) after sentence 2.
B) after sentence 3.
C) after sentence 4.
D) after sentence 5.

STOP
**If you finish before time is called, you may check your work on this section only.
Do not turn to any other section in the test.**

Math Test – No Calculator

25 MINUTES, 20 QUESTIONS

Turn to Section 3 of your answer sheet to answer the questions in this section.

DIRECTIONS

For questions 1–15, solve each problem, choose the best answer from the choices provided, and fill in the corresponding circle on your answer sheet. **For questions 16–20,** solve the problem and enter your answer in the grid on the answer sheet. Please refer to the directions before question 16 on how to enter your answers in the grid. You may use any available space in your test booklet for scratch work.

NOTES

1. The use of a calculator **is not permitted**.
2. All variables and expressions used represent real numbers unless otherwise indicated.
3. Figures provided in this test are drawn to scale unless otherwise indicated.
4. All figures lie in a plane unless otherwise indicated.
5. Unless otherwise indicated, the domain of a given function f is the set of all real numbers x for which $f(x)$ is a real number.

REFERENCE

$A = \pi r^2$
$C = 2\pi r$

$A = \ell w$

$A = \frac{1}{2} bh$

$c^2 = a^2 + b^2$

Special Right Triangles

$V = \ell wh$

$V = \pi r^2 h$

$V = \frac{4}{3}\pi r^3$

$V = \frac{1}{3}\pi r^2 h$

$V = \frac{1}{3}\ell wh$

The number of degrees of arc in a circle is 360.
The number of radians of arc in a circle is 2π.
The sum of the measures in degrees of the angles of a triangle is 180.

CONTINUE

1

When the equation $-5y - 2x = 10$ is graphed in the xy-plane, which of the following is true?

A) Both the slope and the y-intercept of the line are negative.

B) Both the slope and the y-intercept of the line are positive.

C) The slope of the line is negative, and the y-intercept is positive.

D) The slope of the line is positive, and the y-intercept is negative.

2

$$x + 3y = 9$$
$$3x - y = 17$$

What is the value of $x - y$ for the system of equations above?

A) 5

B) 6

C) 10

D) 20

3

$$6(y^3 + y^2) - 2(y^3 + y^2)$$

Which of the following is equivalent to the expression above?

A) $4y^3$

B) $4y^5$

C) $4y^3 - 4y^2$

D) $4y^3 + 4y^2$

4

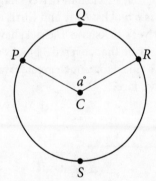

In the circle above with center C, $a = 120$. If the length of arc $\overparen{PSR}$ is 8π, what is the length of $\overparen{PQR}$?

A) 12π

B) 6π

C) 4π

D) 2π

CONTINUE

5

What is the value of a if $300 = \dfrac{12}{a}$?

A)   0.04

B)   25

C)   60

D) 3,600

6

The equation $F = 3b + 6$ gives the cost of the fare F, in dollars, that a rickshaw driver charges for a ride that covers b blocks. Amy and Chris each took a ride in this driver's rickshaw. The rickshaw driver took Chris on a ride that covered 3 blocks more than did Amy's ride. How much greater was Chris's fare than Amy's fare?

A) $15

B) $9

C) $6

D) $3

7

A glass marble is at the top of a flat ramp at a distance of 48 inches from the ground. If the marble rolls down the ramp such that its distance from the ground decreases at a constant rate of 7 inches per second, which of the following equations gives the distance d, in inches, between the glass marble and the ground t seconds after the marble begins rolling down the ramp?

A) $d = \dfrac{155}{48} - 7t$

B) $d = 48 - 7t$

C) $d = 48t - \dfrac{155}{7}$

D) $d = 48t - 7$

8

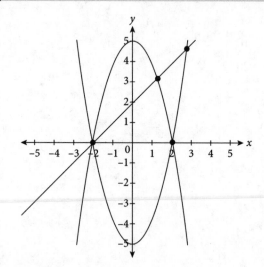

The system of equations graphed in the xy-plane above has exactly n solutions. What is the value of n ?

A) 1

B) 2

C) 3

D) 4

CONTINUE

9

$$9(x + 2) - 3(x + 3) = 3(cx + 5)$$

There is no value of x that satisfies the equation above, in which c is a constant. What is the value of constant c?

A) 2

B) 3

C) 4

D) 6

10

For $x > 1$, which of the following is equivalent to the expression $\dfrac{1}{3x - 2} + 4$?

A) $\dfrac{3x + 2}{3x - 2}$

B) $\dfrac{3x + 4}{3x - 2}$

C) $\dfrac{12x - 7}{3x - 2}$

D) $\dfrac{12x - 8}{3x - 2}$

11

$$4y^3 - 10y^2 - 36y + 48 = (2y + c)(ky^2 + 3y - 6)$$

In the equation above, c and k are constants. If the equation is true for all values of y, what is the value of ck?

A) −2

B) −16

C) −18

D) −24

12

Which of the following is the set of all solutions to the equation $\dfrac{2x + 4}{2} = \dfrac{15}{x}$?

A) {3}

B) {−5, 5}

C) {−5, 3}

D) {0, 3}

CONTINUE

13

$$6y + x \geq -6$$

$$y \leq 3x - 1$$

The solution set of the system of inequalities above is represented by the shaded region of which of the following graphs?

A)

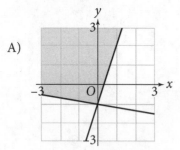

B)

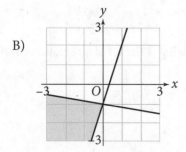

C)

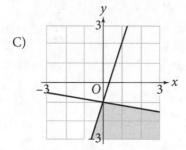

D)

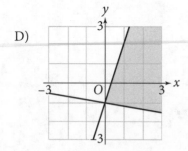

14

$$x = \sqrt{30 - x}$$

Which of the following includes all solutions to the equation above?

A) There are no values of x that satisfy the given equation.

B) −6 and 5

C) −6

D) 5

15

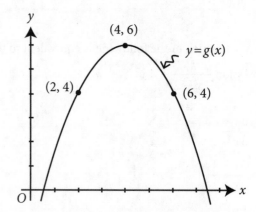

Which of the following equations defines function g graphed in the xy-plane above?

A) $g(x) = -\dfrac{1}{2}(x - 4)^2 - 6$

B) $g(x) = -\dfrac{1}{2}(x - 4)^2 + 6$

C) $g(x) = -\dfrac{1}{3}(x + 4)^2 + 6$

D) $g(x) = -(x + 4)^2 + 6$

CONTINUE

DIRECTIONS

For questions 16–20, solve the problem and enter your answer in the grid, as described below, on the answer sheet.

1. Although not required, it is suggested that you write your answer in the boxes at the top of the columns to help you fill in the circles accurately. You will receive credit only if the circles are filled in correctly.

2. Mark no more than one circle in any column.

3. No question has a negative answer.

4. Some problems may have more than one correct answer. In such cases, grid only one answer.

5. **Mixed numbers** such as $3\frac{1}{2}$ must be gridded as 3.5 or 7/2. (If 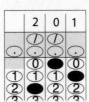 is entered into the grid, it will be interpreted as $\frac{31}{2}$, not as $3\frac{1}{2}$.)

6. **Decimal Answers:** If you obtain a decimal answer with more digits than the grid can accommodate, it may be either rounded or truncated, but it must fill the entire grid.

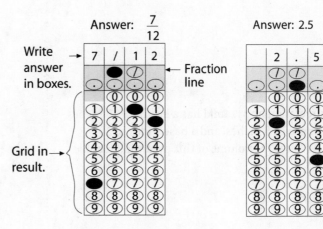

Answer: $\frac{7}{12}$ — Write answer in boxes. Fraction line. Grid in result.

Answer: 2.5 — Decimal point

Acceptable ways to grid $\frac{2}{3}$ are:

Answer: 201 – either position is correct

NOTE: You may start your answers in any column, space permitting. Columns you don't need to use should be left blank.

16

If a satisfies the equation $2a - 6 = 2$, what is the value of $4a - 12$?

17

A right rectangular pyramid has a height of 15 inches, a base length of 5 inches, and a base width of 20 inches. What is the volume of this pyramid, in cubic inches?

18

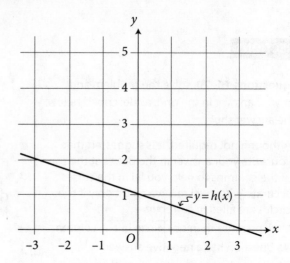

Function h is the linear function graphed in the xy-plane above. When linear function k (not shown) is graphed in the xy-plane, it contains the point $(-1, 2)$. If functions h and k are perpendicular, what is the value of $k(0)$?

CONTINUE

19

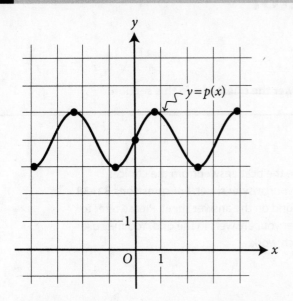

The complete graph of the function p in the xy-plane is shown in the figure above. Function r, which is defined by $r(x) = p(x) - 2$, is not shown. What is the minimum value of the function r?

20

In triangle ABC with right angle B, $\tan C = \dfrac{5}{12}$. What is the value of $\cos A$?

STOP
If you finish before time is called, you may check your work on this section only.
Do not turn to any other section in the test.

Math Test – Calculator

55 MINUTES, 38 QUESTIONS

Turn to Section 4 of your answer sheet to answer the questions in this section.

DIRECTIONS

For questions 1–30, solve each problem, choose the best answer from the choices provided, and fill in the corresponding circle on your answer sheet. **For questions 31–38**, solve the problem and enter your answer in the grid on the answer sheet. Please refer to the directions before question 31 on how to enter your answers in the grid. You may use any available space in your test booklet for scratch work.

NOTES

1. The use of a calculator **is permitted**.
2. All variables and expressions used represent real numbers unless otherwise indicated.
3. Figures provided in this test are drawn to scale unless otherwise indicated.
4. All figures lie in a plane unless otherwise indicated.
5. Unless otherwise indicated, the domain of a given function f is the set of all real numbers x for which $f(x)$ is a real number.

REFERENCE

$A = \pi r^2$
$C = 2\pi r$

$A = \ell w$

$A = \frac{1}{2}bh$

$c^2 = a^2 + b^2$

$x\sqrt{3}$ — Special Right Triangles

$V = \ell w h$

$V = \pi r^2 h$

$V = \frac{4}{3}\pi r^3$

$V = \frac{1}{3}\pi r^2 h$

$V = \frac{1}{3}\ell w h$

The number of degrees of arc in a circle is 360.
The number of radians of arc in a circle is 2π.
The sum of the measures in degrees of the angles of a triangle is 180.

CONTINUE

1

David has a mobile data plan for which the monthly fee is $20.00 and the data usage fee is $2.50 per gigabyte. Which of the following functions expresses David's cost, in dollars, for a month in which he uses g gigabytes of data?

A) $f(g) = 22.50g$

B) $f(g) = 20g + 2.50$

C) $f(g) = 20 + 250g$

D) $f(g) = 20 + 2.50g$

2

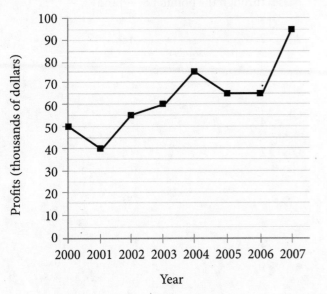

Annual Profits

The line graph above shows the annual profit of a particular clothing store from 2000 to 2007. According to the graph, what was the greatest change (in absolute value) in the annual profit between two consecutive years?

A) $25,000

B) $30,000

C) $35,000

D) $40,000

3

In order to qualify for a fitness competition, a person must be able to complete 30 pull-ups in one minute. Jim can currently do 14 pull-ups in one minute and believes that he can increase that amount by 7 pull-ups each year. Which of the following represents the number of pull-ups that Jim believes he will be able to complete in one minute y years from now?

A) $7y + 14$

B) $7y + 30$

C) $14y + 7$

D) $14 - 7y$

4

$$v = 17 + 2.5t$$

A constantly accelerating particle is moving in a straight line. After t seconds, the particle is moving at a velocity of v, in meters per second, as shown in the equation above. What is t when v is 67 ?

A) 184.5

B) 67

C) 33.6

D) 20

CONTINUE

5

When function h is graphed in the xy-plane, it has x-intercepts at –4, 2, and 4. Which of the following could define h ?

A) $h(x) = (x - 4)(x - 2)(x + 4)$

B) $h(x) = (x - 4)(x + 2)(x + 4)$

C) $h(x) = (x - 4)^2(x + 2)$

D) $h(x) = (x + 2)(x + 4)^2$

6

When three times a number n is added to 9, the result is 3. What is the result when 4 times n is added to 14 ?

A) –2

B) 3

C) 6

D) 22

7

A coffee shop is filling coffee cups from an industrial urn that contains 64 gallons of coffee. At most, how many 16-ounce cups of coffee can be filled from the urn? (1 gallon = 128 ounces)

A)   4

B)   512

C) 1,024

D) 2,048

8

What is the slope of the line in the xy-plane that passes through the points $\left(5, \dfrac{8}{3} \right)$ and $\left(1, -\dfrac{1}{3} \right)$?

A)   –2

B) $-\dfrac{4}{3}$

C) $\dfrac{3}{4}$

D)   2

CONTINUE

9

Number of Fish in Each of 18 Tanks

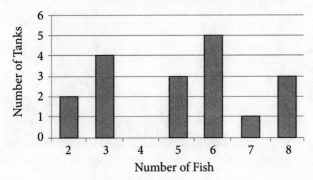

Based on the bar graph above, which of the following is closest to the average (arithmetic mean) number of fish per tank?

A) 5

B) 6

C) 7

D) 8

10

A telephone survey was conducted in order to determine if people in City C are more likely to work 9-to-5 office jobs than other jobs. The research team called 5,000 random people between 12 P.M. and 4 P.M. on a Thursday. Of the 5,000 people called, 3,000 did not answer, and 250 refused to participate. Which of the following was the biggest flaw in the design of the survey?

A) The time the survey was taken

B) Population size

C) Sample size

D) The fact that the survey was done by telephone

11

If the function p has exactly four distinct roots, which of the following could represent the complete graph of $y = p(x)$ in the xy-plane?

A)
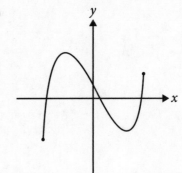

B)
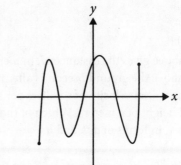

C)
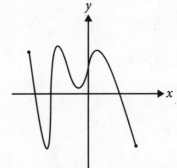

D)
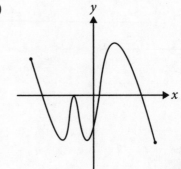

CONTINUE

12

One morning in a particular restaurant, 85 percent of the customers ordered the brunch special. Which of the following could be the total number of customers in the restaurant that morning?

A) 40

B) 42

C) 44

D) 48

13

$$d = -8t^2 + vt + h$$

The equation above gives the distance, d, in meters, a projectile is above the ground t seconds after it is released with an initial velocity of v meters per second from an initial height of h meters. Which of the following gives v, in terms of d, t, and h ?

A) $v = \dfrac{d - h}{t} + 8t$

B) $v = \dfrac{d + h}{t} - 8t$

C) $v = \dfrac{d - h + 8}{t}$

D) $v = d + h - 8t$

14

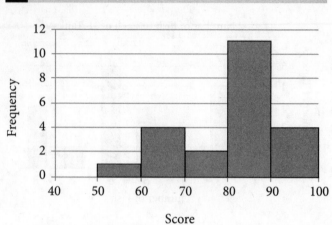

The histogram above shows the distribution of the scores of 22 students on a recent biology test. Which of the following could be the median score of the 22 students represented in the histogram?

A) 68

B) 71

C) 77

D) 84

CONTINUE

Questions 15–17 refer to the following information.

A survey of 130 randomly selected workers in a particular metropolitan area was conducted to gather information about average daily commute times. The data is shown in the table below.

	Commutes by public transit	Does not commute by public transit	Total
Less than 1 hour	22	46	68
At least 1 hour	29	33	62
Total	51	79	130

16

In 2014, the population of the metropolitan area from the survey was about 13 million. If the survey results were used to estimate information about commute times throughout the metropolitan area, which of the following is the best estimate for the number of individuals who used public transit and had an average daily commute of at least one hour?

A) 290,000

B) 2,200,000

C) 2,900,000

D) 6,200,000

15

Which of the following is closest to the percent of those surveyed who commute using public transit?

A) 65%

B) 46%

C) 39%

D) 32%

17

Based on the data, how many times more likely is it for a person with a commute of less than 1 hour NOT to commute by public transit than it is for a person with a commute of at least one hour NOT to commute by public transit? (Round the answer to the nearest hundredth.)

A) 1.39 times as likely

B) 1.27 times as likely

C) 0.78 times as likely

D) 0.72 times as likely

CONTINUE

18

In order to determine the effect that caffeinated beverage C would have on sleep, researchers conducted a study. From a large population of people without sleep disorders, 500 subjects were randomly selected. Half the subjects were randomly selected to consume beverage C and the rest did not consume beverage C. The results of the study showed that the subjects who consumed beverage C slept less than those who did not consume beverage C. Based on the design and results of the study, which of the following statements is the best conclusion?

A) Beverage C will cause more loss in sleep than all other caffeinated beverages.

B) Beverage C will cause a substantial loss in sleep.

C) Beverage C is likely to reduce the amount of sleep of people without sleep disorders.

D) Beverage C will reduce sleep of anyone who consumes it.

19

The sum of four numbers is 1,764. One of the numbers, n, is 40% more than the sum of the other three numbers. What is the value of n ?

A)   287

B)   735

C) 1,029

D) 1,260

20

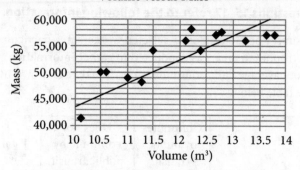

Volume versus Mass

Selin weighs 14 different objects of similar density. The scatterplot shown above shows the volume of each object and the corresponding weight of each object. The line of best fit for the data is shown above. For the object that had a volume of 11.5 m³, the actual mass was about how many kilograms more than the mass predicted by the line of best fit?

A) 1,000

B) 2,000

C) 3,000

D) 4,000

CONTINUE

21

Jessica owns a store that sells only laptops and tablets. Last week, her store sold 90 laptops and 210 tablets. This week, the sales, in number of units, of laptops increased by 50 percent, and the sales, in number of units, of tablets increased by 30 percent. By what percentage did total sales, in units, in Jessica's store increase?

A) 20 percent

B) 25 percent

C) 36 percent

D) 80 percent

22

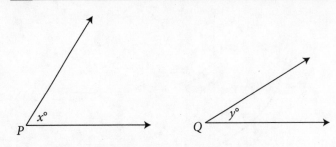

Note: Figures not drawn to scale.

For acute angles P and Q shown above, $\cos(x°) = \sin(y°)$. If $x = 3c - 23$ and $y = 7c - 42$, what is the value of c ?

A) 24.5

B) 15.5

C) 9.0

D) 6.0

CONTINUE

23

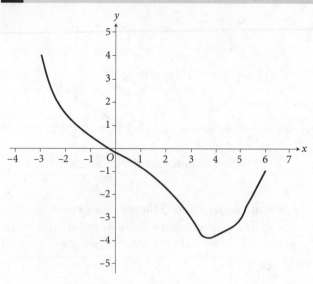

What is the maximum value of the function graphed in the *xy*-plane above, for $-3 \le x \le 6$?

A) 4

B) 5

C) 6

D) ∞

24

Matthew constructs a fence around a patch of grass in his backyard. The patch has a width that is 8 feet more than 4 times the length. What is the perimeter of the fence if Matthew's patch of grass has an area of 5,472 square feet?

A) 364 feet

B) 376 feet

C) 396 feet

D) 400 feet

25

In the *xy*-plane, the line determined by the points $(c, 3)$ and $(27, c)$ intersects the origin. Which of the following could be the value of *c* ?

A) 0

B) 3

C) 6

D) 9

26

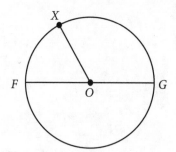

In the circle above, the length of arc $\overset{\frown}{FXG}$ is 14π. If $\overline{FG}$ is a chord that passes through the circle's center, *O*, what is the length of the segment $\overline{XO}$?

A) 7

B) 14

C) 28

D) 56

CONTINUE

27

Let p and q be numbers such that $-|p| < q < |p|$. Which of the following must be true?

    I. $p > 0$

    II. $|p| > -q$

    III. $p > |q|$

A) I only

B) II only

C) II and III only

D) I, II, and III

28

A rectangular container with a base that measures 10 feet by 10 feet is filled with jelly beans. The container is divided into regions each with the same height as the container and a square base with sides that measure 1 foot each. Sherman randomly selects ten of these regions and counts the number of blue jelly beans in each region. The results are shown in the table below.

Region	Blue Jelly Beans	Region	Blue Jelly Beans
I	20	VI	22
II	21	VII	25
III	27	VIII	24
IV	31	IX	28
V	19	X	23

Which of the following is a reasonable approximation of the number of blue jelly beans in the entire container?

A) 25,000

B) 2,500

C) 250

D) 25

CONTINUE

	Flavor	
Product Type	Frozen Yogurt	Ice Cream
Vanilla		
Chocolate		
Total	32	152

The incomplete table above shows the sales for a particular sweet shop by product and flavor. There were 4 times as many vanilla ice creams sold as vanilla frozen yogurts, and there were 6 times as many chocolate ice creams sold as chocolate frozen yogurts. If there were a total of 32 frozen yogurts and 152 ice creams sold, and no flavors other than vanilla and chocolate were available, which of the following is closest to the probability that a randomly selected ice cream sold was vanilla?

A) 0.250

B) 0.435

C) 0.526

D) 0.667

$$\begin{cases} y \geq x \\ 3y < -2x - 3 \end{cases}$$

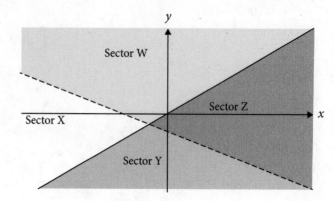

A system of inequalities is graphed above. Which sector or sectors on the graph could represent all of the solutions to the system shown?

A) Sectors Y and Z

B) Sectors W and Y

C) Sector W

D) Sector X

CONTINUE

DIRECTIONS

For questions 31–38, solve the problem and enter your answer in the grid, as described below, on the answer sheet.

1. Although not required, it is suggested that you write your answer in the boxes at the top of the columns to help you fill in the circles accurately. You will receive credit only if the circles are filled in correctly.

2. Mark no more than one circle in any column.

3. No question has a negative answer.

4. Some problems may have more than one correct answer. In such cases, grid only one answer.

5. **Mixed numbers** such as $3\frac{1}{2}$ must be gridded as 3.5 or 7/2. (If $\boxed{3\ |\ 1\ /\ 2}$ is entered into the grid, it will be interpreted as $\frac{31}{2}$, not as $3\frac{1}{2}$.)

6. **Decimal Answers:** If you obtain a decimal answer with more digits than the grid can accommodate, it may be either rounded or truncated, but it must fill the entire grid.

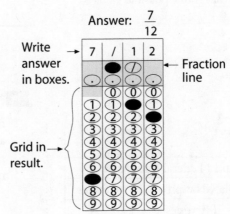

Answer: $\frac{7}{12}$ — Write answer in boxes. ← Fraction line — Grid in result.

Answer: 2.5 ← Decimal point

Acceptable ways to grid $\frac{2}{3}$ are:

Answer: 201 – either position is correct

NOTE: You may start your answers in any column, space permitting. Columns you don't need to use should be left blank.

CONTINUE →

31

At a certain food truck, hamburgers are sold for $5 each and hot dogs are $3 each. If Martina buys one hamburger and *h* hot dogs, and spends at least $20 and no more than $25, what is one possible value of *h* ?

32

Number of States in 14 Federal Nations			
Nation	States	Nation	States
Australia	6	Micronesia	4
Austria	9	Nigeria	36
Brazil	26	Saint Kitts and Nevis	2
Germany	16	South Sudan	10
India	29	Sudan	17
Malaysia	13	United States	50
Mexico	31	Venezuela	23

The table above lists the number of states in each of the 14 federal nations that have subdivisions called states. According to the table, what is the mean number of states of these nations? (Round your answer to the nearest tenth.)

33

In the *xy*-plane, the point (–2, 6) lies on the graph of the function $g(x) = 2x^2 + kx + 18$. What is the value of *k* ?

34

In a certain college dormitory, 108 students are assigned dorm rooms. The dormitory has 26 dorm rooms, each of which is assigned 3 or 5 students. How many of the dorm rooms will be assigned 3 students?

CONTINUE

35

Population of Town A
Each Decade from 1910 to 2000

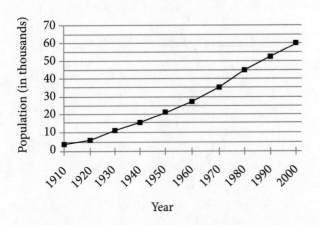

According to the figure shown above, the population of Town A in 1970 was what fraction of the population of Town A in 2000 ?

36

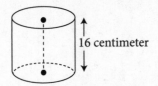

16 centimeter

A wooden block is in the shape of the right circular cylinder shown above. If the volume of the wooden block is 64π cubic centimeters, what is the <u>diameter</u> of the base of the cylinder, in centimeters?

Questions 37 and 38 refer to the following information.

$\omega^2 = \omega_0^2 + 2\alpha\theta$ (angular position – angular velocity)

$\omega = \omega_0 + \alpha t$ (time – angular velocity)

$\theta = \omega_0 t + \dfrac{1}{2}\alpha t^2$ (time – angular position)

A carousel is rotating at an angular velocity of 90 degrees per second. The instant a particular point on the carousel reaches angular position $\theta = 0°$, the carousel operator flips a switch, causing the carousel at a constant angular acceleration to slow down and eventually change direction. The equations above describe the constant-acceleration motion of the carousel, where ω_0 represents the initial angular velocity, ω is the angular velocity as it travels, θ is the angular position of the particular point on the carousel, t is the time since the switch was flipped, and α is the constant angular acceleration ($-12.6°/s^2$).

37

To the nearest degree, at what angular position will the carousel change direction?

38

To the nearest second, how long will it take the carousel to come to a complete stop before it changes direction?

END OF TEST

DO NOT RETURN TO A PREVIOUS SECTION.

Completely darken bubbles with a No. 2 pencil. If you make a mistake, be sure to erase mark completely. Erase all stray marks.

1.

YOUR NAME: _____
(Print)   Last   First   M.I.

SIGNATURE: _____   DATE: ___/___/___

HOME ADDRESS: _____
(Print)   Number and Street

_____
City   State   Zip Code

PHONE NO.: _____
(Print)

IMPORTANT: Please fill in these boxes exactly as shown on the back cover of your test book.

2. TEST FORM

3. TEST CODE

4. REGISTRATION NUMBER

5. YOUR NAME

First 4 letters of last name				FIRST INIT	MID INIT
Ⓐ	Ⓐ	Ⓐ	Ⓐ	Ⓐ	Ⓐ
Ⓑ	Ⓑ	Ⓑ	Ⓑ	Ⓑ	Ⓑ
Ⓒ	Ⓒ	Ⓒ	Ⓒ	Ⓒ	Ⓒ
Ⓓ	Ⓓ	Ⓓ	Ⓓ	Ⓓ	Ⓓ
Ⓔ	Ⓔ	Ⓔ	Ⓔ	Ⓔ	Ⓔ
Ⓕ	Ⓕ	Ⓕ	Ⓕ	Ⓕ	Ⓕ
Ⓖ	Ⓖ	Ⓖ	Ⓖ	Ⓖ	Ⓖ
Ⓗ	Ⓗ	Ⓗ	Ⓗ	Ⓗ	Ⓗ
Ⓘ	Ⓘ	Ⓘ	Ⓘ	Ⓘ	Ⓘ
Ⓙ	Ⓙ	Ⓙ	Ⓙ	Ⓙ	Ⓙ
Ⓚ	Ⓚ	Ⓚ	Ⓚ	Ⓚ	Ⓚ
Ⓛ	Ⓛ	Ⓛ	Ⓛ	Ⓛ	Ⓛ
Ⓜ	Ⓜ	Ⓜ	Ⓜ	Ⓜ	Ⓜ
Ⓝ	Ⓝ	Ⓝ	Ⓝ	Ⓝ	Ⓝ
Ⓞ	Ⓞ	Ⓞ	Ⓞ	Ⓞ	Ⓞ
Ⓟ	Ⓟ	Ⓟ	Ⓟ	Ⓟ	Ⓟ
Ⓠ	Ⓠ	Ⓠ	Ⓠ	Ⓠ	Ⓠ
Ⓡ	Ⓡ	Ⓡ	Ⓡ	Ⓡ	Ⓡ
Ⓢ	Ⓢ	Ⓢ	Ⓢ	Ⓢ	Ⓢ
Ⓣ	Ⓣ	Ⓣ	Ⓣ	Ⓣ	Ⓣ
Ⓤ	Ⓤ	Ⓤ	Ⓤ	Ⓤ	Ⓤ
Ⓥ	Ⓥ	Ⓥ	Ⓥ	Ⓥ	Ⓥ
Ⓦ	Ⓦ	Ⓦ	Ⓦ	Ⓦ	Ⓦ
Ⓧ	Ⓧ	Ⓧ	Ⓧ	Ⓧ	Ⓧ
Ⓨ	Ⓨ	Ⓨ	Ⓨ	Ⓨ	Ⓨ
Ⓩ	Ⓩ	Ⓩ	Ⓩ	Ⓩ	Ⓩ

3. TEST CODE

⓪ Ⓐ Ⓙ ⓪ ⓪
① Ⓑ Ⓚ ① ①
② Ⓒ Ⓛ ② ②
③ Ⓓ Ⓜ ③ ③
④ Ⓔ Ⓝ ④ ④
⑤ Ⓕ Ⓞ ⑤ ⑤
⑥ Ⓖ Ⓟ ⑥ ⑥
⑦ Ⓗ Ⓠ ⑦ ⑦
⑧ Ⓘ Ⓡ ⑧ ⑧
⑨ ⑨ ⑨

4. REGISTRATION NUMBER

⓪ ⓪ ⓪ ⓪ ⓪ ⓪ ⓪
① ① ① ① ① ① ①
② ② ② ② ② ② ②
③ ③ ③ ③ ③ ③ ③
④ ④ ④ ④ ④ ④ ④
⑤ ⑤ ⑤ ⑤ ⑤ ⑤ ⑤
⑥ ⑥ ⑥ ⑥ ⑥ ⑥ ⑥
⑦ ⑦ ⑦ ⑦ ⑦ ⑦ ⑦
⑧ ⑧ ⑧ ⑧ ⑧ ⑧ ⑧
⑨ ⑨ ⑨ ⑨ ⑨ ⑨ ⑨

6. DATE OF BIRTH

Month	Day		Year	
◯ JAN				
◯ FEB	⓪	⓪	⓪	⓪
◯ MAR	①	①	①	①
◯ APR	②	②	②	②
◯ MAY	③	③	③	③
◯ JUN		④	④	④
◯ JUL		⑤	⑤	⑤
◯ AUG		⑥	⑥	⑥
◯ SEP		⑦	⑦	⑦
◯ OCT		⑧	⑧	⑧
◯ NOV		⑨	⑨	⑨
◯ DEC				

7. SEX

◯ MALE
◯ FEMALE

The **Princeton Review**®

Test ❺

Start with number 1 for each new section.
If a section has fewer questions than answer spaces, leave the extra answer spaces blank.

Section 1—Reading

1. Ⓐ Ⓑ Ⓒ Ⓓ
2. Ⓐ Ⓑ Ⓒ Ⓓ
3. Ⓐ Ⓑ Ⓒ Ⓓ
4. Ⓐ Ⓑ Ⓒ Ⓓ
5. Ⓐ Ⓑ Ⓒ Ⓓ
6. Ⓐ Ⓑ Ⓒ Ⓓ
7. Ⓐ Ⓑ Ⓒ Ⓓ
8. Ⓐ Ⓑ Ⓒ Ⓓ
9. Ⓐ Ⓑ Ⓒ Ⓓ
10. Ⓐ Ⓑ Ⓒ Ⓓ
11. Ⓐ Ⓑ Ⓒ Ⓓ
12. Ⓐ Ⓑ Ⓒ Ⓓ
13. Ⓐ Ⓑ Ⓒ Ⓓ
14. Ⓐ Ⓑ Ⓒ Ⓓ
15. Ⓐ Ⓑ Ⓒ Ⓓ
16. Ⓐ Ⓑ Ⓒ Ⓓ
17. Ⓐ Ⓑ Ⓒ Ⓓ
18. Ⓐ Ⓑ Ⓒ Ⓓ
19. Ⓐ Ⓑ Ⓒ Ⓓ
20. Ⓐ Ⓑ Ⓒ Ⓓ
21. Ⓐ Ⓑ Ⓒ Ⓓ
22. Ⓐ Ⓑ Ⓒ Ⓓ
23. Ⓐ Ⓑ Ⓒ Ⓓ
24. Ⓐ Ⓑ Ⓒ Ⓓ
25. Ⓐ Ⓑ Ⓒ Ⓓ
26. Ⓐ Ⓑ Ⓒ Ⓓ
27. Ⓐ Ⓑ Ⓒ Ⓓ
28. Ⓐ Ⓑ Ⓒ Ⓓ
29. Ⓐ Ⓑ Ⓒ Ⓓ
30. Ⓐ Ⓑ Ⓒ Ⓓ
31. Ⓐ Ⓑ Ⓒ Ⓓ
32. Ⓐ Ⓑ Ⓒ Ⓓ
33. Ⓐ Ⓑ Ⓒ Ⓓ
34. Ⓐ Ⓑ Ⓒ Ⓓ
35. Ⓐ Ⓑ Ⓒ Ⓓ
36. Ⓐ Ⓑ Ⓒ Ⓓ
37. Ⓐ Ⓑ Ⓒ Ⓓ
38. Ⓐ Ⓑ Ⓒ Ⓓ
39. Ⓐ Ⓑ Ⓒ Ⓓ
40. Ⓐ Ⓑ Ⓒ Ⓓ
41. Ⓐ Ⓑ Ⓒ Ⓓ
42. Ⓐ Ⓑ Ⓒ Ⓓ
43. Ⓐ Ⓑ Ⓒ Ⓓ
44. Ⓐ Ⓑ Ⓒ Ⓓ
45. Ⓐ Ⓑ Ⓒ Ⓓ
46. Ⓐ Ⓑ Ⓒ Ⓓ
47. Ⓐ Ⓑ Ⓒ Ⓓ
48. Ⓐ Ⓑ Ⓒ Ⓓ
49. Ⓐ Ⓑ Ⓒ Ⓓ
50. Ⓐ Ⓑ Ⓒ Ⓓ
51. Ⓐ Ⓑ Ⓒ Ⓓ
52. Ⓐ Ⓑ Ⓒ Ⓓ

Section 2—Writing and Language Skills

1. Ⓐ Ⓑ Ⓒ Ⓓ
2. Ⓐ Ⓑ Ⓒ Ⓓ
3. Ⓐ Ⓑ Ⓒ Ⓓ
4. Ⓐ Ⓑ Ⓒ Ⓓ
5. Ⓐ Ⓑ Ⓒ Ⓓ
6. Ⓐ Ⓑ Ⓒ Ⓓ
7. Ⓐ Ⓑ Ⓒ Ⓓ
8. Ⓐ Ⓑ Ⓒ Ⓓ
9. Ⓐ Ⓑ Ⓒ Ⓓ
10. Ⓐ Ⓑ Ⓒ Ⓓ
11. Ⓐ Ⓑ Ⓒ Ⓓ
12. Ⓐ Ⓑ Ⓒ Ⓓ
13. Ⓐ Ⓑ Ⓒ Ⓓ
14. Ⓐ Ⓑ Ⓒ Ⓓ
15. Ⓐ Ⓑ Ⓒ Ⓓ
16. Ⓐ Ⓑ Ⓒ Ⓓ
17. Ⓐ Ⓑ Ⓒ Ⓓ
18. Ⓐ Ⓑ Ⓒ Ⓓ
19. Ⓐ Ⓑ Ⓒ Ⓓ
20. Ⓐ Ⓑ Ⓒ Ⓓ
21. Ⓐ Ⓑ Ⓒ Ⓓ
22. Ⓐ Ⓑ Ⓒ Ⓓ
23. Ⓐ Ⓑ Ⓒ Ⓓ
24. Ⓐ Ⓑ Ⓒ Ⓓ
25. Ⓐ Ⓑ Ⓒ Ⓓ
26. Ⓐ Ⓑ Ⓒ Ⓓ
27. Ⓐ Ⓑ Ⓒ Ⓓ
28. Ⓐ Ⓑ Ⓒ Ⓓ
29. Ⓐ Ⓑ Ⓒ Ⓓ
30. Ⓐ Ⓑ Ⓒ Ⓓ
31. Ⓐ Ⓑ Ⓒ Ⓓ
32. Ⓐ Ⓑ Ⓒ Ⓓ
33. Ⓐ Ⓑ Ⓒ Ⓓ
34. Ⓐ Ⓑ Ⓒ Ⓓ
35. Ⓐ Ⓑ Ⓒ Ⓓ
36. Ⓐ Ⓑ Ⓒ Ⓓ
37. Ⓐ Ⓑ Ⓒ Ⓓ
38. Ⓐ Ⓑ Ⓒ Ⓓ
39. Ⓐ Ⓑ Ⓒ Ⓓ
40. Ⓐ Ⓑ Ⓒ Ⓓ
41. Ⓐ Ⓑ Ⓒ Ⓓ
42. Ⓐ Ⓑ Ⓒ Ⓓ
43. Ⓐ Ⓑ Ⓒ Ⓓ
44. Ⓐ Ⓑ Ⓒ Ⓓ

Test 5 Start with number 1 for each new section.
If a section has fewer questions than answer spaces, leave the extra answer spaces blank.

Section 3—Mathematics: No Calculator

1. Ⓐ Ⓑ Ⓒ Ⓓ
2. Ⓐ Ⓑ Ⓒ Ⓓ
3. Ⓐ Ⓑ Ⓒ Ⓓ
4. Ⓐ Ⓑ Ⓒ Ⓓ
5. Ⓐ Ⓑ Ⓒ Ⓓ
6. Ⓐ Ⓑ Ⓒ Ⓓ
7. Ⓐ Ⓑ Ⓒ Ⓓ
8. Ⓐ Ⓑ Ⓒ Ⓓ
9. Ⓐ Ⓑ Ⓒ Ⓓ
10. Ⓐ Ⓑ Ⓒ Ⓓ
11. Ⓐ Ⓑ Ⓒ Ⓓ
12. Ⓐ Ⓑ Ⓒ Ⓓ
13. Ⓐ Ⓑ Ⓒ Ⓓ
14. Ⓐ Ⓑ Ⓒ Ⓓ
15. Ⓐ Ⓑ Ⓒ Ⓓ

16. 17. 18. 19. 20.

Section 4—Mathematics: Calculator

1. Ⓐ Ⓑ Ⓒ Ⓓ
2. Ⓐ Ⓑ Ⓒ Ⓓ
3. Ⓐ Ⓑ Ⓒ Ⓓ
4. Ⓐ Ⓑ Ⓒ Ⓓ
5. Ⓐ Ⓑ Ⓒ Ⓓ
6. Ⓐ Ⓑ Ⓒ Ⓓ
7. Ⓐ Ⓑ Ⓒ Ⓓ
8. Ⓐ Ⓑ Ⓒ Ⓓ
9. Ⓐ Ⓑ Ⓒ Ⓓ
10. Ⓐ Ⓑ Ⓒ Ⓓ
11. Ⓐ Ⓑ Ⓒ Ⓓ
12. Ⓐ Ⓑ Ⓒ Ⓓ
13. Ⓐ Ⓑ Ⓒ Ⓓ
14. Ⓐ Ⓑ Ⓒ Ⓓ
15. Ⓐ Ⓑ Ⓒ Ⓓ
16. Ⓐ Ⓑ Ⓒ Ⓓ
17. Ⓐ Ⓑ Ⓒ Ⓓ
18. Ⓐ Ⓑ Ⓒ Ⓓ
19. Ⓐ Ⓑ Ⓒ Ⓓ
20. Ⓐ Ⓑ Ⓒ Ⓓ
21. Ⓐ Ⓑ Ⓒ Ⓓ
22. Ⓐ Ⓑ Ⓒ Ⓓ
23. Ⓐ Ⓑ Ⓒ Ⓓ
24. Ⓐ Ⓑ Ⓒ Ⓓ
25. Ⓐ Ⓑ Ⓒ Ⓓ
26. Ⓐ Ⓑ Ⓒ Ⓓ
27. Ⓐ Ⓑ Ⓒ Ⓓ
28. Ⓐ Ⓑ Ⓒ Ⓓ
29. Ⓐ Ⓑ Ⓒ Ⓓ
30. Ⓐ Ⓑ Ⓒ Ⓓ

31. 32. 33. 34. 35.

36. 37. 38.

Chapter 12
Practice Test 5:
Answers and
Explanations

PRACTICE TEST 5 ANSWER KEY

Section 1: Reading				Section 2: Writing & Language				Section 3: Math (No Calculator)				Section 4: Math (Calculator)			
1.	C	27.	A	1.	A	23.	D	1.	A	11.	B	1.	D	20.	D
2.	C	28.	B	2.	B	24.	C	2.	A	12.	C	2.	B	21.	C
3.	D	29.	B	3.	C	25.	A	3.	D	13.	D	3.	A	22.	B
4.	A	30.	C	4.	B	26.	C	4.	C	14.	D	4.	D	23.	A
5.	A	31.	D	5.	B	27.	B	5.	A	15.	B	5.	A	24.	B
6.	D	32.	B	6.	D	28.	C	6.	B	16.	4	6.	C	25.	D
7.	A	33.	A	7.	C	29.	C	7.	B	17.	500	7.	B	26.	B
8.	C	34.	D	8.	B	30.	B	8.	A	18.	5	8.	C	27.	B
9.	D	35.	B	9.	B	31.	A	9.	A	19.	1	9.	A	28.	B
10.	B	36.	C	10.	D	32.	A	10.	C	20.	$\frac{5}{13}$, .384, or .385	10.	A	29.	C
11.	D	37.	C	11.	B	33.	C					11.	D	30.	D
12.	C	38.	A	12.	B	34.	D					12.	A	31.	5 or 6
13.	B	39.	B	13.	D	35.	B					13.	A	32.	19.4
14.	B	40.	D	14.	A	36.	D					14.	D	33.	10
15.	A	41.	A	15.	A	37.	D					15.	C	34.	11
16.	C	42.	C	16.	C	38.	A					16.	C	35.	$\frac{7}{12}$
17.	D	43.	A	17.	C	39.	B					17.	B	36.	4
18.	A	44.	D	18.	A	40.	C					18.	C	37.	321
19.	D	45.	A	19.	B	41.	D					19.	C	38.	7
20.	C	46.	B	20.	D	42.	D								
21.	D	47.	D	21.	A	43.	A								
22.	C	48.	C	22.	A	44.	B								
23.	B	49.	B												
24.	D	50.	C												
25.	D	51.	D												
26.	B	52.	C												

Go to PrincetonReview.com to score your exam. Alternatively, for self-assessment tables, please turn to page 909.

PRACTICE TEST 5 EXPLANATIONS

Section 1: Reading

1. **C** The question asks about what happens in the passage as a whole. Because this is a general question, it should be done after all the specific questions. This passage is about a stranger showing up unexpectedly for an unhappy reunion with a former shipmate. Choice (A) might initially look attractive because the narrator and the stranger do hide and then surprise the captain, but there is no *plan* to surprise the captain. Eliminate (A). Choice (B) has nothing to do with the passage and can be eliminated. Choice (C) is a solid paraphrase of the prediction, so keep it. Choice (D) does mention two characters sharing time on a ship, but the passage does not indicate that the two men were reminiscing at all. The correct answer is (C).

2. **C** The question asks for a description of the passage. Because this is a general question, it should be done after all the specific questions. Look at the second part of each answer choice. The *encounter* in the passage is not *enthusiastic*, so (A) can be eliminated. There is no *conference*, so (B) can also be eliminated. Choice (C) looks good because the narrator was worried, and the stranger and the captain fought, so keep (C). There is no *homecoming*, so eliminate (D). The correct answer is (C).

3. **D** The question asks what the word *fancy* means in lines 5 and 10. Go back to the text, find the word *fancy*, and mark it out. Carefully read the surrounding text to determine another word that would fit in the blanks based on the context of the passage. In the first case, the narrator says that he didn't step back inside *quick enough for his fancy*. The correct answer should mean something like "liking." See if that also makes sense in the second occurrence. The stranger tells the narrator that he's *taken quite a fancy* to him because the narrator reminds him of his own son, or *the pride of [his] 'art*. "Liking" definitely fits in that context as well. Choices (A) and (C) can be eliminated immediately. Choice (B) might appear to match the context of the first occurrence of *fancy*, but *impatience* has nothing to do with the prediction of "liking," so (B) can be eliminated. *Preference* means "liking." The correct answer is (D).

4. **A** The question asks about the narrator's sense of the stranger's emotions regarding the coming meeting between him and the captain. Because this is the first question in a paired set, it can be done in tandem with Q5. Consider the answers for Q5 first. In (5A), the narrator observes that *the stranger was certainly frightened himself*, which supports (4A). Choices (5B) and (5D) describe the captain and not the stranger, so eliminate them both. Eliminate (5C) because it does not directly describe any emotional state, leaving (4A) and (5A) as the only possible pair. The correct answers are (4A) and (5A).

5. **A** (See explanation above.)

6. **D** The question asks about how the narrator is addressed by the stranger, so look for evidence in the text to predict what the answer might be. In the text used to answer previous questions, the stranger tells the narrator he has *taken a fancy* to him, but in that same paragraph the stranger swears at the boy *with an oath that made [him] jump*. Eliminate (A) because while the stranger does address the narrator with friendliness at one point, he never addresses him with *respect*. Choice (B) is reversed—the stranger does address the boy with *anger* but he's never violent to him. Choice (C) does not match the prediction. *Affection* in (D) looks good, and later the stranger shows that he does not trust the narrator when he sends him for rum but tells him to leave the door open. The correct answer is (D).

7. **A**   The question asks about the purpose of the first paragraph. Throughout the paragraph, the narrator creates a picture of the stranger, from how he looks to how he acts, which directly supports (A). Eliminate (B) because there is no *belief* to *criticize* in the first paragraph. The paragraph describes an interaction, not a *relationship*, so (C) can be eliminated as well. Last, there is no specific *discrepancy*, eliminating (D). The correct answer is (A).

8. **C**   The question asks what the word *talons* means in line 51. Go back to the text, find the word *talons*, and mark it out. Carefully read the surrounding text to determine another word that would fit in the blank based on the context of the passage. Black Dog says he's lost two talons, and then he holds up *his mutilated hand*. The correct answer should mean something related to a "hand," so eliminate (A), (B), and (D). The correct answer is (C).

9. **D**   The question asks why the narrator uses a particular phrase (*all the brown had gone out of his face*). Use the given line reference to find the window. The narrator uses the phrase to describe the captain's reaction to seeing the stranger. Black Dog surprises the captain, who *spun round on his heel...he had the look of a man who sees a ghost, or the evil one, or something worse, if anything can be; and upon my word, I felt sorry to see him all in a moment turn so old and sick*. The narrator uses the phrase to show that the captain is reacting badly to the surprise of seeing Black Dog. Choice (A) does not match that prediction, so it can be eliminated. Choice (B) might be true, but isn't supported by the text. Choice (C) doesn't have any support in the text, either, so it can be eliminated. The correct answer is (D).

10. **B**   The question is the best evidence question in a paired set. Because Q9 was a specific question, simply look at the lines used to answer Q9. Lines 37–42 were used to answer the previous question. The correct answer is (B).

11. **D**   The question asks why the author mentions certain examples. Use the line reference to find the window and look for the claim the examples are meant to illustrate. The examples of gift-giving are both recent and about Christmas, but they are offered to show that *the ancient practice of gift-giving is still pervasive and significant in modern cultures*. Eliminate (A), as there's no mention of a *recent increase*. Eliminate (B) and (C), since neither *discrepancies* nor *apprehension* is mentioned. The *pervasiveness of gift-giving* in (D) matches the prediction. The correct answer is (D).

12. **C**   The question asks what the word *rich* means in line 20. Go back to the text, find the word *rich*, and mark it out. Carefully read the surrounding text to determine another word that would fit in the blank based on the context of the passage. In this case, *rich* refers to the plethora of information that might help to explain consumer behavior. The correct answer should mean something like "abounding." Choices (A) and (B) are actual definitions of the word *rich*, but they don't make sense based on the context. Both of these answers can be eliminated. Choice (C) could work, because when something is *fertile* it is *abundantly productive*, which fits the context of the passage. Choice (D) might connect with the idea of foods that are rich, but that doesn't make sense in this context. The correct answer is (C).

13. **B**   The question asks what the passage indicates about the *gift-giving described in lines 28–29*. Read a window around the given line reference. Lines 28–29 state, *Mauss concluded that gift-giving is a self-perpetuating system of reciprocity*. The description of the gift-giving system continues through line 53. The window is quite large, and Q13 is the first question in a paired set, so it can be done in tandem with Q14. Look at the answers for Q14. The lines for (14A) state that the *motives* for gift-gifting *become institutionalized...so that under appropriate conditions an individual is socially obligated to give*. Check the answers for Q13 to see whether any of the answers are supported by these lines. At first glance, these lines may seem to support (13A), but the lines for (14A) discuss obligation on the part of gift givers, rather than *gift recipients*. The information in (14A) doesn't

support any of the answer choices for Q13, so eliminate (14A). The lines for (14B) state, *Adequate or overly adequate repayment…creates an obligation to repay on the part of the original giver, and the cycle is reinitiated.* These lines support (13B), so draw a line connecting (13B) with (14B). The lines for (14C) indicate that *acceptance of a particular gift constitutes an acknowledgment and acceptance of the identity that the gift is seen to imply.* At first glance, these lines may seem to support (13A), but the text doesn't actually suggest that it is *oppressive* to accept the identity implied by the gift. These lines do not support any of the answer choices for Q13, so eliminate (14C). The lines for (14D) indicate that the *underlying behavioral questions* related to *gift selection* have *not been addressed by empirical research.* These lines do not support any of the answer choices for Q13, so eliminate (14D). Without any support in the answers from Q14, (13A), (13C), and (13D) can be eliminated. The correct answers are (13B) and (14B).

14. **B** (See explanation above.)

15. **A** The question asks what *Marcell Mauss believes* about *people's reasons for giving gifts.* This is the first question in a paired set, but it is a specific question, so it can be done on its own. Use chronology to find the window for the question. Q13 asked about lines 28–29, so start with line 30 and scan the passage for information about people's reasons for gift-giving. Lines 34–38 list several possible reasons for giving, including *the need to establish or maintain peaceful relations, or simply the expectation of reciprocal giving.* Eliminate answers that don't match this prediction. Keep (A) because it matches the prediction: the need to make and keep peace and the expectation of receiving a gift in return (*reciprocal giving*) are examples of people's *own needs* that motivate gift-giving. Choice (B) is a Could Be True trap answer: while it is possible that people's reasons for giving gifts *change* as they age, the passage doesn't discuss this. Eliminate (B). Choice (C) is a Deceptive Language trap answer: the passage says that Mauss studied *numerous…societies,* but it doesn't discuss any differences in gift-giving between cultures. Eliminate (C). Choice (D) is a Could Be True trap answer: while it is reasonable to think that a person's reason for giving a gift influences the *timing* of the gift, the passage doesn't discuss this. Eliminate (D). The correct answer is (A).

16. **C** The question is the best evidence question in a paired set. Because the previous question was a specific question, simply look at the lines used to answer Q15. Lines 34–38 provided the prediction for Q15. Keep (C) and eliminate (A), (B), and (D). The correct answer is (C).

17. **D** The question asks how *Schwartz* would view the gift-exchanging process. Use the given line reference to find the window. The fourth paragraph presents Schwartz's insights about a gift's ability to reflect the giver's perception of the recipient and the implicit acceptance of that perception when a receiver accepts a gift. This point about the process matches well with (D), symbolic. Though it may be true that such a process could be stressful or unnerving, no evidence is given that Schwartz considers it to be so. Thus, (A) and (B) can be eliminated. While some givers and receivers may act intentional[ly], there's no evidence that the process always operates that way, so (C) can be eliminated. The correct answer is (D).

18. **A** The question asks what the word *function* means in line 65. Go back to the text, find the word *function,* and mark it out. Carefully read the surrounding text to determine another word that would fit in the blank based on the context of the passage. In this case, *function* refers to gift selection. The correct answer should mean something like "objective," which supports (A). The *nevertheless* at the beginning of the sentence shows a continuation from the previous paragraph. The focus of the previous paragraph was how gift-giving *does* something, not *when* the gifts are given. Therefore, *function* in this context does not have to do with an event. Choices (B) and (C) can be eliminated. Choice (D), *occupation,* does not fit the context of the sentence. The correct answer is (A).

19. **D** The question asks why the author mentions *a gift shop's recent advertisement*. Use the given line reference to find the window. The ad does not question any prior claims or counter any explanations, eliminating (A) and (C). Choice (B) can be eliminated because the advertisement does not *offer a motive* for a certain behavior. The ad supports what was said in paragraph 3, a previous window. The correct answer is (D).

20. **C** The question asks about information in both the passage and the graph. Use the passage and the graph to answer it. The *recipient's self-concept* is not included in the graph, nor is the *amount of money the giver spent*, eliminating (A) and (B). Choice (D) does not work because the *thoughtfulness* is not measured by the graph. Rather, the graph shows the implicit communication between the gift-giver and recipient, and the passage supports this information in the last paragraph. The correct answer is (C).

21. **D** The question refers to the *encoding phase represented in the figure* and asks what the author would likely say the gift-giver is attempting to convey during this stage. First, locate the *encoding phase* in the figure. The figure is titled *Gift-Giving as Communication*, and shows the encoding taking place between the *giver* and the *gift*. As is implied by the question, the figure shows the gift-giver encoding the gift with some sort of meaning. Next, look for evidence in the passage regarding the author's views on what information gift-givers convey with gifts. In lines 34–38, the author recounts a theory: *The obligation to give may be based on moral or religious imperatives, the need to recognize and maintain a status hierarchy, the need to establish or maintain peaceful relations, or simply the expectation of reciprocal giving*. In lines 54–57, *the author recounts another finding: Schwartz (1967) noted that beyond the functions served by the general process of gift exchange, the characteristics of the gift itself also act as a powerful statement of the giver's perception of the recipient*. To summarize, the author suggests that by giving gifts, a gift-giver may be communicating information about their status relative to the recipient, a desire for peaceful relations with the recipient, an expectation that the recipient will give a gift in return, or information about how they perceive the recipient. Eliminate answer choices that don't match the passage. Choice (A) is a Right Answer, Wrong Question trap: although the author says *the nature of the occasion* may affect *consumer behavior*, he doesn't indicate that gift-givers use the gift to communicate information about *the occasion for giving*. Eliminate (A). Eliminate (B) because the author never mentions *the giver's personal preferences*. Eliminate (C) because the author never mentions *the location* of the purchase. Keep (D) because *the relationship between the giver and receiver* matches the statements in the passage about *status, peaceful relations,* and *the giver's perception of the recipient*. The correct answer is (D).

22. **C** The question asks for a piece of information that *contradicts* the student's claim that *over half of solar radiation influences the ground temperature*. Read the line references in each of the answer choices. Choice (A) refers to a situation in which the atmosphere is *letting through the light rays of the sun relatively easily*, which would confirm rather than *contradict* the student's claim and should therefore be eliminated. Choice (B) mentions *the temperature of the atmosphere* but does not address *solar radiation* or *ground temperature*, so this answer can be eliminated. Choice (C) should be kept because it specifically contradicts the student's claim with these lines: *Owing to the clouds and dust floating in the atmosphere, this heat is probably only about a third of that derived by using Langley's solar constant*. In other words, the floating particles block the sun's full energy. Choice (D) refers only to the table, not to conceptual information regarding the sun's radiation, so it too can be eliminated. The correct answer is (C).

23. **B** The question asks about the importance of the atmosphere as it influences the temperature of the earth. Use the given line reference to find the window. The relevant information is here: *the atmosphere may act like the glass of a green-house, letting through the light rays of the sun relatively*

easily, and absorbing a great part of the dark rays emitted from the ground, and it thereby may raise the mean temperature of the earth's surface. A second purpose is cited here: *the atmosphere acts as a heat store placed between the relatively warm ground and the cold space, and thereby lessens in a high degree the annual, diurnal, and local variations of the temperature.* In other words, the atmosphere plays a crucial role in allowing certain heat in and trapping that heat so it influences ground temperature. Choice (A) is extreme in its use of the word *all*, particularly given that the text indicates that much of the heat is transferred back out of the atmosphere. Eliminate (A). Choice (B) should be kept because it captures the ideas from both quotations without overstating. Choice (C) can be eliminated because it neglects the role of solar radiation. Choice (D) can be eliminated because the words *free passage* are extreme—the passage indicates that the atmosphere absorbs *a great part of the dark rays emitted from the ground.* The correct answer is (B).

24. **D**   The question asks why the author uses the word *green-house* to describe the effects in this passage. Use the given line reference to find the window. The relevant information is here: *like the glass of a green-house, letting through the light rays of the sun relatively easily, and absorbing a great part of the dark rays emitted from the ground.* In other words, the atmosphere is like a greenhouse in that it lets in more heat than it lets out. Choice (A) may be partially true (though it is extreme in its use of the word *only*), but it does not match the prediction because it does not answer the question as to why the word *green-house* is used. Eliminate (A). Choice (B) can also be eliminated because it neglects the role of solar radiation entirely. Choice (C) is deceptive in that it applies the term *green-house* literally rather than figuratively. Eliminate (C). Choice (D) matches well with the prediction and captures both the idea of solar radiation and the atmosphere's role in absorbing it. The correct answer is (D).

25. **D**   The question asks which of the answers can be supported by the quoted statement and its surrounding context. Use the given line reference to find the window. Read the quotation carefully—the word *principally* indicates that most but not all of this energy comes from solar radiation. Choice (A) states a version of this, but there is no indication in the quotation or the passage that clouds block out solar radiation entirely, nor that ground heat does whatever heating solar energy cannot. Eliminate (A). Choice (B) correctly implies that heat can be generated by the sun and other sources, but this choice then goes on to state that the *heat is held in the atmosphere and released as cool air*, which is untrue. Eliminate (B). Choice (C) may seem plausible, but it overlooks the green-house effect described throughout this passage, which states that solar energy passes relatively unobstructed (not *partially absorbed*) into the earth's atmosphere. Eliminate (C). Choice (D) takes proper account of the word *principally* by stating that the heat in the atmosphere comes from the sun and other sources, and that heat may be generated from non-solar sources. The correct answer is (D).

26. **B**   The question asks why the author uses a few particular words in this context. Use the given line reference to find the window. The conditional language here implies that many factors must be considered when performing the calculations mentioned in the window. Choice (A) overstates the confidence this language implies in the calculations, so this choice should be eliminated. Choice (B) is true, given the author's indication that the calculations will depend on mathematical formulas and constants in combination with some experimental observations. Choice (C) cannot be supported in the passage because it presumes the knowledge that the described calculations are setting out to find. Choice (D) identifies a harsh critique of earlier scientists where none is present in any part of the passage. Choice (D) can thus be eliminated. The correct answer is (B).

27. **A**   The question asks why the author notes the observations of ground temperature. Using the chronology of previous questions, look for the lead words *observations* and *ground temperature* in the last paragraph. They appear in the last part of the last sentence: *assuming a corresponding decrease*

of 0.6°C per 100 meters, we find its temperature to be 46°C lower than that of the ground, and thus the mean temperature of the ground equal to 15°C, as it is according to observations. Taken as a whole, the phrase *as it is according to observations* implies an agreement between the calculated data and the data observed by measurement. In this sense, the author cites the observations as a way to show the correctness of his calculations. Choice (A) captures the importance of the *observations*, so this answer should be kept. Choice (B) would undermine the importance of the mathematical calculations, when in fact the mention of *observations* is used to show the value of mathematical calculations. Eliminate (B). Choice (C) cites a contemporary theory of climate change, one that is not identified in the passage itself, so (C) should be eliminated. Choice (D) can be eliminated because it does not address the importance of the *observations* cited in the question. The correct answer is (A).

28. **B** The question asks for a combination of information from the table and passage. The relevant information in the passage is indicated by the data *1000 gram-calories per square centimeter for 24 hours.* This refers to the *Loss of Heat* columns in the chart, which are given in this unit. A *Loss of Heat* of 300 corresponds to a temperature of approximately −40°C. However, as the passage indicates, the figures given in the chart indicate the temperature at an elevation of *7600 meters.* Therefore, for the numbers given in the chart, *we find its temperature to be 46°C lower than that of the ground.* In other words, when the temperature on the chart is −40°C, the temperature on the ground must be approximately 6°C, or 46°C warmer, which corresponds with (B). Choices (A) and (D) pull the number directly from the chart but do not account for the information in the passage. Choice (C) confuses the negative signs. The correct answer is (B).

29. **B** The question asks whether the table supports the author's claim regarding the atmosphere's *heat store*: *the atmosphere acts as a heat store placed between the relatively warm ground and the cold space.* This information is then expanded upon with the detail that *the higher the [atmospheric] layer, the lower is its temperature relatively to that of the ground.* Since this layer of atmosphere is located between the hot earth and cold space and the earth temperature gets colder with higher elevation, the loss of heat will be less as colder earth temperatures come nearer to space temperatures. Despite this technical explanation, this question can be answered with aggressive POE, particularly by looking at the explanation rather than the "Yes" and "No" component of each answer. Choice (A) can be eliminated because it states that heat loss decreases at larger intervals at lower temperatures, which is not true. For each twenty-degree temperature interval, the heat-loss intervals shrink. In other words, whereas the heat loss at temperatures 100°C and 80°C goes down approximately 400, the heat loss at temperatures −100°C and −120°C goes down only 37. Choice (B) should be kept because it correctly establishes this relationship. Choices (C) and (D) can be eliminated because they cite incorrect relationships between temperature and loss of heat. The correct answer is (B).

30. **C** The question asks for a piece of information that will support the conclusion in the previous question. Because this is the second question in a paired set, it can be done in tandem with Q29. Choice (A) shows a widening gap between two heat-loss values, but it does not show the *smaller and smaller intervals* mentioned in (29B). Eliminate (A). Choice (B) shows large intervals in heat-loss values, which make it difficult to form any conclusion. Eliminate (B). Choice (C) shows adjacent heat-loss values that decrease at *smaller and smaller intervals*, so keep this choice. Choice (D) shows decreasing values, but these are random and cannot be used to support a conclusion. Eliminate (D). The correct answer is (C).

31. **D** The question asks whether the temperature of the atmosphere varies relative to the distance from the ground. The chart does show variations in temperature, but it does not show variations in height. Therefore, the answer cannot be gleaned from the table alone and must be more explic-

itly stated within the passage. Choice (C) does hypothesize that temperatures may be different at the ground and at certain heights, but it does not offer conclusive proof and thus should be eliminated. Choice (D) offers conclusive proof of the relationship: *we find its temperature to be 46°C lower than that of the ground*. Choices (A) and (B) can be eliminated because they do not discuss different distances from the earth. The correct answer is (D).

32. **B** The question asks about the main purpose of the passage. Because this is a general question, it should be done after all the specific questions. In a previous window, Douglass refers to his *early connection with the cause* as well as *having been called upon to do so by one whose voice in this Council we all gladly obey*. Now look for an answer choice that best fits these reasons. Choice (A) reflects a statement in paragraph 2 (*Men have very little business here as speakers, anyhow*), but does not fit the prediction. Choice (B) is consistent with the prediction. Choice (C) does not have support in the passage, which explicitly states that *our cause has passed beyond the period of arguing*. Choice (D) reflects a statement in paragraph 2 (*I say of her, as I say of the colored people, "Give her fair play, and hands off"*), but does not fit the prediction. The correct answer is (B).

33. **A** The question asks for the central claim of the passage. Because this is a general question, it should be done after all the specific questions. Choice (A) has support in paragraph 1 and several points of paragraph 2. Choice (B) contradicts the passage, which says that men *can neither speak for her, nor vote for her, nor act for her*. Choice (C) has support in the end of paragraph 3. Choice (D) slightly contradicts the passage, which indicates that the suffrage movement has become less obscure. It could be true that it should become even less obscure, but the passage doesn't say this, and so this cannot be the passage's central claim. Having eliminated (B) and (D), compare (A) and (C). Since (C) has less support, it is less likely to be the central claim. Eliminate (C). The correct answer is (A).

34. **D** The question asks why Douglass uses the word *cause* throughout the passage. To answer it, find each time the word *cause* appears and take note of what Douglass is doing in each case. The first time, in paragraph 2, Douglass explains why he is speaking at this convention, and refers to his *early connection to the cause*. The second time, also in paragraph 2, he refers to the history of *this woman suffrage cause*. The third time, in paragraph 3, he refers to the convention of women and uses the phrase *our cause*. Putting these ideas together, it is clear that Douglass uses the word *cause* to refer to the women's suffrage movement. Now look for an answer choice that best fits this prediction, and eliminate answer choices that are either false, or true for only one instance of *cause*. (Remember, the question asks how Douglass uses the word *throughout* the passage.) Choice (A) could be true, since it refers to his early connection, but this better fits the first two uses of the word *cause*. Choice (B) goes beyond the scope of the passage: Douglass is not explaining why the movement deserves support; he assumes that it does, and that it is already clear to most people in attendance that it does. Eliminate (B). Choice (C) does not fit any of the uses of the word *cause*. Eliminate (C). Choice (D) could be true, since in each of the three uses of the word *cause*, Douglass is referring to the suffrage movement. Compare (A) and (D). Choice (D) more directly supports all three instances of *cause*. The correct answer is (D).

35. **B** The question asks why *Douglass is hesitant to speak at the gathering*. Use lead words and the order of the questions to find the window. Q35 is the first specific question, and Q38 asks about line 29, so scan the beginning of the passage looking for statements about being hesitant to speak. In lines 8–14, Douglass says, *When I look around on this assembly, and see the many able and eloquent women, full of the subject, ready to speak, and who only need the opportunity to impress this audience with their views...I do not feel like taking up more than a very small space of your time and attention*. In lines 18–23 he says, *Men have very little business here as speakers...For this is an International Council, not of men, but of women, and woman should have all the say in it.*

Eliminate answer choices that don't match the passage. Choice (A) is a Right Words, Wrong Meaning trap answer: Douglass says, *I would not, even now, presume to speak, but for the circumstance of my early connection with the cause.* In other words, his *early connection* with the suffrage movement is what motivates him to speak, not what makes him hesitant. Eliminate (A). Keep (B) because it matches the passage. Choice (C) is a Right Words, Wrong Meaning trap answer: Douglass states that women can speak with more *skill* and *power* than men on the subject of woman suffrage, but he doesn't indicate that *he does not consider himself an eloquent and forceful speaker*. Eliminate (C). Choice (D) is another Right Words, Wrong Meaning trap answer: Douglass says that if men *come here at all they should take back benches and wrap themselves in silence*, but this is a rhetorical device to emphasize his point that women should be featured at this event. He doesn't literally mean that it is *improper to speak from the back benches*. Eliminate (D). The correct answer is (B).

36. **C** The question asks about men according to the passage. Because this is the first question in a paired set, it can be done in tandem with Q37. Consider the answers for Q37 first. In (37A), Douglass says that he doesn't want to take *more than a very small space of...time and attention*. While this could support (36B), it doesn't indicate what Douglass thinks about men in general. Eliminate (37A). Choice (37B) talks about how he ended up speaking at the gathering, which doesn't support any of the answers from Q36. Eliminate (37B). Choice (37C) says that *men have very little business here as speakers* and that they should *take back benches and wrap themselves in silence*. This supports men *primarily listening*, so connect it to (36C). Choice (37D) does not support any of the answers for Q36, so eliminate it. The only possible pair remaining is (36C) and (37C). The correct answers are (36C) and (37C).

37. **C** (See explanation above.)

38. **A** The question asks how the *demands of women* in line 29 are related to some kind of injuries. Use the given line reference to find the window. Douglass says that woman *knows and feels her wrongs as man cannot*, and *she also knows...what measures are needed to redress them*. Look for an answer choice that fits this prediction. Choice (A) paraphrases it, so keep it. Choice (B) can be eliminated because Douglass does not argue for men to speak about these injuries. Choice (C) can be eliminated because there is no evidence anywhere that the *world should support* injuries to women. Choice (D) may be true, but it doesn't fit the prediction. The correct answer is (A).

39. **B** The question is the best evidence question in a paired set. Because Q39 was a specific question, simply look at the lines used to answer Q39. Lines 32–34 were used to answer the previous question. The correct answer is (B).

40. **D** The question asks for the meaning of the word *cradle*, which the passage uses figuratively. Use the given line reference to find the window. *It was when this woman suffrage cause was in its cradle, when it was not big enough to go alone, when it had to be taken in the arms of its mother from Seneca Falls, N.Y., to Rochester, N.Y., for baptism.* Douglass is referring to the history of the movement, so the word *cradle* here means something like "its early years." Choices (A), (B), and (C) have nothing to do with this prediction; eliminate them. Choice (D) fits this prediction exactly. The correct answer is (D).

41. **A** The question asks what the *surprise* referred to in lines 58–74 serves to emphasize. Use the given line reference to find the window. Douglass says that people new to suffrage events *may be surprised that [speakers] do not argue the question* of whether their movement is valid. Look for an answer choice that fits this prediction. Choice (A) mirrors the prediction, so keep it. Choice (B) may be attractive because of the reference to *more arguments than assertions,* but the text does not explicitly say that the audience is male. Eliminate (B). Although the phrase *may not have*

expected might look good on its own, (C) as a whole clearly does not match the prediction. Eliminate (C) and (D) as well because the arguments weren't *unexpected*. It was the lack of arguments that was surprising. The correct answer is (A).

42. **C**   The question asks for some positive aspect of fracking in Passage 1. Because this is the first question in a paired set, it can be done in tandem with Q43. Consider the answers for Q43 first. The lines in (43A) mention that the natural gas from fracking can *accommodate the country's domestic demand for natural gas at current levels of consumption for more than a hundred years*. These lines match with (42C), which paraphrases that information. Choice (43B) details the process of fracking but lacks anything specifically positive, so eliminate it. Choice (43C) completes the description of how fracking extracts natural gas from the shale layer, but the lines have no match in Q42, so (43C) can be eliminated. Like (43C), (43D) fails to support Q42 and can be eliminated, leaving (42C) and (43A) as the only possible pair. The correct answers are (42C) and (43A).

43. **A**   (See explanation above.)

44. **D**   The question asks why the author mentions the number of gallons in discussing fracking. Use the given line reference to find the window. *As many as 25 fracture stages (per horizontal leg) may be involved in preparing a single site for production, each requiring injection of more than 400,000 gallons of water—a possible total of more than 10 million gallons before the well is fully operational.* Phrases like *as many as* and *more than* are there to draw attention to the size and scale of these numbers. Choice (A) can be eliminated because *inevitable* is too extreme and because it does not address the size of the fracking operation. Choice (B) can be eliminated because this passage discusses a single method, fracking, and not a *variety of ways*. Choice (C) can be eliminated because while water might be described as a *basic element*, there is no indication that *only a few* of these basic elements are at play in fracking. Choice (D) should be kept because it reflects the language of the prediction. The correct answer is (D).

45. **A**   The question asks why the author discusses the *aquifer* in the given lines. Use the given line reference to find the window. The passage states that *drillers developing a well must take exceptional care to minimize contact between the wellbore and the surrounding aquifer* and that *it is essential that monitoring be in place to ensure the continuing integrity of the seal isolating the well from the aquifer*. In both cases, the *aquifer* is mentioned as something that must be isolated and protected from the outflowing water used to frack. Choice (A) should be kept because it points to the *significant risk* that the aquifer could be contaminated. Choice (B) may address the concerns of those who worry about fracking, but it does not *dispute* those concerns, so (B) can be eliminated. Choice (C) can also be eliminated because the word *aquifer* does not appear before the final paragraph of Passage 1. Choice (D) can be eliminated because there is no indication that water contamination is a *new finding*. The correct answer is (A).

46. **B**   The question asks what the word *integrity* means in line 44. Go back to the text, find the word *integrity*, and mark it out. Carefully read the surrounding text to determine another word that would fit in the blank based on the context of the passage. Earlier sentences refer to the need to *minimize contact between the wellbore and the surrounding aquifer* and to *failures to isolate the drilling liquids*. The correct answer should therefore mean something like "solidness," or "the opposite of leakiness." Choice (A) does provide one definition of the word *integrity*, but that definition does not agree with the prediction based on the context above, so (A) can be eliminated. Choice (B) matches the prediction, so it should be kept. Choice (C) may be deceptive because this paragraph discusses water at such length, but the word *moisture* does not match the prediction and should be eliminated. Choice (D) provides another possible definition of the word *integrity*, but that definition does not match the context, so (D) can be eliminated. The correct answer is (B).

47. **D** The question asks for some aspect of Passage 2's main idea—something negative, as evidenced by the contrast in the question. Because this is a general question, it should be done after all the specific questions for Passage 2. The first paragraph describes fracking's usefulness, but the remaining two paragraphs discuss its risks. The last paragraph is vicious in its criticism of *Weak safeguards and inadequate oversight*. In short, the author of Passage 2 sees the potential value of fracking, but he does not consider it to be regulated in a way that protects local populations. Choice (A) does not address safety, only cost, so this answer can be eliminated. Choice (B) could be true, but it is not addressed in the passage, so it can be eliminated. Choice (C) is mostly right but slightly wrong because while the author of Passage 2 does believe that industry executives flout the rules, there is no indication that these executives believe *they can mine resources from any place they choose*. This is extreme language that is not supported by the passage. Eliminate (C). Choice (D) effectively paraphrases the evidence presented in the passage. The correct answer is (D).

48. **C** The question asks what the word *oversight* most nearly means as it is used in line 80. Go back to the text, find the word *oversight,* and cross it out. Carefully read the surrounding text to determine another word that would fit in the blank based on the context of the passage. The text says, *Weak safeguards and inadequate oversight have allowed oil and gas producers to run roughshod over communities across the country with their extraction and production activities for too long...Our state and federal leaders have failed to hold them to account, leaving the American people unprotected. Many companies don't play by the few rules that do exist.* Therefore, the word *oversight* could be replaced by a word like "laws" or "governing." Eliminate answer choices that don't match the meaning of the word in context. *Error* doesn't match "laws," so eliminate (A). *Planning* doesn't match "laws," so eliminate (B). Keep (C) because *regulation* matches "laws." An *omission* is something that is neglected or left out; it doesn't match "laws," so eliminate (D). Note that (A) and (D) are Could Be True trap answers based on another meaning of *oversight* that is not supported by the text. The correct answer is (C).

49. **B** The questions asks about the relationship between the two passages. Because this is a general question, it should be done after all the specific questions for both passages. Passage 1 gives an overview of the process of fracking and hints at some of its dangers. Passage 2 is primarily concerned with these dangers and is less admiring of fracking's ability to extract natural resources. Choice (A) can be eliminated because Passage 1's author is not blind to the dangers of fracking and his attitude could not be described as *optimistic confidence*. Choice (B) should be kept because it offers a reasonable paraphrase of the relationship between the two passages. Choice (C) can be eliminated because there is no indication that the author of Passage 1 would disapprove of any particular regulations. Choice (D) can also be eliminated because Passage 2 is less concerned with the process of fracking than is Passage 1. The correct answer is (B).

50. **C** The question asks how the author of Passage 2 might respond to the referenced lines in Passage 1, which discuss both the care that drillers must take to ensure that pollution does not occur and the risks associated with such pollution. Because this is the first question in a paired set, it can be done in tandem with Q51. Consider the answers for Q52 first. The lines in (51A) discuss the expansion of the mining industry. They have no connection to the answer choices in Q50, so (51A) can be eliminated. Choice (51B) discusses the proliferation of fracking. These lines match with (50A), which cites the mining industry's success and growth, but the pair fails to account for how critically the author of Passage 2 would respond. Eliminate (50A) and (51B). The lines for (51C) refer in a general way to increased industrial production, but they do not address the risks of drilling in particular. Choice (51C) can be eliminated because it does not match with any of the answers in Q50. Choice (51D) matches almost exactly with (50C), so these two answers should be connected. The correct answer is (C).

51. **D** (See explanation above.)

52. **C** The question asks for something that is *implicit* (or implied) in Passage 2 and *explicit* (or stated outright) in Passage 1. Consider each answer separately and use POE. Choice (A) can be eliminated because Passage 2 explicitly states that fracking causes air and water pollution, and Passage 1 is concerned only with water pollution. Choice (B) can be eliminated because Passage 2 mentions the *millions of gallons of water used in fracking operations* but doesn't give any indication that it could also be *billions*. Passage 2 also focuses on the effects of fracking rather than the process. Choice (C) should be kept because Passage 2 addresses the effects of fracking on drinking water but does not specifically mention animals, whereas Passage 1 states explicitly, *Serious problems have arisen...including cases where well water used for drinking became so contaminated that human and animal health was threatened.* Choice (D) can be eliminated because neither passage addresses the costs in setting up wells for drilling. The correct answer is (C).

Section 2: Writing and Language

1. **A** The number of words changes in the answer choices, so this question tests concision. Check the shortest answer first: (A) gives a precise meaning to the sentence, so keep it. Choices (B), (C), and (D) are repetitive because they all include both *variety* and a form of *different*, which mean the same thing in this context, so eliminate (B), (C), and (D). The correct answer is (A).

2. **B** The wording of the phrase changes in the answer choices, so this question tests consistency and precision. The answer choices mostly express the same idea, so look for the option that is most consistent in style and tone with the passage. The phrase *something elusive* in (C) is not precise, so eliminate (C). The phrases *the okay* and *the thumbs up* in (A) and (D) are too informal for the passage, so eliminate (A) and (D). Keep (B) because *broader public acceptance* gives a precise meaning to the sentence and is consistent with the formal tone of the passage. The correct answer is (B).

3. **C** Verbs change in the answer choices, so this question tests consistency of verbs. A verb must be consistent with its subject. The subject of the verb is *characteristic movements*, which is plural. To be consistent, the underlined verb must also be plural. Eliminate (A) and (B) because they are singular. Eliminate (D) because it makes the sentence incomplete. The correct answer is (C).

4. **B** Note the question! The question asks whether a sentence should be added, so it tests consistency. If the content of the new sentence is consistent with the ideas surrounding it, then it should be added. The paragraph discusses *hippotherapy* and how it *uses the movement of the horse as a way to treat a specific ailment*. The new sentence describes *therapeutic horseback riding* in comparison to *hippotherapy*. The previous sentence explains hippotherapy's *main difference from therapeutic horseback riding*, and the following sentence explains what one treatment is *more concerned with* as a comparison. The new sentence is consistent with the comparison between hippotherapy and therapeutic horseback riding, so it should be added. Eliminate (C) and (D). Eliminate (A) because the new sentence does not *make the argument* that one therapy is *more effective*. Choice (B) is consistent because both the paragraph and the new sentence are about *the difference between the two disciplines*. The correct answer is (B).

5. **B** Note the question! The question asks which choice *provides a supporting example that reinforces the main point of the sentence*, so it tests consistency. Eliminate answers that are inconsistent with the purpose stated in the question. The paragraph is about how *many fields use the basic tenets of hippotherapy*. The previous sentence explains that *physical therapists* use hippotherapy *to manage...*

disabilities. This sentence discusses how *occupational therapists* use hippotherapy. To be consistent with the previous sentence, this sentence needs to explain occupational therapists' purpose for using hippotherapy. Look for an answer choice that is consistent with the discussion of why people use hippotherapy. Eliminate (A) because *lack of laboratory support* is not consistent with the idea of why hippotherapy is used. Keep (B) because *to develop…skills* explains a reason for using hippotherapy. Eliminate (C) because what therapists *work on* is not consistent with the purpose for hippotherapy. Eliminate (D) because the *backgrounds* (of the therapists) is not consistent with their purpose for using hippotherapy. The correct answer is (B).

6. **D**   Verbs change in the answer choices, so this question tests consistency. A verb must be consistent with its subject and with the other verbs in the sentence. The subject of the sentence is *therapists*; all answer choices are consistent with the subject. The other verb in the sentence is *achieve*, which is in present tense. To be consistent, the underlined verb must also be in present tense. Eliminate (A), because *recommended* is past tense. Eliminate (B) and (C) because *recommending* is not consistent with *achieve*. Choice (D) appropriate uses the present tense *recommend*. The correct answer is (D).

7. **C**   Note the question! The question asks where sentence 5 should be placed, so it tests consistency of ideas. The sentence must be consistent with the ideas that come both before and after it. Sentence 5 says that *as the name suggests, these therapists are concerned mainly with…physical aspects*. The word *these* means that it must come after some mention of the therapists. Since the sentence refers to *the name* and *physical aspects*, *these therapists* must refer to *physical therapists*. *Physical therapists* are mentioned in sentence 2, so this sentence should be placed after sentence 2. The correct answer is (C).

8. **B**   Punctuation changes in the answer choices, so this question tests how to connect ideas with the appropriate punctuation. The first part of the sentence, *Because the discipline is relatively new*, is not an independent clause. The second part, *certified hippotherapists have stringent requirements for staying current on the research within the field*, is an independent clause. Eliminate (D) because a semicolon can only be used between two independent clauses. Eliminate (C) because a comma followed by the word *and* can also only be used between two independent clauses. Eliminate (A) because the word *certified* describes *hippotherapists*, so there should not be a comma between the two. The correct answer is (B).

9. **B**   The wording of a comparison changes in the answer choices, so this question tests idioms. The non-underlined portion contains the phrase *just as*. The correct form of this idiom is *just as… so too*. Eliminate (A), (C), and (D) because they do not contain the phrase *so too*. The correct answer is (B).

10. **D**   Prepositions change in the answer choices, so this question tests idioms. Look at the words before and after the underlined portion to determine the correct idiom. Eliminate (B) because *skeptics* are not *above doctors and researchers*. Eliminate (A) because the word *between* implies that *skeptics* are a separate group than *doctors and researchers*, which does not make the meaning of the sentence clear. Choice (C), *within*, implies that the *skeptics* are physically inside the *doctors and researchers*, which also doesn't make the meaning of the sentence clear. Eliminate (C). Choice (D), *among doctors and researchers*, provides a precise meaning to the sentence. The correct answer is (D).

11. **B**   Note the question! The question asks which choice *restates the main argument of the passage*, so it tests consistency of ideas. Determine the subject of the passage and find the answer that is consistent with that idea. The passage is about hippotherapy, a *relatively new* discipline, and its uses and benefits. Eliminate (A) because the passage's *main argument* is not that *becoming a*

hippotherapist is pretty hard. Choice (B) is consistent with the question and the main argument of the passage because the author explains how hippotherapy can *provide relief* in a new way, so keep (B). Eliminate (C) because the passage is about hippotherapy, not *bloodletting and radiation.* Eliminate (D) because *crazy discovery* is not consistent with the author's position in favor of hippotherapy. The correct answer is (B).

12. **B**   Vocabulary changes in the answer choices, so this question tests precision of word choice. Look for a word with a definition that is consistent with the other ideas in the sentence. The two options in the answer choices are *elicit* and *illicit.* The word *elicit* is a verb that means "to bring out." The word *illicit* is an adjective that means "unlawful." The underlined portion needs to be a verb, not an adjective, as the *responses* are not described as being "unlawful." Eliminate (C) and (D) because *illicit* is not a verb. The difference between (A) and (B) is the verb, so the question also tests consistency of verbs. A verb must be consistent with its subject. The subject of the sentence is *the way,* which is singular. To be consistent, the underlined verb must also be singular. Eliminate (A) because *elicit* is plural. The correct answer is (B).

13. **D**   The length of the phrase surrounding *Marco Polo* changes in the answer choices, so this question could test concision. Choice (B) is the shortest option, but it makes the first part of the sentence, *Marco Polo crossed the desert on his way to China,* an independent clause. The second part of the sentence, *he described the sound he heard as "a variety of musical instruments,"* is also an independent clause. A comma alone cannot be used between two independent clauses, so eliminate (B). Choices (A) and (C) also make the first part of the sentence an independent clause, so eliminate (A) and (C). In (D), the first part of the sentence, *As Marco Polo crossed the desert on his way to China,* is not an independent clause. A comma can be used to separate the two parts of the sentence in (D). The correct answer is (D).

14. **A**   Punctuation changes in the answer choices, so this question tests how to connect ideas with the appropriate punctuation. The first part of the sentence, *Researchers now understand that the curious sound that Polo heard, that odd confluence of pipe organ and cello,* is not an independent clause. The second part of the sentence, *probably resulted from the wind blowing across the sand dunes,* is also not an independent clause. Eliminate (B) because a semicolon can only be used between two independent clauses. Eliminate (C) and (D) because both a dash and a colon must come after an independent clause. Choice (A) correctly uses a comma after the phrase *that odd confluence of pipe organ and cello.* The correct answer is (A).

15. **A**   Punctuation and words change in the answer choices, so this question tests how to connect ideas with the appropriate punctuation. The first part of the sentence, *This variation creates an effect similar to that of a musical instrument,* is an independent clause. In (A) and (B), the second part of the sentence is *a tonal quality coming from the trapping and release of certain frequencies,* which is not an independent clause. Choice (A) correctly connects these ideas with a comma, so keep it. Eliminate (B) because a semicolon can only be used between two independent clauses. In (C), the second part of the sentence, *a tonal quality that is said to be coming from the trapping and release of certain frequencies,* is not an independent clause. This answer choice correctly connects these ideas with a comma. However, (C) uses more words than (A) but does not make the sentence more precise. Eliminate (C) because it is not as concise as (A). In (D), the second part of the sentence, *this quality comes from the trapping and release of certain frequencies,* is an independent clause. Two independent clauses must be connected by some type of punctuation other than a comma, so eliminate (D). The correct answer is (A).

16. **C**   Note the question! The question asks which choice *most smoothly and effectively introduces the writer's discussion of the sounds of the ocean,* so it tests consistency. Eliminate answers that are

inconsistent with the purpose stated in the question. There is also the option to DELETE; consider this choice carefully as it is often the correct answer. The second sentence in the paragraph says *this body of water*. Deleting the underlined sentence would make *this body of water* not refer back to anything, so the sentence should not be deleted. Eliminate (D). Choices (A), (B), and (C) all refer to the *"voice" of the ocean*, so choose the most concise and *smooth* option. Choice (C) is the most concise option and gives the sentence a precise meaning, so eliminate (A) and (B). The correct answer is (C).

17. **C** Note the question! The question asks whether a sentence should be added, so it tests consistency. If the new sentence is consistent with the ideas surrounding it, then it should be added. The paragraph discusses *sounds* in *the ocean* and mentions *deep-sea sound-recording*. The new sentence is about sound but focuses on the lack of sound in the ocean, which is inconsistent with the paragraph's point that there is sound in oceans. Thus, the sentence should not be added. Eliminate (A) and (B). Keep (C) because it accurately states that the sentence *undermines the argument*. Eliminate (D) because the sentence would not *be more appropriately placed at the beginning of the paragraph*. The correct answer is (C).

18. **A** Apostrophes change in the answer choices, so the question tests apostrophe usage. When used with a pronoun, an apostrophe indicates a contraction. *It's* is equal to "it is," which is not necessary in this sentence; eliminate (B). *They're* is equal to "they are," which is not necessary in this sentence; eliminate (D). Both (A) and (C) are possessive pronouns. A pronoun must be consistent in number with the noun it refers to. The underlined portion refers to *the sound of the ocean*, which is singular. In order to be consistent, the underlined pronoun must also be singular. Eliminate (C) because *their* is plural. The correct answer is (A).

19. **B** Words change in the answer choices, so this question tests precision. Look for a phrase that provides the most precise meaning. Choice (A) is not precise because it doesn't indicate what would be *weird* about the sounds. Eliminate (A). Keep (B) because it provides a precise meaning about what the *sound of the ocean* is unwilling to do. Eliminate (C) because the phrase *be normal* is not precise. Eliminate (D) because the words *play* and *others* are imprecise when discussing *the ocean*. The correct answer is (B).

20. **D** Note the question! The question asks which choice *offers the most accurate interpretation of the data in the chart*, so it tests consistency. Read the labels on the graph carefully, and choose an answer that is consistent with the information given in the graph. The solid line shows the number of whales migrating each day in 2012–13, while the dotted line shows the average number per day for the previous ten years. The lines generally follow the same pattern, so it is not true that there is a *lack of any consistency* or an *inverse relationship*; eliminate (A) and (B). The lines do not match exactly, so eliminate (C). The solid line is much higher at some points than the dotted line is, so (D) is consistent with the graph. The correct answer is (D).

21. **A** Note the question! The question asks which choice *offers an accurate interpretation of the data in the chart*, so it tests consistency. Read the labels on the graph carefully, and choose an answer that is consistent with the information given in the graph. Keep (A) because the number indicated by the solid line, which shows the number of whales migrating in 2012–13, is *more than twice* the number indicated by the dotted line, which shows the ten-year average, at a number of points in December, March, and April. Choice (A) is consistent with the graph. Eliminate (B) because the solid line is never *ten times* the dotted line. Eliminate (C) because the solid line is never *less than half* of the dotted line. Eliminate (D) because the graph does not show *the number of shorebirds migrating*. The correct answer is (A).

22. **A** Note the question! The question asks which choice offers *a conclusion that points toward the role that sound might play in future research into different ecosystems,* so it tests consistency. Eliminate answers that are inconsistent with the purpose stated in the question. Keep (A) because the phrase *may clarify* suggests *future research.* Eliminate (B) because it talks about the past, not the *future.* Eliminate (C) and (D) because they don't mention anything related to *future research,* so they are inconsistent with the purpose stated in the question. The correct answer is (A).

23. **D** Punctuation changes in the answer choices, so this question tests how to connect ideas with the appropriate punctuation. The first part of the sentence, *In the 1932 presidential election, up-and-comer Franklin D. Roosevelt won,* is an independent clause. The second part of the sentence, *in a landslide over the incumbent Herbert Hoover, who had done little to avert the crisis that would become known as the Great Depression,* is not an independent clause. Eliminate (B) because a semicolon can only be used between two independent clauses. Eliminate (A) and (C) because there is no reason to break up the phrase *won in a landslide.* The correct answer is (D).

24. **C** Transitions change in the answer choices, so this question tests consistency of ideas. There is also the option to DELETE; consider this choice carefully as it is often the correct answer. Deleting the transition makes the sentence *Hoover took office in 1929, the unemployment rate was a mere 3.2%.* This does not work because the sentence contains two independent clauses separated by only a comma. Eliminate (D) and evaluate the transitions. A transition must be consistent with the relationship between the ideas it connects. Eliminate (A) because the word *and* would indicate that this sentence is making a similar point to the one made in the previous sentence, which is not the case. Eliminate (B) because there is not a causal relationship between Hoover taking office and the low unemployment rate. *When* is consistent with the year *1929* in the non-underlined portion of the sentence. The correct answer is (C).

25. **A** Note the question! The question asks which choice *most effectively sets up the paragraph,* so it tests consistency of ideas. Determine the subject of the paragraph and find the answer that is consistent with that idea. The paragraph draws a contrast with *even so* and states that *no one was quite ready* for the period that was called *Roosevelt's "100 Days."* Look for an answer choice that is consistent with this idea and the contrasting transition *even so.* Keep (A) because the idea that Roosevelt had *a clear mandate* is a contrast with the fact that *no one was quite ready.* Eliminate (B) because it is too general a statement to introduce the paragraph. Eliminate (C) and (D) because they both refer to the previous paragraph but do not mention anything about *Roosevelt,* who is the focus of this paragraph. The correct answer is (A).

26. **C** Transitions change in the answer choices, so this question tests consistency of ideas. A transition must be consistent with the relationship between the ideas it connects. The first part of the sentence states that *he sent government workers to inspect each bank,* and the second part of the sentence says *determining which banks would be safe and sustainable to reopen.* The two ideas agree, and the second part of the sentence is an explanation of what the workers were doing. Eliminate (A) because *although* is a contrasting transition. Eliminate (B) because *for* cannot be used after a comma unless the sentence contains two independent clauses, and the second part of this sentence is not an independent clause. Keep (C) because *thereby* means "through this method," which fits with the meaning of the sentence. Eliminate (D) because *whereupon* means "at this point in time," which is not consistent with the relationship between the parts of the sentence. The correct answer is (C).

27. **B** Note the question! The question asks which choice *provides the most specific information on the areas that Roosevelt hoped to stimulate,* so it tests consistency. Eliminate answers that are inconsistent with the purpose stated in the question. Eliminate (A) because *economy* doesn't explain any

specific areas. Keep (B) because *industrial and agricultural sectors* are *specific areas.* Eliminate (C) because *whole thing* is not a *specific area.* Eliminate (D) because *money flowing and the economy* are not *specific areas.* The correct answer is (B).

28. **C** Prepositions change in the answer choices, so this question tests idioms. Look at the phrase before the preposition to determine the correct idiom. Use POE, and guess if there is more than one answer left. Eliminate (B) and (D) because *level on* and *level to* are not correct idioms. Eliminate (A) because while *level with* is an idiom, it means "be honest with," and *leveling with* is something that could be done to a person, not to a *demand*, so it is inconsistent with the meaning of the sentence. *Level off* means "stop increasing," so keep (C) because it is consistent with the meaning of the sentence. The correct answer is (C).

29. **C** Note the question! The question asks which choice *gives an additional supporting detail that emphasizes the importance of the TVA in Roosevelt's larger economic project*, so it tests consistency. Eliminate answers that are inconsistent with the purpose stated in the question. Eliminate (A) because the explanation of different states does not *emphasize the importance* of the TVA. Eliminate (B) because the fact that farming *is difficult* does not *emphasize the importance* of the TVA. Keep (C) because *electricity for millions of Americans* does *emphasize the importance* of the TVA. Eliminate (D) because the idea that the TVA was *impressive* does not provide a specific *detail* on the TVA's importance. The correct answer is (C).

30. **B** The length of the phrase changes in the answer choices, so this question tests concision. Start with the shortest option. Choice (B) makes the meaning of the sentence precise, so keep it. Choices (A), (C), and (D) all contain phrases that mean the same thing as *future*, so they are all redundant. Eliminate (A), (C), and (D). The correct answer is (B).

31. **A** Pronouns change in the answer choices, so this question tests consistency of pronouns. A pronoun must be consistent in number with the noun it refers to. The underlined pronoun refers to *Roosevelt's "New Deal,"* which is singular. To be consistent, the underlined portion must also be singular. Eliminate (C) because *they* is a plural pronoun. Eliminate (D) because *there* is a directional word that is not consistent with the meaning of the sentence. Apostrophes also change in the answer choices, so this question also tests apostrophe usage. *It's* is a contraction of *it is*, which works in this sentence, so keep (A). Eliminate (B) because it incorrectly uses the possessive pronoun *its*. The correct answer is (A).

32. **A** Apostrophes change in the answer choices, so this question tests apostrophe usage. When used with a noun, an apostrophe indicates possession. In this sentence, *day-to-day lives* belong to *people*, so an apostrophe is needed. Eliminate (C). Eliminate (D) because *peoples's* is not a word that occurs in English. Eliminate (B) because the word *people* is already plural, and choice (B) incorrectly suggests that the lives belong to *peoples* instead of *people*. The correct answer is (A).

33. **C** Note the question! The question asks which choice would *conclude the paragraph effectively without dismissing the debate described in this paragraph*, so it tests consistency. Eliminate answers that are inconsistent with the purpose stated in the question. The paragraph discusses *controversy* related to *Roosevelt's 100 Days* and says that there is *criticism*, but other people see the program as *a model*. Eliminate (A) because the phrase *unadulterated successes* contradicts the *debate* mentioned in the paragraph. Eliminate (B) because the phrase *obvious failures* is inconsistent with the idea of not *dismissing the debate*. Keep (C) because the phrase *in either case* acknowledges the *debate*. Eliminate (D) because stating that *both sides are obviously unfounded* dismisses the debate, which is the opposite of the question's goal.

34. **D**   The length of the phrase changes in the answer choices, so this question tests concision. Choice (D) is the shortest option, and it gives a precise meaning to the sentence, so keep (D). Choices (A), (B), and (C) all express similar ideas but are all less concise than (D). Eliminate (A), (B), and (C). The correct answer is (D).

35. **B**   Transitions change in the answer choices, so this question tests consistency of ideas. A transition must be consistent with the relationship between the ideas it connects. The first part of the sentence says that *The Japanese film industry had divided loyalties*, and the second part of the sentence mentions *its obvious debt to American cinema* and *international tensions*. These ideas agree, so eliminate (A) and (C) because they both contain contrasting transitions. Keep (B) because the second part of the sentence provides *evidence* for the claim that the industry had *divided loyalties*. Eliminate (D) because the second part of the sentence is not what *enabled* the *divided loyalties*. The correct answer is (B).

36. **D**   Note the question! The question asks whether a phrase should be deleted, so it tests consistency. If the content of the phrase is not consistent with the ideas surrounding it, then it should be deleted. The paragraph describes *divided loyalties* and *international tensions*, and the underlined portion explains how the movie used American conventions to lead to *propaganda* for the war. This idea is consistent with the rest of the paragraph, so the phrase should be kept. Eliminate (A) and (B). Eliminate (C) because *propaganda* is mentioned, but a *specific example* is not provided. Keep (D) because the phrase does *clarify an idea central to this paragraph*. The correct answer is (D).

37. **D**   Verbs change in the answer choices, so this question tests consistency of verbs. A verb must be consistent with its subject and with the other verbs in the sentence. The subject of the verb is *various family members*; all answer choices are consistent with the subject. This part of the sentence describes a movie, and the other verbs, *plays* and *is torn*, are in present tense. To be consistent, the underlined verb must also be in present tense. Eliminate (A), (B), and (C) because they are not present tense verbs. The correct answer is (D).

38. **A**   Transitions change in the answer choices, so this question tests consistency of ideas. A transition must be consistent with the relationship between the ideas it connects. The previous sentence explains what Hara could do well as an actor. This sentence explains how her beauty *kept screen audiences…engaged*. The ideas agree, so eliminate (C) and (D) because *nevertheless* and *meanwhile* are contrasting transitions. Keep (A) because *moreover* is used to add on to a previous idea, and the second sentence does add on to the first. Eliminate (B) because *in sum* is used for a conclusion, and this sentence is an additional point rather than a conclusion. The correct answer is (A).

39. **B**   The length of the phrase changes in the answer choices, so this question tests concision. Start with the shortest option. Choice (B) makes the meaning of the sentence precise, so keep it. Eliminate (A) and (D) because the whole passage is about *films*, so there is no need to repeat that idea. Eliminate (C) because the sentence already uses the word *particular*, which means the same thing as *unique to her*. The correct answer is (B).

40. **C**   Commas change in the answer choices, so this question tests comma usage. The sentence contains a list of four things: 1) *office*, 2) *kitchen*, 3) *living room*, and 4) *garden*. There should be a comma after each item in the list. Eliminate (A) because it does not have a comma after *office*. Eliminate (B) because it has a comma after *living* but *living room* is one idea. Keep (C) because it has a comma after each item in the list. Eliminate (D) because it does not have a comma after *kitchen*. The correct answer is (C).

41. **D** Vocabulary changes in the answer choices, so this question tests precision of word choice. Look for a word with a definition that is consistent with the other ideas in the sentence. The word *council* means "a committee of people advising," whereas *counsel* means "advice." The underlined portion should mean "advice" *of her friends and family* as there is no evidence that these people formed a "committee." Eliminate (A) and (B) because they do not mean "advice." Prepositions also change in the answer choices, so this question also tests idioms. Look at the word before the preposition to determine the correct idiom. Use POE, and guess if there is more than one answer left. The phrase *counsel with* means "to talk to someone," but the underlined portion refers to a noun—the advice of *her friends and family*. Eliminate (C). The phrase *counsel of* means "advice of," which is consistent with the meaning of the sentence. The correct answer is (D).

42. **D** Transitions change in the answer choices, so this question tests consistency of ideas. A transition must be consistent with the relationship between the ideas it connects. The first part of the sentence says *The conflict and plot are that simple*, and the second part of the sentence mentions *profound implications*, which is a contrast with something being simple. Eliminate (A), (B), and (C) because they are all same-direction transitions. Choice (D), *yet*, is a contrasting transition. The correct answer is (D).

43. **A** Pronouns change in the answer choices, so this question tests consistency of pronouns. A pronoun must be consistent in number with the noun it refers to. The underlined pronoun refers to *viewers*, which is plural. To be consistent, the underlined pronoun must also be plural. Eliminate (B) and (C) because they are not plural. Choice (A), *their*, is a plural pronoun, so keep it. Choice (D), *your*, could be plural, but it cannot be used to refer to *viewers*. Eliminate (D). The correct answer is (A).

44. **B** Note the question! The question asks where a sentence should be added, so it tests consistency of ideas. The sentence must be consistent with the ideas that come both before and after it. The phrase *others believe* suggests that this sentence must come after a previous belief was mentioned. Sentence 3 explains what *some believe*, so the new sentence should come after that. The correct answer is (B).

Section 3: Math (No Calculator)

1. **A** The question asks about the graph of an equation in the xy-plane. One option is to get the equation into $y = mx + b$ form, where m is the slope and b is the y-intercept. The equation is almost in standard form $Ax + By = C$, though, for which the slope is $-\dfrac{A}{B}$. This equation becomes $-2x - 5y = 10$ in standard form, so $A = -2$ and $B = -5$. The slope is $-\dfrac{-2}{-5} = -\dfrac{2}{5}$. Eliminate (B) and (D), which say that the slope is positive. The y-intercept in standard form is $\dfrac{C}{B}$, and C is 10. The y-intercept is $\dfrac{10}{-5} = -2$. Eliminate (C). The correct answer is (A).

2. **A** The question asks for the value of an expression. There is no obvious way to get the equations into the requested form of $x - y$, so solve for the variables individually. Multiply one equation by

a constant that will make a variable disappear when the equations are added together. Multiply the second equation by 3 to get $9x - 3y = 51$. Stack and add the two equations:

$$\begin{array}{r} x + 3y = 9 \\ + \ 9x - 3y = 51 \\ \hline 10x \qquad = 60 \end{array}$$

Divide both sides of the equation by 10 to get $x = 6$. Plug this value into the first equation to get $6 + 3y = 9$. Subtract 6 from both sides to get $3y = 3$. Divide both sides by 3 to get $y = 1$. The value of $x - y$ is $6 - 1 = 5$. The correct answer is (A).

3. **D**   The question asks for an equivalent form of an expression. There are variables in the answer choices, so plug in. Calculator use is not allowed, so make the math as simple as possible by plugging in $y = 1$. The expression becomes $6(1^3 + 1^2) - 2(1^3 + 1^2) = 6(1 + 1) - 2(1 + 1) = 6(2) - 2(2) = 12 - 4 = 8$. This is the target value; circle it. Now plug $y = 1$ into the answer choices to see which one matches the target value. Choice (A) becomes $4(1^3) = 4(1) = 4$. This does not match the target, so eliminate (A). Choice (B) becomes $4(1^5) = 4(1) = 4$. Eliminate (B). Choice (C) becomes $4(1^3) - 4(1^2) = 4(1) - 4(1) = 4 - 4 = 0$. Eliminate (C). Choice (D) becomes $4(1^3) + 4(1^2) = 4(1) + 4(1) = 4 + 4 = 8$. The correct answer is (D).

4. **C**   The question asks for the length of an arc of the circle. The larger arc $\overset{\frown}{PSR}$ is given and the smaller arc is asked for. The sum of the two arcs makes up the circumference, so try to get the circumference. The parts of a circle have a proportional relationship. In this circle, the degree measure of the central angle is a fraction of the entire 360 degrees, and the arc is the same fraction of the total circumference. Set up the proportion $\dfrac{\text{central angle}}{360} = \dfrac{\text{arc length}}{\text{circumference}}$. The arc given is $\overset{\frown}{PSR}$, but the angle given defines arc $\overset{\frown}{PQR}$, so find the degrees for angle PSR. There are 360° in a circle, so angle $PSR = 360 - 120 = 240°$. Now plug in the given information to get $\dfrac{240}{360} = \dfrac{8\pi}{\text{circumference}}$. Since calculator use is not allowed, reduce the fraction on the left to $\dfrac{2}{3}$ before cross-multiplying to get $2(\text{circumference}) = 24\pi$. Divide both sides of the equation by 2 to get circumference $= 12\pi$. Therefore, $\overset{\frown}{PQR} = 12\pi - 8\pi = 4\pi$. The correct answer is (C).

5. **A**   The question asks for the value of a in the equation. Start by ballparking. If 12 is divided by a value to become the much larger value of 300, it must have been divided into very small pieces. Thus, (A) is the only answer that will work. If this is not apparent, though, plug in the answers, since the question asks for a specific value and the answers contain numbers in increasing order. Begin by labeling the answers as "a" and start with (B), 25. The equation becomes $300 = \dfrac{12}{25}$, which will result in a fraction on the right side. Eliminate (B). The larger numbers in (C) and (D) will only make the fraction on the right side smaller, so eliminate (C) and (D). The correct answer is (A).

6. **B**   The question asks for the difference in two fares and gives an equation for finding the fares. There is no information given about the number of blocks Chris or Amy rode, but the relationship is given: Chris rode 3 more blocks than Amy. Therefore, this is a hidden plug in. For Chris, make $b = 5$. The equation for Chris becomes $F = 3(5) + 6 = 15 + 6 = \$21$. If Chris's ride was 5 blocks, Amy's was $5 - 3 = 2$ blocks. The equation for Amy becomes $F = 3(2) + 6 = 6 + 6 = \$12$. The question asks for the difference in the fares, which is $\$21 - \$12 = \$9$. The correct answer is (B).

7. **B** The question asks for an equation that models a specific situation. Translate the information in bite-sized pieces and eliminate after each piece. One piece of information says that the initial distance from the ground is 48 inches. This value has nothing to do with the time the marble has been rolling, so it should not be associated with t. Eliminate (C) and (D), which multiply 48 by t. Compare the remaining answer choices. The difference between (A) and (B) is the first term on the right side of the equation. The question does not mention the number 155, and there is no reason to divide it by 48, the initial distance. Eliminate (A). The correct answer is (B).

8. **A** The question asks for the number of solutions to a system of equations. Rather than giving the equations, the question shows a graph of the system in the xy-plane. The solution(s) will be any point(s) of intersection of the equations graphed. Be careful to only count points where all three graphs meet. There is a point of intersection of all three graphs around $(-2, 0)$. None of the other points marked on the figure have all three graphs going through them, so there is only one solution. The correct answer is (A).

9. **A** The question asks for the value of a constant in an equation if no value of x will satisfy it. Start by distributing on both sides to determine what is happening with the equation. This becomes $9x + 18 - 3x - 9 = 3cx + 15$. Combine like terms on the left to get $6x + 9 = 3cx + 15$. Because the constants on each side are different, what will cause there to be no solution is if the coefficients on the x terms are the same. For example, there is no solution to $x + 1 = x - 2$ because the x terms cancel out, leaving $1 = -2$. Therefore, $6x = 3cx$. Divide both sides of the equation by $3x$ to get $c = 2$. The correct answer is (A).

10. **C** The question asks for an equivalent form of an expression. There are variables in the answer choices, so plug in. Make $x = 2$. The expression becomes $\frac{1}{3(2) - 2} + 4 = \frac{1}{6 - 2} + 4 = \frac{1}{4} + 4$.

    To get a common denominator, multiply the 4 by $\frac{4}{4}$, so the expression becomes $\frac{1}{4} + 4\left(\frac{4}{4}\right) = \frac{1}{4} + \frac{16}{4} = \frac{17}{4}$. This is the target value; circle it. Now plug $x = 2$ into the answer choices to see which one matches the target value. Choice (A) becomes $\frac{3(2) + 2}{3(2) - 2} = \frac{6 + 2}{6 - 2} = \frac{8}{4} = 2$.

    This does not match the target, so eliminate (A). Choice (B) becomes $\frac{3(2) + 4}{3(2) - 2} = \frac{6 + 4}{6 - 2} = \frac{10}{4}$. Eliminate (B). Choice (C) becomes $\frac{12(2) - 7}{3(2) - 2} = \frac{24 - 7}{6 - 2} = \frac{17}{4}$. Keep (C) but check (D) just in case. Choice (D) has the same denominator as (C) but a different numerator, so it cannot also equal $\frac{17}{4}$. Eliminate (D). The correct answer is (C).

11. **B** The question asks for the value of ck in the provided equation. Although there are variables in the question, plugging in on this question would be difficult, given the lack of calculator use and all the different variables. Instead, see if there is a shortcut to isolate ck somewhere on the right side of the equation. When given a polynomial in factored form, it is often necessary to multiply the factors out to solve the question. Start by multiplying the terms in the two sets of parentheses together, being careful to get every combination. This becomes $2ky^3 + 6y^2 - 12y + cky^2 + 3cy - 6c$. There is a ck as the coefficient of the y^2 term, so collect the y^2 terms on the right side together. This will be $6y^2 + cky^2$, and it is equal to the $-10y^2$ term on the left side. Factor out

y^2 from the terms on the right to make the coefficient easier to see. It becomes $-10y^2 = (6 + ck)y^2$. Therefore, y^2 cancels, and $-10 = 6 + ck$. Subtract 6 from both sides of the equation to get $ck = -16$. The correct answer is (B).

12. **C** The question asks for the solution set of an equation. Since the question asks for a specific value or values and the answers contain numbers, plug in the answers. Begin by labeling the answers as "x" and start with a value that appears in several answer choices, such as $x = 3$. The equation becomes $\frac{2(3) + 4}{2} = \frac{15}{3}$, which simplifies to $\frac{6 + 4}{2} = 5$ or $\frac{10}{2} = 5$. This is true, so 3 is a solution. Eliminate (B), which does not include 3. Now try another value, such as $x = -5$. The equation becomes $\frac{2(-5) + 4}{2} = \frac{15}{-5}$, which simplifies to $\frac{-10 + 4}{2} = -3$ or $\frac{-6}{2} = -3$. This is true, so -5 is also a solution. Eliminate (A) and (D). The correct answer is (C).

13. **D** The question asks for the graph that represents the solution to the system of inequalities. Pick points that are shaded in some graphs but not in others and test them in the given inequalities. To be safe, avoid using points that are on either of the lines. Start with an easy point like (2, 2). The first inequality becomes $6(2) + 2 \geq -6$, which simplifies to $12 + 2 \geq -6$ or $14 \geq -6$. This is true, so try this point in the second inequality. This becomes $2 \leq 3(2) - 1$, which simplifies to $2 \leq 6 - 1$ or $2 \leq 5$. This is also true, so the point (2, 2) should be shaded in the graph of the solution. Eliminate (A), (B), and (C), which do not include this point. The correct answer is (D).

14. **D** The question asks for the solutions to an equation. Since the question asks for a specific value or values and the answers contain numbers, plug in the answers. Begin by labeling the answers as "x" and start with a value that appears in several answer choices, such as $x = 5$. The equation becomes $5 = \sqrt{30 - 5}$, which simplifies to $5 = \sqrt{25}$ or $5 = 5$. This is true, so eliminate (A), which says that there are no values that satisfy the equation, and eliminate (C), which does not include 5. Now try $x = -6$. The equation becomes $-6 = \sqrt{30 - (-6)}$, which simplifies to $-6 = \sqrt{36}$. Be careful: on the SAT, the result of a square root is only positive, so this is not true. The value of $x = -6$ is an extraneous solution, so eliminate (B). The correct answer is (D).

15. **B** The question asks for an equation that represents a graph. Pick a point that is on the graph and plug it into the answer choices to see which ones are true, keeping in mind that $g(x) = y$. The graph contains the point (6, 4), so plug $x = 6$ and $g(x) = 4$ into the answers. Choice (A) becomes $4 = -\frac{1}{2}(6 - 4)^2 - 6$, which simplifies to $4 = -\frac{1}{2}(2)^2 - 6$. This becomes $4 = -\frac{1}{2}(4) - 6$ or $4 = -2 - 6$. This is not true, so eliminate (A). Choice (B) is the same as (A) except that it adds 6 instead of subtracting it. This would make the simplified equation $4 = -\frac{1}{2}(4) + 6$, which becomes $4 = -2 + 6$. This is true, so keep (B), but check the remaining choices just in case. Choice (C) becomes $4 = -\frac{1}{3}(6 + 4)^2 + 6$ or $4 = -\frac{1}{3}(10)^2 + 6$. The value of 10^2 is 100, and this does not divide evenly by 3, so this answer will result in a fraction on the right side. Eliminate (C). Choice (D) becomes $4 = -(6 + 4)^2 + 6$ or $4 = -(10)^2 + 6$. This becomes $4 = -100 + 6$, so eliminate (D). The correct answer is (B).

16. **4** The question asks for the value of an expression. There are two possible approaches to this question. One is to solve for a, and then plug that value into the expression $4a - 12$. The other

approach is to notice that the given expression $2a - 6$ can be multiplied by 2 to get $4a - 12$. Therefore, multiply both sides of the original equation by 2 to get $2(2a - 6) = 2(2)$ or $4a - 12 = 4$. Using either approach, the correct answer is 4.

17. **500** The question asks for the volume of a right rectangular pyramid. Use the geometry basic approach. Start by drawing the figure and labeling it with the given information. The height of the pyramid is 15, and the base of the pyramid is 5 by 20. Now write out the formula for the area of a pyramid, which is given in the reference box at the start of each Math section. That formula is $V = \frac{1}{3}lwh$. Plug in the given values to get $V = \frac{1}{3}(5)(20)(15)$. To make the calculations easier without a calculator, first take $\frac{1}{3}$ of 15 to get 5. The formula becomes $V = (5)(20)(5) = 500$ cubic inches. The correct answer is 500.

18. **5** The question asks for the value of a function. In function notation, the number inside the parentheses is the x-value that goes into the function, and the value that comes out of the function is the y-value. At $x = 0$, the y-value is the y-intercept, so try to determine the equation of the k function. The question states that k is perpendicular to the graphed line for the h function. Perpendicular lines have slopes that are negative reciprocals. To find the slope of h, use the formula $slope = \frac{y_1 - y_2}{x_1 - x_2}$ and the points (0, 1) and (3, 0). The slope of h is $\frac{0 - 1}{3 - 0} = -\frac{1}{3}$, so the slope of k is 3. Plug this into the equation $y = mx + b$, where m is the slope and b is the y-intercept. The equation for k becomes $y = 3x + b$. The values of x and y represent any point on the line, so plug in the point (–1, 2) given in the question. The equation becomes $2 = 3(-1) + b$ or $2 = -3 + b$. Add 3 to both sides of the equation to get $5 = b$, which is the value of $k(0)$. The correct answer is 5.

19. **1** The question asks for the minimum value of function r, which is not shown on the graph. Use the graph of $p(x)$ and the relationship between functions p and r to find the answer. The minimum of a function is the smallest y-value of the function. On the given graph, the smallest y-value is at $y = 3$, which happens at three points on the graph.

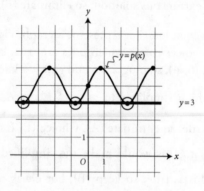

Plug this value for the minimum of $p(x)$ into the equation $r(x) = p(x) - 2$ to get $r(x) = 3 - 2$ or $r(x) = 1$. This is the minimum of function r. The correct answer is 1.

20. $\frac{5}{13}$, **.384, or .385** The question asks for the value of $\cos A$ in triangle ABC. Use the geometry basic approach. Start by drawing the figure and labeling it with the given information. Triangle ABC has a right angle at B, so that angle is 90°. It could look like this:

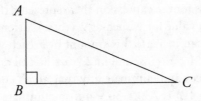

There are trigonometric expressions in the question, so write out SOHCAHTOA to remember the trig functions. The TOA part defines tangent as $\dfrac{opposite}{adjacent}$, so label the side opposite C as 5 and the side adjacent to C as 12.

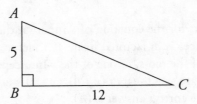

The question asks for the cosine of A, which is defined as $\dfrac{adjacent}{hypotenuse}$. Always set this up before figuring out the remaining side, as it is not always necessary to find it. Here, though, the side adjacent to A is known to be 5, but the hypotenuse is not known yet. The third side of a right triangle can be found by using the Pythagorean Theorem or in this case with the Pythagorean triple 5:12:13. Either way, $AC = 13$. Plug this into the cosine definition to get $\cos A = \dfrac{5}{13}$. This fraction can be gridded in, or it can be expressed as a decimal, which is .384 when lopped off or .385 when rounded. The correct answers are $\dfrac{5}{13}$, .384, or .385.

Section 4: Math (Calculator)

1. **D** The question asks for the function that expresses the cost of David's mobile data plan. Translate the information in the question into an expression one piece at a time. The monthly fee is $20.00 and the data usage fee is $2.50 per gigabyte. Start with the fee for data usage. The usage is $2.50 per gigabyte used, so to get the fee in a month in which David used g gigabytes, multiply g by 2.50 to get 2.50g. Eliminate any answer choice that doesn't include 2.50g: (A), (B), and (C). Thus, only (D) remains. To determine why (D) is correct, note that the word *and* translates to +, so add 20 to 2.50g to get 20 + 2.50g. The correct answer is (D).

2. **B** The question asks for the greatest change in annual profit between consecutive years. Go through each year and determine the change in each. From 2000 to 2001, there is a decrease of $50,000 – $40,000 = $10,000. From 2001 to 2002, there is an increase of $55,000 – $40,000 = $15,000. From 2002 to 2003, there is an increase of $60,000 – $55,000 = $5,000. From 2003 to 2004, there is an increase of $75,000 – $60,000 = $15,000. From 2004 to 2005, there is a decrease of $75,000 – $65,000 = $10,000. From 2005 to 2006, there is no change. From 2006 to 2007, there is an increase of $95,000 – $65,000 = $30,000. The greatest is $30,000, which is (B). Alternatively, Ballpark. Look at the graph and notice that the change from 2006 to 2007 appears to be the steepest, so this difference would have to be the answer. The correct answer is (B).

3. **A** The question asks for the expression that represents the number of pull-ups Jim will be able to do in y years. Pick a value for y, such as 2 years. Currently Jim can do 14 pull-ups in a minute. He believes that he can increase this amount by 7 each year. Therefore, he believes that in 1 year he can do $14 + 7 = 21$ pull-ups, and in 2 years he can do $21 + 7 = 28$ pull-ups. Now plug $y = 2$ into each of the choices and eliminate any that aren't equal to 28. Choice (A) is $7(2) + 14 = 28$, so keep (A). Choice (B) is $7(2) + 30 = 44$, so eliminate (B). Choice (C) is $14(2) + 7 = 35$, so eliminate (C). Choice (D) is $14 - 7(2) = 0$, so eliminate (D). The correct answer is (A).

4. **D** The question asks for the value of t in the equation for a given value of v. Plug in the given value to solve for the value of the other variable. If $v = 67$, the equation becomes $67 = 17 + 2.5t$. Subtract 17 from both sides to get $50 = 2.5t$. Divide both sides by 2.5 to get $t = 20$. The correct answer is (D).

5. **A** The question asks for the equation of a function that could possibly define h. Each of the equations in the choices is in factored form. If a factor of the equation of a function is in the form $(x - r)$, r is one of the roots, or one of the x-intercepts. Since the roots of this function are -4, 2, and 4, the roots are $(x - (-4))$ or $(x + 4)$, $(x - 2)$, and $(x - 4)$. The only equation with all of these factors is (A). The correct answer is (A).

6. **C** The question asks for the result when four times n is added to 14, so determine the value of n. Translate the first statement into an equation. The phrase *three times a number n* translates to $3n$. The phrase *is added to* translates to $+$. The word *is* translates to $=$. Therefore, the sentence translates to $3n + 9 = 3$. Solve this for n: subtract 9 from both sides to get $3n = -6$, then divide both sides by 3 to get $n = -2$. This is (A). However, the question does not ask for the value of n, so (A) is a trap answer. The question asks for *the result when 4 times n is added to 14*. The phrase *4 times n* translates to $4n$. The phrase *is added to 14* translates to $+ 14$. Therefore, *4 times n is added to 14* translates to $4n + 14$. Since $n = -2$, $4n + 14 = 4(-2) + 14 = -8 + 14 = 6$. The correct answer is (C).

7. **B** The question asks how many 16-ounce cups can be filled from a 64-gallon urn. First, convert the 64 gallons into ounces. Use a proportion: $\dfrac{1 \text{ gallon}}{128 \text{ ounces}} = \dfrac{64 \text{ gallons}}{x \text{ ounces}}$. Cross-multiply to get $x = (128)(64) = 8{,}192$. Now determine the number of 16-ounce cups that can be filled from an 8,192-ounce urn. Use another proportion: $\dfrac{1 \text{ cup}}{16 \text{ ounces}} = \dfrac{y \text{ cups}}{8{,}192 \text{ ounces}}$. Cross-multiply to get $16y = 8{,}192$. Divide both sides by 16 to get $y = 512$. The correct answer is (B).

8. **C** The question asks for the slope of a line that passes through the given points. Use the slope formula, $slope = \dfrac{y_2 - y_1}{x_2 - x_1}$. Let $\left(1, -\dfrac{1}{3}\right)$ be (x_1, y_1) and $\left(5, \dfrac{8}{3}\right)$ be (x_2, y_2). The slope is $\dfrac{\dfrac{8}{3} - \left(-\dfrac{1}{3}\right)}{5 - 1} = \dfrac{\dfrac{8}{3} + \dfrac{1}{3}}{4} = \dfrac{\dfrac{9}{3}}{4} = \dfrac{3}{4}$. The correct answer is (C).

9. **A** The question asks for the average number of fish per tank. For averages, use the formula $T = AN$, in which T is the total, A is the average, and N is the number of things. The *things* in this case are the tanks, of which there are 18. The *total* is the number of fish. To determine this, use the bar graph. There are 2 tanks with 2 fish each, so these 2 tanks have a total of $2 \times 2 = 4$ fish. There are 4 tanks with 3 fish, so these 4 tanks have a total of $4 \times 3 = 12$ fish. There are no tanks with 4 fish, so ignore that column. There are 3 tanks with 5 fish, so these 3 tanks

have a total of $3 \times 5 = 15$ fish. There are 5 tanks with 6 fish, so these 5 tanks have a total of $5 \times 6 = 30$ fish. There is 1 tank with 7 fish, so this 1 tank has a total of $1 \times 7 = 7$ fish. There are 3 tanks with 8 fish, so these 3 tanks have a total of $3 \times 8 = 24$ fish. Therefore, all the tanks have a total of $4 + 12 + 15 + 30 + 7 + 24 = 92$ fish. The average formula becomes $92 = A(18)$, so the average number of fish per tank is $A = 5.\overline{1}$. The question asks for the closest choice, which is 5. The correct answer is (A).

10. **A** The question asks for the design flaw in the survey. The survey was conducted to determine whether people in City C are more likely to work 9-to-5 office jobs than other jobs. The survey was conducted exclusively during the time in which people would be working at 9-to-5 office jobs. Therefore, people at this type of job would be less likely to answer the call. Choice (A) matches the prediction, so keep (A). Choice (B) is population size. Population size is not necessarily a design flaw, since the population size is not given. Eliminate (B). Choice (C) is sample size. If the sample size were significantly less than the population size, this fact could lead to unreliable results. However, since population size is not known, sample size cannot be determined to be a design flaw. Eliminate (C). Choice (D) refers to the fact that the telephone was used. Since the question does not mention telephone use by people with different types of jobs, there's no reason to believe that using a telephone to conduct the survey would make the results less reliable. Eliminate (D). The correct answer is (A).

11. **D** The question asks which graph could represent $y = p(x)$ if function p has exactly four roots. A *root* of a function is an x-value for which the y-value is 0. The y-value is 0 for all points on the x-axis, so p has to have exactly four x-intercepts (points where the graph intersects the x-axis). Go through each choice and determine the number of x-intercepts. Choices (A) and (C) have three x-intercepts, so eliminate these. Choice (B) has five intercepts. Since the question states that p has *exactly* four roots rather than *at least* four, eliminate (B) as well. Only (D) has exactly four x-intercepts. The correct answer is (D).

12. **A** The question asks for the possible total number of customers in the restaurant that morning. A percent of customers who ordered the brunch special is given, so take 85% of each of the answer choices. Eliminate any choice that doesn't result in a whole number of customers. Start with (A): 85% of 40 is $(0.85)(40) = 34$. Since this is a whole number, this could be the number of customers. The correct answer is (A).

13. **A** The question asks for the expression that gives v in terms of the other variables. Rather than do complex algebra, choose numbers for the variables. Since an equation is given with d isolated, pick numbers for the other variables, t, v, and h, and calculate d. Let $t = 2$, $v = 10$, and $h = 20$. In this case, $d = -8t^2 + vt + h = -8(2)^2 + (10)(2) + 20 = 8$. The question asks for the value of v, so the target answer is 10. Go through the choices and eliminate any answer that is not 10. Choice (A) is $v = \dfrac{8 - 20}{2} + 8(2) = 10$, so keep (A). Choice (B) is $v = \dfrac{8 + 20}{2} - 8(2) = -2$, so eliminate (B). Choice (C) is $v = \dfrac{8 - 20 + 8}{2} = -2$, so eliminate (C). Choice (D) is $v = 8 + 20 - 8(2) = 12$, so eliminate (D). The correct answer is (A).

14. **D** The question asks for what could be the median of 22 scores. The median of an even number of numbers is the average of the middle two when the numbers are listed in order. In this case, it is the average of the 11th and 12th score. Find the location of the 11th and 12th scores on the histogram. There is 1 score from 50 to 60. There are 4 scores from 60 to 70, so there are 5 scores from 50 to 70. There are 2 scores from 70 to 80, so there are 7 scores from 50 to 80. There are 11 scores from 80 to 90, so there are 18 scores from 50 to 90. Since the 11th and 12th scores were passed at the 80-to-90 interval, they must be in this interval. Therefore, the median must be within this interval, as well. The only choice within this interval is 84. The correct answer is (D).

15. **C**   The question asks for the percent of people in the survey who use public transit. *Percent* is defined as $\frac{\text{part}}{\text{whole}} \times 100$. The *part* is the total number of those surveyed who use public transit, which is 51, and the *whole* is the total number of those surveyed, which is 130. Therefore, the percent is $\frac{51}{130} \times 100 \approx 39$. The correct answer is (C).

16. **C**   The question asks for the best estimate of people in the metropolitan area who would use public transit and commute for at least one hour. The proportion of people who fit the requirements in the survey can be expected to be the same proportion of people who will fit the requirements in the general population. First, find the number of commuters surveyed who used public transit and had an average daily commute of at least 1 hour. According to the table, there were 29 people in this category. Since the total number of those surveyed is 130 and the total population is 13,000,000, set up the proportion $\frac{29}{130} = \frac{x}{13,000,000}$. Cross-multiply to get $130x = 377,000,000$. Divide both sides by 130 to get $x = 2,900,000$. The correct answer is (C).

17. **B**   The question asks how many times more likely it is for a commuter whose average daily commute is less than 1 hour not to take public transit than it is for a commuter whose average daily commute is at least 1 hour not to take public transit. The term *more likely* refers to probability, so determine the probability of each. Go to the table and find the number of commuters who commute less than 1 hour and do NOT commute using public transit. According to the table, there were 46 people in this category, and the total number of commuters who commute less than 1 hour is 68. Therefore, the probability is $\frac{46}{68}$. Now do the same for the probability that someone who commutes at least one hour does not take public transit. According to the table, the number under *Does Not Commute by Public Transit* is 33 and the number under *Total* is 62, so the probability is $\frac{33}{62}$. The question asks *how many times more likely* is the first probability than the second. Set up the equation $\frac{46}{68} = \frac{33}{62}x$. Divide both sides by $\frac{33}{62}$ to get $x \approx 1.27$. The correct answer is (B).

18. **C**   The question asks for the best conclusion from the study. The study takes a random sample of subjects without sleep disorders and gives half of them beverage *C*. The subjects who consume beverage *C* sleep less than the subjects who don't consume it. This would seem to indicate that beverage *C* caused people without sleep disorders to sleep less. Go through each of the choices. Choice (A) is incorrect because the study doesn't compare different caffeinated beverages. It only compares consuming beverage *C* to not consuming it. Choice (B) is incorrect, because the study does not indicate *substantial* loss in sleep. Furthermore, the sample only includes people without sleep disorders, so any conclusion must be restricted to this population. Choice (C) is similar to the prediction, so keep this choice. Choice (D), like (B), does not restrict the conclusion to people without sleep disorders. The correct answer is (C).

19. **C**   The question asks for the value of *n*, which is one of four numbers. First, eliminate any answers that don't make sense: since *n* is 40% larger than the sum of the other three numbers, *n* will have to be greater than half of 1,764. Eliminate (A) and (B). Try one of the remaining answers, such as (D). If *n* = 1,260, then the remaining three numbers would add up to 1,764 – 1,260 = 504. Since 1,260 is not 40% more than 504, eliminate (D) and choose (C). If desired, check (C): if *n* = 1,029, then the other three numbers add up to 735: 735 + 40% (735) = 735 + 294 = 1,029. The correct answer is (C).

20. **D** The question asks how much more the 11.5 m³ object weighed than was predicted by the line of best fit. This question can be solved by determining the actual weight of the object and the weight predicted by the line of best fit. However, finding the actual amounts is not necessary. Instead, simply find the difference between the two. Volume is represented by the horizontal axis, so find 11.5 on the horizontal axis. Trace straight up to the data point. From that point, trace the line downward, counting the number of intervals to the line of best fit. There are four intervals. Go to the vertical axis to determine the number of kilograms per interval. The labels are 5,000 kilograms apart, and there are 5 intervals between each label. Therefore, each interval is $\frac{5,000}{5} = 1,000$, so 4 intervals are 4,000 kg. The correct answer is (D).

21. **C** The question asks for the percent increase in total sales. Since the number of laptops and the number of tablets are different, don't just add the two percent increases. Thus, (D) is a trap answer. A percent change is always equal to the expression $\frac{\text{difference}}{\text{original}} \times 100$. The *original* is the total number of units sold last week, which is 90 + 210 = 300. To get the difference, get the increase in laptops and the increase in tablets separately and then add. There is a fifty percent increase in laptop sales, so the increase is $\frac{50}{100} \times 90 = 45$. There is a thirty percent increase in tablet sales, so the increase is $\frac{30}{100} \times 210 = 63$. Therefore, the total *difference* is 45 + 63 = 108, and the percent increase is $\frac{108}{300} \times 100 = 36\%$. The correct answer is (C).

22. **B** The question asks for the value of c, a constant that determines the values of x and y on the figure. According to the question, $\cos(x°) = \sin(y°)$. This can only be the case if the two angles are complementary, meaning the measures of the two angles have a sum of 90°. Use the values given for c in the answer choices to find the values of x and y, then see if $x + y = 90$. Start with (B). If $c = 15.5$, then $x = 3(15.5) - 23 = 23.5$ and $y = 66.5$, so $x + y = 23.5 + 66.5 = 90$. Thus, the two angles are complementary. The correct answer is (B).

23. **A** The question asks for the maximum value for $-3 \le x \le 6$. This is the domain sketched in the graph, so only worry about the points on the sketch. The value of the function is equal to each y-value. Although the values of the function appear to be increasing toward ∞, they do not actually go to ∞ within the points sketched, so eliminate (D). Since the question asks for the maximum value of the function, which is the maximum y-value, find the highest point on the graph. This appears on the far left. Draw a horizontal line to the y-axis to see that this line crosses the y-axis at 4. Therefore, the y-value at this point, or the maximum value of the function, is 4. The correct answer is (A).

24. **B** The question asks for the perimeter of the fence Matthew will need around his patch of grass. The question says that the width is 8 feet more than 4 times the length. Take this statement and translate it into an equation. Translate *the width* to w. Translate *is* to =. Translate *8 feet more than* to _____ + 8, leaving room on the left for what follows. Translate *4 times the length* to $4l$. Therefore, the statement translates to $w = 4l + 8$. The question also says that the area is 5,472. The area of a rectangle can be found using the formula $A = lw$. Substitute $A = 5,472$ and $w = 4l + 8$ to get $5,472 = l(4l + 8)$. Distribute the l to get $5,472 = 4l^2 + 8l$. Since this is a quadratic equation, get one side equal to 0 by subtracting 5,472 from both sides to get $0 = 4l^2 + 8l - 5,472$. This is a difficult quadratic to factor, so use the quadratic formula, $l = \frac{-b \pm \sqrt{b^2 - 4ac}}{2a}$, where $a = 4$, $b = 8$,

and $c = -5,472$. Substitute these values to get $l = \dfrac{-8 \pm \sqrt{8^2 - 4(4)(-5,472)}}{2(4)}$. Use a calculator to

get $8^2 - 4(4)(-5,472) = 87,616$ and that $l = \dfrac{-8 \pm \sqrt{87,616}}{2(4)}$. Take the square root of 87,616 to get

$l = \dfrac{-8 \pm 296}{2(4)} = \dfrac{-8 \pm 296}{8}$. Since length can only be positive, don't take the negative into account

and $l = \dfrac{-8 \pm 296}{8}$ becomes $l = \dfrac{-8 + 296}{8} = \dfrac{288}{8} = 36$. If $l = 36$, then $w = 4l + 8 = 4(36) + 8 = 152$.

To find the perimeter, use $P = 2l + 2w = 2(36) + 2(152) = 376$. The correct answer is (B).

25. **D** The question asks for the value of c, a coordinate in two points on a line. The line intersects the origin as well as the points $(c, 3)$ and $(27, c)$. Questions about lines in the xy-plane often involve slope, so determine the slope of this line. Any two points can be used to find the equation of a line (including the slope). Note that since the line intersects the origin, it intersects point $(0, 0)$ as well as the other two points. Use points $(0, 0)$ and $(c, 3)$ to calculate the slope: $\dfrac{y_2 - y_1}{x_2 - x_1} = \dfrac{3 - 0}{c - 0} = \dfrac{3}{c}$. The slope can also be determined using points $(0, 0)$ and $(27, c)$: $\dfrac{c - 0}{27 - 0} = \dfrac{c}{27}$. Since these two slopes must be equal, $\dfrac{3}{c} = \dfrac{c}{27}$. Cross-multiply to get $c^2 = 81$. Take the square root of both sides to get $c = \pm 9$. Only 9 is a choice. Therefore, the correct answer is (D).

26. **B** The question asks for the length of the segment $\overline{XO}$. Since $\overline{FG}$ is a chord that includes the center, it is a diameter. Therefore, arc FXG is a semicircle. Since the length of the semicircular arc is 14π, the circumference of the circle is $14\pi \times 2 = 28\pi$. The formula for circumference is $C = 2\pi r$, so $28\pi = 2\pi r$. Divide both sides by 2π to get $r = 14$. Since $\overline{XO}$ is a radius, the length is 14. The correct answer is (B).

27. **B** The question asks for an inequality that must be true, so try out a few different values for p and q. Make sure that all values of p and q satisfy the inequality $-|p| < q < |p|$. Let $p = 4$ and $q = 2$. Go through each statement and eliminate any statement that is false. Statement (I) is $4 > 0$, which is true, so keep (I). Statement (II) is $|4| > -2$, which is true, so keep (II). Statement (III) is $4 > |2|$, which is true, so keep (III). Try other values that might change the results. Since the question involves absolute values, try negative numbers. Let $p = -4$ and $q = -2$. In this case, statement (I) is $-4 > 0$, which is false, so cross out (I). Eliminate (A) and (D), since they include statement (I). Since both remaining choices include (II), it must be true, and no more testing of (II) is necessary. Test (III) using the same values of $p = -4$ and $q = -2$: $-4 > |-2|$. This is false, so cross out (III), and eliminate (C). The correct answer is (B).

28. **B** The question asks for a reasonable estimate for the number of blue jelly beans in the entire container. The number of blue jelly beans is given for each of ten regions. Determine the total number of regions in the container. The container has a base of 10 feet by 10 feet, so the area of the base of the entire container is $A = s^2 = (10)^2 = 100$. Each region has a base of 1 foot by 1 foot, so the area of the base of each region is $A = s^2 = (1)^2 = 1$. To get the number of regions, divide the area of the base of the container by the area of the base of each region to get $\dfrac{100}{1} = 100$. One way to get an estimate of the number of blue jelly beans in the entire container would be to find the average number of blue

jelly beans in the counted regions and multiply that number by 100. The question asks for an approximation, though, and the answer choices are spread apart, so Ballpark. All of the numbers in the table are around 25. Therefore, 25 is a reasonable estimate for the average number of blue jelly beans, and the total number of jelly beans should be about 25 × 100 = 2,500. The correct answer is (B).

29.   **C**   The question asks for the probability that a randomly selected ice cream was vanilla based on an incomplete table, so find a way to complete the table. The question states that there are four times as many vanilla ice creams sold as vanilla frozen yogurts. Let x be the number of vanilla frozen yogurts sold; therefore, $4x$ is the number of vanilla ice creams sold. The question also says that there are six times as many chocolate ice creams sold as chocolate frozen yogurts, so let y be the number of chocolate frozen yogurts sold and $6y$ be the number of chocolate ice creams sold. Since there are a total of 32 frozen yogurts sold, $x + y = 32$. Since there are a total of 152 ice creams sold, $4x + 6y = 152$. Since there are two equations with two variables, it is possible to solve for the variables. Stack and add the two equations, trying to eliminate the chocolates to solve for the vanillas. Multiply both sides of the first equation by −6 to get $-6x - 6y = -192$, then stack and add the equations like this:

$$4x + 6y = \ \ \ 152$$
$$\underline{-6x - 6y = -192}$$
$$-2x \ \ \ \ \ \ \ = -40$$

Divide both sides by −2 to get $x = 20$. The probability that the ice cream was vanilla can be calculated by dividing the number of vanilla ice creams sold ($4x$) by the total number of ice creams sold (152). Since $x = 20$, the number of vanilla ice creams sold is $4x = 4(20) = 80$. The probability is $\frac{80}{152} \approx 0.526$. The correct answer is (C).

30.   **D**   The question asks for the sectors that contain all of the solutions to a system of inequalities. To graph an inequality, start by graphing the equation. If the inequality sign is ≥, draw the equation as a solid line and shade above. If the inequality sign is ≤, draw the equation as a solid line and shade below. If the sign is > or <, use the same rule as ≥ or ≤, respectively, but use a dashed line instead of a solid line. Use the inequalities given. Start with $y ≥ x$. Since the inequality sign is ≥ rather than >, the graph is the one with the solid line. Since the inequality sign is ≥, shade the solution above the line. Therefore, since only Sectors W and X are above the solid line, eliminate any choice that includes Y and Z. Eliminate (A) and (B). Now look at the inequality $3y < 2x - 3$. Divide both sides by 3 to get $y < \frac{2}{3}x - 1$. Since the inequality sign is <, the solution is below the dashed line. Since Sector W is above the dashed line, eliminate (C). The correct answer is (D).

31.   **5 or 6**   The question asks for one possible value of h, the number of hot dogs Martina buys. Martina spends between $20 and $25, inclusive, and she buys one hamburger at a cost of $5. This would leave her at least $20 − $5 = $15 and at most $25 − $5 = $20 for hot dogs. In the first case, $15 total divided by $3 per hot dog would get her 5 hot dogs, so 5 is one possible value for h. If she spent up to $20 on hot dogs, she could get $20 divided by $3 per hot dog for 6.67 hot dogs. She can only buy whole hot dogs, so 6 is another possible value of h. Therefore, the two possible correct answers are 5 and 6.

32.   **19.4**   The question asks for the mean, or average, number of states of the nations listed on the table. For averages, use the formula $T = AN$, in which T is the total, A is the average, and N is the number of things. To get the total, add the number of states for each nation. The total is 6 + 9 + 26 + 16 + 29 + 13 + 31 + 4 + 36 + 2 + 10 + 17 + 50 + 23 = 272. There are 14 nations, so that is the number of things.

The formula becomes $272 = A(14)$, so $A \approx 19.4285714$. Rounded to the nearest tenth, the correct answer is 19.4.

33. **10** The question asks for the value of k given the equation of a function and a point on the graph of the function. Plug the point into the equation. Substitute $x = -2$ and $y = g(x) = 6$ to get $6 = 2(-2)^2 + k(-2) + 18$. Simplify the right side to get $6 = 26 - 2k$. Subtract 26 from both sides to get $-20 = -2k$. Divide both sides by -2 to get $10 = k$. The correct answer is 10.

34. **11** The question asks how many rooms will be assigned three students. Consider the possibility that all rooms have three students. How many leftover students would there be? If 26 rooms are assigned three students, then there are $26 \times 3 = 78$ students. However, the question says that there are 108 students, so there are $108 - 78 = 30$ left. These leftover students have to be assigned to five-student rooms. Since each room already has three students, to make five-student rooms, pair the remaining students and add each pair to one of the three-student rooms. Since there are 30 leftover students, they make 15 pairs, so 15 rooms of three students become five-student rooms. Since there are a total of 26 rooms, there are $26 - 15 = 11$ three-student rooms. The correct answer is 11.

35. $\dfrac{7}{12}$ The question asks what fraction Town A's 1970 population was of Town A's 2000 population. To determine the population in 1970, find 1970 on the horizontal axis, trace straight up to the curve, then straight across to the vertical axis. It hits the vertical axis on the only line between 30 and 40, so the population in 1970 was 35,000. (Note that the vertical axis label indicates that the population is in thousands.) To determine the population in 2000, find 2000 on the horizontal axis, trace straight up to the curve, then straight across to the vertical axis. It hits the vertical axis at 60, so the population in 2000 was 60,000. Therefore, the fraction is $\dfrac{35,000}{60,000} = \dfrac{35}{60} = \dfrac{7}{12}$. This is the correct answer.

36. **4** The question asks for the diameter of the base of a cylinder with a volume of 64π cubic centimeters. The formula for volume of a cylinder is $V = \pi r^2 h$. Plug in $V = 64\pi$ and $h = 16$, as indicated by the figure, to get $64\pi = \pi r^2(16)$. Divide both sides by 16π to get $4 = r^2$. Take the square root of both sides to get $2 = r$. Since the diameter is twice the radius, $d = 2r = 2(2) = 4$. This is the correct answer.

37. **321** This question asks for the angular position at which the carousel will change direction. Angular position is the first equation and represented by θ. Write down known variables and solve. When the carousel changes direction, the angular velocity is 0. Use the first equation, $\omega^2 = \omega_0^2 + 2\alpha\theta$. Plug in $\omega = 0$, $\omega_0 = 90$, and $\alpha = -12.6$ to get $0 = 90^2 + 2(-12.6)\theta$. Simplify the right side to get $0 = 8,100 - 25.2\theta$. Add 25.2θ to both sides to get $25.2\theta = 8,100$. Divide both sides to get $\theta = 321.4286$. Rounded to the nearest degree, the correct answer is 321.

38. **7** The question asks for the time it will take the carousel to completely stop before changing direction. Write down known variables, then choose the equation that gives only time as the unknown. This is the second equation. When the carousel changes direction, the angular velocity is 0. Use the second equation, $\omega = \omega_0 + \alpha t$. Plug in $\omega = 0$, $\omega_0 = 90$, and $\alpha = -12.6$ to get $0 = 90 + (-12.6)t$. Simplify the right side to get $0 = 90 - 12.6t$. Add $12.6t$ to both sides to get $12.6t = 90$. Divide both sides by 12.6 to get $t = 7.1429$. Rounded to the nearest second, the correct answer is 7.

Chapter 13
Practice Test 6

Reading Test

65 MINUTES, 52 QUESTIONS

Turn to Section 1 of your answer sheet to answer the questions in this section.

Questions 1–10 are based on the following passage.

The following passage is from Charlotte Brontë, *Shirley*, originally published in 1849. Robert Moore is a mill owner and Reverend Helstone is the local parson.

Cheerfulness, it would appear, is a matter which depends fully as much on the state of things within as on the state of things without and around us. I
Line make this trite remark, because I happen to know
5 that Messrs. Helstone and Moore trotted forth from the mill-yard gates, at the head of their very small company, in the best possible spirits. When a ray from a lantern (the three pedestrians of the party carried each one) fell on Mr. Moore's face, you could
10 see an unusual, because a lively, spark dancing in his eyes, and a new-found vivacity mantling on his dark physiognomy; and when the rector's visage was illuminated, his hard features were revealed all agrin and ashine with glee. Yet a drizzling night, a somewhat
15 perilous expedition, you would think were not circumstances calculated to enliven those exposed to the wet and engaged in the adventure. If any member or members of the crew who had been at work on Stilbro' Moor had caught a view of this party, they
20 would have had great pleasure in shooting either of the leaders from behind a wall: and the leaders knew this; and the fact is, being both men of steely nerves and steady-beating hearts, were elate with the knowledge.
I am aware, reader, and you need not remind me,
25 that it is a dreadful thing for a parson to be warlike; I am aware that he should be a man of peace. I have
some faint outline of an idea of what a clergyman's mission is amongst mankind, and I remember distinctly whose servant he is, whose message he
30 delivers, whose example he should follow; yet, with all this, if you are a parson-hater, you need not expect me to go along with you every step of your dismal, downward-tending, unchristian road; you need not expect me to join in your deep anathemas, at once so
35 narrow and so sweeping, in your poisonous rancour, so intense and so absurd, against "the cloth;" to lift up my eyes and hands with a Supplehough, or to inflate my lungs with a Barraclough, in horror and denunciation of the diabolical rector of Briarfield.
40 He was not diabolical at all. The evil simply was— he had missed his vocation. He should have been a soldier, and circumstances had made him a priest. For the rest, he was a conscientious, hard-headed, hard-handed, brave, stern, implacable, faithful little man; a
45 man almost without sympathy, ungentle, prejudiced, and rigid, but a man true to principle, honourable, sagacious, and sincere. It seems to me, reader, that you cannot always cut out men to fit their profession, and that you ought not to curse them because their
50 profession sometimes hangs on them ungracefully. Nor will I curse Helstone, clerical Cossack as he was. Yet he was cursed, and by many of his own parishioners, as by others he was adored—which is the frequent fate of men who show partiality in friendship and bitterness
55 in enmity, who are equally attached to principles and adherent to prejudices.

CONTINUE ▶

Helstone and Moore being both in excellent spirits, and united for the present in one cause, you would expect that, as they rode side by side, they would
60 converse amicably. Oh no! These two men, of hard, bilious natures both, rarely came into contact but they chafed each other's moods. Their frequent bone of contention was the war. Helstone was a high Tory (there were Tories in those days), and Moore was a
65 bitter Whig—a Whig, at least, as far as opposition to the war-party was concerned, that being the question which affected his own interest; and only on that question did he profess any British politics at all. He liked to infuriate Helstone by declaring his belief in the
70 invincibility of Bonaparte, by taunting England and Europe with the impotence of their efforts to withstand him, and by coolly advancing the opinion that it was as well to yield to him soon as late, since he must in the end crush every antagonist, and reign supreme.

1

Which choice best summarizes the passage?

A) A character becomes increasingly hostile as he travels with his fellow associate.

B) A character describes his reasons for disliking another character.

C) Two characters in the same profession become increasingly competitive.

D) Two characters traveling together eagerly await confrontation.

2

The main purpose of the opening sentence of the passage is to

A) show the contrast between the clergymen's cheerfulness and the narrator's gloom.

B) provide an allegorical representation of the clergymen's journey.

C) issue a general statement that helps to clarify the characters' emotional states.

D) characterize the narrator's perspective on the characters' violent intentions.

3

During the course of the second paragraph, the narrator's focus shifts from

A) assessment of the reader's sentiment to the desire to chastise the clergymen.

B) acknowledgment that clergymen should be peaceful to admonition for anti-clergy prejudices.

C) reflection on the clergymen's behaviors to identification of their manners and appearance.

D) generalization about peaceful men to the details of two particular clergymen.

4

The references to "rancour" and "denunciation" at the end of the second paragraph mainly have which effect?

A) They reflect the narrator's fear of clergymen.

B) They reveal the reader's empathetic understanding of clergymen.

C) They illustrate the narrator's sense of dismay at clergymen.

D) They capture the reader's potential sense of disapproval of clergymen.

5

The passage indicates that Moore's behavior is mainly characterized by

A) attitudes that do not align with his profession.

B) indignation at his travel partner's political views.

C) a willingness to engage in confrontation.

D) impatience with his travel partner's apparent superiority.

CONTINUE ➡

6

The passage indicates that while the narrator acknowledges a certain evil in the third paragraph, Helstone is actually a

A) sympathetic clergyman.

B) harmless soldier.

C) righteous citizen.

D) ruthless warmonger.

7

Which choice provides the best evidence for the answer to the previous question?

A) Lines 7–14 ("When . . . glee")

B) Lines 24–26 ("I am . . . peace")

C) Lines 42–47 ("For the . . . sincere")

D) Lines 51–56 ("Yet he . . . prejudices")

8

At the end of the third paragraph, the comparison of Helstone to a Cossack mainly has the effect of

A) illustrating his nature as soldier-like.

B) suggesting the likelihood of an altercation.

C) contrasting the natures of the two men.

D) conveying the belligerence of a course of action.

9

The passage indicates that, despite their excellent spirits, the men sometimes found each other's company to be

A) intolerable.

B) mundane.

C) vexing.

D) comforting.

10

Which choice provides the best evidence for the answer to the previous question?

A) Lines 5–7 ("Helstone . . . spirits")

B) Lines 21–23 ("and the . . . knowledge")

C) Lines 60–62 ("These . . . moods")

D) Lines 63–65 ("Helstone . . . Whig")

CONTINUE ➡

Questions 11–21 are based on the following passage and supplementary material.

This passage is excerpted from John W. Murphy and John T. Pardeck, "The Current Political World-View, Education and Alienation," originally published in 1991.

In American society everything is a commodity and education is no exception. Of course, this means that every aspect of life is assumed to have a cash value
Line and can be purchased for the right price. Also, every
5 person is a consumer, who enters the marketplace searching for a bargain. Although this scenario may be appropriate for describing the sale of shoes, when education is approached as a commodity the learning process may be seriously compromised.
10   Nonetheless, most students view education to be a product they are buying. Like good customers, students expect their education to meet their needs and assume a form they find palatable. Accordingly, students demand to have a significant amount of
15 control over their education, so as to guarantee the most favorable outcome possible. On the other hand, administrators must offer a competitive product, or revenues will decrease. Yet is the image of a buyer confronting a seller appropriate to describe how
20 students should relate to their school? The claim at this juncture is that education should not be exchanged in a manner similar to other products. Indeed, the worth of education is depreciated by this demarche.
In what ways do students participate in their
25 education? Usually their desires are voiced in the form of teacher evaluations. What is mostly revealed by this process is that students want, and demand, to be entertained. Like a competent sales representative, a teacher must be attractive, witty and capable of gaining
30 and retaining the attention of students. Additionally, material must not be dull or require much effort, or students will quickly become aggravated. For as every astute businessman knows, customers do not want to be hassled. Securing a favorable evaluation, therefore,
35 requires that a teacher adopt the demeanor of the television personalities who are invoked constantly to sell products to students.
Also similar to wise consumers, students strive to make the best deal possible. Translated into economic
40 terms, this means that the greatest rewards should be gained through the least amount of effort. Hence preparing students to take exams, organizing both their work and leisure time and summarizing their

reading assignments have become very profitable
45 businesses. Entrepreneurs who provide these and other services are well known to students. On the other hand, cheating has become rampant. Consistent with the ethos of consumerism, achieving some sort of advantage is considered to be essential to
50 beating the competition. Unfortunately the view has been conveyed that only through a series of dubious maneuvers can success be attained. In this climate, why should the message that becoming educated is hard work find a receptive audience?
55   From an administrative perspective, the curriculum offered by a school must be competitive. Creating an enticing array of courses is considered to be indispensable to attracting students and keeping enrollment figures high. Hence capitalizing on fads
60 has become normative, as witnessed by the recent proliferation of degrees and courses with captivating titles. In fact, many schools hire high paid advertising consultants to develop promotional material and discover untapped markets.
65   But education is trivialized when it is treated as a commodity. Content, in short, is replaced by form, for flash and glitter sell products. Difficult subjects are avoided, while the term relevant is reserved to describe the trendy courses that administrators have
70 begun to promote. Clearly the integrity of education is jeopardized when educational policies are dictated by the vagaries of the marketplace and ephemeral imagery is used to describe profound ideas that can be understood only through dedicated study.

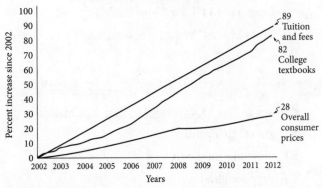

Estimated Increases in New College Textbook Prices, College Tuition and Fees, and Overall Consumer Price Inflation, 2002–2012

Excerpted from the Government Accountability Office report to Congressional Committees from June 2013.

CONTINUE ➡

11

The main purpose of the passage is to

A) advocate for the marketing of education to students.

B) argue a position on a decidedly complex topic.

C) weigh the merits of educational products in the marketplace.

D) evaluate statistics about treating education as a commodity.

12

In the passage, the author makes which concession to the view that every person is a consumer in the marketplace of life?

A) The implied contract which exists between buyer and seller has educational value.

B) It may be valid when one is discussing the sale of some types of goods.

C) Students and administrators benefit from negotiating over the price of higher education.

D) A person engages with all aspects of a product when he or she assigns it monetary value.

13

Which choice provides the best evidence for the answer to the previous question?

A) Lines 2–4 ("Of course . . . price")

B) Lines 6–9 ("Although . . . compromised")

C) Lines 11–13 ("Like . . . palatable")

D) Lines 26–28 ("What . . . entertained")

14

As used in line 13, "assume" most nearly means

A) guess intelligently.

B) pretend grudgingly.

C) suppose blindly.

D) take on readily.

15

The main purpose of the 4th paragraph (lines 38–54) is to

A) concede the logic of an attitude with which the author disagrees.

B) demonstrate that cheating results in serious consequences later in life.

C) provide a contrast to the view of teachers as salesmen.

D) argue against cheating or the use of educational preparation businesses.

16

As used in line 57, "enticing" most nearly means

A) pulling.

B) deceptive.

C) appealing.

D) suggestive.

17

Which choice best supports the authors' claim that schools have already begun to incorporate some facets of the popular marketplace into their educational materials?

A) Lines 16–18 ("On the…decrease")

B) Lines 59–62 ("Hence…titles")

C) Lines 65–66 ("But education…commodity")

D) Lines 67–70 ("Difficult…promote")

CONTINUE

18

The main idea of the final paragraph is that

A) focus on profit can undermine the effectiveness of true education.

B) ephemeral imagery cannot lead to an understanding of complex ideas.

C) education seems unimportant when it is present in the economic marketplace.

D) modern educators ignore difficult subjects in favor of trendy topics.

19

Data in the graph about estimated increases in prices from 2002 to 2012 most strongly supports which of the following statements?

A) Overall consumer prices increased the same amount each year.

B) Overall consumer prices have not increased in the period since 2002.

C) Percent increases in college tuitions and fees exceed those of consumer prices.

D) Prices of college textbooks decreased from 2005 to 2006.

20

Data in the graph indicate that the greatest difference between the percent increase since 2002 of college tuition and fees and that of overall consumer prices occurred during which period?

A) 2004 to 2005

B) 2008 to 2009

C) 2010 to 2011

D) 2011 to 2012

21

Data in the graph provides most direct support for what idea in the passage?

A) Schools are interested in revenue.

B) Students have an expectation that school should be entertaining.

C) Teacher evaluations reflect the students' perceptions.

D) Content is replaced by flashy slogans.

CONTINUE

Questions 22–32 are based on the following passages.

Passage 1 is adapted from Connie Weaver, et al., "Contributions to Nutrition." ©2014 by the American Society for Nutrition. Passage 2 is from David Stuckler and Marion Nestle, "Big Food, Food Systems, and Global Health." ©2012 by PLOS Medicine.

Passage 1

Both fresh and processed foods make up vital parts of the food supply. Processed food contributes to both food security (ensuring that sufficient food is available)
Line and nutrition security (ensuring that food quality
5 meets human nutrient needs) . . . .

Nutrition scientists, public health professionals, agricultural economists, food scientists, and other professionals dedicated to meeting the food and nutritional needs of people around the globe recognize
10 that fresh, local foods cannot meet all nutritional requirements. Food processing is necessary . . . .

Although nutritional security (quality) and food security (quantity) both depend on food processing, in recent years there has been considerable public
15 controversy over the nutritional contribution that processed foods make to the American diet . . . .

If enrichment and fortification were not present, large percentages of the population would have had inadequate intakes of vitamins A, C, D, and E, thiamin,
20 folate, calcium, magnesium, and iron. When nutrients from enrichment and fortification were included, the percentages of the population with inadequate intakes decreased substantially for vitamin A, vitamin D, folate, and iron . . . .

25 Clearly, this type of food processing, of adding nutrients to foods, has greatly benefitted nutrient intakes in the United States . . . .

Thus, processed foods are nutritionally important to American diets. How, then, do we enhance the
30 contribution of processed food to nutritional security and food security? . . .

Rather than limiting processed foods in the diet, it may be more productive to encourage the best available food options, namely, those that provide
35 fewer constituents to limit and more nutrients to encourage for the calories consumed . . . .

One disadvantage of commercial food processing techniques is that they are poorly understood. Commercial food processing involves techniques that
40 are difficult for the general public to grasp and that

are out of their control, thus introducing a lack of transparency and generating suspicion and concerns about safety in some individuals . . . .

In addition, concerns about the nutritional content
45 and other aspects of the production of processed foods, such as sustainability and cost, have led to criticisms of processed foods as "ultra-processed" and not compatible with good nutrition. However, the type and extent of processing do not necessarily correlate
50 with the nutritional content of the product.

Passage 2

Global food systems are not meeting the world's dietary needs. About one billion people are hungry, while two billion people are overweight. Underlying both is a common factor: food systems are not driven
55 to deliver optimal human diets but to maximize profits.

To understand who is responsible for these nutritional failures, it is first necessary to ask: *Who rules global food systems?* By and large it's "Big Food," by which we refer to multinational food and beverage
60 companies with huge and concentrated market power. Three-fourths of world food sales involve processed foods, for which the largest manufacturers hold over a third of the global market.

We see three possible ways to view this debate. The
65 first favors voluntary self-regulation, and requires no further engagement by the public health community. The second view favors partnerships with industry.

The third approach is critical of both. It recognizes the inherent conflicts of interest between corporations
70 that profit from unhealthy food and public health collaborations. Because growth in profit is the primary goal of corporations, self-regulation and working from within are doomed to fail.

We support the critical view, for several reasons.
75 Any partnership *must* create profit for the industry, which has a legal mandate to maximize wealth for shareholders. We also see no obvious, established, or legitimate mechanism through which public health professionals might increase Big Food's profits.

80 Big Food attains profit by expanding markets to reach more people, increasing people's sense of hunger so that they buy more food, and increasing profit margins through encouraging consumption of

CONTINUE

products with higher price/cost surpluses. Although
85 in theory minimal processing of foods can improve
nutritional content, in practice most processing
is done so to increase palatability, shelf-life, and
transportability, processes that reduce nutritional
quality.

90   To promote health, industry would need to make
and market healthier foods so as to shift consumption
away from highly processed, unhealthy foods. Yet,
such healthier foods are inherently less profitable.
The only ways the industry could preserve profit is
95 either to undermine public health attempts to tax and
regulate or to get people to eat more healthy food while
continuing to eat profitable unhealthy foods. Neither is
desirable from a nutritional standpoint.

22

The authors of Passage 1 indicate which of the
following about the addition of nutrients to foods?

A) It has a helpful impact.

B) It should be increased significantly.

C) It may require further investigation.

D) It gives people unnecessary extra vitamins.

23

Which choice provides the best evidence for the
answer to the previous question?

A) Lines 2–5 ("Processed . . . needs")

B) Lines 29–31 ("How, then . . . security")

C) Lines 32–34 ("Rather . . . options")

D) Lines 37–38 ("One disadvantage . . . understood")

24

The authors of Passage 1 indicate that food
enrichment methods

A) often involve industrial machinery.

B) lead to employment opportunities.

C) are the leading source of thiamin.

D) are not comprehended by all people.

25

As used in line 40, "grasp" most nearly means

A) comprehend.

B) clutch.

C) squeeze.

D) reach.

26

The authors of Passage 2 refer to "Big Food" primarily
to suggest that global food systems

A) result from a varied, competitive marketplace.

B) involve regions served by single companies.

C) should be simplified through local markets.

D) are largely dominated by a few extremely
influential companies.

27

According to the authors of Passage 2, what do profit
margins and price/cost surpluses have in common?

A) They typically coincide with ethical practices.

B) They are more important than other concerns
held by companies.

C) They are key elements of economic theory.

D) They are best increased through expanding
markets.

28

The possibilities offered in the final paragraph
(lines 90–98) of Passage 2 have primarily which
effect?

A) They show the only ways that industry could
promote health.

B) They demonstrate the unlikelihood of industry
marketing healthier foods.

C) They refer to government controls to illustrate
excessive regulation.

D) They supply positive steps to emphasize the
impossibility of corporate charity.

CONTINUE ➡

29

The main purpose of each passage is to

A) support a side in an argument about whether to promote vitamin intake through food.

B) discuss the nature of large-scale food production as it relates to nutrition.

C) compare the need for food security with the desire for nutrition security in the American diet.

D) emphasize the importance of sustainable processing in certain foods of the American diet.

30

Which choice best describes the relationship between the two passages?

A) Passage 2 discusses the underlying processes of a solution that Passage 1 describes in specific detail.

B) Passage 2 presents a plan to clarify the several misunderstood processes presented by Passage 1.

C) Passage 2 outlines an objective perspective that clashes with the opinions discussed in Passage 1.

D) Passage 2 explores the problematic nature of a system embraced by Passage 1.

31

On which of the following points would the authors of both passages most likely agree?

A) A thorough discussion of global food systems and content should address adequate nutrition.

B) Well-prepared, non-processed meals are generally more appealing than most processed foods.

C) Previous discussions of nutrition contained less suspicion of processed foods than those discussions do today.

D) People who avoid processed foods due to nutrient concerns are unlikely to be overweight.

32

Which choice provides the best evidence that the authors of Passage 2 would acknowledge some aspect of the statement made in lines 48–50 of Passage 1?

A) Lines 61–63 ("Three-fourths . . . market")

B) Lines 80–84 ("Big Food . . . surpluses")

C) Lines 84–89 ("Although . . . quality")

D) Lines 90–92 ("To promote . . . foods")

CONTINUE

Questions 33–42 are based on the following passage.

This passage is adapted from W.H. Harvey, "A Common Sense Speech," given in 1895. Harvey was an author and political activist who supported bimetallism, a monetary standard in which the value of money is based on the value of both silver and gold.

We believe that bimetallism, that relies on two metals for money, is a better policy than one that relies on only one metal. We do not pretend to say that the
Line intelligence of mankind may not find a better system
5 than both of them, but we do say that to demonetize either of these metals is a step backward and not a step forward.

Bimetallism is the right to use either gold or silver as primary money. Thus, under such a law, if our
10 trade relations or the laws of other nations take our gold away, then we have silver, and no serious injury occurs. And the same saving principle applies if our silver should leave us and gold remained. The vital principle in bimetallism is the right to use either metal.
15 If production grows less on one, we have the other, and the two together furnish a more stable supply of money material than either alone can furnish. With only one of them for money, the contraction and expansion of the world's supply alternating as they will, make
20 an uncertain and unstable supply. Of the two metals, dollar for dollar, sixteen parts of silver to one part of gold, silver is the most useful of the two, is applied to the most uses and is the most serviceable of the two metals.

25 The principle that it is safer to rely for money on two metals than on one, is a principle that we carry into everyday life. We rely on wheat, corn and rice for bread, on beef, pork and mutton for meat. If one is scarce, we use the other. It is also a principle
30 recognized by the Unseen Power that made us. We have two eyes, each to relieve the strain upon the other; two ears, two arms, two legs, for the same reason. We have one head, but two lobes of the brain; one heart, but two ventricles and two sets of veins;
35 one chest, but two lungs; two functions to relieve the organs of digestion; the mouth and nose are both dual in construction. Creation itself is dual in the marriage relation. I remind you of these simple facts in nature to teach the simple lesson, that in providing for money
40 it was simplicity and wisdom to provide that money could be made from two metals, one to relieve the strain upon the other, and the volume of both to be

drawn upon to meet the demand for money.

In 1873, the law was changed and gold only was
45 made primary money. The mints were left open to the free coinage of gold, but closed as to the free coinage of silver. An unlimited demand for gold for use as money was left in operation. The unlimited coinage of silver was stopped. One of the main arteries feeding blood
50 to civilization was cut off. The doctor was to have no option to pay in money made from either of these metals. He was to be limited to gold alone.

One of the fundamental principles of a popular government was violated in making the change. The
55 consent of the people was not obtained—the consent of the governed—that principle pronounced in the Declaration of Independence. It was not discussed in any campaign, and it was not known to the people for over two years afterward. The editors and the
60 newspaper reporters did not know it. It was done surreptitiously. I have not time to dwell upon this dark page of our history and cover what else I want to in this speech. I want to dispose of it in this way: Silver was demonetized February 12, 1873. I now offer
65 a reward of $100 to any man who will find a word about it in any newspaper published in the month of February, 1873. You will find the newspapers of that year in your public library.

Citizens, your country needs your intelligent and
70 unselfish action! You have ears and you can hear! You have eyes and you can see! Our institutions are crumbling around us! Palliatives are being used to make you acquiesce in your poverty! Do not delay your action. We have waited too long already.

CONTINUE →

33

The central problem that Harvey describes in the passage is that the United States government had

A) faced a financial deficit, which negatively impacted the growth of the country's industries.

B) previously made silver the primary money of the country, which led to a decline in gold coinage.

C) publicly announced that it would cease some production of silver coinage, which violated citizen rights.

D) instituted a monetary system in which only one metal was coined, which left the country economically vulnerable.

34

Harvey uses the phrase "saving principle" (line 12) mainly to emphasize what he sees as

A) a check on excessive spending.

B) a consequence of overreliance on one currency.

C) protection against a fluctuating money supply.

D) the U.S. Treasury's current policy.

35

As used in line 13, "vital" most nearly means

A) invigorating.

B) restorative.

C) steady.

D) fundamental.

36

Harvey contends that the decision to rely on one metal for money is unwise because

A) silver's value is sixteen times greater than that of gold.

B) gold has proven more useful than silver.

C) both metals' availability increases and decreases.

D) U.S. trading partners prefer bimetallism.

37

Which choice provides the best evidence for the answer to the above question?

A) Lines 17–20 ("With . . . supply")

B) Lines 20–24 ("Of the . . . metals")

C) Lines 29–30 ("It is . . . us")

D) Lines 72–73 ("Palliatives . . . poverty")

38

The third paragraph (lines 25–43) is primarily concerned with establishing a comparison between

A) the seen and the unseen.

B) nature and economics.

C) symmetrical body parts.

D) gold and silver.

39

As used in line 31, "strain" most nearly refers to

A) an excessive demand.

B) a bodily injury.

C) a forceful action.

D) a specific lineage.

40

Harvey claims that which of the following was a result of government action?

A) The unlimited mining of gold

B) The reduced production of silver coins

C) The reliance of Americans on staple crops

D) The establishment of beneficial trade relations

CONTINUE

Which choice provides the best evidence for the answer to the previous question?

A) Lines 8–12 ("Bimetallism . . . occurs")

B) Lines 27–29 ("We rely . . . other")

C) Lines 44–47 ("In 1873 . . . silver")

D) Lines 50–52 ("The doctor . . . alone")

It can be reasonably inferred that Harvey mentions "a popular government" (lines 53–54) in order to

A) recognize leaders who follow citizens' desires.

B) criticize leaders who conceal actions from the public.

C) applaud leaders who take decisive action.

D) denounce leaders who unfairly tax the poor.

CONTINUE

Questions 43–52 are based on the following passage and supplementary material.

The following excerpt is adapted from Ramez Naam, "Arctic Sea Ice: What, Why, and What Next." ©2012 by *Scientific American*.

On September 19th, NSIDC, the National Snow and Ice Data Center, announced that Arctic sea ice has shrunk as far as it will shrink this summer, and
Line that the ice is beginning to reform, expanding the
5 floating ice cap that covers the North Pole and the seas around it. The Arctic Sea Ice extent this September was far smaller than the previous record set in 2007. At 3.4 million square kilometers of ice coverage, this year's Arctic minimum was 800,000 square kilometers
10 smaller than the 2007 record. That difference between the previous record and this year's is larger than the entire state of Texas. An ice-free summer in the Arctic, once projected to be more than a century away, now looks possible decades from now. Some say that it
15 looks likely in just the next few years.

Conditions in the Arctic change dramatically through the seasons. In the depths of winter, the Earth's tilt puts the Arctic in 24 hour-a-day darkness. Temperatures, cold year round, plunge even lower. The
20 sea surface freezes over. At the height of summer, the opposite tilt puts the Arctic in 24 hour-a-day sunlight. While it's a cold, cold place even at these times, the constant sunshine, warmer air, and influx of warm waters from further south serve to melt the ice. The ice
25 cap usually starts shrinking in March, and then reaches its smallest area in mid-September, before cooling temperatures and shorter days start the water freezing and the ice cap growing once again.

When scientists and reporters talk about an ice-
30 free Arctic, they're usually speaking of the Arctic in *summer*, and especially in September, when ice coverage reaches its minimum. The amount of ice left at that minimum has indeed been plunging. In 1980, the ice shrank down to just under 8 million square
35 kilometers before rebounding in the fall. This year's minimum extent of 3.4 million kilometers is less than half of what we saw in 1980. Strikingly, two thirds of the loss of ice has happened in the 12 years since 2000. The ice is receding, and the process, if anything,
40 appears to be accelerating.

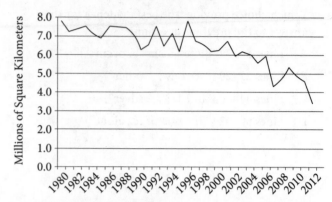

Arctic Sea Ice Minimum Area

Data: NSIDC. Graphic: Ramez Naam

Arctic sea ice coverage in September has dropped by half since 1980, and the drop appears to be accelerating.

As recently as a few years ago, most models of the Arctic ice anticipated that summers would remain icy until the end of the 21st century, and well into the 22nd century. But the trend line above makes that look
45 unlikely. The amount of ice remaining, this year, is about the same as the ice *lost* between the mid-1990s and today. If ice loss continued at that pace, we'd see an ice-free summer sometime around 2030, give or take several years.
50 Is that plausible? Opinions differ substantially, even among climate scientists. At one end of the spectrum are those who see the ice lasting in summer for another 20 or 30 years, or perhaps even a bit longer. For example, Lars-Otto Reierson, who leads the Arctic
55 Monitoring and Assessment Programme told Reuters that most models predict the summer ice disappearing by 2030 or 2040. Similarly, a paper published this year in *Geophysical Research Letters* by multiple scientists, including several from the National Snow and Ice Data
60 Center, found that an ice-free summer in the Arctic in the "next few decades" was a "distinct possibility." A recent assessment from Muyin Wang at the University of Washington and James Overland at the National Oceanographic and Atmospheric Administration,
65 using the most up to date Arctic ice models and data, projected a nearly ice-free Arctic around 2030. And Cecilia Bitz, a professor of Atmospheric Sciences at the University of Washington at part of the Polar Science Center sees a 50/50 chance that the Arctic will be ice-
70 free in summer in the next few decades.

CONTINUE ▶

On the other end of the spectrum are those who think the melt could happen much sooner. Peter Wadhams, who leads the Polar Ocean Physics Group at the University of Cambridge, has predicted since 2008
75 that the Arctic ice could be gone in summer by 2015. He now believes there's a chance that it could happen even sooner. Similarly, Mark Drinkwater, the European Space Agency's senior advisor on polar regions and a mission scientist for the CryoStat satellite that
80 measures arctic ice, believes that the Arctic could be ice-free in September by the end of this decade.

When will the ice melt? While the range of possibilities is wide today, it's shrunk dramatically from just a few years ago, when most climate scientists
85 expected the ice to survive through the 21st century. Now the question is whether it will be gone in decades —or in mere years.

43

The first paragraph serves mainly to

A) inform the reader that Arctic ice is starting to return.

B) compare the size of an Arctic area to a U. S. state.

C) illustrate dramatic changes in polar weather conditions over the last century.

D) present a trend that is occurring differently than expected.

44

As used in line 13, "projected" is closest in meaning to

A) hurled.

B) seen.

C) hypothesized.

D) illuminated.

45

According to Naam, the Earth's tilt is significant primarily because it

A) causes the sea surface to freeze and the ice cap to grow further.

B) accounts for seasonal differences in the Arctic.

C) explains why the ice-free summer is accelerating in recent years.

D) exposes the Arctic to constant daylight and melts portions of ice.

46

Which choice provides the best evidence for the answer to the previous question?

A) Lines 12–15 ("An ice-free . . . years")

B) Lines 16–21 ("Conditions . . . sunlight")

C) Lines 29–32 ("When . . . minimum")

D) Lines 37–40 ("Strikingly . . . accelerating")

47

As used in line 47, "pace" most nearly means

A) walk.

B) loss.

C) rate.

D) measure.

CONTINUE

48

Based on information in the passage, it can reasonably be inferred that climate scientists

A) agree that the polar ice is receding, but disagree about the rate of acceleration.

B) disagree that the polar ice is receding, but agree about the rate of deceleration.

C) are uncertain about whether the polar ice is receding, but agree that it should be studied.

D) are certain that the polar ice is receding, but cannot say whether it will rebound.

49

Which choice provides the best evidence for the answer to the previous question?

A) Lines 50–51 ("Is that . . . scientists")

B) Lines 57–61 ("Similarly . . . possibility'")

C) Lines 66–70 ("And Cecilia . . . decades")

D) Lines 77–81 ("Similarly . . . decade")

50

In the graph, which of the following periods displays the greatest decline in sea ice minimum area?

A) 1986–1987

B) 1995–1996

C) 2005–2006

D) 2011–2012

51

Which concept is supported by the passage and by the information in the graph?

A) The Arctic ice-free summer will be upon us within decades.

B) The Arctic ice-free summer may not be a scientific fact.

C) The Arctic ice-free summer may come sooner than the 22nd century.

D) The Arctic ice-free summer will not come as swiftly as some have predicted.

52

How does the graph support the author's point that Arctic ice is receding?

A) It shows that the change in ice from 2007 to 2012 is similar in size to the state of Texas.

B) It suggests that the amount of ice could drop to zero within a few years.

C) It indicates a loss of 3 million square kilometers of ice from 1980 to 1990.

D) It presents a trend of sharp and noticeable decline since 2000.

STOP
If you finish before time is called, you may check your work on this section only.
Do not turn to any other section in the test.

No Test Material On This Page

Writing and Language Test

35 MINUTES, 44 QUESTIONS

Turn to Section 2 of your answer sheet to answer the questions in this section.

Questions 1–11 are based on the following passage.

A Dirty Job Worth Having

As people become more sensitive to the idea of preserving certain ecosystems, **1** yet more attention must be paid to the land. The central challenge of maintaining an ecosystem, especially by artificial means, is that ecosystems have a tendency to change, particularly with the dual influence of human **2** reacting and a

1

A) NO CHANGE
B) and
C) for
D) DELETE the underlined portion.

2

A) NO CHANGE
B) reacts
C) interacted
D) interaction

CONTINUE →

rapidly altering climate. **3** Still, one career that has grown by leaps and bounds in the last fifty years is that of the soil conservationist, whose land-use surveys guide both public and private entities as to how to work within sustainable ecosystems.

Take, for example, the factors that must be considered **4** when building a beach house. Coastal areas are particularly susceptible to the influence of **5** things eroding because of the water from the ocean and in the air. In this context, a soil conservationist might be asked to conduct a survey of the region in order to determine where it would be safest to build. After all, one's dream house would not be quite so ideal if it were at constant risk of collapsing, shifting, or **6** to deteriorate with the ground beneath it.

3
A) NO CHANGE
B) Nonetheless,
C) Finally,
D) Therefore,

4
Which choice most effectively sets up the subject discussed in this paragraph?
A) NO CHANGE
B) in performing these tasks.
C) with the changes in the seasons.
D) if you are doing soil conservation.

5
A) NO CHANGE
B) erosion
C) what erodes
D) the process of erosion

6
A) NO CHANGE
B) deteriorating
C) deteriorate
D) structures deteriorating

CONTINUE

In more agricultural communities, the work of a soil conservationist might take a different form. Farmers, after all, are not necessarily concerned with building structures on the land—instead, they are concerned with land that will yield reliable crops. [7] In these cases, soil conservationists employ a variety of techniques. Of these techniques each in its way is geared toward preserving or reviving land where crops are grown. The goal in these situations is to mimic the biology of "virgin land," or land that has never been farmed. Soil conservationists might advise on farming techniques [8] or chemical supplements that can help the land produce to its full potential. With the efforts of soil conservationists, no-till farmlands, lands that are not farmed with traditional plowing implements, [9] which has grown dramatically, nearly doubling in the fifteen years since 2000.

7

Which choice most effectively combines the underlined sentences?

A) Soil conservationists, in these cases, are ways of preserving or reviving land where crops are grown, and they will use a variety of techniques to do it.

B) In these cases, each one of them is geared toward the idea of preservation or revival as to crops, and the soil conservationists employ a variety of techniques to that end.

C) Geared toward preserving or reviving land where crops are grown, soil conservationists in these cases employ a variety of different techniques.

D) In these cases, soil conservationists employ a variety of techniques, each in its way geared toward preserving or reviving land where crops are grown.

8

At this point, the writer is considering adding the following information.

    —such as no-till or terrace methods—

Should the writer make this addition here?

A) Yes, because it demonstrates the advantages of the methods described later in the sentence.

B) Yes, because it gives specific instances of the techniques discussed in this sentence.

C) No, because it distracts from the sentence's main focus on soil conservationists.

D) No, because it provides an unnecessary detail that interrupts the sentence's flow.

9

A) NO CHANGE
B) which have
C) have
D) has

CONTINUE

Soil conservation can be applied to any ecosystem, but its details tend to be rather technical. As a result, most people who work as soil conservationists tend to study agricultural science or environmental studies in college. From there, however, the paths diverge. Clearly, someone working on the eastern seaboard would need a different knowledge base from that of someone working in the deserts of the Southwest, the **10** plains of the Midwest, or the forests of the Northwest. **11** In all cases, however, soil conservationists do truly fascinating work, seeking as they do to continue to strike the balance between natural spaces and the people who live in them.

10

A) NO CHANGE

B) areas without trees

C) plains-like ecosystems

D) barren wasteland

11

Which choice most clearly ends the passage with a restatement of the writer's claim?

A) NO CHANGE

B) In all of these places, soil conservationists do essential work, but just as much is required of the builders and contractors who accompany them.

C) Soil conservationists work in both the public and the private sectors, but the public is better because it can be enjoyed by all.

D) Because the desert is unique, the skills that soil conservationists learn in places like Arizona are valuable but difficult to transfer between regions.

CONTINUE

Questions 12–22 are based on the following passage.

A Bigger Piece of the Peace

—1—

Nobel Prizes have been given since 1901 as a way to honor outstanding achievements in Physics, Chemistry, Literature, Medicine, and Economics. There may be some controversy as to who earns these awards in many cases; **12** therefore, there can be no doubt that the winners are always accomplished in their fields and have contributed something significant to their **13** disciplines and the world at large.

12

A) NO CHANGE
B) for example,
C) however,
D) fittingly,

13

A) NO CHANGE
B) disciplines,
C) disciplines, it's
D) disciplines, for example

CONTINUE

—2—

The Nobel Peace Prize may be a good deal more controversial, but it is by no means any less significant. [14] The prize is given each year by the Norwegian Nobel Committee "to the person who shall have done the most or the best work for fraternity between nations, for the abolition or reduction of standing armies and for the holding and promotion of peace congresses." Time and again we see the [15] committee rewarded bravery in the face of adversity. This is a difficult thing to quantify, but the Peace Prize is as important as the other prizes and contributes to [16] their common goal: to make the world a better place.

[14]

At this point, the writer is considering adding the following sentence.

> One of the most important prizes of all time, the 1962 prize in Physiology, was given to Francis Crick, James Watson, and Hugh Wilkins for their discovery of the structure of DNA.

Should the writer make this addition here?

A) Yes, because it cites an important moment in Nobel Prize-giving history.

B) Yes, because it explains the typical genetic makeup of a Nobel Prize winner.

C) No, because it implies that all Peace Prize winners must also be scientists.

D) No, because it distracts from the paragraph's main focus on another prize.

[15]

A) NO CHANGE

B) committee reward

C) committee's rewarding

D) committees' reward

[16]

A) NO CHANGE

B) they're common goal,

C) they're common goal;

D) their common goal;

CONTINUE

—3—

It is probably no surprise that Martin Luther King, Jr., won the award in 1964 amid his non-violent campaign for civil rights in the United States. By 1964, and certainly by the time of his death in 1968, Baptist **17** minister King's, influence spanned the globe, not only for people of color seeking civil rights but also for all **18** those people's friends, family, and loved ones. King was also the first African-American man to gain this particular kind of stature in the United States and on the world stage.

—4—

19 When given to first-year President Barack Obama, there was a good deal more controversy surrounding the award in 2009. In this case as in the others, however, the Nobel Peace Prize seeks to award the intangible, the unquantifiable, and the hopeful. Whether Bunche, King, Obama, or the hundreds of other recipients, all winners provide the important reminder that people work every day to make the world a better place.

17

A) NO CHANGE
B) minister King's
C) minister, King's,
D) minister, King's

18

Which choice gives a specific supporting detail that is most similar to the details already in the paragraph?

A) NO CHANGE
B) the people throughout the world.
C) who thought the Nobel Prize should be awarded to someone who deserved it.
D) those who championed a cause in non-violent ways.

19

A) NO CHANGE
B) There was a good deal more controversy surrounding the award in 2009, when it was given to first-year President Barack Obama.
C) In 2009, when it was awarded, first-year President Barack Obama received the Prize with a good deal more controversy.
D) When it was awarded to first-year President Barack Obama in 2009, a good deal more controversy surrounded the award.

CONTINUE

—5—

King may be the most famous African-American recipient of the Nobel Peace [20] Prize. The honor was first given to a lesser-known but no less illustrious figure, Ralph Bunche, in 1950. After a difficult childhood punctuated by an illustrious educational and political career, Bunche was one of the many tasked with trying to resolve the Arab-Israeli conflict that had erupted after World War II. The work began with a scare, as the UN's appointee, the Swedish Count Folke Bernadotte, was assassinated by members of the underground Lehi group. After this tragic event, Bunche, Bernadotte's chief aide, became the UN's chief mediator, and his long negotiations began with the Israeli representative Moshe Dayan. These negotiations, many of which were done while the two men shot pool, became the 1949 Armistice Agreements, concluding the 1948 Arab-Israeli Conflict and earning Ralph Bunche [21] the Nobel Peace Prize from the year 1950.

Question [22] asks about the previous passage as a whole.

[20]

Which choice most effectively combines the sentences at the underlined portion?

A) Prize: the

B) Prize, while the

C) Prize for the

D) Prize, yet the

[21]

Which choice most closely matches the stylistic pattern established earlier in the sentence?

A) NO CHANGE

B) 1950's Nobel Prize for Peace.

C) the 1950 Nobel Peace Prize.

D) the Nobel Prize for 1950's Peace.

Think about the previous passage as a whole as you answer question 22.

[22]

To make the passage most logical, paragraph 5 should be placed

A) where it is now.

B) after paragraph 1.

C) after paragraph 2.

D) after paragraph 3.

CONTINUE →

Questions 23–33 are based on the following passage and supplementary material.

Conserving the Trees that Conserve the Earth

The most obvious facet of global warming is the rise in global temperatures. What many do not understand quite as well, [23] however, are the factors that contribute to that rise in global temperatures. The rise in carbon dioxide (CO_2) levels, for instance, is commonly cited as a reason, but what exactly does this chemical compound do?

For instance, every time you breathe, you inhale oxygen and a number of other compounds, and you exhale CO_2. Factories, cars, and other heavy machinery perform [24] functions that could be called analogous on a much larger scale. Because of the heavy output from this wide variety of industrial sources, the Earth's atmosphere is bombarded [25] . This excess carbon dioxide creates what is known as a greenhouse effect, wherein heat enters the atmosphere but not all of it leaves. CO_2 does not absorb

---

23

A) NO CHANGE

B) thereby,

C) correspondingly,

D) thus,

24

A) NO CHANGE

B) the functions of an analogy

C) functions that are like analogies

D) analogous functions

25

At this point, the writer is considering adding the following information

> with more CO_2 than it can process or release naturally back into the area outside the Earth's atmosphere

Should the writer make this addition here?

A) Yes, because it defines the role that the trees in the Amazonian rainforest play in modulating the Earth's CO_2 levels.

B) Yes, because it states why high levels of CO_2 can be a problem in the Earth's atmosphere.

C) No, because it mentions the process of absorbing CO_2, which blurs the essay's focus on the Amazonian rainforest.

D) No, because it undermines the passage's central claim that the Earth can absorb CO_2 naturally.

CONTINUE ➤

heat energy from the Sun, but where the compound is concerned, 26 it's always absorbing heat energy released from the Earth. Here's the problem: while the carbon dioxide can release some of that heat into space, it also releases some back to the Earth, creating a kind of self-perpetuating cycle of rising temperatures. Since 1960, carbon dioxide has increased at a steady rate, 27 as temperatures have increased along exactly the same curve.

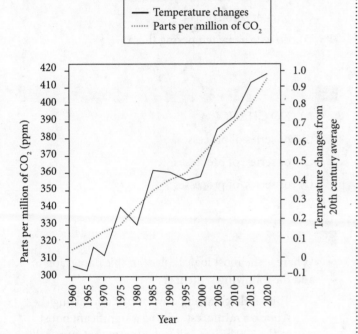

There are some earthly mechanisms to absorb and 28 chill out the levels of carbon dioxide in the atmosphere, but many of these industrial processes have depleted or overwhelmed these mechanisms. For instance, trees need carbon dioxide to perform their basic functions, but the number of trees required to offset carbon emissions is staggering. An independent analysis found that to offset the emissions of one modest coal plant operating in a small city in 29 Connecticut would then require 52 million trees!

26

A) NO CHANGE

B) its

C) they're

D) there

27

Which choice offers an accurate interpretation of the data in the chart?

A) NO CHANGE

B) but the temperatures have shown no general increase despite the rising CO_2 levels.

C) whereas the temperature changes peaked in 1989 for no apparent reason.

D) and although temperatures have fluctuated, those have generally increased as well.

28

A) NO CHANGE

B) kill

C) reduce

D) mellow

29

A) NO CHANGE

B) Connecticut, where it would

C) Connecticut would

D) Connecticut, it would

CONTINUE

Still, there are lots of trees on the Earth, and alongside many of the carbon caps that many countries and industries have begun to impose, people are starting to take the ideas of *re*forestation and conservation more seriously. A team of over 150 researchers produced the first comprehensive map of the Amazon rainforest's ecosystem and **30** said, "that half of the Amazon could be deforested by 2050.

[1] But there is a silver lining to the findings in this research. [2] Because of the team's efforts, as many as 57% of Amazon tree species could be eligible for the International Union for the Conservation of Nature's red list of threatened species. [3] Other polluting behaviors would need to change as well for significant emission reversals, but protecting the Amazon's trees could **31** temper some of those polluting behaviors in the meantime and into the future. [4] This could be a first major step in part of the much longer process, **32** or series, of processes, to get the Earth's carbon levels back to appropriate ranges. **33**

30

A) NO CHANGE
B) said that
C) said, that
D) said—that

31

A) NO CHANGE
B) temper some of them
C) temper some of it
D) do its part by tempering them

32

A) NO CHANGE
B) or series of processes,
C) or series; of processes
D) or series, of processes

33

Where is the most logical place in this paragraph to add the following sentence?

> This could go a long way toward reforesting the Amazon rainforest, adding a significant boost to the 390 billion individual trees that currently grow there.

A) Before sentence 1
B) Before sentence 2
C) Before sentence 3
D) Before sentence 4

Questions 34–44 are based on the following passage.

Original Adaptations and Rewrites

Literary influence can take many forms. Therefore, the results of this influence can take many forms—novels, poems, critiques, and countless others. Every great writer works within a literary tradition established by the great writers who came before. Sometimes that influence is [34] formal, in any case—as in the case of a writer who uses the forms created by an earlier writer to discuss new topics. Sometimes that influence is more literal—as in the case of those writers who take marginal characters from earlier works [35] and sometimes poems or movies are included.

[1] Perhaps the most famous instance of such a work is the epic blank-verse poem *Paradise Lost*, written by John Milton and first published in 1667. [2] It was by this alternate route, Milton claimed, that he could help to "justify the ways of God to men." [3] This work retells the biblical story of Adam and Eve and their exile from the Garden of Eden. [4] With the framework set by the biblical story, *Paradise Lost* offers a unique interpretation, [36] just as the story focuses on the fallen angel Satan rather than on the human characters. [5] As such, *Paradise Lost* is considered essential reading for those interested in matters both aesthetic and theological. [37]

34

A) NO CHANGE
B) formal—
C) formal, nevertheless—
D) formal, therefore—

35

Which choice provides information that best supports the claim made by this sentence?

A) NO CHANGE
B) but don't cite the author's name at all.
C) and build new literary worlds around them.
D) yet still consider it entirely their own.

36

A) NO CHANGE
B) wherein
C) from which
D) into it

37

To make this paragraph most logical, sentence 2 should be placed

A) before sentence 1.
B) before sentence 3.
C) before sentence 4.
D) before sentence 5.

CONTINUE

The practice of adapting literary works, particularly the great classics of a **38** language; to unique ends has continued. The 1966 novel *Wide Sargasso Sea* was British author Jean Rhys's prequel to the 1847 novel *Jane Eyre*. Toward the end of *Jane Eyre*, it is revealed that one of the novel's central characters, Mr. Rochester, has a wife locked away in one of the rooms of his castle. Rhys's novel tells this wife's story, foregrounding the cruelty of British imperialism and the oppressive society that awaited women in England. As Milton had before, Rhys uses a well-known work to **39** overtake an alternate story.

More recently, Algerian writer Kamel Daoud **40** he adapted Albert Camus's novel *The Stranger* into his own unique work, *The Meursault Investigation*, first published in Algeria in 2013. Camus's novel centers on the protagonist Meursault, **41** who kills an anonymous Arab man for vague reasons. Daoud's novel starts with Camus's

38

A) NO CHANGE
B) language
C) language,
D) language—

39

A) NO CHANGE
B) tell
C) manifest
D) ideate

40

A) NO CHANGE
B) adapted
C) he adopted
D) adopted

41

A) NO CHANGE
B) he kills
C) whom killed
D) killing

CONTINUE ➡

basic outline, but *The Meursault Investigation* is [42] more description than *The Stranger* in that it writes the backstory of that man and gives him a name, Musa. [43] Daoud's narrative follows the observations of Musa's brother Harun and offers a critique of European views that refuse to acknowledge the existence of non-Europeans. "By claiming your own name," Daoud said in an interview, "you are also making a claim of your humanity and thus the right to justice."

Although some of these works may not seem quite as "original" as the original texts, they in fact make literal what all other texts merely imply [44] and do not state. Daoud refers to his novel as part of a "dialogue with Camus," but we should not forget that even the greatest works of literature are speaking to someone.

42

A) NO CHANGE

B) more descriptive, than

C) more descriptive then

D) more descriptive than

43

At this point, the writer is considering adding the following sentence.

> The history of Franco-Algerian relations goes back centuries as France was the occupying colonial power in Algeria from 1830 to 1962.

Should the writer make this addition here?

A) Yes, because it situates Daoud's novel in an essential historical context.

B) Yes, because it gives an example of a global conflict that one writer might have drawn upon.

C) No, because it contradicts the passage's larger claim that literature cannot be defined by historical events.

D) No, because it strays from the paragraph's main focus with an idea that is not elaborated upon.

44

A) NO CHANGE

B) as well.

C) similarly.

D) DELETE the underlined portion, and end the sentence with a period.

STOP

If you finish before time is called, you may check your work on this section only.
Do not turn to any other section in the test.

Math Test – No Calculator

25 MINUTES, 20 QUESTIONS

Turn to Section 3 of your answer sheet to answer the questions in this section.

CONTINUE

1

$$2x + 3y = -9$$
$$x - y = -2$$

Which of the following ordered pairs (x, y) satisfies the system of equations above?

A) $(-3, -1)$

B) $(-1, -3)$

C) $(1, 3)$

D) $(3, 1)$

2

$$x = 4(x + y)$$

If (x, y) is a solution to the equation above and $x \neq 0$, what is the value of $\dfrac{y}{x}$?

A) $\dfrac{3}{4}$

B) $\dfrac{1}{4}$

C) $-\dfrac{3}{4}$

D) $-\dfrac{5}{4}$

3

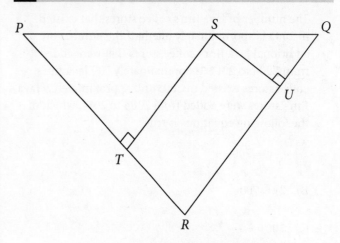

Note: Figure not drawn to scale.

Triangle PQR is isosceles with $PR = QR$ and $PQ = 64$. If the ratio of ST to $SU = 5:3$, what is the length of $\overline{SQ}$?

A) 8

B) 24

C) 32

D) 40

4

Buster estimates the expected profit, in dollars, from one week's operation of his family's chocolate-covered banana stand using the expression $4bd - 200$, where b is the number of bananas expected to be sold at the banana stand each day, and d is the number of days the banana stand will be open during that week. Which of the following is the best interpretation of the number 4 in the expression?

A) There will be 4 chocolate-covered bananas sold at the stand each day.

B) The price of a banana increases by $4 every day.

C) The number of customers will increase by a factor of 4 every day.

D) The banana stand charges $4 for each chocolate-covered banana.

CONTINUE

5

The number of Java Jim's coffee stores that existed in 2003 is approximately one-half the number of additional Java Jim's coffee stores that were added from 2004 to 2014. If approximately 700 Java Jim's coffee stores existed in 2003 and approximately y Java Jim's stores were added from 2004 to 2014, which of the following equations is true?

A) $\dfrac{1}{2} y = 700$

B) $2y = 700$

C) $700y = \dfrac{1}{2}$

D) $700y = 2$

6

Stream Supreme, a streaming movie service, charges a monthly fee of $7 for membership and $1.75 per movie streamed. Another streaming movie service, Download Empire, charges a monthly fee of $4 for membership and $2.25 per movie streamed. If m represents the number of movies streamed in a particular month, what are all the values of m for which Stream Supreme's total monthly charge is less than that of Download Empire?

A) $m < 4$

B) $5 \le m \le 6$

C) $6 \le m \le 7$

D) $m > 6$

7

$$q = \frac{\left(p_e - p_{wf}\right)^k}{\mu d} h$$

The formula above models the productivity index, q, in barrels per day, of an oil well with a pressure differential of $(p_e - p_{wf})$, a permeability of k, a pay zone thickness of h, a viscosity of μ, and a drainage factor of d. Which of the following gives h, in terms of q, p_e, p_{wf}, k, μ, and d?

A) $h = \dfrac{\mu q d}{k}$

B) $h = \dfrac{k}{\mu q d}$

C) $h = \dfrac{\mu q d}{\left(p_e - p_{wf}\right)^k}$

D) $h = \dfrac{\left(p_e - p_{wf}\right)^k}{\mu q d}$

8

$$s = 110 + 4C$$

The equation above is used to model the relationship between the number of scoops, s, of ice cream sold per day at a particular ice cream shop, and the temperature, C, in degrees Celsius. According to the model, what is the meaning of the 4 in the equation?

A) For every increase of 1°C, four more scoops of ice cream will be sold.

B) For every decrease of 1°C, four more scoops of ice cream will be sold.

C) For every increase of 4°C, one more scoop of ice cream will be sold.

D) For every decrease of 4°C, one more scoop of ice cream will be sold.

CONTINUE

9

While saving money to pay for graduate school, Stephan created a plan in which the amount of money he saves each month is increased by a constant amount. If Stephan's savings plan requires that he save $145 during month 3 and that he save $280 during month 12, which of the following describes how the money Stephan saves changes between month 3 and month 12 of his savings plan?

A) Stephan increases the amount he saves by $5 each month.

B) Stephan increases the amount he saves by $15 each month.

C) Stephan increases the amount he saves by $60 every 6 months.

D) Stephan increases the amount he saves by $45 every month.

10

Which of the following equations, when graphed in the xy-plane, will include only values of y that are less than 2 ?

A) $y = -x^2 + 3$

B) $y = |-x| - 1$

C) $y = x^3 - 4$

D) $y = -(x - 1)^2 + 1$

11

If $f(x + 1) = 3x - 4$ for all values of x, what is the value of $f(-4)$?

A) −19

B) −16

C) −13

D) −10

12

$$\frac{5 - i}{2 - 3i}$$

If the expression above is rewritten in the form $a + bi$, where a and b are real numbers, what is the value of a ? (Note: $i = \sqrt{-1}$)

A) −2

B) −1

C) 1

D) $\dfrac{17}{13}$

CONTINUE

13

What is the sum of all values of p that satisfy the equation $3p^2 + 24p - 6 = 0$?

A) $-6\sqrt{2}$

B) -8

C) 8

D) $6\sqrt{2}$

14

The parabola with the equation $y = ax^2 + bx + c$, where a, b, and c are constants, is graphed on the xy-plane. If the parabola passes through the point $(-1, -1)$, which of the following must be true?

A) $a - b + c = -1$

B) $a - b - c = -1$

C) $a + b = 1$

D) $b - c = -1$

15

If $(px + 5)(qx + 3) = 8x^2 + rx + 15$ for all values of x, and $p + q = 6$, what are the two possible values for r ?

A) 2 and 4

B) 7 and 12

C) 22 and 26

D) 29 and 39

CONTINUE

DIRECTIONS

For questions 16–20, solve the problem and enter your answer in the grid, as described below, on the answer sheet.

1. Although not required, it is suggested that you write your answer in the boxes at the top of the columns to help you fill in the circles accurately. You will receive credit only if the circles are filled in correctly.

2. Mark no more than one circle in any column.

3. No question has a negative answer.

4. Some problems may have more than one correct answer. In such cases, grid only one answer.

5. **Mixed numbers** such as $3\frac{1}{2}$ must be gridded as 3.5 or 7/2. (If 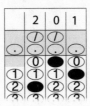 is entered into the grid, it will be interpreted as $\frac{31}{2}$, not as $3\frac{1}{2}$.)

6. **Decimal Answers:** If you obtain a decimal answer with more digits than the grid can accommodate, it may be either rounded or truncated, but it must fill the entire grid.

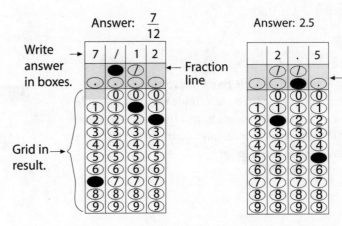

Acceptable ways to grid $\frac{2}{3}$ are:

Answer: 201 – either position is correct

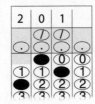

NOTE: You may start your answers in any column, space permitting. Columns you don't need to use should be left blank.

CONTINUE ➡

16

What is the value of y if $(4y + 8) - (7y - 12) = 11$?

17

At a hotel, each double room has 25 more square feet of floor space than each single room. If 2 double rooms and 4 single rooms have a total of 1,400 square feet of floor space, how many square feet of floor space does a double room have?

18

One angle of a right triangle measures $a°$, where $\cos a° = \dfrac{3}{5}$. What is $\sin(90° - a°)$?

19

If $x + 3$ is a factor of $x^2 + kx + 2k$, where k is a constant, what is the value of k ?

CONTINUE →

20

$$x^3 - 3x^2 + 5x - 15 = 0$$

What real value of x is a solution to the above equation?

STOP
If you finish before time is called, you may check your work on this section only.
Do not turn to any other section in the test.

Math Test – Calculator

55 MINUTES, 38 QUESTIONS

Turn to Section 4 of your answer sheet to answer the questions in this section.

DIRECTIONS

For questions 1–30, solve each problem, choose the best answer from the choices provided, and fill in the corresponding circle on your answer sheet. **For questions 31–38**, solve the problem and enter your answer in the grid on the answer sheet. Please refer to the directions before question 31 on how to enter your answers in the grid. You may use any available space in your test booklet for scratch work.

NOTES

1. The use of a calculator **is permitted**.
2. All variables and expressions used represent real numbers unless otherwise indicated.
3. Figures provided in this test are drawn to scale unless otherwise indicated.
4. All figures lie in a plane unless otherwise indicated.
5. Unless otherwise indicated, the domain of a given function f is the set of all real numbers x for which $f(x)$ is a real number.

REFERENCE

$A = \pi r^2$
$C = 2\pi r$

$A = \ell w$

$A = \frac{1}{2} bh$

$c^2 = a^2 + b^2$

Special Right Triangles

$V = \ell wh$

$V = \pi r^2 h$

$V = \frac{4}{3} \pi r^3$

$V = \frac{1}{3} \pi r^2 h$

$V = \frac{1}{3} \ell wh$

The number of degrees of arc in a circle is 360.
The number of radians of arc in a circle is 2π.
The sum of the measures in degrees of the angles of a triangle is 180.

CONTINUE

1

A pizzeria sells pizzas in individual slices or in pies of 8 slices. On a certain day, the pizzeria sold a total of 364 slices, 84 of which were sold as individual slices. Which of the following shows the number of pies, n, sold on that day?

A) $n = \dfrac{364 + 84}{8}$

B) $n = \dfrac{364}{8} + 84$

C) $n = \dfrac{364}{8} - 84$

D) $n = \dfrac{364 - 84}{8}$

2

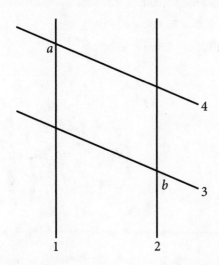

In the figure above, lines 1 and 2 are parallel, and lines 3 and 4 are parallel. If the measure of $\angle a$ is 125°, what is the measure of $\angle b$?

A) 40°

B) 55°

C) 110°

D) 125°

3

	Cream filling	No filling	Total
White chocolate	5	15	20
Dark chocolate	7	3	10
Total	12	18	30

A box contains 30 pieces of chocolate, distributed as shown in the table above. Each piece is made of either white chocolate or dark chocolate, and each piece contains either cream filling or no filling. If one piece is selected at random, what is the probability that the piece is either white chocolate with cream filling or dark chocolate with no filling?

A) $\dfrac{8}{30}$

B) $\dfrac{12}{30}$

C) $\dfrac{20}{30}$

D) $\dfrac{22}{30}$

CONTINUE

4

An isosceles triangle has perimeter T and sides of length x, x, and y. Which of the following represents x, in terms of T and y ?

A) $x = T - y$

B) $x = T - 2y$

C) $x = \dfrac{T - 2y}{2}$

D) $x = \dfrac{T - y}{2}$

5

$$2x + 3y = -6$$
$$x - 4y = 19$$

Which ordered pair satisfies the system of equations shown above?

A) $(-9, 4)$

B) $(-3, 4)$

C) $(-1, -5)$

D) $(3, -4)$

6

When 6 times the number n is subtracted from 8, the result is 20. What is the result when 3 times the number n is subtracted from 5 ?

A) -2

B)   8

C) 11

D) 20

7

At 12 P.M. on Sunday, there are 25,000 people in a football stadium that holds 65,000. Every minute after 12 P.M., the number of people in the stadium increases by 550. If m represents the time, in minutes, after 12 P.M., which of the inequalities below gives the set of minutes in which the football stadium is below capacity?

A) $550m < 25,000$

B) $550m < 65,000$

C) $550m + 25,000 < 65,000$

D) $25,000 - 550m < 65,000$

CONTINUE

Number of United States Residents
With Health Insurance in 2015, in Thousands

Income in dollars	Age in years						Total
	Under 19	19–25	26–34	35–44	45–64	65 and older	
Under 25,000	12,499	4,881	6,146	6,387	13,314	7,359	50,586
25,000–49,999	15,624	6,102	7,683	7,984	16,643	9,200	63,236
50,000–74,999	14,061	5,491	6,915	7,185	14,978	8,278	56,908
75,000–99,999	10,936	4,271	5,378	5,589	11,650	6,439	44,263
100,000 and above	24,998	9,762	12,293	12,774	26,628	14,718	101,173
Total	78,118	30,507	38,415	39,919	83,213	45,994	316,166

The table above shows the number of U.S. residents with health insurance in 2015, in thousands, categorized by age group and annual income. According to these results, if a U.S. resident with health insurance who was 35–64 in 2015 is selected at random, what is the approximate probability that this resident had an income between $50,000 and $74,999 ?

A) 0.20

B) 0.25

C) 0.40

D) 0.80

CONTINUE

9

A truck traveled at an average speed of 70 miles per hour for 4 hours and had a fuel efficiency of 18 miles per gallon. Approximately how many gallons of fuel did the truck use for the entire 4-hour drive?

A)   4

B) 10

C) 16

D) 20

10

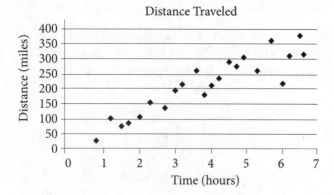

The scatterplot above shows the distances and times spent traveling for 22 trips by a driver. What is the time, in hours, of the trip represented by the data point farthest from the line of best fit (not shown)?

A)   4

B)   6

C)   8

D) 10

11

$$t_b = 212 - 0.0018a$$

The temperature at which water boils varies with altitude. The formula above models the relationship between t_b, the temperature at which water boils, in degrees Fahrenheit, and a, the altitude, in feet. Which of the following equations expresses altitude in terms of the temperature at which water boils?

A) $a = \dfrac{0.0018}{t_b - 212}$

B) $a = \dfrac{t_b + 212}{0.0018}$

C) $a = \dfrac{t_b - 212}{0.0018}$

D) $a = \dfrac{212 - t_b}{0.0018}$

CONTINUE

12

Which scatterplot below expresses a positive association that is not linear? (Note: A positive association between two variables is one in which higher values in one variable correspond to higher values in the other variable, and vice versa.)

A)
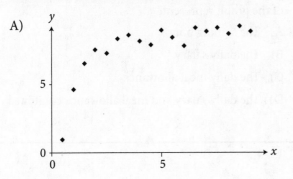

B)
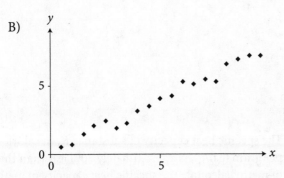

C)
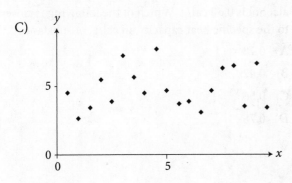

D)
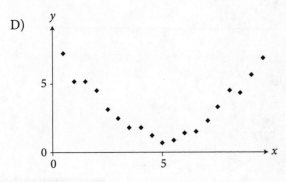

13

$$v = \frac{h - m}{t} + 4.9t$$

For an object thrown straight upward, the formula above gives the relationship between v, the initial speed in meters per second, t, the time in seconds after the object was thrown, h, the height after t seconds, and m, the initial height from which the object was thrown. Which of the following expresses h, in terms of v, t, and m?

A) $h = -4.9t^2 + vt - m$

B) $h = -4.9t^2 + vt + m$

C) $h = -4.9t^2 - vt + m$

D) $h = 4.9t^2 - vt - m$

14

$$65x + y = 455$$

A grocery store receives a shipment of oranges and consistently sells the same number of oranges each day. The equation above models the number of oranges, y, that remain x days after the shipment is received. What does it mean that $(7, 0)$ is a solution to the equation?

A) It takes 7 days after the shipment until none of the oranges are remaining.

B) There are 7 oranges in the shipment.

C) It takes 7 days for oranges to be sold to 455 customers.

D) After the shipment, 7 oranges are sold each day.

CONTINUE

Questions 15 and 16 refer to the following information.

A minor league baseball player is offered a short-term contract by three teams: the Eagles, the Hawks, and the Jays. Each contract consists of a signing bonus, a daily salary, and a daily meal allowance, as shown in the table below.

Team	Signing bonus, b (in dollars)	Salary, s (in dollars per day)	Meal allowance, m (in dollars per day)
Eagles	1,400	140	40
Hawks	1,200	160	50
Jays	1,500	130	30

The player's total compensation, C, for each contract in terms of the number of days, d, is given by the formula $C = b + (s + m)d$.

16

The relationship between the player's total compensation, C, for a contract with the Hawks as a function of the number of days, d, for which the contract lasts is graphed in the xy-plane, with d on the x-axis and C on the y-axis. What does the y-intercept of the graph represent?

A) The signing bonus

B) The daily salary

C) The daily meal allowance

D) The daily salary and meal allowance combined

17

The specific heat capacity of substance K, in calories per gram (cal/g), is approximately 30% less than that of methyl alcohol. The specific heat capacity of methyl alcohol is 0.60 cal/g. Which of the following is closest to the specific heat capacity, in cal/g, of substance K?

A) 0.18

B) 0.42

C) 0.56

D) 0.78

15

For what number of days, d, would the player's total compensation including signing bonus, salary, and meal allowance with the Eagles be greater than the total compensation with the Jays?

A) $d < 5$

B) $d > 5$

C) $d < 6$

D) $d > 6$

CONTINUE

18

In the *xy*-plane, if (–1, 0) is a solution to the system of inequalities $y < x + c$ and $y < -x - d$, which of the following must be true about *c* and *d* ?

A) $c = d$

B) $c = -d$

C) $c < d$

D) $d < c$

19

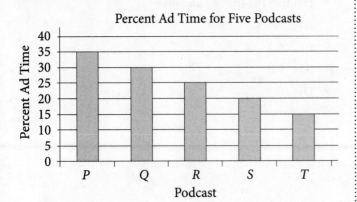

Percent Ad Time for Five Podcasts

A company advertises on five different podcasts: *P*, *Q*, *R*, *S*, and *T*. The graph above shows the amount of time used for the ad on the five different podcasts as a percentage of total run time. Each podcast runs for the same length of time, and the costs to advertise on podcasts *P*, *Q*, *R*, *S* and *T* are $400, $350, $200, $180, and $150, respectively. Which of the following podcasts provides the most ad time per dollar?

A) *Q*

B) *R*

C) *S*

D) *T*

20

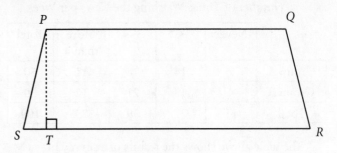

In quadrilateral *PQRS* above, *PS* = *QR*, and $\overline{PQ}$ is parallel to $\overline{SR}$. If *PQ* and *SR* were both decreased by 75% and *PT* were quadrupled, how would the area of *PQRS* change?

A) The area of *PQRS* would be quadrupled.

B) The area of *PQRS* would be increased by 75%.

C) The area of *PQRS* would be decreased by 75%.

D) The area of *PQRS* would be unaffected.

CONTINUE

Number of Times Watching the News per Week

	Never	1–2	3–4	More than 4	Total
Group A	7	14	18	11	50
Group B	4	13	21	12	50
Total	11	27	39	23	100

The table above shows the results of a survey in which 100 people were asked how often they watched the news. Group A consisted of people who were registered voters, and Group B consisted of people who were not registered to vote. If one person is randomly chosen from among those who watch the news fewer than three times a week, what is the probability that the person was a member of Group A?

A) $\dfrac{21}{38}$

B) $\dfrac{4}{50}$

C) $\dfrac{21}{50}$

D) $\dfrac{38}{100}$

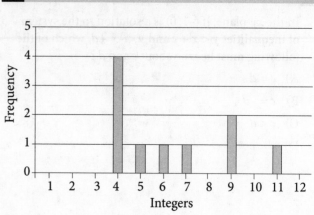

The bar graph above shows the distribution of randomly selected integers from 1 to 12. What is the mean of the list of numbers?

A) 5.5

B) 6.3

C) 7.0

D) 10.0

CONTINUE

Questions 23–25 refer to the following information.

A team of scientists measures the volume of various samples of different gases with a constant pressure of 0.1 atm and a constant temperature of 610 K. The graph below plots the volume of each sample against the amount of the gas.

Volume-Amount Relationship
Among Samples of Gases

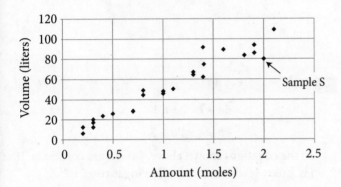

The Ideal Gas Law predicts that at this pressure and temperature, the volume of an ideal gas can be modeled by the equation $V = 50n$, where V is the volume in liters and n is the amount of the substance, measured in moles. Assume that the relationship is valid for greater amounts of the substance than are shown in the graph. (A mole is approximately 6.022×10^{23} molecules.)

23

According to the data provided, what is the volume, in <u>milliliters</u>, of Sample S?

A) 8×10^4

B) 2×10^3

C) 8×10^1

D) 4×10^1

24

There are three samples shown of approximately 1.4 moles. Which of the following is closest to the range of volumes of these three samples, in liters?

A) 30

B) 20

C) 9

D) 3

25

Based on the ideal gas law, what is the volume, in liters, of a sample that contains 1,200 moles?

A) 6,000

B) 24,000

C) 36,000

D) 60,000

CONTINUE

26

Let the polynomials f and g be defined by
$f(x) = 3x^3 + 6x^2 + 11x$ and $g(x) = 8x^2 + 15x + 7$. Which of the following polynomials is divisible by $3x + 7$?

A) $j(x) = 2f(x) + g(x)$

B) $k(x) = f(x) + g(x)$

C) $m(x) = f(x) + 2g(x)$

D) $n(x) = f(x) + 3g(x)$

27

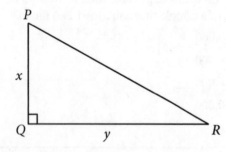

Given the right triangle PQR above, which of the following is equal to $\dfrac{y}{x}$?

A) $\cos P$

B) $\cos Q$

C) $\tan P$

D) $\tan Q$

28

Let the function f be defined by $f(x) = (x - 1)(x + 7)$. Which of the following is an equivalent form of f in which the minimum value of f appears as either a coefficient or a constant?

A) $f(x) = x^2 - 7$

B) $f(x) = x^2 + 6x - 7$

C) $f(x) = (x + 3)^2 - 16$

D) $f(x) = (x - 3)^2 - 20$

29

$$4a - j = 7a + 3$$
$$4b - k = 7b + 3$$

In the equations shown above, j and k are constants. If j is k plus 1, which of the following is true?

A) a is b plus $\dfrac{1}{3}$.

B) a is b minus $\dfrac{1}{3}$.

C) a is b minus 1.

D) a is b minus 3.

CONTINUE

30

If the average (arithmetic mean) of $3x$ and 11 is a, the average of $4x$ and 6 is b, and the average of $5x$ and 7 is c, what is the average of a, b, and c, in terms of x ?

A)　$x + 2$

B)　$x + 3$

C)　$2x + 4$

D)　$4x + 8$

CONTINUE

DIRECTIONS

For questions 31–38, solve the problem and enter your answer in the grid, as described below, on the answer sheet.

1. Although not required, it is suggested that you write your answer in the boxes at the top of the columns to help you fill in the circles accurately. You will receive credit only if the circles are filled in correctly.

2. Mark no more than one circle in any column.

3. No question has a negative answer.

4. Some problems may have more than one correct answer. In such cases, grid only one answer.

5. **Mixed numbers** such as $3\frac{1}{2}$ must be gridded as 3.5 or 7/2. (If [3 1 / 2] is entered into the grid, it will be interpreted as $\frac{31}{2}$, not as $3\frac{1}{2}$.)

6. **Decimal Answers:** If you obtain a decimal answer with more digits than the grid can accommodate, it may be either rounded or truncated, but it must fill the entire grid.

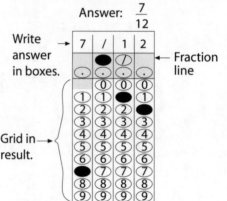

Acceptable ways to grid $\frac{2}{3}$ are:

Answer: 201 – either position is correct

NOTE: You may start your answers in any column, space permitting. Columns you don't need to use should be left blank.

CONTINUE →

31

A scientist estimates that the water level of a lake is dropping by 2.25 inches per year. If this trend continues, how many years will it take for the water level in the lake to drop by 27 inches?

32

A car factory that operates 24 hours a day and 7 days a week produces one car every 20 minutes. How many cars does the factory produce in 3 days?

33

Scores in the game of bowling range from 0 to 300 per game, inclusive. Vito's average score in the first 6 games of a bowling tournament was 200. What is the lowest score he can receive in his 7th game and still have an average score of at least 240 for the entire 12-game tournament?

34

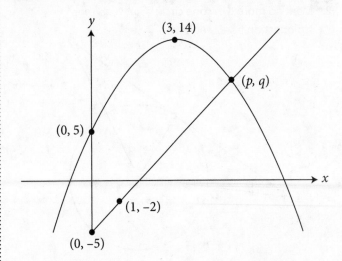

The *xy*-plane shows a point of intersection between a line and a parabola. The point of intersection has coordinates (p, q). If the vertex of the parabola is at $(3, 14)$, what is the value of p ?

CONTINUE ➔

35

To purchase a car, Harry makes a down payment, and every month thereafter, he pays a fixed amount to the car dealer. The total amount, T, in dollars, that Harry has paid after m months can be represented by the equation $T = 175m + 350$. According to this equation, how much, in dollars, was Harry's down payment? (Disregard the $ sign when gridding your answer.)

36

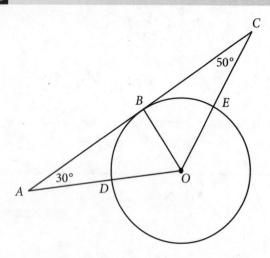

In the figure above, line segment AC is tangent to the circle with center O at point B. Line segments AO and CO intersect the circle at points D and E, respectively. If the circumference of circle O is 72, what is the length of minor arc $\overset{\frown}{DE}$?

Questions 37 and 38 refer to the following information.

The population of a small town is currently 800. A statistician estimates that the population of the town will decline by 14 percent per year for the next five years. The statistician models the population, P, of the town after x years using the equation $P = 800(k)^x$.

37

In the equation above, what value should be used for k ?

38

According to the statistician's model, what will the population of the town be, to the nearest whole number, after five years?

END OF TEST

DO NOT RETURN TO A PREVIOUS SECTION.

Completely darken bubbles with a No. 2 pencil. If you make a mistake, be sure to erase mark completely. Erase all stray marks.

1.

YOUR NAME: _____
(Print)   Last   First   M.I.

SIGNATURE: _____   DATE: ___ / ___ / ___

HOME ADDRESS: _____
(Print)   Number and Street

_____
City   State   Zip Code

PHONE NO.: _____
(Print)

IMPORTANT: Please fill in these boxes exactly as shown on the back cover of your test book.

2. TEST FORM

6. DATE OF BIRTH

Month		Day		Year	
○ JAN					
○ FEB	⓪	⓪	⓪	⓪
○ MAR	①	①	①	①
○ APR	②	②	②	②
○ MAY	③	③	③	③
○ JUN		④	④	④
○ JUL		⑤	⑤	⑤
○ AUG		⑥	⑥	⑥
○ SEP		⑦	⑦	⑦
○ OCT		⑧	⑧	⑧
○ NOV		⑨	⑨	⑨
○ DEC				

3. TEST CODE   **4. REGISTRATION NUMBER**

0	A	J	0	0	0	0	0	0	0	0	0
1	B	K	1	1	1	1	1	1	1	1	1
2	C	L	2	2	2	2	2	2	2	2	2
3	D	M	3	3	3	3	3	3	3	3	3
4	E	N	4	4	4	4	4	4	4	4	4
5	F	O	5	5	5	5	5	5	5	5	5
6	G	P	6	6	6	6	6	6	6	6	6
7	H	Q	7	7	7	7	7	7	7	7	7
8	I	R	8	8	8	8	8	8	8	8	8
9			9	9	9	9	9	9	9	9	9

7. SEX
○ MALE
○ FEMALE

The **Princeton Review**®

5. YOUR NAME

First 4 letters of last name				FIRST INIT	MID INIT
Ⓐ	Ⓐ	Ⓐ	Ⓐ	Ⓐ	Ⓐ
Ⓑ	Ⓑ	Ⓑ	Ⓑ	Ⓑ	Ⓑ
Ⓒ	Ⓒ	Ⓒ	Ⓒ	Ⓒ	Ⓒ
Ⓓ	Ⓓ	Ⓓ	Ⓓ	Ⓓ	Ⓓ
Ⓔ	Ⓔ	Ⓔ	Ⓔ	Ⓔ	Ⓔ
Ⓕ	Ⓕ	Ⓕ	Ⓕ	Ⓕ	Ⓕ
Ⓖ	Ⓖ	Ⓖ	Ⓖ	Ⓖ	Ⓖ
Ⓗ	Ⓗ	Ⓗ	Ⓗ	Ⓗ	Ⓗ
Ⓘ	Ⓘ	Ⓘ	Ⓘ	Ⓘ	Ⓘ
Ⓙ	Ⓙ	Ⓙ	Ⓙ	Ⓙ	Ⓙ
Ⓚ	Ⓚ	Ⓚ	Ⓚ	Ⓚ	Ⓚ
Ⓛ	Ⓛ	Ⓛ	Ⓛ	Ⓛ	Ⓛ
Ⓜ	Ⓜ	Ⓜ	Ⓜ	Ⓜ	Ⓜ
Ⓝ	Ⓝ	Ⓝ	Ⓝ	Ⓝ	Ⓝ
Ⓞ	Ⓞ	Ⓞ	Ⓞ	Ⓞ	Ⓞ
Ⓟ	Ⓟ	Ⓟ	Ⓟ	Ⓟ	Ⓟ
Ⓠ	Ⓠ	Ⓠ	Ⓠ	Ⓠ	Ⓠ
Ⓡ	Ⓡ	Ⓡ	Ⓡ	Ⓡ	Ⓡ
Ⓢ	Ⓢ	Ⓢ	Ⓢ	Ⓢ	Ⓢ
Ⓣ	Ⓣ	Ⓣ	Ⓣ	Ⓣ	Ⓣ
Ⓤ	Ⓤ	Ⓤ	Ⓤ	Ⓤ	Ⓤ
Ⓥ	Ⓥ	Ⓥ	Ⓥ	Ⓥ	Ⓥ
Ⓦ	Ⓦ	Ⓦ	Ⓦ	Ⓦ	Ⓦ
Ⓧ	Ⓧ	Ⓧ	Ⓧ	Ⓧ	Ⓧ
Ⓨ	Ⓨ	Ⓨ	Ⓨ	Ⓨ	Ⓨ
Ⓩ	Ⓩ	Ⓩ	Ⓩ	Ⓩ	Ⓩ

Test ⑥   Start with number 1 for each new section.
If a section has fewer questions than answer spaces, leave the extra answer spaces blank.

Section 1—Reading

1. Ⓐ Ⓑ Ⓒ Ⓓ
2. Ⓐ Ⓑ Ⓒ Ⓓ
3. Ⓐ Ⓑ Ⓒ Ⓓ
4. Ⓐ Ⓑ Ⓒ Ⓓ
5. Ⓐ Ⓑ Ⓒ Ⓓ
6. Ⓐ Ⓑ Ⓒ Ⓓ
7. Ⓐ Ⓑ Ⓒ Ⓓ
8. Ⓐ Ⓑ Ⓒ Ⓓ
9. Ⓐ Ⓑ Ⓒ Ⓓ
10. Ⓐ Ⓑ Ⓒ Ⓓ
11. Ⓐ Ⓑ Ⓒ Ⓓ
12. Ⓐ Ⓑ Ⓒ Ⓓ
13. Ⓐ Ⓑ Ⓒ Ⓓ
14. Ⓐ Ⓑ Ⓒ Ⓓ
15. Ⓐ Ⓑ Ⓒ Ⓓ
16. Ⓐ Ⓑ Ⓒ Ⓓ
17. Ⓐ Ⓑ Ⓒ Ⓓ
18. Ⓐ Ⓑ Ⓒ Ⓓ
19. Ⓐ Ⓑ Ⓒ Ⓓ
20. Ⓐ Ⓑ Ⓒ Ⓓ
21. Ⓐ Ⓑ Ⓒ Ⓓ
22. Ⓐ Ⓑ Ⓒ Ⓓ
23. Ⓐ Ⓑ Ⓒ Ⓓ
24. Ⓐ Ⓑ Ⓒ Ⓓ
25. Ⓐ Ⓑ Ⓒ Ⓓ
26. Ⓐ Ⓑ Ⓒ Ⓓ
27. Ⓐ Ⓑ Ⓒ Ⓓ
28. Ⓐ Ⓑ Ⓒ Ⓓ
29. Ⓐ Ⓑ Ⓒ Ⓓ
30. Ⓐ Ⓑ Ⓒ Ⓓ
31. Ⓐ Ⓑ Ⓒ Ⓓ
32. Ⓐ Ⓑ Ⓒ Ⓓ
33. Ⓐ Ⓑ Ⓒ Ⓓ
34. Ⓐ Ⓑ Ⓒ Ⓓ
35. Ⓐ Ⓑ Ⓒ Ⓓ
36. Ⓐ Ⓑ Ⓒ Ⓓ
37. Ⓐ Ⓑ Ⓒ Ⓓ
38. Ⓐ Ⓑ Ⓒ Ⓓ
39. Ⓐ Ⓑ Ⓒ Ⓓ
40. Ⓐ Ⓑ Ⓒ Ⓓ
41. Ⓐ Ⓑ Ⓒ Ⓓ
42. Ⓐ Ⓑ Ⓒ Ⓓ
43. Ⓐ Ⓑ Ⓒ Ⓓ
44. Ⓐ Ⓑ Ⓒ Ⓓ
45. Ⓐ Ⓑ Ⓒ Ⓓ
46. Ⓐ Ⓑ Ⓒ Ⓓ
47. Ⓐ Ⓑ Ⓒ Ⓓ
48. Ⓐ Ⓑ Ⓒ Ⓓ
49. Ⓐ Ⓑ Ⓒ Ⓓ
50. Ⓐ Ⓑ Ⓒ Ⓓ
51. Ⓐ Ⓑ Ⓒ Ⓓ
52. Ⓐ Ⓑ Ⓒ Ⓓ

Section 2—Writing and Language Skills

1. Ⓐ Ⓑ Ⓒ Ⓓ
2. Ⓐ Ⓑ Ⓒ Ⓓ
3. Ⓐ Ⓑ Ⓒ Ⓓ
4. Ⓐ Ⓑ Ⓒ Ⓓ
5. Ⓐ Ⓑ Ⓒ Ⓓ
6. Ⓐ Ⓑ Ⓒ Ⓓ
7. Ⓐ Ⓑ Ⓒ Ⓓ
8. Ⓐ Ⓑ Ⓒ Ⓓ
9. Ⓐ Ⓑ Ⓒ Ⓓ
10. Ⓐ Ⓑ Ⓒ Ⓓ
11. Ⓐ Ⓑ Ⓒ Ⓓ
12. Ⓐ Ⓑ Ⓒ Ⓓ
13. Ⓐ Ⓑ Ⓒ Ⓓ
14. Ⓐ Ⓑ Ⓒ Ⓓ
15. Ⓐ Ⓑ Ⓒ Ⓓ
16. Ⓐ Ⓑ Ⓒ Ⓓ
17. Ⓐ Ⓑ Ⓒ Ⓓ
18. Ⓐ Ⓑ Ⓒ Ⓓ
19. Ⓐ Ⓑ Ⓒ Ⓓ
20. Ⓐ Ⓑ Ⓒ Ⓓ
21. Ⓐ Ⓑ Ⓒ Ⓓ
22. Ⓐ Ⓑ Ⓒ Ⓓ
23. Ⓐ Ⓑ Ⓒ Ⓓ
24. Ⓐ Ⓑ Ⓒ Ⓓ
25. Ⓐ Ⓑ Ⓒ Ⓓ
26. Ⓐ Ⓑ Ⓒ Ⓓ
27. Ⓐ Ⓑ Ⓒ Ⓓ
28. Ⓐ Ⓑ Ⓒ Ⓓ
29. Ⓐ Ⓑ Ⓒ Ⓓ
30. Ⓐ Ⓑ Ⓒ Ⓓ
31. Ⓐ Ⓑ Ⓒ Ⓓ
32. Ⓐ Ⓑ Ⓒ Ⓓ
33. Ⓐ Ⓑ Ⓒ Ⓓ
34. Ⓐ Ⓑ Ⓒ Ⓓ
35. Ⓐ Ⓑ Ⓒ Ⓓ
36. Ⓐ Ⓑ Ⓒ Ⓓ
37. Ⓐ Ⓑ Ⓒ Ⓓ
38. Ⓐ Ⓑ Ⓒ Ⓓ
39. Ⓐ Ⓑ Ⓒ Ⓓ
40. Ⓐ Ⓑ Ⓒ Ⓓ
41. Ⓐ Ⓑ Ⓒ Ⓓ
42. Ⓐ Ⓑ Ⓒ Ⓓ
43. Ⓐ Ⓑ Ⓒ Ⓓ
44. Ⓐ Ⓑ Ⓒ Ⓓ

The Princeton Review®

Test ⑥ Start with number 1 for each new section.
If a section has fewer questions than answer spaces, leave the extra answer spaces blank.

Section 3—Mathematics: No Calculator

1. Ⓐ Ⓑ Ⓒ Ⓓ
2. Ⓐ Ⓑ Ⓒ Ⓓ
3. Ⓐ Ⓑ Ⓒ Ⓓ
4. Ⓐ Ⓑ Ⓒ Ⓓ
5. Ⓐ Ⓑ Ⓒ Ⓓ
6. Ⓐ Ⓑ Ⓒ Ⓓ
7. Ⓐ Ⓑ Ⓒ Ⓓ
8. Ⓐ Ⓑ Ⓒ Ⓓ
9. Ⓐ Ⓑ Ⓒ Ⓓ
10. Ⓐ Ⓑ Ⓒ Ⓓ
11. Ⓐ Ⓑ Ⓒ Ⓓ
12. Ⓐ Ⓑ Ⓒ Ⓓ
13. Ⓐ Ⓑ Ⓒ Ⓓ
14. Ⓐ Ⓑ Ⓒ Ⓓ
15. Ⓐ Ⓑ Ⓒ Ⓓ

16. 17. 18. 19. 20.

Section 4—Mathematics: Calculator

1. Ⓐ Ⓑ Ⓒ Ⓓ
2. Ⓐ Ⓑ Ⓒ Ⓓ
3. Ⓐ Ⓑ Ⓒ Ⓓ
4. Ⓐ Ⓑ Ⓒ Ⓓ
5. Ⓐ Ⓑ Ⓒ Ⓓ
6. Ⓐ Ⓑ Ⓒ Ⓓ
7. Ⓐ Ⓑ Ⓒ Ⓓ
8. Ⓐ Ⓑ Ⓒ Ⓓ
9. Ⓐ Ⓑ Ⓒ Ⓓ
10. Ⓐ Ⓑ Ⓒ Ⓓ
11. Ⓐ Ⓑ Ⓒ Ⓓ
12. Ⓐ Ⓑ Ⓒ Ⓓ
13. Ⓐ Ⓑ Ⓒ Ⓓ
14. Ⓐ Ⓑ Ⓒ Ⓓ
15. Ⓐ Ⓑ Ⓒ Ⓓ
16. Ⓐ Ⓑ Ⓒ Ⓓ
17. Ⓐ Ⓑ Ⓒ Ⓓ
18. Ⓐ Ⓑ Ⓒ Ⓓ
19. Ⓐ Ⓑ Ⓒ Ⓓ
20. Ⓐ Ⓑ Ⓒ Ⓓ
21. Ⓐ Ⓑ Ⓒ Ⓓ
22. Ⓐ Ⓑ Ⓒ Ⓓ
23. Ⓐ Ⓑ Ⓒ Ⓓ
24. Ⓐ Ⓑ Ⓒ Ⓓ
25. Ⓐ Ⓑ Ⓒ Ⓓ
26. Ⓐ Ⓑ Ⓒ Ⓓ
27. Ⓐ Ⓑ Ⓒ Ⓓ
28. Ⓐ Ⓑ Ⓒ Ⓓ
29. Ⓐ Ⓑ Ⓒ Ⓓ
30. Ⓐ Ⓑ Ⓒ Ⓓ

31. 32. 33. 34. 35.

36. 37. 38.

Chapter 14
Practice Test 6:
Answers and
Explanations

PRACTICE TEST 6 ANSWER KEY

Section 1: Reading		Section 2: Writing & Language		Section 3: Math (No Calculator)		Section 4: Math (Calculator)	
1. D	27. B	1. D	23. A	1. A	11. A	1. D	20. D
2. C	28. B	2. D	24. D	2. C	12. C	2. B	21. A
3. B	29. B	3. D	25. B	3. B	13. B	3. A	22. B
4. D	30. D	4. A	26. A	4. D	14. A	4. D	23. A
5. C	31. A	5. B	27. D	5. A	15. C	5. D	24. A
6. C	32. C	6. B	28. C	6. D	16. 3	6. C	25. D
7. C	33. D	7. D	29. C	7. C	17. 250	7. C	26. C
8. A	34. C	8. B	30. B	8. A	18. $\frac{3}{5}$ or 0.6	8. A	27. C
9. C	35. D	9. C	31. A	9. B		9. C	28. C
10. C	36. C	10. A	32. B	10. D	19. 9	10. B	29. B
11. B	37. A	11. A	33. C		20. 3	11. D	30. C
12. B	38. B	12. C	34. B			12. A	31. 12
13. B	39. A	13. A	35. C			13. B	32. 216
14. D	40. B	14. D	36. B			14. A	33. 180
15. A	41. C	15. B	37. D			15. B	34. 5
16. C	42. B	16. A	38. C			16. A	35. 350
17. B	43. D	17. B	39. B			17. B	36. 20
18. A	44. C	18. D	40. B			18. D	37. 0.86
19. C	45. B	19. B	41. A			19. B	38. 376
20. D	46. B	20. D	42. D				
21. A	47. C	21. C	43. D				
22. A	48. A	22. D	44. D				
23. A	49. A						
24. D	50. C						
25. A	51. C						
26. D	52. D						

Go to PrincetonReview.com to score your exam. Alternatively, for self-assessment tables, please turn to page 909.

PRACTICE TEST 6 EXPLANATIONS

Section 1: Reading

1. **D** The question asks for the best summary of the passage. Because this is a general question, it should be done after all of the specific questions. Choice (A) incorrectly states that a character *becomes increasingly hostile*; eliminate it. Choice (B) incorrectly states that a *character describes* something, so eliminate (B). Choice (C) states that two characters are *in the same profession*, which is not true, and that they *become increasingly competitive*, which is not true; eliminate it. Choice (D) states that two characters are *traveling together*, which is true, and that they *eagerly await confrontation*. This statement could sound extreme, but it does fit the mention of a *frequent bone of contention* and the idea that one character *liked to infuriate* the other. The correct answer is (D).

2. **C** The question asks for the main purpose of the opening sentence. Read the first paragraph and determine the purpose of the first sentence in context. The first sentence describes *cheerfulness* in general before the paragraph moves forward with specific descriptions of the cheerfulness of the characters. Eliminate any answers that are inconsistent with this prediction. Choice (A) incorrectly mentions a *contrast* and the *narrator's gloom*; eliminate it. Choice (B) refers to an *allegorical representation*, which is not present in the text, so eliminate this answer. Choice (C) matches the prediction, so keep it. Choice (D) incorrectly refers to *violent intentions*; eliminate it. The correct answer is (C).

3. **B** The question asks how the narrator's focus shifts in the second paragraph. Carefully read the second paragraph to determine what the shift is. At the beginning of the paragraph, the narrator says that it is *dreadful* for a parson to be *warlike* and that she remembers *distinctly whose servant he is*, so the narrator is referencing a parson being a *man of peace*. In the second half of the paragraph, the narrator continues by saying to the *parson-haters* that she will not go along *every step* of their *dismal, downward-tending, unchristian road*. The correct answer must have something to do with the shift from acknowledging the parson as a man of peace to disagreeing with those who are anti-parson. Eliminate (A) because the narrator does not want to chastise the clergy. Choice (B) matches the prediction, so keep it. Eliminate (C) because the second part of the paragraph does not mention the clergy's *manners and appearance*. The second half of the paragraph does not discuss two clergymen, so eliminate (D). The correct answer is (B).

4. **D** The question asks about the effect of the words *rancour* and *denunciation* in context. Go back to the second paragraph to see how the words are used. The narrator says *if you are a parson-hater*, she's not going to *go along* with the *poisonous rancour* and *horror and denunciation* toward a rector. The correct answer should have something to do with showing strong anti-clergy sentiments. Eliminate (A) because the narrator has no *fear* of clergymen. Choice (B) can be eliminated because it has nothing to do with the prediction. Eliminate (C) because it does not match the prediction because the narrator speaks to those who are anti-clergy, rather than illustrating her own *sense of dismay*. Choice (D) mentions the *disapproval of clergymen* in the prediction, and the *reader* in the answer choice supports the narrator's use of *you*. The correct answer is (D).

5. **C** The question asks about *Moore's behavior*. Look for *Moore* in the passage and read for context about his behavior. In the first paragraph, the narrator says that both of the men knew that there were those who would have had *great pleasure in shooting either of [them]* and that the two men were *elate[d]* with this knowledge. The final paragraph says *you would expect...they would converse amicably. Oh no!* and then goes on to say that Moore *liked to infuriate Helstone*. It's

clear from the text that Moore likes to fight and pick fights, so the correct answer should reflect this. Choice (A) is deceptive: it contains words seen in the text but describes Helstone rather than Moore. Eliminate it. Choice (B) also describes Helstone rather than Moore, so it can be eliminated. Choice (C) is a solid paraphrase of the prediction, so keep it. Choice (D) is deceptive because the word *superiority* seems to match *reign supreme*, but *reign supreme* refers to Bonaparte, not Moore, so eliminate it. The correct answer is (C).

6. **C** The question asks how Helstone might be described and refers to the narrator's acknowledgment of a *certain evil* in the third paragraph. Look in the third paragraph to see that the narrator's larger point about Helstone is that he is not temperamentally suited to being a priest and *should have been a soldier*. On the whole, he is described positively, though some of his limitations are noted. Eliminate (A), as in the text he is described as *a man almost without sympathy*. Eliminate (B) because Helstone is not a *soldier*. Keep (C), as Helstone is described in lines 43–46 as *conscientious…true to principle*, and *honourable*. Eliminate (D) because its tone is negative and there's no evidence to support such an extreme characterization. The correct answer is (C).

7. **C** The question asks for the best evidence to support the correct answer to the previous question. The lines used to answer the previous question are lines 42–47. The correct answer is (C).

8. **A** The question asks about the effect of comparing Helstone to a Cossack. To answer this question, look at the comparison in context. The narrator says, *"Nor will I curse Helstone, clerical Cossack as he was. Yet he was cursed…."* Thus, being a Cossack is something bad. Choice (A) could be true, so keep it. Choice (B) refers to an event, rather than a person; eliminate it. Choice (C) refers to two men, but this paragraph focuses on Helstone only; eliminate it. Choice (D) refers to an action, rather than a person; eliminate it. The only remaining answer is (A), so select it. The correct answer is (A).

9. **C** The question asks how the men found each other's company sometimes, despite their *excellent spirits*. The contrast indicates to look for a negative idea. Use these lead words to read the window at the beginning of paragraph 4, which states in line 62 that they *chafed each other's moods*. Now read the answer choices to see which matches the evidence. Eliminate (A) because there is no evidence that they found each other *intolerable*, only that they annoyed each other. Choice (B) is irrelevant to the text, so it can be eliminated. Choice (C) matches the idea that they annoyed each other, so keep it. Choice (D) can be eliminated because it's a positive word, and the two men were not *comforting* each other. Choice (C) is appropriately negative for the passage. The correct answer is (C).

10. **C** The question asks for the best evidence for the answer to the previous question. The line used to answer the previous question was line 62. The correct answer is (C).

11. **B** The question asks about the main purpose of the passage. Because this is a general question, it should be done after all the specific questions are completed. The passage is about how *education* is treated like a *commodity*, but this treatment ends up *trivializing education*. Eliminate any answer choices that aren't consistent with this idea. Choice (A) can be eliminated because the passage does the opposite of *advocat[ing] for the marketing of education*. Choice (B) is possible, because the topic is *complex*, and the author of the passage has an opinion, so keep it. The author of the passage has a negative opinion about marketing education, so eliminate (C). Choice (D) incorrectly states that the passage's focus is to evaluate statistics, so eliminate it. The correct answer is (B).

12. **B** The question asks about the concession the authors make to the view that people are *consumers in the marketplace of life*. Notice that the following question is a best evidence question, so this ques-

tion and Q13 can be answered in tandem. Look at the answers for Q13 first. The lines in (13A) say that every aspect of life has *cash value* and *can be purchased*. While this does agree with the view presented in the question, these lines do not support any of the answers for Q12, so (13A) can be eliminated. The lines in (13B) say *this scenario may be appropriate for the sale of shoes....* This agrees with the idea that people are consumers, and these lines support (12B). Connect these two answers. The lines in (13C) might initially seem to support (12C) because of the mention of *students* and *customers*, but a careful reading shows these two answers don't actually support each other. Eliminate (13C). The lines in (13D) talk about the students *wanting to be entertained*, which isn't mentioned in any of the choices for Q12. Eliminate (13D). Without any support from Q13, (12A), (12C), and (12D) can be eliminated. The correct answers are (12B) and (13B).

13.　**B**　(See explanation above.)

14.　**D**　The question asks what the word *assume* means in line 13. Go back to the text, find the word *assume*, and mark it out. Carefully read the surrounding text to determine another word that would fit in the blank based on the context of the passage. The text refers to the expectation students have that the education they purchase will *meet their needs* and *assume a form they find palatable*. Something like "adopt" or "accept" could work well for the missing word. Choice (A), *guess intelligently*, could be a possible definition of "assume," but it's not consistent with the context. Eliminate (A). Choice (B), *pretend grudgingly*, is not consistent with the prediction, so it can be eliminated. Choice (C), *suppose blindly*, is another possible definition of *assume*, but it does not fit the context of the passage, so eliminate it. Choice (D), *take on readily*, fits the prediction. The correct answer is (D).

15.　**A**　The question asks about the main purpose of the fourth paragraph. Carefully read the fourth paragraph and determine why the author included it in the passage. In the paragraph, the authors translate the educational experience into economic terms, presenting the idea that *achieving some sort of advantage is considered...essential to beating the competition*. They go on to explain how cheating and *dubious maneuvers*, though *unfortunate*, have become rampant because that is an easier way to achieve success. Choice (A) matches the text because the authors do explain the *logic of an attitude* (cheating) and they do disagree with that attitude. Eliminate (B) because it is something the authors may agree with outside of the text, but that's not what the fourth paragraph is about. Choice (C) has nothing to do with the paragraph and can be eliminated. Although they don't agree with cheating, the fourth paragraph does not argue against cheating, so (D) can be eliminated. The correct answer is (A).

16.　**C**　The question asks what the word *enticing* means in line 57. Go back to the text, find the word *enticing*, and mark it out. Carefully read the surrounding text to determine another word that would fit in the blank based on the context of the passage. The text refers to an *array of courses* being *indispensable to attracting students*. A word similar to "attractive" or "exciting" could work well. Choice (A), *pulling*, is not consistent with that prediction. Choice (B) can be eliminated because the courses are not designed to *deceive*. Choice (C), *appealing*, is consistent with "attractive," so keep it. Eliminate (D) because *suggestive* is not consistent with the text. The correct answer is (C).

17.　**B**　The question asks for the best support for the claim that *schools have already begun to incorporate some facets of the popular marketplace into their educational materials*. Read the lines from each answer choice in the passage. The lines in (A) describe what administrators *must* do, rather than what they have already begun to do, so eliminate it. The lines in (B) describe something that *has become normative*, so this could fit; keep it. The lines in (C) describe an effect of treating education as a business, not an aspect of business that has been incorporated into education, so eliminate it. The lines in (D) refer to courses that administrators *have begun to promote*, so keep that answer. Now read closely around (B) and (D) to compare them to each other. Choice (B) mentions a *proliferation of degrees and courses with captivating titles*, which is closely linked to the idea of *advertising consultants* for schools in the next sentence. Choice (D) mentions *trendy courses that administrators have begun to promote*, but this is linked to the idea that *difficult subjects are avoided*, which is not a concept drawn from the marketplace; eliminate it. The correct answer is (B).

18.   A   The question asks about the main idea of the last paragraph. Carefully read the last paragraph to determine the main idea. The paragraph states that *education is trivialized when it is treated like a commodity*. Look for answers that convey the idea that treating education like a business hurts education. Choice (A) contains both of these ideas from the prediction, so keep it. Choice (B) is true, but it is a secondary point in the last paragraph, too narrow to be the main idea. Eliminate (B). Choice (C) is tempting, but it changes the meaning of *trivial* to *unimportant* in the wrong context. Choice (D) is deceptive, using concepts from the last paragraph to say something that the paragraph itself does not say; eliminate it. The correct answer is (A).

19.   C   The question asks what statement is supported by the data in the graph. Look at the graph and notice units and any obvious trends. All three lines show a positive increase, a small one with overall consumer prices and a big one with college textbooks and tuition and fees. Choice (A) mentions an increase, so keep it. Eliminate (B) because it says there is no increase. Choice (C) mentions an increase, so keep it. Eliminate (D) because it says there is a decrease. Now compare (A) and (C). Choice (A) indicates a consistent rise in overall prices, which does not match the graph, whereas (C) indicates a larger increase for tuition and fees, which matches the information in the graph. The correct answer is (C).

20.   D   The question asks during which period the difference was largest between college tuition and fees and overall consumer prices. Look at the graph and see that the largest increase was in 2012. The correct answer is (D).

21.   A   The question asks which idea in the passage is most directly supported by the graph. To answer this question, note that the graph is measuring prices. Now eliminate answers that do not concern prices, which are (B), (C), and (D). Choice (A) is about revenue, which is related to prices and discussed throughout the passage and the graph. The correct answer is (A).

22.   A   The question asks what the authors of the first passage indicate about the addition of nutrients to food, which is covered throughout the whole passage. Notice that the following question is a best evidence question, so this question and Q23 can be answered in tandem. Look at the answers for Q23 first. Start with (23A). The lines say that processed food contributes to *both food security...and nutrition security*. This could support (22A) because contributing to food and nutrition security is a *helpful impact*. Connect those two answers. The lines in (23B) ask how people could *enhance the contribution to...nutritional...and food security*. These lines ask a question rather than present information, so eliminate (23B). The lines in (23C) present a contrast between *limiting processed foods* and *encouraging best available food options*. These lines don't support any of the answers for Q22, so eliminate (23C). The lines in (23D) mention a *disadvantage* in that the techniques are *poorly understood*. These lines may initially seem to support (22C), but there's no indication from the text that they *may require further investigation*. Even though it might make sense that something poorly understood would need further investigation, that's not in the text. Eliminate (23D). The correct answers are (22A) and (23A).

23.   A   (See explanation above.)

24.   **D**   The question asks about food enrichment methods, which are mentioned throughout the first passage. Use chronology to look for this answer somewhere between the answers to the preceding and following questions. *Food processing techniques* are mentioned in line 37, so carefully read the window, which says that one *disadvantage of commercial food processing techniques* is that they are *poorly understood*. Choice (A) can be eliminated because there is no information about how the food enrichment is done. Choice (B) can be eliminated because there is no mention of *employment opportunities*. Thiamin is mentioned in the fourth paragraph as an enrichment, but the text doesn't actually support choice (C). Eliminate it. Choice (D) is a direct paraphrase of the prediction. The correct answer is (D).

25.   **A**   The question asks what the word *grasp* means in line 40. Go back to the text, find the word *grasp*, and mark it out. Carefully read the surrounding text to determine another word that would fit in the blank based on the context of the passage. The passage talks about the processing techniques that are *difficult for the general public to grasp*. A word like "understand" could work well. Choice (A), *comprehend*, is consistent with that prediction; keep it. Choices (B), *clutch*, (C), *squeeze*, and (D), *reach*, are all possible definitions for *grasp*, but none of them means "understand." The correct answer is (A).

26.   **D**   The question asks what Passage 2's reference to "Big Food" suggests about global food systems. Use lead words to find the window and read carefully. Lines 58–60 state that *"Big Food"* means *multinational food and beverage companies with huge and concentrated market power*. Choices (A) and (C) do not mention companies; eliminate them. Choice (B) refers to single companies that serve individual regions, and (D) refers to a few companies that dominate. Choice (D) is consistent with the prediction. The correct answer is (D).

27.   **B**   The question asks what profit margins and price/cost surpluses have in common in Passage 2. To answer this question, look for the lead words *profit margins* and *price/cost surpluses*; read the window where they are found in paragraph 6 of Passage 2, which states that *Big Food attains profit by expanding markets to reach more people, increasing people's sense of hunger so that they buy more food, and increasing profit margins through encouraging consumption of products with higher price/cost surpluses*. Choice (A) is not supported by this information, as ethics are not brought up; eliminate it. Choice (B) regarding company concerns could be true with regard to *Big Food* companies; keep it. Choice (C) looks relevant because it mentions economics, but the text isn't discussing *economic theory* in general; eliminate it. Choice (D) goes too far; the passage does not indicate how these things are *best increased*; eliminate it. The correct answer is (B).

28.   **B**   The question asks about the effect of the possibilities mentioned in the final paragraph of Passage 2. The last paragraph of the passage states that in order to *promote health, industry would need to make and market healthier foods so as to shift consumption away from highly processed, unhealthy foods. Yet, such healthier foods are inherently less profitable*. Eliminate (A); while it uses words from the paragraph, it suggests the opposite of what the text says. Choice (B) is supported by the idea of this being *inherently less profitable*; keep it. Choices (C) and (D) do not fit the text; eliminate them. The correct answer is (B).

29.   **B**   The question asks about the main purpose of both passages. Because this is a general question about both passages, it should be done after all the questions for each individual passage have been completed. Eliminate choices that are too narrowly focused or that only contain correct information about one passage. Both passages discuss the nutritional concerns of food production. Choice (A) is too specific regarding *vitamin intake* and fits Passage 1 only; eliminate it. Choice (B) is broader and could be true; keep it. Eliminate (C), because it is too specific regarding *nutrition security* and fits some of Passage 1 only. Choice (D) is also too specific regarding *sustainable processing* to be a main idea; eliminate it. The correct answer is (B).

30. **D** The question asks how Passages 1 and 2 are related to each other. Because this is a general question about both passages, it should be done after all the questions for each individual passage have been completed. To answer this question, consider the overall messages of both passages: Passage 1 is positive, saying that American food processing is good, and Passage 2 is more negative, saying that global food systems are problematic. This does not involve *underlying processes* and there is no *solution* in Passage 1, so eliminate (A). Passage 2 does not present a *plan* relating to *processes* presented in Passage 1, so eliminate (B). Each passage seems to have an opinion, rather than *an objective perspective*, so eliminate (C). Choice (D) says that Passage 1 embraces a system, a positive idea, and that Passage 2 explores the problematic nature of a system, a negative idea. The correct answer is (D).

31. **A** The question asks what the authors of both passages would most likely agree on. Because this is a general question about both passages, it should be done after all the questions for each individual passage have been completed. To answer this question, eliminate choices that fit only one or neither passage. Choice (A) mentions adequate nutrition, which both passages examined, so this is possible; keep it. Neither passage discusses whether or not the foods are *appealing*, so eliminate (B). *Suspicion* in (C) is mentioned in Passage 1, but not in Passage 2; eliminate (C). The *nutrient concerns* issue in (D) is absent from Passage 2, and Passage 1 indicates the opposite to be true. The correct answer is (A).

32. **C** The question asks what evidence in Passage 2 matches what is said in lines 48–50 of Passage 1. To answer this question, first review the specific part of Passage 1, and note that it concerns *processing* and *nutritional content*. The lines in (A) discuss processing but not nutrition; eliminate it. The lines in (B) do not discuss processing or nutrition; eliminate it. The lines in (C) discuss both *processing* and nutrition; keep it. Choice (D) has *processing* and mentions *healthier foods*; keep it. To decide between (C) and (D), review the specific part of Passage 1, and note that it focuses on processing and nutrition not necessarily correlating, which means that they might be independent of each other. Choice (C) states that processing *can improve nutritional content*, but that most processing actually serves to *reduce nutritional quality*, suggesting a contrast. Choice (D) states that, for industry to *promote health*, it would need to *shift consumption away from highly processed, unhealthy foods* which indicates that processing and nutrition do correlate. Choice (C) points in two directions, which better fits the prediction. The correct answer is (C).

33. **D** The question asks for the *central problem that Harvey describes in the passage*. Because this is a general question, it should be done after all the specific questions. In lines 1–3, Harvey advocates for *bimetallism*, which is a policy that allows a government to rely on two metals for money. In lines 44–45, Harvey states that *In 1873, the law was changed and gold only was made primary money*. In lines 49–50, he gives a consequence of that action: *One of the main arteries feeding blood to civilization was cut off*. By this metaphor, Harvey implies that the country is economically weakened because the government has ceased production of one of its main sources of currency. Harvey suggests that a return to a system that relies on two metals will fix the economic weakening that has occurred. The change to a new monetary system only reliant on gold is the central problem of his argument. Eliminate answer choices that are not consistent with this prediction. Choice (A) says that the central problem is the government's *financial deficit*, but the passage does not mention a financial deficit. Eliminate (A). Choice (B) says that the government had *previously made silver the primary money of the country*. This is a Mostly Right/Slightly Wrong trap answer; Harvey states that the government made *gold* the primary money, so eliminate (B). Choice (C) says that the central problem is a public announcement made by the government, but the passage does not mention a public announcement by the government; in fact, Harvey indicates that the government did not inform the public about the change. Eliminate (C). Choice (D) says that the central problem is that the government *instituted a monetary system*

in which only one metal was coined, which matches the prediction. Keep (D). The correct answer is (D).

34. **C** The question asks for the reason the speaker *uses the phrase "saving principle"*. Use the given line reference to find the window. Notice that the phrase *saving principle* in lines 12–13 is part of the phrase *the same saving principle applies*. The word *same* indicates that the *saving principle* was previously defined, so look back to the beginning of the window. The first sentence of the paragraph defines *bimetallism*. The second sentence provides a benefit of *bimetallism: if our trade relations... take our gold away, then we have silver, and no serious injury occurs*. Therefore, the saving principle refers to the idea that, under the law of *bimetallism*, the U.S. economy would not be threatened if the supply of one metal should be depleted. Rather, the government would be protected financially. Eliminate answer choices that are not consistent with this idea. *Excessive spending* does not match *financial protection*. This is a Right Words, Wrong Meaning trap answer based on an alternative meaning of "*saving*" that is not supported by the passage: saving money as opposed to spending money. Eliminate (A). The *saving principle* is a protection plan against *overreliance on one currency*, not a *consequence*. Choice (B) is a Mostly Right/Slightly Wrong trap answer; eliminate it. The *saving principle* is a protection plan against a *fluctuating money supply*. Keep choice (C). There is no indication in the passage that the *saving principle* is the U.S. Treasury's *current* policy. Eliminate (D). The correct answer is (C).

35. **D** The question asks what the word *vital* most nearly means in line 13. Go back to the text, find the word *vital*, and mark it out. Then read the window carefully, using context clues to determine another word that would fit in the text. Lines 13–14 discuss the central principle of bimetallism, so the correct word should mean something like "central." Invigorating means "energizing," which does not match "central." Eliminate (A). Restorative means "healing," which does not match "central." Eliminate (B). Both (A) and (B) are Could Be True trap answers based on other meanings of *vital* that are not supported by the text. *Steady* means "stable," which does not match "central." Eliminate (C). *Fundamental* means "essential," which matches "central." Keep (D). The correct answer is (D).

36. **C** The question asks for the reason *Harvey contends that the decision to rely on one metal for money is unwise*. This is the first question in a paired set, but it is a specific question, so it can be done on its own. Q35 asked about line 13, so the window for Q36 most likely begins after this line. Scan the passage beginning with line 15 to find a sentence that discusses *the decision to rely on one metal for money*. Lines 17–20 say that with only one metal for money, the alternating *contraction and expansion* of the world's supply will *make an uncertain and unstable supply*. Therefore, *the decision to rely on one metal for money is unwise* because reliance on one metal will lead to an unstable supply of money material when the world economy fluctuates. Eliminate answers that are not consistent with this idea. Choice (A) says that *silver* has greater *value* than *gold*, but the relative value of silver versus gold does not match the prediction about the unstable money supply. Also, the phrase *sixteen parts of silver to one part of gold* indicates that gold has greater value than silver. Eliminate (A). Choice (B) says that *gold* is *more useful than silver*, but the usefulness of gold does not match the prediction about an unstable supply of money material. Also, this statement is contradicted, since Harvey says, *silver is the most useful of the two*. Eliminate (B). Choice (C) says that *both metals' availability increases and decreases*. This matches the idea that the fluctuation of the world's economy will lead to an unstable supply of money material if only one metal is relied upon. Keep (C). Choice (D) says that *U.S. trading partners prefer bimetallism*. This is a Deceptive Language trap answer because the text mentions *trade relations*, but does not say anything about the preferences of U.S. trading partners. Eliminate (D). The correct answer is (C).

37.   **A**   The question is the best evidence question in a paired set. Because Q36 was a specific question, simply look at the lines used to answer the previous question. Lines 17–20, *With only one of them for money, the contraction and expansion of the world's supply alternating as they will, make an uncertain and unstable supply*, were used in the prediction. The correct answer is (A).

38.   **B**   The question asks for the *comparison* established in the third paragraph. Use the given line reference to find the window. In the third paragraph, Harvey uses a series of metaphors (*bread and meat*, symmetrical body parts, and the *marriage relation*) to emphasize his point that *it is safer to rely on two metals as currency, rather than one*. Therefore, the third paragraph makes a comparison between monetary policy and elements of the natural world. Eliminate answer choices that are not consistent with this prediction. Choice (A) is a Deceptive Language trap answer. Lines 29–30 mention the *Unseen Power*, but the passage does not draw a distinction between things that are seen and things that are unseen. Eliminate (A). Choice (B) matches the prediction, so keep (B). Choice (C) is a Deceptive Language trap answer. Lines 33–37 mention pairs of *symmetrical body parts*, but these are only mentioned as part of an example used to help draw a comparison with the money supply. Eliminate (C). The author is making an argument that the U.S. should use both *gold and silver* in their monetary supply, but the author is not making a comparison between gold and silver. Eliminate (D), which is another Deceptive Language trap answer. The correct answer is (B).

39.   **A**   The question asks what the word *strain* most nearly means in line 42. Go back to the text, find the word *strain*, and mark it out. Then read the window carefully, using context clues to determine another word that would fit in the text. Lines 38–43 say that one metal should *relieve the strain upon the other and that the volume of both should be drawn upon to meet the demand for money*. In this case, the *demand for money* places a *strain* on the supply of both metals. Therefore, *strain* must mean something like "demand." *An excessive demand* matches "demand," so keep (A). A *bodily injury* does not match "demand;" this is a Could Be True trap answer based on another meaning of *strain* that is not supported by the passage. Eliminate (B). A *forceful action* does not match "demand;" this is a Could Be True trap answer based on another meaning of "*strain*" that is not supported by the passage. Eliminate (C). A *specific lineage* does not match "demand;" this is a Could Be True trap answer based on another meaning of "*strain*" that is not supported by the passage. Eliminate (D). The correct answer is (A).

40.   **B**   The question asks for the choice that gives a *result of government action*. Notice that this is the first question in a paired set, so it can be done in tandem with Q41. Look at the answers for Q41 first. The lines for (41A) state, *Bimetallism is the right to use either gold or silver as primary money. Thus, under such a law, if our trade relations or the laws of other nations take our gold away, then we have silver, and no serious injury occurs*. The phrase *laws of other nations take our gold away* is a potential result of government action, so look to see whether these lines supports any of the answer choices in Q40. They do not, so eliminate (41A). The lines for (41B) state, *We rely on wheat, corn and rice for bread, on beef, pork and mutton for meat. If one is scarce, we use the other*. These lines do not mention a result of government action; they do not answer Q40, so eliminate (41B). The lines for (41C) state, *In 1873, the law was changed and gold only was made primary money. The mints were left open to the free coinage of gold, but closed as to the free coinage of silver*. These lines support (40B), *the reduced production of silver coins*. Draw a line connecting (41C) and (40B). The lines for (41D) state, *The doctor was to have no option to pay in money made from either of these metals. He was to be limited to gold alone*. This is a metaphor for a consequence of the 1873 law that made gold alone primary money; however, these lines do not indicate that this was a result of government action, so they do not provide the best support for Q40. Eliminate (41D). The correct answers are (40B) and (41C).

41. **C** (See explanation above.)

42. **B** The question asks why Harvey uses the phrase *a popular government*. Use the given line reference to find the window. In lines 53–57, Harvey states, *One of the fundamental principles of a popular government was violated*: the government did not obtain *the consent of the governed* before it changed the law. In lines 57–59, Harvey further states that this action *was not discussed in any campaign, and it was not known to the people for over two years afterward.* If a fundamental principle of *a popular government* is that such a government must obtain the consent of the people it governs before making actions, it can be inferred that *a popular government* should make its actions known to the public. By calling attention to the fact that this right was *violated*, Harvey is making a criticism of these leaders. Eliminate answer choices that are not consistent with this idea. Both *recognize* and *applaud* are positive verbs that do not match Harvey's negative criticism of government leaders. Eliminate (A) and (C). Choice (B) says that Harvey means to *criticize leaders who conceal actions from the public.* This matches the prediction, so keep (B). Choice (D) says that Harvey means to *denounce leaders who unfairly tax the poor.* Harvey criticizes leaders for being too secretive, not for *unfairly taxing the poor.* Eliminate (D). The correct answer is (B).

43. **D** The question asks for the main purpose of the first paragraph. To answer this question, carefully read the first paragraph, looking for information to indicate the purpose of the paragraph. Several sentences indicate that the amount of ice is shrinking at a rate much faster than what was initially predicted. Look for an answer that matches this idea. Only one sentence talks about the ice reforming, so (A) is too specific; eliminate (A). Although the size is compared to a U.S. state in this paragraph, that's not the paragraph's main purpose; eliminate (B). Choice (C) may be tempting because of the *dramatic changes*, but it is flawed because of the mention of *the last century*; eliminate (C). Choice (D) fits, since the trend of the ice melting is occurring much faster than scientists originally predicted. The correct answer is (D).

44. **C** The question asks what the word *projected* means in line 13. Go back to the text, find the word *projected*, and mark it out. Carefully read the surrounding text to determine another word that would fit in the blank based on the context of the passage. The text talks about the future and when experts "predict" an ice-free summer happening in the Arctic. Choice (A), *hurled*, might initially look attractive because a projectile could be *hurled*, but that meaning isn't consistent with the context. Eliminate (A). Choice (B), *seen*, is not consistent with "predict," nor is (D), *illuminated*. Choice (C), *hypothesized*, is consistent with "predicted." The correct answer is (C).

45. **B** The question asks why the author says the Earth's tilt is significant. To answer this question, find the lead words *Earth's tilt* in paragraph 2, and read the window, which says that the tilt *puts the Arctic in 24-hour-a-day darkness* or *sunlight* in different seasons. The correct answer will have something to do with the tilt affecting sunlight and darkness in different seasons. Choices (A) and (D) are each only true for one season; eliminate them. Choice (C) is inaccurate because there's no mention of the Earth's tilt *accelerating ice-free summers*, but (B) fits the prediction. The correct answer is (B).

46. **B** The question asks for the best evidence for the answer to the previous question. Lines 16–21 were used to answer the previous question. The correct answer is (B).

47. **C** The question asks what the word *pace* means in line 47. Go back to the text, find the word *pace*, and mark it out. Carefully read the surrounding text to determine another word that would fit in the blank based on the context of the passage. The sentence talks about how fast the ice is being lost, so the missing word must mean something like "speed." Choice (A), *walk*, refers to a different meaning of *pace*; eliminate it. Choice (B), *loss*, might initially look good because the passage talks about the ice melting, but *loss* is not consistent with "speed." Eliminate (B). Choice

(C), *rate*, is consistent with "speed," so keep it. Choice (D), *measure*, can be eliminated because it's not consistent with "speed." The correct answer is (C).

48. **A** The question asks what can be inferred about *climate scientists* based on the passage, which is discussed throughout the text. Notice that the following question is a best evidence question, so this question and Q49 can be answered in tandem. Look at the answers for Q49 first. The lines in (49A) state that *opinions differ substantially...among climate scientists*. It's not clear from the line what those opinions are, but (48A) and (48B) have *agree* and *disagree* options, so these lines could work. Keep (49A). The lines in (49B) mention a paper in which *multiple scientists* agree about the possibility of *an ice-free summer*. No disagreement or uncertainty is mentioned, so these lines do not support any answer choices for Q48. Eliminate (49B). The lines in both (49C) and (49D) mention specific scientists by name. Neither of those choices is broad enough to support any answers for Q48, so they can both be eliminated. This leaves (49A), but there is no clear connection to any of the answers in Q48. Go back to the text and read a window around these lines to determine the scientists' differing opinions. Just before that line reference, the text describes the increased loss of ice, stating: *The amount of ice remaining, this year, is about the same as the ice lost between the mid-1990s and today. If ice loss continued at that pace, we'd see an ice-free summer sometime around 2030, give or take several years.* Therefore, the differing opinions have something to do with the increased rate of ice melt. Eliminate (48C) and (48D). Compare the remaining two choices. Choice (48A) correctly matches the information in the text, whereas (48B) suggests the opposite idea. Eliminate (48B). The correct answers are (48A) and (49A).

49. **A** (See explanation above.)

50. **C** The question asks for the period that *displays the greatest decline in sea ice minimum area*. Work through each answer choice using the figure. Eliminate (A) because the graph shows only a slight decrease between 1986 and 1987. Eliminate (B) because the graph shows an increase between 1995 and 1996. Keep (C) because there is a decline of about 1.5 million square kilometers between 2006 and 2007. Eliminate (D) because the decline from 2011 to 2012 is only about 1 million square kilometers. The correct answer is (C).

51. **C** The question asks which concept is supported by the passage and by the information in the graph. Consider both the passage, which indicates that the ice is shrinking and will be gone at some point in the future, and the graph, which shows the amount of ice dropping over a 30-year period. Choices (B) and (D) contradict both the passage and the graph, so eliminate them. Choice (A) is possible but is not necessarily true based on information in the passage or the graph. Choice (C) has the best support from both the main ideas of the passage and the downward trend of the graph. The correct answer is (C).

52. **D** The question asks how the graph supports the author's point that Arctic ice is receding. To answer this question, check each answer against the graph and eliminate those that don't match the graph or aren't supported by the text. The graph doesn't refer to Texas, so eliminate (A). Choice (B) is mentioned in lines 47–49 as a possibility, though not according to the author, and this is not visible in the graph; thus, eliminate it. Choice (C) does not accurately depict the graph; eliminate it. Choice (D) fits both the author's point and the graph. The correct answer is (D).

Section 2: Writing and Language

1. **D** Transitions change in the answer choices, so this question tests consistency of ideas. There is the option to DELETE, which may indicate that the question is also testing concision; consider this choice carefully, as the option to delete is often the correct answer. The transitions in the answer choices are all FANBOYS, or coordinating conjunctions. Note that there's a comma just before the underlined portion; a comma followed by FANBOYS can only be used between two independent clauses. The first part of the sentence, *As people become more sensitive to the idea of preserving certain ecosystems*, is not an independent clause. That means that it should be followed by a comma alone, without one of the FANBOYS. Eliminate (A), (B), and (C). The correct answer is (D).

2. **D** Verbs change in the answer choices, so this question appears to test consistency of verbs. However, the underlined portion actually functions as a noun in this sentence. Eliminate (B) and (C) because *reacts* and *interacted* cannot be nouns. Choices (A) and (D) can both be nouns, so choose the one with the most precise meaning in this context. The passage discusses how *humans* influence the *ecosystem*, so eliminate (A) because *interaction* better captures the sense of interplay between humans and the environment than *reaction* does. The correct answer is (D).

3. **D** Transitions change in the answer choices, so this question tests consistency of ideas. A transition must be consistent with the relationship between the ideas it connects. The sentence before the transition states that *the central challenge of maintaining an ecosystem* is that *ecosystems have a tendency to change*. The sentence that begins with the underlined portion states that *one career that has grown by leaps and bounds in the last fifty years is that of the soil conservationist*, a profession that helps clarify *how to work within sustainable ecosystems*. The second sentence introduces a phenomenon—the growth of the soil conservationists' profession—that is explained by the general situation in the first sentence, so the correct transition will reflect that relationship. Choices (A), *Still*, and (B), *Nonetheless*, suggest that the second sentence challenges or changes direction from the idea in the first sentence, so eliminate (A) and (B). Choice (C), *Finally*, suggests that the second sentence offers the last in a series of events rather than an example of an effect of the idea expressed in the first sentence, so eliminate (C). Choice (D), *Therefore*, correctly reflects the relationship between the two sentences. The correct answer is (D).

4. **A** Note the question! The question asks which choice *most effectively sets up the subject discussed* in the paragraph, so it tests consistency of ideas. Determine the subject of the paragraph and find the answer that is consistent with that idea. The beginning of the sentence that contains the underlined phrase establishes that the paragraph will describe *the factors that must be considered* in a certain situation. The rest of the paragraph describes how *coastal areas are particularly susceptible* to erosion of the soil by ocean water, so *a soil conservationist might be asked to conduct a survey of the region in order to determine where it would be safest to build*. The paragraph also mentions *one's dream house, which would not be quite so ideal if it were at constant risk* from environmental deterioration. Look for an answer choice that is consistent with the discussion of constructing a house in a coastal area. Choice (A) mentions *building a beach house*, so keep (A). Eliminate (B), because the phrase *performing these tasks* does not give a precise indication of the paragraph's subject. Choice (C) mentions *the changes in the seasons*, which is inconsistent with the focus of the rest of the paragraph; eliminate (C). Choice (D) is consistent with the topic of *soil conservation*, but the *subject discussed in this paragraph* is the construction of a house in a coastal area, not soil conservation generally, so eliminate (D). The correct answer is (A).

5. **B** The length of the phrase changes in the answer choices, so this question tests precision and concision. The non-underlined portion of the sentence explains that *coastal areas* are especially *suscepti-*

ble to the influence of particular kinds of changes *because of the water from the ocean and in the air.* All of the answer choices include some variation of the word *erosion.* Choice (B), *erosion,* names the force that affects coastal areas, so keep (B). Choices (A), (C), and (D) all use more words than (B) does. In the case of (A) and (C), the words *things* and *what* make the sentence less precise; eliminate (A) and (C). In the case of (D), *process of* is not needed, so (D) is less concise than (B) without providing any additional information; eliminate (D). The correct answer is (B).

6. **B**   Verbs change in the answer choices. The underlined portion is part of a list in the sentence, so this question tests consistency. All items in a list must be phrased in the same way to be consistent with each other. The first two items in the list are *collapsing* and *shifting,* so the third item must also be in an *-ing* form. Eliminate (A) and (C) because they do not include the necessary *-ing* ending. While (D) uses the word *deteriorating,* it includes the noun *structures,* which is inconsistent with the other phrases in the list; eliminate (D). Choice (B), *deteriorating,* is consistent with the other items in the list. The correct answer is (B).

7. **D**   Note the question! The question asks which answer choice *most effectively combines the underlined sentences,* so it tests precision and concision. In the original underlined sentences, the phrase *each in its way* refers to each of the *techniques* that *soil conservationists employ* in specific *cases;* the correct answer will retain that relationship between ideas. Choice (A) suggests that *soil conservationists* are themselves *ways of preserving or reviving land,* rather than the professionals who use those methods, so eliminate (A). In (B), the phrase *each one of them* appears before any mention of the *variety of techniques* employed by *soil conservationists,* which makes the relationship between those ideas unclear; eliminate (B). Choice (C) describes *soil conservationists,* instead of their *techniques,* as *geared toward preserving or reviving land where crops are grown;* while the conservationists may be interested in preserving or reviving such land, this answer choice does not combine the sentences in a way that maintains the original sentences' stated relationship between ideas, so eliminate (C). Choice (D) correctly suggests that, of the *variety of techniques* that soil conservationists use, *each in its way is geared toward preserving or reviving land.* The correct answer is (D).

8. **B**   Note the question! The question asks whether a phrase should be added, so it tests consistency. If the content of the new phrase is consistent with the ideas surrounding it, the phrase should be added. Prior to the proposed phrase, the sentence describes *farming techniques* on which *soil conservationists might advise* in order to *help the land produce to its full potential.* The new phrase provides specific examples of those techniques, which is consistent with the rest of the sentence, so the phrase should be added. Eliminate (C) and (D). The proposed phrase names *no-till* farming, which is mentioned later in the paragraph, but it does not *demonstrate the advantages of methods described later in the sentence,* so eliminate (A). The proposed phrase does provide *specific instances of the techniques discussed in this sentence,* so keep (B). The correct answer is (B).

9. **C**   Verbs change in the answer choices, so the question tests consistency of verbs. A verb must be consistent in number with its subject. The subject of the verb is *no-till farmlands,* which is plural. To be consistent, the underlined verb must also be plural. Eliminate (A) and (D), because *has* is singular. The difference between (B) and (C) is the presence of the word *which.* Adding the word *which* makes the sentence incomplete, so eliminate (B). The correct answer is (C).

10. **A**   Vocabulary changes in the answer choices. The underlined portion is part of a list in the sentence, so the question tests consistency. All items in a list must be phrased in the same way to be consistent with one another. The other items in this list use a single word to describe a particular kind of ecosystem, then use a prepositional phrase to describe where that ecosystem is located: *deserts of the Southwest* and *forests of the Northwest.* To be consistent, the correct answer should also describe the ecosystem of the *Midwest* using a single word. Eliminate (B), (C), and (D),

because they use multiple words to characterize an ecosystem of the Midwest. Choice (A), *plains*, is consistent with the other items in the list. The correct answer is (A).

11. **A** Note the question! The question asks which answer choice *most clearly ends the passage with a restatement of the writer's claim*, so it tests consistency of ideas. Determine the main claim of the passage and find the answer that is most consistent with that idea. The first paragraph of the passage introduces a soil conservationist as someone whose work guides *both public and private entities as to how to work within sustainable ecosystems*. The subsequent paragraphs provide further explanation of how a soil conservationist's work does that. Choice (A) restates the idea that *soil conservationists* do important work because they *continue to strike the balance between natural spaces and the people who live in them*, so keep (A). Choice (B) claims that while soil conservationists do *essential work, just as much is required of the builders and contractors who accompany them*; *builders and contractors* are not consistent with the main idea of the passage, so eliminate (B). Choice (C) suggests that the public work of soil conservationists is *better because it can be enjoyed by all*, which is not a restatement of the writer's main claim; eliminate (C). Choice (D) claims that *the desert is unique* and that, therefore, the *skills that soil conservationists learn* in desert ecosystems are *difficult to transfer between regions*. While this idea is consistent with a claim made earlier in the final paragraph, choice (D) does not restate the main claim of the passage as a whole, so eliminate (D). The correct answer is (A).

12. **C** Transitions change in the answer choices, so this question tests consistency of ideas. A transition must be consistent with the relationship between the ideas it connects. The part of the sentence that comes before the transition suggests that *there may be some controversy* regarding *who earns these awards*, while the part of the sentence that follows the transition states that *there can be no doubt that the winners are always accomplished in their fields*. The second part of the sentence is in contrast to the first part of the sentence. Eliminate (A), *therefore*, (B), *for example*, and (D), *fittingly*, because all are transitions that suggest the second part of the sentence agrees with the idea in the first part of the sentence. Keep (C), because *however* correctly contrasts the second part of the sentence with the first part. The correct answer is (C).

13. **A** The length of the phrase after *disciplines* changes in the answer choices, so the question tests concision. First, determine whether additional words are necessary. The underlined portion serves to connect *disciplines* and *the world at large*, both of which are realms in which the prize winners *have contributed something significant*. In this case, a word is needed to signal that *disciplines* and *the world* are a pair, and the most concise answer, (B), uses only a comma, so eliminate (B). Choice (A) uses *and* to connect *disciplines* with *the world*, which effectively signals their relationship, so keep (A). Choice (C) adds *it's*, which is a contraction of *it is*. This addition creates an independent clause; since the first part of the sentence is also an independent clause, the comma cannot be used to link them, so eliminate (C). Choice (D) suggests that *the world at large* is an *example* of the *disciplines* within which prize winners work, which is inconsistent with the relationship between the ideas; eliminate (D). The correct answer is (A).

14. **D** Note the question! The question asks whether a sentence should be added, so it tests consistency. If the content of the new sentence is consistent with the ideas surrounding it, then it should be added. The paragraph discusses the significance of the *Nobel Peace Prize*, and the tendency of the prize committee to reward *bravery in the face of adversity*. The new sentence discusses the *1962 prize in Physiology*, so it is not consistent with the rest of the ideas in the paragraph, and the sentence should not be added. Eliminate (A) and (B). Choice (C) inaccurately states that the sentence implies that *all Peace Prize winners must also be scientists*; the sentence under consideration does not mention *Peace Prize winners*, so eliminate (C). Choice (D) accurately states that the new sentence diverges *from the paragraph's main focus on another prize*. The correct answer is (D).

15. **B** Verbs change in the answer choices, so this question tests consistency of verbs. A verb must be consistent with other verbs in the sentence. The other verb in the sentence is the present tense *see*. To be consistent, the underlined verb must also be in the present tense. Eliminate (A) because *rewarded* is past tense. Apostrophes also change in the answer choices, so this question also tests apostrophe usage. When used with a noun, an apostrophe indicates possession. Nothing belongs to the *committee* in this sentence, so no apostrophe is necessary. Eliminate (C) and (D). The correct answer is (B).

16. **A** Pronouns and punctuation change in the answer choices, so this question tests both the consistency of pronouns and how to connect ideas with the appropriate punctuation. When used with a pronoun, an apostrophe indicates a contraction. *They're* is the contraction of *they are*, which is not the possessive pronoun needed in this sentence; eliminate (B) and (C). Both (A) and (D) use the correct pronoun, *their*. The first part of the sentence, *This is a difficult thing to quantify, but the Peace Prize is as important as the other prizes and contributes to their common goal*, is an independent clause. The second part of the sentence, *to make the world a better place*, is not an independent clause. A semicolon can only be used between two independent clauses, so eliminate (D). Choice (A) appropriately uses the possessive pronoun *their* and uses a colon to connect the two ideas in the sentence. The correct answer is (A).

17. **B** Commas change in the answer choices, so this question tests comma usage. There is no need to put a comma after *King's*, as *King's influence spanned the globe* should not be broken up with commas. Eliminate (A) and (C). Choice (D) inserts a comma after *minister*. The phrase *King's influence spanned the globe* is necessary to the main meaning of the sentence, so there is no reason to include that comma; eliminate (D). No commas are necessary. The correct answer is (B).

18. **D** Note the question! The question asks which choice *gives a specific supporting detail that is most similar to the details already in the paragraph*. Eliminate answers that are inconsistent with the purpose stated in the question. The paragraph states that King *won* the Nobel Peace Prize *amid his non-violent campaign for civil rights in the United States*. Look for an answer choice that is consistent with those details. Eliminate (A) because the details already in the paragraph do not reference the *friends, family, and loved ones* of those who were *seeking civil rights*. Eliminate (B) because *the people throughout the world* is not *specific*, especially because the sentence containing the underlined phrase already states that *King's influence spanned the globe*. The paragraph states that *it is probably no surprise* that King won the award, so (C), which states that King's influence was important for *all who thought that the Nobel Prize should be awarded to someone who deserved it*, implies a disagreement with the ideas stated elsewhere in the paragraph: eliminate (C). Choice (D) states that King's influence was important for *those who championed a cause in non-violent ways*, a detail that is both *similar to the details already in the paragraph* and also names a *specific* group of people. The correct answer is (D).

19. **B** The order of phrases in the sentence changes in the answer choices, so this question tests precision. Look for an answer choice that avoids confusion about pronouns and about modifying clauses. In (A), the phrase *when given to first-year President Barack Obama* does not clearly modify a specific noun: the phrase could describe either *controversy* or *the award*. For that reason, eliminate (A). In (B), the pronoun *it* clearly refers to *the award*, and the order of the phrases makes clear that the *good deal more controversy* resulted from the award's being *given to first-year President Barack Obama*: keep (B). In (C), the order of the phrases suggests that the pronoun *it* refers to *first-year President Barack Obama*, instead of *the Prize*; eliminate (C). Finally, the order of phrases in (D) suggests that the pronoun *it*, which describes the object a*warded to first-year President Barack Obama*, refers to the *good deal more controversy*, not to the *award*: eliminate (D). The correct answer is (B).

20. **D** Note the question! The question asks which choice *most effectively combines the sentences at the underlined portion*, and transitions change in the answer choices, so it tests consistency of ideas. The first sentence notes that *King may be the most famous African-American recipient of the Nobel Peace Prize*, while the second sentence explains that *the honor was first given to a lesser-known but no less illustrious figure, Ralph Bunche, in 1950*. The correct answer will effectively signal the shift from talking about King to talking about the lesser-known Bunche. Choice (A) uses a colon to connect the ideas, which incorrectly suggests that the second sentence illustrates or further clarifies, so eliminate (A). Eliminate (C), since the use of *for* also incorrectly suggests that the latter sentence clarifies the former. Eliminate (B), since the *while* suggests that the two statements express parallel ideas—King was famous while Bunche was first—whereas the paragraph is actually transitioning *from* the idea of King's fame *to* a consideration of Bunche. Choice (D) effectively links the two sentences by using *yet* to signal that even though King was *the most famous*, it was Bunch who *first* received *the honor*. The correct answer is (D).

21. **C** Note the question! The question asks which choice *most closely matches the stylistic pattern established earlier in the sentence*, so it tests consistency. The other comparable nouns named in the sentence are the *1949 Armistice Agreements* and *the 1948 Arab-Israeli Conflict*. To be consistent with the *stylistic pattern* used to describe those events, the correct answer should begin with a year. Eliminate (A) and (D), because they begin with the phrase *the Nobel Peace Prize*. Choice (B) uses an apostrophe to indicate that *1950* possesses the *Nobel Peace Prize* won by Bunche; this is inconsistent with the stylistic pattern in the sentence, so eliminate (B). Choice (C) begins with the year *1950* and does not include an apostrophe, and so is consistent with the style used elsewhere in the sentence. The correct answer is (C).

22. **D** Note the question! The question asks where paragraph 5 should be placed, so it tests consistency of ideas. The paragraph must be consistent with the ideas that come both before and after it. Paragraph 5 introduces the example of *Ralph Bunche* as a different kind of Prize winner than *King*, so the paragraph must come after some mention of *King* and his being *the most famous African-American recipient of the Prize*. Martin Luther King, Jr., is not named in the passage until paragraph 3, so paragraph 5 must not come before paragraph 3: eliminate (B) and (C). Paragraph 4 mentions Bunche by only his last name in a list of *winners* of the *Nobel Peace Prize*, so the description of *Ralph Bunche* and his winning of the Prize must come before paragraph 4: eliminate (A). The correct answer is (D).

23. **A** Transitions change in the answer choices, so this question tests consistency of ideas. A transition must be consistent with the relationship between the ideas it connects. The sentence before the transition states that the *most obvious facet of global warming is the rise in global temperatures*. The sentence that includes the underlined transition begins by introducing *what many do not understand quite as well*, and the sentence concludes by naming *the factors that contribute to that rise in global temperatures*. The sentence containing the underlined transition is therefore in contrast to the previous sentence: the *most obvious facet of global warming* is being compared to *what many do not understand quite as well*. Eliminate (B), (C), and (D), because *thereby*, *correspondingly*, and *thus* suggest that the idea in the second sentence is a logical consequence of or agreement with the idea in the first sentence. Choice (A), *however*, correctly indicates that the second sentence introduces a subject that is in contrast with the subject introduced in the first sentence. The correct answer is (A).

24. **D** The length of the underlined phrase changes in the answer choices, so this question tests precision and concision. Check the shortest answer first. Choice (D), *analogous functions*, provides the necessary information that functions performed by *heavy machinery* are *analogous* to the previous sentence's description of what happens *every time you breathe*, so keep (D). Choice (A) states

that the *functions could be called analogous*; the additional words do not make the sentence more precise, so eliminate (A). Choice (B) suggests that *Factories, cars, and other heavy machinery* are working as an analogy, rather than that an analogy can be drawn between their functions and human respiration; eliminate (B). Choice (C) states that the functions are *like analogies*, but the main idea of the sentence is that the functions of the machinery can be related to human respiration by analogy, so eliminate (C). The correct answer is (D).

25. **B** Note the question! The question asks whether a piece of information should be added, so it tests consistency. If the content of the new phrase is consistent with the ideas that surround it, then it should be added. The paragraph discusses the consequences of *excess carbon dioxide* that is emitted as a result of the *heavy output* from a *wide variety of industrial sources*. The new phrase explains why the CO_2 emitted by these industrial sources causes the *Earth's atmosphere to be bombarded*, so it is consistent with the main idea of the sentence: eliminate (C) and (D). The new phrase does not mention *the trees in the Amazonian rainforest*, so eliminate (A). The new phrase does explain *why high levels of CO_2 can be a problem in the Earth's atmosphere*, so keep (B). The correct answer is (B).

26. **A** Pronouns change in the answer choices, so this question tests consistency of pronouns. A pronoun must be consistent in number with the noun it refers to. The underlined pronoun refers to *the compound*, which is singular. To be consistent, the underlined pronoun must also be singular. Eliminate (C), because it contains the plural pronoun *they*. Eliminate (D), since *there* refers to a place or a phenomenon and not to *the compound*. Choice (A), *it's*, is a contraction of *it is*, while (B), *its*, is a possessive. A subject and verb are needed to complete the idea that *the compound* is *always absorbing heat energy*, so eliminate (B). The correct answer is (A).

27. **D** Note the question! The question asks which choice *offers an accurate interpretation of the data in the chart*, so it tests consistency. Read the labels on the graph carefully, and look for an answer that is consistent with the information given in the graph. Choices (A) and (B) are not consistent with the figure, since *temperatures* have not *increased along exactly the same curve* as the *steady rate* by which *carbon dioxide has increased*, but it is also not the case that *temperatures have shown no general increase*. Eliminate (A) and (B). Choice (C) states that the *temperature changes peaked in 1989*. While there was a spike in temperatures around that year, subsequent years have reached the same level, so the levels did not *peak* in 1989; eliminate (C). Choice (D) correctly notes that *although temperatures have fluctuated*, they *have generally increased as well*. The correct answer is (D).

28. **C** Vocabulary changes in the answer choices, so this question tests precision of word choice. Look for a word with a definition that is consistent with the other ideas in the sentence. The sentence says that some *earthly mechanisms* exist that *absorb the levels of carbon dioxide in the atmosphere*, so the correct answer must mean something like "decrease" or "lower." *Chill out* means "relax," so eliminate (A). *Kill* means "destroy," so eliminate (B). *Reduce* means "make smaller," which is consistent with the idea of decreasing the amount of carbon dioxide, so keep (C). *Mellow* means "calm down," so eliminate (D). The correct answer is (C).

29. **C** Commas change in the answer choices, so this question tests comma usage. There is no reason to break up the sentence with a comma, so eliminate (B) and (D). Adding the words *would* and *then*, as in (A), does not make the sentence more precise, so eliminate (A). Choice (C) is concise and gives the sentence a precise meaning. The correct answer is (C).

30. **B** Punctuation changes in the answer choices, so this question tests how to connect ideas with the appropriate punctuation. As written, the first part of the sentence, *A team of over 150 researchers produced the first comprehensive map of the Amazon rainforest's ecosystem and said*, is not an independent clause, and the second part of the sentence, "*that half of the Amazon could be deforested*

by 2050, is also not an independent clause. There is no closing quotation mark at the end of the sentence, so the quotation mark in (A) is incorrect: eliminate (A). A single dash must be used after an independent clause, so eliminate (D). There is no reason to break up the sentence with a comma, so eliminate (C). No punctuation marks are necessary to connect the two parts of the sentence. The correct answer is (B).

31. **A**   Pronouns and nouns change in the answer choices, so this question tests precision. A pronoun can only be used if that pronoun refers clearly to another noun in the sentence. The pronoun *them* could refer to the *Amazon's trees* or to *significant emission reversals*, so the pronoun is not precise: eliminate (B) and (D). There is nothing in the sentence for the pronoun *it* to refer to, so eliminate (C). Choice (A) names the noun that *protecting the Amazon's trees* could *temper*, and the pronoun *those* clearly refers to *polluting behaviors*, so (A) is the most precise option. The correct answer is (A).

32. **B**   Punctuation changes in the answer choices, so this question tests how to connect ideas using the appropriate punctuation. Because the phrase *of processes* describes the noun *series*, there is no reason to break up the phrase *series of processes* with any piece of punctuation, so eliminate (A), (C), and (D). The non-underlined part of the sentence introduces a comma before the word *or*, and the phrase *or series of processes* is unnecessary to the main meaning of the sentence, so the comma inserted after *processes* in (B) is correct. The correct answer is (B).

33. **C**   Note the question! The question asks for *the most logical place in this paragraph to add the following sentence*, so it tests consistency of ideas. The sentence must be consistent with the ideas that come both before and after it. The new sentence describes an action that *could go a long way toward reforesting the Amazon rainforest*, and the new sentence refers to that action as *This*, which means the new sentence must come after the action has been described. Sentence 2 states that *as many as 57% of Amazon tree species could be eligible* for inclusion on a *red list of threatened species*, an action that would, logically, *go a long way toward reforesting the Amazon rainforest*. Consequently, the new sentence should not come before sentence 2: eliminate both (A) and (B). Sentence 3 states that *protecting the Amazon's trees* could be helpful in some ways, but it also introduces the idea that *other polluting behaviors would need to change as well*, so sentence 3 should come after the new sentence: eliminate (D). The correct answer is (C).

34. **B**   The phrase after *formal* changes in the answer choices, so this question tests precision and concision. The first part of the sentence introduces the subject of the sentence as something that *sometimes* happens, while the second part of the sentence includes the phrase *as in the case of a writer* who behaves a certain way. The non-underlined portions of the sentence already establish that this situation only occurs sometimes, so eliminate (A), which suggests the situation can arise *in any case*. Keep (B), because it is the shortest answer and because the sentence does not require a transitional phrase between the two parts of the sentence. Choice (C) suggests that the first part of the sentence is in contrast to the idea introduced in the previous sentence, which is inconsistent with the ideas in the sentence, so eliminate (C). There is no cause-and-effect relationship between the first and second parts of the sentence, so the *therefore* included in (D) is imprecise; eliminate (D). The correct answer is (B).

35. **C**   Note the question! The question asks which option *provides information that best supports the claim made by this sentence*, so it tests consistency. Eliminate answer choices that are not consistent with the purpose stated in the question. The sentence states that sometimes literary influence is *more literal* than the influence described earlier, and it gives the example of when writers *take marginal characters from earlier works*. Choice (A) states that *sometimes poems or movies are included*, which does not support the sentence's main claim about how *influence* can be *more*

literal: eliminate (A). Choice (B) states that writers influenced in this way *don't cite the author's name at all*, which is inconsistent with the discussion of this phenomenon as *influence*: eliminate (B). Choice (C) notes that writers might *build new literary worlds* around the characters taken *from earlier works*, which supports the sentence's main focus on a type of *influence*: keep (C). Choice (D) asserts that writers might *still consider* their work *entirely their own*; since the sentence does not claim that these writers are doing something other than creating their own work, this characterization is inconsistent with the main claim of the sentence, so eliminate (D). The correct answer is (C).

36. **B** Transitions change in the answer choices, so this question tests consistency of ideas. A transition must be consistent with the relationship between the ideas it connects. The first part of the sentence states that *With the framework set by the biblical story*, Paradise Lost *offers a unique interpretation*, and the second part of the sentence describes how *the story focuses on the fallen angel Satan*. The second part of the sentence describes in more detail what happens in the *unique interpretation* offered by *Paradise Lost*. Eliminate (A), *just as*, which suggests that the second part of the sentence is parallel or equivalent to the first part of the sentence. Since the second part of the sentence provides more detail about the *interpretation* offered by *Paradise Lost*, the second part of the sentence is describing what happens in the interpretation, not what happens *from* it, so eliminate (C). *Wherein* means "inside which," so keep (B). Choice (D), *into it*, suggests that the *story* in the second part of the sentence is going *into* the interpretation, rather than that the *story* already exists inside the interpretation, so eliminate (D). The correct answer is (B).

37. **D** Note the question! The question asks where sentence 2 should be placed, so it tests consistency of ideas. The sentence must be consistent with the ideas that come both before and after it. Sentence 2 says that *Milton claimed* that a particular approach allowed him to "*justify the ways of God to men*," so the sentence must come after some mention of John Milton's full name; it cannot come before sentence 1, so eliminate (A). Because sentence 2 describes Milton's approach as *this alternate route*, the sentence must come after an explanation of how Milton's work reinterprets an earlier work. Such an explanation appears in sentence 4, so sentence 2 cannot come before sentence 4: eliminate (B) and (C). The correct answer is (D).

38. **C** Punctuation changes in the answer choices, so this question tests how to connect ideas with the appropriate punctuation. The first part of the sentence, *The practice of adapting literary works, particularly the great classics of a language*, is not an independent clause. The second part of the sentence, *to unique ends has continued*, is also not an independent clause. A semicolon can only be used between two independent clauses, so eliminate (A). A single dash in a sentence must come after an independent clause, so eliminate (D). Note the comma following *works* in the non-underlined portion of the sentence. The phrase *particularly the great classics of a language* is not necessary to the main meaning of the sentence, so it should be set off with a pair of commas. Eliminate (B) because it lacks a comma after *language*. The correct answer is (C).

39. **B** Vocabulary changes in the answer choices, so this question tests precision of word choice. Look for a word with a definition that is consistent with the other ideas in the sentence. The sentence says that *As Milton had before, Rhys uses a well-known work to* provide *an alternate story*, so the correct answer should mean something like "write." *Overtake* means "catch up with," so eliminate (A). *Tell* is close to "write," so keep (B). Choice (C), *manifest*, means "make evident," and (D), *ideate*, means "form an idea." Neither of these meanings works as well as *write* to keep the emphasis of the sentence on how Rhys formulates the story using *a well-known work*, so eliminate (C) and (D). The correct answer is (B).

40. **B** Vocabulary changes in the answer choices, so this question tests precision of word choice. Look for a word with a definition that is consistent with the other ideas in the sentence. *Adapted* means "reworked," while *adopted* means "took as one's own." The word that is consistent with the ideas of the passage is *adapted*; eliminate (C) and (D). In this sentence, *Algerian writer Kamel Daoud* is the subject of the noun *adapted*, so it is unnecessary to repeat the subject with the pronoun *he*: eliminate (A). The correct answer is (B).

41. **A** Verbs and pronouns change in the answer choices, so this question tests consistency of verbs and pronouns. A verb must be consistent with the other verbs in the sentence. The other verb in this sentence is *centers*, which is in present tense, so the correct answer should also include a verb in present tense. Eliminate (C), because *killed* is in past tense. A verb must also be consistent with its subject. The subject of the underlined verb is *the protagonist Meursault*, so eliminate (D), because *killing* would imply that the subject is *Camus's novel*. The difference between (A) and (B) is pronouns. Using the subject pronoun *he* makes the second part of the sentence an independent clause, which would mean that the comma in the non-underlined portion of the sentence is incorrect: eliminate (B). Choice (A) uses the pronoun *who* to indicate that *the protagonist Meursault* is the subject of the verb *kills* without making the second part of the sentence an independent clause. The correct answer is (A).

42. **D** Vocabulary changes in the answer choices, so this question tests precision of word choice. Use POE, and guess if there is more than one answer left. Choice (A) uses the word *description*, while the other answers have *descriptive*. It could be correct to say that the book "has more description than" another book, but the verb in the non-underlined portion is *is*, not *has*, so this phrasing doesn't work. Eliminate (A). The word *then* is used to indicate time, while *than* is used to indicate a comparison or contrast. *Than* is the appropriate word in this context, so eliminate (C). Choices (B) and (D) differ only in the addition of a comma: it is unnecessary here to insert a comma between *descriptive* and the word that follows it, so eliminate (B). The correct answer is (D).

43. **D** Note the question! The question asks whether a sentence should be added, so it tests consistency. If the content of the new question is consistent with the ideas surrounding it, then it should be added. The paragraph discusses how *The Meursault Investigation* provides a name and backstory to a minor character from *The Stranger*. The new sentence discusses the centuries-long *history of Franco-Algerian relations*, so it is not consistent with the ideas in the text: the sentence should not be added. Eliminate (A) and (B). The new sentence does not *contradict the passage's larger claim that literature cannot be defined by historical events*, because the passage does not claim that literature is unrelated to historical events: eliminate (C). Choice (D) states that the new sentence *strays from the paragraph's main focus*, which is consistent with the content of the paragraph and the sentence. The correct answer is (D).

44. **D** Vocabulary changes in the answer choices, so this question tests precision of word choice. There is also the option to DELETE; consider this choice carefully, as it is often the correct answer. The sentence already states that the works that draw on earlier texts *make literal what all other texts merely imply*, so it is unnecessary to repeat the idea that other texts *do not state* what they are doing: eliminate (A). Because the sentence states that *all other texts* also draw on earlier works, it is also unnecessary to repeat that other texts also operate in the same way: eliminate (B) and (C). The underlined portion should be deleted to make the sentence more concise. The correct answer is (D).

Section 3: Math (No Calculator)

1. **A** The question asks for the point that satisfies the system of equations. Rather than doing complex algebra, try out the (x, y) values in each answer to see if they work. Start with (B). Using the values given in (B), the first equation becomes $2(-1) + 3(-3) = -9$. Simplify the left side of the equation to get $-2 - 9 = -9$ or $-11 = -9$. This isn't true, so eliminate (B). Whether to go up or down may not be clear, so just choose a direction. Using the values given in (A), the first equation becomes $2(-3) + 3(-1) = -9$. Simplify the left side of the equation to get $-6 - 3 = -9$, or $-9 = -9$. That works, so plug the values into the second equation to get $-3 - (-1) = -2$. Simplify the left side of the equation to get $-3 + 1 = -2$, and $-2 = -2$. The values given in (A) work in both equations. Therefore, the correct answer is (A).

2. **C** The question asks for the value of $\frac{y}{x}$. Rather than do algebraic manipulation, choose a value for one of the variables and solve for the other. Since there are two instances of the variable x in the equation, select a value for x. Let $x = 4$. Plug this into the equation to get $4 = 4(4 + y)$. Distribute the 4 to get $4 = 16 + 4y$. Subtract 16 from both sides to get $-12 = 4y$. Divide both sides by 4 to get $y = -3$. The question asks for $\frac{y}{x}$, which is $-\frac{3}{4}$. The correct answer is (C).

3. **B** The question asks for the length of line segment $\overline{SQ}$ on the figure. When two triangles have the same angles and sides in a given ratio, they are similar. Check to see if that is the case here. The question gives the ratio of the lengths of $\overline{ST}$ and $\overline{SU}$. Since these two segments are sides of triangles PST and QSU, respectively, determine whether these two triangles are similar. All that is needed to prove that two triangles are similar is to find two pairs of congruent corresponding angles. Since both triangles have a right angle, there is one pair. Also, the question states that triangle PQR is isosceles with $\overline{PR} = \overline{QR}$. In an isosceles triangle, equal angles are opposite equal sides, so $\angle P \cong \angle Q$. Thus, triangles PST and QSU have a second pair of congruent corresponding angles and are similar. Therefore, all corresponding sides have the same ratio. The question asks for the length of $\overline{SQ}$, which is opposite the right angle. Since $\overline{PS}$ is also opposite a right angle, $\overline{PS}$ and $\overline{SQ}$ are corresponding. Therefore, their lengths are in a ratio of 5:3. Therefore, there are 8 parts in the ratio for the total length of $\overline{PQ}$, but the question says that the actual length of $\overline{PQ}$ is 64. The parts of the ratio must be multiplied by 8 to get 64. To find the length of $\overline{SQ}$, multiply the ratio number for $\overline{SQ}$, which is 3, by the multiplier of 8 to get an actual length of 24. The correct answer is (B).

4. **D** The question asks for the meaning of the number 4 in the profit expression. When dealing with profit, it is important to know that Profit = Revenue − Expenses. According to the question, profit $= 4bd - 200$. Therefore, the expression $4bd$ must be related to the revenue the chocolate-covered banana stand brings in. Because b represents the number of bananas sold each day, and d is the number of days, the 4 must be related to revenue dollars. Eliminate (A) and (C) since neither of these answers is related to dollars. The question does not say that the price of bananas increases on any given day, so it's safe to assume that the price of a chocolate-covered banana remains the same irrespective of the day it is bought. Therefore, eliminate (B). The correct answer is (D).

5. **A** The question asks for a true equation regarding y, the number of Java Jim's stores added. Translate the information to find the value of y. According to the question, 700 coffee stores existed in 2003, which is one-half of the number of coffee stores that were added from 2004 to 2014. Therefore, $2 \times 700 = 1,400$ stores were added from 2004 to 2014. Plug $y = 1,400$ into each of the answer choices to see which one works. Choice (A) becomes $\frac{1}{2}(1,400) = 700$, or $700 = 700$.

Since this equation works, keep it, but check the other answers. Choice (B) becomes 2(1,400) = 700, (C) becomes $700(1,400) = \frac{1}{2}$, and (D) becomes 700(1,400) = 2. Even without calculating the exact values, it is easy to see that none of these equations are true. The correct answer is (A).

6. **D** The question asks for values of m for which Stream Supreme's monthly cost is less than Download Empire's. Translate the information in the question into an inequality and solve it. *Less than* translates into <, not ≤, so eliminate (B) and (C). To watch m movies, the cost with Stream Supreme would be $7 for the monthly fee plus $1.75 for each movie, or $7 + 1.75m$. The cost with Download Empire would be $4 + 2.25m$. Therefore, the inequality is $7 + 1.75m$ < $4 + 2.25m$. Subtract $4 from both sides to get $3 + 1.75m$ < 2.25m$, then subtract 1.75m$ from both sides to get $3 < 0.50m$. Divide both sides by $0.50 to get 6 < m. The correct answer is (D).

7. **C** The question asks for the equation to be solved for h in terms of the other variables, so isolate the h. Start by multiplying both sides of the equation by μd to get $q\mu d = (p_e - p_{wf})kh$.

Next, divide both sides by $(p_e - p_{wf})k$ to get $\frac{q\mu d}{(p_e - p_{wf})k} = h$. This does not match any of the

answers exactly, but rewriting the numerator with the q in the middle makes it match (C). The correct answer is (C).

8. **A** The question asks for the meaning of 4 in the equation relating s and C. Unlike many questions of this type, the answers do not refer to different parts of the situation. Instead, they refer to changes in s that will result from changes in C. Try out some values for C to determine the effect on s. To start, plug in $C = 4$ and $C = 0$ to determine what happens when there is an increase or decrease of 4°C. If $C = 0$, then $s = 110 + 4(0) = 110$. If $C = 4$, then $s = 110 + 4(4) = 126$. As the temperature, C, increases by 4 degrees from 0 to 4, there is an increase in s of 126 − 110 = 16, so eliminate (C). Also, as C decreases by 4 degrees from 4 to 0 there is a decrease in s of 16, so eliminate (D). Now, test a temperature change of 1°C. Plug in $C = 1$ to compare the results to those from $C = 0$. If $C = 1$, then $s = 110 + 4(1) = 114$. Therefore, as the temperature decreases from $C = 1$ to $C = 0$, there is a decrease in the number of scoops sold of 114 − 110. Choice (B) says there would be an increase, so eliminate (B). On an increase from $C = 0$ to $C = 1$, there is an increase of 4. This is what is described in (A). The correct answer is (A).

9. **B** The question asks for a description of the changes to the amount Stephan saves over time. Information is given about Stephan's plan over a period of 9 months. Find the increase in savings over that time: $280 − $145 = $135 increase in savings over the 9-month period. Find the increase each month: $135 ÷ 9 = $15 additional savings per month. The correct answer is (B).

10. **D** The question asks for an equation that will only have y-values that are less than 2. Since this is in the No Calculator section, try out some values for x to see what happens to y in each equation. Let $x = 10$. Choice (A) becomes $y = -(10^2) + 3 = -100 + 3 = -97$. Since y is less than 2, leave (A), but check the remaining answers just in case. Choice (B) becomes $y = |-10| - 1 = 10 - 1 = 9$. Since y is greater than 2, eliminate (B). Choice (C) becomes $y = 10^3 - 4 = 1,000 - 4 = 996$. Eliminate (C). Choice (D) becomes $y = -(10 - 1)^2 + 1 = -81 + 1 = -80$. Since this value for y is less than 2, keep (D). Now try a weirder number, such as $x = 0$, in the remaining answer choices. Choice (A) becomes $y = -(0^2) + 3 = 0 + 3 = 3$. Since this is a value greater than 2, eliminate (A). Therefore, the correct answer is (D).

11. **A** The question asks for the value of $f(-4)$. If the function equation were given in $f(x)$ form, -4 would replace x. However, the function is written in $f(x + 1)$ form, so -4 replaces $x + 1$. Since $-4 = x + 1$, subtract 1 from both sides to get $x = -5$. Therefore, $f(-4) = 3(-5) - 4 = -15 - 4 = -19$. The correct answer is (A).

12. **C** The question asks for the value of a when the complex fraction is rewritten in the form $a + bi$. To get rid of the fractions, get the i out of the denominator by multiplying the expression by the conjugate of the denominator. Multiplying the expression by $\dfrac{2 + 3i}{2 + 3i}$ is the same as multiplying by 1, so it won't change the value. This becomes $\dfrac{(5 - i)(2 + 3i)}{(2 - 3i)(2 + 3i)} = \dfrac{10 + 15i - 2i - 3i^2}{4 + 6i - 6i - 9i^2} = \dfrac{10 + 13i - 3i^2}{4 - 9i^2}$.

Since $i = \sqrt{-1}$, $i^2 = -1$. Substitute -1 for i^2 to get $\dfrac{10 + 13i - 3(-1)}{4 - 9(-1)} = \dfrac{10 + 13i + 3}{4 + 9} = \dfrac{13 + 13i}{13}$.

Divide by 13 to get $1 + i$. Therefore, if $a + bi = 1 + i$, then $a = 1$. The correct answer is (C).

13. **B** The question asks for the sum of all the values of p that work in the equation. For all quadratic equations in the form $y = ax^2 + bx + c$, the sum of the roots equals $-\dfrac{b}{a}$. In the equation given, $-\dfrac{b}{a} = -\left(\dfrac{24}{3}\right) = -8$. Without that handy trick, it is still possible to answer the question using the quadratic formula to find the roots. Then add them together to get -8. Either way, the correct answer is (B).

14. **A** The question asks for a true statement regarding a, b, and c in the standard form of a quadratic, which forms a parabola. The parabola passes through the point $(-1, -1)$, so plug $x = -1$ and $y = -1$ into the equation of the parabola. The equation of the parabola is $y = ax^2 + bx + c$, so $-1 = a(-1)^2 + b(-1) + c$. Simplify this equation to get $-1 = a(1) + b(-1) + c$ and $-1 = a - b + c$. The correct answer is (A).

15. **C** The question asks for the possible values for r in an equation. Start by expanding the left side of the equation to get $pqx^2 + 3px + 5qx + 15 = 8x^2 + rx + 15$. Subtract 15 from both sides of the equation to get $pqx^2 + 3px + 5qx = 8x^2 + rx$. The two x terms on the left can be combined as $(3p + 5q)x$. When two quadratics are equal to each other, the coefficients on the x^2 terms on both sides are equal, and the coefficients on the x terms on both sides are equal. From this, it can be determined that $pq = 8$ and $3px + 5qx = rx$. Simplify the second equation by dividing by x to get $3p + 5q = r$. Given that $2 \times 4 = 8$ and that the question states that $p + q = 6$, one of the values for either p or q could be 2 and the other could be 4. If $p = 2$ and $q = 4$, then $3(2) + 5(4) = r$. Simplify the right side of the equation to get $6 + 20 = r$, and $26 = r$. Eliminate (A), (B), and (D), which do not contain this value. The correct answer is (C).

16. **3** The question asks for the value of y in the equation. To solve for y, isolate the variable. First, distribute the negative sign to get $4y + 8 - 7y + 12 = 11$. Combine like terms to get $-3y + 20 = 11$. Subtract 20 from both sides to get $-3y = -9$. Divide both sides by -3 to get $y = 3$. The correct answer is 3.

17. **250** The question asks for the number of square feet of floor space in a double room. Translate the information in the question into equations. Let d represent the square footage of a double room,

and s represent the square footage of a single room. According to the question, $d = s + 25$. Solve the equation for s to get $s = d - 25$. According to the question, $2d + 4s = 1,400$. Substitute $d - 25$ in for s to get $2d + 4(d - 25) = 1,400$. Distribute the 4 to get $2d + 4d - 100 = 1,400$. Combine like terms to get $6d - 100 = 1,400$. Add 100 to both sides of the equation to get $6d = 1,500$, then divide both sides by 6 to get $d = 250$. This is the correct answer.

18. $\frac{3}{5}$ or **0.6**

The question asks for the value of $\sin(90° - a°)$. There is a useful trigonometry rule that states $\cos \theta = \sin(90 - \theta)$. Therefore, $\sin(90 - a°) = \cos a° = \frac{3}{5}$. Without knowing that rule, it is still possible to answer this question. Draw a right triangle and label one of the acute angles as $a°$ and the other as $(90 - a°)$. If $\cos a° = \frac{3}{5}$, the side adjacent to the angle with $a°$ is 3 and the hypotenuse is 5. Now find $\sin(90 - a°)$: it is the value of the side opposite $(90 - a°)$ over the hypotenuse, or $\frac{3}{5}$. The correct answer is $\frac{3}{5}$ or 0.6.

19. **9** The question asks for the value of k and says that $x + 3$ is a factor of $x^2 + kx + 2k$. By definition, this means that $x^2 + kx + 2k = 0$ if $x + 3 = 0$. If $x + 3 = 0$, subtract 3 from both sides to get $x = -3$. Plug this value in for x into the equation $x^2 + kx + 2k = 0$ to get $(-3)^2 + (-3)k + 2k = 0$. Simplify the equation to get $9 - 3k + 2k = 0$. Combine like terms to get $9 - k = 0$. Add k to both sides to get $9 = k$. The correct answer is 9.

20. **3** The question asks for the real value of x in a third-degree polynomial. Look for things to factor out of two or more terms. Factor x^2 out of the first two terms to get $x^2(x - 3) + 5x - 15 = 0$. Factor 5 out of the last two terms to get $x^2(x - 3) + 5(x - 3) = 0$. Factor out the $(x - 3)$ from both parts of the left side and rewrite the equation as $(x^2 + 5)(x - 3) = 0$. If $x^2 + 5 = 0$, then $x^2 = -5$, which results in two imaginary values for x: $\sqrt{-5}$ and $-\sqrt{-5}$. Therefore, the real value of x is when $x - 3 = 0$, and $x = 3$. This is the correct answer.

Section 4: Math (Calculator)

1. **D** The question asks for the number of pies sold. Translate the information in the question into an equation. The store sold a total of 364 slices, 84 of which were individual slices. Since individual slices sold do not affect the number of pies sold, these 84 slices should not be counted. In order not to count them, subtract them from the total to get the total number of slices sold as parts of pies. Therefore, eliminate any choice that does not include $364 - 84$. This eliminates (A), (B), and (C). Only (D) remains. To determine why (D) is correct, note that $364 - 84$ represents the number of slices sold in pies. To get the number of pies, divide this total by the number of slices in each pie, which is 8. Therefore, the number of pies sold is $\frac{364 - 84}{8}$. The correct answer is (D).

2. **B** The question asks for the measure of $\angle b$ in the figure. In this scenario, parallel lines are cut by another set of parallel lines, and two kinds of angles are created—big and small. All the small

angles are equal to each other, all the large angles are equal to each other, and any large angle plus any small angle equals 180°. The given angle, $\angle a$, is a big angle, and $\angle b$ is a small angle. So $125 + \angle b = 180$, and angle $\angle b = 55°$, which is (B). The correct answer is (B).

3.   **A**   The question asks for the probability of selecting a certain type of chocolate from the box. According to the table, there are 5 white chocolate pieces with cream filling, 3 dark chocolate pieces with no filling, and 30 total pieces in the box. Therefore, the probability of selecting a piece that is either white chocolate with cream filling or dark chocolate with no filling is $\dfrac{5+3}{30} = \dfrac{8}{30}$. The correct answer is (A).

4.   **D**   The question asks for the equation that gives x in terms of T and y, where x and y are legs of a triangle with perimeter T. The perimeter of a triangle is the sum of the individual sides. Since no values are given for the sides, assign numbers to the variables. The question says that the sides have length x, x, and y, so let $x = 3$ and $y = 4$. Thus, the perimeter is $T = 3 + 3 + 4 = 10$. Plug $T = 10$, $x = 3$, and $y = 4$ into each choice and eliminate any that are not true equations. Choice (A) is $3 = 10 - 4$. Since this is false, eliminate (A). Choice (B) is $3 = 10 - 2(4)$. Since this is false, eliminate (B). Choice (C) is $3 = \dfrac{10 - 2(4)}{2}$. Since this is false, eliminate (C). Choice (D) is $3 = \dfrac{10 - 4}{2}$. This is true. The correct answer is (D).

5.   **D**   The question asks for the point that satisfies the given system of equations. To solve a system of equations, stack and then add them to try to make a variable disappear. To do this, it may be necessary to manipulate the equations first. In this case, multiply the second equation by -2 to get $-2x + 8y = -38$. Stack and add the equations.

$$
\begin{array}{r}
2x + 3y = {-6} \\
\underline{-2x + 8y = -38} \\
0x + 11y = -44
\end{array}
$$

Therefore, the result is $11y = -44$. Divide both sides by 11 to get $y = -4$. Eliminate any answer choice for which the y-coordinate is not -4: (A), (B), and (C). Only (D) remains. To determine why the x-coordinate is 3, plug $y = -4$ into one of the equations. Try the original form of the second equation. If $x - 4y = 19$, then $x - 4(-4) = 19$, and $x + 16 = 19$. Subtract 16 from both sides to get $x = 3$. The correct answer is (D).

6.   **C**   The question asks for the result when 3 times n is subtracted from 5. Use the information in the question to create an equation to solve for n. The first part of the question indicates that $8 - 6n = 20$. Subtract 8 from both sides of the equation to get $-6n = 12$, then divide both sides by -6 to get $n = -2$. The question is asking for the value of $5 - 3n$. Substitute -2 for n to get $5 - 3(-2) = 5 + 6 = 11$. The correct answer is (C).

7.   **C**   The question asks for the inequality that will show the number of minutes for which the football stadium is below capacity. Given that there are 25,000 attendees at 12 P.M and the number of attendees increases by 550 every minute, the number of attendees m minutes after 12 P.M. can be expressed as $25,000 + 550m$. The full capacity of the stadium is 65,000. To calculate the time prior to the stadium reaching full capacity, the equation would read $25,000 + 550m < 65,000$. The correct answer is (C).

8.   **A**   The question asks for the probability that a chosen resident of age 35–64 has an income between $50,000 and $74,999. According to the table, the total number of residents between the ages of 35 and 64 who have an income between $50,000 and $74,999 is 7,185 + 14,978 = 22,163. These numbers are all in the thousands, and the total will be as well. Those extra zeros cancel out when making the probability, so don't worry about them. The total number of residents between the ages of 35 and 64 is 39,919 + 83,213 = 123,132. Therefore, the approximate probability that a resident randomly selected in this age range has an income between $50,000 and $74,999 is $\frac{22,163}{123,132} = 0.18$. The closest answer is 20%. The correct answer is (A).

9.   **C**   The question asks for the number of gallons of fuel the truck will use in the 4-hour drive. The question says the truck traveled at an average speed of 70 miles per hour for 4 hours. If the speed and time are given, multiply them to get the distance, so d = (70 mph)(4 hours) = 280 miles. The truck has a fuel efficiency of 18 miles per gallon. Set up a proportion: $\frac{1 \text{ gallon}}{18 \text{ miles}} = \frac{g \text{ gallons}}{280 \text{ miles}}$. Cross-multiply to get 280 = 18g. Divide both sides by 18 to get $g \approx 15.56$. The question says *approximately*, so round this to 16. The correct answer is (C).

10.   **B**   The question asks for the time shown by the data point farthest from the line of best fit. No line is given, so draw an estimate of the line of best fit onto the graph itself. It should look something like this.

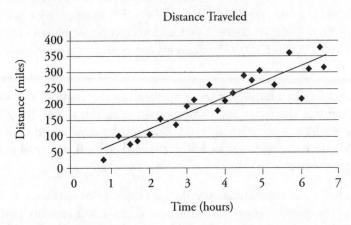

The point farthest away from the line is at about (6, 220). Since time is represented by the x-axis, the time is 6 hours. The correct answer is (B).

11.   **D**   The question asks for the equation that gives altitude in terms of temperature. Isolate the variable a in the given equation. Start by subtracting 212 from both sides of the equation to get $t_b - 212 = -0.0018a$. Multiply both sides of the equation by –1 to get $-t_b + 212 = 0.0018a$. Divide both sides by 0.0018 to get $\frac{-t_b + 212}{0.0018} = a$. Reorder the terms in the numerator to get $\frac{212 - t_b}{0.0018} = a$. The correct answer is (D).

12.   **A**   The question asks for the scatterplot with a positive association that is not linear. First, eliminate any answer that does not have a positive association. In a positive association, y increases as x increases, so eliminate any choice for which this is not true. Eliminate (C), since it doesn't appear to have a clear positive or negative association. Eliminate (D), since it decreases then increases, so it's not consistently increasing. The question asks for the one that is not linear, so eliminate the answer that is

linear. A linear association is one in which a line rather than a curve best fits the data points. In (B), the data points roughly form a linear pattern, so eliminate this choice. The correct answer is (A).

13. **B** The question asks for the equation that gives h in terms of the other variables. Isolate the variable h in the given equation. Start by multiplying the entire equation by t to get $vt = h - m + 4.9t^2$. Isolate the h by adding m and subtracting $4.9t^2$ on both sides to get $vt + m - 4.9t^2 = h$. Reorder the terms to get $-4.9t^2 + vt + m = h$. The correct answer is (B).

14. **A** The question asks for the meaning of the statement that $(7, 0)$ is a solution to an equation. The question says that x refers to the number of days after the shipment is received and y refers to the number of oranges that remain. Therefore, since $(7, 0)$ is a solution, there are 0 oranges remaining 7 days after the shipment. Go through each choice and determine whether it reflects this information. Choice (A) seems to be consistent with this, so keep (A). Choice (B) says that there are 7 oranges, but 7 refers to days rather than oranges, so eliminate (B). Choice (C) refers to 455 customers, but since there is no information about how many oranges are sold to each customer, the number of customers cannot be determined. Eliminate (C). Similar to (B), (D) refers to 7 oranges rather than 7 days, so eliminate (D). The correct answer is (A).

15. **B** The question asks for the number of days at which the player's compensation will be greater playing for the Eagles than for the Jays. There are different values in the answers, so try out a number of days and see what happens. Let $d = 4$. The player's total compensation if he played for the Eagles would be $1,400 + (140 + 40)4 = 1,400 + 720 = 2,120$, and his compensation if he played for the Jays would be $1,500 + (130 + 30)4 = 1,500 + 640 = 2,140$. Given that his compensation would be higher with the Jays, eliminate (A) and (C). Next, try $d = 6$. His compensation with the Eagles would be $1,400 + (140 + 40)6 = 1,400 + 1,080 = 2,480$, and his compensation with the Jays would be $1,500 + (130 + 30)6 = 1,500 + 960 = 2,460$. Given that his compensation is greater with the Eagles, eliminate (D). The correct answer is (B).

16. **A** The question asks for the meaning of the y-intercept on the graph of this situation. The question states that days are on the x-axis and compensation is on the y-axis. The y-intercept is where the line crosses the y-axis, at a point where $x = 0$. Plug in 0 for days, and the function becomes $y = b + (s + m)0$. Simplify the function to get $y = b$. Therefore, when $x = 0$, y is equal to b, which is the signing bonus. The correct answer is (A).

17. **B** The question asks for the approximate specific heat capacity of substance K. Start by using Process of Elimination. The question states that substance K has a heat capacity that is lower than that of methyl alcohol. Eliminate (D) since it is greater than 0.6. To calculate the heat capacity of substance K, find 30% of 0.6, which is $0.3 \times 0.6 = 0.18$. Therefore, the heat capacity of substance K is $0.6 - 0.18 = 0.42$. The correct answer is (B).

18. **D** The question asks for the relationship between c and d, two constants in a pair of linear inequalities. The point $(-1, 0)$ is given as the solution, which means that point is on the graphs of both. Plug $x = -1$ and $y = 0$ into both inequalities and solve them for c and d, respectively. The first inequality becomes $0 < -1 + c$. Add 1 to both sides to get $1 < c$. The second inequality becomes $0 < -(-1) - d$ or $0 < 1 - d$. Add d to both sides to get $d < 1$. If $d < 1$ and $c > 1$, then $d < c$. The correct answer is (D).

19. **B** The question asks for the podcast that had the most ad time per dollar. To get this for each podcast that is an answer choice, divide the amount of ad time by the cost of the ad. To get the amount of ad time, take the percent of ad time multiplied by the length of each podcast. However, since the length of each podcast is the same, the percent can be used rather than the amount itself. The ad times per dollar for Q, R, S, and T, respectively, are $\dfrac{30}{\$350} = 0.086$ per dollar, $\dfrac{25}{\$200} = 0.125$ per dollar,

$\dfrac{20}{\$180}$ = 0.111 per dollar, and $\dfrac{15}{\$150}$ = 0.1 per dollar. Podcast R has the greatest result. The correct answer is (B).

20. **D** The question asks for the effect that changing the dimensions of the quadrilateral will have on the area of the quadrilateral. This quadrilateral is a trapezoid. The formula for the area of a trapezoid is $A = \dfrac{1}{2}(b_1 + b_2)h$, where b_1 and b_2 represent the two bases, or the two parallel sides on the trapezoid, and h represents the height, or the perpendicular distance between the two bases. To see what will happen to the area, pick initial values for the three dimensions. Let $b_1 = 4$, $b_2 = 8$, and $h = 3$. The area is $A = \dfrac{1}{2}(4 + 8)(3) = 18$. The question says that PQ and SR are decreased by 75% and PT is quadrupled. Since PQ and SR are parallel, they are b_1 and b_2. Decrease each of these by 75%. 75% of 4 is $\dfrac{75}{100}(4) = 3$, so decrease by 3 to get $b_1 = 4 - 3 = 1$. 75% of 8 is $\dfrac{75}{100}(8) = 6$, so decrease by 6 to get $b_2 = 8 - 6 = 2$. Since PT is perpendicular to the two bases, it is the height. Since the height is quadrupled, the new height is $4 \times 3 = 12$. Therefore, the new area is $A = \dfrac{1}{2}(1 + 2)(12) = 18$. The area is unchanged. Therefore, the correct answer is (D).

21. **A** The question asks for the probability that someone who watches news fewer than 3 times per week belongs to Group A in the study. According to the table, 11 people never watch the news, and 27 people watch between 1 and 2 times a week, which makes 11 + 27 = 38 people who watch the news fewer than 3 times a week. Of those viewers, there are 7 + 14 = 21 people who belong to Group A. Therefore, the probability that a person randomly chosen from among those who watch fewer than 3 times a week is a member of Group A is $\dfrac{21}{38}$. The correct answer is (A).

22. **B** The question asks for the mean or average of the numbers represented in the bar graph. For averages, use the formula $T = AN$, in which T is the total, A is the average, and N is the number of things. Use the graph to determine the frequency of each integer. There are four 4s, one 5, one 6, one 7, two 9s, and one 11. The sum is 4 + 4 + 4 + 4 + 5 + 6 + 7 + 9 + 9 + 11 = 63. Count the numbers to get that there are 10 numbers. Therefore, the formula becomes 63 = A(10), and $A = 6.3$. The correct answer is (B).

23. **A** The question asks for the volume of Sample S, in milliliters. Find the point representing Sample S on the graph. The volume of the sample is represented by the vertical axis, so trace the horizontal line from Sample S to the vertical axis at 80. However, this is 80 liters and the question asks for milliliters. The answer should begin with an 8, so eliminate (B) and (D). There are 1,000 milliliters in a liter, so set up the proportion $\dfrac{1,000 \text{ mL}}{1 \text{ L}} = \dfrac{x \text{ mL}}{80 \text{ L}}$. Cross-multiply to get $x = 80,000$. The choices are in scientific notation. Since 80,000 is an 8 followed by four 0s, it is equal to 8×10^4. The correct answer is (A).

24. **A** The question asks for the range of the volume of the three samples of approximately 1.4 moles. Range is defined as the difference between the greatest and least values. The horizontal axis represents the amount. Go just to the left of the line representing 1.5 moles, trace a line straight upward and cross

three points. To determine the volume of the sample represented by each point, trace a line directly to the left of each point and see where it crosses the vertical axis, which represents volume. The highest point is between 80 and 100 liters, closer to 100, so it is between 90 and 100. The lowest is between 60 and 80 liters, closer to 60, so it is between 60 and 70. Therefore, the range must be greater than 90 − 70 = 20 and less than 100 − 60 = 40. The only choice in this range is 30. The correct answer is (A).

25. **D** The question asks for the volume of a sample containing 1,200 moles. According to the ideal gas law prediction given, $V = 50n$, where V is the volume and n is the number of moles. The question asks about a sample with 1,200 moles, so the volume is $V = 50(1,200) = 60,000$. The correct answer is (D).

26. **C** The question asks for the polynomial that is divisible by $3x + 7$. Rather than work out complex algebra or factor, select a value for x and determine the values of functions f and g. If $x = 2$, $f(x) = 3(2^3) + 6(2^2) + 11(2) = 24 + 24 + 22 = 70$, $g(x) = 8(2^2) + 15(2) + 7 = 32 + 30 + 7 = 69$, and $3x + 7 = 3(2) + 7 = 13$. In the answers, plug in 70 for $f(x)$ and 69 for $g(x)$ to see which answer is divisible by 13. Choice (A) becomes $j(x) = 2(70) + 69 = 140 + 69 = 209$, which is not divisible by 13. Eliminate (A). Choice (B) becomes $k(x) = 70 + 69 = 139$, which is not divisible by 13. Eliminate (B). Choice (C) becomes $m(x) = 70 + 2(69) = 70 + 138 = 208$. $208 ÷ 13 = 16$. Keep (C), but check (D) just in case. Choice (D) becomes $n(x) = 70 + 3(69) = 70 + 207 = 277$, which is not divisible by 13. Eliminate (D). The correct answer is (C).

27. **C** The question asks for the trigonometric function in the answer choices that is equal to $\frac{y}{x}$. The answer choices include two different functions and two different angles, so use Process of Elimination. The function cosine is equal to $\frac{\text{opposite}}{\text{hypotenuse}}$. Since neither x nor y is the hypotenuse, eliminate the choices that use cosine, (A) and (B). The only two remaining choices use tangent, which is $\frac{\text{opposite}}{\text{adjacent}}$. Therefore, $\frac{\text{opposite}}{\text{adjacent}} = \frac{y}{x}$. Since P is opposite side y, $\frac{y}{x} = \tan P$. The correct answer is (C).

28. **C** The question asks for the form of the function that contains the minimum value as a constant or coefficient. The given equation of $f(x)$ is a quadratic equation which, when graphed, will be a parabola. The minimum value of a parabola is the vertex. The vertex form of a quadratic equation is $y = a(x − h)^2 + k$, where (h, k) is the vertex. Eliminate (B), since it is not in the vertex form of the equation. Expand the function to get $f(x) = x^2 + 7x − x − 7 = x^2 + 6x − 7$. Eliminate (A), since it is not an equivalent form of this quadratic. Set the quadratic equal to 0 to get $x^2 + 6x − 7 = 0$. Complete the square to get $(x^2 + 6x + 9) − 7 = 0 + 9$. Factor the equation to get $(x + 3)^2 − 7 = 9$. Subtract 9 from both sides to get $f(x) = (x + 3)^2 − 16$. The correct answer is (C).

29. **B** The question asks for a true statement about the relationship of a and b. Start by combining like terms in the equations. Simplify the top equation to get $−j = 3a + 3$. Multiply both sides of the equation by −1 to get $j = −3a − 3$. The question says that j is $k + 1$, so substitute $k + 1$ for j to get $k + 1 = −3a − 3$. Subtract 1 from both sides of the equation to get $k = −3a − 4$. Simplify the bottom equation to get $−k = 3b + 3$. Multiply both sides of the equation by −1 to get $k = −3b − 3$. Therefore, $−3a − 4 = −3b − 3$. Add 4 to both sides to get $−3a = −3b + 1$, then divide both sides by −3 to get $a = b − \frac{1}{3}$. The correct answer is (B).

30. **C** The question asks for the average of a, b, and c, which are all defined in terms of x. Rather than deal with all these variables, select a value for x and determine the values of a, b, and c. If $x = 3$, $3x = 9$, $4x = 12$, and $5x = 15$. Use these values to find the values of a, b, and c. *Average = total ÷ number of things*, so $a = \dfrac{9+11}{2} = \dfrac{20}{2} = 10$, $b = \dfrac{12+6}{2} = \dfrac{18}{2} = 9$, and $c = \dfrac{15+7}{2} = \dfrac{22}{2} = 11$. Now take the average of a, b, and c: $\dfrac{10+9+11}{3} = \dfrac{30}{3} = 10$. Plug $x = 3$ into the answers to see which one matches this target number. Choice (A) becomes $3 + 2 = 5$, (B) becomes $3 + 3 = 6$, (C) becomes $2(3) + 4 = 10$, and (D) becomes $4(3) + 8 = 20$. The correct answer is (C).

31. **12** The question asks for the number of years it will take for the lake to drop by a certain amount given the current trend. Translate the information into an equation and solve. Let y represent the number of years. Set up the following equation: $2.25y = 27$. Divide both sides by 2.25 to get $y = 12$. This is the correct answer.

32. **216** The question asks for the number of cars the factory will produce in 3 days. Given that the car factory produces one car every 20 minutes, it produces 3 cars in 1 hour. Since the car factory operates 24 hours a day, the factory produces $3 \times 24 = 72$ cars per day. Therefore, in 3 days, the factory produces $72 \times 3 = 216$ cars. The correct answer is 216.

33. **180** The question asks for the lowest score Vito can get in the 7th game and maintain an average of at least 240. For averages, use the formula $T = AN$, in which T is the total, A is the average, and N is the number of things. To average 240 over all 12 games, Vito must score a total of $T = 240 \times 12 = 2{,}880$ points. In his first 6 games, Vito scored a total of $T = 6 \times 200 = 1{,}200$ points. To find the least number of points he would need to earn on his 7th game, calculate the maximum number of points Vito could get on his last 5 games. If he bowled a perfect game for the last 5 games, he would receive a total of $5 \times 300 = 1{,}500$ additional points. Add this to the total of his first 6 games to get $1{,}200 + 1{,}500 = 2{,}700$ points scored. Therefore, the minimum number of points Vito must score on his 7th game is $2{,}880 - 2{,}700 = 180$ points. The correct answer is 180.

34. **5** The question asks for the value of p, the x-coordinate of the point of intersection between the parabola and the line. The actual values for the coordinates of only two points on the parabola are given. However, one of the points is the vertex, so use the vertex form of the equation of a parabola: $y = a(x - h)^2 + k$, where (h, k) is the vertex. Plug the point $(3, 14)$ in as the vertex to get $y = a(x - 3)^2 + 14$. To determine the value of a, plug in the other point, $(0, 5)$, to get $5 = a(0 - 3)^2 + 14$. Simplify the parentheses to get $5 = a(-3)^2 + 14$, and square -3 to get $5 = 9a + 14$. Subtract 14 from both sides to get $-9 = 9a$. Divide by 9 to get $a = -1$. Therefore, the equation of the parabola is $y = -(x - 3)^2 + 14$. To determine the point of intersection, find the equation of the line, which contains the points $(0, -5)$ and $(1, -2)$. The equation of a line can be put into the form $y = mx + b$, where m is the slope and b is the y-intercept. The y-intercept is the point at which $x = 0$. Since $(0, -5)$ is on the line, the y-intercept is -5. Now get the slope by using the formula $m = \dfrac{y_2 - y_1}{x_2 - x_1}$. Let $(x_1, y_1) = (0, -5)$ and $(x_2, y_2) = (1, -2)$, so $m = \dfrac{-2 - (-5)}{1 - 0} = \dfrac{-2 + 5}{1} = -2 + 5 = 3$. Therefore, the equation of the line is $y = 3x - 5$. Now set the two equations equal to each other to get $-(x - 3)^2 + 14 = 3x - 5$. Use FOIL (First, Outer, Inner, Last) on $(x - 3)^2$ to get $-(x^2 - 6x + 9) + 14 = 3x - 5$. Distribute the negative to get $-x^2 + 6x - 9 + 14 = 3x - 5$. Combine like terms to get $-x^2 + 6x + 5 = 3x - 5$. To solve a quadratic, get

one side equal to 0. Subtract $3x$ and add 5 to both sides to get $-x^2 + 3x + 10 = 0$. Divide both sides by -1 to get $x^2 - 3x - 10 = 0$. Factor to get $(x - 5)(x + 2) = 0$. Set both factors equal to 0 to get $(x - 5) = 0$ and $(x + 2) = 0$. Solve the two equations to get $x = 5$ and $x = -2$. Since the point (p, q) is in Quadrant I, the x-coordinate is positive, so use $x = 5$. Since p is the x-coordinate, the correct answer is 5.

35. **350** The question asks for the amount of Harry's down payment, in dollars. In a situation with a down payment and monthly installments, the total amount paid = monthly payments + down payment. In the function given, $175m$ represents the monthly payments, which means his down payment must have been the 350 dollars. To check this out, try $m = 0$ to see what Harry will pay before the monthly payments begin. The equation becomes $T = 175(0) + 350 = 350$. The correct answer is 350.

36. **20** The question asks for the length of a minor arc on the circle. There is a proportional relationship between the parts and the whole of a circle, so try to determine the "part" of the central angle, $\angle AOC$. A tangent line is always perpendicular to the radius of the circle. Therefore, $\angle ABO = 90°$ and $\angle CBO = 90°$. Given that the interior angles of a triangle add up to $180°$, $\angle AOB = 60°$ and $\angle BOC = 40°$. The interior angle $\angle AOC = 60° + 40° = 100°$. To determine the circumference of minor arc $\overset{\frown}{DE}$, set up the following proportion: $\dfrac{\text{angle}}{360°} = \dfrac{\text{minor arc}}{\text{circumference}}$. In this case, $\dfrac{100°}{360°} = \dfrac{x}{72}$. Cross-multiply to get $360x = 7{,}200$. Divide both sides by 360 to get $x = 20$. This is the correct answer.

37. **0.86** The question asks for the value of k, the variable in parentheses on a population model. The population is decreasing, so use the decay formula, which states that *final amount = original amount* × $(1 - rate)^n$. The rate is 14% per year, which is written as a decimal in the decay formula. Therefore, $k = 1 - 0.14 = 0.86$. This is the correct answer.

38. **376** The question asks for the predicted population of the town after five years. Use the decay formula, *final amount = original amount* × $(1 - rate)^n$, and the value for k found in the last question to find the population in 5 years. Plug 800 in for the original amount, 0.86 in for k, and 5 in for x to get $P = 800(0.86)^5 \approx 376$. Without the formula, it is still possible to get this question right. Just use a calculator to find the population after 1 year, which would be $800 - 0.14(800) = 688$. Then do it again for the population after 2 years: $688 - 0.14(688) = 591.68$. Continue the process three more times to find the population after five years, which will round to 376. This is the correct answer.

Chapter 15
Practice Test 7

Reading Test

65 MINUTES, 52 QUESTIONS

Turn to Section 1 of your answer sheet to answer the questions in this section.

Questions 1–10 are based on the following passage.

The passage is adapted from Saki, "The Background," originally published in 1911.

"That woman's art-jargon tires me," said Clovis to his journalist friend. "She's so fond of talking of certain pictures as 'growing on one,' as though they were a sort of fungus."

"That reminds me," said the journalist, "of the story of Henri Deplis. Have I ever told it to you?"

Clovis shook his head.

"Henri Deplis was by birth a native of the Grand Duchy of Luxemburg. On maturer reflection he became a commercial traveller. His business activities frequently took him beyond the limits of the Grand Duchy, and he was stopping in a small town of Northern Italy when news reached him from home that a legacy from a distant and deceased relative had fallen to his share.

"It was not a large legacy, even from the modest standpoint of Henri Deplis, but it impelled him towards some seemingly harmless extravagances. In particular it led him to patronize local art as represented by the tattoo-needles of Signor Andreas Pincini. Signor Pincini was, perhaps, the most brilliant master of tattoo craft that Italy had ever known, but his circumstances were decidedly impoverished, and for the sum of six hundred francs he gladly undertook to cover his client's back, from the collar-bone down to the waist-line, with a glowing representation of the Fall of Icarus. The design, when finally developed, was a slight disappointment to Monsieur Deplis, who had suspected Icarus of being a fortress taken by Wallenstein in the Thirty Years' War, but he was more than satisfied with the execution of the work, which was acclaimed by all who had the privilege of seeing it as Pincini's masterpiece.

"It was his greatest effort, and his last. Without even waiting to be paid, the illustrious craftsman departed this life, and was buried under an ornate tombstone, whose winged cherubs would have afforded singularly little scope for the exercise of his favourite art. There remained, however, the widow Pincini, to whom the six hundred francs were due. And thereupon arose the great crisis in the life of Henri Deplis, traveller of commerce. The legacy, under the stress of numerous little calls on its substance, had dwindled to very insignificant proportions, and when a pressing wine bill and sundry other current accounts had been paid, there remained little more than 430 francs to offer to the widow. The lady was properly indignant, not wholly, as she volubly explained, on account of the suggested writing-off of 170 francs, but also at the attempt to depreciate the value of her late husband's acknowledged masterpiece. In a week's time Deplis was obliged to reduce his offer to 405 francs, which circumstance fanned the widow's indignation into a fury. She cancelled the sale of the work of art, and a few days later Deplis learned with a sense of consternation that she had presented it to the municipality of Bergamo, which had gratefully accepted it. He left the

CONTINUE ➡

neighbourhood as unobtrusively as possible, and was genuinely relieved when his business commands took
60 him to Rome, where he hoped his identity and that of the famous picture might be lost sight of.

"But he bore on his back the burden of the dead man's genius. On presenting himself one day in the steaming corridor of a vapour bath, he was at once
65 hustled back into his clothes by the proprietor, who was a North Italian, and who emphatically refused to allow the celebrated Fall of Icarus to be publicly on view without the permission of the municipality of Bergamo. Public interest and official vigilance
70 increased as the matter became more widely known, and Deplis was unable to take a simple dip in the sea or river on the hottest afternoon unless clothed up to the collar-bone in a substantial bathing garment. Later on the authorities of Bergamo conceived the idea that
75 salt water might be injurious to the masterpiece, and a perpetual injunction was obtained which debarred the muchly harassed commercial traveller from sea bathing under any circumstances. Altogether, he was fervently thankful when his firm of employers found
80 him a new range of activities in the neighbourhood of Bordeaux. His thankfulness, however, ceased abruptly at the Franco-Italian frontier. An imposing array of official force barred his departure, and he was sternly reminded of the stringent law which forbids the
85 exportation of Italian works of art.

1

Which choice best summarizes the passage?

A) A man is unable to display a work of art.

B) A man is forced to consider whether or not to obey the law.

C) A man finds his choices restricted because of the result of an unpaid debt.

D) A man tries to steal art to please a deceased relative.

2

The passage most clearly suggests that Henri Deplis' financial status before receiving the legacy was

A) chaotic.

B) meager.

C) wealthy.

D) destitute.

3

Which choice provides the best evidence for the answer to the previous question?

A) Lines 8–9 ("Henri . . . Luxemburg")

B) Lines 16–18 ("It was . . . extravagances")

C) Lines 21–25 ("Signor . . . back")

D) Lines 42–44 ("The legacy . . . proportions")

4

In line 38, "exercise" most nearly means

A) express beliefs.

B) increase strength.

C) practice repeatedly.

D) ability to perform.

5

The journalist implies that the cherubs on Pincini's tombstone were

A) artistic subjects.

B) religious icons.

C) particularly tiny.

D) plain stone.

CONTINUE

6

The journalist indicates that Deplis reduced his offer to 405 francs because he

A) thought he could trick Pincini's widow.

B) could no longer afford the 430 francs.

C) wanted to annoy the widow.

D) thought she would accept a lower offer.

7

The author's statement that the widow "cancelled the sale of the work of art" (line 54) chiefly serves to

A) show that Deplis had to return the art.

B) preview Deplis' inability to travel.

C) demonstrate the unpleasant temper of the widow.

D) introduce an unexpected shift in perspective.

8

In line 67, "celebrated" most nearly means

A) welcomed.

B) famous.

C) decorated.

D) endless.

9

As presented in the passage, the trouble Henri Deplis encountered due to his tattoo is most accurately described as

A) socially awkward but well-intended.

B) well-deserved but clearly cruel.

C) obviously absurd but persistently troublesome.

D) uncomfortably restrictive but secretly flattering.

10

Which choice provides the best evidence for the answer to the previous question?

A) Lines 57–61 ("He left . . . of")

B) Lines 62–63 ("But he . . . genius")

C) Lines 78–81 ("Altogether . . . Bordeaux")

D) Lines 82–85 ("An imposing . . . art")

CONTINUE

Questions 11–20 are based on the following passage and supplementary material.

This passage is adapted from Emily Grubert, "'Renewable' natural gas may sound green, but it's not an antidote for climate change." Originally published in 2020 in *The Conversation*: https://theconversation.com/.

Natural gas is a versatile fossil fuel that accounts for about a third of U.S. energy use. Although it produces fewer greenhouse gas emissions and other pollutants
Line than coal or oil, natural gas is a major contributor to
5 climate change, an urgent global problem. Reducing emissions from the natural gas system is especially challenging because natural gas is used roughly equally for electricity, heating, and industrial applications. There's an emerging argument that maybe there could
10 be a direct substitute for fossil natural gas in the form of renewable natural gas (RNG)—a renewable fuel designed to be nearly indistinguishable from fossil natural gas. RNG could be made from biomass or from captured carbon dioxide and electricity.

15 Based on what's known about these systems, however, I believe climate benefits might not be as large as advocates claim. This matters because RNG isn't widely used yet, and decisions about whether to invest in it are being made now, in places like
20 California, Oregon, Washington, Michigan, Georgia and New York. As someone who studies sustainability, I research how decisions made now might influence the environment and society in the future. I'm particularly interested in how energy systems
25 contribute to climate change. Right now, energy is responsible for most of the pollution worldwide that causes climate change. Since energy infrastructure, like power plants and pipelines, lasts a long time, it's important to consider the climate change emissions
30 that society is committing to with new investments in these systems. At the moment, renewable natural gas is more a proposal than reality, which makes this a great time to ask: What would investing in RNG mean for climate change?

35 If RNG could be a renewable replacement for fossil natural gas, why not move ahead? Consumers have shown that they are willing to buy renewable electricity, so we might expect similar enthusiasm for RNG. The key issue is that methane isn't just a fuel—
40 it's also a potent greenhouse gas that contributes to climate change. Any methane that is manufactured

intentionally, whether from biogenic or other sources, will contribute to climate change if it enters the atmosphere. And releases will happen, from
45 newly built production systems and existing, leaky transportation and user infrastructure. For example, the moment you smell gas before the pilot light on a stove lights the ring? That's methane leakage, and it contributes to climate change.

50 To be clear, RNG is almost certainly better for the climate than fossil natural gas because byproducts of burning RNG won't contribute to climate change. But doing somewhat better than existing systems is no longer enough to respond to the urgency of climate
55 change. The world's primary international body on climate change suggests we need to decarbonize by 2030 to mitigate the worst effects of climate change. My recent research suggests that for a system large enough to displace a lot of fossil natural gas, RNG
60 is probably not as good for the climate as is publicly claimed. Although RNG has lower climate impact than its fossil counterpart, likely high demand and methane leakage mean that it probably will contribute to climate change. In contrast, renewable sources such as wind
65 and solar energy do not emit climate pollution directly.

What's more, creating a large RNG system would require building mostly new production infrastructure, since RNG comes from different sources than fossil natural gas. Such investments are both long-term
70 commitments and opportunity costs. They would devote money, political will and infrastructure investments to RNG instead of alternatives that could achieve a zero greenhouse gas emission goal. When climate change first broke into the political
75 conversation in the late 1980s, investing in long-lived systems with low but non-zero greenhouse gas emissions was still compatible with aggressive climate goals. Now, zero greenhouse gas emissions is the target, and my research suggests that large deployments of
80 RNG likely won't meet that goal.

CONTINUE

Figure 1
U.S. Primary Energy Production by Source

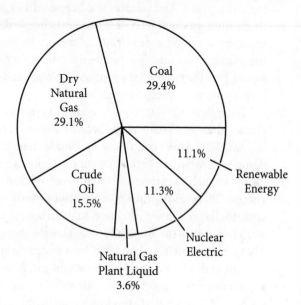

Figure 2
U.S. Primary Energy Consumption by Source

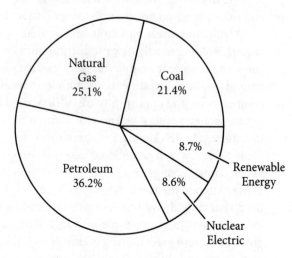

Figure 1 and figure 2 are adapted from U.S. Energy Information Agency data for the year 2010.

What function does the first paragraph (lines 1–14) serve in the passage as a whole?

A) It argues definitively for adopting an alternative which the passage as a whole presents unfavorably.

B) It introduces a potential solution that the author of the passage ultimately rejects.

C) It supports with examples claims made in the last two paragraphs of the passage.

D) It provides a summary of a challenge not fully understood by the consumers mentioned in the passage.

The central idea of the second paragraph (lines 15–34) is that

A) energy systems require a significant investment in infrastructure.

B) several U.S. states are considering implementing RNG systems.

C) the climate impact of RNG should be investigated.

D) RNG will contribute significantly to climate change.

Which choice provides the best evidence for the answer to the previous question?

A) Lines 15–17 ("Based . . . claim")

B) Lines 17–21 ("This . . . York")

C) Lines 23–25 ("I'm particularly . . . change")

D) Lines 27–31 ("Since . . . systems")

CONTINUE

14

Which choice does the author explicitly cite as a disadvantage of using renewable natural gas as an energy source?

A) Energy independence

B) Increased utility costs

C) Safety concerns

D) Escaped gases

15

Which choice provides the best evidence for the answer to the previous question?

A) Lines 31–34 ("At the . . . change")

B) Lines 44–46 ("And releases . . . infrastructure")

C) Lines 50–52 ("To be . . . change")

D) Lines 64–65 ("In contrast . . . directly")

16

As used in line 55, "primary" most nearly means

A) principal.

B) unmediated.

C) simple.

D) first.

17

As used in line 77, "aggressive" most nearly means

A) brash.

B) dominating.

C) ambitious.

D) combative.

18

Which choice best supports the conclusion that preparations for using renewable natural gas could disrupt the development of other energy sources?

A) Lines 66–69 ("What's . . . gas")

B) Lines 69–70 ("Such . . . costs")

C) Lines 70–73 ("They . . . goal")

D) Lines 74–78 ("When . . . goals")

19

Which choice is supported by the data in the first figure?

A) Renewable energy production is equal to energy production from crude oil.

B) Nuclear electric power production exceeds natural gas plant liquid production.

C) The amount of energy produced from renewable sources is greater than the amount of energy produced from coal.

D) Renewable energy is produced less efficiently than energy produced from crude oil.

20

Taken together, the two figures suggest that renewable energy sources

A) are in high demand in urban areas but consumed less frequently in rural areas.

B) are in higher demand in areas where consumers protest the use of fossil fuels.

C) account for less than half of energy production and consumption.

D) account for less than half of total energy production but more than half of total energy consumption.

CONTINUE ➡

Questions 21–30 are based on the following passage.

This passage is adapted from Riley Black, *Fossil Footprints Help Uncover the Mysteries of Bipedal Crocodiles.* ©2020 by *Scientific American.*

More than 113 million years ago, a strange reptile lived in what is now South Korea. It strode around on two legs like many dinosaurs, yet it was not one of them. The tracks it left behind indicate it was a
5 relative of today's crocodiles. And the details of its Cretaceous footfalls resolve one mystery—but open another.

Footprints like these had been found before, though in much older rocks. During the Triassic
10 period (between 252 million and 201 million years ago) crocodile relatives—part of a group known as crocodylomorphs—were the dominant reptiles on land, and they included animals that resembled some dinosaurs by walking on two legs. These forms went
15 extinct at the end of the period, yet the geologically younger tracks from South Korea's Jinju Formation represent a bipedal crocodylomorph that lived long after the Triassic closed.

Paleontologist Kyung Soo Kim of Chinju National
20 University of Education in South Korea, fossil footprint expert Martin Lockley of the University of Colorado Denver and their colleagues describe the puzzling fossil tracks. Lockley calls South Korea a "tracker's heaven" for paleontologists because
25 of the sheer number of fossil footprints found in the country. Last November, he says, Kim had asked for his opinion on large Cretaceous tracks uncovered at the site. The prints looked similar to those attributed to pterosaurs, flying reptiles from
30 the Age of Dinosaurs, that were walking on the ground. But Lockley recognized them as something else. "I immediately saw that they were of the type known as *Batrachopus*," or a form of track attributed to crocodile relatives from the early part of the
35 Jurassic (201 million to 145 million years ago). These footprints not only were much larger than any other known *Batrachopus* tracks, but they also indicated that the animals at the site walked on two legs— and were present for millions of years more in the
40 Cretaceous period.

The presence of bipedal crocs at the fossil site was unexpected. The discovery does help address another fossil mystery, however. At a different South Korean location known as Gain-ri, there are tracks that were
45 also previously believed to be left by large pterosaurs. Tracks found elsewhere in the world indicate that the flying reptiles folded their wings to waddle on all fours while on the ground. But researchers had thought the prints at Gain-ri were made by pterosaurs
50 that moved on two legs to avoid dragging their wings through the muck.

The new fossils have changed the analysis of these tracks—and have undercut interpretations of pterosaurs walking on two legs at other sites.
55 Pterosaur expert Liz Martin-Silverstone of the University of Bristol in England, who was not involved in the new study, agrees that the presumed "pterosaur" tracks at Jinju look much more like prints made by crocodile relatives than those left by
60 pterosaurs. In fact, she notes, "all previously described bipedal 'pterosaur' trackways have come out as crocodilian upon reexamination"—which dovetails with skeletal evidence indicating these prehistoric flappers tottered around on four legs while on the
65 ground.

With the new find, paleontologists now know of at least two fossil sites that apparently record the bipedal footsteps of Cretaceous crocodylomorphs— not those of pterosaurs acting unusually. "This new
70 footprint evidence shows we have to rethink the crocs of yesteryear and regard some as agile land dwellers," Lockley says. Although crocodiles are often cast as "living fossils" that have changed little since their origin in the Triassic, skeletal and track evidence has
75 shown that crocs in the Age of Dinosaurs were varied, active animals that often looked very different from the swimming ambush predators we are familiar with today.

CONTINUE →

21

Which choice best reflects the overall sequence of events in the passage?

A) A discovery is made; comparisons with prior findings reveal new information, and a previous theory is altered to reflect the new understanding.

B) A group of scientists collaborate on their field research; they change their predictions, and the results are verified and published.

C) An expert is consulted; a previous research site is revisited, and scientists retain their original line of thinking.

D) Current research is examined and critiqued; an older theory is revived and confirmed through a new study, and further research is proposed.

22

The passage indicates that South Korea is an ideal site for studying ancient species due to

A) the presence of scientists working there.

B) the nearby university.

C) the abundance of fossils.

D) the ease of fossil excavation.

23

After uncovering the "puzzling fossil tracks," (line 23) Kyung Soo Kim

A) attempted to prove that the tracks belonged to flying reptiles.

B) studied the movements of *Batrachopus*.

C) compared the footprints with modern dinosaur relatives.

D) asked a colleague for assistance in identifying the tracks.

24

As used in line 31, "recognized" most nearly means

A) reinvented.

B) identified.

C) showed appreciation for.

D) gave credit to.

25

In the fourth paragraph (lines 41–51) the description of pterosaurs' behavior mainly serves to

A) present a theory undermined by the identification of the Jinju Formation fossils.

B) outline the hypothesis that Kim intended to disprove.

C) describe a species that is no longer thought to have existed.

D) demonstrate a difference between researchers' methods.

26

Which statement best captures an assumption researchers made in changing their theory that pterosaurs walked on two legs?

A) Tracks of different animals would appear somewhat similar due to geological differences at the Gain-ri and Jinju sites.

B) Insights about tracks at one location can be applied to similar tracks at another location.

C) Flying reptiles of the Cretaceous period were more likely than crocodiles of the same period to walk on two legs.

D) *Batrachopus* and pterosaurs both evolved during the Jurassic period.

CONTINUE ➡

Which choice provides the best evidence for the answer to the previous question?

A) Lines 41–42 ("The presence . . . unexpected")

B) Lines 46–48 ("Tracks . . . ground")

C) Lines 55–60 ("Pterosaur . . . pterosaurs")

D) Lines 69–72 ("This . . . says")

As used in line 72, "cast" most nearly means

A) studied.

B) served.

C) described.

D) molded.

What can reasonably be inferred about modern crocodiles from the passage?

A) They may differ in appearance from their ancient crocodilian relatives.

B) They would be the dominant species on land if they spent less time in the water.

C) Their movement is similar to the movement of their prehistoric counterparts.

D) Their footprints are much larger than those of other reptiles.

Which choice provides the best evidence for the answer to the previous question?

A) Lines 9–14 ("During . . . legs")

B) Lines 35–40 ("These . . . period")

C) Lines 52–53 ("The new . . . tracks")

D) Lines 72–78 ("Although . . . today")

CONTINUE

Questions 31–41 are based on the following passages.

Passage 1 is adapted from a letter from Thomas Jefferson to John Adams, October 28, 1813. Passage 2 is adapted from a letter from John Adams to Thomas Jefferson, November 15, 1813. Jefferson and Adams are discussing whether aristocracy is inherited.

Passage 1

For I agree with you that there is a natural aristocracy among men. The grounds of this are virtue and talents.

Line
5 There is also an artificial aristocracy founded on wealth and birth, without either virtue or talents; for with these it would belong to the first class. The natural aristocracy I consider as the most precious gift of nature, for the instruction, the trusts, and government of society. And indeed it would have
10 been inconsistent in creation to have formed man for the social state, and not to have provided virtue and wisdom enough to manage the concerns of the society. May we not even say that that form of government is the best which provides the most effectually for a pure
15 selection of these natural aristoi into the offices of government? The artificial aristocracy is a mischievous ingredient in government, and provision should be made to prevent its ascendancy.

I think the best remedy is exactly that provided by
20 all our constitutions, to leave to the citizens the free election and separation of the aristoi from the pseudo-aristoi, of the wheat from the chaff. In general, they will elect the really good and wise. In some instances, wealth may corrupt, and birth blind them; but not
25 in sufficient degree to endanger the society. But even in Europe a change has sensibly taken place in the mind of Man. Science had liberated the ideas of those who read and reflect, and the American example had kindled feelings of right in the people. An insurrection
30 has consequently begun, of science, talents and courage against rank and birth, which have fallen into contempt.

This however we have no right to meddle with. It suffices for us, if the moral and physical condition
35 of our own citizens qualifies them to select the able and good for the direction of their government, with a recurrence of elections at such short periods as will enable them to displace an unfaithful servant before the mischief he meditates may be irremediable.

Passage 2

40 We are now explicitly agreed, in one important point, that "there is a natural aristocracy among men; the grounds of which are virtue and talents."

But though we have agreed in one point, in words, it is not yet certain that we are perfectly agreed in
45 sense. Fashion has introduced an indeterminate use of the word "talents." Education, wealth, strength, beauty, stature, birth, marriage, graceful attitudes and motions, gait, air, complexion, and physiognomy are talents, as well as genius and science and learning. Any one of
50 these talents, that in fact commands or influences true votes in society, gives to the man who possesses it the character of an aristocrat, in my sense of the word.

Your distinction between natural and artificial aristocracy does not appear to me well founded. Birth
55 and wealth are conferred on some men as imperiously by Nature, as genius, strength or beauty. The heir is honors and riches, and power has often no more merit in procuring these advantages than he has in obtaining a handsome face or an elegant figure.
60 When aristocracies are established by human laws, and honor, wealth, and power are made hereditary by municipal laws and political institutions, then I acknowledge artificial aristocracy to commence: but this never commences, till corruption in elections
65 becomes dominant and uncontrollable. But this artificial aristocracy can never last. The everlasting envies, jealousies, rivalries and quarrels among them, their cruel rapacities upon the poor ignorant people their followers, compel these to set up Caesar, a
70 demagogue to be a monarch and master. Here you have the origin of all artificial aristocracy, which is the origin of all monarchy. And both artificial aristocracy, and monarchy, and civil, military, political and hierarchical despotism, have all grown out of the
75 natural aristocracy of "virtues and talents."

Your distinction between the aristoi and pseudo aristoi, will not help the matter. I would trust one as soon as the other with unlimited power. The law wisely refuses an oath as a witness in his own cause to the
80 saint as well as to the sinner.

CONTINUE ➡

31

As used in line 20, "free" most nearly means

A) complimentary.

B) available.

C) unrestricted.

D) gratuitous.

32

It can be inferred that the author of Passage 1 believes the best way to prevent the rise of the artificial aristocracy is to

A) allow those with power to pass that power to their children.

B) run America the same way the Europeans run their countries.

C) require voters to vote only for the best and wisest candidates.

D) allow voters to choose their own leaders.

33

Which choice provides the best evidence for the answer to the previous question?

A) Lines 4–6 ("There . . . class")

B) Lines 16–18 ("The artificial . . . ascendancy")

C) Lines 19–22 ("I think . . . chaff")

D) Lines 25–27 ("But even . . . Man")

34

As used in line 45, "fashion" most nearly means

A) convention.

B) demeanor.

C) model.

D) construction.

35

According to the author of Passage 2, an artificial aristocracy begins only when

A) laws give one group power over another.

B) all people are given the right to vote.

C) a democracy turns into a monarchy.

D) those who are virtuous and talented control the government.

36

In Passage 2, the author claims that political advantages come mainly from

A) birth and wealth.

B) a wide range of characteristics.

C) physical attributes.

D) municipal laws and political institutions.

37

Which choice provides the best evidence for the answer to the previous question?

A) Lines 40–42 ("We are . . . talents")

B) Lines 49–52 ("Any one . . . word")

C) Lines 54–56 ("Birth . . . beauty")

D) Lines 60–65 ("When . . . uncontrollable")

38

In lines 76–80, the author of Passage 2 refers to a statement made in Passage 1 in order to

A) question the working vocabulary of the author of Passage 1.

B) argue against the central theme of Passage 1.

C) agree with the logic of the proposal outlined in Passage 1.

D) point out a perceived flaw in the argument made in Passage 1.

CONTINUE

39

Which best describes the overall relationship between Passage 1 and Passage 2?

A) Passage 2 further develops a distinction presented in Passage 1.

B) Passage 2 disagrees with a key assumption of Passage 1.

C) Passage 2 considers the historical context of statements made in Passage 1.

D) Passage 2 redefines key terms used in the argument in Passage 1.

40

The authors of both passages would most likely agree with which of the following statements about advantages people may have over each other?

A) Those born talented and virtuous have an advantage over those who aren't.

B) Wealth and power are more important than beauty and talent.

C) Advantages one gains later in life are more powerful than those one is born with.

D) There is a clear distinction between those who earn their power and those who have it handed to them.

41

How would the author of Passage 1 most likely respond to the points made in Passage 2 (lines 60–75)?

A) Passing power down through families will lead to governments run like those in Europe.

B) Although a few who are unfit may be elected, leaving the decisions in the hands of the voters will ultimately keep the system balanced.

C) Rank and birth are more highly prized than science and talent.

D) The setup of the American system could allow for an unfaithful leader to cause irremediable damage.

CONTINUE

Questions 42–52 are based on the following passage and supplementary material.

This passage is adapted from Nicolaas Bouwes et al., "Ecosystem Experiment Reveals Benefits of Natural and Simulated Beaver Dams to a Threatened Population of Steelhead (*Oncorhynchus mykiss*)." ©2016 by Scientific Reports.

Beaver in Eurasia and North America were once abundant and ubiquitous. Their dense and barbed fur has great felting properties, and as early as the
Line
1500s, intense trapping to provide pelts mainly for
5 making hats occurred throughout Eurasia. When Lewis and Clark explored the Pacific Northwest in 1805, salmon and steelhead coexisted with beavers in very high densities. When the British and United States jointly occupied the Oregon Territories (which
10 included the Columbia River Basin), the Hudson Bay Company implemented their "scorched earth" or "fur desert" policy to eliminate all fur-bearing animals, in an attempt to discourage American settlement. As a result, beaver were nearly extirpated from the region
15 by 1900.

Around this time, a decrease in the great harvests of Pacific salmon and steelhead was first perceived. Anadromous salmon and steelhead populations have since declined precipitously in the Columbia
20 River Basin, leading to their listing under the U.S. Endangered Species Act (ESA). Human activities, including the removal of beaver, have exacerbated the occurrence of stream channel incision, where a rapid down-cutting of the stream bed disconnects
25 the channel from its floodplain. We hypothesized that beaver dams or simulated beaver dams that we construct (referred to as beaver dam analogs or BDAs) can greatly accelerate the incision recovery process.

BDAs were built by pounding wooden fence posts
30 vertically into the channel bed and potential floodplain surfaces. Willow branches were woven between the posts, and bed sediment was used to plug the base of structures. The addition of BDAs into Bridge Creek led to an immediate and rapid increase in the number
35 of natural beaver dams, not only in our treatment areas but throughout much of Bridge Creek. Whether their dam-building activities increased because of a demographic or behavioral response is somewhat immaterial, because the modification of the stream
40 ecosystem, rather than the beavers themselves, likely caused the fish population response.

BDAs and beaver dams led to large changes in both fish and beaver habitat, and the steelhead population response largely followed our hypothesized pathways.
45 We found compelling evidence that beavers increased the quantity of juvenile habitat.

Increasing habitat complexity may also partially explain the observed increase in total juvenile abundance, survival and productivity. Increased
50 habitat complexity provides fish a greater selection of locations at which to forage, rest, and avoid predation and high flow events, while reducing migration distances required to conduct these activities for multiple life-stages. Thus, we suspect that an increase
55 in habitat complexity is partly responsible for the observed positive steelhead population responses.

Number of Dams Over Time

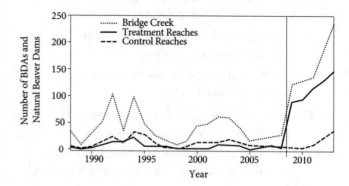

The panel represents the total number of dams for the Bridge Creek (dotted line), the sum of all treatment (solid line), and all control (dashed line) reaches. The black vertical line represents when BDAs were initially installed.

42

As used in line 22, "removal" most nearly means the

A) significant reduction of a population.

B) surgical extraction of an item.

C) complete extinction of a species.

D) physical relocation of an individual beaver.

CONTINUE ➤

43

In line 56, the authors state that certain hypothesized results were largely consistent with "steelhead population responses." According to the passage, which of the following best represents the broader hypothesis the authors tested in order to obtain those results?

A) Artificial beaver dams can be constructed by the placement of wooden posts and cross-woven willow branches without obstructing the development of natural dams.

B) Reconnecting a stream's channel and floodplain can occur more quickly through the construction of natural or artificial beaver dams.

C) The removal of an animal from its habitat can lead to unexpected results throughout an ecosystem.

D) Stream channel incision, caused by the rapid down-cutting of a stream bed, is exacerbated by the presence of unexpectedly large numbers of beaver dams.

44

Which choice provides the best evidence for the answer to the previous question?

A) Lines 16–17 ("Around . . . perceived")

B) Lines 21–25 ("Human . . . floodplain")

C) Lines 25–28 ("We hypothesized . . . process")

D) Lines 29–31 ("BDAs . . . surfaces")

45

The primary purpose of the third paragraph (lines 29–41) is to

A) illustrate methods and results of research to determine the impact of beaver dams on stream ecosystems.

B) detail the findings of research designed to investigate beaver responses to competition from other dams.

C) describe the plan that will be followed by the hypothetical experiment referenced in the fifth paragraph (lines 47–56).

D) suggest a method by which a potential experiment could be carried out in the future in order to test the strength of beaver dams.

46

The passage most clearly indicates that the authors' Bridge Creek BDA building efforts had which of the following indirect effects?

A) They temporarily disturbed the local wildlife populations.

B) They reduced the downstream water flow.

C) They prompted beavers to build more natural dams.

D) They increased local beaver populations.

47

Which choice provides the best evidence for the answer to the previous question?

A) Lines 13–15 ("As a . . . 1900")

B) Lines 33–36 ("The addition . . . Creek")

C) Lines 36–41 ("Whether . . . response")

D) Lines 49–54 ("Increased . . . life-stages")

CONTINUE ➡

48

The words "partially," "suspect," and "partly" in the fifth paragraph (lines 47–56) have which effect on the tone of the paragraph?

A) They indicate an insecure tone that displays the depth of the authors' nervousness about how the new research will be received.

B) They indicate an objective tone that states facts while also allowing for the possibility that other factors may be important.

C) They indicate a conceding tone that grudgingly accepts unwelcome results of the conducted research on the effects of artificial dams.

D) They create a suspicious tone that suggests the authors are afraid that they may have missed crucial implications of their research.

49

An unstated assumption of the experiment described in the passage is that habitat complexity

A) was at its greatest before 1900.

B) is always increased by the addition of dams.

C) is detrimental to most types of predator populations in stream-based ecosystems.

D) was not maximized before the construction of the BDAs.

50

According to the data in the figure, what was the greatest number of dams on Bridge Creek during the twenty years prior to the installation of BDAs?

A) 105 dams

B) 125 dams

C) 150 dams

D) 225 dams

51

Based on the data in the figure, which of the following years represents the last year during which a control reach had a greater number of dams than a treatment reach?

A) 1995

B) 2000

C) 2007

D) 2012

52

Does the graphic support the author's claim that increasing the number of real or simulated beaver dams leads to an increase in steelhead populations?

A) Yes, because the initial construction of BDAs led directly and significantly to steep increases in natural dams along all the treated stream systems.

B) Yes, because the data in the figure indicate that the construction of BDAs led to an increase in the steelhead populations.

C) No, because the data does not provide a link between the number of dams and the quality of steelhead habitats.

D) No, because the data does not show that floodplain access is significantly increased by the presence of dams.

STOP
If you finish before time is called, you may check your work on this section only.
Do not turn to any other section in the test.

No Test Material On This Page

Writing and Language Test

35 MINUTES, 44 QUESTIONS

Turn to Section 2 of your answer sheet to answer the questions in this section.

Questions 1–11 are based on the following passage.

Paternal Instincts: The Case for Paternity Leave

From high-rise office buildings to massive manufacturing plants, the main focus in any workplace is generally on what employees are being paid to do, but **1** the personal needs of workers must also be addressed for a modern company to maximize its potential for success. After all, it is no longer the dawn of the Industrial Age. Children are no longer used as part of the workforce, paid days off are commonplace, and a safe working environment is the rule rather than the exception. Contemporary employers **2** of today understand that providing for the safety and security of an employee, and an employee's family, can improve not only quality of life, but also the company's production.

1

Which choice provides the most appropriate introduction to the passage?

A) NO CHANGE

B) work isn't the only thing.

C) many companies also care about profit as well.

D) companies could do everything possible to make all employees happy.

2

A) NO CHANGE

B) today

C) of right now

D) DELETE the underlined portion.

CONTINUE ➡

There is no more important event for a family than the birth of a child, and many companies offer paid maternity leave to mothers in order to ease the natural burden that families experience during this time. However, significantly fewer companies offer the male equivalent—paid paternity leave. A 2012 study conducted **3** from the United States Department of Labor found that only 13 percent of men who took paternity leave received pay compared to 21 percent of women who took maternity leave. The same study found that maternity leave averages six to twelve weeks in length. Of the men who reported taking leave following the birth of a child, 70 percent indicated that they took a paternity leave **4** they are at most ten days long.

3

A) NO CHANGE
B) by
C) of
D) DELETE the underlined portion.

4

A) NO CHANGE
B) that was
C) they were
D) those being

CONTINUE

This pronounced deficit in leave [5] is important for two reasons. The first is that companies might not only increase the happiness of their workforce, but also retain high-skilled workers who could be tempted to leave for another company offering better paternity benefits. A 2014 study by the U.S. Bureau of Labor and Statistics found that nine out of ten men considered paternity leave to be a factor of at least marginal importance when considering employment opportunities. [6] Others considered it to be less important. [7] Clearly, this is becoming a more important issue to the newest additions to the workforce.

[5]

A) NO CHANGE

B) are

C) is being

D) had been

[6]

Which choice best supports the statement made in the previous sentence?

A) NO CHANGE

B) But not as important as mothers having time off.

C) But others did not seem to think it mattered.

D) Six out of ten considered it to be extremely important.

[7]

At this point, the writer is considering adding the following sentence.

> The younger a male respondent was, the more likely he was to rate the issue of paternity leave as important when considering employment.

Should the writer make this addition?

A) Yes, because it provides a reason for the assertion made in the last sentence of the paragraph.

B) Yes, because it supplies qualitative data that is challenged in the remainder of the paragraph.

C) No, because it interrupts the discussion of what is important to older fathers.

D) No, because it does not take into account whether workers were actually fathers or not.

CONTINUE ➔

8 However, paternity leave is not just about what potential employees want. There is a second reason that paternity leave policies are so important; they bring attention to a larger societal issue. Not enough emphasis has been placed on the importance of both **9** parent's being involved in the earliest stages of a child's life. Paternity leave allows fathers to bond with their children earlier, participate in the household more **10** actively, and, raise children with a greater sense of gender equality. **11** In other words, paternity leave not only benefits a lone employee and his or her family—it improves society as a whole.

8

In context, which choice best combines the underlined sentences?

A) However, another reason that paternity leave is so important is that they bring attention to a larger societal issue that is also what potential employees want.

B) However, a second reason is about what potential employees want and paternity leave having an impact on an entire society.

C) Beyond being something potential employees desire, paternity leave policies are also important because they highlight a larger societal issue.

D) Employees want paternity leave, so another important reason to take it seriously in our society is that these policies involve a larger societal issue.

9

A) NO CHANGE

B) parent's being involved in the earliest stages of a childs

C) parents being involved in the earliest stages of a child's

D) parents being involved in the earliest stages' of a childs

10

A) NO CHANGE

B) active, and raise

C) actively, and raise

D) actively and raising

11

A) NO CHANGE

B) Otherwise,

C) Completely,

D) Alternatively,

CONTINUE ➡

Questions 12–22 are based on the following passage.

The Divided Elections of America

The cyclical nature of American federal elections is one aspect of American life common to all fifty states. However, once you move past the cycle and look at the voting mechanisms themselves, similarities are hard to come by. **12** One major difference among the states pertaining to elections for federal offices, for example presidential or congressional **13** candidates. Is whether a state holds a primary or a caucus. These two systems, primaries and caucuses, are meant to accomplish the same **14** goal; nominate major-party candidates for office.

12

Which choice provides the most logical introduction to the sentence?

A) NO CHANGE

B) All states vote for the same offices on the same cycle

C) The main questions for all democratic nations and their elections,

D) DELETE the underlined portion, and begin the next sentence with a capital letter.

13

A) NO CHANGE

B) candidates:

C) candidates; is

D) candidates, is

14

A) NO CHANGE

B) goal

C) goal, and

D) goal:

CONTINUE

Because the goal of each of these systems is the same, it can be surprising how fundamentally different primaries and caucuses are. Caucuses, for example, are strictly limited to the members of a single political party. If a caucus is the preferred method of election, these state-level party members will convene a meeting, called a caucus, to select candidates or decide policy. At this caucus, members of that single political party meet in person at an appointed time and location to discuss the candidates and debate their merits based on the party platform. **15** The voting for candidates then happens manually.

Primaries, on the other hand, involve an election that narrows the field of major-party candidates before an election for office. Additionally, primaries may be declared as "open," which means that they are not limited to participation by a single political party as caucuses are. In primaries, non-affiliated and affiliated voters may present **16** themselves at their respective precincts and cast their votes privately.

15

The writer is considering revising the underlined sentence to read:

> The voting for candidates then happens manually, either by a raised hand count or by separating into groups for a tally.

Should the writer add this information here?

A) Yes, because it provides examples of why caucuses are more effective than primaries.

B) Yes, because it further explains the assertion made in the sentence.

C) No, because it should be placed later in the passage.

D) No, because it contradicts the main claim of the passage.

16

A) NO CHANGE

B) himself or herself

C) their selves

D) oneself

CONTINUE

Historically, caucuses made a great deal of practical sense. **17** In the late 18th century it was difficult for candidates to share information with potential voters or campaign on a large geographical scale. Much of the voting **18** population had limited, if any, knowledge of the candidates or party platforms before traveling to designated centers to actually cast a vote. Caucuses allowed voters who were limited in their knowledge to learn firsthand from representatives of the candidates what the party platform was and what positions the candidates had on issues within that platform. Voters then selected representatives who were pledged to the candidate the voters had chosen. **19**

17

The writer is considering deleting the previous sentence. Should the writer make this change?

A) Yes, because it does not logically follow from the previous paragraph.

B) Yes, because it introduces information that is irrelevant at this point in the passage.

C) No, because it provides a specific example in support of arguments made elsewhere in the passage.

D) No, because it provides a logical introduction to the paragraph.

18

A) NO CHANGE

B) population, had limited if any knowledge

C) population had, limited, if any, knowledge

D) population had limited if any knowledge,

19

Which choice most logically follows the previous sentence?

A) The man who received the most votes would become president.

B) Of course, not everyone who came voted in the same way.

C) Functionally, voters directly voted for their caucus representatives, not the actual candidates.

D) Local elections rarely used this system because candidates were always well known.

CONTINUE

Over time, especially in this era of mass and social media, primaries have been steadily surpassing caucuses in popularity. Out of the fifty voting states and commonwealths, only 13 currently hold caucuses. This is due in part to the **20** horrid nature of caucuses in comparison to primaries. Not only are they difficult to keep organized, **21** it is also difficult to keep civil. In addition, caucuses have come to be perceived as less democratic because **22** it is an election of representatives rather than direct elections of candidates.

20

Which choice best maintains the tone established in the passage?

A) NO CHANGE

B) deplorable

C) litigious

D) inconvenient

21

A) NO CHANGE

B) but also they are

C) but also being

D) also being

22

A) NO CHANGE

B) it has been an election

C) they are elections

D) those have been an election

CONTINUE

Questions 23–33 are based on the following passage and supplementary material.

The Sloth: Nature's Layabout or Efficient Mammal?

Many people believe that the sloth is an extremely lazy animal. This popular image of the sloth has its roots in both history and etymology. European explorers in South America, **23** they noticed the sloth's slow and **24** lackadaisical movements, named the creature after one of the "Seven Deadly Sins." **25** Recently, the sloth's image is reinforced by Disney's 2016 movie *Zootopia*. In this movie, Flash, a sloth, slows down the main characters by spending hours completing simple tasks. However, while it is true that the sloth typically moves slowly and spends a significant portion of **26** its day sleeping, this slow rate of activity is not due to laziness. Rather, the sloth has evolved this lifestyle in order to adapt to the particular challenges of consuming leaves located high in the rainforest canopy.

23

A) NO CHANGE
B) that
C) which
D) who

24

A) NO CHANGE
B) careless
C) inactive
D) leisurely

25

Which choice most effectively combines the underlined sentences?

A) Flash, a sloth in the 2016 movie *Zootopia*, slows down the main characters by spending hours completing simple tasks, which reinforces the sloth's image recently by Disney.

B) Disney's 2016 movie *Zootopia* reinforces this image by featuring a sloth, Flash, who slows down the main characters by spending hours completing simple tasks.

C) Disney's Flash, a sloth, slows down the main characters by spending hours completing simple tasks recently in *Zootopia*, reinforcing the sloth's image.

D) A sloth, Flash, slows down Disney's 2016 movie *Zootopia*, reinforcing the sloth's image and spending hours completing simple tasks.

26

A) NO CHANGE
B) it's
C) there
D) their

CONTINUE

[1] The sloth is categorized as a folivore because the bulk of its diet consists of the leaves, buds, and tender shoots of *Cercropia*, [27] that is a tree found in the tropical regions of Central and South America. [2] Take the sloth's [28] stomach for example, it is very large with multiple compartments. [3] These compartments contain bacteria that break down the leafy material. [4] It may take a sloth over a month to digest a meal of *Cercropia* leaves. [5] However, leaves and other non-fruit parts of trees are nutritionally poor, so the sloth has various adaptations to help it thrive on this diet. [6] Another, perhaps even more amazing dietary adaptation is the sloth's unusually low body temperature. [29]

27

A) NO CHANGE
B) it is
C) being
D) DELETE the underlined portion.

28

A) NO CHANGE
B) stomach, for example,
C) stomach. For example,
D) stomach, for example:

29

To make this paragraph most logical, sentence 5 should be placed
A) where it is now.
B) after sentence 1.
C) after sentence 3.
D) after sentence 6.

CONTINUE

Most mammals regulate their body temperature in part by creating heat through metabolic processes. Through normal body processes, heat is generated (more in the core organs than in the extremities), and this heat is spread throughout the body. This process of heat generation requires nutrition, and, as mentioned above, the sloth survives predominantly on tree products that are poor in nutrition. As the graph shows, this in part explains why the sloth has a body temperature approximately **30** five degrees Celsius lower than that of the other mammals shown, even when active. Furthermore, the sloth does not keep its body temperature in as limited a range as, for instance, a dog **31** has. A healthy dog's temperature will remain within 0.4 degree Celsius of its average, whereas a healthy sloth's temperature can be as much as 2 degrees Celsius warmer or cooler than its average body temperature when active. This means that a healthy **32** sloth's active body temperature can be greater than that of a healthy dog. This lower body temperature helps the sloth thrive on a nutritionally poor diet. The sloth's slow and steady lifestyle is therefore not the result of laziness, but rather the result of **33** popular culture's stereotypes about this animal as seen through the movie *Zootopia*.

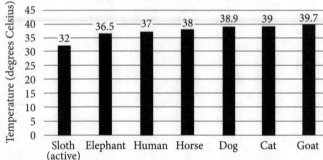

Average Body Temperature of
Various Mammals

Adapted from Gary Meisner, "Golden Ratio in Body Temperatures."
Originally published May 13, 2012 by Goldennumber.net.

30

Which choice offers an accurate interpretation of data in the graph?

A) NO CHANGE

B) equal to

C) five degrees greater than

D) half

31

A) NO CHANGE

B) will.

C) did.

D) does.

32

Which choice offers an accurate interpretation of the data in the graph?

A) NO CHANGE

B) dog's body temperature is greater than that of any mammal shown in the graph.

C) dog's body temperature will be greater than that of a sloth, even when the sloth is active.

D) active sloth will have a body temperature equal to that of a healthy dog.

33

The writer wants a conclusion that conveys how the sloth's inactivity is the result of adaptations to its diet. Which choice best accomplishes this goal?

A) NO CHANGE

B) the unfortunate name given to the sloth by Europeans exploring the South American rainforest.

C) keeping its body temperature lower than that of most other mammals.

D) needing to survive off of a food source that, while abundant, is not a rich source of nutrients.

CONTINUE ➡

Questions 34–44 are based on the following passage.

Milton Babbitt: A Punny Composer

Typically, a pun is a form of word play suggesting that there are multiple interpretations of a word or phrase. Some puns—Oscar Wilde's "The Queen is not a subject," for **34** example use words that have multiple meanings. Other puns, such as the comedian George Carlin's observation that "Atheism is a non-prophet organization," **35** relies on words with different definitions, but that sound alike. From Shakespeare's plays to Abbott and Costello's *Who's on First?* to even the **36** Bible, wordsmiths have used puns for humorous and rhetorical effect. However, puns aren't just limited to words. One **37** punster, American composer, Milton Babbitt, has imported the use of puns into music.

34

A) NO CHANGE

B) example,

C) example;

D) example—

35

A) NO CHANGE

B) rely

C) has relied

D) relying

36

A) NO CHANGE

B) Bible. These wordsmiths

C) Bible. Wordsmiths

D) Bible; these wordsmiths

37

A) NO CHANGE

B) punster, American composer Milton Babbitt,

C) punster, American composer, Milton Babbitt

D) punster American composer Milton Babbitt,

CONTINUE

Two of Babbitt's works for percussion, *Homily* and *Beaten Paths*, show how he **38** writes effectively for the instruments chosen. *Homily*, for snare drum, uses dynamics (how loudly or softly a note is played) and timbre (the "color" of the note, changed by using different drumsticks) to change how similar musical phrases are audibly perceived. The musical phrase is **39** modified in such a way that different interpretations of the phrase are possible, much in the same way that verbal puns rely on concurrent interpretations of a word. Similarly, *Beaten Paths*, for marimba, also uses dynamics to create different musical meanings.

38

Which choice most effectively sets up the examples that follow?

A) NO CHANGE

B) has fun with the music in his compositions.

C) creates puns in music by using the same musical idea in multiple ways.

D) shows the absurdity of translating ideas from one type of work to another.

39

A) NO CHANGE

B) twisted

C) doctored

D) refined

CONTINUE

Beaten Paths uses pitch to not only create repeated musical motifs, but also **40** reshaped the audience's perception of the music. **41** Beyond his music, Babbitt's use of puns even **42** extends to the titles of his works.

A) NO CHANGE

B) reshape

C) have reshaped

D) reshaping

At this point, the writer is considering adding the following sentence.

> Babbitt was one of the first to work in electronic music, producing his *Composition for Synthesizer* in 1961.

Should the writer make this addition here?

A) Yes, because it helps to explain Babbitt's interest in puns.

B) Yes, because it links Babbitt's music to literature.

C) No, because it provides background information that is irrelevant to the paragraph.

D) No, because it fails to indicate whether Babbitt wrote for other instruments besides the synthesizer.

The writer wants to link the second paragraph to the ideas that follow. Which choice best accomplishes this goal?

A) NO CHANGE

B) helps his listeners understand his musical ideas.

C) makes his music both funny and persuasive.

D) makes similar sounding ideas mean different things.

CONTINUE ▶

[1] *Beaten Paths* refers both to the repetition of musical ideas and the use of the marimba, which is struck to create sound. [2] The pun contained in *Homily* is a bit less obvious. [3] The music of both *Beaten Paths* and *Homily* originate in another work of Babbitt's, *My Complements to Roger*, the title of which contains a pun on the word "compliments"/"complements." [4] A homily is a religious sermon, and a quote from a homily by St. John Chrysostom is included in the score: "And why, it is asked, are there so many snares? That we may not fly low, but seek the things that are above." [5] Other works by Babbitt also contain puns, such as *All Set*, *About Time*, and *Autobiography of the Eye*. [6] Milton Babbitt, by 43 using percussion instruments in novel ways, enhances listener enjoyment through the creation of different layers of meaning. 44

43

A) NO CHANGE

B) playing around with the meanings of words,

C) using puns in both the music and titles of his compositions,

D) having his performers use dynamics and timbre in unusual ways,

44

To make this paragraph most logical, sentence 4 should be placed

A) where it is now.

B) after sentence 1.

C) after sentence 2.

D) after sentence 5.

STOP
If you finish before time is called, you may check your work on this section only.
Do not turn to any other section in the test.

No Test Material On This Page

Math Test – No Calculator

25 MINUTES, 20 QUESTIONS

Turn to Section 3 of your answer sheet to answer the questions in this section.

For questions 1–15, solve each problem, choose the best answer from the choices provided, and fill in the corresponding circle on your answer sheet. **For questions 16–20**, solve the problem and enter your answer in the grid on the answer sheet. Please refer to the directions before question 16 on how to enter your answers in the grid. You may use any available space in your test booklet for scratch work.

NOTES

1. The use of a calculator **is not permitted**.
2. All variables and expressions used represent real numbers unless otherwise indicated.
3. Figures provided in this test are drawn to scale unless otherwise indicated.
4. All figures lie in a plane unless otherwise indicated.
5. Unless otherwise indicated, the domain of a given function f is the set of all real numbers x for which $f(x)$ is a real number.

REFERENCE

$A = \pi r^2$
$C = 2\pi r$

$A = \ell w$

$A = \frac{1}{2} bh$

$c^2 = a^2 + b^2$

Special Right Triangles

$V = \ell wh$

$V = \pi r^2 h$

$V = \frac{4}{3}\pi r^3$

$V = \frac{1}{3}\pi r^2 h$

$V = \frac{1}{3}\ell wh$

The number of degrees of arc in a circle is 360.
The number of radians of arc in a circle is 2π.
The sum of the measures in degrees of the angles of a triangle is 180.

CONTINUE

1

Which of the following is equal to $m^{\frac{5}{2}}$, for all values of m ?

A) $\sqrt{m^5}$

B) $\sqrt{m^{\frac{1}{5}}}$

C) $\sqrt[5]{m^2}$

D) $\sqrt[5]{m^{\frac{1}{2}}}$

2

A sealcoating company will seal d driveways with the same size and shape in a subdivision using a specific type of sealant. The company's fee can be calculated by the expression $dClw$, where d is the number of driveways, C is a constant with units in dollars per square meter, l is the length of each driveway in meters, and w is the width of each driveway in meters. If the homeowners' association asks the company to use a less expensive type of sealant, which of the factors in the expression would change?

A) l

B) d

C) w

D) C

3

If $4x = 20$, what is the value of $12x - 4$?

A) 5

B) 36

C) 56

D) 60

4

If $\dfrac{2}{z} = \dfrac{8}{z + 42}$, what is the value of $\dfrac{z}{2}$?

A) 14

B) 7

C) 2

D) $\dfrac{1}{7}$

CONTINUE

5

$$3r - 5s = -17$$
$$5r - 3s = -7$$

If (r, s) is a solution to the system of equations above, what is the value of $r - s$?

A)   10

B)   –3

C)   –10

D)   –24

6

The number of scripted shows produced for streaming services between 2012 and 2013 is triple the number of scripted shows the services produced between 2009 and 2010. If 24 scripted shows were produced between 2012 and 2013 and s shows were produced between 2009 and 2010, which of the following equations is true?

A) $3s = 24$

B) $24s = 3$

C) $\dfrac{s}{3} = 24$

D) $s + 24 = 3$

7

The line $y = cx - 2$, where c is a constant, is graphed in the xy-plane. If the line contains the point (m, n), where $m \neq 0$ and $n \neq 0$, what is the slope of the line, in terms of m and n ?

A) $\dfrac{2 - m}{n}$

B) $\dfrac{2 - n}{m}$

C) $\dfrac{m + 2}{n}$

D) $\dfrac{n + 2}{m}$

8

$$3x - 2y = 5$$
$$cx - 7y = 12$$

In the system of equations above, c is a constant and x and y are variables. For what value of c will the system of equations have no solution?

A) $-\dfrac{21}{2}$

B) $-\dfrac{36}{5}$

C) $\dfrac{36}{5}$

D) $\dfrac{21}{2}$

CONTINUE

9

x	$p(x)$
0	−1
1	0
2	3
5	4

The function p is defined by a polynomial. Some values of x and $p(x)$ are shown in the table above. Which of the following must be a factor of $p(x)$?

A) $x - 1$

B) $x - 2$

C) $x - 3$

D) $x - 4$

10

$$y = a(x - 3)(x + 5)$$

In the quadratic equation above, a is a nonzero constant. The graph of the equation in the xy-plane is a parabola with vertex (s, t). Which of the following is equal to t ?

A) $-2a$

B) $-10a$

C) $-15a$

D) $-16a$

11

In the xy-plane, the parabola with equation $(x - 9)^2$ intersects the line with the equation $y = 36$ at two points, F and G. What is the length of $\overline{FG}$?

A) 10

B) 12

C) 15

D) 25

12

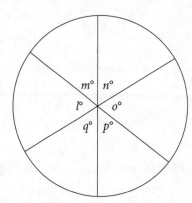

Note: Figure not drawn to scale.

In the figure above, three lines intersect at a point in a circle. If $l + m = n + o$, which of the following statements must be true?

    I. $l = n$

    II. $m = q$

    III. $p = q$

A) I only

B) II only

C) II and III only

D) I, II, and III

CONTINUE

13

What are the solutions to $2x^2 + 12x + 8 = 0$?

A) $-3 \pm \dfrac{\sqrt{58}}{2}$

B) $-3 \pm \sqrt{5}$

C) $-8 \pm \sqrt{5}$

D) $-8 \pm 8\sqrt{5}$

14

$$D = \frac{5}{6}(212 - F)$$

The equation above shows how a temperature F, measured in degrees Fahrenheit, relates to the temperature D, measured in degrees Delisle. Based on the equation, which of the following must be true?

I. A temperature increase of $\dfrac{5}{6}$ degree Fahrenheit is equivalent to a temperature decrease of 1 degree Delisle.

II. A temperature increase of 1 degree Delisle is equivalent to a temperature decrease of 1.2 degrees Fahrenheit.

III. A temperature increase of 1 degree Fahrenheit is equivalent to a temperature decrease of $\dfrac{5}{6}$ degree Delisle.

A) II only

B) III only

C) II and III only

D) I, II, and III

15

The equation $\dfrac{36y^2 + 43y - 25}{ky - 3} = -9y - 4 - \dfrac{37}{ky - 3}$ is true for all values of $y \neq \dfrac{3}{k}$, where k is a constant.

What is the value of k ?

A) 27

B) 4

C) −4

D) −27

CONTINUE ➤

DIRECTIONS

For questions 16–20, solve the problem and enter your answer in the grid, as described below, on the answer sheet.

1. Although not required, it is suggested that you write your answer in the boxes at the top of the columns to help you fill in the circles accurately. You will receive credit only if the circles are filled in correctly.

2. Mark no more than one circle in any column.

3. No question has a negative answer.

4. Some problems may have more than one correct answer. In such cases, grid only one answer.

5. **Mixed numbers** such as $3\frac{1}{2}$ must be gridded as 3.5 or 7/2. (If $\boxed{3\ 1\ /\ 2}$ is entered into the grid, it will be interpreted as $\frac{31}{2}$, not as $3\frac{1}{2}$.)

6. **Decimal Answers:** If you obtain a decimal answer with more digits than the grid can accommodate, it may be either rounded or truncated, but it must fill the entire grid.

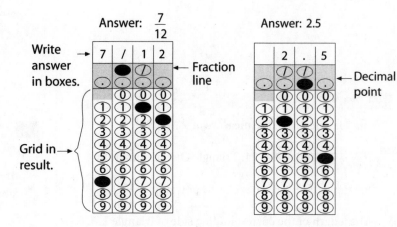

Answer: $\frac{7}{12}$ — Write answer in boxes. — Fraction line — Grid in result.

Answer: 2.5 — Decimal point

Acceptable ways to grid $\frac{2}{3}$ are:

Answer: 201 – either position is correct

NOTE: You may start your answers in any column, space permitting. Columns you don't need to use should be left blank.

CONTINUE ▶

16

If $\dfrac{9}{10}z - \dfrac{7}{10}z = \dfrac{1}{3} + \dfrac{7}{15}$, what is the value of z ?

17

In triangle LMN, the measure of $\angle M$ is 90°,

$LN = 26$, and $MN = 24$. Triangle OPQ is similar to

triangle LMN, where each side of triangle OPQ is $\dfrac{1}{5}$

the length of the corresponding side of triangle LMN

and vertices O, P, and Q correspond to vertices L, M,

and N, respectively. What is the value of $\cos O$?

18

At a bakery, each pecan braid has 30 more milligrams of sodium than each chocolate pastry. If 3 pecan braids and 4 chocolate pastries have a total of 1,840 milligrams of sodium, how many milligrams of sodium does a pecan braid have?

19

$$a^3(a^2 - 25) = -144a$$

If $a > 0$, what is one possible solution to the equation above?

CONTINUE

20

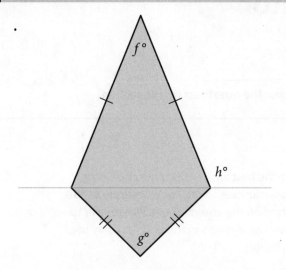

Note: Figure not drawn to scale.

Two isosceles triangles are shown above. If $180 - f = 2g$ and $g = 65$, what is the value of h?

STOP

If you finish before time is called, you may check your work on this section only.
Do not turn to any other section in the test.

Practice Test 7 | **589**

Math Test – Calculator

55 MINUTES, 38 QUESTIONS

Turn to Section 4 of your answer sheet to answer the questions in this section.

DIRECTIONS

For questions 1–30, solve each problem, choose the best answer from the choices provided, and fill in the corresponding circle on your answer sheet. **For questions 31–38**, solve the problem and enter your answer in the grid on the answer sheet. Please refer to the directions before question 31 on how to enter your answers in the grid. You may use any available space in your test booklet for scratch work.

NOTES

1. The use of a calculator **is permitted**.
2. All variables and expressions used represent real numbers unless otherwise indicated.
3. Figures provided in this test are drawn to scale unless otherwise indicated.
4. All figures lie in a plane unless otherwise indicated.
5. Unless otherwise indicated, the domain of a given function f is the set of all real numbers x for which $f(x)$ is a real number.

REFERENCE

$A = \pi r^2$
$C = 2\pi r$

$A = \ell w$

$A = \frac{1}{2}bh$

$c^2 = a^2 + b^2$

Special Right Triangles

$V = \ell wh$

$V = \pi r^2 h$

$V = \frac{4}{3}\pi r^3$

$V = \frac{1}{3}\pi r^2 h$

$V = \frac{1}{3}\ell wh$

The number of degrees of arc in a circle is 360.
The number of radians of arc in a circle is 2π.
The sum of the measures in degrees of the angles of a triangle is 180.

CONTINUE

1

Size	Color		Total
	Red	Blue	
Small	16	6	22
Large	7	21	28
Total	23	27	50

The table above shows the number of marbles of different colors and sizes in a bag of 50 marbles. If a marble is chosen from the bag at random, what is the probability that the marble selected will be either a small red marble or a large blue marble?

A) $\dfrac{9}{50}$

B) $\dfrac{17}{50}$

C) $\dfrac{21}{50}$

D) $\dfrac{37}{50}$

2

The graph below shows the balance of Jerry's bank account, in thousands of dollars, for each month from January through December of 2012.

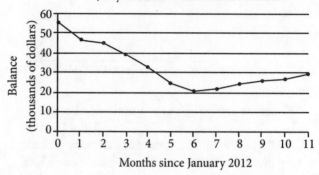

Jerry's Bank Account Balance in 2012

Based on the graph, which of the following best describes the general trend of Jerry's bank account balance in 2012 ?

A) The balance generally decreased each month in 2012.

B) The balance generally decreased until July, then increased.

C) The balance was generally constant throughout 2012.

D) The balance generally increased each month in 2012.

CONTINUE

3

Hot Air Balloon Ride

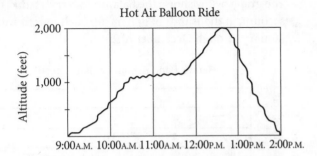

9:00A.M. 10:00A.M. 11:00A.M. 12:00P.M. 1:00P.M. 2:00P.M.

The graph above shows the altitude of a hot air balloon over the course of a 5-hour flight. During the flight, the balloon floated at a constant altitude for 1 hour for the passengers to best view a historic landmark. Based on the graph, what time did the passengers in the hot air balloon begin viewing the historic landmark?

A) 10:30 A.M.

B) 11:30 A.M.

C) 12:30 P.M.

D)   1:00 P.M.

4

Every spring, Lowland High School administers a standardized test that includes only math and science questions at various levels of difficulty. On the standardized test, approximately 6 percent of the math questions and 9 percent of the science questions are categorized as very difficult questions. If the test included 153 math questions and 267 science questions, which of the following is the closest to the total number of very difficult questions on this standardized test?

A)   9

B)   17

C)   24

D)   33

5

What is the sum of $6y^3 - 3y^2 + 7$ and $5y^3 - 2y^2 - 3$?

A) $11y^6 - 5y^4 + 4$

B) $11y^6 + 5y^4 + 4$

C) $11y^3 - 5y^2 + 4$

D) $11y^3 + 5y^2 + 4$

6

x	$g(x)$
2	–4
3	–2
4	0
5	2
6	4

The table above shows some values of the linear function g. Which of the following defines g ?

A) $g(x) = x - 6$

B) $g(x) = 2x - 8$

C) $g(x) = 3x - 10$

D) $g(x) = 4x - 12$

CONTINUE

7

Paul can run 144 meters in 72 seconds. If he runs at this same rate, which of the following is closest to the distance he can run in 16 minutes?

A)   200 meters

B)   500 meters

C) 1,000 meters

D) 2,000 meters

8

If $\frac{2}{7}z = \frac{5}{2}$, what is the value of z ?

A) $\frac{35}{4}$

B) $\frac{5}{7}$

C) $\frac{4}{35}$

D) $\frac{7}{5}$

9

Each year, the average number of legal cases per attorney at Gary's law firm can be modeled by the equation $y = 1.74x + 15.3$, where x represents the number of years that Gary's firm has been in operation since it opened in 2000, and y represents the average number of legal cases per attorney. Which of the following best describes the meaning of the number 1.74 in the equation?

A) The average number of cases per attorney in 2000

B) The approximate increase in the average number of legal cases per attorney each year

C) The total number of legal cases that Gary's firm handled in 2000

D) The approximate difference between the number of legal cases Gary's firm handled in 2000 and in 2005

CONTINUE

10

The function *m* has 4 distinct zeros. Which of the following graphs could represent the graph of *m* in the *xy*-plane?

A)

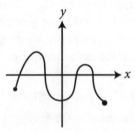

B)

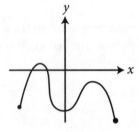

C)

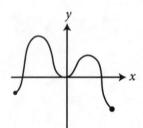

D)

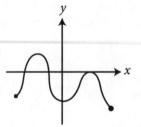

Questions 11 and 12 refer to the following information.

	Spring Constant $\left(\dfrac{N}{m}\right)$
Spring #1	0.7
Spring #2	0.9
Spring #3	1.2
Spring #4	4.7
Spring #5	0.6
Spring #6	3.3
Spring #7	2.1

The chart above shows the spring constants in newtons per meter $\left(\dfrac{N}{m}\right)$ for 7 different springs in a laboratory. The force required to stretch a spring can be found by using the formula $F = km$, where F is the applied force measured in newtons, k is the spring constant measured in $\dfrac{N}{m}$, and m is the distance that the spring is stretched measured in meters.

11

What is the force, in newtons, required to stretch Spring #2 a distance of 5 meters?

A) 3.5

B) 4.5

C) 5.5

D) 6.5

CONTINUE

12

A force of 7 newtons is applied to stretch Spring #4. Which spring would stretch the same distance when a force of 5 newtons is applied?

A) Spring #3

B) Spring #5

C) Spring #6

D) Spring #7

13

A secretarial business bills corporations $0.30 per minute to type reports. Which of the following equations represents the total bill b, in dollars, for a corporation needing t hours of typing?

A) $b = \dfrac{60t}{0.30}$

B) $b = (0.30)(60)(t)$

C) $b = 60t + 0.30$

D) $b = \dfrac{0.30t}{60}$

14

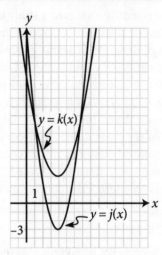

Graphs of the functions j and k are shown in the xy-plane above. For which of the following values of x does $j(x) + k(x) = 0$?

A) 1

B) 2

C) 3

D) 4

15

$$e = 0.5mv^2 + 10mh$$

The equation above gives the approximate energy e in joules associated with a rollercoaster cart that has mass m in kilograms, speed v in meters per second, and height h in meters. Which of the following gives h in terms of e, m, and v ?

A) $h = \dfrac{e}{10m} - 0.05v^2$

B) $\dfrac{e - 0.5v^2}{10m}$

C) $h = e + 0.05v^2 + 1$

D) $h = \dfrac{e}{10m} + 0.05v^2$

CONTINUE

16

A group of scientists designed a study to test the effectiveness of pesticide P at eradicating aphids from rose gardens. From a large group of botanists, 400 participants with aphid-infested rose gardens were randomly selected to participate in the study. Half of the 400 botanists sprayed their rose gardens with pesticide P, and the other half did not. The data showed that the rose gardens sprayed with pesticide P had significantly fewer aphids as compared to those that were not sprayed with pesticide P. Which of the following is an appropriate conclusion of the study?

A) Pesticide P will decrease the number of aphids in any rose garden.

B) Pesticide P is the best pesticide available for decreasing the number of aphids in a garden.

C) Pesticide P will likely decrease the number of aphids in aphid-infested rose gardens.

D) Pesticide P will kill substantial numbers of aphids present in a garden.

Questions 17 and 18 refer to the following information.

$$C(x) = 3x + 75$$
$$R(x) = 8x$$

The cost of manufacturing a product and the revenue generated by that product are functions of the number of products manufactured and sold. The functions above are the cost and revenue functions for a certain product. The function $C(x)$ gives the cost, in dollars, of manufacturing x products and the function $R(x)$ gives the revenue, in dollars, generated when those x products are sold.

17

How many units of product must be manufactured and sold in order for the cost of manufacturing a product to equal the revenue generated by selling the product?

A) 8
B) 10
C) 12
D) 15

18

How will the cost of manufacturing change if 5 additional units of product are manufactured?

A) The cost will decrease by $15.
B) The cost will increase by $3.
C) The cost will increase by $15.
D) The cost will increase by $75.

CONTINUE

19

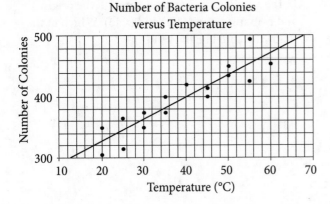

Number of Bacteria Colonies
versus Temperature

Sixteen samples of bacteria were each incubated for 24 hours. The scatterplot above shows the number of colonies present at the end of the incubation period and the temperature of the incubator. The line of best fit for the data is also shown. For the sample incubated at 40°C, the actual number of colonies was about how many more than the number predicted by the line of best fit?

A)   0

B)   10

C)   20

D)   40

20

Of the following four geographically distinct communities, which community would exhibit exponential growth of the population?

A) Each successive year, the community increases by 5% of the original population.

B) Each successive year, the community increases by 4% of the original population and 300 new individuals are added to the community.

C) Each successive year, 300 new individuals are added to the community.

D) Each successive year, the community increases by 3% of the current population.

21

Glucose, which is an important component of growth media for cultured cells, is so energy rich that 1 milliliter can feed up to 9 Petri dishes of cells. If a Petri dish has an area of approximately $7\frac{1}{4}$ square centimeters, about how many square centimeters of cells could 115 milliliters of glucose feed?

A)   140

B)   1,000

C)   6,500

D)   7,500

22

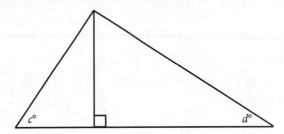

In the triangle shown above, $\sin(c°) = \cos(d°)$. If $c = 6m - 9$ and $d = 8m - 6$, what is the value of m ?

A)   5.4

B)   7.5

C)   10.5

D)   13.5

CONTINUE

23

A behavioral biologist has a bag containing t treats that she is using to train a group of animals. If she gives 4 treats to each animal, she will have 6 treats left over. In order to give each animal 5 treats, she will need an additional 8 treats. How many animals are in the behavioral biologist's training group?

A) 2

B) 8

C) 14

D) 16

24

The sum of three numbers is 738. One of the numbers, k, is 20% less than the sum of the other two numbers. What is the value of k?

A) 328

B) 267

C) 215

D) 144

25

In the xy-plane, line l passes through the origin and contains points $(4, r)$ and $(r, 16)$. Which of the following could be the value of r?

A) 12

B) 8

C) 4

D) 0

26

A triangle was modified by increasing its base by 20 percent and decreasing its height by h percent. If these modifications decreased the area of the triangle by 28 percent, what is the value of h?

A) 48

B) 40

C) 30

D) 28

CONTINUE

27

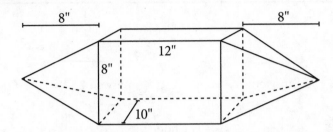

A time capsule is constructed from two rectangular pyramids and a rectangular solid with measurements indicated in the figure above. Of the following, which is the closest to the volume of the time capsule, in cubic inches?

A) 1,386

B) 1,173

C)   960

D)   426

28

$$2a + x = 4a - 8$$

$$2b + y = 4b - 8$$

In the equation above, x and y are constants. If x is y minus $\frac{1}{4}$, which of the following is true?

A) a is b minus $\frac{1}{2}$

B) a is b minus $\frac{1}{4}$

C) a is b minus $\frac{1}{8}$

D) a is b plus $\frac{1}{4}$

29

In order to plan for his family's future, Michael has decided to invest some of his money into a mutual fund that, starting from the present, his broker estimates will increase by 15 percent every 4 years. If Michael invests $20,000 into the mutual fund, which of the following expressions represents his broker's estimate of his mutual fund's worth t years from now?

A) $20,000(1.15)^{\frac{t}{4}}$

B) $20,000(0.15)^{\frac{t}{4}}$

C) $20,000(1.15)^{4t}$

D) $20,000(0.15)^{4t}$

30

	Varsity Soccer	Varsity Basketball
Juniors		
Seniors		
Total	108	32

The unfinished table above shows the number of juniors and seniors at Woodsfield High School who participate in either varsity soccer or varsity basketball. There are 4 times as many varsity soccer players who are juniors as there are varsity basketball players who are juniors, and there are 3 times as many varsity soccer players who are seniors as there are varsity basketball players who are seniors. If there is a total of 108 varsity soccer players and 32 varsity basketball players at Woodsfield High, which of the following is closest to the probability that a randomly chosen varsity basketball player is a junior? (Note: Assume that no student plays both varsity soccer and varsity basketball.)

A) 0.086

B) 0.134

C) 0.247

D) 0.375

CONTINUE

DIRECTIONS

For questions 31–38, solve the problem and enter your answer in the grid, as described below, on the answer sheet.

1. Although not required, it is suggested that you write your answer in the boxes at the top of the columns to help you fill in the circles accurately. You will receive credit only if the circles are filled in correctly.

2. Mark no more than one circle in any column.

3. No question has a negative answer.

4. Some problems may have more than one correct answer. In such cases, grid only one answer.

5. **Mixed numbers** such as $3\frac{1}{2}$ must be gridded as 3.5 or 7/2. (If  is entered into the grid, it will be interpreted as $\frac{31}{2}$, not as $3\frac{1}{2}$.)

6. **Decimal Answers:** If you obtain a decimal answer with more digits than the grid can accommodate, it may be either rounded or truncated, but it must fill the entire grid.

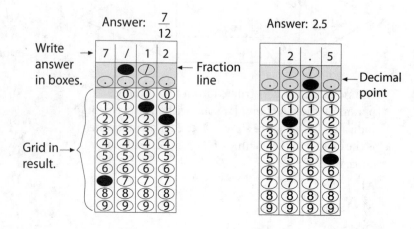

Acceptable ways to grid $\frac{2}{3}$ are:

Answer: 201 – either position is correct

NOTE: You may start your answers in any column, space permitting. Columns you don't need to use should be left blank.

CONTINUE ➤

31

Enrollment per Course at Riverview College—
Spring Semester of 2001

Course	Number of Students Enrolled	Course	Number of Students Enrolled
Sociology	98	U.S. History	27
Psychology	37	Anthropology	33
Economics	85	Marketing	68
Calculus	45	Political Science	79
Biology	42	Linguistics	16
Accounting	64	Chemistry	52

The above table lists the number of students enrolled in 12 different courses at Riverview College during its spring semester of 2001. According to the table, what is the mean class size of these selected courses at Riverview College in the spring semester of 2001 ? (Round your answer to the nearest tenth.)

32

A fruit stand sells pints of blueberries for $3 each and pints of strawberries for $5 each. If John spends at least $23 but no more than $27 on b pints of blueberries and 1 pint of strawberries, what is one possible value of b ?

33

Jasmine's algebra teacher gives pop quizzes that are scored between 0 and 50 points, inclusive. After the first 5 quizzes, Jasmine's quiz average (arithmetic mean) is 35. What is the lowest score Jasmine can receive on the 6th quiz and still be able to have an average of at least 45 for the first 20 quizzes?

34

$$(-4z^2 + 3z - 7) - 3(z^2 - 5z - 2)$$

If the expression above is rewritten in the form $az^2 + bz + c$, where a, b, and c are constants, what is the value of b ?

CONTINUE

35

$$y \geq -12x + 384$$

$$y \geq 4x$$

In the xy-plane, if a point with coordinates (f, g) lies in the solution set of the system of inequalities above, what is the minimum value of g?

36

In a circle with center C, central angle XCY has a measure of $\dfrac{3\pi}{2}$ radians. The major arc XY formed by central angle XCY is what fraction of the circumference of the circle?

Questions 37 and 38 refer to the following information.

In telecommunication networks, the transmission time is the amount of time required for a message to be successfully transmitted from beginning to end. If a message is transmitted at a rate of r bytes per second with a transmission time of T seconds, then the size of the message in b bytes can be found by the formula $b = rT$.

The CEO of Relay Communications estimates that the average global transmission time of a message is 2.5 seconds and that the average transmission rate is 1,000 bytes per second. The CEO uses the above formula to estimate that the average global message size at his company is 2,500 bytes.

37

The CEO of Relay Communications decides to study transmission times in a rural geographical region that his company serves. In this region, the CEO estimates that the average transmission rate rises to 75,000 bytes per <u>minute</u> and that the average transmission time is 1.6 seconds. The average message size in this region is what percent less than the average global message size? (Note: Ignore the percent symbol when entering your answer. For example, if the answer is 24.1%, enter 24.1.)

CONTINUE

38

Transmission times can vary depending on population, geographical region, or the type of material used in the telecommunication wires. The CEO realizes that in a heavily populated city, the transmission rate drops to 45,000 bytes per minute. If the average transmission time of a message being transmitted in this heavily populated city is 4.2 seconds, what is the average size of a message transmitted by Relay Communications in this heavily populated city?

▲

END OF TEST

DO NOT RETURN TO A PREVIOUS SECTION.

Completely darken bubbles with a No. 2 pencil. If you make a mistake, be sure to erase mark completely. Erase all stray marks.

1.

YOUR NAME: _____
(Print)   Last   First   M.I.

SIGNATURE: _____   DATE: ___ / ___ / ___

HOME ADDRESS: _____
(Print)   Number and Street

_____
        City   State   Zip Code

PHONE NO.: _____
(Print)

IMPORTANT: Please fill in these boxes exactly as shown on the back cover of your test book.

2. TEST FORM

_____

6. DATE OF BIRTH

Month	Day		Year	
◯ JAN				
◯ FEB	⓪	⓪	⓪	⓪
◯ MAR	①	①	①	①
◯ APR	②	②	②	②
◯ MAY	③	③	③	③
◯ JUN		④	④	④
◯ JUL		⑤	⑤	⑤
◯ AUG		⑥	⑥	⑥
◯ SEP		⑦	⑦	⑦
◯ OCT		⑧	⑧	⑧
◯ NOV		⑨	⑨	⑨
◯ DEC				

3. TEST CODE

⓪ Ⓐ Ⓙ ⓪
① Ⓑ Ⓚ ①
② Ⓒ Ⓛ ②
③ Ⓓ Ⓜ ③
④ Ⓔ Ⓝ ④
⑤ Ⓕ Ⓞ ⑤
⑥ Ⓖ Ⓟ ⑥
⑦ Ⓗ Ⓠ ⑦
⑧ Ⓘ Ⓡ ⑧
⑨ ⑨

4. REGISTRATION NUMBER

⓪ ⓪ ⓪ ⓪ ⓪ ⓪ ⓪ ⓪
① ① ① ① ① ① ① ①
② ② ② ② ② ② ② ②
③ ③ ③ ③ ③ ③ ③ ③
④ ④ ④ ④ ④ ④ ④ ④
⑤ ⑤ ⑤ ⑤ ⑤ ⑤ ⑤ ⑤
⑥ ⑥ ⑥ ⑥ ⑥ ⑥ ⑥ ⑥
⑦ ⑦ ⑦ ⑦ ⑦ ⑦ ⑦ ⑦
⑧ ⑧ ⑧ ⑧ ⑧ ⑧ ⑧ ⑧
⑨ ⑨ ⑨ ⑨ ⑨ ⑨ ⑨ ⑨

7. SEX
◯ MALE
◯ FEMALE

The Princeton Review®

5. YOUR NAME

First 4 letters of last name				FIRST INIT	MID INIT
Ⓐ Ⓐ Ⓐ Ⓐ				Ⓐ	Ⓐ
Ⓑ Ⓑ Ⓑ Ⓑ				Ⓑ	Ⓑ
Ⓒ Ⓒ Ⓒ Ⓒ				Ⓒ	Ⓒ
Ⓓ Ⓓ Ⓓ Ⓓ				Ⓓ	Ⓓ
Ⓔ Ⓔ Ⓔ Ⓔ				Ⓔ	Ⓔ
Ⓕ Ⓕ Ⓕ Ⓕ				Ⓕ	Ⓕ
Ⓖ Ⓖ Ⓖ Ⓖ				Ⓖ	Ⓖ
Ⓗ Ⓗ Ⓗ Ⓗ				Ⓗ	Ⓗ
Ⓘ Ⓘ Ⓘ Ⓘ				Ⓘ	Ⓘ
Ⓙ Ⓙ Ⓙ Ⓙ				Ⓙ	Ⓙ
Ⓚ Ⓚ Ⓚ Ⓚ				Ⓚ	Ⓚ
Ⓛ Ⓛ Ⓛ Ⓛ				Ⓛ	Ⓛ
Ⓜ Ⓜ Ⓜ Ⓜ				Ⓜ	Ⓜ
Ⓝ Ⓝ Ⓝ Ⓝ				Ⓝ	Ⓝ
Ⓞ Ⓞ Ⓞ Ⓞ				Ⓞ	Ⓞ
Ⓟ Ⓟ Ⓟ Ⓟ				Ⓟ	Ⓟ
Ⓠ Ⓠ Ⓠ Ⓠ				Ⓠ	Ⓠ
Ⓡ Ⓡ Ⓡ Ⓡ				Ⓡ	Ⓡ
Ⓢ Ⓢ Ⓢ Ⓢ				Ⓢ	Ⓢ
Ⓣ Ⓣ Ⓣ Ⓣ				Ⓣ	Ⓣ
Ⓤ Ⓤ Ⓤ Ⓤ				Ⓤ	Ⓤ
Ⓥ Ⓥ Ⓥ Ⓥ				Ⓥ	Ⓥ
Ⓦ Ⓦ Ⓦ Ⓦ				Ⓦ	Ⓦ
Ⓧ Ⓧ Ⓧ Ⓧ				Ⓧ	Ⓧ
Ⓨ Ⓨ Ⓨ Ⓨ				Ⓨ	Ⓨ
Ⓩ Ⓩ Ⓩ Ⓩ				Ⓩ	Ⓩ

Test ⑦   Start with number 1 for each new section.
If a section has fewer questions than answer spaces, leave the extra answer spaces blank.

Section 1—Reading

1. Ⓐ Ⓑ Ⓒ Ⓓ
2. Ⓐ Ⓑ Ⓒ Ⓓ
3. Ⓐ Ⓑ Ⓒ Ⓓ
4. Ⓐ Ⓑ Ⓒ Ⓓ
5. Ⓐ Ⓑ Ⓒ Ⓓ
6. Ⓐ Ⓑ Ⓒ Ⓓ
7. Ⓐ Ⓑ Ⓒ Ⓓ
8. Ⓐ Ⓑ Ⓒ Ⓓ
9. Ⓐ Ⓑ Ⓒ Ⓓ
10. Ⓐ Ⓑ Ⓒ Ⓓ
11. Ⓐ Ⓑ Ⓒ Ⓓ
12. Ⓐ Ⓑ Ⓒ Ⓓ
13. Ⓐ Ⓑ Ⓒ Ⓓ
14. Ⓐ Ⓑ Ⓒ Ⓓ
15. Ⓐ Ⓑ Ⓒ Ⓓ
16. Ⓐ Ⓑ Ⓒ Ⓓ
17. Ⓐ Ⓑ Ⓒ Ⓓ
18. Ⓐ Ⓑ Ⓒ Ⓓ
19. Ⓐ Ⓑ Ⓒ Ⓓ
20. Ⓐ Ⓑ Ⓒ Ⓓ
21. Ⓐ Ⓑ Ⓒ Ⓓ
22. Ⓐ Ⓑ Ⓒ Ⓓ
23. Ⓐ Ⓑ Ⓒ Ⓓ
24. Ⓐ Ⓑ Ⓒ Ⓓ
25. Ⓐ Ⓑ Ⓒ Ⓓ
26. Ⓐ Ⓑ Ⓒ Ⓓ
27. Ⓐ Ⓑ Ⓒ Ⓓ
28. Ⓐ Ⓑ Ⓒ Ⓓ
29. Ⓐ Ⓑ Ⓒ Ⓓ
30. Ⓐ Ⓑ Ⓒ Ⓓ
31. Ⓐ Ⓑ Ⓒ Ⓓ
32. Ⓐ Ⓑ Ⓒ Ⓓ
33. Ⓐ Ⓑ Ⓒ Ⓓ
34. Ⓐ Ⓑ Ⓒ Ⓓ
35. Ⓐ Ⓑ Ⓒ Ⓓ
36. Ⓐ Ⓑ Ⓒ Ⓓ
37. Ⓐ Ⓑ Ⓒ Ⓓ
38. Ⓐ Ⓑ Ⓒ Ⓓ
39. Ⓐ Ⓑ Ⓒ Ⓓ
40. Ⓐ Ⓑ Ⓒ Ⓓ
41. Ⓐ Ⓑ Ⓒ Ⓓ
42. Ⓐ Ⓑ Ⓒ Ⓓ
43. Ⓐ Ⓑ Ⓒ Ⓓ
44. Ⓐ Ⓑ Ⓒ Ⓓ
45. Ⓐ Ⓑ Ⓒ Ⓓ
46. Ⓐ Ⓑ Ⓒ Ⓓ
47. Ⓐ Ⓑ Ⓒ Ⓓ
48. Ⓐ Ⓑ Ⓒ Ⓓ
49. Ⓐ Ⓑ Ⓒ Ⓓ
50. Ⓐ Ⓑ Ⓒ Ⓓ
51. Ⓐ Ⓑ Ⓒ Ⓓ
52. Ⓐ Ⓑ Ⓒ Ⓓ

Section 2—Writing and Language Skills

1. Ⓐ Ⓑ Ⓒ Ⓓ
2. Ⓐ Ⓑ Ⓒ Ⓓ
3. Ⓐ Ⓑ Ⓒ Ⓓ
4. Ⓐ Ⓑ Ⓒ Ⓓ
5. Ⓐ Ⓑ Ⓒ Ⓓ
6. Ⓐ Ⓑ Ⓒ Ⓓ
7. Ⓐ Ⓑ Ⓒ Ⓓ
8. Ⓐ Ⓑ Ⓒ Ⓓ
9. Ⓐ Ⓑ Ⓒ Ⓓ
10. Ⓐ Ⓑ Ⓒ Ⓓ
11. Ⓐ Ⓑ Ⓒ Ⓓ
12. Ⓐ Ⓑ Ⓒ Ⓓ
13. Ⓐ Ⓑ Ⓒ Ⓓ
14. Ⓐ Ⓑ Ⓒ Ⓓ
15. Ⓐ Ⓑ Ⓒ Ⓓ
16. Ⓐ Ⓑ Ⓒ Ⓓ
17. Ⓐ Ⓑ Ⓒ Ⓓ
18. Ⓐ Ⓑ Ⓒ Ⓓ
19. Ⓐ Ⓑ Ⓒ Ⓓ
20. Ⓐ Ⓑ Ⓒ Ⓓ
21. Ⓐ Ⓑ Ⓒ Ⓓ
22. Ⓐ Ⓑ Ⓒ Ⓓ
23. Ⓐ Ⓑ Ⓒ Ⓓ
24. Ⓐ Ⓑ Ⓒ Ⓓ
25. Ⓐ Ⓑ Ⓒ Ⓓ
26. Ⓐ Ⓑ Ⓒ Ⓓ
27. Ⓐ Ⓑ Ⓒ Ⓓ
28. Ⓐ Ⓑ Ⓒ Ⓓ
29. Ⓐ Ⓑ Ⓒ Ⓓ
30. Ⓐ Ⓑ Ⓒ Ⓓ
31. Ⓐ Ⓑ Ⓒ Ⓓ
32. Ⓐ Ⓑ Ⓒ Ⓓ
33. Ⓐ Ⓑ Ⓒ Ⓓ
34. Ⓐ Ⓑ Ⓒ Ⓓ
35. Ⓐ Ⓑ Ⓒ Ⓓ
36. Ⓐ Ⓑ Ⓒ Ⓓ
37. Ⓐ Ⓑ Ⓒ Ⓓ
38. Ⓐ Ⓑ Ⓒ Ⓓ
39. Ⓐ Ⓑ Ⓒ Ⓓ
40. Ⓐ Ⓑ Ⓒ Ⓓ
41. Ⓐ Ⓑ Ⓒ Ⓓ
42. Ⓐ Ⓑ Ⓒ Ⓓ
43. Ⓐ Ⓑ Ⓒ Ⓓ
44. Ⓐ Ⓑ Ⓒ Ⓓ

Test 7 Start with number 1 for each new section.
If a section has fewer questions than answer spaces, leave the extra answer spaces blank.

Section 3—Mathematics: No Calculator

1. Ⓐ Ⓑ Ⓒ Ⓓ
2. Ⓐ Ⓑ Ⓒ Ⓓ
3. Ⓐ Ⓑ Ⓒ Ⓓ
4. Ⓐ Ⓑ Ⓒ Ⓓ
5. Ⓐ Ⓑ Ⓒ Ⓓ
6. Ⓐ Ⓑ Ⓒ Ⓓ
7. Ⓐ Ⓑ Ⓒ Ⓓ
8. Ⓐ Ⓑ Ⓒ Ⓓ
9. Ⓐ Ⓑ Ⓒ Ⓓ
10. Ⓐ Ⓑ Ⓒ Ⓓ
11. Ⓐ Ⓑ Ⓒ Ⓓ
12. Ⓐ Ⓑ Ⓒ Ⓓ
13. Ⓐ Ⓑ Ⓒ Ⓓ
14. Ⓐ Ⓑ Ⓒ Ⓓ
15. Ⓐ Ⓑ Ⓒ Ⓓ

16. 17. 18. 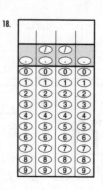 19. 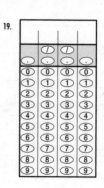 20.

Section 4—Mathematics: Calculator

1. Ⓐ Ⓑ Ⓒ Ⓓ
2. Ⓐ Ⓑ Ⓒ Ⓓ
3. Ⓐ Ⓑ Ⓒ Ⓓ
4. Ⓐ Ⓑ Ⓒ Ⓓ
5. Ⓐ Ⓑ Ⓒ Ⓓ
6. Ⓐ Ⓑ Ⓒ Ⓓ
7. Ⓐ Ⓑ Ⓒ Ⓓ
8. Ⓐ Ⓑ Ⓒ Ⓓ
9. Ⓐ Ⓑ Ⓒ Ⓓ
10. Ⓐ Ⓑ Ⓒ Ⓓ
11. Ⓐ Ⓑ Ⓒ Ⓓ
12. Ⓐ Ⓑ Ⓒ Ⓓ
13. Ⓐ Ⓑ Ⓒ Ⓓ
14. Ⓐ Ⓑ Ⓒ Ⓓ
15. Ⓐ Ⓑ Ⓒ Ⓓ
16. Ⓐ Ⓑ Ⓒ Ⓓ
17. Ⓐ Ⓑ Ⓒ Ⓓ
18. Ⓐ Ⓑ Ⓒ Ⓓ
19. Ⓐ Ⓑ Ⓒ Ⓓ
20. Ⓐ Ⓑ Ⓒ Ⓓ
21. Ⓐ Ⓑ Ⓒ Ⓓ
22. Ⓐ Ⓑ Ⓒ Ⓓ
23. Ⓐ Ⓑ Ⓒ Ⓓ
24. Ⓐ Ⓑ Ⓒ Ⓓ
25. Ⓐ Ⓑ Ⓒ Ⓓ
26. Ⓐ Ⓑ Ⓒ Ⓓ
27. Ⓐ Ⓑ Ⓒ Ⓓ
28. Ⓐ Ⓑ Ⓒ Ⓓ
29. Ⓐ Ⓑ Ⓒ Ⓓ
30. Ⓐ Ⓑ Ⓒ Ⓓ

31.  32. 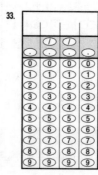 33. 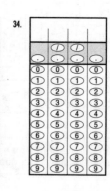 34. 35.

36. 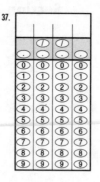 37. 38.

Chapter 16
Practice Test 7:
Answers and
Explanations

PRACTICE TEST 7 ANSWER KEY

Section 1: Reading				Section 2: Writing & Language				Section 3: Math (No Calculator)				Section 4: Math (Calculator)			
1.	C	27.	C	1.	A	23.	D	1.	A	11.	B	1.	D	20.	D
2.	B	28.	C	2.	D	24.	D	2.	D	12.	C	2.	B	21.	D
3.	B	29.	A	3.	B	25.	B	3.	C	13.	B	3.	A	22.	B
4.	D	30.	D	4.	B	26.	A	4.	B	14.	C	4.	D	23.	C
5.	C	31.	C	5.	A	27.	D	5.	B	15.	C	5.	C	24.	A
6.	B	32.	D	6.	D	28.	D	6.	A	16.	4	6.	B	25.	B
7.	D	33.	C	7.	A	29.	B	7.	D	17.	$\frac{5}{13}$	7.	D	26.	B
8.	B	34.	A	8.	C	30.	A	8.	D			8.	A	27.	A
9.	C	35.	A	9.	C	31.	D	9.	A	18.	280	9.	B	28.	C
10.	D	36.	B	10.	C	32.	C	10.	D	19.	3 or 4	10.	A	29.	A
11.	B	37.	B	11.	A	33.	D			20.	115	11.	B	30.	D
12.	C	38.	D	12.	A	34.	D					12.	C	31.	53.8
13.	D	39.	B	13.	D	35.	B					13.	B	32.	6 or 7
14.	D	40.	A	14.	D	36.	A					14.	D	33.	25
15.	B	41.	B	15.	B	37.	B					15.	A	34.	18
16.	A	42.	A	16.	A	38.	C					16.	C	35.	96
17.	C	43.	B	17.	D	39.	A					17.	D	36.	$\frac{3}{4}$ or .75
18.	C	44.	C	18.	A	40.	B					18.	C		
19.	B	45.	A	19.	C	41.	C					19.	C	37.	20
20.	C	46.	C	20.	D	42.	A							38.	3,150
21.	A	47.	B	21.	B	43.	C								
22.	C	48.	B	22.	C	44.	C								
23.	D	49.	D												
24.	B	50.	A												
25.	A	51.	C												
26.	B	52.	C												

Go to PrincetonReview.com to score your exam. Alternatively,
for self-assessment tables, please turn to page 909.

PRACTICE TEST 7 EXPLANATIONS

Section 1: Reading

1. **C** The question asks *for a summary of the passage*. Because it is a general question, it should be done after all of the specific questions. Whether it is referred to as worth *six hundred francs due, 430 francs to offer*, or simply *the burden he bore on his back*, the passage is mainly concerned with Deplis' tattoo and how he would pay for it, so an accurate summary would address this debt and the troubles he faced because of it. Choice (A) says that he is *unable to display a work of art*. Although it does describe his troubles, it is a specific detail and does not mention the debt, which was the prediction. Eliminate (A). Choice (B) mentions *whether or not to obey the law*, which does not match the prediction, so eliminate it. Choice (C) mentions the *unpaid debt* and that he *finds his choices restricted*. Both of these ideas match the prediction, so keep (C). Choice (D) states that he *tries to steal art to please a deceased relative*, which never happened and doesn't match the prediction, so eliminate it. The correct answer is (C).

2. **B** The question asks for *Henri Deplis' financial status before receiving the legacy*. Notice that the question that follows is a best evidence question, so this question and Q3 can be answered in tandem. Look at the answers for Q3 first. The lines in (3A) mention his place of birth, so look to see if those lines support any answers in Q2. His place of birth is not mentioned in any of the answers to Q2. Eliminate (3A). Next, consider the lines for (3B), which mention that his financial situation was *modest*. Choice (2B) is a close match, so draw a line connecting (3B) and (2B). Choice (3C) mentions *impoverished circumstances*, but the lines given refer to Signor Pincini rather than Deplis, so eliminate (3C). Choice (3D) refers to the *legacy dwindling to insignificant proportions*. While (2D) might be tempting, *destitute* is too strong and not supported by the line reference, so eliminate (3D). Deplis' financial status before receiving the legacy was *modest*. The correct answers are (2B) and (3B).

3. **B** (See explanation above.)

4. **D** The question asks what the word *exercise* means in line 38. Go back to the text, find the word *exercise*, and mark it out. Carefully read the surrounding text to determine another word that would fit in the blank based on the context of the passage. According to the text, the tattoo on Deplis' back was *Pincini's masterpiece* and *his greatest effort*, and the text states that the *little scope* of the tombstone cherubs would not be a good place to *exercise his favorite art*—tattooing. A good replacement word in this case would be something like "perform" or "do." Choices (A) and (B) have no relation to performance and can be eliminated. Choice (C) is close, but a *masterpiece* is original and would not be done *repeatedly*; eliminate (C). *Ability to perform* matches the prediction. The correct answer is (D).

5. **C** The question asks about a detail regarding *the cherubs on Pincini's tombstone*. Use the lead words *cherubs* and *tombstone* to find the window to read. Lines 36–37 include the phrase *under an ornate tombstone, whose winged cherubs*. Pincini is a tattoo artist, so *the exercise of his favorite art* refers to tattooing. The passage describes Deplis' tattoo as covering his back, *from the collar-bone down to the waist-line*, which is a big tattoo. The *winged cherubs would have afforded singularly little scope*, offering a surface area much smaller than that of a human back, so the correct answer will have something to do with the small size of the cherubs. Choice (A) might initially look attractive, but the cherubs are not the artistic subjects of the tombstone. Eliminate (A). There is nothing in the text about religion or *religious icons*, so eliminate (B). Choice (C) matches the

prediction, so keep it. Choice (D) is deceptive: while the cherubs are on the tombstone, the passage and the prediction state that they are small. Eliminate it. The correct answer is (C).

6. **B** The question asks why *Deplis reduced his offer to 405 francs*. Look for the lead words *405 francs* in the text and carefully read the window. Earlier in the paragraph, Deplis' *legacy had dwindled* and *there remained little more than 430 francs to offer to the widow*. In this context, *obliged* means he "had to," so Deplis reduced the offer because his funds continued to dwindle. The paragraph indicates that Deplis was running out of money, not that he had an inclination to *trick Pincini's widow*; eliminate (A). Choice (B) states that he couldn't *afford the 430* francs, which matches the prediction, so keep it. Choice (C) could be true, but the text does not state that Deplis wanted to annoy the widow. Eliminate it. While it is true that Deplis wanted Pincini's widow to *accept a lower offer*, there is no indication he *thought she would*, so eliminate (D). The correct answer is (B).

7. **D** The question asks why the author used the phrase *cancelled the sale of the work of art*. The widow *was properly indignant* and Deplis' *offer of 405 francs fanned the widow's indignation into a fury*. However, after the matter-of-fact phrase *she cancelled the sale of the work of art*, there is no further reference to the widow in the entire passage, beyond that *she had presented [the work of art] to the municipality of Bergamo, which had gratefully accepted it*. The tattoo has already been done, so her decision to cancel the sale and give the artwork to Bergamo is unrealistic. The correct answer should reflect this idea of the widow's unrealistic decision. Choices (A) and (B) refer to Deplis, not the widow, and can be eliminated. *The unpleasant temper of the widow* may be mentioned in the passage, but does not match the prediction, so eliminate (C). Choice (D) mentions an *unexpected shift in perspective*, which matches the unexpected idea that the widow has canceled the sale of the completed tattoo and offered the art to Bergamo. The correct answer is (D).

8. **B** The question asks what the word *celebrated* means in line 67. Go back to the text, find the word *celebrated*, and mark it out. Carefully read the surrounding text to determine another word that would fit in the blank based on the context of the passage. The vapour bath proprietor had already been aware of *the celebrated Fall of Icarus*, so the correct answer must mean something like "well known." Choices (A) and (C) might look like possible definitions of *celebrated*, but they do not match the prediction. Eliminate them. Choice (D) does not match the prediction at all and can be eliminated. *Famous* matches the predicted answer of "known." The correct answer is (B).

9. **C** The question asks for a description of the trouble Henri Deplis encountered due to his tattoo. Notice that the question that follows is a best evidence question, so this question and Q10 can be answered in tandem. Look at the answers for Q10 first. Choice (10A) describes how he snuck out *as unobtrusively as possible* and *hoped his identity and that of the famous picture might be lost*, implying that the tattoo was trouble that he hoped to hide. Look to see whether those lines support any answers in Q9. In (9C), the phrase *persistently troublesome* is a good match, but (10A) does not support *obviously absurd*, so it's not a good connection. Choice (10A) does not support any of the other answers for Q9, so it can be eliminated. Choice (10B) mentions that the tattoo is a *burden*, which could support *socially awkward* in (9A) or *persistently troublesome* in (9C), but neither *well-intended* nor *obviously absurd* is supported by (10B), so eliminate it. Choice (10C) says that he was fervently thankful to go to *the neighbourhood of Bordeaux*. Like (10A), this shows that he hoped to get away and hide, so eliminate it for the same reason: it supports *persistently troublesome* but not *obviously absurd*. Choice (10D) states that *an array of official force barred his departure* because of a *stringent law which forbids the exportation of Italian works of art*, which means he couldn't leave the country because the tattoo on his back technically belonged to Italy. These lines support (9C) because *absurd* is a match for *unusual*, and the situation is clearly troublesome. Draw a line to connect (10D) and (9C). Without any support from Q10, (9A), (9B), and (9D) can be eliminated. The correct answers are (9C) and (10D).

10.   **D**   (See explanation above.)

11.   **B**   The question asks about the *function* of the *first paragraph* in the context of *the passage as a whole*. Since this is a general question, it should be done after the specific questions. The first paragraph gives some information about *natural gas* and the challenges of *[r]educing emissions from the natural gas system*. Then, it describes *an emerging argument that maybe there could be a direct substitute for fossil natural gas in the form of renewable natural gas (RNG)*. In the passage as a whole, the author rejects RNG as a solution, stating, *My recent research suggests that for a system large enough to displace a lot of fossil natural gas, RNG is probably not as good for the climate as is publicly claimed* (lines 58–61) and *zero greenhouse gas emissions is the target, and my research suggests that large deployments of RNG likely won't meet that goal* (lines 78–80). Therefore, the function of the first paragraph is to introduce a potential solution that the author argues against. Eliminate answers that don't match this prediction. Choice (A) is a Mostly Right/Slightly Wrong trap answer: the first paragraph does not *argue definitively* for renewable natural gas: the words *could be* and *maybe* are not definitive. Eliminate (A). Keep (B) because it matches the prediction. Eliminate (C) because the last two paragraphs discuss problems with renewable natural gas, and the first paragraph doesn't provide any examples of those problems. Eliminate (D) because, although the first paragraph does mention a *challenge*, (D) does not include the solution that is discussed in the first paragraph. Additionally, there is no evidence that *consumers* have not *understood* the challenge. The correct answer is (B).

12.   **C**   The question asks for the *central idea of the second paragraph*. This is the first question in a paired set, but it is easy to find, so it can be done on its own. Read the second paragraph as the window. The second paragraph states that the *climate benefits* of renewable natural gas *might not be as large as advocates claim* and that *decisions about whether to invest in it are being made now*. In lines 27–31, the author reasons that because *energy infrastructure…lasts a long time, it's important to consider the climate change emissions that society is committing to with new investments in these systems*. The author concludes, *this a great time to ask: What would investing in RNG mean for climate change?* Therefore, the second paragraph's central idea is that it is important to think about renewable natural gas's impact on climate change. Eliminate answers that don't match this prediction. Choice (A) is a Deceptive Language trap answer: the idea in (A) is included in the paragraph, but it is a supporting point rather than the paragraph's central idea. Eliminate (A). The same is true of (B), so eliminate (B). Keep (C) because it matches the prediction. Eliminate (D) because the second paragraph doesn't claim that renewable natural gas *will contribute significantly* to climate change; it argues only for studying how it will contribute. The correct answer is (C).

13.   **D**   The question is the best evidence question in a paired set. Because the previous question was a specific question, simply look at the lines used to answer Q12. Lines 27–34 provided the prediction for Q12. Of these lines, only lines 27–31 are included in the answers for Q13, and they are in (D). Keep (D). Eliminate (A), (B), and (C). The correct answer is (D).

14.   **D**   The question asks what the author *explicitly* mentions *as a disadvantage of using renewable natural gas as an energy source*. This is the first question in a paired set, so it can be done in tandem with Q15. Look at the answer choices for Q15 first. The lines for (15A) state, *At the moment, renewable natural gas is more a proposal than reality, which makes this a great time to ask: What would investing in RNG mean for climate change?* There is no mention of *a disadvantage of using renewable natural gas*, so these lines do not answer Q14. Eliminate (15A). The lines for (15B) state, *And releases will happen, from newly built production systems and existing, leaky transportation and user infrastructure.* In the context of the passage, these lines refer to the fact that greenhouse gases would be released if renewable natural gas were used—a disadvantage of using renewable natural gas. Look to see whether this information supports any of the answers to Q14. It supports (14D),

so draw a line connecting (15B) with (14D). The lines for (15C) state, *To be clear, RNG is almost certainly better for the climate than fossil natural gas because byproducts of burning RNG won't contribute to climate change.* These lines describe an advantage, rather than a disadvantage, of using renewable natural gas, so eliminate (15C). The lines for (15D) state that *renewable sources such as wind and solar energy do not emit climate pollution directly.* These lines give an advantage of *wind and solar energy*, rather than *a disadvantage of using renewable natural gas*. Note that, although these lines imply that using renewable natural gas emits climate pollution, the question asks for something that the author *explicitly* states. Eliminate (15D). Without any support in the answers for Q15, (14A), (14B), and (14C) can be eliminated. The correct answers are (14D) and (15B).

15. **B** (See explanation above.)

16. **A** The question asks what the word *primary* most nearly means in line 55. Go back to the text, find the word *primary*, and cross it out. Then read the window carefully, using context clues to determine another word that would fit in the text. The text says, *doing somewhat better than existing systems is no longer enough to respond to the urgency of climate change. The world's primary international body on climate change suggests we need to decarbonize by 2030 to mitigate the worst effects of climate change.* Therefore, *primary* could be replaced by a word such as "main." Eliminate answers that don't match this prediction. *Principal* matches "main," so keep (A). *Unmediated* means "done without anyone intervening," which does not match "main," so eliminate (B). *Simple* does not match "main," so eliminate (C). *First* does not match "main," so eliminate (D). Note that (B), (C), and (D) are all Could Be True trap answers based on other meanings of *primary* that are not supported by the text. The correct answer is (A).

17. **C** The question asks what the word *aggressive* most nearly means in line 77. Go back to the text, find the word *aggressive*, and cross it out. Then read the window carefully, using context clues to determine another word that would fit in the text. The text says, *When climate change first broke into the political conversation in the late 1980s, investing in long-lived systems with low but non-zero greenhouse gas emissions was still compatible with aggressive climate goals. Now, zero greenhouse gas emissions is the target.* Therefore, having *aggressive* goals could be described as "aiming to achieve large results quickly." Eliminate answers that don't match this prediction. *Brash* means "tactless" or "rash;" it has a negative connotation and doesn't match the author's use of *aggressive* to describe the quick pursuit of large climate change goals, so eliminate (A). *Dominating* means "overbearing;" it doesn't match the prediction, so eliminate (B). *Ambitious* is a good descriptor for aiming to achieve large results quickly, so keep (C). *Combative* means "eager to fight;" it doesn't match the prediction, so eliminate (D). Note that (A), (B), and (D) are all Could Be True trap answers based on other meanings of *aggressive* that are not supported by the text. The correct answer is (C).

18. **C** The question asks for evidence that supports *the conclusion that preparations for using renewable natural gas could disrupt the development of other energy sources*. Look at the line references given in the answer choices, and eliminate the statements that don't support this claim. The lines for (A) state, *creating a large RNG system would require building mostly new production infrastructure, since RNG comes from different sources than fossil natural gas.* RNG refers to renewable natural gas, but these lines don't discuss disrupting *the development of other energy sources*, so eliminate (A). The lines for (B) state, *Such investments are both long-term commitments and opportunity costs.* These lines don't reference *other energy sources*, so eliminate (B). The lines for (C) state, *They would devote money, political will and infrastructure investments to RNG instead of alternatives that could achieve a zero greenhouse gas emission goal.* These lines indicate that the resources devoted to RNG would be taken away from *alternatives* (other energy sources) that emit *zero greenhouse gas*, so keep (C). The lines for (D) state, *When climate change first broke into the political conversation*

in the late 1980s, investing in long-lived systems with low but non-zero greenhouse gas emissions was still compatible with aggressive climate goals. These lines don't mention *renewable natural gas* or how it might *disrupt development of other energy sources,* so eliminate (D). The correct answer is (C).

19. **B**   The question asks for a statement that is *supported by the data in the first figure.* Work through each answer choice using the figure. The percentages shown for *renewable energy* (11.1%) and *crude oil* (15.5%) are not the same, so eliminate (A). The percentage shown for *nuclear electric* (11.3%) is larger than that for *natural gas plant liquid* (3.6%), so keep (B). The percentage shown for *renewable energy* is smaller than that for *coal* (29.4%) so eliminate (C). The first figure shows the percentage of the United States' energy production that comes from various sources; it doesn't show how *efficiently* the energy is produced, so eliminate (D). The correct answer is (B).

20. **C**   The question asks what *the two figures* suggest about *renewable energy sources.* First, locate the information about *renewable energy* in each figure. Figure 1 shows that renewable energy makes up 11.1% of primary energy production in the U.S. Figure 2 shows that renewable energy makes up 8.7% of primary energy consumption in the U.S. Eliminate answers that don't match the data in the figure. Eliminate (A) because the figures don't compare energy use in *urban* versus *rural areas.* Eliminate (B) because the figures don't give information about energy use in *areas where consumers protest the use of fossil fuels.* Keep (C) because 11.1% is *less than half* of total *energy production,* and 8.7% is *less than half* of total *energy consumption.* Eliminate (D) because 8.7% is not *more than half of total energy consumption.* The correct answer is (C).

21. **A**   The question asks about the *overall sequence of events in the passage.* Because this is a general question, it should be done after the specific questions. The passage begins by discussing the discovery of crocodile relatives' footprints in South Korea. It then discusses other similar footprints, once attributed to pterosaurs, that are now attributed to the crocodile relatives. Then the passage explains that, based on the new identification of these footprints, scientists now believe that *pterosaurs* walked *on four legs while on the ground* rather than *walking on two legs,* as researchers previously thought. Eliminate answers that don't match the prediction. Keep (A) because it matches the prediction. Choice (B) is a Mostly Right, Slightly Wrong trap answer: though *a group of scientists collaborate,* there is no mention in the text of *results* being *verified and published.* Eliminate (B). Choice (C) is also a Mostly Right, Slightly Wrong trap answer: though *an expert is consulted* and *previous research* is *revisited,* the scientists changed *their original line of thinking;* they didn't *retain* it. Eliminate (C). Choice (D) states that *further research is proposed,* but there is no mention of *further research* in the passage. Eliminate (D). The correct answer is (A).

22. **C**   The question asks what makes South Korea an *ideal site for studying ancient species.* Since there is no line reference, use lead words and the order of the questions to find the window. Q23 asks about line 23. Scan the first, second, and third paragraphs, looking for the lead words *South Korea* and information about what makes South Korea a good place to study ancient species. Lines 23–26 state that *Lockley calls South Korea a "tracker's heaven" for paleontologists because of the sheer number of fossil footprints found in the country.* Eliminate answers that don't match this prediction. Choice (A) does not match the prediction: in fact, there are scientists working in South Korea because it is a good place to study ancient species, not the other way around. Eliminate (A). Choice (B) is a Deceptive Language trap answer: though a university in South Korea is mentioned in the text, it is never stated that this university makes South Korea an *ideal site for studying ancient species.* Eliminate (B). Keep (C) because it matches the prediction. Eliminate (D) because the text never mentions how easy or difficult it is to excavate fossils in South Korea. The correct answer is (C).

23. **D** The question asks what Kyung Soo Kim did after *uncovering the "puzzling fossil tracks."* Use the given line reference to find the window. Lines 26–28 state that *Kim had asked for [Lockley's] opinion on large Cretaceous tracks uncovered at the site.* Therefore, after discovering the puzzling tracks, Kim asked another scientist for help with the tracks. Eliminate answers that don't match this prediction. Choice (A) is a Deceptive Language trap answer: while *flying reptiles*, specifically *pterosaurs*, are mentioned in the window, Kim did not try to show that the tracks were made by the pterosaurs. Eliminate (A). Choice (B) is also a Deceptive Language trap answer: though the *Batrachopus* is mentioned in the window, the passage never states that Kim was studying their *movements*, only their *footprints*. Eliminate (B). Eliminate (C) because the passage doesn't indicate that Kim *compared the footprints to modern dinosaur relatives.* Keep (D) because it matches the prediction. The correct answer is (D).

24. **B** The question asks what the word *recognized* most nearly means in line 31. Go back to the text, find the word *recognized*, and cross it out. Then read the window carefully, using context clues to determine another word or phrase that would fit in the text. The text says, *Lockley recognized them as something else. "I immediately saw that they were of the type known as Batrachopus."* Therefore, *recognized them* could be replaced by a phrase such as "knew what they were." Eliminate answers that don't match this prediction. *Reinvented* means "remade" or "redid;" it does not match "knew what they were," so eliminate (A). *Identified* matches "knew what they were," so keep (B). *Showed appreciation for* doesn't match "knew what they were," so eliminate (C). *Gave credit to* doesn't match "knew what they were," so eliminate (D). Note that (C) and (D) are Could Be True trap answers based on other definitions of *recognized* that are not supported by the text. The correct answer is (B).

25. **A** The question asks for the purpose of *the description of the pterosaurs' behavior* mentioned in the fourth paragraph. Read the fourth paragraph as the window, and a few lines before and after as needed. The fourth paragraph indicates that fossils found at the Jinju Formation *help address another fossil mystery... At a different South Korean location known as Gain-ri, there are tracks that were also previously believed to be left by large pterosaurs. Tracks found elsewhere in the world indicate that the flying reptiles folded their wings to waddle on all fours while on the ground. But researchers had thought the prints at Gain-ri were made by pterosaurs that moved on two legs to avoid dragging their wings through the muck.* The phrases *previously believed* and *researchers had thought* indicate that the author is explaining a theory that has been disproved or weakened by the new findings. The next sentence confirms this: *The new fossils have changed the analysis of these tracks—and have undercut interpretations of pterosaurs walking on two legs at other sites.* In other words, the author describes pterosaur behavior to explain a theory that changed based on the Jinju Formation fossils. Eliminate answers that don't match this prediction. Keep (A) because it matches the prediction. Choice (B) is a Mostly Right, Slightly Wrong trap answer: while Kim's findings weaken the theory discussed in paragraph four, it is never stated that *Kim intended* to do so. Eliminate (B). Eliminate (C) because the passage does not indicate that researchers no longer believe that pterosaurs *existed*; it indicates only that researchers changed their view of how pterosaurs walked, and which footprints were made by pterosaurs. Eliminate (D) because no *methods* used by researchers are mentioned in this paragraph. The correct answer is (A).

26. **B** The question asks for *an assumption researchers made in changing their theory that pterosaurs walked on two legs.* This is the first question in a paired set, so it can be done in tandem with Q27. The lines for (27A) state, *The presence of bipedal crocs at the fossil site was unexpected.* This information does not support any of the answer choices for Q26, so eliminate (27A). The lines for (27B) may seem to support (26C), as both refer to *flying reptiles*, but the lines for (27B) state that the pterosaurs *waddle on all fours while on the ground* while (26C) states that the pterosaurs were *more likely ... to walk on two legs.* Eliminate (27B). The lines for (27C) state that the *tracks*

at Jinju look much more like the prints made by crocodile relatives than those left by pterosaurs. This information supports (26B) because the researchers changed their theory about supposed pterosaur tracks at several locations based on the discovery of similar-looking fossils at the *Jinju* site. Draw a line connecting (27C) and (26B). The lines for (27D) mention *crocs*, but the question is about *pterosaurs*. Therefore, (27D) does not address Q26. Eliminate (27D). Without any support in the answers from Q27, (26A), (26C), and (26D) can be eliminated. The correct answers are (26B) and (27C).

27. **C** (See explanation above.)

28. **C** The question asks what *cast* most nearly means in line 72. Go back to the text, find the word *cast*, and cross it out. Then read the window carefully, using context clues to determine another word that would fit in the text. The text says *crocodiles are often cast as "living fossils" that have changed little since their origin in the Triassic.* Therefore, *cast* could be replaced with a word such as "portrayed." Eliminate answers that don't match this prediction. *Studied* does not match "portrayed," so eliminate (A). *Served* does not match "portrayed," so eliminate (B). *Described* matches "portrayed," so keep (C). *Molded* does not match "portrayed;" this is a Could Be True trap answer based on another definition of *cast* that is not supported by the text. Eliminate (D). The correct answer is (C).

29. **A** The question asks what can be inferred about *modern crocodiles* based on the passage. This is the first question in a paired set, but it is easy to find, so it can be done on its own. Since there is no line reference, use lead words and the order of the questions to find the window. Q28 asks about line 72, so scan the final paragraph, looking for the lead word *crocodiles*. Lines 72–78 state that *skeletal and track evidence has shown that crocs in the Age of Dinosaurs were varied, active animals that often looked very different from the swimming ambush predators that we are familiar with today.* In other words, modern crocodiles look different from their ancestors. Eliminate answers that don't match this prediction. Keep (A) because it matches the prediction. Eliminate (B) because the passage doesn't discuss the amount of *time* modern crocodiles spend in the water, nor does it discuss what would make modern crocodiles a *dominant species*. Eliminate (C) because it is contradicted by the passage: the crocodilian ancestors discussed in the passage *strode around on two legs*, whereas modern crocodiles are described as *swimming*. Eliminate (D) because the size of modern crocodile *footprints* is not discussed. The correct answer is (A).

30. **D** The question is the best evidence question in a paired set. Because the previous question was easy to find, simply look at the lines used to answer Q29. Lines 72–78 provided the prediction for Q29: *skeletal and track evidence has shown that crocs in the Age of Dinosaurs were varied, active animals that often looked very different from the swimming ambush predators that we are familiar with today.* Eliminate (A), (B), and (C). The correct answer is (D).

31. **C** The question asks what the word *free* means in line 20. Go back to the text, find the word *free*, and mark it out. Carefully read the surrounding text to determine another word that would fit in the blank based on the context of the passage. According to the sentence after line 20, Jefferson believes *In general, [the citizens] will elect the really good and wise.* It is the *free election* that will create this situation, so the correct answer should mean something like "open" or "unhindered." *Complimentary* means without cost, so eliminate (A). While the election would indeed be *available*, the key distinction is that it is available to all, "unrestricted," so eliminate (B). Choice (C), *unrestricted*, matches the prediction, so keep it. The election is not extra, or *gratuitous*, so eliminate (D). The correct answer is (C).

32. **D** The question asks for the *best way to prevent the rise of the artificial aristocracy*. Notice that the question that follows is a best evidence question, so this question and Q33 can be answered in

tandem. Look at the answers for Q33 first. Choice (33A) only defines the term *artificial aristocracy* but provides no *way to prevent the rise*. This doesn't connect to any answer choices in Q32, so eliminate (33A). Similarly, (33B) only says *provision should be made to prevent its ascendancy* without prescribing a *best way*. The answers for Q32 all offer specific plans, so (33B) does not support any of the answers for Q32. Eliminate (33B). Choice (33C) refers to *the best remedy*, which is *to leave to the citizens the free election*. Look to see whether those lines support any answers in Q32. Choice (32D) says to *allow voters to choose their own leaders*, which is a close match. Connect (33C) and (32D). Choice (33D) says *a change has sensibly taken place in the mind of Man*. Look to see whether those lines support any answers in Q32. None of the choices in Q32 mention this idea, so eliminate (33D). Without any support from Q33, (32A), (32B), and (32C) can be eliminated. The correct answers are (32D) and (33C).

33. **C** (See explanation above.)

34. **A** The question asks what the word *fashion* means in line 45. Go back to the text, find the word *fashion*, and mark it out. Carefully read the surrounding text to determine another word that would fit in the blank based on the context of the passage. The author claims that *Fashion has introduced an indeterminate use of the word "talents."* The use of quotes indicates that he doesn't believe them to be talents at all. The next sentence lists the so-called talents, *beauty, stature... graceful attitudes and motions, gait, air, complexion*, which are all more trendy attributes. The correct answer should mean something like "trend." *Convention* matches the prediction, so keep (A). *Demeanor, model*, and *construction* don't mean anything like "trend;" eliminate (B), (C), and (D). The correct answer is (A).

35. **A** The question asks when *an artificial aristocracy begins*. Since there is no given line reference, search for the lead words *artificial aristocracy* in Passage 2. That phrase is mentioned several times in paragraph 7, so read the necessary window around lines 57–68 to predict the correct answer. In the fourth sentence of the paragraph, Adams says that when *aristocracies are established by human laws, and honor, wealth, and power are made hereditary by municipal laws and political institutions, then [he] acknowledge[s] artificial aristocracy to commence*. Therefore, the correct answer will reference this list of conditions. *Laws [that] give one group power over another* matches the prediction, so keep (A). *All people are given the right to vote* does not match the prediction, so eliminate (B). *A democracy turns into a monarchy* does not match the prediction, so eliminate (C). The *virtuous and talented control the government* does not match the prediction, so eliminate (D). The correct answer is (A).

36. **B** The question asks where *political advantages come mainly from*. Notice that the question that follows is a best evidence question, so this question and Q37 can be answered in tandem. Look at the answers for Q37 first. Choice (37A) discusses the *natural aristocracy among men* but not *political advantages*. These lines do not support any of the answers for Q36, so (37A) can be eliminated. Choice (37B) mentions *commands or influences true votes in society* and that the influence comes from *any one of these talents*. Look to see whether those lines support any answers in Q36. Choice (36B) mentions *a wide range of characteristics*, which is a close match. Connect (37B) and (36B). Choice (37C) mentions that some are born with *birth and wealth* and some with *genius, strength or beauty*, but does not relate these attributes to *political advantage*. Because these lines do not support any of the answers for Q36, (37C) can be eliminated. Choice (37D) mentions that the *artificial aristocracy* will take power only when *corruption in elections becomes dominant and uncontrollable*. Look to see whether those lines support any answers in Q36. Choice (36D) might be tempting because it mentions *municipal laws and political institutions*, but that's deceptive language. The author states that it is *corruption* that gives rise to *political advantages*. Elimi-

nate (37D) because it does not have a match. Without any support from Q37, (36A), (36C), and (36D) can be eliminated. The correct answers are (36B) and (37B).

37. **B** (See explanation above.)

38. **D** The question asks why *the author of Passage 2 refers to a statement made in Passage 1*. Return to the passage and read the necessary window around lines 71–80. From the final paragraph, it is clear that Adams would trust neither of the groups defined by Jefferson and believes Jefferson's *distinction…will not help the matter*. Adams refers to the statement in order to disagree with this particular statement by Jefferson. Choice (A) can be eliminated because there is no mention of Jefferson's *working vocabulary*. While Adams takes issue with Jefferson's *distinction between the aristoi and pseudo aristoi*, he is not quarreling with Jefferson's *central theme*. In fact, the second passage begins with *We are now explicitly agreed*. Eliminate (B). Choice (C) begins with *agree,* which is the opposite of the prediction. Eliminate (C). Choice (D) matches the prediction. The correct answer is (D).

39. **B** The question asks *which best describes the overall relationship between Passage 1 and Passage 2*. Because this is a general question, it should be done after all of the specific questions. Adams responds to Jefferson's claim in Passage 1 and in the opening two sentences of Passage 2, Adams outlines his position: *We are now explicitly agreed, in one important point…but…it is not yet certain that we are perfectly agreed in sense*. It can therefore be predicted that Passage 2 provides a qualification, but not a complete alternative to Jefferson's stance in Passage 1. *Further develops* and *considers the historical context* do not match the prediction of a disagreement, so eliminate (A) and (C). While Adams addresses Jefferson's *key terms*, he disagrees with them rather than *redefines* them, so eliminate (D). The correct answer is (B).

40. **A** The question asks what statement the authors of both passages would agree with regarding *advantages people may have over each other*, indicating that it is a general question that should be done after all of the specific questions. In each passage's opening sentence, the authors agree that *there is a natural aristocracy among men*, so it can be predicted that both would agree there are advantages that are innate. Choice (A) mentions *born talented,* which matches the prediction of natural or innate, so keep it. The phrases *Wealth and power* and *beauty and talent* are deceptive language. The authors do not agree that one is *more important* than the other, so eliminate (B). Eliminate (C) because that statement *Advantages one gains later in life are more powerful* is the opposite of the prediction. Eliminate (D) because neither *those who earn their power* nor *those who have it handed to them* matches the prediction of natural or innate advantage. The correct answer is (A).

41. **B** The question asks how *the author of Passage 1 would respond to the points made in* lines 60–75. Since this is a question about both passages, it should be done last. Return to the text and read the necessary window ("Birth and wealth…talents"). Adams's position is that human laws lead to *artificial aristocracy, which is the origin of all monarchy*. Jefferson would disagree because he believes that if we *leave to the citizens the free election…they will elect the really good and wise*. It can be predicted that the correct answer will discuss free elections. Eliminate (A) because *Passing power down through families* is not the same as a free election, so it does not match the prediction. Keep (B) because *leaving the decisions in the hands of the voters will ultimately keep the system balanced* is a direct description of a free election. Eliminate (C) because *Rank and birth, science and talent,* and the order in which they are admired have nothing to do with the prediction. Eliminate (D) because the *American system could allow for an unfaithful leader* is the opposite of the prediction. The correct answer is (B).

42.　**A**　The question asks what the word *removal* means in line 22. Go back to the text, find the word *removal,* and mark it out. Carefully read the surrounding text to determine another word that would fit in the blank based on the context of the passage. According to the end of the paragraph preceding line 22, *the Hudson Bay Company implemented their "scorched earth" or "fur desert" policy to eliminate all fur-bearing animals…As a result, beaver were nearly extirpated*, so the correct answer should mean something like "nearly eliminated." The language in (A), *significant reduction,* closely matches the prediction, so keep it. The *removal* was not *of an individual beaver*, nor was it a *surgical extraction*; eliminate (B) and (D). The phrase *complete extinction* is too extreme, so eliminate (C). The correct answer is (A).

43.　**B**　The question asks for a *broader hypothesis* that was tested to obtain results *consistent with "steelhead population responses."* Notice that the question that follows is a best evidence question, so this question and Q44 can be answered in tandem. Look at the answers for Q44 first. Choice (44A) states that *a decrease…was first perceived*. This is an observation, not a hypothesis, and it does not support any of the answers for Q43, so eliminate (44A). Choice (44B) mentions *the removal of beaver…exacerbated the occurrence of stream channel incision, where a rapid downcutting of the stream bed disconnects the channel from its floodplain*. Look to see whether those lines support any answers in Q43. Choice (43D) may be tempting, but it contains deceptive language. It states that *Stream channel incision…is exacerbated by…large numbers of beaver dams*, which is the opposite of what the passage states. Eliminate (44B) because it has no match in Q43. Choice (44C) mentions what was *hypothesized*, so look to see whether those lines support any answers in Q43. Choice (43B) says *Reconnecting a stream's channel and floodplain can occur more quickly through the construction of natural or artificial beaver dams*, which matches *beaver dams or simulated beaver dams that we construct…can greatly accelerate the incision recovery process* in (44C) and with "the steelhead population responses" because *BDAs and beaver dams led to large changes in both fish and beaver habitat*. Connect (44C) and (43B). Choice (44D) mentions how *BDAs were built* but does not discuss a broader hypothesis, so eliminate it. Without any support from Q44, (43A), (43C), and (43D) can be eliminated. The correct answers are (43B) and (44C).

44.　**C**　(See explanation above.)

45.　**A**　The question asks for *the primary purpose of the third paragraph* in the context of the entire passage. Return to the passage and carefully read the window. The paragraph begins with *BDAs were built*, which describes the experiment that was conducted. It then states that the *addition of BDAs into Bridge Creek led to an immediate and rapid increase in the number of natural beaver dams*, which describes the results of the experiment. The purpose of the paragraph is to describe an experiment and its results. Keep (A) because *illustrate methods and results of research* closely matches the prediction. Choice (B) seems tempting because *detail the findings of research* closely matches the prediction. However, the experiment was not *designed to investigate beaver responses* but rather to investigate *fish population response*. If a choice is slightly wrong, it's all wrong, so eliminate (B). Eliminate (C) because the paragraph does not *describe the plan that will be followed* but an actual experiment with results. For the same reason, eliminate (D). The paragraph does not suggest a *potential experiment could be carried out in the future*. The correct answer is (A).

46.　**C**　This question asks for an indirect effect of building BDAs in Bridge Creek. Notice that the question that follows is a best evidence question, so this question and Q47 can be answered in tandem. Look at the answers for Q47 first. Choice (47A) mentions that *beaver were nearly extirpated*, so look to see whether those lines support any answers in Q46. None of the choices are supported by the lines, so eliminate (47A). Choice (47B) mentions a *rapid increase in the number of natural beaver dams*, so look to see whether those lines support any answers in Q46. Choice (46C) is a close match, so connect (47B) and (46C). Choice (47C) mentions that the BDAs *caused the fish* *population response*, so look to see whether those lines support any answers in Q46. Since none of the answers for Q46 are supported by those lines, eliminate (47C). Choice (47D) mentions that BDAs provide *fish a greater selection of locations…while reducing migration distances*, so look to see whether those lines support any answers in Q46. Since none of the choices matches that idea, eliminate (47D). Without any support from Q47, (46A), (46B), and (46D) can be eliminated. The correct answers are (46C) and (47B).

47. **B** (See explanation above.)

48. **B** The question asks what effect the words *"partially," "suspect," and "partly"* have on the *tone of the paragraph*. Return to the passage and read the window. In the previous paragraph, the experiment provided *compelling evidence that beavers increased the quantity of juvenile habitat*. *Compelling* is directly in contrast to the words *"partially," "suspect," and "partly"* in the fifth paragraph, so these words were used to show the conclusions in this paragraph were less compelling. There is no indication of *the authors' nervousness* or of them being *afraid*, so eliminate (A) and (D). There is also no indication that these are *unwelcome results*, so eliminate (C). *That other factors may be important* matches the prediction stating these conclusions were less compelling. The correct answer is (B).

49. **D** This question asks for an unstated assumption about *habitat complexity*. Even though the question asks for an *unstated assumption,* the correct answer will still be supported by the text. The passage states that an *increase in habitat complexity* is partly responsible for the increases in the steelhead population. Therefore, the correct answer should somehow connect to the idea that increasing complexity positively affects the populations. The complexity increased with the construction of the BDAs, which happened well after 1900, so (A) can be eliminated. Choice (B) might initially look attractive because it mentions *the addition of dams*, but notice the *always* in the answer choice. That is a strong word that is not supported by equally strong wording in the text, so (B) can be eliminated. The prediction has nothing to do with negative effects of habitat complexity on predators, so (C) can be eliminated. Choice (D) is not specifically mentioned, but if increasing habitat complexity increases steelhead population, and the steelhead population increased after the construction of the BDAs, the complexity was not maximized prior to that construction. The correct answer is (D).

50. **A** The question asks for *the greatest number of dams on Bridge Creek during the twenty years prior to the installation of BDAs, according to the figure*. Look at the figure to see the highest point for the Bridge Creek line *before* the black vertical line. The high point is about 100 dams in 1992. Choice (A) at 105 is close, while anything 125 and above is too high, so eliminate (B), (C), and (D). The correct answer is (A).

51. **C** The question asks for *the last year a control reach had a greater number of dams than a treatment reach,* so look at the figure to see the last time the dashed line was above the solid line. The answer will be somewhere between 2005 and 2010. The correct answer is (C).

52. **C** The question asks whether *the graphic [supports] the author's claim that increasing the number of real or simulated beaver dams leads to an increase in steelhead populations*, so look at the figure to see if there are any connections that can be drawn. While the correlation is drawn in the passage, there is no reference at all to steelhead population numbers in the figure, so the correct answer will be "no." Eliminate (A) and (B). Whether or not the graphic mentions *floodplain access* has no relation to the *steelhead populations*, so eliminate (D). That *the data does not provide a link between the number of dams and the quality of steelhead habitats* matches the prediction. The correct answer is (C).

Section 2: Writing and Language

1. **A** Note the question! The question asks what the most appropriate introduction to the passage is, so it is testing consistency. If the content of the underlined portion is consistent with the topics presented in the passage, then it is correct. The passage discusses paternity leave and the need to provide both men and women time off with newborn children. The *personal needs of workers* are discussed in (A), so keep it. Choice (B) is vague and does not address what workers need, so eliminate (B). Choice (C) is focused on profit as opposed to worker needs; eliminate (C). Although (D) addresses worker needs, it is too broad and references *all employees*. Since the passage is focused primarily on paternity leave for male employees, (D) can be eliminated. The correct answer is (A).

2. **D** The phrase after *contemporary workers* is changing in the answer choices, so the question is testing precision and concision. There is also the option to DELETE; consider this choice carefully as it is often the correct answer. First, determine whether the phrase is necessary. The sentence already begins with the words *contemporary employers*, which means the employers of today. There is no need to repeat that idea. Eliminate any choices that are redundant. Choices (A), (B), and (C) each repeat the idea of *contemporary*, so eliminate them. The correct answer is (D).

3. **B** Prepositions change in the answer choices, so this question tests idioms. There is also the option to DELETE; consider this choice carefully as it is often the correct answer. A preposition is necessary to complete the sentence, so eliminate (D). The correct idiom is *conducted by*; eliminate (A) and (C). The correct answer is (B).

4. **B** Pronouns are changing in the answer choices, so the question is testing consistency of pronouns. A pronoun must be consistent in number and case with the noun it is replacing. The pronoun refers to the noun *paternity leave*, which is singular. To be consistent, the underlined pronoun should also be singular. *They* and *those* are plural, so eliminate (A), (C), and (D). The correct answer is (B).

5. **A** Verbs are changing in the answer choices, so the question is testing consistency of verbs. A verb must be consistent with its subject and with the other verbs in the paragraph. The subject of the verb is the *deficit,* which is singular (ignore the prepositional phrase *in leave* between the subject and the verb). To be consistent, the verb in the answer choices must also be singular. Eliminate (B) since *are* is a plural verb. The verb form must also be consistent with the tense of other verbs in the sentence. The sentence immediately following this sentence uses the present verb *is*. Eliminate (D) because *had been* is a past tense verb. Choice (C) is not as concise as (A), so it can be eliminated as well. The correct answer is (A).

6. **D** Note the question! The question asks for the choice that best supports the statement in the previous sentence, so it's testing consistency. If the content of the underlined portion is consistent with the previous sentence in the passage, then it is correct. The previous sentence discusses the results of a study and states that *nine out of ten men considered paternity leave to be a factor of at least marginal importance*, so the best answer should be consistent with that information. Choice (B) discusses mothers having time off and that is not relevant to whether paternity leave is an important factor, so eliminate (B). Choice (C) goes against the claim that paternity leave is important; eliminate (C). Although (A) is consistent with the point being made, (D) offers a more precise supporting statement. Choice (D) is the correct answer.

7. **A** Note the question! The question asks whether the sentence should be added, so it's testing consistency. If the content of the new sentence is consistent with the ideas surrounding it, then it should be added; otherwise, it should not be added. The paragraph discusses the results of a

study conducted by the U.S. Department of Labor. The new sentence indicates that *The younger a male individual respondent was, the more likely he was to rate the issue of paternity leave as important when considering employment,* so it is consistent with the ideas in the paragraph. The sentence should be added. Eliminate (C) and (D). Eliminate (B) because there is no challenge presented to this information in the last sentence of the paragraph. The correct answer is (A).

8. **C** Note the question! The question asks about combining sentences, so it's testing precision and concision. Choice (A) inaccurately combines the *larger societal issue* with *what employees want.* Additionally, *they,* which is plural, refers incorrectly to the singular noun *paternity leave;* eliminate (A). Choice (B) also inaccurately combines *what potential employees want* and *paternity leave having an impact,* so eliminate (B). Choice (D) never mentions that these are reasons paternity leave is important and is therefore not precise; eliminate (D). Choice (C) correctly orders the reasons, so it is the most precise. The correct answer is (C).

9. **C** Apostrophes are changing in the answer choices, so the question is testing apostrophe usage. When used with a noun, an apostrophe indicates possession. In this sentence, the parents are not possessing anything, so eliminate (A) and (B). The *child* does possess its own *life,* so the apostrophe in *child's* is necessary; eliminate (D). The correct answer is (C).

10. **C** Commas are changing in the answer choices, so the question is testing comma usage. The sentence contains a list of three things: 1) *bond with their children earlier,* 2) *participate in their household more actively,* and 3) *raise children with a greater sense of gender equality.* There should be commas between the items in the list, so eliminate (D) because this answer does not include a comma after *actively.* There should not be a comma after *and,* so eliminate (A). In (B), the adverb *actively* has been changed to the adjective *active. Actively* modifies the verb *participate,* so an adverb is needed. Since adjectives can only modify nouns, eliminate (B). The correct answer is (C).

11. **A** Transitions change in the answer choices, so this question tests consistency of ideas. A transition must be consistent with the relationship between the ideas it connects. The sentence states that *paternity leave not only benefits a lone employee and his or her family—it improves society as a whole.* This sentence summarizes the points made in the paragraph, so the answer should be consistent with that summary. Eliminate (B) and (D) as they change direction and are therefore inconsistent with the summary and paragraph. While the passage is in fact complete, nothing rhetorically has been completed, so *completely* is incorrect; eliminate (C). The correct answer is (A).

12. **A** Note the question! The question asks which choice *provides the most logical introduction to the sentence,* so it tests consistency of ideas. There is also the option to DELETE; consider this choice carefully as it is often the correct answer. Deleting the underlined portion makes the sentence incomplete, so eliminate (D). Determine the subject of the sentence and find the answer that is consistent with that idea. The non-underlined portion gives the example of *whether a state holds a primary or a caucus.* The previous sentence says that *similarities [among states] are hard to come by.* Choice (A), which mentions a *difference,* is consistent with these ideas, so keep (A). Choice (B) discusses a similarity rather than a difference, so it is inconsistent with the paragraph; eliminate (B). Choice (C) mentions *all democratic nations,* which is not consistent with *states,* so eliminate (C). The correct answer is (A).

13. **D** Punctuation changes in the answer choices, so this question tests how to connect ideas with the appropriate punctuation. The first part of the sentence, *One major difference among the states pertaining to elections for federal offices, for example, presidential or congressional candidates,* is not an independent clause. The second part of the sentence, *is whether a state holds a primary or a caucus,* is also not an independent clause. Periods and semicolons can only be used between two independent clauses, so eliminate (A) and (C). A colon can only be used after an independent clause, so

eliminate (B). Choice (D) appropriately uses a comma to set off the unnecessary phrase *for example, presidential or congressional candidates* from the rest of the sentence. The correct answer is (D).

14. **D** Punctuation changes in the answer choices, so this question tests how to connect ideas with the appropriate punctuation. The first part of the sentence, *These two systems, primaries and caucuses, are meant to accomplish the same goal,* is an independent clause. The second part of the sentence, *nominate major-party candidates for office,* is not an independent clause. A semicolon can only be used between two independent clauses, so eliminate (A). A comma followed by the word *and* can also only be used between two independent clauses, so eliminate (C). Some type of punctuation is needed to separate the two parts of the sentence, so eliminate (B). Choice (D) appropriately uses a colon to separate the independent clause from a related explanation. The correct answer is (D).

15. **B** Note the question! The question asks if an addition should be made, so it is testing consistency and precision. If the content of the new sentence is consistent with the ideas surrounding it, then it should be added. The paragraph describes how caucuses work, and this new addition to the sentence discusses the two ways votes can be counted at caucuses. This content is consistent with the ideas in the text and provides more precise information. The sentence should be added. Therefore, eliminate (C) and (D). Eliminate (A) because it states that *caucuses are more effective than primaries,* which is not consistent with the information in either the sentence or paragraph. The correct answer is (B).

16. **A** Pronouns are changing in the answer choices, so the question is testing consistency. A pronoun must be consistent in number with the noun it is replacing. The plural pronoun *themselves* refers to the noun *voters,* which is plural. To be consistent, the pronoun in the correct answer choice must also be plural. Eliminate (B) and (D) because both answers present singular pronouns. The pronoun *their* is a possessive pronoun that should not be placed together with the word *selves;* eliminate (C). The correct answer is (A).

17. **D** Note the question! The question asks whether the sentence should be deleted, so it's testing consistency. If the content of the current sentence is consistent with the ideas surrounding it, then it should not be deleted. The paragraph discusses the history and reasoning for caucuses. The sentence at the beginning of the paragraph states that *Historically, caucuses made a great deal of practical sense.* Therefore, the sentence is consistent with the ideas in the paragraph, and the sentence should not be deleted. Eliminate (A) and (B). The sentence does not provide any *specific example,* so eliminate (C). The sentence serves as an introduction to the discussion in this paragraph, so keep (D). The correct answer is (D).

18. **A** Commas are changing in the answer choices, so the question is testing comma usage. The phrase *if any* is unnecessary information, so it should be surrounded by commas. Eliminate (B) and (D) because they each contain only one comma. Eliminate (C) because it includes an unnecessary additional comma after *had.* The correct answer is (A).

19. **C** Note the question! The question asks *which of the following logically follows the previous sentence,* so it is testing consistency. The paragraph discusses the historical reasoning behind and manner in which caucuses function, so the correct answer will further explain one of these two concepts. The previous sentence in particular defines how voters *selected representatives,* not the candidates themselves. The votes discussed in the paragraph are for *representatives,* not for the *president,* so eliminate (A). Choice (B) does not make the paragraph more precise, so eliminate (B). Choice (C) is consistent with the idea of voters voting *for their caucus representatives,* so keep (C). The idea that elections *rarely used this system* is not consistent with the paragraph, so eliminate (D). The correct answer is (C).

20. **D** Note the question! The question asks which choice best maintains the tone established in the passage, so it is testing consistency. The tone of the passage is informative and neutral, so the correct answer should be consistent with that tone. Eliminate (A) and (B) because *horrid* and *deplorable* are both negative words that do not match the neutral tone of the passage. Although (C) is neutral, *litigious* is not consistent with the information provided in the passage as there is no discussion of settling legal disputes in the paragraph. Choice (D) is consistent with the passage, as the paragraph discusses what is difficult about caucuses as compared to primaries. According to the following sentence, caucuses are *difficult to keep organized* and *difficult to keep civil*. The correct answer is (D).

21. **B** Verbs are changing in the answer choices, so the question is testing consistency of verbs. A verb must be consistent with its subject and with the other verbs in the sentence. The subject of the sentence is *caucuses*, which is plural, so the verb must also be plural. Eliminate (A) because of the singular verb *is*. The first part of the sentence states that they *are...difficult*, so the second part of the sentence must use the same structure. Keep (B) because it uses the word *are* and correctly uses the pronoun *they* to refer to the caucuses. Eliminate (C) and (D) because *being* is not consistent with *are...difficult*. The correct answer is (B).

22. **C** Pronouns are changing in the answer choices, so the question is testing consistency of pronouns. A pronoun must be consistent in number with the noun it is replacing. The underlined pronoun *it* refers to the noun *caucuses*, which is plural. To be consistent, the pronoun in the correct answer must also be plural. Eliminate (A) and (B). Verbs change in the answer choices, so this question also tests the consistency of verbs. The rest of the paragraph is in the present tense and there is no reason to change the tense. Choice (D) changes the tense to *have been*, and also incorrectly uses the singular noun *an election*, which is not consistent with *caucuses*, so eliminate (D). The correct answer is (C).

23. **D** Pronouns are changing in the answer choices, so the question is testing consistency of pronouns. The pronouns refer to *European explorers*, so the correct answer must be a plural pronoun that can refer to multiple people in order to be consistent with the non-underlined portion of the sentence. Both (B) and (C) refer to things, not people, so eliminate both. *They* makes the phrase *they noticed the sloth's slow and lackadaisical movements* an independent clause. The commas in this sentence surround unnecessary information, and a phrase providing unnecessary information such as this cannot be an independent clause; eliminate (A). The correct answer is (D).

24. **D** The vocabulary is changing in the answer choices, so this question is testing precision of word choice. Look for a word with a definition that is consistent with the other ideas in the sentence. The sentence describes the sloth's movements as *slow*, and the first sentence describes the sloth as *extremely lazy*. Choice (B), *careless*, can be eliminated because *slow* and *lazy* do not necessarily mean *careless*. *Lackadaisical* means to be carelessly lazy; it can be eliminated for the same reason, so eliminate (A). The sentence is describing *the sloth's slow and ____ movements*; describing *movements* as *inactive* would be contradictory, so eliminate (C). Only (D), *leisurely*, which means lazy, is consistent with *slow*. The correct answer is (D).

25. **B** Note the question! The question asks which option best combines the two sentences, so it's testing precision and concision. Look for the answer that combines the sentences while maintaining the meaning of the originals. The movie *Zootopia* was produced by *Disney*, so these two phrases should be next to each other to make this meaning precise. Eliminate (A) and (C). Choice (D) changes the meaning by stating that *Flash slows down the movie,* not *the main characters.* Eliminate (D). The correct answer is (B).

26. **A** Pronouns are changing in the answer choices, so the question is testing pronoun choice. The pronouns refer to *the sloth*, which is singular, so the underlined pronoun must also be singular. Eliminate (D), *their*, which is plural. Choice (C), *there*, can also be eliminated, as *the sloth* is not a place. With pronouns, apostrophes create contractions. "It is" does not make sense in the sentence, so eliminate (B). The pronoun *Its* is correct because *day* is possessed by *the sloth*, so the possessive form of the pronoun should be used. The correct answer is (A).

27. **D** The length of the phrase changes in the answer choices, so this question tests precision and concision. There is also the option to DELETE; consider this choice carefully as it is often the correct answer. In this case, both (A) and (B) make the phrase after the comma an independent clause. *The sloth is categorized as a folivore because the bulk of its diet consists of the leaves, buds, and tender shoots of Cercropia* is also an independent clause. A comma on its own cannot be used between two independent clauses, so eliminate (A) and (B). Choice (C), *being*, makes the sentence less precise because it confuses whether the subject of the sentence is *the sloth* or *the leaves, buds, and tender shoots of Cercropia*, so eliminate it. Choice (D) is concise and gives the sentence a precise meaning. The correct answer is (D).

28. **D** Punctuation changes in the answer choices, so this question tests how to connect ideas with the appropriate punctuation. The first part of the sentence, *Take the sloth's stomach*, is an independent clause. The second part of the sentence, *it is very large with multiple compartments*, is also an independent clause. The phrase *for example* is unnecessary information that must be set off from the rest of the sentence, so eliminate (A) because there is no punctuation before *for example*. Eliminate (B) because two independent clauses must be separated by some type of punctuation other than commas alone. The *example* given in the sentence is *the sloth's stomach*, which is introduced in the first part of the sentence; the second part of the sentence gives more detail about the stomach. Eliminate (C) because it incorrectly makes *for example* part of the second part of the sentence. Choice (D) correctly places *for example* in the first part of the sentence and appropriately uses a colon to separate the two parts of the sentence. The correct answer is (D).

29. **B** Note the question! The question asks for the best placement of sentence 5, so it tests consistency of ideas. The sentence must be consistent with the ideas that come before and after it. The first part of sentence 5 refers to *leaves* being *nutritionally poor*, so this sentence should come after the reference to eating leaves in sentence 1. The second part refers to *various adaptations*, so sentence 5 should come before any talk about adaptations. Sentence 1 discusses the idea of the sloth eating leaves, and sentence 2 introduces the adaptations of the sloth's stomach. To make the ideas in the paragraph consistent, sentence 5 should go between sentences 1 and 2. The correct answer is (B).

30. **A** Note the question! The question asks for the choice that accurately interprets the graph, so this question is testing consistency. Read the labels on the graph carefully, and look for an answer that is consistent with the information given in the graph. The sentence compares the sloth's body temperature to the other mammals in the graph. In the graph, the other mammals have body temperatures between 36.5 and 39.7 degrees Celsius, whereas the sloth's body temperature is only 32 degrees Celsius. The sloth's body temperature is clearly lower than those of the other mammals in the graph; (B) and (C) are inconsistent with this, so eliminate them. The sloth's temperature is between 4.5 and 7.7 degrees below the temperature of the other mammals, which is consistent with *approximately five degrees Celsius lower*. Keep (A). The sloth's temperature is not *half* that of the other temperatures, so eliminate (D). The correct answer is (A).

31. **D** Verb tense is changing in the answer choices, so the question is testing the consistency of verbs. Select the choice that is consistent with the other verbs in the sentence. The first part of the sentence states *the sloth does not keep its temperature in as limited a range*. Match the tense and mean-

ing closest to *does not*, which is the present tense. Choice (B), *will*, is future tense and (C), *did*, is past tense; eliminate them. *Has* is not consistent with *does not*, so eliminate (A). Choice (D), *does*, is consistent with *does not*. The correct answer is (D).

32. C Note the question! The question asks for the choice that is most consistent with the graph, so it tests consistency. Read the labels on the graph carefully, and look for an answer that is consistent with the information given in the graph. Choice (A) says that *a healthy sloth's active body temperature can be greater than that of a healthy dog*. However, according to the graph, the average body temperature of an active sloth is 32 degrees Celsius, whereas the average body temperature of a healthy dog is 38.9 degrees Celsius. The sentence does say that a sloth's temperature can vary by 2 degrees and a dog's by 0.4 degree, which gives a possible high temperature of 34 degrees Celsius for the sloth and a possible low temperature of 38.5 degrees Celsius for the dog. The dog's temperature is still higher; eliminate (A) because it is inconsistent with the data. Eliminate (D) for the same reason. Choice (B) says that *a healthy dog's body temperature is greater than that of any mammal shown in the graph*, but both the cat's and the goat's body temperatures are higher; eliminate (B). Choice (C) is consistent with the data for a dog's body temperature in comparison to that of the sloth, so keep (C). The correct answer is (C).

33. D Note the question! The question asks for the choice that *conveys how the sloth's inactivity is the result of adaptations to its diet*, so it tests consistency. Eliminate answers that are not consistent with the purpose stated in the question. Choices (A), (B), and (C) do not refer to the sloth's *diet*, so eliminate (A), (B), and (C). Choice (D) discusses the sloth's *food source*, which is consistent with *its diet*, and claims that its diet *is not a rich source of nutrients*, which is the cause of *the sloth's inactivity*. The correct answer is (D).

34. D Punctuation changes in the answer choices, so this question tests how to connect ideas with the appropriate punctuation. Note that there is a dash in the non-underlined portion of the sentence before the phrase *Oscar Wilde's "The Queen is not a subject," for example*. This phrase is not necessary to the main meaning of the sentence, so it should be set off by some type of punctuation. Because there is a dash at the beginning of the phrase, there should also be a dash at the end of the phrase. Eliminate (A), (B), and (C) because none of them uses a dash. The correct answer is (D).

35. B The form of the verb *relies* is changing in the answer choices, so the question is testing consistency of verbs. A verb must be consistent with its subject, which in this case is *puns*. The verb should be plural in order to be consistent with this subject. Eliminate (A), *relies*, and (C), *has relied*, because both are singular. Choice (D), *relying*, makes the sentence incomplete because *relying* cannot be the main verb. Only (B), *rely*, is consistent with the subject and makes the sentence complete. The correct answer is (B).

36. A Punctuation changes in the answer choices, so this question tests how to connect ideas with the appropriate punctuation. The first part of the sentence, *From Shakespeare's plays to Abbott and Costello's* Who's on First? *to even the Bible*, is not an independent clause. The second part of the sentence, *wordsmiths have used puns for humorous and rhetorical effect*, is an independent clause. Periods and semicolons can only be used between two independent clauses, so eliminate (B), (C), and (D). Choice (A) appropriately uses a comma to connect the two parts of the sentence. The correct answer is (A).

37. B Commas are changing in the answer choices, so the question is testing comma usage. When commas surround a phrase, check to see if that phrase is necessary or unnecessary to the sentence. *American composer Milton Babbitt* is unnecessary information; if it is removed from the sentence, the sentence is still grammatically correct and the meaning does not change. Therefore, commas must surround this phrase. Eliminate (C) and (D) because neither of these answers in-

cludes commas both before and after this phrase. There is no reason to place a comma between *composer* and *Milton*; eliminate (A). The correct answer is (B).

38. **C** Note the question! The question asks for the choice that *most effectively sets up the examples that follow*, so it tests consistency. Eliminate any answers that are inconsistent with the purpose stated in the question. The example of *Homily* is used to show how Babbitt *change[s] how similar musical phrases are audibly perceived* and how Babbitt writes the piece so *different interpretations of the phrase are possible, much in the same way that verbal puns rely on concurrent interpretations of a word. Beaten Paths* also *create[s] different musical meanings.* Choice (A) focuses on the instruments, not the different interpretations or meanings; eliminate it. Choice (B) discusses *fun* with the music. Puns may be fun, but fun isn't the point in these examples; eliminate (B). Choice (C) mentions how Babbitt *creates puns...by using the same musical idea in multiple ways.* This is consistent with the examples, so keep (C). The paragraph does not imply that musical puns are *absurd*, so eliminate (D). The correct answer is (C).

39. **A** Vocabulary changes in the answer choices, so this question tests precision of word choice. Look for a word that is consistent with the other ideas in the passage. The previous sentence discusses how Babbitt *change[s] how similar musical phrases are audibly perceived*, so the correct choice will be consistent with *change. Modified* means "to change somewhat in form." This is consistent with the context of the sentence, so keep (A). Choice (B), *twisted*, means "to force out of its natural shape; distort." The changes in the music discussed in the paragraph are positive, not negative, so eliminate (B). Choice (C), *doctored*, means "to change in order to deceive." While different simultaneous interpretations are intended, there is no deception in the music; eliminate (C). Choice (D), *refined*, means "to improve." While the music is being changed, there is no indication that it is being improved. Eliminate (D). The correct answer is (A).

40. **B** Verbs are changing in the answer choices, so the question is testing consistency of verbs. A verb must be consistent with other verbs in the sentence. The sentence contains a list: *not only create repeated musical motifs, but also _____* . The blank should be consistent with the other verb in the list, *create*, which is present tense. Eliminate (A) and (C) because they are both past tense. Keep (B) because *reshape* is consistent with *create*. Eliminate (D) because *reshaping* is not consistent with *create*. The correct answer is (B).

41. **C** Note the question! The question is asking whether to add the proposed sentence to the passage, so it is testing consistency. If the content of the new sentence is consistent with the ideas surrounding it, then it should be added; otherwise, it should not be added, as leaving the sentence out will be the most concise option. The paragraph is about how Babbitt creates puns in his music, whereas the proposed sentence introduces a new composition without discussing puns. Since it does not relate to the rest of the paragraph, the new sentence should not be added. Eliminate (A) and (B). Choice (D) discusses *other instruments,* which is not the reason that the sentence was inconsistent with the paragraph. Eliminate (D). Choice (C) accurately describes how the proposed sentence provides irrelevant information. The correct answer is (C).

42. **A** Note the question! The question is asking for the option that links the second paragraph to the ideas in the following paragraph, so it is testing consistency. The second paragraph is about Babbitt's puns in music, and the following paragraph is about puns in the titles of Babbitt's music. Keep (A), because it discusses the *titles* of Babbitt's compositions. Eliminate (B) because *how listeners understand his musical ideas* is not consistent with the following paragraph. Eliminate (C) because, although puns are often *funny*, neither paragraph mentions anything about whether the music is *persuasive*. Choice (D) defines what a pun does, but is not specific to Babbitt's music, so eliminate (D). The correct answer is (A).

43. **C** The subject of the phrase is changing in the answer choices, so the question is testing consistency. The passage is about how Milton Babbitt uses puns both within his music and in the titles of his works. Choice (A) discusses novel uses of *percussion instruments*. Babbitt used percussion in *Homily* and *Beaten Path*, but the passage doesn't indicate whether it was *novel*, nor is this phrase consistent with the passage overall. Eliminate (A). Choice (B) talks about *playing around with the meanings of words*, but doesn't mention music. This is inconsistent with the passage's point about Babbitt, so eliminate (B). Choice (C) includes puns in both the music and titles, so keep (C). Choice (D), like (A), includes information about *unusual* performance practices, which is not the point of the passage. Eliminate (D). The correct answer is (C).

44. **C** Note the question! The question is asking for the best placement of sentence 4, so it is testing consistency. The sentence must be consistent with the ideas that come both before and after it. Sentence 4 gives information about the word *homily* and a quote contained in the score. This sentence should therefore be near the discussion of *Homily* in sentence 2. Eliminate (A) and (D). Sentence 2 introduces the puns in the meaning of the title *Homily*. Because sentence 4 explains those puns, sentence 4 should be after sentence 2. The correct answer is (C).

Section 3: Math (No Calculator)

1. **A** The question asks for the value of $m^{\frac{5}{2}}$. For fractional exponents, the denominator indicates the root, and the numerator indicates the exponent power. In other words, fractional exponents are Power over Root. Therefore, the 2 in the denominator indicates a square root. Eliminate (C) and (D). The 5 in the numerator indicates that m should be raised to the 5th power. Eliminate (B). The correct answer is (A).

2. **D** The question asks for the factor that would change if a less expensive type of sealant were used. Use Process of Elimination. The length of the driveway, l, the number of driveways, d, and the width of each driveway, w, are values that will remain the same irrespective of what price of sealant is used. Eliminate (A), (B), and (C). The correct answer is (D).

3. **C** The question asks for the value of $12x - 4$ when $4x = 20$. Multiply both sides of this equation by 3 to get $12x = 60$. Subtract 4 from both sides to get $12x - 4 = 56$. The correct answer is (C).

4. **B** The question asks for the value of $\frac{z}{2}$. Cross-multiply to get $2(z + 42) = 8z$. Distribute the 2 to get $2z + 84 = 8z$. Solve for z to get $6z = 84$ and $z = 14$. The question is asking for the value of $\frac{z}{2}$, which is $\frac{14}{2} = 7$. Therefore, the correct answer is (B).

5. **B** The question asks for the value of $r - s$ in the system of equations. Stack and add the equations first to see if that gets closer to the goal. Set the equations on top of each other and add them together to get:

$$3r - 5s = -17$$
$$+ \quad \underline{5r - 3s = -7}$$
$$8r - 8s = -24$$

Divide the resulting equation by 8 to get $r - s = -3$. The correct answer is (B).

6. **A**   The question asks for a true equation for s, which is the number of shows produced between 2009 and 2010. From 2012 to 2013, 24 scripted shows were produced. This is three times the number of scripted shows produced between 2009 and 2010, so $24 \div 3 = 8$ shows were produced between 2009 and 2010. Therefore, $s = 8$. Plug 8 in for s in the answers and eliminate any answer that isn't true. Choice (A) becomes $3(8) = 24$. The equation works, so keep (A). Choice (B) becomes $24(8) = 3$ or $192 = 3$. This is false; eliminate (B). Choice (C) becomes $\frac{8}{3} = 24$, which is false; eliminate (C). Choice (D) becomes $8 + 24 = 3$, or $32 = 3$. This is also false; eliminate (D). The correct answer is (A).

7. **D**   The question asks for the slope of the line that contains point (m, n). The slope-intercept form of the line equation is $y = mx + b$, where m stands for the slope, b stands for the y-intercept, and x and y are points on the line. Therefore, in the equation $y = cx - 2$, the slope is c. Substitute the point (m, n) into the equation given to get $n = cm - 2$. Solve for c to get $n + 2 = cm$ and $c = \frac{n + 2}{m}$. The correct answer is (D).

8. **D**   The question asks for the value of c that will give no solutions for the system of equations. A system of linear equations will have no solution when the lines are parallel, meaning that they have equal slopes. In the equation $Ax + By = C$, the slope is equal to $-\frac{A}{B}$. Therefore, the slope of the first equation given is $-\left(\frac{3}{-2}\right) = \frac{3}{2}$, and the slope of the second equation is $-\left(\frac{c}{-7}\right) = \frac{c}{7}$. Set the slopes of the two equations equal to each other to get $\frac{c}{7} = \frac{3}{2}$. Cross-multiply to get $2c = 21$. Solve for c to get $c = \frac{21}{2}$. Therefore, the correct answer is (D).

9. **A**   The question asks for the binomial that must be a factor of function p. Factors are used to find the roots of a function, which are the places where the function crosses the x-axis. At these places, $y = 0$. For example, if the equation was $y = x^2 - 2x - 3$, factoring it to $(x - 3)$ and $(x + 1)$ and setting those factors equal to 0 would give roots of 3 and -1. On the table, y or $p(x)$ is 0 when $x = 1$. Therefore, $x = 1$ is a solution of $p(x)$, and $(x - 1)$ is a factor of $p(x)$. The correct answer is (A).

10. **D**   The question asks for the value of t, the y-coordinate of the vertex of the parabola. For a quadratic in standard form, it is possible to complete the square to get the vertex. This is trickier with the a in the equation, so try out a value of a. Usually, it is not a good idea to pick 1 to try out. However, the math will be much more straightforward on this particular question if $a = 1$, so try that first. The equation becomes $y = (x - 3)(x + 5)$. Expand the quadratic to get $y = x^2 + 2x - 15$. To answer the question, it is necessary to get this equation into vertex form, $y = (x - h)^2 + k$, in which the vertex is (h, k). To do this, set the equation equal to 0, move the constant over to the left, and complete the square. The equation becomes first $0 = x^2 + 2x - 15$, then $15 = x^2 + 2x$. To complete the square, take half the coefficient on the x-term, square it, and add it to both sides to get $15 + 1 = x^2 + 2x + 1$. Add the numbers on the left side, and convert the right side into the square term, so the equation becomes $16 = (x + 1)^2$. Finally, subtract 16 from both sides and replace the y to get $y = (x + 1)^2 - 16$. The vertex is $(1, -16)$, and the value of t is -16. Plug $a = 1$ into the answer choices to find the one that equals -16. The correct answer is (D).

11. **B**   The question asks for the length of line segment $\overline{FG}$, which connects two points on the parabola. The parabola intersects the line $y = 36$ when the two are equal to one another, so $(x - 9)^2 = 36$. Both sides are squares, so take the square root of both sides to get $(x - 9) = \pm 6$. Now solve the

two equations: if $x - 9 = 6$, then $x = 15$, and if $x - 9 = -6$, $x = 3$. Therefore, the parabola crosses the line $y = 36$ when $x = 15$ and when $x = 3$. In other words, the parabola intersects the line $y = 36$ at the points $(3, 36)$ and $(15, 36)$. The distance between these points will be the difference in the x-values: $15 - 3 = 12$. If taking the square root of both sides of the equation is not an immediately obvious approach, it is also possible to get the values of x using FOIL (First, Outer, Inner, Last). Expand the left side of the equation to get $x^2 - 18x + 81 = 36$. Set the equation equal to 0: $x^2 - 18x + 45 = 0$. Factor the equation to get $(x - 15)(x - 3) = 0$. Either way, the correct answer is (B).

12. **C** The question asks for the statements that must be true given the figure, and the options include pairs of congruent angles. Angles l and o are vertical angles, or opposite angles made by two intersecting lines. Therefore, $l = o$. Since $l + m = n + o$, subtracting l from the left side and o from the right side (which is possible because $l = o$) shows that $m = n$. Since vertical angles are equal to each other, it is also true that $m = p$ and $n = q$. This means that $m = n = p = q$. Therefore, both statements II and III must be true. The correct answer is (C).

13. **B** The question asks for the solutions to the given quadratic. Start by dividing the entire equation by 2 to get $x^2 + 6x + 4 = 0$. This doesn't factor nicely, and the answer choices are simplified versions of the quadratic formula. Therefore, use the quadratic formula, $x = \dfrac{-b \pm \sqrt{b^2 - 4ac}}{2a}$, to solve for x. In this case, $a = 1$, $b = 6$, and $c = 4$. The resulting equation is $x = \dfrac{-6 \pm \sqrt{6^2 - 4(1)(4)}}{2(1)}$. Simplify the right side of the equation to get $x = \dfrac{-6 \pm \sqrt{36 - 16}}{2} = \dfrac{-6 \pm \sqrt{20}}{2} = \dfrac{-6 \pm 2\sqrt{5}}{2} = -3 \pm \sqrt{5}$. The correct answer is (B).

14. **C** The question asks for true statements based on the equation, and the options include changes in temperature measurement. No exact values are given for either variable, so try out numbers to see what happens. To test statement I, plug $F = 2$ into the equation to get $D = \dfrac{5}{6}(212 - 2) = \dfrac{5}{6}(210) = 175$. Plug in again using $F = 2 + \dfrac{5}{6} = \dfrac{17}{6}$. Using this new value, $D = \dfrac{5}{6}(212 - \dfrac{17}{6}) \approx 174.3$. Since the value of D did not decrease by 1 when F increased by $\dfrac{5}{6}$, statement I is not true. Eliminate (D). Go to statement II. Plug $D = 5$ into the equation to get $5 = \dfrac{5}{6}(212 - F)$. Solve for F to get $6 = 212 - F$, and $F = 206$. Next, plug $D = 6$ into the equation to get $6 = \dfrac{5}{6}(212 - F)$. Solve for F to get $7.2 = 212 - F$, and $F = 204.8$. Subtract the two values of F to get $206 - 204.8 = 1.2$. Statement II is true. Therefore, eliminate (B). Finally, test statement III. Plug $F = 2$ into the equation to get $D = \dfrac{5}{6}(212 - 2) = \dfrac{5}{6}(210) = 175$. Next, plug in $F = 3$ to get $D = \dfrac{5}{6}(212 - 3) = \dfrac{5}{6}(209) = 174\dfrac{1}{6}$. Subtract the two values of D to get $175 - 174\dfrac{1}{6} = \dfrac{5}{6}$. Since statement III is true, eliminate (A). The correct answer is (C).

15.　**C**　The question asks for the value of k in the equation. Rather than do complex algebraic manipulation, select a value for y to use in the equation, as any value but $y = \dfrac{3}{k}$ will make the equation true. Since use of a calculator is not allowed on this section, it is especially important to pick an easy number. Try $y = 1$. If $y = 1$, then $\dfrac{36(1)^2 + 43(1) - 25}{k(1) - 3} = -9(1) - 4 - \dfrac{37}{k(1) - 3}$. Simplify to get $\dfrac{36 + 43 - 25}{k - 3} = -9 - 4 - \dfrac{37}{k - 3}$ and then $\dfrac{54}{k - 3} = -13 - \dfrac{37}{k - 3}$. Add $\dfrac{37}{k - 3}$ to both sides to get $\dfrac{54}{k - 3} + \dfrac{37}{k - 3} = -13$. Since the fractions on the left have the same denominator, add both the numerators to get $\dfrac{91}{k - 3} = -13$. Multiply both sides by $(k - 3)$ to get $91 = -13(k - 3)$. Distribute on the right side to get $91 = -13k + 39$. Subtract 39 from both sides to get $52 = -13k$. Divide both sides by -13 to get $k = -4$. The correct answer is (C).

16.　**4**　The question asks for the value of z in the equation. First, clear out the fractions by multiplying the entire equation by 30, the least common multiple of the denominators. The resulting equation is $27z - 21z = 10 + 14$. Combine like terms to get $6z = 24$. Divide both sides by 6 to get $z = 4$. This is the correct answer.

17.　$\dfrac{5}{13}$　The question asks for the value of cosine O on a triangle, but no figure is given. Draw the two triangles and label the sides. Given the information in the question, $PQ = \dfrac{24}{5}$ and $OQ = \dfrac{26}{5}$.

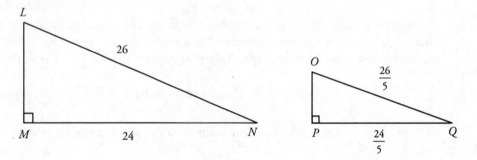

The values for triangle OPQ aren't easy numbers to work with. However, since the triangles are similar, the corresponding angles have the same measurements. Therefore, cos O = cos L. Just work with the larger triangle to find the cosine of L. Cos $\theta = \dfrac{\text{adjacent}}{\text{hypotenuse}}$, so find the length of side LM, which is adjacent to angle L. The Pythagorean Theorem is a way to find the third side of a right triangle, but this is a Pythagorean triple: It's the 5:12:13 triangle with each side doubled. Therefore, $LM = 10$, and cos $L = \dfrac{10}{26} = \dfrac{5}{13}$. Since cos L = cos O, the correct answer is $\dfrac{5}{13}$.

18.　**280**　The question asks for the number of milligrams of sodium in a pecan braid. Translate the information in the question into equations that can be solved. Let p represent the amount of sodium in a pecan braid and c represent the amount of sodium in a chocolate pastry. Then, according to the question, $p = c + 30$. Solve for c to get $c = p - 30$. The question also states that $3p + 4c = 1,840$. Substitute $p - 30$ for c to get $3p + 4(p - 30) = 1,840$. Distribute the 4 to get $3p + 4p - 120 = 1,840$. Solve for p to get $7p - 120 = 1,840$, $7p = 1,960$, and $p = 280$. This is the correct answer.

19. **3 or 4** The question asks for a possible solution to the equation, so isolate a. Divide both sides of the equation by a to get $a^2(a^2 - 25) = -144$. Distribute the a^2 to get $a^4 - 25a^2 = -144$. Set the equation equal to 0 to get $a^4 - 25a^2 + 144 = 0$. Factor the equation to get $(a^2 - 9)(a^2 - 16) = 0$. Factor further to get $(a - 3)(a + 3)(a - 4)(a + 4) = 0$. The question specifies that $a > 0$, so the factors with subtraction will give the possible values of a. Therefore, one of the possible solutions for the equation is $a - 3 = 0$ or $a = 3$. The other possible solution is $a - 4 = 0$ or $a = 4$. The correct answers are 3 and 4.

20. **115** The question asks for the value of h, a labeled angle on the diagram. Substitute 65 in for g in the equation to get $180 - f = 2(65)$. Solve for f to get $180 - f = 130$ and $f = 50$. The three angles in a triangle add up to 180°. Therefore, the other two interior angles of the top triangle will add up to $180 - 50 = 130°$. Because the top triangle is isosceles and the unknown angles are opposite equal sides, the other two angles in the top triangle will be equal to each other. Therefore, each of the other angles in the top triangle is equal to $130 \div 2 = 65°$. Given that a straight line is equal to 180°, $h = 180 - 65 = 115°$. The correct answer is 115.

Section 4: Math (Calculator)

1. **D** The question asks for the probability that the selected marble will be a small red marble or a large blue marble. Probability is defined as $\dfrac{\text{want}}{\text{total}}$. The "want" outcomes are small red marbles and large blue marbles. From the table, there are 16 small red marbles, 21 large blue marbles, and 50 total marbles. So, the probability of getting either a small red marble or a large blue marble is $\dfrac{16 + 21}{50} = \dfrac{37}{50}$. The correct answer is (D).

2. **B** The question asks for the trend in the value of Jerry's bank account over time. Look at trends in the graph and use Process of Elimination. The graph shows a negative slope until month 6, which means that the amount of money in his bank account was decreasing until July, the 6th month after January. Eliminate (C) and (D). After July, the line shows a positive slope, which means that the amount of money in his bank account was increasing. Eliminate (A). The correct answer is (B).

3. **A** The question asks for the time the passengers in the hot air balloon began viewing the landmark. According to the question, the balloon floated at a constant altitude for 1 hour while getting the best view. Since the y-axis is the altitude, the constant altitude is represented by a straight horizontal line. The only horizontal portion of the graph begins at about 10:30 A.M. Therefore, the correct answer is (A).

4. **D** The question asks for the number of very difficult questions on the standardized test. According to the information given, approximately 6 percent of the math questions are very difficult, so there are approximately $\dfrac{6}{100} \times 153 \approx 9$ very difficult math questions. Approximately 9 percent

of the science questions are considered very difficult, so there are approximately $\dfrac{9}{100} \times 267 \approx 24$ very difficult science questions. Therefore, the total number of very difficult questions is 9 + 24 = 33. The correct answer is (D).

5. **C** The question asks for the sum of two polynomials. Rather than work the addition all the way through, do one step at a time and use Process of Elimination after each step. Start by adding the first terms of the two expressions to get $6y^3 + 5y^3 = 11y^3$. Eliminate (A) and (B), which don't contain this term. Next, add the second terms of the two expressions to get $-3y^2 + (-2y^2) = -5y^2$. Eliminate (D). The correct answer is (C).

6. **B** The question asks for the definition of function g based on a table of values, so use the values in the chart to test the equations in the answers. The chart states that when $x = 2$, $g(x) = -4$. Plug 2 into each of the answer choices to see which answer returns a value of -4. Choice (A) becomes $g(x) = 2 - 6 = -4$. Keep (A), but always check the other answers. Choice (B) becomes $g(x) = 2(2) - 8 = -4$. Keep (B). Choice (C) becomes $g(x) = 3(2) - 10 = -4$. Keep (C). Choice (D) becomes $g(x) = 4(2) - 12 = -4$. Keep (D). Since all the answers are true when $x = 2$, try a different value of x, such as $x = 4$. The correct answer will then equal 0, according to the chart. Choice (A) becomes $4 - 6 = -2$. Eliminate (A). Choice (B) becomes $2(4) - 8 = 0$. Keep (B). Choice (C) becomes $3(4) - 10 = 2$. Eliminate (C). Choice (D) becomes $4(4) - 12 = 4$. Eliminate (D). The correct answer is (B).

7. **D** The question asks for the distance Paul can run in 16 minutes. His rate is given in meters per second, so convert the units. There are 60 seconds in one minute. Therefore, 16 minutes = $16 \times 60 = 960$ seconds. To find the distance that Paul can run in that amount of time, set up the following proportion: $\dfrac{x \text{ meters}}{960 \text{ seconds}} = \dfrac{144 \text{ meters}}{72 \text{ seconds}}$. Cross-multiply to get $72x = 138{,}240$. Divide both sides by 72 to get $x = 1{,}920$, which is close to 2,000. The correct answer is (D).

8. **A** The question asks for the value of z in the equation. When given two fractions equal to each other, cross-multiplying will help to solve the equation. In this question, that is tricky with the z multiplied by the first fraction. Rewrite the equation so that the z is in the numerator of the fraction: $\dfrac{2z}{7} = \dfrac{5}{2}$. Now cross-multiply to get $4z = 35$. Divide both sides by 4 to get $z = \dfrac{35}{4}$. Therefore, the correct answer is (A).

9. **B** The question asks for the meaning of the number 1.74 in the equation. Label the parts of the equation and use Process of Elimination. According to the question, y represents the average number of cases per attorney and x represents the years. Eliminate (A) because the average number of cases per attorney is represented by y, not 1.74. Neither the question nor the equation mentions the total number of cases. For this reason, eliminate both (C) and (D). The correct answer is (B).

10. **A** The question asks for the possible graph of function m, which has four distinct zeros. The term *zero* is synonymous with x-intercept, or where the graph intersects the x-axis. Therefore, a function that has 4 distinct zeros will intersect the x-axis at 4 distinct points. Graph (A) intersects the x-axis at 4 distinct points. Graph (B) intersects the x-axis at 2 distinct points. Graphs (C) and (D) intersect the x-axis at 3 distinct points. Therefore, the correct answer is (A).

11. **B** The question asks for the amount of force needed to stretch Spring #2 a distance of 5 meters. According to the information above the question, $F = km$, where F stands for force, k stands for the spring constant, and m stands for the distance the spring is stretched in meters. So, $m = 5$, and for Spring #2, $k = 0.9$. Therefore, $F = (0.9)(5) = 4.5$. The correct answer is (B).

12. **C** The question asks for the spring that will stretch the same amount as Spring #4 when 5 newtons of force are applied. Start by finding the distance that Spring #4 is stretched. According to the question, $F = km$, where F stands for force, k stands for the spring constant, and m stands for the distance the spring is stretched in meters. For Spring #4, $k = 4.7$. To find the distance the spring is stretched, plug $F = 7$ and $k = 4.7$ into the equation $F = km$ to get $7 = 4.7x$. Divide both sides by 4.7 to get $x \approx 1.49$ meters. The question asks for the spring that would stretch the same distance under 5 newtons of force, so plug 5 in for F and 1.49 for m and solve for k. Start with $5 = 1.49k$, then divide both sides by 1.49 to get $k = 3.3$. According to the table, Spring #6 has a spring constant of 3.3. Therefore, the correct answer is (C).

13. **B** The question asks for the equation that represents the total bill. Since no value is given for the number of hours, select a number. Let $t = 3$ hours. Set up the following proportion to convert hours to minutes: $\dfrac{1 \text{ hour}}{60 \text{ minutes}} = \dfrac{3 \text{ hours}}{x \text{ minutes}}$. Cross-multiply to get $x = 180$ minutes. Each minute will cost the corporation 0.30, so multiply 180 by $0.30 to get a cost of $54. Plug 3 in for t in the answer choices to see which answer choice equals $54. Choice (A) becomes $\dfrac{60(3)}{0.3} = 600$. Eliminate (A). Choice (B) becomes $(0.30)(60)(3) = 54$. Keep (B), but always check the remaining answers. Choice (C) becomes $60(3) + 0.30 = 180.30$. Eliminate (C). Choice (D) becomes $\dfrac{0.30(3)}{60} = 0.015$. Eliminate (D). The correct answer is (B).

14. **D** The question asks for the value of x that will make $j(x) + k(x) = 0$. Use the values in the answer choices for x. Start with (B). In (B), $x = 2$. On the graph, $j(2) = 3$ and $k(2) = 6$. Because $3 + 6 \neq 0$, eliminate (B). If it is not clear whether x needs to be larger or smaller, just pick a direction. In (C), $x = 3$, $j(3) \approx -2$, and $k(3) \approx 4$. Because $-2 + 4 \neq 0$, eliminate (C). In (D), $x = 4$, $j(4) = -3$, and $k(4) = 3$. The result is $-3 + 3 = 0$. The correct answer is (D).

15. **A** The question asks for the equation that shows the value of h in terms of the other variables, so isolate h.

Start by subtracting $0.5mv^2$ from both sides of the equation to get $e - 0.5mv^2 = 10mh$. Divide the entire equation by $10m$ to get $\dfrac{e}{10m} - \dfrac{0.5mv^2}{10m} = h$. Simplify the second term to get $\dfrac{e}{10m} - 0.05v^2 = h$.

Therefore, the correct answer is (A).

16. **C** The question asks for the best conclusion based on the study. Questions like this, in which no math is involved, are best handled with Process of Elimination. The word *any* in (A) is problematic. The study does not state whether pesticide P would reduce the number of aphids in a garden that was not infested with aphids. Eliminate (A). The phrase *best pesticide* in (B) is problematic. The study only evaluated pesticide P. It is possible that another pesticide exists that is even better at treating aphid infestation. The phrase *kill substantial numbers of aphids* in (D) is problematic. The study showed that pesticide P led to a reduction in the number of aphids, but this does not necessarily mean that there was a *substantial* decrease in the number of aphids in the gardens that were sprayed with pesticide P.

Furthermore, the answer references *a garden*, not specifically a *rose garden*, which extends the conclusion further than the study would indicate. Therefore, the correct answer is (C).

17. **D** The question asks for the number of units at which the cost will equal the revenue. The information above the question gives equations for cost and revenue in terms of *x*, the number of units. To solve for *x*, set the two equations given equal to each other to get $3x + 75 = 8x$. Subtract $3x$ from both sides to get $75 = 5x$. Divide both sides by 5 to get $x = 15$. The correct answer is (D).

18. **C** The question asks for the change in manufacturing cost when 5 additional units are produced. No starting number of units is given, so select values for the number of products. First, plug in $x = 2$ to find that $C(2) = 3(2) + 75 = 6 + 75 = 81$. Since the question asks for 5 additional units, next plug in $x = 7$ to find that $C(7) = 3(7) + 75 = 21 + 75 = 96$. The cost increased by $96 - 81 = 15$. Therefore, the correct answer is (C).

19. **C** The question asks for the difference between the actual number of colonies and the predicted number of colonies at 40°C. Use the graph to look up the number of bacteria colonies at 40°. The actual number of colonies present, as shown by the dot, was 420. The line of best fit predicts 400 colonies at 40°. The difference is $420 - 400 = 20$ colonies. The correct answer is (C).

20. **D** The question asks for the community that would show exponential growth over time. When a population grows exponentially, it is increasing by a constant percent of the current population, not by a constant amount. Use some actual numbers in the given situations to see how the population would change. Say that the original population is 100 people. In (A), the growth every year would be $100 \times 0.05 = 5$ people. Eliminate (A) since the growth rate does not change. Likewise, in (B), the growth rate would be $(100 \times 0.04) + 300 = 304$ people every year. Eliminate (B). In (C), the growth rate is 300 people every year. Eliminate (C). In (D), the growth rate is $100 \times 0.03 = 3$ people the first year. However, in the second year, the growth rate would be 103×0.03. In subsequent years, the growth rate would continue to increase. The correct answer is (D).

21. **D** The question asks for the number of square centimeters of cells that could be fed by 115 milliliters of glucose. It states that one milliliter of glucose can feed up to 9 Petri dishes of cells. If each Petri dish has an area of $7\frac{1}{4}$ square centimeters, then 9 Petri dishes would have a total area of $9 \times 7\frac{1}{4} = 65\frac{1}{4}$ square centimeters. That is just for 1 milliliter of glucose, but the question asks about 115 milliliters of glucose. Multiply the area 1 milliliter can feed by 115 to get $65\frac{1}{4} \times 115 = 7{,}503.75$ square centimeters. This is close to 7,500. The correct answer is (D).

22. **B** The question asks for the value of *m*, a constant that is used to define *c* and *d*, two angle measurements. Use the values in the answers for *m* to get values for *c* and *d*, then check the relationship between those two numbers. Start with (B). If $m = 7.5$, then $c = 6(7.5) - 9 = 36$, and $d = 8(7.5) - 6 = 54$. Next, use a calculator to see whether $\sin(c°) = \cos(d°)$. Given that $\sin(36°) = \cos(54°)$, it is true that $m = 7.5$. The correct answer is (B).

23. **C** The question asks for the number of animals in the training group. Instead of writing a system of equations, try the numbers in the answers. Start with (B), and assume the biologist has 8 animals. According to the question, if she gives each animal 4 treats, she will have 6 treats left over. This means she has $(8 \times 4) + 6 = 38$ treats. If she gave each of the animals 5 treats, she would need $8 \times 5 = 40$ treats. This would mean she would be $40 - 38 = 2$ treats short. Given that the question states she would be 8 treats short in this second scenario, eliminate (B). It may not be clear which direction to

go from here, so pick a direction. In (C), the biologist has 14 animals. This means she has $(14 \times 4) + 6 = 62$ treats. If she were to give each animal 5 treats, she would need $14 \times 5 = 70$ treats. This would mean that she would be $70 - 62 = 8$ treats short, which matches the information given in the question. The correct answer is (C).

24. **A** The question asks for the value of k. Rather than messing around with the algebra, try the numbers in the answers. Start with (B). If $k = 267$, the sum of the other two numbers is $738 - 267 = 471$. According to the question, k is 20% less than the sum of the other two numbers. This can be calculated as $471 - (0.2)(471) = 376.8$. In this case, the two values for k are not the same, so eliminate (B). It may not be clear which direction to go next, so just pick a direction. In (A), $k = 328$, making the sum of the other two numbers $738 - 328 = 410$. Next, 20% less than 410 is $410 - (0.2)(410) = 328$. The two values for k are equal. Therefore, the correct answer is (A).

25. **B** The question asks for the value of r, which is a coordinate in two points. When given two points on a line, finding the slope of the line is often the key to answering the question. The equation to find the slope of a line containing points (x_1, y_1) and (x_2, y_2) is $slope = \dfrac{y_2 - y_1}{x_2 - x_1}$. Given the point $(4, r)$ and the origin $(0, 0)$, the slope of the line is $\dfrac{r - 0}{4 - 0} = \dfrac{r}{4}$. Given the point $(r, 16)$ and the origin, the slope is $\dfrac{16 - 0}{r - 0} = \dfrac{16}{r}$. Since both points are on the same line, the slopes are equal. Therefore, $\dfrac{r}{4} = \dfrac{16}{r}$. Cross-multiply to get $r^2 = 64$. Take the square root of both sides to find that $r = \pm 8$. The correct answer is (B).

26. **B** The question asks for the value of h, the percent by which the height of the triangle was changed. No information is given about the dimensions of the triangle, so try out some values. Let the base and the height of the original triangle equal 10. The formula for the area of a triangle is $A = \dfrac{1}{2}bh$. The area of the triangle would be $A = \dfrac{1}{2}(10)(10) = 50$. The base of the modified triangle is equal to $10 + (0.2)(10) = 12$. The area of the modified triangle can be calculated as $50 - (0.28)(50) = 50 - 14 = 36$. Plug these values into the formula for the area of a triangle to get $36 = \dfrac{1}{2}(12)(h)$. Solve for h to get $36 = 6h$, and $h = 6$. The formula to find a percent decrease is $\dfrac{\text{difference}}{\text{original}} \times 100$. The height of the original triangle was 10, and the height of the modified triangle is 6. Therefore, the percent decrease $= \dfrac{10 - 6}{10} \times 100 = \dfrac{4}{10} \times 100 = 40$. The correct answer is (B).

27. **A** The question asks for the volume of an unusual shape. To find the volume of the capsule, first find the volume of each part, and then add them together. The formula for the volume of a right rectangular pyramid, found in the reference box at the beginning of each math section, is $V = \dfrac{1}{3}lwh$. Therefore, the volume of each of the pyramids at the ends of the capsule is $V = \dfrac{1}{3}(8)(10)(8) = \dfrac{1}{3}(640)$

≈ 213. The volume of a rectangular solid is given by the formula $V = lwh$. Therefore, the volume of the rectangular solid part of the capsule is $V = (12)(10)(8) = 960$. The total approximate volume of the capsule is $213 + 960 + 213 = 1,386$. The correct answer is (A).

28. **C** The question asks for a true statement about the relationship between a and b. Since information is given about the relationship between x and y, start by solving the two equations for x and y, respectively. Subtract $2a$ from both sides of the first equation to get $x = 2a - 8$. Subtract $2b$ from each side of the second equation to get $y = 2b - 8$. The question states that $x = y - \frac{1}{4}$. Substitute in the expressions for x and y to get $(2a - 8) = (2b - 8) - \frac{1}{4}$. All of the choices are in terms of a, so solve for a. Add 8 to both sides to get $2a = 2b - \frac{1}{4}$. Divide both sides by 2 to get $a = b - \frac{1}{8}$. The correct answer is (C).

29. **A** The question asks for the expression that will estimate the value of the mutual fund. The growth rate formula states that *final amount = initial amount*$(1 \pm rate)^n$, where n is the number of times interest will be calculated. In this question, the initial amount is \$20,000, the rate is 15%, or 0.15 when expressed as a decimal, and interest will be calculated every 4 years. Since the question is asking about interest after t years, $n = \frac{t}{4}$. Plugging all of the values into the growth equation results in the portfolio's worth as $20,000(1.15)^{\frac{t}{4}}$. The correct answer is (A).

30. **D** The question asks for the probability that a randomly selected varsity basketball player is a junior. Probability is defined as $\frac{want}{total}$. The number of varsity basketball players, the *total* in this case, is given as 32. The question gives very few other actual numbers to work with, so create some variables to stand in for the missing numbers. The number of soccer players is given in relation to the number of basketball players. Let j represent the number of varsity basketball players who are juniors and s represents the number of varsity basketball players who are seniors. Fill in the chart according to the information given in the question. In the junior row, fill in $4j$ under varsity soccer and j under varsity basketball. In the senior row, fill in $3s$ in the varsity soccer column and s in the varsity basketball column. Given the information in the chart, $4j + 3s = 108$, and $j + s = 32$. The question asks about juniors, so try to eliminate the seniors in the equations. Multiply the second equation by -3 to get $-3j - 3s = -96$. Stack the two equations on top of each other and add them together.

$$4j + 3s = 108$$
$$\underline{-3j - 3s = -96}$$
$$j \qquad = 12$$

Therefore, there are 12 varsity basketball players who are juniors. Now calculate the probability that a randomly chosen varsity basketball player is a junior: $\frac{\text{varsity basketball players who are juniors}}{\text{total varsity basketball players}} = \frac{12}{32} = 0.375$. The correct answer is (D).

31. **53.8** The question asks for the mean class size of the courses shown on the table. For averages, use the formula $T = AN$, in which T is the total, A is the average, and N is the number of things. Add up all the enrolled students to get a total of 646. There are 12 classes listed, so the formula becomes

646 = A(12), and A = 53.833. The question asks for the number rounded to the nearest tenth, which is 53.8. This is the correct answer.

32. **6** or **7** The question asks for one possible value of b, which is the number of pints of blueberries John bought. The question states that John bought 1 pint of strawberries, which costs \$5, and spent a total amount between \$23 and \$27, inclusive. Therefore, he spent between \$23 − \$5 = \$18 and \$27 − \$5 = \$22 on blueberries. Let b represent a pint of blueberries. Given that a pint of blueberries costs \$3, set up the following equation to solve for the number of pints of blueberries John bought: $18 \le 3b \le 22$. Solve for b to get $6 \le b \le 7.33$. Since he can only buy whole pints of blueberries, John bought either 6 or 7 pints of blueberries. The correct answer is 6 or 7.

33. **25** The question asks for the lowest score Jasmine can get on the 6th quiz to maintain her desired average. For averages, use the formula $T = AN$, in which T is the total, A is the average, and N is the number of things. Over 20 tests, Jasmine wants an average of 45 points. This means that Jasmine will need to score a total of $T = 20 \times 45 = 900$ points. For the first 5 tests, Jasmine has scored a total of $T = 5 \times 35 = 175$ points. This means she needs to score an additional $900 − 175 = 725$ points on the remaining 15 tests. To find the minimum required score on the 6th test, maximize the number of points that Jasmine can score on the other 14 remaining tests. The maximum score for any one test is 50 points, so Jasmine can score a maximum of $14 \times 50 = 700$ on the 14 remaining tests. Since $725 − 700 = 25$, Jasmine can score 25 on the 6th test and keep her average at 45. The correct answer is 25.

34. **18** The question asks for the value of b, which is the coefficient on the z terms. Rather than taking the time to multiply everything out, just focus on the z terms. This becomes $(3z) − 3(−5z) = 3z + 15z = 18z$. Therefore, $b = 18$. This is the correct answer.

35. **96** The question asks for the minimum value of g, which is the y-coordinate of a point in the solution to the system of inequalities. Use a calculator to graph the inequalities to get a better understanding of the relationship. Each inequality will create a line that is shaded on one side. The solution set is the area where the shaded regions overlap. For these inequalities, the solution set forms a "V," so the minimum y-value will be the vertex of the "V" where the two lines intersect. To find the point of intersection, set the two expressions equal to each other: $4x = −12x + 384$. Add $12x$ to both sides to get $16x = 384$. Then divide both sides by 16 to get $x = 24$. Plug this value for x into the second equation to get $y \ge 4(24)$ and $y \ge 96$. Therefore, the smallest value for y is 96. This is the correct answer.

36. $\dfrac{3}{4}$ or **.75**

The question asks about a fraction of the circumference based on the length of the arc. To find the arc, set up the *part to whole* relationship. The total circle has 2π radians, so $\dfrac{\text{part}}{\text{whole}} = \dfrac{\text{arc}}{\text{circumference}} = \dfrac{\text{angle}}{2\pi}$. The angle forming the arc is $\dfrac{3\pi}{2}$ radians, so $\dfrac{\text{arc}}{\text{circumference}} = \dfrac{\text{angle}}{2\pi} = \dfrac{\frac{3\pi}{2}}{2\pi} = \dfrac{3}{4}$. Therefore, the arc is $\dfrac{3}{4}$, or 0.75, of the circumference. Either value can be entered as the correct answer.

37. **20** The question asks about the size of a message, or the value for b, in a certain region relative to the average global message size. The equation for transmission time is $b = rT$, where r represents the rate of transmission and T represents the time. Both r and T are measured in seconds, but the question gives a rate of 75,000 bytes *per minute*, or per 60 seconds. To convert this rate into seconds, set up a

proportion: $\dfrac{75,000 \text{ bytes}}{60 \text{ seconds}} = \dfrac{r \text{ bytes}}{1 \text{ second}}$. Cross-multiply to get $60r = 75,000$. Divide both sides by 60 to get $r = 1,250$. To find the size of the file, plug this value and $T = 1.6$ seconds into the formula to get $b = (1,250)(1.6) = 2,000$ bytes. When asked for a *percent less than* something, use the formula for percent change: $\dfrac{\text{difference}}{\text{original}} \times 100$. The average global transmission time is 2,500 bytes. Therefore, the message size in this region is $\dfrac{2,500 - 2,000}{2,500} \times 100 = \dfrac{500}{2,500} \times 100 = 20\%$ less than the average global message size. The correct answer is 20.

38. **3,150** The question asks for the size of the message, or the value for b, in a particular city. The equation for transmission time is $b = rT$, where r represents the rate of transmission and T represents the time. Both r and T are measured in seconds, but the question gives a rate of 45,000 bytes *per minute*, or per 60 seconds. To convert this rate into seconds, set up a proportion: $\dfrac{45,000 \text{ bytes}}{60 \text{ seconds}} = \dfrac{r \text{ bytes}}{1 \text{ second}}$. Cross-multiply to get $60r = 45,000$. Divide both sides by 60 to get $r = 750$. To find the value of b, plug this value and $T = 4.2$ seconds into the formula to get $b = (750)(4.2) = 3,150$. This is the correct answer.

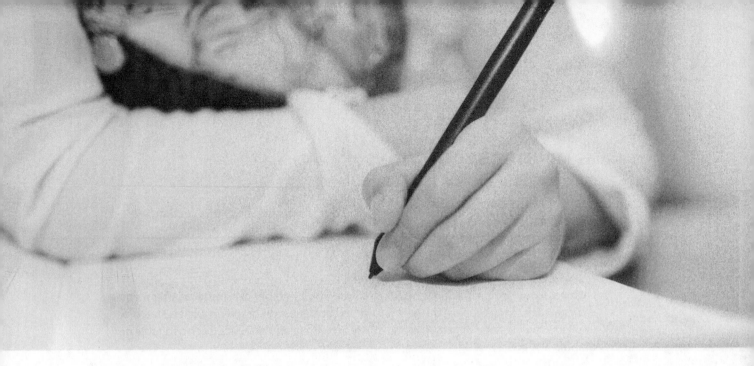

Chapter 17
Practice Test 8

Reading Test

65 MINUTES, 52 QUESTIONS

Turn to Section 1 of your answer sheet to answer the questions in this section.

Each passage or pair of passages below is followed by a number of questions. After reading each passage or pair, choose the best answer to each question based on what is stated or implied in the passage or passages and in any accompanying graphics (such as a table or graph).

Questions 1–10 are based on the following passage.

This passage is adapted from R. O'Grady, "But Once a Year." ©1917 by The Reilly & Britton Co.

A shabby little woman detached herself from the steadily marching throng on the avenue and paused before a shop window, from which solid rows of
Line electric bulbs flashed brilliantly into the December
5 twilight. The ever-increasing current of Christmas shoppers flowed on. Now and then it rolled up, like the waters of the Jordan, while a lady with rich warm furs about her shoulders made safe passage from her car to the tropic atmosphere of the great department store.
10 Wax figures draped with rainbow-tinted, filmy evening gowns caught her passing admiration, but she lingered over the street costumes, the silk-lined coats and soft, warm furs.

With her wistful gaze still fixed upon her favorite,
15 she had begun to edge her way through the crowd at the window. At the same instant, she caught the scent of fresh-cut flowers and looked up into the eyes of a tall young girl in a white-plumed velvet hat, with a bunch of English violets in her brown mink fur. As
20 their glances met, the shabby little woman checked a start, and half-defensively dropped her lids. There had flashed over the mobile face beneath the velvet hat a look of personal interest, an unmistakable impulse to speak.
25 The thrill of response that set the woman's pulses throbbing died suddenly. The red that mottled her grayish cheeks was the red of shame. Through the window, in a mirrored panel cruelly ablaze with light,

she saw herself: her made-over turban, her short,
30 pigeon-tailed jacket of a style long past, and her old otter cape with its queer caudal decorations and its yellowed cracks grinning through the plucked and ragged fur. As the white plume came nearer and nearer, the tremulous little woman regained her self-control.
35 It was but one of the coincidences of the city, she told herself, turning resolutely away.

The door slammed shut behind her. She glanced at her fingers, stained to an oily, bluish grime by the cheap dye of the garments that furnished her daily
40 work. Mechanically, she rose to wash. While her hands were immersed in the lather of rankly perfumed toilet soap, there came a gentle knock at the door.

"Come in," invited the woman, expecting some famine-pressed neighbor for a spoonful of coffee or a
45 drawing of tea.

The woman, having absently hung her towel on the doorknob, stared dazedly at the visitant. She could hardly credit her eyes. It was indeed the girl with the white ostrich plume and the bouquet of violets in her
50 brown mink fur.

"Do you know, I've such a silly excuse for coming." She laughed, and the laugh brought added music to her voice. "I noticed you had a rare fur-piece" her vivid glance returned to the pile of wraps on the chair "and
55 I want to ask a very great favor of you. Now please don't be shocked—I've been ransacking the city for something like it, and," with a determined air of taking the plunge, "I should like to buy it of you!"

CONTINUE ➡

"It, it's a rare pattern, you know," groped the girl,
60 her sweet tones assuming an eloquent, persuasive
quiver, "and you don't know how glad I'd be to have it."

The indignant color faded out of the woman's face.
"If you really want the thing"—abruptly she put her
bizarre possession into her strange visitor's lap—"If
65 you really want it, but I don't see"—yearning crept into
her work-dimmed eyes, a yearning that seemed to
struggle with disillusionment. "Tell me," she broke off,
"is that all you came here for?"

Apparently oblivious to the question, the young
70 woman rose to her feet. "You'll sell it to me then!" she
triumphed, opening her gold-bound purse.

"But, see here," demurred the woman, "I can't, it
ain't worth…"

The girl's gloved hands went fumbling into her
75 purse, while the old fur cape hung limply across one
velvet arm.

"You leave it to me," she commanded, and smiled,
a radiant, winning smile. The girl was gone and all at
once the room seemed colder and dingier than it ever
80 had before. But the woman was not cold. As she sat
huddled on the cot, warmth and vitality glowed within
her, kindled by the memory of a recent kindly human
touch.

The following evening, after working hours, the
85 shabby woman, wearing a faded scarf about her neck
to replace the old fur collar, diffidently accosted a
saleslady at the Sixth Avenue department store.

It was unusual to sell expensive furs to such a
customer. But people might send what freaks of
90 servants they pleased to do their Christmas shopping,
provided they sent the money, too. In this case, the
shabby little woman was prepared. She produced three
crisp ten-dollar bills—the fabulous sum which the
girl had left in her hand at parting—and two dollars
95 more from the savings in her worn little purse. Then,
hugging the big flat box against the tight-fitting bosom
of her jacket, she triumphantly left the store.

1

The author uses the image of the "waters of the Jordan" (line 7) most likely to

A) claim the crowd approaching the window will never ebb.

B) assert that the little woman was drowning in the throng.

C) describe the method and magnitude of the crowd's movement.

D) illustrate how a rich lady arrived at the department store.

2

As used in line 16, "caught" most nearly means

A) chased.

B) grabbed.

C) stopped.

D) noticed.

3

Which choice best supports the claim that the shabby little woman was at first excited by the tall young girl?

A) Lines 16–19 ("At the . . . fur")

B) Lines 19–21 ("As their . . . lids")

C) Lines 25–26 ("The thrill . . . suddenly")

D) Lines 29–33 ("she saw . . . fur")

4

According to the passage, why does the woman invite the visitor to come in?

A) She plans to help someone in need.

B) No one has ever been refused entry.

C) She expects the young girl to drop by.

D) She is dazed and cannot see.

CONTINUE

In the context of the conversation between the young girl and the woman, the girl's comments in lines 51–58 ("Do you . . . you!") mainly serve to

A) persuade the woman to sell the fur at a discount.

B) emphasize the desire that inspired the girl's action.

C) laugh at the shabby woman for being indignant.

D) demand that the shabby woman surrender her wrap.

The girl uses the word "ransacking" (line 56) mainly to emphasize that her search was

A) comprehensive.

B) disruptive.

C) shocking.

D) silly.

It can reasonably be inferred from the passage that the shabby woman initially declines to sell the fur mainly because

A) the young woman is only interested in rare fur pieces.

B) she yearns for the young woman to appreciate her work more.

C) the young woman offers too high of a price.

D) she doesn't believe that it has much value.

Which choice provides the best evidence for the answer to the previous question?

A) Lines 63–67 ("If you . . . disillusionment")

B) Lines 72–73 ("But, see . . . worth")

C) Lines 84–87 ("The following . . . store")

D) Lines 88–89 ("It was . . . customer")

The passage states that after the girl's departure the shabby woman felt

A) cold.

B) dingy.

C) tired.

D) warmth.

The main purpose of the last paragraph is to

A) claim that stores only reluctantly sold to people like the shabby woman.

B) contrast common occurrences with the shabby woman's experience.

C) highlight the shabby woman's greatest triumph.

D) show how servants like the shabby woman go Christmas shopping.

CONTINUE

Questions 11–20 are based on the following passages.

Passage 1 is adapted from Ludwig von Mises, *Bureaucracy*, published in 1944 by Yale University Press and now found through the Liberty Fund. Passage 2 is adapted from Albert Einstein, "Why Socialism?" Originally published by *Monthly Review* in 1949. Von Mises spoke publicly in favor of capitalism.

Passage 1

The main issue in present-day social and
Line political conflicts is whether or not man should
give away freedom, private initiative, and individual
responsibility and surrender to the guardianship of a
5 gigantic apparatus of compulsion and coercion, the
socialist state. Should authoritarian totalitarianism be
substituted for individualism and democracy? Should
the citizen be transformed into a subject, a subordinate
in an all-embracing army of conscripted labor, bound
10 to obey unconditionally the orders of his superiors?
Should he be deprived of his most precious privilege to
choose means and ends and to shape his own life?

Our age has witnessed a triumphal advance of
the socialist cause. As much as half a century ago an
15 eminent British statesman, Sir William Harcourt,
asserted: "We are all socialists now." At that time this
statement was premature as far as Great Britain was
concerned, but today it is almost literally true for that
country, once the cradle of modern liberty. It is no
20 less true with regard to continental Europe. America
alone is still free to choose. And the decision of the
American people will determine the outcome for the
whole of mankind.

The problems involved in the antagonism between
25 socialism and capitalism can be attacked from various
viewpoints. At present it seems as if an investigation
of the expansion of bureaucratic agencies is the
most expedient avenue of approach. An analysis
of bureaucratism offers an excellent opportunity
30 to recognize the fundamental problems of the
controversy.

Passage 2

The economic anarchy of capitalist society as
it exists today is, in my opinion, the real source of
the evil. We see before us a huge community of
35 producers the members of which are unceasingly
striving to deprive each other of the fruits of their
collective labor—not by force, but on the whole in

faithful compliance with legally established rules. In
this respect, is important to realize that the means
40 of production—that is to say, the entire productive
capacity that is needed for producing consumer goods
as well as additional capital goods—may legally be,
and for the most part are, the private property of
individuals.

45 Private capital tends to become concentrated in
few hands, partly because of competition among
the capitalists, and partly because technological
development and the increasing division of labor
encourage the formation of larger units of production
50 at the expense of the smaller ones. The result of
these developments is an oligarchy of private capital
the enormous power of which cannot be effectively
checked even by a democratically organized political
society. This is true since the members of legislative
55 bodies are selected by political parties, largely financed
or otherwise influenced by private capitalists who,
for all practical purposes, separate the electorate
from the legislature. The consequence is that the
representatives of the people do not in fact sufficiently
60 protect the interests of the underprivileged sections of
the population. Moreover, under existing conditions,
private capitalists inevitably control, directly or
indirectly, the main sources of information (press,
radio, education). It is thus extremely difficult,
65 and indeed in most cases quite impossible, for the
individual citizen to come to objective conclusions and
to make intelligent use of his political rights.

This crippling of individuals I consider the worst
evil of capitalism. Our whole educational system
70 suffers from this evil. An exaggerated competitive
attitude is inculcated into the student, who is trained
to worship acquisitive success as a preparation for his
future career.

I am convinced that there is only one way to
75 eliminate these grave evils, namely through the
establishment of the socialist economy, accompanied
by an educational system which would be oriented
toward social goals. Nevertheless, it is necessary to
remember that a planned economy is not yet socialism.
80 A planned economy as such may be accompanied
by the complete enslavement of the individual. The
achievement of socialism requires the solution of some
extremely difficult socio-political problems: how is it

CONTINUE ➡

possible, in view of the far-reaching centralization of
85 political and economic power, to prevent bureaucracy
from becoming all-powerful and overweening? How
can the rights of the individual be protected and
therewith a democratic counterweight to the power of
bureaucracy be assured?

11

In Passage 1, von Mises makes which point about
socialism relative to capitalism?

A) Socialism creates greater equality in incomes,
   but capitalism creates greater disparity in
   incomes.

B) Capitalism is a foundational tenant of democracy,
   but socialism erodes the foundations of
   democracy.

C) Socialism oppresses self-motivation, but
   capitalism allows individuals to retain their
   liberties.

D) Socialism allows men to shape their own lives, but
   socialism also requires men to conscript others
   into employment.

12

Which choice provides the best evidence for the
answer to the previous question?

A) Lines 1–6 ("The main . . . state")

B) Lines 11–12 ("Should . . . life")

C) Lines 13–14 ("Our . . . cause")

D) Lines 14–16 ("As much . . . now")

13

As used in line 13, "advance" most nearly means

A) upgrade.

B) breakthrough.

C) progress.

D) deposit.

14

What is Einstein's central claim in Passage 2?

A) An economic system which allows the wealthy
   to gain disproportionate power is harmful to a
   society.

B) The economic success of a society depends on the
   ability of its citizens to make their own decisions.

C) An economic system that rewards initiative and
   creativity is the most effective way to help all
   members of a society.

D) Different economic systems have different merits
   and disadvantages, and should be considered
   carefully.

15

As used in line 36, "fruits" most nearly means

A) produce.

B) consequences.

C) byproducts.

D) output.

CONTINUE ➡

16

In Passage 2, Einstein implies that an educational system that fosters extreme competition over social goals is

A) idealistic, because it appears beneficial but doesn't work in reality.

B) destructive, because it limits the ability of individuals to exercise their rights.

C) weak, because it heightens differences between social classes.

D) effective, because it effectively prepares the next generation for success.

17

In Passage 2, Einstein makes which point about an improperly attempted socialist economy?

A) It could be more beneficial to society than unchecked freedom.

B) It could eliminate deadly perils and consequences.

C) It could permit the destruction of free choice.

D) It could lead to a capitalist-controlled media.

18

Which choice provides the best evidence for the answer to the previous question?

A) Lines 61–64 ("Moreover . . . education")

B) Lines 68–69 ("This . . . capitalism")

C) Lines 78–79 ("Nevertheless . . . socialism")

D) Lines 80–81 ("A planned . . . individual")

19

Which choice best states the relationship between the two passages?

A) Passage 2 provides social context for the financial system described in Passage 1.

B) Passage 2 elaborates on the pitfalls of the economic system criticized in Passage 1.

C) Passage 2 advocates against the economic system championed in Passage 1.

D) Passage 2 uses specifics to illustrate general ideas put forth in Passage 1.

20

Von Mises would have most likely reacted to lines 74–78 ("I am . . . goals") of Passage 2 with

A) agreement, because he also believes evils of society should be eliminated.

B) hostility, because he believes a socialist society enslaves its citizens and eliminates individualism.

C) impatience, because he believes relying on social goals to fix financial issues is ineffective.

D) reservation, because he agrees social issues are important, but socialism isn't effective.

CONTINUE

Questions 21–30 are based on the following passage and supplementary material.

This passage is adapted from Rob Jackson, Robbie Andrew, Pep Canadell, Pierre Friedlingstein, and Glen Peters, "Natural Gas Use Is Rising: Is that Good News or Bad News for the Climate?" ©2020 by Scientific American.

The best we can say for 2019 is that global carbon dioxide emissions rose "only" 0.6 percent. That's a lot slower than the 1.5 percent and 2.1 percent growth in
Line 2017 and 2018. Is it good news, the start of a transition
5 away from fossil fuels, or is it simply bad news, another record year of fossil carbon dioxide emissions?

Increased natural gas and oil use are driving the increase in carbon dioxide emissions and are outpacing slight declines from global coal use. Oil use around the
10 world has been rising steadily at about a percent and a half per year for the last five or six years. Natural gas use is surging at almost twice that rate, aided by the boom in liquefied natural gas (LNG) that is connecting global gas markets. Emissions from natural gas use
15 rose almost 200 million metric tons of CO_2 in 2019, and were responsible for two thirds of the global emissions increase.

In the United States and Europe, natural gas is replacing coal in electricity generation. Coal
20 consumption in both regions dropped at least 10 percent in 2019. Coal use in the U.S. is down by half from 15 years ago; 500 coal power plants have closed or are scheduled to. In the United Kingdom, the birthplace of the industrial revolution, coal-fired
25 electricity has almost disappeared and now supplies only 5 percent of power. In both countries, the replacement of coal by natural gas and renewables is reducing both CO_2 emissions and air pollution from particulates, mercury, sulfur and lead—saving lives as
30 a result.

While the U.K. and U.S. have some positive news, emissions are rising in many other places around the world. Oil use continues to climb, and the additional natural gas being burned isn't replacing coal in
35 electricity generation. Rather, it's meeting new energy demands for electricity and residential and industrial heating.

With natural gas use surging globally at 2.6 percent a year and with increased emissions from it outpacing
40 decreased emissions from coal globally, we need to reevaluate the role of natural gas as a bridge fuel. Where it replaces coal for electricity generation, it's

reducing carbon dioxide emissions and improving air quality. It still produces carbon pollution, though,
45 and therefore slows, but does not solve, the climate problem. Where it's providing new energy and new emissions—replacing low- and no-carbon technologies or keeping them from being deployed—it is hindering climate solutions.

50 If the world is going to build thousands of new natural gas plants over the next decade—infrastructure that will run for decades—most of the plants should be carbon-capture-ready or use new technologies to produce their power. This is unfortunately not yet
55 happening. One promising new technology is the Allam cycle, which burns natural gas or other fossil fuels in oxygen rather than air, with carbon dioxide as the carrier gas. An Allam cycle power plant produces almost pure CO_2 as a byproduct. This pipeline-
60 quality CO_2 removes the need for CO_2 capture in current technologies that use amines or hydroxides to scrub the CO_2. The CO_2 can then, in principle, be sequestered back underground, like the natural gas or coal it came from. A 50-megawatt Allam Cycle
65 demonstration plant is being built in La Porte, Tex. We hope it succeeds.

This year's likely growth in global CO_2 emissions of approximately 0.6 percent will be slower than the growth in emissions for the past two years. That's good
70 news. But growth is growth, and another year and another decade have been lost to record emissions. We remain far from the 7.6 percent annual declines recommended by a new United Nations report. Current trends don't suggest structural changes are
75 happening that would lead to a peak and decline in global emissions anytime soon. As we welcome the New Year and new decade, some people will celebrate the good news that emissions growth slowed in 2019. Others will bemoan the bad news that growth is
80 growth, with record carbon dioxide emissions reached yet again. What we need is much more radical news: a steep drop in pollution that drains the emissions glass as quickly as a final champagne toast.

CONTINUE ▶

Figure 1
Annual Global CO$_2$ Emissions by Source, in tons

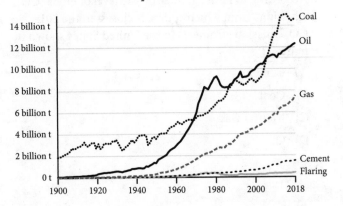

Figure 2
Annual CO$_2$ Emissions from Gas by Country, in tons

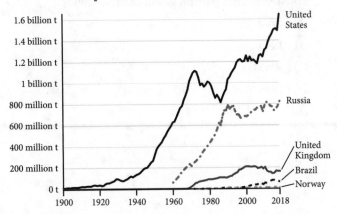

21

The passage is written from the point of view of

A) industry members committed to reducing climate change.

B) scientists proposing potential avenues of research.

C) environmentalists calling consumers to action.

D) citizens concerned with global developments.

22

As used in line 12, "aided by" most nearly means

A) lessened by.

B) relieved of.

C) boosted by.

D) revealed by.

23

The last sentence of the second paragraph (lines 14–17) mainly serves to

A) alert the reader to a troubling trend.

B) evaluate a claim made later in the passage.

C) contrast the results for this year with those of prior years.

D) commend efforts to mitigate climate change.

24

It can most reasonably be inferred from the passage that the authors believe current natural gas production

A) performs better in the American market than in global markets.

B) will be replaced by the Allam Cycle in the near future.

C) is the ultimate solution for clean air technology.

D) pollutes the environment in unsustainable ways.

25

Which choice provides the best evidence for the answer to the previous question?

A) Lines 9–14 ("Oil use . . . markets")

B) Lines 18–19 ("In the . . . generation")

C) Lines 42–44 ("Where . . . quality")

D) Lines 44–46 ("It still . . . problem")

CONTINUE ➤

26

According to the passage, the Allam cycle can improve on current pollution levels by

A) producing fewer carrier gases.

B) storing byproducts almost entirely underground.

C) burning pure oxygen instead of breathable air.

D) eliminating CO_2 capture from the production process.

27

Which choice provides the best evidence for the answer to the previous question?

A) Lines 55–58 ("One . . . gas")

B) Lines 58–59 ("An Allam . . . byproduct")

C) Lines 59–62 ("This . . . CO_2")

D) Lines 62–64 ("The CO_2 . . . from")

28

As used in line 81, "radical" most nearly means

A) fanatical.

B) remarkable.

C) militant.

D) enlightening.

29

According to figure 1, in 2018, the level of global CO_2 emissions from which source is closest to the 2018 CO_2 emissions from gas in the United States shown in figure 2?

A) Cement

B) Coal

C) Natural Gas

D) Oil

30

According to figures 1 and 2, in what year were global CO_2 emissions from oil equal to the U.S. CO_2 emissions from natural gas in the year 2000?

A) 1925

B) 1945

C) 1965

D) 1985

CONTINUE

Questions 31–41 are based on the following passage and supplemental material.

This passage is excerpted from Maxwell T. Boykoff and Jules M. Boykoff, "Balance as bias: global warming and the US prestige press," originally published in 2004 by the University of Colorado Boulder.

The mass media play an important role in the construction of environmental issues and problems. Accordingly, prestige-press coverage of global warming
Line is not just a collection of news articles; it is a social
5 relationship between people that is mediated by news articles. The parameters of this social relationship are defined, in large part, by the many journalistic norms and values that both affect what is deemed news and influence how that news is framed. The
10 United States prestige press—by which we mean the *New York Times*, the *Washington Post*, the *Los Angeles Times*, and the *Wall Street Journal*—has contributed in significant ways to failed discursive translations regarding global warming. These press outlets have
15 done this by adhering to the journalistic norm of balanced reporting, offering a countervailing "denial discourse"—"a voluble minority view [that] argues either that global warming is not scientifically provable or that it is not a serious issue"—roughly equal space
20 to air its suppositions. The 'balancing' of scientific findings and the counter-findings results, in large part, from an accumulation of tactical media responses and practices guided by widely accepted journalistic norms and values.
25 In fact, when it comes to coverage of global warming, balanced reporting can actually be a form of informational bias. Despite the highly regarded United Nations-sponsored Intergovernmental Panel on Climate Change's (IPCC's) consistent assertions
30 that global warming is a serious problem with a "discernible" human component that must be addressed immediately, balanced reporting has allowed a small group of global warming skeptics to have their views amplified.
35 Ross Gelbspan has asserted, "[t]he professional canon of journalistic fairness requires reporters who write about a controversy to present competing points of view. When the issue is of a political or social nature,

fairness—presenting the most compelling arguments
40 of both sides with equal weight—is a fundamental check on biased reporting. But this canon causes problems when it is applied to issues of science. It seems to demand that journalists present competing points of view on a scientific question as though they
45 had equal scientific weight, when actually they do not."

The IPCC has asserted that global warming is a serious problem that has anthropogenic* influences, and that it must be addressed immediately. In the managerial scientific discourse represented by the
50 IPCC, a remarkably high level of scientific consensus has emerged on these two particular issues. D. James Baker, administrator of the US National Oceanic and Atmospheric Administration, has said about global warming that "[t]here's a better scientific consensus on
55 this than on any issue I know—except maybe Newton's second law of dynamics."

However, on December 3, 2002, the *Washington Post* cited "numerous uncertainties [that] remain about global warming's cause and effect," echoing
60 George W. Bush's call "for a decade of research before the government commits to anything more than voluntary measures to stem carbon dioxide and other greenhouse gas emissions." This statement was not only a backhanded swipe at the findings of scientists
65 concerned about global warming, but it was also the spectacular culmination of a complex and perpetually unfolding discursive process propagated by the prestige press in the United States.

The continuous juggling act journalists engage
70 in often mitigates against meaningful, accurate, and urgent coverage of the issue of global warming. Since the general public garners most of its knowledge about science from the mass media, investigating the mass media's portrayal of global warming is crucial. The
75 disjuncture above is one illustration that—through the filter of balanced reporting—popular discourse has significantly diverged from the scientific discourse. To date, this disconnection has played a significant role in the lack of concerted international action to curb
80 practices that contribute to global warming.

* anthropogenic = caused by human beings

CONTINUE

U.S. Prestige-Press Coverage of Action
Regarding Global Warming

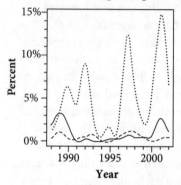

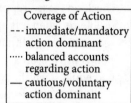
Coverage of Action
- - - immediate/mandatory action dominant
····· balanced accounts regarding action
—— cautious/voluntary action dominant

Credit: Maxwell T. Boykoff and Jules M. Boykoff

Figure 1

31

The main purpose of the passage is to

A) question the journalistic ideal of balanced coverage regarding scientific reporting.

B) demonstrate the bias of scientific journalists covering environmental stories.

C) analyze the antagonistic relationship between the elite press and local news outlets.

D) discuss ideals of objectivity in relation to journalism.

32

According to the passage, which expectation do reporters covering controversy face?

A) They should present only the most objective reporting of the issues.

B) They should persist in unearthing the truth, no matter the consequences.

C) They should offer equal consideration to opposing perspectives.

D) They should promote constructive solutions to environmental problems.

33

Which choice provides the best evidence for the answer to the previous question?

A) Lines 1–2 ("The mass . . . problems")

B) Lines 6–9 ("The parameters . . . framed")

C) Lines 35–38 ("Ross . . . view")

D) Lines 48–51 ("In the . . . issues")

34

As used in line 51, "particular" most nearly means

A) local.

B) specific.

C) appropriate.

D) peculiar.

35

The authors most likely include the quotation in lines 54–56 to

A) contrast the consensus of scientific authorities with the reporting in prestige publications.

B) propose possible models for accurate reporting.

C) criticize the gullibility of readers of partisan media outlets.

D) demonstrate the importance of scientific facts for public discourse.

36

The authors indicate that the work of journalists may involve

A) independent research concerning the trustworthiness of sources.

B) questioning one's own conscience when investigating controversial topics.

C) relating socially to interview subjects for stories.

D) prioritizing balanced reporting of viewpoints over covering the facts.

CONTINUE

37

Which choice provides the best evidence for the answer to the previous question?

A) Lines 3–6 ("Accordingly . . . articles")

B) Lines 57–63 ("However . . . emissions")

C) Lines 63–68 ("This . . . States")

D) Lines 69–71 ("The continuous . . . warming")

38

As used in line 79, "curb" most nearly means

A) bend.

B) limit.

C) delay.

D) edge.

39

Based on the graph, in what year were the percentages of all three types of coverage of action tactics regarding global warming most similar?

A) 1989

B) 1993

C) 1994

D) 1999

40

Which statement is best supported by information in the graph?

A) Between 1989 and 1999, the number of "cautious/ voluntary" accounts of global warming declined dramatically, but then rose significantly.

B) Between 1995 and 2000, the number of "immediate/mandatory" accounts of global warming remained the same.

C) Between 1988 and 2002, the number of "balanced" accounts of global warming tended to increase.

D) Between 1988 and 2001, the number of all accounts of global warming doubled.

41

The 2001 data in the graph best serve as evidence that

A) "coverage of global warming is not just a collection of news articles" (lines 3–4).

B) "balanced reporting can actually be a form of informational bias" (lines 26–27).

C) "global warming is a serious problem that has anthropogenic influences" (lines 46–47).

D) "through the filter of balanced reporting—popular discourse has significantly diverged from the scientific discourse" (lines 75–77).

CONTINUE

Questions 42–52 are based on the following passage.

This passage is adapted from Jef Akst, "Silent Canopies."
©2016 by The Scientist.

In late September, Kimberly Williams-Guillén, an assistant professor at the University of Washington Bothell and a conservation scientist for the Nicaraguan
Line environmental NGO Paso Pacífico, received a report
5 that a handful of howler monkeys (genus Alouatta) had been found dead at an eco-resort in Nicaragua. Bizarrely, the monkeys showed no signs of trauma or disease. "They seemed to be in fairly good condition," she recalls.

10 Over the next couple of months, Williams-Guillén and her colleagues continued to receive news that howler monkeys were dying. Then, around mid-January, the reports really started to flood in.

When it became clear that this was not just an
15 isolated incident, Williams-Guillén hopped on a plane to Nicaragua to see for herself. "I saw many healthy-looking monkeys, but I also saw many visibly unwell monkeys," she says. "They were thin and very lethargic, often solitary and nonresponsive. There were several
20 that I was able to walk up to and grab them out of a bush."

Although the mortality rate seems to have slowed since mid-February, the researchers are anxious to understand what's going on. Williams-Guillén
25 speculates that the deaths may be linked to the drought that has struck Nicaragua and other areas of Central and South America this year. "The deaths are all really concentrated in the areas worst hit by drought," she says. "Even just going to the other side of the
30 mountain, where it's slightly more humid, there's a lot fewer deaths, and there's visibly more potential howler monkey food, whereas the areas that have the highest rates of mortality, the trees are just bare—there's hardly a leaf or flower to be eaten."

35 Kenneth Glander of Duke University agrees that limited food availability is likely a contributing factor, though the cause of death may not be starvation per se. Rather, the lack of food may drive the monkeys to consume plants with high levels of certain toxins
40 that aren't part of their normal diet. In the 1970s,

Glander witnessed a handful of dead or dying howler monkeys in Costa Rica, including two that displayed convulsions similar to those reported in Nicaraguan monkeys this year. "When we did autopsies on them, I
45 was able to determine [that] their stomachs were full of leaves that they'd never eaten before." He then collected a sample of those leaves from trees at his study site and brought them back to Duke for analysis, finding that they were chock-full of toxic alkaloids.

50 A good test of this hypothesis would be to see how other animals in the areas are faring, says Pedro Américo Dias of the University of Veracruz in Mexico. "If there are no reports of deaths in other frugivorous primates and other frugivorous animals, perhaps [food
55 availability] doesn't have to do with it," he says.

Another possible cause for the howler monkey die-offs is disease. Although Nicaragua is currently believed to be free of yellow fever, Dias points out that outbreaks of the viral disease devastated howler
60 monkey populations in the late 1940s and into the 1950s. Some researchers even speculate that yellow fever may be a cause of the relatively low genetic diversity among Central American howler monkeys, Dias says. "Yellow fever in the past could have caused
65 important bottlenecks."

Williams-Guillén thinks that disease is an unlikely cause of the recent monkey deaths, however. While she and her colleagues are still waiting to export blood and tissue samples to U.S. labs for further analysis,
70 she notes that a Nicaraguan researcher has done virus diagnostics on some of the samples. And, so far, none have tested positive for yellow fever, Zika, chikungunya, or dengue viruses. "Between that and the lack of any necrosis of the liver in the dead animals,
75 [disease] is unlikely," Williams-Guillén says.

For now, however, the cause of the recent howler monkey deaths remains a mystery. Williams-Guillén suspects that no one hypothesis will be correct. "There's probably an interaction of factors," she
80 says. "Animals that might have had some clinical or secondary infections that normally aren't that problematic…got into a situation where they were extremely food- and water-stressed, and that might have been enough to tip them into mortality."

CONTINUE ➡

42

The primary purpose of the passage is to

A) portray the concerns, actions, and theories of an investigation.

B) discuss and assess contradictory results regarding an aberration.

C) demonstrate the unusual persistence of a researcher's efforts toward a problem.

D) examine the methodology and questions raised by a hypothesis.

43

According to the passage, Williams-Guillén's ultimate hypothesis rests most strongly on which kind of evidence?

A) Genealogical evidence

B) Authoritative opinions

C) Unreliable descriptions

D) Multiple tests

44

As used in line 15, "hopped on" most nearly means

A) avoided.

B) flew.

C) jumped.

D) entered.

45

Which statement regarding howler monkeys is most strongly supported by the passage?

A) They are less affected by ecological changes than other species would be.

B) They cannot easily be captured by researchers when healthy.

C) They share some known dietary similarities with other species.

D) They prefer the taste of non-toxic foods.

46

According to the author, an early consideration regarding howler monkey deaths was whether they

A) could be prevented through food distribution.

B) were simply random occurrences.

C) impacted howler monkeys of all ages.

D) were impacting the entire population.

47

Which theory provided by the passage supports Williams-Guillén's belief that "no one hypothesis will be correct" (line 78)?

A) The unusual monkey deaths have since ceased to be a problem.

B) The assumption that the impact of drought on the health of the monkey population was more significant than that of any other factor.

C) Lack of food in the past has led some monkeys to consume lethal alkaloids.

D) Yellow fever was the cause of a previous outbreak of disease that had afflicted the howler monkey population.

48

Which choice provides the best evidence for the answer to the previous question?

A) Lines 22–24 ("Although . . . on")

B) Lines 27–29 ("The deaths . . . says")

C) Lines 29–34 ("Even . . . eaten")

D) Lines 35–40 ("Kenneth . . . diet")

CONTINUE

49

The primary purpose of the seventh and eighth paragraphs (lines 56–75) is to

A) define Williams-Guillén's method.

B) demonstrate Williams-Guillén's expertise.

C) underscore Williams-Guillén's assumptions.

D) provide Williams-Guillén's perspective.

50

In indicating that yellow fever may have created "bottlenecks" (line 65), the author most likely means that the fever

A) reduced the monkey's opportunities to breed with genetically different partners.

B) led to the current howler monkey deaths.

C) introduced a prohibitively large number of virus-free monkeys into the ecosystem.

D) caused a greater degree of competition between monkeys.

51

According to the passage, Williams-Guillén's investigation provides an answer to which of the following questions?

A) What factor is unlikely to have contributed to howler monkey deaths?

B) Why do monkeys insist on continuing to consume toxic leaves?

C) How do yellow fever outbreaks affect genetic diversity among howler monkeys?

D) How can howler monkey populations return to normal following this outbreak of deaths?

52

Which choice provides the best evidence for the answer to the previous question?

A) Lines 61–64 ("Some . . . says")

B) Lines 66–67 ("Williams-Guillén . . . however")

C) Lines 71–73 ("And, so . . . viruses")

D) Lines 80–84 ("Animals . . . mortality")

STOP
If you finish before time is called, you may check your work on this section only.
Do not turn to any other section in the test.

No Test Material On This Page

Writing and Language Test

35 MINUTES, 44 QUESTIONS

Turn to Section 2 of your answer sheet to answer the questions in this section.

Questions 1–11 are based on the following passage.

Wake Up!

If you've ever been driving on a long stretch of highway late at **1** night or, early in the morning, you almost certainly know the feeling. Even though you're in a heavy machine hurtling forward at an extraordinary rate, you just can't stay awake. You know that driving requires your full attention, but your eyelids are just too heavy.

If you haven't had this experience, you're lucky, but you're in the minority. Charles Czeisler, from the Division of Sleep Medicine at Harvard, says that as many as 56 million Americans a month "admit that they drive when they haven't gotten enough sleep." This may seem like a harmless enough problem, but as many as one-seventh of these drivers admit to falling asleep at the **2** wheel. Causing more than a million crashes each year, including 50,000 injuries and 6,400 deaths.

1

A) NO CHANGE
B) night or early in the morning you,
C) night or early in the morning, you
D) night, or early in the morning you

2

A) NO CHANGE
B) wheel, causing
C) wheel, this causes
D) wheel. Which causes

CONTINUE

[3] These may sound like drunk-driving numbers and with good cause. At a recent forum, Czeisler suggested that driving on fewer than two hours of sleep is the equivalent of driving while [4] intoxicated. Judgment is—similarly compromised, and reactions are correspondingly slowed. The numbers speak for themselves, so Czeisler and the committee are attempting now to implement changes in the law code to address sleep deprivation. [5]

3

Which choice provides the best transition from the previous paragraph to this one?

A) NO CHANGE

B) Auto-accident fatalities are among the leading causes of death every year.

C) Medical professionals regularly hold forums to share their findings and discover new findings.

D) Drunk driving remains a difficult problem in this country, even though the penalties for it are strict.

4

A) NO CHANGE

B) intoxicated, judgment is

C) intoxicated. Judgment is:

D) intoxicated: judgment is

5

At this point, the writer wants to add a specific proposal that Czeisler's group has made based on the information in this paragraph. Which choice best accomplishes this goal?

A) Some of Czeisler's colleagues have already organized new conferences on sleep apnea and other sleep disorders.

B) The invention of self-driving cars could potentially reduce the risks of sleep-deprived driving.

C) Czeisler has had a long and illustrious career teaching people about how to observe their own unconscious behavior.

D) Czeisler and his colleagues are trying to get sleep-deprived driving added to the list of criminal statutes.

CONTINUE

Some of the group's findings make obvious sense. They argue that people who work night shifts never quite regulate their sleep, regardless of how regular their sleep schedules are. **6** In addition, night-shift workers with sleep disorders are at a particular risk of which they are unaware. One major sleep disorder for which this is especially true is sleep apnea. Czeisler's group estimates that approximately 85% of sleep apnea cases go undiagnosed and untreated. Individuals with sleep apnea don't rest deeply even when they are asleep, and the disorder, given all of its negative side effects, **7** was doubling the risk of sleep-related crashes.

6

Which choice most effectively combines the underlined sentences?

A) In addition, night-shift workers with sleep disorders are at a particular risk of which they are unaware; moreover, one major sleep disorder for which this is especially true is sleep apnea.

B) In addition, night-shift workers with sleep disorders, especially sleep apnea, are at a particular risk of which they are unaware.

C) In addition, night-shift workers with sleep disorders are at a particular risk of which they are unaware: among them are sleep apnea especially.

D) In addition, night-shift workers with sleep disorders are at a particular risk of which they are unaware; one major sleep disorder for which this is especially true is sleep apnea.

7

A) NO CHANGE

B) are doubling

C) is doubling

D) doubles

CONTINUE

The findings regarding young people, [8] for example, were not quite so obvious. Young people have a tendency to think that they can operate at a high level with less sleep. [9] This may be anecdotally true, but the science suggests that in fact quite the opposite is true. A set of chemicals in the hypothalamus region of the brain produces the cells that help the transition from wakefulness to sleep. In younger people, these cells are [10] highly developed, whereas in older people, many of the cells have died or function at a lower level. As a result, a younger person is more at risk for uncontrollable lapses in engagement [11] adding too attention because brain function between wakefulness and sleep is more easily blurred. So next time you think you're okay to drive after a late night, use some of those brain cells and call a cab or take a nap instead.

[8]

A) NO CHANGE
B) however,
C) furthermore,
D) thus,

[9]

Which choice most effectively cites commonly held views while previewing what is to come in this paragraph?

A) NO CHANGE
B) Young people's susceptibility to alcoholism is also much higher than that of adults.
C) It's also well known that young people tend to drive faster than older people.
D) Everyone's different, and maybe you are one of the lucky few who doesn't need that much sleep.

[10]

A) NO CHANGE
B) firing on all cylinders,
C) going off,
D) off the chain,

[11]

A) NO CHANGE
B) and attention lapses also
C) plus attention as well
D) and attention

CONTINUE

Questions 12–22 are based on the following passage.

To Preserve, but Not to Reconstruct

Although the building served a variety of functions, the Parthenon's original construction remained more or less intact for over two millennia. The enormous temple to the goddess Athena Parthenos that stands in ruins today was completed in 432 B.C.E. [12] Nevertheless, it served its original purpose for a thousand years, until it was turned into a church by the Byzantines in the 6th century and then into a mosque by the Ottoman Empire in the mid-15th century. The shift of the building's religious affiliation involved some minor architectural changes, but until the late 17th [13] century, the building, largely retained its majestic, classical profile.

The first major catastrophe in the Parthenon's history came during a war between the Ottoman Empire and the Venetian army in 1687: the Ottomans used the Parthenon as a gunpowder storehouse [14] for storing ammunition, which exploded when it was hit by a Venetian cannon. [15] Additionally, three hundred people died in the explosion.

[12]
A) NO CHANGE
B) Remarkably,
C) As a result,
D) Therefore,

[13]
A) NO CHANGE
B) century, the building largely
C) century: the building largely
D) century the building, largely,

[14]
A) NO CHANGE
B) where they stored ammunition,
C) —a place to store ammunition—
D) DELETE the underlined portion.

[15]
At this point, the writer is considering adding the following sentence.

> The roof of the building collapsed, along with many sculptures and several dozen columns.

Should the writer make this addition here?

A) Yes, because it provides an important detail about the effect of the explosion.
B) Yes, because it helps to explain the facts presented later in the passage.
C) No, because it repeats information presented later in the passage.
D) No, because it is not directly related to the main idea of the paragraph.

CONTINUE

Over the course of the 18th century, the ruins of the Parthenon were largely neglected by the local government, **16** though interest in the building grew in Britain. The first major effort at what might be called preservation came in the years 1801–1812 when Thomas Bruce, the Earl of Elgin, systematically removed most of the extant sculpture from the Parthenon and shipped it all to Britain, where it remains today.

In the 1890s, the first major push to restore the Parthenon began when Nikolaos Balanos was charged with restoring **17** its iconic column's. Unfortunately, Balanos's restoration efforts ultimately caused more harm than good. Most disastrously, the iron clamps that he **18** using holding pieces of masonry together corroded after years of exposure to the **19** weather, eventually it caused even more damage to the already fragile building.

16

Which choice best supports the main point of the paragraph?

A) NO CHANGE

B) which makes it all the more remarkable that the government later sponsored restoration efforts.

C) and the building was even briefly used as an army barracks.

D) but it became a very popular subject of paintings and engravings.

17

A) NO CHANGE

B) it's iconic column's.

C) its iconic columns.

D) it's iconic columns.

18

A) NO CHANGE

B) used to hold

C) using to hold

D) used in the holding of

19

A) NO CHANGE

B) weather; eventually causing

C) weather, eventually causing

D) weather, eventually it causing

CONTINUE →

[1] The most recent restoration effort was begun in 1975, and conservation work continues today. [2] As a result of this painstaking work, the restoration is proceeding at a far slower pace than the original construction, which took only sixteen years. [3] The project has taken so long partly because the first step was to undo the misguided earlier restoration attempt. [4] Workers then catalogued tens of thousands of pieces of marble and used computer programs to try to match each piece to its specific location. [5] The 20 shadows of each column's design are incredibly sophisticated, and pieces match one another by fractions of millimeters. 21

The goal of the current restoration is not, however, to entirely rebuild the structure. "We wanted to preserve the beauty of what has survived these past 2,500 years," says Manolis Korres, 22 who is the project's chief architect. "It's a reminder of man's power to create, as well as to destroy."

20

A) NO CHANGE

B) tininess

C) suggestions

D) nuances

21

To make this paragraph most logical, sentence 2 should be

A) placed after sentence 3.

B) placed after sentence 4.

C) placed after sentence 5.

D) DELETED from the paragraph.

22

A) NO CHANGE

B) being

C) the architect is

D) DELETE the underlined portion.

Questions 23–33 are based on the following passage and supplementary material.

Today is Brought to You by Big Data

Ask anyone what the next big thing in business is, and it's very likely they'll say "big data." The term refers to all the information that the digital age allows companies and organizations to collect: how many items an online shopper looks at before deciding to make a purchase, exactly how much time a delivery truck spends idling in **23** traffic, or, how the weather affects which books patrons check out from the library. Some of this glut of data comes from increasingly sophisticated and connected sensors on everything from cars and trucks to appliances and light bulbs. **24** Consequently, a huge portion of it comes from social media posts that can't be analyzed in traditional ways. This means that new ways of **25** digging online activity for information are constantly being developed.

Data analysts are the people who develop new ways of looking at such information, in fields ranging from healthcare to the nonprofit **26** sector too manufacturing. Although many companies have long employed financial analysts or market research analysts, the need for even more data analysts is quickly growing. Job-seekers with degrees in computer science or mathematics are likely to be attracted to data analysis jobs, because there is no standard requirement for a graduate degree or certification.

23
A) NO CHANGE
B) traffic, or
C) traffic: or
D) traffic; or

24
A) NO CHANGE
B) Additionally,
C) However,
D) Therefore,

25
A) NO CHANGE
B) checking out
C) mining
D) taking a peek at

26
A) NO CHANGE
B) sector to
C) section, to
D) section to

CONTINUE

Salaries are also attractive: the average starting salary of a data analyst is almost $50,000 more than **27** that as a computer programmer.

28 Another draw of the field of data analytics is that specialized knowledge of a particular field is not necessarily a requirement. While it may seem that a background in healthcare would be prerequisite for making sense of medical data, the analyst's job is very much a collaborative one. Doctors and epidemiologists, for example, work alongside data analysts, who can design algorithms tailored to the needs of particular research projects. An expert in statistics can open researchers' eyes to new ways of using **29** his or her information, and such collaborations ultimately lead to innovations that benefit society at large.

30 According to the Bureau of Labor Statistics,

27

A) NO CHANGE

B) that of

C) those of

D) DELETE the underlined portion.

28

Which choice is the best introduction to the paragraph?

A) NO CHANGE

B) More and more schools are offering degree programs in data analytics.

C) Epidemiology is one example of a field in which data analytics is of fundamental importance.

D) Some companies are creating new positions for data analysts, while others are adding the duties to positions that already exist.

29

A) NO CHANGE

B) there

C) they're

D) their

30

At this point, the writer is considering adding the following sentence:

> Since there is no standard certification or job title for those who analyze big data, it can be difficult to quantify exactly how much the field is growing.

Should the writer make this addition here?

A) Yes, because it introduces an issue that is further discussed in the paragraph.

B) Yes, because it offers additional details about a point made in the previous paragraph.

C) No, because it strays from the main focus of the paragraph.

D) No, because it contradicts the ideas presented later in the paragraph.

CONTINUE →

related job **31** titles (including operations research analyst and statistician) have projected growth rates of up to 34% over the next ten years.

32 Big data is already used to schedule our UPS deliveries and to recommend music and movies for us to stream. Within the next decade, it will no doubt become a part of nearly every other aspect of our **33** goings-on.

Projected Increase in Jobs Related to Data Analytics, 2014–2024

	2014 Number	2024 Number (predicted)	Projected Growth Rate
Statistician	30,000	40,100	34%
Operations Research Analyst	91,300	118,900	30%
Market Research Analyst	495,500	587,800	19%
Management Analyst	758,000	861,400	14%
Financial Analyst	277,600	309,900	12%

Data from Bureau of Labor Statistics, Occupational Outlook Handbook, http://www.bls.gov/ooh/

31

A) NO CHANGE

B) titles: including operations research analyst and statistician,

C) titles including operations research analyst, and statistician,

D) titles, including operations research analyst and statistician

32

At this point, the writer is considering adding the following sentence.

> In fact, operations research analyst positions are projected to have the greatest number of jobs in the field by 2024.

Should the writer make this addition?

A) Yes, because it includes surprising data that makes the argument more interesting.

B) Yes, because it summarizes the central thesis of the passage.

C) No, because it is only tangentially related to the main idea of the passage.

D) No, because it is not supported by the data presented in the table.

33

A) NO CHANGE

B) habits.

C) usual procedure.

D) daily lives.

CONTINUE

Questions 34–44 are based on the following passage.

The Near-Death and Rebirth of Rock

Every generation can be defined by its music: the GI Generation is sometimes called the Jazz Generation. The Silent Generation had big band and swing, and Baby Boomers, of course, had rock and roll. But there was a time during the [34] delayed '50s and early '60s when it seemed that rock and roll might be a short-lived fad.

The film *Blackboard* [35] *Jungle,* which featured the song "Rock Around the Clock" by Bill Haley and his Comets—catapulted popular culture into the rock-and-roll era in 1955. The movie sparked controversy, [36] moreover, with some theaters cutting the iconic opening song, others refusing to show it at all, and large crowds of teenagers flocking to see it wherever they could. The following year, Elvis Presley [37] will appear on the Ed Sullivan show, thrilling and scandalizing audiences nationwide with his pompadour and his hip-swiveling dance moves.

34

A) NO CHANGE
B) tardy
C) behind
D) late

35

A) NO CHANGE
B) *Jungle*—
C) *Jungle*:
D) *Jungle*;

36

A) NO CHANGE
B) and,
C) however,
D) as a result,

37

A) NO CHANGE
B) appearing
C) appeared
D) was appearing

CONTINUE

Rock and roll was widely embraced as the [38] symbol, of a new, rebellious generation. Chuck Berry, Little Richard, Buddy Holly, and Jerry Lee Lewis expanded on the groundwork laid by Bill Haley and Elvis, bringing bluesy rhythms and exuberant, danceable energy to popular music. [39] Les Paul's innovations in developing a solid-body electric guitar helped make this kind of music possible.

38

A) NO CHANGE

B) symbol of

C) symbol: of

D) symbol of,

39

The writer wants a conclusion to the paragraph that logically completes the discussion of the popularity of early rock and provides an effective transition into the next paragraph. Which choice best accomplishes these goals?

A) NO CHANGE

B) Popular new dance moves, such as the Hand Jive, popped up alongside the new style of music.

C) The television show American Bandstand, which focused exclusively on Top 40 hits, helped popularize rock music.

D) It seemed as if the rise of rock and roll was unstoppable.

CONTINUE

But in the late 50s, one by one, **40** rock musicians began to expand their musical styles, incorporating elements of gospel and classical music. Buddy Holly was killed in a plane crash. Elvis was drafted. Little Richard abandoned music and became a preacher. Others were marred by scandal: Jerry Lee Lewis married his 13-year-old cousin, and Chuck Berry **41** debuted his signature duck walk, hopping across the stage on one foot while playing the guitar. As the big stars dropped off, it was as if those who viewed rock and roll as dangerous and degenerate had been correct: nothing good was coming of it.

40

Which choice most effectively sets up the main idea of the paragraph?

A) NO CHANGE

B) the icons of early rock disappeared from the music scene.

C) rock musicians began to write their own songs instead of just playing covers of already-established hits.

D) British rock bands began to gain popularity in the United States.

41

Which choice is most consistent with the examples in the previous sentences?

A) NO CHANGE

B) opened some of the first integrated music clubs in St. Louis.

C) served time in jail for having improper relations with a minor.

D) combined blues, country, and R&B in an innovative new way.

CONTINUE

The Beatles changed everything in 1963, when their songs were first aired on American radio. In early 1964, two of The **42** Beatles' album's, were released in the United States, followed quickly by an appearance on the Ed Sullivan show and their first American tour. The Beatles had been inspired by Buddy Holly, and young American audiences loved these new stars even more than they had loved **43** those of the late 50s. **44** Elvis' dance moves had met with disapproval from older generations. The Beatles' shaggy hairdos were seen as a symbol of rebellion by parents of the band's fans. Young fans, however, embraced everything The Beatles stood for, and the band members relished their roles as leaders of a revolutionary youth culture. Over the course of the 1960s, the band's music became increasingly experimental and political, reflecting the changing interests of its audience, but rock's popularity never again waned.

42

A) NO CHANGE

B) Beatles' albums

C) Beatles album's

D) Beatle's album's

43

A) NO CHANGE

B) them

C) these

D) DELETE the underlined portion.

44

Which choice most effectively combines the underlined sentences?

A) Just as Elvis' dance moves had met with disapproval from older generations, The Beatles' shaggy hairdos were seen as a symbol of rebellion by parents of the band's fans.

B) Elvis' dance moves had met with disapproval from older generations, even though The Beatles' shaggy hairdos were seen as a symbol of rebellion by parents of the band's fans.

C) In the same way that Elvis' popular dance moves made older generations disapproving in their style, The Beatles' hairdos, which were seen by many parents as shaggy, were widely taken by the band's fans to be a symbol of rebellion.

D) The Beatles' hairdos were met with disapproval from parents of the band's fans in being shaggy and rebellious, just as Elvis' dance moves had met with disapproval from older generations.

STOP
If you finish before time is called, you may check your work on this section only.
Do not turn to any other section in the test.

Math Test – No Calculator

25 MINUTES, 20 QUESTIONS

Turn to Section 3 of your answer sheet to answer the questions in this section.

DIRECTIONS

For questions 1–15, solve each problem, choose the best answer from the choices provided, and fill in the corresponding circle on your answer sheet. **For questions 16–20,** solve the problem and enter your answer in the grid on the answer sheet. Please refer to the directions before question 16 on how to enter your answers in the grid. You may use any available space in your test booklet for scratch work.

NOTES

1. The use of a calculator **is not permitted**.
2. All variables and expressions used represent real numbers unless otherwise indicated.
3. Figures provided in this test are drawn to scale unless otherwise indicated.
4. All figures lie in a plane unless otherwise indicated.
5. Unless otherwise indicated, the domain of a given function f is the set of all real numbers x for which $f(x)$ is a real number.

REFERENCE

$$A = \pi r^2$$
$$C = 2\pi r$$

$$A = \ell w$$

$$A = \tfrac{1}{2} bh$$

$$c^2 = a^2 + b^2$$

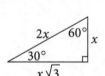
Special Right Triangles

$$V = \ell wh$$

$$V = \pi r^2 h$$

$$V = \tfrac{4}{3} \pi r^3$$

$$V = \tfrac{1}{3} \pi r^2 h$$

$$V = \tfrac{1}{3} \ell wh$$

The number of degrees of arc in a circle is 360.
The number of radians of arc in a circle is 2π.
The sum of the measures in degrees of the angles of a triangle is 180.

CONTINUE

1

What is the sum of the complex numbers $3 + 6i$ and $7 + 2i$, where $i = \sqrt{-1}$?

A) $10 + 8i$

B) $21 + 12i$

C) 18

D) $18i$

2

Abigail creates a pricing plan for her job as a piano instructor. She charges a one-time registration fee to every client in order to begin instruction. The equation $C = 40h + 100$ represents the total amount C, in dollars, that Abigail charges for h hours of lessons. What does 100 represent in the equation?

A) The amount of the registration fee, in dollars

B) The total amount, in dollars, Abigail will charge for one hour

C) The total amount, in dollars, Abigail will charge for any number of hours

D) The price of one hour, in dollars

3

A jeweler obtains two samples of gold. Sample F weighs 220 ounces and Sample G weighs 140 ounces. The samples bought by the jeweler contain a total of 150 ounces of pure gold. Which equation models this relationship, where a is the percent of pure gold, expressed as a decimal, of Sample F and b is the percent of pure gold, expressed as a decimal, of Sample G?

A) $1.4a + 2.2b = 150$

B) $2.2a + 1.4b = 150$

C) $140a + 220b = 150$

D) $220a + 140b = 150$

4

If $a = \frac{4}{5}b$ and $b = 15$, what is the value of $4a - 5$?

A) 8

B) 10

C) 12

D) 43

CONTINUE

5

$$(cy - d)(cy + d) = 25y^2 - 16$$

Which of the following could be the value of c in the equation above, where c and d are constants?

A) 4

B) 5

C) 16

D) 25

6

If $\sqrt{49} = \sqrt{y} - \sqrt{16}$, what is the value of y?

A) 121

B) 65

C) 11

D) $\sqrt{11}$

7

Which of the following is the graph of the equation $y = \dfrac{1}{3}x - 2$ in the xy-plane?

A)

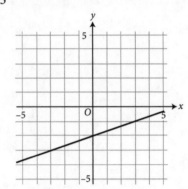

B)

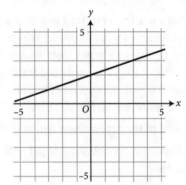

C)

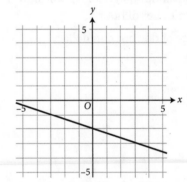

D)

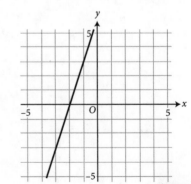

CONTINUE

8

A wedding band uses the equation $F = 300nh$ to estimate the fee F, in dollars, it charges for a wedding that requires n musicians and lasts h hours. Which of the following correctly expresses h, in terms of F and n?

A) $h = \dfrac{F}{300 + n}$

B) $h = \dfrac{F}{300n}$

C) $h = \dfrac{n}{300F}$

D) $h = \dfrac{300}{nF}$

9

s	$r(s)$	$t(s)$
0	−1	−1
1	2	1
2	3	1
3	−1	−3
4	−2	3

The table above shows some values for the functions r and t. For which value of s is $r(s) \times t(s) = s$?

A) 0

B) 1

C) 2

D) 3

10

Which of the following is equivalent to $\dfrac{2y^2 + 5y}{2y + 7}$?

A) $y - 1 + \dfrac{7}{2y + 7}$

B) $\dfrac{7}{2y + 7}$

C) $y + 2$

D) y

11

Renee is taking a calculus class. Her goal is to have the average score on her 3 tests be at least a 90. She scored 99 on the first test and 83 on the second test. Which inequality can be used to represent the score, s, that Renee could receive on the 3rd test to meet her goal?

A) $\dfrac{99}{3} + \dfrac{83}{3} + s \geq 90$

B) $99 + 83 + s \geq 3(90)$

C) $\dfrac{99 + 83}{2} + s \geq 90$

D) $99 + 83 \geq s(90)$

CONTINUE

12

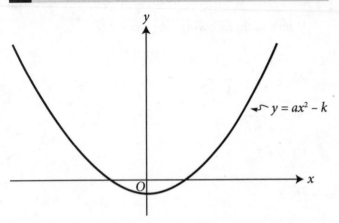

The vertex of the parabola in the xy-plane above is $(0, -k)$. Which of the following is true about the parabola with the equation $y = -a(x + j)^2 - k$?

A) The graph opens downward and the vertex is $(j, -k)$.

B) The graph opens upward and the vertex is $(j, -k)$.

C) The graph opens downward and the vertex is $(-j, -k)$.

D) The graph opens upward and the vertex is $(-j, -k)$.

13

Which of the following is equivalent to $\left(\dfrac{x}{2} - y \right)^2$?

A) $\dfrac{x^2}{2} + y^2$

B) $\dfrac{x^2}{4} + y^2$

C) $\dfrac{x^2}{4} - xy + y^2$

D) $\dfrac{x^2}{2} - \dfrac{xy}{2} + y^2$

14

$$4x^2 - 5x = k$$

In the equation above, k is a constant. If the equation has two real solutions, which of the following could be the value of k ?

A) -4

B) -3

C) -2

D) -1

15

A clothing store owner is buying T-shirts and pairs of jeans from a wholesaler. She wants to buy at least three times as many T-shirts as pairs of jeans. She will spend no more than \$200 on the order. Each T-shirt that is ordered costs the store \$1.25, and each pair of jeans that is ordered costs the store \$9.75. Let t represent the number of T-shirts ordered and j represent the number of pairs of jeans ordered, where t and j are nonnegative integers. Which of the following systems of inequalities best expresses this situation?

A) $t \geq 3j$
$3.75t + 9.75j \leq 200$

B) $3t \geq j$
$3.75t + 9.75j \leq 200$

C) $t \geq 3j$
$1.25t + 9.75j \leq 200$

D) $3t \geq j$
$1.25t + 9.75j \leq 200$

CONTINUE

DIRECTIONS

For questions 16–20, solve the problem and enter your answer in the grid, as described below, on the answer sheet.

1. Although not required, it is suggested that you write your answer in the boxes at the top of the columns to help you fill in the circles accurately. You will receive credit only if the circles are filled in correctly.

2. Mark no more than one circle in any column.

3. No question has a negative answer.

4. Some problems may have more than one correct answer. In such cases, grid only one answer.

5. **Mixed numbers** such as $3\frac{1}{2}$ must be gridded as 3.5 or 7/2. (If is entered into the grid, it will be interpreted as $\frac{31}{2}$, not as $3\frac{1}{2}$.)

6. **Decimal Answers:** If you obtain a decimal answer with more digits than the grid can accommodate, it may be either rounded or truncated, but it must fill the entire grid.

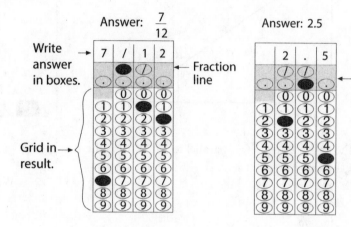

Answer: $\frac{7}{12}$ Answer: 2.5

Write answer in boxes. → Fraction line

Grid in result.

Decimal point

Acceptable ways to grid $\frac{2}{3}$ are:

Answer: 201 – either position is correct

NOTE: You may start your answers in any column, space permitting. Columns you don't need to use should be left blank.

CONTINUE ➡

16

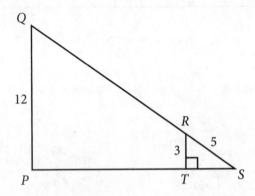

In the figure above, $\overline{PQ}$ is parallel to $\overline{RT}$. What is the length of $\overline{PS}$?

17

If $r^{\frac{s}{2}} = 64$ for positive integers r and s, what is one possible value of s ?

18

Points P and Q lie on a circle with radius 2, and arc $\overset{\frown}{PQ}$ has length $\dfrac{\pi}{6}$. What fraction of the circumference is the length of arc $\overset{\frown}{PQ}$?

19

$$\frac{4}{7}a = \frac{7}{2}$$

What value of a is the solution to the equation above?

CONTINUE

20

How many gallons of a juice mix that is 60% orange juice must be added to 5 gallons of a juice mix that is 30% orange juice to obtain a juice mix that is 40% orange juice?

STOP
If you finish before time is called, you may check your work on this section only.
Do not turn to any other section in the test.

Math Test – Calculator

55 MINUTES, 38 QUESTIONS

Turn to Section 4 of your answer sheet to answer the questions in this section.

DIRECTIONS

For questions 1–30, solve each problem, choose the best answer from the choices provided, and fill in the corresponding circle on your answer sheet. **For questions 31–38**, solve the problem and enter your answer in the grid on the answer sheet. Please refer to the directions before question 31 on how to enter your answers in the grid. You may use any available space in your test booklet for scratch work.

NOTES

1. The use of a calculator **is permitted**.
2. All variables and expressions used represent real numbers unless otherwise indicated.
3. Figures provided in this test are drawn to scale unless otherwise indicated.
4. All figures lie in a plane unless otherwise indicated.
5. Unless otherwise indicated, the domain of a given function f is the set of all real numbers x for which $f(x)$ is a real number.

REFERENCE

$A = \pi r^2$
$C = 2\pi r$

$A = \ell w$

$A = \frac{1}{2} bh$

$c^2 = a^2 + b^2$

Special Right Triangles

$V = \ell wh$

$V = \pi r^2 h$

$V = \frac{4}{3}\pi r^3$

$V = \frac{1}{3}\pi r^2 h$

$V = \frac{1}{3}\ell wh$

The number of degrees of arc in a circle is 360.
The number of radians of arc in a circle is 2π.
The sum of the measures in degrees of the angles of a triangle is 180.

CONTINUE ➡

1

Laura went out for a run. After running for a while, she stopped to sit on a park bench and rest. When she started running again, she was tired, and ran at a slower rate than she had initially. Which of the following graphs could model the distance Laura ran versus time?

A)

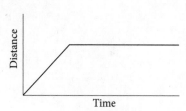

B)

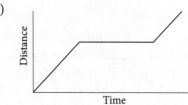

C)

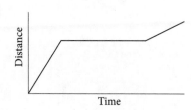

D)

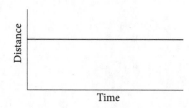

2

What expression is equivalent to
$(3y^2 - 2) - (-5y^2 + 3y - 6)$?

A) $-2y^2 + 3y - 4$

B) $-2y^2 - 3y - 4$

C) $8y^2 + 3y - 4$

D) $8y^2 - 3y + 4$

3

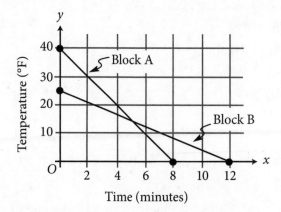

The graph above shows the temperature of two different blocks of metal that are being cooled in a freezer to a temperature of 0 degrees Fahrenheit. Both blocks lose heat at a constant rate, and Block B started at a lower initial temperature to decrease the time required to cool it. Block A took 8 minutes to cool to 0 degrees Fahrenheit and Block B took 12 minutes to cool to 0 degrees Fahrenheit. According to the graph, what was the difference, in degrees Fahrenheit, between the initial temperatures of Block A and Block B?

A) 10

B) 15

C) 20

D) 25

CONTINUE

4

Who is Your Internet Service Provider?

Internet Service Provider	Percent of Households
Corporate Cable	47%
Speedy Connections	21%
Global Networks	17%
Dave's Dial-Up	12%
Other	3%

The table above summarizes a census of 2,800 households within a small community. Based on the table, how many households receive their Internet service from either Corporate Cable or Global Networks?

A) 1,792

B) 1,843

C) 1,904

D) 2,039

5

An office supply vendor that delivers printer ink to companies charges a subscription fee of $230 for its services plus x dollars for each carton of ink. If a company paid $1,364 for 18 cartons of ink, including the subscription fee, what is the value of x?

A) 46

B) 52

C) 63

D) 78

6

$$16a + 20b > 12$$

Which of the following inequalities is equivalent to the inequality above?

A) $5b + 4a > 4$

B) $5a + 4b > 3$

C) $a + b > 4$

D) $4a + 5b > 3$

7

In May of 1937, American aviation pioneer Amelia Earhart attempted to circumnavigate the globe. According to flight logs, the first stage of the trip was 110 nautical miles less than the second stage of the trip, and the two stages combined totaled 676 nautical miles. How many nautical miles was the first stage?

A) 249

B) 283

C) 327

D) 390

CONTINUE

8

The total weight of a carton of oranges is 27.3 pounds, of which 9.6 pounds is the weight of the carton itself. If a fruit vendor pays $46.25 for a carton of oranges, which of the following is closest to the cost of the oranges, in dollars per pound?

A) $6.50

B) $4.80

C) $2.60

D) $1.70

9

The board of directors at a natural history museum decided to survey all of its scientists to determine if the new wing in the museum should feature an aquatic exhibit. The board met with a sample group of 30 marine biologists. The majority of the sample group were in favor of featuring an aquatic exhibit in the new wing. Which of the following is true about the board's survey?

A) The sample group should have included more marine biologists.

B) It concludes that a majority of the scientists are in favor of featuring an aquatic exhibit in the new wing.

C) The sample group is biased because it is not representative of all scientists.

D) The sample group should have consisted only of scientists who are not marine biologists.

10

Adopted Animal Characteristics

		Species	
		Dogs	Cats
Color	Brown	13	9
	Black	21	7

An animal shelter held an adoption event to find new homes for a group of dogs and cats. The table above shows the number and color of dogs and cats that were adopted at the event. Each animal was classified as only one color. Of the cats that were adopted, what fraction were black?

A) $\dfrac{7}{16}$

B) $\dfrac{9}{16}$

C) $\dfrac{7}{50}$

D) $\dfrac{16}{50}$

CONTINUE

Questions 11–13 refer to the following information.

Arctic Sea Ice	
Study Year	Extent (million km²)
0	5.98
1	6.18
2	6.08
3	5.59
4	5.95
5	4.32
6	4.73
7	5.39
8	4.81
9	4.22
10	3.63
11	5.35
12	5.29
13	4.68
14	4.72

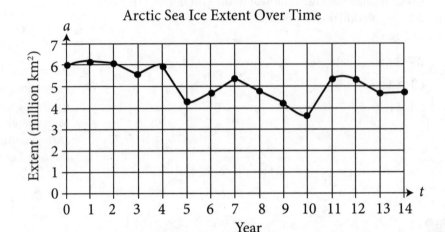

Arctic Sea Ice Extent Over Time

A team of research climatologists conducted a 14-year study to determine the change in the area of the Arctic sea covered with ice, termed the Arctic sea ice extent. The graph and table above model the extent a, in millions of square kilometers, of Arctic sea ice t years after the study began.

11

The function a, defined by $a(t) = c - dt$, where c and d are constants, models the extent, in millions of square kilometers, of Arctic sea ice t years after the start of the study during a period in which the change is approximately linear. What does d represent?

A) The predicted total decrease in extent, in millions of square kilometers, of Arctic sea ice during the period

B) The predicted decrease in extent, in millions of square kilometers, of Arctic sea ice per year during the period

C) The predicted extent, in millions of square kilometers, of Arctic sea ice at the beginning of the period

D) The predicted extent, in millions of square kilometers, of Arctic sea ice at the end of the period

12

The rate of decrease of Arctic sea ice extent from Year 7 to Year 10 is nearly constant. On this interval, which of the following best models the extent a, in millions of square kilometers, of Arctic sea ice t years after the study began?

A) $a = 5 - 0.21t$

B) $a = 7 - 0.13t$

C) $a = 10 - 0.64t$

D) $a = 15 - 1.82t$

13

Over which time period is the average decrease of Arctic sea ice extent the greatest?

A) Year 4 to Year 5

B) Year 7 to Year 8

C) Year 9 to Year 10

D) Year 12 to Year 13

CONTINUE

14

$$9c + 5d = 22$$
$$7c - 5d = 10$$

For the solution (c, d) to the system of equations above, what is the value of $c + d$?

A) $-\dfrac{6}{5}$

B) $\dfrac{6}{5}$

C) $\dfrac{7}{5}$

D) $\dfrac{14}{5}$

15

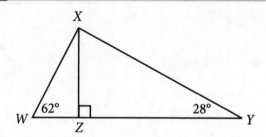

Triangle WXY is shown above. Which of the following is equal to the ratio $\dfrac{WZ}{WX}$?

A) $\dfrac{XZ}{XY}$

B) $\dfrac{XY}{XZ}$

C) $\dfrac{XZ}{YZ}$

D) $\dfrac{YZ}{XY}$

16

s	t
-2	$\dfrac{7}{2}$
-1	$\dfrac{19}{2}$
0	$\dfrac{31}{2}$
1	$\dfrac{43}{2}$
2	$\dfrac{55}{2}$

Which of the following equations relates t to s for the values in the table above?

A) $t = \dfrac{31}{2} \cdot (6)^{s}$

B) $t = 6s + \dfrac{31}{2}$

C) $t = \dfrac{1}{4} \cdot \left(\dfrac{31}{2}\right)^{s}$

D) $t = \dfrac{1}{6}s - 4$

CONTINUE

Questions 17–19 refer to the following information.

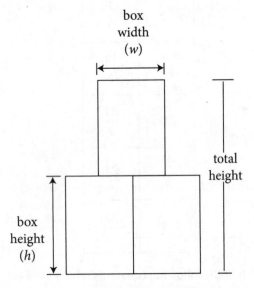

box
width
(w)

total
height

box
height
(h)

Note: Figure not drawn to scale.

When designing stacked displays of different types of crackers for sale, a manufacturer can use the box size formula $h + 3w = 30$, where h is the height of each box of crackers, in inches, and w is the width of each box of crackers, in inches. For any given stacked display, the height and width of each box displayed is the same.

The height of each level in the stacked display is equal to the height of the boxes of crackers in the display. For example, there are 2 levels in the figure above, each with a height of h. The total height of the stacked display is the sum of each level's height as shown in the figure.

17

Some cracker manufacturing companies require that, for wheat crackers, the box height must be at least 12 inches and the box width must be at least 3 inches. According to the box size formula, which of the following inequalities represents the set of all possible values for the box width that meets this size requirement?

A) $6 \le w \le 12$

B) $3 \le w \le 6$

C) $w \ge 3$

D) $0 \le w \le 3$

18

A manufacturer wants to use the box size formula to design a stacked display that has a total height of 7 feet, holds boxes with a height between 8 and 10 inches, and contains an even number of levels. With the manufacturer's constraints, which of the following must be the width, in inches, of the box? (1 foot = 12 inches)

A) 6.8

B) 7.2

C) 8.4

D) 10

19

Which of the following expresses the box width in terms of the box height?

A) $w = \dfrac{1}{3}(30 - h)$

B) $w = \dfrac{1}{3}(30 + h)$

C) $w = -\dfrac{1}{3}(30 - h)$

D) $w = -\dfrac{1}{3}(30 + h)$

CONTINUE

20

A study was done on the circumferences of different types of trees in a forest. A random sample of trees were measured and each tree was marked to guarantee that no tree was measured twice. The sample contained 250 red maple trees, of which 40% had a circumference less than 35 inches. Which of the following conclusions is best supported by the data?

A) The average circumference of all the trees in the forest is approximately 35 inches.

B) Approximately 40% of all the trees in the forest have circumferences less than 35 inches.

C) Approximately 40% of all the red maple trees in the forest have circumferences less than 35 inches.

D) The majority of all the trees in the forest have circumferences larger than 35 inches.

21

What is the product of the solutions to
$(y + 4)(y - 0.3) = 0$?

A) −1.2

B) −3.7

C) 3.7

D) 1.2

22

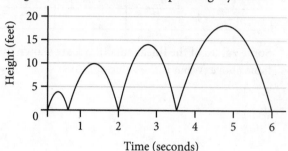

Height versus Time for a Trampolining Gymnast

To break a height record in a trampolining competition, a gymnast repeatedly bounced on a trampoline using increasing amounts of force to achieve greater heights. The graph above represents the relationship between the time elapsed after the start of the jumps and the height of the gymnast above the trampoline. How many times was the gymnast at a height of 15 feet?

A) Three

B) Two

C) One

D) None

23

A writer's salary was $81.34 per assignment. After a promotion and a raise, her salary is now $88.51 per assignment. To the nearest tenth of a percent, by what percent did the writer's salary increase?

A) 7.2%

B) 8.1%

C) 8.8%

D) 9.3%

CONTINUE

24

x	1	3	7
$h(x)$	−3	5	21

Some values of the linear function h are shown in the table above. What is the value of $h(6)$?

A) 14

B) 15

C) 16

D) 17

25

Number of U.S. Presidents Aged 60 or
Younger when Inaugurated

Age	Frequency
42	1
43	1
46	2
47	2
48	1
49	2
50	1
51	5
52	2
54	5
55	4
56	3
57	4
58	1
60	1

There are 35 U.S. Presidents who were 60 years old or younger when they were inaugurated, as shown in the table above. Based on the table, what was the median age for these 35 presidents?

A) 51

B) 52

C) 54

D) 55

26

In the xy-plane, the graph of $4x^2 + 20x + 4y^2 - 12y = 110$ is a circle. What is the radius of the circle?

A) $\sqrt{55}$

B) 34

C) 12

D) 6

27

The resistor ratio $a{:}b$ is the ratio of the current, in amperes, through two resistors connected in a parallel circuit. The ratio of resistance, in ohms, of two resistors connected in a parallel circuit is $b{:}a$. In the diagram below, the circuit is powered by a battery that passes current through Resistors X, Y, and Z.

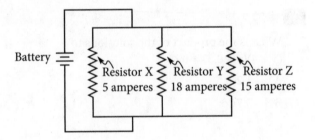

If Resistor X has a resistance of 24 ohms, what is the resistance of Resistor Z?

A) 8

B) 32

C) 72

D) 240

CONTINUE

28

Satellites orbit Earth so that it takes P seconds to complete one orbit when the satellite is a meters from the center of the planet, where $P = 36 \times 10^{-8} \, a\sqrt{a}$. Which of the following gives the approximate orbital ratio, in seconds per meter, for a satellite a meters away from the center of Earth?

A) $6 \times 10^{-4} \sqrt{a}$

B) $\dfrac{36 \times 10^{-8}}{\sqrt{a}}$

C) $36 \times 10^{-8} \, a$

D) $36 \times 10^{-8} \sqrt{a}$

29

The scatterplot below shows the number of soft drinks sold, in thousands of gallons, by fast food restaurants over a 15-year period.

Soft Drinks Sold by Fast Food Restaurants

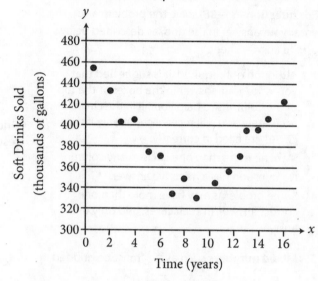

Of the following equations, which best models the data in the scatterplot?

A) $y = 2.138x^2 - 38.44x + 483.27$

B) $y = 2.138x^2 + 38.44x - 483.27$

C) $y = -2.138x^2 - 38.44x - 483.27$

D) $y = -2.138x^2 - 38.44x + 483.27$

30

On a number line, two different points are both 5 units from the point with coordinate −6. The solution to which of the following equations gives the coordinates of both points?

A) $\left| y - 6 \right| = 5$

B) $\left| y + 6 \right| = 5$

C) $\left| y - 5 \right| = 6$

D) $\left| y + 5 \right| = 6$

CONTINUE

DIRECTIONS

For questions 31–38, solve the problem and enter your answer in the grid, as described below, on the answer sheet.

1. Although not required, it is suggested that you write your answer in the boxes at the top of the columns to help you fill in the circles accurately. You will receive credit only if the circles are filled in correctly.

2. Mark no more than one circle in any column.

3. No question has a negative answer.

4. Some problems may have more than one correct answer. In such cases, grid only one answer.

5. **Mixed numbers** such as $3\frac{1}{2}$ must be gridded as 3.5 or 7/2. (If $\boxed{3\ 1\ /\ 2}$ is entered into the grid, it will be interpreted as $\frac{31}{2}$, not as $3\frac{1}{2}$.)

6. **Decimal Answers:** If you obtain a decimal answer with more digits than the grid can accommodate, it may be either rounded or truncated, but it must fill the entire grid.

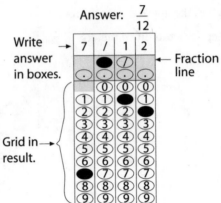

Answer: $\frac{7}{12}$ — Write answer in boxes. Fraction line. Grid in result.

Answer: 2.5 — Decimal point.

Acceptable ways to grid $\frac{2}{3}$ are:

Answer: 201 – either position is correct

NOTE: You may start your answers in any column, space permitting. Columns you don't need to use should be left blank.

CONTINUE ▶

31

A baking company produces ice cream cones, each with an internal radius at the opening of 4 centimeters and an internal height between 14.75 centimeters and 15 centimeters. What is one possible volume, rounded to the nearest cubic centimeter, of an ice cream cone produced by this company?

32

A group of coworkers decided to buy their boss a $400 birthday gift and to split the cost equally among themselves. When three of the coworkers decided not to contribute, those remaining still divided the $400 birthday gift equally, but each coworker's share of the cost increased by $30. How many coworkers were in the group originally?

33

$$3(4k - 10) - (26 + 5k) = 21$$

What value of k satisfies the equation above?

34

The line with the equation $-\dfrac{3}{4}x + \dfrac{5}{6}y = 1$ is graphed in the xy-plane. What is the y-coordinate of the y-intercept of the line?

CONTINUE

35

	Height (feet)				
Robert	3.9	6.1	4.4	5.3	5.8
Louis	h	4.5	5.7	4.2	3.8

Robert and Louis each have five rose bushes, and the heights of the bushes are shown in the table above. The mean of the heights of Robert's rose bushes is 0.3 feet greater than the mean of the heights of Louis's rose bushes. What is the value of h ?

36

In the xy-plane, the graph of $y = -4x^2 + 25x$ intersects the graph of $y = x$ at the points $(0, 0)$ and (c, c). What is the value of c ?

37

John is analyzing the monthly expenditures of his business to determine whether his expenses exceeded his predicted budget. Of the money he spent this month, 10% was for office supplies, 40% was for employee salaries, 35% was for rent, and the remaining \$450 was for utilities. How much more money, in dollars, did John spend on rent than on office supplies? (Ignore the dollar sign when gridding your response.)

38

An elementary school had k kindergarten students enrolled at the beginning of the 2011 school year. The number of kindergarten students enrolled tripled each year until 2014, when the elementary school had 540 kindergarten students enrolled. What is the value of k ?

END OF TEST

DO NOT RETURN TO A PREVIOUS SECTION.

Completely darken bubbles with a No. 2 pencil. If you make a mistake, be sure to erase mark completely. Erase all stray marks.

1.

YOUR NAME: _____
(Print)   Last   First   M.I.

SIGNATURE: _____   DATE: / /

HOME ADDRESS: _____
(Print)   Number and Street

_____
City   State   Zip Code

PHONE NO.: _____
(Print)

IMPORTANT: Please fill in these boxes exactly as shown on the back cover of your test book.

2. TEST FORM

6. DATE OF BIRTH

Month		Day		Year	
○ JAN					
○ FEB	⓪	⓪	⓪	⓪	
○ MAR	①	①	①	①	
○ APR	②	②	②	②	
○ MAY	③	③	③	③	
○ JUN		④	④	④	
○ JUL		⑤	⑤	⑤	
○ AUG		⑥	⑥	⑥	
○ SEP		⑦	⑦	⑦	
○ OCT		⑧	⑧	⑧	
○ NOV		⑨	⑨	⑨	
○ DEC					

3. TEST CODE   **4. REGISTRATION NUMBER**

⓪ Ⓐ Ⓙ ⓪ ⓪ ⓪ ⓪ ⓪ ⓪ ⓪ ⓪ ⓪
① Ⓑ Ⓚ ① ① ① ① ① ① ① ① ①
② Ⓒ Ⓛ ② ② ② ② ② ② ② ② ②
③ Ⓓ Ⓜ ③ ③ ③ ③ ③ ③ ③ ③ ③
④ Ⓔ Ⓝ ④ ④ ④ ④ ④ ④ ④ ④ ④
⑤ Ⓕ Ⓞ ⑤ ⑤ ⑤ ⑤ ⑤ ⑤ ⑤ ⑤ ⑤
⑥ Ⓖ Ⓟ ⑥ ⑥ ⑥ ⑥ ⑥ ⑥ ⑥ ⑥ ⑥
⑦ Ⓗ Ⓠ ⑦ ⑦ ⑦ ⑦ ⑦ ⑦ ⑦ ⑦ ⑦
⑧ Ⓘ Ⓡ ⑧ ⑧ ⑧ ⑧ ⑧ ⑧ ⑧ ⑧ ⑧
⑨ ⑨ ⑨ ⑨ ⑨ ⑨ ⑨ ⑨ ⑨ ⑨

7. SEX
○ MALE
○ FEMALE

The **Princeton Review**®

5. YOUR NAME

First 4 letters of last name				FIRST INIT	MID INIT
Ⓐ	Ⓐ	Ⓐ	Ⓐ	Ⓐ	Ⓐ
Ⓑ	Ⓑ	Ⓑ	Ⓑ	Ⓑ	Ⓑ
Ⓒ	Ⓒ	Ⓒ	Ⓒ	Ⓒ	Ⓒ
Ⓓ	Ⓓ	Ⓓ	Ⓓ	Ⓓ	Ⓓ
Ⓔ	Ⓔ	Ⓔ	Ⓔ	Ⓔ	Ⓔ
Ⓕ	Ⓕ	Ⓕ	Ⓕ	Ⓕ	Ⓕ
Ⓖ	Ⓖ	Ⓖ	Ⓖ	Ⓖ	Ⓖ
Ⓗ	Ⓗ	Ⓗ	Ⓗ	Ⓗ	Ⓗ
Ⓘ	Ⓘ	Ⓘ	Ⓘ	Ⓘ	Ⓘ
Ⓙ	Ⓙ	Ⓙ	Ⓙ	Ⓙ	Ⓙ
Ⓚ	Ⓚ	Ⓚ	Ⓚ	Ⓚ	Ⓚ
Ⓛ	Ⓛ	Ⓛ	Ⓛ	Ⓛ	Ⓛ
Ⓜ	Ⓜ	Ⓜ	Ⓜ	Ⓜ	Ⓜ
Ⓝ	Ⓝ	Ⓝ	Ⓝ	Ⓝ	Ⓝ
Ⓞ	Ⓞ	Ⓞ	Ⓞ	Ⓞ	Ⓞ
Ⓟ	Ⓟ	Ⓟ	Ⓟ	Ⓟ	Ⓟ
Ⓠ	Ⓠ	Ⓠ	Ⓠ	Ⓠ	Ⓠ
Ⓡ	Ⓡ	Ⓡ	Ⓡ	Ⓡ	Ⓡ
Ⓢ	Ⓢ	Ⓢ	Ⓢ	Ⓢ	Ⓢ
Ⓣ	Ⓣ	Ⓣ	Ⓣ	Ⓣ	Ⓣ
Ⓤ	Ⓤ	Ⓤ	Ⓤ	Ⓤ	Ⓤ
Ⓥ	Ⓥ	Ⓥ	Ⓥ	Ⓥ	Ⓥ
Ⓦ	Ⓦ	Ⓦ	Ⓦ	Ⓦ	Ⓦ
Ⓧ	Ⓧ	Ⓧ	Ⓧ	Ⓧ	Ⓧ
Ⓨ	Ⓨ	Ⓨ	Ⓨ	Ⓨ	Ⓨ
Ⓩ	Ⓩ	Ⓩ	Ⓩ	Ⓩ	Ⓩ

Test ⑧   Start with number 1 for each new section.
If a section has fewer questions than answer spaces, leave the extra answer spaces blank.

Section 1—Reading

1. Ⓐ Ⓑ Ⓒ Ⓓ
2. Ⓐ Ⓑ Ⓒ Ⓓ
3. Ⓐ Ⓑ Ⓒ Ⓓ
4. Ⓐ Ⓑ Ⓒ Ⓓ
5. Ⓐ Ⓑ Ⓒ Ⓓ
6. Ⓐ Ⓑ Ⓒ Ⓓ
7. Ⓐ Ⓑ Ⓒ Ⓓ
8. Ⓐ Ⓑ Ⓒ Ⓓ
9. Ⓐ Ⓑ Ⓒ Ⓓ
10. Ⓐ Ⓑ Ⓒ Ⓓ
11. Ⓐ Ⓑ Ⓒ Ⓓ
12. Ⓐ Ⓑ Ⓒ Ⓓ
13. Ⓐ Ⓑ Ⓒ Ⓓ
14. Ⓐ Ⓑ Ⓒ Ⓓ
15. Ⓐ Ⓑ Ⓒ Ⓓ
16. Ⓐ Ⓑ Ⓒ Ⓓ
17. Ⓐ Ⓑ Ⓒ Ⓓ
18. Ⓐ Ⓑ Ⓒ Ⓓ
19. Ⓐ Ⓑ Ⓒ Ⓓ
20. Ⓐ Ⓑ Ⓒ Ⓓ
21. Ⓐ Ⓑ Ⓒ Ⓓ
22. Ⓐ Ⓑ Ⓒ Ⓓ
23. Ⓐ Ⓑ Ⓒ Ⓓ
24. Ⓐ Ⓑ Ⓒ Ⓓ
25. Ⓐ Ⓑ Ⓒ Ⓓ
26. Ⓐ Ⓑ Ⓒ Ⓓ
27. Ⓐ Ⓑ Ⓒ Ⓓ
28. Ⓐ Ⓑ Ⓒ Ⓓ
29. Ⓐ Ⓑ Ⓒ Ⓓ
30. Ⓐ Ⓑ Ⓒ Ⓓ
31. Ⓐ Ⓑ Ⓒ Ⓓ
32. Ⓐ Ⓑ Ⓒ Ⓓ
33. Ⓐ Ⓑ Ⓒ Ⓓ
34. Ⓐ Ⓑ Ⓒ Ⓓ
35. Ⓐ Ⓑ Ⓒ Ⓓ
36. Ⓐ Ⓑ Ⓒ Ⓓ
37. Ⓐ Ⓑ Ⓒ Ⓓ
38. Ⓐ Ⓑ Ⓒ Ⓓ
39. Ⓐ Ⓑ Ⓒ Ⓓ
40. Ⓐ Ⓑ Ⓒ Ⓓ
41. Ⓐ Ⓑ Ⓒ Ⓓ
42. Ⓐ Ⓑ Ⓒ Ⓓ
43. Ⓐ Ⓑ Ⓒ Ⓓ
44. Ⓐ Ⓑ Ⓒ Ⓓ
45. Ⓐ Ⓑ Ⓒ Ⓓ
46. Ⓐ Ⓑ Ⓒ Ⓓ
47. Ⓐ Ⓑ Ⓒ Ⓓ
48. Ⓐ Ⓑ Ⓒ Ⓓ
49. Ⓐ Ⓑ Ⓒ Ⓓ
50. Ⓐ Ⓑ Ⓒ Ⓓ
51. Ⓐ Ⓑ Ⓒ Ⓓ
52. Ⓐ Ⓑ Ⓒ Ⓓ

Section 2—Writing and Language Skills

1. Ⓐ Ⓑ Ⓒ Ⓓ
2. Ⓐ Ⓑ Ⓒ Ⓓ
3. Ⓐ Ⓑ Ⓒ Ⓓ
4. Ⓐ Ⓑ Ⓒ Ⓓ
5. Ⓐ Ⓑ Ⓒ Ⓓ
6. Ⓐ Ⓑ Ⓒ Ⓓ
7. Ⓐ Ⓑ Ⓒ Ⓓ
8. Ⓐ Ⓑ Ⓒ Ⓓ
9. Ⓐ Ⓑ Ⓒ Ⓓ
10. Ⓐ Ⓑ Ⓒ Ⓓ
11. Ⓐ Ⓑ Ⓒ Ⓓ
12. Ⓐ Ⓑ Ⓒ Ⓓ
13. Ⓐ Ⓑ Ⓒ Ⓓ
14. Ⓐ Ⓑ Ⓒ Ⓓ
15. Ⓐ Ⓑ Ⓒ Ⓓ
16. Ⓐ Ⓑ Ⓒ Ⓓ
17. Ⓐ Ⓑ Ⓒ Ⓓ
18. Ⓐ Ⓑ Ⓒ Ⓓ
19. Ⓐ Ⓑ Ⓒ Ⓓ
20. Ⓐ Ⓑ Ⓒ Ⓓ
21. Ⓐ Ⓑ Ⓒ Ⓓ
22. Ⓐ Ⓑ Ⓒ Ⓓ
23. Ⓐ Ⓑ Ⓒ Ⓓ
24. Ⓐ Ⓑ Ⓒ Ⓓ
25. Ⓐ Ⓑ Ⓒ Ⓓ
26. Ⓐ Ⓑ Ⓒ Ⓓ
27. Ⓐ Ⓑ Ⓒ Ⓓ
28. Ⓐ Ⓑ Ⓒ Ⓓ
29. Ⓐ Ⓑ Ⓒ Ⓓ
30. Ⓐ Ⓑ Ⓒ Ⓓ
31. Ⓐ Ⓑ Ⓒ Ⓓ
32. Ⓐ Ⓑ Ⓒ Ⓓ
33. Ⓐ Ⓑ Ⓒ Ⓓ
34. Ⓐ Ⓑ Ⓒ Ⓓ
35. Ⓐ Ⓑ Ⓒ Ⓓ
36. Ⓐ Ⓑ Ⓒ Ⓓ
37. Ⓐ Ⓑ Ⓒ Ⓓ
38. Ⓐ Ⓑ Ⓒ Ⓓ
39. Ⓐ Ⓑ Ⓒ Ⓓ
40. Ⓐ Ⓑ Ⓒ Ⓓ
41. Ⓐ Ⓑ Ⓒ Ⓓ
42. Ⓐ Ⓑ Ⓒ Ⓓ
43. Ⓐ Ⓑ Ⓒ Ⓓ
44. Ⓐ Ⓑ Ⓒ Ⓓ

Test 8

Start with number 1 for each new section.
If a section has fewer questions than answer spaces, leave the extra answer spaces blank.

Section 3—Mathematics: No Calculator

1. Ⓐ Ⓑ Ⓒ Ⓓ
2. Ⓐ Ⓑ Ⓒ Ⓓ
3. Ⓐ Ⓑ Ⓒ Ⓓ
4. Ⓐ Ⓑ Ⓒ Ⓓ
5. Ⓐ Ⓑ Ⓒ Ⓓ
6. Ⓐ Ⓑ Ⓒ Ⓓ
7. Ⓐ Ⓑ Ⓒ Ⓓ
8. Ⓐ Ⓑ Ⓒ Ⓓ
9. Ⓐ Ⓑ Ⓒ Ⓓ
10. Ⓐ Ⓑ Ⓒ Ⓓ
11. Ⓐ Ⓑ Ⓒ Ⓓ
12. Ⓐ Ⓑ Ⓒ Ⓓ
13. Ⓐ Ⓑ Ⓒ Ⓓ
14. Ⓐ Ⓑ Ⓒ Ⓓ
15. Ⓐ Ⓑ Ⓒ Ⓓ

16. 17. 18. 19. 20.

Section 4—Mathematics: Calculator

1. Ⓐ Ⓑ Ⓒ Ⓓ
2. Ⓐ Ⓑ Ⓒ Ⓓ
3. Ⓐ Ⓑ Ⓒ Ⓓ
4. Ⓐ Ⓑ Ⓒ Ⓓ
5. Ⓐ Ⓑ Ⓒ Ⓓ
6. Ⓐ Ⓑ Ⓒ Ⓓ
7. Ⓐ Ⓑ Ⓒ Ⓓ
8. Ⓐ Ⓑ Ⓒ Ⓓ
9. Ⓐ Ⓑ Ⓒ Ⓓ
10. Ⓐ Ⓑ Ⓒ Ⓓ
11. Ⓐ Ⓑ Ⓒ Ⓓ
12. Ⓐ Ⓑ Ⓒ Ⓓ
13. Ⓐ Ⓑ Ⓒ Ⓓ
14. Ⓐ Ⓑ Ⓒ Ⓓ
15. Ⓐ Ⓑ Ⓒ Ⓓ
16. Ⓐ Ⓑ Ⓒ Ⓓ
17. Ⓐ Ⓑ Ⓒ Ⓓ
18. Ⓐ Ⓑ Ⓒ Ⓓ
19. Ⓐ Ⓑ Ⓒ Ⓓ
20. Ⓐ Ⓑ Ⓒ Ⓓ
21. Ⓐ Ⓑ Ⓒ Ⓓ
22. Ⓐ Ⓑ Ⓒ Ⓓ
23. Ⓐ Ⓑ Ⓒ Ⓓ
24. Ⓐ Ⓑ Ⓒ Ⓓ
25. Ⓐ Ⓑ Ⓒ Ⓓ
26. Ⓐ Ⓑ Ⓒ Ⓓ
27. Ⓐ Ⓑ Ⓒ Ⓓ
28. Ⓐ Ⓑ Ⓒ Ⓓ
29. Ⓐ Ⓑ Ⓒ Ⓓ
30. Ⓐ Ⓑ Ⓒ Ⓓ

31. 32. 33. 34. 35.

36. 37. 38.

Chapter 18
Practice Test 8:
Answers and
Explanations

PRACTICE TEST 8 ANSWER KEY

Section 1: Reading		Section 2: Writing & Language		Section 3: Math (No Calculator)		Section 4: Math (Calculator)	
1. C	27. C	1. C	23. B	1. A	11. B	1. C	20. C
2. D	28. B	2. B	24. C	2. A	12. C	2. D	21. A
3. C	29. A	3. A	25. C	3. D	13. C	3. B	22. B
4. A	30. B	4. D	26. B	4. D	14. D	4. A	23. C
5. B	31. A	5. D	27. B	5. B	15. C	5. C	24. D
6. A	32. C	6. B	28. A	6. A	16. 16	6. D	25. C
7. D	33. C	7. D	29. D	7. A	17. 1, 2, 3, 4, 6, or 12	7. B	26. D
8. B	34. B	8. B	30. A	8. B		8. C	27. A
9. D	35. A	9. A	31. A	9. D		9. C	28. D
10. B	36. D	10. A	32. D	10. A		10. A	29. A
11. C	37. D	11. D	33. D		18. $\frac{1}{24}$, .041, or .042	11. B	30. B
12. A	38. B	12. B	34. D			12. C	31. 247, 248, 249, 250, or 251
13. C	39. C	13. B	35. B			13. A	
14. A	40. C	14. D	36. C		19. $\frac{49}{8}$, 6.12, or 6.13	14. D	
15. D	41. D	15. A	37. C			15. A	
16. B	42. A	16. A	38. B			16. B	32. 8
17. C	43. D	17. C	39. D		20. $\frac{5}{2}$ or 2.5	17. B	33. 11
18. D	44. D	18. B	40. B			18. B	34. $\frac{6}{5}$ or 1.2
19. C	45. C	19. C	41. C			19. A	
20. B	46. B	20. D	42. B				35. 5.8
21. D	47. C	21. C	43. A				36. 6
22. C	48. D	22. D	44. A				37. 750
23. A	49. D						38. 20
24. D	50. A						
25. D	51. A						
26. D	52. C						

Go to PrincetonReview.com to score your exam. Alternatively, for self-assessment tables, please turn to page 909.

PRACTICE TEST 8 EXPLANATIONS

Section 1: Reading

1. **C** The question asks why the author uses the image of the *waters of the Jordan*. Use the given line reference to find the window and read carefully. The answer should come from a window of approximately lines 1–10. The passage states that *The ever-increasing current of Christmas shoppers flowed on. Now and then it rolled up, like the waters of the Jordan.* The image is used to describe the movement of the crowd. Find an answer that matches this prediction. Choice (A) includes the word *never,* which is extreme language. The passage does not suggest that the crowd *will never ebb.* Eliminate (A). Choice (B) can be eliminated because there is no indication in the passage that *the little woman was drowning in the throng.* Choice (C) matches the prediction, so hang on to it. The image of the *waters of Jordan* is used to describe the movement of the crowd, not the movements of one person. Eliminate (D). The correct answer is (C).

2. **D** The question asks what the word *caught* means in line 16. Go back to the text, find the word *caught,* and mark it out. Carefully read the surrounding text to determine another word that would fit in the blank based on the context of the passage. The text says the woman *caught the scent of fresh-cut flowers.* In other words, the woman "became aware of" the scent. Find an answer that means something similar to becoming aware of. The only answer that matches this meaning is (D). The other answers might initially look attractive because they all relate to the word "caught," but none of the other three answers match the context of the passage. The correct answer is (D).

3. **C** The question asks about supporting the claim that *the shabby little woman was at first excited by the tall young girl.* Use the line references in the answer choices. The lines for (A) state that the shabby little woman *caught the scent of fresh-cut flowers and looked up into the eyes of a tall young girl in a white-plumed velvet hat, with a bunch of English violets in her brown mink fur.* These lines are an objective description of the young girl. There is no indication in these lines of how the woman feels. Eliminate (A). The lines for (B) state that *As their glances met, the shabby little woman checked a start, and half-defensively dropped her lids.* This description of the woman notes that she is startled and somewhat defensive. However, the question asks which lines show that the woman was excited. Eliminate (B). The lines for (C) state that the *thrill of response that set the woman's pulses throbbing died suddenly.* The phrase *thrill of response that sent the woman's pulses throbbing* indicates that the woman was initially excited. Keep (C). The lines for (D) describe how the woman saw herself. These lines do not relate to how the woman felt at meeting the tall young girl. Eliminate (D). The correct answer is (C).

4. **A** The question asks why the woman invites the visitor to come in. Use chronology to find the answer. The answer to question 3 was in the third paragraph, and the line reference for question 5 is in the seventh paragraph. Therefore, scan between the third and seventh paragraph for a description of the woman inviting a visitor. The fifth paragraph provides the following description. *"Come in," invited the woman, expecting some famine-pressed neighbor for a spoonful of coffee or a drawing of tea.* Look for an answer that matches the idea of the woman *expecting* someone in need. Choice (A) matches that idea, so keep it. Choice (B) can be eliminated because, though she does invite this person in, there's no evidence that the woman allows everyone in. Eliminate (C) because there is no indication that the woman expected *the young girl to drop by.* The passage also does not suggest that the woman *cannot see,* so eliminate (D). The correct answer is (A).

5. **B**   The question asks about the purpose of the girl's comments in lines 51–58. The passage describes the young girl as saying *"I've such a silly excuse for coming.... I noticed you had a rare fur-piece... and I want to ask a very great favor of you. Now please don't be shocked—I've been ransacking the city for something like it, and...I should like to buy it of you."* Find an answer that matches the idea of the girl explaining why she has come to the apartment. Choice (A) can be eliminated: while the girl seeks to persuade the woman to sell her the fur, there is no indication that she wants *a discount*. Choice (B) is a solid paraphrase of the prediction, so keep it. The girl is not laughing at the shabby woman, nor does she demand *the shabby woman surrender her wrap*, so (C) and (D) can both be eliminated. The correct answer is (B).

6. **A**   The question asks why the girl uses the word *ransacking*. In the passage, the young girl says *"I noticed you had a rare fur-piece...and I want to ask a very great favor of you. Now please don't be shocked—I've been ransacking the city for something like it, and...I should like to buy it of you."* In context, *ransacking the city* means that the girl has been looking everywhere in the city for a similar rare fur piece. Find an answer that matches this prediction. Only (A) matches the context of the passage. The girl has searched everywhere in the city for the same fur piece, so her search can be described as *comprehensive*. The correct answer is (A).

7. **D**   The question asks why *the shabby woman initially declines to sell the fur*. In lines 72–73, the woman first expresses confusion about the girl's request, but then says, *"I can't, it ain't worth...."* The woman doesn't think the fur is worth anything. Eliminate (A) because the question asks about the woman's thoughts, not the young girl's. Choice (B) has nothing to do with the passage, so eliminate it. Choice (C) does mention the worth of the piece, but there is no discussion about the actual price. Eliminate (C). Choice (D) is a solid paraphrase of the prediction. The correct answer is (D).

8. **B**   The question asks for the best evidence for the answer to the previous question. Lines 72–73 were used to answer Q8. The correct answer is (B).

9. **D**   The question asks how the shabby woman felt after the girl's departure. Use chronology to find the answer. The answer to question 8 came from lines 72–73. Start reading after these lines to find how the woman felt. According to the passage, *As she sat huddled on the cot, warmth and vitality glowed within her, kindled by the memory of a recent kindly human touch.* Find an answer that is consistent with that prediction. The only answer that matches the positive feeling that the woman has after the young girl leaves is (D), *warmth*. The correct answer is (D).

10. **B**   This question asks what the purpose of the last paragraph is. According to the last paragraph, *It was unusual to sell expensive furs to such a customer. But...[i]n this case, the shabby little woman was prepared. She produced three crisp ten-dollar bills...and two dollars more from the savings in her worn little purse.* Find an answer that matches the idea of the purchase being different than what normally happened. Choice (A) is a detail. Although the first sentence of the paragraph states that *it was unusual to sell expensive furs to such a customer*, this is not the purpose of the paragraph as a whole. Eliminate (A). Choice (B) matches the prediction, so keep it. Choice (C) uses extreme language. While the last paragraph describes the shabby woman as *triumphantly* leaving the store, there is no indication in the passage that the purchase was the shabby woman's *greatest triumph*. Eliminate (C). Choice (D) does not match the prediction. According to the passage, the sale of the furs to the shabby woman is described as *unusual*. Therefore, the last paragraph does not illustrate how servants *go Christmas shopping*. Eliminate (D). The correct answer is (B).

11. **C**   The question asks for a point *von Mises makes about socialism relative to capitalism* in Passage 1. Notice that the following question is a best evidence question, so this question and Q12 can be answered in tandem. Look at the answers for Q12 first. The lines in (12A) mention *present-day*

social and political conflicts and *the socialist state*. Although these lines don't directly mention capitalism, the first sentence of the third paragraph references *the antagonism between socialism and capitalism*, and the blurb states that *von Mises spoke…in favor of capitalism*, which indicates that the *social and political conflicts* are between socialism and capitalism. Look to see whether these lines support any of the answers in Q11. They support (11C): these lines state that surrendering to *the socialist state* means giving up *freedom* and *private initiative*, which supports the claim that *socialism oppresses self-motivation, but capitalism allows individuals to retain their liberties*. Connect these two answers. Next, look at the lines in (12B). These lines don't compare capitalism and socialism, so eliminate (12B). The lines in (12C) mention socialism, but they don't compare it with capitalism, so eliminate (12C). The lines for (12D) also mention socialism, but don't compare it with capitalism, so eliminate (12D). Without support from Q12, (11A), (11B), and (11D) can be eliminated. The correct answers are (11C) and (12A).

12.   **A**   (See explanation above.)

13.   **C**   The question asks what the word *advance* means in line 13. Go back to the text, find the word *advance*, and mark it out. Carefully read the surrounding text to determine another word that would fit in the blank based on the context of the passage. The second paragraph states, *Our age has witnessed a triumphal advance of the socialist cause. As much as half a century ago an eminent British statesman, Sir William Harcourt, asserted: "We are all socialists now."* The correct answer should mean something like "increase" or "furthering." Eliminate (A) because *upgrade* means "improvement," not "increase." Although a *breakthrough* could be related to an *advance*, the context of the passage indicates that socialism is continuously expanding, not "suddenly advancing." Eliminate (B). Keep (C) because *progress* is consistent with "increase." Eliminate (D) because there is no indication of any *deposit* being made. The correct answer is (C).

14.   **A**   The question asks for Einstein's central claim in Passage 2. Because this is a general question, it should be answered after all the specific questions about Passage 2. Einstein says that the *economic anarchy of capitalist society…is…the real source of the evil*. He describes it as *a huge community of producers…unceasingly striving to deprive each other of the fruits of their collective* labor. He goes on to explain how *capital tends to become concentrated in few hands… which results in an oligarchy of private capital…which cannot be effectively checked even by a democratically organized political society*. Eliminate any answers that aren't consistent with the idea of capitalism causing an unequal distribution of resources and power. Choice (A) is a clear paraphrase of the prediction, so keep it. Eliminate (B) because Einstein does not make an argument that the *economic success of a society depends on the ability of citizens to make their own decisions*. Eliminate (C) because Einstein does not mention *initiative and creativity*. Eliminate (D) because Passage 2 discusses *disadvantages* of capitalism and *merits* of socialism; it does not argue that *different economic systems should be considered carefully*. The correct answer is (A).

15.   **D**   The question asks what the word *fruits* means in line 36. Go back to the text, find the word *fruits*, and mark it out. Carefully read the surrounding text to determine another word that would fit in the blank based on the context of the passage. The first paragraph discusses producers who *are unceasingly striving to deprive each other of the fruits of their collective labor*. The correct answer should mean something like "products" or "results." Eliminate (A) because, although *produce* is another word for *fruits,* that definition is not consistent with this context. Eliminate (B), *consequences,* because the *fruits* in the text are intentionally produced and are not negative outcomes of decisions. Eliminate (C), *byproducts,* because the *fruits* are the intended outcome, not "secondary or incidental products." Keep (D) because *output* is consistent with "products." The correct answer is (D).

16. **B** The question asks what *Einstein implies* about *an educational system that fosters extreme competition over social goals* in Passage 2. Look for the lead words *educational system* in the passage. In the second paragraph, Einstein argues that the *whole educational system suffers from this evil. An exaggerated competitive attitude is inculcated into the student, who is trained to worship acquisitive success as a preparation for his future career.* He explains that the problem with those values is that they make it *quite impossible…for the individual citizen to come to objective conclusions and to make intelligent use of his political rights.* Eliminate any answers that aren't consistent with this idea. Choice (A) can be eliminated because there is no indication that an education system that fosters competition *appears beneficial.* Keep (B); such an education system does *limit the ability of individuals to exercise their rights.* Eliminate (C) because the education system is not mentioned as the cause of heightened *differences between social classes.* Eliminate (D) because the passage says that the educational system cripples individuals; therefore, it does not prepare *the next generation for success.* The correct answer is (B).

17. **C** The question asks for a point that Einstein makes *about an improperly attempted socialist economy* in Passage 2. Notice that the following question is a best evidence question, so this question and Q18 can be answered in tandem. Look at the answers for Q18 first. The lines in (18A) do not reference an *improperly attempted socialist economy,* so eliminate (18A). The lines in (18B) do not reference an *improperly attempted socialist economy,* so eliminate (18B). The lines in (18C) do not reference an *improperly attempted socialist economy,* so eliminate (18C). The lines in (18D) come from the fourth paragraph, which states, *Nevertheless, it is necessary to remember that a planned economy is not yet socialism. A planned economy as such may be accompanied by the complete enslavement of the individual.* Look to see whether these lines support any of the answers for Q17. They support (17C): the phrase *could permit the destruction of free choice* is a paraphrase of *may be accompanied by the complete enslavement of the individual.* Connect these two answers. Without support from Q18, (17A), (17B), and (17D) can be eliminated. The correct answers are (17C) and (18D).

18. **D** (See explanation above.)

19. **C** The question asks for *the relationship between the two passages.* Since the question is about both passages, it should be done after the questions that ask about the passages individually. Both passages take a position on the choice of socialism versus capitalism. Passage 1 favors capitalism, stating that the *main issue in present-day social and political conflicts is whether or not man should give away freedom, private initiative, and individual responsibility and surrender to the guardianship of a gigantic apparatus of compulsion and coercion, the socialist state.* Einstein argues against capitalism in Passage 2, saying that *economic anarchy of capitalist society as it exists today is, in my opinion, the real source of the evil.* Eliminate (A) because the passages make opposing arguments for two different economic systems, rather than focusing on *social context* and one *financial system.* Eliminate (B) because Passage 2 advocates for *the economic system criticized in Passage 1* rather than *elaborate[ing] on the pitfalls.* Keep (C) because Passage 2 does advocate *against* capitalism, which is *the economic system championed in Passage 1.* Eliminate (D) because Passage 2 opposes the *ideas put forth in Passage 1* rather than *us[ing] specifics to illustrate the ideas.* The correct answer is (C).

20. **B** The question asks how *von Mises would have most likely reacted to lines 72–76 ("I am…goals") of Passage 2.* Since the question is about both passages, it should be done after the questions that ask about the passages individually. The given lines from Passage 2 state that *the establishment of the socialist economy* would *eliminate these grave evils.* In the first paragraph of Passage 1, von Mises strongly criticizes socialism, saying that to *surrender to the guardianship of a gigantic apparatus of compulsion and coercion, the socialist state* would be to substitute *authoritarian totalitarianism*

for *individualism and democracy.* Eliminate (A) because von Mises is not *in agreement* with the views expressed in Passage 2. Keep (B), because the statement that *a socialist society enslaves its citizens and eliminates individualism* is supported by the first paragraph of Passage 1. Although the language of (B) is strong, it is supported by equally strong wording in the text. Eliminate (C) because von Mises does not discuss *relying on social goals to fix financial issues.* Eliminate (D) because von Mises is strongly opposed to implementing socialism and argues that it would cause serious problems; he would not merely express *reservation* because *socialism isn't effective.* The correct answer is (B).

21. **D** The question asks for *the point of view* of the authors of the passage. Since this is a general question, it should be answered after the specific questions. The passage is about the effects of increased natural gas use on global carbon dioxide emissions. The authors state that where natural gas *replaces coal for electricity generation, it's reducing carbon dioxide emissions and improving air quality. It still produces carbon pollution, though, and therefore slows, but does not solve, the climate problem. Where it's providing new energy and new emissions—replacing low- and no-carbon technologies or keeping them from being deployed—it is hindering climate solutions.* Therefore, the authors are concerned about carbon pollution and its effects on the climate. Eliminate answers that don't match this prediction. There is no evidence that the authors work in the natural gas *industry,* so eliminate (A). Eliminate (B) because the passage is not focused on *avenues of research.* Eliminate (C) because the passage is not directed at *consumers.* Keep (D) because the effects of carbon pollution on the climate are *global developments* that the authors are *concerned* about. The correct answer is (D).

22. **C** The question asks what the phrase *aided by* most nearly means in line 12. Go back to the text, find the phrase *aided by,* and cross it out. Then read the window carefully, using context clues to determine another word that would fit in the text. The text says, *Natural gas use is surging at almost twice that rate, aided by the boom in liquefied natural gas (LNG) that is connecting global gas markets.* Therefore, *aided by* could be replaced by a phrase such as "helped to increase." *Lessened by* does not match "helped to increase," so eliminate (A). *Relieved of* does not match "helped to increase," so eliminate (B). *Boosted by* matches "helped to increase," so keep (C). *Revealed by* does not match "helped to increase," so eliminate (D). The correct answer is (C).

23. **A** The question asks for the purpose of the *last sentence of the second paragraph.* Use the given line reference to find the window. The second paragraph states, *Increased natural gas and oil use are driving the increase in carbon dioxide emissions* and goes on to say, *Natural gas use is surging at almost twice* the rate of oil use. The last sentence of the second paragraph says, *Emissions from natural gas use rose almost 200 million metric tons of CO_2 in 2019, and were responsible for two thirds of the global emissions increase.* Therefore, the last sentence gives specific information about the trend of increasing natural gas use. Eliminate answers that don't match this prediction. Keep (A) because it matches the prediction. Eliminate (B) because the sentence gives data; it does not *evaluate a claim.* Eliminate (C) because only the year 2019 is mentioned in the sentence. Eliminate (D) because the sentence does not mention any *efforts to mitigate climate change.* The correct answer is (A).

24. **D** The question asks what *the authors believe* about *current natural gas production.* Notice that this is the first question in a paired set, so it can be done in tandem with Q25. Look at the answer choices for Q25 first. The lines for (25A) indicate that *[n]atural gas use is surging at almost twice* the rate of oil use, *aided by the boom in liquefied natural gas (LNG) that is connecting global gas markets.* Although these lines mention *natural gas use,* they do not support any of the answers for Q24. Eliminate (25A). The lines for (25B) say, *In the United States and Europe, natural gas is replacing coal in electricity generation.* At first glance, this information may seem to support (24A).

However, these lines indicate that natural gas use in increasing in both the United States and Europe; they do not indicate that *natural gas production performs better in the American market than in global markets*. Eliminate (25B) because it does not support any of the answers for Q24. The lines for (25C) say that when natural gas *replaces coal for electricity generation, it's reducing carbon dioxide emissions and improving air quality*. At first glance, this information may seem to support (24C), but the authors go on to state that natural gas still produces carbon pollution, so the authors do not believe that natural gas is the *ultimate solution for clean air technology*. Eliminate (25C) because it does not support any of the answers for Q24. The lines for (25D) say that natural gas *still produces carbon pollution, though, and therefore slows, but does not solve, the climate problem*. These lines support (24D). Draw a line connecting (24D) and (25D). Without any support in the answers from Q25, (24A), (24B), and (24C) can be eliminated. The correct answers are (24D) and (25D).

25. **D** (See explanation above.)

26. **D** The question asks how *the Allam cycle can improve on current pollution levels*. This is the first question in a paired set, but it is easy to find, so it can be done on its own. Since there is no line reference, use lead words and the order of the questions to find the window. The answer to Q25 came from the fifth paragraph, so scan the sixth paragraph, looking for the lead words *Allam cycle*. Lines 55–56 indicate that the *Allam cycle* is a *promising new technology*. The paragraph then explains, *An Allam cycle power plant produces almost pure CO_2 as a byproduct. This pipeline-quality CO_2 removes the need for CO_2 capture in current technologies that use amines or hydroxides to scrub the CO_2*. Eliminate answers that don't match this prediction. Choice (A) is a Deceptive Language trap answer: although the text mentions *carrier gas*, it does not say that the *Allam cycle* produces *fewer carrier gases*. Eliminate (A). Choice (B) is also a Deceptive Language trap answer; the text indicates that people could sequester the CO_2 that is produced by the Allam cycle underground, but it does not state that the Allam cycle stores its own byproducts underground. Eliminate (B). Choice (C) is also a Deceptive Language trap answer; the text says that the Allam cycle *burns natural gas or other fossil fuels in oxygen rather than air*, not that it burns *pure oxygen*. Eliminate (C). Keep (D) because it matches the prediction. The correct answer is (D).

27. **C** The question is the best evidence question in a paired set. Because the previous question was easy to find, simply look at the lines used to answer Q26. Lines 59–62 provided the prediction for Q26: *This pipeline-quality CO_2 removes the need for CO_2 capture in current technologies that use amines or hydroxides to scrub the CO_2*. Eliminate (A), (B), and (D). The correct answer is (C).

28. **B** The question asks what the word *radical* most nearly means in line 81. Go back to the text, find the word *radical*, and cross it out. Then read the window carefully, using context clues to determine another word that would fit in the text. The last paragraph discusses the *good news* and *bad news* about *emissions*, and then states, *What we need is much more radical news: a steep drop in pollution that drains the emissions glass as quickly as a final champagne toast*. Therefore, *radical news* could be described as news of a large or noteworthy change. Eliminate answers that don't match this prediction. *Fanatical* means "full of zeal" and does not match "noteworthy," so eliminate (A). *Remarkable* matches "noteworthy," so keep (B). *Militant* does not match "noteworthy," so eliminate (C). *Enlightening* does not match "noteworthy," so eliminate (D). Note that (A) and (C) are Could Be True trap answers based on other meanings of *radical* that are not supported by the text. The correct answer is (B).

29. **A** The question asks which source of *global CO_2 emissions in 2018* is closest to *the 2018 CO_2 emissions from gas in the United States*. First locate the *2018* CO_2 emissions from gas in the *United States* on figure 2. Figure 2 shows that in 2018 the CO_2 emissions from gas in the United States were slightly greater than 1.6 billion tons. Then find the source that is closest to 1.6 billion tons

in 2018 on figure 1. Figure 1 shows that the source closest to 1.6 billion tons in 2018 is *cement*. Keep (A) and eliminate (B), (C), and (D). The correct answer is (A).

30. **B** The question asks for the year in which *global CO$_2$ emissions from oil* equal *the U.S. CO$_2$ emissions from natural gas in the year 2000*. First locate CO$_2$ emissions from natural gas for the *United States* in the year *2000* on figure 2. Figure 2 shows that the emissions from natural gas in the United States in 2000 were around 1.2 billion tons. Then find the year when global CO$_2$ emissions from oil were closest to 1.2 billion tons on figure 1. Figure 1 shows that global CO$_2$ emissions from oil were closest to 1.2 billion tons around 1940. Keep (B), *1945*, and eliminate (A), (C), and (D). The correct answer is (B).

31. **A** The question asks for the *main purpose of the passage*. Because this is a general question, it should be done after all the specific questions. Beginning from the opening sentence, the passage states that the *mass media play a role in the construction of environmental issues and problems*. The second paragraph states that *when it comes to coverage of global warming, balanced reporting can be a form of informational bias*. The correct answer will reflect this information. *Question the journalistic ideal of balanced coverage regarding scientific reporting* matches the prediction, so keep (A). The passage does not focus solely on the *bias of scientific journalists*, so eliminate (B). There is no analysis of *the antagonistic relationship between the elite press and local news outlets*, so eliminate (C). The *ideals of objectivity* are not just discussed, they are questioned; eliminate (D). The correct answer is (A).

32. **C** The question asks what expectation *reporters covering controversy face*. Notice that this is the first question in a paired set, so it can be done in tandem with question 33. Start with the best evidence answer choices for Q33. The lines for (33A), (33B), and (33D) talk about *the mass media, journalistic norms and values*, and *scientific consensus*, respectively, but not specifically *reporters*; eliminate (33A), (33B), and (33D). The fact that *journalistic fairness requires reporters who write about a controversy to present competing points of view* in the lines for (33C) matches the idea that *reporters should offer equal consideration to opposing perspectives*. The correct answers are (32C) and (33C).

33. **C** (See explanation above.)

34. **B** The question asks what the word *particular* means in line 51. Go back to the text, find the word *particular*, and mark it out. Carefully read the surrounding text to determine another word that would fit in the blank based on the context of the passage. The passage states that *a remarkably high level of scientific consensus has emerged on these two issues*. In the previous sentence, *these two issues* are defined as the facts *that global warming is a serious problem that has anthropogenic influences, and that it must be addressed immediately*. In the context of the passage, *particular* means something like "defined" or "exact." *Local* can mean "exact," but only in reference to place or position; eliminate (A). *Specific* means "defined" or "exact," so keep (B). *Appropriate* means "suitable," not exact; eliminate (C). *Peculiar* means "strange" or "different," so eliminate (D). The correct answer is (B).

35. **A** The question asks why the authors include the quotation in lines 54–56. Use the given line reference to find the window. The sentence prior to the quotation says that *a remarkably high level of scientific consensus has emerged on these two particular issues*. This references the issues from the prior sentence *that global warming is a serious problem that has anthropogenic influences, and that it must be addressed immediately*, so it can be predicted that the quotation highlights this *remarkably high level of scientific consensus*. This high level of *consensus of scientific authorities* does *contrast... with the reporting in prestige publications*, as mentioned in the beginning of the fifth paragraph, so keep (A). The quote does not *propose models for accurate reporting, criticize readers*, nor *demonstrate the importance of scientific facts*; eliminate (B), (C), and (D). The correct answer is (A).

36. **D** The question asks what *the work of journalists may involve*. Notice that this is the first question in a paired set, so it can be done in tandem with question 37. Start with the best evidence answer choices for Q37. The lines for (37A) discuss *prestige-press coverage of global warming* as *a social relationship between people*. The only paired answer discussing social aspects of journalists' work is (36C), but it specifically mentions an unsupported claim about the journalists *relating socially to interview subjects*; eliminate (37A). The lines for (37B) and (37C) are related to concerned scientists and scientific discourse, not *the work of journalists*; eliminate (37B) and (37C). The lines for (37D) indicate that journalists engage in a *continuous juggling act [that] often mitigates against meaningful, accurate, and urgent coverage of the issue of global warming*. This provides evidence to support (36D), stating that the *work of journalists* is *prioritizing balanced reporting of viewpoints over covering the facts*. The correct answers are (36D) and (37D).

37. **D** (See explanation above.)

38. **B** The question asks what the word *curb* means in line 79. Go back to the text, find the word *curb*, and mark it out. Carefully read the surrounding text to determine another word that would fit in the blank based on the context of the passage. The passage states that a *disconnection has played a significant role in the lack of concerted international action to* do something to the *practices that contribute to global warming*. From the overall passage, it is known that journalism has not helped to stop global warming. Therefore, *curb* must mean something like "stop" or "restrict" in the context of the passage. Neither *bend* nor *edge* matches this prediction, so eliminate (A) and (D). *Limit* means "restrict," so keep (B). *Delay* is a close answer that means "slow down" rather than "stop" or "restrict," so eliminate (C). The correct answer is (B).

39. **C** The question asks *in what year the percentages of all three types of coverage of action tactics regarding global warming were most similar*, based on the graph. Check the answer choices against the graph, looking for a year where the three lines are closest together. In 1989, the lines for balanced accounts and immediate/mandatory action are close together, but the line for cautious/voluntary action is not; eliminate (A). In 1993 and 1999, the lines for cautious/voluntary action and immediate/mandatory action are close together, but the line for balanced accounts is not; eliminate (B) and (D). In 1994, all three lines, for balanced accounts, immediate/mandatory action, and cautious/voluntary action, are close together. The correct answer is (C).

40. **C** The question asks *which statement is best supported by information in the graph*. Check the answer choices against the table. *Between 1989 and 1999, the number of "cautious/voluntary" accounts of global warming* did decline *dramatically*, but then never *rose significantly*; eliminate (A). *Between 1995 and 2000, the number of "immediate/mandatory" accounts of global warming* may not have varied as much as the number of balanced accounts regarding action, but they didn't remain *the same* either; eliminate (B). Overall, *the number of "balanced" accounts of global warming* did increase between 1988 and 2002, so keep (C). There is no indication that the information from the graph includes *all accounts of global warming*, so eliminate (D). The correct answer is (C).

41. **D** The question asks what *the 2001 data in the graph best serve as evidence* of. Check the graph for where the coverage of action lines lie in 2001 to predict that in 2001 balanced accounts regarding global warming action had peaked. The graph provides no information regarding the composition of *coverage of global warming* or *anthropogenic influences;* eliminate (A) and (C). Choice (B) refers to *balanced reporting*, but the graph has no reference to *informational bias*; eliminate (B). Choice (D) also refers to *balanced reporting*, and states that *popular discourse has significantly diverged from the scientific discourse*. According to the passage, *balanced reporting* is the *popular discourse*, and according to the graph, in 2001 the line for *balanced reporting* diverged the most from the other types of reporting. The correct answer is (D).

42. **A** The question asks about the *primary purpose of the passage*. Because this is a general question, it should be done after all the specific questions. The passage starts with the report of the death of howler monkeys in Nicaragua, goes on to present different theories on why the howler monkeys died, and concludes by stating that the *cause of the recent howler monkey deaths remains a mystery* and that there is *probably an interaction of factors*. Choice (A) is consistent with this structure. The passage presents concerns for the howler monkey deaths, portrays the actions of the researchers, and raises several theories for why the howler monkeys died. Choice (B) can be eliminated because there are no *contradictory results* presented in the passage. The passage simply raises various theories as to why the howler monkeys died. Eliminate (C) because there is no indication in the passage that the researchers are *unusual[ly]* persistent. Choice (D) can be eliminated because the passage does not examine the researcher's *methodology*. The correct answer is (A).

43. **D** The question asks what type of evidence *Williams-Guillén's ultimate hypothesis* rests on. In the eighth paragraph of the passage, the author states that *William-Guillén thinks that disease is an unlikely cause of the recent monkey deaths,* and that *she and her colleagues are still waiting to export blood and tissue samples to U.S. labs for further analysis.* Therefore, Williams-Guillén's ultimate hypothesis rests on laboratory tests, which is (D). The correct answer is (D).

44. **D** The question asks what the words *hopped on* mean in line 15. Go back to the text, find the words *hopped on*, and mark them out. Carefully read the surrounding text to determine another word that would fit in the blank based on the context of the passage. According to the passage, *William-Guillén hopped on a plane to Nicaragua.* In this context, *hopped on* would mean something like "boarded" a plane. Look for an answer that could mean "boarded." The only answer that could have a similar meaning is (D), *entered*. Choice (B), *flew,* may seem tempting. However, there is no indication in the passage that William-Guillén is a pilot. The correct answer is (D).

45. **C** The question asks what the passage states about *howler monkeys*. Given that the entire passage is about the howler monkeys, this is a general question that should be done after all the specific questions. For (A), there is no indication in the passage that howler monkeys *are less affected by ecological changes than other species would be.* In fact, the passage states that drought may have played a role in the death of the howler monkeys. Eliminate (A). For (B), although the third paragraph describes sick monkeys being easily captured, it never describes how difficult it is to capture healthy howler monkeys. Eliminate (B). For (C), look to the sixth paragraph of the passage, which states that one way to test whether limited food availability was a factor in the howler monkeys' deaths is to *see how other animals in the area are faring...If there are no reports of deaths in other frugivorous primates and other frugivorous animals, perhaps [food availability] doesn't have to do with it.* This suggests that howler monkeys *share some known dietary similarities with other species.* Keep (C). Choice (D) can be eliminated, because while the passage suggests that the howler monkeys may have eaten toxic food as a result of not having enough food available, it does not indicate whether the howler monkeys *prefer the taste of non-toxic foods.* The correct answer is (C).

46. **B** The question asks for *an early consideration regarding howler monkey deaths*. Given that the question is asking about an *early consideration,* the answer is likely to be found toward the beginning of the passage. According to the first paragraph, in late September Williams-Guillén received the first report that *a handful of howler monkeys...had been found dead at an eco-resort in Nicaragua.* According to the second paragraph, *Over the next couple of months, Williams-Guillén and her colleagues continued to receive news that howler monkeys were dying. Then around mid-January, the reports really started to flood in.* According to the third paragraph, *When it became clear that this was not just an isolated incident, Williams-Guillén hopped on a plane to Nicaragua to see for herself.* Therefore, an early consideration was whether the deaths were an isolated incident. Iso-

lated incidents can also be thought of as *random occurrences,* which matches (B). The passage doesn't provide any suggestions on what could prevent the howler monkey deaths. Eliminate (A). The passage does not state that *all ages* of howler monkeys were impacted. Eliminate (C). The passage does not suggest that *the entire population* of howler monkeys was impacted. Eliminate (D). The correct answer is (B).

47. **C** The question asks which theory provided by the passage *supports William-Guillén's belief that "no one hypothesis will be correct."* Notice that this is the first question in a paired set, so it can be done in tandem with Q48. Start with the best evidence answer choices for Q48. The lines for (48A) state that *although the mortality rate seems to have slowed since mid-February, the research-ers are anxious to understand what is going on.* These lines do not discuss the accuracy of any hypotheses. Eliminate (48A). The lines for (48B) state that *the deaths are all really concentrated in the areas worst hit by drought.* This does not support any of the answers in Q47. Eliminate (48B). The lines for (48C) state that in areas where it is *slightly more humid, there's a lot fewer deaths, and there's visibly more potential howler monkey food, whereas the areas that have the highest rates of mortality, the trees are just bare.* This does not support any of the answers in Q47. Eliminate (48C). The lines for (48D) state that *limited food availability is likely a contributing factor, though the cause of death may not be starvation per se. Rather, the lack of food may drive the monkeys to consume plants with high levels of certain toxins that aren't part of their normal diet.* This supports (47C). Connect (48D) and (47C). Any unsupported answers for Q47 can be eliminated. The correct answers are (47C) and (48D).

48. **D** (See explanation above.)

49. **D** The question asks about the *primary purpose of the seventh and eighth paragraphs (lines 56–75).* The seventh paragraph introduces disease as a possible cause for the howler monkeys' deaths and provides the historical impact of yellow fever on howler monkeys. The eighth paragraph discusses Williams-Guillén's thoughts that *disease is an unlikely cause of the recent monkey deaths.* According to the eighth paragraph, none of the virus diagnostics done tested positive for yellow fever. Find an answer consistent with this prediction. Choice (A) does not match the prediction. Neither paragraph 7 nor paragraph 8 discusses Williams-Guillén's methodology. Choice (B) can be eliminated because there is no discussion of Williams-Guillén's *expertise* in either the seventh or eighth paragraph. Choice (C) can also be eliminated because in the eighth paragraph Williams-Guillén rules out disease as a cause for the howler monkey deaths. However, there is no assumption that is underscored in either paragraph. Choice (D) matches the prediction. Williams-Guillén's perspective is that disease was not responsible for the howler monkey deaths. The seventh paragraph provides background on the historical impact of yellow fever on the howler monkeys, while the eighth paragraph rules yellow fever out as a cause for the current howler monkey deaths. The correct answer is (D).

50. **A** The question asks what the author means when he indicates that *yellow fever may have created bottlenecks* in line 65. According to Dias, *yellow fever may be a cause of the relatively low genetic diversity among Central American howler monkeys. 'Yellow fever could have caused important bottle-necks.'* Find an answer that matches this prediction. Choice (A) matches the prediction. The bottleneck is related to the *relatively low genetic diversity.* Choice (B) can be eliminated because, although the passage states that yellow fever *devastated howler monkey populations into the late 1940s and into the 1950s,* there is no indication that yellow fever *led to the current howler monkey deaths.* In fact, later in the passage yellow fever is specifically ruled out as a cause of the howler monkey deaths. Eliminate (C) because nowhere in the passage is it suggested that a *prohibitively large number of virus-free monkeys* were introduced into the ecosystem. Choice (D) can be eliminated because there is no discussion of *competition between monkeys.* The correct answer is (A).

51. **A** The question asks what question Williams-Guillén's investigation answers. Notice that this is the first question in a paired set, so it can be done in tandem with question 52. Start with the best evidence answer choices for Q52. The lines for (52A) state that *Some researchers even speculate that yellow fever may be a cause of the relatively low genetic diversity among Central American howler monkeys.* It may be tempting to connect this answer with (51C). However, these lines do not relate to the findings of Williams-Guillén's investigation. For this reason, eliminate (52A). The lines for (52B) state that *Williams-Guillén thinks that disease is an unlikely cause of the recent monkey deaths.* This might initially seem to connect with (51A). Keep it if there isn't a clear reason to immediately eliminate it. The lines for (52C) state that *so far, none [of the howler monkeys] have tested positive for yellow fever, Zika, chikungunya, or dengue viruses.* This solidly supports (51A). The listed diseases are unlikely to have contributed to howler monkey deaths. Connect (52C) with (51A). The lines for (52D) state that *Animals that might have had some clinical or secondary infections that normally aren't that problematic…got into a situation where they were extremely food- and water-stressed, and that might have been enough to tip them into mortality.* This does not support any of the answers in Q51. Eliminate (52D). Compare the remaining answers. While both (52B) and (52C) address the issue of whether disease caused the howler monkey deaths, (52B) only provides a hypothesis—*Williams-Guillén thinks.* Choice (52C), on the other hand, provides concrete evidence of disease not being present. The correct answers are (51A) and (52C).

52. **C** (See explanation above.)

Section 2: Writing and Language

1. **C** Commas are changing in the answer choices, so the question tests comma usage. The phrase *or early in the morning* is necessary information, so it should not be surrounded by commas; eliminate (A). There is no reason to break up the phrase *you almost certainly know the feeling* with a comma, so eliminate (B). There is no reason to break up the phrase *late at night or early in the morning* with a comma, so eliminate (D). Choice (C) appropriately uses a comma to separate the phrase *If you've ever been driving on a long stretch of highway late at night or early in the morning* from the main part of the sentence, *you almost certainly know the feeling.*

2. **B** Punctuation changes in the answer choices, so this question tests how to connect ideas with the appropriate punctuation. The first part of the sentence, *This may seem like a harmless enough problem, but as many as one-seventh of these drivers admit to falling asleep at the wheel,* is an independent clause. The second part of the sentence, *causing more than a million crashes each year, including 50,000 injuries and 6,400 deaths,* is not an independent clause. A period can only be used between two independent clauses, so eliminate (A). Adding the word *which* to the beginning of the second part of the sentence does not make it an independent clause, so eliminate (D). Adding the word *this* to the beginning of the second part of the sentence does make it an independent clause. A comma on its own cannot be used between two independent clauses, so eliminate (C). Choice (B) appropriately uses a comma to connect the two parts of the sentence. The correct answer is (B).

3. **A** Note the question! The question asks which sentence *provides the best transition from the previous paragraph*, so it is testing consistency. Determine the subject of the paragraph and find the answer that is consistent with that idea. The end of the previous paragraph states that drivers *falling asleep at the wheel* cause *more than a million crashes each year* and the following sentence says that *driving on fewer than two hours of sleep is the equivalent of driving while intoxicated.* The

statement *these* [numbers] *may sound like drunk driving numbers and with good cause* combines both of these concepts, so keep (A). There is no reason to mention *the leading causes of death every year, medical professionals,* or *drunk driving penalties* in general so eliminate (B), (C), and (D). The correct answer is (A).

4. **D**   Punctuation changes in the answer choices, so this question tests how to connect ideas with the appropriate punctuation. The first part of the sentence, *At a recent forum, Czeisler suggested that driving on fewer than two hours of sleep is the equivalent of driving while intoxicated,* is an independent clause. The second part of the sentence, *Judgement is seriously compromised, and reaction times are correspondingly slowed,* is also an independent clause. A comma on its own cannot be used between two independent clauses, so eliminate (B). Either a period or a colon can be used between two independent clauses, so look at the punctuation at the end of the underlined portion. *Judgement is* is not an independent clause. A colon or a dash can only be used after an independent clause, so eliminate (A) and (C). The correct answer is (D).

5. **D**   Note the question! The question asks which choice best addresses a *specific proposal that Czeisler's group has made,* so it is testing consistency. The previous sentence indicates that *Czeisler and the committee are now attempting to implement changes in the law code to address sleep deprivation,* so the correct answer should provide a legal proposal to address sleep deprivation. *Conferences, risks of sleep-deprived driving,* and *Czeisler's career* are not consistent with the idea of changing the *law code,* so eliminate (A), (B), and (C). *Trying to get sleep-deprived driving added to the list of criminal statutes* is a proposed change *in the law code to address sleep deprivation.* The correct answer is (D).

6. **B**   Note the question! The question asks how to effectively combine the underlined sentences, so it tests precision and concision. Look for the answer that combines the sentences while maintaining the meaning of the originals. Both sentences use the phrase *sleep disorder,* but there is no need to repeat the phrase when the sentences are combined. Choices (A) and (D) repeat the phrase, so eliminate them. *Among them are* redundantly refers to the *sleep disorders,* and the plural verb *are* is not consistent with the singular noun *sleep apnea;* eliminate (C). The correct answer is (B).

7. **D**   Verbs are changing in the answer choices, so the question is testing verb consistency. A verb must be consistent with its subject and with the other verbs in the sentence. The subject of the verb is *the disorder,* which is singular. To be consistent, the underlined verb should also be singular. Eliminate (B) because *are doubling* is plural. The other verb in the sentence is *don't,* which is in simple present tense. To be consistent, the underlined verb should also be in present tense. Eliminate (A) because *was doubling* is past tense. Eliminate (C) because it's less concise than (D) and because *is doubling* is not consistent with *don't. Doubles* is consistent with *don't.* The correct answer is (D).

8. **B**   Transition words are changing in the answer choices, so the question is testing the consistency of ideas. A transition should be consistent with the relationship between the ideas it connects. The sentence with the underlined transition indicates that *the findings regarding young people were not quite so obvious.* These ideas contrast with each other, so look for a contrasting transition. *For example, furthermore,* and *thus* are all same-direction transitions, so eliminate (A), (C), and (D). *However* indicates that the ideas contrast. The correct answer is (B).

9. **A**   Note the question! The question asks which of the following *most effectively cites commonly held views while previewing what is to come in this paragraph,* so it is testing consistency. Eliminate any answers that are not consistent with the purpose stated in the question. Before the underlined portion, it is stated that *young people have a tendency to think that they can operate at a high level with less sleep.* The rest of the paragraph after the underlined portion then explains that this

thought regarding young people and sleep deprivation is actually a misconception, so the correct answer will address this "misconception." That *science suggests the opposite is true* is consistent with this idea, so keep (A). The notions that young people *drive faster* and are susceptible to *alcoholism* are both irrelevant to the paragraph, so eliminate (B) and (C). Whether *you are one of the lucky few who doesn't need sleep* is also not consistent with the paragraph, so eliminate (D). The correct answer is (A).

10. **A** The vocabulary is changing in the answer choices, so this question is testing the precision of word choice. Look for a phrase that has a definition consistent with the other ideas in the sentence. The cells in younger people are compared to the same cells in older people that *have died or function at a lower level*. Therefore, the cells in younger people could accurately be described as "alive" and "high functioning." *Firing on all cylinders, going off,* and *off the chain* are all slang phrases that do not match the formal tone of the passage; eliminate (B), (C), and (D). The correct answer is (A).

11. **D** The length of the phrase changes in the answer choices, so this question tests precision and concision. The words *and* and *also* mean the same thing, so there is no reason to use both words; eliminate (B). Similarly, *plus* and *as well* mean the same thing, so eliminate (C). Choice (D) is both more concise than (A) and makes the meaning of the sentence more precise. Eliminate (A). The correct answer is (D).

12. **B** Transitions change in the answer choices, so the question is testing consistency of ideas. A transition must be consistent with the relationship between the ideas it connects. The previous sentence states that the temple that *stands in ruins today was completed in 432 B.C.E.* The next sentence states that it *served its original purpose for a thousand years*. These ideas are similar but *nevertheless* indicates a contrast, so eliminate (A). There is no cause/effect relationship between the two ideas, so eliminate (C) and (D). Two thousand years is a long time, and is remarkable, as (B) indicates. The correct answer is (B).

13. **B** Punctuation changes in the answer choices, so this question tests how to connect ideas with the appropriate punctuation. The first part of the sentence, *The shift of the building's religious affiliation involved some minor architectural changes, but until the late 17th century,* is not an independent clause. The second part of the sentence, *the building largely retained its majestic, classical profile,* is an independent clause. A colon can only be used after an independent clause, so eliminate (C). There is no need to break up the independent clause in the second part of the sentence with commas, so eliminate (A) and (D). Choice (B) appropriately uses a comma to separate the two parts of the sentence. The correct answer is (B).

14. **D** The words and punctuation are changing in the choices with the option to DELETE. Consider the DELETE option carefully as it is often the correct answer. The sentence already states that the Parthenon was used as a *gunpowder storehouse*. The phrase *for storing ammunition* is redundant, so the phrase should be deleted. Eliminate (A), (B), and (C), which all repeat the idea. The correct answer is (D).

15. **A** Note the question! The question asks whether the sentence should be added, so it's testing consistency. If the content of the new sentence is consistent with the ideas surrounding it, then it should be added; otherwise, it should not be added. The previous sentence states that the Parthenon exploded. The next sentence starts with the word *additionally*, which indicates more information about the results of the explosion. The sentence to be added discusses the results of the explosion. Therefore, it's consistent with the surrounding ideas and should be added. Eliminate (C) and (D). The sentence does not explain later facts, so eliminate (B). The correct answer is (A).

16. **A** Note the question! The question asks for the choice that best supports the main point of the paragraph, so it's testing consistency of ideas. The only other sentence in the paragraph states that Britain took the first steps to preserve the Parthenon, so the correct answer should contain that idea. Only (A) mentions Britain. The correct answer is (A).

17. **C** Apostrophes are changing in the choices, so the question is testing apostrophe usage. When used with a pronoun, an apostrophe indicates a contraction. In this sentence, *it* refers to the Parthenon, which is possessing the *iconic columns*. The possessive pronoun does not use an apostrophe, so eliminate (B) and (D). When used with a noun, an apostrophe indicates possession. In this sentence, the *columns* are plural and are not possessing anything, so the apostrophe is not needed. Eliminate (A). The correct answer is (C).

18. **B** The verbs are changing in the answer choices, so the question is testing verb consistency. A verb must be consistent with the other verbs in the sentence. The verb *corroded* is in the past tense, so the verb *used* must also be in the past tense. Eliminate (A) and (C) because *using* is not past tense. Choices (B) and (D) mean the same thing, but (D) is less concise, so eliminate (D).

19. **C** Punctuation changes in the answer choices, so this question tests how to connect ideas with the appropriate punctuation. The first part of the sentence, *Most disastrously, the iron clamps that he used to hold pieces of masonry together corroded after years of exposure to the weather*, is an independent clause. The second part of the sentence, *eventually it caused even more damage to the already fragile building*, is also an independent clause. A comma on its own cannot be used between two independent clauses, so eliminate (A). Removing the word *it* from the second part of the sentence means it is no longer an independent clause. A semicolon can only be used between two independent clauses, so eliminate (B). Changing the verb in the second part of the sentence to *causing* makes the entire sentence incomplete, so eliminate (D). Choice (C) appropriately uses a comma to separate the two parts of the sentence. The correct answer is (C).

20. **D** The vocabulary is changing in the answer choices, so this question is testing precision of word choice. Look for a word with a definition that is consistent with the other ideas in the sentence. The sentence states that the pieces are *incredibly sophisticated* and *match by fractions of millimeters*, so the word should mean something like "small details." *Shadows* means "areas of less light," so eliminate (A). *Tininess* means "small" but does not capture the intricacies of the details, so eliminate (B). *Suggestions* means "hints" or "possible ideas," so eliminate (C). *Nuances* means "slight difference or variation," so keep (D). The correct answer is (D).

21. **C** Note the question! The question asks where sentence 2 should be placed, so it's testing consistency. The sentence must be consistent with the ideas that come both before and after it. Sentence 2 discusses *a result of this painstaking work*, so it should follow the description of the work. Sentence 5 states that the work is hard because the *design is incredibly sophisticated, and pieces match one another by fractions of millimeters*. Therefore, sentence 2 should be placed after sentence 5. The correct answer is (C).

22. **D** The length of the phrase changes in the answer choices, so this question could test concision. There is also the option to DELETE; consider this option carefully as it is often the correct answer. The sentence contains the name *Manolis Korres* followed by a description of who that person is. Only a comma is needed to link the name and the description, so the sentence could read *Manolis Korres, the project's chief architect*. The correct answer is (D).

23. **B** Punctuation changes in the answer choices, so this question tests how to connect ideas with the appropriate punctuation. The sentence contains a list of three things: 1) *how many items an online shopper looks at before deciding to make a purchase*, 2) *exactly how much time a delivery truck*

spends idling in traffic, and 3) *how the weather affects which books patrons check out from the library*. There should be commas separating the items in the list. Eliminate (C) and (D) because they don't use commas. There is no reason to include a comma after the word *or*, so eliminate (A). The correct answer is (B).

24. **C** Transitions change in the answer choices, so the question is testing consistency of ideas. A transition must be consistent with the relationship between the ideas it connects. The previous sentence discusses one of the sources of the *glut of data: sensors*. The next sentence introduces a different source—*social media posts*—which *can't be analyzed in traditional ways*. This indicates a shift in ideas, so the transition word should indicate a shift. Eliminate (A), (B), and (D) because they all indicate that the ideas agree. The correct answer is (C).

25. **C** The vocabulary is changing in the answer choices, so this question is testing the precision of word choice. Look for a word whose definition is consistent with the other ideas in the sentence. The previous sentence states that *social media posts can't be analyzed in traditional ways*. This sentence highlights that *new ways of "digging" online activity* are needed. Therefore, the word should mean something like "analyzing" or "studying." *Digging* means either "to burrow under the earth" or "to really like something," so eliminate (A). *Checking out* means "to look at," so keep (B). *Mining* means "to extract a desired material or information," so keep (C). *Take a peek at* means "to look at for a brief time," so eliminate (D). *Checking out* is too informal for this passage and doesn't indicate analysis, so eliminate (B). The correct answer is (C).

26. **B** The vocabulary is changing in the answer choices, so this question is testing the precision of word choice. Look for a word whose definition is consistent with the other ideas in the sentence. The sentence uses the comparison *from* this *to* that. The word *too* means "also" and is not correct. Eliminate (A). *Sector* means "a distinct part or area," so keep (B). *Section* means "part that is cut off or separated," so eliminate (C) and (D). The correct answer is (B).

27. **B** The pronouns are changing in the answer choices, so the question is testing consistency and precision of meaning. There is also the option to DELETE; consider this choice carefully as it is often the correct answer. There is a comparison in the sentence, so this question tests consistency. When two things are compared, they should be consistent with each other. The first item in the comparison is *the average starting salary of a data analyst*. Deleting the underlined portion would make the second part of the comparison *a computer programmer*, which is not consistent with *salary*, so eliminate (D). The underlined pronoun refers to *salary*, which is singular. To be consistent, the underlined portion should also be singular. Eliminate (C) because *those* is plural. The phrase *that of* is consistent with the first part of the comparison, so eliminate (A). The correct answer is (B).

28. **A** Note the question! The question asks for the best introduction to the paragraph, so it's testing consistency of ideas. The rest of the paragraph discusses how the analyst works with other experts in the field, so that the analyst doesn't need to be an expert in everything. The correct answer should be consistent with this idea. Stating that *specialized knowledge of a particular field is not necessarily a requirement* is consistent, so keep (A). *Schools are offering degree programs* is not consistent, so eliminate (B). *A field in which data analytics is of fundamental importance* is not consistent, so eliminate (C). *Creating new positions* is not consistent, so eliminate (D). The correct answer is (A).

29. **D** Pronouns are changing in the answer choices, so the question tests consistency of pronouns. A pronoun must be consistent with the noun it refers to. The pronoun refers to *researchers*, which is plural. The pronoun must also be plural, so eliminate (A). *There* does not refer to people, so eliminate (B). The apostrophe in *they're* indicates the conjunction "they are," while the pronoun

their indicates possession. The information belongs to the researchers, so the possessive pronoun is needed. Eliminate (C). The correct answer is (D).

30.   **A**   Note the question! The question asks whether the sentence should be added, so it's testing consistency. If the content of the new sentence is consistent with the ideas surrounding it, then it should be added; otherwise, it should not be added. The sentence to be added discusses *how much the field is growing.* The rest of the paragraph discusses how *related jobs have projected growth rates of up to 34% over the next ten years* and that the *big data will no doubt become a part of nearly every other aspect* of our society. Thus, the sentence is consistent with the rest of the paragraph, so it should be added. Eliminate (C) and (D). The sentence *introduces an issue that is further discussed in the paragraph*, so keep (A). The sentence does not *offer additional details about a point made in the previous paragraph*, so eliminate (B). The correct answer is (A).

31.   **A**   Punctuation changes in the answer choices, so this question tests how to connect ideas with the appropriate punctuation. The first part of the sentence, *According to the Bureau of Labor Statistics, related job titles*, is not an independent clause. Eliminate (B) because a colon can only be used after an independent clause. The phrase *including operations research analyst and statistician* is not necessary to the main meaning of the sentence, so it should be set off by some type of punctuation. Choice (A) appropriately uses parentheses to set off the unnecessary phrase, so keep (A). Eliminate (C) both because it lacks a comma before the unnecessary phrase and because it has an unnecessary comma after *analyst*. Eliminate (D) because it lacks a comma after the unnecessary phrase. The correct answer is (A).

32.   **D**   Note the question! The question asks whether the sentence should be added, so it's testing consistency. If the content of the new sentence is consistent with the ideas surrounding it, then it should be added; otherwise, it should not be added. The sentence to be added states that *operations research analyst positions are projected to have the greatest number of jobs in the field by 2024.* The rest of the paragraph discusses the *projected growth rates* of analysts, so the content is consistent. However, the claim is not supported by the table. The number of *operations research analyst[s]* in 2024 is projected to be 587,800, and the number of *management analysts* is projected to be 861,400. The new sentence is not supported by the table, so it should not be added. Eliminate (A) and (B). The sentence is related to the topic, so eliminate (C). The correct answer is (D).

33.   **D**   The vocabulary is changing in the answer choices, so this question is testing precision of word choice. Look for a word whose definition is consistent with the other ideas in the sentence. The previous sentence states *big data is used in deliveries and to recommend music and movies.* The next sentence discusses how the use of big data will grow in the next decades. The word should mean something like other aspects of our "lives" or "society." *Goings-on* is too informal for this passage, so eliminate (A). *Habits* means "a reoccurring practice," so eliminate (B). *Usual procedures* means "common course of action," so eliminate (C). *Daily lives* means "everyday society," so keep (D). The correct answer is (D).

34.   **D**   The vocabulary is changing in the answer choices, so this question is testing precision of word choice. Look for a word whose definition is consistent with the other ideas in the sentence. The sentence is discussing time periods and mentions the *early 60s.* Therefore, the word must mean something like "late" or "latter." *Delayed* means "postponed," so eliminate (A). *Tardy* means "behind schedule," so eliminate (B). *Behind* means "come after," so eliminate (C). *Late* means "at the end," so keep (D). The correct answer is (D).

35.   **B**   Punctuation changes in the answer choices, so this question tests how to connect ideas with the appropriate punctuation. The first part of the sentence, *The film* Blackboard Jungle, is not an independent clause. The second part of the sentence, *which featured the song "Rock Around*

the Clock" by Bill Haley and his Comets—catapulted popular culture into the rock-and-roll era in 1955, is also not an independent clause. A semicolon can only be used between two independent clauses, so eliminate (D). A colon must come after an independent clause, so eliminate (C). Note that there is a non-underlined dash in the sentence. The phrase that comes before the dash, *which featured the song "Rock Around the Clock" by Bill Haley and his Comets*, is not necessary to the main meaning of the sentence, so it should be set off by some type of punctuation. Since there is a dash at the end of the phrase, there needs to be a dash at the beginning of the phrase also. Eliminate (A). The correct answer is (B).

36. **C**   Transitions change in the answer choices, so the question is testing consistency of ideas. A transition must be consistent with the relationship between the ideas it connects. The previous sentence mentions that the film *catapulted popular culture*. The next sentence states that the *movie sparked controversy*. The two ideas are contrasting, so the conjunction should indicate a contrast. *Moreover, and,* and *as a result* both indicate similar ideas, so eliminate (A), (B), and (D). The correct answer is (C).

37. **C**   Verbs are changing in the choices, so the question is testing verb consistency. A verb must be consistent with the other verbs in the sentence. Both the sentence before and after this one have verbs in the past tense: *movie sparked controversy* and *rock and roll was widely embraced*. To be consistent, the answer choice must also be in the past tense. Eliminate (A) and (B) because they are not past tense. Choice (D) is past tense, but it is less concise than (C), and is not consistent with the other verbs. The correct answer is (C).

38. **B**   Punctuation changes in the answer choices, so this question tests how to connect ideas with the appropriate punctuation. The first part of the sentence, *Rock and roll was widely embraced as the symbol* is not an independent clause. The second part of the sentence, *of a new, rebellious generation,* is also not an independent clause. A colon can only be used after an independent clause, so eliminate (C). There is no reason to break up the phrase *symbol of a new, rebellious generation* with commas before or after *of*, so eliminate (A) and (D). The correct answer is (B).

39. **D**   Note the question! The question asks for the choice that *logically completes the discussion of the popularity of early rock and provides an effective transition into the next paragraph*, so it's testing consistency of ideas. The paragraph discusses the rise in the popularity of rock and roll and the artists that propelled it to popularity. The next paragraph begins with *but in the late 50s*, which indicates a shift in ideas. The paragraph goes on to say that many of the popular artists were disappearing from the rock-and-roll scene. The concluding sentence should end on a very positive note about the popularity of rock and roll. The type of *guitar* is not consistent with the popularity of the music, so eliminate (A). The type of *dance moves* is not consistent with the popularity of the music, so eliminate (B). The information about *American Bandstand* does discuss the *popularity* of rock music, but it does not provide a direct contrast to the next paragraph, so eliminate (C). The *rise of rock and roll was unstoppable* is consistent with the popularity of the music and does provide a contrast to the next paragraph, so keep (D). The correct answer is (D).

40. **B**   Note the question! The question asks for the choice that *most effectively sets up the main idea of the paragraph*, so it's testing consistency of ideas. The paragraph discusses how many of the popular artists were leaving the rock-and-roll scene. The correct answer will be consistent with this idea. *Expand their musical styles* is not consistent with leaving the scene, so eliminate (A). *Icons of early rock disappeared from the music scene* is consistent, so keep (B). *Write their own songs* is not consistent with leaving the scene, so eliminate (C). *British rock bands* are not consistent with leaving the scene, so eliminate (D). The correct answer is (B).

41.   **C**   Note the question! The question asks for the choice that is *most consistent with the examples in the previous sentences*, so it's testing consistency of ideas. All the other examples are negative situations that caused artists to leave the rock-and-roll scene. The correct answer will be consistent with this idea. *Debuted his signature move* is not consistent with leaving the scene, so eliminate (A). *Opened some of the first integrated music clubs* is not consistent with leaving the scene, so eliminate (B). *Served time in jail* is consistent with leaving the scene, so keep (C). *An innovative new way* is not consistent with leaving the scene, so eliminate (D). The correct answer is (C).

42.   **B**   Apostrophes are changing in the choices, so the question is testing apostrophe usage. When used with a noun, an apostrophe indicates possession. In this sentence, The Beatles are possessing the albums, but the albums are not possessing anything. Therefore, *albums* does not need an apostrophe. Eliminate (A), (C), and (D). The correct answer is (B).

43.   **A**   Pronouns change in the answer choices, so this question tests consistency of pronouns. There is also the option to DELETE; consider this choice carefully as it is often the correct answer. There is a comparison in the sentence, so this question tests consistency. When two things are compared, they should be consistent with each other. The first item in the comparison is *these new stars.* Deleting the underlined portion would make the second part of the comparison *of the late 50s*, which is not consistent with *stars*, so eliminate (D). The word *them* cannot be used before the phrase *of the late 50s*, so eliminate (B). *These* indicates something nearby; the stars of the late 50s are not nearby, so eliminate (C). Choice (A) makes the comparison consistent. The correct answer is (A).

44.   **A**   Note the question! The question asks how to effectively combine the underlined sentences, so it tests precision and concision. The first sentence mentions that Elvis was *met with disapproval,* and the second sentence mentions that The Beatles were *seen as a symbol of rebellion.* These two ideas are similar examples of the same phenomenon, so the combination should be consistent with this comparison. *Just as* indicates two similar ideas, so keep (A). *Even though* indicates opposite ideas, so eliminate (B). The sentence is supposed to convey that *parents* not *the band's fans* viewed The Beatles' hairdos as a symbol of rebellion; eliminate (C). In (D), it is unclear what is *shaggy and rebellious*, so eliminate (D). The correct answer is (A).

Section 3: Math (No Calculator)

1.   **A**   The question asks for the sum of two complex numbers, which are numbers with both real and imaginary parts. To do this, add the real parts and the imaginary parts separately. Therefore, $(3 + 6i) + (7 + 2i) = (3 + 7) + (6i + 2i) = 10 + 8i$. The correct answer is (A).

2.   **A**   The question asks for the meaning of a constant in context. Start by reading the full question, which asks for the meaning of the number 100. Then label the parts of the equation with the information given. The question states that C is the total cost and h is the hours. The number 100 is added to the expression for hours, so it must be unrelated to the number of hours. Next, use process of elimination to get rid of answer choices that are not consistent with the labels. Choices (B), (C), and (D) all refer to hours, which is represented by h, not 100, so eliminate these answers. To check (A), plug in some numbers. Choice (A) says that 100 is the registration fee, which must be paid no matter how many hours are charged. Make $h = 0$ to get $C = 40(0) + 100 = 100$. This fits the situation described. The correct answer is (A).

3. **D** The question asks to model a relationship, so figure out one part at a time and eliminate after each step. In all four choices, 150 is given on the right side as a result of addition on the left side. Since 150 is the total number of ounces of gold, determine what is added to get the total number of ounces. Because there are two samples, the number of ounces of gold in each sample is added to get 150. Since a represents the percent, as a decimal, of pure gold in Sample F, which weighs 220 ounces, the number of ounces of gold in Sample F is $220a$. Eliminate any choice that does not include this quantity. Eliminate (A), (B), and (C). Only one choice remains. To better see why (D) is correct, follow a similar line of reasoning to get that the number of ounces of gold in Sample B is $140b$. This must be added to $220a$ to get 150. The correct answer is (D).

4. **D** The question asks for the value of $4a - 5$. Put the value $b = 15$ into $a = \frac{4}{5}b$ to get $a = \frac{4}{5} \times \frac{15}{1}$.

   Cancel a 5 from the numerator and denominator to make the math easier: $a = \frac{4}{1} \times \frac{3}{1} = 12$.

   Now plug this value into $4a - 5$ to get $4(12) - 5 = 48 - 5 = 43$. The correct answer is (D).

5. **B** The question asks for the value of c, which appears on the left side of the question. Notice that the left side is in the form of one of the common quadratics: $a^2 - b^2 = (a + b)(a - b)$ with $a = cy$ and $b = d$. Therefore, $(cy - d)(cy + d) = (cy)^2 - d^2 = c^2y^2 - d^2$. Since $25y^2 - 16 = c^2y^2 - d^2$, $c^2 = 25$ and $d^2 = 16$. The question asks for the value of c, so take the square root of both sides in $c^2 = 25$ to get $c = \pm 5$. Only $+5$ is a choice. The correct answer is (B).

6. **A** The question asks for the value of y, so isolate y in the equation $\sqrt{49} = \sqrt{y} - \sqrt{16}$. Add $\sqrt{16}$ to both sides to get $\sqrt{49} + \sqrt{16} = \sqrt{y}$. Now simplify the equation. Since $\sqrt{49} = 7$ and $\sqrt{16} = 4$, the equation simplifies to $7 + 4 = \sqrt{y}$. Add on the left side to get $11 = \sqrt{y}$. Square both sides to get $y = 121$. The correct answer is (A).

7. **A** The question asks for the graph of the given equation. To find the graph of an equation in the form $y = mx + b$, use the fact that m is the slope and b is the y-intercept. In the equation $y = \frac{1}{3}x - 2$, the y-intercept is -2, so eliminate any choice that crosses the y-axis at a point other than -2. Eliminate (B) and (D). The slope of $y = \frac{1}{3}x - 2$ is $\frac{1}{3}$. Because the slope is positive, the graph increases as it goes from left to right. Eliminate (C), which decreases as it goes from left to right. The correct answer is (A).

8. **B** The question asks for h, in terms of F and n. Isolate h in the equation $F = 300nh$ by dividing both sides by $300n$ to get $\frac{F}{300n} = h$. The correct answer is (B).

9. **D** The question asks for the value of s, and there are numbers in the choices, so use those in the equation. Eliminate any choice for which $r(s) \times t(s)$ is not equal to s. For (A), $s = 0$, so $r(s) \times t(s) = r(0) \times t(0) = (-1) \times (-1) = 1$. Since this is not equal to 0, eliminate (A). For (B), $s = 1$, so $r(s) \times t(s) = r(1) \times t(1) = 2 \times 1 = 2$. Since this is not equal to 1, eliminate (B). For (C), $s = 2$, so $r(s) \times t(s) = r(2) \times t(2) = 3 \times 1 = 3$. Since this is not equal to 2, eliminate (C). For (D), $s = 3$, so $r(s) \times t(s) = r(3) \times t(3) = (-1) \times (-3) = 3$. This is equal to the value of s. Therefore, the correct answer is (D).

10. **A** The question asks for an equivalent expression to the given one. Rather than doing complex algebra, choose a number for y. Let $y = 2$. If $y = 2$, then $\dfrac{2y^2 + 5y}{2y + 7} = \dfrac{2(2)^2 + 5(2)}{2(2) + 7} = \dfrac{2(4) + 5(2)}{4 + 7} = \dfrac{8 + 10}{11} = \dfrac{18}{11}$. Plug $y = 2$ into each of the choices and eliminate any that are not equal to $\dfrac{18}{11}$. Choice (A) is $2 - 1 + \dfrac{7}{2(2) + 7} = 1 + \dfrac{7}{11} = \dfrac{18}{11}$. Keep (A), but try the other answers just in case. Choice (B) is $2 + \dfrac{7}{2(2) + 7} = 2 + \dfrac{7}{11} = \dfrac{29}{11}$. Eliminate (B). Choice (C) is $2 + 2 = 4$. Eliminate (C). Choice (D) is 2. Eliminate (D). The correct answer is (A).

11. **B** The question asks for an inequality to represent the value of s, the score Renee could receive on a test and still maintain her desired average. For averages, use the formula $T = AN$, in which T is the total, A is the average, and N is the number of things. Here, Renee wants her average for the 3 tests to be 90 or more. To find the total, multiply these numbers to get $T = 3(90)$. Renee has already received scores of 99 and 83, so the total can also be represented as $99 + 83 + s$. Since Renee wants at least this much, the full inequality is $99 + 83 + s \geq 3(90)$. The correct answer is (B).

12. **C** The question asks what is true about the parabola given by the equation $y = -a(x + j) - k$. Look at one part of the parabola equation at a time and use Process of Elimination. First, notice $-a$. The negative sign on the a means the parabola opens downwards. Eliminate (B) and (D). The equation $y = -a(x + j)^2 - k$ is in vertex form, so it is straightforward to determine the vertex. In vertex form $a(x - h)^2 + k$, the vertex is (h, k). Therefore, the vertex in the given equation is $(-j, -k)$. Eliminate (A). The correct answer is (C).

13. **C** The question asks for an expression that is equivalent to the given one. Rather than doing complicated algebraic manipulation, try some numbers for the variables. Let $x = 4$ and $y = 5$. The given expression becomes $\left(\dfrac{x}{2} - y\right)^2 = \left(\dfrac{4}{2} - 5\right)^2 = (2 - 5)^2 = (-3)^2 = 9$. Plug $x = 4$ and $y = 5$ into each of the choices, and eliminate any that are not 9. Choice (A) is $\dfrac{4^2}{2} + 5^2 = \dfrac{16}{2} + 25 = 8 + 25 = 33$, so eliminate (A). Choice (B) is $\dfrac{4^2}{4} + 5^2 = \dfrac{16}{4} + 25 = 4 + 25 = 29$, so eliminate (B). Choice (C) is $\dfrac{4^2}{4} - (4)(5) + 5^2 = \dfrac{16}{4} - 20 + 25 = 4 - 20 + 25 = -16 + 25 = 9$, so keep (C). Choice (D) is $\dfrac{4^2}{2} - \dfrac{(4)(5)}{2} + 5^2 = \dfrac{16}{2} - \dfrac{20}{2} + 25 = 8 - 10 + 25 = -2 + 25 = 23$, so eliminate (D). The correct answer is (C).

14. **D** The question asks for the value of k in the equation. Since there are numbers in the answer choices, try them out in the equation to see which one yields two real values of x. Start with one of the middle choices. Try (C). If $k = -2$, then $4x^2 - 5x = -2$. Add 2 to both sides to get $4x^2 - 5x + 2 = 0$. Determine whether this has two real solutions. This may be difficult to factor, so use the quadratic formula. To find the solutions to a quadratic in the form $ax^2 + bx + c = 0$, use the formula $x = \dfrac{-b \pm \sqrt{b^2 - 4ac}}{2a}$. Plug in $a = 4$, $b = -5$, and $c = 2$ to get

$x = \dfrac{-(-5) \pm \sqrt{(-5)^2 - 4(4)(2)}}{2(4)} = \dfrac{5 \pm \sqrt{25 - 32}}{8} = \dfrac{5 \pm \sqrt{-8}}{8}$. However, since $\sqrt{-8}$ does not have

any real values, this does not have any real solutions. Eliminate (C). In order to get a positive number under the square root, a smaller number must be subtracted from b^2. Try (D). If $k = -1$, then $4x^2 - 5x = -1$. Add 1 to both sides to get $4x^2 - 5x + 1 = 0$. Plug in $a = 4$, $b = -5$, and

$c = 1$ into the quadratic formula to get $x = \dfrac{-(-5) \pm \sqrt{(-5)^2 - 4(4)(1)}}{2(4)} = \dfrac{5 \pm \sqrt{25 - 16}}{8} = \dfrac{5 \pm \sqrt{9}}{8}$

$= \dfrac{5 \pm 3}{8}$. Therefore, $x = \dfrac{5 + 3}{8} = \dfrac{8}{8} = 1$ or $x = \dfrac{5 - 3}{8} = \dfrac{2}{8} = \dfrac{1}{4}$. There are two real solutions.

Therefore, the correct answer is (D).

15. **C** The question asks for a system of inequalities to model a situation. Translate one piece at a time and use Process of Elimination. Start with the simplest piece. The store owner wants to buy at least three times as many T-shirts as pairs of jeans. Since the number of T-shirts must be at least 3 times the number of pairs of jeans, $t \geq 3j$. Eliminate (B) and (D), which don't include this inequality. The store owner wants to spend no more than \$200. Set what the store owner spends as ≤ 200. Because the store owner spends \$1.25 on each of the t T-shirts, the store owner spends a total of $1.25t$ dollars on T-shirts. Even though the number of T-shirts is at least 3 times the number of pairs of jeans, there is no need to multiply this number by 3. Eliminate (A), which does not include $1.25t$. Only one choice remains. To better see why (C) is correct, note that the store owner spends \$9.75 on each of the j pairs of jeans she buys, for a total of $9.75j$ dollars spent on jeans. Therefore, she spends a total of $1.25t + 9.75j$ on T-shirts and jeans. Set this sum less than or equal to 200 to get $1.25t + 9.75j \leq 200$. The correct answer is (C).

16. **16** The question asks for the length of $\overline{PS}$, which is the longer leg of the larger triangle. Because $\overline{PQ}$ is parallel to $\overline{RT}$, the two triangles are similar, making their corresponding sides proportional. Notice that the smaller right triangle has a leg with length 3 and a hypotenuse of 5. Therefore, this is a 3:4:5 right triangle with $\overline{ST}$ measuring 4. Since $\overline{PQ}$ corresponds to $\overline{RT}$ and $\overline{PS}$ corre-

sponds to $\overline{ST}$, set up the proportion $\dfrac{PQ}{RT} = \dfrac{PS}{ST}$. Substitute the known lengths to get $\dfrac{12}{3} = \dfrac{PS}{4}$.

To make the math easier, reduce the left fraction to get $4 = \dfrac{PS}{4}$. Multiply both sides by 4 to get

$PS = 16$. The correct answer is 16.

17. **1, 2, 3, 4, 6, or 12**

The questions asks for one possible value of s in an exponential equation. This indicates that there are likely many answers, but only one is needed. Rather than doing complicated algebra, try out a value for r. To make this as easy as possible, put the two sides of the equation in the same form. Because the left side of the equation is a base raised to an exponent, rewrite the right

side as 64^1 to get $r^{\frac{s}{2}} = 64^1$. Since both sides are bases raised to exponents, the two bases could

be equal and the two exponents could be equal, so set $r = 64$ and $\dfrac{s}{2} = 1$. To find the value of s, multiply both sides of $\frac{s}{2} = 1$ by 2 to get $s = 2$. Therefore, one possible answer is 2. There is no

need to continue, but other correct answers are $s = 1$ when $r = 4{,}096$, $s = 3$ when $r = 16$, $s = 4$ when $r = 8$, $s = 6$ when $r = 4$, and $s = 12$ when $r = 2$. All these value of s are correct answers.

18. $\frac{1}{24}$, .041, or .042

The question asks what fraction of the circumference is the length of arc PQ, so set up the fraction $\frac{\text{arc}}{\text{circumference}}$. The question says that the arc length is $\frac{\pi}{6}$, so put this into the numerator to

get $\frac{\frac{\pi}{6}}{\text{circumference}}$. Now find the circumference. The formula for circumference is $C = 2\pi r$. Since

the question says that the radius is 2, plug $r = 2$ into the formula to get $C = 2\pi(2) = 4\pi$. Plug this

into the denominator to get $\frac{\frac{\pi}{6}}{4\pi}$. Rewrite the denominator as a fraction to get $\frac{\frac{\pi}{6}}{\frac{4\pi}{1}}$. To divide

fractions, multiply the numerator by the reciprocal of the denominator to get $\frac{\pi}{6} \times \frac{1}{4\pi} = \frac{\pi}{24\pi}$.

Cancel π in the numerator and denominator to get $\frac{1}{24}$. The correct answer is $\frac{1}{24}$.

19. $\frac{49}{8}$, 6.12, or 6.13

The question asks for the value of a in an equation. To do this, divide both sides by the coefficient of a. Because the coefficient is a fraction, dividing by the coefficient is the same as multiply-

ing by the reciprocal. Multiply both sides by $\frac{7}{4}$ to get $a = \frac{7}{2} \times \frac{7}{4} = \frac{49}{8}$. The correct answer is

$\frac{49}{8}$.

20. $\frac{5}{2}$ or 2.5

The question asks how many gallons of a certain juice mix must be added to another mix to make a final mix that contains 40% juice. The type of juice being added is 60% orange juice. Let this

amount be x. A juice mix of x gallons that contains 60% orange juice has $\frac{60}{100}x$ gallons of orange

juice. The 5 gallons of a juice mix that have 30% orange juice contain $\frac{30}{100}(5)$ gallons of orange

juice. The solutions are added to a new solution that contains $\frac{60}{100}x + \frac{30}{100}(5)$ gallons of orange

juice. Because the combined juice mix has $x + 5$ total gallons and is 40% orange juice, it con-

tains $\frac{40}{100}(x + 5)$ gallons of orange juice. Set the two equal to get $\frac{60}{100}x + \frac{30}{100}(5) = \frac{40}{100}(x + 5)$.

Multiply both sides by 100 to get $60x + 30(5) = 40(x + 5)$. Simplify the left side and distribute the 40 on the right side to get $60x + 150 = 40x + 200$. Subtract $40x$ from both sides to get $20x + 150 = 200$. Subtract 150 from both sides to get $20x = 50$. Divide both sides by 20 to get $x = \dfrac{50}{20}$. Because this requires more than four spaces to grid in, reduce the fraction. Divide the numerator and denominator by 10 to get that the correct answer is $\dfrac{5}{2}$.

Section 4: Math (Calculator)

1. **C** The question asks for the graph that could model a situation. Look at the graphs in the answer choices and use Process of Elimination to find the answer. Choice (D) shows that Laura's distance did not change over time. Since this isn't true, eliminate (D). Choice (A) indicates that after resting on the park bench, Laura didn't run any more. This isn't true either, so eliminate (A). The question states that after resting, Laura *ran at a slower rate than she had initially*. This means that her change in distance over time would be less after she rested. The graph in (B) shows that Laura's change in distance over time before and after resting is the same. This doesn't match the statement in the question, so eliminate (B). In (C), Laura's change in distance is less after resting than it was before resting. The correct answer is (C).

2. **D** The question asks for an expression that is equivalent to the given one. Combine one set of terms at a time and eliminate after each one. Start by finding the first term, which is $3y^2 - (-5y^2) = 3y^2 + 5y^2 = 8y^2$. Eliminate (A) and (B), since neither has $8y^2$ as the first term. Now find the last term, which is $-2 - (-6) = -2 + 6 = 4$. Eliminate (C) since it has -4 as the last term. The correct answer is (D).

3. **B** The question asks for the difference between the initial temperatures of Block A and Block B. Since the temperature is found on the y-axis, look for the temperature of each block at time $t = 0$. Block B has an initial temperature of 40 and Block A has an initial temperature of 25. The difference is $40 - 25 = 15$. The correct answer is (B).

4. **A** The question asks how many households receive their Internet service from either Corporate Cable or Global Networks. Corporate Cable serves 47% of households and Global Networks serves 17% of households. Add these to get $47\% + 17\% = 64\%$. Since the total number of households is 2,800, take 64% of that to get $2{,}800 \times \dfrac{64}{100} = 1{,}792$. The correct answer is (A).

5. **C** The question asks for the value of x, the cost in dollars of each carton of ink. Rather than creating an algebraic equation, try the numbers in the answer choices. Start with (B) and plug in 52 for the value of x. If the cost of the cartridges is $52, 18 cartridges would cost $\$52 \times 18 = \$936$. Add on the subscription fee of $230 to get a total of $\$936 + \$230 = \$1{,}166$. This is not enough, so eliminate (B) and also (A), which is even smaller. The total was only slightly too small, so try (C) next. If the cartridges cost $63 each, 18 cost $\$63 \times 18 = \$1{,}134$. With the subscription fee, the total is $\$1{,}134 + \$230 = \$1{,}364$. This matches the information in the question. The correct answer is (C).

6. **D** The question asks for an inequality that is equivalent to the given one. Simplify the inequality to find the answer. Since each term has a greatest common factor of 4, divide each term by 4 to get $4a + 5b > 3$. This inequality matches (D). The correct answer is (D).

7. **B**   The question asks for the number of nautical miles in the first stage of Amelia Earhart's trip. Rather than creating an algebraic equation, try the numbers in the answer choices. Start with (B) and plug in 283 for the number of nautical miles in the first stage. If the first stage was 283 nautical miles, then the second stage was 283 + 110 = 393 nautical miles. Add the two stages together to get 283 + 393 = 676 nautical miles. This matches the information in the question. The correct answer is (B).

8. **C**   The question asks for the cost of oranges, in dollars per pound. The total weight of the carton of oranges is 27.3 pounds, but 9.6 of those pounds represent the weight of the carton itself. Since 27.3 – 9.6 = 17.7 pounds, the oranges by themselves weigh 17.7 pounds. The cost of the carton is $46.25. Divide to find $\frac{\$46.25}{17.7 \text{ pounds}}$ = $2.61 per pound. This is closest to (C). The correct answer is (C).

9. **C**   The question asks what information is true about the board's survey. Since only marine biologists were included in the sample group, the results of the survey cannot be extrapolated to all scientists. Even though a majority of the marine biologists were in favor of the aquatic exhibit, this does not mean that a majority of all the scientists would also be in favor of the aquatic exhibit. Because of this, eliminate (B). For the survey to be truly representative of all the scientists, the sample group needs to include other scientists besides marine biologists. Adding more marine biologists would not make the sample group more representative, so eliminate (A). Using a sample group that contains no marine biologists at all would also not be representative, so eliminate (D). Since the sample group used in the survey was not representative of all the scientists, the survey was biased. The correct answer is (C).

10. **A**   This question asks for the fraction of adopted cats that were black. First, find the total number of adopted cats, which is 9 + 7 = 16. Of those 16 cats, 7 were black. Therefore, the fraction of adopted cats that were black is $\frac{7}{16}$. The correct answer is (A).

11. **B**   The question asks for the meaning of d in the function $a(t) = c - dt$. Label what is known in the equation. The function a is the extent, in millions of square kilometers, of Arctic sea ice. The variable t represents the number of years since the study began. Next, use Process of Elimination. Constant d is multiplied by t. In a linear equation, the coefficient on the variable is the slope, which is the rate of change. Choices (A), (C), and (D) refer to a specific amount, not the change *per year*. Only (B) indicates that d is the rate of change. The correct answer is (B).

12. **C**   The question asks for the best linear model for the extent from Year 7 to Year 11. Use the equations in the answer choices to try out values from the table during this period. Since the extent in Year 7 was 5.39, plug in $t = 7$ into each choice, and eliminate any for which a is not close to 5.39. Choice (A) is $a = 5 - 0.21(7) = 3.53$. This is not close to 5.39, so eliminate (A). Choice (B) is $a = 7 - 0.13(7) = 6.09$. This is not close to 5.39, so eliminate (B). Choice (C) is $a = 10 - 0.64(7) = 5.4$. This is close to 5.39, so keep (C). Choice (D) is $a = 15 - 1.82(7) = 2.26$. This is not close to 5.39, so eliminate (D). The correct answer is (C).

13. **A**   The question asks for the period for which the average decrease in the ice extent was the greatest. Look at the years from the answer choices on the graph and estimate. A great decrease would be a line that slopes down sharply from left to right. Choice (A) shows a sharp decrease from Year 4 to Year 5, so keep (A). Choice (B) also shows a decrease from Year 7 to Year 8, but it is not as steep as the one in (A). Eliminate (B). Choice (C) shows a decrease from Year 9 to Year 10, but it

is not as steep as the one in (A). Eliminate (C). Choice (D) shows a decrease from Year 12 to Year 13, but it is not as steep as the one in (A). Eliminate (D). The correct answer is (A).

14. **D** This question asks for the sum of the values of c and d in the solution to the system of equations. Since the equations have the same coefficient on the d terms with opposite signs, add the two equations together to eliminate d.

$$\begin{aligned} 9c + 5d &= 22 \\ +\ 7c - 5d &= 10 \\ \hline 16c\quad\ \ &= 32 \end{aligned}$$

Divide both sides by 16 to get $c = 2$. Plug $c = 2$ back into the top equation to get $9(2) + 5d = 22$. Simplify to $18 + 5d = 22$. Subtract 18 from both sides to get $5d = 4$. Divide both sides by 5 to get $d = \dfrac{4}{5}$.

The value of $c + d$ is $2 + \dfrac{4}{5} = \dfrac{10}{5} + \dfrac{4}{5} = \dfrac{14}{5}$. The correct answer is (D).

15. **A** The question asks for the ratio that is equivalent to $\dfrac{WZ}{WX}$. Start this question by filling in the missing angle measurements for $\angle WXZ$ and $\angle YXZ$ by using the rule that there are 180° in a triangle. $\angle WXZ$ is 28° and $\angle YXZ$ is 62°. Since triangle WXZ and triangle XYZ have identical angle measurements, they are similar triangles. Start by determining what the numerator of the ratio represents. Side WZ is the side opposite the 28° angle in triangle WXZ and corresponds to side XZ of triangle XYZ, since side XZ is opposite the 28° angle in triangle XYZ. Therefore, WZ corresponds to XZ. Eliminate (B) and (D), since these answers do not have the correct numerator. As for the denominator of the ratio, side WX represents the hypotenuse of triangle WXZ. In triangle XYZ, the hypotenuse is represented by XY. Therefore, WX corresponds to XY. Taken together, $\dfrac{WZ}{WX} = \dfrac{XZ}{XY}$. The correct answer is (A).

16. **B** The question asks for an equation to model the values in the table. Rather than trying to create an equation, pick a value from the table to test out the answers. Choose an easy number to work with, like $s = 0$, and look for an equation that gives $t = \dfrac{31}{2}$. Choice (A) becomes $t = \dfrac{31}{2} \times (6)^0 = \dfrac{31}{2}(1) = \dfrac{31}{2}$. This equals $\dfrac{31}{2}$, so keep (A). Choice (B) becomes $t = 6(0) + \dfrac{31}{2} = 0 + \dfrac{31}{2} = \dfrac{31}{2}$. This equals $\dfrac{31}{2}$, so keep (B). Choice (C) becomes $t = \dfrac{1}{4} \times \left(\dfrac{31}{2}\right)^0 = \dfrac{1}{4}(1) = \dfrac{1}{4}$. This does not equal $\dfrac{31}{2}$, so eliminate (C). Choice (D) becomes $t = \dfrac{1}{6}(0) - 4 = 0 - 4 = -4$. This does not equal $\dfrac{31}{2}$, so eliminate (D). Test a second value to see if the answer is (A) or (B). Choose another easy value to plug in, like $s = 1$, and look for an equation that gives $t = \dfrac{43}{2}$. Choice (A) becomes $t = \dfrac{31}{2}(6)^1 = \dfrac{31}{2}(6) = \dfrac{186}{2}$. This does not equal $\dfrac{43}{2}$, so eliminate (A). Choice (B) becomes $t = 6(1) + \dfrac{31}{2} = 6 + \dfrac{31}{2} = \dfrac{43}{2}$. Choice (B) equals $\dfrac{43}{2}$. Therefore, the correct answer is (B).

17. **B** The question asks for all the possible values for box width. The question states that the box width must be at least 3 inches. Use this information to eliminate (D), since it allows for box widths that are less than 3 inches. Now, determine what possible box dimensions meet the requirements of a width of at least 3 inches and a height of at least 12 inches using the box size formula, $h + 3w = 30$. If the width of the box is 3 inches, then the height is $h + (3)(3) = 30$, or $h + 9 = 30$. Subtract 9 from both sides to get $h = 21$. This means that when a box has a width of 3 inches, the height of the box is 21 inches. Since 21 inches is more than 12 inches, these dimensions meet the requirement. Therefore, 3 inches is a possible width for this requirement. Use this information to eliminate (A), since 3 inches is not included in this answer choice. According to the box size formula, as the width of the box increases, the height of the box decreases. Therefore, to find the maximum possible width of the box, plug in the least possible height of 12 inches to get $12 + 3w = 30$. Subtract 12 from both sides to get $3w = 18$. Divide both sides by 3 to get $w = 6$. Therefore, 6 inches is a possible box width, and it is also the greatest possible box width given the restrictions in the question. Since 6 inches must be the greatest possible width, eliminate (C), which allows for unlimited box widths. The correct answer is (B).

18. **B** The question asks for the width of the box. Rather than doing complicated algebraic manipulations, try the values in the answer choices. Use the box size formula, $h + 3w = 30$, to find the corresponding height for each answer choice. The question states that this height must be between 8 and 10 inches. Start with (B) and make $w = 7.2$ inches. The box size formula becomes $h + 3(7.2) = 30$, which simplifies to $h + 21.6 = 30$. Subtract 21.6 from both sides to get $h = 8.4$. Since 8.4 is between 8 and 10, keep (B). Now use the other information in the question to determine if the answer is (B). The question says that the stacked display has a total height of 7 feet, which is $7 \times 12 = 84$ inches. Since the height of the boxes is equal to the height of each level, divide the total height of the stacked display by the height of the box to find the number of levels. The question states that the stacked display must have an even number of levels. If the boxes have a height of 8.4 inches, divide to find $\frac{84}{8.4} = 10$ levels. This is an even integer, so the value for the width in (B) satisfies all the requirements in the question. The correct answer is (B).

19. **A** This question asks for the box width in terms of the box height. To find the answer, rearrange the box size formula in terms of w. The formula states that $h + 3w = 30$. Start by subtracting h from both sides to get $3w = 30 - h$. Divide both sides by 3 to get $w = \dfrac{30 - h}{3} = \dfrac{1}{3}(30 - h)$. This matches (A). The correct answer is (A).

20. **C** The question asks for the conclusion that is best supported by the data. The main result of the study was that of the 250 red maple trees measured in the sample, 40% had a circumference less than 35 inches. This data is specific to one type of tree, the red maple tree, and cannot be extrapolated to other types of trees or generalized to all the trees in the forest. Use this logic to eliminate (A), (B), and (D), which draw conclusions for *all the trees in the forest*. The data from the study can only be used to support conclusions about red maple trees. Since (C) is the only choice that specifically references red maple trees, the correct answer is (C).

21. **A** The question asks for the product of the solutions to an equation. To solve the equation in the question, set each binomial equal to 0 and solve. For the first binomial, $y + 4 = 0$, so subtract 4 from both sides to get $y = -4$. For the second binomial, $y - 0.3 = 0$, so add 0.3 to both sides to get $y = 0.3$. Therefore, there are two solutions to the equation, $y = -4$ or 0.3. A *product* is the result of multiplication, so multiply these values to get $-4 \times 0.3 = -1.2$. The correct answer is (A).

22. **B** The question asks how many times the gymnast was at a height of 15 feet. Find 15 feet on the y-axis and draw a line across. Look for the number of times this line intersects with the graph. It intersects twice: once at about 4 seconds and a second time at about 5.5 seconds. Since the gymnast was at a height of 15 feet exactly two times, the correct answer is (B).

23. **C** The question asks by what percent the writer's salary increased. Rather than creating an equation with the awkward numbers given, use the percents in the answer choices, looking for the answer choice that gives the writer's new salary of $88.51. Start with (B). If the writer's original salary of $81.34 increased by 8.1%, her salary would increase by $81.34 $\times$ $\dfrac{8.1}{100}$ = $6.59. Add this increase to her original salary to get a new salary of $81.34 + $6.59 = $87.93. This is not equal to the new salary of $88.51, so eliminate (B). Additionally, since the salary calculated with (B) is too small, eliminate (A) as well. Try (C) next. If the writer's original salary of $81.34 increased by 8.8%, her salary would increase by $81.34 $\times$ $\dfrac{8.8}{100}$ = $7.16. Add this increase to her original salary to get a new salary of $81.34 + $7.16 = $88.50. This is closest to the new salary of $88.51. The correct answer is (C).

24. **D** The question states that the function is a linear function and asks for the value of $h(6)$, or the value of y when $x = 6$. The function is linear, so use two points to find the slope of the line, which is defined as $\dfrac{y_2 - y_1}{x_2 - x_1}$. Using the second and third points on the table, slope = $\dfrac{21 - 5}{7 - 3} = \dfrac{16}{4} = 4$. Plug this value and point (3, 5) into $y = mx + b$ to get 5 = 3(4) + b or 5 = 12 + b. Therefore, $b = -7$ and the equation of the line is $y = h(x) = 4x - 7$. Now find $h(6)$, which is 4(6) – 7 = 24 – 7 = 17. The correct answer is (D).

25. **C** The question asks for the median age, and the median is defined as the middle number in a numerical list. The table contains 35 numbers for age, but displays them as frequency. Because there are 35 numbers for age, the middle age will be the 18th age in the table. Start counting from the left, adding up the frequency for each age: 1 + 1 + 2 + 2 + 1 + 2 + 1 + 5 + 2 = 17. This list includes all ages up to and including 52. The 18th age is 54, so the median age in the table is 54. The correct answer is (C).

26. **D** This question asks for the radius of a circle based on its equation. Start by simplifying the equation by dividing each term by 4 to get $x^2 + 5x + y^2 - 3y = 27.5$. The standard form for the equation of a circle with center (h, k) and radius r is $(x^2 - h)^2 + (y^2 - k)^2 = r^2$. In order to factor this equation into standard form, complete the square. For each x and y, take half of the coefficient of the middle term, square it, and add it to both sides. For the x-terms, $x^2 + 5x$, add $\left(\dfrac{5}{2}\right)^2$ = 6.25 to both sides. For the y-terms, $y^2 - 3y$, add $\left(-\dfrac{3}{2}\right)^2$ = 2.25 to both sides. The new equation will be $(x^2 + 5x + 6.25) + (y^2 - 3y + 2.25)$ = 27.5 + 6.25 + 2.25. The simplified expression in standard form is $(x^2 + 2.5)^2 + (y^2 - 1.5)^2 = 36$. Therefore, $r^2 = 36$ and $r = 6$. The correct answer is (D).

27. **A** The question asks for the resistance of a certain resistor in a circuit diagram. Focus on Resistors X and Z since the question does not ask about Resistor Y. Start with the information in the figure, which shows that the current through Resistor X is 5 amperes and the current through Resistor Z is 15 amperes. According to the question, this means that the current ratio, a:b, is 5:15, which can be reduced to 1:3. Therefore, the current ratio of Resistor X to Resistor Z is 1:3. How-

ever, the question is asking about the resistance. The resistance ratio is defined as $b:a$. Since the current ratio, $a:b$, is 1:3, the resistance ratio, $b:a$, is 3:1. Therefore, the resistance ratio of Resistor X to Resistor Z is 3:1. The question states that the resistance of Resistor X is 24 ohms.

Use the resistance ratio to find the resistance of Resistor Z: $\frac{3}{1} = \frac{24}{x}$. Cross-multiply to get

$3x = 24$, then divide both sides of the equation by 3 to get $x = 8$. The resistance of Resistor Z is 8. The correct answer is (A).

28. **D** The question asks for the orbital ratio, specifically in seconds per meter. Label the variables given in the equation, where P is seconds and a is meters. To get *seconds per meter*, divide P by a to get

$\frac{36 \times 10^{-8} a\sqrt{a}}{a}$. Cancel the a in the numerator and the a in the denominator to get $36 \times 10^{-8}\sqrt{a}$.

The correct answer is (D).

29. **A** This question asks for the equation that best models the data in the scatterplot. All the equations in the answer choices are parabolas, and this matches the shape of the data in the scatterplot. The scatterplot data is shaped as a parabola opening upwards. Since a parabola that opens upwards must have a positive x^2 term, eliminate (C) and (D). Now check the constant term in the equations. For an equation in the xy-plane, a positive constant term means that the graph crosses the y-axis above the x-axis, and a negative constant term means that the graph crosses the y-axis below the x-axis. Since the graph of the scatterplot data would cross the y-axis well above the x-axis, the constant term must be positive. Eliminate (B), since the constant term is −483.27. Choice (A) has a positive constant term of 483.27. The correct answer is (A).

30. **B** The question asks for the coordinates of the two points on the number line. Each point is 5 units away from the point −6. Since −6 + 5 = −1 and −6 − 5 = −11, the two points on the number line must be −1 and −11. Try out these values for y and use Process of Elimination to find the answer. Start with −1. Choice (A) becomes $|-1 - 6| = 5$, which simplifies to $|-7| = 5$. Since this is false, eliminate (A). Choice (B) becomes $|-1 + 6| = 5$, which simplifies to $|5| = 5$. Since this is true, keep (B). Choice (C) becomes $|-1 - 5| = 6$, which simplifies to $|-6| = 6$. Since this is true, keep (C). Choice (D) becomes $|-1 + 5| = 6$, which simplifies to $|4| = 6$. Since this is false, eliminate (D). Now test −11 in (B) and (C). Choice (B) becomes $|-11 + 6| = 5$, which simplifies to $|-5| = 5$. Since this is true, keep (B). Choice (C) becomes $|-11 - 5| = 6$, which simplifies to $|-16| = 6$. Since this is false, eliminate (C). The correct answer is (B).

31. **247, 248, 249, 250, or 251**

This question asks for the volume of the ice cream cone. The reference box at the beginning of the math section gives the formula for the volume of a cone as $V = \frac{1}{3}\pi r^2 h$. The question states that r is 4 centimeters and that h is between 14.75 and 15 centimeters. Choose a value of h to work with, for example, 14.8. Plug the known values into the formula to get $V = \frac{1}{3}\pi(4)^2(14.8)$. Solve to get $V = 247.97$ or 248. Depending on which value is used for height, the correct answer could be 247, 248, 249, 250, or 251.

32. **8** This question asks for the number of coworkers in the original group. Rather than creating an algebraic equation, try out different numbers for this value to solve the question. Try 10, since $400 divides evenly among 10 people. This would make the cost $40 per person. The question states that after 3 people decide not to contribute, the cost increases by $30 per person. In this scenario, that would mean the new cost should be $70 per person. However, after 3 people decide not to contribute, 7 people remain, and the $400 is divided by 7, making each person's share approximately $57. Since $57 is smaller than $70, 10 people is incorrect. Try a smaller number to make each person's share greater. Try 8 people, which would make the original cost per person $50. If 3 people drop out, the cost should increase by $30 per person. In this scenario, that would mean the new cost is $80 per person. After 3 people decide not to contribute, 5 people remain, and the $400 is divided by 5, making each person's share $80. Since $80 is equal to $80, 8 people were in the original group. The correct answer is 8.

33. **11** This question asks for the value of k in the equation. Simplify the equation by distributing the 3 and negative sign to get $12k - 30 - 26 - 5k = 21$. Combine like terms to get $7k - 56 = 21$. Add 56 to both sides to get $7k = 77$. Divide by 7 to get $k = 11$. The correct answer is 11.

34. $\dfrac{6}{5}$ or **1.2**

The question asks for the y-coordinate of the y-intercept of the line. The y-intercept is the point where $x = 0$. To find the y-intercept, plug in 0 for x. This gives $-\dfrac{3}{4}(0) + \dfrac{5}{6}y = 1$, which can be simplified to $\dfrac{5}{6}y = 1$. Multiply both sides by 6 to get $5y = 6$. Divide both sides by 5 to get $y = \dfrac{6}{5}$. The y-intercept is $\left(0, \dfrac{6}{5}\right)$, and its y-coordinate is $\dfrac{6}{5}$. This is the correct answer.

35. **5.8** The question asks for the value of h in the table. Start by finding the mean of the heights of Robert's rose bushes. For averages, use the formula $T = AN$, in which T is the total, A is the average, and N is the number of things. The total is $3.9 + 6.1 + 4.4 + 5.3 + 5.8 = 25.5$, and the number of things is 5. The formula becomes $25.5 = A(5)$, so $A = 5.1$. The mean of the heights of Robert's rose bushes is 5.1, and the question states that this value is 0.3 feet greater than the mean of the heights of Louis's rose bushes. Since $5.1 - 0.3 = 4.8$, the mean of the heights of Louis's rose bushes is 4.8. For Louis, the formula becomes $T = (4.8)(5) = 24$. The total for Louis can also be written as $h + 4.5 + 5.7 + 4.2 + 3.8$, which simplifies to $h + 18.2$. Set these two totals equal to get $h + 18.2 = 24$. Subtract 18.2 from both sides to get $h = 5.8$. The correct answer is 5.8.

36. **6** This question asks for the value of c. Since the point (c, c) can be found on the graph of $y = -4x^2 + 25x$, plug in c for both x and y. This gives $c = -4c^2 + 25c$. Subtract $25c$ from both sides to get $-24c = -4c^2$. Divide both sides by $-4c$ to get $6 = c$. The correct answer is 6.

37. **750** The question asks how much more money John spent on rent than on office supplies. Add up the percents that have already been allocated to get $10\% + 40\% + 35\% = 85\%$. Notice that 15% remains unaccounted for. This 15% represents the $450 that was spent on utilities. This means that 15% of John's total monthly expenditures equaled $450. Set up an equation to find John's total monthly expenditures: $\left(\dfrac{15}{100}\right)total = \$450$. Simplify to get $(0.15)total = \$450$. Divide by 0.15 to get $total = 3,000$.

Now answer the question. John spent 35% of his monthly expenditures on rent, which is $\left(\dfrac{35}{100}\right)(\$3,000) = \$1,050$. He spent 10% of his monthly expenditures on office supplies, which is

$\left(\dfrac{10}{100}\right)$($3,000$) = $300. The difference between rent and office supplies is $1,050 − $300 = $750. The correct answer is $750.

38. **20** The question asks for the value of k, which represents the number of kindergarten students enrolled in 2011. Since the enrollment triples each year, divide by 3 to find the number of students enrolled each year. If there were 540 students enrolled in 2014, then there were $\dfrac{540}{3}$ = 180 students enrolled in 2013. This means that there were $\dfrac{180}{3}$ = 60 students enrolled in 2012 and $\dfrac{60}{3}$ = 20 student enrolled in 2011. The correct answer is 20.

Chapter 19
Practice Test 9

Reading Test

65 MINUTES, 52 QUESTIONS

Turn to Section 1 of your answer sheet to answer the questions in this section.

Questions 1–10 are based on the following passage.

This passage is adapted from *Revolutionary Road* by Richard Yates. ©1961 by Richard Yates.

With parched, hard-breathing mouths, with wobbling heads and shaking limbs, they settled themselves in the car like very old and tired people.
Line He started the engine and drove carefully away, down
5 to the turn at the base of Revolutionary Hill and on up the winding blacktop grade of Revolutionary Road.

This was the way they had first come, two years ago, as cordially nodding passengers in the station wagon of Mrs. Helen Givings, the real-estate broker.
10 She had been polite but guarded over the phone – so many city people were apt to come out and waste her time demanding impossible bargains – but from the moment they'd stepped off the train, as she would later tell her husband, she had recognized them as
15 the kind of couple one did take a little trouble with, even in the low-price bracket. "They're sweet," she told her husband. "The girl is absolutely ravishing, and I think the boy must do something very brilliant in town – he's very nice, rather reserved – and really, it
20 is so refreshing to deal with people of that sort." Mrs. Givings had understood at once that they wanted something out of the ordinary – a small remodeled barn or carriage house, or an old guest cottage – something with a little charm – and she did hate
25 having to tell them that those things simply weren't available any more. But she implored them not to lose heart; she did know of one little place they might like.

"Now of course it isn't a very desirable road down at this end," she explained, her glance twitching
30 birdlike between the road and their pleased, attentive faces as she made the turn off Route Twelve. "As you see, it's mostly these little cinderblocky, pickup-trucky places – plumbers, carpenters, little people of that sort. And then eventually" – she aimed the stiff pistol
35 of her index finger straight through the windshield in fair warning, causing a number of metal bracelets to jingle and click against the steering wheel – "eventually it leads up and around to a perfectly dreadful new development called Revolutionary Hill Estates – great
40 hulking split levels, all in the most nauseous pastels and dreadfully expensive too, I can't think why. No, but the place I want to show you has absolutely no connection with that. One of our nice little local builders put it up right after the war, you see, before all
45 the really awful building began. It's really rather a sweet little house and a sweet little setting. Simple, clean lines, good lawns, marvelous for children. It's right around this next curve, and you see the road is nicer along in here, isn't it? Now you'll see it – there. See the
50 little white one? Sweet, isn't it? The perky way it sits there on its little slope?"

"Oh yes," April said as the house emerged through the spindly trunks of second-growth oak and slowly turned toward them, small and wooden, riding high
55 on its naked concrete foundation, its outsized central window staring like a big black mirror. "Yes, I think it's sort of – nice, don't you, darling? Of course it does

CONTINUE →

have the picture window; I guess there's no escaping that."

60   "I guess not," Frank said. "Still, I don't suppose one picture window is necessarily going to destroy our personalities."

    "Oh, that's *marvelous*," Mrs. Givings cried, and her laughter enclosed them in a warm shelter of flattery

65 as they rolled up the driveway and climbed out to have a look. She hovered near them, reassuring and protective, while they walked the naked floors of the house in whispering speculation. The place did have possibilities. Their sofa could go here and their

70 big table there; their solid wall of books would take the curse off the picture window; a sparse, skillful arrangement of furniture would counteract the prim suburban look of this too-symmetrical living room. On the other hand, the very symmetry of the

75 place was undeniably appealing – the fact that all its corners made right angles, that each of its floorboards lay straight and true, that its doors hung in perfect balance and closed without scraping in efficient clicks. Enjoying the light heft and feel of these doorknobs,

80 they could fancy themselves at home here. Inspecting the flawless bathroom, they could sense the pleasure of steaming in its ample tub; they could see their children running barefoot down this hallway free of mildew and splinters and cockroaches and grit. It did have

85 possibilities. The gathering disorder of their lives might still be sorted out and made to fit these rooms, among these trees; and what if it did take time? Who could be frightened in as wide and bright, as clean and quiet a house as this?

1

Over the course of the passage, the primary focus shifts from

A) the views of Helen Givings to those of Frank and April.

B) an interaction between Frank and April to a monologue by Mrs. Givings.

C) the description of a setting to an evaluation of the characters.

D) tragic past events to possibilities of a hopeful future.

2

The main purpose of the first paragraph is to

A) establish a mood that will be maintained throughout the passage.

B) clarify the ages of the main characters through descriptive imagery.

C) present circumstances that the rest of the passage explains.

D) introduce a setting that is central to the passage.

3

Mrs. Givings's primary impression of her "cordially nodding passengers" (line 8) is that they

A) are unusually troublesome clients.

B) merit some degree of special attention.

C) remind her of herself and her husband.

D) project unique sophistication and charm.

4

Which choice provides the best evidence for the answer to the previous question?

A) Lines 10–16 ("She had . . . bracket")

B) Lines 20–26 ("Mrs. Givings . . . more")

C) Lines 26–27 ("But she . . . like")

D) Lines 41–43 ("No, but . . . that")

5

While describing Revolutionary Hill Estates, Mrs. Givings emphasizes the contrast between the

A) quality of local homes with that of houses in other towns.

B) appearance of one house and that of the nearby homes.

C) affordability of one home and the luxury of another nearby.

D) lifestyles of plumbers and those of her more affluent clients.

CONTINUE

6

Which choice best supports the conclusion that Mrs. Givings prefers older homes?

A) Lines 28–31 ("Now of . . . Twelve")

B) Lines 31–41 ("As you . . . why")

C) Lines 43–45 ("One of . . . began")

D) Lines 47–50 ("It's right...isn't it")

7

It can be reasonably inferred that Frank and April find the "central window" (lines 55–56) to be

A) an aesthetically pleasing piece of architecture.

B) a matter of potential disagreement between them.

C) overly symmetrical but ultimately appealing.

D) out of proportion with other features of the house.

8

The primary impression created by the narrator's description of Mrs. Givings in lines 63–68 ("Oh . . . speculation") is that she is

A) formal and professional.

B) amiable and amusing.

C) anxious and compulsive.

D) doting and attentive.

9

As used in line 80, "fancy" most nearly means

A) elaborate.

B) embellish.

C) envision.

D) enshrine.

10

The main idea of the last paragraph is that the new house

A) can accommodate a great deal of furniture.

B) incorporates perfect symmetry into its design.

C) is somewhere Frank and April can imagine living.

D) causes feelings of ambivalence in Frank and April.

CONTINUE ➡

Questions 11–20 are based on the following passage and supplementary material.

This passage is adapted from John Byers, et al, "The Groupon Effect on Yelp Ratings: A Root Cause Analysis." Submitted to ACM EC '12 ACM X, X, Article X (February 2012).

In previous work examining Groupon, we measured and evaluated aspects of Groupon's operational strategy, as well as observed the impact
Line of customer behaviors including word-of-mouth
5 effects and how running a Groupon offer affects a merchant's reputation. One specific finding that received significant interest and attention was that Yelp reviews that contained the word "Groupon" provided, on average, significantly lower ratings than reviews
10 that did not, to the extent that it significantly lowered the average rating for businesses that used Groupon. In the original paper, we did not examine reasons to explain this finding, leaving it to future work. Our analysis met with a variety of reactions, ranging
15 from disbelief, to a number of plausible explanations for why this phenomenon should be expected: for example, Groupon users are fussy reviewers, Groupon businesses provide worse service than their peers, businesses discriminate by providing worse service
20 specifically to Groupon customers, and Groupon users are less of a good fit for the businesses where they redeem Groupons.
In this paper, we return to our finding of a sharp decline in Yelp ratings scores that coincides with
25 Groupon offers, a phenomenon we term the *Groupon effect*, and consider possible explanations through the lens of data analysis, based on an extensive dataset we gathered from Groupon and Yelp. Through this undertaking, we learn significantly more about the
30 daily deals model, including the behavior of Groupon users and businesses. *A priori*, one or more of the suggested explanations might be valid, and as such we examine where data provides positive and negative evidence for each.
35 However, we also suggest and provide evidence for an alternative explanation that we have not heard previously. It is well known that a potential problem with review sites is that businesses may actively solicit positive reviews for their business, either through
40 unscrupulous means such as hiring people to write positive reviews for them, or by less questionable means such as encouraging reviews from obviously

enthusiastic customers. (In some cases, they may also attempt to place negative reviews for their competitors,
45 although this is arguably a less effective strategy.) Indeed, Yelp filters its reviews to prevent "spam reviews" from affecting its ratings.
Our hypothesis is that one reason for the discrepancy in review scores is that reviews that
50 mention Groupon correspond almost exclusively to reviews written by actual customers who use the service, and that other reviews are significantly more likely to be "fake" or otherwise introduced in an arguably artificial manner. Hence, we suggest that, at
55 least in part, the issue is not that reviews mentioning Groupon are somehow unusually low, but that the baseline of other reviews is on average artificially high, most likely because of actions taken by businesses designed specifically to generate high-scoring reviews.
60 We investigate the question of whether one class of reviewers is generally more critical than another. A more critical class of reviewers would review all businesses more critically on average, irrespective of whether they ran a Groupon. The fairest comparison
65 to isolate this effect is to compare evaluation on non-Groupon businesses. The results are surprising. We do not see strong evidence that Groupon reviewers are much more critical on average. Instead, they are more moderate! They provide fewer 1- and 5-star ratings
70 than their non-Groupon counterparts and more 3- and 4-star ratings.
Our interpretation is that this evidence strongly points not to critical reviewers, but to unrealized expectations between reviewers and merchants.
75 Moreover, while this mismatch appears to occur relatively infrequently, when it does occur, the result is a much more negative review than is typical for that reviewer.
We have examined a number of hypotheses for
80 explaining what we have dubbed the Groupon effect. While there remain challenges in trying to exactly quantify the different issues at play, we have shown that a combination of poor business behavior, Groupon user experimentation, and an artificially high baseline
85 all play a role.
Our compilation of evidence about Groupon users highlights that on average, Groupon users provide detailed reviews that are valued more highly by their Yelp peers. Contrary to what some would believe, the

CONTINUE →

90 evidence suggests that Groupon users are no more
critical than their peers, although they may well be
experimenting with a new business when using a
Groupon. Although it seems obvious, we would advise
businesses to treat Groupon customers as well as (or
95 possibly better than?) their other customers to avoid
negative reputational impact.

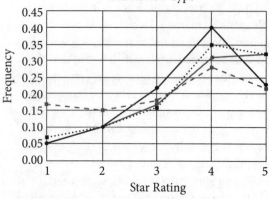

Distribution of Yelp Star-Ratings by User
and Review Type

→— Groupon Businesses, Groupon User, Does Not Mention Groupon
—•— Non-Groupon Businesses, Groupon User
·····■···· Non-Groupon Businesses, Standard User
- ■ - Groupon Businesses, Groupon User, Mentions Groupon

11

Over the course of the passage, the main focus shifts
from describing a known phenomenon and potential
theories for its existence to

A) an evaluation of evidence that addresses the
possibility of several hypotheses.

B) an explanation of the method used to detect the
original observation.

C) a critical review of the research and its implicit
results.

D) an absolute reason for the previously identified
dynamic.

12

The authors of the passage suggest that the *Groupon
effect* may be defined by

A) ascribing great importance to Yelp ratings instead
of multiple reviews.

B) combining disparate causes rather than just a
single factor.

C) providing "spam reviews" more often than honest
customer opinions.

D) speculating about Groupon users' behavior as
compared to that of the general public.

13

Which choice provides the best evidence for the
answer to the previous question?

A) Lines 29–31 ("we learn . . . businesses")

B) Lines 43–45 ("In some . . . strategy")

C) Lines 72–74 ("Our interpretation . . . merchants")

D) Lines 81–85 ("While . . . role")

14

As used in line 53, "fake" most nearly means

A) plastic.

B) imaginary.

C) counterfeit.

D) planted.

15

Which action would best address a concern regarding
the introduction of artificial Yelp reviews?

A) Requiring a verifiable receipt image to submit a
review

B) Decreasing the scale from five stars to three stars

C) Implementing baseline ratings for online
businesses

D) Soliciting only positive opinions of participating
businesses

CONTINUE ➡

16

Which choice best describes the "unrealized expectations" (lines 73–74)?

A) Lines 1–5 ("we measured . . . effects")

B) Lines 17–22 ("Groupon . . . Groupons")

C) Lines 37–43 ("It is . . . customers")

D) Lines 86–89 ("Our compilation . . . peers")

17

As used in line 86, "compilation" most nearly means

A) collection.

B) summary.

C) anthology.

D) yearbook.

18

According to the figure, which category of Yelp user showed the most evenly distributed star ratings?

A) Standard users of non-Groupon businesses

B) Groupon users of Groupon businesses who mention Groupon

C) Groupon users of Groupon businesses who do not mention Groupon

D) Groupon users of non-Groupon businesses

19

In the figure, which Yelp rating is a non-Groupon user most likely to give a business?

A) 1 star

B) 2 stars

C) 4 stars

D) 5 stars

20

Data presented in the figure most directly supports which idea from the passage?

A) The patterns of Yelp star ratings are directly correlated to the type of business the customers are patronizing.

B) The customers most likely to post reviews on Yelp are those that produce "spam reviews."

C) The Yelp scores of Groupon users are more moderate than non-Groupon user reviews of the same businesses.

D) The number of Groupon mentions in a review directly correlates with the relative ranking of that review.

CONTINUE

Questions 21–31 are based on the following passage.

This passage is adapted from Malcolm Macleod, "Some Salt with Your Statin, Professor?" ©2014 by PLOS Biology.

We know that clinical trials sponsored by the pharmaceutical industry are likely to exaggerate benefit and minimize harms. But do these biases extend to
Line their sponsorship of non-human animal research?
5 Are the findings of such studies credible? And how do those findings compare with "proper" research conducted by dispassionate academics?

These are important questions, but how could we find this stuff out? In the same way that it would
10 be difficult to conduct a randomized controlled trial of the effect of living in Scotland on your chance of having a stroke, it is difficult to do an experiment to test whether the funding source for a study influences the outcome. Since clinical trials sponsored by the
15 pharmaceutical industry seem to be at greater risk of bias than others, a lazy assumption might be that their non-human animal research is similarly confounded, as they seek to rush compounds to market to maximize profitability.
20 However, a few straws in the wind hint this might not be the case. One way companies identify drug targets is by reading what's out there in the literature and, if something looks interesting, seeking to replicate the findings. Bayer scientists found inconsistencies
25 in 43 of 65 studies when they tried to replicate them in-house. Implementation of good laboratory practice standards is much more advanced in industry labs, and for some types of experiments these standards are a legal requirement. So, could it be that industry-
30 sponsored research is actually more rigorous than academic research?

Taking the example of statin treatments for atheroma, David Krauth, Andrew Anglemyer, Rose Philipps, and Lisa Bero address this issue head-on.
35 Using systematic review, they identified non-human animal studies describing the efficacy of statins. Focusing on those studies where sponsorship status was known, they found that the results of nine of 19 industry-sponsored studies (43%) and 18 of 28
40 non-industry-sponsored studies (72%) supported

the efficacy of statins. As interesting, however, is the analysis of the interpretation placed on the findings in each of the included studies. Of 19 industry-sponsored studies, the conclusion of 18 favored the use of statins
45 (95%), while of 28 non-industry-sponsored studies, only 21 did so (75%).

It does therefore appear that findings from research sponsored by industry are more conservative than those sponsored by non-industry sources, but
50 the interpretation of those data is, in contrast, less conservative. Why might this be?

In my view it is likely that the impact of approaches to research management and the regulatory environment that apply to some parts of industry—
55 particularly standards for internal reporting—extends to most of the non-human animal research activity with which they are involved, whether or not it is performed in-house. That is, non-human animal work sponsored by industry is likely to be performed and
60 reported to a higher quality, and to be at lower risk of bias, than work sponsored by others. This would explain the difficulty industry has in replicating the results of research conducted in academic labs. However, the interpretation, or "spin," with which
65 industry-sponsored work is presented does appear to be an issue, with exaggeration of the conclusions to favor the drug being tested.

This makes sense—for industry there is a clear financial interest in being absolutely secure in the non-
70 human animal data for a compound before embarking on a clinical trial, so there is a real motivation to get the preclinical data as good as they can be. But when that money has been spent (and for statins it largely has been), the motivation is to present an analysis of
75 the available data that is most supportive for clinical use. So, if a drug is a turkey, try to find that out before spending a fortune taking it to clinical trial—and if it's too late for that, try to convince everyone that the non-human animal and clinical trial data supporting an
80 efficacy for *Meleagris gallopavo* (commonly known as the wild turkey) are more convincing than they might at first appear.

CONTINUE

21

As used in line 3, "extend" most nearly means

A) reach.

B) require.

C) apply.

D) stretch.

22

The questions posed in lines 3–7 are chiefly intended to

A) introduce a set of considerations that may not have been investigated in prior research.

B) show confusion about the nature of results provided by similar forms of research.

C) declare that non-human animal research is an improper method of conducting trials.

D) stir controversy about the quality of research performed by academics.

23

Which question was the research of Bero's team primarily intended to answer?

A) Does industry-sponsored research make it more difficult to analyze statins than academic research sponsored by non-industry sources?

B) Do experiments funded by invested corporations get performed with a greater level of attention to detail than those that are not?

C) What prevents industry-sponsored research from being conducted with the same level of rigor as academic research?

D) Does non-human animal research funded by industry sources lead to fewer clinical trials than research performed by academics?

24

Which choice provides the best evidence for the answer to the previous question?

A) Lines 29–31 ("So, could . . . research")

B) Lines 32–34 ("Taking . . . head-on")

C) Lines 37–41 ("Focusing . . . statins")

D) Lines 61–63 ("This . . . labs")

25

The main purpose of the fourth paragraph (lines 32–46) is to

A) question the implications of the surprising findings of Bero's team.

B) note significant results of Bero's team's study regarding sources of research.

C) shift from a description of Bero's team's study to an overview of a question.

D) connect research performed on human subjects to research performed on non-human animals.

26

As used in line 48, "conservative" most nearly means

A) old-fashioned.

B) dramatic.

C) traditional.

D) reserved.

27

According to the passage, when compared to non-human animal research sponsored by industry, the non-human research sponsored by others

A) shows a lower risk of bias.

B) is easier to accurately reproduce in clinical trials.

C) is not always performed at as high a quality.

D) costs more to complete.

CONTINUE

28

According to the passage, the findings of Bero's team are surprising because they

A) give support to an obvious conclusion.

B) apparently contradict a sensible assumption.

C) undermine the studies of clinical trials.

D) confirm the existence of unknown statistics.

29

Which choice provides the best evidence for the answer to the previous question?

A) Lines 24–26 ("Bayer . . . in-house")

B) Lines 43–46 ("Of 19 . . . (75%)")

C) Lines 47–51 ("It does . . . be")

D) Lines 64–67 ("However . . . tested")

30

The author of the passage would most likely agree that industry-sponsored research may be rigorous because it

A) applies standards of internal reporting to employees who cut corners.

B) hires scientists who excel in their respective fields.

C) risks scrutiny from legislators if it fails to adhere to adequate standards.

D) utilizes elements of documentation that are also applied to purposes other than research.

31

Which choice provides the best evidence for the answer to the previous question?

A) Lines 21–24 ("One way . . . findings")

B) Lines 35–36 ("Using . . . statins")

C) Lines 41–43 ("As interesting . . . studies")

D) Lines 52–58 ("In my . . . in-house")

CONTINUE ➤

Questions 32–42 are based on the following passages.

Passage 1 is adapted from P. G. Hubert, "Occupations for Women," originally published in 1894. Passage 2 is adapted from Virginia Penny, *Think and Act*, originally published in 1869.

Passage 1

The fact that women are paid less than men for apparently the same service seems to disturb a great many people, who find here a conspiracy upon the part
Line of man to keep women out of the wage-earning field
5 so far as this can be done. The maxim, "Business is business," applies here with as much force as anywhere. Both men and women earn, as a rule, just what they are worth. The law of supply and demand comes into play as relentlessly here as elsewhere. If a woman wants
10 more money than a man, she has only to do better and more work in the long run than the man, and she will get more pay as surely as business rules remain in force in the business world.

There are some reasons for the apparent
15 discrepancy between the pay of men and women, which may serve to clear away some of the false impressions that have grown up about this question. In the first place, women as a class of workers are beginners, comparatively speaking, in the great field
20 of industry; they lack the hereditary instinct for such work, and as beginners their wages are low. Woman's preparation for work is seldom so thorough as with a man, and long technical training for any work is often considered superfluous for a woman because she
25 may marry. Even should she remain a wage earner, the woman has seldom the strong incentive of others dependent upon her; the man has a wife and children who will suffer, should he relax his efforts; the woman is usually alone.

30 A curious feature of work by women is that, while in this century and in America work and money-earning have always been considered to be proper in every way for men, there is still some slight social stigma pertaining to money-getting by women. This
35 may be trusted to die out as fast as women show that they can retain all the most attractive attributes of womanhood and yet earn their own living.

The old-time fiction to the effect that woman was a tender flower, blooming only when sheltered from the
40 world, and likely either to droop or lose its fragrance when brought into contact with a vulgar, work-a-day, money-grubbing world, has been called into question before now. Some eminent thinkers and essayists, such as Mr. Frederic Harrison, the English writer, dread
45 the effect of political, professional, and business life upon woman. They fear the appearance of the mannish woman upon the scene.

Passage 2

In woman's work and wages the times are a century or more behind the improvements made in science and
50 art. Society is tardy, dragging, in the matter. A woman may be defined to be a creature that receives half price for all she does, and pays full price for all she needs. She earns as a child—she pays as a man. Besides, her sex, if not barbarous custom, cuts her off from the
55 best rewarded colleges. Her hands, feet, and brain are clogged. We ask our readers to pause and inquire if this is not true.

It requires just as much to support a woman as a man. Her dress requires more. Often infirm, sick, or
60 aged parents are relying on her for a support, or, it may be, orphan brothers and sisters. Or, even if it were not so, a woman needs to lay up something for times of sickness, old age, and want of employment, as well as a man. When men and women are employed in the same
65 establishments, women have not the lightest, most healthy, and most pleasant parts of the labor. They have the hardest, worst paid, and most unhealthy work. In civilized countries it is a remnant of the former degradation of the sex. Over-work and under-pay are
70 the curse of workwomen. While they last, the poverty, and suffering, of women, will continue.

To pay women better prices for labor will give it a dignity in public estimation. The effect will prove beneficial not only to workers, pecuniarily and socially,
75 but its influence will extend to those indirectly affected. If women were paid in proportion to the quality and quantity of their work, at the same rate that men are paid, there could be no reasonable objection to women entering any occupation they desire to. It is unmanly
80 and unjust to cut short a woman's wages merely because she is a woman.

In Passage 1, Hubert makes which point about working women relative to working men?

A) Women make disturbingly less than men, and women also supply more conspiracies than men.

B) Women are able to earn as much as men, but women choose to become parents more often than men.

C) Women are newer to the workforce than men, and women have less training than men.

D) Women can currently perform as well as men, but women receive less pay than men.

Which choice provides the best evidence for the answer to the previous question?

A) Lines 1–5 ("The fact . . . done")

B) Lines 18–25 ("In the . . . marry")

C) Lines 25–29 ("Even . . . alone")

D) Lines 30–34 ("A curious . . . women")

34

In Passage 1, Hubert implies that the wage gap between women and men is

A) inevitable, because women's genes do not prepare them for the same work as men's.

B) avoidable, because women and men can either support themselves or marry.

C) misunderstood, because workers are paid based on experience.

D) regrettable, because women and men deserve fair treatment in the working world.

As used in line 28, "relax" most nearly means

A) lessen.

B) chill.

C) recuperate.

D) calm.

As used in line 30, "curious" most nearly means

A) interested.

B) nosy.

C) mischievous.

D) peculiar.

What is Penny's central claim in Passage 2?

A) Women must protest the gender-based wage gap.

B) Society should progress by reducing the gender-based wage gap.

C) Women should not have to pay full price when they are paid half price.

D) Societies that underpay women while overpaying men will be punished.

In Passage 2, Penny makes which point about women's working conditions?

A) They are similar to the working conditions of children.

B) They may involve lighter tasks than those expected of men in similar jobs.

C) They can involve harder and less pleasant tasks than men are asked to do.

D) They have been improved through acts of civil disobedience.

CONTINUE

39

Which choice provides the best evidence for the answer to the previous question?

A) Line 50 ("Society . . . matter")

B) Lines 59–61 ("Often . . . sisters")

C) Lines 64–66 ("When . . . labor")

D) Lines 73–75 ("The effect . . . affected")

40

Which choice best states the relationship between the two passages?

A) Passage 2 promotes several theories offered in Passage 1.

B) Passage 2 outlines the results of a plan defended in Passage 1.

C) Passage 2 supports changing a discrepancy discussed in Passage 1.

D) Passage 2 offers reasons for a view presented in Passage 1.

41

Based on the passages, both authors would agree with which of the following claims?

A) Businesses often overwork and underpay women.

B) Social disapproval of working women may decline over time.

C) The wage gap between men and women is more apparent than real.

D) Educated women should earn higher salaries.

42

Hubert would most likely have reacted to lines 72–73 ("To pay . . . estimation") of Passage 2 with

A) disagreement, because men and women are paid fairly according to the labor market.

B) panic, because affirmative action amounts to reverse discrimination.

C) empathy, because women deserve this sort of respect as much as men do.

D) elation, because pay raises for working women will remove the stigma that working women currently suffer from.

CONTINUE

Question 43–52 are based on the following passage and supplementary material.

This passage is excerpted from Jane Smith, "Desalination: Is It Really Sustainable?" ©2021 by Jane Smith.

When it comes to our species, nobody would disagree that clean drinking water is essential. It's so elemental to human life that people never challenge
Line the government regulation of this utility, even when
5 they call for resistance to public regulation of other essentials. Clean drinking water allows us to maintain many aspects of public health, which include all the great strides that have been made since the turn of the last century. In a world of rising temperatures,
10 access to clean water is the best way to guarantee a decent quality of life. Everybody in the developing and developed world would agree.

For centuries, relying on traditional sources of water, such as rainfall, has served most of the world
15 well. This has become even easier to do for many regions in the world that are experiencing higher rates of precipitation. According to the National Centers for Environmental Information, 2019 was the second-wettest year in the history of the United
20 States, specifically in the Great Plains and Great Lakes regions. Thanks to climate change, rainfall in Puerto Rico has increased by 33 percent during heavy storms alone. All this added moisture, combined with longer growing seasons owing to higher average yearly
25 temperatures, might seem to contribute to a more stable food supply as well.

But that's not how most advocates of desalination view the changes occurring in the earth's climate. They have embraced desalination as a godsend that is better
30 for the species—making drinkable the vast amounts of saltwater encircling the globe—than depending on what they view as unstable sources of natural water. Noting the increasing municipal, agricultural, and industrial need for fresh water, its proponents cite a
35 recent study concluding that, by 2071, half of the 204 freshwater basins in the United States may be unable to meet demands. In contrast, there are currently 1400 desalination plants in the US alone—and all of them treat the ocean water, brackish water, and wastewater
40 that would otherwise be undrinkable.

However, a new study looking at the numbers shows the hard truth: desalination is expensive.

Desalinated water costs about $2000 per acre foot, which is enough water for a family of five to use in
45 one year. This is four times more expensive than other methods of reducing dependence on traditional water supply, such as giving rebates to homeowners to purchase more efficient toilets, sinks, and showers— and that means that increased desalination may not
50 mean the end of water scarcity.

A study by the Advisian Worley Group analyzed the various factors that contribute to the expense of these desalination plants. It found that the two types of technology used in the process—either thermal
55 or membrane—cost wildly different amounts. Other factors that need to be considered include the location of the plants, the raw water quality, the type of intake and outfall, and others. Furthermore, because of the complexity of the variables, the report advised that it
60 was nearly impossible to make predictions about future costs of desalination.

The main difference between traditional water sourcing and desalination is consistency. In places such as California, having a reliable source of water—even
65 if it is expensive—is sometimes seen as preferable to relying upon melted snowpack from the Sierra Nevada Mountains, or piped-in water from the Colorado River. When we discuss the growing popularity of desalination plants, we're really discussing stability.

70 And traditional water sources are by no means problem-free. Flooding that accompanies once- in-a-century climate events—which are now occurring much more often than that—pollutes watersheds. Many lakes, rivers, and wetlands are being
75 overexploited by human activity and are declining at a rapid rate. Runoff from agriculture is damaging local water supplies. In short, having a lot of fresh water in one's community is no guarantee, in the twenty-first century, that it will be drinkable.

80 All of this simply means that there are a lot of trade-offs. While desalination is more consistent, its cost and relatively small output leads us to conclude that it will be difficult to ever rely fully upon it. In fact, the ideal national water system may borrow from both
85 systems, as different regions of the world consider their own particular needs before subscribing to a top-down

CONTINUE ➡

order from an overarching body. A one-size-fits-all model may have worked in the past, but like the energy grid, the new century may force cities and states to rely
90 upon a patchwork of different solutions.

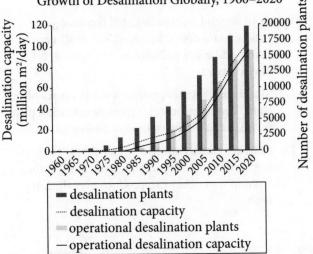

Figure 1
Growth of Desalination Globally, 1960–2020

- desalination plants
- desalination capacity
- operational desalination plants
- operational desalination capacity

Published by DesalData, the Worldwide Desalination Inventory in 2013.

Figure 2

Water Sources for Reverse Osmosis Desalinization

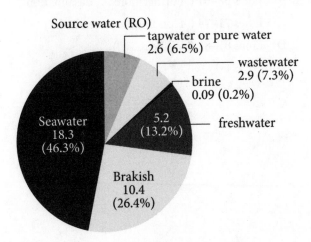

Source water (RO)
- tapwater or pure water 2.6 (6.5%)
- wastewater 2.9 (7.3%)
- brine 0.09 (0.2%)
- 5.2 (13.2%) freshwater
- Seawater 18.3 (46.3%)
- Brakish 10.4 (26.4%)

Published by DesalData, the Worldwide Desalination Inventory in 2013.

The global reverse osmosis desalination capacity (in millions of cubic meters per day) as of June 2013 with regards to source water.

43

According to the passage, one advantage of acquiring water from traditional sources is that they

A) provide high-quality water for drinking and cooking.

B) are sufficient to meet the global demand.

C) are readily accessible in many regions.

D) lessen the demand for desalination plants.

44

As used in line 26, "stable" most nearly means

A) balanced.

B) rational.

C) dependable.

D) fixed.

45

Which choice best reflects the perspective of the "advocates" (line 27) on traditional water sources?

A) The are readily available in many regions and essential for public health.

B) They are not reliable and may not meet people's need for water.

C) They are able to provide a stable supply only temporarily.

D) They depend on climate change but are cost-effective.

46

Which choice provides the best evidence for the answer to the previous question?

A) Lines 27–28 ("But that's . . . climate").

B) Lines 28–32 ("They . . . water")

C) Lines 41–42 ("However . . . expensive")

D) Lines 62–63 ("The main . . . consistency")

CONTINUE

47

According to the Advisian Worley Group (line 51), the desalination process

A) varies based on the amount of water supplied and local demand.

B) is impacted by the quality of the equipment used.

C) may involve unforeseen investments due to its variable components.

D) varies in cost primarily according to plant location.

48

As used in line 57, "raw" most nearly means

A) unprocessed.

B) inexperienced.

C) unchecked.

D) underdone.

49

Which statement best expresses a relationship between traditional sources of water and desalination that is presented in the passage?

A) While traditional water sources provide larger quantities of water at a lower cost, desalination offers a more reliable source.

B) Both depend on sophisticated technology to produce and distribute water, but desalination plants add more pollution to the natural environment.

C) Traditional sources provide a stable source of water, but only the water from desalination plants is consistently safe for human consumption.

D) Both are equally affordable and simple to implement, but they differ significantly in the amount water they can produce over the long term.

50

Which choice provides the best evidence for the answer to the previous question?

A) Lines 1–2 ("When . . . essential"")

B) Lines 58–61 ("Furthermore . . . desalination")

C) Lines 71–74 ("Flooding . . . watersheds")

D) Lines 81–83 ("While . . . it")

CONTINUE

51

Which statement about reverse osmosis desalination capacity in 2013 is best supported by the information provided in figure 2?

A) Seawater yielded 46.3 million cubic meters of water per day.

B) The desalination capacity from brine was greater than that from wastewater.

C) Reverse osmosis desalination was most commonly used to remove salt from water extracted from the ocean.

D) Tap water and pure water together made up 2.6% of the global desalination capacity.

52

Which of the following claims is supported by figure 1?

A) Although desalination is not running at its full capacity, the growth of desalination has been steady since 1960.

B) Operational desalination capacity in 2020 was less than 17,500 cubic meters per day.

C) The number of operational desalination plants was more than 40 for the first time in 2005.

D) Desalination capacity exceeded operational desalination capacity by approximately 20 million cubic meters per day in 2010.

STOP
**If you finish before time is called, you may check your work on this section only.
Do not turn to any other section in the test.**

Writing and Language Test

35 MINUTES, 44 QUESTIONS

Turn to Section 2 of your answer sheet to answer the questions in this section.

DIRECTIONS

Each passage below is accompanied by a number of questions. For some questions, you will consider how the passage might be revised to improve the expression of ideas. For other questions, you will consider how the passage might be edited to correct errors in sentence structure, usage, or punctuation. A passage or a question may be accompanied by one or more graphics (such as a table or graph) that you will consider as you make revising and editing decisions.

Some questions will direct you to an underlined portion of a passage. Other questions will direct you to a location in a passage or ask you to think about the passage as a whole.

After reading each passage, choose the answer to each question that most effectively improves the quality of writing in the passage or that makes the passage conform to the conventions of standard written English. Many questions include a "NO CHANGE" option. Choose that option if you think the best choice is to leave the relevant portion of the passage as it is.

Questions 1–11 are based on the following passage.

Lions and Tigers and... Deer?

A large majority of the six million auto accidents each year are preventable. Many are caused by the traditional risks, like cell phone use, drunk driving, or excessive speed. **1**

1

At this point, the writer is considering adding the following sentence.

> Statistics show that people are 23 times more likely to be involved in collisions when they are texting and driving.

Should the writer make this addition here?

A) Yes, because it provides a useful transition from the previous sentence to the next.

B) Yes, because it provides evidence for a claim made in the paragraph's first sentence.

C) No, because it gives a detail that contradicts the paragraph's main focus.

D) No, because it deviates from the paragraph's main topic and argument.

CONTINUE

A recent set of research findings, however, **2** has been suggesting that nearly one-sixth of these accidents could be prevented by a single factor: mountain lions.

    3 We probably want to start conjuring funny images of mountain lions with speed guns or a taste for cell phones. Before we do that, let's back up a bit. The fact is that nearly 1.2 million collisions each year occur between automobiles and deer. **4** The eastern part of the United States is at a special risk for these collisions because deer tend to roam freely and plentifully around the region. For all their adaptations to human life, deer have not developed a way to deal with traffic. If you drive regularly in the northeast, you know that the proof is usually on the side of the road.

2

A) NO CHANGE

B) would suggest

C) have suggested

D) suggests

3

Which choice most effectively combines the underlined sentences?

A) Before we start conjuring funny images of mountain lions with speed guns or a taste for cell phones, let's back up a bit.

B) Let's back up a bit before we start conjuring images like the funny ones we want of mountain lions with speed guns or a taste for cell phones.

C) We probably want to start conjuring funny images of mountain lions with speed guns or a taste for cell phones; before we do that, however, let's back up a bit.

D) Let's back up a bit before we can talk about mountain lions with speed guns and a taste for cell phones that we conjured in funny ways.

4

The writer is considering deleting the underlined sentence. Should the sentence be kept or deleted?

A) Kept, because it provides a detail that explains the statistic given in the previous sentence.

B) Kept, because it helps to explain why car travel is so dangerous in the United States.

C) Deleted, because it skews the passage's focus on the more serious causes of auto accidents.

D) Deleted, because it undermines the passage's claim that deer are useful members of an ecosystem.

CONTINUE

[1] Part of the reason that deer populations have grown as much as [5] they have is that deer face no natural predators in the eastern states. [2] Large-scale development and hunting have eliminated this threat. [3] In areas where these predators continue to exist, such as California, deer-related collisions are significantly lower. [4] Deer are thus able to reproduce without restriction. [6]

For a kind of natural solution to this problem, University of Washington wildlife biologist Laura Pugh has proposed reintroducing mountain lions into ecosystems along the eastern seaboard. The shock for the carnivorous cats would not be so significant because these species of mountain lion are actually indigenous to the area. Pugh [7] opines the mountain lion populations of the west as evidence [8] that these big cats "can coexist in close proximity with people, with very few conflicts."

5

A) NO CHANGE

B) we have

C) it has

D) one has

6

To make this paragraph most logical, sentence 4 should be placed

A) before sentence 1.

B) after sentence 1.

C) after sentence 2.

D) where it is now.

7

A) NO CHANGE

B) cites

C) says

D) proclaims

8

A) NO CHANGE

B) or

C) which

D) when

CONTINUE

Obviously, it will be difficult to get public sentiment on her side. The thought of encountering mountain lions in the wild chills most of us to the bone, and it doesn't seem that introducing this fierce animal back into the wild would be beneficial enough to offset its terrorizing costs. [9] Therefore, Pugh and her team say, these predators could save approximately five times as many people from deer-related deaths as they might endanger through unprovoked attacks.

The question now is whether the data are [10] sufficiently overcoming public concerns. If we've accepted the risks of driving tons of metal many miles an hour down the road, is it possible that [11] our fear of mountain lions could be the next human instinct to be cast aside?

9

A) NO CHANGE

B) Still,

C) Inevitably,

D) Furthermore,

10

A) NO CHANGE

B) a good amount in overcoming

C) enough to overcome

D) enough for overcoming

11

A) NO CHANGE

B) its

C) one's

D) their

CONTINUE

Questions 12–22 are based on the following passage.

The Original Music of New Orleans

The city of New Orleans, Louisiana, has always been a kind of national treasure with **12** routes in French, American, African, and indigenous cultures. This has become even more apparent since 2005, when Hurricane Katrina nearly wiped the city off the map. **13** For example, Katrina brought new attention to the city, demonstrating how much would be lost if New Orleans were to disappear.

While the city has always been praised as the place to "let the good times roll," its status in the popular imagination has changed significantly over the years and **14** shifts with broader national interests. Today, for instance, New Orleans is seen as the birthplace of jazz music. **15** Louis Armstrong was born in New Orleans in 1901 and began playing trumpet at an early age. The annual Jazzfest celebrates this heritage, and groups like the New Orleans Preservation Hall Jazz Band continue to commemorate the long tradition of jazz in the city.

12

A) NO CHANGE
B) roots in
C) roots of
D) routes of

13

A) NO CHANGE
B) However,
C) Thus,
D) DELETE the underlined portion.

14

A) NO CHANGE
B) have shifted
C) shifted
D) shifting

15

The writer is considering deleting the underlined sentence. Should the sentence be kept or deleted?

A) Kept, because it supports the passage's claim that jazz is a significant part of musical history.

B) Kept, because it adds a crucial detail about a resident of New Orleans that supports the passage's main idea.

C) Deleted, because it suggests that the type of music discussed in the passage is insignificant.

D) Deleted, because it introduces a piece of information that is only vaguely related to the paragraph's main idea.

CONTINUE

The musical history of New Orleans does not stop here, however. In a way, jazz gets the attention because it is a kind of national [16] music has roots all over the American South, the East Coast, and the Midwest. But there is at least one style of music that is unique to New Orleans and the areas to the south: zydeco. [17] Some people find this name curious, and you may be one of them. If you are, you're not alone. Scholars disagree on its origins, though most believe that it comes from some combination of words in creole French, the dialect spoken by the early European settlers of Louisiana.

Wherever the name comes from, one of its earliest recorded uses is on the 1929 recording "It Ain't Gonna Rain No' Mo'" by the Zydeco Skillet Lickers. This song is one of the earliest examples of a genre that has [18] remained and impressively stayed both durable and adaptable with the changing times and technologies. Early zydeco music was primarily performed with a button or piano accordion and a washboard, and it was [19] influenced by the polkas and waltzes of the late nineteenth century.

16

A) NO CHANGE
B) music that it has
C) music, with
D) music, which

17

Which choice most effectively combines the underlined sentences?

A) Finding this name curious as many people do means that you're not alone.
B) If you find this name curious, you're not alone.
C) You're not alone if you find this name a curious one like many people.
D) Like many people who find this name curious, you're not alone if you do.

18

A) NO CHANGE
B) remained, impressively stayed
C) remained
D) remained and stayed

19

A) NO CHANGE
B) influenced, by the polkas and waltzes,
C) influenced by the polkas and waltzes—
D) influenced by the polkas and waltzes,

CONTINUE

The form changed throughout the twentieth century, perhaps crystallizing in the work of the "King of Zydeco" Clifton **20** Chenier. Today, groups like **21** BeauSoleil continue to help zydeco to evolve, incorporating rock and country influences as well. As a testament to the endurance and popularity of zydeco music, the Grammys even introduced a new category in 2007: Best Zydeco or Cajun Music Album.

Zydeco is a pleasure to listen to, but it is just as important as a cultural **22** memorial. Indeed, zydeco provides an important reminder that a region is never merely defined by its most popular exports. Lots of things go into creating "local color," and the "local" in any place is much richer than we typically recognize.

20

Which choice adds the most relevant supporting information to the paragraph?

A) Chenier, born in the Creole-French speaking town of Opelousas, Louisiana.

B) Chenier, who infused the uptempo music with blues and jazz from the region.

C) Chenier; he is best known for how well he played the accordion and once won a Grammy.

D) Chenier, who was greatly respected at the time of his death in 1987.

21

A) NO CHANGE

B) BeauSoleil continue to help zydeco, to evolve

C) BeauSoleil continue, to help zydeco, to evolve

D) BeauSoleil, continue to help zydeco to evolve,

22

A) NO CHANGE

B) agreement.

C) victory.

D) artifact.

CONTINUE

Questions 23–33 are based on the following passage and supplementary material.

Between Land and Sea

The separation between land and water seems a relatively simple one. Land is for walking, for cars, and for trains, whereas water is for swimming, for bathing, and for ships. The two come into contact in riverbeds, on banks, and on beaches, but the separation between them is clear. Or is it?

[23] Excavations in San Francisco, conducted over the past fifty years have revealed that the boundary between land and water is not so distinct. Digging into the surface of San Francisco's downtown Financial District has unearthed some unlikely building foundations: ships. [24] In fact, one of the tunnels for San Francisco's subway system, the BART, passes right through one of these interred ships. How did those massive vessels all get down there?

[25] The answer may seem counterintuitive. San Francisco manufactured a bit of its land. If this seems odd, consider that many cities throughout the world—among them Chicago, Singapore, and New York—have created landmasses in this way. The solution may seem bizarre until we consider that one of the major problem in cities is overcrowding. What better way to ease this problem than to create more land?

[23]

A) NO CHANGE
B) Excavations—in San Francisco conducted over the past fifty years—
C) Excavations, in San Francisco conducted, over the past fifty years,
D) Excavations in San Francisco conducted over the past fifty years

[24]

At this point, the writer is considering adding the following information.

> The area that was to become San Francisco was for many years known as Yerba Buena.

Should the writer make this addition here?

A) Yes, because it gives an interesting detail that delves further into San Francisco's history.
B) Yes, because it explains why so many ships should be buried in San Francisco's downtown.
C) No, because it obscures the focus of the passage by introducing a detail that does not have an obvious connection.
D) No, because the passage is primarily concerned with the importance of mass transit in San Francisco.

[25]

Which choice most effectively combines the underlined sentences?

A) San Francisco, an answer that may seem counterintuitive, manufactured some of its land.
B) The answer may seem counterintuitive, so San Francisco manufactured some of its land.
C) Even though the answer may be seeming counterintuitive, San Francisco was a place that manufactured some of its land.
D) The answer may seem counterintuitive: San Francisco manufactured some of its land.

CONTINUE

[1] One outgrowth of these recent discoveries has been a blurring of traditional scholarly boundaries. [2] Each of these disciplines has historically stuck to **26** its own area of expertise. [3] What happens, though, when geologists want to study landmasses containing man-made items such as ships and building fragments? [4] Both groups of experts are starting to work together on many projects, as it becomes clear that, particularly in the last 150 years, humans have shaped their natural environments to such an extent that nothing can be considered purely "natural" any longer. [5] For example, archaeology focused on human history, while geology concerned itself with natural history. **27**

Researchers have called this new layer of land the "archaeosphere." **28** Because we may think of the ground as something that is relatively constant, the archaeosphere suggests that quite the opposite is true.

26

A) NO CHANGE
B) our
C) their
D) his

27

To make this paragraph most logical, sentence 5 should be placed

A) where it is now.
B) after sentence 1.
C) after sentence 2.
D) after sentence 3.

28

A) NO CHANGE
B) But
C) While
D) Since

CONTINUE

On the one hand, this is disturbing because it shows that the solid ground <u>29 built on by them</u> may not be so solid after all. On the other hand, the classification and study of the archaeosphere could be beneficial and not just for the work of archaeologists and geologists. <u>30 In a sense,</u> some companies in Scandinavia have begun to mine the archaeosphere for <u>31 resources that may have been</u> wasted or discarded in earlier ages. Perhaps the world is not running out of resources in the way that we believed. Maybe it has instead found <u>32 its'</u> own way to recycle those resources, and we just need to catch up.

Cross-section of Waste Deposits

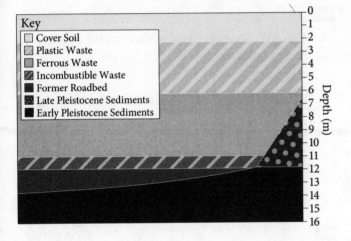

Question 33 asks about the graphic.

29

A) NO CHANGE

B) they build on

C) built on by us

D) we build on

30

A) NO CHANGE

B) Nonetheless,

C) For example,

D) Therefore,

31

A) NO CHANGE

B) resources to have been

C) resources, they have been

D) resources, being

32

A) NO CHANGE

B) they're

C) it's

D) its

33

Which choice offers an accurate interpretation of the data in the figure?

A) The cover soil is made up primarily of human and industrial waste products.

B) The soil as deep as 14 meters below the surface contains traces of human development.

C) The soil above 14 meters deep is made up of approximately 75% human and industrial waste products.

D) At depths of less than 10 meters below the surface, there is some human influence, but at depths greater than 10 meters, there is none.

CONTINUE

Questions 34–44 are based on the following passage.

The Sequence

Advances in the medical sciences have saved countless lives and made the lives of many, even the seriously ill, much more [34] healthy and medical. Since the Human Genome Project declared its work complete in 2003, genetic sequencing has begun to reveal some of its most significant contributions, and the breadth of those contributions is likely to extend well beyond what is currently known.

[35] One affect, genetic sequencing, as it relates to family history and lifetime health, has spawned a whole new field of wellness. Genetic counseling enables expectant parents to estimate the risks of having children based on hereditary patterns. This growing field is primarily concerned with the transmission of potentially harmful genes from parents to their offspring. [36] Children are particularly susceptible to illness just after birth. A large category of patients are expectant mothers, who seek prenatal testing to predict the likelihood of [37] medical risks, transmittable diseases, inborn illnesses, and birth defects for their unborn children.

[34]
A) NO CHANGE
B) tolerable and manageable.
C) complicated and expensive.
D) patient and tolerant.

[35]
A) NO CHANGE
B) An affect
C) Effecting
D) In effect

[36]
Which choice most effectively sets up the examples in the following sentences?
A) NO CHANGE
B) Patients of genetic counselors can be of any age.
C) Little is known about the range of inheritable diseases.
D) Parents' behaviors can often influence their children's health.

[37]
A) NO CHANGE
B) the dark side of medicine,
C) unpleasant things,
D) DELETE the underlined portion.

CONTINUE

If she decides to continue with the pregnancy after a potential risk has been identified, **38** a mother might seek the guidance of a genetic counselor to help manage a child with inborn medical issues. Older parents might even consider genetic testing before trying to conceive, thus reducing the **39** risks associated with: conceptions after the primary maternal or paternal periods of fertility.

As in the case of expectant mothers, genetic counseling has many **40** facets, the two primary divisions are diagnosis and support. The diagnostic side of genetic counseling involves the actual testing of genes and an estimation of risk. The support side involves managing and assessing risks to the child and mother that are associated with certain medical conditions. The work of these groups is often **41** complicated, particularly since modern adults more frequently have children in their 30s and 40s.

38

A) NO CHANGE

B) a genetic counselor who can advise how to manage a child with inborn medical issues may be sought.

C) a child with inborn medical issues may be born to a mother who seeks the help of a genetic counselor.

D) advice of a genetic counselor may be sought by a mother who fears inborn medical issues.

39

A) NO CHANGE

B) risks, associated with

C) risks associated with

D) risks: associated with

40

A) NO CHANGE

B) facet's;

C) facet's—

D) facets:

41

Which choice most effectively suggests that the "two primary divisions" are often not separate from one another?

A) NO CHANGE

B) specialized,

C) intertwined,

D) enriching,

CONTINUE ➤

For all of genetic counseling's benefits, **42** therefore, the field and its accomplishments are still not widely known. The National Society of Genetic Counselors was founded in 1979, and the field has had some breakthroughs (such as prenatal testing for Down syndrome) become popular knowledge. **43** Even so, there remains abundant opportunity for publicity and many genetic counselors are determined to get the word out—not only to patients, but also the general public.

[1] The field is perfect for those with an interest in science and education. [2] How effectively they communicate their findings can, at the most basic level, be a matter of life and death. [3] The technical aspects can be gained with a Master of Science in genetic counseling. [4] The ability to share these findings with patients, however, requires a special skill set. [5] Genetic counselors, like addiction or employment counselors, are fundamentally educators. **44**

42

A) NO CHANGE
B) for instance,
C) thus,
D) however,

43

At this point, the writer is considering adding the following sentence.

> The number of children born with Down syndrome has decreased significantly since this type of genetic prediction became available in the mid-1970s.

Should the writer make this addition here?

A) Yes, because it offers an important reminder for those who believe that genetic counseling is not a morally demanding job.

B) Yes, because it provides evidence that genetic counseling has resulted in new diagnostic possibilities.

C) No, because it gives an example that is inconsistent with the work of genetic counselors as they are described in the passage.

D) No, because it offers an illustration that does not have a significant bearing on this particular paragraph.

44

For the sake of the logic and cohesion of the paragraph, sentence 2 should be

A) placed where it is now.
B) placed before sentence 1.
C) placed after sentence 5.
D) DELETED from the paragraph.

STOP
If you finish before time is called, you may check your work on this section only.
Do not turn to any other section in the test.

No Test Material On This Page

Math Test – No Calculator

25 MINUTES, 20 QUESTIONS

Turn to Section 3 of your answer sheet to answer the questions in this section.

DIRECTIONS

For questions 1–15, solve each problem, choose the best answer from the choices provided, and fill in the corresponding circle on your answer sheet. **For questions 16–20**, solve the problem and enter your answer in the grid on the answer sheet. Please refer to the directions before question 16 on how to enter your answers in the grid. You may use any available space in your test booklet for scratch work.

NOTES

1. The use of a calculator **is not permitted**.
2. All variables and expressions used represent real numbers unless otherwise indicated.
3. Figures provided in this test are drawn to scale unless otherwise indicated.
4. All figures lie in a plane unless otherwise indicated.
5. Unless otherwise indicated, the domain of a given function f is the set of all real numbers x for which $f(x)$ is a real number.

REFERENCE

$A = \pi r^2$
$C = 2\pi r$

$A = \ell w$

$A = \frac{1}{2}bh$

$c^2 = a^2 + b^2$

Special Right Triangles

$V = \ell w h$

$V = \pi r^2 h$

$V = \frac{4}{3}\pi r^3$

$V = \frac{1}{3}\pi r^2 h$

$V = \frac{1}{3}\ell w h$

The number of degrees of arc in a circle is 360.
The number of radians of arc in a circle is 2π.
The sum of the measures in degrees of the angles of a triangle is 180.

CONTINUE

1

What are the solutions of the quadratic equation $-3x^2 - 3x + 18 = 0$?

A) $x = -3$ and $x = 2$

B) $x = -3$ and $x = -2$

C) $x = 3$ and $x = -2$

D) $x = 3$ and $x = 2$

2

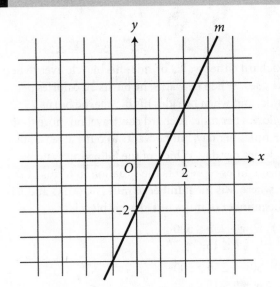

Which of the following is an equation of line m ?

A) $x = -2$

B) $y = -2$

C) $y = 2x - 2$

D) $y = 2x + 2$

3

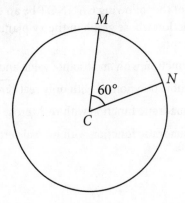

The circle above with center C has an area of 48. What is the area of sector $\overset{\frown}{MN}$?

A) 48

B) 16

C) 12

D) 8

4

Which of the following is equivalent to the sum of the expressions $x^2 + x$ and $-x - 2$?

A) $x - 2$

B) $2x - 2$

C) $x^2 - 2$

D) $x^3 - x^2 - 2$

CONTINUE

5

Which of the following CANNOT be an example of a function whose graph in the xy-plane has two x-intercepts?

A) A function with an absolute value and real zeros

B) A cubic polynomial with only real zeros

C) A quadratic function with real zeros

D) A quadratic function with no real zeros

6

$$\sqrt{c - 1} - t = 0$$

In the equation above, c is a constant. If $t = 4$, what is the value of c ?

A) 17

B) 15

C) 5

D) 3

7

$$x = y^2$$
$$6x + 9 = -3(2y - 3)$$

If (x, y) is a solution to the system of equations above and $y < 0$, what is the value of xy ?

A) −2

B) −1

C) 1

D) 3

8

Richard either walks or rides his bicycle everywhere he goes. When he walks, he burns 50 calories per mile, and when he rides his bicycle, he burns 25 calories per mile. Richard can travel no more than 15 miles per day, but he wants to burn at least 500 calories per day. Which of the following systems of inequalities represents the situation in terms of w and b, where w is the number of miles he walks and b is the number of miles he rides his bicycle?

A) $50w + 25b \leq 500$
   $w + b \leq 15$

B) $50w + 25b \geq 500$
   $w + b \leq 15$

C) $50w + 25b \geq 500$
   $w + b \geq 15$

D) $50w + 25b \leq 500$
   $w + b \geq 15$

CONTINUE

9

The Rankine scale is an alternate scale for measuring temperature where the unit of temperature is a Rankine, R. The conversion from degrees Celsius, C, to degrees Rankine, R, is given by the function $R(C) = 1.8C + 491.67$. Which of the following statements is the best interpretation of the number 491.67 in this context?

A) The increase in degrees Rankine that corresponds to a 1-degree Celsius increase in temperature

B) The increase in degrees Rankine that corresponds to a 1.8-degree Celsius increase in temperature

C) The temperature in degrees Rankine at 1.8 degrees Celsius

D) The temperature in degrees Rankine at 0 degrees Celsius

10

Which of the following is equivalent to $4^{\frac{5}{6}}$?

A) $2\sqrt[3]{4}$

B) $\sqrt[3]{2}$

C) $\sqrt[5]{4}$

D) $\sqrt[6]{4}$

11

If $x^2 + y^2 = c$ and $-xy = b$, which of the following is equivalent to $c + 2b$?

A) $(-2x - y)^2$

B) $(-x - y)^2$

C) $(x - y)^2$

D) $(x + y)^2$

12

The volume of cone C is 12 cubic millimeters. What is the volume, in cubic millimeters, of a cone with one-third the radius and triple the height of cone C?

A) 2

B) 4

C) 12

D) 36

CONTINUE

13

Marcy spends an average of $42 on coffee each month. She buys special pods of coffee that cost $7 each. Recently, Marcy decided that she wanted to reduce the amount of coffee she drinks per month by 9 cups. Assuming these pods can brew four cups of coffee at a time, which equation can Marcy use to determine how many dollars, *d*, she will save each month?

A) $\dfrac{4}{7}d = 9$

B) $\dfrac{4}{7}d = 33$

C) $\dfrac{7}{4}d = 9$

D) $\dfrac{7}{4}d = 33$

14

At a juice bar, *s* servings of banana smoothie are made by adding *b* bananas to a blender. If $s = b - 4$, how many additional servings of banana smoothie can be made with each additional banana?

A) One

B) Two

C) Three

D) Four

15

$$g(x) = 2 - 3^x$$

The function $g(x)$ is defined by the equation above. Which of the following is the graph of $y = -g(x)$ in the *xy*-plane?

A)

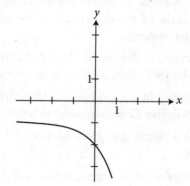

B)

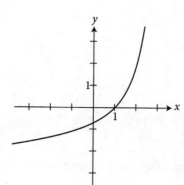

C)

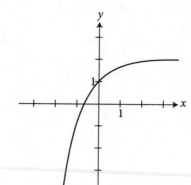

D)

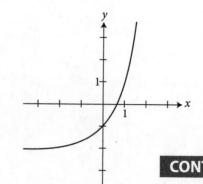

CONTINUE

DIRECTIONS

For questions 16–20, solve the problem and enter your answer in the grid, as described below, on the answer sheet.

1. Although not required, it is suggested that you write your answer in the boxes at the top of the columns to help you fill in the circles accurately. You will receive credit only if the circles are filled in correctly.

2. Mark no more than one circle in any column.

3. No question has a negative answer.

4. Some problems may have more than one correct answer. In such cases, grid only one answer.

5. **Mixed numbers** such as $3\frac{1}{2}$ must be gridded as 3.5 or 7/2. (If ⊞ $3\,1\,/\,2$ is entered into the grid, it will be interpreted as $\frac{31}{2}$, not as $3\frac{1}{2}$.)

6. **Decimal Answers:** If you obtain a decimal answer with more digits than the grid can accommodate, it may be either rounded or truncated, but it must fill the entire grid.

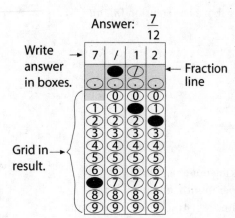

Answer: $\frac{7}{12}$ Write answer in boxes. ← Fraction line. Grid in result. Answer: 2.5 ← Decimal point

Acceptable ways to grid $\frac{2}{3}$ are:

Answer: 201 – either position is correct

NOTE: You may start your answers in any column, space permitting. Columns you don't need to use should be left blank.

CONTINUE ➜

16

$$\frac{1}{3}(5m - n) = \frac{31}{3}$$

$$n = 3m$$

The system of equations above has solution (m, n). What is the value of m ?

17

Asaf plans to start working out at a gym. The gym membership costs $50 per month, and he will also have to pay a $30 one-time registration fee. Asaf wants to spend no more than $555 for the membership and the registration fee. If gym memberships are only available for a whole number of months, what is the maximum number of months for which Asaf can have his gym membership?

18

Intersecting lines l, m, and o are shown below.

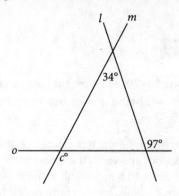

What is the value of c ?

CONTINUE

19

$$9(s - 2) + 3(s + 2) = 7s$$

What value of s is the solution of the equation above?

20

$$\frac{4c + 1}{(2c - 3)^2} - \frac{2}{(2c - 3)}$$

The expression above is equivalent to $\dfrac{x}{(2c - 3)^2}$, where x is a positive constant and $c \neq \dfrac{3}{2}$. What is the value of x?

S T O P

If you finish before time is called, you may check your work on this section only.
Do not turn to any other section in the test.

Math Test – Calculator

55 MINUTES, 38 QUESTIONS

Turn to Section 4 of your answer sheet to answer the questions in this section.

DIRECTIONS

For questions 1–30, solve each problem, choose the best answer from the choices provided, and fill in the corresponding circle on your answer sheet. **For questions 31–38**, solve the problem and enter your answer in the grid on the answer sheet. Please refer to the directions before question 31 on how to enter your answers in the grid. You may use any available space in your test booklet for scratch work.

NOTES

1. The use of a calculator **is permitted**.
2. All variables and expressions used represent real numbers unless otherwise indicated.
3. Figures provided in this test are drawn to scale unless otherwise indicated.
4. All figures lie in a plane unless otherwise indicated.
5. Unless otherwise indicated, the domain of a given function *f* is the set of all real numbers *x* for which *f(x)* is a real number.

REFERENCE

$A = \pi r^2$
$C = 2\pi r$

$A = \ell w$

$A = \frac{1}{2}bh$

$c^2 = a^2 + b^2$

Special Right Triangles

$V = \ell wh$

$V = \pi r^2 h$

$V = \frac{4}{3}\pi r^3$

$V = \frac{1}{3}\pi r^2 h$

$V = \frac{1}{3}\ell wh$

The number of degrees of arc in a circle is 360.
The number of radians of arc in a circle is 2π.
The sum of the measures in degrees of the angles of a triangle is 180.

CONTINUE

1

Sam's Special Hot Chocolate recipe calls for 4.5 fluid ounces of cream for every serving of hot chocolate. How many <u>cups</u> of cream are needed to make 24 servings of hot chocolate?

(1 cup = 8 fluid ounces)

A) 108

B) 36

C) 28.5

D) 13.5

2

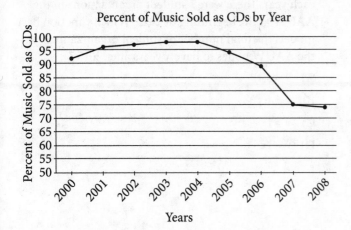

Percent of Music Sold as CDs by Year

According to the line graph above, between which two consecutive years was there the greatest change in the percent of music sold as CDs?

A) 2000–2001

B) 2003–2004

C) 2006–2007

D) 2007–2008

3

x	$g(x)$
2	11
4	17
6	23

Some values of the linear function g are shown in the table above. Which of the following defines g ?

A) $g(x) = 2x + 7$

B) $g(x) = 3x + 5$

C) $g(x) = 4x + 3$

D) $g(x) = 5x + 1$

4

A souvenir store sells postcards and magnets. Each postcard costs $1, and each magnet costs $3. If Annalee purchased a total of 10 postcards and magnets that cost a total of $22 before tax, how many magnets did she purchase?

A) 3

B) 4

C) 5

D) 6

CONTINUE

5

If $7(x - y) = 4$, what is the value of $x - y$?

A) $\dfrac{4}{7}$

B) $\dfrac{7}{4}$

C) 4

D) 7

6

The average annual precipitation in Orlando is approximately $\dfrac{13}{10}$ of the precipitation in Columbus. The average annual precipitation in Saint Cloud is approximately $\dfrac{7}{10}$ of the precipitation in Columbus. If the average annual precipitation in Columbus is 1,000 millimeters, approximately how many more millimeters of precipitation fall in Orlando than in Saint Cloud each year?

A) 600

B) 700

C) 1,150

D) 1,300

7

Which of the following is an equivalent form of $(2.6a - 3.5)^2 - (7.3a^2 - 4.1)$?

A) $-2.1a^2 - 2.9$

B) $-2.1a^2 + 11.1$

C) $-0.54a^2 - 18.2a - 8.15$

D) $-0.54a^2 - 18.2a + 16.35$

8

The American Association of University Women (AAUW) hopes to expand its reach by starting a total of t student organizations on college campuses each year. There were s student organizations in the AAUW at the beginning of 2015. Which function best models the total number of student organizations, y, the AAUW hopes to have x years after 2015 ?

A) $y = s(t)^x$

B) $y = t(s)^x$

C) $y = tx + s$

D) $y = tx - s$

CONTINUE

9

The resistance R of a conductor is found by dividing the voltage V across the conductor by the current I through the conductor. Which of the following gives the voltage V, in terms of R and I ?

A) $V = \dfrac{R}{I}$

B) $V = \dfrac{I}{R}$

C) $V = R - I$

D) $V = IR$

10

In 1893, the Major League Baseball pitching distance from the pitcher's plate to home base was increased from 50 feet to 60.5 feet. Which of the following is closest to the increase in the pitching distance in Major League Baseball, in meters? (1 meter is approximately 3 feet.)

A) 3.50

B) 3.25

C) 3.00

D) 2.75

11

Area of Focus	Highest Level of Education		Total
	Master's Degree	Doctoral Degree	
Pediatric	157	221	378
Adult	129	22	151
Total	286	243	529

In a survey, 529 social workers focusing on pediatric or adult services indicated their highest level of education. If one of the social workers is selected at random, which of the following is closest to the probability that the selected social worker is a pediatric social worker whose highest level of education is a doctoral degree?

A) 0.297

B) 0.418

C) 0.459

D) 0.541

12

$$-3x + 4y = 5$$

In the xy-plane, the graph of which of the following equations is perpendicular to the graph of the equation above?

A) $3x + 6y = 5$

B) $3x + 8y = 2$

C) $4x + 3y = 5$

D) $4x + 6y = 5$

CONTINUE

13

$$2 = -\frac{1}{3}x + y$$

$$6 = \frac{1}{3}x$$

The system of equations above has solution (x, y). What is the value of y ?

A) 8

B) 6

C) $\dfrac{9}{2}$

D) 4

14

A community advocacy group recently polled 500 people who were selected at random from a small town and asked each person, "Are you in favor of the referendum to increase the property tax rate?" Of those surveyed, 67 percent stated that they were opposed to the property referendum. Which of the following statements must be true based on the results of the poll?

   I. If another 500 people selected at random from the town were polled, 67 percent of them would state they are opposed to the property tax referendum.

   II. If 500 people selected at random from a different town were polled, 67 percent of them would report they are opposed to the property tax referendum.

   III. Of all the people in the town, 67 percent are opposed to the property tax referendum.

A) I only

B) I and III only

C) II and III only

D) None

15

$$4x - 1 \leq y$$

$$2 > x + y$$

Which of the following ordered pairs (x, y) satisfies the system of inequalities above?

A) $(-3, -1)$

B) $(2, -5)$

C) $(3, 1)$

D) $(4, -1)$

CONTINUE

Questions 16–18 refer to the following information.

Type of Exercise	Burn Rate
Shooting baskets	3.0
Boxing punching bag	4.5
Light aerobics	2.0
Speed walking	5.0
Doubles tennis	2.5
Yoga	1.5
Moderate walking	3.5
Running sprints	7.5

One method of calculating the calories a person will burn by doing a particular exercise is to multiply the number of minutes doing the exercise by a constant called the burn rate for that exercise. The table above gives the burn rate for a 100-pound person for eight types of exercise.

16

Two 100-pound people have each been exercising for 1 hour, one speed walking and one doing yoga. Which of the following will be closest to the difference of their total exercise times, in minutes, when they have each burned an additional 20 calories? (1 hour = 60 minutes)

A) 9.2

B) 9.3

C) 9.4

D) 9.6

17

According to the information in the table, what is the approximate number of calories that will be burned by a 100-pound person shooting baskets for 30 minutes?

A) 60 calories

B) 70 calories

C) 90 calories

D) 120 calories

18

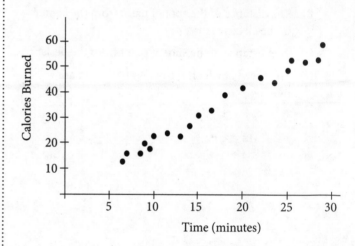

Calories Burned versus Time

The scatterplot above gives the time spent exercising plotted against calories burned for 20 100-pound people doing a particular exercise. The burn rate of this exercise is closest to that of which of the following exercises?

A) Boxing punching bag

B) Light aerobics

C) Moderate walking

D) Running sprints

CONTINUE

19

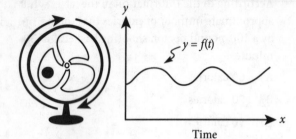

$y = f(t)$

Time

The figure on the left above shows an electric fan with a spot of paint on one of its blades. The electric fan is sitting on a flat desk and is switched on to a constant low setting, causing the blades to rotate in a clockwise direction. The graph of $y = f(t)$ on the right could represent which of the following as a function of time from when the electric fan was turned on?

A) The distance traveled by the spot of paint

B) The distance of the spot of paint from the center of the electric fan

C) The distance of the spot of paint from the desk

D) The speed at which the blades of the fan are moving

20

$$h = \frac{f - g}{g}$$

In the equation above, if f is positive and g is negative, which of the following must be true?

A) $h = 1$

B) $h > 1$

C) $h = -1$

D) $h < -1$

21

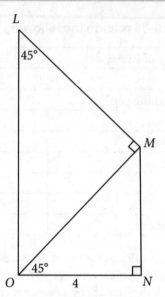

In quadrilateral $LMNO$ above, what is the length of $\overline{LM}$?

A) 8

B) $4\sqrt{3}$

C) $4\sqrt{2}$

D) 4

CONTINUE

Questions 22 and 23 refer to the following information.

Neighborhoods in Forest City		
Neighborhood Name	Population	Area (square miles)
Cedar Vale	12,000	57
Fir Fen	2,000	22
Maple Mall	122,000	442
Old Oaks	85,000	312.5
Poplar Park	78,000	288

Forest City consists of five different neighborhoods, listed in the table above. The table above shows the population of each neighborhood and area, in square miles, as of January 1, 2015. Over the past decade, Forest City has redrawn the borders of its neighborhoods two times in an attempt to balance school enrollments.

22

Due to redrawing of borders, the population of the Maple Mall neighborhood increased by 30% from January 1, 2010 to January 1, 2012. That population then increased a further 20% by January 1, 2014. No other changes in the population of Maple Mall have occurred since 2014. Which of the following best approximates the population of Maple Mall on January 1, 2010 ?

A) 83,700

B) 81,300

C) 78,200

D) 62,500

23

The relationship between the area A, in square miles, and the population n, in <u>thousands</u> of residents, of a neighborhood as of January 1, 2015 can be represented by a linear function. Which of the following functions represents the relationship?

A) $A(n) = 2n + 18$

B) $A(n) = 2.5n - 300$

C) $A(n) = 3.5n + 15$

D) $A(n) = 4.5n - 107$

24

In County C, the 132 employees at the small business Perfect Paper Products were surveyed and 62.9 percent of the employees responded that they had less than $1,000 in savings. The average small business size in the county is 132 employees. If the employees at Perfect Paper Products are representative of employees in the county's small businesses and there are 270 small businesses in the county, which of the following best estimates the number of small business employees in the county who have at least $1,000 in savings?

A) 12,700

B) 13,220

C) 22,400

D) 35,640

CONTINUE

25

The volume of a cube is $V = \dfrac{1}{8}c^3$, where c is a positive constant. Which of the following gives the surface area of the cube?

A) $6\left(\dfrac{c}{2}\right)^2$

B) $6\left(\dfrac{c^2}{2}\right)$

C) $6c^2$

D) $12c^2$

26

The mean weight of 6 people in an elevator is 160.5 pounds. If the person with the lowest weight gets off, the mean weight of the remaining 5 people becomes 168 pounds. What is the weight of the person with the lowest weight, in pounds?

A) 89

B) 123

C) 140

D) 297

27

A sociologist designed an experiment to examine the likelihood of a person to favor members of a group to which that person belongs. In the experiment, 400 students from several different colleges watched a series of video-taped interviews in a random order. Each interview featured an actor identified as a professor from each of those colleges discussing issues affecting students. Each student was then asked to select the most trustworthy interviewee. Of the first 200 students, s students chose the interviewee associated with their college. Among the remaining 200 students, 58 chose the interviewee associated with their college. If less than 25% of all students chose the interviewee associated with their college, which of the following inequalities best describes the possible value of s ?

A) $s - 58 < 0.25(400)$, where $0 \le s \le 200$

B) $s + 58 < 0.25(400)$, where $0 \le s \le 200$

C) $s < 0.25(400 - 58)$, where $0 \le s \le 200$

D) $s < 0.25(400 + 58)$, where $0 \le s \le 200$

28

$$y = c - x^2$$

The graph of the equation above forms a parabola in the xy-plane. If c is a positive constant, which of the following is an equivalent form of the equation?

A) $y = (c - x)^2$

B) $y = (c - x)(c + x)$

C) $y = \left(\dfrac{c}{2} - x\right)\left(\dfrac{c}{2} + x\right)$

D) $y = \left(\sqrt{c} - x\right)\left(\sqrt{c} + x\right)$

CONTINUE

29

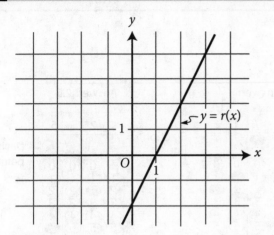

The graph of the linear function r is shown in the xy-plane above. The slope of the graph of the linear function s is $\frac{1}{6}$ the slope of the graph of r. If the graph of s passes through the point $(0, 2)$, what is the value of $s(15)$?

A) 5

B) 7

C) 10

D) 15

30

$$x^2 + 16x + y^2 - 12y = -19$$

The equation above defines a circle in the xy-plane. What are the coordinates of the center of the circle?

A) $(16, -12)$

B) $(8, -6)$

C) $(-8, 6)$

D) $(-16, 12)$

CONTINUE

DIRECTIONS

For **questions 31–38**, solve the problem and enter your answer in the grid, as described below, on the answer sheet.

1. Although not required, it is suggested that you write your answer in the boxes at the top of the columns to help you fill in the circles accurately. You will receive credit only if the circles are filled in correctly.

2. Mark no more than one circle in any column.

3. No question has a negative answer.

4. Some problems may have more than one correct answer. In such cases, grid only one answer.

5. **Mixed numbers** such as $3\frac{1}{2}$ must be gridded

   as 3.5 or 7/2. (If ![3 1 / 2 grid fragment]is entered into

   the grid, it will be interpreted as $\frac{31}{2}$, not as

   $3\frac{1}{2}$.)

6. **Decimal Answers:** If you obtain a decimal answer with more digits than the grid can accommodate, it may be either rounded or truncated, but it must fill the entire grid.

Answer: $\frac{7}{12}$ Answer: 2.5

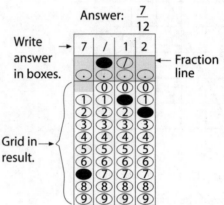

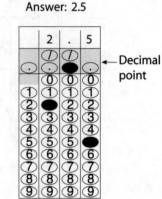

Write answer in boxes. ← Fraction line

Grid in result.

← Decimal point

Acceptable ways to grid $\frac{2}{3}$ are:

Answer: 201 – either position is correct

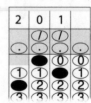

NOTE: You may start your answers in any column, space permitting. Columns you don't need to use should be left blank.

CONTINUE →

31

The flag that was raised in 1814 at Fort McHenry, the original "Star Spangled Banner," was rectangular in shape with height 30 feet and length 42 feet. If a reproduction is made where each dimension is $\frac{1}{9}$ the corresponding original dimension, what is the length of the reproduction, in feet?

32

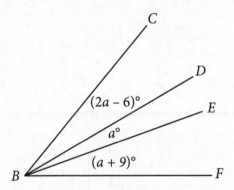

Note: Figure not drawn to scale.

In the figure above, $\angle CBD = \angle EBF$. What is the measure of $\angle CBF$, in degrees?

33

The square mile and the acre are units of measure of land area that are directly proportional. If 7 square miles are equal to 4,480 acres, how much area, in acres, is equal to 4 square miles?

34

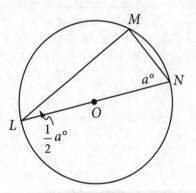

Point O is the center of the circle in the figure above. What is the value of a ?

CONTINUE

35

The point (4, 3) lies on the graph of the function $h(x)$ in the xy-plane. If $h(x) = \dfrac{1}{2}x^2 - a$, where a is a constant, what is the value of a ?

36

An artist is creating a rectangular mural. The height of the mural is to be 4 meters shorter than the width. What will be the height, in meters, of the mural if the area of the mural will be 96 square meters?

CONTINUE

Questions 37 and 38 refer to the following information.

Ms. McQueen's Sprint Triathlon Performance

Segment of triathlon	Average moving speed for segment (mph)	Distance (miles)
From start of race to end of swimming stage	2	0.25
From end of 1st transition to end of biking stage	20	12.4
From end of 2nd transition to end of running stage	8	3.1

Ms. McQueen competes in sprint triathlons consisting of swimming, biking, and running segments, with a transition period between segments. The table above shows the distance, in miles, and her average speed, in miles per hour, when she is between transition periods, for each segment of the sprint triathlon. The transition periods are not included in her speed or distance numbers.

37

When Ms. McQueen uses her triathlon bike to compete, she can complete a sprint triathlon at her average moving speed for each segment of the competition. When her triathlon bike is broken, she must use her hybrid bike instead. In those cases, the time it takes her to complete the biking segment of the sprint triathlon increases by 30% due to increased drag, but the time for each of the other segments of the competition does not change. Based on the table, how many more <u>minutes</u> did Ms. McQueen take to complete a sprint triathlon when she used her hybrid bike than when she used her triathlon bike? (Round your answer to the nearest minute.)

38

At one sprint triathlon, Ms. McQueen completed the course in 75 minutes, not including the time spent in transitions. What was her average speed, in miles per hour, during the sprint triathlon?

END OF TEST

DO NOT RETURN TO A PREVIOUS SECTION.

Completely darken bubbles with a No. 2 pencil. If you make a mistake, be sure to erase mark completely. Erase all stray marks.

1.

YOUR NAME: _____
(Print)
           Last   First   M.I.

SIGNATURE: _____ DATE: ___ / ___ / ___

HOME ADDRESS: _____
(Print)
      Number and Street

_____
   City   State   Zip Code

PHONE NO.: _____
(Print)

5. YOUR NAME

First 4 letters of last name				FIRST INIT	MID INIT

(Bubble columns A–Z for each letter position and initials)

IMPORTANT: Please fill in these boxes exactly as shown on the back cover of your test book.

2. TEST FORM

3. TEST CODE

4. REGISTRATION NUMBER

6. DATE OF BIRTH

Month	Day	Year
JAN		
FEB		
MAR		
APR		
MAY		
JUN		
JUL		
AUG		
SEP		
OCT		
NOV		
DEC		

7. SEX
- MALE
- FEMALE

The **Princeton Review®**

Test 9 Start with number 1 for each new section.
If a section has fewer questions than answer spaces, leave the extra answer spaces blank.

Section 1—Reading

1. Ⓐ Ⓑ Ⓒ Ⓓ
2. Ⓐ Ⓑ Ⓒ Ⓓ
3. Ⓐ Ⓑ Ⓒ Ⓓ
4. Ⓐ Ⓑ Ⓒ Ⓓ
5. Ⓐ Ⓑ Ⓒ Ⓓ
6. Ⓐ Ⓑ Ⓒ Ⓓ
7. Ⓐ Ⓑ Ⓒ Ⓓ
8. Ⓐ Ⓑ Ⓒ Ⓓ
9. Ⓐ Ⓑ Ⓒ Ⓓ
10. Ⓐ Ⓑ Ⓒ Ⓓ
11. Ⓐ Ⓑ Ⓒ Ⓓ
12. Ⓐ Ⓑ Ⓒ Ⓓ
13. Ⓐ Ⓑ Ⓒ Ⓓ
14. Ⓐ Ⓑ Ⓒ Ⓓ
15. Ⓐ Ⓑ Ⓒ Ⓓ
16. Ⓐ Ⓑ Ⓒ Ⓓ
17. Ⓐ Ⓑ Ⓒ Ⓓ
18. Ⓐ Ⓑ Ⓒ Ⓓ
19. Ⓐ Ⓑ Ⓒ Ⓓ
20. Ⓐ Ⓑ Ⓒ Ⓓ
21. Ⓐ Ⓑ Ⓒ Ⓓ
22. Ⓐ Ⓑ Ⓒ Ⓓ
23. Ⓐ Ⓑ Ⓒ Ⓓ
24. Ⓐ Ⓑ Ⓒ Ⓓ
25. Ⓐ Ⓑ Ⓒ Ⓓ
26. Ⓐ Ⓑ Ⓒ Ⓓ
27. Ⓐ Ⓑ Ⓒ Ⓓ
28. Ⓐ Ⓑ Ⓒ Ⓓ
29. Ⓐ Ⓑ Ⓒ Ⓓ
30. Ⓐ Ⓑ Ⓒ Ⓓ
31. Ⓐ Ⓑ Ⓒ Ⓓ
32. Ⓐ Ⓑ Ⓒ Ⓓ
33. Ⓐ Ⓑ Ⓒ Ⓓ
34. Ⓐ Ⓑ Ⓒ Ⓓ
35. Ⓐ Ⓑ Ⓒ Ⓓ
36. Ⓐ Ⓑ Ⓒ Ⓓ
37. Ⓐ Ⓑ Ⓒ Ⓓ
38. Ⓐ Ⓑ Ⓒ Ⓓ
39. Ⓐ Ⓑ Ⓒ Ⓓ
40. Ⓐ Ⓑ Ⓒ Ⓓ
41. Ⓐ Ⓑ Ⓒ Ⓓ
42. Ⓐ Ⓑ Ⓒ Ⓓ
43. Ⓐ Ⓑ Ⓒ Ⓓ
44. Ⓐ Ⓑ Ⓒ Ⓓ
45. Ⓐ Ⓑ Ⓒ Ⓓ
46. Ⓐ Ⓑ Ⓒ Ⓓ
47. Ⓐ Ⓑ Ⓒ Ⓓ
48. Ⓐ Ⓑ Ⓒ Ⓓ
49. Ⓐ Ⓑ Ⓒ Ⓓ
50. Ⓐ Ⓑ Ⓒ Ⓓ
51. Ⓐ Ⓑ Ⓒ Ⓓ
52. Ⓐ Ⓑ Ⓒ Ⓓ

Section 2—Writing and Language Skills

1. Ⓐ Ⓑ Ⓒ Ⓓ
2. Ⓐ Ⓑ Ⓒ Ⓓ
3. Ⓐ Ⓑ Ⓒ Ⓓ
4. Ⓐ Ⓑ Ⓒ Ⓓ
5. Ⓐ Ⓑ Ⓒ Ⓓ
6. Ⓐ Ⓑ Ⓒ Ⓓ
7. Ⓐ Ⓑ Ⓒ Ⓓ
8. Ⓐ Ⓑ Ⓒ Ⓓ
9. Ⓐ Ⓑ Ⓒ Ⓓ
10. Ⓐ Ⓑ Ⓒ Ⓓ
11. Ⓐ Ⓑ Ⓒ Ⓓ
12. Ⓐ Ⓑ Ⓒ Ⓓ
13. Ⓐ Ⓑ Ⓒ Ⓓ
14. Ⓐ Ⓑ Ⓒ Ⓓ
15. Ⓐ Ⓑ Ⓒ Ⓓ
16. Ⓐ Ⓑ Ⓒ Ⓓ
17. Ⓐ Ⓑ Ⓒ Ⓓ
18. Ⓐ Ⓑ Ⓒ Ⓓ
19. Ⓐ Ⓑ Ⓒ Ⓓ
20. Ⓐ Ⓑ Ⓒ Ⓓ
21. Ⓐ Ⓑ Ⓒ Ⓓ
22. Ⓐ Ⓑ Ⓒ Ⓓ
23. Ⓐ Ⓑ Ⓒ Ⓓ
24. Ⓐ Ⓑ Ⓒ Ⓓ
25. Ⓐ Ⓑ Ⓒ Ⓓ
26. Ⓐ Ⓑ Ⓒ Ⓓ
27. Ⓐ Ⓑ Ⓒ Ⓓ
28. Ⓐ Ⓑ Ⓒ Ⓓ
29. Ⓐ Ⓑ Ⓒ Ⓓ
30. Ⓐ Ⓑ Ⓒ Ⓓ
31. Ⓐ Ⓑ Ⓒ Ⓓ
32. Ⓐ Ⓑ Ⓒ Ⓓ
33. Ⓐ Ⓑ Ⓒ Ⓓ
34. Ⓐ Ⓑ Ⓒ Ⓓ
35. Ⓐ Ⓑ Ⓒ Ⓓ
36. Ⓐ Ⓑ Ⓒ Ⓓ
37. Ⓐ Ⓑ Ⓒ Ⓓ
38. Ⓐ Ⓑ Ⓒ Ⓓ
39. Ⓐ Ⓑ Ⓒ Ⓓ
40. Ⓐ Ⓑ Ⓒ Ⓓ
41. Ⓐ Ⓑ Ⓒ Ⓓ
42. Ⓐ Ⓑ Ⓒ Ⓓ
43. Ⓐ Ⓑ Ⓒ Ⓓ
44. Ⓐ Ⓑ Ⓒ Ⓓ

Test 9   Start with number 1 for each new section.
If a section has fewer questions than answer spaces, leave the extra answer spaces blank.

Section 3—Mathematics: No Calculator

1. Ⓐ Ⓑ Ⓒ Ⓓ
2. Ⓐ Ⓑ Ⓒ Ⓓ
3. Ⓐ Ⓑ Ⓒ Ⓓ
4. Ⓐ Ⓑ Ⓒ Ⓓ
5. Ⓐ Ⓑ Ⓒ Ⓓ
6. Ⓐ Ⓑ Ⓒ Ⓓ
7. Ⓐ Ⓑ Ⓒ Ⓓ
8. Ⓐ Ⓑ Ⓒ Ⓓ
9. Ⓐ Ⓑ Ⓒ Ⓓ
10. Ⓐ Ⓑ Ⓒ Ⓓ
11. Ⓐ Ⓑ Ⓒ Ⓓ
12. Ⓐ Ⓑ Ⓒ Ⓓ
13. Ⓐ Ⓑ Ⓒ Ⓓ
14. Ⓐ Ⓑ Ⓒ Ⓓ
15. Ⓐ Ⓑ Ⓒ Ⓓ

16. 17. 18. 19. 20.

Section 4—Mathematics: Calculator

1. Ⓐ Ⓑ Ⓒ Ⓓ
2. Ⓐ Ⓑ Ⓒ Ⓓ
3. Ⓐ Ⓑ Ⓒ Ⓓ
4. Ⓐ Ⓑ Ⓒ Ⓓ
5. Ⓐ Ⓑ Ⓒ Ⓓ
6. Ⓐ Ⓑ Ⓒ Ⓓ
7. Ⓐ Ⓑ Ⓒ Ⓓ
8. Ⓐ Ⓑ Ⓒ Ⓓ
9. Ⓐ Ⓑ Ⓒ Ⓓ
10. Ⓐ Ⓑ Ⓒ Ⓓ
11. Ⓐ Ⓑ Ⓒ Ⓓ
12. Ⓐ Ⓑ Ⓒ Ⓓ
13. Ⓐ Ⓑ Ⓒ Ⓓ
14. Ⓐ Ⓑ Ⓒ Ⓓ
15. Ⓐ Ⓑ Ⓒ Ⓓ
16. Ⓐ Ⓑ Ⓒ Ⓓ
17. Ⓐ Ⓑ Ⓒ Ⓓ
18. Ⓐ Ⓑ Ⓒ Ⓓ
19. Ⓐ Ⓑ Ⓒ Ⓓ
20. Ⓐ Ⓑ Ⓒ Ⓓ
21. Ⓐ Ⓑ Ⓒ Ⓓ
22. Ⓐ Ⓑ Ⓒ Ⓓ
23. Ⓐ Ⓑ Ⓒ Ⓓ
24. Ⓐ Ⓑ Ⓒ Ⓓ
25. Ⓐ Ⓑ Ⓒ Ⓓ
26. Ⓐ Ⓑ Ⓒ Ⓓ
27. Ⓐ Ⓑ Ⓒ Ⓓ
28. Ⓐ Ⓑ Ⓒ Ⓓ
29. Ⓐ Ⓑ Ⓒ Ⓓ
30. Ⓐ Ⓑ Ⓒ Ⓓ

31. 32. 33. 34. 35.

36. 37. 38.

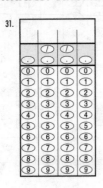
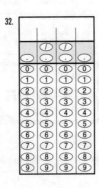
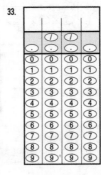

Chapter 20
Practice Test 9:
Answers and
Explanations

PRACTICE TEST 9 ANSWER KEY

Section 1: Reading		Section 2: Writing & Language		Section 3: Math (No Calculator)		Section 4: Math (Calculator)	
1. A	27. C	1. D	23. D	1. A	11. C	1. D	20. D
2. D	28. B	2. D	24. C	2. C	12. B	2. C	21. C
3. B	29. C	3. A	25. D	3. D	13. A	3. B	22. C
4. A	30. D	4. A	26. A	4. C	14. A	4. D	23. C
5. B	31. D	5. A	27. B	5. D	15. D	5. A	24. B
6. C	32. C	6. C	28. C	6. A	16. $\frac{31}{2}$	6. A	25. A
7. D	33. B	7. B	29. D	7. B	or	7. D	26. B
8. D	34. C	8. A	30. C	8. B	15.5	8. C	27. B
9. C	35. A	9. B	31. A	9. D	17. 10	9. D	28. D
10. C	36. D	10. C	32. D	10. A	18. 117	10. A	29. B
11. A	37. B	11. A	33. B		19. $\frac{12}{5}$	11. B	30. C
12. B	38. C	12. B	34. B		or	12. C	31. $\frac{42}{9}$,
13. D	39. C	13. D	35. D		2.4	13. A	$\frac{14}{3}$,
14. D	40. C	14. C	36. B		20. 7	14. D	4.66,
15. A	41. B	15. D	37. D			15. A	or
16. B	42. A	16. C	38. A			16. B	4.67
17. A	43. C	17. B	39. C			17. C	32. 63
18. B	44. C	18. C	40. D			18. B	33. 2,560
19. C	45. B	19. A	41. C			19. C	34. 60
20. C	46. B	20. B	42. D				35. 5
21. C	47. C	21. A	43. D				36. 8
22. A	48. A	22. D	44. C				37. 11
23. B	49. A						38. 12.6
24. A	50. D						
25. B	51. C						
26. D	52. A						

> Go to PrincetonReview.com to score your exam. Alternatively,
> for self-assessment tables, please turn to page 909.

PRACTICE TEST 9 EXPLANATIONS

Section 1: Reading

1. **A**   The question asks how *the primary focus shifts over the course of the passage*. Because this is a general question, it should be done after the specific questions. The passage initially focuses on Mrs. Helen Givings' views of Frank and April, saying that *she had recognized them as the kind of couple one did take a little trouble with*, and proceeds to expand on her views of the couple until it *shifts* to describing Frank and April's positive views about the house that *did have possibilities* such that *they could fancy themselves at home here*. Eliminate answer choices that don't match the passage. Keep (A) because it matches the passage. Choice (B) is a Mostly Right/Slightly Wrong trap answer: although the passage does contain *an interaction between Frank and April* toward the end, it does not contain *a monologue by Mrs. Givings*. Eliminate (B). Choice (C) is a Right Answer, Wrong Question trap answer: though the passage does contain a *description of a setting* and an *evaluation of the characters*, neither of these is the *primary focus* of the passage. Eliminate (C). Eliminate (D) because the passage does not discuss *tragic past events*. The correct answer is (A).

2. **D**   The question asks for *the main purpose of the first paragraph*. Because this is a general question, it should be done after the specific questions. The first paragraph describes Frank and April's drive *down to the turn at the base of Revolutionary Hill and on up the winding blacktop grade of Revolutionary Road*, the location that gives the novel its name and is discussed later in the passage. Eliminate answer choices that do not match the passage. Choice (A) is a Mostly Right/Slightly Wrong trap answer: although the first paragraph does *establish a mood*, that mood is not *maintained throughout the passage*. Eliminate (A). Choice (B) is a Right Words, Wrong Meaning trap answer: though the first paragraph does use *descriptive imagery* to describe the couple as *like very old and tired people*, this phrase is used figuratively, rather than literally. Eliminate (B). Eliminate (C) because the rest of the passage does not *explain* the *circumstances* of the first paragraph. Keep (D) because it matches the passage. The correct answer is (D).

3. **B**   The question asks for *Mrs. Givings's primary impression of her "cordially nodding passengers."* The question is the first question in a paired set, but it is easy to find, so it can be done on its own. Use the given line reference to find the window. Lines 10–16 state that Mrs. Givings, after initially being *polite but guarded* since *so many city people were apt to come out and waste her time*, eventually recognized her passengers as *the kind of couple one did take a little trouble with*. Eliminate answer choices that don't match this answer from the passage. Choice (A) is a Right Answer, Wrong Question trap answer: Mrs. Givings does indicate that *many city people…waste her time demanding impossible bargains*, but she does not describe Frank and April this way. Eliminate (A). Keep (B) because it matches the passage. Eliminate (C) because the passage does not say that Frank and April *remind* Mrs. Givings *of herself and her husband*. Choice (D) is a Right Words, Wrong Meaning trap answer: though Mrs. Givings describes the house she believes Frank and April are looking for as *something with a little charm*, the passage does not describe the couple themselves as projecting *sophistication and charm*. Eliminate (D). The correct answer is (B).

4. **A**   The question is the best evidence question in a paired set. Because the previous question was easy to find, simply look at the lines used to answer Q3. Lines 14–16 provided the evidence for Q3: *she had recognized them as the kind of couple one did take a little trouble with, even in the low-price bracket*. Eliminate (B), (C), and (D). The correct answer is (A).

5. **B** The question asks about the *contrast emphasized* by *Mrs. Givings* while *describing Revolutionary Hill Estates*. Since there is no line reference, use lead words and the order of the questions to find the window. The evidence for Q3 and Q4 came from lines 10–16, so scan the passage beginning with line 16, looking for the lead words *Mrs. Givings* and *Revolutionary Hill Estates*. Starting at line 38, Mrs. Givings describes *a perfectly dreadful new development called Revolutionary Hill Estates – great hulking split levels, all in the most nauseous pastels and dreadfully expensive too*, but then states that the house Frank and April will be shown *has absolutely no connection with that*, instead describing its appearance as *a sweet little house and a sweet little setting* with *simple, clean lines* and *good lawns*. Mrs. Givings is contrasting the appearance of this house with the appearance of nearby houses in *Revolutionary Hill Estates*. Eliminate answer choices that don't match this answer from the passage. Eliminate (A) because the passage does not mention *houses in other towns*. Keep (B) because it matches the passage. Choice (C) is a Right Words, Wrong Meaning trap answer: although Mrs. Givings describes the *Revolutionary Hill Estates* as *dreadfully expensive*, she doesn't mention the *affordability* of another home, nor does she describe a home's *luxury*. Choice (D) is a Right Words, Wrong Meaning trap answer. Though the passage does mention *plumbers, carpenters, little people of that sort*, it does not contrast their *lifestyles* to those of *her more affluent clients*. Eliminate (D). The correct answer is (B).

6. **C** The question asks for evidence that supports the *conclusion that Mrs. Givings prefers older homes*. Look at the line references given in the answer choices, and eliminate the statements that don't support this claim. The lines for (A) say that Mrs. Givings thinks that *Route Twelve* isn't a *very desirable road*, but the lines don't mention *old homes*, so eliminate (A). In the lines for (B), Mrs. Givings describes the homes on Route Twelve as *little cinderblocky, pickup-trucky places*. There is no mention of *old homes*, so eliminate (B). In the lines for (C), Mrs. Givings says, *One of our nice little local builders put it up right after the war, you see, before all the really awful building began.* These lines compare an older home *put up right after the war* to the new *really awful building*, which supports the idea that Mrs. Givings prefers older homes. Keep (C). The lines for (D) say that the *road is nicer along here*, but there is no mention of *homes*, so eliminate (D). The correct answer is (C).

7. **D** The question asks how *Frank and April find the "central window."* Use the given line reference to find the window for the question. Lines 55–56 describe *its outsized central window staring like a big black mirror*. In lines 57–59, April says, *Of course it does have the picture window; I guess there's no escaping that*, and in lines 60–62, Frank says, *Still, I don't suppose one picture window is necessarily going to destroy our personalities*. Eliminate answer choices that don't match this answer from the passage. Eliminate (A) because the reaction to the central window is not positive. Eliminate (B) because Frank and April don't disagree about the window. Choice (C) is a Right Answer, Wrong Question trap: the passage describes the *living room* as *too-symmetrical* but *undeniably appealing*, but this description doesn't refer to the *central window*. Keep (D) because *out of proportion* matches *outsized*. The correct answer is (D).

8. **D** The question asks for the *primary impression created by the narrator's description of Mrs. Givings in lines 63–68*. Use the given line reference to find the window. Lines 64–67 say that Mrs. Givings's *laughter enclosed them in a warm shelter of flattery* and *she hovered near them, reassuring and protective*. Eliminate answer choices that don't match this answer from the text. Eliminate (A) because *formal* does not match her *laughter*. Eliminate (B) because there is no indication that Mrs. Givings is *amusing*. Eliminate (C) because Mrs. Givings is not *compulsive*. Keep (D) because it matches the passage: *doting and attentive* match *reassuring and protective*. The correct answer is (D).

9. **C** The question asks what the word *fancy* most nearly means in line 80. Go back to the text, find the word *fancy*, and cross it out. Then read the window carefully, using context clues to determine another word that would fit in its place. The text says, *Enjoying the light heft and feel of these doorknobs, they could fancy themselves at home here.* Therefore, *fancy* could be replaced by a word such as "imagine." Eliminate answer choices that don't match the way the word is used in context. *Elaborate* means "develop in detail;" it doesn't match "imagine," so eliminate (A). *Embellish* means "add decorative detail;" it doesn't match "imagine," so eliminate (B). *Envision* matches "imagine," so keep (C). *Enshrine* means "put in a place to protect and show respect;" it doesn't match "imagine," so eliminate (D). Note that (A) and (B) are Could Be True trap answers based on another meaning of *fancy* that is not supported by the text. The correct answer is (C).

10. **C** The question asks for the *main idea of the last paragraph*. Use the given paragraph reference to find the window. The paragraph describes Frank and April's thoughts about the house. Lines 68–69 say, *The place did have possibilities* and line 80 says, *they could fancy themselves at home here*. Eliminate answer choices that don't match this answer from the text. Choice (A) is a Right Answer, Wrong Question trap: *furniture* is mentioned, but it is not the main idea. Eliminate (A). Choice (B) is also a Right Answer, Wrong Question trap: the new house is *symmetrical*, but that is not the main idea. Eliminate (B). Keep (C) because the statement *Frank and April can imagine living* in the new house matches the statement *they could fancy themselves at home here*. Choice (D) is a Right Answer, Wrong Question trap: although there are some things about the house that Frank and April don't like, (the *picture window*, for example) as well as things they do like, the main idea of the paragraph is not that they feel ambivalent (which means "having mixed feelings") about the house. The final sentence of the paragraph emphasizes their positive feelings about it: *Who could be frightened in as wide and bright, as clean and quiet a house as this?* Eliminate (D). The correct answer is (C).

11. **A** The question asks how the main focus of the passage shifts. Because this is a general question, it should be done after all the specific questions. The authors evaluate the evidence for whether Groupon users are more critical in their reviews than non-Groupon users, and then suggest some hypotheses about why Groupon reviews yield lower ratings. Choice (A) summarizes this shift, so keep (A). Eliminate (B) because the original observation was that *Yelp reviews that contained the word "Groupon" provided, on average, significantly lower ratings than reviews that did not*. The authors do not discuss the method used to detect this. Choice (C) can be eliminated because the passage provides no review of the research itself. Eliminate (D) because the authors conclude that there are a number of reasons that combine to create the Groupon effect. Hence, there is no *absolute* reason. Note, too, that the word *absolute* is an extreme word that does not have similarly extreme support in the text. The correct answer is (A).

12. **B** The question asks how the *Groupon effect* may be defined. Notice that this is the first question in a paired set, so this question can be done in tandem with Q13. Look at the best evidence answer choices for Q13 first. The lines for (13A) state that by looking at a dataset from Groupon and Yelp, the authors learned *significantly more about the daily deals model*. These lines do not describe the Groupon effect and do not support any of the answers in Q12. Eliminate (13A). The lines for (13B) state that in some cases, businesses *may also attempt to place negative reviews for their competitors*. These lines support (12C), but that pair does not answer the question and can ultimately be eliminated. The lines for (13C) describe *unrealized expectations between reviewers and merchants*. This does not support any of the answers in Q12. Eliminate (13C). The lines for (13D) state that the authors have *shown that a combination of poor business behavior, Groupon user experimentation, and an artificially high baseline all play a role* in describing the Groupon effect. This supports (12B). Connect answers (13D) and (12B). The correct answers are (12B) and (13D).

13.　**D**　(See explanation above.)

14.　**D**　The question asks what the word *fake* means in line 53. Go back to the text, find the word *fake*, and mark it out. Carefully read the surrounding text to determine another word that would fit in the blank based on the context of the passage. The word *fake* in the passage is used in the context of a review being introduced *in an arguably artificial manner*. Look for an answer that means something like "being introduced in an artificial manner." Only (D), *planted*, has that meaning. To "plant information" means "to secretly place the information for publication or dissemination." Choices (A), (B), and (C) may all seem tempting because all of these answers relate to a definition of the word *fake*. However, none of these answers relate to introducing a review *in an arguably artificial manner*. The correct answer is (D).

15.　**A**　The question asks about an action which would *best address a concern regarding the introduction of artificial Yelp reviews*. Use the lead word *artificial* and chronology to find the window and read carefully. The passage states that reviews that mention Groupon are written by actual customers, while other reviews *are significantly more likely to be "fake" or otherwise introduced in an arguably artificial manner*. Therefore, the problem is that not all reviews are being written by actual customers who use the service. Find an answer that addresses this concern. Choice (A) addresses the concern. If a *verifiable receipt image* were required, the reviews would be entirely submitted by customers who used the service. None of the other answers would help ensure that only those who had used the services could write reviews. The correct answer is (A).

16.　**B**　The question asks which choice best describes the *"unrealized expectations"* between reviewers and merchants. Carefully read each line reference in the answer choices and eliminate any that don't address the question. The correct answer should mention both the reviewers and the merchants. The lines for (A) describe the research methodology the author used. This information is unrelated to the *unrealized expectations* between reviewers and merchants. The lines for (B) describe Groupon users as *fussy reviewers* and businesses as *providing worse service specifically to Groupon customers*. This describes a mismatch between reviewers and merchants. Keep (B). The lines for (C) describe how businesses attempt to gain more positive reviews. However, these lines say nothing about the reviewers themselves. Eliminate (C). The lines for (D) state that *Groupon users provide detailed reviews that are valued more highly by their Yelp peers*. However, this answer provides no information about the merchants. Eliminate (D). The correct answer is (B).

17.　**A**　The question asks what the word *compilation* means in line 86. Go back to the text, find the word *compilation*, and mark it out. Carefully read the surrounding text to determine another word that would fit in the blank based on the context of the passage. The word describes a group of data about Groupon users. Look for an answer choice that means "a group." Only (A), *collection*, means a group. Choice (B), *summary*, may seem tempting. However, while the data has been collected, it is not clear from the passage that it has been summarized. The correct answer is (A).

18.　**B**　The question asks *which category of Yelp user showed the most evenly distributed star ratings*, according to the figure. In the figure, the *x*-axis shows the star rating and the *y*-axis shows the frequency of any given star rating. The user group with the flattest line is the one with the most evenly distributed star ratings. The flattest relative line in the graph belongs to the Groupon Businesses, Groupon User, Mentions Groupon, which is (B). The correct answer is (B).

19.　**C**　The question asks which Yelp rating a non-Groupon user is most likely to give. Look at the two lines for non-Groupon businesses. Both lines for the non-Groupon business users peak at 4 stars. The correct answer is (C).

20. **C** The question asks what idea from the passage is most directly supported from the passage. The data in the figure provides no information on the correlation between the type of business and the pattern of Yelp star ratings. Eliminate (A). The data in the figure provides no information on customers who produce "spam reviews." Eliminate (B). The data in the figure provides no information on the number of Groupon mentions in a review. Eliminate (D). The only answer that can be deduced from the figure is (C). The figure shows Yelp scores of Groupon users relative to Yelp scores of non-Groupon users. The correct answer is (C).

21. **C** The question asks what the word *extend* means in line 3. Go back to the text, find the word *extend*, and mark it out. Carefully read the surrounding text to determine another word that would fit in the blank based on the context of the passage. The word *extend* refers to the statement in the previous sentence that *We know that clinical trials sponsored by the pharmaceutical industry are likely to exaggerate benefit and minimize harms* related to *their sponsorship of non-human animal research*. So *extend* should mean something like "relate." *Reach*, *require*, and *stretch* do not mean "relate," so eliminate (A), (B), and (D). *Apply* means "to make relevant," which matches the prediction. The correct answer is (C).

22. **A** The question asks what the questions posed in lines 3–7 chiefly intend to do. Read the window to find that the questions, *do these biases extend to their sponsorship of non-human animal research? Are the findings of such studies credible? And how do those findings compare with "proper" research conducted by dispassionate academics?*, are asked before being described as *important questions* to begin the second paragraph. The questions intend to show what type of information could be determined by the proposed investigation of pharmaceutical clinical trials. *Introduce a set of considerations that may not have been investigated in prior research* matches the prediction, so keep (A). There is no reference to *confusion about the nature of results, an improper method of conducting trials,* or *controversy about the quality of research performed by academics*; eliminate (B), (C), and (D). The correct answer is (A).

23. **B** The question asks which question *the research of Bero's team* primarily intended to answer. Notice that this is the first question in a paired set, so this question can be done in tandem with Q24. Look at the best evidence answer choices for Q24 first. The lines for (24A) ask *could it be that industry-sponsored research is actually more rigorous than academic research?* This matches whether *experiments funded by invested corporations get performed with a greater level of attention to detail than those that are not*, so connect (24A) with (23B). The lines for (24B) and (24C) discuss statins, so they might initially seem to connect to (23A), but neither set of lines actually answers the question in (23A). Eliminate (24B) and (24C). The lines for (24D) address *the difficulty industry has in replicating the results of research conducted in academic labs*, but there is no indication that something explicitly *prevents industry-sponsored research from being conducted with the same level of rigor as academic research* in (23C); eliminate (24D). The correct answers are (23B) and (24A).

24. **A** (See explanation above.)

25. **B** The question asks about the *main purpose of the fourth paragraph*. The fourth paragraph describes the systematic review of statin treatments for atheroma, *focusing on those studies where sponsorship status was known* before presenting the results of the studies. So the main purpose of the fourth paragraph is to show the results of the studies of sponsorship status. The fourth paragraph does not *question the implications of the surprising findings, shift from a description of Bero's team's study to an overview of a question*, or *connect research performed on human subjects to research performed on non-human animals*, so eliminate (A), (C), and (D). *Note significant results of Bero's team's study* matches the prediction. The correct answer is (B).

26. **D**   The question asks what the word *conservative* means in line 48. Go back to the text, find the word *conservative*, and mark it out. Carefully read the surrounding text to determine another word that would fit in the blank based on the context of the passage. The study in the previous paragraph shows *that findings from research sponsored by industry are more conservative than those sponsored by non-industry sources, but the interpretation of those data is, in contrast, less conservative.* Additionally, in the previous paragraph, industry-supported studies find less evidence supporting the use of statins, but are more likely to ultimately favor their use. So *conservative* means something like "reserved in interpretation." Because *old-fashioned*, *dramatic*, and *traditional* do not mean "reserved in interpretation," eliminate (A), (B), and (C). *Reserved* matches the prediction. The correct answer is (D).

27. **C**   The question asks about *non-human research sponsored by others compared to non-human animal research sponsored by industry*. The author states in the sixth paragraph that *non-human animal work sponsored by industry is likely to be performed and reported to a higher quality, and to be at lower risk of bias, than work sponsored by others.* Subsequently, the passage mentions *the difficulty industry has in replicating the results of research conducted in academic labs.* Find an answer choice that matches the information from the text. *Non-human research sponsored by others shows a lower risk of bias* reverses this relationship, so eliminate (A). Choice (B) might initially look attractive because the passage does talk about research that is easier to reproduce, but read the question carefully. The question asks about *non-human research sponsored by others,* which the passage says industry has *difficulty replicating.* Eliminate (B). Choice (C) is directly supported by the passage, so keep that answer. There is no comparison of the *costs,* so (D) can be eliminated. The correct answer is (C).

28. **B**   The question asks why *the findings of Bero's team are surprising*. Notice that this is the first question in a paired set, so this question can be done in tandem with Q29. Look at the best evidence answer choices for Q29 first. The lines for (29A) and (29B) provide the study results alone without any indication as to why they *are surprising*, so eliminate (29A) and (29B). The lines for (29C) indicate that *findings from research sponsored by industry are more conservative than those sponsored by non-industry sources, but the interpretation of those data is, in contrast, less conservative,* before asking *why might this be?* This contradiction indicates the findings are surprising and *apparently contradict a sensible assumption,* so connect (29C) with (28B). The lines for (29D) reference *exaggeration of conclusions,* but this doesn't match any of the choices for Q28; eliminate (29D). The correct answers are (28B) and (29C).

29. **C**   (See explanation above.)

30. **D**   The question asks why the author of the passage would most likely agree that *industry-sponsored research may be rigorous*. Notice that this is the first question in a paired set, so this question can be done in tandem with Q31. Look at the best evidence answer choices for Q31 first. The lines for (31A), (31B), and (31C) make no reference to the level of rigor with which *industry-sponsored research* is conducted; eliminate (31A), (31B), and (31C). *Standards for internal reporting* would refer to the rigor with which *non-human animal research* is conducted by industry and matches *elements of documentation that are also applied to purposes other than research.* The correct answers are (30D) and (31D).

31. **D**   (See explanation above.)

32. **C**   The question asks what point Hubert makes about *working women relative to working men*. Notice that this is the first question in a paired set, so this question can be done in tandem with Q33. Look at the best evidence answer choices for Q33 first. The lines for (33A) state that *women are paid less than men for apparently the same service* which *seems to disturb a great many people*

who find here a conspiracy upon the part of the man to keep women out of the wage-earning field. This supports none of the answers in Q32. It may be tempting to connect this answer with (32A) because (32A) includes both the words *disturbingly* and *conspiracies*. However, the passage does not state that women *supply more conspiracies than men*. Eliminate (33A). The lines for (33B) state that *women as a class of workers are beginners, comparatively speaking in the great field of industry…Woman's preparation for work is seldom so thorough as with a man, and long technical training for any work is considered superfluous for a woman….* This supports (32C). Connect answers (33B) and (32C). The lines for (33C) state that *the woman has seldom the strong incentive of others dependent upon her; the man has a wife and children who will suffer, should he relax his efforts; the woman is usually alone.* This answer supports none of the answers in Q32. Eliminate (33C). The lines for (33D) state that *while in this century and in America work and money-earning have always been considered to be proper in every way for men, there is still some slight social stigma pertaining to money-getting by women.* This supports none of the answers in Q32. Eliminate (33D). The correct answers are (32C) and (33B).

33. **B** (See explanation above.)

34. **C** The question asks what Hubert implies about the *wage gap between women and men*. Scan the passage for where the author discusses the wage gap. The second paragraph discusses the *reasons for the apparent discrepancy between the pay of men and women.* Use the second paragraph as the window to read. According to the second paragraph, *some reasons for the apparent discrepancy between the pay of men and women…may serve to clear away some of the false impressions that have grown up about this question. In the first place, women as a class of workers are beginners comparatively speaking, in the great field of industry; they lack the hereditary instinct for such work, and as beginners their wages are low.* Find an answer that is consistent with this prediction. Choice (A) can be eliminated because at no point in the passage does the author suggest that the wage gap is *inevitable*. In fact, the first paragraph states that *If a woman wants more money than a man, she has only to do better and more work in the long run than the man.* In other words, the author does not preclude a woman from earning as much as a man. Choice (B) can be eliminated because the passage does not indicate that the reason the wage gap is *avoidable* is because *women and men can either support themselves or marry.* Choice (C) matches the prediction. The author states that there are *false impressions* about the apparent discrepancy between the pay of men and women, and that women get paid less because they are *beginners*. The implication is that one gets paid more if one has more experience. Eliminate (D) because the author never indicates that he finds the wage gap *regrettable*. The correct answer is (C).

35. **A** The question asks what the word *relax* means in line 28. Go back to the text, find the word *relax*, and mark it out. Carefully read the surrounding text to determine another word that would fit in the blank based on the context of the passage. The word *relax* is used in the sentence that states *the man has a wife and children who will suffer, should he relax his efforts.* Within the context of the passage *relax his efforts* means something like "reducing" the amount of work he does. Find an answer that has a meaning close to "reduce." Choice (A), *lessen*, is the only answer that means "to reduce." Choices (B), *chill*, and (D), *calm*, may seem tempting because they are alternate definitions of the word *relax*. However, given that *relax* is used in this passage as meaning to "reduce effort", these answers do not work in context. The correct answer is (A).

36. **D** The question asks what the word *curious* means in line 30. Go back to the text, find the word *curious*, and mark it out. Carefully read the surrounding text to determine another word that would fit in the blank based on the context of the passage. The word *curious* is used to describe a feature of *work by women*. The sentence states that *while in this century and in America work and money-earning have always been considered to be proper in every way for men, there is still some*

slight social stigma pertaining to money-getting by women. In context, the word *curious* means "odd." It is odd that it is proper for men to make money by working, but not proper for women to do so. The only answer that means something similar to odd is (D), *peculiar.* Choice (A), *interested,* may seem tempting because that is a definition of *curious,* however, it does not work in the context of the sentence. The correct answer is (D).

37. **B** The question asks what *Penny's central claim* is in Passage 2. Because this is a general question, it should be done after all of the specific questions for Passage 2. In the first paragraph, the author notes that *a woman...receives half price for all she does.* In the second paragraph, the author goes on to state that *It requires just as much to support a woman as a man*, and that when women are employed *they have the hardest, worst paid, and most unhealthy work.* The passage concludes with the author stating that the effect of paying women better *will prove beneficial not only to workers... but its influence will extend to all those directly affected.* Choice (A) can be eliminated because at no point in the passage does the author suggest that *women must protest.* Choice (B) is consistent with the prediction since the central claim of the passage is that women should get paid more. Choice (C) may be tempting because the first paragraph states that *a woman may be defined to be a creature that receives half price for all she does, and pays full price for all she needs.* However, the author does not state that women shouldn't pay full price. The central claim of the passage is that women should be paid more. Choice (D) can be eliminated because there is no call in the passage for punishing *societies that underpay women.* The correct answer is (B).

38. **C** The question asks what point Penny makes about *women's working conditions* in Passage 2. Notice that this is the first question in a paired set, so this question can be done in tandem with Q39. Look at the best evidence answer choices for Q39 first. The line for (39A) states that *Society is tardy, dragging, in the matter.* This does not support any of the answers in Q38. Eliminate (39A). The lines for (39B) state that *often infirm, sick, or aged parents are relying on her for a support, or, it may be, orphan brothers and sisters.* This matches none of the answers in Q38. Eliminate (39B). The lines for (39C) state that *When men and women are employed in the same establishments, women have not the lightest, most healthy, and most pleasant parts of the labor.* This supports (38C). Connect answer (39C) with (38C). The lines for (39D) discuss the beneficial effect of paying women better prices for their labor. This answer is unrelated to women's working conditions. Eliminate (39D). The correct answers are (38C) and (39C).

39. **C** (See explanation above.)

40. **C** The question asks about the *relationship between the two passages.* Because this question is a general question about both passages, it should be done after the questions that pertain to each individual passage have been completed. Passage 1 describes the reasons that women are paid less than men. Passage 2 argues that women should get paid the same as men. Find an answer that connects the two passages. Passage 1 provides several theories of why women do not get paid the same as men, but these theories are not discussed in Passage 2, so eliminate (A). Choice (B) can be eliminated because there is no *plan defended* in Passage 1. Choice (C) matches the passages: Passage 1 discusses the reasons for the discrepancies in the wages between men and women. Passage 2 argues that women should get paid more, which if it came to pass would lessen the discrepancy. Choice (D) can be eliminated because although Passage 1 provides reasons for why women do not get paid as much as men, Passage 2 does not address these reasons. The correct answer is (C).

41. **B** The question asks what both authors would agree on. Because this is a general question about both passages, it should be done after the questions that pertain to each individual passage have been completed. While the author of Passage 2 states that when men and women work in the same establishments, women have *the hardest, worst paid, and most unhealthy work.* The author

of Passage 1 does not state that businesses *overwork* women. For this reason, eliminate (A). The authors of both passages agree that there is a real *wage gap* between men and women. For this reason, eliminate (C). Neither passage discusses whether educated *women should earn higher salaries*. For this reason, eliminate (D). The correct answer is (B).

42. **A**   The question asks how the author of Passage 1 would most likely have reacted to lines 72–73 of Passage 2. Because this question is about both passages, it should be done after the questions that pertain to each individual passage have been completed. According to the author of Passage 1, there are a number of valid reasons that women do not get paid as much as men. These include that *women as a class of workers are beginners;* that *woman's preparation for work is seldom so thorough as with a man*; and that *the woman has seldom the strong incentive of others dependent on her* that a man does. Therefore, the author would not agree with the statement that *pay[ing] women better prices for labor will give it a dignity in public estimation*. Eliminate (C) and (D) because *empathy* and *elation* would suggest that the author of Passage 1 agrees with the author of Passage 2. In (B), *panic* is too extreme. The author of Passage 1 does not indicate that he is in any way panicked. Choice (B) is also incorrect since neither passage discusses reverse discrimination. The correct answer is (A).

43. **C**   The question asks for *one advantage of acquiring water from traditional sources*. Since there is no line reference, use lead words and the order of the questions to find the window. Q44 asks about line 26, so scan the first two paragraphs, looking for the lead words *traditional sources*. Lines 13–17 say, *relying on traditional sources of water... has served most of the world well. This has become even easier to do for many regions in the world that are experiencing higher rates of precipitation*. Eliminate answer choices that don't match this answer from the passage. Eliminate (A) because the *quality* of the water is not discussed in the window. Choice (B) is a Right Words, Wrong Meaning trap answer: the passage says *most of the world*, not all of the *global demand*. Keep (C) because it matches the passage: *readily accessible* is consistent with *even easier to do for many regions in the world*. Eliminate (D) because *desalination plants* are not mentioned in this part of the passage. The correct answer is (C).

44. **C**   The question asks what the word *stable* most nearly means in line 26. Go back to the text, find the word *stable*, and cross it out. Then read the window carefully, using context clues to determine another word that would fit in its place. The text says, *All this added moisture, combined with longer growing seasons owing to higher average yearly temperatures, might seem to contribute to a more stable food supply as well*. Therefore, *stable* could be replaced by a word such as "secure." Eliminate answer choices that don't match the way the word is used in context. *Balanced* does not match "secure," so eliminate (A). *Rational* does not match "secure," so eliminate (B). *Dependable* matches "secure," so keep (C). *Fixed* does not match "secure," so eliminate (D). Note that (A), (B), and (D) are Could Be True trap answers based on other meanings of *stable* that are not supported by the text. The correct answer is (C).

45. **B**   The question asks what *best reflects the perspective of the "advocates" on traditional water sources*. This is the first question in a paired set, but it is easy to find, so it can be done on its own. Use the given line reference to find the window. According to lines 27–32 the *advocates of desalination* view traditional water sources as *unstable sources of natural water*. Lines 34–37 say that the advocates *cite a recent study concluding that, by 2071, half of the 204 freshwater basins in the United States may be unable to meet demands*. Eliminate answer choices that don't match this answer from the passage. Choice (A) is a Right Answer, Wrong Question trap: the first paragraph describes traditional water sources this way, but the *advocates* in the third paragraph view *traditional water sources* in a negative way. Keep (B) because it matches the passage: *not reliable* is consistent with *unstable*. Eliminate (C) because the *advocates* view the *traditional water sources*

as *unstable*; they don't think these sources provide a *stable supply* even *temporarily*. Eliminate (D) because there is no mention of *cost* in the window. The correct answer is (B).

46. **B** The question is the best evidence question in a paired set. Because the previous question was easy to find, simply look at the lines used to answer Q45. Lines 28–37 provided the evidence for Q45: *They have embraced desalination as a godsend that is better for the species—making drinkable the vast amounts of saltwater encircling the globe—than depending on what they view as unstable sources of natural water* and *by 2071, half of the 204 freshwater basins in the United States may be unable to meet demands.* Of the answer choices for Q46, only (B) includes any of these lines. Eliminate (A), (C), and (D). The correct answer is (B).

47. **C** The question asks what *the Advisian Worley Group* indicates about *the desalination process*. Use the given line reference to find the window. Lines 51-53 mention the *Advisian Worley Group* and how it *analyzed the various factors that contribute to the expense of these desalination plants*, and lines 59–61 say that the *report advised that it was nearly impossible to make predictions about future costs of desalination*. Eliminate answer choices that don't match this answer from the passage. Eliminate (A) because the window does not mention *the amount of water supplied* or *local demand*. Eliminate (B) because there is no mention of *quality of equipment*. Keep (C) because it matches the passage: *unforeseen investments* is consistent with *impossible to make predictions about future costs*. Choice (D) is a Right Words, Wrong Meaning trap answer: although the passage does mention *plant location*, it does not say that plant location is the primary factor for determining cost, just one of the factors. Eliminate (D). The correct answer is (C).

48. **A** The question asks what the word *raw* most nearly means in line 57. Go back to the text, find the word *raw*, and cross it out. Then read the window carefully, using context clues to determine another word that would fit in its place. The text discusses factors that impact the cost of desalination: *Other factors that need to be considered include the location of the plants, the raw water quality, the type of intake and outfall, and others*. Therefore, *raw* could be replaced by a word such as "untreated." Eliminate answer choices that don't match the way the word is used in context. *Unprocessed* matches "untreated," so keep (A). *Inexperienced* does not match "untreated," so eliminate (B). *Unchecked* means "free," which does not match "untreated," so eliminate (C). *Underdone* does not match "untreated," so eliminate (D). Note that (B), (C), and (D) are Could Be True trap answers based on other meanings of *raw* that are not supported by the text. The correct answer is (A).

49. **A** The question asks about the relationship between *traditional sources of water and desalination* as presented in the passage. This is the first question in a paired set, so it can be done in tandem with Q50. Look at the answer choices for Q50 first, reading with the question in mind. The lines for (50A) say that *nobody would disagree that clean drinking water is essential*. These lines do not refer to *traditional water sources* or *desalination*, so eliminate (50A). The lines for (50B) say, *Furthermore, because of the complexity of the variables, the report advised that it was nearly impossible to make predictions about future costs of desalination.* While these lines mention *desalination*, there is no discussion of its relationship to *traditional water sources*; eliminate (50B). The lines for (50C) say, *Flooding that accompanies once-in-a-century climate events—which are now occurring much more often than that—pollutes watersheds.* Since there is no mention of *traditional water sources* or *desalination*, eliminate (50C). The lines for (50D) say, *While desalination is more consistent, its cost and relatively small output leads us to conclude that it will be difficult to ever rely fully upon it.* These lines discuss *desalination* as compared to *traditional water sources*. Check the answer choices for Q49 to see whether any of the choices are supported by these lines. These lines support (49A). Draw a line connecting (49A) and (50D). Without any support in the answer choices from Q50, (49B), (49C), and (49D) can be eliminated. The correct answers are (49A) and (50D).

50. **D** (See explanation above.)

51. **C** The question asks *which statement about reverse osmosis desalination capacity in 2013 is best supported by the information in figure 2*. Work through each answer choice using the figure. Eliminate (A) because *seawater* yielded 46.3% of the water for reverse osmosis desalination, not *46.3 million cubic meters*. This answer choice is a trap based on mixing up the desalination capacity of seawater (measured in millions of cubic meters per day) with the percentage of the source water for desalination that comes from seawater. Eliminate (B) because *wastewater* provided *2.9* million cubic meters of water per day while *brine* provided only *0.09* million cubic meters of water per day, so the desalination capacity of wastewater was greater. Keep (C) because *seawater* was the source that provided the most water through desalination. Eliminate (D) because *tap water* and *pure water* together provide 2.6 million cubic meters of water per day, which is 6.5% of the capacity. This answer choice is a trap based on mixing up the desalination capacity of tap or pure water with the percentage of the source water for desalination that comes from tap or pure water. The correct answer is (C).

52. **A** The question asks which claim *is supported by figure 1*. Work through each answer choice using the figure. Keep (A) because the figure does show steady growth of desalination. Furthermore, the fact that *desalination capacity* is greater *than operational desalination capacity* indicates that *desalination is not running at its full capacity*. Eliminate (B) because *operational desalination capacity*—which is represented by the solid line and shown on the left vertical axis—was a little less than 100 million m³/day in 2020. This answer choice is a trap based on mixing up the *desalination capacity* with the *number of desalination plants*, which is shown on the right vertical axis. Eliminate (C) because the number of *operational desalination plants*—which is represented by the light grey bar and shown on the right vertical axis—was well over 40 before 2005; in 2000 the number of *operational desalination plants* was over 5,000. This answer choice is a trap based on mixing up the *desalination capacity* (shown on the left axis) with the *number of desalination plants* (shown on the right axis). Eliminate (D) because the difference between *desalination capacity* and *operational desalination capacity*—represented by the dotted and solid lines, respectively—was considerably less than 20 million cubic meters per day in 2010. This answer choice is a trap based on mixing up the *desalination capacity* with the *number of desalination plants* (represented by the bars). The correct answer is (A).

Section 2: Writing and Language

1. **D** Note the question! The question asks whether the sentence should be added, so it is testing consistency. If the content of the new sentence is consistent with the topics presented in the passage, then it should be added. The previous sentences discuss preventable auto accidents and lists their causes; the following sentence introduces *A recent set of research findings* pertaining to a single potential preventative factor, mountain lions. The proposed sentence would add information stating that *Statistics show that people are 23 times more likely to be involved in collisions when they are texting and driving*, which is not relevant to the topic of research findings on mountain lions; eliminate (A) and (B). The sentence does not *contradict the paragraph's main focus*, so eliminate (C). The additional sentence does *deviate from the paragraph's main topic*. The correct answer is (D).

2. **D** Verbs change in the answer choices, so this question tests consistency of verbs. A verb must be consistent with its subject and with the other verbs in the paragraph. The subject of the verb is *a recent set of research findings*, which is singular. To be consistent, the underlined verb must also be singular. Eliminate (C) because *have suggested* is plural. The paragraph is in present tense, so the underlined verb should also be in present tense. Eliminate (A) and (B) because they are not present tense. Choice (D) appropriately uses a singular, present tense verb. The correct answer is (D).

3. **A** Note the question! The question asks which option best combines the two sentences, so it's testing precision and concision. Look for the answer that combines the sentences while maintaining the meaning of the originals. The sentences use the repetitive phrasing *We probably want to start* and *before we do that*, so the correct answer will eliminate this redundancy without introducing another. Choice (A) eliminates the redundancy without introducing any other errors, so keep it. *Images* and *funny ones* are redundant, so eliminate (B). Choice (C) does not eliminate the original redundancy, so eliminate it. Choice (D) uses the subject *we* twice, so eliminate it. The correct answer is (A).

4. **A** Note the question! The question asks whether the sentence should be kept or deleted, so it is testing consistency. If the content of the underlined sentence is not consistent with the topics presented in the passage, then it should be deleted. The sentence states that *The eastern part of the United States is at a special risk for these collisions because deer tend to roam freely and plentifully around the region.* The sentence mentions *these collisions*, which refers directly to the *1.2 million collisions each year between automobiles and deer* from the previous sentence. Therefore, the sentence should be kept; eliminate (C) and (D). The sentence is only about accidents involving deer, not why all *car travel is so dangerous in the United States*; eliminate (B). The information in the sentence *does provide a detail that explains the statistic in the previous sentence*. The correct answer is (A).

5. **A** Pronouns are changing in the answer choices, so the question is testing consistency of pronouns. A pronoun must be consistent in number with the noun it refers to. The pronoun refers to the plural *deer populations*. To be consistent, the underlined pronoun must also be plural. *They* is a plural pronoun, so keep (A). *We* is a first person pronoun that cannot be used to refer to *deer populations*, so eliminate (B). *It* and *one* are singular, so eliminate (C) and (D). The correct answer is (A).

6. **C** Note the question! The question asks where sentence 4 should be placed, so it's testing consistency. The sentence must be consistent with the ideas that come both before and after it. Sentence 4 states that *Deer are thus able to reproduce without restriction*, so this sentence should come after the reason deer can reproduce freely. Sentence 2 states *development and hunting have eliminated this threat*, mentioned in sentence 1, *that deer face no natural predators in the eastern states*. Sentence 4 must come directly after the elimination of the threat, allowing for increased reproduction. The correct answer is (C).

7. **B** The vocabulary is changing in the answer choices, so this question is testing precision of word choice. Look for a word whose definition is consistent with the other ideas in the sentence. According to the context of the sentence, *the mountain lion populations of the west* are mentioned *as evidence*, so the underlined word should mean something like "uses" or "references." *Opines* means "express an opinion," so eliminate (A). *Cites* means "quotes," which matches the prediction, so keep (B). *Says* means "states," which is not the same as "uses," so eliminate (C). *Proclaims* means "announces," so eliminate (D). The correct answer is (B).

8. **A** Transitions change in the answer choices, so this question tests consistency of ideas. A transition must be consistent with the relationship between the ideas it connects. The first part of the sentence says that *Pugh cites the mountain lion populations as evidence*, and the second part says what the evidence shows: *these big cats "can coexist in close proximity with people, with very few conflicts."* The word *that* appropriately indicates that the second part of the sentence is what the evidence shows, so keep (A). The second part of the sentence is not an alternative to the first part, so eliminate (B). Eliminate (C) because it makes the sentence incomplete. There is no indication of time in the sentence, so eliminate (D). The correct answer is (A).

9. **B** Transitions change in the answer choices, so the question is testing the consistency of ideas. A transition must be consistent with the relationship between the ideas it connects. The sentence before the transition states that *it doesn't seem that introducing this fierce predator into the wild*

would be beneficial enough to offset its terrorizing costs. The sentence that starts with the underlined transition states that *Pugh and her team say these predators could save approximately five times as many people from deer-related deaths as they might endanger through unprovoked attacks.* These ideas contrast, so eliminate (A), (C), and (D), which would all indicate that the ideas agree. *Still* appropriately indicates a contrast. The correct answer is (B).

10. **C** Prepositions change in the answer choices, so this questions tests idioms. Because the phrase *data are* is plural, the phrase *a good amount*, which is singular, is inconsistent; eliminate (A). The correct idiom is *enough to overcome*, so eliminate (A) and (D). The correct answer is (C).

11. **A** Pronouns are changing in the answer choices, so the question is testing consistency of pronouns. A pronoun must be consistent in number with the noun it refers to or with other pronouns in the sentence. The sentence contains the pronoun *we*, which is first-person plural. To be consistent, the underlined pronoun should also be first-person plural. Eliminate (B) and (C), which contain singular pronouns. Eliminate (D) because *their* is third person. Choice (A) appropriately uses the first-person plural pronoun *our*. The correct answer is (A).

12. **B** The vocabulary is changing in the answer choices, so this question is testing precision of word choice. Look for a phrase whose definition is consistent with the other ideas in the sentence. The sentence states that *New Orleans has always been a kind of national treasure with* "bases" *or* "origins" *in French, American, African, and indigenous cultures. Routes* means "way" or "manner of travel," but New Orleans does not include a way through these various cultures; eliminate (A) and (D). *Roots* in context means "origins" that reside *in* the various cultures, not *of* them; eliminate (C). The correct answer is (B).

13. **D** Transitions change in the answer choices, so this question tests consistency of ideas. There is also the option to DELETE; consider this choice carefully, as it is often correct because it is the most concise answer. The previous sentence says that *This*, which refers to the status of New Orleans as a *national treasure, has become even more apparent since 2005, when Hurricane Katrina nearly wiped the city off the map.* The sentence that starts with the underlined portion says that *Katrina brought new attention to the city.* This sentence is not an *example* of the idea in the previous sentence, so eliminate (A). The two sentences do not contrast with each other, so eliminate (B). This sentence is not a conclusion based on the previous idea, so eliminate (C). There is no need for a transition. The correct answer is (D).

14. **C** Verbs are changing in the answer choices, so the question is testing the consistency of verbs. A verb must be consistent with its subject and with the other verbs in the sentence. The subject of the verb is *status*, which is singular. To be consistent, the underlined verb must also be singular. Eliminate (B) because *have shifted* is plural. The other verbs in the sentence, *has...been praised* and *has changed*, are past tense. To be consistent, the underlined verb must also be past tense. Eliminate (A) and (D) because they are not past tense. The underlined verb is the second in a list of two (*has changed* and *shifted*); the helping verb *has* at the beginning of the list can refer to both *changed* and *shifted*. Choice (C) is consistent with the sentence. The correct answer is (C).

15. **D** Note the question! The question asks whether the sentence should be kept or deleted, so it is testing consistency. If the content of the underlined sentence is not consistent with the topics presented in the passage, then it should be deleted. The sentence states that *Louis Armstrong was born in New Orleans in 1901 and began playing trumpet at an early age.* This is the only reference to Louis Armstrong in the entire passage and is not consistent with the paragraph, so eliminate (A) and (B). The sentence does not *suggest that the type of music discussed in the passage is insignificant*, so eliminate (C). Choice (D) accurately states that the sentence *is only vaguely related to the paragraph's main idea.* The correct answer is (D).

16. **C**   Transitions change in the answer choices, so this question tests consistency of ideas. A transition must be consistent with the relationship between the ideas it connects. The first part of the sentence states that *jazz gets the attention because it is a kind of national music*, and the second part gives a description of jazz. Choice (A) lacks any kind of transition that would indicate the relationship between these ideas, and it also makes the sentence incomplete; eliminate (A). Choices (B), (C), and (D) all include transition words that indicate that the second part of the sentence describes the first part. Since *that* in (B) refers to *music*, there is no need to also use the pronoun *it*; eliminate (B). For (D) to work, the verb *has* would need to be included after *which*. Since it is not included, eliminate (D). The correct answer is (C).

17. **B**   Note the question! The question asks which option best combines the two sentences, so it's testing precision and concision. Look for the answer that combines the sentences while maintaining the meaning of the originals. The phrases *you may be one of them* and *you aren't alone* use repetitive phrasing, so the correct answer will eliminate this redundancy without introducing another. Choices (C) and (D) don't get rid of the redundancy, so eliminate them. Choices (A) and (B) both express the same idea, but (B) is more concise. Eliminate (A). The correct answer is (B).

18. **C**   The phrase after *remained* is changing in the answer choices, so the question is testing precision and concision. First, determine whether the phrase is necessary. The sentence already states that the genre *has remained…durable and adaptable*, so there is no need to repeat that idea. Eliminate any choices that are redundant. Choices (A), (B), and (D) each repeat the idea of *remained* by adding *stayed*, so eliminate them. The correct answer is (C).

19. **A**   Commas are changing in the answer choices, so the question is testing comma usage. The phrase *by the polkas and waltzes* is necessary information that shouldn't be bracketed by commas, so eliminate (B). There is no need to break up the phrase *the polkas and waltzes of the late nineteenth century* with any punctuation, so eliminate (C) and (D). The correct answer is (A).

20. **B**   Note the question! The question asks *which choice adds the most relevant supporting information*, so it is testing consistency. Eliminate any answer choices that are not consistent with the purpose stated in the question. The start of the paragraph says that *the work of the "King of Zydeco" Clifton Chenier* changed (musical) forms, so the correct choice will explain how Chenier changed zydeco music. The choices that acknowledge that Chenier was *born in…Opelousas*, that he *once won a Grammy*, and that he *was greatly respected at the time of his death* do not explain how he changed zydeco music; eliminate (A), (C), and (D). That he *infused the uptempo music with blues and jazz* explains how Chenier changed zydeco music. The correct answer is (B).

21. **A**   Commas are changing in the answer choices, so this question is testing comma usage. The phrase *groups like BeauSoleil continue to help zydeco to evolve* is a complete idea that does not need to be broken up by any commas, so keep (A). Choices (B) and (C) add a comma after *zydeco*, so eliminate them. Choice (D) adds a comma after BeauSoliel, so eliminate (D). The correct answer is (A).

22. **D**   The vocabulary is changing in the answer choices, so this question is testing precision of word choice. Look for a word whose definition is consistent with the other ideas in the paragraph. The sentence before the underlined portion states that *Zydeco is a pleasure to listen to, but it is just as important* culturally. The next sentence continues to state that *zydeco provides an important reminder*. The correct choice will be something like "important cultural thing." *Memorial* means "monument" or "tribute" and can be important culturally, but a memorial is mostly about the person or thing it commemorates; eliminate (A). *Agreement* means "accordance in opinion," so eliminate (B). *Victory* means "triumph," so eliminate (C). A *cultural artifact* is in fact something important to a culture. The correct answer is (D).

23. **D** Commas are changing in the answer choices, so the question is testing comma usage. In (C), the phrase *in San Francisco conducted* is surrounded by commas. This phrase is necessary to the main meaning of the sentence, so eliminate (C). A pair of dashes can also surround unnecessary information, but the phrase *in San Francisco conducted over the past fifty years* is necessary to the main meaning of the sentence, so eliminate (B). There is no need to break up the phrase *Excavations in San Francisco conducted over the past fifty years* with a comma, so eliminate (A). The correct answer is (D).

24. **C** Note the question! The question asks whether a sentence should be added, so it is testing consistency. If the content of the new sentence is consistent with the topics presented in the passage, then it should be added. The surrounding sentences discuss *unlikely building foundations: ships,* and that *San Francisco's subway...passes right through one.* The proposed sentence would add information stating that *San Francisco was for many years known as Yerba Buena,* which is not relevant to the main topic of the paragraph, so eliminate (A) and (B). The passage isn't *primarily concerned with mass transit,* so eliminate (D). Choice (C) accurately states that the new sentence *obscures the focus of the passage by introducing a detail that does not have an obvious connection.* The correct answer is (C).

25. **D** Note the question! The question asks which option best combines the two sentences, so it's testing precision and concision. Choice (A) refers to San Francisco as *an answer,* but San Francisco is the location of the question posed at the end of the previous paragraph, not an answer. Eliminate (A). The word *so* between the parts of the sentence in (B) inaccurately make it seem like San Francisco manufactured land because of *the answer.* Eliminate (B). Choice (C) includes the phrase *Even though,* but a contrast is not needed. Eliminate (C). Choice (D) states *The answer* to the question at the end of the previous paragraph in a way that connects the ideas precisely. The correct answer is (D).

26. **A** Pronouns are changing in the answer choices, so the question is testing consistency of pronouns. A pronoun must be consistent in number and gender with the noun it refers to. The pronoun refers to *each of these disciplines,* which is singular—the word *each* is singular, and the prepositional phrase *of these disciplines* modifies *each* but is not what the pronoun refers to. To be consistent, the underlined pronoun must also be singular. *Our* and *their* are plural pronouns, so eliminate (B) and (C). *His* refers to a male and *each of these disciplines* lacks gender specificity, so eliminate (D). Choice (A) appropriately uses the gender-neutral, singular pronoun *its.* The correct answer is (A).

27. **B** Note the question! The question asks where sentence 5 should be placed, so it's testing consistency. The sentence must be consistent with the ideas that come both before and after it. Sentence 5 starts with the transition *for example,* and the example is *archaeology focused on human history, while geology concerned itself with natural history.* There is nothing in sentence 4 that sentence 5 could be an *example* of, so eliminate (A). Sentence 5 could be an example of *traditional scholarly boundaries* mentioned in sentence 1, and it also introduces two disciplines, which provides a point of reference for the phrase *each of these disciplines* in sentence 2. Sentence 5 belongs between sentences 1 and 2. The correct answer is (B).

28. **C** Transitions are changing in the answer choices, so the question tests consistency of ideas. A transition must be consistent with the relationship between the ideas it connects. The sentence that starts with the transition says that *we may think of the ground as something that is relatively constant,* but after a comma the sentence changes direction to say that *the archaeosphere suggests that the opposite is true.* Therefore, there needs to be an introduction indicating this change of direction. *Because* and *since* both indicate that ideas agree, so eliminate (A) and (D). *But* would indicate that this sentence contrasts with the one before it, rather than that the two ideas in

this sentence contrast with each other, so eliminate (B). *While* appropriately indicates a contrast within the sentence. The correct answer is (C).

29. **D** Pronouns change in the answer choices, so this question tests consistency of pronouns. A pronoun must be consistent with the noun it refers to or with other pronouns. The pronouns *them* and *they* in (A) and (B) do not clearly refer to anything, so they are imprecise. Eliminate (A) and (B). The previous sentence uses the first-person plural pronoun *we*, and both *us* and *we* are consistent with that. Choices (C) and (D) both express the same idea, but (D) is more concise. Eliminate (C). The correct answer is (D).

30. **C** Transitions are changing in the answer choices, so the question is testing the consistency of ideas. A transition must be consistent with the relationship between the ideas it connects. The sentence that starts with the underlined transition says *some companies in Scandinavia have begun to mine the archaeosphere*, which is provided to support information in the prior sentence stating that *the classification and study of the archaeosphere could be beneficial and not just for the work of archaeologists and geologists*. This sentence is not an interpretation of the previous sentence, as *in a sense* would indicate, so eliminate (A). This sentence does give an *example* of the idea stated in the previous one, so keep (C). This sentence is not a conclusion based on the previous one, so eliminate (D). The correct answer is (C).

31. **A** The length of the phrase after *resources* changes in the answer choices, so this question could test concision. Choice (D) is the shortest option, but *being* is present tense, which is not consistent with the phrase *in earlier ages*, which indicates the past. Eliminate (D). The phrase *to have been wasted* is also inconsistent with *in earlier ages*, so eliminate (B). The first part of the sentence, *some companies in Scandinavia have begun to mine the archaeosphere for resources*, is an independent clause. In (C), the second part of the sentence, *they have been wasted or discarded in earlier ages*, is also an independent clause. A comma alone cannot be used between two independent clauses, so eliminate (C). Choice (A) appropriately connects the two parts of the sentence and gives the sentence a precise meaning. The correct answer is (A).

32. **D** Pronouns are changing in the answer choices, so the question is testing consistency of pronouns. A pronoun must be consistent with the noun it refers to or with other pronouns in the sentence. The sentence contains the singular pronoun *it*. To be consistent, the underlined pronoun should also be singular. Eliminate (B) because *they* is plural. *Its'* is not a word that occurs in English, so eliminate (A). *It's* is a contraction of *it is*, which is not necessary in this context; eliminate (C). Choice (D) appropriately uses the singular possessive pronoun *its*. The correct answer is (D).

33. **B** Note the question! The question asks for the choice which *offers an accurate interpretation of the data in the figure*, so it tests consistency. Read the labels on the graph carefully, and look for an answer that is consistent with the information given in the graph. There is no information in the figure regarding the proportion *of human and industrial waste products* in the *cover soil* or in the soil at any depth, so eliminate (A) and (C). The figure indicates that ferrous waste, incombustible waste, and former roadbed are all present below 10 meters. These are all examples of *traces of human development*, so (B) is consistent with the figure. Eliminate (D) because there is *human influence* below 10 meters. The correct answer is (B).

34. **B** The vocabulary is changing in the answer choices, so this question is testing precision of word choice. Look for a phrase whose definition is consistent with the other ideas in the sentence. The opening of the passage states that scientific endeavors purporting to better the human condition *have saved countless lives* and that this science in turn has done something similar for *the lives of many, even the seriously ill*. From the context of the passage, the phrase should be something like "better their personal condition." *Healthy* matches this prediction, but *medical* means "pertain-

ing to medicine" instead of the patient's own condition; eliminate (A). *Tolerable and manageable* matches, so keep (B). Neither *complicated and expensive* nor *patient and tolerant* match "better their personal condition," so eliminate (C) and (D). The correct answer is (B).

35. **D** Vocabulary changes in the answer choices, so this question tests precision of word choice. *Affect* as a noun means "feeling" or "emotion," which is not consistent with the sentence's focus on *genetic sequencing*, so eliminate (A) and (B). The word *effecting* can only be used in certain contexts to mean "bring about a desired result," which is also not consistent with the sentence's focus; eliminate (C). The phrase *in effect* is a transition that means "essentially," which appropriately introduces the statement in the rest of the sentence about *genetic sequencing*. The correct answer is (D).

36. **B** Note the question! The question asks which *most effectively sets up the examples in the following sentences*, so it is testing consistency. Eliminate answers that are not consistent with the purpose stated in the question. The example after the underlined sentence is *a large category of patients—expectant mothers*, so the correct choice will be related to the category of *expectant mothers*. *Children* and *inheritable diseases* are not related to the category of *expectant mothers*, so eliminate (A) and (C). *Patients…of any age* could include *expectant mothers*, so keep (B). *Parents' behaviors* are not mentioned in the passage, so eliminate (D). The correct answer is (B).

37. **D** The length of the phrase changes in the answer choices, so this question tests concision. There is also the option to DELETE; consider this choice carefully, as it is often correct. *Medical risks* is redundant because each of the items in the subsequent list—*transmittable diseases, inborn illnesses, and birth defects*—is a medical risk; eliminate (A). *The dark side of medicine* is unrelated and *unpleasant things* is also redundant, so eliminate (B) and (C). Choice (D) is concise and gives the sentence a precise meaning. The correct answer is (D).

38. **A** The subject of the underlined portion changes in the answer choices, so this question tests consistency. The subject of the underlined section should match *she* in the non-underlined beginning of the sentence. The beginning of the sentence indicates that she could *continue with… pregnancy*, so look for an answer that is consistent with the idea of *pregnancy*. Neither *a child* nor *advice of a genetic counselor* is consistent with someone who could be pregnant, so eliminate (C) and (D). While a *genetic counselor* could be pregnant, (A) is more precise than (B) is because (A) specifies that the *mother* is the one who might seek *the guidance of a genetic counselor*. Eliminate (B). The correct answer is (A).

39. **C** Punctuation changes in the answer choices, so this question tests how to connect ideas with the appropriate punctuation. The first part of the sentence, *Older parents might even consider genetic testing before trying to conceive, thus reducing the risks associated with* is not an independent clause. A colon can only be used after an independent clause, so eliminate (A). There is no reason to break up the phrase *the risks associated with conceptions* with any punctuation, so eliminate (B) and (D). The correct answer is (C).

40. **D** Punctuation changes in the answer choices, so this question tests how to connect ideas with the appropriate punctuation. The first part of the sentence, *As in the case of expectant mothers, genetic counseling has many facets*, is an independent clause. The second part of the sentence, *the two primary divisions are diagnosis and support*, is also an independent clause. A comma on its own cannot be used between two independent clauses, so eliminate (A). Apostrophes also change in the answer choices, so this question also tests apostrophe usage. When used with a noun, an apostrophe indicates possession. Nothing belongs to *facets*, so no apostrophe is necessary. Eliminate (B) and (C). The correct answer is (D).

41.   **C**   Note the question! The question asks *which most effectively suggests that the "two primary divisions" are not often separate* with different vocabulary in the answer choices, so it is testing precision of word choice. *Complicated* means "difficult to understand," which is not consistent with *not separate*, so eliminate (A). *Specialized* means "specifically tailored," which is also not consistent with *not separate*, so eliminate (B). *Intertwined* means "tied together," which is consistent with *not separate*, so keep (C). *Enriching* means "adding value to," which is not consistent with the question, so eliminate (D). The correct answer is (C).

42.   **D**   Transitions are changing in the answer choices, so the question is testing the consistency of ideas. A transition must be consistent with the relationship between the ideas it connects. The part of the sentence before the transition talks about *genetic counseling's benefits*, and the part of the sentence after the transition states that *the field and its accomplishments are still not widely known*. Therefore, a change-of-direction transition is necessary. *Therefore* and *thus* both indicate that ideas agree, so eliminate (A) and (C). The fact that *the field and its accomplishments are not widely known* is not an example of a phenomenon, so eliminate (B). *However* appropriately indicates a contrast. The correct answer is (D).

43.   **D**   Note the question! The question asks whether the sentence should be added, so it is testing consistency. If the content of the new sentence is consistent with the topics presented in the passage, then it should be added. The surrounding sentences discuss *the work of genetic counselors* in general and how this work is *still not widely known*. The proposed sentence would add information stating that *the number of children born with Down syndrome has decreased significantly since this type of genetic prediction became available in the mid-1970s*. The sentence is not relevant to the main topic of the paragraph, so eliminate (A) and (B). The example is not *inconsistent with the work of genetic counselors*, so eliminate (C). Choice (D) accurately states that the new sentence *does not have a significant bearing on this paragraph*. The correct answer is (D).

44.   **C**   Note the question! The question asks where sentence 2 should be placed, so it tests consistency. There is also the option to DELETE; consider this choice carefully, as it is often correct. The sentence must be consistent with the ideas that came both before and after it. Determine the subject matter of the sentence, and determine if there are other sentences also discussing that information. Sentence 2 says that *How effectively they communicate their findings can...be a matter of life and death*. Based on the context of the passage, the *they* in this sentence refers to *genetic counselors*, so look for another sentence about *genetic counselors*. Sentence 5 is the only sentence in the paragraph to mention *genetic counselors*, so eliminate (A) and (B). Sentence 2 provides new information directly related to the content of sentence 5, so eliminate (D). The correct answer is (C).

Section 3: Math (No Calculator)

1.   **A**   The question asks for the solutions to a quadratic. Rather than do complicated algebraic manipulation, try out the numbers in the answer choices. Pick a value that appears in more than one answer, such as $x = -3$. Plug -3 into the equation for x to get $-3(-3)^2 - 3(-3) + 18 = 0$ or $-3(9) + 9 + 18 = 0$. This becomes $-27 + 27 = 0$, which is true. Eliminate (C) and (D), which do not contain the value $x = -3$. Now try $x = 2$ to get $-3(2)^2 - 3(2) + 18 = 0$ or $-3(4) - 6 + 18 = 0$. This becomes $-12 + 12 = 0$, which is true, so eliminate (B). The correct answer is (A).

2.   **C**   The question asks for the equation of the line shown in the graph. To determine this, plug an x-value from the graph into the equation and see if it gives the correct y-value. The point $(1, 0)$ is on the graph of m, so plug in $x = 1$ and $y = 0$. Choice (A) becomes $1 = -2$, which is not true, so

eliminate (A). Choice (B) becomes $0 = -2$, so eliminate (B). Choice (C) becomes $0 = 2(1) - 2 = 2 - 2 = 0$. This is true, so keep (C), but check (D) just in case. Choice (D) becomes $0 = 2(1) + 2 = 2 + 2 = 4$, so eliminate (D). The correct answer is (C).

3. **D** The question asks for the area of a sector of a circle. The parts of a circle all have the same proportional relationship, so use the given information to determine the part:whole relationship for circle C. A full circle is 360°, and angle MCN measures 60°. Set up the proportion $\frac{60°}{360°} = \frac{\text{sector}}{48}$. Reduce the fraction on the left to get $\frac{1}{6} = \frac{\text{sector}}{48}$, then cross-multiply to get $6(\text{sector}) = 48$. Divide both sides by 6 to get sector $= 8$. The correct answer is (D).

4. **C** The question asks for the answer that is equivalent to the sum of two expressions. The word *sum* indicates addition, so add the two expressions to get $x^2 + x - x - 2 = x^2 - 2$. The correct answer is (C).

5. **D** The question asks for the function whose graph CANNOT have two x-intercepts, so eliminate those that can. Zeros, which are mentioned in the answers, are also known as x-intercepts, so find the answer choice that cannot have two zeros. An absolute-value function with real zeros will have two x-intercepts. Eliminate (A). Cubic functions can have up to three real zeros, so eliminate (B). A quadratic function with real zeros can have up to two real zeros, so eliminate (C). Only a function with no real zeros or just one real zero CANNOT have two x-intercepts. The correct answer is (D).

6. **A** The question asks for the value of c for a certain value of t, so put $t = 4$ into the given equation to get $\sqrt{c - 1} - 4 = 0$. Now, rather than doing complicated algebra, try out the answers to see which one makes this equation true. Start with (B) and plug in 15 for c. The equation becomes $\sqrt{15 - 1} - 4 = 0$, or $\sqrt{14} - 4 = 0$. This is not true, so eliminate (B). The square root of 14 would be less than the square root of 16, or less than 4, so the left side of the equation would give a negative value with (B). A larger value is needed for c, so eliminate (C) and (D). The correct answer is (A).

7. **B** The question asks for the value of xy, the product of the coordinates of a possible solution to the system of equations. To solve this system, substitute y^2 into the second equation for x to get $6y^2 + 9 = -3(2y - 3)$. Distribute the -3 across the terms on the right side to get $6y^2 + 9 = -6y + 9$. Subtract 9 from both sides to get $6y^2 = -6y$. Divide both sides by $6y$ to get $y = -1$. Now, plug the value for y back into the first equation to get $x = (-1)^2 = 1$. To find the value of xy, multiply the two values: $(-1)(1) = -1$. The correct answer is (B).

8. **B** The question asks for a system of inequalities to represent the situation. Rather than try to translate a whole inequality at once, deal with one piece of information at a time. Start with a straightforward piece of information, such as the total number of miles. This value will be made up of the miles Richard walks, w, and the miles he bikes, b, so it translates to $w + b$. The total miles must be *no more than 15*, which translates to $w + b \leq 15$. Eliminate (C) and (D) because they do not include this inequality. Now compare the remaining answers. Both have the same numbers and variables, and the only difference is the direction of the inequality sign. These inequalities relate to the other part of the question, the calories burned, which should be *at least 500*. *At least* is represented by the $\geq$ symbol, so eliminate (A). The correct answer is (B).

9. **D** The question asks for the meaning of the number 491.67 in context. Label what is known about the equation. The left side is Rankine degrees and the C on the right side is Celsius degrees. The number 491.67 is on the right side, so it has something to do with Rankine degrees. However, all the answers refer to Rankine degrees, so it is difficult to eliminate anything at this time. Try out some different values in the equation to see how the variables relate. Since this is the No Calculator section, start with the easiest plug in, which will be in (D). If $C = 0$, then $R(0) = 1.8(0) + 491.67 = 491.67$. Therefore, at 0 degrees Celsius, the temperature in degrees Rankine is 491.67. This matches the information in (D). The correct answer is (D).

10. **A** The question asks for an expression that is equivalent to the given exponential one. The key to solving exponent questions is often to rewrite the base in a different form. The number 4 can be rewritten as 2^2, so the expression becomes $\left(2^2\right)^{\frac{5}{6}}$. To raise an exponential expression to a power, multiply the exponents, so this becomes $2^{\frac{10}{6}} = 2^{\frac{5}{3}}$. With fractional exponents, the numerator is the power and the denominator is the root, so this can be rewritten as $\sqrt[3]{2^5}$. There are five 2s under the root sign, and for every three, one of them can come out. The expression becomes $2\sqrt[3]{2^2} = 2\sqrt[3]{4}$. The correct answer is (A).

11. **C** The question asks for the value of $c + 2b$. Start by multiplying the second equation by 2 to get the value of $2b$, which is $2b = -2xy$. Add that to the expression for c, $x^2 + y^2$, to get $x^2 + y^2 - 2xy$. None of the answer choices are in this form, so factor the expression to make it look like the answers. It becomes $x^2 - 2xy + y^2 = (x - y)^2$. The correct answer is (C).

12. **B** The question asks for the volume of a cone. The formula for this is given at the beginning of the Math sections as $V = \frac{1}{3}\pi r^2 h$. There aren't explicit values for the radius and height given in the question, so ratios will be necessary to find the new value. The new radius is one-third the original, so the value will be written as $\frac{r}{3}$. The new height is triple the original, so it will be written as $3h$. Plug these new values in the formula for the volume of a cone to get $V = \frac{1}{3}\pi r^2 h = \frac{1}{3}\pi\left(\frac{r}{3}\right)^2(3h) = \frac{1}{3}\pi\left(\frac{1}{9}\right)r^2(3)h = \frac{1}{3}\pi r^2 h\left(\frac{1}{9}\right)(3) = \frac{1}{3}\pi r^2 h\left(\frac{1}{3}\right)$. The value of $\frac{1}{3}\pi r^2 h$ is the volume of the original cone, 12 cubic millimeters. Plug this value into the formula for the new cone to get $(12)\left(\frac{1}{3}\right) = 4$. The correct answer is (B).

13. **A** The question asks for the equation that will represent how much money Marcy will save each month by drinking 9 fewer cups of coffee. The question says that one coffee pod costs $7 and brews 4 cups of coffee. Set up a proportion of $\frac{\text{cups}}{\text{dollars}}$ to figure out how much 9 cups of coffee will cost her: $\frac{4}{7} = \frac{9}{d}$. To make this look like the answer choices, multiply both sides by d to get $\frac{4}{7}d = 9$. The correct answer is (A).

14. **A** The question asks how many additional servings of smoothies can be made for each additional banana. Try some numbers in the equation to see how the variables are related in order to solve

this question. Start with b = 6 bananas and solve for the number of servings of smoothie. The equation becomes s = 6 − 4 = 2. Now plug in b = 7 for the additional banana to get s = 7 − 4 = 3. The difference in number of servings of smoothie from 2 bananas to 3 bananas is 3 − 2 = 1 serving. The correct answer is (A).

15. **D** The question asks for the graph of $y = -g(x)$ given the equation of $g(x)$. Start by getting some idea of what the original graph of $g(x)$ will look like. Take advantage of the fact that the equation has been given and plug in x = 0 to find the y-intercept of the function. The equation becomes $2 - 3^0 = 2 - 1 = 1$. The y-intercept of $g(x)$ is 1, so multiply this value by −1 to find the y-intercept of $-g(x)$: (−1)(1) = −1. The only graph that has a y-intercept at −1 is (D). Therefore, the correct answer is (D).

16. $\dfrac{31}{2}$ or **15.5**

The question asks for the value of m in a system of equations. To get just one equation in terms of m, plug the value of n given in the second equation into the first equation to get $\dfrac{1}{3}(5m - 3m)$ = $\dfrac{31}{3}$. Multiply both sides of the equation by 3 to eliminate the fractions, and combine like terms to get $2m$ = 31. Divide both sides by 2 to get m = $\dfrac{31}{2}$. The correct answer is $\dfrac{31}{2}$.

17. **10** The question asks for the maximum number of months Asaf can have his gym membership. Use the information given in the question to set up an inequality to solve. Asaf must pay a rate of $50 per month for the membership, so this must be multiplied by a number of months, and the first piece of the inequality is $50m$. Next, Asaf must pay a one-time fee of $30, so this must be added to the first piece to get $50m + 30$. Finally, the total must not exceed $555, so the complete inequality is $50m + 30 \le 555$. Subtract 30 from both sides to get $50m \le 525$, and divide both sides by 50 to get $m \le 10.5$. The question asks for an answer as a whole number of months, so round down to 10. The correct answer is 10.

18. **117** The question asks for the value of c, an angle measure on the diagram. There are 180° in a line, so use this to find the angle to the left of the one that measures 97°: 180° − 97° = 83°. The sum of the internal angles of a triangle must equal 180°, so add 83° and 34° and subtract this from 180° to find the measure of the third angle, which is 180° − (83° + 34°) = 63°. The angle marked $c°$ is next to the one that is 63°, so they add up to 180, and 180° − 63° = 117°. The correct answer is 117.

19. $\dfrac{12}{5}$ or **2.4**

The question asks for the solution to the equation. To begin to simplify the equation, distribute the numbers across the terms on the left-hand side of the equation to get $9s - 18 + 3s + 6 = 7s$. Next, combine like terms on the left to get $12s - 12 = 7s$. Subtract $7s$ from both sides to get $5s - 12$ = 0, then add 12 to both sides to get $5s$ = 12. Divide both sides by 5 to get s = $\dfrac{12}{5}$. This fits in the grid-in box, so enter it in. The correct answer can also be entered as 2.4.

20. **7** The question asks for the value of x, a variable in two equivalent expressions. The word *equivalent* means that these two expressions need to be equal, so write an equation to show this:

$\dfrac{4c + 1}{(2c - 3)^2} - \dfrac{2}{(2c - 3)} = \dfrac{x}{(2c - 3)^2}$. Multiply $\dfrac{2}{(2c - 3)}$ by $\dfrac{(2c - 3)}{(2c - 3)}$, so that the two expressions

on the left have a common denominator and can be combined. The left side of the equation be-

comes $\dfrac{4c + 1}{(2c - 3)^2} - \dfrac{4c - 6}{(2c - 3)^2}$ or $\dfrac{4c + 1 - 4c + 6}{(2c - 3)^2}$. Combine like terms in the numerator to get

$\dfrac{7}{(2c - 3)^2}$. The left side of the equation must equal the right, so $\dfrac{7}{(2c - 3)^2} = \dfrac{x}{(2c - 3)^2}$. Because

both sides have the same denominator, set the numerators equal to one another, so $x = 7$. The
correct answer is 7.

Section 4: Math (Calculator)

1. **D** The question asks for the number of cups of cream needed to make 24 servings of hot chocolate. Start by determining how many fluid ounces are needed for 24 servings of hot chocolate
by multiplying: $4.5 \times 24 = 108$ fluid ounces. Next, convert to cups by making a proportion:

$\dfrac{1 \text{ cup}}{8 \text{ fluid ounces}} = \dfrac{x \text{ cups}}{108 \text{ fluid ounces}}$. Cross-multiply to get $8x = 108$. Divide both sides by 8 to get

$x = 13.5$ cups of cream. The correct answer is (D).

2. **C** The question asks for the two consecutive years with the greatest change in percent. The percents
are shown on the vertical axis, so a large change in percent will result in a steep slope on the
graph. There are many small changes on the graph, but there is a steep one from 2006 to 2007.
The correct answer is (C).

3. **B** The question asks for the equation that defines function g based on the table of values. Try out
values of x from the table and eliminate choices that do not match the given value of $g(x)$. Start
with the first row. When $x = 2$, $g(2) = 11$. Choice (A) becomes $2(2) + 7 = 4 + 7$, which is 11. Keep
(A). Choice (B) becomes $3(2) + 5 = 6 + 5$, which is 11. Keep (B). Choice (C) becomes $4(2) + 3$
$= 8 + 3$, which is 11. Keep (C). Choice (D) becomes $5(2) + 1 = 10 + 1$, which is 11. Keep (D).
Since all the answers worked, try another pair of numbers from the table. When $x = 4$, $g(x) = 17$.
Choice (A) becomes $2(4) + 7 = 8 + 7$, which is 15. This doesn't match the target value of 17, so
eliminate (A). Choice (B) becomes $3(4) + 5 = 12 + 5$, which is 17. This matches the target value,
so keep (B). Choice (C) becomes $4(4) + 3 = 16 + 3$, which is 19. Eliminate (C). Choice (D) becomes $5(4) + 1 = 20 + 1$, which is 21. Eliminate (D). The correct answer is (B).

4. **D** The question asks for the number of magnets Annalee purchased. Rather than do complicated
algebra, try out the values in the answer choices to see if they fit the situation. Start with (B),
which indicates that Annalee purchased 4 magnets. Those 4 magnets would cost $\$3(4) = \$12$.
She bought 10 items, so if she bought 4 magnets, she bought 6 postcards. Those cost $\$1$ each,
so that adds $\$6$ to her total cost to get $\$12 + \$6 = \$18$. The question states that she paid $\$22$,
so this value is not enough. Annalee must have purchased more magnets to increase the total
cost. Eliminate (A) and (B). Try (C) and assume she bought 5 magnets. The magnets would cost
$\$3(5) = \$15$. She would also buy 5 postcards, adding $\$5$ to her total to get $\$20$. This is still not
enough, so eliminate (C). The correct answer is (D).

5.　**A**　The question asks for $x - y$, so look to isolate that expression. Clear the 7 by dividing both sides of the equation by 7 to get $\frac{7(x - y)}{7} = \frac{4}{7}$, so $x - y = \frac{4}{7}$. The correct answer is (A).

6.　**A**　The question asks for the difference in annual precipitation between Orlando and Saint Cloud. To find the average annual precipitation in Orlando, multiply the precipitation in Columbus by $\frac{13}{10}$ to get $\frac{13}{10}(1,000) = 1,300$ millimeters. To get the average annual precipitation in Saint Cloud, multiply the precipitation in Columbus by $\frac{7}{10}$ to get $\frac{7}{10}(1,000) = 700$ millimeters. The difference in precipitation in the two cities is $1,300 - 700 = 600$ millimeters. The correct answer is (A).

7.　**D**　The question asks for an equivalent form of an expression. Rather than doing complicated algebraic manipulation, work on one term at a time and look for opportunities to eliminate answers. Start with the first term of the squared expression: $(2.6a)^2 = 6.76a^2$. Next, subtract the a^2 term from the second expression to get $6.76a^2 - 7.3a^2 = -0.54a^2$. Eliminate (A) and (B) because they do not contain this term. Next, find another term in the expression. Both (C) and (D) have the term $-18.2a$, so find the terms without a: $(-3.5)^2 = 12.25$, and $12.25 - (-4.1) = 12.25 + 4.1 = 16.35$. This only appears in (D), so eliminate (C). The correct answer is (D).

8.　**C**　The question asks for an equation to model a situation. Translate one piece of information at a time and look for opportunities to eliminate answers. The AAUW plans to increase the number of student organizations by t per year for x years, so multiply t by x to get tx. Since (A) and (B) do not include tx, eliminate those answers. The number of student organizations is increasing, so the value tx must be added to the total number of student organizations. The equation needs to include addition, so eliminate (D). The correct answer is (C).

9.　**D**　The question asks for the equation that represents voltage in terms of resistance and current. According to the question, the resistance, R, of a conductor is found by dividing the voltage, V, by the current, I. Therefore, $R = \frac{V}{I}$. To solve this equation in terms of V, it is necessary to get V by itself. Multiply both sides by I to get $IR = V$. Flip the equation to get $V = IR$. The correct answer is (D).

10.　**A**　The question asks for the difference in pitching distance in meters but gives measurements in feet. The pitching distance increased from 50 feet to 60.5 feet, for an increase of $60.5 - 50 = 10.5$ feet. To convert this to meters, set up a proportion: $\frac{1 \text{ meter}}{3 \text{ feet}} = \frac{x \text{ meters}}{10.5 \text{ feet}}$. Cross-multiply to get $3x = 10.5$. Divide both sides by 3 to get $x = 3.5$ meters. The correct answer is (A).

11.　**B**　The question asks for the probability that a social worker in a survey has a pediatric focus and a doctoral degree. Probability is defined as $\frac{\text{want}}{\text{total}}$. Since the social worker is selected at random, the total number of possible outcomes is the total number of social workers: 529. The question asks for the probability that the social worker is a pediatric social worker whose highest level of education is a doctoral degree, so find this number on the chart, which is 221. Put this into the probability definition to get $\frac{221}{529} \approx 0.418$. The correct answer is (B).

12. **C**   The question asks for the equation of a line that is perpendicular to the given line. Perpendicular lines have slopes that are negative reciprocals. The given equation and the answer choices are all in standard form: $Ax + By = C$. In standard form, the slope of the line is $-\dfrac{A}{B}$. Therefore, the slope of the given line is $-\dfrac{(-3)}{4}$ or $\dfrac{3}{4}$. The perpendicular slope will be $-\dfrac{4}{3}$. Determine the slope of each answer choice to see which one matches this value. For (A), the slope is $-\dfrac{3}{6} = -\dfrac{1}{2}$. This is not equal to the target slope, so eliminate (A). For (B), the slope is $-\dfrac{3}{8}$. Eliminate (B). For (C), the slope is $-\dfrac{4}{3}$, which matches the target slope. The correct answer is (C).

13. **A**   The question asks for the value of y in a system of equations, so look for the most direct way to find that. The goal is to make the x-terms disappear. In the two equations, the coefficients of the x-terms have the same value with opposite signs. Therefore, if the two equations were added together, the x-terms would cancel each other out. Stack and add the equations:

$$
\begin{array}{r}
2 = -\dfrac{1}{3}x + y \\
+\,6 = \dfrac{1}{3}x \\
\hline
8 = \phantom{-\dfrac{1}{3}x +\;} y
\end{array}
$$

Therefore, the correct answer is (A).

14. **D**   The question asks for a statement that *must be true* based on the results of a poll. With statistics, the only things that can definitively be stated are about the survey or poll itself. Statement (I) says that another poll would have the exact same results, but there is no way to know this, so eliminate (A) and (B). Next, statement (II) says that another survey conducted with people in a different town would have the same results, but again, there is no way to know this. Eliminate (C). Thus, the correct answer is (D).

15. **A**   The question asks for the point that satisfies a system of inequalities. Rather than doing complicated algebraic manipulation or trying to sketch the graphs, use the points in the answers to see if they fit the inequalities. Start with (B) and plug in $x = 2$ and $y = -5$ in the first inequality to get $4(2) - 1 \le -5$ or $8 - 1 \le -5$. This is not true, so eliminate (B). The number on the left side of the inequality was too big, so the value of x needs to be smaller. Choice (A) has a negative value for x, so try it next. The first inequality becomes $4(-3) - 1 \le -1$ or $-12 - 1 \le -1$. This is true, so check the second inequality, which becomes $2 > -3 + (-1)$ or $2 > -4$. This is also true. Thus, the correct answer is (A).

16. **B**   The question asks for the difference in time it takes for the two people to burn an additional 20 calories each. The 1 hour that the people have already exercised is irrelevant; only the time it takes to burn an additional 20 calories matters. Use the formula *calories* = (*time in minutes*) × (*burn rate*) to calculate the time for each person. For the person who is speed walking, the formula becomes $20 = $ (*time in minutes*) × (5.0). Divide both sides of the formula by 5 to get *time in minutes* = 4. For the person who is doing yoga, the formula becomes $20 = $ (*time in minutes*) × (1.5). Divide both sides by 1.5 to get *time in minutes* $= 13\dfrac{1}{3}$. The difference between these times is $13\dfrac{1}{3} - 4 = 9\dfrac{1}{3}$. This is closest to 9.3. Therefore, the correct answer is (B).

17. **C** The question asks for the number of calories burned by a 100-pound person shooting baskets for 30 minutes. According to the information above the question, the number of calories burned is equal to the time in minutes multiplied by the burn rate for that exercise. The time is given as 30 minutes, and the burn rate for shooting baskets is 3.0. Therefore, *calories burned* = (30)(3.0) = 90 calories. The correct answer is (C).

18. **B** The question asks for the exercise with a burn rate closest to that of the exercise shown on the graph. There are a lot of data points on the graph, but just focus on one. Pick any point that looks like it intersects a known value on each axis, such as 15 minutes and 30 calories. To calculate the burn rate in calories per minute, divide the calories by the time to get $\dfrac{30 \text{ calories}}{15 \text{ minutes}} = 2.0$. This value is closest to the burn rate of light aerobics. Therefore, the correct answer is (B).

19. **C** The question asks for the variable that could be shown on the vertical axis of the graph. With no label on that axis, the best approach is to read each answer and eliminate those that do not make sense. Choice (A) considers the total distance traveled by the spot of paint, which should always be increasing. The graph of $f(t)$ oscillates, so this does not match. Eliminate (A). Choice (B) describes the distance the spot of paint is from the center of the fan, but the spot is traveling in a circular path with the center of the fan as its center. Therefore, the distance between the spot and the center will not change. Eliminate (B). If (C) is true, it indicates that in this scenario the spot would start at a certain distance above the table, go a maximum distance from the table, decrease to a minimum distance close to the table, and return toward the starting point. This matches the graph on the right, so keep (C), but check out (D) just in case. Choice (D) mentions the speed of the fan blades, but the question states that the fan is at a constant low setting, meaning the speed does not change. Eliminate (D). Therefore, the correct answer is (C).

20. **D** The question asks what must be true about h given an equation. To get a sense of the possible values for h, use the information given about f and g to try out values for those. Make $f = 2$ and $g = -2$. The equation becomes $h = \dfrac{2 - (-2)}{-2} = \dfrac{2 + 2}{-2} = \dfrac{4}{-2} = -2$. Of the given ranges or values for h, only the range in (D) fits this value of $h = -2$. The correct answer is (D).

21. **C** The question asks for the length of a line segment on a figure with two 45° angles and two 90° angles. At the beginning of the Math sections, the relationship between the sides of a 45°:45°:90° triangle is listed. Use this information whenever a triangle question contains these values for angles. The hypotenuse is opposite the 90° angle, and its length is the length of one of the legs multiplied by $\sqrt{2}$. The leg given is 4, so *MO* is $4\sqrt{2}$. Sides *MO* and *LM* are legs of a second 45°-45°-90° triangle, so they are congruent. Therefore, the length of *LM* is also $4\sqrt{2}$. The correct answer is (C).

22. **C** The question asks for the approximate population of Maple Mall at the beginning of 2010. Rather than create an algebraic equation with multiple percents, try out the answer choices. Start with (B) and calculate the increase of 30 percent: $81,300 + \dfrac{30}{100}(81,300) = 81,300 + 24,390 = 105,690$. Next, calculate the increase of 20 percent: $105,690 + \dfrac{20}{100}(105,690) = 105,690 + 21,138 = 126,828$. Choice (B) is too big, since the chart indicates a current population of 122,000 for Maple Mall. Eliminate (B) and also (A), which is even bigger. Since the population wasn't too far off with (B), try (C) next using the same steps. If the 2011 population was 78,200, the 30% increase would bring it to 101,660.

The 20% increase would bring the population to 121,992. This is very close to 122,000. Therefore, the correct answer is (C).

23. **C** The question asks for the equation that best approximates the relationship between population and area. Select a set of data from the table to test out the equations in the answer choices. Choose the data for Fir Fen because it has the smallest population, making it easier to work with. Use Bite-Sized Pieces to translate the question. The population n is actually in terms of <u>thousands</u> of people, so convert the population of Fir Fen to thousands, which would be 2. Plug 2 into the answer choices to see which one results in the target answer of 22. Choice (A) becomes $A(2) = 2(2) + 18 = 4 + 18 = 22$. This matches the target value of 22, so keep (A), but check the remaining answers just in case. Choice (B) becomes $A(2) = 2.5(2) - 300 = 5 - 300 = -295$. Eliminate (B). Choice (C) becomes $A(2) = 3.5(2) + 15 = 7 + 15 = 22$. Keep (C). Choice (D) becomes $A(2) = 4.5(2) - 107 = 9 - 107 = -98$. Eliminate (D). Since both (A) and (C) worked, try another point, such as Cedar Vale's $n = 12$ and $A(12) = 57$. Choice (A) becomes $A(12) = 2(12) + 18 = 24 + 18 = 42$. This doesn't match the target value of 57, so eliminate (A). The correct answer is (C).

24. **B** The question asks for the best estimate of the number of small business employees with at least $1,000 in savings. There is a lot of information in the question, so read carefully. It is stated that 62.9 percent of the employees at the small business have less than $1,000 in savings. To find the percentage of employees who have *at least* that much in savings, subtract 62.9% from the total to get 100% − 62.9% = 37.1%. Now, calculate the total number of employees working at small businesses in the county by multiplying the number of small businesses by the average number of employees at each small business to get $270 \times 132 = 35,640$ total small business employees. Now take 37.1% of this total: $\frac{37.1}{100}(35,640) \approx 13,222$. This is closest to (B). The correct answer is (B).

25. **A** The question asks for an expression for the surface area of a cube based on the formula for its volume. The reference box at the start of the Math sections gives the formula for the volume of a rectangular solid as $V = lwh$, but on a cube, all the dimensions are the same, so the volume of a cube is $V = s^3$. There are variables in the question and answers, so plug in a value for c to find the volume of the cube. If $c = 4$, the volume is $V = \frac{1}{8}(4^3) = \frac{1}{8}(64) = 8$. Set this equal to the volume formula for a cube to solve for s. If $V = s^3 = 8$, take the cube root of both sides to get $s = 2$. Now find the surface area of the cube, which is the area of one face times the number of faces. For this cube, that value is $SA = (2 \times 2) \times 6 = 24$. This is the target value. Plug $c = 4$ into the answer choices to see which one equals 24. Choice (A) becomes $6\left(\frac{4}{2}\right)^2 = 6(2)^2 = 24$. This matches the target, so keep (A), but check the remaining answers just in case. Choice (B) becomes $6\left(\frac{4^2}{2}\right) = 6\left(\frac{16}{2}\right) = 6(8) = 48$. Eliminate (B). Choice (C) becomes $6(4^2) = 6(16) = 96$. Eliminate (C). Choice (D) will be even larger, so eliminate (D). The correct answer is (A).

26. **B** The question asks for the lowest weight of the people in the elevator. Use the given information about the average weights before and after that person gets off the elevator to find the total weight of all people. For averages, use the formula $T = AN$, in which T is the total, A is the average, and N is the number of things. The initial total weight was $T = (160.5)(6) = 963$ pounds. After the lightest person got off, the total weight was $T = (168)(5) = 840$. The change in total is $963 - 840 = 123$. Because the only difference between the two groups is the weight of the person that gets off the elevator, the weight of that person must have been 123 pounds. Thus, the correct answer is (B).

27. **B** The question asks for the inequality that best represents possible values of s, the number of students in an experiment that chose the interviewee associated with their college. This is a long question with a lot of information, so deal with one piece at a time and look for opportunities to eliminate answers. The first piece of information is that s students chose the interviewee associated with their college, so the correct answer choice needs to include s. All the choices have s, so nothing can be eliminated. The question also states that 58 more people chose the interviewee associated with their college, so that translates to $s + 58$. This eliminates all choices except for (B). The correct answer is (B).

28. **D** The question asks for an equivalent form of the given equation. The word *equivalent* means "the same," so the expressions in the answer choices need to equal $y = c - x^2$ when expanded. Start with (A) and use FOIL (First, Outer, Inner, Last) to get $y = (c - x)(c - x) = c^2 - cx - cx + x^2$. This does not match the given expression, so eliminate (A). Choice (B) becomes $y = (c - x)(c + x) = c^2 + cx - cx - x^2$. Eliminate (B). Choice (C) becomes $y = \left(\dfrac{c}{2} - x\right)\left(\dfrac{c}{2} + x\right) = \dfrac{c^2}{4} + \dfrac{cx}{2} - \dfrac{cx}{2} - x^2$. Eliminate (C). Therefore, the correct answer is (D).

29. **B** This question asks for the value of $s(15)$. There is a graph of $r(x)$, but no equation is given for $s(x)$. The slope of s is described in terms of the slope of r, so start there. The graph shows line r going through points $(1, 0)$ and $(0, -2)$. To calculate the slope of $s(x)$, use slope $= \dfrac{y_2 - y_1}{x_2 - x_1}$. Therefore, the slope is $\dfrac{0 - (-2)}{1 - 0} = \dfrac{2}{1} = 2$. The slope of $s(x)$ is $\dfrac{1}{6}$ times the slope of $r(x)$, or $\dfrac{1}{6}(2) = \dfrac{2}{6} = \dfrac{1}{3}$. Now, find the equation for $s(x)$. The slope-intercept form is $y = mx + b$, where m is the slope and b is the y-intercept. The y-intercept is the y-value when $x = 0$. The question states that s passes through the point $(0, 2)$, so the y-intercept is 2. Therefore, $s(x) = \dfrac{1}{3}x + 2$. To find the value of $s(15)$, plug in 15 for x. The equation becomes $s(15) = \dfrac{1}{3}(15) + 2 = 5 + 2 = 7$. Thus, the correct answer is (B).

30. **C** The question asks for the coordinates of the the center of a circle. The standard equation of a circle is $(x - h)^2 + (y - k)^2 = r^2$, where the center is point (h, k). In order to find the center, convert this equation to standard form by completing the square. First, group the x- and y-terms together to get $(x^2 + 16x) + (y^2 - 12y) = -19$. Next, divide the coefficient on the x-term, 16, by two and square it to get 64. Add this number to the x-terms and to the other side of the equation to get $(x^2 + 16x + 64) + (y^2 - 12y) = -19 + 64$. Divide the coefficient on the y-term, -12, by two and square it to get 36. Now, add this number to the y-terms and to the other side of the equation to get $(x^2 + 16x + 64) + (y^2 - 12y + 36) = -19 + 64 + 36$. Factor the x and y expressions to get $(x + 8)^2 + (y - 6)^2 = -19 + 64 + 36$. According to the standard form, $h = -8$ and $k = 6$, so the center must be $(-8, 6)$. The correct answer is (C).

31. $\dfrac{42}{9}, \dfrac{14}{3}$, **4.66**, or **4.67**

The question asks for the length of a reproduction of a flag where both dimensions of the flag are multiplied by $\dfrac{1}{9}$. Use this information, and multiply the original length by the fraction to get $\dfrac{1}{9}(42) = \dfrac{42}{9}$. This fits in the grid-in box, so the correct answer is $\dfrac{42}{9}$.

32. **63** The question asks for the measure of $\angle CBF$ in the figure. The question states that $\angle CBD = \angle EBF$, so $2a - 6 = a + 9$. Add 6 to both sides to get $2a = a + 15$. Subtract a from both sides to get $a = 15$. Use

this value for *a* to find the value of either ∠*CBD* or ∠*EBF*, since they are equal. It is easier to find ∠*EBF*, which is 15 + 9 = 24. Add the three angles together to get the measure of ∠*CBF*, which is 24 + 15 + 24 = 63. The correct answer is 63.

33. **2,560** The question asks how much area, in acres, is equal to 4 square miles. The measurements are proportional, so use the information given in the question to set up a proportion: $\dfrac{7 \text{ square miles}}{4,480 \text{ acres}} = \dfrac{4 \text{ square miles}}{x \text{ acres}}$. Cross-multiply to get $7x = 17,920$, then divide both sides by 7 to get $x = 2,560$ acres. The correct answer is 2,560.

34. **60** The question asks for the value of *a* in the figure. In the given triangle, ∠*LMN* is inscribed in the circle, with points *L* and *N* as its endpoints. Points *L* and *N* are also the endpoints of a diameter of the circle, since line $\overline{LN}$ passes through center *O*. When this happens, the inscribed angle has a measure of 90°, so ∠*LMN* = 90°. There are 180° in a triangle, so set up an equation to solve for *a*: $\dfrac{1}{2}a + a + 90 = 180$. Combine like terms to get $\dfrac{3}{2}a + 90 = 180$, then subtract 90 from both sides to get $\dfrac{3}{2}a = 90$. Multiply both sides by $\dfrac{2}{3}$ to get $a = 60$. The correct answer is 60.

35. **5** The question asks for the value of *a* in the function *h*. When dealing with functions, *x*-values are the inputs, and *y*-values are the outputs of the function. Plug in 4 for *x* and 3 for *h*(*x*) to get $3 = \dfrac{1}{2}(4^2) - a$ or $3 = 8 - a$. Add *a* to both sides to get $3 + a = 8$. Subtract 3 from both sides to get $a = 8 - 3 = 5$. Therefore, the correct answer is 5.

36. **8** The question asks for the height of a mural. There is no figure provided, so draw a rectangle and label the sides in terms of the height. The height is 4 meters shorter than the width, so label the height *h* and label the width *h* + 4. Write any of the formulas that are mentioned in the question, so *area = height × width*. The area is given as 96 square meters, so the formula becomes 96 = *h*(*h* + 4). Expand the right side of the equation to get $96 = h^2 + 4h$, then subtract 96 from both sides to get $0 = h^2 + 4h - 96$. Now, factor the right side of the equation into 0 = (*h* − 8)(*h* + 12). Set each factor equal to 0 and solve to get *h* = 8 and *h* = −12. Since the value for height must be positive, the correct answer is 8.

37. **11** The question asks for the difference in time it took Ms. McQueen to complete a sprint triathlon using a hybrid bike and a triathlon bike. Because only one portion of the sprint triathlon has a different time to complete, it is only necessary to calculate the time it takes Ms. McQueen to complete the biking stage. If she uses her triathlon bike, she can complete the distance of the biking stage, 12.4 miles, at her average speed in miles per hour, which is 20. When dealing with rates, use the formula *D* = *RT*, in which *D* is distance, *R* is rate, and *T* is time. The formula becomes 12.4 = (20)(*T*), then divide both sides by 20 to get *T* = 0.62 hour. Multiply this by 60 to get a time of about 37.2 minutes. If Ms. McQueen uses her hybrid bike, the biking stage will take 30% more time, so multiply 37.2 × 0.3 to get an additional time of about 11.2 minutes. Since the question says to round the answer to the nearest minute, the correct answer is 11.

38. **12.6** The question asks for Ms. McQueen's average speed in miles per hour over the course of the sprint triathlon. To calculate this, start by finding the total number of miles she traveled, which is 0.25 + 12.4 + 3.1 = 15.75 miles. To find the average speed in miles per hour, first convert 75 minutes to hours by dividing by 60 to get a time of 1.25 hours. When dealing with rates, use the formula *D* = *RT*, in which *D* is distance, *R* is rate, and *T* is time. The formula becomes 15.75 = *R*(1.25), then divide both sides by 1.25 to get *R* = 12.6 miles per hour. The correct answer is 12.6.

Chapter 21
Practice Test 10

Reading Test

65 MINUTES, 52 QUESTIONS

Turn to Section 1 of your answer sheet to answer the questions in this section.

DIRECTIONS

Each passage or pair of passages below is followed by a number of questions. After reading each passage or pair, choose the best answer to each question based on what is stated or implied in the passage or passages and in any accompanying graphics (such as a table or graph).

Questions 1–10 are based on the following passage.

This passage is excerpted from Gloria Steinem, *My Life on the Road.* ©2015 by Random House. The narrator, a writer, recalls her childhood in the United States of America.

There were only a few months each year when my father seemed content with a house-dwelling life. Every summer, we stayed in the small house he had built across the road from a lake in rural Michigan, where he ran a dance pavilion on a pier over the water. Though there was no ocean within hundreds of miles, he had named it Ocean Beach Pier, and given it the grandiose slogan "Dancing Over the Water and Under the Stars."

On weeknights, people came from nearby farms and summer cottages to dance to a jukebox. My father dreamed up such attractions as a living chess game, inspired by his own love of chess, with costumed teenagers moving across the squares of the dance floor. On weekends, he booked the big dance bands of the 1930s and 1940s into this remote spot. People might come from as far away as Toledo or Detroit to dance to this live music on warm moonlit nights. Of course, paying the likes of Guy Lombardo or Duke Ellington or the Andrews Sisters meant that one rainy weekend could wipe out a whole summer's profits, so there was always a sense of gambling. I think my father loved that, too.

But as soon as Labor Day had ended this precarious livelihood, my father moved his office into his car. In the first warm weeks of autumn, we drove to nearby

country auctions, where he searched for antiques amid the household goods and farm tools. After my mother, with her better eye for antiques and her reference books, appraised them for sale, we got into the car again to sell them to roadside antique dealers anywhere within a day's journey. I say "we" because from the age of four or so, I came into my own as the wrapper and unwrapper of china and other small items that we cushioned in newspaper and carried in cardboard boxes over country roads. Each of us had a role in the family economic unit, including my sister, nine years older than I, who in the summer sold popcorn from a professional stand my father bought her.

But once the first frost turned the lake to crystal and the air above it to steam, my father began collecting road maps from gas stations, testing the trailer hitch on our car, and talking about such faraway pleasures as thin sugary pralines from Georgia, all-you-can-drink orange juice from roadside stands in Florida, or slabs of salmon fresh from a California smokehouse.

Then one day, as if struck by a sudden whim rather than a lifelong wanderlust, he announced that it was time to put the family dog and other essentials into the house trailer that was always parked in our yard, and begin our long trek to Florida or California.

Sometimes this leave-taking happened so quickly that we packed more frying pans than plates, or left a kitchen full of dirty dishes and half-eaten food to greet us like Pompeii on our return. My father's decision

CONTINUE

always seemed to come as a surprise, even though
his fear of the siren song of home was so great that
he refused to put heating or hot water into our small
60 house. If the air of early autumn grew too chilly for us
to bathe in the lake, we heated water on a potbellied
stove and took turns bathing in a big washtub next to
the fireplace. Since this required the chopping of wood,
an insult to my father's sybaritic soul, he had invented
65 a wood-burning system all his own: he stuck one end
of a long log into the fire and let the other protrude
into the living room, then kicked it into the fireplace
until the whole thing turned to ash. Even a pile of
cut firewood in the yard must have seemed to him a
70 dangerous invitation to stay in one place.

After he turned his face to the wind, my father did
not like to hesitate. Only once do I remember him
turning back, and even then my mother had to argue
strenuously that the iron might be burning its way
75 through the ironing board. He would buy us a new
radio, new shoes, almost anything rather than retrace
the road already traveled.

Over the course of the passage, the main focus shifts
from

A) a description of the narrator's father to a portrayal
of a significant place the family often visited.

B) a depiction of the family's settled life to a
description of the family's life on the road.

C) an allegorical display of domesticity to an example
of its rejection by the narrator's father.

D) an anecdote about the poverty of the narrator's
childhood to a speculation concerning the causes
of that poverty.

The main purpose of the second paragraph (lines
10–23) ("On weeknights . . . too") is to

A) analyze the source of the father's compulsive
desire to travel.

B) introduce the figures who play a role in the
narrator's remembrances.

C) illustrate the father's delusions of grandeur that
harmed the family's financial well-being.

D) describe the father's unique approach to living life
that is expanded upon later in the passage.

The word "precarious" is used in line 24 to

A) emphasize the danger inherent to dancing over
the water.

B) caution against burning firewood in an
unapproved manner.

C) underscore the joy that this dancehall brought to
so many.

D) highlight the uncertainty regarding the summer
profits.

The narrator indicates that she participated in the
family business

A) in a way that matched her age and abilities.

B) much less than her older siblings.

C) despite not being paid for her work.

D) on a volunteer basis until her teenage years.

CONTINUE

5

With which of the following statements about her father would the narrator most likely agree?

A) He objected to train travel as a mode of transportation.

B) He had no consideration for his family's wishes.

C) He feared the expense of installing a heater into the family home.

D) He seemed mostly discontent with a settled, domestic life.

6

Which choice provides the best evidence for the answer to the previous question?

A) Lines 1–2 ("There . . . life")

B) Lines 22–23 ("I think . . . too")

C) Lines 36–39 ("Each . . . her")

D) Lines 59–60 ("he refused . . . house")

7

As used in line 48, "struck" most nearly means

A) battered.

B) boycotted.

C) inspired.

D) disturbed.

8

It can reasonably be inferred from the passage that the main reason that the narrator's father started the cross-country trip is because

A) he was struck by a sudden desire to escape the monotony of the house.

B) his desire to travel stemmed from a basic personality trait.

C) the family had already depleted the resources at one site.

D) he was surprised by the sudden change in the weather.

9

Which choice provides the best evidence for the answer to the previous question?

A) Lines 25–28 ("In the . . . tools")

B) Lines 40–47 ("But once . . . smokehouse")

C) Lines 48–52 ("Then . . . California")

D) Lines 53–56 ("Sometimes . . . return")

10

Which statement best characterizes the mother's role in the family?

A) She resented the father's impulsive nature.

B) She shared the father's wanderlust equally.

C) She sometimes played a more practical role than the father did.

D) She rescued the family's possessions from the flames.

CONTINUE

Questions 11–21 are based on the following passage and supplementary material.

This passage is adapted from "Stanford researchers uncover patterns in how scientists lie about their data," by Bjorn Carey, originally published in November 2015 by Stanford University.

Even the best poker players have "tells" that give away when they're bluffing with a weak hand. Scientists who commit fraud have similar, but even more subtle,
Line tells, and a pair of Stanford researchers have cracked
5 the writing patterns of scientists who attempt to pass along falsified data. The work, published in the *Journal of Language and Social Psychology*, could eventually help scientists identify falsified research before it is published.

10 There is a fair amount of research dedicated to understanding the ways liars lie. Studies have shown that liars generally tend to express more negative emotion terms and use fewer first-person pronouns. Fraudulent financial reports typically display higher
15 levels of linguistic obfuscation—phrasing that is meant to distract from or conceal the fake data—than accurate reports.

To see if similar patterns exist in scientific academia, Jeff Hancock, a professor of communication
20 at Stanford, and graduate student David Markowitz searched the archives of PubMed, a database of life sciences journals, from 1973 to 2013 for retracted papers. They identified 253, primarily from biomedical journals, that were retracted for documented fraud and
25 compared the writing in these to unretracted papers from the same journals and publication years, and covering the same topics.

They then rated the level of fraud of each paper using a customized "obfuscation index," which
30 rated the degree to which the authors attempted to mask their false results. This was achieved through a summary score of causal terms, abstract language, jargon, positive emotion terms and a standardized ease of reading score.

35 "We believe the underlying idea behind obfuscation is to muddle the truth," said Markowitz, the lead author on the paper. "Scientists faking data know that they are committing a misconduct and do not want to get caught. Therefore, one strategy to evade this may be
40 to obscure parts of the paper. We suggest that language can be one of many variables to differentiate between

fraudulent and genuine science."

The results showed that fraudulent retracted papers scored significantly higher on the obfuscation index
45 than papers retracted for other reasons. For example, fraudulent papers contained approximately 1.5 percent more jargon than unretracted papers. "Fraudulent papers had about 60 more jargon-like words per paper compared to unretracted papers," Markowitz said.
50 "This is a non-trivial amount."

The researchers say that scientists might commit data fraud for a variety of reasons. Previous research points to a "publish or perish" mentality that may motivate researchers to manipulate their findings or
55 fake studies altogether. But the change the researchers found in the writing, however, is directly related to the author's goals of covering up lies through the manipulation of language. For instance, a fraudulent author may use fewer positive emotion terms to curb
60 praise for the data, for fear of triggering inquiry.

In the future, a computerized system based on this work might be able to flag a submitted paper so that editors could give it a more critical review before publication, depending on the journal's threshold
65 for obfuscated language. But the authors warn that this approach isn't currently feasible given the false-positive rate. "Science fraud is of increasing concern in academia, and automatic tools for identifying fraud might be useful," Hancock said. "But much more
70 research is needed before considering this kind of approach. Obviously, there is a very high error rate that would need to be improved, but also science is based on trust, and introducing a 'fraud detection' tool into the publication process might undermine that trust."

Frequencies of Language Categories in Publications, Reviewed by Markowitz and Hancock

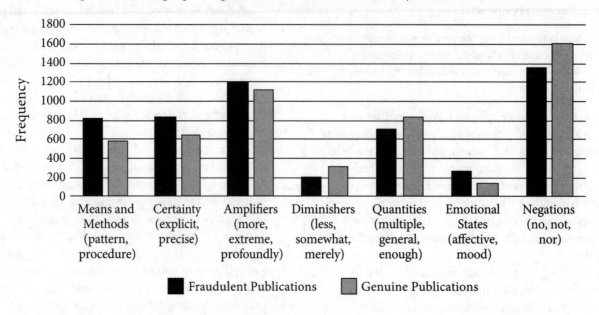

Data sourced from "Linguistic Traces of a Scientific Fraud: The Case of Diederik Stapel," © David M. Markowitz and Jeffrey T. Hancock, August 25, 2014. http://journals.plos.org/plosone/article/figure?id=10.1371/journal.pone.0105937.t001

The primary purpose of this passage is to

A) defend scientists who have incorporated fraudulent data into their reports in order to succeed in a competitive field.

B) contrast various methodologies for spotting false information in different industries and research fields.

C) describe an experiment designed to find the differences between fraudulent and genuine scientific data and caution against a possible solution.

D) reveal the secrets of those who successfully convince others of the veracity of false information.

The first paragraph serves mainly to

A) introduce a concept at the foundation of the research discussed in the passage.

B) propose additional applications for the results of the study in the passage.

C) introduce the development of general methods of fraud detection.

D) present an idea about scientific development that will be questioned later in the passage.

As used in line 10, "fair" most nearly means

A) ample.

B) lawful.

C) equal.

D) favorable.

CONTINUE

14

As used in line 40, "obscure" most nearly means

A) hide.

B) blind.

C) distort.

D) characterize.

15

The passage indicates that scientific papers with fraudulent data can potentially be spotted by looking for

A) references to research studies that did not happen.

B) writing that uses deliberately distracting and confusing words and phrases.

C) results that differ from those of other studies by more than 1.5 percent.

D) authors who have published more than 60 papers in academic journals.

16

Which choice provides the best evidence for the answer to the previous question?

A) Lines 31–34 ("This . . . score")

B) Lines 43–45 ("The results . . . reasons")

C) Lines 58–60 ("For instance . . . inquiry")

D) Lines 61–65 ("In the . . . language")

17

Which hypothetical situation would Hancock most likely agree could be a consequence of action without further research into science fraud?

A) A scientist runs his paper through a computer program to check for confusing language before publication.

B) A scientist includes fraudulent data in a paper that does not affect the conclusion of the experiment.

C) A scientist publishes a genuine paper in a journal that has been known to publish fraudulent papers.

D) A scientist is less likely to submit a paper to a journal that uses automatic tools to detect fraud.

18

Which choice provides the best evidence for the answer to the previous question?

A) Lines 39–40 ("Therefore . . . paper")

B) Lines 52–55 ("Previous . . . altogether")

C) Lines 65–67 ("But the . . . rate")

D) Lines 71–74 ("Obviously . . . trust")

19

According to the graph, the greatest difference between the language used in fraudulent and genuine research occurred in which category?

A) Means and Methods

B) Amplifiers

C) Quantities

D) Emotional States

CONTINUE

Which of the following statements is supported by the graph?

A) Scientists who published fraudulent data were more likely to use quantities-related language in their papers than were scientists who published genuine data.

B) Scientists who published fraudulent data used means and methods-related language nearly as often as they used certainty-related language.

C) Scientists who used more negation-related language were more likely to have published fraudulent data than scientists who used less negations-related language.

D) Scientists who used more amplifiers and diminishers were more likely to publish genuine data than scientists who used fewer amplifiers and diminishers.

Based on information in the graph and passage, which statement from the passage best supports the claim that jargon would be classified as "means and methods?"

A) Lines 2–6 ("Scientists . . . data")

B) Lines 11–13 ("Studies . . . pronouns")

C) Lines 47–49 ("Fraudulent . . . said")

D) Lines 69–71 ("But much . . . approach")

CONTINUE

Questions 22–31 are based on the following passage and supplementary material.

This passage is adapted from "The Story of YInMn Blue," originally published by Mas Subramanian, Joseph Tang, and Oregon State University.

YInMn Blue, or "MasBlue" as it is commonly referred to at Oregon State University ("OSU"), is a serendipitous discovery of a bright blue pigment
Line by scientists led by Mas Subramanian at OSU while
5 researching materials for electronics applications. The pigment contains the elements Yttrium, Indium, Manganese, and Oxygen.

In 2009, graduate student Andrew Smith was exploring the electronic properties of manganese oxide
10 by heating it to approximately 1,200°C (~2,000°F). Instead of a new, high-efficiency electronic material, what emerged from the furnace was a brilliant blue compound—a blue that Subramanian knew immediately was a research breakthrough. "If I hadn't
15 come from an industry research background—DuPont has a division that developed pigments and obviously they are used in paint and many other things—I would not have known this was highly unusual, a discovery with strong commercial potential," he says.
20 Blue pigments dating back to ancient times have been notoriously unstable—many fade easily and contain toxic materials. The fact that this pigment was synthesized at such high temperatures signaled to Subramanian that this new compound was extremely
25 stable, a property long sought in a blue pigment, he says. . . .

The chemical formula of YInMn Blue is $YIn_{1-x}Mn_xO_3$. These compositions adopt a crystal structure in which the chromophore responsible for
30 the intense blue color (Mn^{3+}) resides in the trigonal bipyramidal site. The intensity of the color can be systematically tuned by adjusting the In:Mn ratio. . . .

By measuring the spectral properties of this series, it was found that $YIn_{1-x}Mn_xO_3$ exhibits high absorbance
35 in the UV region and high reflectivity in the near-infrared region when compared to currently-used Cobalt Blue pigments. . . .

In May 2012, the Subramanian team received a patent with the U.S. Patent Office for the new pigment
40 (US82822728). Shepherd Color Co. subsequently began rigorous testing of the pigment. They concluded that the increased UV absorbance and stability in outdoor weathering and heat buildup tests

demonstrate that YInMn blue is superior to Cobalt
45 Blue ($CoAl_2O_4$). In addition, the high solar reflectance (compared to similarly colored pigments) indicates that this 'cool pigment' can find use in a variety of exterior applications by reducing surface temperatures, cooling costs, and energy consumption. As a result of
50 this testing, Shepherd Color Co. has licensed the patent for commercialization efforts.

Recently, several local artists (including OSU art students) have used this pigment in their own professional endeavors, utilizing it in watercolors and
55 drypoint.

The excitement of discovering a brilliant blue, heat reflecting, thermally stable, and UV absorbing pigment did not stop them from exploring beyond the blues. Since then, Subramanian and his team have expanded
60 their research and have made a range of new pigments to include almost every color, from bright oranges to shades of purple, turquoise and green.

They continue to search for a new stable, heat reflecting, and brilliant red, the most elusive color to
65 synthesize.

CONTINUE

Reflectance vs. Wavelength

Figure 1

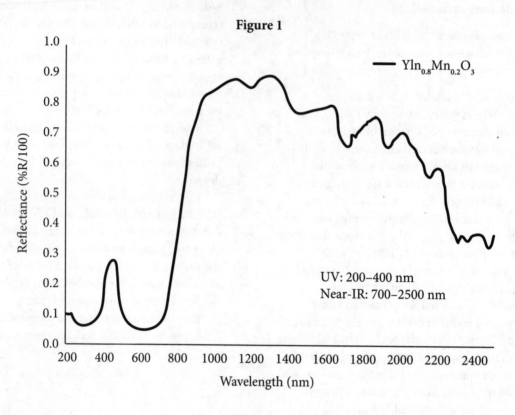

Figure 2

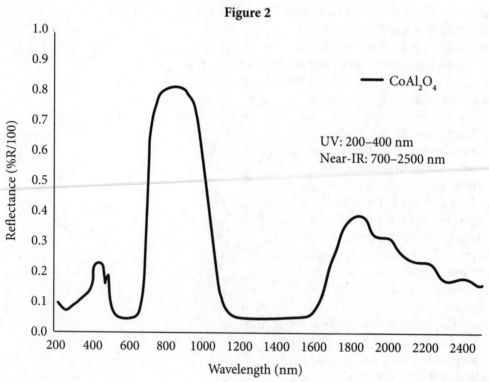

Images provided courtesy of Oregon State University.

CONTINUE ➤

22

One main idea of the passage is that

A) chemically engineered substances can be both beneficial and dangerous.

B) unexpected findings can have significant implications.

C) pigments can be described most effectively in terms of chemical composition.

D) increased UV absorbance is directly related to pigment stability.

23

Which choice best describes the overall structure of the passage?

A) A description of a discovery, a scientific explanation, and the practical applications of the discovery

B) A comparison of the properties of a synthetic compound and the presentation of a natural compound alternative

C) A historical account of several accidental discoveries and an unbiased critique of the resulting products

D) A listing of chemical compounds, a description of how those compounds work together, and a comparison of the benefits of each compound

24

As used in line 5, "applications" most nearly means

A) requests.

B) forms.

C) uses.

D) industries.

25

Which choice provides the best evidence for the claim that Smith did not intend for his experiment to produce the results that it did?

A) Lines 6–7 ("The pigment . . . Oxygen")

B) Lines 11–14 ("Instead . . . breakthrough")

C) Lines 49–51 ("As a . . . efforts")

D) Lines 63–65 ("They . . . synthesize")

26

As used in line 21, "unstable" most nearly means

A) impermanent.

B) threatening.

C) careless.

D) antiquated.

27

According to the passage, researchers have identified which of the following factors as most indicative of stable pigments?

A) Toxic materials

B) Oxygenated indium

C) Extreme temperatures

D) High pressure

CONTINUE

28

Based on the passage, which choice best describes the relationship between the new YInMn Blue pigment and the Cobalt Blue pigment currently used?

A) Cobalt Blue is superior for exterior conditions, while YInMn Blue is preferred for interior conditions.

B) YInMn Blue was specifically engineered to provide a color that can be chemically adjusted for intensity, while Cobalt Blue was not.

C) YInMn Blue pigment is as hard to synthesize as purple pigment is, while Cobalt Blue is simpler.

D) Cobalt Blue has a lower UV absorbency and infrared reflectivity than does YInMn Blue.

29

Which choice provides the best evidence for the answer to the previous question?

A) Lines 20–22 ("Blue . . . materials")

B) Lines 34–37 ("$YIn_{1-x}Mn_xO_3$ . . . pigments")

C) Lines 41–45 ("They . . . ($CoAl_2O_4$)")

D) Lines 56–58 ("The excitement . . . blues")

30

According to figure 2, at which of the following wavelengths does $CoAl_2O_4$ have a reflectance of 0.4%?

A) 2400 nm

B) 1800 nm

C) 1200 nm

D) 600 nm

31

Based on information in the passage and the graph, which of the following ranges of wavelengths most clearly illustrates the thermal advantages of YInMn Blue over Cobalt Blue?

A) 200–400

B) 400–600

C) 800–1000

D) 1200–1400

CONTINUE

Questions 32–41 are based on the following passages.

Passage 1 is adapted from President Grover Cleveland's *1895 Annual Message to the Congress of the United States*. Passage 2 is adapted from William Jennings Bryan's speech at the 1896 Democratic National Convention. The Coinage Act of 1873 ended the United States' federal policy of accepting both gold- and silver-backed currency, establishing a gold monetary standard. This decision was a primary point of contention in the 1896 presidential race.

Passage 1

While I have endeavored to make a plain statement of the disordered condition of our currency and the present dangers menacing our prosperity and to
Line suggest a way which leads to a safer financial system, I
5 have constantly had in mind the fact that many of my countrymen, whose sincerity I do not doubt, insist that the cure for the ills now threatening us may be found in the single and simple remedy of the free coinage of silver. They contend that our mints shall be at once
10 thrown open to the free, unlimited, and independent coinage of both gold and silver dollars of full legal-tender quality, regardless of the action of any other government and in full view of the fact that the ratio between the metals which they suggest calls for 100
15 cents' worth of gold in the gold dollar at the present standard and only 50 cents in intrinsic worth of silver in the silver dollar.

Were there infinitely stronger reasons than can be adduced for hoping that such action would secure for
20 us a bimetallic currency moving on lines of parity, an experiment so novel and hazardous as that proposed might well stagger those who believe that stability is an imperative condition of sound money.

No government, no human contrivance or act of
25 legislation, has ever been able to hold the two metals together in free coinage at a ratio appreciably different from that which is established in the markets of the world.

Those who believe that our independent free
30 coinage of silver at an artificial ratio with gold of 16 to 1 would restore the parity between the metals, and consequently between the coins, oppose an unsupported and improbable theory to the general belief and practice of other nations; and to the
35 teaching of the wisest statesmen and economists of the world, both in the past and present, and, what is far more conclusive, they run counter to our own actual experiences.

Twice in our earlier history our lawmakers,
40 in attempting to establish a bimetallic currency, undertook free coinage upon a ratio which accidentally varied from the actual relative values of the two metals not more than 3 per cent. In both cases, notwithstanding greater difficulties and cost
45 of transportation than now exist, the coins whose intrinsic worth was undervalued in the ratio gradually and surely disappeared from our circulation and went to other countries where their real value was better recognized.
50 Acts of Congress were impotent to create equality where natural causes decreed even a slight inequality.

Passage 2

If they tell us that the gold standard is the standard of civilization, we reply to them that this, the most enlightened of all nations of the earth, has never
55 declared for a gold standard, and both the parties this year are declaring against it. If the gold standard is the standard of civilization, why, my friends, should we not have it? So if they come to meet us on that, we can present the history of our nation. More than that, we
60 can tell them this, that they will search the pages of history in vain to find a single instance in which the common people of any land ever declared themselves in favor of a gold standard. They can find where the holders of fixed investments have.
65 Mr. Carlisle said in 1878 that this was a struggle between the idle holders of idle capital and the struggling masses who produce the wealth and pay the taxes of the country; and my friends, it is simply a question that we shall decide upon which side the
70 Democratic Party shall fight. Upon the side of the idle holders of idle capital, or upon the side of the struggling masses? That is the question that the party must answer first; and then it must be answered by each individual hereafter. The sympathies of the
75 Democratic Party, as described by the platform, are on the side of the struggling masses, who have ever been the foundation of the Democratic Party.

There are two ideas of government. There are those who believe that if you just legislate to make the
80 well-to-do prosperous, that their prosperity will leak through on those below. The Democratic idea has been that if you legislate to make the masses prosperous

CONTINUE →

their prosperity will find its way up and through every class that rests upon it.

85   You come to us and tell us that the great cities are in favor of the gold standard. I tell you that the great cities rest upon these broad and fertile prairies. Burn down your cities and leave our farms, and your cities will spring up again as if by magic. But destroy our farms
90 and the grass will grow in the streets of every city in the country.

32

As used in line 3, "present" most nearly means

A) prompt.

B) current.

C) instant.

D) gifted.

33

What does Passage 1 suggest about the proponents of implementing a bimetallic system of currency?

A) They doubt the use of gold to back a currency in any situation.

B) They have an honest belief in the potential of their proposed solution.

C) They would rather Congress become impotent than submit to bimetallic currency.

D) They resent the great cities that are pushing the gold standard on the people of the prairies.

34

Which choice provides the best evidence for the answer to the previous question?

A) Lines 4–9 ("I have . . . silver")

B) Lines 9–13 ("They . . . government")

C) Lines 29–34 ("Those . . . nations")

D) Lines 37–38 ("they . . . experiences")

35

In the final sentence of Passage 1, the main purpose of Cleveland's reference to "Acts of Congress" is to

A) emphasize a disparity between government forces and market forces.

B) summarize Congress's argument for implementing the gold standard.

C) propose a natural alternative to the complex problem facing the nation.

D) assert that only the passage of a law could solve a seemingly intractable debate.

36

As used in line 66, "idle" most nearly means

A) abandoned.

B) ambitious.

C) inactive.

D) cheap.

37

Based on Passage 2, Bryan would be most likely to agree with which claim about the controversy over the gold standard?

A) It would only be settled if gold were the preferred standard of civilization.

B) It has consistently lacked support from large segments of society.

C) It motivated further investigation of the silver standard worldwide.

D) It could have been avoided if Congress had not listened to the prosperous.

CONTINUE

38

Which choice provides the best evidence for the answer to the previous question?

A) Lines 56–58 ("If the . . . it")

B) Lines 59–63 ("More . . . standard")

C) Lines 74–77 ("The sympathies . . . Party")

D) Lines 78–81 ("There . . . below")

39

Both passages discuss the issue of the gold standard in relation to

A) Congress.

B) the Democratic Party.

C) economists.

D) other nations.

40

In the context of each passage as a whole, the historical references in line 39 of Passage 1 and line 65 of Passage 2 primarily function to help each speaker

A) establish that a debate has been ongoing.

B) cite established precedent to support a position.

C) challenge the gold standard status quo.

D) question whether progress has been made.

41

Which choice identifies a central tension between the two passages?

A) Cleveland advocates for new legislation to enact the gold standard, but Bryan questions the necessity of such a move without elite support.

B) Cleveland questions the validity of a proposed solution, but Bryan argues that the alternative is an even more unreasonable path forward.

C) Cleveland demands gold standard proponents reconsider their position, and Bryan defends the specifics of that position.

D) Cleveland presents studies in support of the gold standard, and Bryan asserts that the sources of the evidence are biased.

CONTINUE

Questions 42–52 are based on the following passage.

This passage is adapted from "Zombie ant fungi 'know' brains of their hosts," originally published on August 22, 2014 by Chuck Gill, Penn State College of Agricultural Sciences.

A parasitic fungus that reproduces by manipulating the behavior of ants emits a cocktail of behavior-controlling chemicals when encountering the brain
Line of its natural target host, but not when infecting other
5 ant species, a new study shows. The findings, which suggest that the fungus "knows" its preferred host, provide new insights into the molecular mechanisms underlying this phenomenon, according to researchers. "Fungi are well known for their ability to secrete
10 chemicals that affect their environment," noted lead author Charissa de Bekker, a Marie Curie Fellow in Penn State's College of Agricultural Sciences, and Ludwig Maximilian of the University of Munich. "So we wanted to know what chemicals are employed to
15 control so precisely the behavior of ants."

The research focused on a species from the genus *Ophiocordyceps*—known as "zombie ant fungi"—which control their ant hosts by inducing a biting behavior. Although these fungi infect many insects,
20 the species that infect ants have evolved a mechanism that induces hosts to die attached by their mandibles to plant material, providing a platform from which the fungus can grow and shoot spores to infect other ants. To study this mechanism, the researchers combined
25 field research with a citizen-scientist in South Carolina, infection experiments under laboratory conditions, and analysis using metabolomics, which is the study of the chemical processes associated with the molecular products of metabolism. The scientists used a newly
30 discovered fungal species from North America—initially called *Ophiocordyceps unilateralis sensu lato* while it awaits a new name—that normally controls an ant species in the genus *Camponotus*. To test whether a species of fungus that has evolved to control the
35 behavior of one ant species can infect and control others, they infected nontarget hosts from the same ant genus and another genus (*Formica*).

They found that this obligate killer can infect and kill nontarget ants, but it cannot manipulate their
40 behavior. "The brain of the target species was the key to understanding manipulation," de Bekker said. The researchers next removed ant brains, keeping the organs alive in special media. The fungus then

was grown in the presence of brains from different
45 ant species to determine what chemicals it produced for each brain. "This was 'brain-in-a-jar' science at its best," said co-author David Hughes, assistant professor of entomology and biology, Penn State. "It was necessary to reduce the complexity associated
50 with the whole, living ant, and just ask what chemicals the fungus produces when it encounters the ant brain. "You don't get to see a lot of behavior with fungi," he said. "You have to infer what they are doing by examining how they grow, where they grow and most
55 important, what chemicals they secrete."

"We could see in the data that the fungus behaved differently in the presence of the ant brain it had co-evolved with," said de Bekker, whose Penn State co-authors also included Andrew Patterson, assistant
60 professor of molecular toxicology, and Phil Smith, director of the Metabolomics Core Facility. The researchers found thousands of unique chemicals, most of them completely unknown. This, according to Hughes, is not surprising, since little previous work has
65 mined these fungi for the chemicals they produce. But what did stand out were two known neuromodulators, guanobutyric acid (GBA) and sphingosine. These both have been reported to be involved in neurological disorders and were enriched when the fungus was
70 grown in the presence of brains of its target species. "There is no single compound that is produced that results in the exquisite control of ant behavior we observe," de Bekker said. "Rather, it is a mixture of different chemicals that we assume act in synergy. "But
75 whatever the precise blend and tempo of chemical secretion," she said, "it is impressive that these fungi seem to 'know' when they are beside the brain of their regular host and behave accordingly."

Noted Hughes, "This is one of the most complex
80 examples of parasites controlling animal behavior because it is a microbe controlling an animal—the one without the brain controls the one with the brain. By employing metabolomics and controlled laboratory infections, we can now begin to understand how the
85 fungi pull off this impressive trick." The research also is notable, the scientists contend, because it is the first extensive study of zombie ants in North America.

CONTINUE

42

The primary purpose of the passage is to

A) correct a misconception about the interactions between fungi and host organisms.

B) present the findings of a study that is one of the first of its kind.

C) detail a research study that discovered a new genus of ant.

D) explain the difference between a symbiotic relationship and a parasitic relationship.

43

According to the passage, which statement best explains why the fungi have evolved to control the behavior of the ants?

A) When the infected ant bites a non-infected ant, the fungus is able to spread and grow.

B) When an infected ant dies while biting a plant, the fungus can reproduce more easily.

C) When the infected ant dies on the ground, its corpse is an ideal breeding ground for the fungus.

D) There is no evolutionary benefit for the fungus to control the ant's behavior.

44

In line 37, the mention of the *Formica* genus primarily serves to

A) introduce another ant genus newly discovered to be controlled by the fungus.

B) provide the scientific name of the ant genus most affected by the fungus.

C) present a new finding about a specific genus of fungus.

D) name a genus of ant that scientists tested to extend their research on the fungus.

45

The use of phrases such as "exquisite control" (line 72), "most complex examples" (lines 79–80), and "impressive trick" (line 85) in the passage communicate a tone that is

A) amused.

B) informative.

C) critical.

D) admiring.

46

Which choice describes a scenario in which the zombie ant fungi would NOT successfully reproduce?

A) Fungus spores infect both *Camponotus* and *Formica* ants.

B) An infected *Camponotus* ant attaches to a twig and dies.

C) A spore-releasing stalk grows from the head of a dead, infected *Camponotus* ant.

D) An infected *Formica* ant dies on a plant-free patch of soil.

47

As used in line 43, "media" most nearly means

A) communications.

B) material.

C) channels.

D) periodicals.

CONTINUE

48

Based on the passage, which part of the research process was the most effective for obtaining an unprecedented amount of information?

A) The researchers grew the fungus in the presence of isolated ant brains.

B) The researchers infected ants not normally targeted by the fungus.

C) The researchers removed the brains from the ants.

D) The researchers observed how the fungus behaved while in the ant brains.

49

Which choice provides the best evidence for the answer to the previous question?

A) Lines 29–33 ("The scientists . . . *Camponotus*")

B) Lines 43–46 ("The fungus . . . brain")

C) Lines 61–63 ("The researchers . . . unknown")

D) Lines 65–67 ("But what . . . sphingosine")

50

Based on the passage, a unique outcome of the chemicals produced by the fungus is

A) a reaction from the host organism that could only be reproduced in the lab.

B) a contagious infection that could not be controlled in the lab.

C) a parasitic relationship notably different from those usually found in nature.

D) a result that can be applied to neurological disorders in human patients.

51

Which choice provides the best evidence for the answer to the previous question?

A) Lines 16–19 ("The research . . . behavior")

B) Lines 38–40 ("They . . . behavior")

C) Lines 56–58 ("We could . . . de Bekker")

D) Lines 79–82 ("This . . . brain")

52

Based on the passage, in studying the zombie ants, the research team made the most extensive use of which type of evidence?

A) Observation of the interplay between the ant and the fungus in the natural world

B) Predictions based on research obtained from experiments with a different genus of ant

C) Chemical analysis of the brains of fungi

D) Data obtained from laboratory experiments designed to isolate particular factors

STOP
**If you finish before time is called, you may check your work on this section only.
Do not turn to any other section in the test.**

No Test Material On This Page

Writing and Language Test

35 MINUTES, 44 QUESTIONS

Turn to Section 2 of your answer sheet to answer the questions in this section.

Questions 1–11 are based on the following passage and supplementary material.

Fast Fashion Slows Down

In most U.S. cities, the presence of blue recycling bins alongside the ubiquitous black trash bins is no longer [1] an innovation. Most people are used to separating recyclable materials from their landfill-bound trash, even in public waste bins. In many cities, composting is even becoming a standard third component of waste separation, but one area that is just [2] kicking off is textile recycling.

[1]
A) NO CHANGE
B) a deviation.
C) a novelty.
D) a miracle.

[2]
Which choice best maintains the style and tone of the passage?
A) NO CHANGE
B) fixing to start
C) getting in gear
D) gaining traction

CONTINUE ➡

A few cities have begun to collect textiles as part of their curbside recycling programs, along with the more customary cardboard and glass, but such programs generally require specially designed multi-compartment recycling **3** trucks—(which most cities don't have). Many areas that don't have curbside textile recycling instead have designated drop-off bins where residents can recycle unwanted clothing and other household textiles, such as sheets and towels.

Textile recycling is in its infancy, but it has the potential to make a big impact. The average American discards 70 pounds of **4** clothing each year, only 15% of which is recycled. Of the most commonly recycled materials, only **5** rubber and leather are recycled at a higher rate than is clothing. Not only can cities save on trash pick-up and disposal costs by encouraging their residents to recycle unwanted textiles, **6** and re-using clothing can also save resources by reducing the amount of new clothing that needs to be manufactured.

7 For example, producing enough virgin cotton for one pair of jeans requires 1,800 gallons of water; buying a pair of jeans second-hand saves that water.

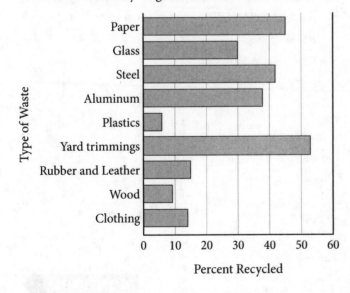

Estimated Recycling Rates in the United States

Type of Waste

Percent Recycled

3

A) NO CHANGE
B) trucks which
C) trucks—which
D) trucks (which

4

The writer wants to include information from the graph that is consistent with the description of textiles in the passage. Which choice most effectively accomplishes this goal?

A) NO CHANGE
B) paper each year, only 45%
C) rubber and leather each year, only 15%
D) wood each year, only 9%

5

The writer wants to support the paragraph's main idea with accurate, relevant information from the graph. Which choice most effectively accomplishes this goal?

A) NO CHANGE
B) plastic and wood are recycled at a lower
C) yard trimmings are recycled at a higher
D) glass is recycled at a higher

6

A) NO CHANGE
B) yet
C) but
D) for

7

A) NO CHANGE
B) Surprisingly,
C) However,
D) Moreover,

CONTINUE ►

So-called "fast fashion" chains that produce trendy, low-cost (and, according to critics, low-quality) clothing, are often singled out as one of the primary causes of the increase in clothing waste in the United States in recent decades. But at least one such chain, the Swedish retailer H&M, is also trying to [8] rain in, clothing waste by offering 15%-off coupons to consumers who bring unwanted clothing, of any brand, to their stores for recycling. Since the program began in 2013, H&M has collected over 44,000 tons of clothing to recycle. The company's goal is to eventually collect 25,000 tons of clothing for recycling each year.

[9] Hopefully other retailers will institute similar programs. The first step is reuse: any items still in useable condition are sold second-hand. Non-useable items are shredded for use as insulation, [10] they are repurposed as cleaning rags, or recycled to make fabric for new clothing.

The technology for recycling textile fibers into new fabrics [11] are currently limited, however. The ultimate goal of H&M and other environmentally conscious retailers is to establish a "closed loop" manufacturing system, in which 100% of the fibers they use to create their clothing can be recycled into new clothing. This may seem like a lofty goal, but it is worth pursuing.

8

A) NO CHANGE
B) rain in
C) rein in,
D) rein in

9

Which choice provides the most effective transition from the previous paragraph?

A) NO CHANGE
B) Recycling that quantity of clothing is done in several steps.
C) Low-quality fast fashion should make that goal easily attainable.
D) Offering a bigger discount might help H&M meet its goal.

10

A) NO CHANGE
B) repurposed as cleaning cloths,
C) cleaning cloths are repurposed,
D) alternatively they are repurposed as cleaning cloths,

11

A) NO CHANGE
B) is
C) were
D) have been

CONTINUE

Questions 12–22 are based on the following passage.

Celebrating Death

At dusk on the night of November 1, Lake Pátzcuaro in the southern Mexican state of Michoacán begins to glow as residents float across the lake in candlelit boats. The people are going to the island of Janitzio for an all-night vigil at the cemeteries where **12** its loved ones are buried. This vigil is the culmination of the Day of the Dead celebrations that begin with the construction of **13** ofrendas. Ofrendas are altars that honor the dead. The festivities begin in early October, when towns host markets **14** dedicated to the bright skeleton decorations and colorful flowers used to adorn the altars.

[1] The origins of the Mexican Day of the Dead tradition date back nearly 3,000 years to pre-Columbian times, when dead ancestors were celebrated in rituals that lasted for an entire month in the late summer of the Aztec calendar. [2] After Europeans brought Catholicism to North America, the Aztec rituals were combined with the Christian tradition of All Souls Day and moved to November 1–2. [3] During these two days, the spirits of the dead are believed to come back to the land of the living to visit their families. [4] The Aztec tradition was that the dead would be offended by mourning, **15** but it's sad when family members die. [5] The *ofrendas* that help to

12

A) NO CHANGE
B) it's
C) they're
D) their

13

Which choice most effectively combines the sentences at the underlined portion?
A) *ofrendas*, in Spanish; those are
B) *ofrendas*; the Spanish word *ofrendas* means
C) *ofrendas*,
D) *ofrendas*; moreover, *ofrendas* are

14

A) NO CHANGE
B) dedicated, to the bright skeleton decorations,
C) dedicated to the bright, skeleton, decorations,
D) dedicated to the bright skeleton decorations—

15

Which choice most effectively completes the explanation of the Aztec tradition?
A) NO CHANGE
B) so they are remembered in a spirit of celebration rather than sadness.
C) though it can be difficult to tell whether an invisible spirit is offended.
D) and the Aztec didn't want to disrespect the wishes of the dead.

CONTINUE

celebrate the dead often have items similar to **16** those found on church altars, such as candles and pictures. **17**

Many Day of the Dead altars are built in private homes, but they can also be found in cemeteries, at churches, in government buildings, and in public squares. Some public altars are meant to call attention to a specific cause. Others are built by local artists, **18** of which many are best known for their elaborate *ofrendas*.

For many families, preparing an *ofrenda* is similar to preparing for a visit from living relatives. The bright colors and fragrance of marigolds are said to lead spirits back to their families. Altars are loaded with food and drink **19** (which smell delicious) and sometimes include pillows and blankets (which provide a resting spot for the spirits). Some families put personal items that belonged to the deceased on the altars, and altars dedicated to children

16

A) NO CHANGE

B) church

C) churches and

D) the structures of church

17

To make this paragraph most logical, sentence 3 should be placed

A) where it is now.

B) before sentence 1.

C) before sentence 2.

D) before sentence 5.

18

A) NO CHANGE

B) many

C) many of whom

D) many of them

19

Which choice provides information that is most consistent in style and content with the information about why pillows and blankets are included on the altars?

A) NO CHANGE

B) (including *pan de muerto*)

C) (which are often homemade)

D) (which provide sustenance for the travelling spirits)

CONTINUE ➡

often include toys. [20] It's more work to provide food for living relatives than for dead ones.

Many of the same items that decorate altars are also part of the cemetery vigils on Janitzio. Graves are covered with candles and [21] marigolds, and families bring ample picnics to sustain both themselves and the spirits of the departed through the night. Living family members spend the night eating, drinking, singing, and telling stories. Rather than focusing on the finality of death, [22] the people's merriment celebrates life.

Which choice most effectively concludes the paragraph?

A) NO CHANGE

B) Regardless of what specifically is included on an altar, the dead are always welcomed home, just as they were when they were alive.

C) The toys for children can be new or old.

D) Some altars include religious items such as crucifixes and images of saints.

A) NO CHANGE

B) marigolds just as altars are,

C) marigolds like those that also decorate altars,

D) marigolds that attract spirits with their bright colors,

A) NO CHANGE

B) life is celebrated by the people through their merriment.

C) the merriment of the people celebrates life.

D) the people celebrate life through their merriment.

CONTINUE

Questions 23–33 are based on the following passage and supplementary material.

Bank Tellers: Machine v. Human

When automated teller machines (ATMs) were first installed in the 1970s, there were widespread predictions that the machines would replace human bank tellers. Such predictions did not immediately come true, however. **23** In fact, throughout the 1990s, as the number of ATMs increased most quickly, the number of human bank tellers also increased.

[1] While many simple bank transactions now happen at ATMs, people still rely on human tellers to cash **24** checks, transfer money between accounts; provide specific bill denominations, and dispense information about bank products and services. [2] Some of these duties, particularly the marketing aspect of advising customers about bank services, have changed with the advent of ATMs. [3] They also limit the amount of cash a customer can get in a single day, place restrictions on how soon funds from deposits are available, and generally don't offer much choice in currency denominations. [4] Before the rise of banking machines, tellers were primarily responsible for handling cash, but machines have proven to be faster and **25** more rock solid with cash than people are.

23

A) NO CHANGE
B) As a result,
C) For example,
D) Therefore,

24

A) NO CHANGE
B) checks; transfer money between accounts;
C) checks; transfer money between accounts,
D) checks, transfer money between accounts,

25

Which choice best fits with the tone of the rest of the passage?
A) NO CHANGE
B) more impeccable
C) more reliable
D) safer

CONTINUE

26 [5] On the other hand, ATMs are far more vulnerable to theft. **27**

26

At this point, the writer is considering adding the following graph.

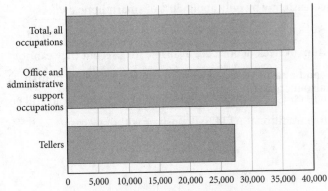

Annual Wage Comparison:
Tellers versus Other Occupations
Median annual wages, May 2016

Note: All Occupations includes all occupations in the U.S. Economy.
Source: U.S. Bureau of Labor Statistics, Occupational Employment Statistics

Should the writer make this addition here?

A) Yes, because it provides evidence that supports the idea that the number of bank tellers is rising.

B) Yes, because it effectively contradicts the idea that ATMs are faster at counting money than people are.

C) No, because it does not make a comparison between wages for tellers and those for loan officers.

D) No, because it gives information that distracts from the paragraph's focus on the duties performed by tellers.

27

To make this paragraph most logical, sentence 3 should be placed

A) where it is now.

B) after sentence 1.

C) after sentence 4.

D) after sentence 5.

CONTINUE

With the rise of tech-savvy customers who are increasingly 28 custom to using their smartphones in all aspects of life, mobile banking apps are the latest mechanized challenge to the need for human bank tellers. Apps are also beginning to improve upon some banking functions that had largely been taken over by ATMs. Mobile apps 29 are used consistently by only about 50% of smartphone owners. Apps also usually offer less waiting time before funds from a check deposit are available for use, but they cannot handle cash. That doesn't mean there's a need for human tellers, 30 though. Without a teller, customers can still go to a traditional ATM to deposit or withdraw cash.

28

A) NO CHANGE
B) accustomed for
C) accustomed to
D) custom at

29

Which choice provides the best supporting example for the main idea of the paragraph?

A) NO CHANGE
B) can quickly and easily perform the more complex balance inquiries and transfers that not all ATMs are capable of.
C) are not always designed well, though user ratings through an app store can help consumers decide which one is best.
D) are also highly susceptible to theft or fraud, particularly when they are used over public Wi-Fi networks.

30

Which choice most effectively combines the sentences at the underlined portion?

A) though:
B) though, because it's true that
C) though, without them
D) though; it's the case that

CONTINUE

Physical banks have begun to respond to the rising popularity of mobile banking by replacing their old-fashioned teller windows **31** with an automated kiosk that combine all the functions of both mobile banking apps and ATMs.

Such kiosks are not replacing ATMs, nor are they replacing humans altogether. What they are doing is changing, again, the job description of human bank employees. Todd Barnhart, head of branch distribution for PNC bank, stresses the continued need for humans in bank branches. Employees are now trained to answer questions about how to use mobile apps, **32** as well as trained to handle deposits and provide loan advice. "We're not building branches with teller lines but with places where customers and employees can have meaningful conversations," he said. So while the old-fashioned notion of a bank teller may be on the way **33** out, machines are not yet close to replacing human bank employees altogether.

31

A) NO CHANGE
B) to an automated kiosk
C) each for automated kiosks
D) with automated kiosks

32

A) NO CHANGE
B) as well as handle
C) also to answer questions about
D) and in addition to handle

33

A) NO CHANGE
B) out; machines
C) out. Machines
D) out, nevertheless machines

Questions 34–44 are based on the following passage.

Bacteria in Space

Ever since antibiotics began to be widely used in the 1940s, scientists have been engaged in an arms race against bacteria. Bacteria continue to evolve and develop resistance to antibiotics; 34 as a result, scientists must continually develop newer, stronger antibiotics to overcome the resistant bacteria. Since scientists generally want to 35 count the number of bacteria mutations, it may seem strange that they would intentionally make bacteria more aggressive, but researchers from Arizona State University (ASU) are doing just that by sending some strains of bacteria to the International Space Station to be studied.

NASA scientists first began studying bacteria and other pathogens in space because they wanted to keep astronauts healthy. Extended trips to space 36 that last a long time have long been understood to weaken astronauts' immune systems, so studies were designed to determine whether pathogens, including bacteria, are similarly affected by microgravity. Scientists were surprised

---

34

A) NO CHANGE

B) however,

C) nevertheless,

D) for example,

35

Which choice most effectively establishes the scientists' goal, related to information presented earlier in the paragraph?

A) NO CHANGE

B) facilitate

C) stay ahead of

D) shoot at

36

A) NO CHANGE

B) that are extensive

C) continuing for many weeks

D) DELETE the underlined portion.

CONTINUE

to find that pathogens of any kind [37] mutated more rapidly and became more virulent in space. A team led by Cheryl Nickerson of the Biodesign Institute at ASU [38] speculated that microgravity would cause a fluid shear stress reduction (the friction between cells and the fluids they interact with). Fluid shear stress affects gene expression in pathogens, and reducing it allows mutations to occur more quickly. The ASU scientists believe that microgravity mimics the reduced fluid shear stress conditions that bacteria encounter inside the human body [39].

37

A) NO CHANGE
B) had mutated more rapidly and had become
C) mutates more rapidly and becomes
D) mutate more rapidly and becomes

38

A) NO CHANGE
B) thought that fluid shear stress would be reduced by microgravity
C) speculated that microgravity reduces fluid shear stress
D) believed that microgravity lessens the shear stress caused by fluid

39

At this point, the writer is considering adding the following:

so that studying something like *Salmonella* in space allows, in effect, a glimpse into how that pathogen behaves in the human digestive tract

Should the writer make this addition here?

A) Yes, because it makes clear that researchers cannot actually see inside the human digestive tract.
B) Yes, because it further explains the benefits of conducting bacteria studies in space.
C) No, because it repeats information stated earlier in the paragraph.
D) No, because it is not relevant to the discussion of what fluid shear stress is.

CONTINUE

Although pathogen studies in space were initially intended just to help protect astronauts' health during flight, the implications of these **40** subjects now have a much broader application. Scientists are looking more closely at the specific mechanics of various pathogens' mutations so that they **41** could have developed treatments, especially vaccines, that attack those changes. Nickerson and her team are working on developing a vaccine for *Salmonella*. The virus is one of the leading **42** causes of food-borne illness, in the United States and one of the leading causes of infant mortality worldwide, so an effective vaccine has the potential to have a major impact on public health.

40

Which choice provides the most precise description of the proceeding depicted in the first part of the sentence?

A) NO CHANGE

B) examinations

C) experiments

D) tests

41

A) NO CHANGE

B) can develop

C) were developing

D) developed

42

A) NO CHANGE

B) causes of food-borne illness in the United States

C) causes, of food-borne illness in the United States

D) causes of food-borne illness, in the United States,

CONTINUE

43 *Salmonella* is already playing an important role in vaccine research, though in an unexpected way. A promising new vaccine technology, recombinant attenuated *Salmonella* vaccine (RASV), uses a genetically modified form of *Salmonella* as a delivery vehicle. RASVs quickly and efficiently deliver **44** antigens, substances, that stimulate the production of antibodies to multiple body systems with just a single dose, and can be taken orally, eliminating the need for more expensive vaccine shots. Such a vaccine already exists for *Streptococcus pneumonia*, the bacterium responsible for pneumonia and meningitis among other things. Next up on the researchers' list: an RASV to guard against *Salmonella* itself.

43

Which choice provides the most effective transition between ideas in the paragraph?

A) NO CHANGE

B) Such a vaccine hasn't yet been developed for *Salmonella*, however.

C) Researchers would also like to be able to develop better vaccines against a number of other particularly nasty bacteria.

D) This potential positive impact is part of the reason the *Salmonella* studies have expanded beyond the International Space Station.

44

A) NO CHANGE

B) antigens, substances that stimulate the production of antibodies, to multiple body systems

C) antigens, substances that stimulate the production of antibodies to multiple body systems,

D) antigens substances that stimulate the production of antibodies to multiple body systems

STOP
If you finish before time is called, you may check your work on this section only.
Do not turn to any other section in the test.

Math Test – No Calculator

25 MINUTES, 20 QUESTIONS

Turn to Section 3 of your answer sheet to answer the questions in this section.

DIRECTIONS

For questions 1–15, solve each problem, choose the best answer from the choices provided, and fill in the corresponding circle on your answer sheet. **For questions 16–20**, solve the problem and enter your answer in the grid on the answer sheet. Please refer to the directions before question 16 on how to enter your answers in the grid. You may use any available space in your test booklet for scratch work.

NOTES

1. The use of a calculator **is not permitted**.
2. All variables and expressions used represent real numbers unless otherwise indicated.
3. Figures provided in this test are drawn to scale unless otherwise indicated.
4. All figures lie in a plane unless otherwise indicated.
5. Unless otherwise indicated, the domain of a given function f is the set of all real numbers x for which $f(x)$ is a real number.

REFERENCE

$A = \pi r^2$
$C = 2\pi r$

$A = \ell w$

$A = \frac{1}{2} bh$

$c^2 = a^2 + b^2$

Special Right Triangles

$V = \ell wh$

$V = \pi r^2 h$

$V = \frac{4}{3}\pi r^3$

$V = \frac{1}{3}\pi r^2 h$

$V = \frac{1}{3}\ell wh$

The number of degrees of arc in a circle is 360.
The number of radians of arc in a circle is 2π.
The sum of the measures in degrees of the angles of a triangle is 180.

CONTINUE

1

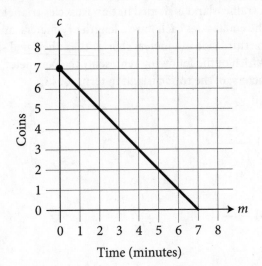

Time (minutes)

In a certain game, players start with a certain number of coins and then spend their coins. The graph above shows the number of coins, c, possessed by Erica at m minutes. Which of the following equations correctly relates c and m ?

A) $c = -\dfrac{1}{7}m$

B) $c = -m$

C) $c = -m + 7$

D) $c = -7m + 7$

2

$$\dfrac{2A + B + 2C}{5} = D$$

Based on the number of pages of algebra homework, A, biology homework, B, and chemistry homework, C, she is assigned, Katerina uses the above formula to determine the amount of time, D, in hours, she spends per page of homework assigned by her teachers. Which of the following correctly gives B, in terms of A, C, and D ?

A) $B = \dfrac{2A + 2C - D}{5}$

B) $B = \dfrac{D - 2A - 2C}{5}$

C) $B = 2A + 2C - 5D$

D) $B = 5D - 2A - 2C$

3

$$a + a - 9 = 4a + a + a - 3 - 1$$

In the equation above, what is the value of a ?

A) -1

B) $\dfrac{9}{4}$

C) $\dfrac{13}{5}$

D) 5

CONTINUE ▶

4

$$3y < 7$$

$$x < 3y + 4$$

Which of the following consists of the *x*-coordinates of all the points that satisfy the system of inequalities above?

A) $x < \dfrac{7}{3}$

B) $x < 3$

C) $x < \dfrac{19}{3}$

D) $x < 11$

5

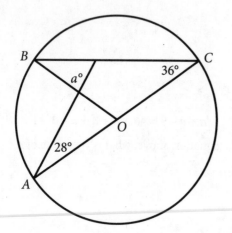

In the figure above, *O* is the center of the circle. What is the value of *a* ?

A) 100

B) 80

C) 72

D) 64

6

A traffic island is shaped like an isosceles triangle. The equal sides each have a length of *s* meters, and the third side is 4 meters shorter than the equal sides. Which of the following represents the perimeter, in meters, of the traffic island in terms of *s* ?

A) $2s - 4$

B) $\dfrac{s^2 - 4s}{2}$

C) $3s - 4$

D) $\dfrac{s - 4}{2}$

7

Point *A* has coordinates $(-11, 1)$, point *B* has coordinates $(-11, 7)$, and $\overline{AB}$ is the diameter of a circle. What is the equation of that circle?

A) $(x - 11)^2 + (y + 4)^2 = 9$

B) $(x + 11)^2 + (y - 1)^2 = 36$

C) $(x - 11)^2 + (y - 7)^2 = 36$

D) $(x + 11)^2 + (y - 4)^2 = 9$

8

$$a - 6 = \sqrt{8a - 7} - 4$$

What is the solution set of the equation above?

A) $\{0\}$

B) $\{1\}$

C) $\{11\}$

D) $\{1, 11\}$

CONTINUE

9

$$h(a) = a^2 + a - 20$$
$$k(a) = a^3 - 16a$$

Which of the following is equal to $\dfrac{h(a)}{k(a)}$, for $a > 4$?

A) $\dfrac{a+5}{a(a+4)}$

B) $\dfrac{a+5}{a(a-4)}$

C) $\dfrac{a+5}{a+4}$

D) $a + 5$

10

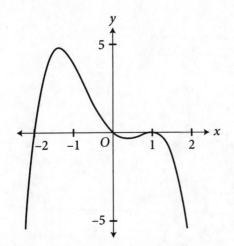

Which of the following could be the equation of the graph above?

A) $y = -x(x-1)(x+2)$

B) $y = -x(x+1)(x-2)$

C) $y = -x(x-1)^2(x+2)$

D) $y = -x(x+1)^2(x-2)$

11

If $\dfrac{x}{3y} = 3$, what is the value of $\dfrac{y}{x}$?

A) $\dfrac{1}{9}$

B) $\dfrac{1}{3}$

C) 3

D) 9

12

Taylor's garden produced 296 tomatoes, and he is preserving all the tomatoes in jars that hold either 3 or 5 tomatoes each. Taylor has a total of 80 jars. If he fills all the jars and preserves all the tomatoes, exactly how many of the jars hold 3 tomatoes?

A) 50

B) 52

C) 54

D) 56

13

$$f(x) = 2 - [g(x)]^2$$
$$g(x) = 3x - 3$$

The functions f and g are defined above. Which of the following is the value of $f(0)$?

A) -7

B) -3

C) 2

D) 11

CONTINUE

14

The population of Bulgaria was approximately 9 million people in 1989. Bulgaria's population decreased to 7.4 million people in 2011. If the decrease in population was linear, which of the following linear functions P best models the population of Bulgaria, in millions of people x years after the year 1989 ?

A) $P(x) = -\dfrac{74}{220}x + 9$

B) $P(x) = -\dfrac{16}{220}x + 9$

C) $P(x) = \dfrac{16}{220}x + 9$

D) $P(x) = \dfrac{74}{220}x + 9$

15

$$y = x^2 + 2x + k$$
$$y = 2x$$

If the system of equations above has exactly one real solution, which of the following is the value of k ?

A) −4

B) 0

C) 2

D) 4

CONTINUE

DIRECTIONS

For questions 16–20, solve the problem and enter your answer in the grid, as described below, on the answer sheet.

1. Although not required, it is suggested that you write your answer in the boxes at the top of the columns to help you fill in the circles accurately. You will receive credit only if the circles are filled in correctly.

2. Mark no more than one circle in any column.

3. No question has a negative answer.

4. Some problems may have more than one correct answer. In such cases, grid only one answer.

5. **Mixed numbers** such as $3\frac{1}{2}$ must be gridded as 3.5 or 7/2. (If $\boxed{3\ 1\ /\ 2}$ is entered into the grid, it will be interpreted as $\frac{31}{2}$, not as $3\frac{1}{2}$.)

6. **Decimal Answers:** If you obtain a decimal answer with more digits than the grid can accommodate, it may be either rounded or truncated, but it must fill the entire grid.

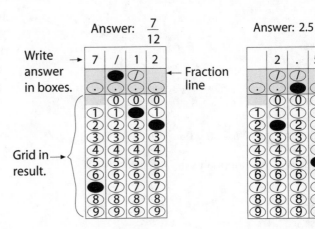

Acceptable ways to grid $\frac{2}{3}$ are:

Answer: 201 – either position is correct

NOTE: You may start your answers in any column, space permitting. Columns you don't need to use should be left blank.

CONTINUE ➤

16

When $a^2 + 2a + 4$ is subtracted from $3a^2 - 4a + 27$, the result can be written in the form $xa^2 + ya + z$, where x, y, and z are constants. What is the value of $y + z$?

17

$$n^2 - n - 30 = 0$$

What is the positive solution to the equation above?

18

A student is modeling the number of assignments she has completed in a semester. She models the number of completed assignments by writing an equation in the form $y = mx + b$, where y is the number of assignments she has completed and x is the number of weeks since the start of the month. If at the start of the month she has completed 12 assignments and she completes 3 assignments per week, what is the value of m ?

CONTINUE

19

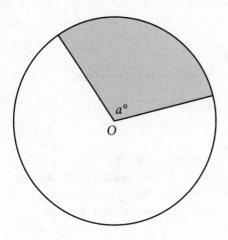

Note: Figure not drawn to scale.

In the figure above, O is the center of the circle and $a = 110$. If the area of the circle is 72, what is the area of the shaded region?

20

$$9x + 2y = 17.75$$
$$x + 2y = 3.75$$

If (x, y) is the solution to the system of equations above, what is the value of x ?

STOP
If you finish before time is called, you may check your work on this section only.
Do not turn to any other section in the test.

Math Test – Calculator

55 MINUTES, 38 QUESTIONS

Turn to Section 4 of your answer sheet to answer the questions in this section.

DIRECTIONS

For questions 1–30, solve each problem, choose the best answer from the choices provided, and fill in the corresponding circle on your answer sheet. **For questions 31–38,** solve the problem and enter your answer in the grid on the answer sheet. Please refer to the directions before question 31 on how to enter your answers in the grid. You may use any available space in your test booklet for scratch work.

NOTES

1. The use of a calculator **is permitted**.
2. All variables and expressions used represent real numbers unless otherwise indicated.
3. Figures provided in this test are drawn to scale unless otherwise indicated.
4. All figures lie in a plane unless otherwise indicated.
5. Unless otherwise indicated, the domain of a given function f is the set of all real numbers x for which $f(x)$ is a real number.

REFERENCE

$A = \pi r^2$
$C = 2\pi r$

$A = \ell w$

$A = \frac{1}{2}bh$

$c^2 = a^2 + b^2$

Special Right Triangles

$V = \ell w h$

$V = \pi r^2 h$

$V = \frac{4}{3}\pi r^3$

$V = \frac{1}{3}\pi r^2 h$

$V = \frac{1}{3}\ell w h$

The number of degrees of arc in a circle is 360.
The number of radians of arc in a circle is 2π.
The sum of the measures in degrees of the angles of a triangle is 180.

CONTINUE

4   **4**

1

The figure below shows the total number of tenants living in an apartment building between January 1ˢᵗ of 2005 and January 1ˢᵗ of 2010.

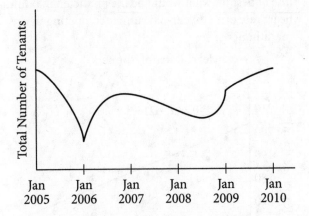

During which of the following years of operation does the number of tenants in the building increase the fastest?

A) 2005

B) 2006

C) 2007

D) 2009

2

A doctor randomly selects 500 residents of an island and finds that 4 of these residents have a specific gene mutation. Based on these results, approximately how many of the island's 15,000 residents likely have this mutation?

A)   75

B)   90

C)   105

D)   120

3

Chris buys one box of cookies for n dollars. At this rate, how much does he pay, in dollars, for 4 boxes of cookies?

A) $\dfrac{n}{4}$

B) $\dfrac{4}{n}$

C) $4n$

D) $n + 4$

4

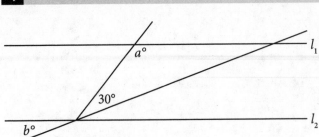

In the figure above, lines l_1 and l_2 are parallel and $a = 110$. What is the value of b ?

A)   40

B)   70

C)   80

D)   140

CONTINUE

5

A newspaper sells both paper and digital subscriptions. The newspaper reports that 1,800 total subscriptions were sold last month and the total revenue from those subscription sales was $20,760. The digital subscriptions, d, cost $8 a month, and the paper subscriptions, p, cost $20 a month. Which of the following systems of equations could be used to solve for the number of each type of subscription that was sold by the newspaper last month?

A) $d + p = 1,800$
$20d + 8p = 20,760$

B) $d + p = 1,800$
$8d + 20p = 20,760$

C) $d + p = 20,760$
$8d + 20p = 1,800$

D) $d + p = 1,800$
$8d (20p) = 20,760$

6

A study tracked the maximum heart rate for runners competing in a marathon. The data and line of best fit are shown in the scatterplot below. Based on the line of best fit, what would be the predicted maximum heart rate of a 60-year-old runner competing in the marathon?

Heart Rates of Runners

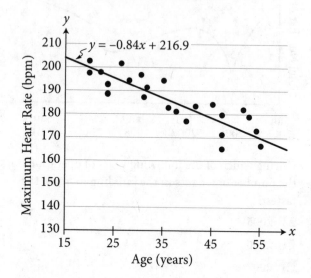

A) 166.5

B) 170.7

C) 183.4

D) 216.9

7

$$\frac{3}{c-2} = c - 2$$

Which of the following values of $c - 2$ satisfies the equation above?

A) 5

B) 3

C) $\sqrt{3}$

D) $\sqrt{3} - 2$

CONTINUE

8

Which of the following equations, when graphed in the xy-plane, results in a line with a y-intercept of -1 ?

A) $y = x - \dfrac{1}{2}$

B) $y = \dfrac{1}{2}x - 1$

C) $y = -x$

D) $y = 2x + 1$

9

Sarah works at an art school and is purchasing canvases for $6 each and bottles of paint for $4 each. She budgets a total of $1,700 for canvases and paint. She goes over-budget, but purchases more than 360 items. Which of the following systems of inequalities represents all the possible values for the number of canvases, a, and the number of paint bottles, b, that she buys?

A) $6a + 4b < 1,700$
    $a + b > 360$

B) $6a + 4b < 1,700$
    $a + b < 360$

C) $6a + 4b > 1,700$
    $a + b < 360$

D) $6a + 4b > 1,700$
    $a + b > 360$

Questions 10–12 refer to the following information.

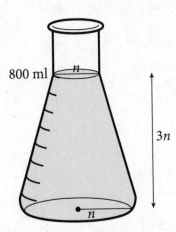

A beaker that can be filled to a maximum volume of 800 milliliters is shown above. For safety reasons, it cannot be filled above the 800-milliliter line. The radius of the base is equal to the diameter of the top, and the volume in cubic inches of the beaker is given by the equation $V = \dfrac{21\pi n^3}{12}$.

10

How many beakers of this size, filled to the 800-milliliter line, would be needed to hold 4 liters of a solution? (1 liter = 1,000 mL)

A) 2

B) 4

C) 5

D) 8

CONTINUE

11

Given that the volume of 800 milliliters of liquid is approximately 13.2 cubic inches, which of the following is closest to the radius of the base of the beaker?

A) 1.34 inches

B) 2.28 inches

C) 4.23 inches

D) 8.04 inches

12

The beaker is filled with a solution to the 800-milliliter line and then left outside in the sun where the solution evaporates at a constant rate. The graph of the height of the solution remaining in the beaker over time would have which of the following shapes?

A)
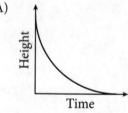

B)
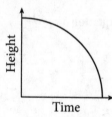

C)
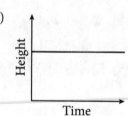

D)
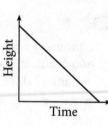

13

The amount of work done to move an object is equal to the product of the mass of the object, in kilograms; the distance the object moves, in meters; and the gravitational constant of 9.8 meters per second squared. What is the power rating of a machine that can move a 100-kilogram object 3.6 meters in 18 seconds? (Power is work per unit time.)

A) 196

B)   54

C)   19.6

D)   5.4

14

If $y = \dfrac{1}{x^3}$, which of the following gives x in terms of y?

A) $y^{\frac{1}{3}}$

B) $y^{-\frac{1}{3}}$

C) $-y^3$

D) y^3

CONTINUE

15

The function $f(x) = \dfrac{5}{x^2 - 5x + 4}$ is graphed in the

xy-plane. Which of the following values of x is NOT

in the domain of $f(x)$?

A) −1

B) 0

C) 1

D) 5

16

Number of Eggs Laid by Chickens

Number of Eggs	8	7	6	5	4	2
Frequency	1	3	8	5	2	5

A farmer has 24 chickens. At the end of a week, he counts the total number of eggs each chicken laid that week. The table above shows the distribution of the number of eggs laid by the chickens. Which of the following statements about the mean, median, and mode of the number of eggs laid is true?

A) The mean is greater than both the mode and the median.

B) The mean is less than both the mode and the median.

C) The mean is greater than the mode but less than the median.

D) The mean is equal to both the mode and the median.

17

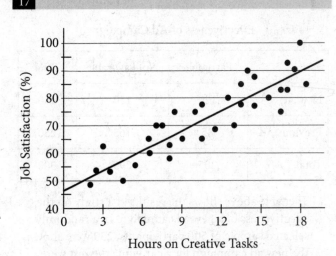

Hours on Creative Tasks

A Human Resources department seeking to increase employee retention commissioned a study to determine the relationship between job tasks and employee satisfaction. The scatterplot above shows the relationship for employees in a particular field between the number of work hours spent on creative tasks per week and their overall job satisfaction. The line of best fit is shown on the figure.

An employee that works in the same field but was not part of the study indicates that he spends 12 hours a week on creative tasks. Which of the following is the best approximation of his predicted job satisfaction based on the line of best fit?

A) 68%

B) 75%

C) 80%

D) 84%

CONTINUE

18

Effectiveness of Ad Campaign

	Favorable	Not Favorable	Total
New Ad	120	130	250
Previous Ad	85	165	250
Total	205	295	500

The table above shows the results of a study on the effectiveness of a new ad campaign. In a randomly selected sample of 500 participants, 250 were shown the new ad campaign for a car while the rest were shown the previous ad campaign. The participants then reported whether their opinion of the car was favorable or not. What proportion of participants who watched the new ad campaign had a favorable opinion?

A) $\dfrac{12}{25}$

B) $\dfrac{41}{100}$

C) $\dfrac{6}{25}$

D) $\dfrac{24}{41}$

Questions 19 and 20 refer to the following information.

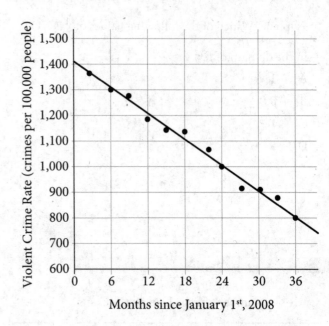

Months since January 1st, 2008

On January 1st, 2008, a city implemented a new program to combat crime. The graph above shows the violent crime rate in the city, measured in violent crimes per 100,000 residents, from January 1st, 2008, to the end of 2010. The line of best fit has the equation $y = 1,412 - 16.8x$, where y is the violent crime rate and x is the number of months since the implementation of the program.

19

Which of the following is closest to the percent decrease in the violent crime rate in the city from January 1st, 2010, to January 1st, 2011 ?

A)   8%

B)   20%

C)   80%

D)   140%

CONTINUE

20

What does the coefficient 16.8 represent in the line of best fit equation?

A) The number of months since the crime reduction program was implemented

B) The average crime rate per month since January 2008

C) The average monthly reduction in the violent crime rate during the first three years that the crime reduction program was in place

D) The violent crime rate in January 2008

21

Samuel's annual salary is \$49,500. If he completes an MBA program with a tuition of \$73,320, his annual salary will be \$64,500. If n represents the number of years that Samuel works at his job after completing his MBA, which of the following inequalities demonstrates the value of n for which his total additional income exceeds the cost of the tuition?

A) $n > \dfrac{73,320}{(64,500 - 49,500)}$

B) $n < \dfrac{73,320}{(64,500 - 49,500)}$

C) $n > \dfrac{(73,320 - 49,500)}{64,500}$

D) $n < \dfrac{(73,320 - 49,500)}{64,500}$

22

Polynomial function g is graphed in the xy-plane. This function has zeros at -4 and 2, and its range is the set of all real numbers such that $g(x) \geq -3$. Which of the following graphs represents function g?

A)

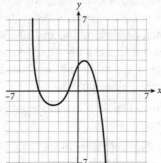

B)

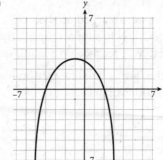

C)

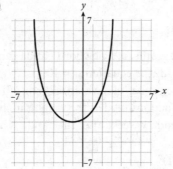

D)

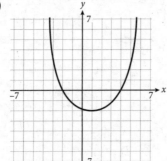

CONTINUE

23

To determine support for a proposition on the state ballot, residents were called on the phone. Of those residents called, 20% did not answer the phone. Approximately 35% of the residents who did answer were contacted on a landline and the other 65% were contacted on a cell phone. Approximately 55% of the respondents contacted on a landline and 30% of the respondents contacted on a cell phone supported the proposition. Which of the following conclusions is best supported by the poll results?

A) The proposition will pass if voter turnout is high on Election Day.

B) Voters over 35 years old were more likely to support the proposition than voters between 18 and 35 were.

C) Participants that were reached on their cell phones were less likely to support the bill than participants that were reached on a landline.

D) If only voters that own a landline vote on Election Day, the proposition will pass.

24

The weight w, in grams, of a newborn panda can be approximated with the equation $w = 109(1.12)^n$, where n represents the number of days since birth. Which of the following equations models the weight, in grams, of a newborn panda x weeks after the panda is born?

A) $w = 109(2.21)^{\frac{x}{7}}$

B) $w = 109(1.12)^{\frac{x}{7}}$

C) $w = 109(1.84)^x$

D) $w = 109(1.12)^{7x}$

25

An activist group wants to determine how frequently the average resident of a county uses the library. The group plans to ask everybody that enters one of the library branches on a Saturday to estimate how many times per year they visit a library. Based on these responses, the group will estimate the number of library visits that the average resident makes each year. Which of the following statements is true?

A) The proposed survey has a small sample size and therefore the results will likely be an unreliable estimate of the average library use of the county's residents.

B) The proposed survey will likely produce a reliable estimate of the average library use of the county's residents only if the group conducts it on both a Saturday and a weekday.

C) The proposed survey will likely produce a reliable estimate of the average library use of the county's residents if the group conducts the survey at the busiest library in the county.

D) Due to a flawed sampling method, the proposed survey will likely produce a biased estimate of the average library use of the county's residents regardless of the sample size and the days of the week on which the survey is conducted.

CONTINUE ➡

26

The point (c, d) lies on a line with a slope of 2 in the xy-plane. The point $(3, 2d)$ lies on a different line with a slope of -3. If the two lines have the same y-intercept and $\dfrac{c}{d} = \dfrac{3}{2}$, what is the value of d ?

A) $-\dfrac{9}{4}$

B) $-\dfrac{2}{3}$

C) $\dfrac{3}{2}$

D) $\dfrac{9}{2}$

27

Unemployment Rate in Country X

Year	2010	2013
Unemployment Rate	11.5%	13%

The table above shows the unemployment rate for Country X in 2010 and 2013. If the unemployment rate and year have a linear relationship, which of the following expressions best approximates the unemployment rate of the country n years after 2010 ?

A) $1.5n + 11.5$

B) $0.5(n - 2{,}010) + 11.5$

C) $0.5n + 11.5$

D) $-1.5n + 11.5$

28

A pool has 750 gallons of water in it when a hose begins adding water at a constant rate. The pool contains 60% more water after the hose has run for 5 hours. Which of the following expressions gives the number of gallons of water in the pool after the hose has run for a total of t hours?

A) $750 + 90t$

B) $750 + 5t$

C) $750(1.6)^{\frac{t}{5}}$

D) $750(1.6)^{5t}$

CONTINUE

29

A table of values for function $f(x)$ and the graph of function $h(x)$ are shown below. If the vertex of $h(x)$ is (a, b), what is $f(h(a))$?

x	−3	−2	−1	0	1	2	3
$f(x)$	11	8	5	2	−1	−4	−7

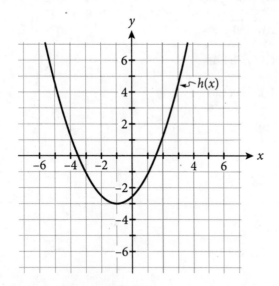

A) −1

B) 2

C) 5

D) 11

30

Researchers allowed 15 participants in a study to get a full night's sleep, while another 15 were awoken after only 3 hours of sleep. The researchers then gave the participants a series of mental tasks and calculated each participant's average completion time. The results are shown below.

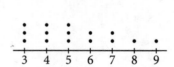

Completion time (sec)
Normal Sleep

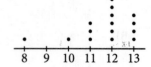

Completion time (sec)
Reduced Sleep

If the participants with normal sleep make up Group A and the participants with 3 hours of sleep make up Group B, which of the following statements regarding the standard deviations and ranges of the groups is true?

A) The range of Group B is larger than the range of Group A.

B) The standard deviation of Group B is smaller than the standard deviation of Group A.

C) The standard deviation of Group B is equal to the standard deviation of Group A.

D) The range of Group B is equal to the range of Group A.

CONTINUE

DIRECTIONS

For questions 31–38, solve the problem and enter your answer in the grid, as described below, on the answer sheet.

1. Although not required, it is suggested that you write your answer in the boxes at the top of the columns to help you fill in the circles accurately. You will receive credit only if the circles are filled in correctly.

2. Mark no more than one circle in any column.

3. No question has a negative answer.

4. Some problems may have more than one correct answer. In such cases, grid only one answer.

5. **Mixed numbers** such as $3\frac{1}{2}$ must be gridded as 3.5 or 7/2. (If $\boxed{3\ 1\ /\ 2}$ is entered into the grid, it will be interpreted as $\frac{31}{2}$, not as $3\frac{1}{2}$.)

6. **Decimal Answers:** If you obtain a decimal answer with more digits than the grid can accommodate, it may be either rounded or truncated, but it must fill the entire grid.

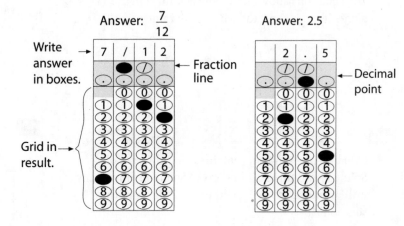

Answer: $\frac{7}{12}$ Answer: 2.5

Write answer in boxes. ← Fraction line

Grid in result.

Decimal point →

Acceptable ways to grid $\frac{2}{3}$ are:

Answer: 201 – either position is correct

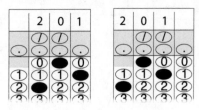

NOTE: You may start your answers in any column, space permitting. Columns you don't need to use should be left blank.

CONTINUE →

31

$$nx - 8y = 18$$
$$7x - 4y = 9$$

The equations above both represent line l in the xy-plane. If n is a constant, what is the value of n ?

32

One liter of a solution contains one milligram of Solute A and three milligrams of Solute B. How many milligrams of Solute B are there in 22 liters of the solution?

33

$$\frac{1}{3}c + x = 0$$

The equation above is true when $x = -3$. What is the value of c ?

34

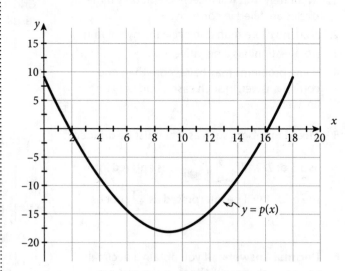

The function p is defined by the equation

$p(x) = \frac{1}{3}(x - 9)^2 - 18$. A portion of the graph of p

is shown above. Function q (not shown) is defined

by the equation $q(x) = 15 - 5x$. If $p(x)$ intersects the

graph of $q(x)$ at the point (r, s) where $r > 0$, what

is the value of r ?

CONTINUE

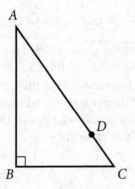

In the figure above, if cos (∠*DBA*) = 0.3, what is the value of cos (∠*DBA*) + sin (∠*DBC*) ?

October 28 and 29, 1929, are known as Black Monday and Black Tuesday, respectively. During two days of trading, the Dow Jones Industrial Average lost 68.9 points. If there were 5 hours of trading during each of the two days, on average how many points per <u>minute</u>, to the nearest hundredth, did the Dow Jones Industrial Average lose during those two days?

CONTINUE ➡

Questions 37 and 38 refer to the following information.

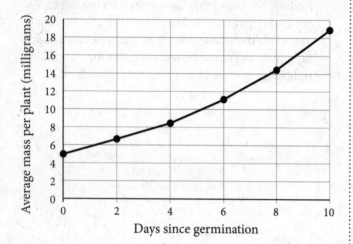

Days since germination	0	2	4	6	8	10
Average mass per plant (milligrams)	5.0	6.6	8.4	11.1	14.4	18.8

Once a seed has germinated and the first leaves begin producing carbohydrates through photosynthesis, a plant grows rapidly until it begins flowering or its growth is restricted by a lack of nutrients or light. An agriculture class grew *Zea mays L.* (sweet corn) in its greenhouse and measured the mass of each plant every other day. The average mass per plant was determined and presented in the graph and table above.

$$H(d) = 5.0r^{\frac{d}{2}}$$

The students in the class modeled the average mass per plant using the above function H, where H is average mass in grams d days after germination, and r is a constant. The students found their model matched the data collected within 0.1 gram. To the nearest tenth, what is the value of r ?

38

According to the table, what is the positive difference on average, in grams, between a group of 4 plants that germinated 4 days ago and a group of 3 plants that germinated 8 days ago?

STOP
If you finish before time is called, you may check your work on this section only.
Do not turn to any other section in the test.

Experimental: Writing and Language Skills

20 MINUTES, 18 QUESTIONS

Turn to Section 5 of your answer sheet to answer the questions in this section.

CONTINUE

Questions 1–18 are based on the following passage.

Metric Mayhem

[1] In the fall of 1999, the metric system caused the $125 million Mars Climate Orbiter to crash on Mars 1 . [2] Somehow, neither group realized the units were different, and the result was that the trajectory of the probe was miscalculated and it crashed. [3] This, at least, is the argument of 2 people who are against adopting the metric system in the United States. [4] The problem was that two different groups that worked on the project used different systems of measurement. [5] One group used pounds of force per second, a U.S. Customary measurement, and the other group 3 uses newtons, the equivalent metric measurement of force. 4

1

At this point, the writer is considering adding the following.

   instead of going into orbit around the planet to collect and transmit data

Should the writer make this addition here?

A) Yes, because it gives details that clarify that the crash was unexpected.

B) Yes, because it establishes an important shift in focus in the paragraph's discussion of the Mars Climate Orbiter.

C) No, because it contains information that is not directly related to the main focus of the paragraph.

D) No, because it repeats information given later in the paragraph.

2

A) NO CHANGE

B) them

C) they

D) those ones

3

A) NO CHANGE

B) had used

C) used

D) will have used

4

To make this paragraph most logical, sentence 2 should be placed

A) where it is now.

B) after sentence 3.

C) after sentence 4.

D) after sentence 5.

CONTINUE

The history of the metric system in the Western world began soon after the replacement of Roman numerals with the base-ten Arabic numbering **5** system. The replacement of Roman numerals with Arabic numerals happened in the 15th century. The earliest known treatise promoting the **6** idea, of a decimal, or base-ten system of measurement was printed in 1586. The foundations of the metric system as we know it today were developed over the next two **7** centuries, as commerce, across great distances, became more common. A universal system makes trade vastly simpler because weights and prices can be easily understood, **8** so cheating is difficult.

5

Which choice most effectively combines the sentences at the underlined portion?

A) system; this replacement

B) system, which

C) system—the adoption of Arabic numerals

D) system, an occurrence that largely

6

A) NO CHANGE

B) idea of a decimal, or base-ten,

C) idea, of a decimal or base-ten,

D) idea of a decimal—or base-ten,

7

A) NO CHANGE

B) centuries as commerce, across great distances

C) centuries as commerce, across great distances,

D) centuries as commerce across great distances

8

Which choice most effectively completes the explanation of how the metric system was important for trade over long distances?

A) NO CHANGE

B) since different currencies make long-distance trade hard enough.

C) regardless of whether buyers and sellers are from the same place.

D) whether the goods are spices, wine, or textiles.

CONTINUE

France was the first country to officially adopt the metric system in the late 18th century, and **9** they organized several international conferences to establish what the universal standards would be. Much of Europe **10** got on board with the metric system quickly on the heels of France, with the exception of Britain. **11** Since the American colonies were part of the British Empire, they used the British Imperial System of measurement. When the United States was established, the Constitution specified that Congress had the power to "fix the Standard of Weights and Measures," and Thomas Jefferson and Ben Franklin were both among the proponents of **12** sacrificing the British system in favor of the metric system.

9

A) NO CHANGE
B) they were organizing
C) it organized
D) it had organized

10

Which choice best maintains the style and tone of the passage?
A) NO CHANGE
B) singled out
C) adopted
D) pinned down

11

A) NO CHANGE
B) Although
C) Therefore,
D) Nevertheless,

12

A) NO CHANGE
B) ducking
C) evading
D) abandoning

CONTINUE

In the late 18th century, **13** for example, politics and distance turned out to be insurmountable roadblocks to adopting the metric system in the United States. Although France had been an American ally during the Revolutionary **14** War. It quickly turned hostile towards the United States as diplomatic relations between the United States and Britain warmed after the war. There was also concern in the United States about the cost of sending a delegation to France **15** for learn about the metric system and worry that political upheaval within France might mean the quick demise of the new system. In the end, the British system was retained, though we now know it as the United States Customary System.

16 There have been multiple attempts over the years to establish the metric system in the United States. In fact, the metric system was made legal (though not mandatory) by Congress in 1866, and our standards for yards and pounds are defined as fractions of meters and

13

A) NO CHANGE
B) moreover,
C) thus,
D) however,

14

A) NO CHANGE
B) War, it
C) War; it
D) War: it

15

A) NO CHANGE
B) to
C) by
D) of

16

Which choice provides the best introduction to this paragraph?

A) NO CHANGE
B) The metric system continued in France, despite Napoleonic rule.
C) Congress deals with a lot of issues that might not seem like they have a big impact on everyday life.
D) Political upheaval also happens in the United States.

CONTINUE

kilograms, respectively. When Congress passed the Metric Conversion Act in 1975, [17] metric enthusiasts who admired that system were optimistic that the United States was finally going to make the switch. But the bill was later amended to make metric conversion voluntary, [18] which is why our speed limit signs are in miles per hour instead of kilometers per hour, and at least in part why the Mars Climate Orbiter crashed.

[17]

A) NO CHANGE

B) those in enthusiastic favor of the metric system

C) metric enthusiasts

D) enthusiastic metric system admirers

[18]

Which choice most effectively concludes the essay?

A) NO CHANGE

B) but even though it isn't official, many school children learn about the metric system from an early age.

C) so some businesses have opted to go metric, while most government agencies haven't fully made the switch.

D) which means no one is motivated to make the change even though it wouldn't be that hard.

END OF TEST

DO NOT RETURN TO A PREVIOUS SECTION.

Completely darken bubbles with a No. 2 pencil. If you make a mistake, be sure to erase mark completely. Erase all stray marks.

1.

YOUR NAME: _____
(Print)   Last   First   M.I.

SIGNATURE: _____   DATE: __/__/__

HOME ADDRESS: _____
(Print)   Number and Street

_____
City   State   Zip Code

PHONE NO.: _____
(Print)

IMPORTANT: Please fill in these boxes exactly as shown on the back cover of your test book.

2. TEST FORM

6. DATE OF BIRTH

Month	Day		Year	
○ JAN				
○ FEB	⓪	⓪	⓪	⓪
○ MAR	①	①	①	①
○ APR	②	②	②	②
○ MAY	③	③	③	③
○ JUN		④	④	④
○ JUL		⑤	⑤	⑤
○ AUG		⑥	⑥	⑥
○ SEP		⑦	⑦	⑦
○ OCT		⑧	⑧	⑧
○ NOV		⑨	⑨	⑨
○ DEC				

3. TEST CODE 	**4. REGISTRATION NUMBER**

⓪	Ⓐ	Ⓙ	⓪	⓪	⓪	⓪	⓪	⓪	⓪	⓪
①	Ⓑ	Ⓚ	①	①	①	①	①	①	①	①
②	Ⓒ	Ⓛ	②	②	②	②	②	②	②	②
③	Ⓓ	Ⓜ	③	③	③	③	③	③	③	③
④	Ⓔ	Ⓝ	④	④	④	④	④	④	④	④
⑤	Ⓕ	Ⓞ	⑤	⑤	⑤	⑤	⑤	⑤	⑤	⑤
⑥	Ⓖ	Ⓟ	⑥	⑥	⑥	⑥	⑥	⑥	⑥	⑥
⑦	Ⓗ	Ⓠ	⑦	⑦	⑦	⑦	⑦	⑦	⑦	⑦
⑧	Ⓘ	Ⓡ	⑧	⑧	⑧	⑧	⑧	⑧	⑧	⑧
⑨			⑨	⑨	⑨	⑨	⑨	⑨	⑨	⑨

7. SEX
○ MALE
○ FEMALE

The **Princeton Review**®

5. YOUR NAME

First 4 letters of last name				FIRST INIT	MID INIT
Ⓐ	Ⓐ	Ⓐ	Ⓐ	Ⓐ	Ⓐ
Ⓑ	Ⓑ	Ⓑ	Ⓑ	Ⓑ	Ⓑ
Ⓒ	Ⓒ	Ⓒ	Ⓒ	Ⓒ	Ⓒ
Ⓓ	Ⓓ	Ⓓ	Ⓓ	Ⓓ	Ⓓ
Ⓔ	Ⓔ	Ⓔ	Ⓔ	Ⓔ	Ⓔ
Ⓕ	Ⓕ	Ⓕ	Ⓕ	Ⓕ	Ⓕ
Ⓖ	Ⓖ	Ⓖ	Ⓖ	Ⓖ	Ⓖ
Ⓗ	Ⓗ	Ⓗ	Ⓗ	Ⓗ	Ⓗ
Ⓘ	Ⓘ	Ⓘ	Ⓘ	Ⓘ	Ⓘ
Ⓙ	Ⓙ	Ⓙ	Ⓙ	Ⓙ	Ⓙ
Ⓚ	Ⓚ	Ⓚ	Ⓚ	Ⓚ	Ⓚ
Ⓛ	Ⓛ	Ⓛ	Ⓛ	Ⓛ	Ⓛ
Ⓜ	Ⓜ	Ⓜ	Ⓜ	Ⓜ	Ⓜ
Ⓝ	Ⓝ	Ⓝ	Ⓝ	Ⓝ	Ⓝ
Ⓞ	Ⓞ	Ⓞ	Ⓞ	Ⓞ	Ⓞ
Ⓟ	Ⓟ	Ⓟ	Ⓟ	Ⓟ	Ⓟ
Ⓠ	Ⓠ	Ⓠ	Ⓠ	Ⓠ	Ⓠ
Ⓡ	Ⓡ	Ⓡ	Ⓡ	Ⓡ	Ⓡ
Ⓢ	Ⓢ	Ⓢ	Ⓢ	Ⓢ	Ⓢ
Ⓣ	Ⓣ	Ⓣ	Ⓣ	Ⓣ	Ⓣ
Ⓤ	Ⓤ	Ⓤ	Ⓤ	Ⓤ	Ⓤ
Ⓥ	Ⓥ	Ⓥ	Ⓥ	Ⓥ	Ⓥ
Ⓦ	Ⓦ	Ⓦ	Ⓦ	Ⓦ	Ⓦ
Ⓧ	Ⓧ	Ⓧ	Ⓧ	Ⓧ	Ⓧ
Ⓨ	Ⓨ	Ⓨ	Ⓨ	Ⓨ	Ⓨ
Ⓩ	Ⓩ	Ⓩ	Ⓩ	Ⓩ	Ⓩ

Test ⑩ Start with number 1 for each new section.
If a section has fewer questions than answer spaces, leave the extra answer spaces blank.

Section 1—Reading

1. Ⓐ Ⓑ Ⓒ Ⓓ
2. Ⓐ Ⓑ Ⓒ Ⓓ
3. Ⓐ Ⓑ Ⓒ Ⓓ
4. Ⓐ Ⓑ Ⓒ Ⓓ
5. Ⓐ Ⓑ Ⓒ Ⓓ
6. Ⓐ Ⓑ Ⓒ Ⓓ
7. Ⓐ Ⓑ Ⓒ Ⓓ
8. Ⓐ Ⓑ Ⓒ Ⓓ
9. Ⓐ Ⓑ Ⓒ Ⓓ
10. Ⓐ Ⓑ Ⓒ Ⓓ
11. Ⓐ Ⓑ Ⓒ Ⓓ
12. Ⓐ Ⓑ Ⓒ Ⓓ
13. Ⓐ Ⓑ Ⓒ Ⓓ
14. Ⓐ Ⓑ Ⓒ Ⓓ
15. Ⓐ Ⓑ Ⓒ Ⓓ
16. Ⓐ Ⓑ Ⓒ Ⓓ
17. Ⓐ Ⓑ Ⓒ Ⓓ
18. Ⓐ Ⓑ Ⓒ Ⓓ
19. Ⓐ Ⓑ Ⓒ Ⓓ
20. Ⓐ Ⓑ Ⓒ Ⓓ
21. Ⓐ Ⓑ Ⓒ Ⓓ
22. Ⓐ Ⓑ Ⓒ Ⓓ
23. Ⓐ Ⓑ Ⓒ Ⓓ
24. Ⓐ Ⓑ Ⓒ Ⓓ
25. Ⓐ Ⓑ Ⓒ Ⓓ
26. Ⓐ Ⓑ Ⓒ Ⓓ
27. Ⓐ Ⓑ Ⓒ Ⓓ
28. Ⓐ Ⓑ Ⓒ Ⓓ
29. Ⓐ Ⓑ Ⓒ Ⓓ
30. Ⓐ Ⓑ Ⓒ Ⓓ
31. Ⓐ Ⓑ Ⓒ Ⓓ
32. Ⓐ Ⓑ Ⓒ Ⓓ
33. Ⓐ Ⓑ Ⓒ Ⓓ
34. Ⓐ Ⓑ Ⓒ Ⓓ
35. Ⓐ Ⓑ Ⓒ Ⓓ
36. Ⓐ Ⓑ Ⓒ Ⓓ
37. Ⓐ Ⓑ Ⓒ Ⓓ
38. Ⓐ Ⓑ Ⓒ Ⓓ
39. Ⓐ Ⓑ Ⓒ Ⓓ
40. Ⓐ Ⓑ Ⓒ Ⓓ
41. Ⓐ Ⓑ Ⓒ Ⓓ
42. Ⓐ Ⓑ Ⓒ Ⓓ
43. Ⓐ Ⓑ Ⓒ Ⓓ
44. Ⓐ Ⓑ Ⓒ Ⓓ
45. Ⓐ Ⓑ Ⓒ Ⓓ
46. Ⓐ Ⓑ Ⓒ Ⓓ
47. Ⓐ Ⓑ Ⓒ Ⓓ
48. Ⓐ Ⓑ Ⓒ Ⓓ
49. Ⓐ Ⓑ Ⓒ Ⓓ
50. Ⓐ Ⓑ Ⓒ Ⓓ
51. Ⓐ Ⓑ Ⓒ Ⓓ
52. Ⓐ Ⓑ Ⓒ Ⓓ

Section 2—Writing and Language Skills

1. Ⓐ Ⓑ Ⓒ Ⓓ
2. Ⓐ Ⓑ Ⓒ Ⓓ
3. Ⓐ Ⓑ Ⓒ Ⓓ
4. Ⓐ Ⓑ Ⓒ Ⓓ
5. Ⓐ Ⓑ Ⓒ Ⓓ
6. Ⓐ Ⓑ Ⓒ Ⓓ
7. Ⓐ Ⓑ Ⓒ Ⓓ
8. Ⓐ Ⓑ Ⓒ Ⓓ
9. Ⓐ Ⓑ Ⓒ Ⓓ
10. Ⓐ Ⓑ Ⓒ Ⓓ
11. Ⓐ Ⓑ Ⓒ Ⓓ
12. Ⓐ Ⓑ Ⓒ Ⓓ
13. Ⓐ Ⓑ Ⓒ Ⓓ
14. Ⓐ Ⓑ Ⓒ Ⓓ
15. Ⓐ Ⓑ Ⓒ Ⓓ
16. Ⓐ Ⓑ Ⓒ Ⓓ
17. Ⓐ Ⓑ Ⓒ Ⓓ
18. Ⓐ Ⓑ Ⓒ Ⓓ
19. Ⓐ Ⓑ Ⓒ Ⓓ
20. Ⓐ Ⓑ Ⓒ Ⓓ
21. Ⓐ Ⓑ Ⓒ Ⓓ
22. Ⓐ Ⓑ Ⓒ Ⓓ
23. Ⓐ Ⓑ Ⓒ Ⓓ
24. Ⓐ Ⓑ Ⓒ Ⓓ
25. Ⓐ Ⓑ Ⓒ Ⓓ
26. Ⓐ Ⓑ Ⓒ Ⓓ
27. Ⓐ Ⓑ Ⓒ Ⓓ
28. Ⓐ Ⓑ Ⓒ Ⓓ
29. Ⓐ Ⓑ Ⓒ Ⓓ
30. Ⓐ Ⓑ Ⓒ Ⓓ
31. Ⓐ Ⓑ Ⓒ Ⓓ
32. Ⓐ Ⓑ Ⓒ Ⓓ
33. Ⓐ Ⓑ Ⓒ Ⓓ
34. Ⓐ Ⓑ Ⓒ Ⓓ
35. Ⓐ Ⓑ Ⓒ Ⓓ
36. Ⓐ Ⓑ Ⓒ Ⓓ
37. Ⓐ Ⓑ Ⓒ Ⓓ
38. Ⓐ Ⓑ Ⓒ Ⓓ
39. Ⓐ Ⓑ Ⓒ Ⓓ
40. Ⓐ Ⓑ Ⓒ Ⓓ
41. Ⓐ Ⓑ Ⓒ Ⓓ
42. Ⓐ Ⓑ Ⓒ Ⓓ
43. Ⓐ Ⓑ Ⓒ Ⓓ
44. Ⓐ Ⓑ Ⓒ Ⓓ

Completely darken bubbles with a No. 2 pencil. If you make a mistake, be sure to erase mark completely. Erase all stray marks.

Test ⑩ Start with number 1 for each new section.
If a section has fewer questions than answer spaces, leave the extra answer spaces blank.

Section 3—Mathematics: No Calculator

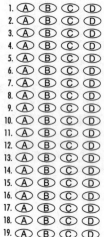

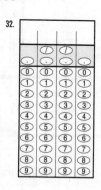

Section 4—Mathematics: Calculator

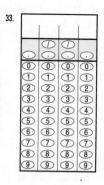

Section 5—Experimental: Writing and Language Skills

1. Ⓐ Ⓑ Ⓒ Ⓓ   10. Ⓐ Ⓑ Ⓒ Ⓓ
2. Ⓐ Ⓑ Ⓒ Ⓓ   11. Ⓐ Ⓑ Ⓒ Ⓓ
3. Ⓐ Ⓑ Ⓒ Ⓓ   12. Ⓐ Ⓑ Ⓒ Ⓓ
4. Ⓐ Ⓑ Ⓒ Ⓓ   13. Ⓐ Ⓑ Ⓒ Ⓓ
5. Ⓐ Ⓑ Ⓒ Ⓓ   14. Ⓐ Ⓑ Ⓒ Ⓓ
6. Ⓐ Ⓑ Ⓒ Ⓓ   15. Ⓐ Ⓑ Ⓒ Ⓓ
7. Ⓐ Ⓑ Ⓒ Ⓓ   16. Ⓐ Ⓑ Ⓒ Ⓓ
8. Ⓐ Ⓑ Ⓒ Ⓓ   17. Ⓐ Ⓑ Ⓒ Ⓓ
9. Ⓐ Ⓑ Ⓒ Ⓓ   18. Ⓐ Ⓑ Ⓒ Ⓓ

Chapter 22
Practice Test 10:
Answers and
Explanations

PRACTICE TEST 10 ANSWER KEY

Section 1:	**Section 2:**	**Section 3:**	**Section 4:**
Reading	Writing & Language	Math (No Calculator)	Math (Calculator)

Section 1: Reading

1. B	27. C		
2. D	28. D		
3. D	29. B		
4. A	30. B		
5. D	31. D		
6. A	32. B		
7. C	33. B		
8. B	34. A		
9. C	35. A		
10. C	36. C		
11. C	37. B		
12. A	38. B		
13. A	39. D		
14. C	40. A		
15. B	41. B		
16. B	42. B		
17. D	43. B		
18. D	44. D		
19. A	45. D		
20. B	46. D		
21. C	47. B		
22. B	48. A		
23. A	49. B		
24. C	50. C		
25. B	51. D		
26. A	52. D		

Section 2: Writing & Language

1. C	23. A
2. D	24. D
3. D	25. C
4. A	26. D
5. B	27. D
6. C	28. C
7. A	29. B
8. D	30. A
9. B	31. D
10. B	32. B
11. B	33. A
12. D	34. A
13. C	35. C
14. A	36. D
15. B	37. A
16. A	38. C
17. A	39. B
18. C	40. C
19. D	41. B
20. B	42. B
21. A	43. A
22. D	44. B

Section 3: Math (No Calculator)

1. C	13. A
2. D	14. B
3. A	15. B
4. D	16. 17
5. B	17. 6
6. C	18. 3
7. D	19. 22
8. C	20. $\frac{14}{8}$, $\frac{7}{4}$, or 1.75
9. A	
10. C	
11. A	
12. B	

Section 4: Math (Calculator)

1. B	20. C
2. D	21. A
3. C	22. C
4. A	23. C
5. B	24. D
6. A	25. D
7. C	26. A
8. B	27. C
9. D	28. A
10. C	29. D
11. A	30. B
12. A	31. 14
13. A	32. 66
14. B	33. 9
15. C	34. 6
16. B	35. 0.6
17. B	36. 0.11
18. A	37. 1.3
19. B	38. 9.6

Section 5:
Experimental (Writing & Language)

1. A	6. B	11. A	16. A
2. A	7. D	12. D	17. C
3. C	8. C	13. D	18. A
4. D	9. C	14. B	
5. B	10. C	15. B	

Go to PrincetonReview.com to score your exam. Alternatively, for self-assessment tables, please turn to page 909.

PRACTICE TEST 10 EXPLANATIONS

Section 1: Reading

1. **B** The question asks how the main focus of the passage shifts from the beginning to the end. Because this is a general question, it should be done after the specific questions. The passage begins with the narrator's description of her family's *house-dwelling life* in a house built *across the road from a lake*. She continues with a description of the family's business running a *dance pavilion* with live music and dancing throughout the summer. In the third paragraph, the story focus changes when her father *moved his office into his car* and they drove around buying and selling antiques. The narrator describes her father's *lifelong wanderlust* and how he would suddenly decide it was time to go somewhere else. Eliminate any answer choices that are not consistent with this structure. Choice (A) can be eliminated because there is no *portrayal of a significant place the family often visited* in the passage. Choice (B) is consistent with the shift from her description of life in the summer house to life on the road. Choice (C) can be eliminated because the descriptions in the first part of the passage are concrete descriptions of the narrator's childhood rather than an *allegorical display of domesticity*. Choice (D) can be eliminated because the passage is not an examination of the narrator's childhood financial situation. The correct answer is (B).

2. **D** The question asks about the main purpose of the second paragraph. Carefully read the paragraph to determine the central focus. Throughout the paragraph, the narrator describes the dance pavilion her father ran during the summer. He *dreamed up such attractions as a living chess game* and *booked the big dance bands of the 1930s and 1940s*. She says that people would come from *as far away as Toledo or Detroit*, but that *paying the likes of Guy Lombardo or Duke Ellington...meant that one rainy weekend could wipe out a whole summer's profits*. This paragraph establishes the idea that the narrator's father is a man with big ideas who doesn't always play it safe. Eliminate any answer choices that aren't consistent with this idea. Choice (A) can be eliminated because there is no discussion of the father's *compulsive desire to travel* in this paragraph. Choice (B) can also be eliminated, because no one important to the *narrator's remembrances* is *introduced* in this paragraph. Choice (C) might initially look good, but the father is actually bringing in the famous acts rather than suffering *delusions of grandeur*, and while his decisions *could wipe out the summer's profits*, that's a risk that is being described rather than an actual negative outcome. Eliminate (C). Choice (D) is consistent with the prediction. The correct answer is (D).

3. **D** The question asks what the word *precarious* means in line 24. Go back to the text, find the word *precarious*, and mark it out. Carefully read the surrounding text to determine another word that would fit in the blank based on the context of the passage. The narrator describes the family's livelihood as *precarious* after saying that her father's business decisions could *wipe out a whole summer's profits*, which always gave them *a sense of gambling*. The word *precarious* describes their livelihood as "risky" or "a gamble." Eliminate anything that is not consistent with this prediction. Choices (A) and (B) can be eliminated because there is no mention of their family's financial situation in either answer. Choice (C) might be true in the life of the narrator, but the word *precarious* is used here to highlight the riskiness of the financial situation, so eliminate (C). Choice (D) is a clear paraphrase of the prediction. The correct answer is (D).

4. **A** The question asks about the narrator's participation in the *family business*. Use chronology to find the window that talks about the family business and read carefully. The narrator says that *from the age of four*, she *came into [her] own as the wrapper and unwrapper of china*. She goes on to say that each of the family members *had a role in the family economic unit*, including her older

sister, who *sold popcorn from a professional stand*. The correct answer should be consistent with the idea of the narrator having her own job within the family business from a young age. Choice (A) is consistent with this idea, so keep it. Choice (B) might be initially attractive, but there is no mention in the text of the time either sister spent doing her job. Choices (C) and (D) can be eliminated because there is no mention in the passage of money, getting paid, or volunteering. The correct answer is (A).

5. **D** The question asks which statement the narrator's father would most likely agree with. Notice that this is the first question in a paired set, so it can be done in tandem with Q6. Begin with the answers to Q6. The lines for (6A) say that there were only *a few months each year* when her father was *content with a house-dwelling life*. These lines support (5D), so draw a line connecting those two answer choices. The lines for (6B) say that her father loved the risks of the summer business. These lines do not support any of the answer choices for Q5, so eliminate (6B). The lines for (6C) say that everyone *had a role in the family economic unit* and then go on to explain her sister's role. These lines don't support any of the answers for Q5, so eliminate (6C). The lines for (6D) say that he *refused to put heating or hot water* in their house. Those lines might initially seem to support (5C), but read carefully. The father is not concerned about *the expense* of the water heater; he is concerned about the permanence of it. Eliminate (6D). Without support from Q6, (5A), (5B), and (5C) can all be eliminated. The correct answers are (5D) and (6A).

6. **A** (See explanation above.)

7. **C** The question asks what the word *struck* means in line 48. Go back to the text, find the word *struck*, and mark it out. Carefully read the surrounding text to determine another word that would fit in the blank based on the context of the passage. The narrator describes how her father is preparing to travel by *collecting road maps…, testing the trailer hitch…, and talking about faraway pleasures*. Then she says he announces it's time to go *as if struck by a sudden whim rather than a lifelong wanderlust*. The missing word must mean "suddenly decided" or "just realized." Eliminate anything that isn't consistent with this prediction. Choice (A), *battered*, is a definition of *struck*, but it doesn't mean "suddenly decided." Eliminate (A). Choice (B), *boycotted*, means "abstained from buying," which does not match the prediction. Eliminate (B). Choice (C), *inspired*, is consistent with the prediction, so keep it. Choice (D), *disturbed*, can be eliminated because it does not mean "suddenly decided" or "just realized." The correct answer is (C).

8. **B** The question asks why the father started the cross-country trip. Notice that it is the first question in a paired set, so it can be done in tandem with Q9. Begin with the answers to Q9. The lines for (9A) refer to the family's antiquing business, driving to *nearby country auctions* to search for antiques. There is no mention of the *cross-country trip*, so these lines do not support any of the answers for Q8. Eliminate (9A). The lines for (9B) describe the father's specific actions as he prepares for the trip, including *collecting road maps…, testing the trailer hitch…, and talking about faraway pleasures*. These lines provide details about the trip, but they do not give the *reason* the trip started. Eliminate (9B). The lines for (9C) refer to the father's *lifelong wanderlust* when he announces it's time to go. These lines support (8B), so draw a line connecting those two answers. The lines for (9D) describe the speed of the *leave-taking*, but do not offer a reason for it. Eliminate (9D). Without support from Q9, (8A), (8C), and (8D) can all be eliminated. The correct answers are (8B) and (9C).

9. **C** (See explanation above.)

10. **C** The question asks about the mother's role in the family. Carefully read the window where the mother is mentioned. She is first mentioned in line 28 when the narrator discusses the family antiquing business. She says that her mother had a *better eye for antiques and reference books* and

was the one who *appraised them for sale*. Then, in the last paragraph (lines 71–77), the narrator again mentions her mother as the one who remembered the iron was still on and *might be burning its way through the ironing board*. The correct answer should have something to do with the mother being reasonable and practical in the family. Choice (A) can be eliminated because there is no evidence that she *resented* her husband's *impulsive nature*. Choice (B) can also be eliminated because she goes along with her husband, but there is no evidence in the text that she *shared the… wanderlust equally*. Choice (C) is consistent with the prediction, so keep it. Choice (D) can be eliminated because, although she was worried about the iron, it did not actually set the house on fire. The correct answer is (C).

11.   **C**   The question asks about the primary purpose of the passage. Because it is a general question, it should be done after the specific questions have been completed. The passage begins by introducing the idea that liars and bluffers have *tells* that indicate when they aren't being truthful. The passage then expands this idea into a discussion about a pair of Stanford researchers who identified patterns that show up in reports with falsified data and could potentially be used to spot fraudulent papers. The passage ends with a warning that systems designed to detect fraudulent papers by simply counting words could have negative repercussions. The correct answer should be consistent with this prediction. Eliminate (A) because this passage is not *defend[ing]* anyone. Choice (B) can also be eliminated because the passage is focused on scientific publications, not *different industries and research fields*. Choice (C) is consistent with the prediction, so keep it. Eliminate (D) because the passage is about research into detecting fraud, not *reveal[ing] secrets* of those who successfully lie. The correct answer is (C).

12.   **A**   The question asks about the function of the first paragraph. Carefully read the paragraph to determine the author's reason for including the given information. The paragraph begins by mentioning how *poker players* have "tells" that give away *when they're bluffing*. The paragraph goes on to say that this idea of *tells* can also happen with *scientists* who *commit fraud* by attempting to *pass along falsified data*. The paragraph ends by saying *a pair of Stanford researchers* have *cracked the writing patterns* of the tells, which could help *identify falsified research* before it is published. The paragraph is there to provide context for research discussed later in the passage. Eliminate any answer choices that are not consistent with that prediction. Choice (A) is consistent with the prediction, as the paragraph introduces the concept of *tells*, which is what the later research is about. Keep (A). Choice (B) can be eliminated because there is no mention in the paragraph of *additional applications* of the research results. Choice (C) can be eliminated: although there is mention of *fraud detection*, the paragraph does not introduce *general methods* of fraud detection. Choice (D) can be eliminated because the idea is not *questioned* later in the passage, but expanded upon. The correct answer is (A).

13.   **A**   The question asks what the word *fair* means in line 10. Go back to the text, find the word *fair*, and mark it out. Carefully read the surrounding text to determine another word that would fit in the blank based on the context of the passage. The text says that there is a *fair amount of research* dedicated to understanding how liars lie. The text continues with a mention of the results of some of these studies. The missing word must mean something like "enough" or "plenty." Eliminate any answer choices that aren't consistent with that prediction. Choice (A), *ample*, is consistent with "plenty," so keep it. Choice (B), *lawful*, can be eliminated because there is no mention in the text about the legality of the evidence. Choice (C) can be eliminated because the amount of research is not compared to anything else, so it can't be *equal*. Choice (D) can be eliminated because the text focuses on the amount of research, not the quality of the research or whether the outcomes were positive or negative. The correct answer is (A).

14. **C** The question asks what the word *obscure* means in line 40. Go back to the text, find the word *obscure*, and mark it out. Carefully read the surrounding text to determine another word that would fit in the blank based on the context of the passage. The passage says that scientists who don't want to get caught *committing a misconduct* may *obscure parts of the paper*. The text also says that these same fraudsters may *muddle the truth*. Therefore, the missing word must mean something like "muddle" or "confuse." Eliminate anything that isn't consistent with this prediction. Choice (A) might initially look good because the scientists would want to *hide* the fact that they are lying. However, *hide* does not mean "muddle" or "confuse," and the scientists aren't actually hiding parts of their papers. Eliminate (A). Choice (B), *blind*, can be eliminated because the scientists are trying to make parts of their papers "confusing," not *blind[ing]*. Choice (C), *distort*, is consistent with "muddle" or "confuse," so keep it. Choice (D), *characterize*, is not consistent with the predictions at all. Eliminate (D). The correct answer is (C).

15. **B** The question asks how papers with fraudulent data can be spotted. Notice that this is the first question in a paired set, so it can be done in tandem with Q16. Begin with the answers to Q16 first. The lines for (16A) say that the [rating] was done through *summary score of causal terms, abstract language, jargon, positive emotion terms and…an ease of reading score*. These lines explain how the obfuscation index was determined, but there are no specifics about how to spot the papers that are fraudulent. These lines do not support any of the answers for Q15, so eliminate (16A). The lines for (16B) say that *fraudulent retracted papers scored significantly higher on the obfuscation index*. These lines indicate that a fraudulent paper will have a higher obfuscation index, which would mean more *abstract language and jargon*. These lines could support (15B), so draw a line connecting those two answers. The lines for (16C) say that a *fraudulent author* may use *fewer positive emotion terms*. While this could be a way to spot a fraudulent paper, these lines do not support any of the answer choices for Q15. Eliminate (16C). The lines for (16D) talk about a *computerized system* that might be able to *flag a submitted paper*. These lines don't give any specifics about how to spot the paper, so these lines don't support any of the answers for Q15. Eliminate (16D). Without support from Q16, eliminate (15A), (15C), and (15D). The correct answers are (15B) and (16B).

16. **B** (See explanation above.)

17. **D** The question asks which hypothetical situation Hancock would most likely agree could be a consequence of action without further research. Notice that this is the first question in a paired set. Although *Hancock* could be a good lead word, the whole passage is about his experiment, so his ideas are not in once place. Do this question in tandem with Q18. Begin with the answer choices for Q18. The lines for (18A) refer to avoiding getting caught publishing fraudulent data by *obscur[ing] parts of the paper*. These lines don't support any of the answers for Q17, so eliminate (18A). The lines for (18B) talk about the *publish or perish* mentality that motivates researchers to publish manipulated or fake findings. These lines do not support any of the answers for Q17, so eliminate (18B). The lines for (18C) warn of the *false-positive rate* of the computerized fraud-detection system. These lines might seem to connect to (17A) because both mention *computer programs*, but there is no connection between the ideas or to the question. Eliminate (18C). The lines for (18D) refer back to the *high error rate*, and also say that *science is based on trust* and if a publication introduces a *fraud detection tool*, it might *undermine that trust*. These lines support (17D), so draw a line connecting those two answers. Without support from Q18, (17A), (17B), and (17C) can all be eliminated. The correct answers are (17D) and (18D).

18. **D** (See explanation above.)

19.   **A**   The question asks which category of language had the greatest difference between the *language used in fraudulent research and* that used in *genuine research,* according to the graph. The difference between the two in Means and Methods is a little over 200, so keep (A) for now. The difference between them in Amplifiers is less than 100, so eliminate (B). Quantities has a difference of about 125, so eliminate (C). Emotional States has a difference of about 75, so eliminate (D). The correct answer is (A).

20.   **B**   The question asks which of the statements is supported by the graph. Go through each of the answer choices and eliminate anything not supported by the graph. Eliminate (A) because *Quantities* is higher in Genuine Publications rather than Fraudulent ones. Keep (B) because the bars for *Means and Methods* and *Certainty* are about the same for Fraudulent publications. Eliminate (C) because the Genuine publications have higher occurrences of *Negations* than the Fraudulent publications. Eliminate (D) because there is no consistency for *Amplifiers* and *Diminishers.* The correct answer is (B).

21.   **C**   The question asks which statement supports the idea that *jargon* could be classified as *means and methods,* using both the graph and the passage. Carefully read each answer choice and eliminate any that do not address the connection between *jargon* and *means and methods.* Choice (A) can be eliminated because it is only a general statement that scientists who falsify data have certain writing patterns they use. There is no specific connection to *jargon* or the graph. Choice (B) mentions a specific characteristic of the writing of liars in general, but there is no connection to the study discussed in the passage. Eliminate (B). Choice (C) says that the *fraudulent papers* had *60 more jargon-like words per paper.* The graph shows that fraudulent papers contain more *Means and Methods* language than genuine papers, so that could support the idea in question. Keep (C). Choice (D) simply says that *more research is needed,* with no specifics about types of language or types of papers. Eliminate (D). The correct answer is (C).

22.   **B**   The question asks about a main idea of the passage. Because this is a general question, it should be done after the specific questions have been completed. The passage begins with an introduction of a new, blue pigment, a *serendipitous discovery* made while *researching materials for electronics applications.* The passage then goes on to describe how the pigment was discovered, what makes the pigment particularly notable, and ends with a discussion of further discoveries that have resulted from the discovery of this pigment. Eliminate any answers that are inconsistent with the ideas in the passage. Choice (A) can be eliminated because there is no discussion of how the pigment is *dangerous.* Choice (B) is consistent with the idea of a *serendipitous discovery* of a *superior* new pigment. Choice (C) is consistent with the passage naming the new pigment by its chemical composition, but that is not the *main idea* of the passage, nor is there mention of the chemical composition being the *most effective* way to describe a pigment. Eliminate (C). Choice (D) can be eliminated because it is too narrow: the relationship between *UV absorbance* and *pigment stability* is mentioned in the passage, but it is not the *main idea.* The correct answer is (B).

23.   **A**   The question asks about the *overall structure of the passage.* Because this is a general question, it should be done after the specific questions have been completed. The passage begins with an introduction of a new pigment, goes on to describe how the pigment was discovered and what makes the pigment particularly notable, and then ends with a discussion of further discoveries that have resulted from the discovery of this pigment. Eliminate any answer choices that aren't consistent with this prediction. Choice (A) is similar to the prediction, so keep it. Choice (B) can be eliminated because the focus of the passage is the new, synthetic pigment. There is no *natural alternative* presented. Choice (C) can also be eliminated because only one accidental discovery is mentioned, rather than *several accidental discoveries.* Choice (D) can be eliminated because there is no discussion about how compounds *work together* in the passage. The correct answer is (A).

24. **C** The question asks what the word *applications* means in line 5. Go back to the text, find the word *applications*, and mark it out. Carefully read the surrounding text to determine another word that would fit in the blank based on the context of the passage. The text says that a scientist discovered the pigment while *researching materials for electronics applications*. It goes on to say that the researchers were trying to create a *high-efficiency electronic material*. The missing word must mean something like "functions" or "materials." Eliminate (A), *requests*, because it does not mean "functions." Choice (B), *forms*, can also be eliminated because it is not consistent with the prediction. Choice (C), *uses*, is consistent, so keep it. Choice (D), *industries*, might initially look attractive, but the text says that they were trying to develop *material* rather than "businesses." Eliminate (D). The correct answer is (C).

25. **B** The question asks for the best evidence that Smith did not intend for his experiment to produce the results it did. Carefully read each of the lines provided and eliminate any that do not answer the question. Choice (A) can be eliminated because the lines simply describe the pigment, not an experiment or results. Choice (B) answers the question, saying that *instead of…high-efficiency material, what emerged…was a brilliant blue compound*. Keep (B). Choice (C) can be eliminated because the patent process is not related to the discovery process. Choice (D) can also be eliminated because those lines indicate the researchers are continuing to research the accidental discovery, hoping to find additional new pigments. The correct answer is (B).

26. **A** The question asks what the word *unstable* means in line 21. Go back to the text, find the word *unstable*, and mark it out. Carefully read the surrounding text to determine another word that would fit in the blank based on the context of the passage. The text describes blue pigments as *notoriously unstable* and then goes on to say that they *fade easily*. The missing word must mean something like "fades easily" or "doesn't last." Eliminate any answer choices that are inconsistent with this prediction. Choice (A), *impermanent*, means "doesn't last." Keep (A). Choice (B) can be eliminated because the pigments are not *threatening*. Choice (C) can be eliminated because *careless* does not mean the same thing as "doesn't last." Choice (D) might initially look attractive because the passage does mention *ancient times*, but *antiquated* does not mean "doesn't last." Eliminate (D). The correct answer is (A).

27. **C** The question asks which factor has been identified as *most indicative of stable pigments*. In lines 22–25, the author says that the fact that *this pigment was synthesized at such high temperatures* signaled to researchers that *this new compound was extremely stable*. Therefore, synthesis at high temperatures indicates a stable compound. The correct answer is (C).

28. **D** The question asks about the relationship between the *YInMn Blue pigment and the Cobalt Blue pigment currently used*. The fifth paragraph, lines 33–37, discusses the relationship between the two pigments. The paragraph says that $YIn_{1-x}Mn_xO_3$ exhibits high absorbance in the UV region and high reflectivity in the near-infrared region when compared to currently-used Cobalt Blue pigments. Therefore, Cobalt Blue has *lower UV absorbency* and *lower reflectivity in the near-infrared region*. Eliminate any answer choices that aren't consistent with this prediction. Eliminate (A): although the text mentions *outdoor weathering*, YInMn is superior to Cobalt Blue for exterior applications. Choice (B) can be eliminated because, although *YInMn* can be *chemically-adjusted*, it was not *specifically engineered* to be so. Choice (C) can be eliminated because there is no discussion of the comparative difficulty of engineering purple, YInMn, or Cobalt Blue. Choice (D) is consistent with the prediction. The correct answer is (D).

29. **B** The question asks for the best evidence for the answer to the previous question, so simply look at the lines used to answer Q28: $YIn_{1-x}Mn_xO_3$ exhibits high absorbance in the UV region and high reflectivity in the near-infrared region when compared to currently-used Cobalt Blue pigments. This statement is in lines 34–37. The correct answer is (B).

30. **B**   The question asks at which wavelength $CoAl_2O_4$ has a reflectance of 0.4%. Go to Figure 2 and find the reflectance of 0.4. Draw a line across the graph and see which wavelengths correspond to that reflectance. There are several places where $CoAl_2O_4$ has a reflectance of 0.4%, but the only one that is an answer choice is 1800 nm. The correct answer is (B).

31. **D**   The question asks which range of wavelengths illustrates the thermal advantages of YInMn Blue over Cobalt Blue based on both the graph and the passage. The passage says that *high solar reflectance [of YInMn Blue] indicates that this 'cool pigment' can find use in a variety of exterior applications by reducing surface temperatures, cooling costs, and energy consumption.* Eliminate any answer choices that aren't consistent with this prediction. Choices (A), (B), and (C) all offer wavelength ranges in which the reflectance for YInMn Blue and Cobalt Blue are similar. This would not give YInMn Blue any thermal advantages, so eliminate all three. Choice (D), 1200–1400, gives a range in which the reflectance of YInMn Blue is much higher than Cobalt Blue, which, according to the passage, would give YInMn Blue an advantage. The correct answer is (D).

32. **B**   The question asks what the word *present* means in line 3. Go back to the text, find the word *present*, and mark it out. Carefully read the surrounding text to determine another word that would fit in the blank based on the context of the passage. The author says that he is trying to be clear about the *disordered condition of...currency and the present dangers*, while also trying to *suggest a way which leads to a safer financial system.* He is contrasting the current situation with what he hopes will be a better situation in the future. The missing word must mean something like "at this moment" or "at this time." Eliminate any answers that aren't consistent with that prediction. Choice (A), *prompt*, means that something happens right away, but not necessarily "at this time." Eliminate (A). Eliminate (C) for the same reason. Choice (B), *current*, is consistent with "at this time," so keep (B). Choice (D) can be eliminated because *present* and *gifted* might seem similar, but *gifted* does not mean "at this time." The correct answer is (B).

33. **B**   The question asks what Passage 1 suggests about those who support implementing the bimetallic system of currency. Notice that this is the first question in a paired set, so it can be done in tandem with Q34. Read the lines for Q34 first. The lines for (34A) say that *many countrymen... insist that the cure for the ills* is *the free coinage of silver.* These lines support (33B), so draw a line connecting those two answers. The lines for (34B) say that those who support the bimetallic system think *mints shall be...thrown open to the free, unlimited, and independent coinage of both gold and silver.* These lines don't support any of the answers to Q33, so eliminate (34B). The lines for (34C) say that those who believe *independent coinage...would restore the parity between the metals...oppose an unsupported and improbable theory.* While these lines do describe those who support the bimetallic system, these lines don't support any of the answers for Q33. Eliminate (34C). The lines for (34D) say that the ideas *run counter to our own actual experiences.* These lines give the author's feelings about the system, but not about those who support the system. The lines don't support any of the answers for Q33, so eliminate (34D). Without support from Q34, (33A), (33C), and (33D) can be eliminated. The correct answers are (33B) and (34A).

34. **A**   (See explanation above.)

35. **A**   The question asks why Cleveland refers to Acts of Congress, which is in line 50. Go back to the text and carefully read the window to determine why he mentions them. The line says that the Acts of Congress were *impotent to create equality where natural causes decreed even a slight inequality.* The correct answer must have something to do with the idea that the Acts of Congress could not create equality when outside forces set up an inequality. Choice (A) is a direct paraphrase of this prediction, so keep it. Choice (B) can be eliminated, because Cleveland mentions the acts to show a contrast, not to *summarize* anything. Choice (C) can be eliminated because the acts

would not be a viable *alternative* if they are *impotent to create equality*. Choice (D) can be eliminated for the same reason as (C). The correct answer is (A).

36. **C**   The question asks what the word *idle* means in line 66. Go back to the text, find the word *idle*, and mark it out. Carefully read the surrounding text to determine another word that would fit in the blank based on the context of the passage. The text contrasts the *idle holders of idle capital* with the *struggling masses who produce the wealth and pay the taxes*. Therefore, the missing word must mean something like "not working" or "not producing anything." Eliminate any answer choices that aren't consistent with that prediction. Choice (A) can be eliminated, because the holders of the capital have not *abandoned* anything. Choice (B) might initially make sense, because those who hold a great deal of money are likely to be *ambitious*, but *ambitious* does not mean "not producing anything." Eliminate (B). Choice (C), *inactive*, is consistent with "not working." Keep (C). Choice (D), *cheap*, is not consistent with the prediction, so it can be eliminated. The correct answer is (C).

37. **B**   The question asks which claim Bryan would most likely agree with about the gold standard controversy. Notice that this is the first question in a paired set, so it can be done in tandem with Q38. Begin with the answers to Q38 first. The lines for (38A) say that if the gold standard is the standard of civilization, *should we not have it?* Those lines could support (37A), so draw a line connecting those two answers. The lines for (38B) say that a person could *search the pages of history in vain to find a single instance in which the common people...declared themselves in favor of a gold standard*. Those lines support (37B), so draw a line connecting those two answer choices. The lines for (38C) say that *the sympathies of the Democratic Party...are on the side of the struggling masses*. These lines don't mention anything about Bryan's views about the gold standard controversy, and these lines don't support any of the answer choices for Q37. Eliminate (38C). The lines for (38D) say what others believe about legislation to make the *well-to-do prosperous*, but there is no mention of Bryan's thoughts about the gold standard controversy. Eliminate (38D). Go back to the remaining pairs of answer choices and reread the question. The question asks which statement *Bryan would be most likely to agree with*. Choices (37A) and (38A) present an idea that Bryan refutes later in the passage, so eliminate those two answer choices. The correct answers are (37B) and (38B).

38. **B**   (See explanation above.)

39. **D**   The question asks how both passages discuss the issue of the gold standard. Because this question asks about both passages, it should be done after the questions are done for each individual passage. Use POE to go through the answers one passage at a time. Passage 1 mentions *Acts of Congress* in line 50, *economists* in line 35, and *other nations* in line 34. Because Passage 1 does not mention *the Democratic Party*, eliminate (B). Now look for the remaining three answers in Passage 2. Passage 2 does not mention *Congress* or *economists*, so eliminate (A) and (B). Passage 2 mentions *all nations of the earth* in line 54. The correct answer is (D).

40. **A**   The question asks how the two historical references mentioned help each speaker. The reference in Passage 1 says that *twice in our earlier history* and the Passage 2 reference says that someone *said in 1878 that this was a struggle*. Both of these references show this debate occurring in the past, which allows both speakers to say something to the effect of, "We've been talking about this for a while now." Eliminate any answer choice that is not consistent with this prediction. Choice (A) is a direct paraphrase of the prediction, so keep it. Choice (B) can be eliminated because there is no *established precedent*, just an idea that's been discussed previously. Choices (C) and (D) can be eliminated because the lines neither *challenge* nor *question* any of the ideas in the debate. The correct answer is (A).

41. **B** The question asks about a *central tension* between the passages. Because this is a general question about both passages, it should be done after all the other questions have been completed. Use POE to go through the answers one passage at a time. Choice (A) can be eliminated because Cleveland is not advocating for *new legislation to enact the gold standard*. He is against the gold standard and says that *Acts of Congress were impotent to create equality* when the market said otherwise. Choice (B) looks good for Passage 1, because Cleveland is *questioning* the validity of the *free coinage bimetallic* proposal, so keep (B) for now. Choice (C) can be eliminated because Cleveland does not *demand gold standard proponents reconsider their position*. Choice (D) can be eliminated, because Cleveland never *presents studies*. The correct answer is (B).

42. **B** The question asks about the primary purpose of this passage. Because this is a general question, it should be done after the specific questions are complete. The passage begins with introducing the discovery of *a parasitic fungus* that manipulates *the behavior of ants*. The passage goes on to describe the research and the fungus. The primary purpose of the passage is to explain a new discovery. Eliminate any answers that aren't consistent with this prediction. Choice (A) can be eliminated because the passage was not written to *correct* any *misconception*. The first part of (B), *present the findings*, is consistent with the prediction, and the second part of the answer choice is supported by the final sentence of the passage (*The research also is…the first extensive study of zombie ants in North America*). Choice (C) can be eliminated because a new fungus has been discovered, not a new ant. Choice (D) can be eliminated because the passage does not explain differences between types of relationships. The correct answer is (B).

43. **B** The question asks why fungi have evolved to control the behavior of the ants. Go back to the text and find the window in which the author discusses how the fungi works. In the second paragraph, the author says that the fungus species that infects ants *induces hosts to die attached by their mandibles to plant material*. The author goes on to say that the dead ant attached to the plant provides *a platform from which the fungus can grow and shoot spores to infect other ants*. Find an answer that is consistent with this information. Choice (A) can be eliminated because the fungus spreads through spores, not through bite wounds. Choice (B) is consistent with the information in the text, so keep it. Choice (C) can be eliminated because the text says the fungus wants the ant to die attached to a plant. Choice (D) can be eliminated because it is the opposite of what the text says. The correct answer is (B).

44. **D** The question asks about the role of the *Formica* ant in the passage. Use the lead word to find the window and read carefully to determine why the author mentions the *Formica* ant. In line 37, the author mentions the *Formica* ant as *another genus* of ant not normally targeted by the fungus. Researchers infected the *Formica* ants as well as ants from the *Camponotus* genus, the genus typically targeted by the fungus. Eliminate any answer choices that aren't consistent with the prediction. Choice (A) can be eliminated because the scientists already know that the *Formica* ants are *nontarget ants*. Choice (B) can be eliminated for the same reason as (A): *Formica* ants aren't *most affected* because they are *nontarget ants*. Choice (C) can be eliminated because it doesn't address the role of the ant in the research. Choice (D) is consistent with the prediction. The correct answer is (D).

45. **D** The question asks what tone the author communicates with the use of phrases such as *exquisite control…, most complex examples…,* and *impressive trick*. Use the lines provided to find the window, and read carefully for context. The phrases come from a quote from one of the researchers talking about how evolved the fungus is. The use of the words *exquisite* and *impressive* gives a positive tone, so eliminate (B) and (C). There is no evidence that the researcher is *amused* by the fungus, but he is impressed. Eliminate (A). The correct answer is (D).

46. **D** The question asks about a scenario in which zombie ant fungi would not successfully reproduce. Carefully read the second paragraph, in which the fungus reproduction is explained. The fungus infects *Camponotus* ants and *induces [them] to die attached by their mandibles to plant material*. The dead ant, attached to the plant, provides *a platform from which the fungus can grow and shoot spores to infect other ants*. Because this is a *NOT* question, cross out the *NOT* and mark each answer choice as "true" or "false." Choice (A) is true. Although the fungus cannot control the *Formica* ant, it can infect and kill it. Keep (A). Choice (B) is true, so keep it. Choice (C) is true, so keep it. Choice (D) is false. A *Formica* ant that doesn't die on a plant will not provide any sort of platform for the fungus to grow from. The correct answer is (D).

47. **B** The question asks what the word *media* means in line 43. Go back to the text, find the word *media*, and mark it out. Carefully read the surrounding text to determine another word that would fit in the blank based on the context of the passage. The text describes the experiment and how the researchers *removed ant brains* and then kept them *alive in special media*. The missing word must mean something like "material" or "substance." Eliminate anything that is not consistent with this prediction. Choice (A), *communications*, might initially seem to be consistent with the word *media*, but it does not mean "substance" or "material." Eliminate (A). Choice (B) is consistent with the prediction, so keep it. Choice (C), *channels*, and (D), *periodicals*, may also be tempting because of the connection with *media*, but neither of those words is consistent with the prediction. The correct answer is (B).

48. **A** The question asks which part of the research was *most effective for obtaining an unprecedented amount of information*. The text says that the *researchers found thousands of unique chemicals, most of them completely unknown*. That is the *unprecedented information*, but remember that the question is asking about the *part of the research* that allowed them to obtain that information. Carefully read the window. The researchers were able to find out this information by growing the fungus *in the presence of brains from different ant species to determine what chemicals it produced for each brain* (lines 44–46). Eliminate any answer choice that is not consistent with this prediction. Choice (A) is an exact paraphrase of the prediction, so keep it. Choice (B) was a part of the process, but not the one that allowed them to obtain all the information. Eliminate it. Choice (C), as with (B), was a part of the research, but not the key piece. Eliminate (C). Choice (D) might initially look attractive, but the scientists weren't actually looking at the fungus *in the ant brains*. Eliminate (D). The correct answer is (A).

49. **B** Lines 44–46 were used to answer the previous question. The correct answer is (B).

50. **C** The question asks about a unique outcome of the chemicals produced by the fungus. Notice that this is the first question in a paired set, so it can be done in tandem with Q51. Consider the answer for Q51 first. The lines for (51A) introduce the fungus, but don't mention anything about the chemicals the fungus produces. Eliminate (51A). The lines for (51B) say that the killer *can infect and kill nontarget ants* but cannot *manipulate their behavior*. These lines do not support any of the answers for Q50. Eliminate (51B). The lines for (51C) say *the fungus behaved differently in the presence of the ant brain it had co-evolved with*. These lines could look attractive on their own, but they do not support any of the answers for Q50. Eliminate (51C). The lines for (51D) say that the fungus/ant relationship is *one of the most complex examples of parasites controlling animal behavior*. These lines support the idea in (50C) that the complexity of this relationship is different than those *usually found in nature*. Draw a line connecting those two answers. Without support from Q51, (50A), (50B), and (50D) can be eliminated. The correct answers are (50C) and (51D).

51. **D** (See explanation above.)

52.   **D**   The question asks what type of evidence the team mostly used while studying the zombie ants. Most of their work took place in the lab, so eliminate (A). Choice (B) can also be eliminated because researchers were making observations rather than *predictions*. Choice (C) might initially look attractive, but the researchers were using the brains of *ants* in their research. Choice (D) is consistent with information in the passage. The correct answer is (D).

Section 2: Writing and Language

1.   **C**   The vocabulary is changing in the answer choices, so this question is testing precision of word choice. Look for a word whose definition is consistent with the other ideas in the passage. The sentence discusses the *presence of blue recycling bins*, and the next sentence says that *most people are used to separating recyclable materials*. The underlined portion is preceded by *no longer*, so the definition should mean "out of the ordinary." An *innovation* is "a new way of doing something." While this is close, it is not the bins themselves that were an innovation, so eliminate (A). A *deviation* is "a departure from the norm." While this is close, the bins were not "going against the system," so eliminate (B). A *novelty* is "something new and unusual." The presence of the bins is now a normal, everyday sight, so keep (C). A *miracle* is "an extraordinary event," so eliminate (D). The correct answer is (C).

2.   **D**   Note the question! The question asks for the choice that *best maintains the style and tone of the passage*, so it tests consistency. Eliminate any answer choices that are inconsistent with the purpose stated in the question. The tone of the passage is somewhat formal, so eliminate any answer choices that are informal or slangy. *Kicking off*, *fixing to start*, and *getting in gear* are all too informal for the passage, so eliminate (A), (B), and (C). *Gaining traction* matches the tone of the passage. The correct answer is (D).

3.   **D**   The punctuation is changing in the answer choices, so the question tests how to connect ideas with the appropriate punctuation. Note that the sentence ends with a closed parenthesis. Therefore, the phrase must start with an open parenthesis; eliminate (B) and (C). There is no reason to use a dash to separate an idea already separated by parentheses, so eliminate (A). The correct answer is (D).

4.   **A**   Note the question! The question asks for information that is *consistent with the description of textiles*. *Clothing* is a type of textile, so keep (A). *Paper*, *rubber*, and *wood* are not textiles, so eliminate (B), (C), and (D). The correct answer is (A).

5.   **B**   Note the question! The question asks for information that is supported by the graph, so it tests consistency. Read the labels on the graph carefully, and look for an answer that is consistent with the information given in the graph. The sentence is comparing the recycling rate of clothing to that of the other items in the graph. First, look up clothing on the graph and find that its rate is about 15%. Then look up each choice to see whether it's true, keeping in mind that the underlined part follows the word *only*. The rate for rubber and leather is about 16%, which is higher than that of clothing, but many other materials are also recycled at higher rates than clothing. Since rubber and leather aren't the only ones with higher rates, eliminate (A). The rate for plastic is 5% and wood is 9%, which is lower than that of clothing, so keep (B). The rate for yard trimmings is 53%, which is higher than that of clothing. Again, it is not the only higher rate, so eliminate (C). The rate for glass is 30%, which is another rate higher than that of clothing, so eliminate (D). It is true that *only* plastics and wood are lower. The correct answer is (B).

6. **C** Transitions change in the answer choices, so the question is testing consistency of ideas. A transition must be consistent with the relationship between the ideas it connects. The sentence begins with *Not only*, which should be followed by *but also*. The correct answer is (C).

7. **A** Transitions change in the answer choices, so the question is testing consistency of ideas. A transition must be consistent with the relationship between the ideas it connects. The previous sentence says that *re-using clothing can also save resources*. The sentence that starts with the underlined transition says that *buying a pair of jeans second-hand saves that water*. The second sentence is similar in idea to the first, so eliminate (B) and (C) because they indicate a change of idea. *Moreover* indicates a new idea that is similar to the first, but the second sentence is a specific example of the general idea in the first sentence; eliminate (D). The correct answer is (A).

8. **D** Commas change in the answer choices, so this question tests comma usage. The sentence does not contain a list, and the phrase *clothing waste by offering 15%-off coupons to consumers who bring unwanted clothing* is a necessary part of the sentence. Therefore, there is no reason to use a comma; eliminate (A) and (C). Vocabulary also changes in the answer choices, so this question also tests precision of word choice. Look for a word with a definition that is consistent with the other ideas in the sentence. *Rain* means "water that falls from clouds;" *rein* means to "control." The correct answer is (D).

9. **B** Note the question! The question asks for the most effective transition from the previous paragraph, so it tests consistency. Determine the subject of each paragraph and find the answer that is consistent with the relationship between those ideas. The previous paragraph discusses H&M's desire to reduce clothing waste and the beginning of its plan to collect and recycle unwanted clothing. The paragraph that starts with the underlined portion discusses the specific steps taken to recycle the clothing. The correct answer will connect these two ideas. Introducing *other retailers* does not connect the ideas, so eliminate (A). Introducing the *several steps* of recycling does connect the ideas, so keep (B). Introducing *low-quality fast fashion* does not connect the ideas, so eliminate (C). Introducing *a bigger discount* does not connect the ideas, so eliminate (D). The correct answer is (B).

10. **B** The length of the phrase changes in the answer choices. The underlined portion is part of a list in the sentence, so this question tests consistency. All items in a list must be phrased the same way to be consistent with one another. The other items in the list are *shredded for use as insulation* and *recycled to make fabric for new clothing*. Each item starts with a past tense verb, so eliminate (A), (C), and (D) because they do not start with *repurposed*. The correct answer is (B).

11. **B** Verbs are changing in the answer choices, so the question is testing consistency of verbs. A verb must be consistent with its subject. The subject of the verb is *the technology*, which is singular. To be consistent, the verb in the answer choices must also be singular. Eliminate (A), (C), and (D) because they are plural. The correct answer is (B).

12. **D** Pronouns and apostrophes change in the answer choices, so this question tests consistency of pronouns and apostrophe usage. A pronoun must be consistent in number with the noun it refers to. The underlined pronoun refers to *the people*, which is plural. To be consistent, the underlined pronoun must also be plural. Eliminate (A) and (B) because *it* is singular. *They're* is a contraction of *they are*, which is not necessary in this sentence; eliminate (C). Choice (D) appropriately uses the possessive pronoun *their*. The correct answer is (D).

13. **C** Note the question! The question asks for the choice that combines the sentences, so it's testing precision and concision. Select the choice that keeps the intended meaning of the sentences using the fewest words. Consider (C) first because it's the shortest. The choice ends with *ofrendas*,

followed by a comma, and the non-underlined portion is a modifier that describes the *ofrendas*. This creates a sentence that is both precise and concise. Eliminate (B) and (D) because they both unnecessarily repeat the word *ofrendas*. Eliminate (A) because it is unclear what the phrase *in Spanish* refers to. The correct answer is (C).

14.   **A**   Commas are changing in the answer choices, so the question is testing comma usage. There is no need to break up the phrase *markets dedicated to the bright skeleton decorations* with a comma. Eliminate (B) and (C). The long dash cannot be followed by *and*, so eliminate (D). No punctuation is necessary. The correct answer is (A).

15.   **B**   Note the question! The question asks for the explanation of the Aztec tradition, so it's testing consistency. Eliminate any answer choices that are inconsistent with the purpose stated in the question. The first part of the sentence says that *the dead would be offended by mourning*. The correct answer must be consistent with a "tradition" that would not offend the dead. Eliminate (A) because it describes an emotion (*sad*) but not a tradition. Keep (B) because it describes a tradition of *celebration rather than sadness*. Eliminate (C) and (D) because neither knowing *whether an invisible spirit is offended* nor the fact that *the Aztec didn't want to disrespect the wishes of the dead* describes a tradition. The correct answer is (B).

16.   **A**   The length of the phrase changes in the answer choices. There is a comparison in the sentence, so this question tests consistency. When two things are compared, they should be consistent with each other. The sentence says that *ofrendas...have items*. Thus, the correct answer must be consistent with the "items" on *church altars*. The pronoun *those* could refer to the *items*, so keep (A). Choices (B) and (C) only mention the *altars* and not the *items* on the altars, so eliminate them both. Eliminate (D) because it mentions the *structures* and not the *items*. The correct answer is (A).

17.   **A**   Note the question! The question asks where sentence 3 should be placed, so it's testing consistency. The sentence must be consistent with the ideas that come both before and after it. Sentence 3 says *During these two days*, so it should be placed after a sentence that references two days. Sentence 2 discusses *November 1–2*, so sentence 3 should be placed after sentence 2. The correct answer is (A).

18.   **C**   The pronouns are changing in the answer choices, so the question is testing consistency of pronouns. The pronoun must be consistent with the noun it is referring to. The phrase *are best known for their elaborate ofrendas* refers to the *local artists*, so the pronoun should also refer to the artists. Eliminate (A) because *which* refers to things, and not people. The first part of the sentence, *Others are built by local artists*, is an independent clause. In (B), the second part of the sentence, *many are best known for their elaborate ofrendas*, is also an independent clause. A comma alone cannot be used between two independent clauses, so eliminate (B). Keep (C) because *whom* can refer to people, and the second part of the sentence is not an independent clause. Although *them* can refer to people, (D) makes the second part of the sentence an independent clause; eliminate (D). The correct answer is (C).

19.   **D**   Note the question! The question asks for information *that is most consistent in style and content with the information about why pillows and blankets are included on the altars*, so it's testing consistency. Eliminate any answer choices that are inconsistent with the purpose stated in the question. The sentence includes the phrase *pillows and blankets (which provide a resting spot for the spirits)*, which describes their function or use. *Smells delicious* describes a characteristic but not a function, so eliminate (A). *Pan de muerto* is an example but not a function, so eliminate (B). *Homemade* describes a characteristic but not a function, so eliminate (C). *Provide sustenance* describes a function, so keep (D). The correct answer is (D).

20. **B** Note the question! The question asks for the choice that best concludes the paragraph, so it's testing consistency of ideas. Determine the subject of the paragraph and find the answer that is consistent with that idea. The first sentence of the paragraph says that the celebration of the dead is *similar to preparing for a visit from living relatives.* The remaining sentences discuss the many items placed on the altars. Therefore, a concluding sentence should be consistent with each of those ideas. Claiming that it is *more work* would highlight how the situations are different, not similar; since it's not consistent, eliminate (A). Mentioning both what is *included on an altar* and the similarity to *when they were alive* is consistent, so keep (B). Mentioning the *toys* is consistent with the items on the altars but does not conclude the paragraph by discussing the similarities for *preparing for a visit from living relatives*; eliminate (C). Eliminate (D) for the same reason as (C). The correct answer is (B).

21. **A** The length of the phrase changes in the answer choices, so the question is testing precision and concision. Select the shortest answer with a precise meaning. Keep (A) because it is concise and makes the meaning of the sentence clear. The first sentence in the paragraph states that *Many of the same items that decorate altars are also part of the cemetery vigils,* so there's no need to repeat that idea. Eliminate (B) and (C) because they unnecessarily repeat the comparison between graves and altars. The phrase *that attract spirits with their bright colors* does not play a precise role in the sentence, so eliminate (D). The correct answer is (A).

22. **D** The subject of the phrase changes in the answer choices, so the question is testing precision. The beginning of the sentence (*focusing on the finality of death*) is a modifying phrase that does not have a subject. Therefore, the subject must be placed immediately after the comma. In (A) and (C), it is the *merriment* that is *focusing on the finality of death*; this is not the correct meaning, so eliminate (A) and (C). In (B), it is *life* that is *focusing on the finality of death*; this is not the correct meaning, so eliminate (B). In (D), it is *the people* who are *focusing on the finality of death*, which makes the meaning of the sentence precise. The correct answer is (D).

23. **A** Transitions change in the answer choices, so the question is testing consistency of ideas. A transition must be consistent with the relationship between the ideas it connects. The previous sentence states that the *predictions that the machines would replace human bank tellers...did not immediately come true.* The sentence that starts with the underlined transition states that *the number of human bank tellers also increased.* The second idea supports the first with evidence. *In fact* indicates support, so keep (A). *As a result* indicates an effect of a previous cause, so eliminate (B). *For example* is close, but the second sentence is not a specific example but rather general evidence; eliminate (C). *Therefore* indicates causality, so eliminate (D). The correct answer is (A).

24. **D** The punctuation is changing in the answer choices, so the question is testing how to connect ideas with the appropriate punctuation. There is a list in the sentence. The non-underlined portion of the list is separated by a comma: *provide specific bill denominations, and dispense information.* Therefore, all the items in the list must be separated by commas. Eliminate (A), (B), and (C) because they contain semicolons. The correct answer is (D).

25. **C** Note the question! The question asks for the choice that *best fits with the tone of the rest of passage,* so it tests consistency. Eliminate any answer choices that are inconsistent with the purpose stated in the question. The tone of the passage is somewhat formal, so eliminate any answer choices that are informal or slangy. *Rock solid* is too informal for the passage, so eliminate (A). The underlined word describes how machines handle cash. The word *safer* cannot be used to describe how a machine is *with cash,* so eliminate (D). *Impeccable* means "without fault," while *reliable* means "accurate." There is no discussion in the paragraph of fault or blame, so eliminate (B). Choice (C) is consistent with the paragraph. The correct answer is (C).

26. **D** Note the question! The question asks whether the graph should be added, so it's testing consistency of ideas. The graph should be added only if the information in the graph is consistent with the information in the passage. The passage compares and contrasts the services provided by human tellers and ATMs. The graph shows the income for different groups of people. The information is not consistent, so the graph should not be added; eliminate (A) and (B). The passage does not contrast *tellers and loan officers*, so eliminate (C). The wage data does *distract from the paragraph's focus*. The correct answer is (D).

27. **D** Note the question! The question asks where sentence 3 should be placed, so it's testing consistency. The sentence must be consistent with the ideas that come both before and after it. Sentence 3 says that *They also limit the amount of cash...*, which lists another downside of ATMs. Thus, sentence 3 should follow another sentence about the downside of ATMs. Sentence 5 gives a downside when it states *ATMs are far more vulnerable to theft*. The correct answer is (D).

28. **C** The vocabulary is changing in the answer choices, so the question is testing precision of word choice. *Custom* means "personalized" and *accustomed* means "familiar with" or "used to." *Accustomed* is the appropriate word in this context, so eliminate (A) and (D). Prepositions also change in the answer choices, so this question also tests idioms. The correct answer is (C).

29. **B** Note the question! The question asks for a supporting example for the main idea of the paragraph, so it's testing consistency. Eliminate any answer choices that are inconsistent with the purpose stated in the question. The paragraph as a whole compares and contrasts human tellers, ATMs, and mobile apps. The previous sentence says that *Apps are...beginning to improve upon some banking functions that had largely been taken over by ATMs*, so the underlined portion must be consistent with that idea. The percentage of people using the app is not consistent, so eliminate (A). Comparing the mobile apps to what *ATMs are capable of* is consistent, so keep (B). Stating that mobile apps are *not always designed well* and stating that they are *highly susceptible to theft or fraud* is not consistent with the apps outperforming ATMs, so eliminate (C) and (D). The correct answer is (B).

30. **A** Note the question! The question asks for the most effective combination of the two sentences, so it's testing precision and concision. Select the shortest answer that makes the meaning of the sentence precise. Choice (A) is the shortest answer, and it gives the sentence a precise meaning. Eliminate (C) because it inappropriately connects two independent clauses with a comma. The additional words in (B) and (D) do not make the meaning of the sentence more precise, so eliminate (B) and (D). The correct answer is (A).

31. **D** Nouns change from singular to plural in the answer choices, so this question tests consistency of nouns. A noun must be consistent in number with the other nouns or pronouns in the sentence. The sentence contains the noun *teller windows*, which is plural. To be consistent, the underlined noun must also be plural. Eliminate (A) and (B) because they contain the singular noun *kiosk*. Next, the adjoining phrase is changing, so the question is testing precision of language. The proper idiom is *replacing...with*, so the banks are *replacing* teller windows *with* kiosks; eliminate (C). The correct answer is (D).

32. **B** The length of the phrase changes in the answer choices, so this question tests concision. The non-underlined portion of the sentence states that *employees are...trained to answer questions*. Eliminate (A) because it unnecessarily repeats *trained*, and eliminate (C) because it repeats *answer questions*. The phrase *in addition* means the same thing as *and*, so there is no reason to use both terms; eliminate (D). Choice (B) is concise and gives the sentence a precise meaning. The correct answer is (B).

33.　**A**　Punctuation changes in the answer choices, so this question tests how to connect ideas with the appropriate punctuation. The first part of the sentence, *So while the old-fashioned notion of a bank teller may be on the way out*, is not an independent clause. The second part of the sentence, *machines are not yet close to replacing human bank employees altogether*, is an independent clause. Periods and semicolons can only be used between two independent clauses, so eliminate (B) and (C). The sentence starts with the contrasting transition *while*, so there is no reason to also use *nevertheless*; eliminate (D). Choice (A) is concise and appropriately uses a comma to connect the two parts of the sentence. The correct answer is (A).

34.　**A**　Transitions change in the answer choices, so the question is testing consistency of ideas. A transition must be consistent with the relationship between the ideas it connects. The first sentence states that there is *an arms race against bacteria*. Then it says that *Bacteria…develop resistance to antibiotics* and follows with *scientists must continually develop newer, stronger antibiotics*. The second is an effect of the first. *As a result* indicates an effect, so keep (A). *However* and *nevertheless* indicate opposite ideas, so eliminate (B) and (C). Developing new antibiotics is not an *example* of bacterial resistance, so eliminate (D). The correct answer is (A).

35.　**C**　Note the question! The question asks for the *scientists' goal*, so it's testing consistency. Eliminate any answer choices that are inconsistent with the purpose stated in the question. Earlier in the paragraph it says that *scientists have been engaged in an arms race against bacteria* and that they need to *overcome the resistant bacteria*, so the correct answer must be consistent with "outcompete." *Count the number* is not consistent, so eliminate (A). *Facilitate* means "to help," which is not consistent, so eliminate (B). *Stay ahead of* is consistent, so keep (C). *Shoot at* is too literal of the arms race and is not consistent with "outcompete," so eliminate (D). The correct answer is (C).

36.　**D**　The length of the phrase changes in the answer choices, so this question tests consistency. There is also the option to DELETE; consider this choice carefully, as it is often correct. The sentence already says *extended trips*, so there's no reason to repeat that idea. Eliminate (A), (B), and (C) because they all repeat the idea of *extended trips*. Choice (D) is concise and gives the sentence a precise meaning. The correct answer is (D).

37.　**A**　Verbs are changing in the answer choices, so the question is testing consistency of verbs. A verb must be consistent with its subject and with the other verbs in the sentence. The subject of the verb is *pathogens*, which is plural. To be consistent, the underlined verbs must also be plural. *Becomes* is singular, so eliminate (C) and (D). The non-underlined verb in the phrase *were surprised* is past tense, so the correct answer should also be in the past tense. *Mutated* and *became* are past tense, so keep (A). *Had mutated* and *had become* are the past perfect tense, but the non-underlined verb does not contain *had*. Eliminate (B) because it's not consistent with the sentence. The correct answer is (A).

38.　**C**　The order of the phrases is changing in the answer choices, so the question is testing precision. Note that the underlined portion is followed by a descriptive phrase set off by parentheses. The descriptive phrase must be adjacent to the thing it describes. The parenthetical phrase, *the friction between cells and the fluids they interact with*, cannot describe a *reduction*, so eliminate (A). It also does not accurately describe *microgravity*, so eliminate (B). The phrase could accurately describe *fluid shear stress*, so keep (C). The phrase cannot describe *fluid*, so eliminate (D). The correct answer is (C).

39.　**B**　Note the question! It asks whether a phrase should be added, so it's testing consistency and concision. The phrase should be added only if the information is consistent with the information in the passage and makes the meaning of the sentence more precise. The first part of the sentence states how scientists believe microgravity will affect *bacteria inside the human body*. The new phrase says that studying this allows for *a glimpse into how that pathogen behaves in the human digestive tract*. The idea is consistent with the sentence, so it should be added. Eliminate (C) and (D). Eliminate (A) because the new phrase does not *make it clear that researchers cannot actually see inside the human digestive tract*. Choice (B) accurately states that the new phrase *further explains the benefits of conducting bacteria studies in space*. The correct answer is (B).

40. **C** Note the question! It asks for *the most precise description of the proceeding depicted in the first part of the sentence*, so it's testing precision of word choice. The first part of the sentence discusses the *studies*, so the correct answer should match that idea. *Subject* could mean "ideas" or "participants." Neither matches *studies*, so eliminate (A). *Examinations* means "inspections," so eliminate (B). *Experiments* means "studies" or "acts of discovery," so keep (C). *Tests* means "methods to assess," so eliminate (D). The correct answer is (C).

41. **B** Verbs are changing in the answer choices, so the question is testing consistency of verbs. A verb must be consistent with its subject and with the other verbs in the sentence. The subject of the verb is *they*, which is plural. Since all the answers are plural, check the other verbs. The other verbs in the sentence are *are looking* and *attack*, which are present tense. Choices (A), (C), and (D) are past tense, so eliminate them. The correct answer is (B).

42. **B** Commas are changing in the answer choices, so the question is testing comma usage. There is no need to break up the phrase *one of the leading causes of food-borne illness in the United States*, so eliminate (A), (C), and (D). No commas are necessary. The correct answer is (B).

43. **A** Note the question! The question asks for the most effective transition, so it's testing consistency of ideas. Determine how the ideas before and after the sentence relate to each other and select the appropriate transition. The previous sentences discuss the need for *developing a vaccine for* Salmonella. The following sentences discuss using Salmonella *as a delivery vehicle* for another vaccine. The correct transition will shift from needing a vaccine to cure *Salmonella* to using *Salmonella* as a vaccine to cure some other illness. Salmonella...*playing an important role in vaccine research...in an unexpected way* connects the two ideas, so keep (A). Stating that a *vaccine hasn't yet been developed* does not connect to the second part, so eliminate (B). Wanting to *develop better vaccines against...other* illnesses connects to the second part, but doesn't mention *Salmonella*, so eliminate (C). *Studies...beyond the International Space Station* do not connect the ideas, so eliminate (D). The correct answer is (A).

44. **B** Commas are changing in the answer choices, so the question is testing comma usage. The sentence does not contain a list, so check for unnecessary information. The phrase *substances that stimulate the production of antibodies* gives a definition of *antigens*. The phrase is not necessary to the main meaning of the sentence and should be set off by commas. Eliminate (D) because it lacks commas altogether. Eliminate (A) because it only sets off the word *substances*, which incorrectly makes the phrase *that stimulate the production of antibodies* describe *antigens*. Eliminate (C) because it incorrectly includes the phrase *to multiple body parts* in the unnecessary phrase. Choice (B) correctly sets off the unnecessary phrase with commas. The correct answer is (B).

Section 3: Math (No Calculator)

1. **C** The question asks for an equation that represents a graph. To find the best equation, compare features of the graph to the answer choices. The graph for this question has a y-intercept of 7 and a negative slope. Eliminate answer choices that do not match this information. All the choices are already in $y = mx + b$ form, in which m is the slope and b is the y-intercept. Choices (A) and (B) have y-intercepts of 0; eliminate (A) and (B). The difference between (C) and (D) is the slope, so calculate slope using the formula $slope = \frac{y_2 - y_1}{x_2 - x_1}$. The graph goes through the points (0, 7) and (7, 0), so $slope = \frac{0-7}{7-0}$, which is $\frac{-7}{7}$ or –1. Eliminate (D). The correct answer is (C).

2. **D** The question asks for an equation in terms of a specific variable. To begin to isolate B, start by multiplying both sides by 5 to get $2A + B + 2C = 5D$. Next, subtract $2A$ and $2C$ from both sides to get $B = 5D - 2A - 2C$. The correct answer is (D).

3. **A** The question asks for the value of a. To begin to isolate a, combine like terms on both sides of the equation to get $2a - 9 = 7a - 4$. Next, subtract $2a$ from both sides to get $-9 = 5a - 4$. Add 4 to both sides to get $-5 = 5a$. Divide both sides to get $-1 = a$. The correct answer is (A).

4. **D** The question asks for the value of a variable in a system of inequalities. There are variables in the answer choices, so try out some values for them. Find a value of y that works in the first equation, such as $y = 2$. Plug this in to the second inequality to get $x < 3(2) + 4$, which is $x < 10$. Use this inequality to find a value for x. Make $x = 9$. Next, plug in this value for x into each answer choice and eliminate any choice that is not true when $x = 9$. Choice (A) becomes $9 < \frac{7}{3}$. This is false; eliminate (A). Choice (B) becomes $9 < 3$; eliminate (B). Choice (C) becomes $9 < \frac{19}{3}$; eliminate (C). Choice (D) becomes $9 < 11$; keep (D). The correct answer is (D).

5. **B** The question asks for the value of an angle on a figure. Start by labeling the figure with the given information. Because O is the center of the circle, BO and CO are both radii, so $BO = CO$, and triangle BOC is an isosceles triangle. Therefore, angle CBO is also equal to 36°; mark this in the figure. The angles in a triangle add up to 180°, so the third angle in the triangle with angles 28° and 36° must equal $180 - 28 - 36 = 116°$. Label this angle in the diagram:

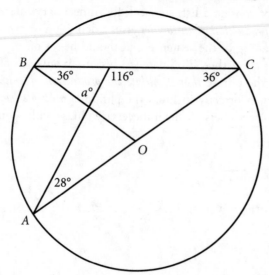

A straight angle has 180°, so the angle adjacent to the 116° angle must be 180 − 116 = 64°; label this in the diagram. Finally, the triangle containing the angle with measure $a°$ has 180°, so a must be 180 − 36 − 64 = 80°. The correct answer is (B).

6. **C** The question asks for the perimeter of the traffic island. Start by drawing an isosceles triangle. Next, label the figure. Because there are variables for the side lengths, pick a value for s. Make $s = 6$. Label the two equal sides as having a length of 6. The third side is *4 meters shorter than the equal sides*, so the third side must be 6 − 4 = 2 meters. Label that side. The perimeter is the sum of the sides: 6 + 6 + 2 = 14. This is the target value; circle it. Next, make $s = 6$ in each answer and eliminate any answer that does not equal the target value. Choice (A) becomes 2(6) − 4, which is 12 − 4 or 8. This does not equal the target value; eliminate (A). Choice (B) becomes $\frac{(6)^2 - 4(6)}{2}$, which is $\frac{36 - 24}{2}$ or $\frac{12}{2}$, which is 6. Eliminate (B). Choice (C) becomes 3(6) − 4, which is 18 − 4 or 14. Keep (C), but check (D) just in case. Choice (D) becomes $\frac{6-4}{2}$, which is $\frac{2}{2}$ or 1. Eliminate (D). The correct answer is (C).

7. **D** The question asks for the equation of a circle given the endpoints of the diameter. The equation of a circle in standard form is $(x − h)^2 + (y − k)^2 = r^2$, where (h, k) is the center and r is the radius. Since the endpoints have the same x-coordinate, the length of the diameter is the difference in the y-coordinates. Therefore, the diameter is 7 − 1 = 6, and the radius is 3. This means that $r^2 = 9$. Eliminate (B) and (C), which have $r^2 = 36$. Be careful of sign changes with the coordinates of the center of the circle. In this circle equation, h is −11, so the first part of the equation is $[x − (−11)]^2$, or $(x + 11)^2$. Eliminate (A). The correct answer is (D).

8. **C** The question asks for the solution set of the equation. Rather than doing complicated algebraic manipulations, try out the numbers in the answers. Begin by labeling the answers as a and start with (B). If $a = 1$, the equation becomes $1 − 6 = \sqrt{8(1) − 7} − 4$, which is $−5 = \sqrt{1} − 4$ or $−5 = −3$. This is false; eliminate (B) and (D) because both answers include 1. There must be a positive number or 0 under the square root; eliminate (A) because if $a = 0$, there would be a negative number under the radical. Only one choice remains, but test it to be sure. If $a = 11$, then the equation becomes $11 − 6 = \sqrt{8(11) − 7} − 4$, which is $5 = \sqrt{81} − 4$ or $5 = 9 − 4$. This is true. The correct answer is (C).

9. **A** The question asks for an equivalent form of an expression when one function is divided by another. Rather than doing complicated algebraic manipulations, pick a number to use in the functions. Make $a = 5$. The first function becomes $h(5) = 5^2 + 5 − 20 = 25 + 5 − 20 = 10$. The second function becomes $k(5) = 5^3 − 16(5) = 125 − 80 = 45$. The question asks for $\frac{h(a)}{k(a)}$, so plug these values in to get $\frac{10}{45}$. This is the target value; circle it. Now plug $a = 5$ into the answer choices to see which one matches the target value. Choice (A) becomes $\frac{5 + 5}{5(5 + 4)} = \frac{10}{5(9)} = \frac{10}{45}$. This matches the target, so keep (A) but check the remaining answers just in case. Choice (B)

becomes $\dfrac{5+5}{5(5-4)} = \dfrac{10}{5(1)} = \dfrac{10}{5}$. Eliminate (B). Choice (C) becomes $\dfrac{5+5}{5+4} = \dfrac{10}{9}$. Eliminate (C). Choice (D) becomes $5 + 5 = 10$. Eliminate (D). The correct answer is (A).

10. **C** The question asks for an equation that represents a graph. One option would be to pick a point that is on the graph and plug it into the answer choices to see which ones are true. The answers are all in factored form, however, which shows the roots or solutions of a function. If $(x - a)$ is a factor of a polynomial, then a is a solution, and the graph will cross the x-axis at a. This graph crosses the x-axis at -2, 0, and 1, so the factors must include $(x + 2)$, x, and $(x - 1)$. Eliminate (B) and (D) because they do not contain these factors. Compare the remaining answers, (A) and (C). They have the same factors, so plugging in the points will result in true statements for both. Instead, pick an x-value that is not a root, such as $x = -1$. The exact y-value is not clear, but it must be positive. Choice (A) becomes $y = -(-1)(-1 - 1)(-1 + 2)$ or $y = 1(-2)(1)$. This becomes $y = -2$, which does not match the graph. Eliminate (A). The correct answer is (C).

11. **A** The question asks for the value of an expression given an equation. Because the question includes a relationship between the variables without providing actual values, select values to use. Start by plugging in for y and solving for x in the first equation. Make $y = 2$. The equation becomes $\dfrac{x}{3(2)} = 3$, which is $\dfrac{x}{6} = 3$. Multiply both sides by 6 to get $x = 18$. Next, plug $y = 2$ and $x = 18$ into $\dfrac{y}{x}$ to get $\dfrac{2}{18}$, which is $\dfrac{1}{9}$. The correct answer is (A).

12. **B** The question asks for the number of jars that hold 3 tomatoes. Rather than creating a system of equations, use the numbers in the answer choices. Begin by labeling the answers as "jars with 3 tomatoes" and start with (B), 52. If 52 jars hold 3 tomatoes each, then these jars hold a total of $52 \times 3 = 156$ tomatoes. Because there are 80 jars, there are $80 - 52 = 28$ jars that hold 5 tomatoes each, for a total of $28 \times 5 = 140$ tomatoes in these jars. This gives a total of $156 + 140 = 296$ tomatoes, which matches the value given in the question, so stop here. The correct answer is (B).

13. **A** The question asks for the value of a function. In function notation, the number inside the parentheses is the x-value that goes into the function, and the value that comes out of the function is the y-value. Plug $x = 0$ into the f function to get $f(0) = 2 - [g(0)]^2$. Now plug $x = 0$ into the g function to get $g(0) = 3(0) - 3 = 0 - 3 = -3$. Plug this value into the f function for $g(0)$ to get $f(0) = 2 - [-3]^2 = 2 - (9) = -7$. The correct answer is (A).

14. **B** The question asks for an equation that models a specific situation. Translate the question one piece at a time and eliminate after each piece. One piece of information says that the population of Bulgaria is decreasing. This will translate to a negative slope, so eliminate (C) and (D), which have positive slopes. Compare the remaining answers. The difference between (A) and (B) is the slope, so calculate slope using the formula $slope = \dfrac{y_2 - y_1}{x_2 - x_1}$. The question states that the population was *approximately 9 million people in 1989* and *7.4 million people in 2011*. Because x is *years after the year 1989* and $P(x)$ is in *millions of people*, the points are $(0, 9)$ and $(22, 7.4)$. Use the slope formula to get $slope = \dfrac{7.4 - 9}{22 - 0}$, which is $-\dfrac{1.6}{22}$. Both answers have slopes with a denominator of 220, so multiply by $\dfrac{10}{10}$ to get a slope of $-\dfrac{16}{220}$. The correct answer is (B).

15. **B** The question asks for the value of k in the system of equations. Rather than doing complicated algebraic manipulation, use the numbers in the answer choices. With two equations, it may be hard to tell if a value that doesn't work is too big or too small, so start with any of the answers. Since 0 is an easy number to work with, start with (B). If $k = 0$, the first equation becomes $y = x^2 + 2x + 0$ or $y = x^2 + 2x$. The second equation states that $y = 2x$, so the right sides of the two equations can be set equal to get $2x = x^2 + 2x$. Subtract $2x$ from both sides to get $x^2 = 0$. Take the square root of both sides to get $x = 0$. There is only one solution when $k = 0$. The correct answer is (B).

16. **17** The question asks for the sum of y and z, which are two of the coefficients in the expression $xa^2 + ya + z$. This expression comes from subtracting the first polynomial $(a^2 + 2a + 4)$ from the second polynomial $(3a^2 - 4a + 27)$, so the resulting expression is $(3a^2 - 4a + 27) - (a^2 + 2a + 4)$. Work one piece at a time. It is unnecessary to know what x is to solve the question, so ignore the a^2 terms. Subtracting the a terms gives $-4a - 2a = -6a$, so $y = -6$. Subtracting the constants gives $27 - 4 = 23$, so $z = 23$. Therefore, $y + z = -6 + 23$, which is 17. The correct answer is 17.

17. **6** The question asks for the positive solution of a quadratic. When given a quadratic in standard form, which is $ax^2 + bx + c$, it is often necessary to factor it to solve the question. Find two numbers that add to -1 and multiply to -30. These are -6 and 5. Therefore, the equation factors to $(n - 6)(n + 5) = 0$. Set each factor equal to 0 and solve to find the solutions. If $n - 6 = 0$, then $n = 6$. If $n + 5 = 0$, then $n = -5$. The question asks for the positive solution, so $n = 6$. The correct answer is 6.

18. **3** The question asks for the value of a variable in the context of a model. In the form $y = mx + b$, m is the slope and b is the y-intercept. Therefore, this question asks for the slope of the equation, so calculate slope using the formula $slope = \dfrac{y_2 - y_1}{x_2 - x_1}$. The question states that *at the start of the month she has completed 12 assignments* and x is *the number of weeks since the start of the month*, so when $x = 0$, $y = 12$. Additionally, the question states that *she completes 3 assignments per week*, so when $x = 1$, $y = 12 + 3$, or 15. Therefore, two points are $(0, 12)$ and $(1, 15)$. The slope formula gives $slope = \dfrac{15 - 12}{1 - 0}$, which is $\dfrac{3}{1}$ or 3. The correct answer is 3.

19. **22** The question asks for the area of a sector of the circle. The parts of a circle have a proportional relationship, so the fraction of the degrees in the shaded region is the same as the fraction of the sector area out of the total area. Set up the proportion $\dfrac{\text{degrees}}{360} = \dfrac{\text{sector area}}{\text{total area}}$, then plug in the given information to get $\dfrac{110}{360} = \dfrac{\text{sector area}}{72}$. Since calculator use is not allowed, reduce the fraction on the left to $\dfrac{11}{36}$ before cross-multiplying to get $11(72) = 36(\text{sector area})$. Rather than doing the awkward multiplication on the left, divide both sides by 36 first to get $11(2) = \text{sector area}$. Therefore, the shaded region has an area of 22. The correct answer is 22.

20. $\dfrac{14}{8}$, $\dfrac{7}{4}$, or **1.75**

The question asks for the value of a variable given a system of equations. Try to make the other variable disappear. Because the unwanted variable has the same coefficient in both equations, multiply the second equation by -1 to get opposite signs on the y terms. The second equation becomes $-x - 2y = -3.75$, then stack and add the equations.

$$\begin{aligned} 9x + 2y &= 17.75 \\ -x - 2y &= -3.75 \\ \hline 8x \qquad\;\; &= 14 \end{aligned}$$

Divide both sides by 8 to get $x = \dfrac{14}{8}$. Since this answer fits in the grid, there is no need to reduce. The correct answer is $\dfrac{14}{8}$, $\dfrac{7}{4}$, or 1.75.

Section 4: Math (Calculator)

1. **B** The question asks for the year when the number of tenants in the building increased the fastest. Use Ballparking and estimation to eliminate incorrect answers. The graph represents the total number of tenants on the y-axis and years on the x-axis. For the number of tenants to increase the fastest, the line should have a great positive slope. In 2005 and 2007, the slope is negative; eliminate (A) and (C). In 2006, the slope of the line is steeper than in 2009; eliminate (D). The correct answer is (B).

2. **D** The question asks about population based on information about a study of a sample from that population. Since the residents were randomly selected, the incidence of the gene mutation found in the study should match that of the larger population. To extrapolate the study results, set up a proportion. In this case, the proportion is based on the number of mutations out of the total of each group: $\dfrac{4}{500} = \dfrac{x}{15,000}$. Cross-multiply to get $500x = 60,000$. Divide both sides by 500 to get $x = 120$. The correct answer is (D).

3. **C** The question asks for an algebraic expression to represent a situation. Rather than creating an algebraic equation, pick a number for n. Make $n = 2$. If each box of cookies costs \$2, then 4 boxes of cookies will cost \$2 × 4 = \$8. This is the target value; circle it. Now plug $n = 2$ into the answer choices to see which one matches the target value. Choice (A) becomes $\dfrac{2}{4}$, which reduces to $\dfrac{1}{2}$. This does not match the target, so eliminate (A). Choice (B) becomes $\dfrac{4}{2}$, which reduces to 2. Eliminate (B). Choice (C) becomes $4(2) = 8$. Keep (C), but check (D) just in case. Choice (D) becomes $2 + 4 = 6$. Eliminate (D). The correct answer is (C).

4. **A** The question asks for the value of an angle on a figure. Start by labeling the figure with the given information. Mark lines l_1 and l_2 as parallel and the angle marked $a°$ as 110. It may not be immediately obvious how to get the value of b, so see what else can be determined. There are 180° in a triangle, so the angle to the right of a is $180 - 110 - 30 = 40°$. When two parallel lines like l_1 and l_2 are cut by a third line, like the one to the right of the 40° angle and the angle marked

$b°$, two kinds of angles are created: big and small. All small angles are equal, and both of these angles are small angles. Therefore, $b = 40$. The correct answer is (A).

5. **B**   The question asks for a system of equations that models a specific situation. Translate the question one piece at a time and eliminate after each piece. One piece of information says that the total number of digital and paper subscriptions was 1,800, so one of the equations must be $d + p = 1,800$. Eliminate (C), which does not contain this equation. Compare the remaining answer choices. All are equal to 20,760, which is the total revenue from the sale of subscriptions. Find the other information related to money. Digital subscriptions cost $8, so $8d$ must be part of the equation. This does not appear in (A), so eliminate it. The revenue from the digital subscriptions must be added to the revenue from the paper subscriptions to get the total revenue, but (D) multiplies the values. Eliminate (D). The correct answer is (B).

6. **A**   The question asks for the predicted value given a graph. This specific value will be based on the line of best fit, but the maximum heart rate of a 60-year-old runner is not on the graph. Use either the equation or the graph of the line of best fit to determine the value. In the equation, the x-value is the age and the y-value is the heart rate. The equation becomes $y = -0.84(60) + 216.9$ or $y = -50.4 + 216.9 = 166.5$. To use the graph instead, continue the line of best fit off the right side of the graph a bit, then estimate where an age of 60 years would fall along the horizontal axis. From this point, trace up to find the intersection with the line of best fit, using the answer sheet as a straight edge if necessary. It is between the horizontal gridlines for 160 and 170 on the maximum heart rate axis. Only the value in (A) falls between 160 and 170. The correct answer is (A).

7. **C**   The question asks for the value of $c - 2$ in the given equation. Rather than doing algebraic manipulation, use the numbers in the answer choices. Begin by labeling the answers as "$c - 2$" and start with (B), 3. If $c - 2 = 3$, then the equation becomes $\frac{3}{3} = 3$ or $1 = 3$. This is not true, so eliminate (B). A smaller value of $c - 2$ is needed to make the two sides of the equation closer to the same value, so try (C) next. If $c - 2 = \sqrt{3}$, the equation becomes $\frac{3}{\sqrt{3}} = \sqrt{3}$. Multiply both sides by $\sqrt{3}$ to get $3 = \sqrt{3} \times \sqrt{3}$ or $3 = 3$. This is true. The correct answer is (C).

8. **B**   The question asks for an equation with a y-intercept of -1. To find the equation, look for the y-intercept in each answer choice. Each answer choice is already in slope-intercept form: $y = mx + b$, where m represents the slope and b represents the y-intercept. Therefore, the correct answer must have a b term of -1. Choices (A), (C), and (D) have y-intercepts of $-\frac{1}{2}$, 0, and 1, respectively; eliminate them. The correct answer is (B).

9. **D**   The question asks for a system of inequalities that models a specific situation. Translate the question one piece at a time and eliminate after each piece. One piece of information says that Sarah purchases *more than 360 items*. The items she purchases are canvases (a) and paint bottles (b), so one inequality must be $a + b > 360$. Eliminate (B) and (C) because they do not contain this inequality. Compare the remaining answer choices. The difference between (A) and (D) is which way the inequality sign is pointing. The question states that Sarah *goes over-budget*, so she spent more than $1,700. The expression on the left is therefore greater than the cost. This does not fit (A), so eliminate it. The correct answer is (D).

10. **C**   The question asks for the number of beakers needed to hold 4 liters of solution. The note after the question indicates that 1 liter is equivalent to 1,000 milliliters. Therefore, 4 liters is equivalent to 4(1,000) = 4,000 milliliters. Divide this by the amount each beaker can hold, which is 800 milliliters, to get 4,000 ÷ 800 = 5. The correct answer is (C).

11. **A**   The question asks for the radius of the beaker, in inches. Rather than doing algebraic manipulation, use the numbers in the answer choices. Begin by labeling the answers as "radius" and start with (B), 2.28 inches. If $n = 2.28$, the volume becomes $\dfrac{21\pi(2.28)^3}{12} \approx \dfrac{21\pi(11.85)}{12} \approx \dfrac{782}{12} \approx 65$ cubic inches. The question states that the volume of 800 milliliters is 13.2 cubic inches, so this is much too large. Eliminate (B), (C), and (D). The correct answer is (A).

12. **A**   The question asks for the graph that models a specific situation. To find the best graph, read the question carefully and compare features of the graphs in the answer choices, then use Process of Elimination. The question states that the beaker was full of a solution which then evaporated over time. Therefore, the height of the solution in the beaker must be decreasing. Choice (C) shows a constant height over time. Eliminate (C). Choice (D) shows a linear decrease over time. Although the solution evaporates at a constant rate, the odd shape of the beaker would make the height of the solution change in a non-linear way. Eliminate (D). Since the beaker is narrower at the top, the height of the solution will decrease quickly at first then more slowly near the wide base of the beaker. Eliminate (B), which shows the height decreasing more quickly near the end of the evaporation period. The correct answer is (A).

13. **A**   The question asks for the power rating of a machine given that power is work per unit time. Set up the power equation: $power = \dfrac{work}{time}$. Now find the information about work and time. Work is defined as *the product of the mass of the object, in kilograms; the distance the object moves, in meters; and the gravitational constant of 9.8 meters per second squared*. Put this into the power formula to get $power = \dfrac{(mass)(distance)\left(9.8\,\frac{m}{s^2}\right)}{time}$. The time is given as 18 seconds, the mass as 100 kilograms, and the distance as 3.6 meters. Plug these values into the formula to get $\dfrac{(100\text{ kg})(3.6\text{ m})\left(9.8\,\frac{m}{s^2}\right)}{18\text{ s}}$ $= \dfrac{3,528}{18} = 196$. The correct answer is (A).

14. **B**   The question asks for one variable in terms of another. Rather than doing algebraic manipulation, pick a number for x. Make $x = 2$. This is the target value; circle it. Use this to find the value of y: $y = \dfrac{1}{2^3} = \dfrac{1}{8}$. Now plug $y = \dfrac{1}{8}$ into the answer choices to see which one matches the target value. Use a calculator if needed to find the values. Choice (A) becomes $\left(\dfrac{1}{8}\right)^{\frac{1}{3}} = \sqrt[3]{\dfrac{1}{8}} = \dfrac{1}{2}$. This does not match the target value, so eliminate (A). A negative exponent flips the base to its reciprocal, so (B) becomes $\left(\dfrac{1}{8}\right)^{-\frac{1}{3}} = (8)^{\frac{1}{3}} = \sqrt[3]{8} = 2$. Keep (B), but check the remaining answer choices

just in case. Choice (C) becomes $-\left(\dfrac{1}{8}\right)^3 = -\left(\dfrac{1}{512}\right)$, and (D) becomes $\left(\dfrac{1}{8}\right)^3 = \left(\dfrac{1}{512}\right)$. Eliminate (C) and (D). The correct answer is (B).

15. **C** The question asks for the value of x that is not in the domain of $f(x)$, which is a value of x that does not work in the equation. Rather than doing algebraic manipulation, use the numbers in the answer choices. Begin by labeling the answers as x and start with (B), 0. If $x = 0$, the function becomes $f(0) = \dfrac{5}{0^2 - 5(0) + 4}$, which is $\dfrac{5}{4}$. This is a value for $f(x)$ that works, so $x = 0$ is in the domain of $f(x)$; eliminate (B). It can be tricky to determine whether a larger or smaller number is needed when working with quadratics, so just pick a direction. Try (C). If $x = 1$, the function becomes $f(1) = \dfrac{5}{1^2 - 5(1) + 4}$, which is $\dfrac{5}{1-5+4}$ or $\dfrac{5}{0}$. This is undefined, so $x = 1$ must not be in the domain of $f(x)$. The correct answer is (C).

16. **B** The question asks about the mean, median, and mode of a set of data. For averages, use the formula $T = AN$, in which T is the total, A is the average, and N is the number of things. The number of things is 24, since the farmer took the total for each of the 24 chickens for the week. To find the total, take each number of eggs times the frequency for that number, then add all the results together. The total is $8(1) + 7(3) + 6(8) + 5(5) + 4(2) + 2(5) = 8 + 21 + 48 + 25 + 8 + 10 = 120$. Therefore, the formula becomes $120 = A(24)$, and $A = 5$. The median of a list of numbers is the middle number when all values are arranged in order. In lists with an even number of items, the median is the average of the middle two numbers. There are 24 chickens, so the median number of eggs will be the average of the eggs laid by the 12th and 13th chickens. The number of eggs are already listed in order, so start counting from the 1st chicken, which laid 8 eggs. The 2nd, 3rd, and 4th chickens laid 7 eggs each. The next 8 chickens, the 5th through the 12th, laid 6 eggs and the 13th chicken laid 5 eggs. Therefore, the median number of eggs is $\dfrac{6+5}{2} = 5.5$. This is greater than the mean, so eliminate (A) and (D). Now find the mode, which is the most common number in a set of data. In this set, the number of eggs with the highest frequency is 6, so the mode is 6. This is also greater than the mean, so eliminate (C). The correct answer is (B).

17. **B** The question asks for a certain value on a graph. *Hours* are listed along the horizontal axis, so find 12 on that axis. From this point, trace up to find the intersection with the line of best fit, using the answer sheet as a straight edge if necessary. It is between the horizontal gridlines for 70% and 80% on the *Job Satisfaction* axis. Only the value in (B) falls between 70% and 80%. The correct answer is (B).

18. **A** The question asks for a proportion, which is defined as $\dfrac{\text{part}}{\text{whole}}$. Read the table carefully to find the numbers to make the proportion. There were 250 participants who watched the new ad, so that is the *whole*. Of these participants, 120 had a favorable opinion, so that is the *part*. Therefore, the proportion is $\dfrac{120}{250} = \dfrac{12}{25}$. The correct answer is (A).

19. **B**   The question asks for a percent decrease based on data. Percent change is defined as $\dfrac{\text{difference}}{\text{original}} \times 100$.

Set it up, then find the numbers on the table. The question asks *for the percent decrease...from January. 1st, 2010, to January 1st, 2011*. The graph lists time as *Months since January 1st, 2008*. There are two years or 24 months from January 1st, 2008 to January 1st, 2010, so the crime rate for January 1st, 2010 is at 24 months on the horizontal axis. From this point, trace up to find the intersection with the line of best fit, using the answer sheet as a straight edge if necessary. It is at a crime rate of 1,000. There is one more year, or an additional 12 months, between January 1st, 2010 and January 1st, 2011, so the crime rate for January 1st, 2011 is at 36 months on the vertical axis. This intersects the line of best fit at a crime rate of 800. Therefore, the percent decrease is $\dfrac{1,000 - 800}{1,000} \times 100 =$ $\dfrac{200}{1,000} \times 100 = 0.2 \times 100 = 20\%$. The correct answer is (B).

20. **C**   The question asks for the meaning of a coefficient in context. Start by reading the full question, which asks for the meaning of the number 16.8. Then label the parts of the equation with the information given. The question states that y is the violent crime rate in the city and x is the number of months since the crime prevention program began. The number 16.8 is multiplied by months and subtracted from 1,412, so it must have something to do with the decrease in the crime rate over time. Next, use Process of Elimination to get rid of answer choices that are not consistent with the labels. Choice (A) refers to the number of months, but x represents time in the equation, so eliminate (A). Choice (B) refers to the average crime rate, but y represents the crime rate in the equation, so eliminate (B) also. Choice (C) refers to a *reduction* in the crime rate over time, so keep (C). Choice (D) refers to the exact crime rate in 2008, when the program began. To check this, plug in $x = 0$. The equation becomes $y = 1,412 - 16.8(0) = 1,412 - 0 = 1,412$. Therefore, the crime rate at the start of the program in January 2008 was 1,412. Eliminate (D). The correct answer is (C).

21. **A**   The question asks for an inequality that models a specific situation. Translate the question one piece at a time and eliminate after each piece. One piece of information says that Samuel's salary will increase from $49,500 to $64,500 once he completes the MBA program. Therefore, the *additional income* each year will be (64,500 − 49,500), so eliminate (C) and (D), which do not include this term. Compare the remaining answer choices. The difference between (A) and (B) is the direction of the inequality symbol. The question states that the *total additional income* should *exceed the cost of tuition*. Therefore, the additional income per year times the number of years will be greater than the tuition. This translates to $(64,500 - 49,500)n > 73,320$. The answer choices isolate n, so divide both sides by $(64,500 - 49,500)$ to get $n > \dfrac{73,320}{(64,500 - 49,500)}$. The correct answer is (A).

22. **C**   The question asks for the graph of a function given a description of that function. The *zeros* of a polynomial are the points where it crosses the x-axis, or where $y = 0$. Therefore, the graph of this polynomial will contain the points $(-4, 0)$ and $(2, 0)$. Look at the graphs and eliminate any that do not include these points. Choice (A) has zeros at $(-4, 0)$, $(-1, 0)$, and $(2, 0)$. Choice (A) also has a third zero not mentioned in the question, so check the remaining answers. Choice (B) has zeros at $(-4, 0)$ and $(2, 0)$. Keep (B) as well. Choice (C) has zeros at $(-4, 0)$ and $(2, 0)$. Keep (C) as well. Choice (D) has zeros at $(-2, 0)$ and $(4, 0)$. Eliminate (D). The question also states that the graph should only contain values for y that are greater than or equal to -3. Choices (A) and (B) contain values of y less than -3. Eliminate (A) and (B). The correct answer is (C).

23. **C** The question asks for a statement that is supported based on the results of a poll that was conducted. Read each answer carefully and use Process of Elimination. Choice (A) refers to high voter turn-out on Election Day. It is impossible to know whether additional voters will be for or against the proposition, since only one poll was conducted. Furthermore, no information is given regarding the number of people polled or how they were selected. The poll sample may be too small or too biased to draw conclusions about the larger population. Eliminate (A). Choice (B) refers to the ages of voters. No information was given about the ages of the poll participants, so no conclusion can be drawn about voters based on age. Eliminate (B). Choice (C) refers to the method in which the poll participants were reached. This applies directly to the poll, so it could contain a reasonable conclusion. The percent of participants contacted by cell phone who supported the proposition was 30%, whereas 55% of all participants contacted by landline supported it. Since the percent is higher for landline participants, (C) is true. Keep it, but check (D) just in case. Choice (D) refers to only the landline users, but it has the same problem as (A) in that no information is given to determine if these participants make up a representative sample. Eliminate (D). The correct answer is (C).

24. **D** The question asks for an equation that models a specific situation. There are variables in the answer choices, so plug in. Make $n = 14$ days in the original equation, so $x = 2$ weeks in the answer choices. The original equation becomes $w = 109(1.12)^{14} \approx 109(4.887) \approx 532.7$. This is the target value; circle it. Now plug $x = 2$ into the answer choices to see which one matches the target value. Choice (A) becomes $w = 109(2.21)^{\frac{2}{7}} \approx 109(1.254) \approx 137$. This does not match the target, so eliminate (A). Choice (B) becomes $w = 109(1.12)^{\frac{2}{7}}$, which will be even smaller than (A). Eliminate (B). Choice (C) becomes $w = 109(1.84)^2 = 109(3.3856) \approx 369$. Eliminate (C). Choice (D) becomes $w = 109(1.12)^{7(2)} \approx 109(4.887) \approx 532.7$. The correct answer is (D).

25. **D** The question asks for a true statement regarding the results of a study that was conducted. Read each answer carefully and use Process of Elimination. Choice (A) refers to the size of the sample. Generally, the larger the sample, the more reliable the study results. No numbers are given regarding the sample size or number of residents, so this is difficult to determine. Keep (A) for now, but check the other answers. Choice (B) refers to the days that the study was conducted. While doing the study two days instead of one would improve the results, there is no way to tell if that will make the result completely reliable. Keep (B) but see if there is a better answer. Choice (C) refers to the location of the study. A busier location may help get more respondents, but it is unclear if that will make the study reliable. Eliminate (C). Choice (D) refers to bias in the study, which means that the group involved might be more inclined to a certain outcome. Since the study only involved people entering the library, the results are likely to favor library use more than if randomly selected people had participated. Since exact numbers were not given, the sample size is less of a problem than the bias in the sample. Eliminate (A). The correct answer is (D).

26. **A** The question asks for the value of d in point (c, d). Start by determining the value of c in terms of d. The question states that $\dfrac{c}{d} = \dfrac{3}{2}$. Cross-multiply to get $2c = 3d$. Divide both sides by 2 to get $c = \dfrac{3d}{2}$.

Next, use the given information to determine the equation of the lines. Use slope-intercept form: $y = mx + b$, where (x, y) is a point on the line, m is the slope, and b is the y-intercept. The first line contains point (c, d) and has a slope of 2, so its equation is $d = 2c + b$. Substitute $\dfrac{3d}{2}$ for c to get $d = 2\left(\dfrac{3d}{2}\right) + b$, which becomes $d = 3d + b$ or $-2d = b$. The second line contains the point $(3, 2d)$, has a slope of –3, and the same y-intercept as the first equation, so its equation is $2d = -3(3) + b$, or $2d = -9 + b$. Substitute $-2d$ for b to get $2d = -9 - 2d$. Add $2d$ to both sides to get $4d = -9$. Divide both sides by 4 to get $d = -\dfrac{9}{4}$. The correct answer is (A).

27. **C** The question asks for the relationship between two variables. When given a table of values and asked for the correct equation, plug values from the table into the answer choices to see which one works. In the answers, n is *years after 2010*. Therefore, according to the table, $n = 3$ when the unemployment rate was 13%. Choice (A) becomes $1.5(3) + 11.5$, which is $4.5 + 11.5$, or 16. This does not match the unemployment rate; eliminate (A). Choice (B) becomes $0.5(3 - 2,010) + 11.5$, which is $0.5(-2,007) + 11.5$ or $-1,003.5 + 11.5$, which is -992. Eliminate (B). Choice (C) becomes $0.5(3) + 11.5$, which is $1.5 + 11.5$, or 13. Keep (C), but check (D) just in case. Choice (D) becomes $-1.5(3) + 11.5$, which is $-4.5 + 11.5$, or 7. Eliminate (D). The correct answer is (C).

28. **A** The question asks for the model that best fits the data. The question states that water is added *at a constant rate*. Therefore, the rate of increase is linear rather than exponential. Eliminate (C) and (D), which are equations for exponential growth. Next, find a value from the data to plug in to the remaining answers. The pool *contains 60% more water after the hose has run for 5 hours*. The pool initially contained 750 gallons, so after 5 hours it contains $750 + 750 \times \dfrac{60}{100} = 1,200$ gallons. Therefore, when $t = 5$, the answer should equal 1,200. Choice (A) becomes $750 + 90(5)$, which is $750 + 450$ or 1,200. This is true, so the correct answer is (A).

29. **D** The question asks for the value of a function. In function notation, the number inside the parentheses is the x-value that goes into the function, and the value that comes out of the function is the y-value. The vertex of the graph of function h is at $(-1, -3)$, so $a = -1$ and $h(a) = h(-1) = -3$. Substitute to get $f(h(a)) = f(-3)$. Use the table to determine that $f(-3) = 11$. The correct answer is (D).

30. **B** The question asks for a true statement based on the data. Consider each answer and use Process of Elimination. Choice (A) compares the ranges of Group A and Group B. The range of a list of values is the greatest value minus the least value. In Group A, the greatest value is 9 and the least value is 3, so the range is $9 - 3$, which is 6. In Group B, the greatest value is 13 and the least value is 8, so the range is $13 - 8 = 5$. Eliminate (A), which says the range of Group B is larger. Also eliminate (D), which says the ranges are equal. Choices (B) and (C) compare the standard deviation of the two groups. Standard deviation is a measure of how close together the data points are in a group of numbers; a list with numbers close together has a small standard deviation, whereas a list with numbers spread out has a large standard deviation. In Group A, the data points are evenly distributed, whereas in Group B most of the data points are around 12. Therefore, the standard deviation of Group B must be less than the standard deviation of Group A. Eliminate (C). The correct answer is (B).

31. **14** The question asks for the value of n if the two equations represent the same line. Make the second equation equal to the first by multiplying the second equation by 2 to get $14x - 8y = 18$. Both equations are equal, so n must equal 14. The correct answer is 14.

32. **66** The question asks for a measurement and gives conflicting units. When dealing with unit conversion, make a proportion, being sure to match up units. The proportion is $\dfrac{1 \text{ liter}}{3 \text{ milligrams}} = \dfrac{22 \text{ liters}}{x \text{ milligrams}}$. Cross-multiply to get $x = 66$. The correct answer is 66.

33. **9**   The question asks for the value of c in the equation. Start by substituting -3 for x to get $\frac{1}{3}c + (-3) = 0$. Add 3 to both sides of the equation to get $\frac{1}{3}c = 3$. Multiply both sides by 3 to get $c = 9$. The correct answer is 9.

34. **6**   The question asks for the value of a variable in a system of equations. Since $p(x) = q(x)$ where the two functions intersect, one way to solve this would be to graph both functions on a graphing calculator and trace to find the intersections. Another method is to solve algebraically by setting the equations equal to one another. This gives $15 - 5x = \frac{1}{3}(x - 9)^2 - 18$. Add 18 to both sides to get $33 - 5x = \frac{1}{3}(x - 9)^2$. Clear the fraction by multiplying both sides by 3 to get $99 - 15x = (x - 9)^2$. Use FOIL (First, Outer, Inner, Last) on the right side to get $99 - 15x = x^2 - 9x - 9x + 81$, which is $99 - 15x = x^2 - 18x + 81$. Add $15x$ to both sides to get $99 = x^2 - 3x + 81$. Subtract 99 from both sides to get $0 = x^2 - 3x - 18$. Factor by finding two numbers that add to -3 and multiply to -18. Those numbers are -6 and 3, so the equation becomes $0 = (x - 6)(x + 3)$. Set each factor equal to 0 and solve to get $x - 6 = 0$ or $x = 6$ and $x + 3 = 0$ or $x = -3$. The question asks for the positive x-value. The correct answer is 6.

35. **0.6**   The question asks for the value of the sum of two trigonometric functions. The functions of sine and cosine usually apply to right angles and give the ratio of the side opposite or adjacent to the angle, respectively, to the hypotenuse. This question has a right angle, but the angles in question are not the other two angles of triangle ABC. The angles $\angle DBA$ and $\angle DBC$ add together to make the right angle, so use the fact that $\sin(x°) = \cos(90° - x°)$. If $\angle DBC$ is $x°$, then $\angle DBA$ is $(90° - x°)$ and $\sin(\angle DBC) = \cos(\angle DBA) = 0.3$. Therefore, $\cos(\angle DBA) + \sin(\angle DBC) = 0.3 + 0.3 = 0.6$. The correct answer is 0.6.

36. **0.11**   The question asks for a rate in terms of points per minute. Begin by reading the question to find information on the average number of points lost. The question states that *during two days of trading, the Dow Jones Industrial Average lost 68.9 points* and that *there were 5 hours of trading during each of the two days combined*. Therefore, there were $2 \times 5 = 10$ hours of trading. There are 60 minutes in an hour, so 10 hours is $60 \times 10 = 600$ minutes. To determine rate, divide amount by time: $\frac{68.9 \text{ points}}{600 \text{ minutes}} \approx 0.1148$ points per minute. The question asks for the rate to the nearest hundredth of a point per minute, so round to 0.11. The correct answer is 0.11.

37. **1.3**   The question asks for the value of r in the function. Use the table to fill in the other variables and solve. Choose a point that makes the math easier. Because the exponent is divided by 2 in the function, choose 2 days. At 2 days after germination, the plants weighed 6.6 grams, so $d = 2$ and $H(2) = 6.6$. The function becomes $6.6 = 5.0r^{\frac{2}{2}}$, which is $6.6 = 5.0r^1$ or $6.6 = 5.0r$. Divide both sides by 5.0 to get $r = 1.32$. The question asks for the value of r rounded to the nearest tenth, so round 1.32 to 1.3. The correct answer is 1.3.

38. **9.6** The question asks for the difference between the masses of two groups of plants. Start by determining the mass of the 4 plants that germinated 4 days ago. According to the table, plants that germinated 4 days ago have a mass of 8.4 grams per plant, so 4 plants would have a mass of $4 \times 8.4 = 33.6$ grams. Next, find the mass of the 3 plants that germinated 8 days ago. These plants have an average mass of 14.4 grams, so their total mass is $3 \times 14.4 = 43.2$ grams. To find the difference, subtract: $43.2 - 33.6 = 9.6$ grams. The correct answer is 9.6.

Section 5: Experimental

1. **A** Note the question! The question asks whether the phrase should be added, so it's testing consistency of ideas and precision. If the phrase is consistent with the first part of the sentence and it plays a precise role, then it should be added. The first part of the sentence states that the Orbiter crashed on Mars. The new phrase states that it should have gone *into orbit around the planet to collect and transmit data*. This explains what the Orbiter's mission was supposed to be, so it's consistent and plays a precise role. The phrase should be added, so eliminate (C) and (D). The phrase does *give details that clarify that the crash was unexpected*, so keep (A). The phrase does not *establish an important shift in focus*, so eliminate (B). The correct answer is (A).

2. **A** The change in the answer choices is from a noun to different pronouns, so the question is testing precision. Determine the subject of the pronoun, and choose an answer that makes the meaning consistent and precise. The underlined portion must establish who is *against adopting the metric system*. At this point in the passage, no specific party has been established, so the most precise answer will be the specific noun, not the general pronoun. *People* is a specific noun, so keep (A). *They, them,* and *those* are general pronouns, so eliminate (B), (C), and (D). The correct answer is (A).

3. **C** Verbs are changing in the answer choices, so the question is testing consistency of verbs. A verb must be consistent with its subject and with the other verbs in the sentence. All the answer choices are consistent with the subject of the verb, *the other group*, so look for other verbs. The first part of the sentence states that *one group used*, so the underlined portion must be consistent with that verb. Only *used* is consistent. Eliminate (A), (B), and (D). The correct answer is (C).

4. **D** Note the question! The question asks where sentence 2 should be placed, so it's testing consistency. Determine the subject matter of the sentence, and find the other sentence that also discusses that information. Sentence 2 states that *neither group realized*, so it should be placed after the sentence that mentions the two groups. Only sentence 5 mentions *one group* and *the other group*, so sentence 2 should be placed after sentence 5. The correct answer is (D).

5. **B** Note the question! The question asks for the best combination, so it's testing concision. Select the shortest choice that eliminates the redundancy present in the original sentences. Evaluate (B) first because it's the shortest. The pronoun *which* refers to the *replacement of Roman numerals with the base-ten Arabic numbering* in the first part of the sentence. Because *which* replaces that same phrase in the second part of the sentence, the redundancy has been eliminated and the answer is concise. The correct answer is (B).

6. **B** The number and placement of the commas is changing in the answer choices, so the question is testing comma usage. The commas are changing in two places (and there's a dash), so check for unnecessary information. Because *decimal* and *base-ten* mean the same thing, it is unnecessary to say it twice. Therefore, there should be either commas or dashes before and after the phrase *or base-ten*. The comma and the dash cannot be used together, so eliminate (D). Eliminate (A) and (C) because the commas are in the wrong place. The correct answer is (B).

7. **D** The number and placement of the commas is changing in the answer choices, so the question is testing comma usage. The sentence does not contain a list, so check for unnecessary information. Removing any of the phrases between the commas creates an incomplete sentence. Therefore, all the phrases are necessary, and there is no reason to use a comma. The correct answer is (D).

8. **C** Note the question! The question asks for the explanation of how the metric system was important for trade over long distances, so it's testing consistency of ideas. Select the choice that is consistent with *important for trade over long distances. Cheating* is not consistent with *long distances*, so eliminate (A). Although (B) mentions *long-distance, different currencies* is not consistent with the *metric system*; eliminate (B). The *buyers and sellers* not being *from the same place* is consistent with *trade over long distances*, so keep (C). The type of *goods* is not consistent, so eliminate (D). The correct answer is (C).

9. **C** First, the pronouns are changing in the answer choices, so the question is testing consistency. The pronoun must be consistent in number with the noun it is replacing. The noun is *France*, which is singular. Thus, the pronoun must also be singular. Eliminate (A) and (B), which are plural. Next, the verbs are changing, so the question is testing consistency. A verb must be consistent with its subject and with the other verbs in the sentence. The sentence states that *France was*, which is the simple past tense. Thus, the underlined portion must also be in the simple past tense. *Organized* is the simple past tense, so keep (C). *Had organized* includes the unnecessary helping verb *had*, so eliminate (D). The correct answer is (C).

10. **C** Note the question! The question asks for the choice that maintains the style and tone of the passage, so it's testing consistency. The overall tone of the passage is semi-formal and educational, so the correct answer should be consistent with this tone. Choices (A), (B), and (D) are too informal. The correct answer is (C).

11. **A** The transition phrase is changing in the answer choices, so the question is testing consistency of ideas. The sentence contains two phrases separated by a comma, so evaluate those two ideas to determine how they should be connected. The first part states that *the American colonies were part of the British Empire*, and the second part states that *they used the British Imperial System of measurement*. These ideas are similar, so eliminate (B) and (D) because they indicate opposite ideas. Using *therefore* would create two complete ideas separated by a comma. GO punctuation cannot separate two complete ideas, so eliminate (C). The correct answer is (A).

12. **D** The vocabulary is changing in the answer choices, so this question is testing word choice. Look for a word whose definition is consistent with the other ideas in the sentence. The sentence is trying to state that both Jefferson and Franklin were proponents of "getting rid of" the British system, so the correct answer must be consistent with this idea. *Sacrificing* means "to kill or destroy something as an offering," so eliminate (A). *Ducking* means "to get out of the way of something," so eliminate (B). *Evading* means "to avoid something," so eliminate (C). *Abandoning* means to "give something up" or to "leave something behind." This is consistent with the rest of the sentence. The correct answer is (D).

13. **D** The transition phrase is changing in the answer choices, so the question is testing consistency of ideas. Evaluate the ideas that come before and after the transition to determine how they should be connected. The prior idea is that both Jefferson and Franklin were proponents of adopting the metric system. The next idea is that there were *insurmountable roadblocks to adopting the metric system*. These are opposite ideas, so a transition that changes direction is needed. *For example, moreover*, and *thus* all indicate the same direction, so eliminate (A), (B), and (C). *However* indicates a change in direction. The correct answer is (D).

14. **B** The punctuation is changing in the answer choices, so the question is testing STOP and GO punctuation. Use the vertical line test, and identify the ideas as complete or incomplete. Draw the vertical line between the words *War* and *it*. The first phrase is an incomplete idea, and the second phrase is a complete idea. STOP punctuation can only come between two complete ideas, so eliminate (A) and (C), which both contain STOP punctuation. HALF-STOP punctuation must come after a complete idea, so eliminate the colon in (D). A comma is GO punctuation, which can separate an incomplete idea from a complete idea. The correct answer is (B).

15. **B** The vocabulary is changing in the answer choices, so the question is testing word choice. The correct choice will match the idea of *sending a delegation to France* to the purpose of the trip. The purpose was not *by learn* or *of learn*, so eliminate (C) and (D). If the word *for* is used, the phrase should say *for learning*, so eliminate (A). The purpose was *to learn about the metric system*. The correct answer is (B).

16. **A** Note the question! The question asks for the best introduction to this paragraph, so it's testing consistency of ideas. The previous paragraph ends by stating that the United States kept the British system. This paragraph discusses a few times that the United States tried and failed to convert to the metric system. The correct answer will be consistent with this idea. *Multiple attempts...to establish the metric system* is consistent, so keep (A). Discussing *France* is not consistent, so eliminate (B). Eliminate (C) because it does not mention the metric system. The topic of *political upheaval* is not consistent, so eliminate (D). The correct answer is (A).

17. **C** The phrases are changing in the answer choices, so the question is testing concision and precision. Select the shortest choice whose meaning is precise. The terms *enthusiasts* and *admirers* mean the same thing, so that idea should not be repeated. Eliminate (A) and (D) because they are redundant. Choices (B) and (C) mean the same thing, so select the more concise choice. The correct answer is (C).

18. **A** Note the question! The question asks for the conclusion of the essay, so it's testing consistency of ideas. The essay started by stating that some people believe the metric system caused the Mars Climate Orbiter to crash, and it ended by stating that the United States had been unable to make the metric system mandatory. The correct answer must be consistent with these ideas. Choice (A) states that our *speed limit signs are* not in *kilometers per hour* and revisits the *Mars Climate Orbiter crash*, so keep it. Stating what *school children learn* is not consistent, so eliminate (B). Discussing *businesses* in relation to *government agencies* is not consistent, so eliminate (C). Stating that *no one is motivated to make the change* is not consistent, so eliminate (D). The correct answer is (A).

RAW SCORE CONVERSION TABLE SECTION AND TEST SCORES

Raw Score (# of correct answers)	Math Section Score	Reading Test Score	Writing and Language Test Score
0	200	10	10
1	200	10	10
2	210	10	10
3	230	11	10
4	240	12	11
5	260	13	12
6	280	14	13
7	290	15	13
8	310	15	14
9	320	16	15
10	330	17	16
11	340	17	16
12	360	18	17
13	370	19	18
14	380	19	19
15	390	20	19
16	410	20	20
17	420	21	21
18	430	21	21
19	440	22	22
20	450	22	23
21	460	23	23
22	470	23	24
23	480	24	25
24	480	24	25
25	490	25	26
26	500	25	26
27	510	26	27
28	520	26	28
29	520	27	28

Raw Score (# of correct answers)	Math Section Score	Reading Test Score	Writing and Language Test Score
30	530	28	29
31	540	28	30
32	550	29	30
33	560	29	31
34	560	30	32
35	570	30	32
36	580	31	33
37	590	31	34
38	600	32	34
39	600	32	35
40	610	33	36
41	620	33	37
42	630	34	38
43	640	35	39
44	650	35	40
45	660	36	
46	670	37	
47	670	37	
48	680	38	
49	690	38	
50	700	39	
51	710	40	
52	730	40	
53	740		
54	750		
55	760		
56	780		
57	790		
58	800		

*Please note that these scores are best approximations and that actual scores on the SAT may slightly vary, depending on individual adaptations made by the College Board.

CONVERSION EQUATION 1 SECTION AND TEST SCORES

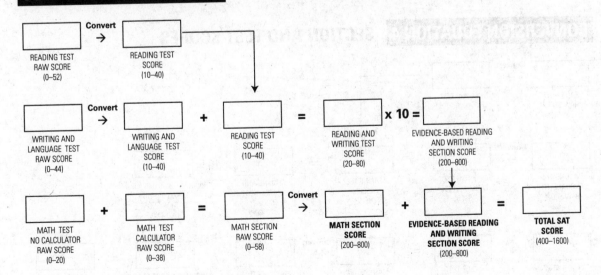

CONVERSION EQUATION 2 SECTION AND TEST SCORES

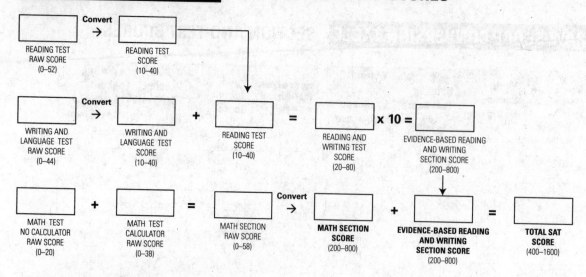

CONVERSION EQUATION 3 SECTION AND TEST SCORES

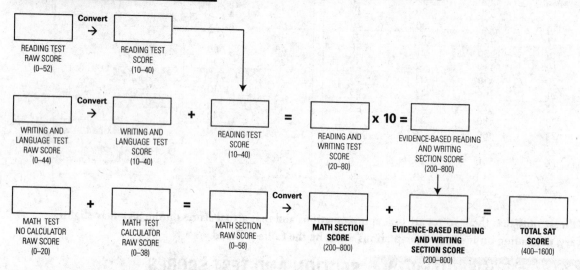

CONVERSION EQUATION 4 SECTION AND TEST SCORES

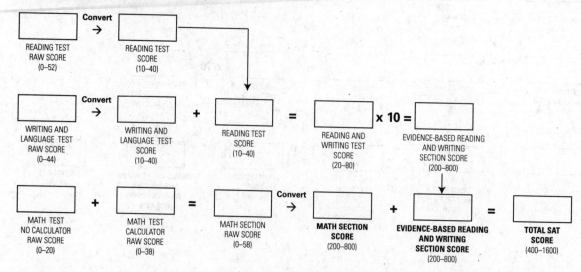

CONVERSION EQUATION 5 SECTION AND TEST SCORES

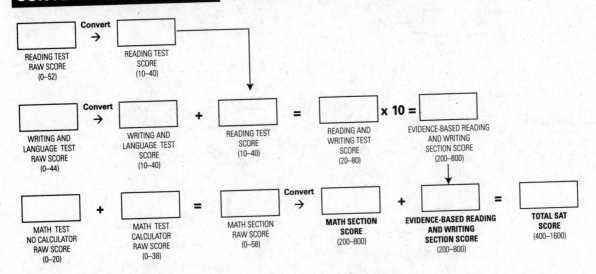

CONVERSION EQUATION 6 SECTION AND TEST SCORES

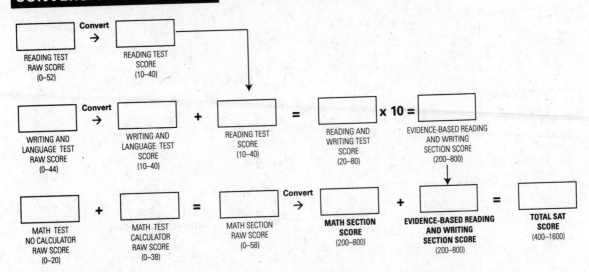

CONVERSION EQUATION 7 SECTION AND TEST SCORES

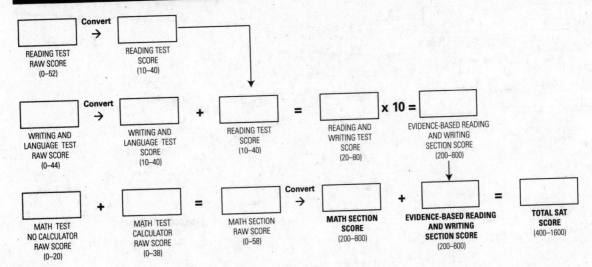

CONVERSION EQUATION 8 SECTION AND TEST SCORES

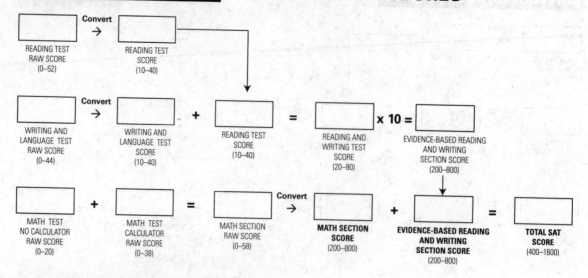

CONVERSION EQUATION 9 SECTION AND TEST SCORES

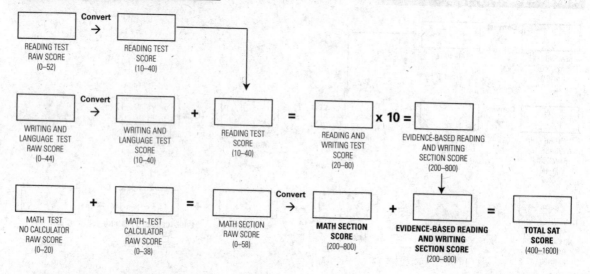

CONVERSION EQUATION 10 SECTION AND TEST SCORES

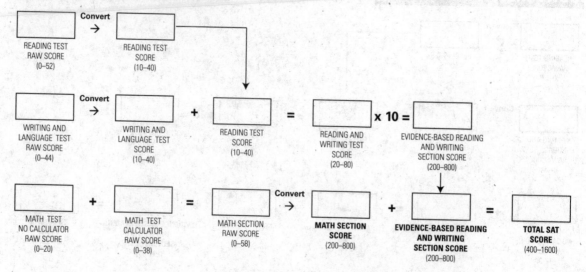

The Princeton Review®

Permissions

NOTES

NOTES

NOTES

NOTES

NOTES

NOTES

NOTES